MANHATTAN PREP

5 lb. Book of ACT®
Practice Problems

ACT® Strategy Guide Supplement

ACT success lies in consistent performance, which requires the deep
familiarity with ACT questions that can only be gained with practice.
This guide provides that practice.

Book of ACT® Practice Problems, First Edition

git International Standard Book Number: 1-941234-50-X
it International Standard Book Number: 978-1-941234-50-1
e 978-1-941234-49-5

Copyright © 2015 MG Prep, Inc.

10 6 5 4

Note registered trademark of ACT, Inc., which neither sponsors nor is affiliated
in any way with this product.

Layout: Dan McNaney
Production Manager: Derek Frankhouser
Production Designers: Cathy Huang and Belen Ferrer
Cover: Dan McNaney and Frank Callaghan

MORE TITLES BY MANHATTAN PREP

GMAT

STRATEGY GUIDES

GMAT ROADMAP
FRACTIONS, DECIMALS, & PERCENTS
ALGEBRA
WORD PROBLEMS
GEOMETRY
NUMBER PROPERTIES
CRITICAL REASONING
READING COMPREHENSION
SENTENCE CORRECTION
INTEGRATED REASONING & ESSAY

SUPPLEMENTS

FOUNDATIONS OF GMAT MATH
FOUNDATIONS OF GMAT VERBAL
GMAT ADVANCED QUANT
OFFICIAL GUIDE COMPANION
OFFICIAL GUIDE COMPANION FOR SENTENCE CORRECTION
TEST SIMULATION BOOKLET

LSAT

STRATEGY GUIDES

LOGIC GAMES
LOGICAL REASONING
READING COMPREHENSION

SUPPLEMENTS

10 REAL LSATS GROUPED BY QUESTION TYPE

GRE

STRATEGY GUIDES

ALGEBRA
FRACTIONS, DECIMALS, & PERCENTS
GEOMETRY
NUMBER PROPERTIES
WORD PROBLEMS
QUANTITATIVE COMPARISONS & DATA INTERPRETATION
READING COMPREHENSION & ESSAYS
TEXT COMPLETION & SENTENCE EQUIVALENCE

SUPPLEMENTS

5 LB. BOOK OF GRE PRACTICE PROBLEMS
500 ESSENTIAL WORDS: GRE VOCABULARY FLASH CARDS
500 ADVANCED WORDS: GRE VOCABULARY FLASH CARDS
500 GRE MATH FLASH CARDS

MANHATTAN PREP

June 2nd, 2015

Dear Student,

Thank you for picking up a copy of the 5 lb. Book of ACT® Practice Problems. We hope this meaty tome provides just the right practice—a workout for both your mind and your biceps!—as you prepare for the ACT.

A great number of people were involved in the creation of the book you are holding. First and foremost is Zeke Vanderhoek, the founder of Manhattan Prep. Zeke was a lone tutor in New York when he started our company in 2000. Now, well into its second decade, the company contributes to the successes of thousands of students around the globe every year.

Our Manhattan Prep resources are based on the continuing experiences of our instructors and students. As the primary editor of this book, I had tons of help from a fantastic team. Passages and questions were written and edited by me, Mary Adkins, Jesse Cotari, Taylor Dearr, Whitney Garner, Rina Goldfield, Ben Ku, Dan Lerman, Emily Madan, and Tate Shafer. As I headed up the English section, Tate led Math, Mary and Rina split leadership duties on Reading, and Dan oversaw Science. Outside contributors Carlota Dwyer and Haven Reininger provided valuable writing and editing, and Cheryl Duckler shared her copy editing chops. Additional editing was provided by Whitney, Emily, Chelsey Cooley, and Julia Van Dyke.

Meanwhile, Dan McNaney, Derek Frankhouser, Cathy Huang, and Belen Ferrer provided design and layout expertise as Dan and Derek managed book production. Liz Krisher made sure that all the moving pieces came together at just the right time. I am deeply grateful to each of these wonderful people.

Finally, we are all indebted to all of the Manhattan Prep students who have given us feedback over the years. This book wouldn't be half of what it is without your voice.

At Manhattan Prep, we aspire to provide the best instructors and resources possible, and we hope that you will find our commitment manifest in this book. We strive to keep our books free of errors, but if you think we've goofed, please visit manhattanprep.com/ACT/errata. If you have any questions or comments in general, please email our Student Services team at act@manhattanprep.com. Or give us a shout at 212-721-7400 (or 800-576-4628 in the U.S. or Canada). I look forward to hearing from you.

Thanks again, and best of luck preparing for the ACT!

Sincerely,

Chris Ryan
Vice President of Academics
Manhattan Prep

HOW TO ACCESS YOUR ONLINE RESOURCES

IF YOU PURCHASED A PHYSICAL COPY OF THIS BOOK

1. Go to: **www.manhattanprep.com/act/access**
2. Follow the instructions on the screen.

Your one year of online access begins on the day that you register your book at the above URL.

You only need to register your product ONCE at the above URL. To use your online resources any time AFTER you have completed the registration process, log in to the following URL:
www.manhattanprep.com/act/studentcenter

Please note that online access is nontransferable. This means that only NEW and UNREGISTERED copies of the book will grant you online access. Previously used books will NOT provide any online resources.

IF YOU PURCHASED A DIGITAL VERSION OF THIS BOOK

1. Create an account with Manhattan Prep at this website:
www.manhattanprep.com/act/register

2. Email a copy of your purchase receipt to **act@manhattanprep.com** to activate your resources. Please be sure to use the same email address to create an account that you used to purchase the book.

For any questions, email **act@manhattanprep.com** or call **800-576-4628**.
Please refer to the following page for a description of the online resources that come with this book.

YOUR ONLINE RESOURCES
YOUR PURCHASE INCLUDES ONLINE ACCESS TO THE FOLLOWING:

SUPPLEMENTAL QUESTION BANKS

Take your studies even further with our question banks. These banks include extra ACT practice problems fine-tuned by our curriculum team to simulate real exam questions. Every question comes with a detailed answer explanation. These problems are an excellent practice resource for dedicated ACT students.

SCIENCE VOCABULARY LIST

This list features over 150 terms that have been used in official ACT Science passages. Many of these terms are not defined within the passage, so you must know them in advance. Other terms in our list are defined within the passage, but the more familiar you are with the specialized vocabulary that is typically used in Science passages, the faster you'll go and the better you'll do on this section of the ACT.

ONLINE UPDATES TO THE CONTENT IN THIS BOOK

The content presented in this book is updated periodically to ensure that it reflects the ACT's most current trends. You may view all updates, including any known errors or changes, upon registering for online access.

The above resources can be found in your Student Center at manhattanprep.com/act/studentcenter

TABLE *of* CONTENTS

TABLE *of* CONTENTS

Chapter *of* 1

5lb. Book of ACT® Practice Problems

Introduction

In This Chapter...

Chapter 1

Introduction

You didn't buy this book to read introductions. You bought this book for 5 pounds of problems that will help you get ready for the ACT.

So let's keep this intro short and useful.

What the ACT Is

The ACT contains 4 multiple-choice sections containing 215 questions. You'll be given just under 3 hours for those 4 sections. There is a fifth, optional section.

Section 1: English

You have 45 minutes for 75 questions, spread across 5 passages. Apply grammar rules, choose the best sentence to add at some point, etc.

Section 2: Math

You have 60 minutes for 60 questions. Solve short problems involving pre-algebra, algebra, geometry, even a little trigonometry. You can use an approved calculator here.

Section 3: Reading

You have 35 minutes for 40 questions, spread across 4 passages. Answer questions about details, big-picture themes, etc.

Section 4: Science

You have 35 minutes for 40 questions, spread across 7 passages. Interpret charts and tables, evaluate theories, etc.

1

Section 5: Writing (Optional)

Surprise: you write a half-hour essay. Some colleges require this section. Others do not.

Here's an obvious point that's worth remembering. **The content of the ACT is at the high school level.** The ACT is meant to measure skills you've gained over the years from your English classes, math classes, etc.

That said, before you encounter the real exam, you ought to **exercise your skills on a lot of good ACT-style problems.** That's why this book exists.

Go to ***www.actstudent.org*** for more details and logistics. At the ACT's official site, you can sign up for the test, get the latest information directly from the test makers, and find even more practice problems. The printed *Real ACT Prep Guide* is another great source of both information and practice.

What's in This Book

This book contains over 1,800 problems that mirror the content and format of the ACT. The proportions of various problem types, topics, and difficulties reflect the proportions of the exam.

Chapter 2 contains a short diagnostic test with 49 problems in English, Math, Reading, and Science. With this test, you can figure out where to focus your efforts, if you're not sure.

Chapters 3 and 4 contain 160 English problems grouped by topic. Most of these problems are tied to single sentences, so that you can efficiently practice a particular set of skills—say, correctly punctuating a sentence. Each chapter is followed by an answer key and a full set of explanations (this is the case throughout the book).

Chapters 5 through 10 contain 450 English problems in 25 passages. Each of these chapters contains 75 questions across 5 passages, the same as a standard English section. The English topics tested in these passages are mixed together, just as on the real ACT. However, answer keys will help you track how you're doing on specific skills.

Chapters 11 through 16 contain 500 Math problems. These chapters are arranged by the broad areas of mathematics that the ACT defines: Pre-Algebra, Elementary & Intermediate Algebra, Coordinate & Plane Geometry, and Trigonometry. The number of problems in each chapter follows the percentage of problems in each broad area on the exam. You can track subtopics using the answer keys.

Chapters 17 through 20 contain 346 Reading problems. These chapters are arranged by the types of Reading passages you'll face on the ACT: Literary Narrative, Humanities, Social Studies, and Natural Sciences. Question types (e.g., details, generalizations) are mixed together throughout the passages, but you can track your performance by question type using the answer keys.

Chapters 21 through 23 contain 343 Science problems. These chapters are arranged by the types of Science passages you'll face on the ACT: Life Sciences, Physical Sciences, and Earth Sciences. In each chapter, you'll find a mix of passage styles (e.g., data representation, research summaries) and corresponding question types.

Chapter 24 provides guidance for the optional Writing section.

4 Ways to Use This Book

1. Practice.

Now that you've opened the book, put pen to paper. Do some problems. You can't do them all at once, of course. But go ahead and get started.

If you just flip through this book, it's as if you're watching someone else work out at the gym. If you actually do problems, you're the one working out. That's how you get stronger.

Do a little bit consistently—every day, if you can. As long as you're actually doing the problems, the exact way that you practice matters less than the fact that you're practicing.

2. Practice in Various Ways.

Here are a few ideas.

1. Do some problems untimed, and do others timed.

By doing some problems without timing yourself, you give your brain a chance to wrestle with the issues in a less stressful way. That can be good for learning. But you should also do some problems under time pressure. After all, you need to do them that way on the real exam, and ultimately, you should practice as you play.

Here are some average timing guidelines:

English: 36 seconds per problem. If you are doing a whole passage, do the 15 questions in 9 minutes.

Math: 60 seconds per problem.

Reading: 53 seconds per problem. If you are doing a whole passage, do the 10 questions in 9 minutes. (A few passages have 9 questions, in which case, do the passage in 8 minutes.)

Science: 53 seconds per problem. If you are doing a whole passage (the passages in this book all have 7 questions), do the 7 questions in 6 minutes. On the ACT, some passages will have just 6 or even 5 questions. To practice under those constraints, drop 1–2 questions and do the passage in 5 minutes (if you drop 1 question) or in 4 minutes (if you drop 2 questions).

2. Do some problems individually, and do others in sets.

Especially when you're starting out, you might want to stop after each problem and check your answer. That's okay. As you progress, though, shift more and more of your work to sets. You don't have to do huge numbers of problems at once, but doing a full passage, or doing 5–10 math problems in a row, is a more realistic workout.

3. Do some sets of problems and/or passages by topic, and do other sets that are mixed.

The traditional way to develop a skill is to drill it: do the same kind of problem/passage, or nearly the same kind, repeatedly. This approach works up to a point. Be sure to do a good number of "mixed" sets, in which you do problems or read passages that are not so closely related to each other. After all, the exam will present material in a random way to you. Doing mixed sets forces you to become better at switching gears and distinguishing cases—knowing when to apply which technique.

3. Practice, Review, and Redo.

Don't just do a problem once. To get the most out of this book, do your work in a separate notebook. Then you can come back later and redo passages and problems under time pressure. You can then be sure that you can tackle similar material on the real exam. You have lots of problems available to you, but don't always be in search of what's new and untouched. Going back over the same ground again—really forcing yourself to redo the work—may be the most valuable part of your preparation.

4. Put This Book down and Rest Your Feet on It. Then Go Get a Different Book: The Real ACT Prep Guide, from the Makers of the ACT.

Why on earth would we recommend that you use a different book from this one? The reason is that every third-party ACT preparation book—every book written by people like us who are *not* the test makers—must fall a little short. Only the Real ACT Prep Guide (or materials that you get from www.actstudent.org) can provide *actual* problems retired from the ACT.

At a couple of points along the way, especially toward the end of your preparation, you should **do a timed practice test using real ACT problems**. Make sure that you apply test-room conditions as best you can—turn off your cell phone, close the door, use a no. 2 pencil, etc. Then score your results.

Such practice tests give you the most authentic measure of what you would go and get on the real exam that day. No practice test is perfect, even one with retired ACT questions in it, but you want to be able to trust your practice test score as much as possible. That score is not destiny—far from it! A practice test is not a crystal ball. But you need to know the current state of affairs as accurately as you can, so that you can actually *change* that state.

A great one-two punch for the ACT is **this 5-pound book for your workouts, plus the Real ACT Prep Guide for practice exams**.

4 Tips for Test Week—and Test Day

1. Do Less New—Redo Old.

The week before the test, avoid doing too many new problems or passages. In fact, it's totally fine just to redo problems and passages you've already seen. You need to rehearse what you know and feel good about it. Don't try to cram in a lot of new experiences that you won't be able to reflect on.

2. Sleep Enough.

There is no substitute for sleep. Your brain absolutely needs it. Prioritize the ACT over other commitments the week before the test, so that you don't run yourself ragged. Find a way to get enough shut-eye that you aren't sabotaging yourself on the exam.

3. Take a Shot and Move On.

During the test, avoid getting bogged down on any one problem. Take your best guess, mark the problem in your test booklet (so you can come back if you have time), and proceed to the next problem. Steel yourself mentally to make some sacrifices in pursuit of your higher goal—the best score you can get that day. Be ready to lose a few battles to win the war.

4. During the Breaks, Get up and Drink a Little Sugar.

The exam is a physical marathon as much as it is a psychic ordeal. By getting up and walking around, you re-energize your body, which is what your brain rides around in. On long standardized tests that tax you physically and mentally, use your breaks to gain ground on all the other kids who just put their heads down on their desks. Their brains are sinking into sleepy mush, while yours is getting re-fired up.

The other key move to make is to drink a few gulps of something with sugar in it. This way, you deliver glucose to your brain as efficiently as you can without an IV drip.

Why is glucose important? It's the only food your brain eats. And quick delivery of glucose to your brain has been shown to counteract *decision fatigue*—the stupefied mental state you get into after you've made a whole bunch of decisions, for example, when you're taking a long standardized test.

Don't chug a giant soda or some weird energy drink. You don't need that much sugar, and you should stay away from caffeine or other additives that mysteriously appear in various beverages. A few sips of orange or apple juice will do.

Get rid of that decision fatigue, and you'll start the next section in a much stronger and readier state of mind.

That's enough introduction. Onto the problems!

Chapter *of* 2

5lb. Book of ACT® Practice Problems

Diagnostic Test

In This Chapter...

Chapter 2
Diagnostic Test

The following diagnostic test is a miniature version of the ACT. End to end, it will take you just 40 minutes (versus 3 hours for a full 4-section practice test). The purpose of this short diagnostic is to expose you to the material and help you focus your studies, not to predict how you will do on the ACT. Do the best you can, of course, but interpret the results as guidance for your work, not as destiny.

Here is the format of the diagnostic:

Section	Area	Questions	Time
1	English	15 (1 passage)	9 minutes
2	Math	10	10 minutes
3	Reading	10 (1 passage)	9 minutes
4	Science	14 (2 passages)	12 minutes

Set a timer for each section and do just that section. Write down your answers on a separate sheet of paper. If you finish early, don't go back or forward to another section; instead, just check your work until the clock runs down. That's how the real ACT works, too. Do the sections in order and without breaks in between.

When you're ready, set a timer to count down 9 minutes[1]. Turn the page and begin Section 1: English.

---

1   If you qualify for accommodations such as extra time, then adjust these time limits accordingly.

2

SECTION 1: ENGLISH, 9 MINUTES, 1 PASSAGE, 15 PROBLEMS

The Origins of Corn

[1]

[1] One of today's staple crops is corn, called
—————————
1
maize in scientific contexts. [2] It is a direct source of
nourishment for humans and animals. [3] In addition,

it supplies oils, starches, as well as providing sugars to
                        ————————————————
                                    2
make other products, from penicillin to ethanol.

[4] However, details of it's origins have remained
                        ————
                         3
shrouded. [5] Over the last few decades, happily, some

new light has been shed on the mystery, in part through
              ————————
                  4

the research of Mary Eubanks. [5]

[2]

Trained in anthropology, Eubanks' studies
                          ———————————
                               6
originally were of ancient Mexican pottery that featured
———
                                    6
impressions of corncobs. These artifacts led her to
——————————————————
        6

1. A. NO CHANGE
    B. Today, one of the most staplest
    C. Today, the most staple
    D. Today's staple

2. F. NO CHANGE
    G. as well as sugars
    H. and sugars, too
    J. and sugars

3. A. NO CHANGE
    B. its
    C. its'
    D. corns

4. Which of the following alternatives to the under-
    lined portion would NOT be acceptable?
    F. illuminated
    G. been shed by
    H. been cast upon
    J. been thrown on

5. Upon reviewing this paragraph and finding that
    some information has been left out, the writer com-
    poses the following sentence incorporating that
    information:
        Thousands of years ago, corn was domesticated
        in Mexico.
    This sentence would most logically be placed after
    Sentence:
    A. 1.
    B. 2.
    C. 3.
    D. 4.

6. F. NO CHANGE
    G. ancient Mexican pottery featuring impressions of
        corncobs was what Eubanks studied originally.
    H. Eubanks originally studied ancient Mexican
        pottery that featured impressions of corncobs.
    J. Eubanks originally studied impressions of corn-
        cobs, featuring ancient Mexican pottery.

MANHATTAN
PREP

collaborate with retired biologist Paul <u>Mangelsdorf to</u>
<u>7</u>
<u>investigate the ancestry of corn.</u>
7

[3]

The closest relative of corn is a certain wild

grass. <u>It was teosinte and, unlike</u> corn, teosinte produces
8
just a few hard, small kernels on scattered stalks. Recent

genetic studies have revealed that teosinte and corn are

in fact the same species. Differences in just a few genes

within the species lead to highly variable appearance

and behavior, much <u>as the single species of domestic</u>
9
<u>dog, includes</u> Chihuahuas, Dachshunds, and Great
9
Danes.

[4]

Eubanks' key discovery was that gamagrass [10]

could be crossbred with teosinte. That is, these species

could be mated to produce fertile offspring, which

resemble the tiny ears of <u>maize she observed: in the</u>
11
pottery.

7. Given that all are true, which one would most effec-
tively connect to the subject of the essay?
A. NO CHANGE
B. Mangelsdorf, who was living in the same area.
C. Mangelsdorf, though Eubanks' doctorate was
not in biology.
D. Mangelsdorf over the course of many produc-
tive years.

8. F. NO CHANGE
G. grass. Known as teosinte and unlike
H. grass, known as teosinte. Unlike
J. grass; known as teosinte, unlike

9. A. NO CHANGE
B. as the single species of domestic dog includes
C. as the single species of domestic dog includes:
D. as, the single species of domestic dog includes

10. At this point, the writer is considering adding the
following parenthetical phrase:
    —a slightly more distant cousin of corn—
Given that it is true, would this addition be relevant
to make here?
F. Yes, because it relates an unfamiliar plant,
newly mentioned, to the topic of the essay.
G. Yes, because it proves that gamagrass and teosinte could be successfully crossbred.
H. No, because it does not specify the precise genetic
relationship between gamagrass and corn.
J. No, because such asides about the connection
between species are irrelevant to the essay.

11. A. NO CHANGE
B. maize she observed;
C. maize she observed
D. maize, she observed

[5]

Eubanks has contended that crossbreeding in the wild transferred key traits from gamagrass to teosinte, helping modify the latter into the highly useful form of modern corn. [12] However, the studies that demonstrate the essential genetic unity of teosinte and corn argue against this theory.

[6]

The precise development of this important crop may never be traced exactly, and the scientific debate continues. Nevertheless, Eubanks has not sat around bashing heads with naysayers. She is using gamagrass
                                                13

hybrids to infuse corn with additional valuable traits, such as: resistance to drought and to insects.
                                                14

12. The writer is considering deleting the following phrase from the preceding sentence (placing a period after the word *teosinte*):

> helping modify the latter into the highly useful form of modern corn

Should the writer make this deletion?

F. Yes, because the information duplicates that which has been provided earlier in the essay.
G. Yes, because the information is irrelevant to the topic of this paragraph, which is the conflict between theories.
H. No, because the information undermines the argument that Eubanks has proposed.
J. No, because the information explains the potential impact of this transfer on corn's development.

13. A. NO CHANGE
B. simply engaged in scholarly disputation, arguing with other researchers.
C. just bandied barbs with complainers.
D. contented herself with academic arguments.

14. F. NO CHANGE
G. traits such as resistance to drought,
H. traits, such as resistance to drought,
J. traits, such as resistance to drought

Question 15 asks about the preceding passage as a whole.

---

15. Suppose the writer's goal had been to write a brief essay outlining a theory about how modern corn emerged. Would this essay successfully fulfill that goal?

A. Yes, because the essay describes Eubanks' research and its impact on hypotheses about corn's origins.
B. Yes, because the essay asserts that modern corn resulted from a wild hybrid of teosinte and gamagrass.
C. No, because the essay leaves the discussion inconclusive as to the definitive origins of the crop.
D. No, because the essay fails to provide enough archaeological detail to support the theory.

END OF SECTION 1

DO NOT GO ON TO THE NEXT SECTION UNTIL THE 9 MINUTES FOR SECTION 1 ARE OVER.

ONCE THOSE 9 MINUTES ARE OVER, SET YOUR TIMER TO COUNT DOWN 10 MINUTES.

TURN THE PAGE AND BEGIN SECTION 2: MATH.

2

SECTION 2: MATH, 10 MINUTES, 10 PROBLEMS

1. A taxi service charges $2.60 per passenger ride plus $0.60 for each $\frac{1}{4}$ of a mile driven. If a passenger takes a taxi trip r miles in length, what will be the total fare for the trip in terms of r?

   A. $3.20

   B. $3.20 + r

   C. 3.20r$

   D. $2.60 + 0.60r$

   E. $2.60 + 2.40r$

2. What is the least common multiple of 4, 8, 12, and 27?

   F. 1

   G. 48

   H. 72

   J. 216

   K. 324

3. The degree measures of the interior angles of 4-sided polygon $ABCD$, shown below, form an arithmetic sequence with common difference 30°. What is the degree measure of the second smallest angle in the polygon?

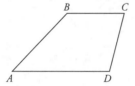

   A. 45°

   B. 75°

   C. 90°

   D. 105°

   E. 120°

4. For right triangle $\triangle ABC$ shown below, what is cos A?

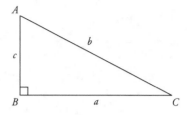

   F. $\dfrac{a}{b}$

   G. $\dfrac{a}{c}$

   H. $\dfrac{b}{c}$

   J. $\dfrac{c}{b}$

   K. $\dfrac{c}{a}$

5. In the standard (x, y) coordinate plane, what is the distance, in coordinate units, between $(8, 6)$ and $(-2, -3)$?

   A. $\sqrt{181}$

   B. $\sqrt{45}$

   C. $\sqrt{19}$

   D. 19

   E. 9

MANHATTAN
PREP

6. Shown below is the graph of the equation $y = 1 - \dfrac{1}{2}x$, for values of x such that $-2 \le x \le 2$. Which of the statements that follow are true?

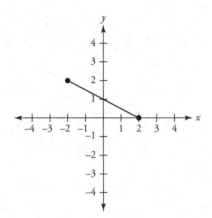

I. The graph has a constant slope of $-\dfrac{1}{2}$.

II. The graph's x-intercept lies at the point $(2, 0)$.

III. The range of the graph contains all values of y such that $-2 \le y \le 2$.

   F. I only

   G. II only

   H. III only

   J. I and II only

   K. II and III only

7. The growth of a particular bacterial colony, P, in a Petri dish can be modeled by the equation $P = \dfrac{3^{2t-1}}{h} + 200$, where t is time measured in days, such that $0 < t$. The variable h represents a growth coefficient, such that $0 < h \le 10$. In ideal heat and moisture conditions, $h = 0.5$. Which of the following expressions represents the population of the bacterial colony after 5 days of growth under ideal heat and moisture conditions?

   A. $\dfrac{3^9}{2} + 200$

   B. $2 \cdot 3^{11} + 200$

   C. $2 \cdot 3^9 + 200$

   D. $6^9 + 200$

   E. 6^9

8. The global probability of a person being a carrier of a certain genetic disorder is 3.7×10^{-8}. If in Country X the likelihood of carrying the genetic disorder is 1,000 times the likelihood among the global population, what is the probability of a randomly selected person from Country X being a carrier of the genetic disorder?

   F. 3.7×10^{-11}

   G. 3.7×10^{-5}

   H. $3.7 \times 10^{-\frac{8}{3}}$

   J. 3.7×10^{-24}

   K. 3.7×10^{-108}

9. $\left(2x - \dfrac{1}{3}\right)^2$ is equivalent to:

   A. $4x^2 - \dfrac{4}{3}x + \dfrac{1}{9}$

   B. $4x^2 - \dfrac{2}{3}x - \dfrac{1}{9}$

   C. $4x^2 + \dfrac{2}{3}x + \dfrac{1}{9}$

   D. $4x^2 - \dfrac{1}{9}$

   E. $4x^2 + \dfrac{1}{9}$

10. Which of the following sets of numbers could be the lengths of the 3 sides of a $45°$–$45°$–$90°$ triangle?

   F. $1, 1, 2$

   G. $\sqrt{2}, \sqrt{2}, 2$

   H. $2, 2, \sqrt{3}$

   J. $1, \sqrt{3}, 2$

   K. $3, 3, 4$

END OF SECTION 2

DO NOT GO ON TO THE NEXT SECTION UNTIL THE 9 MINUTES FOR SECTION 2 ARE OVER.

ONCE THOSE 9 MINUTES ARE OVER, SET YOUR TIMER TO COUNT DOWN 9 MINUTES.

TURN THE PAGE AND BEGIN SECTION 3: READING.

2

SECTION 3: READING, 9 MINUTES, 1 PASSAGE, 10 PROBLEMS

LITERARY NARRATIVE: This passage is adapted from a memoir by a Nicaraguan-American author. The story is set in the late 1990s.

My mother knew right away what the old man meant, when he told her to turn right *donde fue la farmacia Ixchen*—where the Ixchen pharmacy used to be. Directions in this country are for those in the know, not for outsiders. Street addresses may exist on a government map, but no one uses them. Instead, everyone describes a path using landmarks, and you had better know that "toward the lake" means north, and that the pharmacy used to be on that corner, where now only grass and trees grow amid the rubble.

We trudged forward under the blazing sun. "Mom, when was the last time it rained here?" I asked. She made no response; her pace slowed, as she stared at a high concrete wall across the dirt road.

"Mom! Does it ever rain in Nicaragua?" I repeated.

"Look," she said, pulling my hand. As we crossed over to the wall, I kicked pebbles, annoyed that she was ignoring my questions.

She knelt down and traced her forefinger across the uneven concrete. "See these marks, Yesenia?" she murmured. I remained silent, just as she had.

"These were made by bullets. There was a lot of fighting along this street. A lot of people…" Her voice trailed off sadly.

With that, it was as if someone else was resentful, someone else was hot and tired and hungry. I tried to think of a man I had never met, who had died in this fighting just before I was born. My memories of him were not even my own. I could only picture a worn photograph that my mother always carried, its edges tattered from being touched over and over. In it, my father smiles conspiratorially, as if he has just told a joke but is trying to look serious for the camera. Next to him, my mother's head is turned, both indignant and amused. I had always wondered what joke he told at that moment, but never dared to ask, sensing that the memory would be too private.

This was our first trip back to the country since we left just after the war. My father had fought on the winning side, so with speeches and ceremonies we were honored, along with other bereft families, for our sacrifice. But the hole in my mother was too big to fill with speeches. Her brother, my uncle Carlos, was living in the United States and invited her north to start over again.

I was too young to remember the journey, which was not in an air-conditioned plane, but rather on the roof of a freight train chugging precariously up the map. I never learned the details of our crossing, or of the first several years after we arrived. What most evokes my early childhood is a smell: the scent of pine trees, artificially replicated by air fresheners. My mother would religiously hang those dark green pine trees from the rear-view mirror of the unpleasantly pungent station wagon we shared with Uncle Carlos. This all-American aroma surrounded us protectively at all times.

A decade, then almost another, passed. Now we were back to see Don Lorenzo, my father's uncle and my oldest living relative, a modest, stately man who was very ill.

"You found this new house okay?" he asked in a light, raspy Spanish like fine sandpaper, as we sat on his porch.

"Yes, they told me to turn where the pharmacy used to be. What happened to it?" my mother replied.

They continued to talk. My Spanish was not quite good enough for me to participate fully. Lost in my own thoughts, I sipped my soda and watched the one-eyed cat creep along the wall behind Don Lorenzo, stalking some kind of giant spindly bug. Meanwhile, Necio, the slavering pit bull, never took its menacing eyes off the cat.

Out of nowhere an albino rabbit, all white fur and vampire red eyes, crossed nonchalantly in front of the pit bull. What is this, a zoo? Why isn't that thing being eaten? I snorted at the absurdity of the scene, only to suppress a laugh with a blush as Don Lorenzo and my mother turned.

"There it is," said Don Lorenzo, looking right at me. "The smile. The same as your father had." I froze. My childish reactions were suddenly tiny compared to something huge and strange as a planet inside me. I watched my mother's hand slip into her purse unconsciously; I knew she was touching the photograph.

At that moment, I felt more connected to my father than ever before or since. I no longer needed to know the joke; in fact, I knew that I would probably not understand it. At the same time, I somehow knew the joke completely. It was not a vampire rabbit, but something else equally ridiculous and touching, that had provoked my father's sense of humor, a sense probably amplified in "serious" situations, as I realized with another leap. Like me, he laughed inappropriately and was reprimanded frequently, or so I imagined.

Later, we visited the cemetery; there were plenty of carved letters in stone, but no picture, no new information about the man and his secret smile. Before long a rain shower burst from the sky, sending us running for cover and turning the dusty roads into streams of mud.

1. It can be reasonably inferred that the narrator's mother doesn't complete her sentence at the concrete wall because:
   A. she forgets what she was going to say.
   B. she is overcome by her recollections.
   C. she changes her mind about sharing her thoughts.
   D. she is tired and hungry.

2. When the narrator says, "or so I imagined" (line 94), she most likely means that:
   F. the narrator and her father had a similar sense of humor.
   G. the narrator's father was often reprimanded for laughing inappropriately.
   H. the narrator felt, rather than knew, that her father had certain traits.
   J. the narrator realized that the specific content of the joke was unimportant.

3. In describing how she finally understood her father's joke, the narrator draws an important contrast between:
   A. serious situations that required formality and lighter moments that permitted frivolity.
   B. the vampire rabbit on the porch and the cause of the joke in the photograph.
   C. inappropriate laughter and the frequent reprimands that resulted.
   D. the literal words that remained unknown and the joke's wry stance on life that was familiar.

4. According to the passage, the reason why the narrator and her mother have returned to Nicaragua is to visit:
   F. their ill relative.
   G. the grave of the narrator's father.
   H. landmarks of the war.
   J. the site of the photograph.

5. The passage states that just before examining the concrete wall with her mother, the narrator feels all of the following EXCEPT:
   A. exhaustion.
   B. resentment.
   C. hunger.
   D. thirst.

6. It can be reasonably inferred that the person whom the narrator "never dared to ask" (line 36) is:
   F. her father.
   G. her mother.
   H. Uncle Carlos.
   J. Don Lorenzo.

7. Which of the following statements best describes the way the second-to-last paragraph (lines 85–94) functions in the passage as a whole?
   A. It separates the passage into two parts, one focused on life in Nicaragua, the other focused on life in the United States.
   B. It resolves the mystery of the photograph, by revealing the hidden source of the father's joke.
   C. It explains the sense of connection that the narrator was at last able to feel with her father through a shared characteristic.
   D. It emphasizes the difficulty of understanding jokes literally, while acknowledging the similar conditions that give rise to humor.

8. The passage suggests that all of the following are potential reasons why the narrator's mother hung pine-scented air fresheners EXCEPT:
   F. to remind herself of her home country.
   G. to mask unpleasant odors.
   H. to create an American surrounding.
   J. to provide a sense of protection.

2

9. The main theme of this passage could best be described as:

   A. the narrator's passage from ignorance to deep knowledge of her father.
   B. the narrator's struggle to adapt to her mother's native culture.
   C. the tension between the narrator and her mother over the narrator's father.
   D. the narrator's efforts to separate herself from her Nicaraguan relatives.

10. It can most reasonably be concluded from the passage that:

    F. the Ixchen pharmacy was destroyed in the war.
    G. it had not rained for weeks before the shower at the cemetery.
    H. it had been too painful for the narrator's mother to return to Nicaragua before now.
    J. the narrator's mother is an insider, as far as Nicaraguan directions are concerned.

END OF SECTION 3

DO NOT GO ON TO THE NEXT SECTION UNTIL THE 9 MINUTES FOR SECTION 3 ARE OVER.

ONCE THOSE 9 MINUTES ARE OVER, SET YOUR TIMER TO COUNT DOWN 12 MINUTES.

TURN THE PAGE AND BEGIN SECTION 4: SCIENCE.

2

SECTION 4: SCIENCE, 12 MINUTES, 2 PASSAGES, 14 PROBLEMS

PASSAGE 1

Photosynthesis is the process by which organisms use sunlight to synthesize food from carbon dioxide and water. Most plants, algae, and *cyanobacteria*, or blue bacteria, perform photosynthesis and for this reason are called *autotrophs*. The chemical reaction for photosynthesis is represented below:

$$6CO_2 + 6H_2O \xrightarrow{\text{light}} C_6H_{12}O_6 + 6O_2$$

Experiment 1

A student created a laboratory setup to demonstrate the effects of photosynthesis. Using a fern plant submerged in water and the equipment pictured in Figure 1, the student observed the plant over 9 hours. She then counted the number of oxygen bubbles collecting in the test tube, and her results are summarized in Table 1.

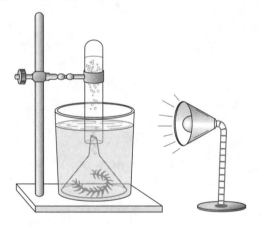

Figure 1

Table 1

Hour of Experiment	Number of O$_2$ Bubbles Observed (Cumulative)
1	5
3	19
5	33
7	48
9	49

Experiment 2

The more CO_2 is added to an environment, the more acidic it becomes. A common measure of acidity is pH. As the pH of a substance increases, it becomes less acidic.

The pH of a solution can be measured by an *indicator,* or a substance that changes color at a specific pH. *Phenol red* is an indicator of pH. A student repeated the setup from Experiment 1, but she added phenol red to the water for this trial. She then observed the color of the solution as well as the pH of the solution, which she measured with a pH meter.

Table 2

Hour of Experiment	Color of Phenol Red	pH of Solution
1	Yellow	6.8
3	Orange	7.2
5	Red	7.6
7	Pink	8.0
9	Pink	8.0

1. According to Table 1, the number of O$_2$ bubbles observed 4 hours after the experiment began was most likely closest to:

   A. 19
   B. 26
   C. 32
   D. 33

2. According to Table 2, which phenol red color would indicate the most acidic solution?

   F. Yellow
   G. Orange
   H. Red
   J. Pink

MANHATTAN
PREP

3. In order to witness photosynthesis in action, the student in Experiment 1 could have replaced the fern with any of the following EXCEPT:

    A. algae
    B. a specific type of bacteria
    C. a salamander
    D. a pea plant

4. Which of the following is NOT one of the ways this experimental setup differs from the manner in which plants conduct photosynthesis in the real world?

    F. Plants do not generally use artificial light in their natural environments.
    G. Plants are not generally kept in glass containers in their natural environments.
    H. Plants are generally not confined to such small spaces in their natural environments.
    J. Plants do not perform photosynthesis in their natural environments.

5. According to Table 2, which of the following is the most plausible reason that the pH stopped increasing after 7 hours?

    A. All of the CO_2 had been used up, so the plant stopped performing photosynthesis.
    B. All of the O_2 had been used up, so the plant stopped performing photosynthesis.
    C. All of the $C_6H_{12}O_6$ had been used up, so the plant stopped performing photosynthesis.
    D. All of the H_2O had been used up, so the plant stopped performing photosynthesis.

6. Most animals perform a process called *respiration,* in which they use O_2 and glucose to create CO_2. Suppose the student modified Experiment 2 after 9 hours by removing the fern and replacing it with a small fish. Which of the following is most likely to be the pH of that solution after 2 additional hours?

    F. 8.8
    G. 8.4
    H. 8.2
    J. 7.8

7. The chemical formula for *glucose*, a simple sugar, is $C_6H_{12}O_6$. According to the chemical reaction for photosynthesis, if a plant were given 60 molecules of CO_2 and 60 molecules of H_2O, as well as an adequate amount of light, how many molecules of glucose could be produced?

    A. 10
    B. 12
    C. 60
    D. 360

PASSAGE 2

Two students explain the source of *lift*, the upward force on the wings of an airplane as it moves forward through the air. They also discuss how changing the *angle of attack*, the angle of the wing relative to horizontal, affects lift.

Student 1

Planes fly because of differences in air pressure. As the plane moves forward, the air rushes backward over the fixed wings. Because the wings are shaped to be humped on top, the air moving over the top of the wings gets squeezed together. Just like water through a pinched hose, the air therefore squirts over the wings faster than it does under the wings, where the air was not squeezed. Air is a fluid; fluids that move faster exert less *pressure*, or force, over an area. Since the air above is moving faster than the air underneath, the air above exerts less pressure down on the wings than the air underneath exerts up on the wings. This imbalance in pressures results in lift. The faster the plane moves forward (all else being equal), the greater the imbalance in pressures, and therefore the greater the lift. If this lift is greater than the plane's *weight* (the downward *force of gravity* acting on the plane), the plane ascends; if the lift is less than the plane's weight, the plane descends.

As the angle of attack increases from horizontal to about 15 degrees, lift increases because the air moving over the top of the wing is forced to go faster and faster. Beyond 15 degrees, though, the air on top no longer flows smoothly along the wing. Instead, it flows *turbulently*, in chaotic whirlwinds. The effective speed of this turbulent air is not as high as it is in smooth flow, so the pressure above increases and lift decreases from its peak at an angle of 15 degrees.

Student 2

Planes fly because of action and reaction. The wings of the plane, as they move forward through the air, push down on that air. This process is enhanced by the smoothly curved shape of the wings, which actually draw air upward as they approach. The air is then bent around the top of the wings and sent forcefully downward, as can be seen when a plane travels over a bank of clouds, leaving holes in those clouds from the down-rushing air behind the plane. Since the wings are exerting a force downward on the air, the air has to exert an equal and opposite force upward on the wings, by the principle of action and reaction. This force that the air exerts on the wings is lift. The faster the plane moves forward (all else being equal), the faster and more forcefully the air is pushed down, resulting in greater lift. If this lift is greater than the plane's weight, the plane ascends; if the lift is less than the plane's weight, the plane descends.

As the angle of attack increases from horizontal to about 15 degrees, lift increases because the air is thrust more effectively downward at higher angles. Beyond 15 degrees, though, the air on top of the wings no longer curls effectively down around those wings. Instead, the air flows turbulently. Since this air is no longer flowing smoothly downward, it does not push back on the wings as much upward force, so lift decreases from its peak at an angle of 15 degrees.

MANHATTAN
PREP

8. According to Student 1, which of the following quantities is less for the air on top of an airplane wing in flight than for the air underneath the wing?

   F. Pressure
   G. Speed
   H. Area
   J. Angle of attack

9. When two identical planes were flown under identical conditions but at different speeds, the lift on Plane Y was found to be greater than the lift on Plane X. What conclusion would each student draw about the relative speeds of the two planes?

   A. Both Student 1 and Student 2 would conclude that Plane X was going faster.
   B. Both Student 1 and Student 2 would conclude that Plane Y was going faster.
   C. Student 1 would conclude that Plane X was going faster; Student 2 would conclude that Plane Y was going faster.
   D. Student 1 would conclude that Plane Y was going faster; Student 2 would conclude that Plane X was going faster.

10. Which student(s), if either, would predict that an airplane wing NOT moving through the air will experience lift?

   F. Student 1 only
   G. Student 2 only
   H. Both Student 1 and Student 2
   J. Neither Student 1 nor Student 2

11. Which student(s), if either, would clearly predict that a plane flying over a grassy field would flatten the grass behind it with down-rushing air?

   A. Student 1 only
   B. Student 2 only
   C. Both Student 1 and Student 2
   D. Neither Student 1 nor Student 2

12. When the angle of attack of a particular plane's wings was decreased from 15 degrees to 0 degrees (horizontal), the plane, which had been in level flight, started to descend. Based on Student 1's explanation, the reason the plane descended is most likely that:

   F. the increased lift force became stronger than the downward force of gravity acting on the plane.
   G. the decreased downward force of gravity was no longer as strong as the constant lift force.
   H. the decreased lift force was no longer as strong as the downward force of gravity acting on the plane.
   J. the increased downward force of gravity became stronger than the constant lift force.

13. As the angle of attack is increased from horizontal to 30 degrees, what would each student predict will happen to the lift force?

   A. Both students would predict that the lift force will increase at first, then decrease.
   B. Both students would predict that the lift force will decrease at first, then increase.
   C. Student 1 would predict that the lift force will increase; Student 2 would predict that the lift force will decrease.
   D. Student 1 would predict that the lift force will decrease; Student 2 would predict that the lift force will increase.

14. Based on Student 2's explanation, the reason that a helicopter is able to fly is that the blades of the helicopter's main rotor act like airplane wings by:

   F. decreasing the angle of attack from 15 degrees to horizontal.
   G. remaining motionless relative to the surrounding air.
   H. pushing air downward and therefore being pushed up by that air.
   J. causing air above the blades to move faster and therefore exert less downward pressure.

Scoring

Count up the number you got right in each section, using the answer keys below.

Section 1: English

Problem #	Correct Answer	Your Answer	Right? Put 1 if yes
1	A		
2	J		
3	B		
4	G		
5	C		
6	H		
7	A		
8	H		
9	B		
10	F		
11	C		
12	J		
13	D		
14	J		
15	A		
		Total	

Section 2: Math

Problem #	Correct Answer	Your Answer	Right? Put 1 if yes
1	E		
2	J		
3	B		
4	J		
5	A		
6	J		
7	C		
8	G		
9	A		
10	G		
		Total	

Section 3: Reading

Problem #	Correct Answer	Your Answer	Right? Put 1 if yes
1	B		
2	H		
3	D		
4	F		
5	D		
6	G		
7	C		
8	F		
9	A		
10	J		
		Total	

Section 4: Science

2

Science Problem #	Correct Answer	Your Answer	Right? Put 1 if yes
1	B		
2	F		
3	C		
4	J		
5	A		
6	J		
7	A		
8	F		
9	B		
10	J		
11	B		
12	H		
13	A		
14	H		
		Total	

Put the total you got right for each section into the following table:

	English	Math	Reading	Science
Number Right	——— out of 15	——— out of 10	——— out of 10	——— out of 14

Circle the level you achieved: Fundamentals, Fixes, or Tweaks.

	English	Math	Reading	Science
3. Tweaks (76–100% right)	12–15 right	8–10 right	8–10 right	11–14 right
2. Fixes (50–75% right)	7–11 right	5–7 right	5–7 right	7–10 right
1. Fundamentals (0–49% right)	0–6 right	0–4 right	0–4 right	0–6 right

MANHATTAN
PREP

Again, these levels have little to do with the score you'll eventually achieve on the ACT. Rather, they should just help you focus your efforts. Plan to spend the most time and energy on the Fundamentals, a moderate amount on the Fixes, and the least on the Tweaks.

1. Fundamentals (0–49% right)

You have a solid amount of work ahead of you in this area. You might need to learn the principles behind these problems. Or you might need to apply your knowledge more effectively in the context of this particular standardized test. If you're like most people, you'll need to do some of both: learn new content and get more comfortable with the process of answering ACT-style questions in a timed setting. Either way, you have to work on the fundamentals.

Good news: you have this book. You have hundreds of practice problems to work out with. Reread the end of Chapter 1 to get ideas about how to plan your workouts.

Keep your chin up. Focus on this area and commit to improving your performance, and over time you can make real improvements.

2. Fixes (50–75% right)

You have the basics down and can rack up points in this area, but there are clear fixes to make. Perhaps certain topics threw you. Maybe your process has some holes in it, or you had to rush at the end, causing you to miss problems that you know how to do.

Again, good news: you have this book. You can make your fixes by working out with the practice problems in the following chapters.

3. Tweaks (76–100% right)

Nice job! At most, you just got a few wrong in this area. To progress further, you just need to make some tweaks on a particular type of question or an aspect of your problem-solving process.

Here is some great news: you can spend the majority of your time elsewhere. Don't completely ignore this area, of course. Do a little work here and there: it will confirm your mastery and make you feel good about this whole ACT business.

Diagnostic Test Solutions

Before diving into these solutions (let alone the rest of the book), go back and take a look at the diagnostic problems again. Try your hand at them again, untimed. See whether you can figure any out that you missed the first time. Only then should you take a look at the solutions below.

Section 1: English Solutions

1.   **(A)** One of today's staple crops is corn …

Usage/Mechanics   Grammar & Usage   Subject–Verb Agreement

The verb in the sentence is singular (*is*), so the subject cannot be the plural noun *crops*. Thus, the choices that do not use *one of* (thereby making the subject *one,* not *crops*) must be incorrect. To decide between the remaining choices, look at the word *staple*, here used as an adjective. No adjective should ever get both superlatives (*most* and *–est*); a construction such as *most staplest* is always wrong. In fact, *staple* rarely gets any modification (even *most staple* would be awkward). When *staple* is an adjective, use it by itself. The correct answer is (A).

2.   **(J)** In addition, it supplies oils, starches, and sugars to make other products …

Usage/Mechanics   Grammar & Usage   Parallelism

What does corn supply? It supplies a list of three items: oils, starches, and sugars. This kind of parallel list should follow the *X, Y, and Z* pattern. You should not use *as well as* in place of *and*; nor should you compound the error by adding in *providing* (you already have *supplies* up front). The *too* in choice (C) is both unnecessary and poorly punctuated (you would need commas on both sides). The correct answer is (J).

3.   **(B)** … details of its origins …

Usage/Mechanics   Punctuation   Apostrophes

The possessive form of *it* is *its,* without an apostrophe. The form *it's* always means *it is*; if you substitute *it is* in place of *it's,* you'll immediately see that *details of it is origins* makes no sense. There is no valid form *its'* in English. Finally, the possessive of *corn* is *corn's*, with an apostrophe, so *corns origins* is punctuated incorrectly. The correct answer is (B).

4.   **(G)** Not acceptable: … some new light has been shed by the mystery …

Usage/Mechanics   Sentence Structure   Verb Voice

The acceptable variations of *light has been shed on the mystery* (that is, something or someone has shed light on the mystery) are *light has illuminated the mystery, light has been cast upon the mystery,* and *light has been thrown on the mystery.* Each of these versions means essentially the same thing. However, if you write *light has been shed by the mystery,* then you are saying that the mystery itself has shed light on something. That is not at all what the writer intends. Used after a passive voice verb (such as *has been shed*), the preposition *by* indicates the agent that performs the action on the subject. The prepositions *on* or *upon* are the right ones here (indicating where the light has fallen). The correct answer is (G).

MANHATTAN
PREP

5.   **(C)** This sentence would most logically be placed after Sentence 3.

Rhetorical Skills   Organization   Sentence Order

Examine the content and function of each sentence, paying special attention to transitions:

>   S1: Corn is a staple crop.
>   S2: It's a source of food.
>   S3: It also supplies oils, etc., for other products.
>   S4: However, details of its origins are mysterious.
>   S5: New light has been shed on this mystery.

The flow through the first three sentences is tight, with S2 and S3 supporting S1. S3 also has the logical *In addition* opener, tying it more closely to S2. The logical place to put S3 is near the sentence that already mentions its origins: S4. Should the new sentence go before or after? If before, then the contrasting *However* makes sense—the new sentence provides a very general picture of corn's origins, but details remain a mystery. This logical flow is best. Placing the new sentence before S4 also preserves the good link between S4 and S5 (S4 proposes a mystery, while S5 indicates that *new light has been shed on the mystery*). If the new sentence goes after S4, then this link is broken. The correct answer is (C).

6.   **(H)** Trained in anthropology, <u>Eubanks originally studied ancient Mexican pottery that featured impressions of corncobs.</u>

Usage/Mechanics   Sentence Structure   Modifier Placement

The leading modifier *Trained in anthropology* gives you a strong constraint: the subject must be *Eubanks* (not *Eubanks' studies* or anything else), because she is the only one who could be so trained. This constraint eliminates choices (A) and (B). The final answer is dictated by the logical relationship between the *ancient Mexican pottery* and the *impressions of corncobs*. It was the pottery that *featured* the impressions of corncobs, not the other way around (how could these impressions feature the pottery?). The correct answer is (H).

7.   **(A)** These artifacts led her to collaborate with retired biologist Paul <u>Mangelsdorf to investigate the ancestry of corn.</u>

Rhetorical Skills   Writing Strategy   Choice of Content

The subject of the essay is clearly indicated by its title: *The Origins of Corn*. To tie this sentence back to that subject, you can identify the purpose of the scientists' collaboration: *to investigate the ancestry of corn*. The alternatives are all irrelevant (e.g., the fact that they lived in the same area, or that Eubanks' doctorate was not in biology, or that the collaboration lasted many years). None of these address the essay's topic. The correct answer is (A).

2

8.   **(H)** The closest relative of corn is a certain wild grass, known as teosinte. Unlike corn, teosinte produces …

Usage/Mechanics   Sentence Structure   Modifier Placement

Rather than start another sentence with the weak clause *It was teosinte*, simply tack onto the end of the prior sentence a modifier that does the job: *a certain wild grass, known as teosinte*. Then close out that sentence with a period and start the next one with *Unlike corn …*, which is a good leading modifier for the subject *teosinte*. Choices (G) and (J) weirdly modify *teosinte* with *known as teosinte*, a modifier that should clearly be attached to *a certain wild grass* in order to name it. The correct answer is (H).

9.   **(B)** Differences … lead to highly variable appearance and behavior, much as the single species of domestic dog includes Chihuahuas, Dachshunds, and Great Danes.

Usage/Mechanics   Punctuation   Commas

The subordinate clause at the end of the sentence begins with the conjunction *much as* (a variation on *just as*). The subject of this clause is *the single species of domestic dog*, the verb is *includes*, and the object is *Chihuahuas, Dachshunds, and Great Danes*. Just as in any other typical subject–verb–object sequence, no commas, colons, or other punctuation should be used anywhere here to interrupt the logical flow. It does not matter that the object is a list—do not put a colon in front of it. The correct answer is (B).

10.   **(F)** Would this addition be relevant? Yes, because it relates an unfamiliar plant, newly mentioned, to the topic of the essay.

Rhetorical Skills   Writing Strategy   Additions

Consider the sentence with the addition made: *Eubanks' key discovery was that gamagrass—a slightly more distant cousin of corn—could be crossbred with teosinte*. It is certainly possible to introduce *gamagrass* cold, expecting that the reader will infer that it's some kind of plant (the "grass" component of the name helps). However, you shouldn't make your reader work for this point when you want him or her to concentrate on what's new and truly important here: Eubanks' key discovery that this plant could be crossbred with teosinte. By adding in a quick parenthetical to connect gamagrass to corn, you help the reader assimilate a new detail easily.

Note that this aside does not prove that the two plants could be successfully crossbred, as suggested by (G). Proof is a very high standard. The fact that gamagrass and teosinte are on the same family tree perhaps suggests that the plants can be crossbred, but that suggestion does not rise to the level of proof. The correct answer is (F).

11.   **(C)** … fertile offspring, which resemble the tiny ears of maize she observed in the pottery.

Usage/Mechanics   Punctuation   Commas

The correct version has no punctuation at all. The phrase *the tiny ears of maize* is modified by the essential modifier *she observed in the pottery*. This clause could also be written as *that she observed in the pottery*. No comma should be placed between an essential modifier and the noun it modifies.

Likewise, no colon or semicolon should be placed between *observed* and *in the pottery*. For stylistic effect, you might be able to get away with a comma there, since you could end the sentence reasonably with *the tiny ears of maize she observed*. However, this choice would be risky—and it's not available anyway. Each essential modifier answers a key question that has just been raised:

… *resemble the tiny ears of maize.* (Which tiny ears of maize?)
… *resemble the tiny ears of maize she observed.* (Where did she observe them?)
… *resemble the tiny ears of maize she observed in the pottery.*

The correct answer is (C).

12.   **(J)**   Should the writer make this deletion? No, because the information explains the potential impact of this transfer on corn's development.

Rhetorical Skills   Writing Strategy   Deletions

Take a look at the sentence (and its neighbor) before and after the proposed deletion:

Before: *Eubanks has contended that crossbreeding in the wild transferred key traits from gamagrass to teosinte, helping modify the latter into the highly useful form of modern corn. However, the studies that demonstrate the essential genetic unity of teosinte and corn argue against this theory.*

After: *Eubanks has contended that crossbreeding in the wild transferred key traits from gamagrass to teosinte. However, the studies that demonstrate the essential genetic unity of teosinte and corn argue against this theory.*

The underlined portion is crucial, giving Eubanks' theory its purpose. After all, Eubanks is not hypothesizing that two random plants crossbred in the wild for no reason. She is arguing that this process is how corn developed. Another hint that you need the phrase is in the next sentence, which discusses *the essential genetic unity of teosinte and corn.* If you haven't even mentioned corn directly in the prior sentence, where you have outlined Eubanks' theory, then you're forcing the reader to guess at the result of the crossbreeding. Spell it out with the underlined phrase. The correct answer is (J).

13.   **(D)** Nevertheless, Eubanks has not contented herself with academic arguments.

Rhetorical Skills   Style   Word Choice

The original version (*sat around bashing heads with naysayers*) and choice (C) (*just bandied barbs with complainers*) are both far too casual and emotional for the formal tone established throughout the essay. The writing in this passage overall is direct, academic, and neutral: keep to that style. Choice (B), meanwhile, goes too far in the other direction and falls into pompous redundancy. *Scholarly disputation* and *arguing with other researchers* mean essentially the same thing. The correct answer is (D).

2

14. **(J)** ... infuse corn with additional valuable <u>traits, such as resistance to drought</u> and to insects.

Usage/Mechanics   Punctuation   Commas

The modifier *such as ... insects* is not essential, so it should be set off from *additional valuable traits* by a comma. The *resistance* mentioned is two-fold: it is *to drought and to insects*. Do not put a comma after *drought*, improperly splitting this two-part list. The correct answer is (J).

15. **(A)** Does the essay fulfill the goal of outlining a theory about how modern corn emerged? Yes, because the essay describes Eubanks' research and its impact on hypotheses about corn's origins.

Rhetorical Skills   Writing Strategy   Goal of Essay

The essay fulfils the proposed goal well. The first paragraphs put forward the importance of corn, the mystery of its origin, and the background of Eubanks. Then the essay explores the relationship between teosinte and corn, as well as Eubanks' theory of how gamagrass may have helped teosinte evolve into modern corn. These paragraphs do little besides *outline a theory about how modern corn emerged*. Note that the essay does not assert the truth of the theory; in the second-to-last paragraph, both Eubanks' theory and opposing evidence are presented, and the final paragraph reinforces that the kernel of the mystery, so to speak, may always remain. The correct answer is (A).

Section 2: Math Solutions

1. **(E)** $2.60 + 2.40r$ Elementary Algebra   Expressing Relationships

The initial fare for a passenger is just $2.60. If a passenger rides for $\frac{1}{4}$ of a mile, the additional charge will be $0.60. Therefore, if a passenger rides for 1 mile, the additional charge will be $0.60 × 4 = $2.40. Similarly, if a passenger rides for r miles, the additional charge will be 2.40r$.

The correct answer is therefore $2.60 + 2.40r$.

Note that $2.60 + 0.60r$ is incorrect because the charge is $0.60 per $\frac{1}{4}$ of a mile, not per mile. The correct answer is (E).

2. **(J)** 216   Pre-Algebra   Number Properties and Operations (Multiples and Factors)

The least common multiple of 4, 8, 12, and 27 is the smallest number that is divisible by all of these numbers. To solve for this number, express the numbers in prime-power form as 2^2, 2^3, $2^2{\cdot}3$, and 3^3. The least common multiple must include all of the prime factors that appear, and it must include those primes to the highest power that each appears in the list of prime-power expressions of the numbers in the list.

To demonstrate: the prime factor 2 appears three times in the prime-power form of 8, which is 2^3; the prime factor 3 appears three times in the prime-power form of 27, which is 3^3. Those are the only prime factors that appear, and 3 is the highest power to which each prime number appears in the prime-power expression of the list of numbers. Therefore, the least common multiple must consist of 2^3 and 3^3. Finally, $2^3{\cdot}3^3 = 6^3 = 216$.

MANHATTAN
PREP

The number 216 is divisible by all of the numbers in the list, 4, 8, 12, and 27 (you can test each individually and verify this), and no smaller number is divisible by all of the numbers in this list. Therefore, 216 is the least common multiple. The correct answer is (J).

3.   (B) 75°   Plane Geometry   Polygons (Lines & Angles)

What does it mean that the angles of the given rectangle form an "arithmetic sequence with common difference 30°"? It means that when ordered from smallest to largest, each angle of the polygon increases in size by exactly 30°. Therefore, the smallest angle can be labeled as x, the next smallest as $x + 30°$, the next as $x + 30° + 30°$, and the largest as $x + 30° + 30° + 30°$. Since the angles of a 4-sided polygon sum to 360°, you can add up these terms and solve for the value of x:

$x + (x + 30°) + (x + 60°) + (x + 90°) = 360°$
$4x + 180° = 360°$
$4x = 180°$
$x = 45°$

The second smallest angle is $45° + 30° = 75°$. The correct answer is (B).

4.   (J) $\dfrac{c}{b}$ Trigonometry   Triangle Ratios

The cosine of an angle in a right triangle is the adjacent (or touching) side, divided by the hypotenuse (the longest side, shown as the diagonal in the diagram). The adjacent side to angle A is c, while the hypotenuse is b. So the cosine of A, or $\cos A$, is $\dfrac{\text{Adjacent}}{\text{Hypotenuse}} = \dfrac{c}{b}$:

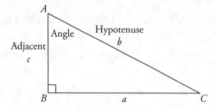

The correct answer is (J).

5.   (A) $\sqrt{181}$ Coordinate Geometry   Distance & Area

To find the distance, you can use the distance formula:

$$d = \sqrt{\left(x_2 - x_1\right)^2 + \left(y_2 - y_1\right)^2} = \sqrt{\left(-2 - 8\right)^2 + \left(-3 - 6\right)^2}$$
$$= \sqrt{\left(-10\right)^2 + \left(-9\right)^2} = \sqrt{100 + 81} = \sqrt{181}$$

Alternatively, you can graph the points and use the Pythagorean theorem, from which the distance formula is derived:

2

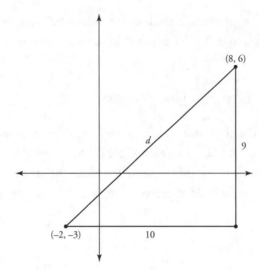

$$d^2 = (9)^2 + (10)^2 = 181, \text{ so } d = \sqrt{181}$$

The correct answer is (A).

6. **(J)** I and II only   Coordinate Geometry   Equations of Lines

From examining both the graph and the linear equation $y = -\frac{1}{2}x + 1$ (written here in $y = mx + b$ form), you can see that the slope is $-\frac{1}{2}$, which validates conclusion I. By setting the equation's y value equal to 0, you can solve for the x-intercept, which is located at (2, 0). This validates conclusion II. You can also examine the graph of the line segment to find the x-intercept.

Conclusion III, however, is incorrect. The range of the equation (for domain $2 \leq x \leq 2$) is $0 \leq y \leq 2$, inclusive. This does not include the values for $-2 \leq y < 0$, which will occur for values of x such that $2 < x \leq 6$. The correct answer is (J).

7. **(C)** $2 \cdot 3^9 + 200$ Intermediate Algebra   Formulas, Functions, Sequences

It is given in the problem that $h = 0.5$ under ideal growing conditions, and t is equal to 5, so the resulting equation is $P = \dfrac{3^{2(5)-1}}{0.5} + 200$. This equation can be simplified as follows:

$$P = \frac{3^{10-1}}{\frac{1}{2}} + 200 = (2)3^9 + 200 = 2 \cdot 3^9 + 200$$

The correct answer is (C).

8. **(G)** 3.7×10^{-5} Pre-Algebra   Fractions, Decimals, Percents (Scientific Notation)

The global probability of carrying the disorder is 3.7×10^{-8}. If in Country X the probability is 1,000 times higher than the global probability, then in Country X the probability will be $1,000 \times (3.7 \times 10^{-8})$.

MANHATTAN
PREP

Note that when you are working with scientific notation, it is best to separate the digit terms (in this case, 3.7) from the exponential terms (in other words, the powers of 10). Then, work on each piece separately and bring the results together at the end:

$$1{,}000 \times (3.7 \times 10^{-8}) = 3.7 \times (1{,}000 \times 10^{-8})$$
$$3.7 \times (1{,}000 \times 10^{-8}) = 3.7 \times (10^3 \times 10^{-8})$$
$$3.7 \times (10^3 \times 10^{-8}) = 3.7 \times 10^{(3-8)} = 3.7 \times 10^{-5}$$

In the final step, don't forget that $a^b \cdot a^c = a^{b+c}$, not a^{bc}. The correct answer is (G).

9. **(A)** $4x^2 - \dfrac{4}{3}x + \dfrac{1}{9}$ Elementary Algebra   Simple Quadratics

$\left(2x - \dfrac{1}{3}\right)^2$ can be rewritten as $\left(2x - \dfrac{1}{3}\right)\left(2x - \dfrac{1}{3}\right)$. To expand this quadratic expression, use the FOIL method (first, outer, inner, last). Use the distributive property to expand the expression and group common terms to get:

$$\left(2x - \frac{1}{3}\right)\left(2x - \frac{1}{3}\right) = (2x)(2x) - \frac{1}{3}\cdot(2x) - \frac{1}{3}\cdot(2x) + \left(\frac{1}{3}\right)^2$$
$$= 4x^2 + \left(-\frac{2}{3}x - \frac{2}{3}x\right) + \frac{1}{9}$$
$$= 4x^2 - \frac{4}{3}x + \frac{1}{9}$$

The correct answer is (A).

10. **(G)** $\sqrt{2}, \sqrt{2}, 2$ Plane Geometry   Triangles (Right Triangles)

The lengths of the sides of a 45°–45°–90° triangle will always be in the ratio $1:1:\sqrt{2}$. You can test whether this ratio holds for each answer choice by dividing each set of numbers by the smallest number in the set:

$\dfrac{1}{1}, \dfrac{1}{1}$, and $\dfrac{2}{1} = 1, 1,$ and 2 NOT in the ratio $1:1:\sqrt{2}$

$\dfrac{\sqrt{2}}{\sqrt{2}}, \dfrac{\sqrt{2}}{\sqrt{2}}$, and $\dfrac{2}{\sqrt{2}} = 1, 1,$ and $\sqrt{2}$ CORRECT: in the ratio $1:1:\sqrt{2}$

$\dfrac{2}{2}, \dfrac{2}{2}$, and $\dfrac{\sqrt{3}}{2} = 1, 1,$ and $\dfrac{\sqrt{3}}{2}$ NOT in the ratio $1:1:\sqrt{2}$

$\dfrac{1}{1}, \dfrac{\sqrt{3}}{1}$, and $\dfrac{2}{1} = 1, \sqrt{3},$ and 2 NOT in the ratio $1:1:\sqrt{2}$

$\dfrac{3}{3}, \dfrac{3}{3}$, and $\dfrac{4}{3} = 1, 1,$ and $\dfrac{4}{3}$ NOT in the ratio $1:1:\sqrt{2}$

The correct answer is therefore $\sqrt{2}, \sqrt{2},$ and 2. The correct answer is (G).

Section 3: Reading Solutions

1.   **(B)** she is overcome by her recollections.

Relationships (Cause–Effect)

The voice of the narrator's mother "trailed off *sadly*" (line 24). Even without the next paragraph, which describes the mother's photograph of her dead husband, you can conclude from the use of *sadly* that the reason is *not* that she forgets or changes her mind or is tired and hungry, as in choices (A), (C), and (D). The only reason given that really fits *sadly* is choice (B), that she is overcome by her recollections. Moreover, the verb *trailed off* does not fit with changing her mind, which would cause a more abrupt break. During the entire episode at the concrete wall, the mother was reliving the past distractedly, as she "stared" (line 13) while ignoring her daughter's questions (lines 11–15). Choice (B) is correct.

2.   **(H)** the narrator felt, rather than knew, that her father had certain traits.

Meaning of Words

Reread the entire sentence: "Like me, he laughed inappropriately and was reprimanded frequently, or so I imagined." Without the tag line *or so I imagined*, the narrator would be asserting that her father definitely laughed inappropriately and was reprimanded frequently. But she does not know these facts for sure. She only feels "connected" (line 85) to her father; she does not have any additional knowledge of his behavior. Earlier, the narrator provides another hedge: "… a sense *probably* amplified in "serious" situations…" (lines 91–92). With these phrases, the narrator acknowledges the limits of what she believes to be true. Choice (H) is correct.

3.   **(D)** the literal words that remained unknown and the joke's wry stance on life that was familiar.

Relationships (Comparisons)

Early in the second-to-last paragraph, the narrator writes "I no longer needed to know the joke; in fact, I knew that I would probably not understand it. *At the same time*, I somehow knew the joke completely." The phrase *At the same time* indicates the contrast. Before that transition, the narrator states that she did not literally know the joke; however, she then says that she "knew the joke completely." The paradox is resolved as she explains that it was the same *kind* of "ridiculous and touching" moment that made her father laugh. In other words, she and her father had similar senses of humor and a "wry stance on life," as choice (D) correctly puts it.

She does not contrast serious and less serious situations, as in choice (A). She connects the vampire rabbit and the cause of the joke in the photograph, but to point out their essential similarity, not their differences, as choice (B) incorrectly claims. Finally, the inappropriate laughter and resulting reprimands are linked by *and* in the last sentence of the paragraph, indicating a cause–effect relationship, not a contrast, as choice (C) asserts. Again, choice (D) is correct.

4.   **(F)** their ill relative.

Relationships (Cause–Effect)

The intentions of the narrator and her mother are made clear in lines 58–59: "Now we were back *to see Don Lorenzo*, my father's uncle and my oldest living relative…" The words *to see Don Lorenzo* mean that this action is the reason for their being "back" in Nicaragua.

It is strongly implied that the narrator and her mother visit the father's gravesite in lines 95 and following: "Later, we visited the cemetery… no new information about the man and his secret smile." However, this visit to the grave is not indicated as the purpose of the trip, as choice (G) incorrectly states. Along the way, the narrator and her mother encounter "landmarks of the war" (that is, bullet marks in the concrete wall), but this is never given as a reason for their return. The site of the photograph is never mentioned. Choice (F) is correct.

5.   **(D)** thirst.

Details

What the narrator felt just before examining the wall with her mother is listed explicitly in lines 25–26: "…it was as if someone else was *resentful*, someone else was hot and *tired* and *hungry*." *Tired* is an adjective synonym for the noun *exhaustion*. Thus, choices (A), (B), and (C) are all incorrect. Thirst is never mentioned, here or elsewhere. The narrator is certainly *hot*, and she repeatedly asks about rain, but the passage does not *state* that the narrator feels thirsty. Choice (D) is correct.

6.   **(G)** her mother.

Relationships (Cause–Effect)

Only two people are in the photograph, namely the father and the mother. Moreover, it is not known who took the photograph, so Uncle Carlos and Don Lorenzo, choices (H) and (J), can be ruled out. Finally, since her father is dead, the only person it would make sense for the narrator to ask is her mother, for whom "the memory would be too private" (lines 36–37). Choice (G) is correct.

7.   **(C)** It explains the sense of connection that the narrator was at last able to feel with her father through a shared characteristic.

Main Ideas/Author's Approach

The first sentence of the paragraph in question captures its purpose: "At that moment, I felt more connected to my father than ever before or since." The paragraph goes on to explain how and why that sense of connection occurred—namely, through the sense of humor that father and daughter shared. This function corresponds to choice (C).

The paragraph does not separate the passage into two parts focused on Nicaragua and the U.S., as choice (A) incorrectly asserts. Neither does the paragraph reveal the hidden source of the father's joke: the narrator says that she does not know the literal content of the joke. All she knows is that the source is "something… ridiculous and touching" (line 90). Thus, choice (B) is wrong. Finally, choice (D) is too general. The narrator is not making a statement about all jokes; rather, she uses *this* joke and *this* situation to highlight the connection between her father's sense of humor and her own. Choice (C) is correct.

2

8.   **(F)** to remind herself of her home country.

Relationships (Cause–Effect)

Since this is an EXCEPT question, the three wrong answers must be suggested in the passage. Choice (G), "to mask unpleasant odors," has a basis in line 54 (*the unpleasantly pungent station wagon*). Choice (H), "to create an American surrounding," is supported by the adjective *all-American* in line 55. Choice (J), "to provide a sense of protection," is suggested by the adverb *protectively* in line 56. All of these choices are therefore incorrect.

Only choice (F), "to remind herself of her home country," has no support in the text. In fact, the adjective *all-American* implies a contrast: this scent is *not* Nicaraguan, according to the narrator. Choice (F) is correct.

9.   **(A)** the narrator's passage from ignorance to deep knowledge of her father.

Main Ideas/Author's Approach

Early in the passage, the narrator acknowledges her ignorance about her father, "a man I had never met… My memories of him were not even my own" (lines 27–29). She had always "wondered what joke he had told" in the photograph (line 35). The epiphany or breakthrough comes toward the end of the passage, when Don Lorenzo points out that the narrator's smile is "the same as [her] father had" (line 80). She then recognizes her father in herself, in her sense of humor. Although she does not know the literal content of the joke, it no longer matters. She "felt more connected to my father than ever before or since" (line 85–86).

This transition from ignorance to knowledge is captured in choice (A). The other choices are either not central to the passage or not even mentioned. The narrator hardly struggles "to adapt to her mother's native culture"; for instance, she does not really participate in the conversation with Don Lorenzo and is soon "lost in [her] own thoughts" (lines 67–68). What minor tension there is between the narrator and her mother (the incident at the wall) is not really about the narrator's father: in fact, as soon as the narrator realizes that her mother is remembering her father, her resentment vanishes (line 25). Finally, the narrator never attempts to "separate herself from her Nicaraguan relatives" at all. Hence, choices (B), (C), and (D) are all wrong. Choice (A) is correct.

10.   **(J)** the narrator's mother is an insider, as far as Nicaraguan directions are concerned.

Generalizations

Everywhere within the passage is fair game, since the question stem is wide open. Regardless, the right answer must be 100% provable from the text, so challenge every answer choice. Was the Ixchen pharmacy definitely destroyed in the war? You know from lines 9–10 that it "used to be on that corner, where now only grass and trees grow amid the rubble." Later, the narrator's mother asks what happened to the pharmacy (line 65). However, you are never told that the pharmacy was destroyed in the war; perhaps it was demolished or fell down for some other reason. Thus, eliminate choice (F).

Moving on: do you know for sure that it had not rained for weeks before the shower at the cemetery? No. All you know is that it had not rained for some period of time (otherwise, the narrator would not ask "Does it ever rain in Nicaragua?" in line 15), but you do not know that this period of time is weeks. Cut choice (G). Next, had it definitely been too painful for the narrator's mother to return to Nicaragua before now? You don't know for sure: all you know is that "this was

[her] first trip back to the country since… the war" (lines 38–39), but you don't know the reason for the delay. So eliminate choice (H).

Finally, is the narrator's mother an insider with regard to Nicaraguan directions? Yes. Line 1 states that "My mother knew right away what the old man meant"; lines 4–5 explain that "Directions in this country are for those in the know, not for outsiders." Because the mother knew how to interpret the directions, she is "in the know" and not an "outsider"—therefore, she is an insider. Choice (J) is correct.

Section 4: Science Solutions

PASSAGE 1 SOLUTIONS

1. **(B)** 26

Scientific Investigation

Looking at Table 1, 19 bubbles were observed after 3 hours and 33 bubbles were observed after 5 hours. After 4 hours, you would expect a value somewhere between 19 and 33 bubbles. Since 26 bubbles is exactly halfway between 19 and 33, just as 4 hours is halfway between 3 and 5 hours, 26 bubbles is a more reasonable estimate than 32 (which is much closer to 33). The correct answer is (B).

2. **(F)** Yellow

Scientific Investigation

The passage states that an environment with a lower pH is more acidic, so you want to look for a solution that has the lowest pH. According to Table 2, the point at which the pH is lowest is after the first hour of the experiment, and the color of the phenol red in the solution at that time is yellow. The correct answer is (F).

3. **(C)** a salamander.

Scientific Investigation

The passage states that "most plants, algae, and cyanobacteria . . . perform photosynthesis." A salamander is an animal and would not perform photosynthesis. The correct answer is (C).

4. **(J)** Plants do not perform photosynthesis in their natural environments.

Scientific Investigation

In a natural environment, plants use natural light (not artificial) and are not confined in small containers made of glass. However, plants do perform photosynthesis in their natural environments. The correct answer is (J).

5. **(A)** All of the CO_2 had been used up, so the plant stopped performing photosynthesis.

Scientific Investigation

2

In Experiment 2, when the pH stops increasing after 7 hours, the amount of CO_2 in the environment is no longer changing, so there is evidence that photosynthesis has stopped. According to the chemical equation for photosynthesis, photosynthesis would stop if all available CO_2 or H_2O in the environment had been used up. Because the fern is sub-merged in water, H_2O would not be used up. So perhaps all of the CO_2 had been used up. The correct answer is (A).

6.   **(J)** 7.8

Scientific Investigation

In respiration, CO_2 is produced by an animal. If a fish were to replace the fern, then the fish would create CO_2, and therefore increase the acidity of the solution. If the acidity were to increase, then the pH would decrease from its level at 9 hours, which is 8.0. Among the answer choices, only 7.8 is less than 8.0. The correct answer is (J).

7.   **(A)** 10

Scientific Investigation

The reaction for photosynthesis is represented by the chemical equation given in the passage: $6\,CO_2 + 6\,H_2O \longrightarrow C_6H_{12}O_6 + 6\,O_2$. The coefficients in this equation tell you that for every 6 molecules of CO_2 and 6 molecules of H_2O that are used, 1 molecule of $C_6H_{12}O_6$ is produced. If there are 60 molecules of CO_2 and 60 molecules of H_2O, then 10 molecules of $C_6H_{12}O_6$ will be produced. The correct answer is (A).

PASSAGE 2 SOLUTIONS

8.   **(F)** Pressure

Evaluation of Models, Inferences, and Experimental Results

Toward the end of the first paragraph, Student 1 writes that "the air above exerts *less pressure* down on the wings than the air underneath exerts up on those wings." Since you are looking for a quantity that is less for the air on top, that quantity must be pressure. The correct answer is (F).

9.   **(B)** Both Student 1 and Student 2 would conclude that Plane Y was going faster.

Evaluation of Models, Inferences, and Experimental Results

Near the end of the first paragraph of each student's explanation, different reasoning is given, but the same conclusion is reached: the faster a plane is flown, the greater the lift on the wings. The correct answer is (B).

10.   **(J)** Neither Student 1 nor Student 2

Evaluation of Models, Inferences, and Experimental Results

MANHATTAN
PREP

Both students start their explanations by describing an airplane moving forward through the air. Since each explanation of lift depends on that motion, it is reasonable to conclude that neither student would predict that a *motionless* wing will experience lift. The correct answer is (J).

11.   **(B)** Student 2 only

Evaluation of Models, Inferences, and Experimental Results

In the middle of the first paragraph, Student 2 describes the holes in a cloudbank created by "the down-rushing air behind the plane." The same down-rushing air would also flatten grass. In contrast, Student 1 never mentions any such effect. The correct answer is (B).

12.   **(H)** the decreased lift force was no longer as strong as the downward force of gravity acting on the plane.

Evaluation of Models, Inferences, and Experimental Results

Student 1 states that lift force increases as the angle of attack increases from horizontal to 15 degrees. Therefore, if the angle of attack decreases from 15 degrees to horizontal, then the lift force decreases, according to Student 1. The most likely rationale, then, that Student 1 would give for the plane's descent is that this decreased lift force is no longer strong enough to overcome the downward force of gravity. The correct answer is (H).

13.   **(A)** Both students would predict that the lift force will increase at first, then decrease.

Evaluation of Models, Inferences, and Experimental Results

The students give different lines of reasoning, but in the second paragraph of both explanations, the claim is made that lift increases at first, as the angle of attack increases from horizontal to 15 degrees, then lift decreases from its peak beyond that angle. The correct answer is (A).

14.   **(H)** pushing air downward and therefore being pushed up by that air.

Evaluation of Models, Inferences, and Experimental Results

Student 2's explanation of lift is based on the idea that the wings push air downward; the air, in turn, pushes back up on the wings. Student 2 would apply the same principle to the helicopter's blades. The correct answer is (H).

Chapter 3

of

5lb. Book of ACT® Practice Problems

English:
Usage/Mechanics

In This Chapter...

Chapter 3

English: Usage/Mechanics

The English problems in this chapter test your skills in "Usage/Mechanics"—that is, in grammar. The three major subtopics in Usage/Mechanics are as follows:

1. Punctuation. Mostly commas, but also colons, semicolons, and so on.

2. Grammar & Usage. Subject–verb agreement, pronoun forms and agreement, modifier & verb forms, parallelism, comparisons, and idioms.

3. Sentence Structure. "Whole sentences" (versus fragments and run-ons), modifier placement, and verb Tense & voice.

How should you use this chapter? Here are some recommendations, according to the level you've reached in ACT English.

1. Fundamentals. It's good to start with a topically focused chapter, such as this one. Do at least some of these problems untimed. This way, you give yourself a chance to think deeply about the principles at work. Review the solutions closely, and articulate what you've learned. Redo problems as necessary.

2. Fixes. Do a few problems untimed, examine the results, learn your lessons, then test yourself with longer timed sets.

3. Tweaks. Confirm your mastery by doing longer sets of problems under timed conditions. Aim to improve the speed and ease of your solution process. Mix the problems up by jumping around in the chapter.

Good luck on the problems!

PUNCTUATION PROBLEMS

1. Although the term "hoppin' john" may not seem appetizing, the <u>dish itself</u> is quite tasty.
   A. NO CHANGE
   B. dish, itself,
   C. dish itself,
   D. dish, itself

2. To avoid the harmful effects of cold weather, every winter each <u>plant</u> according to its species and condition, is either moved indoors or pretreated against frost.
   F. NO CHANGE
   G. plant,
   H. plant;
   J. plant which,

3. The process of describing a <u>culture's development</u> seems tricky to me, because it may assume a particular idea of "progress."
   A. NO CHANGE
   B. cultures' development
   C. cultures development
   D. culture's development,

4. Fourteen-year-old Bill wanted to stay out late on Thursdays. His <u>parents argued, however</u> that an early curfew on school nights was reasonable, given the importance of his grades.
   F. NO CHANGE
   G. parents argued, however,
   H. parents, argued however,
   J. parents argued however,

5. My neighbor's oldest daughter, who had <u>been invited to study, in Mexico City for a semester,</u> had to find additional funds when her scholarship ran out early.
   A. NO CHANGE
   B. been invited to study in Mexico City for a semester
   C. been invited to study in Mexico City for a semester,
   D. been invited, to study in Mexico City for a semester,

6. The influence of classical mythology on the naming of certain chemical elements can be seen in the names <u>themselves:</u> tantalum, niobium, cadmium, and mercury.
   F. NO CHANGE
   G. themselves
   H. themselves,
   J. themselves;

7. If you consider all the objects that orbit the Sun, the bounds of the solar system <u>stretch far beyond</u> Pluto.
   A. NO CHANGE
   B. stretch far, beyond
   C. stretch, far beyond,
   D. stretch, far beyond

8. When my sister makes brownies in the kitchen, each of the <u>ingredients, in front of her sails</u> into the mixing bowl as if by magic.
   F. NO CHANGE
   G. ingredients in front of her sails,
   H. ingredients in front of her, sails
   J. ingredients in front of her sails

9. The <u>one, crucial, aspect of a good tent</u> is that it should keep you dry in a storm.
   A. NO CHANGE
   B. one crucial, aspect of a good tent
   C. one crucial aspect of a good tent,
   D. one crucial aspect of a good tent

10. Some people prefer bright yellow mustard on their hot <u>dogs; others,</u> prefer ketchup, relish, onions, or even chili.
    F. NO CHANGE
    G. dogs others
    H. dogs; others
    J. dogs, others

11. Because of <u>it's having</u> ability to absorb or reflect ultraviolet light, zinc oxide is used in many sunscreens.
    A. NO CHANGE
    B. its
    C. it's
    D. its'

12. On the first day of each month, on a large calendar in the kitchen, Janet posts the <u>month's social events,</u> day by day.
   F. NO CHANGE
   G. months social events,
   H. months social events
   J. social event's for the month,

13. The committee took a long time to evaluate the <u>benefits, and the drawbacks</u> of the first proposal.
   A. NO CHANGE
   B. benefits and, the drawbacks,
   C. benefits and the drawbacks
   D. benefits and the drawbacks,

14. Borrowing from a nearby culture, the Japanese began to use simplified forms of Chinese <u>characters, in their own syllabic alphabets,</u> *hiragana* and *katakana*.
   F. NO CHANGE
   G. characters in their own syllabic alphabets,
   H. characters, in their own syllabic alphabets
   J. characters in their own syllabic alphabets

15. Our hometown newspaper's <u>editor, and resident visionary Daniel Rivera,</u> argues that a free press is now more important than ever.
   A. NO CHANGE
   B. editor, and resident visionary Daniel Rivera
   C. editor and resident visionary Daniel Rivera,
   D. editor and resident visionary, Daniel Rivera,

16. Lucy Maud Montgomery taught in several schools on Prince Edward Island during her early adult <u>life before</u> publishing her first book, *Anne of Green Gables.*
   F. NO CHANGE
   G. life, before,
   H. life before,
   J. life; before

17. Dissatisfaction with standard Igbo led Achebe to use English to <u>write</u> *Things Fall Apart* and its less famous sequel, *No Longer at Ease.*
   A. NO CHANGE
   B. write:
   C. write;
   D. write,

18. <u>Cities</u> typical attempts to deal with increased traffic by building highways only worsens the problem, as more and more cars from far-flung suburbs populate the streets.
   F. NO CHANGE
   G. City's
   H. Citys
   J. Cities'

19. Among the honorees at the club's annual awards <u>banquet, will be</u> those who are unable to attend because of old age or illness.
   A. NO CHANGE
   B. banquet; will be
   C. banquet will be
   D. banquet will be:

20. My uncle comes from <u>Malta a small Mediterranean island nation,</u> with historical ties not only to the rest of Europe but also to Africa and the Middle East.
   F. NO CHANGE
   G. Malta, a small Mediterranean island, nation
   H. Malta, a small Mediterranean island nation
   J. Malta; a small Mediterranean island nation

21. Several months <u>ago, her husband David,</u> decided to go back to graduate school for a master's degree in journalism.
   A. NO CHANGE
   B. ago, her husband, David,
   C. ago, her husband, David
   D. ago her husband David,

22. Nevertheless, if a nuclear reactor's core heats up too <u>much. It</u> could experience a meltdown and break through the containment barriers.

    F. NO CHANGE
    G. much; it
    H. much and it
    J. much, it

23. Within their community, a new <u>hope arose; based on</u> renewed trust and a shared sense of responsibility for the mistakes of the past.

    A. NO CHANGE
    B. hope arose based on
    C. hope arose based on,
    D. hope, arose based on

24. All metals share certain characteristics. Not every <u>metal though,</u> is a hard, shiny solid at room temperature.

    F. NO CHANGE
    G. metal; though,
    H. metal, though
    J. metal, though,

25. In 1981, <u>designer and artist</u> Maya Lin won the public competition to design the national Vietnam Veterans Memorial when she was only 21 years old.

    A. NO CHANGE
    B. designer, and artist
    C. designer and artist,
    D. designer, and artist,

Punctuation Answer Key

Write in whether you got each problem right or wrong (or left it blank). If your answer was correct, put a 1 in every blank to the right of that problem. Many problems test more than one type of punctuation. Sum up each column and compare your total to the total possible "Out Of" points in each column.

Problem	Correct Answer	Right/Wrong/ Blank	Commas	Apostrophes	Semicolons	Colons	Periods
1	A		—				
2	G		—		—		
3	A		—	—			
4	G		—				
5	C		—				
6	F		—		—	—	
7	A		—				
8	J		—				
9	D		—				
10	H		—		—		
11	B			—			
12	F			—			
13	C		—				
14	G		—				
15	D		—				
16	F		—		—		
17	A		—		—	—	
18	J			—			
19	C		—		—	—	
20	H		—		—		
21	B		—				
22	J		—		—		—
23	B		—		—		
24	J		—		—		
25	A		—				
Total							
Out Of		25	22	4	10	3	1

3

Punctuation Solutions

1.   **(A)** … the <u>dish itself</u> is quite tasty.

Commas

Don't place a comma between the subject (*dish*) and the verb (*is*). Moreover, when you have a "-self" pronoun right after a noun to single out that noun (*the dish itself, the Queen herself, the people themselves*), don't place commas around the pronoun. The correct answer is (A).

2.   **(G)** … each <u>plant,</u> according to its species and condition, is …

Commas, Semicolons

You need to have commas on both sides of the interrupting phrase *according to its species and condition*. Stylistically, this phrase would probably be better at the end of the sentence, removing the interruption between *each plant* and *is*, but you don't have that choice. The correct answer is (G).

3.   **(A)** The process of describing a <u>culture's development</u> seems tricky …

Apostrophes, Commas

The phrase in question means "the development of a [single] culture." The word *culture* is singular, so when you put it in front of *development*, you must add an *'s*: *culture's development*. Don't place a comma after that phrase, because you don't need a comma between subject and verb. The correct answer is (A).

4.   **(G)** His <u>parents argued, however,</u> that …

Commas

To create a contrast with the previous sentence, you can use the word *however* (or similar transitions). If you place that transition in the middle of your new sentence, put commas on both sides of the transition. These commas indicate the break or change in tone you would put in speech. The correct answer is (G).

5.   **(C)** My neighbor's oldest daughter, who had <u>been invited to study in Mexico City for a semester,</u> had to …

Commas

The whole modifier *who had been invited to study in Mexico City for a semester* should be set off by commas on both ends, because it is not needed to identify *my neighbor's oldest daughter*. Notice that you don't have a choice about the first comma, so you definitely need the second. No commas should be inserted within this modifier, however, since there would be none inserted in a similar stand-alone sentence: *She had been invited to study in Mexico City for a semester.* The correct answer is (C).

3

6.   **(F)** The influence … can be seen in the names <u>themselves:</u> tantalum, niobium …

Colons, Commas, Semicolons

If you want to list the specific examples of *the names themselves* (or of any other noun phrase), use a colon (:) after the noun phrase to introduce the list. The colon acts like the word "namely." What comes after the colon explains what comes before the colon. The correct answer is (F).

7.   **(A)** … the bounds of the solar system <u>stretch far beyond</u> Pluto.

Commas

The original form with no commas is correct. How far do these bounds *stretch? Beyond Pluto.* To what degree beyond Pluto? *Far beyond Pluto.* Inserting a comma between *far* and *beyond,* as in choice (B), is theoretically possible, but doing so is both unnatural and subtly different in meaning from the original: the bounds *stretch far* … And where is far? *Beyond Pluto.* It's even less natural to pause after *stretch,* as in choice (D). The correct answer is (A).

8.   **(J)**   each of the <u>ingredients in front of her sails</u> into the mixing bowl …

Commas

No commas should be used anywhere here. Which *ingredients?* The ones *in front of her.* You need to identify which ingredients, so do not insert a comma between *ingredients* and *in.* Moreover, no comma should go between the subject phrase (*each of the ingredients in front of her*) and the verb (*sails*), because you do not separate the subject from the verb by a comma. Finally, you must indicate where each ingredient *sails* (namely, *into the mixing bowl*), so don't use a comma after *sails* either. The correct answer is (J).

9.   **(D)** The <u>one crucial aspect of a good tent</u> is that …

Commas

Leave out all commas from the underlined portion. Do not put a comma between *one* and *crucial,* because you are counting *crucial aspects* (there's only *one* of them), not all aspects. Never put a comma between an adjective (*crucial*) and a noun immediately following (*aspect*). Finally, do not put a comma after *tent,* because you should not separate the subject phrase (*the one crucial aspect of a good tent*) from the verb (*is*) with a comma. The correct answer is (D).

10.   **(H)** Some people prefer bright yellow mustard on their hot <u>dogs; others</u> prefer ketchup …

Semicolons, Commas

The part before the semicolon can stand alone as a complete sentence (*Some people prefer bright yellow mustard on their hot dogs*). Likewise, the part *after* the semicolon can stand alone (*Others prefer ketchup, etc.*). So the semicolon is correctly used. You cannot use a comma by itself, as in choice (J). Furthermore, you should not place a comma after *others* (the subject of the "sentence" after the semicolon), separating it from its verb (*prefer*). The correct answer is (H).

11.   **(B)** Because of <u>its</u> ability to absorb …

Apostrophes

The form *its* (without an apostrophe) is the correct possessive. The contraction *it's* is never possessive: it always means *it is*. Before using *it's*, check whether *it is* would make sense. There is no form *its'* that ends in an apostrophe. Choice (A) also contains a redundant *having*, which should be eliminated (*its* indicates possession just fine by itself). The correct answer is (B).

12.   **(F)** … Janet posts the <u>month's social events,</u> day by day.

Apostrophes

The word *month* must be followed by an *'s* (not a plain *s*) to indicate that the month "possesses" the social events. Do not use *'s* to indicate plurals, however. The word *events* is plural and is correctly written without an apostrophe. Finally, a comma correctly follows *events* to separate the extra phrase *day by day*. The correct answer is (F).

13.   **(C)** … to evaluate the <u>benefits and the drawbacks</u> of the proposal.

Commas

In a list of two items, don't use commas. What did the committee evaluate? Two things: *the benefits and the drawbacks*. Moreover, don't put a comma after *drawbacks*. The benefits and the drawbacks of what? *Of the first proposal*. This prepositional phrase is required to tell you which benefits and drawbacks, so don't separate that phrase with a comma. The correct answer is (C).

14.   **(G)** … use simplified forms of Chinese <u>characters in their own syllabic alphabets,</u> *hiragana* and *katakana*.

Commas

No comma should go between *characters* and *in*, because you need to specify where the Japanese used these characters (namely, *in their own syllabic alphabets*). However, you do need a comma after *alphabets*, because the two additional terms (*hiragana and katakana*) just provide extra information—the names of these alphabets. You could omit these terms and have a complete, sensible sentence. Most appositive phrases, such as this one, are non-essential and so should be set off by commas. The correct answer is (G).

15.   **(D)** Our hometown newspaper's <u>editor and resident visionary, Daniel Rivera,</u> argues that …

Commas

Don't put commas within a two-item list, such as *editor and resident visionary*. However, place the personal name in commas, because the name (*Daniel Rivera*) is a non-essential piece of information. You could leave out this name and have a fine sentence (*Our hometown newspaper's editor and resident visionary argues that …*). Most appositive phrases (such as *Daniel Rivera* in this case) are surrounded by commas, because they can be omitted without causing the sentence to break down. The correct answer is (D).

3

16.   **(F)** Lucy Maud Montgomery taught in several schools on Prince Edward Island during her early adult <u>life before</u> publishing her first book ...

Commas, Semicolons

No punctuation at all should be used in the underlined portion. *She taught in X on Y during Z before doing W.* Each of these prepositional phrases (*in ... on ... during ... before ...*) serves an essential purpose in the sentence, so don't separate any of them with a comma—or with a semicolon, as is the case in choice (J). Moreover, never put a comma between a preposition (*before*) and its object (*publishing*), as choice (H) incorrectly does. The correct answer is (F).

17.   **(A)** Dissatisfaction ... led Achebe to use English to <u>write</u> *Things Fall Apart* and its less famous sequel ...

Commas, Semicolons, Colons

Use no punctuation between a verb (*write*) and its object (*Things Fall Apart*). This italicized phrase is the title of a literary work. When used by themselves in a sentence, titles require no special punctuation. The correct answer is (A).

18.   **(J)** <u>Cities'</u> typical attempts to deal with increased traffic ...

Apostrophes

The subject could be reworded as *The typical attempts of cities.* Since *cities* is plural, to make the word possessive and place it in front of *typical attempts,* you add an apostrophe *after* the plural *-s* of *cities* to make *Cities' typical attempts ...* This possessive apostrophe, although not pronounced, is required in writing. The singular form *City's* doesn't work, because you would need an article in front (*A city's* or *The city's*). The correct answer is (J).

19.   **(C)** Among the honorees at the club's annual awards <u>banquet will be</u> those who are unable to attend ...

Commas, Semicolons, Colons

No punctuation should be used in the underlined portion. The reason may be easier to see if you flip the sentence around, putting the subject before the verb: *Those who are unable to attend because of old age or illness will be among the honorees at the club's annual awards banquet.* In both versions of the sentence, you don't use any comma, colon, or semicolon to separate the subject (*those ...*) from the verb (*will be*) or the verb from the prepositional phrase *among the honorees ...* The correct answer is (C).

20.   **(H)** My uncle comes from <u>Malta, a small Mediterranean island nation</u> with historical ties ...

Commas, Semicolons

The word *Malta* is the name of a place: *My uncle comes from Malta.* This place is then described with a long appositive phrase (*a small Mediterranean island nation with historical ties ...*). That phrase should be separated from *Malta* by a comma, as most appositives are, but not by a semicolon. Within the phrase itself, no commas are necessary. Certainly no comma should come between *island* and *nation*, because *island* is acting as an adjective for the noun *nation*. A comma after *nation* and before *with* is possible but not required. The correct answer is (H).

21. **(B)** Several months <u>ago, her husband, David,</u> decided to go back to graduate school …

Commas

You need several commas in this sentence. First, you need to separate the introductory phrase (*Several months ago*) from the subject (*her husband*). Next, you need to surround the name *David* with commas on both sides. Some grammarians feel that this pair of commas isn't necessary, but regardless, you cannot keep one of the two commas and leave out the other, as choices (A) and (C) do. The correct answer is (B).

22. **(J)** Nevertheless, if a nuclear reactor's core heats up too <u>much, it</u> could experience a meltdown …

Commas, Semicolons, Periods

As written, the first sentence (up to *much*) is a fragment. An *if* statement by itself is a dependent clause. To have a complete thought, you have to join that *if* clause to the second sentence using a comma (not an *and* or a semicolon). *If X happens, Y could happen.* The correct answer is (J).

23. **(B)** Within their community, a new <u>hope arose based on</u> renewed trust and …

Commas, Semicolons

The best choice of those available is the one with no punctuation. The phrase beginning with *based on* modifies *a new hope*. Do not use a semicolon to punctuate a modifier, as choice (A) does; only use a comma or nothing at all. Moreover, no comma should interrupt the flow from subject (*hope*) to verb (*arose*) or from preposition (*on*) to object (*renewed trust …*). These commas make choices (C) and (D) wrong. The correct answer is (B).

24. **(J)** Not every <u>metal, though,</u> is a hard, shiny solid …

Commas, Semicolons

When you use *though* in the middle of a sentence to emphasize a contrast with the previous sentence, put commas on both sides of the *though*. This principle also applies to *however, on the other hand,* and other contrastive words and phrases. The correct answer is (J).

25. **(A)** In 1981, <u>designer and artist</u> Maya Lin won the public competition …

Commas

When you place a role or roles (such as *designer and artist*) with no article before someone's name, don't put any commas around the role or roles. Think of these roles as adjectives before the name. This technique is common in newspaper writing. *Designer Maya Lin won the competition.* If you use *the*, the same rule applies, as long as the name is essential to the meaning of the sentence. *The designer Maya Lin won the competition.* If you use *a*, you will need to rephrase: *A designer named Maya Lin won.* Finally, do not interrupt a two-item list (*designer and artist*) with a comma. The correct answer is (A).

3

GRAMMAR & USAGE PROBLEMS

26. After a short illness, Marta was again back in the office, <u>she worked</u> 12-hour shifts without a break.
    - F. NO CHANGE
    - G. to work
    - H. working
    - J. and while working

27. Upon arriving at the site, members of the construction crew shout slightly off-color comments to each other while making silly gestures, <u>slap</u> one another on the back, and grabbing food from anyone too slow to defend it.
    - A. NO CHANGE
    - B. slapping
    - C. slapped
    - D. they slap

28. In many cases, targeted pesticides can be applied that <u>homes in on and then neutralizes</u> the reproductive capacity of rootworms.
    - F. NO CHANGE
    - G. home in on and neutralizes
    - H. homes in on and neutralizes
    - J. home in on and neutralize

29. Above <u>their doorway theirs</u> a sign that says "Welcome" in five languages.
    - A. NO CHANGE
    - B. the doorway their is
    - C. they're doorway that's
    - D. that doorway there's

30. If Paolo wants to succeed in chemistry, he <u>had start to work better and</u> more diligently.
    - F. NO CHANGE
    - G. had start better to work
    - H. had better start to work
    - J. better had start to work

31. As soon as the other candidates dropped out of the race, Alison became the <u>presumptuously</u> nominee.
    - A. NO CHANGE
    - B. presumptively
    - C. presumptive
    - D. presume

32. Over time, several alchemists took a new approach to their work, abandoning mysticism, adopting clarity and rigor, concentrating on repeatable experiments based in the scientific method, and sharing their results openly with other investigators who had also left medievalism behind. <u>It was now truly chemistry and</u> became a dominant strand of modern science.
    - F. NO CHANGE
    - G. This approach, now truly chemistry,
    - H. Now truly being chemistry, it
    - J. It being now truly chemistry

33. The Green Revolution also modernized agricultural <u>practices, around the world,</u> provided a template for applying academic knowledge to real-life problems.
    - A. NO CHANGE
    - B. practices around the world and
    - C. practices around the world
    - D. practices, around the world, it

34. Before the grand reopening, Lee had assumed that the restaurant would be much more impressive than it actually was and that the new owners <u>would of</u> taken more care in their renovations.
    - F. NO CHANGE
    - G. would have
    - H. would of been
    - J. DELETE the underlined portion

35. We asked the manufacturer to support its assertion <u>that</u> its rugs were essentially impervious to stains.
    - A. NO CHANGE
    - B. which
    - C. in which
    - D. where

36. The potential issues with the nation's infrastructure are <u>more concerning than</u> ever before.
    - F. NO CHANGE
    - G. the most concerning than
    - H. of more concern then
    - J. more concerning then

MANHATTAN
PREP

37. Even before her fever broke, Jessica's illness <u>had in essence ran</u> its course.

   A. NO CHANGE
   B. have essentially ran
   C. would in essence of run
   D. had essentially run

38. Once the new wooden furniture has been unloaded, I will <u>rearrange it</u> into subgroups by type and destination.

   F. NO CHANGE
   G. will rearrange them
   H. rearranged them
   J. rearranged those

39. Neurotransmitters are chemicals that have a powerful <u>affect on</u> the way our brains work.

   A. NO CHANGE
   B. affect in
   C. effect of
   D. effect on

40. There has never been a period in history during which wars could have been avoided entirely and <u>only peaceful activities pursued</u> everywhere.

   F. NO CHANGE
   G. only there were peaceful activities pursued then
   H. peaceful activities were pursued only at that time
   J. the pursuit of only peaceful activities

41. <u>One of the catchiest</u> advertising slogans of all time, in my opinion, is Taco Bell's "Think Outside the Bun."

   A. NO CHANGE
   B. One of the most catchiest
   C. The most catchy
   D. The catchiest

42. The geographic area that may benefit most from the action of the Gulf Stream is northern Europe, <u>in which</u> water heated by the Caribbean sun travels in a strong current from the Gulf of Mexico, keeping the coastline of Norway nearly 100% ice-free.

   F. NO CHANGE
   G. from which
   H. when
   J. to which

43. Javier thought about his father and his uncle in the workshop, each carefully constructing his own tackle box out of polished hardwoods over the course of many weeks, each drawing deeply on his knowledge both of carpentry and of fishing. <u>That box</u> represented skill and care.

   A. NO CHANGE
   B. This box
   C. His boxes
   D. Those boxes

44. Photons are in a class of particles called bosons, named for physicist Satyendra Bose, which under appropriate conditions <u>actually occupies</u> the same quantum state as each other, as if they were mysteriously in the same place at the same time.

   F. NO CHANGE
   G. has actual ability to occupy
   H. can actually occupy
   J. is able to actually occupy

45. According to some neurologists, speech problems later in life can stem <u>as</u> hearing impediments in early childhood that hinder the development of auditory processing pathways in the brain.

   A. NO CHANGE
   B. from
   C. of
   D. on

46. Ask ten people what their favorite ice-cream flavor is, and you'll hear twelve different replies. <u>There is</u> the addict who swears by nothing but pure chocolate, unadulterated by nuts or marshmallows, to the adventurer who craves butter-pecan-bacon-peanut-butter-swirl, lovers of ice cream come in all shapes, sizes, and opinions.

   F. NO CHANGE
   G. Given
   H. From
   J. With

47. Graphene is a novel form of carbon <u>who's</u> incredible strength derives from the "chicken wire" lattice of tough covalent bonds linking every atom together into a thin sheet.

    A. NO CHANGE
    B. whose
    C. of which its
    D. that's

48. Whenever you convert a photographic image from one file format to another, some portion of the information is usually lost, and <u>you must consider</u> whether the lower resolution is acceptable.

    F. NO CHANGE
    G. you needed to consider
    H. one must consider
    J. one need consider

49. In their single-minded quest for sudden wealth, these particular wildcatters have forsaken practically every other activity, driven their families and friends to near madness, and <u>breaking</u> local, state, and federal laws restricting drilling on public lands.

    A. NO CHANGE
    B. they broke
    C. even break
    D. even broken

50. Obsessed with birds of prey, the mayor believed that a new falconry center just outside of town would boost both tourism and <u>its</u> chances for re-election.

    F. NO CHANGE
    G. it's
    H. his
    J. their

51. Winter fell early that year. After the third week of November, the shipping lanes <u>had froze</u> over, and the final shipments were rerouted onto freight trains traveling overland.

    A. NO CHANGE
    B. frozen
    C. froze
    D. freeze

52. Living in what is now Mongolia and northern China, the Khitan were a nomadic people who had developed an impressive ability <u>for surviving</u> in the semi-arid steppe.

    F. NO CHANGE
    G. surviving
    H. to survive
    J. of surviving

53. One of the most influential figures in the history of blues music was McKinley Morganfield, <u>who</u> was nicknamed "Muddy" by his grandmother and later became known as Muddy Waters.

    A. NO CHANGE
    B. he who
    C. whom
    D. which

54. Certain apes called gibbons resemble monkeys more than other apes do, at least in behavior. <u>Gibbons brachiate, or swing by their arms,</u> to travel quickly through trees, obtain otherwise inaccessible food sources for themselves and their young, and avoid predators.

    F. NO CHANGE
    G. Brachiation, which is also known as arm-swinging, is employed
    H. Brachiation, otherwise known as arm-swinging, is used
    J. Brachiation, or arm-swinging, is a way

55. According to geologists, a fossil fuel deposit of truly game-changing size—whether a giant pocket of natural gas trapped within a shale formation or an enormous reservoir of crude oil deep beneath the ocean waves—<u>have</u> become increasingly difficult to discover, if any even still exist.

    A. NO CHANGE
    B. are
    C. has
    D. OMIT the underlined portion

Grammar & Usage Answer Key

Write in whether you got each problem right or wrong (or left it blank). If your answer was correct, put a 1 in every blank to the right of that problem. A few problems test more than one type of grammar issue. Sum up each column and compare your total to the total possible "Out Of" points in each column.

Problem	Correct Answer	Right/ Wrong/ Blank	Comparisons	Idioms	Modifier Forms	Parallelism	Pronouns	Subject–Verb Agreement	Verb Forms
26	H				—				
27	B					—			
28	J							—	
29	D						—		
30	H			—					
31	C				—				
32	G						—		
33	B					—			
34	G								—
35	A				—				
36	F		—						
37	D								—
38	F						—		
39	D			—					
40	F					—			
41	A							—	
42	J				—				
43	D						—		
44	H							—	
45	B			—					
46	H					—			
47	B				—				
48	F						—		—
49	D					—			—
50	H						—		

(continued)

3

Problem	Correct Answer	Right/ Wrong/ Blank	Comparisons	Idioms	Modifier Forms	Parallelism	Pronouns	Subject–Verb Agreement	Verb Forms
51	C								—
52	H			—					
53	A				—				
54	F						—		
55	C							—	
Total									
Out Of		30	1	4	6	5	7	4	5

Grammar & Usage Solutions

26. **(H)** … Marta was again back in the office, <u>working</u> 12-hour shifts …

Modifier Forms

The underlined portion answers the question "What was Marta doing when she *was again back in the office?*" The *-ing* form *working* is appropriate in this case. The words *she worked* are a new subject and a new verb, so they cannot be glued on as a second sentence with simply a comma to the first sentence. The infinitive *to work* does not fit, because *to work* implies that her purpose was to work those shifts without a break (and an infinitive of purpose should not be placed after a comma). *And while working* creates a list of two actions that are not parallel (*was* and *while working*). The correct answer is (H).

27. **(B)** … members … shout … while making silly gestures, <u>slapping</u> one another on the back, and grabbing food …

Parallelism

An "X, Y, and Z" list of three parallel actions follows the word *while*: *making, slapping,* and *grabbing.* The two end items are fixed (*making* and *grabbing*), so the middle item must also be an *-ing* form. The correct answer is (B).

28. **(J)** … targeted pesticides can be applied that <u>home in on and neutralize</u> the reproductive capacity …

Subject–Verb Agreement

The subject of the verbs *home in on* and *neutralize* is *targeted pesticides*, which is a plural noun. Thus, the verbs must both take a plural form as well. Ignore the intervening verb *can be applied*; the sentence is written this way to distract you. The correct answer is (J).

29. **(D)** Above <u>that doorway there's</u> a sign …

Pronoun Forms

Before the word *doorway*, many choices are possible, including *their* ("belonging to them"), *the*, or *that*. However, you can't use *they're*, which means *they are*. Before the words *a sign*, to indicate the existence of this sign, you can write *there is* or *there's*. You can't write, however, *theirs* ("belonging to them") or *their is*. The correct answer is (D).

30. **(H)** If Paolo wants …, he <u>had better start to work</u> more diligently.

Idioms

The idiom *had better* is fixed; it is followed by the bare infinitive form of the verb to indicate a strong recommendation: *you had better be here on time.* The word *better* cannot be placed in any position other than directly after *had*. That's just the way this idiom works. The correct answer is (H).

3

31. **(C)** … Alison became the <u>presumptive</u> nominee.

Modifier Forms

To get this problem right, you don't even have to know the exact definitions of *presumptuous* (= arrogant) or *presumptive* (= probable, presumed). You just need to recognize that the *-ly* ending on those words turns them from adjectives into adverbs, and adverbs can never modify nouns such as *nominee*. Moreover, *presume* is a verb form that can't work as an adjective as is. So the only possibility is *presumptive*. The correct answer is (C).

32. **(G)** … <u>This approach, now truly chemistry,</u> became a dominant strand of modern science.

Pronouns

The three wrong answers all suffer from the same problem: the pronoun *it* does not have a clear antecedent (= noun it refers to) in the previous sentence. The intended antecedent, *a new approach*, is so far away that other possible nouns in between confuse the reader. Does *it* refer to *medievalism*, the closest noun, or *the scientific method*, etc.? It is clearly better to repeat the noun *approach* in the underlined portion. The wrong answers also suffer from wordiness (*being* is unnecessary here) and from loose assembly of ideas (*it was now truly chemistry and became* … connects the two ideas with *and*, but the second idea can be stressed better if you put the first idea into an appositive phrase, as in the correct answer). The correct answer is (G).

33. **(B)** The Green Revolution also modernized agricultural <u>practices around the world and</u> provided a template

Parallelism

The sentence contains two verbs that should be in parallel: *modernized* and *provided*. This list of two items needs to follow the "X and Y" pattern. There should be an *and* between the two items, but no unnecessary commas. For instance, the phrase *around the world* ought to be joined to the first thought without commas. The correct answer is (B).

34. **(G)** Lee had assumed … that the new owners <u>would have</u> taken more care …

Verb Forms

It is never correct to write *would of*. Always use *would have* instead. The sentence must contain *would have taken* rather than *taken* by itself, since you need a full verb here. *The new owners taken more care* is not a complete thought. The correct answer is (G).

35. **(A)** … its assertion <u>that</u> its rugs were essentially impervious …

Modifier Forms

When you want to indicate the content of an *assertion*, a *report*, or anything similar, use *that*. You would also use *that* after the verb forms: *the manufacturer asserted that its rugs were impervious* … *the spokesperson reported that the threat was over.* Rewritten with *report* as a noun, the second example might be this: *the spokesperson released a report that the threat was over.* In these situations, do not use *which, in which, where,* or any other relative pronoun. The correct answer is (A).

MANHATTAN
PREP

36.   **(F)** The potential issues … are <u>more concerning than</u> ever before.

Comparisons

In a comparison, never use *then*; always use *than* instead. *This is better than that.* When you are comparing two things, as in the given sentence, use *-er, more, less,* and so on. Only use *-est* or *-st, most,* and *least* when you are comparing three or more things, and never use these forms together with *than.* Instead, use *of.* Example: *Of all the issues we considered, this one is the most concerning.* The correct answer is (F).

37.   **(D)** Even before her fever broke, Jessica's illness <u>had essentially run</u> its course.

Verb Forms

The past tense of *run* is *ran*; it cannot be used with *have, has,* or *had.* With the *have* verbs, use *run: The illness had run its course.* Never write *would of* (the correct form is *would have*). Either *essentially* or *in essence* can be used in this circumstance. Finally, *have* is wrong because it would only agree with a plural subject, but *illness* is singular. *Had run* is the correct form of the past-perfect tense, which places this action even further in the past, before the breaking of the fever. The correct answer is (D).

38.   **(F)** Once the new wooden furniture has been unloaded, I <u>will rearrange it</u> into subgroups …

Pronouns

Furniture is a singular noun, whether the furniture consists of one piece or several pieces. So you should use a singular pronoun such as *it* (not *them* or *those*) to refer to *furniture.* The pronoun issue is sufficient to solve the problem, but as an additional point, the verb *rearrange* should not be in past tense (*rearranged*), because the other verb in the sentence is in present perfect tense (*has been unloaded*), which is really a tense about the current (or possibly future) state of affairs. Thus, the main verb *rearrange* should either be in present tense (if these actions take place repeatedly) or in future tense (*will rearrange*) to indicate a single set of actions in the future ("The furniture is coming tomorrow. Once it has been unloaded, I will rearrange it."). The correct answer is (F).

39.   **(D)** Neurotransmitters … have a powerful <u>effect on</u> the way our brains work.

Idioms (also Word Choice in Rhetorical Skills)

Affect and *effect* are easy to mix up. Here's a good rule of thumb: to *affect* something is to *have an effect on* that thing. If X *affects* Y, then X has an *effect* (= influence) on Y. *Affect* is more commonly used as a verb, while *effect* is more commonly used as a noun. (You *can* use *affect* as a noun to mean "a fake feeling, for show," and you *can* use *effect* as a verb to mean "bring about, cause to happen," but these meanings are less common.)

After *effect,* use the preposition *on* to indicate the thing that is affected. *Effect of* has a different meaning: *the effect of* X *on* Y means that X is affecting Y. Since the neurotransmitters affect the way the brain works, according to the sentence, use *on.* The correct answer is (D).

3

40. **(F)** There has never been a period in history during which wars could have been avoided entirely and <u>only peaceful activities pursued</u> everywhere.

Parallelism

The original sentence pulls an interesting trick. The sentence starts with *There has never been a period in history during which …*, and now two actions are placed in parallel: *wars could have been avoided entirely* and *only peaceful activities [could have been] pursued everywhere*. The second action leaves out the helping verbs *could have been*, which are implied by the parallel structure. This omission is very formal and literary, but it is perfectly legal. The wrong answers break the parallelism (*were pursued* has a different meaning than *could have been pursued* does). Moreover, *only* belongs in front of *peaceful* to modify just that word; be careful when *only* floats around the sentence. The correct answer is (F).

41. **(A)** <u>One of the catchiest</u> advertising slogans … is Taco Bell's "Think Outside the Bun."

Subject–Verb Agreement

The verb in this sentence is *is,* which is singular. Thus, the subject must be singular as well. *One of the slogans* is singular, but *slogans* itself is plural, so you have to keep the *One of* at the beginning of the sentence. Next, you can argue about whether *catchiest* or *most catchy* is better (*catchiest* is actually preferred), but you should never double down with *most catchiest*. Every adjective takes just one superlative form (*most* or *-est*), not both. The same is true for *more* and *-er:* no matter what, only use one or the other. The correct answer is (A).

42. **(J)** The geographic area … is northern Europe, <u>to which</u> water heated by the Caribbean sun travels in a strong current from the Gulf of Mexico …

Modifier Forms

To make the right decision about the modifier form, make the second part of the sentence stand alone and insert *northern Europe*:

Water heated by the Caribbean sun travels in a strong current from the Gulf of Mexico _____ northern Europe.

What preposition should go in the blank? *To* or *toward,* since northern Europe is the destination of the water. The prepositions *in* and *from* do not fit, and *when* is only appropriate if attached to a time period, not a place. The correct answer is (J).

43. **(D)** Javier thought about his father and his uncle in the workshop, each carefully constructing his own tackle box … <u>Those boxes</u> represented skill and care.

Pronouns

The key here is to recognize that there is more than one tackle box. Two people (Javier's father and Javier's uncle) each was constructing a box, so there are two boxes. Simply writing *That box* or *This box* leaves the reference ambiguous: whose box are you talking about? Moreover, *His boxes* acknowledges the plurality of the boxes, but leaves ambiguous the antecedent of *His*—father or uncle?—and also fails to recognize that there are two people. The right answer simply points out the boxes: *Those boxes*. It would also be correct to write *These boxes* or *Their boxes*. The correct answer is (D).

MANHATTAN
PREP

44. (H) Photons are … bosons, … which under appropriate conditions <u>can actually occupy</u> the same quantum state as each other …

Subject–Verb Agreement

The plural noun *bosons* is the logical subject of the clause beginning with *which*. Moreover, the phrase *each other* reinforces that the subject is plural. So the verb in this clause must be plural, rather than singular. This result knocks out every wrong answer: *occupies, has,* and *is* are all singular. *Can occupy* can be either singular or plural (the helping verbs *can, may, must,* etc. do not have different singular and plural forms), so it works with *bosons*. The correct answer is (H).

45. (B) … speech problems later in life can stem <u>from</u> hearing impediments in early childhood …

Idioms

The verb *stem* can only be followed by the preposition *from*. An effect *stems from* a cause. This use is the correct one in this situation (the problems later in life *can stem from* impediments in early childhood). *Stem as, stem of,* and *stem on* are all idiomatically incorrect. The correct answer is (B).

46. (H) <u>From</u> the addict … to the adventurer …, lovers of ice cream come in all shapes …

Parallelism

In such a long sentence, it can be easy to miss the parallel structure. The pattern is *From [this person] to [that person]*; it's used here to show the range of *lovers of ice cream*. The *to*, which is not underlined, forces the underlined portion to be *From*. The correct answer is (H).

47. (B) Graphene is a novel form of carbon <u>whose</u> incredible strength derives from …

Modifier Forms

You can use *whose* after any noun or noun phrase (including non-persons such as *carbon* or *form of carbon*) to indicate something that the noun possesses. *Graphene is a novel form of carbon + The incredible strength of this form of carbon derives from … = Graphene is a novel form of carbon whose incredible strength …*

The contraction *who's* means *who is*; the contraction *that's* means *that is*. Neither is appropriate here. *Of which its* doesn't make sense when inserted. You could correctly write *Graphene is a novel form of carbon, the incredible strength of which derives from …,* but you have to insert a comma, place the phrase *of which* after *strength*, and use *the*, not *its*. The correct answer is (B).

48. (F) Whenever you convert … some portion … is usually lost, and <u>you must consider</u> …

Pronouns (also Verb Tenses, placed here under Verb Forms)

In generalizations, be consistent in your use of pronouns. If you start by using *you*, as in the sentence above, stick with *you* all the way through. Don't switch to *one*.

To decide between the remaining answer choices (which both have *you*), keep the verb tense consistent. The other verbs in the sentence (*convert, is lost*) are both in the present tense, and there is no reason to switch to past tense (*needed*). The present tense phrase *must consider* is appropriate. The correct answer is (F).

49.   **(D)** … these particular wildcatters have forsaken …, driven …, and <u>even broken</u> local, state, and federal laws …

Parallelism (and Verb Tenses)

The wildcatters have done three things in the sentence. They *have forsaken, [have] driven,* and *[have] broken. The have* is implied in the second and third actions. The three past participles (*forsaken, driven,* and *broken*) are parallel to one another; with the *have* in front, all three actions are in present perfect tense (*have done*). None of the wrong answer choices fit in this list of three parallel actions. *Breaking* is just an *-ing* form, not a full tense; *broke* is past tense; *break* is present tense. The correct answer is (D).

50.   **(H)** … the mayor believed that a new falconry center … would boost both tourism and <u>his</u> chances for re-election.

Pronouns

The question you should immediately ask is this: *Whose chances for re-election?* Logically, the only noun in the sentence that can be re-elected is the mayor, who is a singular person. Thus, either *her* or *his* could work; only *his* is available. *Their* requires a plural noun to refer to, and *its* can only refer to a non-person. *It's* means *it is* and is actually not a possessive form. The correct answer is (H).

51.   **(C)** … the shipping lanes <u>froze</u> over, and the final shipments were rerouted …

Verb Forms

The plain past tense form *froze* is the correct choice, because it matches the past tense of *were rerouted.* The phrase *had froze* is never correct: the helping verb *had* must be followed by past participles (which, for many irregular verbs such as *freeze*, are not the same as the plain past tense form). *Frozen* is just a past participle and cannot function by itself as a complete verb. Finally, in another context, *freeze* might work, but the second part of the main sentence (as well as the first sentence, *Winter fell early that year*) pushes all the action into the past. The correct answer is (C).

52.   **(H)** … an impressive ability <u>to survive</u> …

Idioms

The noun *ability* is always followed by infinitive forms (*to survive, to hunt,* etc.). Other nouns follow different rules (e.g., *capability of surviving*), but the idiomatic rule for *ability* forces the sentence to read *ability to survive.* The correct answer is (H).

53.   **(A)** … McKinley Morganfield, <u>who</u> was nicknamed …

Modifier Forms

McKinley Morganfield is the name of a person, so you must use *who* or *whom* (not *which*) to refer to this person. *Who* is needed because it functions as the subject of the clause (*who was nicknamed …*); *whom* would only be used if it were the object of a verb or preposition. Finally, *he who* is stylistically poor, creating an overdramatic reading of the clause, as if the nicknaming were the crowning of a monarch. It's much more normal (and also more concise) to simply use *who* here. The correct answer is (A).

54. **(F)** Gibbons brachiate, or swing by their arms, to travel …, obtain … food sources for themselves and their young …

Pronouns

You might have trouble deciding whether the subject of the sentence should be *Gibbons* or *Brachiation*. After all, *Gibbons brachiate to travel quickly* and *Brachiation is a way to travel quickly* are both grammatically correct, even if you might slightly prefer the active voice of *Gibbons brachiate*. However, the later part of the sentence settles the issue. The pronouns *themselves* and *their* require the subject to be the plural noun *Gibbons*, which is the only logical antecedent (= noun the pronouns refer to). All the wrong answer choices can be eliminated in this fashion. The correct answer is (F).

55. **(C)** … a fossil fuel deposit … has become increasingly difficult to discover …

Subject–Verb Agreement

The subject of the sentence is *a fossil fuel deposit*, which is a singular noun. Thus, the verb must also be singular. *Have become* and *become* (by itself, a present-tense verb) are both plural. *Are become* is both plural and archaic. The only viable possibility among the choices is *has become*. The correct answer is (C).

3

SENTENCE STRUCTURE: WHOLE SENTENCES PROBLEM SET

56. Herodotus is known as the "Father of <u>History." He chronicled</u> the wars between the ancient Greeks and the Persian Empire.

  F. NO CHANGE
  G. History" chronicling,
  H. History" he chronicled
  J. History," and chronicling

57. Every summer, our town throws a parade to honor <u>firefighters, the volunteers</u> protect our property and our lives.

  A. NO CHANGE
  B. volunteer firefighters,
  C. volunteer firefighters, who
  D. volunteer firefighters, they

58. Cooperative enterprises are intended in fact to be <u>cooperative—the members typically</u> work alongside each other in some way and even share in the financial results.

Which of the following alternatives to the underlined portion would NOT be acceptable?

  F. cooperative; the members typically
  G. cooperative, the members typically
  H. cooperative. The members typically
  J. cooperative; typically, the members

59. One of Russia's tsars in the nineteenth <u>century being</u> Alexander II, a strong-willed reformer who freed the serfs in 1861.

  A. NO CHANGE
  B. century,
  C. century, named
  D. century was

60. In 1805 the Lewis and Clark Expedition crossed from what is now Montana into present-day Idaho at Lemhi <u>Pass, it is</u> a mountain pass marking both the continental divide and a former western border of the United States.

  F. NO CHANGE
  G. Pass
  H. Pass,
  J. Pass, being

61. If you aren't careful, your to-do list can become over-cluttered with homework assignments and household <u>chores that you will need to</u> confront and tackle at some point anyway.

  A. NO CHANGE
  B. chores unless you
  C. chores, these you must
  D. chores, you need to;

62. Grinding the beans every time rather than using pre-ground coffee, <u>Rhona has made</u> a delicious beverage, hot or cold, and takes great pride in doing so.

  F NO CHANGE
  G. Rhona makes
  H. Rhona making
  J. making

63. The serene silence in the bedroom was broken <u>when</u> the alarm clock, noisy and relentless in its sudden, angry chiming.

  A. NO CHANGE
  B. while
  C. as
  D. by

64. Spiral galaxies whirling like pinwheels and supernovas <u>exploded</u> into cosmic gas clouds amazed the visitors to the planetarium.

  F. NO CHANGE
  G. were exploding
  H. exploding
  J. DELETE the underlined portion.

65. One of the British battlecruisers, or giant warships, sunk in the Battle of Jutland during World War I was the first such ship ever built, named the <u>*Invincible* that her</u> sister ship with a similarly grand name of *Inflexible* survived both the battle and the war.

  A. NO CHANGE
  B. *Invincible*, her
  C. *Invincible* and her
  D. *Invincible*. Her

MANHATTAN
PREP

66. I was just about to sit down on a stump next to the fire <u>upon spotting</u> an enormous caterpillar, nearly as long as my hand, crawling across my intended seat.

  F. NO CHANGE
  G. when I spotted
  H. when spotting
  J. when

67. The usual tip is ten <u>percent,</u> Yolanda usually gives her driver twenty percent—and makes that offer up front so that the extra money is motivational during the ride.

  A. NO CHANGE
  B. percent, however,
  C. percent, but
  D. percent, just the same

68. I stopped running and looked up at the horizon, lit by the <u>sunset against the eastern sky</u> in the distance loomed storm clouds, piled threateningly high.

  F. NO CHANGE
  G. sunset. Against the eastern sky
  H. sunset, against the eastern sky
  J. sunset against the eastern sky,

69. In the narrow streets of the ancient city of Kairouan, Tunisia, <u>where</u> you can wander for hours, ducking into shops crowded with porcelain teacups, plush carpets, and intricate brassware.

  A. NO CHANGE
  B. is where
  C. it is there that
  D. DELETE the underlined portion

70. After surveying the landscape, the platoon of <u>soldiers crossed</u> the swollen river with care, surveying the underbrush along the banks for potential foes.

  F. NO CHANGE
  G. soldiers that crossed
  H. soldiers, who crossed
  J. soldiers, crossing

71. Sara considered what she had done all day. <u>She had written</u> a dozen or so long emails to prospective clients, reorganized all the active files, and held five or six meetings with each of her salespeople—and yet, by 6pm what had really been accomplished?

  A. NO CHANGE
  B. When she wrote
  C. Having written
  D. As she wrote

72. Among the vast variety of ant species in the world are the attine <u>ants, tending</u> and harvesting particular kinds of fungus for food within their nests, they can be said to practice agriculture.

  F. NO CHANGE
  G. ants, which tend
  H. ants. Tending
  J. ants, which are tending

73. Reducing the depletion of the protective ozone layer through limitations on the production of destructive chemicals has been a somewhat forgotten environmental success <u>story, it happened over</u> the last couple of decades.

  A. NO CHANGE
  B. story, it has happened over
  C. story that it has happened in
  D. story of

74. It is fascinating to consider that many writing systems from the Bronze Age, such as the Indus <u>script. And even</u> more modern forms, such as rongorongo writing from Easter Island, have never been deciphered.

  F. NO CHANGE
  G. script, and that even
  H. script. Even
  J. script, and even

75. The assumption that the liquid phase and the gaseous phase of a material can always be clearly <u>distinguished being</u> contradicted by the existence of supercritical fluids, which merge the two phases at high temperatures and pressures.

  A. NO CHANGE
  B. distinguished is
  C. distinguished,
  D. distinguished, having been

3

76. During the First World War, <u>Europe was</u> mired in deadly conflict and much of its academic progress was disrupted, German mathematician Emmy Noether proved a theorem that would be fundamental to the progress of particle physics.

  F. NO CHANGE
  G. Europe
  H. Europe was being
  J. while Europe was

77. Some people in Chicago fear that the Cubs will never win a World Series in their <u>lifetime; others</u> regard the long-standing drought with indifference or even amusement.

  A. NO CHANGE
  B. lifetime others
  C. lifetime, others
  D. lifetime; others,

78. A former officer in the United States Navy, Coach Parker has practice extremely well organized. Without being told, freshmen put out the <u>goals, and sophomores</u> set up the cones automatically.

Which of the following alternatives to the underlined portion would NOT be acceptable?

  F. goals. Sophomores
  G. goals, sophomores
  H. goals; sophomores
  J. goals, while sophomores

79. The website demands enormous amounts of attention on a continual <u>basis. Every</u> week writers must upload new articles to the blog, graphic artists must create original, catchy images to accompany those articles, and technical experts must check for broken links and defend against hacker attacks.

  A. NO CHANGE
  B. basis every
  C. basis, every
  D. basis, and every

80. As I wandered further through the outskirts of the town, with the sky growing steadily darker, yellow streetlights that were curved over like <u>showerheads starting</u> to flicker to life and illuminate oval patches of sidewalk pavement and asphalt.

  F. NO CHANGE
  G. showerheads, starting
  H. showerheads started
  J. showerheads, which were starting

MANHATTAN
PREP

Sentence Structure: Whole Sentences Answer Key

Write in whether you got each problem right or wrong (or left it blank). If your answer was correct, put a 1 in every blank to the right of that problem. Since every problem in this set tests the same topic, there is only one column. Sum up each column and compare your total to the total possible "Out Of" points in each column.

Problem	Correct Answer	Right/Wrong/Blank	Whole Sentences
56	F		—
57	C		—
58	G		—
59	D		—
60	H		—
61	A		—
62	G		—
63	D		—
64	H		—
65	D		—
66	G		—
67	C		—
68	G		—
69	D		—
70	F		—
71	A		—
72	H		—
73	D		—
74	J		—
75	B		—
76	J		—
77	A		—
78	G		—
79	A		—
80	H		—
Total			
Out Of		25	25

Sentence Structure: Whole Sentences Solutions

56. **(F)** Herodotus is known as the "Father of <u>History." He chronicled</u> the wars …

The two sentences, as written, are complete. They each have a perfectly good subject and verb. It is possible to combine the sentences, but not by simply removing the period and thereby creating a run-on sentence. The attempted link *and chronicling* is also unworkable, because *and* requires a parallel list, and *chronicling* by itself isn't parallel to anything in the first sentence. The closest miss is *chronicling,* but the comma usage is off. The sentence would have to read … *History," chronicling the wars* … Even then, you could argue against this variation, since it implies that the action of chronicling is taking place right now—and it surely isn't. The best choice of those available is the original one: keep the two sentences apart. The correct answer is (F).

57. **(C)** … our town throws a parade to honor <u>volunteer firefighters, who</u> protect our property …

The subject of the main clause is *our town*; the verb is *throws*. Since there is another verb later on (*protect*) that needs to go with *firefighters* (a different subject) somehow, you need to create a subordinate clause. *Who* does just that. Avoid comma splices (jamming two complete sentences together with just a comma, as choices (A) and (D) do). Fragments such as choice (B) are also wrong: *protect* has no subject.

Note: Either *volunteer firefighters, who* … or *volunteer firefighters who* … would be correct in theory. The form with the comma means that the parade honors all volunteer firefighters (and it so happens that what these folks do is *protect our property* …). The form without the comma means that the parade is singling out a subgroup of volunteer firefighters—those who *protect our property* … The form with the comma is more logical in this case, because there are probably no volunteer firefighters who do *not* protect our property and our lives. The correct answer is (C).

58. **(G)** NOT acceptable: Cooperative enterprises are intended … to be <u>cooperative, the members typically</u> work … and even share …

The original sentence consists of two independent clauses connected by a dash. Each of these clauses could stand on its own as a sentence. In fact, it's a perfectly acceptable choice to split the sentence into two stand-alone pieces. You can also join the two clauses with a semicolon. What is unacceptable is to join them with a comma (the dreaded comma splice). If two clauses can each stand alone, never join them with just a comma. The correct answer is (G).

59. **(D)** One of Russia's tsars in the nineteenth <u>century was</u> Alexander II, a strong-willed reformer who freed …

Without *was*, the sentence has no main verb. The verb *freed* is trapped in a subordinate clause (*who freed* …) and so cannot be the primary engine. In this context, *named* is not a full verb (as it would be in *She named her son Jack*) but rather a participle, acting as an adjective (as in *Her son, named Jack, is a nice guy*). *Being* is not a full verb either—no *-ing* form is. You need *was* to be the sentence's main verb, linking *One of Russia's tsars* … and *Alexander II*. The correct answer is (D).

60. **(H)** … the Lewis and Clark Expedition crossed … at Lemhi <u>Pass,</u> a mountain pass …

In theory, the sentence could end with the phrase *at Lemhi Pass*, but the writer chooses to continue. The appositive phrase *a mountain pass … the United States* describes Lemhi Pass. Like most appositive phrases (and any lengthy one), this phrase should be set off from the noun it describes (*Lemhi Pass*) by a comma. *Being* is unnecessary and wordy, while *it is* creates a run-on sentence. The correct answer is (H).

3

61.   **(A)** … your to-do list can become over-cluttered with … household <u>chores that you will need to</u> confront and tackle … anyway.

There are two thoughts in the sentence: *your to-do list can become over-cluttered with assignments and chores,* and *you will need to confront and tackle these assignments and chores at some point anyway.* To combine these two thoughts, use a subordinate clause, as in this simplified example: *your list is cluttered with chores that you need to confront.* The possibility of *unless* is interesting, but you would need a *them* later on, as in this case: *your list can become cluttered with chores, unless you confront them.* As always, avoid comma splices (… *chores, these you must* … and … *chores, you need to* …) that inappropriately link two independent clauses. The correct answer is (A).

62.   **(G)** Grinding the beans every time …, <u>Rhona makes</u> a delicious beverage … and takes great pride …

The sentence needs a subject (*Rhona*) and a verb (*makes*). *Making* is not a complete verb and cannot run the sentence by itself. The remaining issue is one of tense: should the verb be *has made* or *makes*? The answer comes most clearly in the phrase *and takes.* The verb *takes* is present tense, and there's no reason to deviate from that choice. The words *every time* suggest the present tense as well (as a rule, Rhona makes a delicious beverage). The correct answer is (G).

63.   **(D)** The serene silence … was broken <u>by</u> the alarm clock, noisy and relentless …

You can write *The silence was broken by the alarm clock* or *The silence was broken when the alarm clock went off.* In the first case, there is only one verb (*was broken*), and the word *by* tells you what did the breaking (the alarm clock). In the second case, *when* introduces a clause, which must contain a verb (such as *went off*). The original sentence in the problem is equivalent to *The silence was broken when the alarm clock.* This choice is a fragment, because you are missing a necessary verb in the subordinate clause starting with *when.*

The phrase beginning with *noisy* is just a long, fancy modifier that describes the *alarm clock* in more detail. The correct answer is (D).

64.   **(H)** Spiral galaxies whirling like pinwheels and supernovas <u>exploding</u> into cosmic gas clouds amazed the visitors …

The main verb of the sentence is *amazed.* Everything that comes before it is actually part of the subject, which is a list of two items connected by *and.* The first item is *Spiral galaxies* (modified by *whirling like pinwheels*), while the second item is *supernovas* (modified by *exploding into cosmic gas clouds*). No other reading makes sense. The underlined portion cannot be a full verb such as *exploded* or *were exploding,* and you can't simply omit the idea either, because *supernovas into cosmic gas clouds* is illogical. The correct answer is (H).

65.   **(D)** One of the British battlecruisers … sunk in the Battle of Jutland during World War I was the first such ship ever built, named the <u>*Invincible.* Her</u> sister ship with a similarly grand name of *Inflexible* survived both the battle and the war.

The two lengthy thoughts here should be put into separate sentences. You cannot link the second to the first with *that* (which would modify *Invincible*), because the second thought does not describe the *Invincible;* rather, it describes the sister ship (it *survived both the battle and the war*). In theory, you could turn *her* into *whose* and link the two clauses, but at risk of creating a very ungainly sentence. Moreover, a comma splice does not suffice to join these sentences. Finally, an *and* can generally link two independent clauses, but in this case, you would definitely form a huge sentence that would be difficult to follow. Notice also the lack of a comma before the *and.* Stylistically, an *and* without a comma should only join two very short sentences (*She is tall and I am short*). The correct answer is (D).

MANHATTAN
PREP

66.   **(G)** I was just about to sit down … <u>when I spotted</u> an enormous caterpillar … crawling …

The correct answer acknowledges that the main clause (*I was just about to sit down … fire*) is the set-up for a dramatic event expressed in the subordinate *when* clause (*when I spotted an enormous caterpillar*). You need a subject (*I*) and a verb (*spotted*) in that *when* clause. *When* would only work by itself if the form *crawling* were a true verb, such as *crawled* (*when an enormous caterpillar crawled …*), so that *caterpillar* could be the subject. *Upon spotting* means "just after spotting" or "on the occasion of spotting"; this expression should logically be used for a set-up action, not for the main event (*Upon sitting down on the stump, I spotted an enormous caterpillar*). The correct answer is (G).

67.   **(C)** The usual tip is ten <u>percent, but</u> Yolanda usually gives her driver twenty percent …

The two independent clauses here cannot be linked by just a comma. *However* would work, but there needs to be a semicolon, not a comma, in front (*The tip is ten percent; however, Yolanda …*). *Just the same* works just the same. The only viable option among those given is a simple *but* after a comma. The correct answer is (C).

68.   **(G)** I … looked up at the horizon, lit by the <u>sunset. Against the eastern sky</u> in the distance loomed storm clouds …

It may not be immediately apparent which thought the prepositional phrase *against the eastern sky* belongs to. As you read along (… *lit by the sunset against the eastern sky …*), the phrase might seem to attach to *sunset,* if a little awkwardly. But then you get to *loomed storm clouds*, and the assumption collapses. The second thought is expressed in a somewhat literary order: prepositional phrase, then verb, then subject (*Against the sky loomed the storm clouds*). This second thought is an independent clause: it can be a complete sentence. If not, it must be joined to the prior thought by a semicolon, a dash, or other appropriate device that can join two independent clauses. (Stylistically, you would probably not use comma-*and* to join these sentences, since the second clause is not logically parallel to the first; rather, it is the outcome of the action in the first. The narrator *looked up at the horizon*. Result: *against the eastern sky loomed the storm clouds*.) The correct answer is (G).

69.   **(D)** DELETE the underlined portion: In the narrow streets of the ancient city of Kairouan, Tunisia, you can wander for hours …

The core of the sentence is *you can wander. You* is the subject and *can wander* is the verb. This core is modified by the prepositional phrase at the start of the sentence. Where can you wander? *In the narrow streets of the ancient city of Kairouan, Tunisia*. The rest of the sentence modifies the core as well. For how long can you wander? *For hours*. What can you be doing as you wander? You can be *ducking into shops …*

The original choice would be fine if another clause were the main, independent clause. *In Kairouan, where I wandered for hours the other day, I lost my clipboard*. Here, the main clause is *I lost my clipboard*. Choice (B) incorrectly keeps a comma (*In Kairouan, is where you can wander …*), and even without the comma this option would be unnecessarily wordy. Finally, *it is there that* creates a run-on sentence. The correct answer is (D).

70.   **(F)** … the platoon of <u>soldiers crossed</u> the swollen river …

The subject of the sentence is *the platoon* (or *the platoon of soldiers*). The main verb is *crossed*. If you place this verb into a subordinate clause by means of *that* or *who*, then the sentence lacks a verb and becomes a fragment. (By the way, *who* is much preferred to *that* with human subjects, such as *soldiers*.) If you convert the verb *crossed* into the *-ing* form *crossing*, again the sentence loses its only verb. The correct answer is (F).

71. **(A)** Sara considered what she had done all day. <u>She had written</u> a dozen …, reorganized …, and held … —and yet, by 6pm what had really been accomplished?

The first part of the second sentence (from the underlined portion to the dash) needs to be an independent clause, one that could work as a stand-alone sentence. Thus, it needs a subject (*She*) and a true verb (*had written*, not *having written* by itself). Moreover, you cannot start the clause with a subordinating word (such as *When* or *As*) that would turn the whole thing into a subordinate clause. The only possible option is *She had written*. The past perfect tense here (*had written*) indicates that the actions of writing, reorganizing, etc. all took place before the "narrative" time (*Sara considered*), which is also in the past. The correct answer is (A).

72. **(H)** Among the vast variety of ant species in the world are the attine <u>ants. Tending</u> and harvesting particular kinds of fungus for food within their nests, they can be said to practice agriculture.

The text properly has two independent clauses: the best option is to split them. The first clause is *Among … the ant species … are the attine ants.* The subject is *attine ants* and the verb is *are*. Reading uncritically, you might think that *tending and harvesting …* are fine additions to *attine ants*, until you reach *they can be said*. This is the core of the second independent clause (subject is *they*, verb is *can be said*), which is separated from the prior phrase by just a comma. As a result, this phrase (*Tending and harvesting*) needs to be expressed as a leading modifier in the second sentence, not as a tag-along modifier in the first sentence. The correct answer is (H).

73. **(D)** … a somewhat forgotten environmental success <u>story of</u> the last couple of decades.

If there were a period right after *story*, the sentence would end correctly. *This reduction has been a success story.* Thus, if you append a comma and attach a new independent clause, such as *it happened …* or *it has happened,* you create an improper comma splice. The subordinate clause *that it has happened* is incorrect as well, because *that* and *it* cannot refer to *story* at the same time. The only possible option is also the most concise: *of* does the trick. The correct answer is (D).

74. **(J)** … many writing systems from the Bronze Age, such as the Indus <u>script, and even</u> more modern forms, such as …, have never been deciphered.

The initial part of the sentence is just a frame. Technically, the subject of the sentence is *It*, and the verb is *is*. However, what you really have to analyze is the text after *consider that*, which has to be an independent clause: *It is fascinating to consider that [new subject – new verb]*. Don't skip over the *that*! *It is fascinating to consider many writing systems* is fine as a sentence. *It is fascinating to consider that many writing systems* is not: you should be asking "That many writing systems do what?"

The verb in the embedded clause is at the end of the whole sentence (*have never been deciphered*). The subject of that verb is the list *many writing systems … and even more modern forms.* You should not split up this clause. The correct answer is (J).

75. **(B)** The assumption that the liquid phase and the gaseous phase … can always be clearly <u>distinguished is</u> contradicted by the existence …

The subject of the sentence is *assumption*; the main verb is *is contradicted*. Other verbs, such as *can be distinguished* and *merge*, lurk in subordinate clauses. Don't let the presence of those junior verbs distract you from the need for a main verb in the independent clause. *Being contradicted, having been contradicted,* or plain old *contradicted (by …)* are not complete verbs. You need to add a form of the verb *be* in a tense, as in the correct answer (*is contradicted* is in the present tense), to make a complete verb in the passive voice. The correct answer is (B).

76.   **(J)**   During the First World War, <u>while Europe was</u> mired …, German mathematician Emmy Noether proved a theorem …

The main clause of this sentence comes at the end: *German mathematician Emmy Noether proved a theorem* … The subject is *German mathematician Emmy Noether*, and the verb is *proved*. You are not given the choice to alter this part of the sentence. As a result, the other verbs in the sentence must be relegated to subordinate clauses. By putting *while* in front of *Europe was mired … and much of its academic progress was disrupted*, you successfully make that clause subordinate (it then can expand on the phrase *During the First World War*, adding more color).

If instead you leave out the *while*, at best you wind up with an independent clause (*Europe was mired …*) that is joined incorrectly via a comma to the *German mathematician* clause. Moreover, *Europe mired* is not even a clause, and *Europe was being mired* is needlessly wordy. The correct answer is (J).

77.   **(A)**   Some people … fear that the Cubs will never win a World Series in their <u>lifetime; others</u> regard the long-standing drought …

The sentence is correct as written. The text before the semicolon can stand alone as a complete sentence, with subject *Some people* and main verb *fear*. Likewise, the text after the semicolon (*others regard …*) is an independent clause, and a comma should not be placed between the subject *others* and the verb *regard*. The two independent clauses cannot be smashed together with nothing but a space or a comma between them. If punctuation alone is used to create one sentence, the proper mark is either a semicolon or a dash. The correct answer is (A).

78.   **(G)**   NOT acceptable: … freshmen put out the <u>goals, sophomores</u> set up the cones …

The text from *Without* to *goals* is an independent clause, with *freshmen* as the subject and *put* as the main verb. Likewise, *sophomores … automatically* is another independent clause. The meaning of these two clauses is parallel: they each explain what a group of students does at the start of practice. Thus, you have many legitimate choices for these independent clauses, as shown below:

> *Clause, and clause.*   *Clause. Clause.*   *Clause; clause.*   *Clause, while clause.*

The one choice that is *not* acceptable is to join the two clauses with just a comma, forming an illegitimate comma splice:

> NOT acceptable: *Clause, clause.*

The correct answer is (G).

79.   **(A)**   The website demands … attention on a continual <u>basis. Every</u> week writers must upload …, graphic artists must create …, and technical experts must check …

The website demands … basis is a perfectly fine stand-alone sentence. The subject is *The website*, while the main verb is *demands*. What's tricky is that the following sentence has three parallel independent clauses joined in a list: *Clause, clause, and clause*. In this sort of list, you *can* actually separate the first two clauses with just a comma (just ensure that

the three clauses are all relatively short and simple). What you are not allowed to do, however, is join *The website …*
basis to that list with just a comma—or with no punctuation at all. Either option creates a run-on sentence.

Using a "comma *-and*" to attach that first clause may seem acceptable. However, doing so breaks parallelism: *Clause,*
and clause, clause, and clause. Even if the four clauses were all internally parallel to each other, the structure of this list
is unworkable. The correct answer is (A).

80. **(H)** … yellow streetlights that were curved over like <u>showerheads started</u> to flicker to life …

In the original sentence, there is no independent clause. *As I wandered … darker* is an introductory subordinate clause
(because of the word *As*), so it cannot be the backbone of the sentence. The clause *that were curved over like showerheads*
is also subordinate. The only option for the subject of the sentence is *yellow streetlights;* this subject needs a real verb,
such as *started.* The *-ing* form *starting*, whether separated by a comma or not, cannot by itself be the main verb of the
sentence. *Which were starting* would create yet another subordinate clause. The correct answer is (H).

SENTENCE STRUCTURE: MODIFIERS
AND VERBS PROBLEMS

81. Austrian sculptor Theodor Friedl <u>has been commissioned</u> to create a number of figures for the opening in 1877 of the Vienna Stock Exchange, including a full quadriga or a Roman chariot drawn by four horses.

   A. NO CHANGE
   B. is commissioned
   C. was commissioned
   D. has been commissioning

82. Aggregating by the hundreds and even thousands at a time, <u>and</u> olive ridley sea turtles suddenly land on certain beaches in simultaneous nesting swarms known as *arribadas.*

   F. NO CHANGE
   G. as
   H. when
   J. DELETE the underlined portion.

83. *Lactobacillus acidophilus* is a strain of what you might call friendly bacteria, naturally occurring in our gastrointestinal <u>tract and used</u> in the production of yogurt.

   A. NO CHANGE
   B. tract and using
   C. tract that used
   D. tract that is used

84. As our altitude lessened with our approach, on either side of the tiny runway I <u>can see</u> the famous Red Rocks of Sedona.

   F. NO CHANGE
   G. am able to see
   H. have seen
   J. could see

85. Actively connecting native Shinto elements to ones imported with the new religion, <u>buddhas were claimed by some people to appear as local deities.</u>

   A. NO CHANGE
   B. some people claimed that buddhas appeared as local deities.
   C. local deities were how buddhas were claimed by some people to appear.
   D. the claim of some people was that local deities were the appearance of buddhas.

86. The coffee shop that Teresa recently opened has been a hit. <u>Opening eyes—and mouths—to the subtleties of bean origination, roasts, and grinds, her customers have rewarded her by coming in droves.</u>

   F. NO CHANGE
   G. Rewarding her by coming in droves, she has opened her customers' eyes—and mouths—to the subtleties of bean origination, roasts, and grinds.
   H. Rewarded by coming in droves, her customers have had their eyes—and mouths—opened by her to the subtleties of bean origination, roasts, and grinds.
   J. She has opened eyes—and mouths—to the subtleties of bean origination, roasts, and grinds; her customers have rewarded her by coming in droves.

87. In 1845, landscape painter Henry Mark Anthony <u>had been</u> elected to the Society of British Artists; only seven years later, he resigned, although he had exhibited five paintings at the Society that same year.

   A. NO CHANGE
   B. were to have been
   C. was
   D. is

88. The movie theater that my friends and I like to go to keeps rather strange hours for a business that you'd think ought to make a profit. On weekends it <u>opened</u> well after noon, missing the opportunity for a normal matinee.

   F. NO CHANGE
   G. opens
   H. was open
   J. had opened

89. <u>Seeing bears and moose in my mind, it is that they will one day be</u> repopulating areas that we will have returned to the wild.

   A. NO CHANGE
   B. In my mind, I see bears and moose one day
   C. Seen in my mind one day, bears and moose
   D. Seeing bears and moose in my mind will be one day

3

90. Before graduating from high school, DeAnn had put in many hours guiding her Junior R.O.T.C. class-mates and winning their respect, so it was not a sur-prise that as a new cadet at the Academy, <u>she ably exercised her leadership skills</u> to be elected to a posi-tion at the head of her platoon.

   F. NO CHANGE
   G. her skills in leadership were ably exercised
   H. her leadership skills ably were exercised
   J. the exercise of her leadership skills was able

91. Modern hygienic practices have taken hold in all healthcare occupations. Not only because of the development of new medicines and devices, but be-cause of the improved application of simple, well-known practices such as hand-washing, hospitals <u>are</u> safer places than ever for patients.

   A. NO CHANGE
   B. were
   C. had been
   D. would have been

92. Troops of howler monkeys patrol the steep forests surrounding Apoyo Lake, <u>estimated to be 600 feet deep</u> a volcanic crater lake.

The best placement for the underlined phrase would be:

   F. where it is now.
   G. before the word *Troops* (revising the capitaliza-tion accordingly).
   H. after the word *forests*.
   J. after the word *lake* (ending the sentence with a period).

93. The whole downtown area has been truly rejuve-nated. Out-of-towners <u>that local entrepreneurs have stimulated who visit the wonderful shopping district will be impressed.</u>

   A. NO CHANGE
   B. that local entrepreneurs have stimulated will be impressed, who visit the wonderful shopping district.
   C. who visit the wonderful shopping district that local entrepreneurs have stimulated will be impressed.
   D. will be impressed by visiting the wonderful shopping district to which local entrepreneurs have stimulated.

94. To hinder enemy gunners from getting fixes on their targets, the British Admiralty asked modern-ist artist Edward Wadsworth, among others, <u>re-markably</u> to design so-called "dazzle camouflage" schemes that would not conceal warships, but rather make them look confusing.

The best placement for the underlined word would be:

   F. where it is now.
   G. before the phrase *To hinder* (revising the capi-talization accordingly).
   H. before the word *fixes.*
   J. before the word *asked.*

95. By the time the sixteenth-century German scholar Valentinus Otho proposed the fraction 355/113 as an excellent approximation to the value of pi, Zu Chongzhi, the Chinese mathematician who had first discovered this approximation, <u>was dead</u> for over a millennium.

   A. NO CHANGE
   B. had been dead
   C. dead
   D. died

96. <u>In 1786 and 1787, Daniel Shays led a rebellion of small farmers in western Massachusetts against the state and federal governments,</u> a time when the new nation was still finding its economic, social, and po-litical feet.

   F. NO CHANGE
   G. Daniel Shays led a rebellion of small farmers in western Massachusetts against the state and federal governments in 1786 and 1787,
   H. Daniel Shays led a rebellion of small farmers in 1786 and 1787 against the state and federal governments in western Massachusetts,
   J. In the western Massachusetts of 1786 and 1787, Daniel Shays led a rebellion of small farmers against the state and federal governments,

MANHATTAN
PREP

97. When zoos <u>change their hours to accommodate working parents, as ours did earlier this month,</u> more families are able to take advantage of available programs and resources.

    A. NO CHANGE
    B. change their hours earlier this month to accommodate working parents, as ours did,
    C. earlier this month change their hours, as ours did, to accommodate working parents,
    D. change their hours, as ours did, to accommodate working parents earlier this month,

98. The cheetah is built for speed: if necessary, it <u>accelerated</u> from standstill to speeds as high as 65 miles per hour in just three seconds.

    F. NO CHANGE
    G. accelerating
    H. accelerates
    J. had accelerated

99. <u>Even when the central government disagrees, Elyse declares that to argue cities can essentially do what they wish is to pave a road to dissolution for nations.</u>

    A. NO CHANGE
    B. For nations, Elyse declares what cities can essentially wish to do, even when the central government disagrees, is arguing to pave a road to dissolution.
    C. Elyse declares that to argue cities can essentially do what they wish, even when the central government disagrees, is to pave a road to dissolution for nations.
    D. Essentially doing what they wish, Elyse declares cities argue is to pave a road to dissolution for nations, even when the central government disagrees.

100. The polyrhythmic beating of drums in the distance signaled the start of a concert that we <u>knew</u> would be special, a one-night-only gathering of important Garifuna musicians from around the Caribbean.

    F. NO CHANGE
    G. know
    H. had been known
    J. will have known

3

Sentence Structure: Modifiers and Verbs Answer Key

Write in whether you got each problem right or wrong (or left it blank). If your answer was correct, put a 1 in every blank to the right of that problem. Problems may be categorized in more than one column. Sum up each column and compare your total to the total possible "Out Of" points in each column.

Problem	Correct Answer	Right/Wrong/ Blank	Modifier Placement	Verbs: Tense and Voice
81	C			—
82	J		—	
83	A		—	
84	J			—
85	B		—	
86	J		—	
87	C			—
88	G			—
89	B		—	
90	F		—	
91	A			—
92	J		—	
93	C		—	
94	J		—	
95	B			—
96	G		—	
97	A		—	
98	H			—
99	C		—	
100	F			—
Total				
Out Of		20	12	8

Sentence Structure: Modifiers and Verbs Solutions

81.   **(C)** Austrian sculptor Theodor Friedl <u>was commissioned</u> to create … figures for the opening in 1877 of the Vienna Stock Exchange …

Usage/Mechanics   Sentence Structure   Verb Tenses

The proper tense here for the verb is past: *was commissioned*. A specific point in time in the past is mentioned (*in 1877*), so you need to use the past tense (*was*), not the present tense (*is*). Avoid using the present perfect (*has been* …) with a specific past time, since the present perfect is really a tense about the present state of affairs (which first came into being at some indefinite point in the past that you don't care about). Finally, the passive voice is correct in this case: it makes sense that a sculptor *was commissioned* (by someone) to do something, not that he or she *commissioned* or *was/has been commissioning* (someone unnamed?) to do that thing. In fact, you must name the object (the person being commissioned) in the latter case, and that object is absent from all the options above. The correct answer is (C).

82.   **(J)** Aggregating by the hundreds and even thousands at a time, olive ridley sea turtles suddenly land on certain beaches …

Usage/Mechanics   Sentence Structure   Modifier Placement

The phrase *Aggregating … at a time* is a leading modifier. As such, it must modify the subject, and that subject has to immediately follow the modifier. The intervention of any conjunction (such as *and, as,* or *when*) breaks this rule among others. (In addition, *and* here creates bad parallelism, while *as* and *when* turn the sentence into a fragment by subordinating the only independent clause in town.) The correct answer is (J).

83.   **(A)** *Lactobacillus acidophilus* is a strain of … friendly bacteria, naturally occurring in our gastrointestinal <u>tract and used</u> in the production …

Usage/Mechanics   Sentence Structure   Modifier Placement

The sentence contains two phrases that modify *a strain of … friendly bacteria*: (1) *naturally occurring in our gastrointestinal tract* and (2) *used in the production of yogurt*. Each of these modifiers would work with "that is": *This is a friendly strain that is naturally occurring …* and *This is a friendly strain that is used in the production …* Therefore, these modifiers can be linked by *and* and placed parallel to each other after the noun phrase they modify.

Using does not make sense: the *friendly bacteria* are not *using* but *used*. Putting in *that* makes the second modifier improperly modify *gastrointestinal tract*, a meaning that also does not reflect the author's intention. The correct answer is (A).

84.   **(J)** As our altitude lessened …, on either side … I <u>could see</u> the famous Red Rocks.…

Usage/Mechanics   Sentence Structure   Verb Tenses

The first verb in the sentence (*lessened*) places the action squarely in the past. There is no reason to change tenses: in fact, the subordinate clause beginning with *as* tells you explicitly to make the main verb the same tense. Besides the correct answer (*could see*), legal alternatives involving the same verb *to see* include *saw* and *was able to see*. (*Was seeing* would technically work too, although this past progressive tense is a bit awkward to use with *see*.)

You can tell a story about the past using the present tense, in fact, but you must be consistent throughout the story. Thus, *can see* and *am able to see* both fail to work, because the normal past tense has already been deployed. The present perfect tense (*have seen*) does not mix well with narratives in the past tense. *I have seen the Red Rocks* means that at some *indefinite* point in the past, you saw these rocks (you're really making a statement about yourself right now: you are a person who has seen …). However, a story in the past tense creates a definite past time. Avoid using the present perfect tense with definite points in the past. The correct answer is (J).

85.   **(B)**   Actively connecting native Shinto elements to ones imported with the new religion, <u>some people claimed that buddhas appeared as local deities.</u>

Usage/Mechanics   Sentence Structure   Modifier Placement

Who or what was *actively connecting native Shinto elements to ones imported with the new religion*? The best choices are people (*some people*) or some kind of statement or system of beliefs. One of these should therefore be the subject of the sentence, immediately following the leading modifier *Actively connecting …* The best choice among those given is *some people.*

Neither *local deities* nor *buddhas* work as cleanly with the modifier—these are elements themselves of the religions in question. Using *the claim* might be acceptable, but the clause *local deities were the appearance of buddhas* is wordy and unclear (does *appearance* mean the act of appearing or the outer surface or look?). The correct answer is (B).

86.   **(J)**   The coffee shop that Teresa recently opened has been a hit. <u>She has opened eyes—and mouths—to the subtleties of bean origination, roasts, and grinds; her customers have rewarded her by coming in droves.</u>

Usage/Mechanics   Sentence Structure   Modifier Placement

Each of the wrong choices contains an illogically placed modifier at the beginning of the sentence. The original text reads *Opening eyes … her customers.* However, the customers are not the ones opening eyes—it's Teresa, or her shop. *Rewarding her … she* is likewise nonsensical: the customers are the ones doing the rewarding (*by coming in droves*), not Teresa. Finally, *Rewarded … her customers* fails the logic test as well. Teresa is the one rewarded, not the customers.

The only viable option, in fact, avoids the use of a leading modifier altogether. Instead, two independent clauses, joined by a semicolon, contain the two thoughts (*She has opened eyes …; her customers have rewarded her*). The correct answer is (J).

87.   **(C)**   In 1845, landscape painter Henry Mark Anthony <u>was</u> elected …

Usage/Mechanics   Sentence Structure   Verb Tenses

For an event in the past with a date, the default is to use the plain past tense (*was*). Only use the past perfect (*had been*) if you are talking about something even further back in time than that past event. For instance, *By 1845 Anthony had already achieved success.* In other words, Anthony's achievement happened at some point before 1845. This sort of use shows up later in the sentence: *he resigned, although he had exhibited …* emphasizes that the exhibitions took place before the resignation.

In a narrative about the past, you can use plain past tense in a sequence of verbs, as long as the order is clear: *he was elected … later he resigned …* The correct answer is (C).

88. **(G)** The movie theater that my friends and I like to go to keeps rather strange hours... On weekends it <u>opens</u> well after noon …

Usage/Mechanics   Sentence Structure   Verb Tenses

The first sentence sets up the governing tense of the story in the first sentence: *the movie theater … keeps rather strange hours* and *that my friends and I like to go to.* The verbs *keeps* and *like* are both in the present tense. Thus, since there is no reason to change the tense in the second sentence (which is talking about a general situation *on weekends*), the verb there should be *opens,* not *opened, was,* or *had opened.* The correct answer is (G).

89. **(B)** <u>In my mind, I see bears and moose one day</u> repopulating areas that we will have returned to the wild.

Usage/Mechanics   Sentence Structure   Modifier Placement

The original text fails because the leading modifier *Seeing bears and moose in my mind* is not immediately followed by the only possible subject: *I.* Other incorrect options break logic (*Seeing bears and moose* cannot be the subject of *will be repopulating*—it should be the bears and moose themselves) or sentence structure (*bears and moose repopulating … has no verb*). Small modifiers also get lost in the shuffle: for instance, *one day* should be clearly attached to the action of *repopulating,* not the action of seeing.

The correct answer simply relates the three actions: *In my mind, I see [present tense] bears and moose one day [in the future] repopulating areas that we will have returned [future perfect] to the wild.* The correct answer is (B).

90. **(F)** … it was not a surprise that as a new cadet at the Academy, <u>she ably exercised her leadership skills</u> to be elected …

Usage/Mechanics   Sentence Structure   Modifier Placement

After *it was not a surprise that,* a new "mini-sentence" is required, a clause that could stand alone as a sentence. Thus, the modifier *as a new cadet at the Academy* should be considered a leading modifier, and as such, it must be followed by the right logical subject: *she,* meaning DeAnn. Neither her leadership skills nor the exercise of these skills is the new cadet; she is. All of the wrong answers fail in this respect. The correct answer is (F).

91. **(A)** Modern hygienic practices have taken hold … hospitals <u>are</u> safer places than ever …

Usage/Mechanics   Sentence Structure   Verb Tenses

The prior sentence uses the present perfect tense (*have taken*), which indicates an action that started or took place in the past, but whose effect is still felt today. That is, saying that *modern hygienic practices have taken hold* is really saying that these modern practices are currently in a strong state, they are being used, etc. In general, the present perfect tense refers to the present more than to the past.

The next sentence gives no reason to change time periods. As a result, it should not be in the past tense (*were*), but rather in the present tense (*are*). The past perfect (*had been*) and the conditional perfect (*would have been*) are both inappropriate here. The correct answer is (A).

92. **(J)** The best placement for the underlined phrase would be after the word *lake* (ending the sentence with a period).

Usage/Mechanics   Sentence Structure   Modifier Placement

The modifier *estimated to be 600 feet deep* seems to modify *Apoyo Lake*, but then you come across *a volcanic crater lake*, which is dangling out on its own at the end of the sentence. This noun phrase needs to be closer to *Apoyo Lake*, which it modifies as an appositive. Then *estimated …* can be tacked onto *a volcanic crater lake,* as follows:

> Troops of howler monkeys patrol the steep forests surrounding Apoyo Lake, a volcanic crater lake estimated to be 600 feet deep.

Neither the *troops of howler monkeys* nor *the steep forests* should be modified by the phrase in question. The correct answer is (J).

93. **(C)** Out-of-towners <u>who visit the wonderful shopping district that local entrepreneurs have stimulated will be impressed.</u>

Usage/Mechanics   Sentence Structure   Modifier Placement

The sequence of modifying clauses in this sentence matters a great deal. You can analyze the correct sentence in one of two ways.

Outside in: *Out-of-towners will be impressed.* Which out-of-towners? The ones *who visit the wonderful shopping district.* Which wonderful shopping district? The one *that local entrepreneurs have stimulated.*

Inside out: What *have local entrepreneurs stimulated?* A wonderful shopping district. What else is true about this shopping district? *Out-of-towners who visit* this district *will be impressed.*

Either way, the modifiers *who visit …* and *that local …* need to be arranged in the right order. It's okay for the subject *Out-of-towners* and the verb *will be impressed* to be separated by the necessary modifiers in between, but you can't separate the modifiers from the nouns they should be attached to. The correct answer is (C).

94. **(J)** To hinder enemy gunners from getting fixes on their targets, the British Admiralty <u>remarkably</u> asked modernist artist Edward Wadsworth, among others, to design so-called "dazzle camouflage" schemes that would not conceal warships …

Usage/Mechanics   Sentence Structure   Modifier Placement

The adverb *remarkably* has to be positioned close to a reasonable verb—that is, one that *remarkably* would make the most unambiguous sense with—and in a spot that idiomatically sounds all right. In the correct answer, the phrase *remarkably asked* means "it is remarkable that the British Admiralty asked." This is a very sensible reading, and the best one available.

The alternatives make odd juxtapositions. For instance, *Remarkably to hinder enemy gunners …* fails because it is not clear whether *remarkably* here means "it is remarkable that the goal was to hinder these gunners" or "to hinder these gunners to a remarkable extent." Moreover, placing *Remarkably* before the infinitive *to hinder* at the beginning of the sentence is unusual and awkward. Writing … *from getting remarkably fixes …* should sound strange as well: in English, avoid putting

MANHATTAN
PREP

3

adverbs between verbs and their objects, if at all possible. The meaning of *remarkably* doesn't really fit here, either. Finally, if you put *The British Admiralty asked the artist, among others, remarkably to design* ..., it is not clear which verb you mean to attach *remarkably* to (*asked* or *design*), and if the latter, the meaning is also muddled (is it remarkable to design these schemes, or is it that the schemes were designed to be remarkable?). The correct answer is (J).

95.   **(B)**   By the time … Otho proposed …, Zu Chongzhi … <u>had been dead</u> for over a millennium.

Usage/Mechanics   Sentence Structure   Verb Tenses

The past perfect tense (*had been*) is most appropriate here, since it takes the action of the sentence back to a prior past time. *By the time Otho proposed* … is in plain past tense, setting up an action in the past. *Zu Chongzhi had been dead* takes you back to an even earlier time. *Was dead* is less apt. As for *died*, the issue is not only tense but meaning: *died for over a millennium* is not possible (the act of dying did not take more than a thousand years). Finally, choosing *dead* by itself deprives the sentence of a working verb in its main clause. The correct answer is (B).

96.   **(G)**   <u>Daniel Shays led a rebellion of small farmers in western Massachusetts against the state and federal governments in 1786 and 1787,</u> a time when the new nation …

Usage/Mechanics   Sentence Structure   Modifier Placement

As is so often the case, the key to this problem is the non-underlined portion, which begins *a time when the new nation* … This is a modifying phrase that describes a *time*. Therefore, the very last part of the underlined portion (that joins to this modifier) must be a time. Only *1786 and 1787* qualify. All of the wrong answer choices place something else against that fixed modifier (*the state and federal governments* or *western Massachusetts*). The correct answer is (G).

97.   **(A)**   When zoos <u>change their hours to accommodate working parents, as ours did earlier this month,</u> more families are able …

Usage/Mechanics   Sentence Structure   Modifier Placement

The position of the time modifier *earlier this month* is the issue at stake. Logically, this past-time phrase must be clearly attached to the past tense verb *did*, not the present tense verb *change*. The clause *When zoos change their hours* … is in the general present and should not be modified by a specific past-time modifier such as *earlier this month*. The correct answer is (A).

98.   **(H)**   The cheetah is built for speed: if necessary, it <u>accelerates</u> from standstill …

Usage/Mechanics   Sentence Structure   Verb Tenses

The first part of the sentence is in the present tense, indicating a general truth (*the cheetah is built for speed*). There is no reason to switch tenses in the second clause, which also presents a general fact. Thus, the present tense *accelerates* should be chosen. *Can accelerate* would also be fine, but this option is not available. The correct answer is (H).

99. **(C)** <u>Elyse declares that to argue cities can essentially do what they wish, even when the central government disagrees, is to pave a road to dissolution for nations.</u>

Usage/Mechanics   Sentence Structure   Modifier Placement

This sentence is very difficult to analyze. The correct answer assembles the parts in the right order:

Elyse declares something. What does she declare? She declares *that to argue* something *is to* do something else. Okay, what is the argument? That *cities can essentially do what they wish, even when the central government disagrees.* So she declares that to argue this point is to do something else. What is that other thing? To *pave a road to dissolution for nations.*

The wrong answers create a tossed salad of thoughts, keeping all the pieces but mixing them up thoroughly. For this very reason, when the whole sentence is underlined, some of the wrong answers are typically very hard to make sense of. Don't get bogged down; rather, scan the choices and look for one that simply seems easier to read. Study that choice closely. You may well already be looking at the right answer. The correct answer is (C).

100. **(F)** The polyrhythmic beating ... signaled the start of a concert that we <u>knew</u> would be special ...

Usage/Mechanics   Sentence Structure   Verb Tenses

The main verb in the sentence is *signaled,* which is past tense. Thus, the underlined verb can either be *knew* (meaning at the same time as *signaled*) or *had known* (meaning at some earlier time). Those are the only two simple possibilities. *Had known* is not available—*had been known* is the right tense but the wrong voice (the passive voice *we had been known* means that someone else was doing the knowing). The correct answer is (F).

Chapter 4 *of*

5lb. Book of ACT® Practice Problems

English:
Rhetorical Skills

In This Chapter...

Chapter 4

English: Rhetorical Skills

The English problems in this chapter test your "Rhetorical Skills"—that is, how well you choose the content of an essay, how well you organize that content, and how well you choose your words. The three major subtopics in Rhetorical Skills are as follows:

1. Writing Strategy. General choice of content, additions, deletions, and whether the passage achieves certain goals.

2. Organization. Transitions, choice of opening/closing content, sentence order, paragraph order, and paragraph breaks.

3. Style. Concision, choice of particular words.

How should you use this chapter? Here are some recommendations, according to the level you've reached in ACT English.

1. Fundamentals. It's good to start with a topically focused chapter, such as this one. Do at least some of these problems untimed. This way, you give yourself a chance to think deeply about the principles at work. Review the solutions closely, and articulate what you've learned. Redo problems as necessary.

2. Fixes. Do a few problems untimed, examine the results, learn your lessons, then test yourself with longer timed sets.

3. Tweaks. Confirm your mastery by doing longer sets of problems under timed conditions. Aim to improve the speed and ease of your solution process. Mix the problems up by jumping around in the chapter.

Good luck on the problems!

PASSAGE 1: WRITING STRATEGY

Food Truck

When I am home for the summer between terms, I work where I did in high school: on a food truck called Wunderbare Wurst, which means "Wonderful Sausage." ☐1 This truck was started several years ago by

two adults <u>with driver's licenses</u>, Sabine and Ferdinand,
          ²
who realized that Miami was generally overflowing with culinary riches, particularly the cuisine of Cuba and other Latin American countries, but authentic bratwurst, sauerkraut, and other real German dishes

were missing. ☐3 The two caught the wave of gourmet food trucks, which are in a different category—and

1. At this point, the writer is considering adding the following sentence:

   > People usually pronounce the ending of the first word like "bare" or "bear," but it should be pronounced "bah-ruh."

   Should the writer make this addition?

   A. Yes, because the sentence provides the right guidance for pronouncing an unfamiliar word.
   B. Yes, because the sentence reveals the narrator's familiarity with the culture on which the truck is based.
   C. No, because the sentence fails to identify the language in which the truck's title is expressed.
   D. No, because the content of the sentence strays from the main focus of the paragraph.

2. Given that all the choices are true, which one provides the most relevant background information on Sabine and Ferdinand?

   F. NO CHANGE
   G. dedicated entrepreneurs,
   H. married German immigrants,
   J. people not born in this country,

3. The writer is considering deleting the words "authentic bratwurst, sauerkraut, and other" from the previous sentence. If the writer were to make this deletion, the sentence would primarily lose:

   A. information that contrasts German dishes with those of other cultures.
   B. examples of the German dishes to which the narrator is referring.
   C. details that support a point made earlier in the paragraph.
   D. information that provides a logical transition to the next sentence.

MANHATTAN
PREP

ought to be distinguished—from hot dog carts or
₄
other low-end providers. Sabine and Ferdinand charge
₄

a premium for their products, but their ingredients are
₅
expensive, as is gasoline.
₅

  I started working with Sabine and Ferdinand very soon after they launched their business. As the president of my high school's German club, I invited their then-unknown truck to park outside a Friday night home football game. [6] It was the truck's best night to date, and Sabine offered me a job the next day. I arranged for brats to be sold after all our remaining games,

and enrollment in the German club actually went up
₇
during that time, too. Over the course of that year,
₇

4. Which choice makes the most effective comparison by describing what Sabine and Ferdinand's operation could be most reasonably confused with?

  F. NO CHANGE
  G. high-end stationary restaurants
  H. tractor-trailers and other large transport trucks
  J. specialty grocery stores and delicatessens.

5. Which choice most effectively illustrates the popularity of the food truck's offerings?

  A. NO CHANGE
  B. I believe that customers are getting a great value.
  C. they don't seem to be primarily motivated by money.
  D. wherever they take the truck, they sell out.

6. The writer is considering deleting the following phrase from the preceding sentence:

  As the president of my high school's German club,

If the writer were to make this deletion, the essay would primarily lose:

  F. a detail that suggests a rationale for the invitation made by the narrator.
  G. an explanation of why the narrator took a risk for the truck's owners.
  H. details about what Sabine and Ferdinand thought of the narrator.
  J. broad background information on active clubs at the narrator's high school.

7. Given that all of the choices are true, which one is most relevant at this point in the essay?

  A. NO CHANGE
  B. and my friends were pleased with our improved Friday night meals.
  C. though some students were upset about lower sales at the concession stand.
  D. and in the truck itself, I started operating the cash register.

4

I took on more and more responsibilities, learning the ins and outs of running a small business. ⑧ Of course, Sabine and Ferdinand have taught me how to grill sausages properly, but more importantly, they have taught me how to serve customers with a smile, even when you don't feel like smiling. They have helped me learn how to manage crises calmly and improvise solutions. They have been excellent mentors to me, and

I hope that <u>later in life,</u> I can provide the same kind of
                        9
guidance to my employees.

8. At this point, the writer is considering adding the following true statement:

   > My college doesn't have a business major exactly, so I'm studying economics.

   Should the writer make this addition here?

   F. Yes, because it explains the narrator's desire to acquire hands-on experience in business.
   G. Yes, because it reminds the reader of the narrator's need to pay tuition and earn money.
   H. No, because it distracts the reader from the main focus of the paragraph.
   J. No, because it is inconsistent with the tone and style of the rest of the essay.

9. Which choice would provide the most appropriate context for the rest of the sentence?

   A. NO CHANGE
   B. when I start my own business someday,
   C. at some point in the future,
   D. whether I feel like smiling or frowning,

   > Question 10 asks about the preceding passage as a whole.

10. Suppose the writer had chosen to write a brief essay describing the evolution of a professional relationship between a small enterprise and an employee. Would this essay successfully fulfill the writer's goal?

    F. Yes, because the narrator outlines his or her own process of becoming a valued employee of the food truck.
    G. Yes, because the narrator continues to work in the same food truck in which he or she began to work in high school.
    H. No, because the food truck has reached a level of success that disqualifies it from being considered a small enterprise.
    J. No, because the relationship has been unable to progress further while the narrator has been attending college.

PASSAGE 2: WRITING STRATEGY

Ella Fitzgerald

[1]

I once kissed Ella Fitzgerald, the "First Lady of Song," on the cheek. She was getting an honorary degree, ⑪ and a member of the a-cappella group in which I sang had a family connection to Ella's road

manager, who happened to be called Val Valentine. We
_____
12

lay in wait for the grande dame outside of the reception

hall, built in honor of graduates fighting for the Union
_____
13

during the American Civil War. As Ella and Val slowly
_____
13

climbed a ramp toward the hall, we greeted them in white tie and tails, singing a song Ella made famous: "The Lady Is a Tramp."

[2]

Quite elderly at that point, yet energetic and smiling, Ella appeared delighted with our performance.

---

11. At this point, the writer is considering removing the comma from after the word *degree* and adding the following phrase:

> at my university,

Would this be a relevant addition to make here?

A. Yes, because it provides academic credibility for assertions made later in the essay.
B. Yes, because it justifies the narrator's connection to the place where Fitzgerald would be.
C. No, because it consists of unnecessary personal information that detracts from the narrative.
D. No, because it offers insufficient detail, such as the name of the university itself.

12. Which choice most effectively conveys the narrator's perspective on the name of Fitzgerald's manager?

F. NO CHANGE
G. a man whose real name was
H. the wonderfully named
J. OMIT the underlined portion.

13. Given that all of the choices are true, which one provides the most logical cause for the events described in the next sentence?

A. NO CHANGE
B. where she was due for a dinner the night before the degree ceremony.
C. which contains a theater in which we ourselves had often sung.
D. an immense Gothic building used for many purposes over the years.

Afterwards, we lined up and each gave her a kiss. ☐14 The only danger was that she was really leaning on each of us, a realization not shared by the last singer in line. When he pulled away, this national treasure started to topple. Only Val Valentine's quick reactions saved Ella from a

bad spill, and thankfully, the scare was quickly over.
15
[3]

Born in 1917, Ella Fitzgerald overcame a difficult

childhood ☐16 to win an "Amateur Night" while still a teenager at the famous Apollo Theater in Harlem, New

York, which was built in 1914 but wasn't opened to
17
African-American audiences until the 1930s. By 1940,
17
she was the bandleader of her own jazz orchestra.

14. If the writer were to delete the preceding sentence, the paragraph would primarily lose:
F. a description of the context needed to make sense of the next few sentences.
G. insight into the formation and composition of the singing group.
H. supporting evidence for the impact that Fitzgerald had on the narrator.
J. details that could be safely omitted without harming the rest of the story.

15. Given that all of the choices are true, which one gives the clearest glimpse into possible repercussions for the singing group if Fitzgerald had actually fallen?
A. NO CHANGE
B. spill, although many of us leapt to her aid.
C. spill—and us from terrible shame.
D. spill—and who knows how bad that could have been.

16. At this point, the writer is considering placing a comma after the word *childhood* and adding the following phrase:
one that included time in an orphanage and a reformatory school,
Given that it is true, should the writer make this addition here?
F. Yes, because it illustrates more specifically the obstacles to Fitzgerald's achievements
G. Yes, because it explains the source of Fitzgerald's emotional power as a singer.
H. No, because it makes an already long sentence even longer and more unwieldy.
J. No, because it is inconsistent with the positive tone established in the rest of the essay.

17. Given that all of the choices are true, which one provides the most detailed and effective explanation of the cultural importance of the venue referred to in this sentence?
A. NO CHANGE
B. which frequently competed with its neighbor, the Lafayette Theatre, for top acts.
C. an establishment.
D. the launching pad for many prominent African-American performers for more than eighty years.

Other contemporaneous big bands were led by

such greats as Count Basie and Duke Ellington.

Recording countless hits and jazz standards over the next few decades, Ella became known for her agility in scat singing, which imitates the improvised solos of trumpets and saxophones by means of nonsense syllables. [19] As for me, I will always remember and treasure the experience of singing for one of the greatest vocalists in history.

18. **F.** NO CHANGE
    G. Count Basie and Duke Ellington were among the great leaders of other big bands around the same time.
    H. Leaders of other big bands at the same time included the great Count Basie and Duke Ellington.
    J. OMIT the underlined portion.

19. Which of the following true statements, if added here, would most effectively emphasize the public's recognition of Fitzgerald's accomplishments?
    A. Perhaps because of her upbringing, Ella generously supported organizations that help underprivileged children.
    B. In her lifetime, Ella won fourteen Grammy Awards and dozens of other honors from groups around the world.
    C. Passionate fan Marilyn Monroe helped Ella make her debut for Hollywood celebrities at the Mocambo night club.
    D. Later in life, Ella underwent several complicated surgeries and sang her final concert at Carnegie Hall in 1991.

Question 20 asks about the preceding passage as a whole.

---

20. Suppose the writer's goal had been to write a brief essay demonstrating how a musical icon influenced the subsequent career of a younger performer after a short meeting. Would this essay successfully fulfill that goal?
    F. Yes, because it is evident that the narrator highly values the memory of his or her encounter with Fitzgerald.
    G. Yes, because the career achievements of Fitzgerald have had a profound effect on American musical culture.
    H. No, because the essay omits any mention of the narrator's later career, whether as a performer or otherwise.
    J. No, because the episode described in the essay is too brief to have had lasting influence on the narrator.

Writing Strategy Answer Key

Write in whether you got each problem right or wrong (or left it blank). If your answer was correct, put a 1 in every blank to the right of that problem. Many problems test more than one type of punctuation. Sum up each column and compare your total to the total possible "Out Of" points in each column.

Problem	Correct Answer	Right/Wrong/ Blank	Additions	Choice of Content	Deletions	Goal of Essay
1	D		—			
2	H			—		
3	B				—	
4	F			—		
5	D			—		
6	F				—	
7	D			—		
8	H		—			
9	B			—		
10	F					—
11	B		—			
12	H			—		
13	B			—		
14	F				—	
15	C			—		
16	F		—			
17	D			—		
18	J				—	
19	B			—		
20	H					—
Total						
Out Of		20	4	10	4	2

Rhetorical Skills Solutions

Passage 1

1.   **(D)** Should the writer make this addition? No, because the content of the sentence strays from the main focus of the paragraph.

Rhetorical Skills   Writing Strategy   Additions

The proposed addition is a digression into the pronunciation of the last part of the word *Wunderbare*. The name of the food truck (*Wunderbare Wurst*) has already been translated for the reader (*Wonderful Sausage*), so there is no need to dive further into the intricacies of the original words. The focus of the paragraph is on the food truck itself, not the language of the name. This addition would be a distraction from that focus. The correct answer is (D).

2.   **(H)** Provides the most relevant background information on Sabine and Ferdinand: This truck was started several years ago by two <u>married German immigrants,</u> Sabine and Ferdinand, who realized that Miami was generally overflow-ing with culinary riches … but authentic bratwurst … and other real German dishes were missing.

Rhetorical Skills   Writing Strategy   Choice of Content

The most relevant background information is that Sabine and Ferdinand are "German immigrants"; that is, they came from Germany to live in Miami. This fact helps explain why they realized *authentic bratwurst … and other real German dishes were missing*—most likely because they had been raised in Germany with such dishes. The information is relevant to constructing a sensible narrative.

The incorrect choices do not provide the same level of explanatory power for Sabine's and Ferdinand's actions. It doesn't help the story to know that Sabine and Ferdinand are *adults with driver's licenses*, *dedicated entrepreneurs*, or *people not born in this country*. Sure, they can drive a food truck because they have driver's licenses, but this characteristic is not at all remarkable. Being a German immigrant in the U.S. is much less common than having a driver's license. The correct answer is (H).

3.   **(B)** If the writer were to make this deletion, the sentence would primarily lose examples of the German dishes to which the narrator is referring.

Rhetorical Skills   Writing Strategy   Deletions

The possible deletion is of the words "authentic bratwurst, sauerkraut, and other," which would leave the relevant part of the sentence as this: *who realized that Miami was generally overflowing with culinary riches, particularly the cui-sine of Cuba and other Latin American countries, but real German dishes were missing*. The deleted terms *authentic brat-wurst* and *sauerkraut* are examples of the *real German dishes* that are missing. Their role is just to illustrate this broader term. By themselves, these examples do not provide contrast with dishes from other cultures, support an earlier point, or lead logically to the next sentence (about catching the wave of gourmet food trucks). The correct answer is (B).

MANHATTAN
PREP

4.   **(F)**   Makes the most effective comparison by describing what Sabine and Ferdinand's operation could be most reasonably confused with: … gourmet food trucks, which are in a different category—and ought to be distinguished— from hot dog carts or other low-end providers.

Rhetorical Skills   Writing Strategy   Choice of Content

Sabine and Ferdinand's *operation* is a food truck that sells *Wonderful Sausage* and is in the category of *gourmet food trucks*. Of the available options, the one that describes what this food truck could most reasonably be confused with is *hot dog carts or other low-end providers*. From a distance, both are mobile vehicles (perhaps of somewhat different size) that park somewhere busy and sell food to passersby. In fact, this truck and hot dog carts both sell sausages. It is much less likely that the food truck would be confused either with a huge transport truck (that sells nothing to retail customers) or with any building, such as a gourmet restaurant or specialty delicatessen, regardless of whether the food truck serves similar dishes. The correct answer is (F).

5.   **(D)**   Most effectively illustrates the popularity of the food truck's offerings: Sabine and Ferdinand charge a premium for their products, but wherever they take the truck, they sell out.

Rhetorical Skills   Writing Strategy   Choice of Content

The fact that Sabine and Ferdinand always "sell out" is the best indicator of the "popularity of the food truck's offerings"— these offerings are so popular, in fact, that the truck always runs out of food.

The other options present interesting, valid contrasts to the first point in the sentence (that the products are expensive), but these options do not illustrate how popular those products are. The original sentence justifies the price premium by noting that the *ingredients are expensive, as is gasoline*. The other incorrect choices state that the narrator believes *customers are getting a great value* for the price they're paying, or that the owners *don't seem to be primarily motivated by money* (even though they charge a lot). None of these facts illustrate the desired point. The correct answer is (D).

6.   **(F)**   If the writer were to make this deletion, the essay would primarily lose a detail that suggests a rationale for the invitation made by the narrator.

Rhetorical Skills   Writing Strategy   Deletions

The phrase in question is *As the president of my high school's German club*, which would be deleted from before this text: "I invited their then-unknown truck to park outside a Friday night home football game." According to the correct answer, the phrase *suggests a rationale for the invitation*—that is, the truck sells German food, so it makes sense that the president of a high school's German club (who would theoretically be looking for ways to promote German culture) might seek out this truck to provide food at a school event.

The other choices do not correctly describe the role of the phrase in the sentence. Choice (B) states that the narrator *took a risk for the truck's owners*, but there is no reason to believe that the invitation constituted a risk. The phrase does not reveal what Sabine and Ferdinand thought of the narrator, as choice (C) puts it; the two entrepreneurs might be predisposed to think nicely of the narrator because he is the president of the German club, but no firm conclusions can actually be drawn. Finally, the phrase provides no *broad background information on active clubs*. All that the phrase implies is that there is an active German club. The correct answer is (F).

7.   **(D)** Most relevant at this point: I arranged for brats to be sold after all our remaining games, <u>and in the truck itself, I started operating the cash register.</u> Over the course of that year, I took on more and more responsibilities, learning the ins and outs of running a small business.

Rhetorical Skills   Writing Strategy   Choice of Content

The essay goes on to outline how the narrator *took on more and more responsibilities*, that is, for the operation of the truck. Thus, it's very logical that the underlined portion would introduce a first responsibility that the narrator took on: *operating the cash register.*

The incorrect choices refer to irrelevant events that do not prepare the reader for the next part of the paragraph. These events include changes in the German club's enrollment, the happiness expressed by the narrator's friends about the food, and the unhappiness expressed by other students (because of lower sales at the concession stand). None of these events propel the narrative forward. The correct answer is (D).

8.   **(H)** Should the writer make this addition here? No, because it distracts the reader from the main focus of the paragraph.

Rhetorical Skills   Writing Strategy   Additions

The proposed addition reads as follows: *My college doesn't have a business major exactly, so I'm studying economics.* This addition would come right after the text that describes how the narrator *took on more and more responsibilities, learning the ins and outs of running a small business.* The proposed addition is not very relevant to the paragraph, which focuses on how the narrator started working with the owners of the food truck and how he or she has progressed under their guidance. The fact that the narrator is majoring in economics because he or she can't major in business may demonstrate the narrator's interest in the general area, but this aside interrupts the storyline about the food truck. It's better not to make this addition. Its tone and style are fine, but its content is distracting. The correct answer is (H).

9.   **(B)** Most appropriate context for the rest of the sentence: They have been excellent mentors to me, and I hope that <u>when I start my own business someday,</u> I can provide the same kind of guidance to my employees.

Rhetorical Skills   Writing Strategy   Choice of Content

The last words in the sentence are *my employees.* The way to have employees is to own a business. Since the narrator does not now own his or her own business, the underlined portion should not just vaguely refer to *later in life* or *some point in the future,* but rather create a specific context in which the narrator would have employees. The right answer creates this context explicitly: *when I start my own business someday.* Choice (D) makes a nice reference back to an earlier point about smiling when you don't feel like it, but the choice does not create a context in which the narrator would have employees. The correct answer is (B).

10. **(F)** Fulfill the goal of describing the evolution of a professional relationship between a small enterprise and an employee? Yes, because the narrator outlines his or her own process of becoming a valued employee of the food truck.

Rhetorical Skills   Writing Strategy   Goal of Essay

The essay does describe *the evolution of a professional relationship between a small enterprise and an employee*. The *small enterprise* is the food truck (which at one point is referred to as a *small business*), and the *employee* is the narrator. The professional relationship is the working arrangement the narrator has with the owners of the truck, and the relationship has demonstrably evolved. The narrator first invited the truck to a football game; the success of that night led to a job offer, and the narrator *took on more and more responsibilities over time*. By the end of the essay, the narrator certainly comes across as a trusted, valued employee, one to whom the truck's owners have been *excellent mentors*.

The fact that the narrator continues to work at the same food truck now is not evidence of the evolution of the professional relationship. Plenty of people continue to work at jobs without the professional relationship between employee and employer evolving, unfortunately. The correct answer is (F).

Passage 2

11. **(B)** Would this be a relevant addition to make here? Yes, because it justifies the narrator's connection to the place where Fitzgerald would be.

Rhetorical Skills   Writing Strategy   Additions

The essay begins with the statement that the narrator once kissed Ella Fitzgerald. The next sentence answers the implied question: How did the narrator manage to meet, let alone kiss, Fitzgerald? Without the addition of *at my university*, the second sentence fails to close the gap between the narrator and Fitzgerald: *She was getting an honorary degree, and a member of the a-cappella group in which I sang had a family connection to Ella's road manager …* Where was she getting the honorary degree—and more importantly, how does that provide context for the kiss? The phrase *at my university* supplies the missing logic: the narrator and Fitzgerald would be on the same campus. The correct answer is (B).

12. **(H)** Most effectively conveys the narrator's perspective on the name of Fitzgerald's manager: Ella's road manager, the wonderfully named Val Valentine.

Rhetorical Skills   Writing Strategy   Choice of Content

The only choice from among those available that conveys any perspective or opinion is the right answer, which contains the word *wonderfully*. This adverb expresses the narrator's pleasure in Val Valentine's name. The other choices are all generally neutral: *who happened to be called* and *a man whose real name was* might both be said to put a slight emphasis on the fact that the name is unusual, but this effect is small in comparison to that created by *wonderfully*. The choice to eliminate the underlined portion is completely neutral and conveys no perspective whatsoever. The correct answer is (H).

MANHATTAN
PREP

13.   **(B)**   Provides the most logical cause for the events described in the next sentence: We lay in wait for the grande dame outside of the reception hall, <u>where she was due for a dinner the night before the degree ceremony.</u> As Ella and Val slowly climbed a ramp toward the hall, we greeted them …

Rhetorical Skills   Writing Strategy   Choice of Content

The correct choice supplies the most logical cause for the events that followed: *As Ella and Val slowly climbed a ramp toward the hall …* The fact that Fitzgerald *was due for a dinner* at that hall provides motivation for her and her manager to be coming to the hall at that time. The reference to *the reception hall* might be able to stand on its own (it's reasonable to assume that when receiving an honorary degree, at some point you might go to a reception hall), but the right choice makes the chain of cause and effect much clearer than otherwise.

The incorrect options actually make that causal sequence less clear by adding in irrelevant information. It doesn't help the story much to note that the hall was an immense Gothic building built to honor Civil War dead, or that it contains a theater in which the singing group had performed. Perhaps these details add some color, but they do not relate at all to the events that happened afterwards. The correct answer is (B).

14.   **(F)**   If the writer were to delete the preceding sentence, the paragraph would primarily lose a description of the context needed to make sense of the next few sentences.

Rhetorical Skills   Writing Strategy   Deletions

The preceding sentence is this: *Afterwards* [= after the performance], *we lined up and each gave her a kiss.* Without this sentence, the paragraph would go straight from the performance to this situation: *The only danger was that she was really leaning on each of us, a realization not shared by the last singer in line.* This narrative jump would be mysterious: why was she *leaning on each of us* during the performance? And why is there a *last singer in line*?

The sentence being considered for deletion is a key moment in the story, one that should not be deleted because it would make subsequent events harder to understand. The correct answer is (F).

15.   **(C)**   Gives the clearest glimpse into possible repercussions for the singing group if Fitzgerald had actually fallen: Only Val Valentine's quick reactions saved Ella from a bad spill—and us from terrible shame.

Rhetorical Skills   Writing Strategy   Choice of Content

Only one choice suggests particular consequences for the group if Fitzgerald had actually fallen. Combined with the first part of the sentence (which gives the subject and verb), this choice would read: "Only Val Valentine's quick reactions saved us [the group] from terrible shame." That is, at least one of the specific repercussions for the singing group would have been "terrible shame."

Choice (D) raises the specter of unknown repercussions (*who knows how bad that* [spill] *could have been*), but this is not the "clearest glimpse" into any of those repercussions. The other two choices do not hint at consequences at all. Choice (A) smooths over the situation (*thankfully, the scare was quickly over*), while choice (B) portrays a simultaneous action (*many of us leapt to her aid*). The correct answer is (C).

16.   **(F)** Should the writer make this addition here? Yes, because it illustrates more specifically the obstacles to Fitzgerald's achievements.

Rhetorical Skills   Writing Strategy   Additions

Without the addition, the text is adequate but somewhat bland: *Ella Fitzgerald overcame a difficult childhood to win an 'Amateur Night'* … The phrase *difficult childhood* can mean many different things. Adding in specific elements of Fitzgerald's difficult childhood—*one that included time in an orphanage and a reformatory school*—not only makes the vague term *difficult childhood* concrete, but also highlights the magnitude of Fitzgerald's achievement to overcome those obstacles.

It is likely that these experiences contributed to *Fitzgerald's emotional power as a singer*. However, the essay never alludes to this power, so no connection is ever drawn between her childhood experiences and this force behind her singing. As for the issue of the sentence's length, the addition does make the sentence longer, but the sentence is built in a cumulative, easily digestible fashion, so this addition is acceptable. Finally, mentioning the orphanage and reformatory school does not clash with the *positive tone established in the rest of the essay*. Even if there were such a clash, the addition lends dramatic power to the paragraph and should be made. The correct answer is (F).

17.   **(D)** Provides the most detailed and effective explanation of the cultural importance of the venue referred to in this sentence: … at the famous Apollo Theater in Harlem, New York, <u>the launching pad for many prominent African-American performers for more than eighty years.</u>

Rhetorical Skills   Writing Strategy   Choice of Content

The correct answer "provides the most detailed and effective explanation of the cultural importance of the venue," namely the Apollo Theater, by describing it as *the launching pad for many prominent African-American performers for more than eighty years*. That is, over that long span of time, numerous African-American performers started out at the Apollo and ultimately achieved prominence; as a result of this fact, the theater has cultural importance.

Choice (C) does state that the Apollo is *associated with African-American success on stage*, but that statement is just an assertion, and a rather weak one at that—not a detailed or effective explanation of why the theater is so associated. Little rationale for the theater's cultural importance is given here; a much stronger explanation is provided in the correct answer. The other incorrect choices offer historical details about the Apollo, but these details are inconsequential to the theater's cultural importance. The correct answer is (D).

18.   **(J)** By 1940, she was the bandleader of her own jazz orchestra. {Omitted sentence.} Recording countless hits and jazz standards over the next few decades, Ella became known for her agility in scat singing …

Rhetorical Skills   Writing Strategy   Deletions

The point of this short paragraph is to sketch Ella Fitzgerald's career in a rapid, yet meaningful way. The mention of Count Basie and Duke Ellington—in a way that is hardly related to Fitzgerald—is distracting. It could be worth highlighting that Fitzgerald performed with other luminaries, but the simple fact that these other people led other big bands at the same time is not relevant to the subject at hand. The best option is to delete the content altogether. The correct answer is (J).

MANHATTAN
PREP

19.   **(B)** Most effectively emphasizes the public's recognition of Fitzgerald's accomplishments: In her lifetime, Ella won fourteen Grammy Awards and dozens of other honors from groups around the world.

Rhetorical Skills   Writing Strategy   Choice of Content

The key to this question is to articulate the goal precisely: emphasizing "the public's recognition of Fitzgerald's accomplishments." That is, the additional sentence should not just emphasize her accomplishments but indicate how the public recognized those accomplishments. The correct answer states that Fitzgerald won numerous awards *from groups around the world*; this fact certainly qualifies as recognition of achievement by the public.

The other choices give insight into various achievements of Fitzgerald (her support of certain organizations, her debut at a particular night club, her surgeries, and her final concert at Carnegie Hall), but public recognition of these achievements is nowhere emphasized. The correct answer is (B).

20.   **(H)** Fulfill goal of demonstrating how a musical icon influenced the subsequent career of a younger performer after a short meeting? No, because the essay omits any mention of the narrator's later career, whether as a performer or otherwise.

Rhetorical Skills   Writing Strategy   Goal of Essay

Taken as a whole, the essay recounts a "short meeting" between the narrator (a "younger performer," since he or she is singing and is probably not as old as Fitzgerald) and Ella Fitzgerald (a "musical icon"). The essay also gives a quick summary of Fitzgerald's career and ends with a return to the personal: "As for me, I will always remember and treasure the experience of singing for one of the greatest vocalists in history."

This essay almost fulfills each condition of the goal, but a crucial element is left out. The goal is to demonstrate how a musical icon influenced a career, but the "subsequent career" of the narrator is never described. The personal impact of the encounter is certainly emphasized in the final sentence; however, no professional or career impact is ever mentioned, because the reader learns nothing about the narrator's career after the event. Thus, the essay does not fulfill the goal as stated. The correct answer is (H).

PASSAGE 3: ORGANIZATION

Bolivian Lithium

[1]

A salt flat, or dried-out lake, in a high-altitude desert in Bolivia may unlock riches for that country. This enormous and forbidding place, which may appear barren and worthless, just in case holds vast quantities of lithium, a valuable metal.
₂₁

[2]

Lithium-based greases were first used in airplane engines during World War II. However, consumption of the element is chiefly growing because of another use: batteries. Commercially introduced in 1991, lithium-ion batteries have demonstrated several excellent characteristics. These batteries are light, and they leak more slowly than many other kinds of batteries.

In addition, they can be recharged without first having
₂₃

to be drained completely. In contrast, nickel-cadmium batteries permanently lose storage capacity if they are recharged when still partially full.
₂₄

[3]

[1] The explosion in the popularity of mobile devices is not the only factor triggering increased demand for lithium, though. [2] Automobiles using hybrid gas-electric or all-electric motors currently require lithium-ion batteries. [3] Unsurprisingly, an automobile uses far more lithium than a cell phone.

21. **A.** NO CHANGE
    B. likewise
    C. in summary
    D. in fact

22. Given that all of the choices are true, which one provides the most effective introduction to this paragraph?
    F. NO CHANGE
    G. The United States government has sold the lithium hydroxide it had stockpiled for hydrogen bombs.
    H. Lithium is the lightest metallic element and the third lightest element on the periodic table.
    J. The largest current use of lithium is in the manufacture of glass and ceramic materials.

23. **A.** NO CHANGE
    B. Therefore,
    C. However,
    D. For example,

24. Given that all the choices are true, which one most effectively concludes this paragraph and offers the best transition to the next paragraph?
    F. NO CHANGE
    G. As a result of these advantages, lithium-ion is the preferred battery type for cellular phones and other portable electronic devices.
    H. Moreover, lithium-ion batteries contain less toxic material than do lead-acid batteries and many other rechargeable kinds.
    J. At the same time, lithium-ion batteries can discharge so quickly that they can catch fire if built-in safeguards fail.

MANHATTAN
PREP

[4] For this reason, even if the market for hybrid and
25
electric automobiles only grows gradually in the future,

the industrial need for lithium will soar. 26

[4]

[1] In the Salar de Uyuni, the Bolivian salt flat,
a crust just a few feet thick covers a briny soup rich

in lithium compounds. [2] So, extraction of lithium
27

from this brine has been limited. [3] Nevertheless,
28
the government recently collaborated with a Chinese
company to build a battery-manufacturing plant.
[4] The Bolivian government is wary of possible

exploitation and thus has maintained tight control over
29
its lithium resources. [5] The hope is to develop Bolivia's
production of lithium, not only as raw ore, but also as a

component of finished batteries for export. 30

25. **A.** NO CHANGE
    B. even so,
    C. although
    D. as

26. Upon reviewing the third paragraph and realizing that some information has been left out, the writer composes the following sentence:

    Only these kinds of batteries are light enough to store energy efficiently inside a vehicle.

    The most logical placement for this sentence would be:

    F. before Sentence 1.
    G. after Sentence 1.
    H. after Sentence 2.
    J. after Sentence 3.

27. **A.** NO CHANGE
    B. So far,
    C. Then,
    D. Therefore,

28. Which of the following alternatives to the underlined portion would be LEAST acceptable?
    F. However,
    G. Still,
    H. Except,
    J. At the same time,

29. **A.** NO CHANGE
    B. since
    C. otherwise
    D. in reality

30. For the sake of the logic and coherence of Paragraph 4, Sentence 3 should be placed:
    F. where it is now.
    G. after Sentence 1.
    H. after Sentence 4.
    J. after Sentence 5.

4

PASSAGE 4: ORGANIZATION

Animal Tales

[1]

[1] It is probably impossible to identify a human culture in which stories are or were not told about talking animals. [2] <u>Therefore</u>, in the modern world,
₃₁
such stories are technically reserved for children—

<u>because</u> anyone attending an animated movie in which
₃₂
penguins speak would likely see as many engrossed

adults as kids. [3] <u>However</u>, these kinds of stories have
₃₃
a long, broad, and distinguished history with audiences of all ages around the globe. [4] What role or roles do

stories about talking animals play in society? ▢34

[2]

[1] <u>Think back to your own childhood, to a
₃₅
time when you heard an animal speak in a story.</u>
₃₅
[2] Somehow, a tale that introduces a talking animal becomes fascinating and even magical to its listeners, transporting them to "Once upon a time," a very different world from the everyday one. [3] In many

31. A. NO CHANGE
   B. In addition,
   C. Furthermore,
   D. Of course,

32. F. NO CHANGE
   G. whether
   H. although
   J. unless

33. Which of the following alternatives to the underlined portion would be LEAST acceptable?
   A. That said,
   B. Nevertheless,
   C. Yet
   D. OMIT the underlined portion (capitalizing the following word appropriately).

34. Upon reviewing the prior paragraph and realizing that some information has been left out, the writer composes the following sentence:

> The reason seems to be that tales in which animals talk like humans are not now regarded as serious, important fare for intelligent adults.

The most logical and effective place to add this sentence would be after Sentence:
   F. 1.
   G. 2.
   H. 3.
   J. 4.

35. Given that all the choices are true, which one provides the most effective transition from the previous paragraph and opens this paragraph most clearly?
   A. NO CHANGE
   B. One obvious role of animal stories is entertainment: providing a diversion from normal reality.
   C. The term "talking animal" is intended to exclude humans, who are animals that actually talk.
   D. It is difficult to catalog all the functions that animal stories can serve within a culture.

MANHATTAN
PREP

traditional cultures, animal stories often have an explicit spiritual or religious meaning as well, one that strives to make sense of the cosmos. [4] For example, some Native American groups recount legends of their wolf or bear ancestors. [5] Sometimes, the associated explanations are focused. [6] For instance, the Lenape people, who once lived in what would become Delaware, Pennsylvania, and New York, tell a story explaining why the rabbit's shoulders are narrow. [7] Other stories paint a bigger picture, describing the creation of the world and connecting people to the natural environment. [8] This connection can be perfectly literal. 36

[3]

[1] Animal stories often have other important social uses, such as imparting personal moral lessons. [2] Aesop's Fables are meant to teach moral judgment safely by using animal characters. [3] The medicine is a little easier to swallow when it's a fox, not a person, who complains about sour grapes. [4] Likewise, tales of a trickster animal, such as Coyote, abound in Native American cultures, often serving up morals as warnings. [5] Animals have <u>then</u> been used in satires to
₃₇
criticize powers-that-be or current events in a disguised way. [6] Perhaps the most famous example in modern times is *Animal Farm*, in which British author George Orwell represents the Russian Revolution of 1917 and its aftermath in a veiled way, relating the tale of English farm animals who free themselves of their evil master, only to fall under the yoke of the pigs. [7] <u>Even with</u>
₃₈
this camouflage, Orwell had trouble finding a publisher during World War II. [8] The parallels were too obvious—and controversial—for some contemporary

36. For the sake of the logic and coherence of the preceding paragraph, Sentence 4 should be placed:

   F. where it is now.
   G. after Sentence 2.
   H. after Sentence 6.
   J. after Sentence 8.

37. A. NO CHANGE
   B. still
   C. also
   D. soon

38. F. NO CHANGE
   G. Because of
   H. Other than
   J. To illustrate

readers. [9] <u>After all, the Soviet Union (represented</u>
<u>by a pig dictatorship in the book) was an ally of Great</u>
<u>Britain at the time.</u>
₃₉

39. Given that all of the choices are true, which one most effectively concludes this paragraph by providing the best explanation of why Orwell struggled to have *Animal Farm* published?

A. NO CHANGE

B. Today, though, the book is read annually by hundreds of thousands of students worldwide.

C. One of Orwell's other novels, *Nineteen Eighty-Four*, had a smoother road to publication.

D. The fictional pigs could be matched up to specific human leaders of the Russian Revolution.

> Question 40 asks about the preceding passage as a whole.

40. The writer has decided to divide the final paragraph in two. The best place to add the new paragraph break would be at the beginning of Sentence:

F. 4, because it would distinguish between the example of Aesop's Fables and that of Native American trickster tales in an appropriate manner.

G. 5, because it would reinforce that the essay shifts from describing the role of animal stories as morality tales to describing their role as satires.

H. 6, because it would provide clear separation and emphasis to the closing example of the essay, Orwell's satirical novel *Animal Farm*.

J. 7, because it would signal that the essay is going to conclude with a dramatic case of how a modern animal story can ignite controversy.

Organization Answer Key

Write in whether you got each problem right or wrong (or left it blank). If your answer was correct, put a 1 in every blank to the right of that problem. Many problems test more than one type of punctuation. Sum up each column and compare your total to the total possible "Out Of" points in each column.

Problem	Correct Answer	Right/Wrong/ Blank	Opening/ Closing Content	Paragraph Break	Sentence Order	Transitions
21	D					—
22	J		—			
23	A					—
24	G		—			
25	A					—
26	H				—	
27	B					—
28	H					—
29	A					—
30	H				—	
31	D					—
32	H					—
33	D					—
34	G				—	
35	B		—			
36	J				—	
37	C					—
38	F					—
39	A		—			
40	G			—		
Total						
Out Of		20	4	1	4	11

Organization Solutions

Passage 3

21.   **(D)** This enormous and forbidding place, which may appear barren and worthless, <u>in fact</u> holds vast quantities of lithium, a valuable metal.

Rhetorical Skills   Organization   Transitions

The transition here needs to signal a contrast between appearances (*barren and worthless*) and the underlying reality (*holds vast quantities of lithium, a valuable metal*). The best choice is *in fact*, which stresses exactly such a contrast: this desert may seem worthless, but *in fact* it contains riches. The other choices (*just in case, likewise,* and *in summary*) do not signal a contrast at all, let alone one between appearance and reality. The correct answer is (D).

22.   **(J)**   Most effective introduction to this paragraph: <u>The largest current use of lithium is in the manufacture of glass and ceramic materials.</u> However, consumption of the element is chiefly growing because of another use: batteries.

Rhetorical Skills   Organization   Opening/Closing Content

The second sentence provides the necessary clues for determining the right first sentence for this paragraph. The transition *However* tells you that the sentences are in contrast with each other. Next, the second sentence states that *consumption of the element [lithium] is chiefly growing because of another use* … If this sentence is pointing out "another" use, then the first sentence should be pointing out some use of the element. Moreover, the tense of the verb (*is … growing*) is present, indicating that the first use ought to be in the present as well. It should be an important use as well, because the *However* means that before reading the second sentence, you might expect growth in lithium consumption to come from that first use.

Putting all these deductions together, you can predict the general shape of the first sentence: *Here is an important way lithium is used at present. However, consumption of the element is chiefly growing because of another use: batteries.* The correct answer provides just such an important current use ("in the manufacture of glass and ceramic materials").

Choices (F) and (G) provide uses of lithium, but these are stated as *historical* uses—airplane grease during World War II and hydrogen bomb production (*had stockpiled*). Thus, these uses do not form the best contrast to the second sentence, which seeks to explain the growth in current consumption of lithium. Choice (G) in fact emphasizes the sale of lithium material, as if its use in hydrogen bombs were no longer relevant. Finally, choice (H) does not list a use of lithium at all. The correct answer is (J).

23.   **(A)** … lithium-ion batteries have demonstrated several excellent characteristics. These batteries are light, and they leak more slowly than many other kinds of batteries. <u>In addition,</u> they can be recharged without first having to be drained completely.

Rhetorical Skills   Organization   Transitions

The best transition for the beginning of the sentence in question is one that essentially means "also." The prior sentence lists two excellent characteristics of lithium-ion batteries: light weight and slow leakage. The sentence in question lists a third characteristic related to recharging the batteries. For the next item in a list, a transition such as *In addition* is appropriate.

The other available transitions do not serve the right need. *Therefore* would work if the recharging capability (the fact that these batteries can be recharged without first draining them completely) logically followed from either of the first two properties, but it does not. *However* would indicate a contrast, but no contrast is required here. Finally, *For example* would indicate an example, and in fact, this list is one of examples. However, you would need to use *For example* at the beginning of the list, not toward the end. The correct answer is (A).

24.   **(G)** Most effectively concludes this paragraph and offers the best transition to the next paragraph: These batteries are light, and they leak more slowly than many other kinds of batteries. In addition, they can be recharged without first having to be drained completely. <u>As a result of these advantages, lithium-ion is the preferred battery type for cellular phones and other portable electronic devices.</u>

Rhetorical Skills   Organization   Opening/Closing Content

The correct choice provides a key implication of the various beneficial characteristics of lithium-ion batteries: they are *preferred* for use in *cellular phones and other portable electronic devices*. However, it's not necessary that the last sentence in a paragraph provide an implication of earlier statements. In fact, all of the incorrect choices are suitable as the final sentence of this paragraph, if this paragraph is only considered by itself.

What differentiates the correct choice is that it links properly to the first sentence of the next paragraph, which begins as follows: *The explosion in the popularity of mobile devices is not the only factor triggering increased demand for lithium, though.* The *though* means that this sentence must contrast to the end of the previous paragraph. Therefore, the final sentence of that paragraph must have alluded to *mobile devices* and how they are *triggering increased demand for lithium.* Otherwise, it would not make sense to say that this is *not the only factor* having that effect. The correct answer makes the right connection: these batteries are preferred for use in mobile devices.

As was already mentioned, the incorrect choices are all at least decent conclusions to the prior paragraph, each with different content (another advantage of these batteries, a disadvantage of them, and a contrast with another kind of battery). However, none of these choices work well with the beginning of the following paragraph, because none of them mention mobile devices at all, let alone how these devices are driving demand for lithium. The correct answer is (G).

25.   **(A)** Unsurprisingly, an automobile uses far more lithium than a cell phone. For this reason, <u>even if</u> the market for hybrid and electric automobiles only grows gradually in the future, the industrial need for lithium will soar.

Rhetorical Skills   Organization   Transitions

The logical conjunction to use here is *even if*, which precedes a condition that surprisingly leads to some result. "Even if you eat all the ice cream, I will still be nice to you." You might expect the opposite result, but the word *even* stresses the fact that you still get the stated result (I will be nice to you) under the given condition (you eat all the ice cream). In the text, the condition is *the market for hybrid and electric automobiles only grows gradually in the future.* Under that condition, you might expect that the need for lithium will also grow gradually, but in fact, that need *will soar.* Thus, *even if* creates the correct relationship between the parts of the sentence.

The incorrect choices all create illogical or non-grammatical relationships. *Even so* is not even a conjunction, so the sentence becomes a run-on (with two independent clauses joined by a comma). *Although* might seem to work (it creates a contrast), but *although* doesn't precede a condition; it precedes a fact. "Although you eat all the ice cream (in general), I am still nice to you." The problem is that what follows is not known to be a fact ("the market … only grows gradually in the future"). Rather, it's a condition: a possible future occurrence. *Although the market only grows gradually in the future* probably sounds strange, because it would mean that the writer knows the market will grow gradually in the future, but such things can't be known. Finally, *as* also precedes facts and fails to set up any contrast or surprise. The correct answer is (A).

26. **(H)** The most logical placement for this sentence would be after Sentence 2.

Rhetorical Skills   Organization   Sentence Order

The proposed addition begins with *Only these kinds of batteries*. Thus, the sentence should immediately follow a reference to some kind or kinds of batteries. Sentence 2 ends with *lithium-ion batteries*, so you should try placing the addition after Sentence 2. Here is what you get:

> *Automobiles using hybrid gas-electric or all-electric motors currently require lithium-ion batteries. Only these kinds of batteries are light enough to store energy efficiently inside a vehicle.*

The result makes narrative sense. The addition explains Sentence 2, which states that certain vehicles *currently require lithium-ion batteries*. Why are these particular batteries required? The reason is given in the addition: only lithium-ion batteries are *light enough to store energy efficiently inside a vehicle*. The reference to *a vehicle* is also sensible now, because it follows a sentence about hybrid and electric automobiles.

In any other position, the addition fails to connect to the prior sentence, which lacks a reference to lithium-ion batteries, automobiles, or both. Moreover, the addition performs its explanatory role only in the correct position. The correct answer is (H).

27. **(B)** In the Salar de Uyuni, the Bolivian salt flat, a crust just a few feet thick covers a briny soup rich in lithium compounds. <u>So far,</u> extraction of lithium from this brine has been limited.

Rhetorical Skills   Organization   Transitions

The only reasonable transition among the choices is *So far*, meaning "up to now." Other transitions would be possible, but the wrong choices are all impossible. *So* and *therefore* would mean that the second sentence logically follows from the first. However, the crust that *covers a briny soup rich in lithium compounds* is *just a few feet thick* (that is, not very thick), so you would expect that it would be easy to extract the lithium. Extraction "has been limited," though. So the second sentence is actually in contrast to the first sentence, and a causal transition, such as *so* or *therefore,* should be avoided. Finally, *then* would indicate either a causal relationship (like *So* or *Therefore*) or a temporal one (when *then* means "at that time" or "next"). Neither relationship is appropriate here. The correct answer is (B).

28. **(H)** Least acceptable: <u>Except,</u> the government recently collaborated with a Chinese company to build a battery-manufacturing plant.

Rhetorical Skills   Organization   Transitions

The original transition is *Nevertheless,* so the acceptable transitions should all indicate contrast (just as *Nevertheless* does). In fact, all of the choices do or can indicate contrast: *However, Still, Except,* and *At the same time.* The difference is grammatical. *Except* is a preposition and so must be followed by a noun or pronoun ("I know everyone here *except him*"). In standard written English, *Except* cannot be used by itself at the beginning of a sentence to indicate general contrast with the previous sentence in the way that *Nevertheless* and the other transitions here can be used. Since you are looking for the least acceptable alternative, *Except* is the right answer to the question. The correct answer is (H).

29. **(A)** The Bolivian government is wary of possible exploitation and <u>thus</u> has maintained tight control over its lithium resources.

Rhetorical Skills   Organization   Transitions

The relationship between the two parts of the sentence is causal. That is, the first part (*The Bolivian government is wary of possible exploitation*) logically leads to the second part (that government *has maintained tight control over its lithium resources*). Therefore, a causal transition is appropriate. Among the choices, only *thus* fits the bill.

Since in this position would mean "since then," and even if it preceded an entire clause to take on a causal meaning, that meaning is exactly opposite of what you want. "I like ice cream; *thus,* I eat a lot of it" means something very different from "I like ice cream *since* I eat a lot of it." Cause and effect are reversed. The other two choices, *otherwise* ("or else, in other circumstances") and *in reality* ("in fact"), do not signify the correct relationship between the parts of the sentence. The correct answer is (A).

30. **(H)** For the sake of the logic and coherence of this paragraph, Sentence 3 should be placed after Sentence 4.

Rhetorical Skills   Organization   Sentence Order

The subject of Sentence 3 is *the government,* while the subject of Sentence 4 is "the Bolivian government." This slight difference in reference is a useful clue to the correct relative position of the two sentences. Logically, the first reference should be the most specific, in order to make sure that the reader knows which government is intended: the Bolivian government. After that, the term can be safely shortened to *the government,* as long as no other government is introduced. Thus, Sentence 3 should happen somewhere after Sentence 4. The position immediately after Sentence 4 makes the most sense, as can be seen in the corrected order:

[4] The Bolivian government is wary of possible exploitation and thus has maintained tight control over its lithium resources.

[3] Nevertheless, the government recently collaborated with a Chinese company to build a battery-manufacturing plant.

[5] The hope is to develop Bolivia's production of lithium, not only as raw ore, but also as a component of finished batteries for export.

MANHATTAN
PREP

The contrast transition *Nevertheless* is sensible: the Bolivian government has maintained tight control over lithium resources, but it recently collaborated with a Chinese company. Moreover, Sentence 5 makes much more sense now. *The hope* in Sentence 5 is evidently the hope for the battery-manufacturing plant in Sentence 3—that it will *develop Bolivia's production of lithium ... as a component of finished batteries for export.* Sentence 3 closes a logic gap that now exists between Sentences 4 and 5.

No other position for Sentence 3 is as reasonable as the one after Sentence 4. The original position may seem okay for the *Nevertheless*, but the gap between Sentences 4 and 5 would remain unclosed. The correct answer is (H).

Passage 4

31.   **(D)** It is probably impossible to identify a human culture in which stories are or were not told about talking animals. <u>Of course,</u> in the modern world, such stories are technically reserved for children ...

Rhetorical Skills   Organization   Transitions

The second sentence qualifies, or limits, the scope of the first sentence, since the first sentence claims that animal stories are everywhere, while the second sentence points out that these stories are *technically reserved for children* in today's world. Thus, the two sentences are in contrast with each other to some extent.

The only transition among the choices that works is *Of course*, which can function to limit a broad claim ("I am the best basketball player in the world; *of course*, by 'the world,' I mean my driveway"). The original version of the sentence uses *Therefore*, which would indicate that the second sentence flows logically from the first. The other two choices, *In addition* and *Furthermore,* would suggest that the second sentence is at least aligned with the first. However, since these two sentences are actually in conflict, all three alternatives are inappropriate. The correct answer is (D).

32.   **(H)** ... in the modern world, such stories are technically reserved for children—<u>although</u> anyone attending an animated movie in which penguins speak would likely see as many engrossed adults as kids.

Rhetorical Skills   Organization   Transitions

The two parts of this sentence are meant to be in contrast with each other. The first part claims that animal stories are *for children*, while the second part points out that you would see *as many engrossed adults as kids* at a movie that involves talking penguins. The first point remains the most important; the second point is intended to be just a concession, not a full reversal. For concessions, the conjunction *although* works perfectly.

The other choices are not as appropriate as *although*. *Because* signals a cause, not a concession. *Whether* doesn't signal a concession; rather, it signals that a possible condition is unimportant ("I'm eating this ice cream, *whether* you like it or not"). This meaning doesn't fit the scenario of the animated film very well—it's easier to read that scenario as an actual fact than as a condition that may or may not hold. Finally, *unless* means "if not." Placed into the sentence, this conjunction would make the following statement: *if* you are *not* likely to see as many engrossed adults as children at an animated film, then these stories are reserved for children. How, though, would that observation prove the point (that the stories are for children)? This claim is unreasonable. The correct answer is (H).

33. **(D)** Least acceptable: … in the modern world, such stories are technically reserved for children … [omitted] These kinds of stories have a long, broad, and distinguished history with audiences of all ages around the globe.

| Rhetorical Skills | Organization | Transitions |

The underlined portion should signal a contrast, as the original transition (*However*) does, because the coming thought is at odds with the prior one. These stories are now reserved for children; *however*, these stories have a long history with audiences of all ages. Proper alternatives to *However* include *That said, Nevertheless,* and *Yet*, all of which indicate a reversal. The option that is least acceptable is to omit the underlined portion completely and put no contrast signal at all. Since you are looking for the least acceptable option, this choice is correct. The correct answer is (D).

34. **(G)** The most logical and effective place to add this sentence would be after Sentence 2.

| Rhetorical Skills | Organization | Sentence Order |

The sentence in question is this: *The reason seems to be that tales in which animals talk like humans are not now regarded as serious, important fare for intelligent adults.* Since the subject is *The reason*, the rest of the sentence needs to be the reason for, or an explanation of, the previous sentence. *Animal stories are not considered serious enough for adults* is a reasonable summary of the explanation. This point would most logically explain the main clause of Sentence 2, which asserts that today, animal stories are meant for children. In this position, the addition also works well with Sentence 3 (which would follow afterward):

[2] … in the modern world, such stories are technically reserved for children … [Addition] The reason seems to be that tales in which animals talk like humans are not now regarded as serious, important fare for intelligent adults. [3] However, these kinds of stories have a long … history with audiences of all ages …

No other position in this paragraph is suitable for the proposed addition. Sentence 1 claims that animal stories are universal; very similarly, Sentence 3 claims that these stories have a long history with audiences of all ages. Neither of these claims is explained by "animal stories are not serious enough for adults"; if anything, this point is incompatible with those claims. Finally, Sentence 4 poses a question: What roles do these stories play in society? The addition fails to answer this question; it also would interfere with the question's purpose, which is to set up the rest of the essay. The correct answer is (G).

35. **(B)** Most effective transition from previous paragraph and clearest opening to this paragraph: One obvious role of animal stories is entertainment: providing a diversion from normal reality.

| Rhetorical Skills | Organization | Opening/Closing Content |

The first paragraph closes with a rhetorical question: What role (or roles) do stories about talking animals play in society? In this position at the end of the first paragraph, the question is evidently meant to be answered throughout the rest of the essay. Almost certainly, more than one role will be outlined. Thus, a fitting transition sentence (such as the right answer) would introduce a first role of animal stories: *One obvious role of animal stories is entertainment* … The next sentence explores this entertainment role further.

The original sentence (*Think back to your own childhood* …) is nicely engaging and works in isolation with the next sentence, but the first role is not directly named or identified. Thus, within the essay, this choice does not serve the clear *signpost* function that the correct answer does. Choice (C), which clarifies the term *talking animal* to mean non-humans, is a distracting aside. Choice (D), which claims that it is *difficult to catalog all the functions* of animal stories, answers the previous question in a wishy-washy way, without plainly indicating the first such function. The correct answer is (B).

36. **(J)** For the sake of the logic and coherence of the preceding paragraph, Sentence 4 should be placed after Sentence 8.

Rhetorical Skills   Organization   Sentence Order

Sentence 4 reads thus: *For example, some Native American groups recount legends of their wolf or bear ancestors.* To some degree, it fits in its current position: it provides an example of animal stories having spiritual meaning that *strives to make sense of the cosmo*s. The real problem is the gap at the end of the paragraph. The last two sentences (7 and 8) make assertions that cry out for an example:

> [7] Other stories paint a bigger picture, describing the creation of the world and connecting people to the natural environment. [8] This connection can be perfectly literal.

What is meant by a *literal* connection to the natural environment? As currently structured, the paragraph doesn't explain, and the next paragraph moves on to *other important social uses* of animal stories. Sentence 4, if moved to the end of the paragraph, supplies the missing example—having wolf or bear ancestors certainly qualifies as being literally connected to the natural environment. Shifting Sentence 4 to the end does remove the example from its current position, but the transition from Sentence 3 to Sentence 5 works without an example:

> [3] In many traditional cultures, animal stories often have an explicit spiritual or religious meaning as well, one that strives to make sense of the cosmos. [5] Sometimes, the associated explanations are focused.

No other position for Sentence 4 works as well as the end of the paragraph, where the example most clearly fits the prior point, and that point would otherwise be left hanging. The correct answer is (J).

37. **(C)** Animal stories often have other important social uses, such as imparting personal moral lessons. Aesop's Fables are meant to teach moral judgment safely by using animal characters … Animals have <u>also</u> been used in satires to criticize powers-that-be or current events in a disguised way.

Rhetorical Skills   Organization   Transitions

The first example of *other important social uses* is named in the opening sentence: *imparting personal moral lessons*. The following few sentences elaborate on this point. Finally, the sentence in question introduces another important social use of animal stories: satires that *criticize powers-that-be or current events*. The best available transition to this new use is *also*, which signals that the use of animal stories as satires is one more example, following the prior example of moral lessons.

The alternatives (*then, still,* and *soon*) do not indicate that this sentence is next on the list. Perhaps the closest wrong answer is *then*, but whether *then* is taken to mean "at that time" or "as a result," the meaning of this transition is not in tune with the sentence's content, which is just another example in a list. The correct answer is (C).

38. **(F)** ... British author George Orwell represents the Russian Revolution of 1917 and its aftermath in a veiled way ... <u>Even with</u> this camouflage, Orwell had trouble finding a publisher during World War II. The parallels were too obvious for some contemporary readers.

| Rhetorical Skills | Organization | Transitions |

The preposition before *this camouflage* should point out the contrast: although the book had this camouflage, Orwell had trouble finding a publisher. The best choice from among the answer choices is *Even with*. Good alternatives would be *Despite* and *In spite of*.

The incorrect choices suggest illogical relationships between the camouflage and the publishing trouble Orwell had. *Because of* would make the camouflage the cause of the trouble, but the trouble happened in spite of the camouflage. *Other than* creates a contrast of sorts, but the meaning of *besides* is out of place. Finally, *To illustrate* would wrongly mean that the trouble was an example of the camouflage. The correct answer is (F).

39. **(A)** Most effectively concludes this paragraph by providing the best explanation of why Orwell struggled to have *Animal Farm* published: <u>After all, the Soviet Union (represented by a pig dictatorship in the book) was an ally of Great Britain at the time.</u>

| Rhetorical Skills | Organization | Opening/Closing Content |

The two sentences before the final paragraph read as follows: *Even with this camouflage, Orwell had trouble finding a publisher during World War II. The parallels were too obvious—and controversial—for some contemporary readers.* The question asks for the conclusion that provides the best explanation for Orwell's trouble. The correct answer gives the most compelling argument: the Soviet Union (the target of the satire) was "an ally of Great Britain at the time [during World War II]." That is, the political environment in time of war undermined Orwell's ability to publish his book, in which the parallels to real life "were too obvious—and controversial—for some contemporary readers."

Choices (B) and (C) do not provide explanations for *Animal Farm*'s trouble at all—rather, they describe the current readership of the book and the publication of a different book by Orwell. Choice (D) does provide an explanation for some readers' discomfort (the fictional pigs could be matched up to specific humans), but this choice is clearly weaker than the correct answer. The fact that the pigs could be identified with humans would make the book uncomfortable for some, perhaps even controversial, but many books are published that cause some controversy. Moreover, the text indicates elsewhere that the camouflage was rather thin, so this choice does not yield much new information. The more effective explanation for Orwell's trouble is based in the political atmosphere of the time, in which criticism of the Soviet Union could be seen as weakening the British war effort. The correct answer is (A).

40. **(G)** The best place to add the new paragraph break would be at the beginning of Sentence 5, because it would reinforce that the essay shifts from describing the role of animal stories as morality tales to describing their role as satires.

| Rhetorical Skills | Organization | Paragraph Break |

The final paragraph is very long, so it makes sense that the writer might want to break this paragraph in two. The most natural place to make this break is before Sentence 5. Sentences 1 through 4 concentrate on how animal stories can convey *personal moral lessons*, as seen in the examples of Aesop's Fables and Native American trickster tales. Sentence 5

MANHATTAN
PREP

provides a pivot to another use of animal stories: as satires that *criticize powers-that-be or current events in a disguised way.* The rest of the paragraph describes *Animal Farm*, an example of such a satire. Logically, then, Sentences 1 through 4 can form their own coherent paragraph about animal stories as morality tales; meanwhile, in a different paragraph, Sentences 5 through 9 focus on the satirical use of animal stories.

No other paragraph break makes as much sense. Sentence 5, which introduces the idea of animal satires, should be kept with the *Animal Farm* example in the following sentences. Likewise, the examples of morality tales earlier in the paragraph should be kept together. The correct answer is (G).

4

STYLE PROBLEMS

41. In 628, a prominent Indian mathematician named Brahmagupta described the use of negative numbers, which were generally opposed in Europe for the following ten or so centuries, which is about a thousand years.

    A. NO CHANGE
    B. centuries—approximately one thousand years.
    C. centuries, the rough duration of a millennium.
    D. centuries.

42. Among historians of science, there is consensus that Isaac Newton and Gottfried Leibniz each discovered and subsequently developed modern calculus independently of the other. Even their notation and terminology vary in such a way that it is hard to conceive of outright plagiarism. However, the matter of who first "invented" the field was historically a matter of strong debate; today, the issue may plain stump folks for good.

    F. NO CHANGE
    G. may never be resolved satisfactorily.
    H. might just be one of those things you have to shrug about.
    J. is a mysterious conundrum that may never be solved and put to rest to everyone's satisfaction.

43. Author and Nobel laureate Toni Morrison is known for her masterful ability to represent, describe, and portray in her writing the subtle, winding currents of feelings that her characters experience.

    A. NO CHANGE
    B. represent and portray
    C. describe and represent
    D. represent

44. At a certain point, solid state memory became so cheap that flash drives that had earlier been loaded with music or video files beforehand could be given away as promotional items.

    F. NO CHANGE
    G. previously
    H. before that time
    J. OMIT the underlined portion.

45. In a renewed effort to win the state contract, Callie and her team worked around the clock to prepare what would turn out to be a persuasive presentation to government officials.

    Which choice would be LEAST likely to suggest that Callie's endeavor was successful?

    A. NO CHANGE
    B. compelling
    C. rousing
    D. convincing

46. In the 1930s and '40s, "Little" Ann Little Rothschild recorded the voice of Betty Boop, a well-liked cartoon character modeled on the flapper women of the Roaring Twenties.

    F. NO CHANGE
    G. really rather well-liked cartoon character
    H. well-liked, it might be said, cartoon character
    J. well-liked cartoon character who was popular and

47. After a few months, Sheila began to distrust her office mate, who frequently made flattering statements excessively praising her and her work in private but undercut her in public meetings.

    A. NO CHANGE
    B. statements to compliment her work often, though to an extreme
    C. statement after statement of insincere admiration of her work
    D. statements about her work

48. It was the fulfillment of a lifelong dream for Emily to receive her Ph.D. and begin teaching public health to first-generation college students at her new university.

    F. NO CHANGE
    G. start instructing
    H. commence educating
    J. embark on inculcating

49. The management team of the nonprofit organization found it difficult to <u>champion and defend a position that stirred such controversial debate.</u>

    A. NO CHANGE
    B. defend and support a divisive position that stirred such controversy.
    C. support and champion such a contentious, divisive position.
    D. defend such a controversial position.

50. Early researchers studying the nervous system used electric—or, as they were then called, galvanic—currents to <u>induce</u> a physiological response in dissected nerve cells.

    Which of the following alternatives to the underlined word would be LEAST acceptable?

    F. generate
    G. evoke
    H. entice
    J. produce

51. On the heels of an engineering breakthrough, the prospects of the solar-cell company have dramatically risen the last several weeks, <u>and during this recent period up to now</u> investors have poured into the stock, sending the price skyrocketing.

    A. NO CHANGE
    B. so during these weeks of good fortune
    C. and things have been looking up, so
    D. so

52. Michael has been reluctant to address the poor working conditions at his job. Unfortunately, no one else is going to fight his battle for him; he needs to search within himself and find the right personal <u>catalyst that will provide a stimulus,</u> so that he can seize the opportunity to resolve these issues at work.

    F. NO CHANGE
    G. catalyst to give him impetus,
    H. catalyst to be a spur to action,
    J. catalyst

53. Just as the application of mechanical stress to a piezoelectric crystal causes it to develop an electric voltage, the application of a voltage to the same crystal can cause it to <u>contract or multiply</u> in various directions.

    A. NO CHANGE
    B. shrink or enlarge
    C. shrivel or amplify
    D. lessen or escalate

54. The water here is safe for swimming, <u>due to the capability that</u> you can always see the bottom and easily resist the gentle current.

    F. NO CHANGE
    G. thanks to the ability that you have that
    H. since
    J. so

55. It is an unfortunate consequence of the current state of medical knowledge that <u>occasionally,</u> the initial symptoms of viral infections that pose low threats to most of the population can seldom be distinguished from those of much more serious illnesses.

    A. NO CHANGE
    B. rarely,
    C. infrequently,
    D. OMIT the underlined portion.

56. Incorporating appropriate safety mechanisms, the chain-link fence properly folded over when <u>a numerous multitude</u> pressed against it and spilled onto the soccer field.

    Which of the following would provide the MOST specific estimate of the size of the crowd?

    F. NO CHANGE
    G. a mass of several hundred people
    H. a swarming, teeming throng
    J. a mob of countless fans

4

57. Architects of any plan to rescue a failing bank need to pose tough questions. Overall, is the plan plausible? <u>Believable?</u> What resources will be required to implement the plan, under both optimistic and pessimistic scenarios? How long will the plan take to put into effect, and when can its goals be expected to be achieved?

   A. NO CHANGE
   B. Can it be believed?
   C. Or is it incredible?
   D. OMIT the underlined portion.

58. The annals of history are filled with examples of extinct realms whose legacy survives, perhaps primarily, in words. The Spanish language frequently refers to itself as *castellano,* or Castilian, and in fact the Spanish monarch has, among other designations, the <u>exalted</u> title of King of Castile, but this title is in name only: the medieval state as a living entity has vanished.

Which choice would be MOST consistent with the academic tone established elsewhere in this passage?

   F. NO CHANGE
   G. quality
   H. top-notch
   J. fabulous

59. Suddenly he realized that to attempt to flee in his car to the mainland would be nearly impossible, and certainly dangerous, <u>in</u> the chaos of the hurricane sweeping across the island town and its environs.

Which of the following alternatives to the underlined portion would NOT be acceptable?

   A. amid
   B. during
   C. between
   D. in the midst of

60. To alleviate the effects of the spike in oil prices on a population struggling with an unusually cold winter, the minister temporarily put into effect a series of small measures and <u>programs that were only short-lived.</u>

   F. NO CHANGE
   G. programs.
   H. programs limited in both scope and duration.
   J. programs that did not last very long.

Style Answer Key

Write in whether you got each problem right or wrong (or left it blank). If your answer was correct, put a 1 in every blank to the right of that problem. Problems may be categorized in more than one column. Sum up each column and compare your total to the total possible "Out Of" points in each column.

Problem	Correct Answer	Right/ Wrong/Blank	Concision	Word Choice
41	D		—	
42	G			—
43	D		—	
44	J		—	
45	C			—
46	F		—	
47	D		—	
48	F			—
49	D		—	
50	H			—
51	D		—	
52	J		—	
53	B			—
54	H		—	
55	D		—	
56	G			—
57	D		—	
58	F			—
59	C			—
60	G		—	
Total				
Out Of		20	12	8

By the way, if it seems to you that a lot of the right answers above are D's or J's, then congratulations: you have noticed a real pattern in the ACT that is deliberately mimicked in this practice set. In the Second Edition of the Real ACT Prep Guide, D or J occurs 50% of the time with Style questions, an outcome that is 99.99% likely not to have occurred by chance. That is, a preference for making the last choice right seems to be built into these questions, especially ones testing Concision. Bottom line: if you encounter what you recognize as a Concision question and you're not sure of the answer, guess D or J.

Style Solutions

41. (D) ... for the following ten or so <u>centuries.</u>

Rhetorical Skills   Style   Concision

The word *century* means "one hundred years," so nothing is added by restating the phrase *ten or so centuries* as *about a thousand years, approximately one thousand years,* or *the rough duration of a millennium* (which is exactly 1,000 years). Delete the redundant language. The correct answer is (D).

42. (G) ... today, the issue <u>may never be resolved satisfactorily.</u>

Rhetorical Skills   Style   Word Choice

The paragraph is formal in tone throughout, with academic language (e.g., *consensus, subsequently, conceive of*) and phrasing. It's jarring, therefore, to end with *plain stump folks for good,* which is far too colloquial for the rest of the text. Likewise, ... *one of those things you have to shrug about* is both too informal and too vague: if you *shrug about* this issue, does that mean you can't resolve it or that you don't care about it?

The other wrong answer choice fails the concision standard with a double redundancy: *mysterious conundrum* (that's like saying *mysterious mystery*) and *solved and put to rest* (just write one or the other). The right answer is both concise and tonally appropriate. The correct answer is (G).

43. (D) ... her masterful ability to <u>represent</u> in her writing the ... currents of feelings ...

Rhetorical Skills   Style   Concision

In this context, the words *represent, describe,* and *portray* all mean the same thing. You don't get any closer to Toni Morrison by using two or three of these words at the same time. There are no extra layers of subtle meaning in *represent and portray.* Avoid redundancy by picking just one word for the job. The correct answer is (D).

44. (J) ... flash drives that had earlier been loaded with music or video files [omitted] could be ...

Rhetorical Skills   Style   Concision

You don't need the underlined portion at all. Each of the wrong answer choices (*beforehand, previously, before that time*) means "earlier"—but you already have *earlier* in the same clause, modifying the same verb (*had been loaded*). All of these choices are redundant, so the best option is just to drop the word altogether. The correct answer is (J).

45. (C) Least likely to suggest success: ... a <u>rousing</u> presentation ...

Rhetorical Skills   Style   Word Choice

The other three choices (*persuasive, compelling, convincing*) indicate a successful result: if you say you have persuaded, compelled, or convinced someone to do your laundry, then you are saying that that person has done or will definitely do your laundry. As a result, a presentation that is *persuasive, compelling,* or *convincing* is successful at achieving its desired ends. A *rousing* presentation, on the other hand, may *rouse* (= excite) the audience, perhaps to action, but that action may only be applause. There is no indication that the result is success. The correct answer is (C).

46. **(F)** … Betty Boop, a <u>well-liked cartoon character</u> modeled on …

Rhetorical Skills   Style   Concision

As additions to *well-liked,* the phrases *really rather* and *it might be said* are not only unnecessary but actively harmful: they weaken the strength of the adjective. Simply say *well-liked.* Moreover, the modifier *who was popular* is redundant, if you already have *well-liked.* The dead horse can be kicked once more: *popular and modeled* is not a parallel list, because *popular* is a static adjective, whereas *who was modeled on the flapper women* … can be read as a passive-voice action. *He was unhappy and hit by a ball* is a simpler example of the problem. The correct answer is (F).

47. **(D)** … who frequently made flattering <u>statements about her work</u> in private …

Rhetorical Skills   Style   Concision

The word *flattering* means "praising excessively and insincerely," so it is redundant to write that these *flattering statements* were *excessively praising,* or were *of insincere admiration,* or were made *to compliment her work … though to an extreme.* A second redundancy shows up as well: the sentence already has *frequently,* so you can omit *often* and avoid the over-the-top phrasing of *statement after statement.* The correct answer is (D).

48. **(F)** … for Emily to … <u>begin teaching</u> public health to first-generation college students …

Rhetorical Skills   Style   Word Choice

Which *-ing* form to use is determined by the objects after it. You can *teach* a subject (such as *public health*) to people (such as *first-generation college students*). You cannot, however, *instruct* or *educate* that subject to anyone. Rather, you instruct or educate people in a subject. The verb *inculcate* is a little different, but it also fails to pass muster. You can *inculcate* a quality (not so much a subject) in or into someone, or you can inculcate that person with the quality. But you cannot inculcate a subject to anyone.

Begin and its synonyms here (*start, commence, embark on*) are all fine. These variations are red herrings (that is, meaningless distractions). The correct answer is (F).

49. **(D)** … found it difficult to <u>defend such a controversial position.</u>

Rhetorical Skills   Style   Concision

This problem is loaded with redundancy to strip away. First, pick just one verb, since whether you *champion, defend,* or *support a position,* you're really doing the same thing. Nothing is gained by doubling up on these verbs. Next, you only need one word meaning *debate, controversial, divisive,* or *contentious* to modify *position.* The right answer uses *controversial,* but which word is used is less important than the fact that only one is used. The correct answer is (D).

50. **(H)** Least acceptable: … to <u>entice</u> a physiological response …

Rhetorical Skills   Style   Word Choice

In the original verb phrase *induce a response*, you can substitute *generate, evoke,* or *produce* without a hitch. Many other verbs, such as *cause,* also work neutrally. However, you cannot *entice* a response, technically speaking: you entice a person. Synonyms for *entice,* which has an emotional component, include *tempt* and *lure.* You *entice* someone with a temptation of some kind. Even if you could theoretically *entice* a response, these galvanic currents are not a temptation. The correct answer is (H).

51. **(D)** … the prospects of the solar-cell company have dramatically risen the last several weeks, <u>so</u> investors have poured into the stock …

Rhetorical Skills   Style   Concision

The only connection you need between the two thoughts is *so*, indicating result. *During this recent period up to now* is not only wordy in and of itself, but also redundant with *the last several weeks.* Granted, that phrase is in the previous clause, which in theory doesn't have to involve the same period of time, but both clauses use the present perfect tense—*have risen, have poured*—to indicate that the time period is the same: up to and including the present. *During these weeks* is redundant for the same reason.

Finally, you can remove bloat by cutting out the vague restatement that *things have been looking up.* This clause adds nothing to the discussion. The correct answer is (D).

52. **(J)** … he needs to search within himself and find the right personal <u>catalyst,</u> so that he can seize the opportunity …

Rhetorical Skills   Style   Concision

In a non-scientific setting, the word *catalyst* means "something that causes change, provides a stimulus or impetus or a spur to action." Thus, it's redundant to write *a catalyst that will provide a stimulus* or *a catalyst to give him impetus* or *to be a spur to action.* All the meaning you need is captured in the word *catalyst* itself. Use it here alone. The correct answer is (J).

53. **(B)** … the application of a voltage to the same crystal can cause it to <u>shrink or enlarge</u> in various directions.

Rhetorical Skills   Style   Word Choice

You need a pair of verbs that can both fit the framework: the voltage can cause the crystal to X. These verbs should be opposites of each other. The first verb is either *contract, shrink, shrivel,* or *lessen.* Evidently, the desired meaning is "physically get smaller" (*lessen* doesn't really fit by itself, and that discrepancy is enough to reject this answer choice, but something can *lessen in size*). Thus, the second verb should mean "physically get bigger." Only *enlarge* is suitable. As an intransitive verb, *multiply* means "increase in number" (*our problems multiplied*), not "increase in size." Several crystals could therefore *multiply* in number, but a single crystal can't *multiply* in a particular direction.

Amplify means "make louder or bigger in strength, impact, etc." but not in physical size, and it's not intransitive (a sound doesn't just *amplify* on its own). Finally, *escalate* can certainly mean "get bigger," but it does not work with physical things. Rather, what can escalate is international tension or other abstractions (usually problems). Only the correct answer *shrink or enlarge* means "physically get smaller or bigger." The correct answer is (B).

54. **(H)** The water here is safe for swimming, <u>since</u> you can always see the bottom …

Rhetorical Skills   Style   Concision

The best choice you have to indicate causality here is *since*. The phrase *due to* … would require *the fact that*, at minimum, and even then is a wordy, controversial replacement for *since* or *because*. Likewise, *thanks to* would also require *the fact that* and still be far wordier than necessary. The use of *capability* or *ability* in place of *fact* is redundant (with *can*) and awkward as well.

Don't jump to the last choice with the fewest letters, just because it's the last choice with the fewest letters! *So* indicates causality, but in the wrong direction. *A so B* means *A* is the cause of *B*. But you want *A since B*, because clause *B* (*you can always see the bottom and easily resist the gentle current*) is the cause of *A* (*the water here is safe for swimming*). The correct answer is (H).

55. **(D)** … [omitted] the initial symptoms … can seldom be distinguished from …

Rhetorical Skills   Style   Concision

The main verb *can be distinguished* is modified by the adverb *seldom*, which means "only rarely." Thus, you should not duplicate that meaning by using *occasionally, rarely,* or *infrequently* at the start of the clause. In fact, the meaning is muddied, because *occasionally* has a positive sense (= a few times), but *seldom* has a negative sense (= few times, *only* occasionally). Drop the underlined portion completely. The correct answer is (D).

56. **(G)** Most specific estimate of size of crowd: … <u>a mass of several hundred people</u> …

Rhetorical Skills   Style   Word Choice

The correct answer is the only one with any real numbers in it (*several hundred*), so it provides the most specific estimate of the crowd's size. Other choices may supply more insight into the crowd's behavior (*swarming, teeming throng*) or the people themselves (*fans* is more descriptive than *people*), but the question asks about the size of the group. By the way, *numerous* should not modify a singular noun such as *multitude,* as it does in the original sentence. The correct answer is (G).

57. **(D)** … Overall, is the plan plausible? [omitted] What resources will be required …

Rhetorical Skills   Style   Concision

The first question is whether the plan is *plausible,* which means "believable." Thus, if your second question is *Believable?* or *Can it be believed?*, you have succumbed to pure redundancy. *Incredible* means "unbelievable," so asking *Or is it incredible?* is also unnecessary, as if you were asking of an apple *Is it red? Or is it not red?*

The best option is to drop the underlined portion altogether. The correct answer is (D).

58. **(F)** Most consistent with academic tone: … the Spanish monarch has, among other designations, the <u>exalted</u> title of King of Castile …

Rhetorical Skills   Style   Word Choice

Of all the choices, *exalted* is the most appropriate as an adjective meaning "lofty, grand" in a piece of academic writing. *Quality* as an adjective meaning "great" or "of high quality" is too informal, as are *top-notch* and *fabulous*. You can use *fabulous* in its literal sense (= mythical) in an academic paper, but in the sense of "wonderful, great," the adjective is colloquial. The correct answer is (F).

59. **(C)** Not acceptable: … to attempt to flee … would be nearly impossible … <u>between</u> the chaos of the hurricane sweeping across the island town and its environs.

Rhetorical Skills   Style   Word Choice

The preposition *between* requires two objects connected by *and*, as in the phrase *between you and me* or *between a rock and a hard place*. Thus, *between the chaos* … does not work, since the *and* much later on is evidently meant to link *town* and *environs*, not *chaos* and *environs*.

The prepositional phrases *in the chaos, amid the chaos,* and *in the midst of the chaos* all mean the same thing (imagining *chaos* almost as a physical thing). *During the chaos* has a slightly different connotation, implying *chaos* is an event or a period of time, but that's a perfectly acceptable reading as well. The correct answer is (**C**).

60. **(G)** the minister temporarily put into effect a series of small measures and <u>programs.</u>

Rhetorical Skills   Style   Concision

The clause already has *temporarily* (= for a short time) and *small* (= limited in scope). Thus, the modifiers *that were only short-lived, that did not last very long,* and *limited in both scope and duration* are unnecessary additions to *programs*. You should use the noun by itself. The correct answer is (G).

Chapter *of* 5

5lb. Book of ACT® Practice Problems

English:
Passage Set 1

In This Chapter...

Set 1 Passages & Solutions

Chapter 5

English: Passage Set 1

The English problems in this chapter are distributed across five passages, just as they will be on the ACT itself. Every topic is up for grabs, so expect a little of everything. The answer key and the solutions classify the problems for you, so you can pinpoint strengths and weaknesses.

How should you use this chapter? Here are some recommendations, according to the level you've reached in ACT English.

1. Fundamentals. If you haven't done any topical work yet, consider working in Chapters 3 and 4 first. Otherwise, do a passage or two untimed to begin with. As you become more comfortable, put the clock on. In all cases, review the solutions closely, and articulate what you've learned. Redo problems as necessary.

2. Fixes. Do one passage at a time under timed conditions. Examine the results, learn your lessons, then test yourself with more passages at once.

3. Tweaks. Confirm your mastery by doing a few passages at once under timed conditions. A full set of five is the ultimate goal. Aim to improve the speed and ease of your solution process.

Good luck on the problems!

PASSAGE 1

A Pioneering Author

[1]

Ursula K. Le Guin has broken ground as an
award-winning author and writer of science fiction and
₁
fantasy. However, she resists being pigeonholed. After

all, she might ask, when the wizard Prospero commands
₂
spirits in *The Tempest,* isn't Shakespeare writing fantasy

as well? As Le Guin argues that these genres let authors
₃

explore the implications of a high intriguing premise.
₄

In this way, new light can be shed on the human
₅
condition.

[2]

[1] Written at a time when traditional roles in
₆
American society were being contested, Le Guin's
celebrated novel *The Left Hand of Darkness* contains a
fascinating sentence: "The king was pregnant." [2] In
this book, the inhabitants of a planet, normally without
₇
gender become male or female once a month—and not
₇
always the same way each time. [3] Le Guin originally
used "he" to refer to these people in their genderless
phase, but later questioned that choice. [4] Le Guin

1. **A.** NO CHANGE
   B. award-winning author who has received honors in
   C. award-winning author
   D. author and writer who has won awards in

2. **F.** NO CHANGE
   G. might ask when
   H. might, ask when
   J. might ask, when,

3. **A.** NO CHANGE
   B. When Le Guin argues
   C. Le Guin, arguing
   D. Le Guin argues

4. **F.** NO CHANGE
   G. highly intriguing
   H. highly intrigued
   J. high intrigue

5. Which of the following alternatives to the under-lined portion would NOT be acceptable?
   A. In this fashion
   B. Thus
   C. In contrast
   D. As a result

6. **F.** NO CHANGE
   G. Writing
   H. Having written
   J. Having been writing

7. **A.** NO CHANGE
   B. planet, normally without gender,
   C. planet—normally genderless
   D. planet genderless normally

MANHATTAN
PREP

was one of the first <u>writers, of any kind</u> to investigate
                        ₈
what is left when gender is transformed. [5] She is also
progressive with the concept of race, giving many of her

protagonists dark skin. <u>9</u> [6] As she has explained, she
challenges her mostly white readers to overcome their
possible resistance to identifying with these characters.
[7] She even rewrote the opening chapter with a neutral

pronoun "e" instead. <u>10</u>

[3]

<u>11</u> One invention of Le Guin's, the ansible, is so
interesting that other authors use it as well. There are

8. F. NO CHANGE
   G. writers of any kind
   H. writers of any kind;
   J. writers of any kind:

9. Which of the following true statements, if added
here, would LEAST exemplify the assertion about
Le Guin's approach to race?
   A. In *The Left Hand of Darkness*, the only person
   from Earth is subtly revealed to be black partway through the novel.
   B. The first three books of Le Guin's *Earthsea* tril-
   ogy revolve around a wizard with a red-brown
   complexion.
   C. Le Guin's later *Earthsea* novels raise the profile
   of Tenar, a pale-skinned priestess who has lost
   her power.
   D. The androgynous lords in *The Left Hand of
   Darkness* are generally brown-skinned and
   short.

10. For the sake of the logic and coherence of this para-
graph, Sentence 7 should be placed:
   F. where it is now.
   G. after Sentence 1.
   H. after Sentence 3.
   J. after Sentence 5.

11. Given that all the sentences are true, which one, if
added here, would offer the best transition to Paragraph 3 from Paragraph 2?
   A. As the daughter of a famous anthropologist,
   Le Guin grew up sensitive to issues of race and
   gender.
   B. Le Guin does not seem enamored of technology in and of itself, but as premises for sociological exploration, imaginary technical advances
   play an important role in her writing.
   C. Le Guin's mother published a bestselling book
   about Ishi, a family friend who was one of the
   last survivors of his Native American tribe.
   D. A person of strong principles, Le Guin has
   turned down awards and resigned from writers'
   organizations in protest over a variety of issues.

many science fiction milieus <u>into which</u> Einstein's ban
¹²
on faster-than-light speeds is broken. Spaceships hop

through the galaxy <u>as if they have flown</u> from Europe
¹³
to Asia. Le Guin cleverly imagines a universe in which
instant communication, but not instant travel, among

the stars <u>might of</u> take place. Her interstellar telephone,
¹⁴
the ansible, links distant planets, but people on these
separated islands cannot physically reach each other
without serious personal consequences. For instance,
a mother journeys to a nearby star <u>and returns</u> much
¹⁵
younger than her daughter.

12. **F.** NO CHANGE
    G. by which
    H. when
    J. in which

13. **A.** NO CHANGE
    B. as though flew
    C. as though having flew
    D. as if flying

14. **F.** NO CHANGE
    G. might have
    H. may be
    J. may

15. **A.** NO CHANGE
    B. in return
    C. and returned
    D. and returning

MANHATTAN
PREP

PASSAGE 2

Noodles Everywhere

[1]

My favorite dish has always been spaghetti with

meatballs. My parents each make it <u>slight different—</u>
                                        16
my father sprinkles in less oregano—but I love it both

ways. At restaurants, <u>where my family knew that if the</u>
                          17
option is available, they may as well order for me. I'm

particular even about how I eat <u>spaghetti:</u> I always use a
                                    18
spoon to get a nice, tight spool around my fork. In the

last few months, though, I <u>become</u> curious about the
                              19
wider world of noodles, resolving to venture out more

boldly.

[2]

[1] What makes a noodle a noodle? [2] <u>For example,</u>
                                          20
the dough out of which the noodle is made must be

unleavened: it must lack yeast, baking powder, or any

other agent to puff out the dough as it cooks.

[3] Second, the dough must be rolled out into thin

sheets. [4] <u>A machine is often employed at this point,</u>
                                              21
<u>because the dough can be very tough.</u> [5] Boiling the
              21
strips in water or broth is customary; alternatively,

16. **F.** NO CHANGE
    G. slightly different
    H. slightly differently
    J. slight differently

17. **A.** NO CHANGE
    B. my family knows that if
    C. which my family knows that
    D. in which my family is known,

18. **F.** NO CHANGE
    G. spaghetti, I
    H. spaghetti that I
    J. spaghetti, which I

19. **A.** NO CHANGE
    B. had became
    C. have become
    D. am become

20. **F.** NO CHANGE
    G. First,
    H. In any event,
    J. Granted,

21. Given that all of the choices are true, which one would provide the most effective link between Sentences 3 and 5?
    A. NO CHANGE
    B. From that point, the sheets are often cut into long, narrow strips and dried.
    C. Rolling noodles by hand takes true physical strength and endurance.
    D. For some types of wide, flat noodles, such as lasagna, you're almost done.

noodles may or may not also be fried in oil. [6] Despite
          ——————————————————
                22
these commonalities, noodles vary in innumerable ways,

from the doughs grain constituent to the shape and size
         ——————————————————
               23
of the noodle itself, enabling highly diverse dishes in

5 cuisines around the globe. [24]

[3]

As I have learned in my research, even Italian
pasta, a single culture's noodles, comes in far more

than a few classic types. Each tiny region of Italy seems
                          ——————————————————
                                25
to have its own specialty in this regard. Pasta varieties

reveal a sense of humor when you translate it's names:
                                          ————————
                                            26
little tongues, twins, pens, wheels, butterflies, ears, and
bridegrooms. Now I think of little strings when I eat
spaghetti, since *spago* means "string."

[4]

Pasta was brought back from China to Italy by
———
                      27
Marco Polo, so the story goes, where four-thousand-
————————————————————————————
        27
year-old noodles have been dug up. Noodles are
prevalent in Chinese and other Asian dishes and are

made not only of regular wheat but also buckwheat,
——
                    28

22. F. NO CHANGE
   G. might
   H. are potentially able to
   J. in addition might in fact

23. A. NO CHANGE
   B. constituent grain dough
   C. dough's constituent grain
   D. constituent of the dough of the grain

24. The writer is considering adding the following true statement to this paragraph:

> Out of a desire to cut carbohydrates or possibly gluten from their diets, some people no longer eat noodles at all.

Should the sentence be added to this paragraph, and if so, where should it be placed?

   F. Yes, after Sentence 3.
   G. Yes, after Sentence 5.
   H. Yes, after Sentence 6.
   J. The sentence should NOT be added.

25. A. NO CHANGE
   B. Each tiny region of Italy, however,
   C. Nonetheless, each tiny region of Italy
   D. Granted, each tiny region of Italy

26. F. NO CHANGE
   G. its
   H. there
   J. their

27. A. NO CHANGE
   B. The story goes that China was where Marco Polo brought pasta back to Italy from,
   C. Marco Polo brought back pasta from China to Italy, so goes the story,
   D. The story goes that Marco Polo brought pasta back to Italy from China,

28. F. NO CHANGE
   G. made of not only regular wheat but also
   H. not only made of regular wheat but also of
   J. made of not only regular wheat but also of

rice, potato starch, and even mung bean to make translucent sheets or strips. <u>Currently</u> my family and
₂₉
I are now making the rounds of neighborhood Asian

restaurants, <u>where I order whatever looks least like</u>
₃₀
<u>spaghetti and meatballs.</u>
₃₀

29. **A.** NO CHANGE
    B. These days
    C. At present
    D. OMIT the underlined portion (adjusting the capitalization accordingly).

30. At this point in the essay, the writer wants to show that the narrator has made progress in his or her plan to eat in a more adventurous manner. Given that all of the choices are true, which one BEST conveys that message?
    F. NO CHANGE
    G. which are about as expensive as the local Italian eateries.
    H. one of which is run by the family of a friend of mine.
    J. although they are always packed, even on weeknights.

PASSAGE 3

Business Casual

[1]

What is acceptable to wear to work in an office? Over the years, the answer has become more complicated. <u>Every day, employees face tough daily decisions</u> to meet the hazy guidelines of "business casual."
₃₁

[2]

<u>After World War II, the United States entered a period of growth and prosperity.</u> White-collar
₃₂
workplaces were dominated by conventional business outfits, such as gray flannel suits and cautiously long,

dark skirts. <u>Nevertheless,</u> electronics manufacturer
₃₃

Hewlett-Packard broke with convention <u>and instituted</u> dress-down Fridays, so that office workers could pitch
₃₄

in at the warehouse preparing shipments. [35]

31. A. NO CHANGE
  B. Employees face everyday tough decisions nowadays on a daily basis
  C. Every day, nowadays, every employee faces a tough daily decision
  D. Nowadays, employees face tough decisions daily

32. Given that all of the choices are true, which one would MOST effectively introduce this paragraph?
  F. NO CHANGE
  G. In the 1950s, standards of corporate dress in the U.S. were quite uniform.
  H. The term itself is a recent creation, after the middle of the past century.
  J. The trend toward less serious office attire may reflect a cultural decline since the 1950s.

33. A. NO CHANGE
  B. Thus,
  C. Furthermore,
  D. For example,

34. F. NO CHANGE
  G. but instituted
  H. and instituting
  J. that instituted

35. At this point, the writer is considering adding the following true statement:

  > Hewlett-Packard is commonly regarded as a corporate founder of Silicon Valley, the high-technology area around San Jose, California.

  Should the writer make this addition here?
  A. Yes, because it positions the company within a broader geographic and economic context.
  B. Yes, because it reinforces the impression that the company is a risk-taking pioneer.
  C. No, because it is not in step with the style and tone of the essay as a whole.
  D. No, because it diverts attention from the clear narrative path of the paragraph.

MANHATTAN PREP

[3]

The next step toward casual wear was also taken for hardheaded business reasons. To boost its sales: the Hawaiian garment industry in the 1960s promoted

"Aloha Fridays," on which aloha or Hawaiian shirts, could be worn to the office. Once the president of the Bank of Hawaii started wearing an aloha shirt on Fridays, the tradition caught on in Hawaiian places and locations and probably contributed to the rise of "Casual Fridays" on the mainland.

[4]

By the 1990s, Fridays in a typical office setting presented a hodgepodge of styles, leading to confusion

among workers and managers alike. Observing this disordered turmoil while seeking to supplement its revenues from denim jeans, Levi's developed a "Guide to Casual Businesswear," which naturally featured its own line of Dockers khaki pants and button-down shirts. The company sent this guide to thousands of human resources managers around the country. Suddenly, "business casual" became a style adopted

widely, even if few could define them.

---

36. **F.** NO CHANGE
G. its sales,
H. it's sales:
J. it's sales,

37. **A.** NO CHANGE
B. aloha or Hawaiian, shirts
C. aloha, or Hawaiian, shirts,
D. aloha, or Hawaiian, shirts

38. **F.** NO CHANGE
G. locally, as far as Hawaii is concerned,
H. in the localities of Hawaii
J. locally

39. Given that all of the choices are true, which one would provide the clearest examples of the range of clothing worn on casual Fridays?
A. NO CHANGE
B. although the possibilities varied by employer and job type.
C. from traditional corporate attire to flip-flops and shorts.
D. as employees took advantage of tentative and unclear rules.

40. **F.** NO CHANGE
G. Observing this turmoil
H. Sensing and perceiving this disarray
J. Perceiving this disarray and disorder

41. **A.** NO CHANGE
B. Deliberately,
C. Incidentally,
D. In moderation,

42. **F.** NO CHANGE
G. few could define it.
H. they could not define it.
J. it was not to be defined.

[5]

Benchmarks are far more harder now to discern
                          43

than ever. Some major companies lack a written dress

code altogether. Certain industries, such as finance,

take a conservative view, generally decreeing suits for

men and women. Other sectors revel in their opposition
                          44

to such clothing. [45]

43. A. NO CHANGE
  B. now more harder
  C. now far harder
  D. now the hardest

44. F. NO CHANGE
  G. sectors reveled,
  H. sectors, revel
  J. sectors reveled

45. Which of the following sentences, if added here, would provide the best conclusion to the paragraph and is most consistent with the rest of the essay?

  A. Of course, certain professions, such as those in the medical field, demand another sort of dress entirely.
  B. Technology leader Mark Zuckerberg of Facebook, with his trademark hoodie sweatshirts, may embody this stance most publicly.
  C. After studying many aspects of this complex issue, I am still not sure which side I will embrace when I enter the workforce.
  D. Nonetheless, in the future greater conformity can be expected, as technology improves lives and cultural expectations converge.

PASSAGE 4

Mama Dip's Kitchen

[1]

If you are in Chapel Hill, North Carolina and are hungry for Southern home-style cooking, then look no

46. **F.** NO CHANGE
    G. cooking, therefore
    H. cooking, however,
    J. cooking

farther than Mama Dip's Kitchen, an unpretentious, restaurant that has been featured in the New York Times.

47. **A.** NO CHANGE
    B. Kitchen an unpretentious restaurant, that
    C. Kitchen; an unpretentious restaurant that
    D. Kitchen, an unpretentious restaurant that

[2]

Mama Dip is an actual person named Mildred Council born in 1929, she grew up on a farm as the youngest of seven children. When she was only two years old, her mother died, and she had to work hard to survive. Along the way, she learned to cook "dump" style. That is, she relied on her experience not on recipes for guidance, as she "dumped" the right amount of flour and other ingredients together.

48. **F.** NO CHANGE
    G. Council. Born in 1929, she
    H. Council, born in 1929, she
    J. Council; born in 1929 she,

49. **A.** NO CHANGE
    B. experience, not on, recipes
    C. experience not, on recipes
    D. experience, not on recipes,

[3]

[1] As an adult, Mama Dip made food in various establishments around Chapel Hill and was therefore already well known when she struck out on her own in 1976. [2] However, she certainly took a risk opening "Dip's Country Kitchen" with $64, just enough to buy grits, eggs, and bacon for that first Sunday breakfast and to make change.

50. Given that all the choices are true, which one provides the MOST specific information about the intentions for the money?
    F. NO CHANGE
    G. which she had saved over the course of many months by working extra shifts elsewhere.
    H. split between large and small bills and kept carefully in her apron pocket as she cooked.
    J. effectively a much larger amount of money decades ago, due to inflation.

MANHATTAN
PREP   163

[3] At every table is devoured sweet potatoes, fried
                                    ‾51‾

chicken, and black-eyed peas as the cash register
                          ‾‾‾‾‾52‾‾‾‾
filled up. [4] A true entrepreneur, Mama Dip had

bootstrapped her way to financial independence.

[5] Breakfast went so well that she purchased food to

make lunch, then dinner. 53

[4]

In 1985, a customer ordered "chittlins," an

unusual item on the menu. Double-checking that the

customer was serious, a plate of fried pig's intestines
                        ‾‾‾‾‾‾‾‾‾‾‾‾‾‾‾‾‾‾‾‾‾‾‾‾‾‾‾‾
was brought. Some might have fainted, but this
‾‾‾‾‾‾‾‾‾‾‾‾ 54
customer wolfed the chittlins down with

gusto—then complained about
            ‾‾‾‾‾‾‾‾‾‾‾‾‾‾‾‾
                  55

them in the *New York Times*. This mysterious customer
‾‾‾‾‾‾‾‾
   56
turned out to be none other than Craig Claiborne.

[5]

When Mama Dip expanded her business beyond
‾‾‾‾‾‾‾‾‾‾‾‾‾‾
         57
her restaurant to local stores and the Internet, where

51. A. NO CHANGE
    B. are
    C. was being
    D. were being

52. Which of the following alternatives to the underlined portion would be LEAST acceptable?
    F. peas; as a result,
    G. peas while
    H. peas because
    J. peas; meanwhile,

53. For the sake of the logic and coherence of this paragraph, Sentence 5 should be placed:
    A. where it is now.
    B. at the start of the paragraph, before Sentence 1.
    C. after Sentence 1.
    D. after Sentence 2.

54. F. NO CHANGE
    G. fried pig's intestines were brought on a plate,
some
    H. the server brought a plate of fried pig's intes-
tines. Some
    J. pig's intestines were fried and brought on a
plate. Some

55. Which choice would be MOST consistent with the
description of the customer provided elsewhere in
this paragraph?
    A. NO CHANGE
    B. raved
    C. thought
    D. grumbled

56. F. NO CHANGE
    G. those on
    H. it on
    J. them over

57. A. NO CHANGE
    B. As Mama Dip
    C. Having
    D. Mama Dip has

she sells cornbread mix, poppy seed dressing, and both
kinds of North Carolina barbecue sauce: vinegar-based
and tomato-based. Mama Dip has even written two

cookbooks with her smiling face on the cover. ⁵⁹ This
way, people who never learned to cook "dump" style
can create at home the taste of Mama Dip's.

58. **F.** NO CHANGE
　　G. cornbread, mix poppy, seed, dressing
　　H. cornbread mix poppy seed, dressing,
　　J. cornbread, mix poppy, seed dressing

59. If the writer were to delete the phrase "with her smiling face on the cover" from the preceding sentence, the sentence would primarily lose:
　　A. a detail that compares Mama Dip's mood to that of her readers.
　　B. information that highlights Mama Dip's attitude toward her readers.
　　C. a description that reiterates a point made at the beginning of the passage.
　　D. nothing valuable, since this detail is already stated elsewhere in the passage.

> Question 60 asks about the preceding passage as a whole.

60. Upon reviewing the essay and realizing that some key information has been left out, the writer composes the following sentence incorporating that information:

> He was a famous food critic who became a passionate supporter of the restaurant.

This sentence would most logically be placed after the last sentence in Paragraph:
　　F. 1.
　　G. 2.
　　H. 3.
　　J. 4.

PASSAGE 5

Strange Sports

[1]

The United States has just a few sports that dominate the culture. Think about the lead stories on the sports page or the TV show *SportsCenter*. ESPN's home page, based on it's tabs for football, basketball,
61

baseball, hockey, NASCAR, and soccer, featuring both
62
men's and women's leagues on college and professional
62
levels. However, your curiosity might lead you to the catchall link to "More Sports." Imagine clicking through to find "Even More Sports"; now, keep going.
63
What strange sports might you uncover seven or eight

levels down? 64

[2]

You might come across real tennis, which

is different from the version of tennis you see on
65
television. In fact, regular "lawn" tennis descended from real, meaning royal, tennis that was always played

inside. The latter adjective is appropriate, though Louis X,
66
king of France in the early 1300s, was a devoted

61. A. NO CHANGE
B. having its'
C. with its
D. whose

62. F. NO CHANGE
G. soccer featured both mens' and womens'
H. soccer, both featuring mens, and womens,
J. soccer, features both men's and women's

63. A. NO CHANGE
B. Sports," now
C. Sports" now
D. Sports" now,

64. The writer is considering deleting the preceding sentence from this paragraph. If the writer made this deletion, the paragraph would primarily lose:
F. a difficult hypothetical challenge posed to the reader.
G. a mystery whose solution ultimately evades the writer.
H. a prompt to spur thinking about the theme of the essay.
J. a rhetorical question that has already been answered.

65. A. NO CHANGE
B. you see it
C. so you see
D. that as seen

66. F. NO CHANGE
G. appropriate, whether or not
H. appropriate; for instance,
J. appropriate; as a result,

player. [67] Real tennis has intricate rules, special terms

and equipment, and courts with odd asymmetries and

openings that is to be defended, including one with
                     ‾‾‾‾‾‾‾‾‾‾‾‾
                          68

a unicorn painted inside. The aristocrats who came

up with this game centuries ago must have been both

bored and creative. Today, there are only about fifty real

tennis courts in the world.

[3]

A variety that is unique to sports can be found
‾‾‾‾‾‾‾‾‾‾‾‾‾‾‾‾‾‾‾‾‾‾‾‾‾‾‾‾‾‾‾‾
                     69

at British private schools. One of these sports, the

Eton Wall Game, is only ever played at one place: a wall

at Eton College. Scoring a goal is so difficult that

they have not done it in the big annual match in over
‾‾‾‾‾‾‾‾‾‾‾‾‾‾‾‾‾‾‾
        70

one hundred years.

[4]

As you examine these specialty sports, you might

find them more interesting than ones you watch or
         ‾‾‾‾‾‾‾‾‾‾‾‾‾‾‾‾‾
                 71

play. You might even come to the same conclusion I

did—every sport is weird, involving arbitrary rules

that can seem silly. Even soccer, my personal favorite, is

formally known as association football; it developed at
                                 ‾‾‾‾‾‾‾‾‾‾‾
                                      72

Cambridge University as a compromise among students

who had played different versions of football while

67. Given that all of the following statements are true, which one would provide the MOST relevant information, if added at this point in the essay?

    A. After a long, exhausting game, however, he supposedly fell ill and died.

    B. Another aficionado, King Henry VIII of England, built at least one court in a palace.

    C. Some of the terminology of the sport comes from medieval French.

    D. Before he ruled France, he was the king of Navarre for eleven years.

68. F. NO CHANGE

    G. must be defended,

    H. demands defense,

    J. are demanded to be defended,

69. A. NO CHANGE

    B. A variety that is unique of sports

    C. Uniquely, a variety of sports

    D. A variety of unique sports

70. F. NO CHANGE

    G. it has not been done

    H. it is not so done

    J. they have not done so

71. A. NO CHANGE

    B. interesting, more than

    C. more of interest then

    D. of more interest compared to

72. Which of the following alternatives to the underlined portion would be LEAST acceptable?

    F. football; it was

    G. football. It was

    H. football: the game

    J. football, the game

growing up. Now this sport, <u>with its strange rules made</u>
<u>up by college kids,</u> has billions of fans.
                          73

73. The writer wants to provide a phrase or clause here that will tie the ending of the essay to its major themes. Which choice does that BEST?

   A. NO CHANGE

   B. although not as popular in the United States as American football,

   C. whose World Cup happens once every four years,

   D. which can be played almost anywhere, unlike real tennis,

---

Questions 74 and 75 ask about the preceding passage as a whole.

---

74. The writer is considering deleting the last sentence of the second paragraph of the essay. If the writer were to make this deletion, the essay would primarily lose:

   F. a historical summary of the cultural impact of the sport in question.

   G. a necessary conclusion of a series of statements made earlier in the paragraph.

   H. a contemporary detail that underlines the unfamiliarity of the paragraph's example.

   J. a description that provides visual imagery of where the sport in question is played.

75. Suppose the writer's goal had been to write an essay focusing on the essential differences between strange and familiar sports. Would this essay fulfill that goal?

   A. Yes, because the two major examples of strange sports reveal fundamental peculiarities in those sports.

   B. Yes, because the essay describes how some familiar sports originated from what might be called strange ancestors.

   C. No, because the essay does not adequately describe familiar sports that would be the basis for comparison.

   D. No, because the essay reaches the conclusion that all sports are strange in some ways.

Passage Set 1 Answer Key

Write in whether you got each problem right or wrong (or left it blank). If your answer was correct, put a 1 in every blank to the right of that problem. Sum up each column and compare your total to the total possible "Out Of" points in each column.

Problem	Correct Answer	Right/ Wrong/ Blank	Usage/Mechanics			Rhetorical Skills		
			Grammar & Usage	Punctuation	Sentence Structure	Organization	Style	Writing Strategy
1	C						—	
2	F			—				
3	D				—			
4	G		—					
5	C					—		
6	F		—					
7	B			—				
8	G			—				
9	C							—
10	H					—		
11	B					—		
12	J		—					
13	D		—					
14	J		—					
15	A		—					
16	H		—					
17	B				—			
18	F				—			
19	C				—			
20	G					—		
21	B							—
22	G						—	
23	C			—				
24	J							—
25	A					—		
26	J		—					

MANHATTAN
PREP

5

Problem	Correct Answer	Right/ Wrong/ Blank	Usage/Mechanics			Rhetorical Skills		
			Grammar & Usage	Punctuation	Sentence Structure	Organization	Style	Writing Strategy
27	D				—			
28	G		—					
29	D						—	
30	F							—
31	D						—	
32	G					—		
33	A					—		
34	F		—					
35	D							—
36	G			—				
37	D			—				
38	J						—	
39	C							—
40	G						—	
41	A					—		
42	G		—					
43	C		—					
44	F				—			
45	B					—		
46	F					—		
47	D			—				
48	G				—			
49	D			—				
50	F							—
51	D		—		—			
52	H					—		
53	D					—		
54	H				—			
55	B							—
56	F		—					

Problem	Correct Answer	Right/ Wrong/ Blank	Usage/Mechanics			Rhetorical Skills		
			Grammar & Usage	Punctuation	Sentence Structure	Organization	Style	Writing Strategy
57	D			—				
58	F			—				
59	B							—
60	J					—		
61	C			—				
62	J				—			
63	A				—			
64	H							—
65	A				—			
66	H					—		
67	B							—
68	G		—					
69	D				—			
70	G		—					
71	A		—					
72	J				—			
73	A							—
74	H							—
75	D							—
Total								
Out Of		75	17	11	13	14	6	14

Passage Set 1 Solutions

Passage 1

1. **(C)** … Le Guin has broken ground as an <u>award-winning author</u> of science fiction and fantasy.

Rhetorical Skills   Style   Concision

It is redundant to include both *author* and *writer*; they are equivalent in this context. Likewise, it is needlessly wordy to say both that Le Guin is *award-winning* and that she *has received honors* in the same sentence. The concise phrase *award-winning author* is both sufficient and superior. The correct answer is (C).

2. **(F)** After all, she <u>might ask, when</u> the wizard Prospero commands spirits in *The Tempest*, isn't Shakespeare writing fantasy …

Usage/Mechanics   Punctuation   Commas

The parenthetical phrase *she might ask* needs to be surrounded by commas, because it is inserted to provide context for the rest of the sentence, which is the question *she might ask*. She is not asking *when*; she is asking whether Shakespeare is writing fantasy.

No commas should be inserted within *she might ask*. Likewise, the word *when* should not be separated from the rest of the clause it governs (*when the wizard Prospero commands …*). The correct answer is (F).

3. **(D)** <u>Le Guin argues</u> that these genres let authors explore the implications …

Usage/Mechanics   Sentence Structure   Whole Sentences

The main clause of the sentence is simply *Le Guin argues X*, with *Le Guin* as the subject and *argues* (not *arguing*) as the verb. The presence of *As* or *When* turns this main clause into a subordinate clause, rendering the whole sentence a fragment. The correct answer is (D).

4. **(G)** … the implications of a <u>highly intriguing</u> premise.

Usage/Mechanics   Grammar & Usage   Modifier Forms

Intriguing as an *-ing* form should be used here as an adjective modifying the noun *premise*: an *intriguing premise* (= a premise that intrigues someone). *Highly* is an adverb and so can modify the adjective *intriguing*. An adjective (*high*) cannot normally modify another adjective (*intriguing*). The correct answer is (G).

5. **(C)** Not acceptable: … these genres let authors explore the implications of a highly intriguing premise. <u>In contrast</u>, new light can be shed on the human condition.

Rhetorical Skills   Organization   Transitions

The two thoughts on either side of the transition are closely aligned: (1) *these genres let authors explore the implications* … (2) *new light can be shed on the human condition*. In fact, the second follows from the first. Thus, the transition *In contrast* misleads the reader. The alternatives *In this fashion, Thus,* and *As a result* indicate the causal link and are all acceptable. The correct answer is (C).

6.   **(F)** <u>Written</u> at a time when … , Le Guin's celebrated novel …

Usage/Mechanics   Grammar & Usage   Modifier Forms

The opening phrase of this sentence (up to the comma) is a modifier that describes Le Guin's novel. A novel can be *written*; it cannot be *writing, having written,* or *having been writing*. In theory, these modifiers could describe Le Guin herself, but the subject of the sentence is *novel*, not *Le Guin's*. The 's prevents the modifier from referring to Le Guin herself. The correct answer is (F).

7.   **(B)**   … the inhabitants of a <u>planet, normally without gender,</u> become male or female once a month …

Usage/Mechanics   Punctuation   Commas

The phrase *normally without gender* is inserted parenthetically to modify the subject phrase *the inhabitants of a planet*. Thus, *normally without gender* must be surrounded by commas to properly set it apart. In theory, you could use dashes to accomplish the same feat, but you would have to put a dash both before and after the phrase. The correct answer is (B).

8.   **(G)** Le Guin was one of the first <u>writers of any kind</u> to investigate …

Usage/Mechanics   Punctuation   Commas

The most neutral and normal choice in this situation is to avoid punctuation altogether. It would be possible to emphasize the phrase *of any kind* dramatically by surrounding it with dashes or to de-emphasize it by putting it in parentheses. However, you are given neither of these options. Even separating the phrase *of any kind* with just commas could be confusing. You certainly cannot follow the phrase with a semicolon or colon (just before *to investigate*). The correct answer is (G).

9.   **(C)** Le Guin's later *Earthsea* novels raise the profile of Tenar, a pale-skinned priestess who has lost her power.

Rhetorical Skills   Writing Strategy   Additions

Le Guin's approach to race is asserted in the prior sentence: *She is also progressive with the concept of race, giving many of her protagonists dark skin*. Examples of such protagonists would then be appropriate. Tenar, described as *pale-skinned*, does not fit. The alternatives all match the condition (*the only person from Earth is subtly revealed to be black … The first three books … revolve around a wizard with a red-brown complexion … The androgynous lords … are generally brown-skinned*). The correct answer is (C).

10.   **(H)** For the sake of the logic and coherence of this paragraph, Sentence 7 should be placed after Sentence 3.

Rhetorical Skills   Organization   Sentence Order

Examine the sentence in question: *She even rewrote the opening chapter with a neutral pronoun "e" instead.* The word *even* emphasizes the connection to the prior sentence, since this action of rewriting using a neutral pronoun somehow goes beyond a just-mentioned action somewhere. Which sentence provides that springboard? Sentence 3: *Le Guin originally used "he" to refer to these people in their genderless phase, but later questioned that choice.* The very first action is Le Guin using "he"; then she questions that choice; finally, she rewrites the opening chapter with a neutral pronoun. The correct answer is (H).

11.   **(B)** Le Guin does not seem enamored of technology in and of itself, but as premises for sociological exploration, imaginary technical advances play an important role in her writing.

Rhetorical Skills   Organization   Opening/Closing Content

Paragraph 2 describes how Le Guin challenges assumptions about race and gender. This paragraph is in the service of the theme of the whole passage: how Le Guin explores *the implications of a highly intriguing premise … [so that] new light can be shed on the human condition.* As written, however, Paragraph 3 starts rather abruptly, diving right into this invention of Le Guin's, the ansible. Why is this important, and how is this related to the big picture? The right answer provides the proper context: *as premises for sociological exploration, imaginary technical advances play an important role in her writing.* The ansible now emerges sensibly as one of her *imaginary technical advances.* The correct answer is (B).

12.   **(J)** There are many science fiction milieus <u>in which</u> Einstein's ban on faster-than-light speeds is broken.

Usage/Mechanics   Grammar & Usage   Modifier Forms

A *milieu* is an environment or world. The ban on faster-than-light travel can be broken *in* a milieu (that is, within that milieu), but not *into* a milieu. It does not make sense for the ban to be broken *by* these milieus, because that would wrongly imply that the ban is broken everywhere, including in the real world. As potent as science fiction may be, its imaginary worlds lack this power. Finally, a milieu is a place, so theoretically it could be followed by *where*, but not by *when*. The correct answer is (J).

13.   **(D)** Spaceships hop through the galaxy <u>as if flying</u> from Europe to Asia.

Usage/Mechanics   Grammar & Usage   Verb Forms & Tenses

The main verb *hop* is present tense, describing the general action of these spaceships. The correct answer, *as if flying*, doesn't actually have a tense or otherwise make a statement about time, so this choice works fine. *As if they have flown* changes tense oddly. This choice implies that the action of flying from Europe to Asia is over, but you want to compare hopping through the galaxy with flying, not with the state of having flown.

As if they were flying is a legitimate possibility (notice the past tense, which here captures the hypothetical nature of the action: the spaceships are not actually flying from Europe to Asia, but they hop about *as if they were doing so*). You are not given this extended version as a choice, however.

Having flew is an incorrect form: *having* must always be followed by *flown,* not *flew. As though flew* lacks a needed subject. The correct answer is (D).

14. **(J)** Le Guin cleverly imagines a universe in which instant communication … among the stars <u>may</u> take place.

Usage/Mechanics   Grammar & Usage   Verb Forms

Might of is never right. Never put *of* after a helping verb such as *might, may, could,* or *would* when you mean to say *have.* That doesn't mean that *might have* is right in this circumstance, however. The verb immediately after the underlined portion is *take,* which is the bare present-tense form. For *might have* to be correct, you would need to have *taken* there (*might have taken*). *May be take* is absolutely incorrect: if you mean *maybe* (= possibly), then you need to write it as one word, and in this situation you would have to change *take* to *takes* or *took* (and stylistically, *maybe takes place* is still inferior). The best option is simply *may,* giving you *may take place.* The correct answer is (J).

15. **(A)** … a mother journeys to a nearby star <u>and returns</u> much younger than her daughter.

Usage/Mechanics   Grammar & Usage   Parallelism

The two present-tense verbs in the sentence, *journeys* and *returns,* should be parallel to each other. There is no need to change tense or form. The correct answer is (A).

Passage 2

16. **(H)** My parents each make it <u>slightly differently</u> …

Usage/Mechanics   Grammar & Usage   Modifier Forms

Both words must be adverbs here, with *-ly* on the end. *Differently* modifies the verb *make*: how do they each make it? Differently. Likewise, *slightly* modifies the adverb *differently*: how differently? Slightly differently. The adjective forms (*slight, different*) can only be used to modify nouns, either directly or after linking verbs (*it seemed different, but it wasn't different*). The correct answer is (H).

17. **(B)** At restaurants, <u>my family knows that if</u> the option is available, they may as well order for me.

Usage/Mechanics   Sentence Structure   Whole Sentences

In the correct version of the sentence, the main clause is *my family knows,* in which *my family* is the subject and *knows* is the verb. What does the family know? They know *that if the option is available, they may as well order for me.* This logic has layers, but they make sense.

The incorrect answers destroy the sentence in various ways. In choice (A), putting *where* in front causes the sentence to lack a main clause altogether. The past tense (*knew*) is also wrong. Choice (C), *which my family knows that,* creates confusion by having both *which* and *that*: it's not clear what the family knows. Finally, choice (D) changes the meaning of the verb radically by shifting *knows* to *is known*; more unforgivably, it turns the rest of the sentence into two independent clauses joined by just a comma. That's a run-on. The correct answer is (B).

18.   **(F)** I'm particular even about how I eat <u>spaghetti: I</u> always use a spoon to get a nice, tight spool around my fork.

Usage/Mechanics   Sentence Structure   Whole Sentences

The two clauses (before and after the colon) are each able to stand alone. A period or a semicolon would be acceptable here. The colon also works, because the second clause is an explanation of the specific way in which the narrator eats spaghetti.

What doesn't work is simply to use a comma, which can never on its own join two independent clauses. Moreover, using *that* or *which* after *spaghetti* means that this noun could have a legal place in the second clause. However, there's no spot where a missing *spaghetti* could go in *I always use a spoon to get a nice, tight spool around my fork.* Of course, the writer is referring indirectly to spaghetti with this clause, but the word *spaghetti* cannot be inserted in a way that *that* or *which* would create. The correct answer is (F).

19.   **(C)** In the last few months, though, I <u>have become</u> curious …

Usage/Mechanics   Sentence Structure   Verb Tense & Forms

The phrase *In the last few months* indicates a past time leading up to the present. In this case, the present perfect tense (*have become*) is ideal, because it means that the narrator is still curious. The present (*become*) is not suitable here. *Became* cannot be used after *had* (the past is *became*, while the past perfect is *had become*). *Am become* is archaic and inappropriate for a normal piece of modern expository writing. The correct answer is (C).

20.   **(G)** What makes a noodle a noodle? <u>First,</u> the dough out of which the noodle is made must be unleavened … Second, the dough …

Rhetorical Skills   Organization   Transitions

The rhetorical question that launches the paragraph demands a direct answer. The writer gives two conditions for being a noodle, flagging these conditions with *First* and *Second,* both of which are clear signposts. The later use of *Second* should guide you toward *First* (it's not an absolute necessity to have the *First,* perhaps, but call it a strong preference). The other transition phrases (*For example, In any event, Granted*) are all out of place. It would be better to use no transition at all than to use any of these distracting, misplaced signposts. The correct answer is (G).

21.   **(B)** Most effective link between Sentences 3 and 5: From that point, the sheets are often cut into long, narrow strips and dried.

Rhetorical Skills   Writing Strategy   Choice of Content

The correct answer yields this simplified logical sequence:

     Sentence 3:   The dough must be rolled into sheets.
     Sentence 4:   Then the sheets are cut into long, narrow strips and dried.
     Sentence 5:   Boiling the strips in water or broth is customary …

Notice how the *strips* of Sentence 5 need to be referred to earlier, and *strips* and *sheets* are not the same thing (strips are narrow, sheets are wide). The correct answer introduces the strips in a sensible way; the wrong answers do not do so. The correct answer is (B).

22. **(G)** … alternatively, noodles <u>might</u> be fried in oil.

Rhetorical Skills   Style   Concision

The most concise choice here is the best. If you can just say *might,* why say the wordy *may or may not* or *are potentially able to*? Likewise, *in fact* is a needless tag here that can be snipped away; there's no need for such emphasis.

Also and *in addition* are worse than redundant when combined with *alternatively;* they're downright confusing. Do they mean that you fry the noodles rather than boil them or in addition to boiling them? Omitting these terms leaves the case clear—the noodles might be fried rather than boiled. The correct answer is (G).

23. **(C)** noodles vary in innumerable ways, from the <u>dough's constituent grain</u> to

Usage/Mechanics   Punctuation   Apostrophes

The possessive of *dough* is *dough's*, with an 's. Thus, you cannot correctly write *the doughs grain*. The right answer uses the proper form to mean *the constituent grain of the dough*—that is, the grain that makes up the dough.

Modifier form and placement matter here as well. Choice (B), *constituent grain dough*, is hard to dissect and make sense of. Likewise, choice (D), *constituent of the dough of the grain*, mixes up the modifiers to little sensible result. The correct answer is (C).

24. **(J)** The sentence should NOT be added.

Rhetorical Skills   Writing Strategy   Additions

The sentence in question discusses people who do not eat noodles:

> *Out of a desire to cut carbohydrates or possibly gluten from their diets, some people no longer eat noodles at all.*

However, this sentence does not belong anywhere in this paragraph, which describes the key characteristics of noodles and declares that noodles still vary in many ways around the world. The fact that some people no longer eat noodles at all is irrelevant.

With small tweaks, this sentence could be very relevant. For instance, it could indicate that some people are abandoning certain types of noodles (say, wheat-based) in favor of other types that are gluten-free. Nevertheless, as written, the proposed sentence should not be added to the paragraph. The correct answer is (J).

25. **(A)** … even Italian pasta, a single culture's noodles, comes in far more than a few classic types. <u>Each tiny region of Italy</u> seems to have its own specialty in this regard.

Rhetorical Skills   Organization   Transitions

The thoughts in the two sentences are openly in accord with each other. If anything, the transition would provide emphasis or reinforcement: *In fact* or *Indeed* would work. The choice to use no transition here is the best of those available.

Any contrasting transition, such as *however* or *nonetheless,* would be unsuitable. *Granted* provides a subtler form of contrast, an unwilling concession to the other side of an argument, but a contrast all the same. The correct answer is (A).

26.　**(J)**　Pasta varieties reveal a sense of humor when you translate <u>their</u> names …

Usage/Mechanics　　　　Grammar & Usage　　　　Pronoun Forms

The possessive pronoun *their* refers back correctly to the plural noun *Pasta varieties*, so that the end of the sentence means *the names of the pasta varieties.* The word *there* means *in that place* and is completely incorrect in this context.

Since the noun *pasta varieties* is plural, you should not use the singular form *its.* By the way, the form *it's* always means *it is*, never *of it.* The correct answer is (J).

27.　**(D)**　<u>The story goes that Marco Polo brought pasta back to Italy from China,</u> where four-thousand-year-old noodles have been dug up.

Usage/Mechanics　　　　Sentence Structure　　　　Modifier Placement

The non-underlined portion of the sentence is a modifying clause beginning with *where.* Thus, the underlined portion must end with a place, specifically the place where these ancient noodles could have been dug up. The correct answer ends with *China,* a place that makes a great deal of sense. None of the other choices even properly end with a place; on the basis of this factor, you should eliminate all the incorrect answers. For choice (C), you could make the weak argument that the parenthetical *so goes the story* could be dropped, so that the modifier attaches to *Italy.* However, this argument is further weakened by the logic of the rest of the paragraph, which discusses *Chinese and other Asian dishes.* The focus of the passage has moved from Italy to Asia; thus, it only makes sense for the modifier to attach to *China,* even if you had minimal knowledge of the history of the two regions. The correct answer is (D).

28.　**(G)**　Noodles … are <u>made of not only regular wheat but also</u> buckwheat, rice, …

Usage/Mechanics　　　　Grammar & Usage　　　　Parallelism

The *not only … but also …* framework enforces parallelism. What follows *not only* must be parallel to what follows *but also,* as illustrated in the following legal examples:

> *Noodles are made of {not only <u>regular wheat</u> but also <u>buckwheat</u>}.*

> *Noodles are made {not only <u>of regular wheat</u> but also <u>of buckwheat</u>}.*

> *Noodles are {not only <u>made of regular wheat</u> but also <u>made of buckwheat</u>}.*

If you put the preposition *of* in one of the two places, you have to put it in the other. Likewise, if you put *made* after *not only,* you also have to put it after *but also.* The wrong answers mix and match these variations. The correct answer is (G).

MANHATTAN
PREP

29. **(D)** [omitted] My family and I are now making the rounds …

Rhetorical Skills   Style   Concision

The word *now* is already modifying the main verb *are making*, so you should not redundantly add *Currently*, *These days*, or *At present*. Time modifiers are tricky, because they can often be slipped into various nooks throughout the sentence. Pay attention to such modifiers whenever you spot them. The correct answer is (D).

30. **(F)** Best conveys that the narrator is eating more adventurously: My family and I are now making the rounds of neighborhood Asian restaurants, <u>where I order whatever looks least like spaghetti and meatballs.</u>

Rhetorical Skills   Writing Strategy   Choice of Content

The narrator begins the essay by naming spaghetti and meatballs as his or her favorite meal. At the end of the first paragraph, though, the narrator states that *in the last few months … I have become curious about the wider world of noodles, resolving to venture out more boldly.* Thus, it makes sense that *ordering whatever looks least like spaghetti and meatballs* would constitute progress toward the goal of more adventuresome eating (at least as far as noodles are concerned). None of the wrong answers convey this message at all—they simply describe the expense of these restaurants, their popularity, or the ownership of one of them. The correct answer is (F).

Passage 3

31. **(D)** <u>Nowadays, employees face tough decisions daily</u> to meet the hazy guidelines …

Rhetorical Skills   Style   Concision

The original version redundantly includes both the phrase *Every day* and the word *daily*, as does choice (C). Similarly, choice (B) uses both *everyday* and *on a daily basis*. The only non-redundant choice includes only *daily*. Notice that *Nowadays* has a different meaning altogether (it means "these days, at present"). The correct answer is (D).

32. **(G)** Most effective introduction: In the 1950s, standards of corporate dress in the U.S. were quite uniform.

Rhetorical Skills   Organization   Opening/Closing Content

The correct answer sets the stage well for the rest of the paragraph. The sentence begins with the time period (*In the 1950s*), then provides a general statement about the *standards of corporate dress* at that time. This statement (they were *quite uniform*) is backed up by the next sentence (the *conventional business outfits*), after which a first counterexample is given (when *Hewlett-Packard broke with convention*). The rest of the essay continues this narrative from uniformity in the 1950s to today's situation, in which almost anything goes.

The incorrect choices fail in various ways. The original version paints too broad a picture of the U.S. after the Second World War. *A period of growth and prosperity* is not obviously connected to attire in the workplace. The main clause in choice (H) asserts that *the term itself* [business casual] *is a recent creation*. You would then expect the rest of the paragraph to explain how the term came about, but this expectation is never fulfilled. Likewise, choice (J) is irrelevant to the rest of the paragraph and does not clearly place the reader in the 1950s. The correct answer is (G).

33.   **(A)** White-collar workplaces were dominated by conventional business outfits … <u>Nevertheless,</u> electronics manu-facturer Hewlett-Packard broke with convention and instituted dress-down Fridays …

Rhetorical Skills   Organization   Transitions

The previous sentence states that *conventional business outfits* were dominant in offices. So, to introduce the thought that *Hewlett-Packard broke with convention and instituted dress-down Fridays*, you should use a contrasting transition, such as *Nevertheless*. The wrong answers (*Thus, Furthermore, For example*) create various illogical relationships between the first thought and the second thought. The correct answer is (A).

34.   **(F)**   … Hewlett-Packard broke with convention <u>and instituted</u> dress-down Fridays …

Usage/Mechanics   Grammar & Usage   Parallelism

The two verb phrases *broke with convention* and *instituted dress-down Fridays* are in alignment with each other, logically, so they ought to be structurally parallel. The conjunction joining the two phrases should be *and*, not *but*, and the second verb form should be the past tense *instituted*, not *instituting*. Finally, using *that* in place of *and* incorrectly means that the convention was what instituted the dress-down Fridays. Of course, it was the company itself that did so, breaking convention. The correct answer is (F).

35.   **(D)** Should the writer make this addition here? No, because it diverts attention from the clear narrative path of the paragraph.

Rhetorical Skills   Writing Strategy   Additions

The proposed addition reads *Hewlett-Packard is commonly regarded as a corporate founder of Silicon Valley, the high-technology area around San Jose, California*. This sentence provides irrelevant information about the company. The important point has already been made: Hewlett-Packard broke convention and changed its office dress code on Fridays for a specific reason (having office workers help with shipments). The next paragraph picks up the narrative immediately: *The next step toward casual wear* … Any further background on Hewlett-Packard distracts the reader from that narrative. The sentence's tone and style are fine, but its content is extraneous. The correct answer is (D).

36.   **(G)** To boost <u>its sales,</u> the Hawaiian garment industry …

Usage/Mechanics   Punctuation   Apostrophes (and Commas)

To indicate that the sales belong to the garment industry, write *its sales*. The possessive form of *it* is *its*. The form with the apostrophe (*it's*) means "it is," which would make no sense here.

After *sales*, a comma should be used. Only use a colon in a sentence if the part before the colon could stand alone as a complete sentence. *To boost its sales* would be a fragment. The correct answer is (G).

37.   **(D)** … the Hawaiian garment industry … promoted "Aloha Fridays," on which <u>aloha, or Hawaiian, shirts</u> could be worn to the office.

Usage/Mechanics   Punctuation   Commas

MANHATTAN
PREP

The writer uses the word *aloha* as an adjective, first to modify *Fridays,* then to modify *shirts.* The term is defined for the reader: *aloha shirts* are Hawaiian shirts. The proper way to punctuate the explanatory phrase *or Hawaiian* is to put commas on both sides, as in the correct answer. These commas indicate that this phrase is just an aside. There are not two different kinds of shirts.

No comma should follow *shirts,* separating this subject from its verb *could be worn.* The correct answer is (D).

38.   **(J)**   Once the president of the Bank of Hawaii … the tradition caught on <u>locally</u> …

Rhetorical Skills   Style   Concision

The word *locally* is sufficient in this context. *In Hawaiian places and locations* is wordy, since *places* and *locations* are synonyms, and even *in Hawaiian places* could be more simply expressed as *in Hawaii.* This sentence and the one prior are both evidently set in Hawaii, so you do not need to write both *locally* and *as far as Hawaii is concerned.* Finally, the phrase *in the localities of Hawaii* is an unnecessarily wordy way of saying "in Hawaii" or "locally." The correct answer is (J).

39.   **(C)**   Clearest examples of the range of casual Friday clothing: By the 1990s, Fridays in a typical office setting presented a hodgepodge of styles, <u>from traditional corporate attire to flip-flops and shorts.</u>

Rhetorical Skills   Writing Strategy   Choice of Content

Only the correct answer presents a range of clothing: *from* one type of attire *to* a different type, exemplified by *flip-flops and shorts.* In fact, the wrong answers lack examples of clothing entirely. Instead, they add other information that the reader may or may not find useful and interesting, but that information does not contain examples of clothing worn on casual Fridays. The correct answer is (C).

40.   **(G)**   <u>Observing this turmoil</u> while seeking …

Rhetorical Skills   Style   Concision

The word *turmoil* already contains the meanings of *disorder* and *disarray,* so there's no need to use more than one of these words. Likewise, *sensing* and *perceiving* together are redundant. Either by itself, or *observing* for that matter, would be fine. The correct answer is (G).

41.   **(A)**   The company sent this guide to thousands of human resources managers around the country. <u>Suddenly,</u> "business casual" became a style adopted widely …

Rhetorical Skills   Organization   Transitions

The only acceptable transition among the choices is the original *Suddenly.* The word *Deliberately* has the seemingly appropriate meaning of "on purpose," but it doesn't match the verb *became.* The style can be *suddenly* adopted widely, but the only way it could become *deliberately* adopted widely is for a single decision maker to pull the strings everywhere. As much as Levi's may have influenced the human resources managers, they each made their separate decisions. Choice (C), *Incidentally,* would imply that the result is disconnected from the prior sentence, but the writer wants to show a causal connection. Finally, choice (D), *In moderation,* does not make sense in context: how can a style be adopted both *widely* and *in moderation*? The correct answer is (A).

42. **(G)** … "business casual" became a style adopted widely, even if <u>few could define it.</u>

Usage/Mechanics   Grammar & Usage   Pronoun Agreement

In the corrected version, the pronoun *it* refers back to the noun *style* (or to its name, *business casual*). The word *few* by itself means "few people" here.

Two of the wrong answers use *them* or *they,* plural pronouns that have no plural noun to refer back to. Finally, choice (J) uses *it* correctly, but the verb form ("was not to be defined") is unclear: does it mean that the style never wound up being defined, or that the style was not supposed to be defined? Such vagueness in meaning is unacceptable. The correct answer is (G).

43. **(C)** Benchmarks are <u>now far harder</u> to discern than ever.

Usage/Mechanics   Grammar & Usage   Comparisons

The correct comparative form of *hard* is *harder,* not *more harder.* You should never make a comparative form with both *more* and *-er.* The word *far* here is used as an adverb: how much harder? *Far harder.* The comparative (*harder*), not the superlative (*hardest*), is required, because the sentence ends with *than ever.* With *than,* you have to use the comparative form: "This is harder than that," not "This is the hardest than that." The correct answer is (C).

44. **(F)** Benchmarks are now … Some major companies lack … Certain industries … take a conservative view … Other <u>sectors revel</u> in their opposition …

Usage/Mechanics   Sentence Structure   Verb Tense

The whole paragraph is set in the present tense, as indicated by the verbs *are, lack,* and *take.* These verbs indicate general facts about the present day. There is no reason to change tenses; in fact, parallelism demands that if *certain industries lack …,* then *other sectors revel,* not *reveled.*

There should be no comma between the subject *other sectors* and the verb *revel.* The correct answer is (F).

45. **(B)** Best conclusion to the paragraph and most consistent with the rest of the essay: Technology leader Mark Zuckerberg of Facebook, with his trademark hoodie sweatshirts, may embody this stance most publicly.

Rhetorical Skills   Organization   Opening/Closing Content

The conclusion to the paragraph should be related to the topic sentence: *Benchmarks are now far harder to discern than ever.* Of the possibilities available to you, the best answer gives an example of the point made in the prior sentence (*Other sectors revel in their opposition to such clothing*). That point was an illustration of the overall message (that benchmarks are now very unclear), so the example of Zuckerberg and his hoodies fits neatly within the paragraph. Granted, it doesn't wrap up the essay with a grand insight, but the addition fits logically.

In contrast, the wrong answers each take off in a different inappropriate direction. Choice (A) introduces, for the first time anywhere in the essay, a work environment that doesn't even exist on the spectrum between business attire and business casual. This introduction is completely misplaced at this point in the essay. Choice (C) suddenly breaks into

MANHATTAN
PREP

personal voice (*I am* …), for another unsuitable introduction in the final sentence. Finally, choice (D) makes an un-warranted assertion about the future, claiming that the trend established throughout the essay will reverse because of random generalities such as "technology improves lives." Such a reversal cannot be brought out at the last second, even if it were well-supported. The correct answer is (B).

Passage 4

46.   **(F)** If you … are hungry for Southern home-style <u>cooking, then</u> look no farther …

Rhetorical Skills   Organization   Transitions (within a sentence)

After an *if* condition (*If you … are hungry …*), place the result (*look no farther*). Between the *if* condition and the result, you can either have just a comma or a comma plus *then* (*If you are hungry, then look no farther…*). Do not use other transitions, even causal ones such as *therefore*. The correct answer is (F).

47.   **(D)** … Mama Dip's <u>Kitchen, an unpretentious restaurant that</u> has been featured …

Usage/Mechanics   Punctuation   Commas

The words *Mama Dip's Kitchen* is the name of a restaurant: *Look no farther than Mama Dip's Kitchen*. This restaurant is then described by a long appositive phrase (*an unpretentious restaurant that has been featured in the New York Times*). Separate this phrase from *Kitchen* by a comma, but don't put a comma within the phrase anywhere. The correct answer is (D).

48.   **(G)** Mama Dip is an actual person named Mildred <u>Council. Born in 1929, she</u> grew up …

Usage/Mechanics   Sentence Structure   Whole Sentences

The first sentence should end either after *Council* or after *1929*, if the modifier *born in 1929* is attached to *Mildred Council* with a comma. Either way, *she* is the subject of the second sentence. The modifier *Born in 1929* could start that sentence, if separated from *she* with a comma. The two sentences cannot be joined by a comma; a semicolon would have to be used. Finally, *she* should not be separated from its verb *grew up* by any punctuation. The correct answer is (G).

49.   **(D)** … she relied on her <u>experience, not on recipes,</u> for guidance

Usage/Mechanics   Punctuation   Commas

The core of the sentence is *she relied on her experience for guidance*. This sentence requires no commas. To insert a contrasting point (what she didn't rely on), surround the contrasting phrase *not on recipes* with two commas. Don't put any commas anywhere in the middle of that phrase, however. The correct answer is (D).

50. **(F)** … with $64, <u>just enough to buy grits, eggs, and bacon for that first Sunday breakfast and to make change</u>.

Rhetorical Skills   Writing Strategy   Purpose of Words

The *intentions* or purposes for the money are best captured in *to* infinitive phrases, as in the existing sentence (… *to buy grits … and to make change*). The alternative choices may all be true and interesting, but they do not explain what the money will be used for. The correct answer is (F).

51. **(D)** At every table <u>were being</u> devoured sweet potatoes, fried chicken, and black-eyed peas …

Usage/Mechanics   Grammar & Usage   Subject–Verb Agreement
                       Sentence Structure   Verb Tense

This question tests two topics. First, is the subject singular or plural? The subject (*sweet potatoes, fried chicken, and black-eyed peas*) actually comes after the verb in this sentence, so it might be hard to spot; however, it is definitely plural, so the verb should be *are* or *were*, not *is* or *was*. You might recognize the point better if you flip the sentence: *Sweet potatoes, fried chicken, and black-eyed peas were being devoured around the room.*

Next, should the verb be *are* (present tense) or *were being* (past tense)? Every action in this sentence took place in the past, so the verb should be *were being*. The correct answer is (D).

52. **(H)** Least acceptable alternative: … sweet potatoes, fried chicken, and black-eyed <u>peas because</u> the cash register filled up.

Rhetorical Skills   Organization   Transitions

This choice is *least* acceptable of the alternatives to the original version. Consider the relationship between the two actions. In the first part of the sentence, food was being devoured; in the second part of the sentence, *the cash register filled up*. These two actions were happening at the same time, and the first was causing the second. So the transition can indicate the "same time" relationship (*as, while,* or *meanwhile*), or it could indicate the causal relationship *in the right direction* (from first to second, as *as a result* does). The least acceptable alternative reverses the causal arrow. The food wasn't being devoured *because* the cash register was filling up. The correct answer is (H).

53. **(D)** … that first Sunday breakfast and to make change. <u>Breakfast went so well …</u>

Rhetorical Skills   Organization   Sentence Order

The sentence in question starts with *Breakfast*, so the prior sentence should explain the context of that breakfast. Sentence 2 does just that: the money was enough to buy food to make that first breakfast. Then that *breakfast went so well* that Mama Dip could buy food to make subsequent meals. The existing Sentence 3 explains what happened at those meals, and then the paragraph ends with a generalization about Mama Dip: that she was a *true entrepreneur* and *had bootstrapped her way to financial independence.* The correct answer is (D).

MANHATTAN
PREP

54. **(H)** Double-checking that the customer was serious, <u>the server brought a plate of fried pig's intestines. Some …</u>

Usage/Mechanics   Sentence Structure   Modifier Placement

The sentence begins with *Double-checking*. Therefore, the subject of the sentence must logically be doing the double-checking. Neither the *plate* nor the *pig's intestines* fit the bill; only *the server* was performing that action. The correct answer is (H).

55. **(B)** … this customer wolfed the chittlins down with gusto—then <u>raved</u> about them …

Rhetorical Skills   Writing Strategy   Choice of Content

If the customer *wolfed* the food down *with gusto* (= enthusiasm), then he must have liked them a lot. It would make the most sense, then, if he subsequently *raved* (= wrote a very positive review) about them. The choices *complained* or *grumbled* indicate the opposite opinion. The other choice *thought* is too neutral, and it also doesn't make sense that the customer would just "think" about them in the New York Times. The correct answer is (B).

56. **(F)** … then raved about <u>them in</u> the *New York Times*.

Usage/Mechanics   Grammar & Usage   Pronoun Forms; Idioms

First, the pronoun should be *them*, not *it*, because *chittlins* (the noun that the pronoun is referring to) is plural. *Those* is also plural, but as a point of style, you should avoid using *those* by itself unless you are making a comparison (*I prefer these clothes to those over by the door*).

Next, the preposition should be *in*, not *on* or *over*. The *New York Times* is a newspaper, and content is *in* a newspaper, not *on* it or *over* it. The correct answer is (F).

57. **(D)** <u>Mama Dip has</u> expanded her business … to local stores and the Internet, where she sells …

Usage/Mechanics   Sentence Structure   Whole Sentences

The main clause of the sentence is the first thought: *Mama Dip has expanded her business.* The second part of the sentence is a subordinate clause: *where she sells …* This second thought cannot stand alone as written, so the first part of the sentence needs to be an independent clause, with a subject (*Mama Dip*) but no subordinators (*When, As*). The correct answer is (D).

58. **(F)** … she sells <u>cornbread mix, poppy seed dressing,</u> and both kinds of North Carolina barbecue sauce …

Usage/Mechanics   Punctuation   Commas

The list consists of three items: (1) *cornbread mix,* (2) *poppy seed dressing,* and (3) *both kinds of North Carolina barbecue sauce.* Commas need to be inserted between the items, with an *and* before the last item. Within item 1, *cornbread mix* is a single noun phrase, in which *cornbread* is acting like an adjective (indicating that the mix is for cornbread). Thus, *cornbread mix* should have no commas. Likewise, *poppy seed dressing* is a single noun phrase (*poppy* modifies *seed*, and then *poppy seed* modifies *dressing*), so there should be no commas within this phrase. The alternative choices make much less logical sense (e.g., what would *mix poppy* be?). The correct answer is (F).

59.   (B) If the writer were to delete the phrase "with her smiling face on the cover" from the preceding sentence, the sentence would primarily lose *information that highlights Mama Dip's attitude toward her readers.*

Rhetorical Skills   Writing Strategy   Deletions

What is the impact of including the phrase *with her smiling face on the cover*? This phrase is the first place in which Mama Dip's smile is mentioned. The position of her smile on the cover of her cookbooks indicates her positive attitude toward the people looking at or buying her book—that is, her readers. The correct answer is (B).

60.   (J) The sentence *He was a famous food critic who became a passionate supporter of the restaurant* most logically belongs after the last sentence in Paragraph 4.

Rhetorical Skills   Organization   Additions

Who could *He* be in the sentence given? Look for a person to whom the pronoun could be referring. At the end of Paragraph 4, you'll find this sentence: *This mysterious customer turned out to be none other than Craig Claiborne.* The additional sentence fits like a jigsaw puzzle piece. *He* is *Craig Claiborne.* The new sentence explains who Craig Claiborne is, an important piece of omitted information. The correct answer is (J).

Passage 5

61.   (C) ESPN's home page, <u>with its</u> tabs for football, …

Usage/Mechanics   Punctuation   Apostrophes

The possessive form of *it* is *its.* The contraction *it's* always means "it is" and is incorrect in this position. The form *its'* is never correct. *Whose* can work here on its own (*whose tabs* means *the tabs of which*). However, the modifier would need a verb, something for *whose tabs* to do, and don't forget that the subject *home page* needs a verb as well: *The home page, whose tabs are wonderful, is working.* In the sentence in question, unfortunately, there are not enough verbs to go around. Use *with its*, which requires no verb. The correct answer is (C).

62.   (J) ESPN's home page, with its tabs for football, basketball, … and <u>soccer, features both men's and women's</u> leagues …

Usage/Mechanics   Sentence Structure   Whole Sentences

The subject of the sentence is *ESPN's home page.* This subject needs a verb, if the sentence is to avoid being a fragment. The *-ing* form *featuring* is not a complete verb; the best option is *features* in the present tense, since the rest of the paragraph is in the general present.

In addition, the possessive forms of *men* and *women* are *men's* and *women's*, respectively. *Mens, mens', womens,* and *womens'* are all incorrect forms. Finally, the modifier that begins right after *home page* ends after *soccer.* This modifier should be set off by commas. The correct answer is (J).

MANHATTAN
PREP

63. **(A)** Imagine clicking through to find "Even More <u>Sports"; now,</u> keep going.

Usage/Mechanics   Sentence Structure   Whole Sentences

There are two verbs expressed as commands: *Imagine* and *keep*. The first verb runs an independent clause that goes up through "*Even More Sports*." The second verb governs a different independent clause: *now, keep going.* (The comma after the *now* is optional.) These two clauses can either stand alone as separate sentences or be linked, like any two related independent clauses, by a semicolon. The latter method is used in the correct answer.

What is not allowed is to jam these two clauses together with either just a comma or no punctuation at all. These errors condemn the wrong choices. The correct answer is (A).

64. **(H)** If the writer made this deletion, the paragraph would primarily lose a prompt to spur thinking about the theme of the essay.

Rhetorical Skills   Writing Strategy   Deletions

The sentence on the chopping block is *What strange sports might you uncover seven or eight levels down?* This question serves as a set-up device for the examples of such sports in the next two paragraphs. Since the topic of the essay is *Strange Sports,* as given in the title, the question focuses the reader's thinking on this theme.

The question is not meant to pose *a difficult hypothetical challenge to the reader.* After all, the question is given an immediate answer in the next sentence (*You might come across real tennis …*). You are not meant to puzzle over this question. Likewise, the *mystery* is raised, but its *solution* doesn't *ultimately evade the writer.* By the end of the essay, there's no lingering mystery about these sports. Finally, the question is *rhetorical* (that is, for effect), but at that point in the passage, it has not yet been answered. The correct answer is (H).

65. **(A)** … which is different from the version of tennis <u>you see</u> on television.

Usage/Mechanics   Sentence Structure   Whole Sentences

The original sentence has *you see on television* as a modifier to *the version of tennis.* In English, you can drop the *that* at the beginning of such a modifier if you have a different subject: *This is the table I bought.* In this short example, *I bought* is really the same as *that I bought.* So the sentence in the problem could read this way: … *the version of tennis that you see …* Either form is fine, because the writer is describing the version of tennis: you see that version on television.

The other answer choices create run-ons or incorrect forms of modifiers. The *it* in *you see it* turns those words into a whole new sentence: they're no longer a modifier for *the version of tennis.* Now you have a run-on, just as if you wrote *This is the table I bought it.* Likewise, the other wrong answers (*so you see* and *that as seen*) can no longer serve as proper modifiers, certainly not in the sense intended. The correct answer is (A).

66. **(H)** … descended from real, meaning royal, tennis … The latter adjective is <u>appropriate; for instance,</u> Louis X, king of France in the early 1300s, was a devoted player.

Rhetorical Skills   Organization   Transitions

MANHATTAN
PREP   187

Examine the thoughts on either side of the transition in question. How are these thoughts related? First, you have the definition of *real* as *royal* in this context. Then you read that *the latter adjective [i.e., royal] is appropriate.* Finally, after the transition, you learn that an early king of France liked to play the sport. This last fact is an example that helps justify the claim that the word *royal* is appropriate for this type of tennis. Of all the available transitions in the choices, only *for instance* works here. The correct answer is (H).

67.   **(B)** Most relevant addition: Another aficionado, King Henry VIII of England, built at least one court in a palace.

Rhetorical Skills   Writing Strategy   Choice of Content

The best option here is to add another example of a royal patron or player of real tennis, and King Henry VIII fits the bill. This addition provides reinforcement for the claim that the adjective *royal* is appropriate for real tennis. After all, if just one king played the game, that could be a fluke, but two kings? Now you've got a case.

The wrong answers give information that is not only true but related to King Louis X. The problem is that these facts detract from the point of the paragraph: to describe real tennis as a strange, special sport. The king's death (even if perhaps caused by the game) and his prior kingdom are distracting topics. Even the fact that some of the terms come from medieval French does not advance the story right here. Maybe that point could be slipped into the next sentence as an aside about the *special terms*, but it does not deserve its own full sentence. The correct answer is (B).

68.   **(G)** … courts with odd asymmetries and openings that <u>must be defended,</u> …

Usage/Mechanics   Grammar & Usage   Subject–Verb Agreement

The subject of the verb in the *that* clause is *openings* (or potentially *asymmetries and openings*). Either way, you have a plural subject. So the verb cannot be *is* or *demands*; these verbs are both singular. *Must* is the same in singular or plural: *she must* and *they must* are both right. So *must be defended* is correct. The option *are demanded to be defended* is slightly but definitively off. The text would have to read "… openings that demand to be defended," not *are demanded*. The correct answer is (G).

69.   **(D)** <u>A variety of unique sports</u> can be found at British private schools.

Usage/Mechanics   Sentence Structure   Modifier Placement

To make sense, the adjective *unique* needs to be placed to modify either *sports* or *variety;* these two nouns should be related through *of,* as in the phrase *A variety of sports.* Either *A variety of unique sports* or *A unique variety of sports* would do.

The original version (*unique to sports*) would illogically mean that some *variety* (of what?) was only found in sports. Likewise, *Uniquely* would mean that *a variety of sports* could not be found anywhere but in British private schools. Lastly, *A variety that is unique* does mean *A unique variety*, but the necessary addition of the phrase *of sports* makes the former not only wordy but awkward (it seems that *unique of sports* is meant to mean something). The correct answer is (D).

70.   **(G)** Scoring a goal is so difficult that <u>it has not been done</u> in the big annual match …

Usage/Mechanics   Grammar & Usage   Pronoun Agreement

The original version, as well as one other incorrect choice, mentions *they*. Who or what is *they*? No noun in this or any prior sentence is suitable—the writer seems to mean "players," but this noun needs to be explicitly stated somewhere. Thus, you have to go without *they* (and active voice in the verb). The correct answer uses *it* to refer to the action of *Scoring a goal*.

The other wrong answer (*it is not so done*) employs the present tense (*is*) incorrectly in place of the present perfect (*has been*). Also, *not so done*, an awkwardly arranged phrase, seems to mean "not done in this way." However, the intended meaning of the writer is that the act of scoring a goal has simply not been done at all. The correct answer is (G).

71. **(A)** … you might find them <u>more interesting than</u> ones you watch or play.

Usage/Mechanics   Grammar & Usage   Comparisons

The correct way to write a comparison with a long adjective such as *interesting* is to put *more* (or *less*) in front of the adjective and *than* behind it: *this is more interesting than that*.

Do not use *then* or *compared to* in place of *than*. Also, avoid the stilted pause created by putting a comma and *more* after the adjective: revise *this is interesting, more than that* to be *this is more interesting than that*. The correct answer is (A).

72. **(J)** Least acceptable: Even soccer … is formally known as association <u>football, the game</u> developed …

Usage/Mechanics   Sentence Structure   Whole Sentences

The segment of text *Even soccer … association football* is an independent clause. So is the segment from *it* (or *it was* or *the game*) through *while growing up*. Thus, you must either split these two independent clauses into two separate sentences or join them properly. A semicolon is fine; a colon will also work here, because the second sentence explains the first (the term *association* is a result of the *compromise among students*). However, it is not acceptable to use just a comma, which creates a run-on. The correct answer is (J).

73. **(A)** Best tie to major themes: Now this sport, <u>with its strange rules made up by college kids,</u> has billions of fans.

Rhetorical Skills   Writing Strategy   Choice of Content

In the first paragraph, the essay mentions sports popular in the U.S., then raises the question: what about the "strange sports" of the title? The next two paragraphs give examples of such sports, and then the writer confesses in the last paragraph that he or she has come to believe that *every sport is weird, with arbitrary rules that can seem silly*. This conclusion unifies the strange and the popular sports, so the final sentence should ideally do something similar. The non-underlined portion mentions the *billions of fans* that soccer has, certainly qualifying it as popular. The correct answer brings in the *strange rules*, creating the right marriage of popular and strange.

The wrong answers fail to make the same connection. Mentioning that soccer *can be played anywhere* or when its *World Cup happens* or that it is *not as popular in the United States as American football* does not emphasize that soccer, like every other sport, is played with *arbitrary rules that can seem silly*. The correct answer is (A).

74.   **(H)** If the writer were to make this deletion, the essay would primarily lose a contemporary detail that underlines the unfamiliarity of the paragraph's example.

Rhetorical Skills   Writing Strategy   Deletions

The sentence in question (the last one of the second paragraph) is *Today, there are only about fifty real tennis courts in the world*. This fact is not *a historical summary* of anything (it's hardly historical), nor is it *a necessary conclusion* of any prior statements (unless those statements were mathematical, such as *There used to be fifty-one courts, and then one closed*). Moreover, this sentence does not provide any *visual imagery* of the courts: the only descriptor is the number *fifty*. The only choice that fits is the one indicating that this sentence provides *a contemporary [i.e., today] detail that underlines the unfamiliarity of the paragraph's example [real tennis]*. That is, the fact that only about fifty courts exist today reinforces the idea that this sport is unfamiliar to most people. The correct answer is (H).

75.   **(D)** Does the essay fulfill the goal of focusing on the essential differences between strange and familiar sports? No, because the essay reaches the conclusion that all sports are strange in some ways.

Rhetorical Skills   Writing Strategy   Goal of Essay

In the final paragraph, the writer comes right out and names his or her *conclusion—every sport is weird, involving arbitrary rules that can seem silly*. In other words, the big "aha" of the essay is that these strange sports that *seem* to be so different from "everyday" sports are in reality not so different, because those everyday sports are also strange, when you really think about them. Thus, the writer is opposed to the idea of *focusing on the essential differences between strange and familiar sports*, as the question puts the hypothetical goal. This goal is not fulfilled because the writer concludes the opposite. The correct answer is (D).

MANHATTAN
PREP

Chapter 6
of

5lb. Book of ACT® Practice Problems

English:
Passage Set 2

In This Chapter...

Set 2 Passages & Solutions

Chapter 6
English: Passage Set 2

The English problems in this chapter are distributed across five passages, just as they will be on the ACT itself. Every topic is up for grabs, so expect a little of everything. The answer key and the solutions classify the problems for you, so you can pinpoint strengths and weaknesses.

How should you use this chapter? Here are some recommendations, according to the level you've reached in ACT English.

1. Fundamentals. If you haven't done any topical work yet, consider working in Chapters 3 and 4 first. Otherwise, do a passage or two untimed to begin with. As you become more comfortable, put the clock on. In all cases, review the solutions closely, and articulate what you've learned. Redo problems as necessary.

2. Fixes. Do one passage at a time under timed conditions. Examine the results, learn your lessons, then test yourself with more passages at once.

3. Tweaks. Confirm your mastery by doing a few passages at once under timed conditions. A full set of five is the ultimate goal. Aim to improve the speed and ease of your solution process.

Good luck on the problems!

PASSAGE 1

The Number Four

[1]

I barely speak Japanese. Most of my great-grandparents came to the United States from Japan, but through the <u>generations, our family</u> has preserved only
¹
some cultural aspects. My mother makes better sushi

than any <u>restaurant, and at</u> home we often have miso
²

soup. However, we also frequently <u>ate</u> American food. If
³
I am Japanese-American, I would stress the second half
of the term.

[2]

One element of Japanese culture, though, <u>have</u>
⁴
been kept unchanged in our house: the number four

<u>being avoided and shunned.</u> Since the word for "four"
⁵
sounds just like the word for "death" in the Japanese

language, <u>dishes and chocolates are never boxed in sets</u>
⁶
<u>of four.</u> If this practice seems strange, consider that
⁶
hotels in the United States also leave out a floor—the
thirteenth. My parents have never decorated our house

1. **A.** NO CHANGE
    B. generations our family,
    C. generations, our family,
    D. generations: our family

2. Which of the following alternatives to the underlined portion would NOT be acceptable?
    F. restaurant; at
    G. restaurant. At
    H. restaurant, at
    J. restaurant; moreover, at

3. **A.** NO CHANGE
    B. eat
    C. had eaten
    D. could eat

4. **F.** NO CHANGE
    G. has
    H. is
    J. OMIT the underlined portion

5. **A.** NO CHANGE
    B. were avoided
    C. avoided and shunned
    D. is shunned

6. At this point, the writer wants to make a statement that would logically lead into the sentence that follows it. Given that all of the choices are true, which one would BEST accomplish this purpose?
    F. NO CHANGE
    G. hotels in Japan skip directly from the third to the fifth floor.
    H. even related numbers such as 42 are considered unlucky.
    J. several other Asian societies take the same dim view of this number.

in any way that could symbolize the number four. ⟦7⟧

[3]

Last year, my high school hosted an exchange student, Shawn, who came from another nation but not another country. A Navajo, Shawn grew up in Chinle,

which is in Apache County, Arizona, but <u>Chinle is also part</u> of the Navajo Nation.
          8
   8

[4]

[1] My chemistry teacher made Shawn and me lab partners. [2] At first, we hardly talked. [3] One day, however, when the experiment called <u>on</u> four test tubes, I muttered, "I bet one breaks." [4] Staring at me, Shawn asked why. [5] I replied, "Four is unlucky." [6] In response, he shook his head forcefully and said, "No, it's sacred," <u>explained</u> that the number four holds a special place in Navajo culture. [7] For instance, the four primary directions are each associated with a different <u>color and correspond to north, south, east,</u>
          11

7. Which of the following sentences, if added at this point, would both articulate a major theme of the essay and create an effective transition to the next paragraph?
   A. As I found out, though, radically different perspectives on this number exist.
   B. Especially sensitive to the connotations, Japanese hospitals never label rooms as number four.
   C. My high school offers a greater variety of languages for study than other schools in our district.
   D. My grandparents were instrumental in arranging my nursery right after I was born.

8. F. NO CHANGE
   G. Chinle, is also part
   H. Chinle is, also part,
   J. Chinle: is also part

9. A. NO CHANGE
   B. for
   C. at
   D. OMIT the underlined portion

10. F. NO CHANGE
    G. explains
    H. having explained
    J. explaining

11. Given that all of the choices are true, which one would provide information that is MOST relevant and meaningful to the passage as a whole?
    A. NO CHANGE
    B. color: black, white, blue, or yellow.
    C. color and indicated by a holy mountain in the ancestral Navajo homeland.
    D. color, in contrast to the five cardinal directions recognized in Japan.

6

and west. [12]
11

[5]

Right then we became friends, forgetting about the test tubes, and his ideas have since influenced mine. Shawn has returned home for his senior year, but we keep in touch by email. Hashke Dilwo'ii, his birth name, had meant Angry Runner, so now Shawn and I
13

are currently designing a video game called Four Angry
14
Runners. We're hoping for Navajo, not Japanese, luck to hold.

12. For the sake of the logic and coherence of this paragraph, Sentence 7 should be placed:
   F. where it is now.
   G. after Sentence 2.
   H. after Sentence 4.
   J. after Sentence 5.

13. A. NO CHANGE
    B. has meant
    C. means
    D. meaning

14. F. NO CHANGE
    G. at present designing
    H. designing presently
    J. designing

Question 15 asks about the preceding passage as a whole.

---

15. Suppose the writer had chosen to write a brief essay about an example of how people from different cultures can affect each other's perspectives. Would this essay successfully fulfill the writer's goal?
    A. Yes, because the essay compares traditional features of Navajo and Japanese cultures to modern innovations such as video games.
    B. Yes, because the essay illustrates how someone with a traditional Japanese belief has acquired a more complex viewpoint after exposure to Navajo beliefs.
    C. No, because although Shawn and the narrator may have both learned something new, their respective cultures each remained unaltered as a whole.
    D. No, because these ideas about the number four, whether positive or negative, have not been adequately tested according to the scientific method.

PASSAGE 2

Television Displays

[1]

When you're watching your favorite show, you probably don't stop thinking about how the television set or computer monitor works—unless, of course, it breaks down. Recently, my laptop screen acquired bright spots. Now, when I scroll down a document or watch a video, those areas are always lit up, revealing the proverbial "man behind the curtain" who

metaphorically operates the lamps behind the screen. [18] This computer mishap has prompted me to look into

the technology of television displays and computer monitors.

[2]

All such displays, as well as film projectors, depend on an optical illusion called the phi phenomenon. If your eye sees a series of related snapshots quickly enough, one after the other, your

16. **F.** NO CHANGE
    G. stop while thinking
    H. stop thoughts
    J. stop to think

17. Which of the following alternatives to the under-lined portion would be LEAST acceptable?
    A. As a result,
    B. So now,
    C. Now, however,
    D. Thus,

18. At this point, the writer is considering adding the following true statement:

    Naturally, the quotation refers to the Wizard of Oz, who frantically generates a magical illusion for Dorothy and her companions from behind a curtain before that illusion is spoiled by Doro-thy's dog.

    Should the writer add this sentence here?
    F. Yes, because it provides critical background information about the quotation.
    G. Yes, because it explains how the man behind the curtain operated his illusion.
    H. No, because it distracts the reader from the main point of the example.
    J. No, because it does not give specific enough details about how the illusion worked.

19. **A.** NO CHANGE
    B. and those of
    C. and to
    D. into

20. **F.** NO CHANGE
    G. snapshots, quickly
    H. snapshots quickly,
    J. snapshots; quickly

MANHATTAN
PREP   197

brain perceives motion. You can flip through pages of

similar doodles to witness this thing.
                          21

[3]

For television screens, the technical challenge

is how to redraw fast: the display has to paint each
22

snapshot, hold it for a split second, and then replace
                                          23
it with the next snapshot. To achieve the illusion of

motion, as many as twenty-five to thirty frames are

drawn every second.

[4]

[1] For decades after the birth of television, a more
                                        24
controversial event than you might realize, the pen with
                   24
which theses frames were drawn was primarily a beam

of electrons, or cathode ray. [2] In cathode ray tubes, or

CRTs, this beam sweeps over an array of dots that glow

when the beam strikes them. [3] As if interrupting and
                                                  25
releasing a spray of water, the television signal rapidly
                25
turns the beam on and off, synchronizing the electrons

to hit exactly the dots that make up for the proper
                                  26
picture. [4] As the glow from one sweep fades, another

sweep begins. [5] In consumer applications, cathode

ray tubes have been largely replaced by liquid crystal

displays and are thinner, lighter, and potentially bigger.
        27
[6] However, as technology marches on, these displays

21. A. NO CHANGE
  B. the effect.
  C. all that.
  D. OMIT the underlined portion (ending the
      sentence with a period).

22. F. NO CHANGE
  G. is, how to redraw fast—
  H. is how to redraw, fast,
  J. is, how to redraw fast

23. Which of the following alternatives to the under-
    lined portion would be LEAST acceptable?
  A. immediately
  B. originally
  C. finally
  D. OMIT the underlined portion.

24. F. NO CHANGE
  G. television, although sets were not widespread in
      the U.S. until the mid-1950s,
  H. television (and many people, correctly or not,
      claimed parenthood),
  J. television,

25. Given that all the choices are true, which one MOST
    effectively describes the origin of the television signal?
  A. NO CHANGE
  B. Arriving over the airwaves or through a cable,
  C. A complex sequence of electrical instructions,
  D. In order to create an image temporarily,

26. F. NO CHANGE
  G. make up
  H. made for
  J. made

27. A. NO CHANGE
  B. displays because
  C. displays, which are
  D. displays,

may <u>soon be surpassed</u> by organic light-emitting diodes
28

28. F. NO CHANGE
    G. soon be surpassed,
    H. soon, be surpassed,
    J. soon, be surpassed

or by the more <u>mysteriously</u> named "quantum dots." [7]
29

29. Which choice would MOST clearly indicate that the name "quantum dots" is of interest?
    A. NO CHANGE
    B. puzzlingly
    C. secretively
    D. intriguingly

These dots produce pure and bright colors at low power. [30]

30. The writer has decided to divide this closing paragraph into two. The best place to add the new paragraph break would be at the beginning of Sentence:
    F. 4, because it would signal the essay's shift from the first sweep of the electron beam to the following sweep.
    G. 4, because it would indicate that the essay is now going to address how the picture on a CRT screen changes.
    H. 5, because it would signal the essay's shift from the operation of CRTs to their replacement by newer displays.
    J. 5, because it would indicate that the essay is now going to focus on consumer applications of these technologies.

6

PASSAGE 3

Checkers

[1]

For years during my childhood Pop-pop my
  <u>   </u>
                                        31
<u>grandfather</u>, and I went to the park twice a week,
        31

usually <u>Monday and Wednesday evenings</u>, and laid out
        32
his little plastic checkers set. He had been using it for so

long that the black and red squares had begun to wear

off, showing the brown paper <u>underneath</u>. The surface
                                        33

was worn to the point that you could almost see <u>some</u>
                                                      34
<u>of Pop-pops</u> favorite strategies, hinted at by faded paths
        34
where checkers had slid back and forth over and over,

<u>at ceaseless war in the unending battle</u> between black
                              35
and red.

[2]

The best parts of checkers with Grandpa were his

quirks. On even-numbered days he always played red,

and on odd days, black—heaven help you if you tried to

play with his color. We stood <u>after each game</u>, bowed to
                                        36
each other, and switched sides of the table. Of course,

first every single piece had to be neatly cleared. While I

31. A. NO CHANGE
   B. childhood, Pop-pop my grandfather
   C. childhood Pop-pop, my grandfather
   D. childhood, Pop-pop my grandfather,

32. F. NO CHANGE
   G. in the evenings on Mondays and also Wednes-day evenings,
   H. evenings on Mondays and Wednesdays were when we would go,
   J. Mondays and Wednesdays, typically going in the evenings,

33. Which of the following alternatives to the under-lined portion would be LEAST acceptable?
   A. beneath
   B. beneath them
   C. below
   D. under

34. F. NO CHANGE
   G. some, of Pop-pops
   H. some, of Pop-pop's
   J. some of Pop-pop's

35. A. NO CHANGE
   B. battling endlessly and without ceasing
   C. waging the unending war
   D. never ceasing to wage the endless war

36. The LEAST acceptable placement for the underlined portion in the sentence would be:
   F. where it is now.
   G. before the word *we* (appropriately changing capitalization and putting a comma after *stood*).
   H. after the word *sides* (putting a comma after *stood* and deleting the comma after *game*)
   J. after the word *table* (putting a comma after *stood* and ending the sentence with a period, not a comma).

appreciated all of his tics. The strangest by far was the king-crowning ritual.
[37]

[3]

[1] Whenever I advanced a man to his side for a king, Pop-pop picked up a discarded piece of mine, which had been taken off of the board, and licked one side. [2] He also licked a side of my new king-worthy piece, as if it were the other half of an Oreo. [3] Finally, he stuck the two circles together and the pair entitled
[38] [38]
[39]

a proper king. [4] But he had already taught myself, and I never forgot. [5] Sometimes he added, "The spit helps 'em stay stacked up," as if worried that I had
[40]

forgotten. [41]

[4]

Each week we sat in the park, engrossed in sliding, hopping, double-jumping, licking, king-making, and capturing. When a solitary checker was all that remained, we started all over again. On a good day, we got in eleven or twelve games while the sun dipped lower and lower in the sky.
[42]

[5]

The last game of the day was always my favorite, with the sun barely streaming over the horizon, my grandfather glowing slightly around the edges, and the stubby checkers casting long shadows. During these
[43]

---

37. A. NO CHANGE
   B. tics and the
   C. tics, the
   D. tics, but the

38. F. NO CHANGE
   G. my own, which I had thrown away,
   H. mine that had belonged to me
   J. mine

39. A. NO CHANGE
   B. called the pair
   C. gave the pair
   D. the pair was raised

40. F. NO CHANGE
   G. me,
   H. me myself,
   J. him myself,

41. For the sake of the logic and coherence of the paragraph, Sentence 5 should be placed:
   A. where it is now.
   B. after Sentence 1.
   C. after Sentence 2.
   D. after Sentence 3.

42. Which of the following alternatives to the underlined portion would NOT be acceptable?
   F. as the sun dipped
   G. that the sun dipped
   H. while the sun kept dipping
   J. as the sun continued to dip

43. A. NO CHANGE
   B. was glowing
   C. glowed
   D. glows

times, the games took on an epic quality, <u>lasting for</u> <u>what felt unfortunately like hours.</u>
₄₄

44. Which choice would BEST reinforce the themes in this paragraph, using an appropriate tone?

  F. NO CHANGE

  G. soon to be vanquished with the fall of night.

  H. becoming twilight tales of strategy and defeat.

  J. but onlookers would have seen nothing special.

> Question 45 asks about the preceding passage as a whole.

---

45. After finishing the essay, the writer composes the following sentence:

> I once asked whether we could replace the board, but he only shot me a quizzical look in reply.

If the writer were to include this sentence, the most logical place to add it would be at the end of Paragraph:

  A. 1.

  B. 2.

  C. 3.

  D. 5.

PASSAGE 4

Electronic Music

[1]

In the second half of the nineteenth century, two developments opened the door to true electronic music. One will be the creation of vibrating circuits called
46
oscillators. The other was the invention of loudspeakers that could turn these electronic vibrations into actual

sounds. Once these two components are paired, a
47
simple musical instrument is born.
47

[2]

Soon after World War I, a young Russian physicist named Lev Termin devised an electronic device whose unique auditory impact on the ears is still recognizable
48
today: the theremin, after the German form of Termin's

name. Interestingly, you play the theremin by touching
49
it. The position of your hands in the air near the two

antennas controls the pitch and the volume of the sound
50
an eerie warble that provided the sonic setting for a
50
dozen science-fiction movies and television shows in the 1950s. If you imagine a black-and-white flying saucer flitting across the screen on poorly hidden wires. The
51
soundtrack in your mind is supplied by the theremin.

46. F. NO CHANGE
   G. is
   H. was
   J. had been

47. Given that all of the choices are true, which one provides the BEST conclusion to this paragraph?
   A. NO CHANGE
   B. Both oscillators and loudspeakers have become much more sophisticated since then.
   C. More advances were necessary, of course, before this music was more than a novelty.
   D. Microphones do the opposite: they turn sounds into electrical signals.

48. F. NO CHANGE
   G. sonic products in the air are
   H. environmental characteristics aurally are
   J. sound is

49. A. NO CHANGE
   B. without touching
   C. touching
   D. having touched

50. F. NO CHANGE
   G. sound, an eerie, warble
   H. sound, an eerie warble
   J. sound; an eerie warble

51. A. NO CHANGE
   B. wires and the
   C. wires; the
   D. wires, the

[3]

Since even tiny variations in the proximity of
your hands <u>causes noticeable effects to occur,</u> the
                        52
theremin is difficult to play consistently. Moreover,

only one tone <u>really created.</u> Musical pioneers
              53

craved more tractable and versatile machines built
54
makeshift prototypes of what would later become

synthesizers. By the sixties and seventies, <u>Mellotron, and</u>
                                            55
<u>Moog synthesizers</u> produced the signature backdrop for
                   55
much jazz, rhythm & blues, and rock music.

[4]

[1] Amplified instruments, <u>such as electric guitars</u>
                           56
<u>and the Clavinet keyboard,</u> also became widespread
           56
in popular songs. [2] Unlike synthesizers, amplified
instruments first generate sound in a traditional way,

perhaps by vibrating a metal string. [3] <u>For example, this</u>
                                         57

tiny sound, though <u>too weak to travel far, is than</u> picked
                   58

52. F. NO CHANGE
   G. causes noticeable effects as their results,
   H. result in the occurrence of noticeable effects,
   J. cause noticeable effects,

53. A. NO CHANGE
   B. had been really created.
   C. is really created.
   D. really created it.

54. F. NO CHANGE
   G. craving
   H. were craving
   J. craved by

55. A. NO CHANGE
   B. Mellotron and Moog synthesizers
   C. Mellotron and, Moog synthesizers
   D. Mellotron and Moog synthesizers,

56. At this point, the writer would like to provide illus-
trative examples of specific devices. Given that all
the choices are true, which one BEST accomplishes
this purpose?
   F. NO CHANGE
   G. condemned by some and celebrated by others,
   H. that is to say ones made electronically louder,
   J. which depend upon electricity as well,

57. A. NO CHANGE
   B. In contrast, this
   C. Therefore, this
   D. This

58. F. NO CHANGE
   G. the weakest to travel farther than is
   H. far weaker to travel, is then
   J. too weak to travel far, is then

up by electronic sensors called, unsurprisingly, "pickups."

[4] The amplified result can be big enough to fill a

football stadium. [59]

59. For the sake of the logic and coherence of this paragraph, Sentence 4 should be placed:

    A. where it is now.
    B. before Sentence 1.
    C. after Sentence 1.
    D. after Sentence 2.

Question 60 asks about the preceding passage as a whole.

---

60. Suppose the writer's goal had been to write a brief essay charting milestones in the development of electronic music. Would this essay successfully fulfill that goal?

    F. Yes, because it suggests possible directions that this music will take in the future.
    G. Yes, because it highlights relevant advances in the field over the course of decades.
    H. No, because it neglects similar developments in music that do not involve electronics.
    J. No, because the dates given in the essay for certain events are not specific enough.

PASSAGE 5

Dollar Coins

[1]

Coins with the value of one dollar have been issued throughout United States history from the perspective of the government, coins have a crucial

61. **A.** NO CHANGE
    B. history, from
    C. history: from
    D. history. From

advantage over bills: coins last longer and so are cheaper to make. The Treasury could save almost two

62. Which of the following alternatives to the underlined word would be LEAST acceptable?
    F. endure
    G. survive
    H. persist
    J. take

hundred million dollars a year if they switched to dollar

63. **A.** NO CHANGE
    B. they're
    C. it
    D. its

coins. The American public, however, has not taken to recent experiments with dollar coins, preferring lighter and thinner bills. Dollar coins would likely be broadly adopted only if the Treasury stopped printing equivalent bills.

64. **F.** NO CHANGE
    G. public; however,
    H. public however,
    J. public, however

65. **A.** NO CHANGE
    B. bills, which are less bulky and heavy than coins.
    C. bills, which are favored by the U.S. population.
    D. bills that have the same value as the coins do.

[2]

[1] The U.S. Mint first produced silver dollar coins in 1794, but stopped in 1804. [2] Any of these 1804 dollars is now worth millions. [3] In fact, the coins minted that year bore the date of 1803, since the dies had been reused. [4] The only authentic silver dollars dated 1804 were created decades afterward, special gifts

66. **F.** NO CHANGE
    G. afterward, where
    H. afterward, when
    J. afterward, which

for foreign rulers were needed. [5] Later, an employee of the Mint made a few more copies to sell illegally. [67]

[3]

In the 1800s and early 1900s, several distinct types of dollar coins were produced. The face value of the coin, the underlying value of the metal, and the exchange rate with other coins <u>was</u> sometimes different,
<u>68</u>
resulting in odd behavior. For instance, speculators swapped lighter coins for heavier ones and extracted

the excess metal, <u>or did other things like that to make</u>
<u>69</u>
<u>money from money.</u>
<u>69</u>

[4]

Nowadays, dollar coins are not melted down; they are ignored. [70] Vending machines rarely accept the giant Eisenhower dollar of the 1970s. In turn, the Susan B. Anthony coin was made to resemble a quarter,

confusing users. <u>Mostly recent,</u> the brass Sacagawea
<u>71</u>
coin, designed in honor of the Native American guide of the Lewis and Clark expedition, and its Presidential

cousin have <u>fallen short of success and failed to win</u>
<u>72</u>

67. For the sake of the logic and coherence of this paragraph, Sentence 2 should be placed:
   A. where it is now.
   B. before Sentence 1.
   C. after Sentence 3.
   D. after Sentence 5.

68. F. NO CHANGE
   G. were
   H. is
   J. has been

69. Given that all the choices are true, which one would BEST conclude the sentence with another illustration of speculator behavior?
   A. NO CHANGE
   B. or brought coins from Asia to the U.S. for a profit.
   C. or tried to manipulate the system in various other ways.
   D. which was then a free source of gold or silver.

70. The writer is considering deleting the preceding sentence from the essay. The sentence should NOT be deleted because it:
   F. explains why dollar coins have not been widely accepted by the American public.
   G. proposes that melting down coins is less advantageous than simply not using them.
   H. creates a transition from the more distant past to the recent history of these coins.
   J. suggests that dollar coins had been melted down at times for their metallic content.

71. A. NO CHANGE
   B. Most recent,
   C. Mostly recently,
   D. Most recently,

72. F. NO CHANGE
   G. failed to win
   H. fallen short of success and of winning
   J. failed to succeed at winning

acceptance, at least in the U.S. private sector. Some

mass-transit systems have given Sacagaweas as change,
                        —————
                          73

whether these coins are desired or not, although
                                     ————————
                                        74
typically, commuters try to get rid of these coins as
———
                        74
quickly as possible.
————————————
      74

73. A. NO CHANGE
   B. would of gave
   C. been given
   D. had gave

74. Given that all the choices are true, which one would MOST effectively illustrate a current and accepted use of dollar coins?
   F. NO CHANGE
   G. and in Ecuador and El Salvador, which use the U.S. dollar, Sacagawea coins circulate widely and without comment.
   H. while Sacagaweas and Susan B. Anthony coins have the same electrochemical properties, a useful feature for coin machines.
   J. though the bright brass finish of Sacagaweas unfortunately tarnishes to a dull gray or brown more quickly than expected.

Question 75 asks about the preceding passage as a whole.

---

75. Suppose the writer's goal had been to write a brief essay tracing the history and current status of a certain kind of coin in the United States. Would this essay fulfill that goal?
   A. Yes, because the essay highlights milestones in the development of dollar coins and assesses their present level of acceptance.
   B. Yes, because the essay demonstrates that dollar coins will not be accepted by the public until bills are withdrawn from circulation.
   C. No, because the essay focuses on the process of minting dollar coins, not on their distribution or their use over time.
   D. No, because the essay implies that the face value of dollar coins should not deviate from the value of their metallic content.

Passage Set 2 Answer Key

Write in whether you got each problem right or wrong (or left it blank). If your answer was correct, put a 1 in every blank to the right of that problem. Sum up each column and compare your total to the total possible "Out Of" points in each column.

Problem	Correct Answer	Right/ Wrong/ Blank	Grammar & Usage	Punctuation	Sentence Structure	Organization	Style	Writing Strategy
				Usage/Mechanics			Rhetorical Skills	
1	A			—				
2	H				—			
3	B				—			
4	G		—					
5	D						—	
6	G					—		
7	A					—		
8	F			—				
9	B		—					
10	J		—					
11	C							—
12	F					—		
13	C				—			
14	J						—	
15	B							—
16	J		—					
17	C					—		
18	H							—
19	A		—					
20	F			—				
21	B						—	
22	F			—				
23	B					—		
24	J						—	
25	B							—
26	G		—					

Problem	Correct Answer	Right/ Wrong/ Blank	Usage/Mechanics			Rhetorical Skills		
			Grammar & Usage	Punctuation	Sentence Structure	Organization	Style	Writing Strategy
27	C				—			
28	F			—				
29	D						—	
30	H					—		
31	B			—				
32	F						—	
33	D		—					
34	J			—				
35	C						—	
36	H				—			
37	C				—			
38	J						—	
39	B						—	
40	G		—					
41	D					—		
42	G		—					
43	A		—					
44	H					—		
45	A					—		
46	H				—			
47	A					—		
48	J						—	
49	B						—	
50	H			—				
51	D				—			
52	J						—	
53	C				—			
54	G				—			
55	B			—				
56	F							—

Problem	Correct Answer	Right/ Wrong/ Blank	Usage/Mechanics			Rhetorical Skills		
			Grammar & Usage	Punctuation	Sentence Structure	Organization	Style	Writing Strategy
57	D					—		
58	J		—					
59	A					—		
60	G							—
61	D				—			
62	J						—	
63	C		—					
64	F			—				
65	A						—	
66	H		—					
67	D					—		
68	G		—					
69	B							—
70	H							—
71	D		—					
72	G						—	
73	A		—					
74	G							—
75	A							—
Total								
Out Of		75	16	10	11	13	15	10

Passage Set 2 Solutions

Passage 1

1. **(A)** … but through the <u>generations, our family</u> has preserved … cultural aspects.

Usage/Mechanics   Punctuation   Commas

This part of the sentence could stand alone (after *but*) as a complete sentence. The core of this sentence is *our family has preserved*, with *our family* as the subject and *has preserved* as the verb. The object of the verb is *aspects*. There should be no commas or any other punctuation anywhere in this subject–verb–object sequence. The lead-in prepositional phrase (*through the generations*) would typically be separated from the subject *our family* by a comma, but in the case of a short leading prepositional phrase, you can sometimes omit that comma. However, you cannot use a colon in place of that optional comma. The correct answer is (A).

2. **(H)** NOT acceptable: … better sushi than any <u>restaurant, at</u> home we often have …

Usage/Mechanics   Sentence Structure   Whole Sentences

The sentence up through *restaurant* is an independent clause: it can stand alone as a legitimate sentence: *My mother makes better sushi than any restaurant.* Likewise, from *at home* onward, the clause can stand alone: *At home we often have rice and miso soup.*

With two independent clauses whose ideas are aligned, as in this case, you have several options. You can link the two clauses with "comma-and" (*Clause, and clause.*) as is done in the original text. You can link the two by a semicolon alone (*Clause; clause.*) or by a semicolon and an appropriate transition word or phrase (*Clause; moreover, clause.*). You can even make two sentences with a period (*Clause. Clause.*). What you cannot legally do is simply put the two clauses together by themselves (*Clause clause*) or via a comma (*Clause, clause*). The correct answer is (H).

3. **(B)** My mother makes … we often have miso soup … However, we frequently <u>eat</u> American food.

Usage/Mechanics   Sentence Structure   Verb Tenses

The previous sentence uses present-tense verbs (*makes, have*) to indicate that these actions take place in the general present. There is no reason to change tenses. The verb should be plain present (*eat*), not past (*ate*), past perfect (*had eaten*), or the past/conditional form *could eat* (=*were able to eat* or *would be able to eat*). The correct answer is (B).

4. **(G)** One element of Japanese culture … <u>has</u> been kept unchanged …

Usage/Mechanics   Grammar & Usage   Subject–Verb Agreement & Verb Forms

The subject of the verb is *element*, a singular noun, so the verb should be singular (*has been kept*), not plural (*have been kept*). No other options are possible: *is been kept* would never be correct, and *been kept* by itself cannot function as the main verb of a sentence. The correct answer is (G).

MANHATTAN
PREP

5.   **(D)** One element … kept unchanged in our house: the number four <u>is shunned</u>.

Rhetorical Skills   Style   Concision
                                                     also Verb Tense & Voice and Whole Sentences

Since *avoid* and *shun* are essentially synonyms, it is redundant to use both. Moreover, the idea following the colon is most clearly expressed as a full clause (with a verb such as *is*) rather than as a fragment. Finally, the verb should be singular (because the subject *number* is singular) and in present tense, because the prior clause, which is in the present perfect (*has been kept*) is really talking about the present day. The correct answer is (D).

6.   **(G)** … hotels in Japan skip directly from the third to the fifth floor. If this practice seems strange, consider that hotels in the United States also leave out a floor—the thirteenth.

Rhetorical Skills   Organization   Transitions

The next sentence says that hotels in the United States *also* leave out a floor. Therefore, the sentence in question should indicate a kind of hotel that leaves out a floor; otherwise, the *also* makes little sense. According to the correct answer, hotels in Japan leave out the fourth floor. The correct answer is (G).

7.   **(A)** As I found out, though, radically different perspectives on this number exist.

Rhetorical Skills   Organization   Transitions

The added sentence should form a good transition between a paragraph that ends *My parents have never decorated our house in any way that could symbolize the number four* to a very different paragraph. This paragraph introduces a brand-new character, Shawn, who turns out to have a nearly opposite point of view about the number four (that it is sacred, in fact). So the right transition should set up the reader for Shawn's story by signaling that a big contrast is coming. Nicely, the right answer does so in a very general way (*radically different perspectives on this number exist*), fulfilling the other request of the problem—to articulate a major theme of the essay. The correct answer is (A).

8.   **(F)** A Navajo, Shawn grew up in Chinle, which is in Apache County, Arizona, but <u>Chinle is also part</u> of the Navajo Nation.

Usage/Mechanics   Punctuation   Commas

The words after *but* should form an independent clause, which could stand alone as a sentence: *Chinle is also part of the Navajo Nation.* No commas or other punctuation should intervene anywhere in here. The subject *Chinle* should be followed immediately by the verb *is,* then by the adverb *also*, then by the object or complement *part,* and finally by the preposition *of* and its object *the Navajo Nation.* The correct answer is (F).

9.   **(B)** … the experiment called <u>for</u> four test tubes …

Usage/Mechanics   Grammar & Usage   Idioms

The idiom *call for* means "require" or "ask for": *This situation calls for new thinking.* This meaning is the one that is, well, called for in the text. The experiment asked for, or required, four test tubes.

In contrast, the idiom *call on* either means "pay a visit to" or "draw on" (a resource): *She was able to call on reserves of strength she didn't know she had.* The phrase *call at* could only mean something like *shout at.* Finally, *call* by itself in this context would mean *summon.* None of these meanings make sense. The correct answer is (B).

10.   (J)   … he shook his head forcefully and said, "No, it's sacred," <u>explaining</u> that …

Usage/Mechanics   Grammar & Usage   Modifier Forms

The proper form of *explain* here is *explaining,* which can then modify the prior verb phrase that begins with *said.* An *-ing* form used in this way indicates what the subject went on to do as an outgrowth of what went before. That's exactly what you want here: the explanation is an outgrowth of the statement *"No, it's sacred."*

Explained and *explains* both create broken lists of verbs. The two main verbs of the sentence are *shook* and *said.* These verbs are already linked in a two-item list: *he shook … and said …* It would be possible to write *he shook … , said … , and explained … ,* but that's now how the writer put the non-underlined portion. So *he shook … and said … , explained* creates a run-on; *explains* adds the insult of the wrong tense to the injury of the run-on. Finally, *having explained* is at least an *-ing* form, but it incorrectly forces the explanation into the past, as if the explanation took place *prior* to the statement *"No, it's sacred."* That timeline isn't sensible. The correct answer is (J).

11.   (C)   Most relevant to the passage: In response, he … and said, "No, it's sacred," explaining that the number four holds a special place in Navajo culture. For instance, the four primary directions are each associated with a different <u>color and indicated by a holy mountain in the ancestral Navajo homeland.</u>

Rhetorical Skills   Writing Strategy   Choice of Content

In the prior sentence, Shawn states that the number four is *sacred* and that it *holds a special place in Navajo culture.* The current sentence starts with *For instance,* so you know that an illustration of *how* the number four is sacred and special must follow.

Simply stating that the four primary directions correspond to north, south, east, and west is not that interesting, nor illustrative of the necessary point. Naming the associated colors is perhaps marginally more interesting, but it still doesn't show how four is sacred. Likewise, the *contrast with the five cardinal directions recognized in Japan* is irrelevant to this goal. Only the correct answer connects the number four with anything sacred (*a holy mountain in the ancestral Navajo homeland*). The correct answer is (C).

12.   (F)   For the sake of the logic and coherence of this paragraph, Sentence 7 should be placed where it is now.

Rhetorical Skills   Organization   Sentence Order

By beginning with *For instance,* Sentence 7 announces itself as an example of an immediately preceding point. Notice that it will help you to have solved the prior problem, so that you can be sure of the content of this sentence! However, even if you were unsure, the transition phrase *For instance* and the rest of the non-underlined portion (*the four primary directions are each associated with a different color*) tell you clearly that this sentence is an example of something about the number four. Moreover, you don't want to interrupt the earlier narrative, with the quick back-and-forth dialogue between Shawn and the narrator. The only possible attachment point is the generalization *the number four holds a special place in Navajo culture.* This broad statement is begging for a subsequent illustrative example; Sentence 7 is meant to provide that example in its current position. The correct answer is (F).

13.   **(C)**   … we keep in touch … Hashke Dilwo'ii, his birth name, <u>means</u> Angry Runner, so now Shawn and I are …

Usage/Mechanics   Sentence Structure   Verb Tenses

The tenses of the verbs surrounding the underlined verb (*keep* and *are*) are both present. The time frame of the action doesn't need to change here. Moreover, the meaning of a name is generally permanent, so present tense would be expected. *Had meant* would imply that the name no longer has this meaning; in fact, even *has meant* would have this unjustified implication too. Finally, *meaning* incorrectly turns this clause into a fragment, because *meaning* is not a full verb and cannot run a sentence or a clause on its own. The correct answer is (C).

14.   **(J)**   … so now Shawn and I are <u>designing</u> …

Rhetorical Skills   Style   Concision

The prior use of the word *now* makes *currently, at present,* and *presently* redundant. No such duplicate padding should be used in or around *are designing*. The correct answer is (J).

15.   **(B)**   Fulfill this goal? Yes, because the essay illustrates how someone with a traditional Japanese belief has acquired a more complex viewpoint after exposure to Navajo beliefs.

Rhetorical Skills   Writing Strategy   Goal of Essay

The question proposes a goal—*write a brief essay about an example of how people from different cultures can affect each other's perspectives*—and asks whether this essay fulfills that goal. The answer is yes. Regarding Shawn's impact, the narrator writes in the final paragraph: *his ideas have since influenced mine*. Together the narrator and Shawn are now *designing a video game called Four Angry Runners … hoping for Navajo, not Japanese, luck to hold*. That's a change from the narrator's prior view that four was unlucky. This vignette is an example of "how someone with a traditional belief [about the number four] has acquired a more complex viewpoint [about that number, acknowledging that both Navajo and Japanese luck may exist] after exposure to Navajo beliefs [in chemistry class]." The correct answer is (B).

Passage 2

16.   **(J)**   When you're watching your favorite show, you probably don't <u>stop to think</u> about how the television set or computer monitor works—unless, of course, it breaks down.

Usage/Mechanics   Grammar & Usage   Idioms

The correct form to follow the verb *stop* is the infinitive *to think*. "Stop to think" is the appropriate meaning: if you are watching your favorite show, you become engaged in the show and forget about the television or computer monitor itself. In other words, you do not *stop* your activities in order *to think* about how the display works.

Stop thinking has exactly the opposite meaning. "You never stop to think about X" means that you never think about X, but "you never stop thinking about X" means that you always think about X. *Stop thoughts* would mean something similar, as would *stop while thinking*. The correct answer is (J).

17. **(C)** Least acceptable: Recently, my laptop screen acquired bright spots. <u>Now, however,</u> when I scroll down a document or watch a video, those areas are always lit up …

Rhetorical Skills   Organization   Transitions

The idea before the transition is that the laptop screen *acquired bright spots* recently. After the transition, the result is described: *those areas are always lit up*. So the transition should lead directly from the first thought to the next. A time marker is appropriate to bring the reader from *recently* to *now*. Causation markers are also appropriate, such as *so*, *thus*, and *as a result*. What is not appropriate is a contrast signal, as in the correct answer *however*. The correct answer is (C).

18. **(H)** Should the writer add this sentence here? No, because it distracts the reader from the main point of the example.

Rhetorical Skills   Writing Strategy   Additions

The writer is proposing to add a sentence after the period in the following text: … *those areas are always lit up, revealing the proverbial "man behind the curtain" who metaphorically operates the lamps behind the screen.* [Add here] *This computer mishap has prompted me to look into the technology of television displays* …

The proposed sentence describes in great detail the origin of the quotation "man behind the curtain"; it is a reference to the Wizard of Oz. As interesting as the sentence may be, adding it would be a mistake. The next sentence begins with *This computer mishap,* by which the writer is referring to the bright spots on the laptop screen. The proposed sentence, however, ends with "… before that illusion is spoiled by Dorothy's dog." It would be natural, and completely misleading, then to read *This computer mishap* as the spoiling of the wizard's illusion. The paragraph already adequately explains the quotation with *proverbial* and *who metaphorically operates the lamps behind the screen.* Digressing into the wonderful world of Oz to explain the quotation further would be a distraction from the point of the example, which is simply to motivate the narrator's investigation of television displays. The correct answer is (H).

19. **(A)** … has prompted me to look into the technology of television displays <u>and</u> computer monitors.

Usage/Mechanics   Grammar & Usage   Parallelism

The simple conjunction *and* works best here, linking the parallel noun phrases *television displays* and *computer monitors.* The narrator has been looking into the technology of both of these kinds of displays, so a two-item list within the prepositional phrase (*of X and Y*) is appropriate.

The phrase *and those of* does not fit, because plural *those* does not agree in number with singular *technology,* which is the sensible noun that *those* would be referring to. Both *and to* and *into* would break the parallelism of the list. The correct answer is (A).

20. **(F)** If your eye sees a series of related <u>snapshots quickly</u> enough, …

Usage/Mechanics   Punctuation   Commas

There should be no commas or semicolons in the underlined portion. The object of the verb *see* is *a series of related snapshots*. This object should be followed by the adverbial phrase *quickly enough* without any pause (and this phrase should not itself be interrupted). "Your eye sees these snapshots quickly enough" would not demand any commas; neither does the corresponding text in the essay. The correct answer is (F).

21. **(B)** … your brain perceives motion. You can flip through pages … to witness <u>the effect.</u>

Rhetorical Skills   Style   Word Choice

The original phrase *this thing* and the alternative *all that* are both unacceptably vague. The correct answer uses a more specific noun: *the effect*. This phrase properly indicates that what you would witness as you flip pages is the perception of motion—that's *the effect* in question. Finally, you have to put an object after *witness*; you can't just leave that verb hanging. The correct answer is (B).

22. **(F)** … the technical challenge <u>is how to redraw fast:</u> the display has to paint each snapshot …

Usage/Mechanics   Punctuation   Colons

In the correct sentence, the subject of the first independent clause is *the technical challenge*, the verb is *is*, and the object or complement of that verb is the phrase *how to redraw fast*. No punctuation belongs anywhere between these elements of the clause. Moreover, the phrase *how to redraw fast* does not require any punctuation internally.

The second clause is also independent; it starts with *the display*. The two independent clauses need to be separated by a suitable punctuation mark. The colon works, because the second clause explains the first. A dash (or a semicolon, for that matter) would also be acceptable, but a mere comma is not enough. The correct answer is (F).

23. **(B)** Least acceptable: … the display has to paint each snapshot, hold it for a split second, and <u>originally</u> replace it with the next snapshot.

Rhetorical Skills   Organization   Transitions

The display has to do three things in sequence: (1) *paint each snapshot*, (2) *hold it for a split second*, and (3) *replace it with the next snapshot*. The original sentence puts *then* in front of the third action. Alternatively, you could use *immediately* (to emphasize the speed of the action) or *finally* (to stress the release that the third step represents, as the last step after holding the snapshot for a short period of time). In fact, you could even leave out a transition altogether. The steps make sense as a straightforward list of three actions (*paint, hold, and replace*).

What is unacceptable, however, is to use the adverb *originally*. It's not clear what this adverb would even mean in this context; the idea of *originally* (= "at first, initially") doesn't fit in front of the last step of the sequence. Thus, this choice is correct. The correct answer is (B).

24.   **(J)**   For decades after the birth of <u>television,</u> the pen with which theses frames were drawn was primarily a beam of electrons …

Rhetorical Skills   Style   Concision

All of the incorrect answer choices introduce irrelevant comments about the "birth of television." This part of the essay is meant to describe the operation of cathode ray tubes (the technology behind most older television sets). Therefore, it is a distraction to mention that the birth of television was "a more controversial event than you might realize," or that "sets were not widespread in the U.S." until a certain time, or that "many people, correctly or not, claimed parenthood [of television]." Leaving out this sort of side comment altogether is the best choice. The correct answer is (J).

25.   **(B)**   Most effectively describes the origin of the signal: <u>Arriving over the airwaves or through a cable,</u> the television signal rapidly turns the beam on and off …

Rhetorical Skills   Writing Strategy   Choice of Content

The alternatives to the correct answer are all fine grammatically, and they are even interesting and relevant to the essay as a whole. However, none of them accomplish the stated purpose—describe the origin of the signal—as well as the right choice, which indicates how the signal arrives at the television set (*over the airwaves or through a cable*). The correct answer is (B).

26.   **(G)**   … the dots that <u>make up</u> the proper picture.

Usage/Mechanics   Grammar & Usage   Idioms (and Verb Tense)

In this context, the verb phrase *make up* means "compose, be the parts of": *The dots make up the picture.* The verb *make* by itself would also be acceptable, since you could say that the dots make, or produce, the picture.

The verb phrase *make up for* means something completely different ("compensate, make recompense"). *Make for* would also be unacceptable, since the closest meanings of this phrase ("move toward, aim for" and "contribute to, promote, usually result in") do not fit. The dots don't "make for" the picture; they make up the picture or they make the picture.

Finally, the verb tense should be present, since the writer describes the general operation of the cathode ray tube using present tense (*sweeps, glow, strikes, turns, fades, begins*). So *made* and *made for* are both wrong for this reason alone. The correct answer is (G).

27.   **(C)**   … cathode ray tubes have been largely replaced by liquid crystal <u>displays, which are</u> thinner, lighter, and potentially bigger.

Usage/Mechanics   Sentence Structure   Modifier Placement

The correct answer appropriately connects the list of comparative adjectives (*thinner, lighter, and potentially bigger*) to the noun they ought to be describing, namely *liquid crystal displays.* This connection is accomplished by means of the relative pronoun *which* and the verb *are.*

The original sentence incorrectly states that the *cathode ray tubes* (the subject of the sentence) are thinner, lighter, and bigger. This assertion makes no sense. The other alternatives do not properly attach the adjectives to *liquid crystal displays.*

MANHATTAN
PREP

You can't put the conjunction *because* in front of the list of adjectives, since that list lacks both a subject and a verb. Nor can you simply put a comma between the noun phrase and the list that follows. In English, adjectives normally go before nouns. A list of adjectives following a noun is confusing. The correct answer is (C).

28. **(F)** … these displays may <u>soon be surpassed</u> by organic light-emitting diodes …

Usage/Mechanics   Punctuation   Commas

No commas belong anywhere in the underlined portion. The verb is *may be surpassed*. The adverb *soon* is inserted between *may* and *be* without commas. Finally, this passive-voice verb is followed by the preposition *by* (to indicate what may soon surpass *these displays*). A comma should not normally separate a passive-voice verb from its *by* phrase, even if the verb makes sense on its own (*these displays may soon be surpassed*). Such commas are melodramatic and stylistically poor ("This record will soon be broken, by me.") The correct answer is (F).

29. **(D)** Most clearly indicate that the name is of interest: … or by the more <u>intriguingly</u> named "quantum dots."

Rhetorical Skills   Style   Word Choice

The word *intriguing* means "interesting," so *intriguingly* here means that the name is interesting. *Mysteriously, puzzlingly,* and *secretively* all indicate that the name is a mystery, but mysteries aren't necessarily interesting. Some mysteries are boring. The correct answer is (D).

30. **(H)** The best place to add the new paragraph break would be at the beginning of Sentence 5, because it would signal the essay's shift from the operation of CRTs to their replacement by newer displays.

Rhetorical Skills   Organization   Paragraph Break

Sentences 1 through 4 all describe how cathode ray tubes (CRTs) work: an electron beam sweeps over an array of dots, causing them to glow. Sentence 4 is a key part of this description (*As the glow from one sweep fades, another sweep begins*), so it should be kept with the previous sentences.

Sentence 5, however, begins an entirely different thought: how CRTs *have been largely replaced* by a newer technology. The remaining sentences continue in the same vein, discussing even newer technologies. Thus, the best paragraph break would come at the beginning of Sentence 5. The reason is that the topic transitions from how CRTs work to how they have been replaced. The correct answer is (H).

Passage 3

31. **(B)** For years during my <u>childhood, Pop-pop my grandfather</u> and I went to the park …

Usage/Mechanics   Punctuation   Commas

The opening phrase *For years during my childhood* should be set off from the rest of the sentence by a comma. The subject is a list of two people: *Pop-pop my grandfather and I*. No comma should separate these two people. As for the use of commas within the words *Pop-pop my grandfather*, you can either surround *my grandfather* with commas (although this risks making the list seem to contain three people) or leave out commas altogether, as is done in the correct answer. A name

(*Pop-pop*) and a short title in apposition (*my grandfather*) does not always require commas, though appositives generally do take commas. The correct answer is (B).

32. **(F)** … went to the park twice a week, usually <u>Monday and Wednesday evenings,</u> and …

Rhetorical Skills   Style   Concision

The correct answer uses four words to get the meaning across clearly and efficiently. Why use 8–10 words that convey no additional nuance and in fact clutter up the page? Go with the short and sweet option here. The correct answer is (F).

33. **(D)** Least acceptable: … the black and red squares had begun to wear off, showing the brown paper <u>under</u>.

Usage/Mechanics   Grammar & Usage   Idioms

All of the choices are very close in meaning to each other, but *under* is clearly least acceptable. *Under* is best as a preposition (*under the table*) or as a directional adverb (if something is traveling down). But to indicate a position by itself, *under* doesn't work so well. In fact, *showing the brown paper under* almost sounds as if you are pushing the brown paper down somewhere, instead of revealing where it is.

Consider: *There is a shelf on top, and another one _____.* The options *underneath, beneath,* and *below* are all fine on their own, but saying *under* by itself is strange—you would normally extend the word to *underneath* or *under it.* This issue is purely idiomatic; trust your ear. The correct answer is (D).

34. **(J)**   … you could almost see <u>some of Pop-pop's</u> favorite strategies …

Usage/Mechanics   Punctuation   Apostrophes and Commas

The possessive form of almost every singular noun ends in 's, as this one does: *Pop-pop's* (meaning that the strategies belong to Pop-pop). No commas belong anywhere in this phrase. *Some* should be followed immediately by *of.* The correct answer is (J).

35. **(C)** … where checkers had slid back and forth over and over, <u>waging the unending war</u> between black and red.

Rhetorical Skills   Style   Concision

The wrong answer choices are all redundant in some fashion. You don't need to write both *war* and *battle* or both *ceaseless* and *unending* (or both *endlessly* and *without ceasing* or both *never ceasing* and *endless*). *Waging the unending war* has no extra words; pick this choice. The correct answer is (C).

36. **(H)** Least acceptable: We stood, bowed to each other, and switched sides <u>after each game</u> of the table.

Usage/Mechanics   Sentence Structure   Modifier Placement

The modifying phrase *after each game* tells you when this whole sequence of events occurred. Nothing else in the sentence describes time, so you do have some flexibility around where to place this phrase. You can put it at the beginning of the sentence: *After each game, we stood, bowed to each other, and switched sides of the table.* Stylistically, this position is probably best within the paragraph (so that the time phrase functions as a transition), but you can certainly leave the phrase where it is in the original essay, after *stood*. You can even put it at the end of the sentence, since the sentence is not too long: *We stood, bowed to each other, and switched sides of the table after each game.* What you absolutely cannot do, however, is interrupt the tight noun phrase *sides of the table* by inserting *after each game* before the *of*. In general, *of* phrases are essential modifiers of the previous noun, as in this case (Which sides? *Sides of the table*), so avoid separating *of* phrases from the noun they ought to modify. The correct answer is (H).

37.   **(C)**   While I appreciated all of his <u>tics, the</u> strangest by far was the king-crowning ritual.

Usage/Mechanics   Sentence Structure   Whole Sentences

The conjunction *While* subordinates the clause *I appreciated all of his tics*, so that it cannot stand on its own as a sentence. It needs to be joined with a comma to the proper independent clause that follows: *the strangest … was the king-crowning ritual.* Nothing else (such as *and* or *but*) should be inserted into the seam between the dependent clause and the independent clause. The correct answer is (C).

38.   **(J)**   … Pop-pop picked up a discarded piece of <u>mine</u> and …

Rhetorical Skills   Style   Concision

Since the piece has already been described as *discarded,* there is no need to add modifiers such as *which had been taken off the board* or *which I had thrown away.* Likewise, each option describes the piece as *mine* (or *my own*), so the additional modifier *that had belonged to me* is redundant. The phrase *a discarded piece of mine* is complete and concise. The correct answer is (J).

39.   **(B)**   Finally, he stuck the two circles together and <u>called the pair</u> a proper king.

Rhetorical Skills   Style   Word Choice

The right choice here fits the intended meaning like a glove: *he called the pair a proper king.*

The word *entitled* is used as an adjective to mean "given the right to" (*you are entitled to a reward*) or "formally named" (*the picture entitled "The Scream" is frightening*). Perhaps you can *entitle* something a name, but in the given sentence you would have to say *entitled the pair* or *the pair was entitled* (and even then this use of the verb *entitle* is archaic and no longer viable). The other choices require words that are missing. *Gave the pair a proper king* would have to be *gave the pair the name of king properly* or something like that. Likewise, to be at all sensible, *the pair was raised a proper king* would have to be *the pair was raised to a proper king* or *to be a proper king* or *to the level of king*. The correct answer is (B).

40.   **(G)**   … he had already taught <u>me,</u> …

Usage/Mechanics   Grammar & Usage   Pronoun Forms

The subject of the clause is *he*, so the correct form of the object is *me* (*he had taught me*). You can only use *myself* if the subject is *I* (*I had taught myself to fish*). It would be possible to add *himself* to *me* for emphasis: *he had taught me himself.* This option, however, isn't available. The correct answer is (G).

41. **(D)** For the sake of the logic and coherence of the paragraph, Sentence 5 should be placed after Sentence 3.

Rhetorical Skills   Organization   Sentence Order

Sentences 4 and 5 should be flipped. The current Sentence 4 reads *But he had already taught me, and I never forgot.* Never forgot what? What had Pop-pop taught? Why is there a *But* here? These questions should not even need to be asked, because the answers would be in the prior sentence, the current Sentence 5 (*Sometimes he added, "The spit helps 'em stay stacked up," as if worried that I had forgotten*). When you move Sentence 5 to its proper position after Sentence 3, then *But he had already taught me, and I never forgot* makes sense. The correct answer is (D).

42. **(G)** Not acceptable: On a good day, we got in eleven or twelve games <u>that the sun dipped</u> lower and lower in the sky.

Usage/Mechanics   Grammar & Usage   Modifier Forms

The original sentence and the acceptable alternatives all create a "same-time" relationship between the subordinate action (the sun dipping lower) and the main action (*we got in eleven or twelve games*). The games happened *while* or *as* the sun was dipping lower. The unacceptable option in the correct answer creates a very different relationship between the actions: *we got in … games that the sun dipped lower and lower in the sky* means that the sun somehow dipped these games lower. What would that even mean? This choice makes little sense. The correct answer is (G).

43. **(A)** … with the sun barely streaming …, my grandfather <u>glowing</u> slightly …, and the stubby checkers casting long shadows.

Usage/Mechanics   Grammar & Usage   Verb Forms

The appropriate form of the verb *glow* here is the *-ing* form *glowing*. This form makes the list of actions after *with* parallel to each other: *with the sun streaming, my grandfather glowing, and the checkers casting shadows.*

A verb form that could be the main verb of a sentence, such as *was glowing, glowed,* or *glows,* would also cause this sentence to be a run-on. You already have the independent clause: *The last game of the day was always my favorite,* in which the verb is *was.* The preposition *with* and everything after it are technically just modifiers to that main clause. The correct answer is (A).

44. **(H)** Best reinforces the themes in this paragraph, using an appropriate tone: During these times, the games took on an epic quality, <u>becoming twilight tales of strategy and defeat.</u>

Rhetorical Skills   Organization   Opening/Closing Content

The main idea of this paragraph is stated up front: *The last game of the day was always my favorite.* Since the paragraph should end in a way that shows the narrator's appreciation for the memory, you should eliminate the options that incorrectly indicate the narrator's dislike or boredom: *lasting for what unfortunately felt like hours* and *but onlookers would have seen nothing special.* The remaining two options are both heroic in tone, but *soon to be vanquished with the fall of night* has an unclear, unsuitable meaning. Were the games themselves *soon to be vanquished* or the epic quality? Neither makes sense. Only the right answer fits both theme and tone. The correct answer is (H).

45.   **(A)** If the writer were to include this sentence, the most logical place to add it would be at the end of Paragraph 1.

Rhetorical Skills   Organization   Placement of Additions

The proposed addition talks about replacing the checkerboard (*I once asked whether we could replace the board …*), so the right paragraph should be discussing the board—in fact, its state of disrepair. Paragraph 1 focuses on just such a discussion: *He had been using it for so long that the black and red squares had begun to wear off … The surface was worn to the point that …* It would be natural to add the proposed sentence here. The correct answer is (A).

Passage 4

46.   **(H)** In the second half of the nineteenth century, two developments opened the door … One <u>was</u> the creation … The other was the invention of loudspeakers …

Usage/Mechanics   Sentence Structure   Verb Tense

The first sentence uses plain past tense (*opened*) to indicate an event in the nineteenth century. The *two developments* then are each named. To be consistent not only with *opened* but also with *was* in the next sentence (about the other development), you should use *was* (plain past tense) in the underlined portion as well. The correct answer is (H).

47.   **(A)** Best conclusion: <u>Once these two components are paired, a simple musical instrument is born.</u>

Rhetorical Skills   Organization   Opening/Closing Content

The paragraph starts by asserting that *two developments opened the door to true electronic music.* You then are told what each development was. As written, the conclusion of this paragraph appropriately puts the two developments together and connects back to the goal of music mentioned in the first sentence.

The alternatives do not tie up the first paragraph anywhere as neatly. Bringing up microphones is a distraction. It might seem important to state that the devices have become *much more sophisticated since then* or that *more advances were necessary*, but neither one provides an especially strong bridge to the next paragraph about the theremin. Moreover, these options would each weaken the first paragraph. The correct answer is (A).

48.   **(J)** … a young Russian physicist … devised an electronic device whose unique <u>sound is</u> still recognizable …

Rhetorical Skills   Style   Concision

The single word *sound* captures all the meaning you want here. The alternatives (*auditory impact on the ears, sonic products in the air,* and *environmental characteristics aurally*) are all wordy to the point of redundancy. In addition, they are pompous, calling unnecessary attention to themselves. Stick with the simple word *sound* that gets the job done. The correct answer is (J).

49. **(B)** Interestingly, you play the theremin <u>without touching</u> it. The position of your hands in the air near the two antennas controls the pitch and the volume …

Rhetorical Skills   Style   Word Choice

Even if you've never played a theremin before (and it's assumed that you haven't), the essay provides two clear clues to indicate that you play a theremin *without* touching it. One clue is that the next sentence describes how you play in more detail: *the position of your hands in the air near the two antennas …* In other words, you are not touching the theremin itself, because your hands are in the air. The other clue is that the sentence containing the underlined portion begins with *Interestingly.* Since you typically play musical instruments by touching them, it would not be interesting to say so. The most interesting alternative given is that you play the instrument *without* touching it. The correct answer is (B).

50. **(H)** … the pitch and the volume of the <u>sound, an eerie warble</u> that provided the sonic setting …

Usage/Mechanics   Punctuation   Commas

The noun *sound* is modified by the appositive phrase *an eerie warble that provided …* This long appositive phrase must be separated from the noun it modifies by a comma, but it does not require any internal commas; in fact, it should contain none. The semicolon does not work as a separator, because the text on each side of the semicolon must be able to stand alone as a complete sentence. You should not use a semicolon between an appositive phrase and the noun it modifies. The correct answer is (H).

51. **(D)** If you imagine a black-and-white flying saucer flitting across the screen on poorly hidden <u>wires, the</u> soundtrack in your mind is supplied by the theremin.

Usage/Mechanics   Sentence Structure   Whole Sentences

If a sentence begins with an *if* (as this very one does), then after the subordinate *if* clause you have to have an independent *then* clause, although you don't always have to include the word *then* itself. *If you imagine a flying saucer, the soundtrack is supplied by the theremin.* These two clauses must be in the same sentence. Moreover, you cannot use an *and* or a semicolon to mark off the *if* clause; use a comma instead. The correct answer is (D).

52. **(J)** Since even tiny variations in the proximity of your hands <u>cause noticeable effects,</u> …

Rhetorical Skills   Style   Concision

Of those available, the most concise option is *cause noticeable effects.* The alternatives all contain redundancies: *cause effects to occur* is simply wordier than *cause effects,* as is *result in the occurrence of effects. Cause effects as their results* is not idiomatic English.

The issue of subject–verb agreement also allows you to eliminate two of the wrong answer choices. The subject of the clause is *variations,* a plural noun, so the verb should be plural as well: *variations cause,* not *causes.* The correct answer is (J).

53.   **(C)** Since … variations … cause noticeable effects, the theremin is difficult to play … Moreover, only one tone <u>is really created.</u>

Usage/Mechanics   Sentence Structure   Verb Tense & Voice

Although the active voice is often preferred to the passive voice, in this case you must use the passive. The *tone* doesn't do the creating; it *is created* (by the theremin). So the active choices ("really created" and "really created it") are both inappropriate. As for which tense to use, notice that the nearby sentences describing similar characteristics of the theremin contain the present tense (*cause, is*). Even though the theremin is a device associated with an era in the past, the writer has chosen to describe the general operation of the theremin using the generalized present tense. So you should say *is created,* not *had been created.* The correct answer is (C).

54.   **(G)** Musical pioneers <u>craving</u> more tractable and versatile machines built makeshift prototypes …

Usage/Mechanics   Sentence Structure   Whole Sentences

If you keep the underlined portion as *craved,* then you get a two-verb sentence without an *and* between them: *Musical pioneers craved machines built prototypes.* This structure is not grammatical. You must turn the first thought into a modifier, such as *craving* (or *who craved,* although that's not an option here). *Were craving* has the same problem as *craved.* As for *craved by,* this form is certainly a modifier, but it reverses the meaning: the musical pioneers weren't being craved. They were doing the craving. The correct answer is (G).

55.   **(B)** By the sixties and seventies, <u>Mellotron and Moog synthesizers</u> produced the signature backdrop …

Usage/Mechanics   Punctuation   Commas

The subject of the sentence is *Mellotron and Moog synthesizers.* The words *Mellotron and Moog* are evidently functioning as adjectives modifying the noun *synthesizers,* describing different brands or types of synthesizers. No commas belong within this subject phrase, which should also not be separated from the verb (*produced*) by a comma or any other punctuation. The correct answer is (B).

56.   **(F)** Best provides illustrative examples of specific devices: Amplified instruments, <u>such as electric guitars and the Clavinet keyboard,</u> also became widespread in popular songs.

Rhetorical Skills   Writing Strategy   Choice of Content

If the writer wants to provide *illustrative examples of specific devices,* then he or she can simply name relevant devices, as in the original sentence: *such as electric guitars and the Clavinet keyboard.*

Defining *Amplified instruments* with *that is to say ones made electronically louder* may help the reader, but that phrase doesn't provide *examples.* The other options provide "nice-to-know" information that is unrelated to the purpose stated in the question. The correct answer is (F).

57.   **(D)** Unlike synthesizers, amplified instruments first generate sound in a traditional way, perhaps by vibrating a metal string. This tiny sound, though too weak to travel far, is then picked up by electronic sensors …

Rhetorical Skills   Organization   Transitions

This narrative about how amplified instruments work is already sufficiently signposted: *Unlike synthesizers* (contrast with an earlier topic), *amplified instruments first* (step 1) *generate … this tiny sound … is then* (step 2) *picked up …* The words *first* and *then* do all the work you need here. None of the proposed transitions are suitable: the second step is not an example, not a contrast, and not even necessarily a logical consequence of the first step (as *Therefore* would have it). The second step just happens next. The correct answer is (D).

58.   **(J)**   … this tiny sound, though too weak to travel far, is then picked up

Usage/Mechanics   Grammar & Usage   Comparisons

The proper word to use here is *then* (meaning "next" or "at that time"), not *than*, which must be used in a comparison (*this tree is taller than that bush*). In addition, the correct way to express the weakness of the sound is to say that it is *too weak to travel far*. The adjective *weak* should not be in its comparative (*weaker*) or superlative (*weakest*) form, but rather in its bare form *weak* to be modified by *too*.

Likewise, *far* in this context should simply be *far*, meaning "a great distance," not the comparative *farther* or the metaphorical *far* in *far weaker* (where it simply means "a great deal"). The correct answer is (J).

59.   **(A)** For the sake of the logic and coherence of this paragraph, Sentence 4 should be placed where it is now.

Rhetorical Skills   Organization   Sentence Order

Sentence 4 reads *The amplified result can be big enough to fill a football stadium.* As the *result* of something earlier, this sentence is evidently some kind of conclusion—the image is a dramatic finale. What is this sentence the conclusion of? The operation of *amplified instruments,* which are first mentioned in Sentence 1 (a good place to mention such a broad topic first). Sentence 2 details the *first* step in the operation of these instruments, which *generate sound in a traditional way.* Sentence 3 outlines the next step: *this tiny sound … is then picked up by electronic sensors …* In its current position, Sentence 4 provides the natural ending to the process of amplifying sound. The correct answer is (A).

60.   **(G)** Suppose the writer's goal had been to write a brief essay charting milestones in the development of electronic music. Would this essay successfully fulfill that goal? Yes, because it highlights relevant advances in the field over the course of decades.

Rhetorical Skills   Writing Strategy   Goal of Essay

Review each paragraph and articulate its main point.

Paragraph 1: Sometime in 1850–1900, two developments open the door to true electronic music.

Paragraph 2: The spooky-sounding theremin is invented after WW1 and used in movies in the 1950s.

Paragraph 3: Dissatisfied with the theremin, pioneers build synthesizers that become important in music in the 1960s and 1970s.

Paragraph 4: Amplified instruments also become widespread around this time.

This essay certainly *charts milestones in the development of electronic music*: this is its primary effect. It does not suggest anything about the future of this kind of music, but it does highlight *relevant advances*—namely, the invention of oscillators, of loudspeakers, of the theremin, of synthesizers, and of equipment necessary for amplification. These inventions took place *over the course of decades*. The correct answer is (G).

Passage 5

61.   **(D)** Coins with the value of one dollar have been issued throughout United States <u>history. From</u> the perspective of the government, coins have a crucial advantage over bills: coins last longer …

Usage/Mechanics   Sentence Structure   Whole Sentences

The underlined portion is at the juncture of two independent clauses. The first clause is *Coins … have been issued throughout United States history*. The second clause is *From the perspective … coins have a crucial advantage …* in which the subject is *coins* and the verb is *have*. These two independent clauses can be separated into different sentences, as in the correct answer. However, they cannot be run together without any punctuation or with just a comma.

A colon can sometimes join two independent clauses, but only if the second is an explanation of the first. Whether that condition is true here, the worse sin is that the second sentence already uses a colon in this way (*coins last longer …* is a clause that explains why "coins have a crucial advantage"). You can't use a colon twice in the same sentence this way. The correct answer is (D).

62.   **(J)** Least acceptable alternative to *last*: … coins <u>take</u> longer …

Rhetorical Skills   Style   Word Choice

The original sentence uses *last* as a verb, meaning "endure, survive, persist in existence." Thus, *endure, survive,* or *persist* are all acceptable substitutes for *last*. However, *take* cannot express the same meaning. You would need to say something such as "take longer to wear out," but without the tacked-on infinitive, "take longer" doesn't mean the same thing as "last longer." Since you are looking for the least acceptable alternative, *take* is the correct answer. The correct answer is (J).

63.   **(C)** The Treasury could save almost two hundred million dollars a year if <u>it</u> switched to dollar coins.

Usage/Mechanics   Grammar & Usage   Pronoun Agreement

In American English, nouns that refer to organizations are singular. Thus, the noun *Treasury* is singular ("The Treasury *is* in charge of printing money"), and the singular pronoun *it* must be used, not the plural pronoun *they* (whether by itself or in the contraction *they're*).

The pronoun *its* is a possessive and is normally followed by a noun. You should ask "Its what?", and there is no good answer. The subject of the verb *switched* should be either *the Treasury* or the corresponding pronoun *it*. The correct answer is (C).

64. **(F)** The American <u>public, however,</u> has not taken to recent experiments with dollar coins …

Usage/Mechanics   Punctuation   Commas

When the word *however* indicates contrast from the prior sentence (as it does here), surround the word with commas on both sides. The same principle holds for any other contrast transition. If the transition is at the start of the sentence, follow it with a comma; if it is embedded within the sentence (as it is here), surround it with two commas. The correct answer is (F).

65. **(A)** The American public, however, has not taken to recent experiments with dollar coins, preferring lighter and thinner bills. Dollar coins would likely be broadly adopted only if the Treasury stopped printing equivalent <u>bills.</u>

Rhetorical Skills   Style   Concision

The only word needed here is *bills* itself. All of the wrong choices add on language that just repeats what has already been said. Choice (B), "bills, which are less bulky and heavy than coins," is redundant with *lighter and thinner bills* in the previous sentence. Choice (C), "bills, which are favored by the U.S. population," is redundant with *The American public … preferring lighter and thinner bills*. Finally, choice (D), "bills that have the same value as the coins do," is redundant with the adjective *equivalent*. The correct answer is (A).

66. **(H)** The only authentic silver dollars dated 1804 were created decades <u>afterward, when</u> special gifts for foreign rulers were needed.

Usage/Mechanics   Grammar & Usage   Modifier Forms

The original sentence is a run-on, with two independent clauses (*The only … dollars … were created decades afterwards* and *special gifts … were needed*) joined by only a comma. The correct answer fixes the issue by inserting *when*, which makes the second clause dependent. The proper relative pronoun is *when*, because *decades afterward* is a time. The pronoun *where* can only follow places. *At which* would be possible, but *which* by itself does not work. The pronoun *which* by itself plays the role of subject or object, but neither role is open in the second clause. The correct answer is (H).

67. **(D)** For the sake of the logic and coherence of this paragraph, Sentence 2 should be placed after Sentence 5.

Rhetorical Skills   Organization   Sentence Order

Sentence 2 is *Any of these 1804 dollars is now worth millions*. The verb phrase *is now* indicates that the sentence is referring to the present time. The rest of the story in the paragraph follows chronological order: 1794, then 1804, *the coins minted that year*, then *decades afterward*, then *later*. Since all those events took place in the past, the best place for Sentence 2 is after Sentence 5 at the end of the paragraph. This way, the sentence can refer back to *any of these 1804 dollars* (there were two kinds made) and state a current fact about them all. The correct answer is (D).

68. **(G)** The face value of the coin, the underlying value of the metal, and the exchange rate with other coins <u>were</u> sometimes different …

Usage/Mechanics   Grammar & Usage   Subject–Verb Agreement

The subject of the verb is a three-item list: *The face value …, the underlying value …, and the exchange rate …* This compound subject is plural, so the verb must be plural as well. The only plural option is *were;* the other choices (*was, is,* and *has been*) are all singular. The tense should be past, but you don't need that issue to make the right call here. The correct answer is (G).

69.   **(B)** Best concludes the sentence with another illustration of speculator behavior: For instance, speculators swapped lighter coins for heavier ones and extracted the excess metal, <u>or brought coins from Asia to the U.S. for a profit.</u>

Rhetorical Skills   Writing Strategy   Choice of Content

The question asks for "another illustration of speculator behavior," since the first part of the sentence provides one such illustration (swapping coins and extracting excess metal). The correct answer choice provides a specific additional example: importing coins from Asia.

Two of the wrong choices, (A) and (C), allude to *other things* the speculators did or *other ways* they tried to make money, but these choices are not as specific as the correct answer. The remaining wrong choice, (D), does not provide another example at all; rather, it just continues the first example. The correct answer is (B).

70.   **(H)** The sentence should NOT be deleted because it creates a transition from the more distant past to the recent history of these coins.

Rhetorical Skills   Writing Strategy   Deletions

The sentence in question is this: *Nowadays, dollar coins are not melted down; they are ignored.* This sentence takes the reader from the 1800s and early 1900s (the topic of earlier paragraphs) to the recent past and present day, which are the subject of the final paragraph.

The sentence does not explain anything (e.g., why dollar coins have not been widely accepted). It does not compare the actions of melting down coins and ignoring them. Finally, it does imply that dollar coins had been melted down previously, but this implication is not the purpose of the sentence. Rather, the purpose is to transition the reader from an earlier time (characterized by strange speculator behavior) to the more recent past (characterized by indifference toward the coins). The correct answer is (H).

71.   **(D)** <u>Most recently,</u> the brass Sacagawea coin … and its Presidential cousin have failed to win acceptance …

Usage/Mechanics   Grammar & Usage   Modifier Forms

The word *recently* is an adverb, modifying the action of the whole sentence. *Recent* is an adjective and would have to modify a noun directly. The superlative word *most* modifies *recently*: how recently? *Most recently,* meaning "in the most recent past." The word *mostly* means something else entirely, namely "in large part, generally, frequently." So *mostly recently* would mean "generally recently, although not always." This meaning is not what the writer intends. The correct answer is (D).

72.   **(G)** … the brass Sacagawea coin … and its Presidential cousin have <u>failed to win</u> acceptance …

Rhetorical Skills   Style   Concision

The right choice expresses the thought completely and concisely: *failed to win*. The wrong answer choices all fall into redundancy. There is no need to say both *failed to win* and *fallen short of success,* or both *fallen short of success* and [fallen short] *of winning,* or *failed to succeed at winning,* when you can just say *failed to win.* The correct answer is (G).

73. **(A)** Some mass-transit systems <u>have given</u> Sacagaweas …

Usage/Mechanics   Grammar & Usage   Verb Forms

The only grammatically correct choice is the right answer, *have given.* The phrase *would of* is always wrong (the correct form is *would have*). *Been given* is not a complete verb: you would need a *have, has,* or *had* in front, and even so, the voice would be wrong (the transit systems have not been *given* Sacagaweas; the systems have been *giving* the coins). Finally, *had gave* is always wrong as well. The form of *give* after *have, has,* or *had* is the past participle *given,* not the past tense *gave.* The correct answer is (A).

74. **(G)** Most effectively illustrates a current and accepted use of dollar coins: Some mass-transit systems have given Sacagaweas as change, whether these coins are desired or not, <u>and in Ecuador and El Salvador, which use the U.S. dollar, Sacagawea coins circulate widely and without comment.</u>

Rhetorical Skills   Writing Strategy   Choice of Content

The correct choice describes a "current and accepted use of dollar coins"—namely, their wide and natural circulation in Ecuador and El Salvador. The wrong choices fail to describe such a situation. The original version points out that *commuters try to get rid of these coins as quickly as possible,* an action that might barely qualify as a "current use," but it is certainly not "accepted." Choice (H) states that *Sacagaweas and Susan B. Anthony coins have the same electrochemical properties, a useful feature for coin machines,* but this fact is not a true "use." At most, it implies that these coins may be accepted by coin machines, but again, this implication is hardly "accepted." Finally, choice (J) mentions an unfortunate characteristic of Sacagawea coins (they tarnish quickly), but this characteristic is not a use. The correct answer is (G).

75. **(A)** Fulfill goal of tracing the history and current status of a certain kind of coin in the United States? Yes, because the essay highlights milestones in the development of dollar coins and assesses their present level of acceptance.

Rhetorical Skills   Writing Strategy   Goal of Essay

To determine whether the essay meets the goal, examine the content and role of each paragraph. The first paragraph indicates that dollar coins have been issued throughout U.S. history, but recent experiments with these coins have failed. The second paragraph describes early silver dollars, touching on the strange story of the 1804 dollar. The third paragraph moves forward over the next 100–150 years, revealing the *odd behavior* of speculators with regard to dollar coins. Finally, the fourth paragraph explains how dollar coins are now generally ignored in the U.S.

This recap of the essay fits the correct answer well: *highlights milestones in the development of dollar coins and assesses their present level of acceptance.* The essay does meet the goal of "tracing the history and current status of a certain kind of coin," namely the dollar coin.

Incorrect choice (B) gives a wrong reason that the goal is fulfilled. Nowhere does the essay *demonstrate* that dollar coins will not be accepted by the public until bills are withdrawn from circulation. The last sentence of the first paragraph, which addresses this issue, only states that this is *likely* to be the case, and no evidence is given. The correct answer is (A).

Chapter 7

of

5lb. Book of ACT® Practice Problems

English:
Passage Set 3

In This Chapter...

Set 3 Passages & Solutions

Chapter 7
English: Passage Set 3

The English problems in this chapter are distributed across five passages, just as they will be on the ACT itself. Every topic is up for grabs, so expect a little of everything. The answer key and the solutions classify the problems for you, so you can pinpoint strengths and weaknesses.

How should you use this chapter? Here are some recommendations, according to the level you've reached in ACT English.

> **1. Fundamentals.** If you haven't done any topical work yet, consider working in Chapters 3 and 4 first. Otherwise, do a passage or two untimed to begin with. As you become more comfortable, put the clock on. In all cases, review the solutions closely, and articulate what you've learned. Redo problems as necessary.

> **2. Fixes.** Do one passage at a time under timed conditions. Examine the results, learn your lessons, then test yourself with more passages at once.

> **3. Tweaks.** Confirm your mastery by doing a few passages at once under timed conditions. A full set of five is the ultimate goal. Aim to improve the speed and ease of your solution process.

Good luck on the problems!

PASSAGE 1

Maps of the World

[1]

The central library in my city has a collection of rare old books that I have permission to look at from time to time. For years I have been a student volunteer at the library, helping out with a pre-school program that builds literacy and ensures that the other high-school students show up when they're supposed to.

[2]

As a result of my work in this program, the childrens librarians have persuaded other staff to trust me. I have been granted my own scholar-level library card myself, which allows me to examine rare books under supervision.

[3]

The most fascinating of all, are the historical maps and atlases. Geography or history alone may seem dull, but the two together inspires awe. The antique maps are always distorted, but the cartographers did the best they could with the technology of the time. Think about how difficult it would be to draw an accurate map of your neighborhood, let alone of a coastline, without GPS.

1. **A.** NO CHANGE
    B. books, and
    C. books and
    D. books,

2. **F.** NO CHANGE
    G. literacy, ensuring
    H. literacy and ensuring
    J. literacy, which ensures

3. **A.** NO CHANGE
    B. children's librarians
    C. childrens librarians,
    D. childrens' librarians

4. **F.** NO CHANGE
    G. card of mine,
    H. card, myself,
    J. card,

5. **A.** NO CHANGE
    B. all:
    C. all are
    D. all are:

6. **F.** NO CHANGE
    G. inspires awe and wonder.
    H. inspires wonder.
    J. inspire awe.

7. Which one of the following choices provides the MOST relevant hypothetical situation at this point in the essay?
    A. NO CHANGE
    B. how long it would take to sail the coast of Africa in a sixteenth-century galleon—or in an ancient Phoenician ship.
    C. how different it would be today if Columbus had not mistakenly computed the circumference of the earth.
    D. how strange it would be for the sailors of yesteryear to have had access to modern navigational equipment.

MANHATTAN
PREP

[4]

Nevertheless, now that our society has agreed
8
upon a common view of our landscape, the personal
perspective of the mapmaker is sadly lost. Why did the

ancient Greeks put south at the top of they're maps?
9
Why did Europeans believe that California was an

island, despite evidence to the contrary? In the latter case,
10
perhaps they wanted in some fashion to envisage an isle
11
of wonders on earth.

[5]

Crossing the reading room and opening the
closed door that reads "Rare Books and Antiquities,"

the book I've requested, as I slide a pair of white cotton
12
gloves onto my hands, is retrieved by Mrs. Hernandez.
12
Under her watchful eye, I page right to the plates. Her

nervousness is understandable; our library the story goes,
13
was one of many around the country victimized by
a thief who sliced precious maps out of books with a
razor. I feel physically ill thinking of that crime: no
person was hurt, yet the damage to our heritage was

8. Which of the following alternatives to the under-
lined portion would be LEAST acceptable?
   F. given that
   G. it is true that
   H. because
   J. since

9. A. NO CHANGE
   B. they are
   C. there
   D. their

10. F. NO CHANGE
    G. investigation,
    H. container,
    J. argument,

11. The underlined phrase could be placed in all the following locations EXCEPT:
    A. where it is now.
    B. after the word *envisage*.
    C. after the word *isle*.
    D. after the word *earth* (ending the sentence with a
       period).

12. F. NO CHANGE
    G. a pair of white cotton gloves slides onto my
       hands as Mrs. Hernandez retrieves the book
       that I've requested.
    H. I slide a pair of white cotton gloves onto my
       hands, as the book that I've requested is re-
       trieved by Mrs. Hernandez.
    J. while I've requested the book that Mrs. Her-
       nandez retrieves, I slide a pair of white cotton
       gloves onto my hands.

13. A. NO CHANGE
    B. library, the story goes
    C. library the story goes—
    D. library, the story goes,

7

irreparable. [14] I am lucky to be able to examine these

maps, which provide mapmakers of the past with a
window into their worldviews.

14. If the writer were to delete the preceding sentence, the essay would primarily lose:

 F. a perspective on the narrator's emotional stance toward rare books.

 G. a description of a serious ailment that periodically afflicts the narrator.

 H. a reflection on the possibility of similar criminal acts occurring again.

 J. an assertion that violations of historical artifacts are more serious than personal injuries.

15. A. NO CHANGE

 B. a window into the worldviews of mapmakers of the past.

 C. the mapmakers with a window of the past's worldviews.

 D. a window into mapmakers of the worldviews of the past.

PASSAGE 2

Fixing Nitrogen

[1]

Well over half of the atmosphere we breathe is nitrogen. This nearly inactive gas passes in and out of our lungs with little effect. <u>Nevertheless,</u> many organic
16
molecules necessary to life, such as the genetic code-carrier

DNA and every kind of <u>protein, contain nitrogen</u> as
17
a building block. How, then, is atmospheric nitrogen "fixed" so that it can be included in organic compounds by plants and animals?

[2]

One interesting contributor is <u>lightning it</u> pries
18
apart nitrogen's tough internal bond. The main sources of naturally fixed nitrogen, however, are certain strains

of bacteria and similar creatures called archaea. [19] Most of these microorganisms live in the roots of soybeans and other legumes, where the organisms convert nitrogen

to ammonia in return for nutrients. <u>It</u> can then turn
20
this ammonia into other nitrogen compounds within their roots and elsewhere. Animals and other

16. Which of the following alternatives to the underlined portion would be LEAST acceptable?
   F. At the same time,
   G. Likewise,
   H. On the other hand,
   J. Despite this fact,

17. A. NO CHANGE
   B. protein, contain nitrogen,
   C. protein contain nitrogen,
   D. protein contain nitrogen

18. F. NO CHANGE
   G. lightning, it
   H. lightning, which
   J. lightning,

19. At this point, the writer is thinking about adding the following true statement:

   > One of the most famous nitrogen-fixers is a common bacterium that can cause pneumonia and other infections requiring intensive care.

   Should the writer make this addition here?
   A. Yes, because it provides additional information about microorganisms that fix nitrogen.
   B. Yes, because it helps to explain the complex role of these organisms in the environment.
   C. No, because it fails to include the specific name of the bacterium in question.
   D. No, because it distracts the reader from the primary focus of this paragraph.

20. F. NO CHANGE
   G. They
   H. Those
   J. The legumes

plants <u>are capable of feeding</u> on the legumes, absorb the
₂₁
fixed nitrogen, and spread that element throughout the

ecosystem. Eventually, as it <u>decomposes and</u> organic
₂₂
material returns the nitrogen to the atmosphere.

[3]

Before a <u>long time</u> ago, society relied on this
₂₃
sort of organic material for nitrates, a type of nitrogen

compound used in fertilizers, explosives, <u>and there was</u>
₂₄
<u>an early plastic called celluloid.</u> In fact, bat droppings
₂₄

in Chile <u>would of provided</u> a large quantity of nitrates
₂₅
to industry. As World War I began, the British navy

blockaded the European <u>continent,</u> cutting off Chilean
₂₆
nitrate supplies. Germany could have run out of both

food and gunpowder, <u>bringing the fighting to a halt.</u>
₂₇
However, prominent German chemist Fritz Haber had

<u>just shook</u> the scientific world by inventing a method for
₂₈
artificially fixing nitrogen. His invention singlehandedly

extended the war.

21. **A.** NO CHANGE
　　B. are feeding
　　C. feed
　　D. have fed

22. **F.** NO CHANGE
　　G. decomposes,
　　H. decomposed,
　　J. decomposing,

23. Which choice provides the MOST specific information?
　　A. NO CHANGE
　　B. good while
　　C. number of years
　　D. century

24. **F.** NO CHANGE
　　G. celluloid, as well as other materials, such as early plastics.
　　H. and early plastics, such as celluloid.
　　J. celluloid, such as early plastics.

25. **A.** NO CHANGE
　　B. would have provided
　　C. used to have provided
　　D. provided

26. **F.** NO CHANGE
　　G. continent
　　H. continent:
　　J. continent;

27. Given that all the choices are true, which one MOST effectively outlines the relevant consequence of the first part of the sentence?
　　A. NO CHANGE
　　B. although supplies of these materials would have been rationed.
　　C. which had previously depended greatly on nitrates from Chile.
　　D. which is typically a mixture of sulfur, carbon, and potassium nitrate.

28. **F.** NO CHANGE
　　G. just shaken
　　H. shook just
　　J. shaken just

[4]

The Haber process has altered human history in another way, too. Some estimate that half of the world's, living population is here because of the agricultural productivity enabled by Haber.

No researchers have ever found a suitable replacement for the process, which won Haber the Nobel Prize.

29. **A.** NO CHANGE
    B. worlds living,
    C. world's living
    D. worlds living

30. Given that all the choices are true, which one BEST illustrates the level of Haber's achievement described earlier in the essay?
    F. NO CHANGE
    G. Haber was criticized by many, however, for his leadership in developing chemical weapons, such as chlorine gas.
    H. Less successfully, Haber also tried to separate gold from seawater, which contains tiny but measurable amounts of the metal.
    J. With the rise of the Nazi Party, Haber was ultimately forced to leave his beloved Germany, because of his Jewish heritage.

7

PASSAGE 3

Dropping an Egg

[1]

My freshman teacher, Ms. Windham, of physics, did not like to be sitting down. After greeting us at

the door, she sprang around the room, acting out the motion of a projectile according to Newton's Laws or

the behavior of gas particles under pressure. We were taking a test, she moved silently among our desks,

examining our performance intently. She regarded tests as assessments of both our learning and her own teaching.

[2]

With her contagious and infectious enthusiasm, Ms. Windham did not want us to be sitting for

long, either. We were often the gas particles or the

projectiles—although not literally, of course. The catapults that we painstakingly calibrated, to twisted rolling tracks in the style of Dr. Seuss, we built various

31. A. NO CHANGE
   B. Ms. Windham my freshman teacher of physics
   C. My freshman physics teacher, Ms. Windham,
   D. My physics teacher, Ms. Windham, for freshmen,

32. Which choices MOST effectively conveys the high level of energy with which Ms. Windham taught?
   F. NO CHANGE
   G. twitched
   H. sauntered
   J. tottered

33. A. NO CHANGE
   B. Although we
   C. During the time when we
   D. Even when we

34. Given that all the choices are true, which one is MOST relevant to the statement that follows this sentence?
   F. NO CHANGE
   G. a practice that effectively kept anyone from cheating.
   H. which were old and squeaky in that classroom.
   J. so you weren't always sure exactly where she was.

35. A. NO CHANGE
   B. infectious zeal that spread from person to person,
   C. zealous, eager enthusiasm that infected us all,
   D. contagious enthusiasm,

36. F. NO CHANGE
   G. particles:
   H. particles;
   J. particles—

37. A. NO CHANGE
   B. Whether
   C. Given
   D. From

MANHATTAN
PREP

devices for small steel balls. ⟨38⟩ In the gymnasium, we floated on a noisy hovercraft that she and the rest of

the science department <u>constructed a contraption</u> of
                                        39
plywood and garbage bags powered by leaf blowers. That was one time I saw her smile while seated, as she glided across the gym floor.

[3]

The highlight of the year was the egg drop in May. Much prestige was associated <u>at</u> this contest,
                                                    40
which involved building a capsule that, when dropped from the roof of the science wing, would protect a raw egg nestled inside. As Ms. Windham explained, the top <u>prize was for a combination of speed and accuracy would</u>
                                        41
be awarded to the capsule that fell fastest and landed closest to the target, while still preserving its egg.

Another prize <u>had went</u> to the pod that took the longest
                    42
to land. The "Disaster Miracle" trophy would be for the capsule that broke apart most dramatically, in Ms. Windham's judgment, but still kept its contents safe.

38. The writer is considering adding the following true information to the end of the preceding sentence:

> that Ms. Windham issued to each lab group with mock ceremony.

Should the writer make this addition?

- **F.** Yes, because it distinguishes these steel objects from the particles mentioned earlier.
- **G.** Yes, because it provides an interesting detail about Ms. Windham's personality.
- **H.** No, because it interrupts the discussion of lab experiments that the class conducted.
- **J.** No, because it raises questions about such issues as the ceremony that remain unanswered.

39. A. NO CHANGE
- **B.** constructed, a contraption
- **C.** constructed a contraption,
- **D.** constructed a contraption:

40. F. NO CHANGE
- **G.** for
- **H.** to
- **J.** with

41. A. NO CHANGE
- **B.** prize was for a combination of speed and accuracy, would
- **C.** prize would be for a combination of speed and accuracy, to
- **D.** prize, for a combination of speed and accuracy, to

42. F. NO CHANGE
- **G.** goes
- **H.** would go
- **J.** has gone

[4]

Before this class, I had never operated power tools.
43
My lab partner and I had decorated our "Egg-splorer"

module like a lunar lander, which glinted in the bright

sun. On impact it shattered beautifully, and our egg

survived. Years later, my old partner and I still take
44

turns with our trophy. [45]

43. Given that all the choices are true, which one BEST
    leads from the preceding paragraph to the subject of
    this paragraph?
    A. NO CHANGE
    B. On the day of the drop, the weather was gorgeous.
    C. Earlier in the spring, I had watched a movie
       about the first landing on the moon.
    D. Deciding which prize to strive for was far from
       straightforward.

44. F. NO CHANGE
    G. Afterwards,
    H. In the meantime,
    J. So far,

45. The writer is considering ending the essay with the
    following statement:

    I credit Ms. Windham with sparking my love for
    science and engineering, subjects I intend to pur-
    sue in college.

    Should the writer add this sentence here?

    A. Yes, because it provides needed insight into the
       narrator's plans for the future.
    B. Yes, because it underscores the impact
       Ms. Windham has had on the narrator.
    C. No, because it does not sufficiently specify
       which field or fields interest the narrator.
    D. No, because it omits mention of other benefi-
       cial influences in the narrator's life.

PASSAGE 4

The Fire of Fireflies

[1]

The thought of seeing flashes in a field on a summer night may awaken nostalgia in city dwellers
_____
46

who grew up in suburban or rural areas catching fireflies.

Unfortunately, the nostalgia is not felt only by urbanites.
___
47

Firefly populations have been declining worldwide, and
_____
48

unless measures are taken, these insects could disappear.
_____
48

[2]

More than 2,000 species of firefly are known, some of them not bioluminescent. That is, these kinds

have not been emitting the "cold light" for which fireflies
_____
49

are famous. In most nocturnal species, though, an intricate

chain of chemical reactions leads to the result of
_____
50

a nearly complete conversion of energy to light, with

46. F. NO CHANGE
   G. night, may awaken nostalgia,
   H. night may awaken nostalgia,
   J. night, may awaken nostalgia

47. All of the following would be acceptable placements for the underlined portion EXCEPT:
   A. where it is now.
   B. before the word *the*.
   C. after the word *by*.
   D. after the word *urbanites* (ending the sentence with a period).

48. Which of the following alternatives to the under-lined portion would NOT be acceptable?
   F. worldwide; unless measures are
   G. worldwide, unless measures are
   H. worldwide; if measures are not
   J. worldwide. If measures are not

49. A. NO CHANGE
   B. were not emitting
   C. are not emitted
   D. do not emit

50. F. NO CHANGE
   G. causes in those species
   H. causes as its effect
   J. results in

little wasted heat. 51 In contrast, if you have ever touched a glowing incandescent, fluorescent, or even

LED bulb, it becomes quite apparent as you realize
52
these invented light sources release a great deal of heat.

Scientists have been studying ways to duplicate practically,
53
the cold light of fireflies, but the goal is still distant.

[3]

As larvae, fireflies flicker to warn away predators. Other animals and plants that lack bioluminescence use colorful markings for the same purpose: to announce they're poisonous or just distasteful.
54

Living for 1 to 2 years, the transformation of firefly
55
larvae is into adults that fly and mate, but generally
55
do not eat. During their few weeks before death, adult

fireflies glimmer to find mates, sometimes becoming
56
synchronized in great waves of light. The females of one
56
genus, however, can mimic the specific sequences of other species.

51. At this point, the writer is considering adding the following true statement:

> The reactions involve a class of enzymes called luciferases, from the Latin term for "light-carrier."

Should the writer make this addition here?

A. Yes, because the sentence emphasizes that the chemical reactions produce light.
B. Yes, because the sentence provides important information about the biology of fireflies.
C. No, because the sentence distracts from the logical flow of other sentences nearby.
D. No, because the sentence fails to explain these chemical reactions in more detail.

52. F. NO CHANGE
G. you well know the evident truth that
H. as you well know, it's rather obvious
J. you know that

53. A. NO CHANGE
B. ways, to duplicate practically
C. ways to duplicate, practically
D. ways to duplicate practically

54. F. NO CHANGE
G. their
H. there
J. there's

55. A. NO CHANGE
B. After living for 1 to 2 years, firefly larvae transform into adults that
C. Transformed from firefly larvae, after living for 1 to 2 years, adults
D. Firefly larvae living for 1 to 2 years are transformed into adults,

56. Given that all of the choices are true, which one is MOST relevant at this point in the paragraph?
F. NO CHANGE
G. although some researchers posit secondary rationales.
H. signaling to each other in unique patterns.
J. otherwise a difficult task in a dark forest.

MANHATTAN
PREP

[4]

Fireflies are under assault by habitat loss, as forests are cut down and marshes drained. Even when woods and streams are preserved, the encroachment of human civilization via light pollution takes a toll.

A car's headlights disorients fireflies, disrupting their short mating window. It is hoped that the Dark Sky Initiative and similar efforts can combat light pollution, allowing summer nights again to be lit: solely by the moon, stars, and lightning bugs.

57. A. NO CHANGE
 B. marshes draining
 C. draining marshes
 D. drain marshes

58. F. NO CHANGE
 G. The headlights of a car have disoriented
 H. A car's headlights can disorient
 J. The headlights of a car disorienting

59. A. NO CHANGE
 B. lit
 C. lit;
 D. lit,

7

Question 60 asks about the preceding passage as a whole.

---

60. Upon reviewing this essay and finding that some information has been left out, the writer composes the following sentence incorporating that information:

> When hopeful males arrive, the females devour them.

This sentence would most logically be placed after the last sentence in Paragraph:

 F. 1.
 G. 2.
 H. 3.
 J. 4.

PASSAGE 5

The Humble Harmonica

[1]

You won't find many harmonica players in orchestras. Although composers as respected, esteemed, and admired as Ralph Vaughan Williams have written

61

61

pieces for the instrument, the harmonica is still not seen as serious in classical-music circles. Only the kazoo is less appreciated. 62

[2]

On the other hand, snobbery is probably at work.

63

A cheap instrument that is easy to start playing may not be exclusive enough for social climbers. For everyone else, however, low cost and low difficulty are attractions. A pocket tool for tunes the harmonica has provided a

64

cornerstone to American popular music, influencing styles from folk and blues to jazz and rock & roll.

Vibrating reeds produce the sound of harmonicas.

65

[3]

Trossingen, Germany, is not where the harmonica was born, but it has been the instrument's spiritual home

66

for over 150 years, since Matthias Hohner started manufacturing "mouth organs" there. The company

---

61. A. NO CHANGE
    B. respected and admired
    C. admired and esteemed
    D. respected

62. Upon reviewing this paragraph, the writer considers deleting the preceding sentence. If the writer were to delete the sentence, the paragraph would primarily lose:
    F. a defense of the kazoo as a serious instrument.
    G. a comparison reinforcing the point of the prior sentence.
    H. an assessment of the general strength of music appreciation.
    J. a demand for the classical music world to perform a re-evaluation.

63. A. NO CHANGE
    B. Otherwise,
    C. Sadly,
    D. Therefore,

64. F. NO CHANGE
    G. tunes,
    H. tunes;
    J. tunes:

65. A. NO CHANGE
    B. Harmonicas work on the same principles as pitch pipes.
    C. The two major types of harmonicas are diatonic and chromatic.
    D. OMIT the underlined portion.

66. F. NO CHANGE
    G. instruments spiritual home
    H. instruments' spiritual home,
    J. instrument's spiritual home,

who bears his name is still the worldwide leader in
$\overline{}$
67
harmonica sales. Today, the World Harmonica Festival

draws thousands to Trossingen each year.
     $\overline{}$
       68

[4]

     How did Hohner harmonicas become so popular?
Spotting an opportunity faster than competitors,
Matthias Hohner shipped harmonicas to the United

States through relatives. 69 The country, then in the

throes of the Civil War, may have seemed as an unlikely
                                 $\overline{}$
                                  70
market, but soldiers quickly adopted and circulated the
handy instrument.

[5]

     By the 1920s, the harmonica was embedded
throughout American roots music, including folk,
blues, and country. Influential African-American
blues players pioneered the use of "crossharp" scales
                 71
and note-bending to create a famously mournful
sound. Decades later, the instrument became

unforgettably linked when musicians as distinct and
                       72

67. **A.** NO CHANGE
     B. that
     C. this
     D. whose

68. Given that all the choices are true, which one would MOST clearly communicate the positive feelings shared by the attendees of the festival?
     F. NO CHANGE
     G. thousands of people of different ages
     H. thousands of eager fans
     J. thousands of residents of various countries

69. The writer is considering deleting the following phrase from the preceding sentence:
     Spotting an opportunity faster than competitors,
   If the writer were to make this deletion, the sentence would primarily lose:
     A. a sense of the business urgency behind Hohner's action.
     B. an evaluation of Hohner's ability to meet commitments.
     C. a formal and measured tone.
     D. an element of surprise.

70. **F.** NO CHANGE
     G. to
     H. in
     J. OMIT the underlined portion.

71. **A.** NO CHANGE
     B. prepared
     C. colonized
     D. speculated

72. **F.** NO CHANGE
     G. by
     H. with
     J. in

7

irregular as Stevie Wonder and Bob Dylan. Even
___
73
the first song performed live in space was played on

a harmonica and some bells, smuggled aboard the

Gemini Six mission. Its lowly instrument was thus
___
74

literally heightened above its classical cousins.
___
75

73. **A.** NO CHANGE
    B. exceptional
    C. peculiar
    D. disqualified

74. **F.** NO CHANGE
    G. One's
    H. Their
    J. This

75. **A.** NO CHANGE
    B. increased
    C. elevated
    D. upgraded

Passage Set 3 Answer Key

Write in whether you got each problem right or wrong (or left it blank). If your answer was correct, put a 1 in every blank to the right of that problem. Sum up each column and compare your total to the total possible "Out Of" points in each column.

Problem	Correct Answer	Right/ Wrong/ Blank	Grammar & Usage	Punctuation	Sentence Structure	Organization	Style	Writing Strategy
			Usage/Mechanics			**Rhetorical Skills**		
1	A				—			
2	H				—			
3	B			—				
4	J						—	
5	C			—				
6	J		—					
7	A							—
8	G				—			
9	D		—					
10	F						—	
11	C				—			
12	H				—			
13	D			—				
14	F							—
15	B				—			
16	G					—		
17	A			—				
18	H				—			
19	D							—
20	J		—					
21	C		—					
22	G				—			
23	D							—
24	H		—					
25	D		—					
26	F			—				

7

Problem	Correct Answer	Right/Wrong/Blank	Usage/Mechanics			Rhetorical Skills		
			Grammar & Usage	Punctuation	Sentence Structure	Organization	Style	Writing Strategy
27	A							—
28	G		—					
29	C			—				
30	F							—
31	C				—			
32	F						—	
33	D				—			
34	F							—
35	D						—	
36	F			—				
37	D		—					
38	G							—
39	B			—				
40	J		—					
41	C				—			
42	H				—			
43	B					—		
44	F					—		
45	B							—
46	F			—				
47	B				—			
48	G				—			
49	D				—			
50	J						—	
51	C							—
52	J						—	
53	D			—				
54	F		—					
55	B				—			
56	H							—

Problem	Correct Answer	Right/ Wrong/ Blank	Usage/Mechanics			Rhetorical Skills		
			Grammar & Usage	Punctuation	Sentence Structure	Organization	Style	Writing Strategy
57	A		—					
58	H		—					
59	B			—				
60	H					—		
61	D						—	
62	G							—
63	C					—		
64	G			—				
65	D							—
66	F			—				
67	B		—					
68	H							—
69	A							—
70	J		—					
71	A						—	
72	H				—			
73	B						—	
74	J		—					
75	C						—	
Total								
Out Of		75	15	13	17	5	10	15

7

Passage Set 3 Solutions

Passage 1

1.   **(A)** The central library … has a collection of rare old <u>books that</u> I have permission to look at …

Usage/Mechanics   Sentence Structure   Whole Sentences

The central library is the subject of the sentence; *has* is the main verb. The independent clause runs from *The central library* to *rare old books*. In the correct version of the sentence, the clause *I have permission to look at* … is attached with the word *that* to modify *rare old books*. These are books *that I have permission to look at*. The incorrect choices all create fragments that are wrongly glued to the main clause, since *I have permission to look at from time to time* is not a complete thought: *look at* what? You need an object after *at* if you don't have *that* at the beginning of the clause. The correct answer is (A).

2.   **(H)** For years I have been a student volunteer at the library, helping out with a pre-school program that builds <u>literacy and ensuring</u> that the other high-school students show up …

Usage/Mechanics   Sentence Structure   Modifier Placement

The problem revolves around a key question: what or who is logically doing the *ensuring*? It doesn't make sense for the *pre-school program that builds literacy* to be *ensuring* that the other high-school students show up. It's even less logical for *literacy* itself to perform this action.

Rather, the logical subject of *ensures* or *ensuring* is *I* (who has been *a student volunteer at the library*). *I have been ensuring that the other high-school students show up*. The only way to have this action be done by *I* (the faraway subject of the sentence) is to make it into a modifier *-ing* form, so that it is parallel to *helping: I have been a volunteer, helping … and ensuring. …* The correct answer is (H).

3.   **(B)** … the <u>children's librarians</u> …

Usage/Mechanics   Punctuation   Apostrophe

The possessive form of *children* is always *children's*, meaning "of or for children." Many irregular plural nouns in English work the same way: just add 's to get *men's shoes, women's shoes, children's shoes*, etc. The correct answer is (B).

4.   **(J)** … I have been granted my own scholar-level library <u>card,</u> which allows me …

Rhetorical Skills   Style   Concision

The words *my own* earlier in the sentence are enough to emphasize that the card belongs to the narrator and to no one else. Adding *myself* or *of mine* after the word *card*, with or without commas, is redundant. The correct answer is (J).

5.   **(C)** The most fascinating of <u>all are</u> the historical maps and atlases.

Usage/Mechanics   Punctuation   Commas, Colons

This sentence has a reversed structure: Adjective–Verb–Subject. The subject is *the historical maps and atlases,* the verb is *are,* and the adjective is *fascinating.* There should be no punctuation anywhere within the sentence. Flip the sentence back to see why: *The historical maps and atlases are the most fascinating of all.* Neither a comma nor a colon should intervene before the subject in the original sentence. If you omit the *are,* then you are left with a fragment of a sentence, one that has no verb. The correct answer is (C).

6.   **(J)** … the two together <u>inspire awe.</u>

Usage/Mechanics   Grammar & Usage   Subject–Verb Agreement

The words *the two* are plural: *The two of them are here.* Adding *together* after *two* doesn't change that fact. Thus, the verb needs to be *inspire,* not *inspires.* It's irrelevant whether you write *awe* or *wonder* (just avoid the wordiness of using both). The correct answer is (J).

7.   **(A)** Most relevant hypothetical situation: Think about <u>how difficult it would be to draw an accurate map of your neighborhood, let alone of a coastline, without GPS.</u>

Rhetorical Skills   Writing Strategy   Choice of Content

The prior sentence provides direction about which choice you should make. It reads as follows: *The antique maps are always distorted, but the cartographers did the best they could with the technology of the time.* The sentence in question, then, should reinforce how difficult the task of making undistorted maps was, given the technology of the time. The correct choice gives a hypothetical example that brings this difficulty home to the reader. The other choices give irrelevant situations. The length of time it would have taken to sail the African coastline is not directly applicable to the issue of accuracy: it might have taken a long time to sail this coastline, but perhaps a very accurate map would be the result. The correct answer is (A).

8.   **(G)** Least acceptable alternative: Nevertheless, <u>it is true that</u> our society has agreed upon a common view of our landscape, the personal perspective of the mapmaker is sadly lost.

Usage/Mechanics   Sentence Structure   Whole Sentences

The acceptable alternatives do not all mean exactly the same thing. *Because* and *since* both indicate direct causality (the personal perspective of the mapmaker is lost *because* or *since* our society has agreed upon a common view). *Now that* and *given that* suggest more indirect causality: these are the circumstances in which that perspective is lost. Nevertheless, these options are all acceptable, because they all create subordinate clauses that are also sensible. The option *it is true that* may seem like a logical alternative, but it creates a run-on sentence with a comma splice: *Independent clause, independent clause.* The correct answer is (G).

9.   **(D)** Why did the ancient Greeks put south at the top of <u>their</u> maps?

Usage/Mechanics   Grammar & Usage   Pronoun Forms

The word *their* is the possessive of *they*. In this case, it indicates that the maps are *of the Greeks*. The contraction *they're* always means *they are*; both options are nonsensical here. The word *there* means *in that place* and also makes no sense in this context. The correct answer is (D).

10. **(F)** Why did the ancient Greeks …? Why did Europeans …? In the latter <u>case,</u> perhaps they …

Rhetorical Skills   Style   Word Choice

Here, the words *latter case* mean "the second situation or instance." That is, this point refers to the second question (*they = Europeans*, not *the ancient Greeks*). In other contexts, *case* can mean "investigation" (*a criminal case*), "argument" (*make your case*), or even "container" (*a plastic case*), but not here. The correct answer is (F).

11. **(C)** The underlined phrase cannot be placed here: … they wanted to envisage an isle <u>in some fashion</u> of wonders on earth.

Usage/Mechanics   Sentence Structure   Modifier Placement

The phrase *in some fashion* means *somehow* and functions as an adverb, modifying either the verb *wanted* or the infinitive *to envisage*. Thus, there is some flexibility about where to put this phrase. You can write any of the following:

> They wanted <u>in some fashion</u> to envisage an isle of wonders on earth.

> They wanted to envisage <u>in some fashion</u> an isle of wonders on earth.

> They wanted to envisage an isle of wonders on earth <u>in some fashion</u>.

The different positions are stylistically distinct and even create subtle variations in meaning or connotation, but they are all acceptable. What is not acceptable, however, is to break up the tight unit *an isle of wonders* with *in some fashion*. If you read the right answer aloud, it seems as if you mean something by the phrase *fashion of wonders*, whereas that phrase in fact means nothing.

Generally, *of* phrases are closely bound to what they modify. Try never to separate an *of* phrase from the noun it should be bound to. The correct answer is (C).

12. **(H)** Crossing the reading room and opening the closed door …, <u>I slide a pair of white cotton gloves onto my hands, as the book that I've requested is retrieved by Mrs. Hernandez.</u>

Usage/Mechanics   Sentence Structure   Modifier Placement

The sentence begins with a leading modifier: *Crossing … and opening …* Therefore, the subject must be logically the one crossing and opening. Neither *the book* nor *a pair of white cotton gloves* is suitable. The subject can only be *I* (or, in theory, *Mrs. Hernandez,* but that option is not given to you). This subject should immediately follow the modifier; it should not be separated by a subordinate clause (*while I've requested …*). Furthermore, the choice that makes this separation creates an illogical time sequence (the requesting happened prior to the present, but *while I've requested* puts the action in the present). The correct answer is (H).

13.   **(D)** … our <u>library, the story goes,</u> was one of many …

Usage/Mechanics   Punctuation   Commas

This part of the sentence could be rewritten this way: *The story goes that our library was one of many …* If you want to take the "frame" (*the story goes*) and move it inside, then delete the *that* and surround the insertion by commas on both sides, as is done in the correct answer. Theoretically, you could use a pair of dashes, but not just one. The correct answer is (D).

14.   **(F)** If the writer were to delete the preceding sentence, the essay would primarily lose a perspective on the narrator's emotional stance toward rare books.

Rhetorical Skills   Writing Strategy   Deletions

The sentence in question reads *I feel physically ill thinking of that crime: no person was hurt, yet the damage to our heritage was irreparable.* The narrator here is expressing powerful emotions about what the thief did to some rare books (that is, cut maps out of them). The right answer properly indicates that this sentence provides *a perspective on the narrator's emotional stance toward rare books.* This option does not go into any detail about what that stance is, but this generic statement cannot be argued with. The narrator is not describing a *serious ailment,* nor is he or she reflecting on the *possibility of similar criminal acts occurring again* (the narrator only is thinking *of that crime* in particular). Finally, you would be stretching the text significantly if you think that the narrator is asserting that *violations of historical artifacts are more serious than personal injuries.* The narrator just points out that *no person was hurt* in the crime, yet it is still serious. The correct answer is (F).

15.   **(B)** … examine these maps, which provide <u>a window into the worldviews of mapmakers of the past.</u>

Usage/Mechanics   Sentence Structure   Modifier Placement

Logically, the proper sequence is this: *mapmakers* lived in the past, so you should write *mapmakers of the past.* These mapmakers had worldviews, so you should write *worldviews of mapmakers of the past.* Now, these maps can *provide a window into* these worldviews. To whom is this window being provided? The text doesn't say, but the implication is the present-day world, or society in general. Regardless, the maps are certainly not providing the *mapmakers* with this window. The correct answer is (B).

Passage 2

16.   **(G)** Least acceptable alternative: This nearly inactive gas passes in and out of our lungs with little effect. <u>Likewise,</u> many organic molecules necessary to life … contain nitrogen as a building block.

Rhetorical Skills   Organization   Transitions

The idea before the underlined portion and the idea after that portion are in contrast, as the original transition (*Nevertheless*) indicates. Nitrogen doesn't get absorbed when you breathe, *but* you need nitrogen in many of your molecules. Three of the transitions express this contrast: *At the same time, On the other hand,* and *Despite this fact.* The only transition that doesn't express the contrast is *Likewise,* which means "in a similar way." Since you are looking for the least appropriate transition, *Likewise* is the right answer. The correct answer is (G).

MANHATTAN
PREP   255

17.   **(A)**   … many organic molecules necessary to life, such as the genetic code-carrier DNA and every kind of <u>protein, contain nitrogen</u> as a building block.

Usage/Mechanics   Punctuation   Commas

The phrase *such as … every kind of protein* is a parenthetical aside that gives a couple of examples of the *organic molecules necessary to life*. Therefore, this parenthetical phrase should be separated on both sides from the rest of the sentence with commas; in other words, a comma belongs between *protein* and *contain*. However, no comma should go after *nitrogen*, since the phrase *as a building block* is a natural extension of the verb phrase *contain nitrogen*. *This molecule contains nitrogen as a building block* is a clause that needs no commas within. The correct answer is (A).

18.   **(H)** One interesting contributor is <u>lightning, which</u> pries apart nitrogen's tough internal bond.

Usage/Mechanics   Sentence Structure   Whole Sentences

The corrected version of the sentence turns the second clause into a modifier with the word *which*. The main clause is then *One interesting contributor is lightning*.

The original sentence and choice (G) both use *it*, creating a second independent clause (*it pries apart …*). However, you cannot use just a comma (or nothing at all) to join these two independent clauses, as these choices attempt to do. The result in either case is a run-on. Finally, choice (J) omits the second subject altogether, turning the sentence into a run-on as well (*One interesting contributor is lightning, pries apart …*). The correct answer is (H).

19.   **(D)** Should the writer make this addition here? No, because it distracts the reader from the primary focus of this paragraph.

Rhetorical Skills   Writing Strategy   Additions

The proposed addition is this sentence: "One of the most famous nitrogen-fixers is a common bacterium that can cause pneumonia and other infections requiring intensive care." However, the paragraph's focus is on how nitrogen fixation works, most importantly the kind performed by microorganisms. Thus, adding a random fact about a particular nitrogen-fixer—namely, that it can also cause diseases in humans—would be a mistake. The writer should keep this paragraph well-focused, so that the reader can concentrate on understanding how nitrogen is fixed. The correct answer is (D).

20.   **(J)** Most of these microorganisms live in the roots of soybeans and other legumes, where the organisms convert nitrogen to ammonia in return for nutrients. <u>The legumes</u> can then turn this ammonia …

Usage/Mechanics   Grammar & Usage   Pronoun Agreement

The pronoun *It* is the wrong number (singular) to refer to a plural noun phrase (*soybeans and other legumes*). The obvious solution is to use *They* instead, but there are several plural nouns in the previous sentence, besides the phrase already mentioned (*microorganisms, roots, organisms, nutrients*). At least some of these nouns (especially *microorganisms/organisms*) might seem to be reasonable subjects of the next sentence, so the antecedent (the noun a pronoun refers to) for *They* is not clear. *Those* has the same issue (and some people argue that *those* should not stand by itself anyway). What definitively clarifies that the logical subject ought to be "legumes" is that the sentence refers to *their roots*, which properly belong to

MANHATTAN
PREP

the *soybeans and other legumes.* The best solution is to use a shortened version of the noun phrase the writer intends to refer to: *The legumes.* This choice removes all confusion about the meaning of the sentence. The correct answer is (J).

21.   **(C)** Animals and other plants <u>feed</u> on the legumes, absorb the fixed nitrogen, and spread that element ...

Usage/Mechanics   Grammar & Usage   Parallelism

As indicated by the commas and the *and,* the sentence contains a three-item list of verbs: *feed ...,* *absorb ...,* *and spread ...* These verbs should be parallel to each other in form as much as possible. Since you cannot change the last two items, the first must be changed to match the simple present tense of *absorb* and *spread.* The correct answer is (C).

22.   **(G)** Eventually, as it <u>decomposes,</u> organic material returns the nitrogen to the atmosphere.

Usage/Mechanics   Sentence Structure   Whole Sentences (and Verb Tense)

In the correct sentence, the main clause is *organic material returns the nitrogen ...,* in which *organic material* is the subject and *returns* is the verb. There is a subordinate clause at the beginning: *as it decomposes,* which tells you the context in which the main clause happens.

Using *and* in place of the comma after *decomposes* (as in the original sentence) converts the sentence into a fragment. There would no longer be a main clause; what had been that clause would now fall under the dominion of the conjunction *as.* Choice (J) removes the working verb from the subordinate clause, also causing the sentence to fail. Finally, choice (H) retains a functional verb (*decomposed*) in the proper position, but the tense is wrong. The process of nitrogen fixation has been described in present tense consistently; there is no reason to change to the past. The correct answer is (G).

23.   **(D)** Most specific information: Before a <u>century</u> ago ...

Rhetorical Skills   Writing Strategy   Choice of Content

The wrong choices (*long time, good while, number of years*) are grammatically correct, but they are all much vaguer than *century,* which means "one hundred years." Thus, the most specific choice is *century.* The correct answer is (D).

24.   **(H)** ... nitrates, a type of nitrogen compound used in fertilizers, explosives, <u>and early plastics, such as celluloid.</u>

Usage/Mechanics   Grammar & Usage   Parallelism

Where are nitrates used? According to the passage, they are used in three things. These things should be in a parallel list: *fertilizers, explosives, and early plastics.* This list follows the standard *X, Y, and Z* structure. An example of the final item in the list is given with the phrase *such as celluloid.*

The original sentence breaks the parallel structure: *in X, Y, and there was Z.* The other two wrong answers leave out the necessary *and* before the last item. Choice (G) creates a four-item list but uses *as well as,* which can't substitute for *and* in the list: *in X, Y, Z, as well as W.*

Note that you don't have to know anything about chemistry here, but the correct answer makes more sense: *early plastics* are a general type of thing (and a plural noun, like *fertilizers* and *explosives*), whereas *celluloid* seems to be more specific. The correct answer is (H).

25. **(D)** … society relied on this sort of organic material for nitrates … In fact, bat droppings in Chile <u>provided</u> a large quantity of nitrates to industry. As World War I began, the British navy blockaded the European continent, cutting off Chilean nitrate supplies.

Usage/Mechanics	Grammar & Usage	Verb Forms & Tenses

Never write *would of*. The only possible form is *would have*. However, that doesn't mean that *would have provided* is automatically correct in context. The right tense to use here is plain past (*provided*), matching the verbs used to tell the surrounding story (*relied, began, blockaded*). The phrase *would have provided* would indicate that these nitrates were *not* actually provided to industry ("I would have gone to the store for you … but I fell asleep" = I didn't go to the store). However, the next sentence indicates that these nitrate supplies were *cut off*, and they can only be cut off if they had been provided previously. So the bat droppings actually did provide the nitrates.

Finally, *used to have provided* is an improper verb form. *Used to provide* would be fine in this context (meaning that the nitrates were provided at one time, but no longer are). Don't combine *used* with a perfect infinitive (*to have provided*). The correct answer is (D).

26. **(F)** … the British navy blockaded the European <u>continent,</u> cutting off Chilean nitrate supplies.

Usage/Mechanics	Punctuation	Commas

The correct comma after *continent* indicates that the result of the blockade was to cut off the nitrate supplies. The modifier *cutting off* … properly modifies the verb *blockaded* and shares its subject (*the British navy*).

If no comma is used, the implication is that *cutting off* modifies *continent,* as if the continent itself is doing the cutting off. That reading makes no sense here. No other punctuation (e.g., a colon or a semicolon) is possible in this position before the modifier *cutting off*. The correct answer is (F).

27. **(A)** Most effectively outlines the consequence of the first part of the sentence: Germany could have run out of both food and gunpowder, <u>bringing the fighting to a halt.</u>

Rhetorical Skills	Writing Strategy	Choice of Content

The previous sentence discusses the British naval blockade of the European continent that was intended to cut off nitrate supplies. The first part of the current sentence states what could have happened: *Germany could have run out of both food and gunpowder*. You are asked for the choice that outlines the most relevant consequence of this event: that is, what is the most important result that would have happened? The correct answer indicates that result: *bringing the fighting* [that is, the war] *to a halt*.

The incorrect choices do not list major consequences, or in the case of choices (C) and (D), any consequences at all. The correct answer is (A).

28.   **(G)**   … Fritz Haber had <u>just shaken</u> the scientific world …

Usage/Mechanics   Grammar & Usage   Verb Forms & Idioms

The irregular verb *shake* becomes *shaken* after *had or have*: "I have shaken the rattle." The phrase *had shook* is always wrong. *Shook* is the stand-alone past-tense form: "I shook the rattle."

The other issue at work in this problem is the word *just*, whose meaning depends on its placement. In the middle of a verb phrase such as *had shaken,* the word *just* almost always means "recently," which is the intended meaning here: "I have just shaken the rattle" (= Moments ago, I shook the rattle). However, if placed after the verb and before the object, the word *just* means "only": "I have shaken just the rattle" (= I haven't shaken anything else). That meaning is illogical in the context of the essay. Fritz Haber didn't shake *only* the scientific world. After all, his process "singlehandedly extended the war." The correct answer is (G).

29.   **(C)**   … half of the <u>world's living</u> population is here …

Usage/Mechanics   Punctuation   Apostrophes & Commas

The possessive form of the word *world* is *world's*, with an apostrophe. *The world's population* means "the population of the world." The form *worlds* is just the plural of *world*, meaning "more than one world."

No comma should ever go between a possessive (such as *world's*) and the noun phrase following (such as *living population*). Moreover, don't put a comma between *living* and *population*. You do place commas between certain adjectives in a series ("my tall, handsome friend"), but only when *and* works between the adjectives ("my tall and handsome friend"). This principle explains why you don't put a comma after the possessive ("the world's and living population" is nonsensical). Likewise, never put a comma between the last adjective and the noun, because you would never put *and* there ("the world's living and population" is also nonsensical). The correct answer is (C).

30.   **(F)**   Best illustrates the level of Haber's achievement: <u>No researchers have ever found a suitable replacement for the process, which won Haber the Nobel Prize.</u>

Rhetorical Skills   Writing Strategy   Choice of Content

The correct answer points out both the difficulty of Haber's achievement (no one has ever found a substitute for the Haber process) and a result of that achievement (Haber won the Nobel Prize). These facts certainly "illustrate the level" of his accomplishment.

The wrong answers do not highlight the level of this achievement; in fact, they do not refer to this particular achievement at all, but rather other events in Haber's life. The correct answer is (F).

Passage 3

31. **(C)** <u>My freshman physics teacher, Ms. Windham,</u> did not like …

Usage/Mechanics   Sentence Structure   Modifier Placement

There are two noun phrases that indicate the same person: *Ms. Windham* and *my freshman physics teacher.* Either one could theoretically be the subject, with the other placed next to that subject (and separated by commas). The correct answer has *My freshman physics teacher* as the subject; this could also have been expressed as *My teacher of freshman physics.* However, you should not break apart this phrase by inserting *Ms. Windham,* as the original version incorrectly does.

Choice (D) causes a similar violation (in addition, *physics teacher for freshmen* is phrased less clearly). Finally, choice (B) lacks any comma separation between the noun phrases; it also oddly modifies *teacher* with *freshman.* The correct answer is (C).

32. **(F)** Most effectively conveys high energy: … she <u>sprang</u> around the room …

Rhetorical Skills   Style   Word Choice

This problem revolves around the specific meaning of the verbs in the choices. The original *sprang* is best, indicating that Ms. Windham leaped around the room (perhaps not literally, but with a similar impression of speed and energy). *Twitched* may indicate high energy, but it would portray restricted, spasmodic movements, similar to *shudder* or *shake.* *Sauntered* would mean that Ms. Windham strolled around the room in a slow, casual way—certainly not conveying energy. *Totter* means "stagger, teeter," as if she were barely able to keep her balance. The correct answer is (F).

33. **(D)** <u>Even when we</u> were taking a test, she moved silently among our desks …

Usage/Mechanics   Sentence Structure   Whole Sentence

The main clause in this sentence is *she moved silently among our desks.* The underlined portion, which together with the rest of its clause is only separated from the main clause by a comma, must therefore contain a subordinator. That is, the word *We* by itself cannot start the sentence. The next question is which subordinator is most appropriate. The correct answer, *Even when,* creates a right relationship of time, making the test and Ms. Windham's movement around the room simultaneous. The *Even* is an appropriate intensifier (i.e., *even* under these testing conditions, she didn't sit down).

During the time when is needlessly wordy, and *although* sets up an unsuitable contrast between the two clauses. The correct answer is (D).

34. **(F)** Most relevant to the following statement: … she moved silently among our desks, <u>examining our performance intently.</u> She regarded tests as assessments of both our learning and her own teaching.

Rhetorical Skills   Writing Strategy   Choice of Content

The statement after the underlined portion reveals how Ms. Windham thought about tests: she considered them *assessments of both our learning and her own teaching.* This attitude is set up well by the correct choice, which depicts matching behavior on Ms. Windham's part (*examining our performance intently*).

The wrong answers do not lead into the next sentence. Rather, they bring up irrelevant points: the prevention of cheating, the age of the desks, or the mystery of Ms. Windham's location. None of these describe any actions Ms. Windham took that would point to her attitude toward tests. The correct answer is (F).

35.   **(D)** With her <u>contagious enthusiasm,</u> Ms. Windham did not want …

Rhetorical Skills   Style   Concision

The words *contagious* and *infectious* mean the same thing as the modifiers *that spread from person to person* and *that infected us all.* The right answer deploys only one option from this group. Likewise, only one of the words *enthusiasm, zeal, zealous,* and *eager* needs to be used. The other answers repeat themselves unnecessarily. The correct answer is (D).

36.   **(F)** We were often the gas <u>particles</u> or the projectiles—although not literally, of course.

Usage/Mechanics   Punctuation   Colons, Semicolons, Dashes

The right answer uses no punctuation at all. The core of the sentence is *We were X or Y.* No marks, not even a comma, belongs after the first item in the list (here, *the gas particles*). The dash is tempting, but only use a pair of dashes as an emphatic insertion. The phrase *or the projectiles* is not such an insertion: acting like projectiles would not be significantly different from acting like gas particles in a science class. The parallelism of the *X or Y* construction should not be broken. The correct answer is (F).

37.   **(D)** <u>From</u> catapults that we painstakingly calibrated, to twisted rolling tracks …, we built various devices for small steel balls.

Usage/Mechanics   Grammar & Usage   Parallelism

The main clause in this sentence is *we built various devices.* The opening phrase, which illustrates the range of devices built, has the parallel structure *From X to Y.* Thus, the underlined word must be *From.* By the way, what goes in the positions of *X* and *Y* is long enough to merit a comma after *X* (*catapults that we painstakingly calibrated*).

Whether might be acceptable in other circumstances, but the structure would have to be *Whether X or Y.* The other wrong choices, *The* and *Given,* do not fit the sentence as written. The correct answer is (D).

38.   **(G)** Should the writer make this addition? Yes, because it provides an interesting detail about Ms. Windham's personality.

Rhetorical Skills   Writing Strategy   Additions

The proposed addition would make the end of the sentence read as follows: *we built various devices for small steel balls that Ms. Windham issued to each lab group with mock ceremony.* Without this addition, the sentence lacks some context for the *small steel balls,* but these objects are not so out of place in a science classroom that they absolutely require explanation. Rather, the main effect of this addition is to gain additional insight into the personality of Ms. Windham, the central figure in the passage. She issued the steel balls *with mock ceremony.* That is, she handed these items out formally in some way, but she did so with a wink, acknowledging a degree of silliness. This detail enriches the reader's understanding of Ms. Windham, and the proposed modifier should be added.

MANHATTAN
PREP

The addition of this modifier is not necessary to distinguish the steel balls from the gas particles mentioned earlier (which were only mimicked by humans running around). The modifier does not interrupt the flow of description for long; indeed, it adds to that flow. Finally, the modifier does not really raise any questions—the reader is not left wondering about the specifics of the way in which Ms. Windham issued the steel balls to each lab group. The phrase *with mock ceremony* does not demand further exposition. The correct answer is (G).

39.   **(B)**   … we floated on a noisy hovercraft that she and the rest of the science department constructed, a contraption of plywood and garbage bags …

Usage/Mechanics   Punctuation   Commas

The phrase *a contraption of plywood* is an appositive that modifies *a noisy hovercraft*, so it should be separated from that noun phrase (and the modifier following it, *that she … constructed*) by a comma. If there is no comma, then the modifier turns into a run-on: *… hovercraft that she constructed a contraption …* incorrectly creates two objects for the verb *constructed* (*hovercraft* and *contraption*). No punctuation belongs between *contraption* and its essential modifier *of plywood*. The correct answer is (B).

40.   **(J)**   Much prestige was associated with this contest …

Usage/Mechanics   Grammar & Usage   Idioms

The verb *associate* normally takes the preposition *with*: *Good grades are associated with hard work*. The preposition *to* may be possible, but idiomatically it's clearly worse in general contexts. Neither *at* nor *for* are suitable at all. The correct answer is (J).

41.   **(C)**   As Ms. Windham explained, the top prize would be for a combination of speed and accuracy, to be awarded to the capsule that fell fastest …

Usage/Mechanics   Sentence Structure   Whole Sentences

The original phrasing creates a run-on, with two working verbs tied to the subject *prize* without an *and* or other conjunction linking those verbs: *the top prize was for … would be awarded …* The correct answer fixes this issue by keeping just one form as a complete verb (*would be*), while turning the other into an infinitive (*to be awarded*).

Just placing a comma between *was for …* and *would be awarded …*, as in choice (B), is not enough to correct the mistake. Choice (D) goes too far with the surgery, however, removing all working verbs from the sentence, which is thus reduced to a fragment. The correct answer is (C).

42.   **(H)**   As Ms. Windham explained, the top prize would be for … Another prize would go to the pod that took … The "Disaster Miracle" trophy would be for the capsule …

Usage/Mechanics   Sentence Structure   Verb Tense & Forms

The nearby verbs describing the various prizes are all in the conditional tense (*would go*), which here indicates what was going to happen. This use is known as "future in the past": *Today he says he will go to the store. Yesterday he said he would go to the store.* In the first sentence, *will go* is normal future tense; moving present tense *says* to past tense *said* also brings the *will go* into conditional *would go.* The same pattern occurs in the passage, so the verb should be *would go.*

The original version *had went* is always wrong: *had* should be followed by *gone* (past participle), not *went* (past tense). Present tense *goes* and past perfect *had gone* are correct in form but wrong in context. The correct answer is (H).

43. **(B)** Best leads from preceding paragraph: The "Disaster Miracle" trophy would be for the capsule … <u>On the day of the drop, the weather was gorgeous.</u> My lab partner and I had decorated our "Egg-splorer" module like a lunar lander, which glinted in the bright sun. On impact it shattered beautifully …

Rhetorical Skills   Organization   Opening/Closing Content

It is helpful to think about the logical sequence of events here, with the assistance of verb tense. The prior paragraph ends with a description of what the "Disaster Miracle" trophy *would be* for. That is, the point in time of the discussion is still far back in time, when *Ms. Windham explained* what the prizes would be. The correct answer leaps forward to the *day of the drop,* when *the weather was gorgeous.* The next sentence dips back in time to describe how the team *had decorated* the module (past perfect), then returns to the contest itself, continuing the narrative with regular past tense: *glinted in the bright sun* and *shattered beautifully.* Perhaps ironically, the best transition here is a jump from the prior paragraph all the way to the contest, providing the right setting for the rest of the final paragraph.

The original version (*Before this class, I had never operated power tools*) might be appropriate if the rest of the paragraph focused on the construction of the egg-drop module, emphasizing how much those tools were needed and what the narrator learned as a result. However, the paragraph only describes the decoration before quickly moving to the day of the contest itself and the outcome. Notice that the detail *glinted in the bright sun* is left hanging if the stage is not clearly set for the day of the contest. The other wrong answers share similar flaws, creating disjointed narrative flows. The correct answer is (B).

44. **(F)** … and our egg survived. <u>Years later,</u> my old partner and I still take turns with our trophy.

Rhetorical Skills   Organization   Transitions

As in the previous problem, verb tense is helpful here to decode the timeline. The narrative of the contest ends in the past tense: *our egg survived.* The new sentence, however, is in present tense: *still take turns.* Therefore, the transition must bring the reader forward swiftly to the present day. *Years later* does the trick.

Choice (G), *Afterwards,* would move the narration forward but keep it in the past (you expect a post-contest celebration or some other activity directly after the contest). Choice (H), *In the meantime,* would in fact keep the narration at the same time as the prior action, and Choice (J), *So far,* meaning "up to this point in time, probably against the odds," is redundant with *still.* Moreover, *so far* carries an implication that the continued action is unexpected or even a struggle ("I robbed a bank. *So far,* I have not been caught."). This implication is not desirable here. The correct answer is (F).

45. **(B)** Should the writer add this sentence? Yes, because it underscores the impact Ms. Windham has had on the narrator.

Rhetorical Skills   Writing Strategy   Additions

7

The focus of the essay is Ms. Windham, who evidently impressed the narrator in a positive way. The proposed addition provides an appropriate capstone for the passage by indicating that this impact continues to the present day (and perhaps into the future). The correct answer makes this point.

The reason that the addition is appropriate is not that it sheds light on the narrator's future plans, which by themselves are only illustrative of Ms. Windham's influence on the narrator. It is unimportant that the sentence does not specify the future plans more precisely, or that it omits mention of other beneficial influences. The spotlight of the text is really on Ms. Windham, and the correct answer explains why the addition works. The correct answer is (B).

Passage 4 Solutions

46. **(F)** The thought of seeing flashes in a field on a summer <u>night may awaken nostalgia</u> in city dwellers …

Usage/Mechanics   Punctuation   Commas

No commas should be placed anywhere in the underlined portion. The subject phrase is *The thought of seeing flashing in a field on a summer night*. The verb is *may awaken* and the object of that verb is *nostalgia*. Commas do not belong between the subject and the verb, or between the verb and its object. The correct answer is (F).

47. **(B)** Not acceptable placement: Unfortunately, <u>only</u> the nostalgia is not felt by urbanites.

Usage/Mechanics   Sentence Structure   Modifier Placement

The adverb *only* needs to go near or within the phrase *by urbanites*, indicating that this nostalgia is felt by more people than just the urbanites. The original position (*not felt only by urbanites*) and the positions described by choices (C) and (D), namely *not felt by only urbanites* and *not felt by urbanites only*, all convey this meaning. However, *only the nostalgia was not felt …* means that every other emotion besides nostalgia was in fact felt. That reading makes little sense. The correct answer is (B).

48. **(G)** Not acceptable alternative: Firefly populations have been declining <u>worldwide, unless measures are</u> taken, these insects could disappear.

Usage/Mechanics   Sentence Structure   Whole Sentences

The unacceptable variation attempts to connect the two sentences with just a comma. This kind of comma splice is illegal. The first independent clause is *Firefly populations have been declining worldwide;* the second independent clause is *these insects could disappear.* That second clause is preceded by a dependent clause, expressed either as *unless measures are taken* or as *if measures are not taken* (these clauses are synonymous). You can connect these two sentences with a comma and an *and*, as in the original version, or with a semicolon. You can even keep the sentences separate. You cannot, however, simply join the sentences with a comma. The correct answer is (G).

49. **(D)** More than 2,000 species of firefly are known … That is, these kinds <u>do not emit</u> the "cold light" for which fireflies are famous.

Usage/Mechanics   Sentence Structure   Verb Tense & Voice

The verbs near the underlined portion—*are known, are (famous)*—are all in the present tense. This tense is appropriate, as it is here, for expressing general facts (e.g., about the behavior of insects). Thus, *do not emit* is the correct choice. As written, *have not been emitting* (the present perfect tense, with the progressive *-ing* form) implies wrongly that these insects have not been emitting light for some reason lately, but that they normally do. *Were not emitting* (the past progressive tense), likewise turns the action into a specific event, not a general truth. The passive voice *are not emitted* clashes with the surrounding words: *these kinds are not emitted the "cold light,"* which is not sensible English. The correct answer is (D).

50.   **(J)**   In most nocturnal species, though, an intricate chain of chemical reactions <u>results in</u> a nearly complete conversion …

Rhetorical Skills   Style   Concision

The incorrect answers are all redundant in various ways. Instead of *leads to the result of,* you would just put *leads to* or *results in*. Similarly, *causes as its effect* would be trimmed to *causes*. Since the sentence begins with *In most nocturnal species,* you should not also put *in those species* right next to the verb. The correct answer does all the work you need done: *results in*. The correct answer is (J).

51.   **(C)**   Should the addition be made? No, because the sentence distracts from the logical flow of other sentences nearby.

Rhetorical Skills   Writing Strategy   Additions

The proposed addition reads *The reactions involve a class of enzymes called luciferases, from the Latin term for "light-carrier."* To see whether this sentence deserves a place in the essay, check the nearby sentences. Before the proposed insertion point, the text describes the *nearly complete conversion of energy to light, with little wasted heat* that fireflies are able to accomplish. After the proposed insertion point, the contrast with human sources of light (*incandescent, fluorescent,* etc.) is drawn clearly with the transition *In contrast*: that is, these sources *release a great deal of heat*. These two sentences need to be kept right next to each other.

The proposed addition is just an extra detail about the chemical reactions; the name of some enzymes involved is unimportant. You should not break the sequence of thinking as it is already expressed in the passage. The correct answer is (C).

52.   **(J)**   … if you have ever touched a glowing … bulb, <u>you know that</u> these invented light sources release … heat.

Rhetorical Skills   Style   Concision

The wrong answers each contain redundancy around the idea of knowing or realizing something. *It becomes quite apparent as you realize* does not need both the *becomes apparent* clause and the *realize* clause. Likewise, *you well know the evident truth that* and *as you well know, it's rather obvious* can each be drastically shortened to the tight, concise version *you know that*. There's no reason to linger over this part of the sentence. The correct answer is (J).

53.   **(D)**   Scientists have been studying <u>ways to duplicate practically</u> the cold light of fireflies …

Usage/Mechanics   Punctuation   Commas

No comma belongs between *ways* and *to duplicate*, since the former is defined by the latter: *I know a way to get to Cleveland*. Perhaps the tougher case is whether to put a comma or commas near the word *practically*, which seems slightly awkward where it is. The reason it does is that usually in English, you place an adverb after the object of a verb, not before it. For instance, you would typically say *I ate the hamburger quickly,* not *I ate quickly the hamburger.* However, it's acceptable to put the adverb first if the object is long (*the cold light of fireflies*), and in any event, you don't have the choice to move the adverb. Despite its unusual position between the verb and its object, the adverb should be free from commas. Some might argue for surrounding it on both sides by commas for emphasis, but you don't have that option either; what you should absolutely avoid doing is placing a comma on just one side of the adverb. The correct answer is (D).

54.　**(F)**　Other animals and plants … use colorful markings for the same purpose: to announce <u>they're</u> poisonous or just distasteful.

Usage/Mechanics　　　　　　Grammar & Usage　　　　　Pronoun Forms

The correct form here, *they're,* means *they are* (i.e., these *other animals and plants are poisonous*). The forms that sound like the correct answer, *their* and *there,* are each inappropriate: *their* would have to be followed by a noun possessed by these animals and plants, and *there* means *in that place,* which is nonsensical if inserted. *There's,* meaning *there is,* also would require a noun (e.g., *there's poison*). The correct answer is (F).

55.　**(B)**　<u>After living for 1 to 2 years, firefly larvae transform into adults that</u> fly and mate, but generally do not eat.

Usage/Mechanics　　　　　　Sentence Structure　　　　　Modifier Placement

In the original sentence, the opening modifier *Living for 1 to 2 years* illogically modifies the noun *transformation*; instead, it should modify *firefly larvae,* as in the correct answer. Choice (C) awkwardly strings together two leading modifiers, leaving the situation unclear: does *after living for 1 to 2 years* modify *larvae* or *adults*? Logically, it should really modify *larvae,* but by position, it modifies the subject *adults.* Finally, in choice (D), the verbs *fly and mate* have as their subject *Firefly larvae,* supposedly in parallel with *are transformed.* This list, however, doesn't make much sense. It is the adults that *fly and mate,* not the larvae. Put these verbs into a modifier with *that* and attach this modifier to *adults.* The correct answer is (B).

56.　**(H)**　Most relevant: During their few weeks before death, adult fireflies glimmer to find mates, <u>signaling to each other in unique patterns.</u> The females of one genus, however, can mimic the specific sequences of other species.

Rhetorical Skills　　　　　　Writing Strategy　　　　　Choice of Content

The key to this problem is in the following sentence, which tells you that some insects, *however, can mimic the specific sequences of other species.* The *however* must be indicating a contrast with the prior point; thus, that prior point must be something to the effect that each species has its own specific sequence. The correct answer describes *unique patterns,* which in this context is synonymous with the *specific sequences* belonging to various kinds of fireflies. The wrong answers provide interesting tidbits but fail to contrast well with the following sentence. The correct answer is (H).

57.　**(A)**　… as forests are cut down and <u>marshes drained.</u>

Usage/Mechanics　　　　　　Grammar & Usage　　　　　Parallelism

The existing sentence has the parallelism right: *forests are cut down and marshes [are] drained.* Notice that you do not need to repeat the *are* in the second clause. The other choices put the second thought into a form that doesn't match *forests are cut down,* in which the verb is present tense, passive voice. The correct answer is (A).

58.   **(H)** Even when woods and streams are preserved, the encroachment of human civilization … takes a toll. <u>A car's headlights can disorient</u> fireflies …

Usage/Mechanics   Grammar & Usage   Subject–Verb Agreement

The original version has a mismatch between plural *headlights* as the subject and the singular verb *disorients.* The corrected version uses *can disorient,* which works with either singular or plural subjects. Choice (G) uses an illogical verb tense (the present perfect *have disoriented*), which here implies that a particular car's headlights have had this disorienting effect at some point in the past. Nearby verbs properly keep the action in the present tense, which is suitable for general facts. Finally, choice (J), by using the *-ing* form *disorienting,* robs the sentence of its only complete verb and turns it into a fragment. The correct answer is (H).

59.   **(B)** … allowing summer nights again to be <u>lit</u> solely by the moon …

Usage/Mechanics   Punctuation   Commas (also Colons & Semicolons)

The past participle *lit* should not be followed by any punctuation at all. The passive-voice phrase *to be lit solely by the moon* requires no commas, colons, or semicolons anywhere. Each part of the phrase is necessary, so no pauses should be taken. The correct answer is (B).

60.   **(H)** This sentence would most logically be placed after the last sentence in Paragraph 3.

Rhetorical Skills   Organization   Sentence Order

The sentence in question may be mysterious: *When hopeful males arrive, the females devour them.* Which females is this sentence referring to? The use of the word *the* before *females* means "you know which females I mean," so you should look for a paragraph that currently ends with a discussion of the behavior of some female fireflies. Paragraph 3 is that paragraph, ending *The females of one genus, however, can mimic the specific sequences of other species.* Placed after this sentence, the proposed addition now makes sense. When these females mimic the flash sequences of other species, hopeful males of those species arrive, only to be devoured. The correct answer is (H).

Passage 5 Solutions

61.   **(D)** Although composers as <u>respected</u> as Ralph Vaughan Williams …

Rhetorical Skills   Style   Concision

The words *respected, esteemed,* and *admired* hardly differ at all in meaning. To avoid redundancy, use just one of the three. The correct answer is (D).

62. **(G)** If the writer were to delete the sentence, the paragraph would primarily lose a comparison reinforcing the point of the prior sentence.

Rhetorical Skills   Writing Strategy   Deletions

The sentence on the chopping block is *Only the kazoo is less appreciated*. The implied remainder of the comparison is *than the harmonica*. This comparison between the harmonica and the kazoo is another way of saying that the harmonica *is still not seen as serious in classical-music circles*. The reason the writer makes the point again (though in a different and more dramatic way) is to emphasize it.

The sentence does none of the things in the wrong answer choices. It does not defend the kazoo as a serious instrument—in fact, it puts the kazoo forward as an even less respected instrument. The sentence does not assess *the general strength of music appreciation* (whatever that might mean), nor does it demand that the classical music world *perform a re-evaluation* (either of the kazoo or of the harmonica). The correct answer is (G).

63. **(C)** … the harmonica is still not seen as serious in classical-music circles. Only the kazoo is less appreciated. [New paragraph] <u>Sadly,</u> snobbery is probably at work. A cheap instrument … may not be exclusive enough for social climbers.

Rhetorical Skills   Organization   Transitions

Of the available transitions, only *Sadly* works in context. The original option (*On the other hand*) indicates a contrast between what comes before and what comes after the transition. However, the sentence *snobbery is probably at work* is a possible explanation for the earlier point (i.e., that the harmonica is regarded with contempt). So a contrast is inappropriate. Choice (B), *Otherwise,* means "in other circumstances" and indicates an alternative scenario. This transition also doesn't work. Finally, choice (D), *Therefore,* makes too strong of a claim, suggesting that snobbery explanation must follow from the lack of appreciation. However, the writer uses softening language (*probably, may not be*), implying that the case is not this strong. Furthermore, the paragraph moves on from this topic, but more support would be demanded to prove the *Therefore* relationship.

The correct answer, *Sadly,* simply makes a comment on the situation, calling it sad. This answer is impossible to contradict. The correct answer is (C).

64. **(G)** A pocket tool for <u>tunes,</u> the harmonica has provided …

Usage/Mechanics   Punctuation   Commas

The subject of the sentence is *the harmonica* and its verb is *has provided*. The subject is preceded by a leading modifier: *A pocket tool for tunes*. This appositive phrase should be separated from the subject by a comma. No other punctuation is a suitable replacement for that comma. The correct answer is (G).

65. **(D)** … the harmonica has provided a cornerstone to American popular music, influencing styles from folk and blues to jazz and rock & roll. [Omit the underlined portion.]

Rhetorical Skills   Writing Strategy   Choice of Content

MANHATTAN
PREP

Every sentence needs a reason to be in the passage and should be clearly related to its neighbors. The original sentence (*Vibrating reeds produce the sound of harmonicas*) is the only sentence in the whole passage about the physics of harmonicas. Tacked onto the end of this paragraph (and failing to connect to the next), this sentence is completely out of place. The potential replacements suffer from the same lack of connection to the rest of the passage. The best option available to you is to cut the underlined portion entirely. The correct answer is (D).

66.   **(F)** ... is not where the harmonica was born, but it has been the <u>instrument's spiritual home</u> for over 150 years ...

Usage/Mechanics   Punctuation   Apostrophes and Commas

The possessive forms of the word *instrument* are *instrument's* (singular) and *instruments'* (plural). Since the sentence uses the singular form *harmonica*, you should continue with singular.

In addition, there should be no comma after the word *home*. The clause has the structure *It has been X for a period of time*. The *for* phrase is necessary, so it should not be separated by a comma. The correct answer is (F).

67.   **(B)** The company <u>that</u> bears his name is still ...

Usage/Mechanics   Grammar & Usage   Modifier Forms

The noun *company* is a thing, not a person, so the modifier form should be *that*, not *who*. The full subordinate clause is *that bears his name*. The word *this* cannot be used to introduce such a clause. *Whose* can introduce a subordinate clause, but it must be followed by a noun (e.g., "the company *whose name* is Hohner is still ..."). By the way, for future reference, note the difference: *who* must refer only to people, but *whose* can refer to any kind of noun. The correct answer is (B).

68.   **(H)** Most clearly communicates the positive feelings of the festival attendees: ... draws <u>thousands of eager fans</u> to Trossingen ...

Rhetorical Skills   Writing Strategy   Choice of Content

The words *eager fans* declare that these attendees enthusiastically like harmonica music. Thus, this choice conveys the positive feelings of the attendees.

The alternatives are neutral, simply listing numbers (*thousands*) and other qualities (*different ages, residents of various countries*) that do not indicate feelings one way or the other. The correct answer is (H).

69.   **(A)** If the writer were to make this deletion, the sentence would primarily lose a sense of the business urgency behind Hohner's action.

Rhetorical Skills   Writing Strategy   Deletions

The phrase in question (*Spotting an opportunity faster than competitors*) raises the "business urgency" around Hohner's decision to ship harmonicas to the United States. The reader is told about *competitors* here; Hohner spotted the opportunity faster than they did, essentially winning the competition. Without this phrase, the sentence loses the sense that Hohner had to act quickly.

If the phrase is deleted, however, the sentence does not lose any "evaluation of Hohner's ability to meet commitments," as in choice (B). This phrase does not provide such an evaluation; in fact, no part of the text does so. The deletion would not cause the sentence to lose "a formal and measured tone," either—the sentence does not shift in formality one way or the other. Likewise, there is no "element of surprise" in the sentence, either way. The correct answer is (A).

70.   **(J)**   The country … may have seemed [omitted] an unlikely market …

Usage/Mechanics   Grammar & Usage   Idioms

After the verb *seem*, only certain options are possible before a noun:

> "The suggestion seems *like* a good idea."
> "The suggestion seems *to be* a good idea."
> "The suggestion seems a good idea."

The third option (inserting nothing at all after *seem*) is a little more unusual than the first two, but it's perfectly correct and it's the only one available to you. *Seems as, seems to,* and *seems in* are all incorrect idiomatically. The correct answer is (J).

71.   **(A)**   Influential African-American blues players pioneered the use of "crossharp" scales …

Rhetorical Skills   Style   Word Choice

The correct verb in context is *pioneer*, meaning "break new ground with, be the first to do something." The alternatives do not fit. The musicians did not *prepare* the use of these scales; they were the first to use these scales. *Colonize* means "establish a colony"; the object must be the place where the colony is established, so *colonize the use* makes little sense. Finally, *speculate* means "make guesses about" or "gamble, invest in a risky venture." Neither meaning is suitable. The correct answer is (A).

72.   **(H)**   … the instrument became unforgettably linked with musicians as distinct … as Stevie Wonder and Bob Dylan.

Usage/Mechanics   Sentence Structure   Whole Sentences

The original version (*when*) leaves the verb form *linked* hanging. The instrument became linked with or to what? Asking the question reveals the right preposition among the choices: *with*. The instrument became linked *with* these musicians. *When* would also require a full clause after it—that is, there would need to be a verb after *musicians* somewhere. The correct answer is (H).

73.   **(B)**   … the instrument became unforgettably linked with musicians as distinct and exceptional as Stevie Wonder and Bob Dylan.

Rhetorical Skills   Style   Word Choice

Throughout the essay, the writer takes a positive stance toward the harmonica. Thus, when the writer describes musicians with whom the harmonica *became unforgettably linked*, the description is going to be positive, not negative. The wrong choices (*irregular, peculiar,* and *disqualified*) all have negative meanings when applied to people. Only *exceptional* has a positive meaning, namely "remarkable, extraordinary, one of a kind." The correct answer is (B).

74.   **(J)**   Even the first song performed live in space was played on a harmonica and some bells, smuggled aboard the Gemini Six mission. <u>This</u> lowly instrument was thus …

Usage/Mechanics   Grammar & Usage   Pronoun Forms

The best option among those available is *This*, pointing back to the harmonica (which has been the subject of the entire essay). The possessive pronouns *Its* and *Their* are both inappropriate, because they do not have possible nouns to refer back to: whose lowly instrument would the harmonica be? The same question dooms the other wrong choice *One's*. The simplest option is also the correct one: *This.* The correct answer is (J).

75.   **(C)**   This lowly instrument was thus literally <u>elevated</u> above its classical cousins.

Rhetorical Skills   Style   Word Choice

The only choice that can refer to an actual, literal increase in elevation is *elevate*, meaning "raise, lift." The verb *heighten* can only be used metaphorically ("my sense of smell was heightened.") Note that the verb *increase* doesn't work either: the harmonica itself can't increase. The harmonica's *height* has to increase. Finally, saying that the harmonica was *upgraded* would mean that it was improved in some way. Rather, the writer means to say here that the "lowly" harmonica was, in a real sense, lifted above other instruments into outer space. The correct answer is (C).

Chapter *of* 8

5lb. Book of ACT® Practice Problems

English:
Passage Set 4

In This Chapter...

Set 4 Passages & Solutions

Chapter 8
English: Passage Set 4

The English problems in this chapter are distributed across five passages, just as they will be on the ACT itself. Every topic is up for grabs, so expect a little of everything. The answer key and the solutions classify the problems for you, so you can pinpoint strengths and weaknesses.

How should you use this chapter? Here are some recommendations, according to the level you've reached in ACT English.

1. Fundamentals. If you haven't done any topical work yet, consider working in Chapters 3 and 4 first. Otherwise, do a passage or two untimed to begin with. As you become more comfortable, put the clock on. In all cases, review the solutions closely, and articulate what you've learned. Redo problems as necessary.

2. Fixes. Do one passage at a time under timed conditions. Examine the results, learn your lessons, then test yourself with more passages at once.

3. Tweaks. Confirm your mastery by doing a few passages at once under timed conditions. A full set of five is the ultimate goal. Aim to improve the speed and ease of your solution process.

Good luck on the problems!

PASSAGE 1

"The" Los Angeles Freeway

[1]

When my family moved from New York City
to Los Angeles, I expected many changes in my
surroundings, and my expectations matched reality.

Possibly, the weather was different; in fact, it appeared
that my new home actually lacked weather. At school,

I was presented to earthquake drills and a much bigger
sky in the windows. The surface roads running straight

for miles made the grid of Manhattan, seem minuscule.

[2]

One of the differences that struck me most,
however, was a linguistic quirk, an oddity in the use

of language involving the way to refer to roadways.
In New York, you would call them expressways or
parkways. Elsewhere on the East Coast, you might
hear "highway," while some roads are designated

as turnpikes. In Los Angeles however, people say
"freeway," a weird yet sensible term, because there are
no tolls.

1. **A.** NO CHANGE
    B. on
    C. of
    D. for

2. **F.** NO CHANGE
    G. Certainly,
    H. Therefore,
    J. Furthermore,

3. **A.** NO CHANGE
    B. got friendly with
    C. was down with
    D. was introduced to

4. **F.** NO CHANGE
    G. grid of Manhattan
    H. grid, of Manhattan
    J. grid, of Manhattan,

5. **A.** NO CHANGE
    B. quirk in how people oddly talk about certain things
    C. quirk, which may or may not be a quirk to some,
    D. quirk

6. Given that all of the choices are true, which one would MOST specifically define the kinds of roads to which the writer is referring?
    F. NO CHANGE
    G. roadways: namely, paved routes built for cars.
    H. fast roadways with exits but no stoplights.
    J. roadways, on which society depends so much.

7. **A.** NO CHANGE
    B. In Los Angeles, however, people
    C. In Los Angeles, however people,
    D. In Los Angeles however people

[3]

Even stranger to me than the word "freeway"
is the use of the word "the." At lunch one day, a new
friend of mine describing how to get to the Santa
Monica Pier said, "You take the 405 to the 10."
I couldn't help interrupting her. "*The* 405?" Everywhere

else, in the country so it seems, when you refer to a

highway by number, you say just its number. Southern
Californians, on the other hand, add the word "the"
in front. Perhaps this use of the definite article reflects
the idea that freeways are vast living beings, even
eccentric deities, to Angelenos. The coiling, multi-lane
serpent of "the" 405 looms in L.A.'s collective psyche,
since residents have little alternative to deal with this
freeway's whims.

[4]

Of course, the freeways are not literally gods to
residents of Los Angeles, any more than expressways
are to New Yorkers. Both sets of overcrowded highways

8. Given that all of the choices are true, which one
would MOST effectively introduce the main idea of
this paragraph?
   F. NO CHANGE
   G. When I arrived in L.A., I set about making
      friends as soon as I could.
   H. In our new city, my family and I adjusted to
      the need to drive more often.
   J. Freeways in L.A. have both names and num-
      bers, which are used interchangeably.

9. A. NO CHANGE
   B. else in the country, so it seems,
   C. else, in the country so it seems
   D. else in the country so it seems,

10. F. NO CHANGE
    G. it's
    H. ones
    J. their

11. A. NO CHANGE
    B. which
    C. in which
    D. where

12. F. NO CHANGE
    G. for dealing
    H. to dealing
    J. of dealing

13. Which choice would MOST effectively open this
paragraph?
    A. NO CHANGE
    B. It must be admitted that highways around the
       world all share certain characteristics, both
       positive and negative.
    C. All that said, the similarities between express-
       ways in New York and freeways in Los Angeles
       outnumber the differences.
    D. After a year of living—and driving—in Los
       Angeles, I feel more at home than I expected,
       having been born and raised in New York.

8

MANHATTAN
PREP   277

demand real driving skills. On either coast, <u>by knowing</u>
¹⁴
how to take surface roads past the next congested
stretch or how to slip ahead in the exit lane without
actually exiting is crucial. I've committed to mastering
"the" L.A. freeway before I graduate from high school.

14. **F.** NO CHANGE
    G. when knowing
    H. if you know
    J. knowing

Question 15 asks about the preceding passage as a whole.

---

15. Suppose the writer's goal had been to write a brief persuasive essay urging the use of Los Angeles terminology for roadways. Would this essay fulfill that goal?

    A. Yes, because the narrator has evidently adopted such terminology in his or her own writing.
    B. Yes, because the narrator makes a comparison of regional terms and draws a clear conclusion.
    C. No, because the narrator rejects the personal use of this terminology in his or her new city.
    D. No, because the narrator makes no recommendations about which way to refer to roadways.

MANHATTAN
PREP

PASSAGE 2

Rear Admiral Grace Hopper

[1]

I once saw Grace Hopper speak at a science summer camp. This <u>diminutive, elderly person talked on</u> the stage in a formal military uniform; her rank in the Navy was Commodore, later renamed Rear Admiral. At one point, she passed out foot-long lengths of wire. Once they were fully distributed, she clarified what they <u>represented the distance</u> light travels in a nanosecond, or one billionth of a second.

[2]

Nothing can move faster than light in a <u>vacuum, so</u> electrons in a wire can at best move a fraction of a foot in a nanosecond. As Hopper explained, this speed limit forces modern computers, which perform billions of operations a second, to be <u>physical small.</u> Hopper certainly had the authority to speak on this matter. ☐20 She played a formative role in the development of computer science.

[3]

Intellectually curious from an early age, Hopper studied mathematics at Vassar College and Yale University. She obtained a Ph.D. in <u>1934, as she taught</u> at Vassar. During World War II, she joined the Navy,

16. Given that all the choices are true, which one would MOST logically and effectively emphasize Hopper's dynamism?
F. NO CHANGE
G. short, powerful woman commanded
H. older naval officer appeared on
J. woman of limited stature came onto

17. A. NO CHANGE
B. represented; the distance
C. represented, the distance:
D. represented: the distance

18. F. NO CHANGE
G. vacuum, this means that
H. vacuum, because of this,
J. vacuum,

19. A. NO CHANGE
B. physical and small.
C. physically, small.
D. physically small.

20. If the writer were to delete the preceding sentence, the essay would primarily lose:
F. a transition between the camp scene and a statement of Hopper's impact.
G. a reason why the narrator was attending the summer camp.
H. a contrast between Hopper's appearance and her effect on society at large.
J. nothing at all; this sentence is irrelevant to the essay.

21. Which of the following alternatives to the underlined portion would NOT be acceptable?
A. 1934 while teaching
B. 1934 and at the same time taught
C. 1934, teaching simultaneously
D. 1934, taught at the same time

although with difficulty: she weighed less than the
<u>   </u>
                22
standard minimum. Assigned to work on Harvard

University's gigantic Mark I computer, Hopper famously

once "debugged" the <u>computer by removing a moth,</u>
                                    23
<u>and taping it</u> into a notebook. The Mark I ran many
    23
critical computations for the war effort, including ones

related to building the first atomic bomb.

[4]

<u>After the war,</u> Hopper worked at a variety of
            24
corporations, including Remington Rand, where she

wrote the <u>worlds</u> first compiler. Compilers are essential
          25
computer programs that take instructions intelligible to

humans <u>and translate</u> them into the elemental code that
        26
computers can understand. All current programming

depends on Hopper's work.

[5]

<u>Because she also served</u> in the Naval Reserve for
              27
decades, and she was called out of retirement twice.

A motivational speaker and educator, Hopper gave

thousands of <u>them</u> her nanosecond wires. My computer
            28
has <u>it</u> proudly fastened to it.
    29

---

22. Which of the following alternatives to the under-
    lined portion would be LEAST acceptable?
    F. difficulty—she
    G. difficulty; she
    H. difficulty, she
    J. difficulty, because she

23. A. NO CHANGE
    B. computer by removing a moth and taping it
    C. computer by removing a moth and, taping it
    D. computer, by removing a moth and taping it,

24. Which choice MOST effectively leads into the new
    subject of this paragraph?
    F. NO CHANGE
    G. A versatile scientist,
    H. After a divorce,
    J. OMIT the underlined portion.

25. A. NO CHANGE
    B. world's
    C. worlds'
    D. worlds's

26. F. NO CHANGE
    G. that translate
    H. who translate
    J. translate

27. A. NO CHANGE
    B. Due to the additional fact that she served
    C. She also served
    D. Also serving

28. F. NO CHANGE
    G. those
    H. people
    J. OMIT the underlined portion.

29. A. NO CHANGE
    B. them
    C. theirs
    D. mine

MANHATTAN
PREP

Question 30 asks about the preceding passage as a whole.

---

30. Suppose the writer's goal had been to write an essay describing the achievements and influence of a pioneering scientist. Would this essay fulfill that goal?

  F. Yes, because it offers a detailed account of Hopper's work at Harvard during World War II.

  G. Yes, because it outlines Hopper's career as both a groundbreaking programmer and a teacher.

  H. No, because it provides evidence only of Hopper's personal impact on the narrator.

  J. No, because it focuses primarily on the technical aspects of Hopper's accomplishments.

8

PASSAGE 3

Inventing an Alphabet

[1]

The creation of writing <u>thought to be</u> one of the
                                31
leading achievements of our species. Without writing,

it would be almost impossible to store and retrieve

<u>our societies knowledge</u> in sufficient quantities. In 1821,
           32

recognizing the usefulness of writing, <u>in a singlehanded
                                                    33
achievement possibly unique in history, the Cherokee
                          33
language had an alphabet invented for it by Sequoyah, a
                          33
Cherokee smith.</u>
         33

[2]

Writing exists in many forms. Symbols described

as "logographic" <u>displayed</u> meaning not directly linked
                       34
to sound: consider numerals or emoticons such as the

smiley face :-). <u>At the other extreme,</u> alphabetic symbols
                          35
indicate pronunciation only. For instance, the letters "g"

and "o," which don't <u>signify, anything, by themselves</u>
                              36
must be combined to form the meaningful word "go."
Some alphabets are syllabic—that is, each character has

31. A. NO CHANGE
   B. thinks it to be
   C. is thought to be
   D. thought that it was

32. F. NO CHANGE
   G. our society knowledge
   H. our society's knowledge
   J. our knowledge of society

33. A. NO CHANGE
   B. the Cherokee smith Sequoyah invented an
       alphabet for his language, a singlehanded
       achievement that may be unique in history.
   C. Sequoyah, a Cherokee smith who made a
       singlehanded achievement, invented for his
       language an alphabet that is possibly unique in
       history.
   D. the singlehanded achievement of Sequoyah, a
       Cherokee smith, inventing an alphabet for his
       language may be unique in history.

34. F. NO CHANGE
   G. display
   H. had displayed
   J. were displaying

35. A. NO CHANGE
   B. In the same fashion,
   C. As a further example,
   D. Broadly speaking,

36. F. NO CHANGE
   G. signify anything, by themselves
   H. signify, anything by themselves,
   J. signify anything by themselves,

a vowel and a consonant or two. This kind of alphabet

is what Sequoyah <u>invented</u> for the Cherokee language.
                  37

[3]

Little is known for certain about Sequoyah's early

<u>life;</u> stories of his upbringing in Tennessee conflict. It
 38

is largely agreed, though, that he had a leg <u>disability,</u>
                                                      39
<u>this problem</u> may have led him to the forge for work.
 39
As a successful silversmith, he had customers of various

backgrounds and <u>likely heard a mix of languages</u>
                                          40
<u>besides Cherokee.</u> Inspired, he decided to come up with
 40
a writing system for his own language.

[4]

At first, he tried to represent <u>each word with</u>
                                          41
<u>a different symbol.</u> However, logographic systems,
 41
such as Chinese, contain thousands of characters

and require many years to <u>master to the point of true</u>
                                          42
<u>fluency.</u> Finally abandoning this approach, he devised
 42
a syllabic alphabet with only 86 characters. The ability

37. Three of these choices indicate that Sequoyah's work
    on the Cherokee writing system was original. Which
    choice does NOT do so?
    A. NO CHANGE
    B. designed
    C. replicated
    D. contrived

38. Which of the alternatives to the underlined portion
    would be LEAST acceptable?
    F. life, as
    G. life, but
    H. life, so
    J. life, since

39. A. NO CHANGE
    B. disability, it is possible that it
    C. disability that
    D. disability, it

40. Given that all the choices are true, which one pro-
    vides the MOST relevant information with regard to
    the conclusion of the paragraph?
    F. NO CHANGE
    G. was considered a skilled craftsman in his field.
    H. used silver coins brought to him by traders to
       make jewelry.
    J. undoubtedly encountered many "talking
       leaves," or written pages, in books he saw.

41. A. NO CHANGE
    B. each word with a different symbol, distinct
       from any other.
    C. words or ideas as individual wholes, each with
       its own sign or icon.
    D. words.

42. F. NO CHANGE
    G. master, such that one is in full command.
    H. master beyond a beginner's level of control.
    J. master.

8

of his <u>daughter, who was his first student,</u> to read aloud
43
convinced Cherokee leaders to give tentative support

to his syllabary. In just a few years, literacy among the

Cherokee soared. In fact, since the Cherokee <u>alphabet,</u>
                                               44
<u>being</u> closely suited to the language, Cherokee is easier
  44

to learn to read than English. ☐45

43. A. NO CHANGE
   B. daughter, which
   C. daughter whom
   D. daughter, she who

44. F. NO CHANGE
   G. alphabet is
   H. alphabet having been
   J. alphabet,

45. Which of the following true sentences, if inserted
     here, would BEST conclude the essay?

   A. After all, English spelling, which is notoriously
        opaque, was not masterminded by one person.
   B. At the same time, English is more widely spoken,
        not only in the U.S. but around the world.
   C. A few symbols, such as D and W, are shared by
        the languages but have different sounds.
   D. If you drive through the town of Cherokee,
        North Carolina, you'll see bilingual signs.

8

PASSAGE 4

The Uses of Sound

[1]

[1] What can sound be used to do? [2] The answer seems <u>evident to</u> communicate. [3] From spoken words
₄₆
and wordless shouts to mechanical beeps and police

sirens, our society <u>is</u> flooded with sounds that have
₄₇
meaning, which, to be fair, may not always be explicit.
[4] What does a saxophone solo exactly mean? [5]
Indeed, in more than one religion, the universe begins
with a hum or an uttered command—perhaps the
most profound message of all. [6] Regardless, we
feel that with the physical vibrations <u>are transmitted</u>
₄₈

something deep. 49

[2]

<u>In the modern world, sound has many uses</u>
₅₀
<u>besides communication.</u> Underwater sonar, for instance,
₅₀
is not just a way for submarines to talk; it allows us to
map the ocean floor. Likewise, ultrasound scans probe the

health of a growing fetus with <u>little risk of harm.</u> In this
₅₁

46. F. NO CHANGE
   G. evident in order to
   H. evident; to
   J. evident: to

47. A. NO CHANGE
   B. will be
   C. would be
   D. is to be

48. F. NO CHANGE
   G. is
   H. were
   J. have been

49. For the sake of logic and coherence, Sentence 6
   should be placed:
   A. where it is now.
   B. after Sentence 2.
   C. after Sentence 3.
   D. after Sentence 4.

50. Which choice MOST effectively guides the reader
   from the preceding paragraph into this new para-
   graph?
   F. NO CHANGE
   G. The formless waters in some creation tales
      conceal another use of sound.
   H. Sonar, which is based on sound rather than on
      radio waves like radar, has many applications.
   J. Sound travels much better through solids and
      liquids, such as ocean water, than through air.

51. A. NO CHANGE
   B. less risky harm.
   C. less harmful risk.
   D. little risk and even less harm.

regard, we are like our mammalian cousins who are bats.
52
We fling out a sound signal and catch it on its return; in

the process, we learn about whatever reflected the signal.

[3]

Even more exotic uses of sound have been

dreamed up. An astrophysics major, Meredith Berry,
53
and recent college graduate has founded a company whose
53

ultrasound transmitters recharge wireless devices. 54

Having demonstrated that the technology is viable,

she has attracted several prominent investors who are
55
known to back companies financially and plans to sell
55
consumer products soon.

[4]

On a grimmer note, sonic cannons have been

deployed against protestors and pirates. These cannons
56
being immense loudspeakers, they have the ability to
56

52. F. NO CHANGE
   G. our mammalian cousins, which are bats.
   H. bats, our mammalian cousins.
   J. the bats that are our mammalian cousins.

53. A. NO CHANGE
   B. An astrophysics major, a recent college gradu-
       ate, and Meredith Berry,
   C. An astrophysics major and recent college
       graduate, Meredith Berry
   D. Meredith Berry: an astrophysics major and
       recent college graduate,

54. At this point, the writer wants to add a sentence
    that would further describe the company's transmit-
    ters. Which of the following sentences would BEST
    accomplish this?
   F. Her thin, unobtrusive panels send sonic energy
       through the air to phones and tablets equipped
       with receivers.
   G. At an industry trade fair, Berry displayed a
       prototype employing frequencies that could not
       be heard.
   H. Berry had the idea while pondering both entre-
       preneurial opportunities and the location of her
       phone charger.
   J. Some critics worry about inundating public
       spaces, such as restaurants, with ultrasonic
       frequencies.

55. A. NO CHANGE
   B. prominent investors who are recognized for
       putting significant funds into companies
   C. prominent, well-known investors who are
       providing monetary support
   D. prominent investors

56. F. NO CHANGE
   G. Being immense loudspeakers, the ability of
       these cannons is to
   H. Immense loudspeakers, these cannons can
   J. Immense, these cannons, which are
       loudspeakers, can

communicate a warning in words or in a beam of

deafening noise that fewer too long can withstand.
57

[5]

Perhaps the strangest use of sound is not by

humans, but by certain crustaceans. The claw of the

pistol shrimp is designed to snap together and shoots
58

a bubble at prey. Innocuous as it may seem, this

bubble collapses in a sonic shockwave that can stun

or even kill. 59 In the lab, similar bubbles generated

and crushed by ultrasound emit flashes of light in

a mysterious process. One that, according to some
60

scientists, may involve nuclear fusion.

57. A. NO CHANGE
    B. that few can long
    C. which longer can too few
    D. which can fewer longer

58. F. NO CHANGE
    G. shoot
    H. shot
    J. shooting

59. The writer is considering deleting the following phrase from the preceding sentence and adjusting the capitalization accordingly:

    Innocuous as it may seem,

If the writer were to make this deletion, the essay would primarily lose:

    A. a measured assessment of the danger of the bubble.
    B. a contrast between the appearance and the essence of the bubble.
    C. a detail that foreshadows the end of the paragraph.
    D. a restatement of the fundamental purpose that the bubble serves.

60. F. NO CHANGE
    G. process one, which
    H. process, one that,
    J. process,

8

PASSAGE 5

Edward James Olmos

[1]

Mexican-American actor, director, and producer Edward James Olmos has accomplished much on stage and screen. He has a well-known face and manner from the many television shows and movies he has been in. In addition, he has been nominated for a Tony, the loftiest prize in American theater, and for a Hollywood

equivalent the Academy Award for Best Actor. Olmos

may be most proud however, of his many honors for social activism.

[2]

Born in 1947 in East Los Angeles, Olmos gravitated in his youth to baseball and to rock music.

He was enough successful in the latter pursuit to front a band as its lead singer. After a few acting classes he took to improve his voice, he realized he was a better

61. In this paragraph, the writer intends to list several specific achievements of Olmos. Given that all of the choices are true, which one would BEST accomplish the writer's intention?
- **A.** NO CHANGE
- **B.** won both a Golden Globe and an Emmy for his iconic work on the 1980s television show "Miami Vice."
- **C.** has a quiet, yet commanding presence and thoroughly inhabits the roles he plays.
- **D.** is highly praised by critics, by fans, and by fellow actors who respect the craft with which he works.

62. F. NO CHANGE
- **G.** equivalent, the Academy Award:
- **H.** equivalent: the Academy Award
- **J.** equivalent; the Academy Award,

63. A. NO CHANGE
- **B.** proud, however
- **C.** proud, however,
- **D.** proud; however,

64. F. NO CHANGE
- **G.** was gravitationally attracted in his youth toward
- **H.** as an adolescent was attracted youthfully to
- **J.** gravitated during his childhood and youth toward

65. The BEST placement for the underlined portion would be:
- **A.** where it is now.
- **B.** after the word *successful.*
- **C.** after the word *pursuit.*
- **D.** after the word *band.*

MANHATTAN
PREP

actor than singer, <u>except</u> he changed direction. In 1978,
his break came with his starring role as the boastful
narrator in the play "Zoot Suit," which earned Olmos
his Tony nomination.

[3]

<u>Offers began to arrive more rapidly.</u> Negotiating a
rare degree of creative control for himself, Olmos joined
the cast of "Miami Vice" as Lieutenant Martin Castillo;
a few years later, he played Jaime Escalante in the film

"Stand and Deliver." This <u>adaptation, of Escalante's true
story portrays</u> his inspiring efforts to teach advanced
math in a deeply underprivileged school. Olmos was
nominated for the Academy Award for his skilled
depiction of Escalante.

[4]

A younger generation of fans has become
acquainted with Olmos in his role as Commander
William Adama in the reboot of Battlestar Galactica.
<u>Much of Olmos's time,</u> though, is now consumed
by advocacy. Various organizations that he founded

or co-founded <u>supports Latinos and also promotes</u>
Latino culture, such as the L.A. Latino International
Film Festival, Latino Literacy Now, and Latino

Public Broadcasting. <u>As for</u> a more ordinary level,

66. F. NO CHANGE
   G. so
   H. but
   J. unless

67. Given that all of the choices are true, which one
   would be the MOST effective first sentence of Para-
   graph 3?
   A. NO CHANGE
   B. Originally expected to close in two weeks, the
      play ran for well over a year.
   C. Olmos is the first Latino born in the U.S. to
      receive an Academy Award nomination for Best
      Actor.
   D. Then Olmos performed in various films and
      television movies, many of which are largely
      forgotten today.

68. F. NO CHANGE
   G. adaptation of Escalante's true story, portrays
   H. adaptation of Escalante's true story portrays,
   J. adaptation of Escalante's true story portrays

69. A. NO CHANGE
   B. The use of much of Olmos's time,
   C. The way Olmos's time is mostly spent,
   D. Olmos's current use of much of his time,

70. F. NO CHANGE
   G. supports Latinos and promotes
   H. support Latinos and promotes
   J. support Latinos and promote

71. A. NO CHANGE
   B. According to
   C. On
   D. In

his response to the 1992 Rodney King riots in Los
——————
72
Angeles by walking into the streets alone with a broom

to start sweeping up the mess. Hundreds followed,

galvanized by the example Olmos set.

72. F. NO CHANGE
    G. he responded
    H. his responding
    J. responding

Questions 73–75 ask about the preceding
passage as a whole.

---

73. This essay is written without the use of first-person
singular pronouns (*I, me, my*). If the essay were revised to include first-person opinion clauses, such as
I think and *I believe*, but otherwise left unchanged,
the essay would primarily:

    A. gain important personal perspectives on the
actor and his work.
    B. gain a more balanced tone, appropriate to the
subject of the essay.
    C. lose any sense of objectivity that it now
establishes.
    D. lose some measure of its direct, assertive style.

74. Upon reviewing this essay and realizing that some information has been left out, the writer composes the
following sentence, incorporating that information:

> In fact, he would likely consider his imprisonment
> after a protest in Puerto Rico a badge of honor.

The most logical and effective place to add this sentence would be after the last sentence of Paragraph:

    F. 1.
    G. 2.
    H. 3.
    J. 4.

75. Suppose the writer had decided to write an essay assessing the ethical positions that Olmos has taken
in his advocacy work. Would this essay successfully
fulfill the writer's goal?

    A. Yes, because the essay details what Olmos
thought and felt about a variety of social issues.
    B. Yes, because the essay explains both sides of con-
troversies in which Olmos has been involved.
    C. No, because the essay limits itself to broadly de-
scribing the causes that Olmos has supported.
    D. No, because the essay discusses only the opinions
expressed by Olmos, not those of his opponents.

8

Passage Set 4 Answer Key

Write in whether you got each problem right or wrong (or left it blank). If your answer was correct, put a 1 in every blank to the right of that problem. Sum up each column and compare your total to the total possible "Out Of" points in each column.

Problem	Correct Answer	Right/ Wrong/ Blank	Usage/Mechanics			Rhetorical Skills		
			Grammar & Usage	Punctuation	Sentence Structure	Organization	Style	Writing Strategy
1	A		—					
2	G					—		
3	D						—	
4	G			—				
5	D						—	
6	H							—
7	B			—				
8	F					—		
9	B			—				
10	F		—					
11	A		—					
12	H		—					
13	C					—		
14	J				—			
15	D							—
16	G							—
17	D			—				
18	F					—		
19	D		—					
20	F							—
21	D				—			
22	H				—			
23	B			—				
24	F					—		
25	B			—				
26	F				—			

8

Problem	Correct Answer	Right/ Wrong/ Blank	Usage/Mechanics			Rhetorical Skills		
			Grammar & Usage	Punctuation	Sentence Structure	Organization	Style	Writing Strategy
27	C				—			
28	H		—					
29	D		—					
30	G							—
31	C				—			
32	H			—				
33	B				—			
34	G				—			
35	A					—		
36	J			—				
37	C						—	
38	G					—		
39	C				—			
40	J							—
41	A							—
42	J						—	
43	A		—					
44	G				—			
45	A					—		
46	J			—				
47	A				—			
48	G		—					
49	D					—		
50	F					—		
51	A		—					
52	H		—					
53	C				—			
54	F							—
55	D						—	
56	H				—			

MANHATTAN
PREP

Problem	Correct Answer	Right/ Wrong/ Blank	Usage/Mechanics			Rhetorical Skills		
			Grammar & Usage	Punctuation	Sentence Structure	Organization	Style	Writing Strategy
57	B		—					
58	G		—					
59	B							—
60	H				—			
61	B							—
62	H			—				
63	C			—				
64	F						—	
65	B		—					
66	G					—		
67	A					—		
68	J			—				
69	A						—	
70	J		—					
71	C		—					
72	G				—			
73	D							—
74	F					—		
75	C							—
Total								
Out Of		75	16	12	15	13	7	12

8

Passage Set 4 Solutions

Passage 1

1.　**(A)** … I expected many changes <u>in</u> my surroundings …

Usage/Mechanics　　　　　Grammar & Usage　　　　Idioms

The best preposition to use here is *in*. After the phrase *many changes*, the preposition *in* tells you where the changes are taking place: in this case, *in my surroundings.*

None of the other prepositions fit as well as *in*. It is also possible to use *of* after *change* to indicate what is changing: *we have a change of plans* (= "our plans have changed"). In the passage, however, *many changes of my surroundings* would imply that the background scenery changed over and over, as if in a frenzied music video. Rather, the writer means that various aspects of the surroundings changed (e.g., the weather). *Change for* would signify the reason for or goal of the change (*a change for the better*). Finally, *change on* could only be used with a restricted set of objects, such as time indicators (*a change on the count of three*). The correct answer is (A).

2.　**(G)** … I expected many changes in my surroundings, and my expectations matched reality. <u>Certainly,</u> the weather was different; in fact, it appeared that my new home actually lacked weather.

Rhetorical Skills　　　　　Organization　　　　Transitions

The best transition of the available options, *Certainly*, emphasizes a particular example (*the weather was different*) of the previous generalization (*my expectations matched reality*). This transition conveys that this example is *certainly* representative of the trend, even if other examples may be less so.

The other transitions fail to link the first thought to the second in a logical way. *Possibly* does the opposite of *Certainly*; it in fact undermines the example, as well as the general trend. *Therefore* would suggest that the weather was different *because* the narrator's expectations matched reality. This suggestion is not reasonable, unless the narrator has power over the weather. Finally, *Furthermore* would only be appropriate if the two thoughts were on the same level of generality (for instance, if they were both examples of the trend). This transition doesn't work to lead from a generalization to a specific, emphatic example. The correct answer is (G).

3.　**(D)** At school, I <u>was introduced to</u> earthquake drills and a much bigger sky in the windows.

Rhetorical Skills　　　　　Style　　　　　　　Word Choice

The original verb phrase, *was presented to*, implies that someone presented the narrator to earthquake drills, as if these drills were a visiting dignitary. The proper correction, *was introduced to*, is much more appropriate for non-human objects (such as *earthquake drills and a much bigger sky*) that a person can become familiar with.

Even though this essay is personal, even informal in ways, the phrases *got friendly with* and *was down with* are too vague and colloquial for the prevalent tone of the essay. The correct answer is (D).

MANHATTAN
PREP

4.   **(G)** The surface roads … made the <u>grid of Manhattan</u> seem minuscule.

Usage/Mechanics   Punctuation   Commas

No commas should be used anywhere in this phrase. The word *grid* should not be separated from the prepositional phrase *of Manhattan*, which defines which grid is being talked about. Moreover, when you "make X do something," you should not place a comma after *X* (in this case, *X* is the phrase *the grid of Manhattan*). The correct answer is (G).

5.   **(D)** One of the differences that struck me most, however, was a linguistic <u>quirk</u> involving the way to refer to …

Rhetorical Skills   Style   Concision

The word *quirk* means "oddity," so it is redundant to use *oddity* or *oddly* as well. The word *linguistic* means "having to do with language," and the non-underlined portion also contains the words *the way to refer to*, so you should not also say the *use of language* or *how people talk about certain things*. Finally, the aside *which may or may not be a quirk to some* adds no real value; it's not actually saying much of anything. In context, it's filler that should be discarded. The correct answer is (D).

6.   **(H)** Most specifically defines the kinds of roads: … the way to refer to <u>fast roadways with exits but no stoplights.</u>

Rhetorical Skills   Writing Strategy   Choice of Content

The correct answer uses descriptive language that specifies particular kinds of roads: *fast* ones that have *exits but no stoplights*. These modifiers distinguish the roadways in question from other kinds of roadways (e.g., ones with stoplights).

Just using the word *roadways* by itself doesn't do the job as well (you can imagine a roadway with stoplights). The modifier *namely, paved routes built for cars* does eliminate unpaved roads, but doesn't narrow down the possibilities as much as the right answer does. Finally, the modifier *on which society depends so much* adds a fact, perhaps, but not one that restricts the kinds of roadways in any way. The correct answer is (H).

7.   **(B)** <u>In Los Angeles, however, people</u> say "freeway," …

Usage/Mechanics   Punctuation   Commas

A contrasting transition that's put into the middle of a sentence, such as *however* or *though,* should always be separated from the surrounding sentence by commas. Thus, you need commas on both sides of *however* here. After the subject *people*, however, you should not put a comma, which would inappropriately separate this subject from its verb *say*. The correct answer is (B).

8.   **(F)** Most effectively introduces the main idea: <u>Even stranger to me than the word "freeway" is the use of the word "the."</u>

Rhetorical Skills   Organization   Opening/Closing Content

The prior paragraph described the different words used to refer to fast roadways with no stoplights: expressways, parkways, highways, turnpikes, and—in Los Angeles—freeways. The current paragraph describes the use of the word *the* in front of freeway numbers. The correct answer makes a clear transition between these paragraphs, while the incorrect options fail to name the topic of the current paragraph. The correct answer is (F).

8

9.   **(B)** Everywhere <u>else in the country, so it seems,</u> when you refer to a highway by number, …

Usage/Mechanics   Punctuation   Commas

The phrase *so it seems* is a parenthetical aside inserted into the middle of this sentence. Therefore, it ought to be sur-rounded on both sides by commas. The opening phrase *Everywhere else in the country* should not have any internal com-mas (especially not between *else* and *in,* as in two of the wrong answers). The correct answer is (B).

10.   **(F)** … when you refer to a highway by number, you say just <u>its</u> number.

Usage/Mechanics   Grammar & Usage   Pronoun Forms

The correct form of the possessive pronoun is *its,* meaning *the highway's* here. An *'s* attached to a noun is the way to indi-cate possession by that noun. This is why it's so hard to keep *its* and *it's* straight, because the situation is exactly reversed. The form *it's* never means possession; it always means "it is," which is nonsensical here. The pronoun *their* is possessive, but the noun would need to be plural (*highways,* not *highway*). The word *ones* is not possessive. The correct answer is (F).

11.   **(A)** Perhaps this use … reflects the idea <u>that</u> freeways are vast living beings, …

Usage/Mechanics   Grammar & Usage   Modifier Forms

If you want to indicate what the *idea* is with a modifier, you have to use *that.* This rule holds true for any noun that can indicate a full thought, such as *claim* or *report:* "the claim that the Earth is flat" or "the report that Martians landed on the moon" are both correct.

The pronoun *which* can only be used if you want to add an extra modifier about the idea: "The idea that freeways are vast living beings is odd. This idea, *which* I had just the other day, is not one I'd announce at school." The phrase *in which* would work the same way. Finally, *where* would never be appropriate after *idea,* because an idea is not a place. The correct answer is (A).

12.   **(H)** … residents have little alternative <u>to dealing</u> with this freeway's whims.

Usage/Mechanics   Grammar & Usage   Idioms

After the noun *alternative,* the word *to* is a preposition and so must be followed by a noun: "We have no alternative to starvation." Here, *starvation* is the noun. An *-ing* form of a verb can be used as a noun, so this example sentence could be rewritten as "We have no alternative to starving."

The *to* after *alternative* is not the *to* of an infinitive verb (*to deal*). No other preposition (e.g., *for* or *of*) works in place of *to.* The correct answer is (H).

13.   **(C)** Most effectively opens the paragraph: <u>All that said, the similarities between expressways in New York and freeways in Los Angeles outnumber the differences.</u>

Rhetorical Skills   Organization   Opening/Closing Content

The next two sentences in the paragraph point out specific similarities between New York expressways and L.A. freeways: *Both sets of overcrowded highways demand real driving skills. On either coast, knowing how to take surface roads …* Since the prior two paragraphs have emphasized differences between the two sets of roadways (involving the names and the use of the word "the"), you should clearly pivot from talking about differences to talking about similarities. The correct answer explicitly makes this pivot, as signaled by the opening transition *All that said.*

The original sentence does draw a parallel between L.A. freeways and New York expressways (neither are *literally gods*), but this offhand similarity does not make a strong enough contrast with the earlier part of the essay. Choice (B) spreads the focus too wide, including highways around the world, when the comparison should still be mostly restricted to Los Angeles and New York. Finally, choice (D) does not set up the underlying similarities that the rest of the paragraph lists. The correct answer is (C).

14. **(J)** On either coast, <u>knowing</u> how to take surface roads … or how to slip ahead … is crucial.

Usage/Mechanics   Sentence Structure   Whole Sentences

The main verb in the sentence is *is,* in the phrase *is crucial* at the very end. What is crucial? *Knowing* how to do X or how to do Y. The *-ing* form *knowing* is used as a noun here, playing the role of subject.

In each of the wrong choices, there is no subject. Placing a preposition in front of *knowing,* such as *by* or *when,* means that *knowing* could not be the subject. Likewise, the clause *if you know* cannot be the subject of a sentence. The correct answer is (J).

15. **(D)** Fulfill the persuasive goal of urging the use of L.A. terminology? No, because the narrator makes no recommendations about which way to refer to roadways.

Rhetorical Skills   Writing Strategy   Goal of essay

The essay does not contain any judgments about which terminology is ultimately best to use. The narrator does say that the use of the term *freeway* and of *the* in front of highway numbers is *a quirk, weird,* or *strange* in the body of the essay. Then, the end of the essay hints at some measure of acceptance on a linguistic level: *I've committed to mastering "the" L.A. freeway.* However, the essay never claims that one set of terms is better or worse than any other. The narrator never urges the reader to adopt any terms, so the essay would not fulfill a persuasive goal in this regard (and not because the narrator rejects the personal use of L.A. terminology—no such rejection takes place). The correct answer is (D).

Passage 2

16. **(G)** Most emphasizes Hopper's dynamism: This <u>short, powerful woman commanded</u> the stage …

Rhetorical Skills   Writing Strategy   Choice of Content

"Dynamism" means "energy, enthusiasm, power." The right answer uses words that echo this concept: *powerful* and *commanded.* In contrast, the wrong choices do not contain words that convey dynamism. The correct answer is (G).

17.   **(D)** … she clarified what they represented: the distance light travels in a nanosecond …

Usage/Mechanics   Punctuation   Colons (as well as Semicolons and Commas)

In the main clause of this sentence, the subject is *she* (Hopper) and the verb is *clarified*. What did she clarify? She clarified what they (the foot-long wires) represented. The sentence could end right there, in theory. However, the writer continues by explaining what the wires represented: the distance light travels in a nanosecond. This explanation is properly preceded by a colon in the correct answer. A comma could instead be used, but you must use either a colon or a comma (not a semicolon).

Finally, the word *distance* should not be followed by a colon (or any other punctuation), because it is followed by an essential clause that defines the distance: *the distance [that] light travels in a nanosecond*. The correct answer is (D).

18.   **(F)**   Nothing can move faster than light in a vacuum, so electrons in a wire can at best move a fraction of a foot in a nanosecond.

Rhetorical Skills   Organization   Transitions

The first thought leads into the second thought, so a suitable "causal" transition (such as *so*) should be used, as in the original sentence. Choices (G) and (H) provide versions of *so*, but there are two problems. First, these versions are too colloquial, using *this* without a noun following. Second, these versions cannot follow a comma; they would have to come after a semicolon. Of the "causal" transitions (*so, thus, therefore,* etc.), only *so* can link two independent clauses using only a comma. Thus, choices (G) and (H) create run-on sentences.

Choice (J) is also a run-on, since the two independent clauses are joined by only a comma (and nothing else). The correct answer is (F).

19.   **(D)** … this speed limit forces modern computers, … to be physically small.

Usage/Mechanics   Grammar & Usage   Modifier Forms

The adverb *physically* correctly modifies the adjective *small*. In what way must modern computers be small? Physically, meaning "in a physical way." The form *physical* is an adjective meaning "material, bodily" and is not intended to be applied to the computers.

There should not be a comma between *physically* and *small*. A single adverb (*physically*) followed by an adjective it modifies (*small*) should not be separated from that adjective by a comma. The correct answer is (D).

20.   **(F)**   If the writer were to delete the preceding sentence, the essay would primarily lose a transition between the camp scene and a statement of Hopper's impact.

Rhetorical Skills   Writing Strategy   Deletions

Here is the sentence on the chopping block: *Hopper certainly had the authority to speak on this matter*. The *matter* in question is the design of computers, and she was speaking on this matter at the summer camp the narrator attended. So this sentence connects back to the camp scene previously described in the essay. The sentence also reaches forward: *certainly had the authority …* What *authority*? Where did that authority come from? The questions are answered in the following sentence: *She played a formative role in the development of computer science.*

Putting all these observations together, you can see that the sentence provides "a transition between the camp scene and a statement of Hopper's impact" (namely, her *formative role*). None of the other choices fit the content of the sentence, which is certainly relevant to the essay. The correct answer is (F).

21.   **(D)** Not acceptable alternative: She obtained a Ph.D. in <u>1934, taught at the same time</u> at Vassar.

Usage/Mechanics   Sentence Structure   Whole Sentences

The correct answer is the only one that is grammatically unacceptable. You cannot connect two complete verbs with just a comma. "I walked to the store, ate an apple" is incorrect; any list of two things or actions joined by just a comma is wrong in standard academic English. You must connect the two verbs with an *and* ("I walked to the store and ate an apple"), or you must change the second verb to an *-ing* form ("I walked to the store, eating an apple"). Other options are possible as well (e.g., *while*). These options may have slightly different nuances, but they are grammatically fine, in contrast to the comma splice between two verbs in the correct answer (which is chosen because you are looking for the unacceptable option). The correct answer is (D).

22.   **(H)** Least acceptable alternative: … she joined the Navy, although with <u>difficulty, she</u> weighed less …

Usage/Mechanics   Sentence Structure   Whole Sentences

As in the previous question, the correct answer is the one that creates an ungrammatical sentence—namely, a comma splice between two independent clauses (*she joined the Navy* and *she weighed less …*). Either a semicolon or a dash is acceptable here to join these two related thoughts, and *because* also works (since the phrase *with difficulty* is explained by *she weighed less …*). The correct answer is (H).

23.   **(B)** … Hopper famously once "debugged" the <u>computer by removing a moth and taping it</u> into a notebook.

Usage/Mechanics   Punctuation   Commas

Hopper once debugged the computer. How did she do so? By taking two actions. This two-item list (*removing a moth and taping it into a notebook*) should not have any internal commas. When you connect two things with an *and*, only put a comma before the *and* if the two things are independent clauses ("I saw that movie, and I enjoyed it"). Otherwise, don't insert a comma.

Moreover, there should not be a comma between *computer* and *by* or between *it* and *into*. Normally, if you put a prepositional phrase after the object of a verb, do not separate the prepositional phrase from the object with a comma. "She debugged the computer by removing a moth" and "She taped it into a notebook" should each lack commas. The correct answer is (B).

24. **(F)** Most effectively leads into new paragraph: The Mark I ran many critical computations for the war effort, including ones related to building the first atomic bomb. [New paragraph] <u>After the war,</u> Hopper worked at a variety of corporations …

Rhetorical Skills   Organization   Opening/Closing Content

The prior paragraph ends with a description of activities during World War II. The phrase *After the war* moves the reader forward from the war in a natural and logical way—that is, chronologically.

The phrase *A versatile scientist* is not as effective a lead-in. *Versatile* means "skilled in various ways, adaptable, resourceful." Hopper probably had this trait, but there is little specific reinforcement nearby in the text. So this phrase doesn't function so well as a transition. Likewise, *After a divorce* introduces a brand-new element from Hopper's personal life, instead of leading seamlessly from the prior topic (the war effort) to the current paragraph. Finally, if no transitional phrase is used at all, the timeline is hard to decode: does *Hopper worked …* happen during the war or after the war? The best option is to clarify the sequence of activities with *After the war.* The correct answer is (F).

25. **(B)** … she wrote the <u>world's</u> first compiler.

Usage/Mechanics   Punctuation   Apostrophes

The possessive form of the singular noun *world* is *world's.* The correct answer means "the first compiler in the world." *Worlds* is the plural noun and cannot be used as a possessive. The form *worlds'* would mean "in or of the worlds," and despite tales from science fiction or fantasy, it is customary to refer to our planet as a single *world.* Yes, this compiler was the first of its kind on many worlds, if you count other planets, but this interpretation is unnecessarily distracting. Finally, there is no such word as *worlds's.* The correct answer is (B).

26. **(F)** Compilers are essential computer programs that take instructions intelligible to humans <u>and translate</u> them into the elemental code that computers can understand.

Usage/Mechanics   Sentence Structure   Modifier Placement

The correct logic of the sentence is as follows: Compilers are essential computer programs that do two things. First, they take instructions intelligible to humans (in order to do something else with them). Second, the programs translate those instructions into the elemental code that computers can understand. The structure is "Compilers are essential computer programs that take … and translate …"

If the *and* is changed to *who* or *that*, then the sentence would be saying that the humans translate the instructions. This reading makes much less sense than the one outlined above. (Moreover, *that* should not be used with human subjects.) Finally, *translate* by itself creates a run-on, since this verb would be floating freely, without an obvious subject or relationship to other verbs in the sentence. The correct answer is (F).

27.   **(C)** <u>She also served</u> in the Naval Reserve for decades, and she was called out of retirement twice.

Usage/Mechanics   Sentence Structure   Whole Sentences

The second part of the sentence (… *and she was called out* …) provides the key to how the first part must work. Since that second part is an independent clause (*she was* …) after a comma-*and*, the first part of the sentence must also be an independent clause. The only possible choice, then, is *She also served*.

Starting the sentence with *Because* or *Due to the additional fact that* makes the first clause subordinate. Choice (D) removes the subject altogether and hobbles the verb (an *-ing* form such as *serving* is not a complete verb). The correct answer is (C).

28.   **(H)** … Hopper gave thousands of <u>people</u> her nanosecond wires.

Usage/Mechanics   Grammar & Usage   Pronoun Agreement

In the original sentence, the pronoun *them* lacks a noun it can refer to. The same issue occurs in choice (G)—*those* has no antecedent (the noun that a pronoun refers to). As a result, you must use *people* as the object of *thousands of.* Thousands of whom? Of people.

Choice (J) may seem okay at first: she gave thousands of her wires. However, the verb *give* by itself requires an indirect object: to whom did she give thousands of wires? *Give away* can have just a direct object ("she gave away thousands of wires"), but there is no *away* here. The correct answer is (H).

29.   **(D)** Hopper gave thousands of people her nanosecond wires. My computer has <u>mine</u> proudly fastened to it.

Usage/Mechanics   Grammar & Usage   Pronoun Agreement

The original pronoun *it* is confusing: what exactly is fastened to my computer? There is no singular noun that *it* can refer to (the later *it* refers back to *My computer*). The pronoun *them* has the opposite problem: are tons of wires or thousands of people fastened to my computer? And even if you decide on the wires, it still doesn't make sense that all the thousands of wires Grace Hopper gave away are now attached to my computer. *Theirs* suffers from the same illogic.

The only sensible possibility is *mine,* meaning "my wire." In other words, this wire is the one that the narrator received at the summer camp described at the beginning of the essay, when Hopper *passed out foot-long lengths of wire.* The writer closes the essay neatly this way, by touching back on the personal encounter the narrator had with Hopper. The correct answer is (D).

30.   **(G)** Fulfill the goal of describing the achievements and influence of a pioneering scientist? Yes, because it outlines Hopper's career as both a groundbreaking programmer and a teacher.

Rhetorical Skills   Writing Strategy   Goal of Essay

The essay describes the achievements and influence of a pioneering scientist, namely Grace Hopper. The achievements include her work on the Mark I computer during World War II and her invention of the world's first compiler, as high-lighted in the second and third paragraphs. Her influence is stated or strongly suggested in many parts of the text, including the following: *She played a formative role in the development of computer science, Hopper famously once "debugged" the computer …, All current programming depends on Hopper's work,* and *A motivational speaker and educator …*

It is debatable whether the essay offers a "detailed account" of her work at Harvard. Only the *debugging* incident is mentioned as particularly connected with Hopper. The computer ran *many critical computations for the war*, but the two sentences on the subject do not go very far into specifics. This short account, even if it were more detailed, by itself would not be enough to fulfill the goal, which the essay achieves by outlining Hopper's career and influence more broadly throughout all five paragraphs. The correct answer is (G).

Passage 3

31.   **(C)** The creation of writing <u>is thought to be</u> one of the leading achievements …

Usage/Mechanics   Sentence Structure   Whole Sentences

The original version lacks a complete verb: *thought to be* is only a modifying phrase, in essence. You need to add *is* to make the sentence whole. Using *thinks …* or *thought that …* strangely turns *the creation of writing* into the subject, but that creation isn't doing the thinking; people are. The correct answer is (C).

32.   **(H)** … to store and retrieve <u>our society's knowledge</u> …

Usage/Mechanics   Punctuation   Apostrophes

The right form of the possessive of *society* is *society's*, not *societies*. A correct alternative would be *societies',* the possessive of the plural noun *societies*. Do not use *society* by itself as an adjective unless you are talking about high society or culture: *our society knowledge* would mean "the knowledge we have about sophisticated society." *Knowledge of society* suffers from the same shift in meaning. You have to use another possessive, such as *our*, to mean "society in general." *Our society's knowledge* means "the knowledge of our society, the knowledge that our society possesses." This is the writer's intention. The correct answer is (H).

33.   **(B)** In 1821, recognizing the usefulness of writing, <u>the Cherokee smith Sequoyah invented an alphabet for his language, a singlehanded achievement that may be unique in history.</u>

Usage/Mechanics   Sentence Structure   Modifier Placement

The phrase *recognizing …* must be immediately followed by whoever did the recognizing—namely, *the Cherokee smith Sequoyah,* or just *Sequoyah.* Thus, the original version, as well as choice (D), can be eliminated. Among the two remaining choices, only choice (B) retains the correct indication that the *achievement* is what *may be unique in history,* not the alphabet (although that was also certainly unique). Choice (C) also contains an oddly structured modifier: *who made a singlehanded achievement.* The achievement is not specified until later, unnecessarily raising questions for the reader. Instead, the correct answer puts the phrase *singlehanded achievement* after the clause *invented an alphabet for his language.* This way, the achievement is clearly and immediately defined. The correct answer is (B).

34. **(G)** Writing exists in many forms. Symbols described as "logographic" <u>display</u> meaning not directly linked to sound …

Usage/Mechanics   Sentence Structure   Verb Tenses

Most of this paragraph is in present tense, in order to discuss generally how *writing exists in many forms.* Thus, the underlined verb should be *display,* not *displayed, had displayed,* or *were displaying.* Note that the modifiers *described as* and *not directly linked to* contain past participles (*described, linked*) that only look like past tense. The correct answer is (G).

35. **(A)** Symbols described as "logographic" display meaning not directly linked to sound … <u>At the other extreme,</u> alphabetic symbols indicate pronunciation only.

Rhetorical Skills   Organization   Transitions

The thought before the underlined transition defines logographic symbols: they *display meaning,* not sound. The thought after the underline defines alphabetic symbols: they *indicate pronunciation only.* In other words, the second kind of symbol displays sound, not meaning. These two types are opposites of each other, so the transition should indicate a contrast. *At the other extreme* does the job.

Of the wrong choices, perhaps the most tempting is choice (B), *In the same fashion.* You could make an argument that these two kinds of symbols are similar, in that they each only show one aspect (meaning or sound), not both. The problem is that this is a rather subtle argument that would not be apparent to most readers on the first pass of the text. In the position between the two definitions, the writer absolutely needs to emphasize the contrast in the specific features, so that the simple message can get across: logographic = meaning, whereas alphabetic = sound. The correct answer is (A).

36. **(J)** … the letters "g" and "o," which don't <u>signify anything by themselves,</u> must be combined …

Usage/Mechanics   Punctuation   Commas

The nonessential modifier *which don't signify anything by themselves* must be set off by commas from the sentence it is embedded in. Within the modifier itself, however, no commas should be used between the verb (*signify*) and its object (*anything*) or between that object and the prepositional phrase (*by themselves*). After all, a simple sentence expressing that thought would contain no commas: *These letters don't signify anything by themselves.* The correct answer is (J).

37. **(C)** Does not indicate that Sequoyah's work was original: This kind of alphabet is what Sequoyah <u>replicated</u> for the Cherokee language.

Rhetorical Skills   Style   Word Choice

To *replicate* is to duplicate or mimic. Of course, there can be elements of originality in any replication, but by saying that Sequoyah *replicated* the alphabet, you are emphasizing that he copied it in some essential way. The verbs *invent, design,* and *contrive,* although they have different nuances, would all mean that the work was original. The correct answer is (C).

38. **(G)** Least acceptable alternative: Little is known for certain about Sequoyah's early <u>life, but</u> stories of his upbringing in Tennessee conflict.

Rhetorical Skills   Organization   Transitions

The two facts given are very much in concert: *little is known* … and *stories conflict.* In fact, these two statements are so closely aligned that many transitions are possible. You can link them with a semicolon, as in the original sentence. You can use *as* or *since,* indicating that little is known because these stories conflict. That is, the conflicting stories cause little to be known for certain.

You can even use *so,* indicating that little is known for certain, and *as a result* of little being known, these stories conflict. All of these versions make sense. What doesn't make sense (and is therefore the correct answer here) is the use of *but,* indicating a contrast in meaning. The correct answer is (G).

39. **(C)** … he had a leg <u>disability that</u> may have led him …

Usage/Mechanics   Sentence Structure   Whole Sentences

The three wrong answers all suffer from the same comma-splice problem: they all join two independent clauses with just a comma. The correct answer fixes the issue by making the second clause dependent with a *that.* The correct answer is (C).

40. **(J)** Most relevant to the conclusion of the paragraph: … he had customers of various backgrounds and <u>undoubtedly encountered many "talking leaves," or written pages, in books he saw.</u> Inspired, he decided to come up with a writing system for his own language.

Rhetorical Skills   Writing Strategy   Choice of Content

The paragraph's final sentence describes Sequoyah as *inspired … to come up with a writing system for his own language.* What would have most logically inspired him is writing that he must have seen on pages of books, newspapers, and the like. The correct answer makes the proper allusion. Even hearing other languages would not be as appropriate as seeing physical writing. The correct answer is (J).

41. **(A)** At first, he tried to represent <u>each word with a different symbol.</u> However, logographic systems … contain thousands of characters …

Rhetorical Skills   Writing Strategy   Choice of Content

Two of the wrong answers suffer from redundancy, using both *different* and *distinct from any other,* both *individual wholes* and *each with its own …,* or both *sign* and *icon.* These choices can be safely rejected. However, you've gone too far if you simply write *At first, he tried to represent words.* After all, there are many ways to represent words, including by alphabets. The critical point is that he tried at first to represent each word *with a different symbol,* as in the logographic systems. Cutting *with a different symbol* from the original sentence leaves the description too ambiguous. The correct answer is (A).

42. **(J)** … logographic systems … contain thousands of characters and require many years to <u>master.</u>

Rhetorical Skills   Style   Concision

The word *master* is sufficient on its own here. The tacked-on phrases *to the point of true fluency, such that one is in full command,* or *beyond a beginner's level of control* are all wastefully redundant, adding nothing to the meaning of *master* except padding. Trim the waste and stick with just *master.* The correct answer is (J).

43. **(A)** … his <u>daughter, who</u> was his first student,

Usage/Mechanics   Grammar & Usage   Modifier Forms

The relative pronoun *who,* not *which,* should be used with human subjects. Since the relative pronoun is also the subject of the rest of the clause (*was his first student*), the form should be *who,* not *whom* (which would be appropriate only as an object of a verb or preposition: *his daughter, whom he loved*). Finally, *she who* in place of *who* is unnecessarily dramatic. Go with the simpler version stylistically. The correct answer is (A).

44. **(G)** … since the Cherokee <u>alphabet is</u> closely suited to the language, Cherokee is easier …

Usage/Mechanics   Sentence Structure   Whole Sentences

The main clause of this sentence is *Cherokee is easier* … The subordinate clause *since … the language* requires a complete verb, such as *is.* Using the forms *being* or *having been* (or nothing at all) makes this sentence a fragment. In the phrase *closely suited to the language,* note that *suited* is not a complete verb; rather, it's a past participle, here used as an adjective to describe the Cherokee alphabet. The correct answer is (G).

45. **(A)** Best conclusion: After all, English spelling, which is notoriously opaque, was not masterminded by one person.

Rhetorical Skills   Organization   Opening/Closing Content

As indicated by the title "Inventing an Alphabet," the essay focuses on the creation of an alphabet by one person, Sequoyah, for his language. Thus, the best conclusion would remind the reader of the fact that Sequoyah singlehandedly created an alphabet. The correct answer does so in a neat reverse, emphasizing that English spelling *was not masterminded by one person.* That cannot help but emphasize that another system of spelling was in fact "masterminded by one person."

The wrong answers focus on irrelevancies, such as the prevalence of the English language, the overlap in symbols between the two languages, or the fact that you can see bilingual signs in Cherokee, North Carolina. None of these choices reinforce the central theme of the passage. The correct answer is (A).

8

MANHATTAN
PREP   305

Passage 4

46. **(J)** What can sound be used to do? The answer seems <u>evident: to</u> communicate.

Usage/Mechanics   Punctuation   Commas & Colons

The first part of the sentence should be able to stand alone as *The answer seems evident.* The colon properly functions as a device to add explanation—what is the answer to the question? The answer is *to communicate;* that is, sound can be used to communicate, but you don't have to repeat *sound can be used.*

You must use some kind of punctuation here, because *The answer seems evident to communicate* has an entirely different meaning: it is evident to communicate the answer. However, the following sentences should then give the answer, rather than give examples of an answer already provided (as they now do). The answer is not obvious to communicate; the answer is obvious, and the answer is to communicate.

Adding *in order* in front of the *to* actually destroys the *evident to communicate* reading. Only use *in order to* when a subject is performing the verb for this purpose. It doesn't make sense to claim that the answer is seeming evident so that it can communicate. Finally, do not use a semicolon here, because the part before *and* the part after a semicolon must be able to stand alone as sentences. *To communicate* would be a fragment. The correct answer is (J).

47. **(A)** The answer seems evident: to communicate … our society <u>is</u> flooded with sounds that have meaning … which, to be fair, may not always be …

Usage/Mechanics   Sentence Structure   Verb Tenses

The sentence is embedded in a paragraph that is consistently in present tense, in order to express general truths. In fact, even the beginning of the universe is expressed in the present: *the universe begins.* With *seems, have,* and *may be* nearby, you'd need a strong justification to change the *is* to any other tense. No such justification exists in the sentence. The correct answer is (A).

48. **(G)** … we feel that with the physical vibrations <u>is</u> transmitted something deep.

Usage/Mechanics   Grammar & Usage   Subject–Verb Agreement

After the *feel that*, you need a clause that could stand alone as a sentence. (Most verb-*that* combinations have the same requirement.) As written, the mini-sentence is in a flipped state, with the verb before the subject. If you restore normal order, you get *something deep is transmitted with the physical vibrations.* Now it's probably easier to see that *something deep* is the subject, not *physical vibrations* (which are in the prepositional phrase formed by *with*). Since *something* is singular, the verb must be singular as well. Only *is* fits the bill, among the available options. Present tense is ideal as well, but you don't need to apply that issue here, since subject–verb agreement takes you all the way. The correct answer is (G).

49. **(D)** For the sake of logic and coherence, Sentence 6 should be placed after Sentence 4.

Rhetorical Skills   Organization   Sentence Order

The sentence whose position is at stake is this: *Regardless, we feel that with the physical vibrations is transmitted something deep.* The *Regardless* transition tells you that there should be a contrast with the prior sentence, which must have raised an issue that the writer doesn't want to pursue further. However, in the current position, the previous sentence is Sentence 5, which ends with *the most profound message of all.* That ending might work with the main content of Sentence 6, but the *Regardless* is completely out of place—you would want *the most profound message* and *something deep* to reinforce each other.

The correct position of Sentence 6 is after Sentence 4, which reads *What does a saxophone solo exactly mean?* This is the issue the writer wants to dismiss quickly with *Regardless.* Now the *something deep* can lead to the *profound message,* because the current Sentence 5 begins with *Indeed*—that is, the new sentence reinforces the prior point, perhaps even more than expected.

In the end, the correct order is this: *What does a saxophone solo even mean? Regardless, we feel that with the physical vibrations is transmitted something deep. Indeed, in more than one religion, the universe begins with a hum or an uttered command—perhaps the most profound message of all.* The correct answer is (D).

50. **(F)** Most effectively guides into new paragraph: In the modern world, sound has many uses besides communication.

Rhetorical Skills   Organization   Opening/Closing Content

The essay is titled "The Uses of Sound," and the first paragraph explores the most common use of sound: to communicate. It would be natural, then, to introduce other uses of sound at this point. The correct answer does so in an explicit, simple manner: *sound has many uses besides communication.* In line with expectations, the rest of the essay outlines some of these other uses. The next sentence indicates one of those uses (*underwater sonar*) and suggests that the opening sentence proposed more than one use of sound—after all, there's no other reason to write *for instance.*

Choice (G) connects the end of the previous paragraph and the rest of this one, but in an abrupt way. If the subject of this sentence is *The formless waters in some creation tales,* then you have to stay in the world of the tales; they do not literally *conceal another use of sound,* as if submarines were plumbing the depths of those waters with sonar. Choice (H) proposes *many applications,* but they are of *sonar,* not sound itself. Finally, choice (J) is a fact about sound, but does not assert anything about its uses. The correct answer is (F).

51. **(A)** … ultrasound scans probe the health of a growing fetus with <u>little risk of harm.</u>

Usage/Mechanics   Grammar & Usage   Modifier Forms

The proper relation between the ideas is expressed in the original version. The scans probe the health of a fetus *with little risk.* Risk of what? *Of harm.* In other words, there is not much risk that harm will occur. The incorrect versions scramble the forms themselves and their order, creating confusion. It is not the harm that is risky (as in *risky harm*), nor the risk that is harmful (as in *harmful risk*); rather, there is a risk (a small one), and the risk is that harm can occur. Moreover, the use of *less* before either *risky harm* or *harmful risk* is ambiguous. Does *less risky harm* mean "harm that is less risky" or "less harm that is risky"? Stick with the original version, which has a clear, logical construction. The correct answer is (A).

52. (H) … we are like <u>bats, our mammalian cousins.</u>

Usage/Mechanics Grammar & Usage Modifier Forms

The correct answer places *bats* in the core of the sentence: *we are like bats*. Then an appositive phrase (*our mammalian cousins*) further describes bats. Similarly, you could also write *we are like bats, which are our mammalian cousins*.

You cannot use *who* with a non-human noun, so choice (F) is out. By putting *our mammalian cousins* in the core of the sentence and pushing *bats* to a *which* clause, choice (G) implies that all of our mammalian cousins are bats. This implication is nonsensical. In a similarly illogical fashion, choice (J) implies that only some bats are our mammalian cousins; moreover, there is no reason anywhere for focusing on some subset of bats. Keep the sentence simple with *bats, our mammalian cousins*. The correct answer is (H).

53. (C) <u>An astrophysics major and recent college graduate, Meredith Berry</u> has founded a company …

Usage/Mechanics Sentence Structure Modifier Placement

In the corrected version, the subject is *Meredith Berry,* who *has founded a company*. You might naturally ask who she is or what else is known about her. The opening modifier, which is an appositive noun phrase, supplies that information: *An astrophysics major and recent college graduate*. Note that the use of one article (*An*) means that the two nouns following (*major* and *graduate*) are both descriptors of the same person, namely *Meredith Berry*.

Choices (B) and (C) mix up the positions of the nouns, such that you are not sure whether the sentence is describing one person, two people, or even three people. Choice (D) begins with *Meredith Berry:* and so creates a fragment (the part before a colon in a standard sentence must be able to stand alone grammatically as an independent clause). The correct answer is (C).

54. (F) Further describe company's transmitters: Her thin, unobtrusive panels send sonic energy through the air to phones and tablets equipped with receivers.

Rhetorical Skills Writing Strategy Additions

Additional description of the transmitters is found in the correct answer: the *panels* are *thin* and *unobtrusive*. Now you can picture these transmitters in your mind. (The fact that they *send sonic energy through the air to phones and tablets* is perhaps implied by the prior sentence, in which *ultrasound transmitters recharge wireless devices*.) None of the other choices provide any description of the transmitters themselves, focusing instead on the origin of the idea, a concern of critics, or a particular trade fair (where a *prototype* was displayed, but this prototype is not described except by its function—moreover, this prototype was not necessarily the same as the transmitters in general). The correct answer is (F).

55. (D) … she has attracted several <u>prominent investors</u> and plans to sell …

Rhetorical Skills Style Concision

The words *prominent investors* by themselves contain all you need. *Prominent* means "well-known, recognized," and *investors* means "those who invest money, who back companies or others financially, who provide monetary support, who put in funds" (to write a definition that covers all the redundancies that appear in the wrong answers).

You might argue that, in some contexts, *investors* are those who *could* invest, but don't: for instance, *she scared off investors*. But in the actual sentence, the clause *she has attracted investors* very strongly suggests that these investors have actually invested in her company, so you don't need additional modifiers to say so. The correct answer is (D).

56. **(H)** Immense loudspeakers, these cannons can communicate a warning …

Usage/Mechanics   Sentence Structure   Modifier Placement (also Style: Concision)

The clearest and most concise option here is to use the verb *can* in place of wordier alternatives and to open the sentence with an appositive phrase (*Immense loudspeakers*) to modify the subject (*these cannons*). The incorrect options with *being* are bloated and unclear. In fact, choice (G) wrongly suggests that *the ability* itself is *immense loudspeakers*. Choice (J) creates extra stutter-step pauses for no reason. The correct answer is (H).

57. **(B)** … a beam of deafening noise that few can long withstand.

Usage/Mechanics   Grammar & Usage   Modifier Forms

The correct form to mean "not many people" is *few,* not *fewer* (than what?) or *too few* (implying that more should be able to withstand?). Likewise, use *long* to mean "for a long time." *Longer* means "for additional time."

Word order in the right answer is sensible: *this is noise that few can long withstand*, that is, not many people can withstand this noise for a long time. The wrong answers make a jumble of the words, resulting in orders that are at best archaic and at worst meaningless. The correct answer is (B).

58. **(G)** The claw of the pistol shrimp is designed to snap together and shoot a bubble at prey.

Usage/Mechanics   Grammar & Usage   Parallelism

What is the claw of the pistol shrimp designed to do? It is designed to *snap together and shoot a bubble at prey.* The verb forms *snap* and *shoot* are in parallel, as indicated by the conjunction *and*. You can argue that *shoot* could or even should be a result or purpose: the claw is designed to snap together *to shoot* or *in order to shoot* a bubble. However, you do not have the option to change the *and* to *to*. Either way, the verb form has to be *shoot*. The present tense *shoots* awkwardly forces the parallelism to extend back to *is designed*, a construct that makes less sense. Past tense *shot* and *-ing* form *shooting* do not have any possible partner in the sentence. The correct answer is (G).

59. **(B)** If the writer were to make this deletion, the essay would primarily lose a contrast between the appearance and the essence of the bubble.

Rhetorical Skills   Writing Strategy   Deletions

The proposed deletion is the phrase *Innocuous as it may seem*. Without reading on, you are set up to expect that, while this bubble may *seem* innocuous to the reader, it really isn't. That expectation is borne out in the rest of the sentence. If the phrase is deleted, the text reads as follows: *The claw of the pistol shrimp is designed to snap together and shoot a bubble at prey. This bubble collapses in a sonic shockwave that can stun or even kill.* This version entirely loses the contrast between the bubble's appearance (it may seem to be *innocuous*) and its essence (that it *can stun or even kill*). The correct answer is (B).

MANHATTAN
PREP   309

60. **(H)** … similar bubbles … emit flashes of light in a mysterious <u>process, one that,</u> according to some scientists, may involve nuclear fusion.

Usage/Mechanics   Sentence Structure   Whole Sentences

The original version leaves the last thought as a fragment. *One that … may involve nuclear fusion* lacks a main verb. More than one fix is possible. You can write *a mysterious process that … may involve* or *a mysterious process, which … may involve*. In general, *that* and *which* are not completely interchangeable, but the phrase *a mysterious process* can be modified either by an essential modifier (defining which mysterious process you're talking about, with *that*) or by a non-essential modifier (simply giving more information about that process, with *which*). A third alternative is taken by the right answer: *a mysterious process, one that …* This nonessential modifier is equivalent in meaning to *which*.

The word *one* must be separated from *process* by a comma and be followed immediately by *that*. There is no flexibility in the format. Finally, you cannot simply leave out the relative pronoun (*that* or *which*) here. In doing so, choice (J) creates a run-on: *bubbles emit light in a mysterious process, according to scientists, may involve nuclear fusion.* You have jammed together two verbs improperly. The correct answer is (H).

Passage 5

61. **(B)** Best accomplishes intention of listing specific accomplishments of Olmos: … won both a Golden Globe and an Emmy for his iconic work on the 1980s television show "Miami Vice."

Rhetorical Skills   Writing Strategy   Choice of Content

The correct answer lists specific accomplishments of Olmos, naming particular awards he won for his work on a particular television show. The alternatives all describe positive characteristics of Olmos, but none of these characteristics are as specific as the awards listed in the correct answer. In addition, these awards are a better fit for the concept of "accomplishments" or achievements than the various characteristics in the wrong choices. The correct answer is (B).

62. **(H)** … he has been nominated for a Tony … and for a Hollywood <u>equivalent: the Academy Award</u> for Best Actor.

Usage/Mechanics   Punctuation   Colons & Commas

The phrase *the Academy Award for Best Actor* should not have a comma or a colon between *Award* and *for*, because the prepositional phrase *for Best Actor* defines which Academy Award you're talking about. (Even if you weren't sure whether there is more than one Academy Award, the phrase *for Best Actor* shouldn't be tacked on with just a comma.)

The punctuation to use between *equivalent* and *the* should be either a colon or a comma. The phrase *a Hollywood equivalent* is clarified and defined—that is, modified—by the following phrase (*the … Actor*), so a comma is perfectly appropriate. The colon, which is used in the correct answer, is a nice stylistic variation, given that the sentence already contains three commas. What comes after a colon must explain what came before it; that condition holds true here. The correct answer is (H).

63.   **(C)** Olmos may be most <u>proud, however,</u> of the plentiful honors …

Usage/Mechanics   Punctuation   Commas

The word *however* is used here as a transition from the previous sentence. Since the word is inserted in the middle of this sentence, it must be separated on both sides by commas. The correct answer is (C).

64.   **(F)** … Olmos <u>gravitated in his youth to</u> baseball and to rock music.

Rhetorical Skills   Style   Concision

In the original, correct version, the verb *gravitated* is used metaphorically to mean that Olmos was attracted to these activities and participated in them. In choice (G), the phrase *was gravitationally attracted* is not only wordy but also misleading: the author surely does not mean that the force of gravity literally pulled Olmos toward baseball. This choice and choice (J) also suffer from a lack of parallelism between *toward baseball* and *to rock music*. Finally, choices (H) and (J) express the idea of youth redundantly. The phrase *in his youth* by itself is sufficient. The correct answer is (F).

65.   **(B)** The best placement for the underlined portion would be after the word *successful*.

Usage/Mechanics   Grammar & Usage   Idioms

In this sort of sentence (containing an adjective, *successful*, and an infinitive, *to front*), the best position for the word *enough* is right after the adjective: "He was successful *enough* to front a band." Idiomatically, the word is less suitable anywhere else. The correct answer is (B).

66.   **(G)** After a few acting classes he took to improve his voice, he realized he was a better actor than singer, <u>so</u> he changed direction.

Rhetorical Skills   Organization   Transitions

Review the story on basic terms. Olmos was originally a rock singer. Then he took some acting classes and realized he was better at acting than at singing. The final thought is he *changed direction* (that is, to become an actor). How does this thought relate to what came before? Olmos's change of direction is the result of his realization, so you should use the one "result" transition you have available: *so*.

The wrong choices (*except*, *but*, and *unless*) all indicate contrast in some fashion. Contrast is inappropriate here, because the change in direction was a direct consequence. The correct answer is (G).

67.   **(A)** Most effective first sentence: <u>Offers began to arrive more rapidly.</u>

Rhetorical Skills   Organization   Opening/Closing Content

The previous paragraph ends with Olmos's *break*, meaning his breakthrough performance in the play "Zoot Suit." The current paragraph shows how the actor's upward trajectory continued (to "Miami Vice" and "Stand and Deliver"). The correct answer provides a good bridge to this paragraph from the prior breakthrough.

Choice (B) might be appropriate if the current paragraph went into more detail about the play, but it doesn't. Choice (C) interrupts the narrative flow, inserting a fact out of chronological order. Finally, choice (D) does continue the narration in a sense, but by pointing out that many of these films and television movies *are largely forgotten today*, the sentence muddies the clear picture of Olmos's upward path. The next sentence begins *Negotiating a rare degree of creative control for himself*, which should come directly on the heels of a positive statement about Olmos's career. The correct answer is (A).

68.   **(J)**   This <u>adaptation of Escalante's true story portrays</u> his inspiring efforts …

Usage/Mechanics   Punctuation   Commas

No commas belong anywhere in the underlined section. The subject is the entire noun phrase *This adaptation of Escalante's true story*. This subject should not be separated from its verb (*portrays*) by a comma, nor should the verb be separated from its object (*his inspiring efforts*) by a comma. Finally, the noun *adaptation* is defined by the following prepositional phrase (*of Escalante's true story*), so there should not be a comma between *adaptation* and *of*. The correct answer is (J).

69.   **(A)**   <u>Much of Olmos's time,</u> though, is now consumed by advocacy.

Rhetorical Skills   Style   Concision

The verb in this sentence is *is consumed*. What can logically be consumed? Time itself. You can't consume the *use* of time; you consume time or you use time. So the subject should not be *the use of time* or *the way time is spent*. These subjects are not only redundant but illogical.

An additional redundancy shows up in choice (D) with the word *current*. The non-underlined portion contains the word *now*, making the word *current* unnecessary. The correct answer is (A).

70.   **(J)**   Various organizations that he founded or co-founded <u>support Latinos and promote</u> Latino culture …

Usage/Mechanics   Grammar & Usage   Subject–Verb Agreement

The subject of the sentence is *Various organizations,* a plural noun, so the verbs *support* and *promote* should both be in the plural form (*they support,* not *it supports*). The correct answer is (J).

71.   **(C)**   <u>On</u> a more ordinary level …

Usage/Mechanics   Grammar & Usage   Idioms

The right preposition to use with the word *level* is *on* or *at*. You can be *on* a certain level or *at* a certain level. Only *on* is available here. By *level*, the writer means "level of existence or of life." The phrase *On a more ordinary level* transitions the reader from grand activity (founding or co-founding organizations) to the everyday action of picking up a broom, as the rest of the sentence describes. The correct answer is (C).

72. **(G)** … <u>he responded</u> to the 1992 Rodney King riots in Los Angeles by walking into the streets …

Usage/Mechanics   Sentence Structure   Whole Sentences

The correct option is the only one that gives the sentence a complete verb: *responded,* which has the subject *he.* Neither the noun *response* nor the *-ing* form *responding* can do the job of the verb *responded.* The incorrect answers are all sentence fragments. The correct answer is (G).

73.   **(D)** If the essay were revised to include first-person opinion clauses, such as *I think* and *I believe,* but otherwise left unchanged, the essay would primarily lose some measure of its direct, assertive style.

Rhetorical Skills   Writing Strategy   Additions

As currently written, the essay narrates the career achievements of Edward James Olmos in a way that is both objective and positive (e.g., including a few value-laden words as *skilled*). There is no need to interject first-person opinion clauses, such as *I think,* as padding in front of these mostly factual statements. Opinion clauses would simply weaken the essay, if the writer adds no actual thoughts or judgments beyond what is already written. The primary casualty would be the *direct, assertive style,* but the essay would not lose *any sense of objectivity that it now establishes,* as choice (C) incorrectly claims. The correct answer is (D).

74.   **(F)** The most logical and effective place to add this sentence would be after the last sentence of Paragraph 1.

Rhetorical Skills   Organization   Sentence Order

The new sentence is *In fact, he would likely consider his imprisonment after a protest in Puerto Rico a badge of honor.* The transition *In fact* means that this sentence agrees with, and goes even further than, the prior sentence. The best candidate for that attachment point should be something to the effect that Olmos is proud of his advocacy work—and the last sentence of Paragraph 1 fits the bill: *Olmos may be most proud, however, of the plentiful honors he has received for social activism.* The correct answer is (F).

75.   **(C)** Fulfill the goal of assessing the ethical positions that Olmos has taken in his advocacy work? No, because the essay limits itself to broadly describing the causes that Olmos has supported.

Rhetorical Skills   Writing Strategy   Goal of Essay

The essay does not even describe the *ethical positions that Olmos has taken in his advocacy work,* let alone assess those positions. The essay simply lists some of the organizations he has *founded or co-founded* to *support Latinos and promote Latino culture.* His grassroots response to the 1992 riots is mentioned, as is the fact that he is proud of his advocacy work. However, none of this constitutes an assessment (or really even a description) of Olmos's *ethical positions*—that is, his philosophy on these issues, his judgments that could be either defended or argued with. The essay does not provide Olmos's opinions directly on any matter. The correct answer is (C).

8

Chapter *of* 9

5lb. Book of ACT® Practice Problems

English:
Passage Set 5

In This Chapter...

Set 5 Passages & Solutions

Chapter 9
English: Passage Set 5

The English problems in this chapter are distributed across five passages, just as they will be on the ACT itself. Every topic is up for grabs, so expect a little of everything. The answer key and the solutions classify the problems for you, so you can pinpoint strengths and weaknesses.

How should you use this chapter? Here are some recommendations, according to the level you've reached in ACT English.

1. Fundamentals. If you haven't done any topical work yet, consider working in Chapters 3 and 4 first. Otherwise, do a passage or two untimed to begin with. As you become more comfortable, put the clock on. In all cases, review the solutions closely, and articulate what you've learned. Redo problems as necessary.

2. Fixes. Do one passage at a time under timed conditions. Examine the results, learn your lessons, then test yourself with more passages at once.

3. Tweaks. Confirm your mastery by doing a few passages at once under timed conditions. A full set of five is the ultimate goal. Aim to improve the speed and ease of your solution process.

Good luck on the problems!

PASSAGE 1

Delivering the Paper

[1]

Warren Buffett, who is one of the richest people in the world, and I, have something in common. Many decades ago, he used to perform a task

1. **A.** NO CHANGE
   B. world and I,
   C. world, and I
   D. world and I

that every morning at 5 a.m. I now do, a time when my friends are asleep—deliver newspapers.

2. **F.** NO CHANGE
   G. that I now do every morning at 5 a.m.,
   H. and now I, at 5 a.m. every morning, am doing it,
   J. but, every morning at 5 a.m., that's what I now do,

[2]

To its credit, my hometown newspaper is still in the belief of traditional paper routes for kids, perhaps because Buffett's company has invested in the newspaper. The industry is in crisis: readership is declining, costs are rising, and in sight these trends have no end. In response, many papers have let go of staff and lowered standards.

3. **A.** NO CHANGE
   B. is still of the belief that
   C. still believes that
   D. still believes in

4. The BEST placement for the underlined portion would be:
   F. where it is now.
   G. after the word *industry*.
   H. after the word *declining* (but before the comma).
   J. after the word *end* (ending the sentence with a period).

[3]

However, our local paper has made a series of smart adjustments. It focuses more clearly now on reporting regional issues, and its website looks fresh. Maybe most importantly, our paper has developed strong partnerships with school districts, libraries, Scout troops, and other organizations who's interest in our area is unquestioned. These organizations have become vested in supporting the paper. As a symbol

5. **A.** NO CHANGE
   B. They focus
   C. It focused
   D. They have focused

6. **F.** NO CHANGE
   G. that's
   H. whose
   J. where their

of our town, the wholesome image is the newspaper's presentation of teenagers earning pocket money and learning the value of work by delivering papers to their neighbors. Almost no other paper still employs

teenagers this way. [8]

[4]

I've had my route for four years and usually enjoy it. The hardest part is getting up early, especially if I had to stay up late doing homework the night before. Once I'm outside, though, I'm fine—except if it's pouring

rain. It's tough to keep the papers dry and completely free of water while I bike, half-blinded, through a

downpour. [10]

7. A. NO CHANGE
  B. the newspaper presents the wholesome image
  C. it is wholesome for the newspaper to present the image
  D. the wholesome image is presented via the newspaper

8. The writer is considering deleting the words "Almost" and "still" from the preceding sentence, adjusting the capitalization as needed. If the writer were to delete these words, would the meaning of the sentence change?
  F. Yes, because without these words, the reader would conclude that the number of other papers employing teenagers as carriers is exactly zero.
  G. Yes, because without these words, the reader would think that many teenagers were employed as carriers by other newspapers.
  H. No, because these words are unnecessary redundancies that can be eliminated safely from the sentence.
  J. No, because although these words provide interesting nuances about the newspapers in question, the words are not vital to the meaning of the sentence.

9. A. NO CHANGE
  B. water from completely soaking and drenching the papers
  C. papers from becoming completely sopping wet in the water
  D. papers completely dry

10. Given that all of the following sentences are true, which one would MOST effectively conclude this paragraph?
  F. On the other hand, a crisp autumn morning just before dawn, with the sky still showing stars, is glorious.
  G. It's even worse when the plastic arrives torn and some of the papers are already ruined.
  H. Snowstorms also test my fortitude, especially when school is canceled but newspaper delivery is not.
  J. Since we have a lot of agriculture in this region, though, I try to remember to be grateful for the precipitation.

9

[5]

Most of all, I have always liked earning my own money, like my hero Warren Buffett. Each year, his company, Berkshire Hathaway hosts in Omaha,
                                      ‾‾‾‾‾‾‾‾‾‾‾‾‾‾‾‾‾‾‾‾‾‾‾‾
                                              11

Nebraska an annual shareholders' meeting, known
        ‾‾‾‾‾‾‾‾‾‾‾‾‾‾‾‾‾‾‾‾
                12
as the "Woodstock of capitalism," with all kinds of

activities. ⬜13 Buffett now regularly challenges visitors to

a newspaper-throwing contest. He probably won most
                                              ‾‾‾
                                              14
of the time, but I bet I could give him a run for his

money.

11. A. NO CHANGE
  B. company, Berkshire Hathaway,
  C. company Berkshire, Hathaway
  D. company, Berkshire, Hathaway

12. F. NO CHANGE
  G. an annual shareholders
  H. a shareholders
  J. a shareholders'

13. At this point, the writer is considering adding the following true sentence:

> Locals who bought in at $20 or $30 per share in the mid-1960s now hold shares that are each worth around $200,000.

Should the writer make this addition?

  A. Yes, because the additional information explains why the narrator admires Warren Buffett so much.
  B. Yes, because if readers understand the dramatic increase in the share price, they will also understand why the meeting is called the "Woodstock of capitalism."
  C. No, because this detail distracts the reader from the focus of both the paragraph and the essay as a whole.
  D. No, because it does not acknowledge that because of inflation, $20 was worth more in the mid-1960s than the same sum is worth today.

14. F. NO CHANGE
  G. had won
  H. wins
  J. would have won

> Question 15 asks about the preceding passage as a whole.

15. For the sake of logic and coherence, Paragraph 2 should be placed:

  A. where it is now.
  B. before Paragraph 1.
  C. after Paragraph 3.
  D. after Paragraph 4.

PASSAGE 2

Stax Records

[1]

In the 1960s, Stax Records did not give its name
to an entire trend in popular music, as its rival Motown
Records did. However, the influence of Stax on the
development of rhythm and blues was arguably as

extensive as Motowns. The sound of Southern soul was
largely born at the Stax studio in Memphis, Tennessee.
There, luminaries such as Otis Redding and Isaac Hayes

recorded numerous songs that become radio sensations
during the heyday of Stax.

[2]

Many credit the session musicians at Stax with the
achievements of the record label. However, these musicians,
several of whom formed the successful band Booker
T. & the M.G.'s, were no less skilled and experienced

than the Funk Brothers, the house players at Motown. [20]

Regrettably, both sets of performers, who were
under-appreciated and underpaid, even as they laid

16. F. NO CHANGE
   G. music. As
   H. music; as
   J. music, and as

17. A. NO CHANGE
   B. Motown's.
   C. Motowns'.
   D. that of Motowns'.

18. F. NO CHANGE
   G. have become
   H. became
   J. had became

19. A. NO CHANGE
   B. Thus, these
   C. At first, these
   D. These

20. The writer is considering deleting the following from
the preceding sentence, revising the punctuation accordingly:

   several of whom formed the successful band
   Booker T. & the M.G.'s

If the writer were to delete this phrase, the essay
would primarily lose:
   F. support for the sentence's assertion about the
      skill level of the Stax musicians.
   G. a comparison between two groups of artists at
      different record labels.
   H. an explanation of the name chosen for the band
      by the session players.
   J. a judgment of the ultimate cultural impact of
      Stax Records in the 1960s.

21. A. NO CHANGE
   B. performers were
   C. performers,
   D. performers

MANHATTAN
PREP   321

down the sound for dozens and dozens of hits of

                                   22
the era.

[3]

Another reason Stax found success is that
partial owner and entrepreneur, Estelle Axton also

                23
ran a record store. Playing rough drafts of songs for
her teenaged customers and observing their reactions,
Axton quickly discovered what would sell and what
wouldn't. 24

[4]

One duo, Sam & Dave, achieved its greatest feats

                          25
at Stax, recording chart-toppers such as "Soul Man."
Unfortunately, the pair was on loan from Atlantic
Records, with which Stax had signed a distribution
deal. After that arrangement ended bitterly, Sam &

                                  26
Dave returned to Atlantic, never to reach the same
stature as before.

[5]

The divorce from Atlantic in 1968, with legal
custody of almost all the hits going to the other side, led
to a downturn and decline for Stax. In 1975, the label

                27
declared bankruptcy. Even after its corporate rebirth
shortly afterward, Stax struggled for decades, surviving

only by reissuing the music under there control. In

                                 28
recent years, however, a rejuvenated Stax Records has
signed new artists and brought back old favorites such

22. **F.** NO CHANGE

    G. dozens of hits, maybe fifty or sixty, or even more

    H. multiple dozen hits

    J. dozens of hits

23. **A.** NO CHANGE

    B. partial owner, and entrepreneur

    C. partial owner and entrepreneur

    D. partial owner, and entrepreneur,

24. If the writer were to delete the preceding sentence, the paragraph would primarily lose:

    F. an explanation of how the store added to the label's success.

    G. background information about one of the owners of Stax.

    H. an overview of typical leisure activities of teenagers at the time.

    J. an observation that weighs against a claim made earlier.

25. **A.** NO CHANGE

    B. reached

    C. obtained

    D. succeeded

26. Which of the following alternatives to the underlined portion would be LEAST acceptable in terms of the context of this sentence?

    F. came to a bitter conclusion,

    G. bitterly culminated,

    H. came to a bitter end,

    J. concluded bitterly,

27. **A.** NO CHANGE

    B. decline downward

    C. decline to a lower position

    D. downturn

28. **F.** NO CHANGE

    G. their

    H. its

    J. it's

as Isaac Hayes. Meanwhile, <u>dedicated to American soul</u>
<u>music, the legendary recording studio once stood where</u>
<u>there is now a museum.</u>
     29

29. **A.** NO CHANGE
    B. a museum dedicated to American soul music stands where the legendary recording studio once did.
    C. where the legendary recording studio once stood is dedicated to American soul music, a museum standing.
    D. standing where there now stands a museum, dedicated to American soul music, the legendary recording studio once was.

Question 30 asks about the preceding passage as a whole.

---

30. Suppose the writer had intended to write a brief essay that describes the complete process that Stax went through to write, record, and release a hit song. Would this essay successfully fulfill the writer's goal?
    F. Yes, because it highlights the skill of the musicians and the label's marketing prowess.
    G. Yes, because it lists in detail each step in creating and promoting a successful song.
    H. No, because the essay focuses more broadly on the history and characteristics of Stax.
    J. No, because the essay does not catalog sufficient examples of hits recorded at Stax.

9

PASSAGE 3

Anne of Green Gables

[1]

Driving through the smallest Canadian province, Prince Edward Island, in the <u>summertime, traffic can leave you stuck</u> behind tour buses filled with visitors from as far away as Japan. These tourists are not primarily on the island to touch its <u>dirt, this is so red-colored</u> because of its high iron content. The rolling green meadows and the bright blue water of the Gulf of St. Lawrence <u>by itself is</u> not the draw. Rather, <u>the buses have brought the tourists</u> to get closer, in some personal way, to the fictional home of their literary hero, Anne of Green Gables.

[2]

Over a century ago, <u>local schoolteacher Lucy Maud Montgomery,</u> who had been born on the island, published *Anne of Green Gables*, a novel about a red-haired orphan who has been taken in by an elderly brother and <u>sister to help around the farm.</u> Having sent to a <u>distant, faraway orphanage</u> for a boy, the pair is at

31. **A.** NO CHANGE
    B. summertime, you had been stuck in traffic
    C. summertime, leaving you stuck in traffic
    D. summertime can leave you stuck in traffic

32. **F.** NO CHANGE
    G. red dirt, so colored
    H. dirt so red, in color,
    J. such red dirt

33. **A.** NO CHANGE
    B. is, in itself,
    C. by themselves are
    D. are, on themselves,

34. **F.** NO CHANGE
    G. the tourists have arrived on their buses
    H. the arrival of the tourists by buses is
    J. in arriving on their buses, the tourists are brought near

35. **A.** NO CHANGE
    B. local, and schoolteacher, Lucy Maud Montgomery,
    C. Lucy Maud Montgomery a local schoolteacher
    D. Lucy Maud Montgomery, schoolteacher, and local,

36. Given that all of the choices are true, which one provides the closest and MOST logical connection to the statement immediately following this underlined portion?
    F. NO CHANGE
    G. sister inadvertently.
    H. sister, named Matthew and Marilla Cuthbert.
    J. sister, neither of whom has been married.

37. **A.** NO CHANGE
    B. distant orphanage, far and away,
    C. far-off orphanage where parentless children live
    D. distant orphanage

9

first reluctant to keep Anne, but in the end she charms
them in spite of themselves with her strong will, good
heart, and passion for the world around her, expressed
almost nonstop in effusive declamations.

[3]

Anne's qualities are not all perfect. One of these, her
quick temper, manifesting itself on her first day
of school, when she breaks a boy's slate over his head.
Her scrapes make her even more appealing, though.

Most likely, she reminded Mark Twain of his own
creations Tom Sawyer and Huck Finn when Twain
praised her as the best child in fiction "since the
immortal Alice."

[4]

Just as she has her neighbors in fictional Avonlea,
readers in Canada and further afield have long been
charmed by Anne. Today, the Anne industry on the

island is healthy, with theme parks, gift shops hawk
kitschy items adorned with the girl's image, and even
musicals that have run for decades. The place other
than Canada that are the most in love with Anne is
Japan, which, as the country struggled to rebuild after

World War II, warmly took to the orphan. There is even

38. Which of the following alternatives to the under-
lined portion would be the LEAST acceptable?
  - **F.** Anne; however, she eventually
  - **G.** Anne. Nevertheless, over time, she
  - **H.** Anne. All the while, she endlessly
  - **J.** Anne; finally, though, she

39. A. NO CHANGE
  - **B.** One, her
  - **C.** One, having a
  - **D.** One of them is her

40. F. NO CHANGE
  - **G.** In contrast
  - **H.** Granted,
  - **J.** Accidentally,

41. A. NO CHANGE
  - **B.** Anne's charm has long been of readers in
    Canada and further afield.
  - **C.** Anne has long charmed readers in Canada and
    further afield.
  - **D.** Canada and further afield have long had
    readers charmed by Anne.

42. F. NO CHANGE
  - **G.** hawked
  - **H.** hawking
  - **J.** have hawked

43. A. NO CHANGE
  - **B.** are, more than any other, in love with Anne
  - **C.** love Anne most
  - **D.** loves Anne the most

44. F. NO CHANGE
  - **G.** tepidly
  - **H.** heatedly
  - **J.** ferociously

9

a Japanese school of <u>nursing, named for</u> and deeply

inspired by, Anne.

45

45. A. NO CHANGE
  B. nursing named for,
  C. nursing named, for
  D. nursing named for

PASSAGE 4

A Sweet Sixteen-añera

[1]

[1] My best friend Dee and I have parallel lives in many ways. [2] Almost everyone in her extended <u>family shows</u> up on Sunday mornings at the same
46
church that my own big family goes to. [3] Sunday dinners at her house are also well-attended affairs, with

<u>them</u> crowding around to fill plates and then dispersing
47
into various rooms, because there's not space for

everyone to sit in one location. [4] <u>However, a</u> similar
48

scene takes place at my house most Sunday evenings. ⁴⁹

46. **F.** NO CHANGE
    G. family show
    H. family showing
    J. family shown

47. **A.** NO CHANGE
    B. relatives
    C. it
    D. the crowd inside the place

48. **F.** NO CHANGE
    G. On the contrary, a
    H. Thus, a
    J. A

49. Upon reviewing Paragraph 1 and realizing that some information has been left out, the writer composes the following sentence:

    > All that's different is that in Dee's kitchen you would hear English, whereas in mine, you'd usually hear Spanish.

    The MOST logical placement for this sentence would be:

    A. after Sentence 1.
    B. after Sentence 2.
    C. after Sentence 3.
    D. after Sentence 4.

[2]

<u>Less than a week apart but in the same grade,</u>
50
<u>Dee and I have birthdays that make her almost</u>
50
<u>exactly a year older than I am.</u> For this reason, as
50
freshmen we knew that November of our sophomore year had an important milestone in store for both

50. **F.** NO CHANGE
    G. Almost exactly a year older than I am, Dee and I are in the same grade but were born less than a week apart.
    H. Dee and I are in the same grade, but she is almost exactly a year older than I am; our birthdays are less than a week apart.
    J. Dee, who is almost exactly a year older than I am and in the same grade, and I are less than a week apart in the days we were born.

of us. Together we decided, that her Sweet Sixteen
51

party and my *quinceañera* a celebration held for girls
52

of my heritage who turn fifteen, would have been
53
combined.

[3]

Our families were initially skeptical, but our enthusiasm won them over—not that the planning was always easy. Our fathers were cordial but had a rough time connecting on a personal level at first. Their difficulty in understanding each other's speech was really a symptom of this issue. Each of them, feeling responsible for "his little girl," seemed reluctant to compromise on any issue in public. For example, our mothers sent them
54
off to a supply store together to design the archway Dee

and I would pass through. We didn't ask for this archway,
55
but our mothers were right: building something together

allowed these two gruff men to bond. When the party
56
rolled around, they were fast friends.

51. A. NO CHANGE
  B. decided that
  C. decided that,
  D. decided,

52. F. NO CHANGE
  G. party, and my *quinceañera*
  H. party and my *quinceañera*,
  J. party, together with my *quinceañera*

53. A. NO CHANGE
  B. will be
  C. would be
  D. should of been

54. F. NO CHANGE
  G. Incidentally,
  H. On the other hand,
  J. Finally,

55. A. NO CHANGE
  B. through not asking
  C. through, we didn't ask
  D. through, although we didn't ask

56. F. NO CHANGE
  G. bond when
  H. bond, when
  J. bond,

MANHATTAN
PREP

[4]

The party itself had the theme of Thanksgiving, with Irish and Mexican decorations everywhere throughout the hall. Of course, the food was both abundant and delicious. 57 Dee and I made a simultaneous grand entrance through the arch

at the same time as each other and our dates, and in the back of the hall I could see my father and Dee's shaking
58

hands, smiling, and chatting excitedly. A good reason to be thankful was that their joint handiwork held up all night.
59

57. Given that all are true, which of the following additions to the preceding sentence (replacing "food") would be MOST relevant?
   A. food, which we had trouble keeping hot throughout the event,
   B. food, which represented our two cultures as well as the holiday,
   C. food, which had been set out in innumerable casserole dishes,
   D. food, which would have cost far too much to have catered,

58. F. NO CHANGE
    G. with our dates, all at once,
    H. synchronized with our dates
    J. with our dates

59. Which of the choices would provide an ending MOST consistent with the essay as a whole?
    A. NO CHANGE
    B. Our mothers, on the other hand, were each too busy with guests even to wave to each other.
    C. Afterwards, our fathers dismantled the structure and used the wood for other projects.
    D. Neither of our fathers is a very skilled carpenter, and the arch was evidence of that fact.

Question 60 asks about the preceding passage as a whole.

60. The writer is considering deleting the first sentence of Paragraph 3. If the writer removed this sentence, the essay would primarily lose:
    F. an explanation for the initial skepticism of each family.
    G. an effective transition from the idea of the party to its planning.
    H. a detailed outline of how Dee and the narrator won over their relatives.
    J. a statement reinforcing the importance of culture in the lives of two teenagers.

PASSAGE 5

Surprising Aluminum

[1]

The next time you pluck a baked potato out of an aluminum foil jacket, remember that it is touching— and probably discarding—a piece of metal that was once more valuable than gold. "Tinfoil" is nowadays made of aluminum, not tin.

[2]

Aluminum is widely used throughout society. Strong, light, and durable, the metal shows up in materials from laptop cases to airplane wings. Aluminum is crucial to modern industry, but it is not a precious metal any more. The fact that millions of tons that are produced annually should be expected, since in the Earth's crust one of the most abundant elements are lucky number 13 on the periodic table, with symbol Al.

[3]

[1] Why, then, did it take until 1827 for aluminum to be discovered? [2] The element is highly reactive, forming a sturdy bond with oxygen. [3] Thus, nuggets of pure aluminum are never found

61. A. NO CHANGE
   B. we are
   C. you are
   D. people are

62. F. NO CHANGE
   G. Nowadays, "tinfoil" is not really tin, but aluminum instead.
   H. Aluminum has nowadays replaced tin in "tinfoil."
   J. OMIT the underlined portion.

63. A. NO CHANGE
   B. up, in materials
   C. up in materials,
   D. up, in materials,

64. F. NO CHANGE
   G. which have been
   H. are
   J. DELETE the underlined portion

65. A. NO CHANGE
   B. is
   C. were
   D. have been

66. Which choice would MOST effectively and appropriately lead the reader from the topic of Paragraph 2 to that of Paragraph 3?
   F. NO CHANGE
   G. In certain applications, aluminum is being replaced by even stronger and lighter carbon fiber.
   H. Used in welding, the thermite reaction between iron oxide and aluminum illustrates the metal's inherent volatility.
   J. Why is aluminum so much more common than even iron at the surface of the Earth?

MANHATTAN
PREP

in rivers, and if you simply heat rocks doesn't work
                    67
to extract the metal, as it does for copper and iron.
[4] Ironically, the very reactivity of aluminum is
what makes aluminum components resistant to wear.
[5] On contact with air, the surface of the pure metal
becomes instantly coated with a thin but tough layer
of aluminum oxide, preventing further corrosion. 68

[4]

The process discovered in 1827 for isolating
aluminum was difficult and costly, for several decades
                    69
thereafter, aluminum was likely the most valuable metal
on the planet. The emperor of France supposedly served
his best guests on aluminum plates, and the pyramid
atop the Washington Monument, where it serves as an
                    70
imperfect lightning rod, was formed from this once-
70
precious metal.

[5]

Then, in 1886, the price fell through the
floor. That year, two simultaneous young inventors
                    71
determined how to separate aluminum from its ore
using electric current. The raw material had always been

plentiful in its unprocessed form; now, extraction was
                    72
cheap. Aluminum plates were no longer worth small

fortunes. Incidentally, the same collapse in cost could
            73
happen to diamonds one day. After all, they're also

---

67. A. NO CHANGE
B. rivers; if one simply heats
C. rivers, and simply heating
D. rivers, and simply heated

68. For the sake of the logic and cohesion of Paragraph 3, Sentence 4 should be:
F. placed where it is now.
G. placed after Sentence 1.
H. placed after Sentence 2.
J. OMITTED, because the paragraph focuses only on the difficulty of discovering aluminum.

69. A. NO CHANGE
B. difficult, costly, and for
C. difficult and costly. For
D. difficult, costly, for

70. F. NO CHANGE
G. Monument, serving as an imperfect lightning rod,
H. Monument, serving imperfectly as a lightning rod,
J. Monument

71. A. NO CHANGE
B. young inventors simultaneously
C. inventors, simultaneously young,
D. inventors, young and simultaneous,

72. F. NO CHANGE
G. plentiful as unprocessed ore;
H. plentiful in an unprocessed state,
J. plentiful;

73. Which of the following alternatives to the underlined portion would be LEAST acceptable?
A. On the contrary,
B. By the way,
C. It is interesting to note that
D. Jewelry investors might take heed:

9

made from an <u>extreme and common</u> element: carbon,
the primary ingredient of coal.

74

74. F. NO CHANGE
  G. extremely common
  H. extreme, common
  J. extremely commonly

Question 75 asks about the preceding passage
as a whole.

---

75. Suppose the writer had chosen to write an essay that traces the historical evolution of the value of aluminum. Would this essay fulfill the writer's goal?

  A. No, because the writer fails to describe the actual discovery of aluminum in 1827.
  B. No, because the writer makes distracting predictions about the price of diamonds.
  C. Yes, because the writer compares the price of aluminum to those of precious metals.
  D. Yes, because the writer connects prices to events affecting the supply of aluminum.

Passage Set 5 Answer Key

Write in whether you got each problem right or wrong (or left it blank). If your answer was correct, put a 1 in every blank to the right of that problem. Sum up each column and compare your total to the total possible "Out Of" points in each column.

Problem	Correct Answer	Right/ Wrong/ Blank	Grammar & Usage	Punctuation	Sentence Structure	Organization	Style	Writing Strategy
			Usage/Mechanics			Rhetorical Skills		
1	C			—				
2	G				—			
3	D		—					
4	J				—			
5	A		—					
6	H		—					
7	B				—			
8	F							—
9	D						—	
10	F					—		
11	B			—				
12	J						—	
13	C							—
14	H				—			
15	A					—		
16	F			—				
17	B			—				
18	H				—			
19	D					—		
20	F							—
21	B				—			
22	J						—	
23	C			—				
24	F							—
25	A						—	
26	G						—	

9

Problem	Correct Answer	Right/ Wrong/ Blank	Usage/Mechanics			Rhetorical Skills		
			Grammar & Usage	Punctuation	Sentence Structure	Organization	Style	Writing Strategy
27	D						—	
28	H		—					
29	B				—			
30	H							—
31	D				—			
32	G				—			
33	C		—					
34	G		—					
35	A			—				
36	G							—
37	D						—	
38	H					—		
39	D				—			
40	F					—		
41	C		—					
42	H				—			
43	D		—					
44	F						—	
45	B			—				
46	F				—			
47	B		—					
48	J					—		
49	D					—		
50	H				—			
51	B			—				
52	H			—				
53	C				—			
54	J					—		
55	A				—			
56	F				—			

MANHATTAN
PREP

Problem	Correct Answer	Right/ Wrong/ Blank	Usage/Mechanics			Rhetorical Skills		
			Grammar & Usage	Punctuation	Sentence Structure	Organization	Style	Writing Strategy
57	B							—
58	J						—	
59	A					—		
60	G							—
61	C		—					
62	J							—
63	A			—				
64	H				—			
65	B		—					
66	F					—		
67	C				—			
68	F					—		
69	C				—			
70	J							—
71	B		—					
72	J						—	
73	A					—		
74	G		—					
75	D							—
Total								
Out Of		75	13	10	19	12	10	11

9

Passage Set 5 Solutions

Passage 1

1.   **(C)** Warren Buffett, who is one of the richest people in the <u>world, and I</u> have something in common.

Usage/Mechanics   Punctuation   Commas

The nonessential modifier *who is … world,* which describes *Warren Buffett,* needs to be set off by commas. The subject of the sentence is the compound phrase *Warren Buffett and I.* This subject should not be separated from its verb (*have*) by a comma: *Warren Buffett and I have something in common.* The correct answer is (C).

2.   **(G)** … he used to perform a task <u>that I now do every morning at 5 a.m.,</u> a time when my friends …

Usage/Mechanics   Sentence Structure   Modifier Placement

The underlined portion is followed by an appositive phrase: *a time when.* This appositive needs to modify *a time,* and that time needs to be placed directly next to the appositive. Thus, the underlined portion has to end with *every morning at 5 a.m.,* as in the correct answer. None of the wrong answer choices place the time at the end, so this issue is sufficient to solve the problem.

In addition, answer choices (H) and (J) succumb to wordiness. The tightest way to express the thought is to attach it as a modifier to *a task,* so that you are indicating right there which task you're talking about. The correct answer is (G).

3.   **(D)** … my hometown newspaper <u>still believes in</u> traditional paper routes for kids, perhaps because …

Usage/Mechanics   Grammar & Usage   Idioms

In the original sentence, the phrase *in the belief of* is an incorrect idiomatic use of the word *belief.* You can be *of the belief that* something is true (this phrase is often seen with *opinion*) or you can act *in the belief that* something is true, but *in the belief of* is definitely wrong.

If you choose *of the belief that* or *believes that,* then the *that* has to be followed by what could be an independent clause, one that could stand alone as a sentence: *I believe that the Eagles will win the Super Bowl.* However, the words following the underlined portion do not constitute a complete clause, since *traditional paper routes for kids* has no verb. The *perhaps because* starts a separate subordinate clause, so you can ignore that. Thus, you must choose the form *believes in,* so that the *traditional paper routes* is the object of *in,* and you're done. The correct answer is (D).

4.   **(J)** The best placement for the underlined portion would be after the word *end* (ending the sentence with a period).

Usage/Mechanics   Sentence Structure   Modifier Placement

The sentence should read … *these trends have no end in sight.* You can think of the issue as an idiom: *have an end in sight* is a relatively fixed expression. The prepositional phrase *in sight* should always go after *end.* It makes little sense to keep the phrase where it is now (after *and*) or to move it anywhere else in the sentence. The correct answer is (J).

5.   **(A)** … our local paper has made a series of smart adjustments. <u>It focuses</u> more clearly now on reporting regional issues, and its website looks fresh.

Usage/Mechanics   Grammar & Usage   Pronoun Agreement

The pronoun should be *it* (referring to *our local paper*), not *they* (referring to *adjustments*). The sentence only makes sense if it means *Our local paper focuses more clearly now on reporting regional issues …* (the *adjustments* cannot do the focusing or reporting). Moreover, the *its* before *website* refers to the *local paper* as well.

Between *focuses* and *focused,* choose the present tense *focuses*. This tense agrees with *has made* (present perfect, which is really a present-like tense) and with *looks*. There is no reason to change to the past tense. The correct answer is (A).

6.   **(H)** … and other organizations <u>whose</u> interest in our area is unquestioned.

Usage/Mechanics   Grammar & Usage   Modifier Forms

The proper form here is *whose*, which you should use as a possessive: *whose interest* = the interest of these other organizations. The contraction *who's* always means *who is*, and the contraction *that's* always means *that is*. Neither is correct in this context. Before you use *who's* or *that's*, make sure the expanded form makes sense.

Finally, *where* should only be used after places, and *where their* is an inadequate substitute for *whose*—it fails to define the organizations the writer is talking about: the ones that have an unquestioned interest in the area, or the ones *whose interest in our area is unquestioned.* The correct answer is (H).

7.   **(B)** As a symbol of our town, <u>the newspaper presents the wholesome image</u> of teenagers earning pocket money …

Usage/Mechanics   Sentence Structure   Modifier Placement

The sentence begins with *As a symbol of our town*. Therefore, the subject of the sentence must follow directly and be *a symbol of our town*. Of the available choices, only *the newspaper* qualifies: not the *wholesome image* or *it is wholesome*.

In both speech and writing, people frequently begin sentences with *As X*, but fail to make the subject equivalent to X. Here's an example that sounds okay but is absolutely incorrect: *As a taxpayer, this issue concerns me.* The issue is not the taxpayer; I am! You must rephrase to *As a taxpayer, I am concerned by this issue.* The correct answer is (B).

8.   **(F)** If the writer were to delete the words "Almost" and "still," would the meaning of the sentence change? Yes, because without these words, the reader would conclude that the number of other papers employing teenagers as carriers is exactly zero.

Rhetorical Skills   Writing Strategy   Deletions

Actually make the deletion and compare the result to the original:

    Original: Almost no other paper still employs teenagers this way.
    After deletion: No other paper employs teenagers this way.

The key difference is the *almost*. With that word in place, the writer is allowing for the possibility that a few other papers employ teenagers this way. Without that word, though, that possibility is zeroed out. The claim is much stronger without the *almost*, and thus, the meaning changes dramatically. (The absence of *still* also creates a shift in meaning, but a smaller one.). The correct answer is (F).

9.　**(D)**　It's tough to keep the <u>papers completely dry</u> while I bike …

Rhetorical Skills　　　　　Style　　　　　　　　Concision

The wrong answers here all suffer from redundancy. The original version does not need both *dry* and *completely free of water*. The other wrong answers do not need to repeat themselves with *soaking and drenching* or with *sopping wet in the water*. The correct answer is sufficient. Note that the adverb *completely* is fine: it adds nuance and emphasis that are worth preserving, even if you had the option to delete *completely*. The correct answer is (D).

10.　**(F)**　Most effective conclusion: On the other hand, a crisp autumn morning just before dawn, with the sky still showing stars, is glorious.

Rhetorical Skills　　　　　Organization　　　　　Opening/Closing Content

This paragraph begins with the statement *I've had my route for four years and usually enjoy it*. The narrator wants to give the overall impression of his or her positive attitude toward the paper route. Thus, the paragraph should also end in an upbeat manner, especially given some switchbacks in the text.

The current end of the paragraph is rather grim, with the narrator biking, *half-blinded, through a downpour*. The choices that continue the grim tone (with the scene of ruined papers or snowstorms) are all inappropriate. The other wrong choice (… *I try to remember to be grateful for the precipitation*) does turn positive, but it doesn't reinforce the narrator's optimistic take on the paper route itself. Thus, a completely different scene, one that is positive about the route (… *a crisp autumn morning before dawn, with the sky still showing stars, is glorious*) is the best choice. The correct answer is (F).

11.　**(B)**　… his <u>company, Berkshire Hathaway,</u> hosts …

Usage/Mechanics　　　　　Punctuation　　　　　Commas

The words *Berkshire Hathaway* represent the name of the company. As an appositive phrase describing *his company,* the name should be surrounded by commas. Each of the wrong answers fails to put a comma after *Hathaway,* as must be done. (You don't have to know whether the name has a comma within it, although two-word company names rarely contain commas in modern times. It turns out that "Berkshire Hathaway" has no internal comma.) The correct answer is (B).

12.　**(J)**　Each year, his company, Berkshire Hathaway, hosts in Omaha, Nebraska <u>a shareholders'</u> meeting …

Rhetorical Skills　　　　　Style　　　　　　　　Concision

The phrase *annual shareholders' meeting* is an expression you might encounter in the business press. The annual meeting of a company's shareholders is a special event. However, the sentence begins with the phrase *Each year*, so you should not also use the word *annual. Each year, the company holds an annual meeting* is redundant. Drop the word *annual.*

As for the form of the word *shareholders* to use, add the apostrophe on the end to indicate possession: *shareholders' meeting* means "meeting of the shareholders." The correct answer is (J).

13.   **(C)** Should the writer make this addition? No, because this detail distracts the reader from the focus of both the paragraph and the essay as a whole.

Rhetorical Skills   Writing Strategy   Additions

The proposed fact is interesting and even astounding in its own right: *Locals who bought in at $20 or $30 per share in the mid-1960s now hold shares that are each worth around $200,000.* Remember, however, the theme and purpose of the essay—to explore the narrator's job of delivering newspapers. The enormous wealth that Warren Buffett's company has generated with the increasing share price would only be a diversion.

The narrator certainly admires Buffett and considers him a role model, but the reason for bringing up the company and its annual meeting is to give context for the *newspaper-throwing contest* that Buffett participates in. In turn, that contest is a way to reinforce the connection between the narrator and Buffett—that is, they both deliver, or delivered, newspapers. The correct answer is (C).

14.   **(H)** Buffett now regularly challenges visitors to a newspaper-throwing contest. He probably <u>wins</u> most of the time …

Usage/Mechanics   Sentence Structure   Verb Tenses

The verb should be in the present tense (*wins*), not in the past tense (*won*), the past perfect (*had won*), or the conditional perfect (*would have won*). The prior sentence is in the present tense (*challenges*), and there is no reason to change tenses from the challenging to the winning. The correct answer is (H).

15.   **(A)** For the sake of logic and coherence, Paragraph 2 should be placed where it is now.

Rhetorical Skills   Organization   Paragraph Order

Examine the paragraph in question, and think about whether it should go somewhere else. Paragraph 2 says essentially three things: (1) the local paper still believes in paper routes for kids, (2) the newspaper industry is in crisis, and (3) in response, many papers have lowered standards.

Paragraph 3 begins with a natural segue from the third point above, drawing a contrast with *our local paper,* which *has made a series of sharp adjustments.* These two paragraphs fit together well. Likewise, Paragraph 1 ends with a point (the narrator delivers newspapers, just like Warren Buffett used to) that fits very well next to the first point of Paragraph 2 (the local newspaper still believes in paper routes for teenagers). On either side, Paragraph 2 fits. Right where it is, it contributes best to the narrative as a whole. The correct answer is (A).

Passage 2

16. **(F)** … Stax Records did not give its name to an entire trend in popular <u>music, as</u> its rival Motown Records did.

Usage/Mechanics   Punctuation   Commas

The clause *as its rival Motown Records did* is subordinate, so it must be attached to the main clause (*Stax Records did not give its name* …) by a comma. It cannot stand on its own, and neither a semicolon nor a comma plus *and* should be used to link this subordinate clause to the independent clause in front. The correct answer is (F).

17. **(B)** … the influence of Stax … was arguably as extensive as <u>Motown's.</u>

Usage/Mechanics   Punctuation   Apostrophes

The possessive form of *Motown* is *Motown's*. Here, the word *influence* does not have to be repeated after *Motown's*, just as you can omit the second *car* in *My car is as nice as Joan's* [*car*]. The forms *Motowns* and *Motowns'* do not exist. Choice (D) would be fine if it read *that of Motown*. Both this altered version and *Motown's* are equally correct. The correct answer is (B).

18. **(H)** The sound of Southern soul was largely born at the Stax studio … There, luminaries … recorded numerous songs that <u>became</u> radio sensations during the heyday of Stax.

Usage/Mechanics   Sentence Structure   Verb Tense

The other verb in this sentence (*recorded*) is in simple past tense, as is every verb in the rest of this paragraph. The clause containing the underlined portion gives no reason to change the tense; the time phrase *during the heyday of Stax* in fact reinforces the consistent narrative choice of past tense. Thus, the verb should be *became,* not *become* (present) or *have become* (present perfect). By the way, if you were going to use the past perfect tense (*had* + past participle), you would need *become* (the irregular past participle), not *became,* after *had.* The correct answer is (H).

19. **(D)** Many credit the session musicians at Stax with the achievements of the record label. <u>These</u> musicians … were no less skilled and experienced than the Funk Brothers …

Rhetorical Skills   Organization   Transitions

The first sentence of the paragraph names *the session musicians* as a key factor in the success of Stax. The full sentence after the underlined portion supports that assertion, explaining that the musicians *were no less skilled and experienced than the Funk Brothers.* The best available option is to use no transition at all. Begun just with *These,* the second sentence naturally backs up the first.

The incorrect choices all warp the intended meaning. *However* would indicate contrast rather than support. *Thus* would suggest that the second point follows from the first; it does not. *At first* would be appropriate if the second sentence were part of a small narrative, with a change over time (*At first … but then …*). However, there is no such narrative. The correct answer is (D).

20.   **(F)**   If the writer were to delete this phrase, the essay would primarily lose support for the sentence's assertion about the skill level of the Stax musicians.

Rhetorical Skills   Writing Strategy   Deletions

The main clause of the sentence in question declares that the session musicians at Stax *were no less skilled and experienced than the Funk Brothers, the house players at Motown.* The phrase that could be deleted indicates that several of the Stax musicians *formed the successful band …* This detail provides support for the main clause's assertion. After all, these musicians were skilled enough to form a successful band in their own right.

There is a comparison happening *between two groups of artists at different record labels*, as choice (G) has it, but that comparison is in the main clause, not the phrase on the chopping block. That phrase also does not explain the band name or provide *a judgment of the ultimate cultural impact of Stax Records*: the fact that the session musicians were able to form a successful band is too small to affect the *ultimate cultural impact* of the label. The correct answer is (F).

21.   **(B)**   … both sets of <u>performers were</u> under-appreciated and underpaid, even as they laid down the sound …

Usage/Mechanics   Sentence Structure   Whole Sentences

The correct version of this sentence has an independent clause. The subject is *both sets of performers,* and the compound, passive-voice verb is *were under-appreciated and underpaid.* The rest of the sentence is a subordinate clause (*even as … the era*) and so cannot provide the main verb.

The incorrect choices each turn the sentence into a fragment. The original version subordinates the verb (*were …*) by placing it after *who.* The other choices discard the key word *were,* without which the verb phrase is not complete. The correct answer is (B).

22.   **(J)**   … they laid down the sound for <u>dozens of hits</u> of the era.

Rhetorical Skills   Style   Concision

The original version, *dozens and dozens of hits,* is unnecessarily wordy and dramatic. You can just write *dozens of hits.* Choice (G) is even wordier, tacking on phrases (*maybe fifty or sixty, or even more*) that seem to add precision but don't. Finally, the phrase *multiple dozen* is colloquial; use the standard plural *dozens* instead. The correct answer is (J).

23.   **(C)**   … <u>partial owner and entrepreneur</u> Estelle Axton also ran a record store.

Usage/Mechanics   Punctuation   Commas

The words *partial owner and entrepreneur* indicate Axton's roles relative to Stax. When placed before a proper name, this sort of phrase should not be separated by a comma from the name. Nor should there be any commas inside the phrase. The lack of articles (*a, an,* or *the*) indicate that, at least as far as punctuation goes, the words *partial owner and entrepreneur* ought to be treated more as adjectives than as nouns.

If you did have articles, then you would separate the phrase from the name by a comma, just as you normally would with appositives. *A partial owner of the label, Estelle Axton ran a record store.* You could also put the name first, in which case you would surround the appositive phrase with commas. *Estelle Axton, a partial owner of the label, also ran a record store.* The correct answer is (C).

24. **(F)** If the writer were to delete the preceding sentence, the paragraph would primarily lose an explanation of how the store added to the label's success.

Rhetorical Skills   Writing Strategy   Deletions

The sentence in question is this: *Playing rough drafts of songs for her teenaged customers and observing their reactions, Axton quickly discovered what would sell and what wouldn't.* This sentence helps explain how the store was *another reason Stax found success*, as the previous sentence claims: Axton was able to test-market early versions of songs with potential customers, so that the label could make timely adjustments.

The other options are all provably wrong. The sentence provides little information about Axton, other than that she engaged in these actions (a detail that hardly qualifies as "background"). Likewise, the sentence sheds little light on *typical leisure activities of teenagers at the time*, except that at least some shopped for records in stores. That point is not an *overview*. Finally, this sentence can be seen as an *observation*, but it does not weigh against a claim made earlier; rather, it supports the earlier claim that the record store was a reason for the success of Stax. The correct answer is (F).

25. **(A)** One duo ... <u>achieved</u> its greatest feats at Stax ...

Rhetorical Skills   Style   Word Choice

The key to this question is the word *feat,* which means "great deed or act." This noun restricts the possible verbs. You can *achieve* a feat (or *accomplish* or *perform* it), but you cannot *reach* a feat, *obtain* a feat, or *succeed* a feat. The correct answer is (A).

26. **(G)** Least acceptable alternative: After that arrangement <u>bitterly culminated,</u> ...

Rhetorical Skills   Style   Word Choice

The original text reads *After that arrangement ended bitterly.* Acceptable replacements for the verb and adverb include *came to a bitter end* (using the same word *end,* but as a noun) and the versions with *conclude/conclusion,* which are synonyms for *end* in this context. However, *culminate,* which here would mean "reach a final peak or most extreme stage," is inappropriate. To use this verb, you would need to choose a different subject from *arrangement* and add a prepositional phrase *in* to describe the final result: *The increasingly vicious arguments over the arrangement culminated in a bitter breakup.* The arrangement itself did not culminate in anything; it just ended or concluded in a bitter way. The correct answer is (G).

27. **(D)** The divorce from Atlantic ... led to a <u>downturn</u> for Stax.

Rhetorical Skills   Style   Concision

In this context, the words *downturn* and *decline* mean the same thing. Just use one of them. Moreover, the modifiers *downward* and *to a lower position* are redundant, since their meaning is already captured within the words *decline* and *downturn.* After all, you can't decline upward or have a downturn to a higher position. The correct answer is (D).

28. **(H)** Even after its corporate rebirth … Stax struggled for decades, surviving only by reissuing the music under <u>its</u> control.

Usage/Mechanics   Grammar & Usage   Pronoun Agreement (& Forms)

The forms *there* and *it's* are not possessives. *There* means "in that place," and *it's* means "it is." Neither is appropriate to mean "of Stax."

The remaining question is whether to use *their* or *its,* which are both valid possessive pronouns. *Their* refers to a plural noun, whereas *its* refers to a singular noun. The fact that *Stax* is singular is reiterated within this sentence by the phrase *Even after its corporate rebirth.* There may have been more than one person working at the record company, but as an entity, the company is singular. *Stax is in Memphis. Stax has music under its control.* The correct answer is (H).

29. **(B)** Meanwhile, <u>a museum dedicated to American soul music stands where the legendary recording studio once did.</u>

Usage/Mechanics   Sentence Structure   Modifier Placement

The corrected version of the sentence places the modifiers in a sensible order. *A museum …* Which museum? One *dedicated to American soul music.* Okay, what is that museum doing? It *stands.* Where does it stand? The museum stands *where the legendary recording studio once did.* Each of the questions you might raise is answered quickly, easily, and correctly.

In contrast, the incorrect versions separate the modifiers from what they should be modifying or otherwise destroy the proper order. In the original sentence, *dedicated to American soul music* is inappropriately placed next to the *studio* rather than the *museum.* Choices (C) and (D) unnaturally split the verb form *standing* from the rest of the complete verb (*is* or *was*), creating confusion. The correct answer is (B).

30. **(H)** Fulfill goal of describing the complete process of writing, recording, and releasing a hit song at Stax? No, because the essay focuses more broadly on the history and characteristics of Stax.

Rhetorical Skills   Writing Strategy   Goal of Essay

Nowhere does the essay describe the *complete process that Stax went through to write, record, and release a hit song.* Only a few aspects of this process are mentioned throughout the essay. For instance, the session musicians were involved certainly in recording songs. But you learn nothing about how songs were written. Likewise, the paragraph about the record store sheds some light on how Stax refined songs, and you know that there was a distribution deal with Atlantic, but the essay describes nothing else about how a song would be released.

Rather, the essay focuses more on Stax's history (from the 1960s to now) and special characteristics (two factors that led to its success, namely the session musicians and the record store). The fact that only one hit is mentioned by name ("Soul Man") is irrelevant to the question of whether this essay fulfills the stated goal. The correct answer is (H).

Passage 3

31.   **(D)** Driving through the smallest Canadian province … in the <u>summertime can leave you stuck in traffic</u> behind tour buses …

Usage/Mechanics   Sentence Structure   Modifier Placement

In the original sentence, the phrase *Driving through … in the summertime* functions as a leading modifier, since it is set off by a comma. This use of the phrase would be fine, except that the noun modified (*traffic*) is not the one driving. The subject of the sentence would have to be *you*, but the only option that fixes the error that way, choice (B), introduces another error in verb tense (past perfect *had been* should be in general present, probably with the verb *can*). Choice (C) contains no working verb at all, turning the sentence into a fragment.

The corrected version turns *Driving through … in the summertime* into a noun phrase (*-ing* forms used as nouns are called gerunds). This noun phrase is the subject of the verb *can leave*. The correct answer is (D).

32.   **(G)** These tourists are not primarily on the island to touch its <u>red dirt, so colored</u> because of its high iron content.

Usage/Mechanics   Sentence Structure   Whole Sentences

The sentence contains two thoughts:

> (1) The tourists are not primarily on the island to touch its red dirt.
> (2) This dirt is so colored, or colored in this way, because of its high iron content.

The correct version positions the second thought as a nonessential modifier, tacked onto *red dirt* by a comma.

The original sentence creates a run-on by expressing the thoughts as independent clauses and linking them with a comma. The other incorrect answers do not clearly distinguish the thoughts, implying that the reason these tourists are not there to touch the dirt is its high iron content. This iron content is the reason for the color only. The correct answer is (G).

33.   **(C)** The rolling green meadows and the bright blue water of the Gulf of St. Lawrence <u>by themselves are</u> not the draw.

Usage/Mechanics   Grammar & Usage   Subject–Verb Agreement

The subject of the sentence is the plural phrase *The rolling green meadows and the bright blue water of the Gulf of St. Lawrence*. Stripped of modifiers, the phrase is *The meadows and the water*. Any subject containing *and* is plural and thus requires a plural verb (*are*) rather than a singular one (*is*). The correct idiom is *by themselves* (meaning "alone"), not *on themselves*. The correct answer is (C).

34.   **(G)** … <u>the tourists have arrived on their buses</u> to get closer … to the fictional home of their literary hero, Anne of Green Gables.

Usage/Mechanics   Grammar & Usage   Pronoun Agreement

MANHATTAN
PREP

One way to see that *tourists* must be the subject is to consider the pronoun *their* in the phrase *their literary hero*. Since *their* needs to refer back to *tourists* in order to make sense, the best position for *tourists* is in the most prominent place for a noun in the sentence: the subject. In the corrected version, *their* is used in the underlined portion to refer to *tourists*, making the later reference even more evident. The infinitive *to get closer* also tells you that the subject must be *tourists*, since this infinitive indicates the reason or purpose for which the subject does its action: *the tourists have arrived … to get closer* is sensible. *The buses have brought the tourists to get closer* would nonsensically mean that the buses wanted to get closer to Anne.

Choice (J) also makes *tourists* the subject, but the result is wordy and weak. The passive voice (*are brought*) does not work well with the infinitive of purpose (*to get closer*); with such an infinitive, you should favor the active voice (*have arrived*). The correct answer is (G).

35.   **(A)** Over a century ago, <u>local schoolteacher Lucy Maud Montgomery,</u> who had been born on the island, published …

Usage/Mechanics   Punctuation   Commas

The original sentence properly puts a comma after the name *Lucy Maud Montgomery* (separating the nonessential modifier *who had been … island*). There should be no comma between *local schoolteacher* and the name. A proper name preceded by a title or profession without an article (*a, an,* or *the*) becomes one unit: *local schoolteacher Lucy Maud Montgomery published a novel*. Here, the profession is acting somewhat like an adjective. If the article is present, then you need commas around the name: *a local schoolteacher, Lucy Maud Montgomery, published a novel*.

Local can be used as a noun to mean "local person," but if you make a list of two nouns (*local* and *schoolteacher*), don't put a comma in the middle of that list. Choices (B) and (D) both make this error. Finally, choice (C) would work if there were a comma after *Montgomery* (turning *a local schoolteacher who … island* into a giant modifier), but there is no comma there. The correct answer is (A).

36.   **(G)** Closest and most logical connection to the next statement: … a novel about a red-haired orphan who has been taken in by an elderly brother and <u>sister inadvertently.</u> Having sent to a distant orphanage for a boy, the pair is at first reluctant to keep Anne …

Rhetorical Skills   Writing Strategy   Choice of Content

The next statement (the one you want to make a close logical connection to) tells you that the elderly brother and sister originally *sent to a distant orphanage for a boy* and are *at first reluctant to keep Anne*. That is, a mistake has been made. *Inadvertently*, which means "by mistake, accidentally," sets up the next statement nicely: you learn that the pair has taken in Anne *inadvertently*, and then you learn more details about the mistake (they had sent for a boy, not a girl).

The wrong answers give you "nice to know" information but do not provide the foreshadowing that *inadvertently* does. The correct answer is (G).

37.   **(D)** Having sent to a <u>distant orphanage</u> for a boy …

Rhetorical Skills   Style   Concision

There is no need to use more than one word meaning "distant"; use only one such adjective. Incidentally, *far and away* does not mean "faraway," but rather "by a wide margin" (*they are far and away the nicest people I know*), which is out of place in this sentence. Finally, an *orphanage* is, by definition, a place *where parentless children live*, so it is redundant to use this modifier with *orphanage.* The correct answer is (D).

38.   **(H)** Least acceptable alternative: … the pair is at first reluctant to keep <u>Anne. All the while, she endlessly</u> charms them in spite of themselves …

Rhetorical Skills   Organization   Transitions

The original version has two key transitions: *but,* showing contrast in general, and *in the end,* showing the transition from the reluctance *at first* to the later situation, in which Anne has charmed the pair. Acceptable replacements for the underlined portion must replicate these meanings. The conjunction *but* can be replaced by *however, nevertheless,* or *though,* but not by *all the while* (which means "meanwhile" and does not necessarily indicate a contrast). Likewise, *in the end* can be replaced by *eventually, over time,* or *finally,* but not by *endlessly* (which means "without end, incessantly, over and over"). This "least acceptable" answer is fine grammatically, and it even makes a certain degree of sense on its own, but it does not mean the same thing as the original version or any of the acceptable replacements. The correct answer is (H).

39.   **(D)** Anne's qualities are not all perfect. <u>One of them is her</u> quick temper, manifesting itself on her first day of school, when she breaks …

Usage/Mechanics   Sentence Structure   Whole Sentences

The original sentence is a disguised fragment; there is no independent clause with a working verb in it. *Manifesting* is an -*ing* form (which can never be a complete verb by itself), and *breaks* is in the subordinate clause *when she breaks.* The only choice that fixes this issue is the correct answer, which employs the complete verb *is,* turning *One of them is her quick temper* into a legitimate main clause. The correct answer is (D).

40.   **(F)** Her scrapes make her even more appealing, though. <u>Most likely,</u> she reminded Mark Twain of his own creations Tom Sawyer and Huck Finn when Twain praised her …

Rhetorical Skills   Organization   Transitions

The transition used in the original, *Most likely,* is justifiable: it indicates that the author believes, but cannot guarantee, that Mark Twain was reminded of his own fictional creations by Anne.

The alternatives, in contrast, lack support in the text. *In contrast* would mean that the current sentence was going to oppose what came before. However, Anne's "appealing" nature and Twain's praise for Anne as a character are in alignment, not opposition. The transition *Granted* would suggest that the author is making an unwilling concession about Twain, but there's no reason to cast the statement in this odd way. Finally, *Accidentally* would indicate that when Twain praised Alice, he was unintentionally reminded of his own creations, but again, there is no justification for this peculiar stance. The correct answer is (F).

MANHATTAN
PREP

41.   **(C)** Just as she has her neighbors in fictional Avonlea, <u>Anne has long charmed readers in Canada and further afield.</u>

Usage/Mechanics   Grammar & Usage   Parallelism

In the subordinate clause at the beginning of the sentence, the subject is *she*, the verb is *has*, and the object is *her neighbors*. The main clause should mimic this structure: the subject should be *Anne* (parallel to *she*), the verb should be *has* [*done something*] (in this case, it is *has charmed*), and the object should be another group Anne has charmed, namely *readers*. Simplified, the sentence reads *Just as she has [charmed] her neighbors, Anne has charmed readers.* The past participle *charmed* does not have to be repeated in the initial clause.

The incorrect answers all fail to present a parallel structure. For instance, they make *readers, Anne's charm,* or *Canada and further afield* the subject of the main clause. The correct answer is (C).

42.   **(H)** … the Anne industry on the island is healthy, with theme parks, gift shops <u>hawking</u> kitschy items …, and even musicals …

Usage/Mechanics   Sentence Structure   Whole Sentences

The main clause of the sentence is *the Anne industry … is healthy.* After that point, the preposition *with* initiates a list of three signs of that health: *theme parks, gift shops,* and *musicals.* In turn, the noun phrase *gift shops* is modified by the *-ing* form *hawking*, which is equivalent here to the clause *that hawk.* The word *hawking* tells you what those gift shops are doing, but in a grammatically fitting way: you need to use a modifier.

The wrong answers put a full verb in place of *hawking* (*hawk, hawked, have hawked*), creating a run-on sentence with an independent clause (e.g., *gift shops hawk kitschy items*) thrown incorrectly in the middle. The correct answer is (H).

43.   **(D)** The place other than Canada that <u>loves Anne the most</u> is Japan …

Usage/Mechanics   Grammar & Usage   Subject–Verb Agreement

The noun *place* is singular, so a singular verb must be used. *Are* and *love* are both plural verbs, so on this issue alone, the correct answer (with singular verb *loves*) can be chosen. In addition, the verb *to love* is more appropriate in meaning than *to be in love with* for the relationship that the country of Japan has with the character of Anne. The correct answer is (D).

44.   **(F)** … is Japan, which, as the country struggled to rebuild after World War II, <u>warmly</u> took to the orphan.

Rhetorical Skills   Style   Word Choice

The most suitable word of those available is *warmly*, which indicates the positive degree of affection with which Japan *took to the orphan.* The word *tepidly* means "in a lukewarm way" and would put a negative spin on the sentence: if you take to something *tepidly*, you aren't so thrilled. *Heatedly* and *ferociously* would also be negative, although they would indicate a great deal of excitement: they are too intense for the context. The correct answer is (F).

45.   **(B)** There is even a Japanese school of <u>nursing named for,</u> and deeply inspired by, Anne.

Usage/Mechanics   Punctuation   Commas

This sentence is punctuated in an unusual way: it has a comma between *by* and *Anne* in a non-underlined portion. This odd placement of a comma means that the phrase *and deeply inspired by* must have been inserted by the writer as a point that could be pulled out, leaving *There is even a Japanese school of nursing named for Anne.* The writer has chosen to add the phrase *and deeply inspired by* with commas on either side for emphasis (a pair of dashes would also work). The presence of a comma after this phrase demands the presence of another comma before the phrase. The correct answer is (B).

Passage 4

46.   **(F)** Almost everyone in her extended <u>family shows</u> up …

Usage/Mechanics   Sentence Structure   Whole Sentence (and Subject–Verb Agreement)

The subject of the sentence is *everyone*, which is singular (*everyone is here*, not *everyone are here*). So the verb in question should be a singular *shows*, not a plural *show*. Moreover, *showing* and *shown* are not complete verbs that can run the sentence. These choices produce sentence fragments. The correct answer is (F).

47.   **(B)** Sunday dinners at her house are also well-attended affairs, with <u>relatives</u> crowding around to fill plates …

Usage/Mechanics   Grammar & Usage   Pronouns

If you stick with *them* (in the original sentence), you have to find the noun *them* is referring to. There is no such good noun: neither *dinners* nor *affairs* makes sense. The writer assumes that you know *them* refers to "people in Dee's family, relatives, etc.," but without one of those nouns in the sentence, you're stuck. The pronoun *it* likewise lacks a noun it can properly refer to. *The crowd inside the place crowding around …* is awkward: not only is *crowd … crowding* repetitive, the phrase *inside the place* is also redundant (you have *at her house*) and unnecessary. Go with the simple choice *relatives*. The correct answer is (B).

48.   **(J)** <u>A</u> similar scene takes place at my house …

Rhetorical Skills   Organization   Transitions

None of the given transitional phrases work; you're better off without any of them. Look at the paragraph as a whole. The opening sentence asserts that *Dee and I have parallel lives.* The next few sentences explain that assertion with specific examples of the parallels. The third sentence describes Sunday dinners at Dee's house. All you need in this fourth sentence, then, is to say *A similar scene takes place at my house.* The word *similar* does all the work you need done in order to draw the correct parallel.

The incorrect choices actually confuse matters by signaling the wrong relationship between Sentence 3 and Sentence 4. *However* and *On the contrary* indicate a contrast, not a parallel. *Thus* would mean that Sentence 4 is somehow the result of Sentence 3, but there's no reason to believe that's the case. It would be odd for the narrator's family to have big Sunday dinners *because* Dee's family has them. The correct answer is (J).

MANHATTAN
PREP

49.   **(D)** The most logical placement for this sentence would be after Sentence 4.

Rhetorical Skills   Organization   Sentence Order

The proposed addition begins with *All that's different …* and goes on to delineate a contrast between Dee's kitchen (where *you would hear English*) and the narrator's (where *you'd usually hear Spanish*). The only way such a sentence fits into a paragraph that seems to be all about something completely opposite—how *Dee and [the narrator] have parallel lives*—is to put the sentence at the very end. In fact, by leading with *All that's different*, the sentence states that there's only this one difference between their lives. In that sense, it reinforces the strength of the parallels—as long as it's placed at the very end, where it will best fit the logical flow: Assertion that the lives are parallel → Examples of how they're parallel → *All that's different* is which language is spoken. The correct answer is (D).

50.   **(H)** Dee and I are in the same grade, but she is almost exactly a year older than I am; our birthdays are less than a week apart.

Usage/Mechanics   Sentence Structure   Modifier Placement

The wrong answers here are very confusing, because the modifiers are placed illogically. In the original sentence, how can *Less than a week apart* describe *Dee and I*? Their *birthdays* should be described as such. This issue is enough to nullify this choice, but you also have awkward phrasing in *Dee and I have birthdays that make her almost exactly a year older …* It would be better to simply say that Dee *is* almost exactly a year older.

If you start the sentence with *Almost exactly a year older than I am*, then the subject must be the word *Dee* by itself. Since *Dee and I* are the subject in choice (G), this choice illogically claims that both Dee and I are exactly a year older than I am. Even with time travel, that would be hard to arrange. Finally, choice (J) starts off on shaky but legal ground with a long modifier (*who is almost exactly a year older than I am and in the same grade*) separating the two parts of the compound subject. The fatal flaw, however, is the core of the sentence: *Dee and I are less than a week apart in the days we were born*. This is at best clunky and at worst nonsensical. The correct answer simply states each fact with its proper subject and predicate: *Dee and I are in the same grade. She is almost exactly a year older than I am. Our birthdays are less than a week apart*. With a minimal amount of glue, the full sentence is properly built. The correct answer is (H).

51.   **(B)** Together we <u>decided that</u> her Sweet Sixteen …

Usage/Mechanics   Punctuation   Commas

If you put a mini-sentence after the verb *decide* (or after similar verbs such as *say, claim, state,* and *agree*), do not put any commas on either side of the *that. We decided that the parties would be combined* has the correct non-punctuation around *decided* and *that*. The correct answer is (B).

52.   **(H)** … her Sweet Sixteen <u>party and my *quinceañera,*</u> a celebration held for girls of my heritage who turn fifteen, would …

Usage/Mechanics   Punctuation   Commas

The subject of the clause is a compound list with two items: *her Sweet Sixteen party and my quinceañera*. No comma belongs in this *X and Y* list. The verb comes after an appositive phrase (*a celebration held for girls … fifteen*) modifying and defining the noun *quinceañera*. This modifying phrase should be surrounded by commas, so a comma must be placed after *quinceañera*. The correct answer is (H).

53.   **(C)**   Together we decided that her Sweet Sixteen party and my *quinceañera* … <u>would be</u> combined.

Usage/Mechanics   Sentence Structure   Verb Tenses & Forms

The right tense in this situation is conditional (*would be*), because the verb *decided* is in the past tense. Here's how the tense sequence works. If *decide* is in the present tense, then the tense of *be combined* is future (*will*): *We decide that our parties will be combined.* This holds true with *are deciding* or even *have decided* (present perfect, which is really a tense about the present time). When you pick up the whole idea, though, and put it in the past, then you move *decide* to *decided* and *will be* to *would be*. The same pattern works with any other verb (such as *say*) that is often followed by a mini-sentence: *He says he will take out the trash. He said he would take out the trash.*

Do not use the conditional perfect tense *would have been*, which would mean that the parties were never actually combined. *I would have taken out the trash, but I was tired and didn't feel like it.* As for *should of,* never ever use *of* when you mean *have*. *Would, should,* and *could* should never be followed by *of*. This error is caused by the similar sounds of the words *of* and *have* (when not stressed). The correct answer is (C).

54.   **(J)**   Our fathers were cordial but had a rough time connecting on a personal level at first … Each of them … seemed reluctant to compromise on any issue in public. <u>Finally,</u> our mothers sent them off to a supply store together …

Rhetorical Skills   Organization   Transitions

The sentences before the underlined portion describe how the fathers initially didn't connect personally. But then, the mothers *sent them off to a supply store together*. By the end of the paragraph, you learn that this move was intended to bring the two men together—and it worked, making them *fast friends*. So you need a transition that shows forward movement in this narrative. *Finally* does the trick.

The other options are like bad road signs, causing mental accidents. *For example* leads you to expect that the trip to the supply store turned out badly (as an example of how the fathers were reluctant to compromise). Instead, though, the trip was a success. *Incidentally* is a detour off the highway, to use the analogy again, but you want to stay on the highway. And *On the other hand* would indicate a contrast, but it is not appropriate for a sequence of events (it indicates a judgment or comparison happening in a kind of vacuum). The correct answer is (J).

55.   **(A)**   … our mothers sent them off to a supply store together to design the archway Dee and I would pass <u>through.</u> <u>We didn't ask</u> for this archway, but our mothers were right: building something together allowed …

Usage/Mechanics   Sentence Structure   Whole Sentences

The first thought, expressed in a complete sentence, ends at *through*. The fathers were sent to a supply store to design an archway, one that Dee and the narrator *would pass through*. The next two thoughts are *We didn't ask for this archway, but our mothers were right*. The conjunction *but* links these two thoughts, which are each in a perfectly acceptable independent clause. That sentence in fact goes on with a colon, so you had better be sure that you want to join these sentences into an even larger one. As it turns out here, if you try to do so, you will make a run-on. Putting a comma or *although*

MANHATTAN
PREP

between *through* and *we* creates a logjam of independent and/or dependent clauses. Changing *We didn't ask* to *not asking* and joining that phrase to *through* creates an even less intelligible set of words. The correct answer is (A).

56. **(F)** … our mothers were right: building something together allowed these two gruff men to bond. When the party rolled around, they were fast friends.

Usage/Mechanics   Sentence Structure   Whole Sentences

In the previous sentence, the part after the colon is a complete sentence that explains the prior statement *our mothers were right*. The subject is *building something together* (an *-ing* form of a verb used as a noun, as in this case, is called a gerund). The verb is *allowed*, and the sentence properly ends with *bond*. The next sentence begins with a dependent clause *When the party rolled around*, and ends with its core independent clause *they were fast friends*.

The verb *bond* at the end of the first sentence should not be connected to the *when* at the beginning of the next sentence, with or without a comma. The *when* is already connected to the clause *they were fast friends*, so if you read the *when* clause as attached to the prior sentence, then *they were fast friends* is a run-on appendage, without a logical place or home. Dropping the *when* to make the connection only creates a longer sequence of independent clauses joined improperly by commas. The correct answer is (F).

57. **(B)** Most relevant addition: Of course, the food, which represented our two cultures as well as the holiday, was both abundant and delicious.

Rhetorical Skills   Writing Strategy   Additions

According to the opening sentence of the paragraph, *The party itself had the theme of Thanksgiving, with Irish and Mexican decorations everywhere throughout the hall*. The most relevant addition, then, in the next sentence is one that echoes those points: *the food, which represented our two cultures* [Irish and Mexican] *as well as the holiday* [Thanksgiving].

The alternatives present facts that might well be accurate but that distract from the paragraph's message. Who cares whether *we had trouble keeping [the food] hot*, or whether the food *had been set out in innumerable casserole dishes* or *would have cost far too much to have catered*? None of these factoids speak to the happy joining of cultures that the Sweet Sixteen-añera represented. The correct answer is (B).

58. **(J)** Dee and I made a simultaneous grand entrance through the arch with our dates, …

Rhetorical Skills   Style   Concision

The word *simultaneous* means "at the same time," so the choices including *at the same time, all at once*, or *synchronized* are all redundant. You can just say *with our dates* and be done. The correct answer is (J).

59. **(A)** Ending most consistent with the whole essay: <u>A good reason to be thankful was that their joint handiwork held up all night.</u>

Rhetorical Skills   Organization   Opening/Closing Content

A good ending should tie back to earlier themes and, at the very least, not jar with them. The correct answer echoes the theme of the Thanksgiving holiday (*a good reason to be thankful*), as well as the theme of people coming together in a positive way (*their joint handiwork held up all night*). Note that the ending of a story such as this one doesn't have to summarize everything that came before in some grand moral; that can be unwise even to attempt. But there should be some reinforcement of story elements.

The alternatives all clash with those prior story elements and wrap the tale on a down note. It's unhelpful and in fact depressing to learn, without any further comment, that the mothers were too busy even to wave to each other, or that the archway, symbolic of the budding friendship of the fathers, was afterwards dismantled for its scrap value, or that the archway was evidence of poor carpentry. If any of these points were to be made, then the story would have to counter them subsequently with even greater reassurance of its core themes of personal bonding across cultures. The correct answer is (A).

60. **(G)** If the writer removed the first sentence of Paragraph 3, the essay would primarily lose an effective transition from the idea of the party to its planning.

Rhetorical Skills   Writing Strategy   Deletions

Paragraph 2 ends with the decision to combine the Sweet Sixteen and the *quinceañera*. Paragraph 3's opening sentence gives the reaction of the families to that decision (*initially skeptical*), states that this reaction was overcome (*our enthusiasm won them over*), and notes that the process had some difficulties (*not that the planning was always easy*). Thus, this sentence transitions the reader from the idea stage to the planning stage, which is the focus of Paragraph 3.

The sentence does not explain why the families were skeptical; that fact is just stated. Nor does the sentence provide a *detailed outline* of how the relatives were won over (all you know is that it was the *enthusiasm* of Dee and the narrator). Finally, the sentence does not refer to culture at all, so it cannot be *reinforcing the importance of culture in the lives of two teenagers*. The correct answer is (G).

Passage 5

61. **(C)** The next time you pluck a baked potato out of an aluminum foil jacket, remember that <u>you are</u> touching—and probably discarding—a piece of metal …

Usage/Mechanics   Grammar & Usage   Pronoun Forms

The baked potato is, or was, *touching* the foil, but not *probably discarding* it. A person has to be the subject of the verb forms *touching* and *discarding*. Since the writer has already made the choice to address the reader as *you* (*you pluck …* and *remember* is a direct command), you should stick with that choice and write *you are touching*. The correct answer is (C).

62. **(J)** OMIT the underlined portion (*"Tinfoil" is nowadays made of aluminum, not tin.*)

Rhetorical Skills   Writing Strategy   Choice of Content

The underlined sentence is an interesting little fact in its own right, but it distracts from the narrative of the essay. The prior sentence, which opens the essay, points out that aluminum was *once more valuable than gold*. This fact demands explanation. Of course, such an explanation will take time—readers will expect to be given background about aluminum, namely its discovery, its uses, and its history—but another sentence in the same paragraph had better set the stage for that explanation. Instead, this sentence's content (no matter how it is written) is irrelevant to the story of aluminum. Deleting the sentence altogether is the best choice. The correct answer is (J).

63. **(A)** … the metal shows <u>up in materials</u> from laptop cases to airplane wings.

Usage/Mechanics   Punctuation   Commas

The underlined portion should have no commas anywhere, since each part is essential: *the metal shows up* (where?) *in materials* (which?) *from laptop cases to airplane wings*. Each question must be answered, so you keep the text going without pause. The correct answer is (A).

64. **(H)** The fact that millions of tons <u>are</u> produced annually should be expected …

Usage/Mechanics   Sentence Structure   Whole Sentences

The core of the sentence is *The fact … should be expected*, with *The fact* as the subject and *should be expected* as the main verb. Now, immediately after *The fact that*, you need to embed a mini-sentence, answering the question "Which fact?" This mini-sentence needs a subject and a full verb, just like a true independent clause that could stand alone: *millions of tons are produced annually*. The subject is *millions of tons*, and the complete verb is *are produced*. The correct answer is (H).

65. **(B)** … one of the most abundant elements <u>is</u> lucky number 13 …

Usage/Mechanics   Grammar & Usage   Subject–Verb Agreement

The subject of this clause is *one*, which is singular. Note that *of the most abundant elements* is a prepositional phrase, which you can eliminate here to determine the subject. Thus, the verb should be *is*, not *are*, *were*, or *have been* (all plural). Don't be distracted by the phrase *lucky number 13*—that's not plural either. It's just a label that the writer uses for the element aluminum. The correct answer is (B).

66. **(F)** <u>Why, then, did it take until 1827 for aluminum to be discovered?</u>

Rhetorical Skills   Organization   Opening/Closing Content

The essay as a whole poses a mystery: how is it that aluminum was once more valuable than gold? Paragraph 2 gives necessary background on aluminum's uses, emphasizes that it is *not* a precious metal nowadays, and in fact heightens the surprise by pointing out that *millions of tons are produced annually* and that aluminum is *in the Earth's crust one of the most abundant elements*.

In its lead-off position in Paragraph 3, the correct answer raises a question that brings the reader closer to solving the mystery: why, then, did it take so long to discover aluminum? The next part of this paragraph answers that question (aluminum is tightly bound to oxygen in rocks); this answer, in turn, leads to the ultimate reason for the initial high price of aluminum (the process for extracting aluminum was difficult and costly).

The wrong choices bring up irrelevant facts and fail to advance the storyline. You don't care about carbon fiber, about the thermite reaction, or even about why aluminum is so abundant. The correct answer is (F).

67.   **(C)**   Thus, nuggets of pure aluminum are never found in <u>rivers, and simply heating</u> rocks doesn't work …

Usage/Mechanics   Sentence Structure   Whole Sentences

The verb *doesn't work* demands a subject. The only possibility among the choices is *simply heating rocks*, which is a gerund (an *-ing* form used as an action noun, as in *Swimming is fun*). An *if* clause cannot serve as the subject. *Simply heated rocks*, as a subject, would not agree with *doesn't work* in number; moreover, the meaning is askew (it should be the action of *heating rocks* that doesn't work, not *heated rocks* themselves). The correct answer is (C).

68.   **(F)**   For the sake of the logic and cohesion of Paragraph 3, Sentence 4 should be placed where it is now.

Rhetorical Skills   Organization   Sentence Order

9

The original order of the sentences in the paragraph is ideal. (1) *Why, then, did it take …* raises the key question about the delay in discovering aluminum. (2) *The element …* asserts that aluminum is very reactive. (3) *Thus, nuggets …* provides an implication of Sentence 2: you don't find free aluminum in nature, and in fact it's hard to separate from the ore. (4) *Ironically …* adds an aside that only makes sense after you know that aluminum is very reactive, and it both connects back to Paragraph 2 and leads clearly to the next sentence. (5) *On contact with air …* explains why aluminum can be so reactive and yet so useful (e.g., in structures) in its metallic form—as Sentence 4 indicated, the reactivity *causes* the protection against corrosion. Any other position for Sentence 4 (or its deletion) would damage the flow of logic. The correct answer is (F).

69.   **(C)**   The process … was <u>difficult and costly. For</u> several decades thereafter, aluminum was likely the most valuable metal …

Usage/Mechanics   Sentence Structure   Whole Sentences

The only grammatical option among those given is to separate the two thoughts into different sentences. The first thought is *The process … was difficult and costly.* That is, the process has these two parallel features. The second thought is *For several decades thereafter, aluminum was likely the most valuable metal …*, in which the subject is *aluminum* and the predicate is *was likely the most valuable metal …* The prepositional phrase *For several decades thereafter* modifies the second thought: it tells you how long aluminum was so valuable.

You can't just group these two sentences together with a comma, whether you adjust the *difficult and costly* list or not. Choice (B) creates false parallelism in an apparent three-part list that should not be: *The process was difficult, costly, and for several decades …* The correct answer is (C).

70. **(J)** … the pyramid atop the Washington <u>Monument</u> was formed from this once-precious metal.

Rhetorical Skills   Writing Strategy   Choice of Content

Good choice of content includes not choosing irrelevant or distracting content. What is the purpose of this sentence? Consider the prior sentence: *For several decades thereafter, aluminum was likely the most valuable metal on the planet.* Thus, the examples with the emperor of France and the Washington Monument should cleanly support that point. Making a side comment that the pyramid on top of the monument *serves as an imperfect lightning rod* is detrimental to the power of the sentence. Delete this aside altogether.

You could call the issue concision at the level of thoughts: which points should you include, and which should you omit, in order to make your case most cogently? The correct answer is (J).

71. **(B)** That year, two <u>young inventors simultaneously</u> determined how to …

Usage/Mechanics   Grammar & Usage   Modifier Forms

The adverb *simultaneously* modifies the verb *determined*, indicating that these two inventors made their discoveries at the same time. *Simultaneous* should not modify the inventors themselves (two events can be simultaneous, but not two people). Moreover, *simultaneously* should not modify *young* to mean, awkwardly, that the inventors are young at exactly the same time. This is not the author's intention. The correct answer is (B).

72. **(J)** The raw material had always been <u>plentiful;</u> now, …

Rhetorical Skills   Style   Concision

The word *raw* in this context means "unprocessed," so adding *in its unprocessed form, as unprocessed ore,* or *in an unprocessed state* is redundant. Delete these extra words. The correct answer is (J).

73. **(A)** Least acceptable alternative: Aluminum plates were no longer worth small fortunes. <u>On the contrary,</u> the same collapse in cost could happen to diamonds one day.

Rhetorical Skills   Organization   Transitions

Before the underlined portion, the paragraph describes how *the price fell through the floor* after the discovery of a cheap extraction process, concluding with the effect on aluminum's value: *aluminum plates were no longer worth small fortunes.* After the underlined portion, the text pivots to a different material that the same price collapse could one day happen to diamonds, which are *also made from an extremely common element.*

The original text uses *Incidentally* to signal that the point about diamonds is an aside. Choice (B), with *By the way,* performs the same task. *It is interesting to note that …* is a longer way to introduce an incidental comment (a *note*), but the result is similar. Choice (D), with *Jewelry investors might take heed,* does not explicitly flag the next point in the same way, but the quick cut to *Jewelry investors* works, immediately transitioning to a different but evidently parallel case.

The only choice that does *not* work (and that is thus the right answer) is *On the contrary,* which creates too stark a contrast between the history of aluminum prices and the possible scenario with diamond prices. In fact, the text reads *the same collapse in cost* …, indicating that the following hypothetical case is meant to align with the prior example. The correct answer is (A).

74.   **(G)** … they're also made from an <u>extremely common</u> element …

Usage/Mechanics   Grammar & Usage   Modifier Forms

The adverb *extremely* is meant to modify *common*. How common is the element? Extremely common. The element itself is not extreme. Meanwhile, the adjective *common* is meant to modify *element*. What is the element like? It's common. *Commonly*, which is the adverbial form, cannot modify a noun. The correct answer is (G).

75.   **(D)** Suppose the writer had chosen to write an essay that traces the historical evolution of the value of aluminum. Would this essay fulfill the writer's goal? Yes, because the writer connects prices to events affecting the supply of aluminum.

Rhetorical Skills   Writing Strategy   Goal of Essay

In the first paragraph, the essay presents an interesting, little-known fact: aluminum *was once more valuable than gold*. Since aluminum is *not a precious metal any more* according to Paragraph 2, the purpose of the essay is to explain why aluminum was once so valuable, and why it is not any more.

The writer succeeds in that purpose by *connecting prices to events affecting the supply of aluminum*. The first such event is the discovery itself of the metal; since the process discovered was *difficult and costly*, it is likely that aluminum at that time (and for decades afterwards) was *the most valuable metal on the planet*. Then *the price fell through the floor* when two inventors found a cheap way to extract aluminum (the second historical event affecting prices). So the writer has certainly succeeded in tracing the historical evolution of the value of aluminum. The correct answer is (D).

Chapter *of* 10

5lb. Book of ACT® Practice Problems

English:
Passage Set 6

In This Chapter...

Set 6 Passages & Solutions

Chapter 10
English: Passage Set 6

The English problems in this chapter are distributed across five passages, just as they will be on the ACT itself. Every topic is up for grabs, so expect a little of everything. The answer key and the solutions classify the problems for you, so you can pinpoint strengths and weaknesses.

How should you use this chapter? Here are some recommendations, according to the level you've reached in ACT English.

1. Fundamentals. If you haven't done any topical work yet, consider working in Chapters 3 and 4 first. Otherwise, do a passage or two untimed to begin with. As you become more comfortable, put the clock on. In all cases, review the solutions closely, and articulate what you've learned. Redo problems as necessary.

2. Fixes. Do one passage at a time under timed conditions. Examine the results, learn your lessons, then test yourself with more passages at once.

3. Tweaks. Confirm your mastery by doing a few passages at once under timed conditions. A full set of five is the ultimate goal. Aim to improve the speed and ease of your solution process.

Good luck on the problems!

PASSAGE 1

A Perfect World

[1]

<u>Like</u> a director, Clint Eastwood has often presented
  1

nature as a vital part of his films. <u>An example includes</u>
  the shots of the African countryside in *White Hunter*
  2

Black Heart and the beautiful panoramas of the

Wyoming landscape in <u>*Unforgiven. A Perfect World*</u>
  3
continues to elevate nature to great importance, using

it to guide viewers through the subtle and complex

relationships that appear in the film.

[2]

<u>The protagonist of *A Perfect World* at first appears</u>
  4
<u>relaxed, although this impression is undermined later.</u>
  4
Kevin Costner lies in a verdant field, the sun shining

<u>down upon</u> him as a hawk circles overhead.
  5

[3]

A Perfect World tells the tale of escaped convict

Butch Haynes (Costner), <u>who runs</u> from the law,
  6
kidnaps and then befriends an eight-year-old boy

1. **A.** NO CHANGE
    B. As
    C. Just as
    D. Such as

2. **F.** NO CHANGE
    G. Its examples include
    H. Their examples include
    J. Examples include

3. **A.** NO CHANGE
    B. *Unforgiven A*
    C. *Unforgiven, A*
    D. *Unforgiven,* and *A*

4. Given that all of the choices are true, which one
    would MOST effectively lead the reader from the
    previous paragraph to this one and provide a suitable
    transition to the description that follows?
    F. NO CHANGE
    G. Eastwood both directs and acts in this film, but
    is absent from the first scene.
    H. The natural world is clearly valued in the open-
    ing shot of the film.
    J. The start of the film may seem boring, but it's
    actually very beautiful.

5. Which of the following alternatives to the under-
    lined portion would NOT be acceptable?
    A. down on
    B. down
    C. above
    D. upon

6. **F.** NO CHANGE
    G. who, while running
    H. who ran
    J. running

named Phillip. [7] Butch is pursued by Eastwood's character, a Texas Ranger named Red Garnett.

[4]

This split narrative involving two main characters presents a conflict for the audience. With whom should
                                                    8
we identify, the criminal or the officer of the law? Still,
                                                      9
Eastwood helps us make our choice with a delicate use of the natural world. It is easy for viewers to anchor themselves to Butch as an essentially good man, because he connects with nature, although some of his actions
                                    10
break the law. Whenever Butch is on screen, the color
  10
palette immediately widens. As Butch drives through
                                              11
the countryside in a car that always has the windows
  11
rolled down, the scenes saturated with lush greens
                    12
and blues.

7. The writer is considering revising the preceding sentence by deleting the phrase "and then befriends" from it. If the writer did this, the paragraph would primarily lose:
   A. a comparison of Butch's journey to those made by other escaped convicts.
   B. a detail that establishes the setting of the story, putting events in their proper time and place.
   C. a detail that illuminates the character of Butch and the evolution of a relationship.
   D. interesting but ultimately irrelevant information about Butch and Phillip.

8. F. NO CHANGE
   G. As
   H. To
   J. In

9. A. NO CHANGE
   B. Thus,
   C. In short,
   D. OMIT the underlined portion.

10. The writer wants to present an implication of an earlier statement, in order to reinforce the main point of the sentence. Given that all of the choices are true, which one BEST accomplishes this goal?
    F. NO CHANGE
    G. nature and is thus associated with freedom, purity, and light.
    H. nature, his behavior with regard to society's rules notwithstanding.
    J. nature; we forget, of course, about the violence in ecological systems.

11. Given that all of the choices are true, which one provides information most relevant to the main focus of the paragraph?
    A. NO CHANGE
    B. at deceptively normal speeds
    C. with a soda bottle in hand,
    D. with a cigarette in his mouth,

12. F. NO CHANGE
    G. scenes saturate
    H. scenes that saturated
    J. scenes are saturated

10

MANHATTAN
PREP   361

[5]

This rich, attractive backdrop is in clear contrast to that given to the lawman, whom for more of the₁₃ film rides inside a metallic camper with covered windows. He is always filmed in a narrow palette of dark beiges. The stark difference in presentation assists the audience's identification of Butch as the unlikely₁₄ protagonist.

[6]

This technique is just one of the nuanced aspects of *A Perfect World*, which succeeds through its careful control of artistic elements. It is a film in which, a₁₅ kidnapper and convict can be a hero.

13. **A.** NO CHANGE
    B. who for more
    C. whom for most
    D. who for most

14. **F.** NO CHANGE
    G. the identification of the audience of Butch
    H. the identification of the audience by Butch
    J. Butch's identification of the audience

15. **A.** NO CHANGE
    B. film, in which a kidnapper,
    C. film in which a kidnapper
    D. film in which, a kidnapper,

PASSAGE 2

A Prima Ballerina

[1]

Until the late 1940s, no other ballerinas in the world were as prominent than the best Europeans,
₁₆
particularly Russians. In 1949, however, American Maria Tallchief danced the lead in "The Firebird,"

staged by celebrated choreographer George Balanchine
₁₇
for the New York City Ballet. With this performance,

Tallchief vaulted to international stardom.
₁₈

[2]

Born in 1925 to a Native American father of the Osage Nation and a Scottish-Irish mother, Tallchief began dancing ballet at the age of three. Elizabeth
₁₉
Marie Tall Chief, as she was then named, also studied

other subjects, [20] while her grandmother took her to

16. **F.** NO CHANGE
    G. as
    H. then
    J. of

17. **A.** NO CHANGE
    B. and staged
    C. since staged
    D. thus staged,

18. **F.** NO CHANGE
    G. vaults
    H. vaulting
    J. who vaulted

19. If the underlined word were deleted, the sentence would primarily lose a detail that:
    A. is necessary for the sentence to be grammatically complete.
    B. duplicates information found elsewhere in the paragraph.
    C. provides new and relevant information to the sentence.
    D. is needlessly specific for the sentence.

20. The writer is thinking of inserting the following phrase here:

    such as piano and gymnastics,

    Should the writer make this addition here?
    F. Yes, because it explains the dedication with which the young Tallchief studied.
    G. Yes, because it provides pertinent examples that help to make a broad term relevant.
    H. No, because it distracts from the paragraph's focus on Tallchief's ballet training.
    J. No, because it provides only two examples of these subjects, rather than a full list.

10

traditional Osage dance ceremonies. <u>These experiences</u> <u>probably provided for Tallchief's later belief the basis</u> <u>that ballet should be grounded in movement and</u> <u>musicality.</u>
21

[3]

Moving to Los Angeles to further her studies, Tallchief resolved in her teenage years <u>that would devote</u> her life to the craft of ballet. She moved again in 1942, this time to New York City. Soon, despite her relative inexperience, she was accepted into the prestigious Ballet Russe de Monte Carlo, <u>partly that,</u> with her American passport, she could travel abroad. Tallchief resisted pressure to "Russify" her name to "Tallchieva," but went by Maria and combined the words Tall and Chief.

[4]

When Balanchine began to coach the company, he and Tallchief clicked artistically. He designed ballets to highlight her technical prowess, easy energy, and regal <u>grace through his designs.</u> In response, her body actually elongated. The two also connected romantically, marrying in 1946. Although the marriage

<u>didn't last.</u> The professional relationship did, resulting

in <u>productions</u> such as "The Nutcracker," previously little known. The Sugar Plum Fairy in Balanchine's

21. **A.** NO CHANGE
B. These experiences should be grounded in movement and musicality for Tallchief's later belief that ballet probably provided the basis.
C. These experiences for the basis probably provided Tallchief's later belief that ballet should be grounded in movement and musicality.
D. These experiences probably provided the basis for Tallchief's later belief that ballet should be grounded in movement and musicality.

22. **F.** NO CHANGE
G. that devoted
H. to devote
J. devoting

23. **A.** NO CHANGE
B. in part because,
C. in that partly,
D. since the part,

24. **F.** NO CHANGE
G. grace that she would show.
H. grace, all qualities of hers.
J. grace.

25. **A.** NO CHANGE
B. last, the
C. last; the
D. last—the

26. The writer wants to suggest that the professional relationship of Tallchief and Balanchine led to success. Which choice BEST accomplishes this goal?
F. NO CHANGE
G. performances
H. triumphs
J. works

reinvented ballet was the soaring Tallchief, who helped
immortalize this staple of the art form.

[5]

Retiring in 1965, Tallchief founded ballet schools
and companies in Chicago. In contrast, Oklahoma

remembers her as one of the "Five Moons," five,
illustrious, Native American ballerinas from that state,

all of whom were born in the 1920s.

27. **A.** NO CHANGE
    B. were
    C. were to be
    D. OMIT the underlined portion.

28. **F.** NO CHANGE
    G. Therefore,
    H. Today,
    J. At last,

29. **A.** NO CHANGE
    B. five, illustrious
    C. illustrious five
    D. five illustrious

30. **F.** NO CHANGE
    G. each of whom were
    H. all of which was
    J. all were

10

PASSAGE 3

Juggling for Fun and War

[1]

I learned how to juggle: clubs, sticks, and knives
from an Irish Traveller who called himself Jimi Juggle. [A]
Travellers, usually spelled with two l's, are ethnically

distinct nomads, some of them may be genetically
related to the Roma people (commonly known as
gypsies).

[2]

[1] I already knew how to juggle three balls with
a certain measure of skill, but the director wanted me

to perform harder tricks. [2] I was living in Galway, a
town on the west coast of Ireland, and had won the part
of a magician in a play. [3] Spotting one of Jimi's flyers,
she arranged for me to train with his troupe, which was

staying on the outskirts of town. [35]

[3]

Jimi and the other performers welcomed me warmly
and then thrust me right away into a rapidly passing
exercise, in which I had to catch clubs from one person

and toss them to another. [B] That took a lot of patient
coaching to make progress, but I improved greatly
over time.

31. **A.** NO CHANGE
    B. juggle, clubs,
    C. juggle, clubs
    D. juggle clubs,

32. **F.** NO CHANGE
    G. of who
    H. of whom
    J. DELETE the underlined portion.

33. **A.** NO CHANGE
    B. three balls, tossing them in the air
    C. three balls, all three at the same time,
    D. DELETE the underlined portion.

34. Which choice would MOST effectively conclude the
    sentence by indicating MOST specifically what was
    desired of the narrator?
    F. NO CHANGE
    G. try new things.
    H. stretch myself.
    J. do more.

35. Which of the following sequences of sentences
    makes the previous paragraph MOST logical?
    A. NO CHANGE
    B. 1, 3, 2
    C. 2, 1, 3
    D. 3, 1, 2

36. **F.** NO CHANGE
    G. rapid passing
    H. pass rapid
    J. rapidly pass

37. **A.** NO CHANGE
    B. He took
    C. It took
    D. With

MANHATTAN
PREP

[4]

While working with Jimi, I found out more about the history of juggling. [C] No one knows when the craft was <u>invented</u> ancient Egyptian paintings and Roman statuettes portray jugglers. The activity was often regarded as light entertainment or even as deceptive trickery; genuine agility is required to juggle well, <u>however,</u> and some tales hint at a connection with

martial arts. [D] The Chinese <u>warrior, Xiong Yiliao is</u> said to have ended a battle before it began by stepping between the drawn lines of hostile soldiers and juggling nine balls. [41] The other army was so intimidated by this

feat of talent that it fled. On October 14, <u>1066; English troops</u> watched the Norman knight Taillefer juggle his sword before the Battle of Hastings. Challenged by an English knight, Taillefer cut him down, only to be swarmed by enemy soldiers <u>from the English side.</u>

38. F. NO CHANGE
  G. invented,
  H. invented by
  J. invented;

39. A. NO CHANGE
  B. that is,
  C. for example,
  D. therefore,

40. F. NO CHANGE
  G. warrior Xiong Yiliao
  H. warrior Xiong Yiliao,
  J. warrior—Xiong Yiliao

41. The writer is concerned about the length of the preceding sentence and is considering deleting the clause "before it began" from it. If the writer were to make this deletion, the paragraph would primarily lose information that:
  A. clarifies the time at which the battle started.
  B. reveals that the battle never actually took place.
  C. suggests that the battle lasted longer than expected.
  D. indicates which side won the battle.

42. F. NO CHANGE
  G. 1066; English troops,
  H. 1066, English troops
  J. 1066 English troops

43. A. NO CHANGE
  B. who were fighting the Normans.
  C. after that.
  D. DELETE the underlined portion and end the sentence with a period.

[5]

My own date with destiny arrived: opening night. Sure enough, I instantly dropped the knives—and thankfully, no warrior or knight was trying to kill me. As Jimi had said, though, everybody drops, and I just picked the knives up and kept going. 44

44. The writer wishes to add a sentence that emphasizes in a positive way the ultimate impact of Jimi Juggle's training. Given that all the following statements are true, which one, if added here, would MOST effectively accomplish the writer's goal?

  F. I never dropped them again.
  G. I did not ever get the chance to try flaming clubs on stage, though.
  H. On another night, an audience member handed me back an apple I had dropped.
  J. The play was sparsely attended, unfortunately, and closed after a week.

> Question 45 asks about the preceding passage as a whole.

45. Upon reviewing the essay and finding that some information has been left out, the writer composes the following sentence incorporating that information:

> Of course, I dropped the clubs more than a few times, but Jimi reassured me that "everybody drops."

If the writer were to add this sentence to the essay, the sentence would most logically be placed at Point:

  A. A.
  B. B.
  C. C.
  D. D.

MANHATTAN
PREP

PASSAGE 4

The Genius of Ramanujan

[1]

The word "genius" originally meant something like "genie," a divine being that inspired one's best work,

more a muse than a guardian angel. Whether truly having such guidance or he may not have, Srinivasa Ramanujan certainly earned the title of genius in the modern sense.

[2]

He was born in 1887 in southern India, Ramanujan soon showed great promise in mathematics and an unswerving dedication to the field. At the age of 16, having

won the awarding of many scholastic prizes at school, he

obtained a copy of Carr's *Synopsis of Pure Mathematics,* filled with thousands of equations but no proofs. The first equation, showing how the difference of two squares

could be factored, struck Ramanujan deeply. He set about devouring the book and creating his own proofs of its contents.

[3]

Unfortunately, since Ramanujan could focus only on mathematics, he flunked out of college twice. While working as an accounting clerk, he did math whenever he could and even published investigations in

46. **F.** NO CHANGE
    G. at most one's good work,
    H. ones' work best as well,
    J. at best the work of one,

47. **A.** NO CHANGE
    D. Truly having such guidance, or maybe not,
    C. Whether he truly had such guidance or not,
    D. If he had, or if he didn't have, such true guidance,

48. **F.** NO CHANGE
    G. Born in 1887
    H. In 1887 being born
    J. The year 1887, in which he was born

49. **A.** NO CHANGE
    B. been awarded at school a great number of scholarly prizes,
    C. competed for and won a numerous amount of awards in school,
    D. won numerous school awards,

50. **F.** NO CHANGE
    G. *Mathematics,* this was full of
    H. *Mathematics* were filled up with
    J. *Mathematics* was filled with

51. Which choice should the writer use to create the clearest and MOST logical ending for Paragraph 2?
    A. NO CHANGE
    B. Today, students in algebra classes worldwide routinely learn how to factor this difference.
    C. He was not physically hurt by this revelation, but he did have a frail constitution all his life.
    D. Some people might find such dense mathematical material to be less than gripping, though.

an academic journal. However, he remained desperately poor. As a high-caste Brahmin, his marriage was commonly arranged. At last, he wrote impassioned letters to professors at Cambridge University in

England. One of the professors, G. H. Hardy, is awestruck by the enclosed material. Ramanujan, mostly self-taught, didn't know that some of his equations had already been discovered; others though, lacked accompanying derivations.

[4]

In 1914, Hardy convinced Ramanujan to come to Cambridge. For almost five years, the two mathematicians collaborated in England; theirs even a number named theirs. Unfortunately, Ramanujan, who had long been sickly, was at that time, diagnosed with tuberculosis. He returned to India and died at the age of only 32.

[5]

A devout man, Ramanujan had insight of his claims coming from Namagiri, his family's goddess, sometimes in dreams. He had a close relationship with

52. F. NO CHANGE
    G. It was the case, as was common, that he had an arranged marriage.
    H. As was common for high-caste Brahmins, his marriage was arranged.
    J. OMIT the underlined portion.

53. A. NO CHANGE
    B. was
    C. had been
    D. OMIT the underlined portion

54. F. NO CHANGE
    G. discovered others,
    H. discovered; others,
    J. discovered: others

55. Given that all are true, which of the choices creates the MOST logical and appropriate contrast in this sentence and provides the best transition to Paragraph 4?
    A. NO CHANGE
    B. puzzled and even baffled Hardy.
    C. were stunning breakthroughs.
    D. involved strange summations.

56. F. NO CHANGE
    G. their is even a number named for them.
    H. they're is even a number named there's.
    J. there's even a number named for them.

57. A. NO CHANGE
    B. was diagnosed during that time
    C. in those days were diagnosed
    D. doctors then diagnosed him

58. F. NO CHANGE
    G. believed that his insights came
    H. came to believe insightfully
    J. claimed his insights that came

59. A. NO CHANGE
    B. the goddess sometimes of his family's
    C. his families goddess sometimes,
    D. sometimes goddess of his families'

MANHATTAN
PREP

numbers and worked by intuition—or perhaps divine

inspiration. One of his four notebooks was lost for

decades but then found and published in 1976.

60. **F.** NO CHANGE
   G. He kept four notebooks, one of which was lost for decades and then found and published in 1976.
   H. Lost for decades, but then found and published in 1976, was one of his four notebooks.
   J. OMIT the underlined portion.

PASSAGE 5

At the Bodega

[1]

If you look up the word "bodega" in a Spanish-English dictionary, the first definition will probably be "wine cellar." That's not what "bodega" means to me, <u>however</u>; anyone who spends some time in my
_61_
neighborhood knows that our bodega is the local

meeting <u>place, which</u> you'll eventually see everyone who
_62_

lives nearby. Why? It's the <u>little corner grocery</u> store.
_63_

[2]

The bodega is open 24 hours a day, 7 days a week. Sometimes, these kinds of stores are called "convenience" stores, and indeed, they are very convenient for <u>customers who shop for and purchase</u>
_64_
<u>food and other items.</u> It is true that the apples might
_64_

not be the freshest, but you can <u>arbitrarily</u> find almost
_65_
anything you might want in our bodega, where the prices are only a little higher than at the big grocery

store several blocks away. [66]

61. **A.** NO CHANGE
    B. consequently;
    C. accordingly;
    D. in other words;

62. **F.** NO CHANGE
    G. place, where
    H. place, when
    J. place,

63. **A.** NO CHANGE
    B. little corner, grocery
    C. little, corner grocery
    D. little, corner, grocery

64. **F.** NO CHANGE
    G. customers that visit these stores to buy food.
    H. customers who shop there, purchasing food items.
    J. customers.

65. The best placement for the underlined word would be:
    A. where it is now.
    B. before the word *true*.
    C. before the word *want*.
    D. before the word *higher*.

66. Which of the following true statements, if added here, would provide the MOST effective transition to the next paragraph?
    F. Coupons issued by that grocery store are not accepted at the bodega.
    G. That store is owned by some distant corporation, not by people I know.
    H. In addition, the grocery store offers a monthly set of special discounts.
    J. Friendly workers at that store walk you home or help you load your car.

[3]

Daoud is always there at the register when I go
in after school. He and his family own the bodega,
                         _____
                            67
although you might think that their cat Asheeb
actually does. Stark white and missing an eye, it curls

up wherever there is sunlight. [68] Eli, who is from El
Salvador, usually works the grill. He knows exactly how

burnt I like my grilled cheese sandwich. [69]

[4]

Many years ago, Daoud emigrated from Tunisia.
Every so often, he tells me about his hometown of

Kairouan, it is the fourth holiest city in Islam. For
_____
  70
instance, he said that in some tiny building in that city,

a blind camel walks in an endless circle, it pumps water
                                        _____
                                           71
from a sacred well discovered over 1,300 years ago. Eli

also has amazing stories. He grew up near an extinct
                                ____
                                 72
volcano, where his brothers and sisters still live.

67. Which of the following alternatives to the under-
    lined portion would be LEAST acceptable?
    A. Together with his family, he owns
    B. He, along with his family, owns
    C. His family and he own
    D. They own

68. If the writer were to delete the preceding sentence,
    the essay would primarily lose details that:
    F. reveal why the narrator prefers to spend time at
       the bodega.
    G. describe the cat physically and explain a previ-
       ous statement about it.
    H. suggest that the cat's behavior is linked to its
       unusual characteristics.
    J. contradict an earlier assertion about the true
       ownership of the store.

69. At this point, the writer is thinking about adding the
    following true statement:

       His name is not pronounced as you might
       guess from the spelling; it sounds like "Ellie."

    Should the writer make this addition here?
    A. Yes, because it is aligned with the narrator's
       interest in foreign languages.
    B. Yes, because it proves that the narrator is
       friends with the bodega's staff.
    C. No, because it does not provide an explanation
       for this pronunciation.
    D. No, because it distracts the reader from the
       main focus of this paragraph.

70. F. NO CHANGE
    G. Kairouan,
    H. Kairouan to be
    J. Kairouan

71. A. NO CHANGE
    B. and while pumping
    C. pumping
    D. pumps

72. F. NO CHANGE
    G. growed
    H. had grew
    J. grown

10

[5]

I am not stating that I am an expert in Tunisia
73
or El Salvador because I shop at our neighborhood
bodega. When I say "shukran" to Daoud or "gracias"

to Eli, though, I mean what I'm saying, expressed
74
sincerely from the heart a "thank you." I'm grateful
74
to them for providing not only great grilled cheese
sandwiches, but a place where all the many cultures in
our neighborhood can mingle in a positive way.

73. Which of the following alternatives to the under-
lined word would be LEAST acceptable?
   A. claiming
   B. asserting
   C. disputing
   D. arguing

74. The best placement for the underlined phrase would be:
   F. where it is now.
   G. before the word *When* (revising the capitaliza-
   tion accordingly).
   H. after the word *mean*.
   J. after the phrase *"thank you"* (ending the sen-
   tence with a period).

> Question 75 asks about the preceding passage
> as a whole.

75. Suppose the writer's goal had been to write an essay
making a detailed comparison between a neighborhood bodega and a bigger grocery store. Would this
essay successfully fulfill that goal?
   A. Yes, because it compares prices and ownership
   of the two stores.
   B. Yes, because it reveals the personal connection
   the narrator has to the bodega.
   C. No, because it focuses almost exclusively on the
   features of the bodega.
   D. No, because it demonstrates little appreciation
   for the positive qualities of bigger stores.

Passage Set 6 Answer Key

Write in whether you got each problem right or wrong (or left it blank). If your answer was correct, put a 1 in every blank to the right of that problem. Sum up each column and compare your total to the total possible "Out Of" points in each column.

Problem	Correct Answer	Right/ Wrong/ Blank	Usage/Mechanics			Rhetorical Skills		
			Grammar & Usage	Punctuation	Sentence Structure	Organization	Style	Writing Strategy
1	B		—					
2	J		—					
3	A				—			
4	H					—		
5	B		—					
6	G		—					
7	C							—
8	F		—					
9	D					—		
10	G							—
11	A							—
12	J				—			
13	D		—					
14	F				—			
15	C			—				
16	G		—					
17	A		—					
18	F				—			
19	C							—
20	G							—
21	D				—			
22	H		—					
23	B					—		
24	J						—	
25	B				—			
26	H						—	

10

Problem	Correct Answer	Right/ Wrong/ Blank	Usage/Mechanics			Rhetorical Skills		
			Grammar & Usage	Punctuation	Sentence Structure	Organization	Style	Writing Strategy
27	A		—					
28	H					—		
29	D			—				
30	F		—					
31	D			—				
32	H		—					
33	A						—	
34	F							—
35	C					—		
36	G		—					
37	C		—					
38	J				—			
39	A					—		
40	G			—				
41	B							—
42	H			—				
43	D						—	
44	F							—
45	B					—		
46	F		—					
47	C		—					
48	G				—			
49	D						—	
50	F				—			
51	A					—		
52	J							—
53	B				—			
54	H			—				
55	C					—		
56	J		—					

MANHATTAN
PREP

Problem	Correct Answer	Right/ Wrong/ Blank	Usage/Mechanics			Rhetorical Skills		
			Grammar & Usage	Punctuation	Sentence Structure	Organization	Style	Writing Strategy
57	B			—				
58	G						—	
59	A			—				
60	J							—
61	A					—		
62	G		—					
63	A			—				
64	J						—	
65	C				—			
66	G					—		
67	D		—					
68	G							—
69	D							—
70	G				—			
71	C				—			
72	F		—					
73	C						—	
74	J				—			
75	C							—
Total								
Out Of		75	20	9	14	11	8	13

10

Passage Set 6 Solutions

Passage 1

1.   **(B)** <u>As</u> a director, Clint Eastwood has often presented nature as a vital part of his films.

Usage/Mechanics   Grammar & Usage   Idioms

Used as a preposition, the word *as* means "in the role of." This meaning is the correct one for this sentence.

The wrong choices all have meanings that do not fit the context. *Like* means "similar to," but Clint Eastwood is actually a director, as the phrase *his films* reveals. *Just as* is generally only appropriate when paired with *so too*, and these conjunctions both need to introduce clauses ("Just as Eastwood is an accomplished director, so too is he a well-known actor"). Finally, *such as* introduces examples ("He is known for his Westerns, such as *Unforgiven*"). The correct answer is (B).

2.   **(J)** Clint Eastwood has often presented nature as a vital part of his films. <u>Examples include</u> the shots of the African countryside … and the beautiful panoramas …

Usage/Mechanics   Grammar & Usage   Parallelism

The previous sentence states that Eastwood *has often* done something in *his films*. That is, the phenomenon has happened many times. It would be fine to give just one example of this phenomenon, but the next sentence gives many such examples (*the shots … and the beautiful panoramas*), following the verb *include*. Thus, the subject must be even more numerous, because these multiple examples are only *included* in the subject. Thus, the subject must be plural (*Examples*), not singular (*An example*).

No possessive pronoun should go in front of the word *Examples*. You could modify *Examples* with a prepositional phrase (e.g., "Examples of this inclusion of nature"), but that phrase has to refer to the whole prior sentence (the fact that Eastwood often presents nature as a vital part of his films). A short possessive, such as *Its* or *Their*, can't capture the entire thought. The best choice of those available is just to leave the word *Examples* unmodified, so that the reader can draw the correct inference (these examples are of the phenomenon discussed in the previous sentence). The correct answer is (J).

3.   **(A)** Examples include the shots of the African countryside … and the beautiful panoramas … in <u>*Unforgiven. A Perfect World*</u> continues to elevate nature to great importance …

Usage/Mechanics   Sentence Structure   Whole Sentences

The text from *Examples include* to *Unforgiven* is a long independent clause. The title *A Perfect World* begins a new independent clause as its subject, followed by the verb *continues*. These two independent clauses cannot be joined by just a comma, as in choice (C), or by nothing at all, as in choice (B).

Grammatically, the two clauses can be joined by a comma plus *and*, as in choice (D). However, this choice is stylistically poor. The two clauses are each very long, making the combined sentence unwieldy and rambling. As large, distinct thoughts in their own right, the clauses are best punctuated as separate sentences, allowing for a real pause between them. The correct answer is (A).

MANHATTAN
PREP

4.   **(H)** Most effectively leads into this paragraph and provides a suitable transition to the description that follows: *The natural world is clearly valued in the opening shot of the film.*

Rhetorical Skills   Organization   Opening/Closing Content

The first paragraph ends with the assertion that Eastwood's film *"A Perfect World" continues to elevate nature to great importance*. This point comes just before the underlined portion, which is followed by a description of Kevin Costner lying *in a verdant field … as a hawk circles overhead*. Thus, the underlined sentence should transition the reader from a general point about the importance of nature in this film to the particular context in which Costner is shown lying in the field. The correct choice does exactly this task, reiterating the value of nature and setting the context (*the opening shot of the film*).

The incorrect choices fail to make this connection from the general argument to the particular example. None of them even mention *nature* or a synonymous phrase. Moreover, they introduce irrelevancies (e.g., *this impression is undermined later*, or *Eastwood both directs and acts …*, or *The start of the film may seem boring*). All of these points distract the reader from making the straightforward shift from the prior paragraph to the example of the opening shot (reflecting the importance of nature). The correct answer is (H).

5.   **(B)** Not acceptable: … the sun shining <u>down</u> him …

Usage/Mechanics   Grammar & Usage   Idioms

The one preposition that does not work here on its own is *down*. The sun can shine *down* a hole or some other kind of cavity, but it cannot shine *down* a person. Because you are looking for the unacceptable option, *down* by itself is the correct answer.

The wrong choices are all acceptable alternatives to *down upon*. The sun can shine *down on* a person or it can shine *upon* a person. The sun can even shine *above* a person, with a slightly different but equally acceptable meaning (here, the emphasis is on the light in the sky around the sun, not on the person). The correct answer is (B).

6.   **(G)** *A Perfect World* tells the tale of escaped convict Butch Haynes (Costner), <u>who, while running</u> from the law, kidnaps and then befriends an eight-year-old boy named Phillip.

Usage/Mechanics   Grammar & Usage   Parallelism

The original sentence phrases the modifier this way: *who runs from the law, kidnaps and then befriends an eight-year-old boy …* This phrasing seems to be parallel, but it's not. There is a list of three verbs (*runs, kidnaps,* and *befriends*), but the last two have the same object (the *boy*), throwing off the list. You would have to rewrite the modifier as "runs from the law, kidnaps an eight-year-old boy, and befriends him." Another issue is that the verbs are not logically parallel. Butch kidnaps and then befriends the boy *while* running from the law; that is, the kidnapping and befriending are parallel, but the running is the background action. The correct answer allows *kidnaps* and *befriends* to be properly parallel, while putting the *running* action in the background.

Choice (H), *who ran,* has the same parallelism issue as the original sentence; in addition, the verb is in the wrong tense (past, rather than the present tense used throughout the rest of the essay to tell the story). Finally, choice (J) creates a run-on sentence by removing *who,* the grammatical subject of *kidnaps* and *befriends.* The correct answer is (G).

7.   **(C)** If the writer deleted the phrase "and then befriends," the paragraph would primarily lose a detail that illuminate the character of Butch and the evolution of a relationship.

Rhetorical Skills   Writing Strategy   Deletions

The phrase *and then befriends* plays two critical roles in the sentence. First, it indicates a positive action that Butch takes; without this phrase, Butch is only a convict and kidnapper on the run from the law. In this fashion, the phrase *illuminates the character of Butch.* Second, the phrase reveals a change in Butch's relationship to Phillip. Butch doesn't just kidnap Phillip; he later befriends him. Thus, the phrase *illuminates … the evolution of a relationship* as well. These roles are described in the correct answer.

Choice (A) claims that the phrase draws a comparison between Butch's journey and those made by other escaped convicts, but this phrase makes no such comparison. In fact, nowhere in the essay are any such other journeys mentioned. The phrase does not establish the setting, either, as is asserted in choice (B). No mention is made of time or place. Finally, it is not true that this information is "ultimately irrelevant," as choice (D) claims. The light that the phrase *and then befriends* sheds on Butch's character and his relationship with Phillip is crucial to the reader's understanding of the film. The correct answer is (C).

8.   **(F)** <u>With</u> whom should we identify …

Usage/Mechanics   Grammar & Usage   Idioms

When used to mean "connect, bond personally, see through the eyes of," the verb *identify* takes the preposition *with*: "We should identify with Butch." The phrase *identify as* would need a direct object (you identify *something* as something else) and would mean a literal statement of identity: "She identified herself as a police officer." Neither *identify to* nor *identify in* are idiomatic English. The correct answer is (F).

9.   **(D)** With whom should we identify, the criminal or the officer of the law? [No transition] Eastwood helps us make our choice with a delicate use of the natural world.

Rhetorical Skills   Organization   Transitions

The sentence before the underlined portion asks a rhetorical question of the reader. The best transition to choose from among those available is nothing at all. That is, the next sentence should just start with the subject *Eastwood* and continue right into what he does (*help us make our choice,* meaning between the criminal and the officer of the law as described in the rhetorical question). The reference back to the question via *our choice* is sufficient to connect this sentence to the previous text.

The original transition *Still* implies some degree of contrast that is unsuitable; no contrast whatsoever should be suggested. *Thus* (indicating a result) and *In short* (indicating a summary) are also inappropriate for an immediate answer to a rhetorical question. The correct answer is (D).

MANHATTAN
PREP

10. **(G)** Best accomplishes goal of presenting an implication of an earlier statement, in order to reinforce the main point of the sentence: It is easy for viewers to anchor themselves to Butch as an essentially good man, because he connects with <u>nature and is thus associated with freedom, purity, and light.</u>

Rhetorical Skills   Writing Strategy   Choice of Content

The main point of the sentence is the first clause: *It is easy for viewers to anchor themselves to Butch as an essentially good man*. The sentence goes on to explain why: *because he connects with nature*. The correct answer provides an implication, or logical consequence, of this statement: … *and is thus associated with freedom, purity, and light*. This last part of the sentence effectively reinforces the main point (the fact that viewers see Butch as a good man), because *freedom, purity, and light* are positive qualities.

None of the other choices present positive qualities of Butch that could reinforce the main point. The original sentence and choice (H) both repeat that Butch is a lawbreaker. Choice (J) makes an unrelated point about *violence in ecological systems*. The correct answer is (G).

11. **(A)** Most relevant to the main focus of the paragraph: As Butch drives <u>through the countryside</u> in a car that always has the windows rolled down …

Rhetorical Skills   Writing Strategy   Choice of Content

The main focus of the paragraph is how Butch's connection with nature, as portrayed subtly in the film, helps the audience identify with him. Thus, the best detail to include in the underlined portion is one that underscores that connection between Butch and his natural surroundings. *Through the countryside* is the most fitting of the available options. None of the other options (*at deceptively normal speeds*, *with a soda bottle in hand*, or *with a cigarette in his mouth*) make any reference to nature. The correct answer is (A).

12. **(J)** As Butch drives through the countryside in a car that always has the windows rolled down, the <u>scenes are saturated</u> with lush greens and blues.

Usage/Mechanics   Sentence Structure   Whole Sentences

The main clause of the sentence is *the scenes are saturated with lush greens and blues*, in which *the scenes* is the subject, and *are* is the verb. Here, *saturated* (which means "soaked, drenched, filled") acts more as an adjective than as part of a passive-voice verb (since the preposition that follows is *with*, not *by*), but whichever interpretation you prefer, *saturated* cannot stand alone here as a main verb. To be a main verb, it would have to have a subject and an object (e.g., "lush greens and blues *saturated* the scenes").

The original phrasing (*the scenes saturated with …*) makes this clause a fragment. Since the initial clause (*As Butch drives …*) is dependent, the whole sentence collapses. The same issue arises with choice (H), *scenes that saturated*. Finally, choice (G) is not grammatical, since you can *saturate* something *with* something else, but you cannot simply *saturate with* something. The correct answer is (J).

10

13. **(D)** … the lawman, <u>who for most</u> of the film rides inside a metallic camper …

Usage/Mechanics   Grammar & Usage   Modifier Forms & Comparisons

The modifying clause should begin with *who*, not *whom*, because the *who* acts as the subject in that clause (*who rides inside* …). *Whom* is only appropriate as the object of a verb or preposition.

The word following *for* should be *most*, not *more*. *Most* can stand on its own (*most of the film* = "the majority of the film"), but *more* should be part of a comparison: *more than* something. No comparison is made here. The correct answer is (D).

14. **(F)** … assists <u>the audience's identification of Butch</u> as the unlikely protagonist.

Usage/Mechanics   Sentence Structure   Modifier Placement

If expressed as a sentence, the thought in the underlined portion and just afterward is this: "The audience identifies Butch as the unlikely protagonist." To convert this thought into a noun phrase, you turn *identifies* into *identification*. The subject of *identifies* (*the audience*) becomes either *the audience's* or *by the audience*. Finally, the object *Butch* becomes *of Butch*. The correct answer obeys these rules.

In contrast, the incorrect choices deliberately mix up these transformations. By using two *of* phrases, choice (G) confuses the meaning. Choices (H) and (J) would actually mean that Butch identifies the audience as the protagonist. The proper meaning is the other way around. The correct answer is (F).

15. **(C)** It is a <u>film in which a kidnapper</u> and convict can be a hero.

Usage/Mechanics   Punctuation   Commas

No commas belong anywhere in the underlined portion. The phrase *a film* should not be separated from *in which* by a comma, because this clause is essential—it defines the phrase *a film*. (In other circumstances, the phrase *in which* could be preceded by a comma, but the clause would have to be nonessential.)

Under no circumstances should *in which* be separated from the subject *a kidnapper and convict* by a comma. No pause should be taken before a subject that immediately follows *which*. Finally, the subject *a kidnapper and convict* deserves to have no commas inside it. Only put a comma before *and* if the list contains three or more items (or if the *and* is joining two independent clauses). Here, the list is just of two nouns. The correct answer is (C).

Passage 2

16. **(G)** … no other ballerinas in the world were as prominent <u>as</u> the best Europeans …

Usage/Mechanics   Grammar & Usage   Comparisons

The proper form of an *as* comparison is *as [adjective] as:* "I am as tall as Maria." No other word can be used in place of the second *as*. The comparison word *than* is used with *more* or *less:* "Maria is more accomplished than Michael." The word *then* means "at that time, or afterwards" and is not used to make comparisons. Finally, *of* is used with superlatives: "Maria is the best dancer of all." The correct answer is (G).

MANHATTAN
PREP

17.   **(A)** ... Maria Tallchief danced the lead in "The Firebird," <u>staged</u> by celebrated choreographer ... With this performance ...

Usage/Mechanics   Grammar & Usage   Modifier Forms

In the original, correct version of the sentence, the noun phrase *"The Firebird"* is directly modified by the past participle *staged* to mean "which was or had been staged."

In choice (B), the additional word *and* throws off the modification, since *and* always implies a list of some kind. However, there is no viable first item in this list; the most natural reading initially would be *danced* (as another verb form), but "Tallchief staged by ..." doesn't make sense (and isn't grammatically complete anyway). *Since staged* is grammatically fine, but with its meaning of "which has been staged since then," this phrase takes you forward in time, interrupting the narration and making the modifier an irrelevant aside. Instead, the writer evidently intends to remain focused on the "Firebird" event, writing *With this performance ...*, so *since staged* is inappropriate. Finally, *thus staged* introduces the transition word *thus* (meaning "for this reason, in this way"), which is unnecessary and distracting here. There is no earlier reason or way for *thus* to refer to. The correct answer is (A).

18.   **(F)**   In 1949 ... Tallchief danced the lead ... With this performance, Tallchief <u>vaulted</u> to international stardom.

Usage/Mechanics   Sentence Structure   Whole Sentences & Verb Tenses

The correct form, *vaulted*, is a complete verb that can run a sentence, unlike *vaulting* ("Tallchief vaulting" is a fragment). *Who vaulted* contains the same complete verb, but the *who* turns the phrase into a modifier, depriving the sentence of a main verb and making it a fragment as well. Finally, *vaults* is complete but in the wrong tense (present rather than past). The event took place in the past, however, and in standard English, the past tense is used to narrate such events. This essay obeys that past-tense convention, as can be seen in the prior sentence (*danced*). The correct answer is (F).

19.   **(C)**   If the underlined word were deleted, the sentence would primarily lose a detail that provides new and relevant information to the sentence.

Rhetorical Skills   Writing Strategy   Deletions

The relevant portion of the sentence reads as follows: ... *Tallchief began dancing ballet at the age of three.* If you delete the word *ballet*, you get this: *Tallchief began dancing at the age of three.* This edited clause is grammatically fine, eliminating choice (A), because the verb *dance* does not require a direct object (such as *ballet*). However, the word *ballet* conveys important information; after all, Tallchief could have begun dancing any kind of dance at the age of three. The fact that she began studying ballet in particular at that young age is not duplicated anywhere else in the paragraph, and it is not "needlessly specific." Rather, it is specific in a very relevant way, because Tallchief later became a professional ballet dancer. The correct answer is (C).

20.   **(G)**   Should the writer make this addition here? Yes, because it provides pertinent examples that help to make a broad term relevant.

Rhetorical Skills   Writing Strategy   Additions

With the addition, the sentence in question would look thus: *Elizabeth Marie Tall Chief, as she was then named, also studied other subjects, such as piano and gymnastics, while her grandmother took her to traditional Osage dance ceremonies.* This addition is valuable, because the phrase *other subjects* by itself could mean many different things unrelated to dance. For instance, she could have been studying chemistry and pottery. The examples of piano and gymnastics "help to make a broad term" namely *other subjects*.

These examples do not, however, explain *the dedication with which the young Tallchief studied*, as choice (F) incorrectly puts it. The subjects of piano and gymnastics may be famously difficult, but plenty of people study them in an undedicated way. As for choices (H) and (J), the examples are too quick to be very distracting, and it is unimportant that only two examples are provided. A full list is unnecessary and, if very long, could in fact be distracting. The correct answer is (G).

21.   **(D)** <u>These experiences probably provided the basis for Tallchief's later belief that ballet should be grounded in movement and musicality.</u>

Usage/Mechanics   Sentence Structure   Modifier Placement

The correct version of the sentence puts all the modifier ducks in a logical row. Work your way forward from the beginning of the sentence. What did these experiences probably provide? The basis for something. Okay, the basis for what? For Tallchief's later belief. What was that belief? The belief that ballet should be grounded in movement and musicality. This ordering makes the most sense by far. The other versions of the sentence mix up the modifier positions, making illogical word salads that cannot be broken down anywhere as reasonably as the correct option. The correct answer is (D).

22.   **(H)** … Tallchief resolved in her teenage years <u>to devote</u> her life to the craft of ballet.

Usage/Mechanics   Grammar & Usage   Modifier Forms & Idioms

Both the original version (*that would devote*) and choice (G) (*that devoted*) are modifiers attached to the noun phrase *her teenage years*. These options both incorrectly state that the teenage years themselves would devote Tallchief's life to ballet.

Instead, the correct answer makes the object of the verb *resolved* the infinitive *to devote*. Tallchief resolved *to devote* her life to ballet. The infinitive form is idiomatically correct. You cannot resolve *doing* something; you resolve *to do* something (meaning that you decide to do it). The correct answer is (H).

23.   **(B)** Soon she was accepted into the Ballet Russe de Monte Carlo, <u>in part because,</u> with her American passport, she could travel abroad.

Rhetorical Skills   Organization   Transitions

The best logical connector between the first thought (*she was accepted …*) and the second (*with her American passport, she could travel abroad*) is *because* or *since*. This connector can then be modified by *partly, partially,* or *in part* (placed before the connector so that it does not accidentally become absorbed by the second thought). Thus, several variations on the correct answer (*in part because*) would be perfectly fine.

Of course, none of the wrong choices include any of those variations. Choice (A) uses *that* by itself, which can never mean *because* or *since* in normal modern English. Choice (C) uses *in that*, which, as a substitute for *because*, is both

MANHATTAN
PREP

pompous and vague. Moreover, the *partly* is in the wrong position. Finally, choice (D) uses a valid connector (*since*), but the phrase *the part* cannot work in place of *partly* or *in part*. The correct answer is (B).

24.   **(J)**   He designed ballets to highlight her technical prowess, easy energy, and regal <u>grace.</u>

Rhetorical Skills   Style   Concision

The incorrect choices are all redundant. In the original sentence, the phrase *through his designs* is unnecessary, since the sentence begins with *He designed ballets to highlight* … , which certainly means that the highlighting would happen through his designs. Choices (G) and (H) are made superfluous by the possessive pronoun *her* in the phrase … *her technical prowess, easy energy, and regal grace.* The reader already knows, therefore, that these are qualities of Tallchief's that she would show in her performances.

The best choice is to eliminate all the excess and finish the sentence with the word *grace.* The correct answer is (J).

25.   **(B)**   Although the marriage didn't <u>last, the</u> professional relationship did …

Usage/Mechanics   Sentence Structure   Whole Sentences

The sentence begins with a subordinate clause: *Although the marriage didn't last.* Subordinate clauses cannot stand alone as sentences, as in the incorrect choice (A). These clauses must be joined to their main clauses by commas, not in general by any other kind of punctuation. In this case, the main clause *the professional relationship did* must be preceded by a comma. The dash is inappropriately emphatic here; it can only work if the subordinate clause follows the main clause. The correct answer is (B).

26.   **(H)**   Best accomplishes the goal of suggesting that the professional relationship led to success: Although the marriage didn't last, the professional relationship did, resulting in <u>triumphs</u> such as "The Nutcracker," …

Rhetorical Skills   Style   Word Choice

The word *triumph,* meaning "victory, lofty achievement," contains within it the meaning of "success." As a result, calling the productions *triumphs* effectively suggests that the professional relationship led to success. The other choices (*productions, performances,* and *works*) are much more neutral descriptions and do not imply anything about how successful these productions were. The correct answer is (H).

27.   **(A)**   The Sugar Plum Fairy in Balanchine's reinvented ballet <u>was</u> the soaring Tallchief …

Usage/Mechanics   Grammar & Usage   Subject–Verb Agreement

The subject of the sentence is the singular noun phrase *The Sugar Plum Fairy.* To match, the verb must also be singular. Thus, *was* must be chosen instead of *were* or *were to be.* Omitting the underlined portion would delete the only verb in the main clause of this sentence, turning the sentence into a fragment. The correct answer is (A).

MANHATTAN
PREP

28. **(H)** Retiring in 1965, Tallchief founded ballet schools and companies in Chicago. <u>Today,</u> Oklahoma remembers her as one of the "Five Moons," …

Rhetorical Skills　　　　　Organization　　　　　Transitions

The first thought (*Retiring in 1965, Tallchief founded ballet schools and companies in Chicago*) and the second thought (*Oklahoma remembers her as one of the "Five Moons,"*) are only related chronologically. That is, the first thought describes what Tallchief did after she retired from active dancing; the action takes place at the end of her career. The second thought moves forward to a situation in the present time (how Oklahoma now remembers Tallchief). Thus, the best transition of those available is *Today*, which swiftly and easily brings the reader forward to the present day.

The two thoughts are not really in contrast. The fact that she founded these schools and companies in Chicago is not in opposition to the fact that she was born and raised in Oklahoma, so *In contrast* is not an appropriate transition. The second thought does not follow logically from the first, so *Therefore* is not fitting either. Finally, *At last* implies the long-awaited fulfillment of an expectation, as if Oklahoma had been expected to remember Tallchief in this particular way but had not done so until just recently. This implication is unwarranted. The correct answer is (H).

29. **(D)** … one of the "Five Moons," <u>five illustrious</u> Native American ballerinas …

Usage/Mechanics　　　　　Punctuation　　　　　Commas

The words *five, illustrious,* and *Native American* are all adjectives (or adjectival phrases) modifying the noun *ballerinas*. If you use a string of adjectives to modify a noun, commas do not always belong between the adjectives. The best test is to see whether the word *and* would work between the adjectives in question. If *and* works (signaling that the adjectives are of the same type), then a comma belongs between the adjectives. For instance, "thin, tall trees" is correct, because "thin and tall trees" works. In contrast, "tall, oak trees" is incorrect, because "tall and oak trees" doesn't work. *Tall* and *oak* are qualitatively different kinds of adjectives, so it does not make sense to put them at the same level.

In the sentence in question, no comma belongs between *five* and *illustrious*, because "five and illustrious ballerinas" does not make sense. More generally speaking, a quantifier (such as *five*) is fundamentally different from a descriptive adjective (such as *illustrious*). Likewise, no comma belongs between *illustrious* and *Native American*, because "illustrious and Native American ballerinas" is also imperfect. A "type" adjective (such as *Native American*) functions like *oak* in *oak tree*. The ballerinas in question were illustrious among all ballerinas, it turns out, but that is not the issue at hand. *Illustrious Native American ballerinas* is the correct formulation, without any commas. The correct answer is (D).

30. **(F)** … Oklahoma remembers her as one of the "Five Moons," five illustrious Native American ballerinas from that state, <u>all of whom were</u> born in the 1920s.

Usage/Mechanics　　　　　Grammar & Usage　　　　　Subject–Verb Agreement & Modifier Forms

The modifier could start either with *all of whom* or with *each of whom*. However, *all* is plural, matching the plural verb *were*. The word *each* is singular, so the underlined portion would have to read *each of whom was* (with the singular *was*) to be correct.

The word *ballerinas* refers to humans, so you must use *who* or *whom* (not *which*) to refer to *ballerinas*. Finally, dropping *of whom* to have *all were* creates a new independent clause ("all were born in the 1920s") that is improperly joined to the previous clause by just a comma. *All* by itself would be fine, but the presence of *were* creates a run-on. The correct answer is (F).

Passage 3

31.   **(D)** I learned how to juggle clubs, sticks, and knives from an Irish Traveller …

Usage/Mechanics   Punctuation   Commas & Colons

The object of the verb *juggle* is a three-item list (*clubs, sticks, and knives*). No punctuation should separate a verb from an object that directly follows. You may be tempted to use a colon before the list (as in the original, incorrect sentence), but lists do not always require colons before them.

The list itself needs to contain a comma after the first item (*clubs*), as in the correct answer. Incidentally, the ACT also follows the convention that a comma belongs before the *and* in a list of three items or more. This comma is known as the "Oxford comma." The correct answer is (D).

32.   **(H)** Travellers … are ethnically distinct nomads, some of whom may be genetically related …

Usage/Mechanics   Grammar & Usage   Pronoun Forms

In the original version, the part of the sentence after the comma (*some of them may be …*) is an independent clause, one that could stand alone as a sentence. Unfortunately, the part before the comma (*Travellers … are ethnically distinct nomads*) is also an independent clause, and two independent clauses cannot legally be joined by just a comma.

The correct answer fixes the issue by changing the second clause from independent to dependent. The *whom* makes this clause a proper modifier, which can be attached to *nomads* by a comma.

The phrase *of who* is incorrect; the form *whom* is used as the object of prepositions (such as *of*) and of verbs. Finally, deleting the underlined portion makes the second clause independent again (*some may be …*), creating the same run-on issue as in the original sentence. The correct answer is (H).

33.   **(A)** I already knew how to juggle three balls with a certain measure of skill, …

Rhetorical Skills   Style   Concision

The original sentence is appropriately concise and specific. The narrator says that he or she *already knew how to juggle three balls*. The additional phrase *tossing them in the air* is redundant, because the verb *juggle* already includes that meaning (you juggle things by tossing them in the air repeatedly and catching them). Likewise, the phrase *all three at the same time* is unnecessary. To juggle three balls means to juggle all three of them at the same time.

At the same time, the option to delete the object of *juggle* goes too far. It is true that the verb *juggle* does not grammatically require an object: you can just say "I can juggle" in some contexts. The object *three balls* is necessary, however, to draw the right contrast with the first sentence of the passage: *I learned how to juggle clubs, sticks, and knives … It would* be confusing to state afterwards that the narrator *already knew how to juggle* without saying what specifically besides *clubs, sticks, and knives* the narrator already knew how to juggle. The correct answer is (A).

34.   **(F)**   Indicates most specifically what was desired of the narrator: ... the director wanted me to <u>perform harder tricks.</u>

Rhetorical Skills   Writing Strategy   Choice of Content

The four options are *perform harder tricks, try new things, stretch myself,* and *do more.* The phrase that best meets the goal is *perform harder tricks,* since the object (*harder tricks*) contains a specific noun (*tricks*) and adjective (*harder*). In the context of the sentence, it's clear that these tricks are juggling tricks and are meant to be harder than juggling three balls.

Try new things has a specific adjective (*new*), but *things* is very broad: "trying new things" could include sliding down the side of a volcano, for instance. *Stretch myself* is similarly vague, and *do more* begs the question "do more what, in what way?" The first sentence of the passage does tell the reader what the narrator learned how to do (*juggle clubs, sticks, and knives*), but since the goal here is to conclude the sentence most effectively "by indicating most specifically what was desired of the narrator," the best choice out of those available is *perform harder tricks.* The correct answer is (F).

35.   **(C)**   Which of the following sequences of sentences makes the previous paragraph most logical? 2, 1, 3

Rhetorical Skills   Organization   Sentence Order

Placed in correct order, the sentences of the paragraph are as follows:

[2] I was living in Galway, a town on the west coast of Ireland, and had won the part of a magician in a play.
[1] I already knew how to juggle three balls with a certain measure of skill, but the director wanted me to perform harder tricks.
[3] Spotting one of Jimi's flyers, she arranged for me to train with his troupe, which was staying on the outskirts of town.

Sentence 2, placed first, sets the broadest background (*I was living in Galway ... and had won the part of a magician in a play.*) Without the context of *a play,* the phrase *the director* in Sentence 1 does not make sense. With Sentence 1 placed after Sentence 2, however, the reader knows that *the director* is the director of the play mentioned in Sentence 2. Finally, Sentence 3 uses the pronoun *she,* which must refer to *the director.* Therefore, Sentence 3 must still come last. The correct answer is (C).

36.   **(G)**   Jimi and the other performers ... thrust me right away into a <u>rapid passing</u> exercise, in which I had to catch clubs from one person and toss them to another.

Usage/Mechanics   Grammar & Usage   Modifier Forms

The exercise is a *passing* exercise. This phrase does not mean "an exercise that passes," any more than *swimming pool* means "a pool that swims." Rather, a *passing exercise* is an exercise that involves the activity of passing something around (in this case, clubs), just as the sentence explains. Since the passing exercise is rapid, it can be described as a *rapid passing exercise,* not a *rapidly passing exercise* (which would necessarily mean "an exercise that passes rapidly"), as in the original sentence. In the same way, you would write a "deep swimming pool," not a "deeply swimming pool."

If *rapid pass exercise* were available, this option would be acceptable, but *pass rapid exercise* in choice (H) puts the adjectives in the wrong order. A "pass exercise," like a "passing exercise," would be a type of exercise, which you could then modify with an adjective just as *rapid* by writing *rapid pass exercise*, but you couldn't break up *pass exercise* by putting the adjective *rapid* in the middle. Finally, *rapidly pass exercise* is incorrect, because the adverb *rapidly* can only modify a verb, but in the phrase *pass exercise*, the word *pass* is being used as a noun to modify another noun, like *apple* in *apple pie*. You cannot modify nouns with adverbs, even if the nouns are being used as a kind of adjective (like *pass* in *pass exercise* or *apple* in *apple pie*). The correct answer is (G).

37.   **(C)** It took a lot of patient coaching to make progress, but I improved greatly over time.

Usage/Mechanics   Grammar & Usage   Pronoun Forms

The form *it* is required, because the real subject is *to make progress.* The sentence could be rewritten this way: "To make progress (or making progress) took a lot of patient coaching." It is both common and correct in English to move infinitive subjects to the back of the sentence and put an *it* at the beginning as a placeholder; in fact, this very sentence (before the semicolon) demonstrates this maneuver. *It* is the only possible subject if the infinitive is the true subject.

The verb *took* can take other subjects. "I took a lot of coaching" is the same as "I required a lot of coaching," so you can say "I took a lot of coaching to get better" or "This building took work to knock down," but only if the subject of *took* is the subject or object of the infinitive.

"I took a lot of coaching to get better" = I needed a lot of coaching, in order that I could get better.

"This building took work to knock down" = To knock down this building took, or required, work.

The infinitive in the original sentence is *to make progress*, which can only refer to the narrator. Thus, pronouns such as *That* in choice (A) or *He* in choice (B) do not work.

Finally, choice (D), *With*, creates a transition problem: *With a lot of patient coaching to make progress, but I improved greatly …* The *but* is now out of place, and even the infinitive *to make progress* is awkward. A corrected version would be *With a lot of patient coaching, I improved greatly …*, but this option is not available. The correct answer is (C).

38.   **(J)** No one knows when the craft was invented; ancient Egyptian paintings and Roman statuettes portray jugglers.

Usage/Mechanics   Sentence Structure   Whole Sentences

The correct version of the sentence properly joins the two independent clauses with a semicolon. *No one knows … invented* could stand alone as a sentence, as could *ancient Egyptian paintings … jugglers.* Thus, these two clauses cannot be just pushed together with just a comma, as in choice (G), or with no punctuation at all, as in the original sentence. Choice (H) introduces the word *by*, which makes an illogical connection between the clauses (the *ancient Egyptian paintings* did not invent the craft of juggling). The correct answer is (J).

39.   **(A)** The activity was often regarded as light entertainment or even as deceptive trickery; genuine agility is required to juggle well, however, and some tales hint at a connection with martial arts.

Rhetorical Skills   Organization   Transitions

10

The semicolon joins clauses that are in opposition to each other. According to the first clause, juggling *was often regarded as light entertainment or even as deceptive trickery*. That is, the activity was considered unserious, deceptive, or both. The second clause states that juggling requires *genuine agility*. The word *genuine* (= "true, authentic") stands in contrast to *deceptive*. Finally, the sentence ends with *a connection to martial arts*, which contrasts with the *light entertainment* mentioned in the first clause. The paragraph goes on to describe legendary scenes of war (the word *martial* means "having to do with war") that involved juggling.

Because the first part and the second part of the sentence are in logical contrast, the transition should indicate that contrast. *However* is the only viable choice. *That is* rephrases and explains what came before, *for example* gives an example, and *therefore* provides a consequence. None of these transitions offers the contrast needed in this sentence. The correct answer is (A).

40. **(G)** The Chinese <u>warrior Xiong Yiliao</u> is said to have ended a battle …

Usage/Mechanics   Punctuation   Commas & Dashes

The noun phrase *The Chinese warrior* is fairly general: many people have been Chinese warriors throughout history. When you put a name after a general phrase such as *The Chinese warrior* to specify which warrior you're talking about, don't use commas or any other kind of punctuation (including dashes). The name is an essential piece of information and cannot be sensibly removed from the sentence.

You are allowed to start a sentence with an appositive noun phrase, separated by a comma from the subject: "A wonderful cook, Xiong Yiliao was also known for his juggling prowess." However, that appositive would need to be extra information about the subject (notice that the phrase starts with the indefinite article "a" rather than the definite article "the"). This case does not apply in this problem, since the phrase *The Chinese warrior* is not extra information.

It is appropriate to surround the name on both sides by commas when the noun phrase is specific enough, making the name nonessential to the sentence: "The first person to set foot on the moon, Neil Armstrong, uttered some famous words …" The answer choices in this problem do not give you the option to surround the name with commas, however, and if one of them did so, it would be incorrect. The phrase *The Chinese warrior* is not specific enough to make the name unnecessary. The correct answer is (G).

41. **(B)** If the writer were to make this deletion, the paragraph would primarily lose information that reveals that the battle never actually took place.

Rhetorical Skills   Writing Strategy   Deletions

Here is a simplified version of the sentence before the deletion: *Xiong Yiliao is said to have ended a battle before it began by doing* blah-blah. Here is the same sentence with the clause "before it began" deleted: "Xiong Yiliao is said to have ended a battle by doing blah-blah." The natural implication in the latter case is that the battle had already been going before Xiong Yiliao ended it.

However, he actually ended the battle *before it began*—that is, the battle was just about to happen, but it never actually happened. Without the words *before it began*, the reader would not conclude that the battle never happened.

MANHATTAN
PREP

The wrong choices make incorrect claims about what the clause *before it began* conveys. It does not convey the time at which the battle started (the battle never did start). Nor does the clause suggest that the battle lasted longer than expected (it actually lasted much less time than expected). Finally, the clause does not suggest which side won the battle. The correct answer is (B).

42. **(H)** On October 14, <u>1066, English troops</u> watched the Norman knight Taillefer …

Usage/Mechanics   Punctuation   Commas & Semicolons

At the beginning of a sentence, a prepositional phrase indicating a date should be separated from the subject by a comma: *On October 14, 1066, English troops …* The date is *October 14, 1066*, so the year *1066* should be followed by a comma. A semicolon does not work here; a semicolon should only be used to join independent clauses (or, in theory, to separate items in a list, when those items themselves contain commas). If no comma is used to separate the year *1066* from *English troops,* then the date could be misinterpreted as a number of troops.

Finally, no comma should intervene between the subject *English troops* and the verb *watched.* The correct answer is (H).

43. **(D)** On October 14, 1066, English troops watched the Norman knight Taillefer juggle his sword before the Battle of Hastings. Challenged by an English knight, Taillefer cut him down, only to be swarmed by enemy soldiers [deleted].

Rhetorical Skills   Style   Concision

The best choice of those available is to end the sentence right after *enemy soldiers.* This sentence and the prior one have established that the English and the Normans are enemies of each other in this battle. Thus, by this point it is redundant to write both *enemy soldiers* and *from the English side* (or *who were fighting the Normans*). Finally, there is no need to write *after that.* The sequence of actions is clearly laid out by the sentence: first Taillefer was challenged by an English knight, then Taillefer cut him down, and finally Taillefer was swarmed by enemy soldiers. The correct answer is (D).

44. **(F)** Most effectively emphasizes in a positive way the ultimate impact of Jimi Juggle's training: I never dropped them again.

Rhetorical Skills   Writing Strategy   Additions

As it is now written, the final paragraph of the essay describes the narrator's *date with destiny*, on which he or she immediately dropped the knives and was grateful that no enemy warrior was around. Then the narrator remembered Jimi's advice ("everybody drops"), picked up the knives, and kept going.

At that point, if the writer wishes to emphasize the ultimate impact of Jimi's training in a positive way, the best choice is to end with *I never dropped them again.* This outcome is certainly positive. The other choices are either neutral about Jimi's training (*I did not ever get the chance to try flaming clubs …* or *The play was sparsely attended …*) or somewhat negative (*On another night, an audience member handed me back an apple I had dropped*). The correct answer is (F).

45. **(B)** If the writer were to add this sentence to the essay, the sentence would most logically be placed at Point B.

Rhetorical Skills   Organization   Sentence Order

10

The sentence in question is this: "Of course, I dropped the clubs more than a few times, but Jimi reassured me that 'everybody drops.'" The best place to insert this sentence is at Point B in the third paragraph, right after the narrator is pushed into joining *a rapid passing exercise, in which I had to catch clubs from one person and toss them to another*. The additional sentence refers to *the clubs*, meaning "clubs already mentioned," so the preceding text has to mention clubs. This constraint eliminates both Points C and D.

At Point A, the preceding sentence mentions clubs: *I learned how to juggle clubs, sticks, and knives from an Irish Traveller who called himself Jimi Juggle*. The additional sentence makes some sense here; however, it's strange that the narrator would just mention dropping the clubs, as if he or she didn't also drop the sticks and knives (an improbable outcome). Another strike against this position is that adding the sentence delays the definition of *Travellers* that now comes immediately after the first sentence (which introduces the term).

Finally, at Point A, there is no follow-up on the *everybody drops* reassurance that the narrator receives from Jimi. In contrast, at Point B, the following sentence is, *It took a lot of patient coaching to make progress, but I improved greatly over time*. This sentence wraps up the addition better than the sentence after Point A, which goes to a completely different subject (defining *Travellers*). The correct answer is (B).

Passage 4

46. **(F)** … a divine being that inspired <u>one's best work,</u> …

Usage/Mechanics   Grammar & Usage   Modifier Forms

In this problem, you need to match the modifier *best* (the superlative form of *good*) to what the author evidently meant. The original sentence is correct as written: what was inspired? *One's best work*, that is, the best or most perfect work that one could do.

The wrong answer choices mix up the modifiers and, with them, the meaning. Choice (G) makes *best* merely *good* and puts the superlative into the phrase *at most*, leading to a highly unlikely meaning: the divine being inspires *at most* the good work of someone. Such a being would not be very effective at its job. Choice (J) suffers from a similar issue, with *at best* making the inspiration rather uninspiring. Finally, in choice (H), *ones'* is incorrectly punctuated, and the *as well* is out of place (there's no prior point for this to be the additional comment for). The correct answer is (F).

47. **(C)** <u>Whether he truly had such guidance or not,</u> Srinivasa Ramanujan certainly earned …

Usage/Mechanics   Grammar & Usage   Modifier Forms

The proper way to introduce the hypothetical statement *he truly had such guidance* is with *Whether*. This subordinate clause appropriately modifies the main clause (*Srinivasa Ramanujan certainly earned the title of genius …*), indicating that the existence of such divine guidance doesn't matter to the main point. *If … or if not …* is not idiomatic English.

The *or not*, which should generally be deleted in *whether* clauses after verbs or prepositions (*I cannot decide whether to go*), can be safely used when the *whether* clause means "it does not matter whether," as in this case. The alternatives to *or not* in the wrong answers (*or he may not have, or maybe not, or if he didn't have*) are all incorrect forms. Just use *or not*. The correct answer is (C).

MANHATTAN
PREP

48. **(G)** <u>Born in 1887</u> in southern India, Ramanujan soon showed ...

Usage/Mechanics   Sentence Structure   Whole Sentences

The original sentence is a flawed run-on: *He was born in 1887 ... , Ramanujan soon showed promise ...* These two independent clauses cannot just be connected by a comma. Instead, turn the first thought into a simple modifier: *Born in 1887 ..., Ramanujan ...*

The other choices make the modifier needlessly wordy (*being born, the year 1887*) and even misleading. After all, it is improbable that actually within the year Ramanujan was born, he *showed great promise in mathematics and an unswerving dedication to the field*—he was a prodigy, not a superhero from another planet). The correct answer is (G).

49. **(D)** ... having <u>won numerous school awards,</u> he obtained ...

Rhetorical Skills   Style   Concision

The correct choice makes every word count, whereas the wrong answers are riddled with redundancies and general wordiness: *won the awarding of ... prizes; scholastic ... school ... scholarly; competed for and won; numerous amount of.* Instead simply write *won awards.* Write *school* once. Write *numerous* by itself. The correct answer is (D).

50. **(F)** ... he obtained a copy of Carr's *Synopsis of Pure Mathematics*<u>, filled with</u> thousands of equations ...

Usage/Mechanics   Sentence Structure   Whole Sentences

The main clause of the sentence is *he obtained a copy,* which you don't have the choice to change. In the original, correct version of the sentence, the modifier *filled with thousands of equations* is properly attached to the title of the book (*Synopsis of Pure Mathematics*) with a comma. The wrong choices turn that simple modifier into a monstrosity by wedging in a verb (*were* or *was*) and even a subject (*this*). Each of these choices creates a run-on, because the main clause remains unaltered. The correct answer is (F).

51. **(A)** Clearest and most logical ending: <u>He set about devouring the book and creating his own proofs of its contents.</u>

Rhetorical Skills   Organization   Opening/Closing Content

The point of Paragraph 2 is revealed in the first sentence: *Ramanujan soon showed great promise in mathematics and an unswerving dedication to the field.* The correct answer to this question illustrates these qualities of Ramanujan—someone who *set about devouring* a book of thousands of equations shows *dedication to the field*, and *creating his own proofs* is an indication of *promise.*

The incorrect choices are irrelevancies that weaken the thesis of the paragraph. It does not matter whether students today *routinely learn* this first equation, or whether Ramanujan *had a frail constitution,* or whether some people might consider this book *less than gripping.* None of these points reinforce the key theme of Ramanujan's unusual ability and passion. The correct answer is (A).

10

52.   **(J)**   However, he remained desperately poor. [omitted sentence stating that his marriage was arranged] At last, he wrote impassioned letters …

Rhetorical Skills   Writing Strategy   Deletions

Three of the choices here rearrange the words of the statement about Ramanujan's marriage. Choice (H) is the best of the lot: sensible, reasonably concise, and grammatically correct. What's wrong with this choice, however, is its content. Mentioning at this point in the narrative that Ramanujan had an arranged marriage disrupts the logic flow entirely: it connects neither to the prior thought that he was *desperately poor*, nor to the next thought that he *at last wrote impassioned letters to professors.*

The point could easily be edited to make the connection to poverty: now he had a spouse to support. However, as written, the sentence fits poorly and should be deleted. The correct answer is (J).

53.   **(B)**   At last, he wrote … One of the professors, G. H. Hardy, <u>was</u> awestruck by the enclosed material.

Usage/Mechanics   Sentence Structure   Verb Tense

The story is correctly set in the past tense, which should be maintained in the underlined portion (*was*). The past perfect *had been* would take the reader back to an even earlier time, but the events of this sentence happened after those of the prior sentence: first Ramanujan wrote the letters, then Hardy was awestruck by the material. If the underlined word is deleted altogether, the sentence becomes a fragment (*awestruck* by itself can only act as a modifier). The correct answer is (B).

54.   **(H)**   Ramanujan, mostly self-taught, didn't know that some of his equations had already been <u>discovered; others,</u> though, [did something specified in the next question].

Usage/Mechanics   Punctuation   Commas & Semicolons

In the correct choice, the semicolon properly connects two independent clauses. It's a little tricky that you don't know the exact content of the second clause until you solve the next problem, but in all possible cases, the text from *others* on would be an independent clause.

In the second clause, you need to surround *though* with commas, because it is placed almost parenthetically in the middle of that clause to indicate contrast with the preceding thought. For this reason, you need a comma after *others*. The correct answer is (H).

55.   **(C)**   Ramanujan, mostly self-taught, didn't know that some of his equations had already been discovered; others, though, <u>were stunning breakthroughs.</u> [Next paragraph] In 1914, Hardy convinced Ramanujan to come to Cambridge.

Rhetorical Skills   Organization   Opening/Closing Content

First, you need a contrast to the first part of the sentence, which states that some of Ramanujan's equations *had already been discovered.* On this basis, you can get rid of the original version: the fact that some equations *lacked accompanying derivations* is not opposite in any way to the fact that others had already been discovered. Each of the other choices, though, could be seen as a contrast to this idea of prior discovery. Hardy would be familiar with equations discovered

MANHATTAN
PREP

earlier, so if these others *puzzled or even baffled* him, this contrast is clear. Likewise, *stunning breakthroughs* are in stark contrast to earlier discoveries, and even *strange summations* would be unfamiliar.

The key is further afield. In the next paragraph, you read that *Hardy convinced Ramanujan to come to Cambridge.* The only reasonable motivation would be if the unfamiliar equations were not just strange, puzzling, or baffling, but *stunning breakthroughs.* You can also hark back to an even earlier sentence, in which Hardy was *awestruck by the enclosed material.* In other words, this material had to be more than just strange; it had to be positively amazing. The correct answer is (C).

56.   **(J)**   … there's even a number named for them.

Usage/Mechanics   Grammar & Usage   Pronoun Forms

The correct form at the beginning of this clause is *there's,* meaning "there is." *Their* means "of them," *theirs* means "their thing or things," and *they're* means "they are." Do not mix these forms up. In addition, *named for them* is a slightly more apt expression than *named theirs,* which would imply that the two mathematicians own the number as the result of some decree. Rather, it's more sensible to assume that the number was named in their honor. (Incidentally, this number is 1729.) The correct answer is (J).

57.   **(B)**   Ramanujan, who had long been sickly, was diagnosed during that time with tuberculosis.

Usage/Mechanics   Punctuation   Commas

The original version is incorrect, because a comma follows the phrase *at that time* but does not precede it. You can either leave out both commas or put both in, but you can't have just one.

This problem also tests Subject–Verb Agreement (*were* should be *was,* because Ramanujan is singular) and Whole Sentences (*doctors then diagnosed him* is a complete, independent clause, but you already have a subject in *Ramanujan, who had long been sickly*). The correct answer avoids all of these pitfalls. The correct answer is (B).

58.   **(G)**   A devout man, Ramanujan believed that his insights came from Namagiri …

Rhetorical Skills   Style   Word Choice

The correct answer uses the words *believe, insights,* and *came* in a sensible way. Ramanujan *believed* something about the *insights* that he had about mathematics. Namely, he believed that those *insights came* from Namagiri.

The wrong answers jumble up the words in such a way that they don't correspond to a reasonable reality. What does *Ramanujan had insight of his claims coming from Namagiri* even mean? Or that he *came to believe insightfully from Namagiri* or that he *claimed his insights that came from Namagiri*? All of these uses of these common words fail to make much sense. The correct answer is (G).

59.   **(A)**   A devout man, Ramanujan believed that his insights came from Namagiri, his family's goddess, sometimes in dreams.

Usage/Mechanics   Punctuation   Apostrophes

You can write either *the goddess of his family* or *his family's goddess*. If you use the *of* phrase, then don't put an apostrophe in at all (as some of the wrong answers do). If *family* comes before *goddess,* conversely, you must use the 's form (*family's*), not the plural noun (*families*).

Finally, *sometimes* should be separated from *goddess* by a comma but not from *in dreams.* The intended meaning is not that the goddess sometimes belongs to his family, but that the insights sometimes come in dreams. The correct answer is (A).

60.   **(J)**   He had a close relationship with numbers and worked by intuition—or perhaps divine inspiration. [omitted sentence about his lost notebook.]

Rhetorical Skills   Writing Strategy   Choice of Content

Originally, the whole essay ends with this sentence: *One of his four notebooks was lost for decades but then found and published in 1976.* The decision to delete this sentence is the best option. The last sentence should wrap up the essay well, echoing themes encountered before. Here, the sentence about the notebook is a pure distraction, referring back to no prior motif or idea. Its only possible benefit is that the date is closer to present day, but that's a thin thread on which to hang hopes for this sentence.

In contrast, the previous sentence functions remarkably well as a closer. The final reference to *divine inspiration* closes the loop resoundingly, not only on this paragraph (which opens with a description of Ramanujan's religious beliefs) but also on the whole essay, which begins with the observation that the word "genius" originally referred to *a divine being that inspired one's best work.* The correct answer is (J).

10 Passage 5

61.   **(A)**   If you look up the word "bodega" … the first definition will probably be "wine cellar." That's not what "bodega" means to me, <u>however;</u> …

Rhetorical Skills   Organization   Transitions

The second sentence (*That's not what "bodega" means to me …*) is meant to contrast with the first sentence, which gives a dictionary definition of the word *bodega.* Thus, you need a transition word that indicates contrast. The only available option that meets the need is *however.* The other three choices (*consequently, accordingly,* and *in other words*) all indicate alignment of some kind between the sentences, not contrast. The correct answer is (A).

62.   **(G)**   … our bodega is the local meeting <u>place, where</u> you'll eventually see everyone who lives nearby.

Usage/Mechanics   Grammar & Usage   Modifier Forms

The bodega is the place *where* you'll eventually see everyone. In other words, you'll eventually see everyone … where? At this bodega place. So the modifying clause should be led by the word *where.*

The word *which* would only be appropriate if *place* were the logical subject in the next clause (e.g., " … the local meeting place, which hosts everyone in the neighborhood") or the object (e.g., " … the local meeting place, which everyone loves"). However, in the actual sentence, the word *place* has neither of these roles in the modifier; rather, it is *where* "you'll eventually see everyone."

The word *when* could only work if it were not modifying *place* directly, but rather telling the reader *when* the whole previous thought happened. Again, this is not the case here. Finally, if no relative pronoun (*which, where, when*) is used, then the sentence becomes a run-on, with two independent clauses linked by only a comma. The correct answer is (G).

63.   **(A)**   It's the <u>little corner grocery</u> store.

Usage/Mechanics   Punctuation   Commas

Adjectives only take commas between them if they are logically at the same level. However, these adjectives are all at different nested levels, as you can see in the following sequence of questions: What kind of store is it? A *grocery* store. What particular kind of grocery store? A *corner* grocery store (one on a corner). How would you describe this corner grocery store? It's a *little* corner grocery store.

The adjectives are added one at a time, so they're not at the same logical level. Another way to see this is that *and* does not work between any two adjacent adjectives: Little *and* corner grocery store? No. Corner *and* grocery store? No. So there should be no commas in the underlined portion. The correct answer is (A).

64.   **(J)**   Sometimes, these kinds of stores are called "convenience" stores, and indeed, they are very convenient for <u>customers.</u>

Rhetorical Skills   Style   Concision

The word *customers* means "people who shop somewhere and typically buy things," and since the bodega is a grocery store, the strong implication is that the purchased items are food. So the word *customers* by itself is all you need in this context. The wrong choices tack on various redundant modifiers, such as *who shop for and purchase food and other items*, *that visit these stores to buy food*, and *who shop there, purchasing food items*. These modifiers are all unnecessary. The correct answer is (J).

65.   **(C)**   The best placement for the underlined word would be before the word *want*.

Usage/Mechanics   Sentence Structure   Modifier Placement

The word in question is *arbitrarily*, which means "at random, based on impulse, whim, or individual preference." This word goes best with the verb *might want*, so that the sentence reads: … *you can find almost anything you might arbitrarily want in our bodega* … That is, you can find almost anything you might want, based on your own individual preference or impulse, in the bodega.

The adverb does not make sense modifying other parts of the sentence, such as "It is true," "you can find," or "prices are only a little higher." Adding in the idea of "based on individual preference" does not work for these clauses. The correct answer is (C).

66.   **(G)**   Most effective transition to the next paragraph: That store is owned by some distant corporation, not by people I know.

Rhetorical Skills   Organization   Opening/Closing Content

The next paragraph begins with *Daoud is always there at the register … goes on to describe this man, his cat, and his employee Eli*. The correct answer states that the big grocery store *is owned by some distant corporation, not by people I know*. Since the contrast has already been set up between the big grocery store and the bodega, the implication is that the bodega *is* owned by *people I know*. Thus, the transition to describing those people (Daoud and Eli) is made as smoothly as possible.

The incorrect choices do not provide any connection to the people who own or work at the bodega. Choices (H) and (J) continue to focus on the big grocery store (in fact, they do so in a positive way, which clashes with the essay's focus on the "good" local bodega). Choice (F) asserts that the big store's coupons are not accepted at the bodega, but this unsurprising revelation is irrelevant to the next paragraph. The correct answer is (G).

67.   **(D)**   Least acceptable alternative: Daoud is always there at the register when I go in after school. <u>They own</u> the bodega …

Usage/Mechanics   Grammar & Usage   Pronoun Agreement

The one unacceptable alternative (which is therefore the right answer) is *They own*, because the pronoun *They* has no good noun or noun phrase to refer to. Daoud is mentioned in the prior sentence, but not his family, so the best possible interpretation is that Daoud and his register own the bodega—and that interpretation makes no sense.

The other choices can each substitute for *He and his family own*. Choices (A) and (B) put the subject and verb as "he owns," incorporating the reference to "his family" through prepositional phrases (*Together with his family* or *along with his family*). Choice (C) puts the compound subject in an unusual order (*His family and he*, rather than *He and his family*), but this order is grammatically acceptable. The correct answer is (D).

68.   **(G)**   If the writer were to delete the preceding sentence, the essay would primarily lose details that describe the cat physically and explain a previous statement about it.

Rhetorical Skills   Writing Strategy   Deletions

The sentence in question is this: *Stark white and missing an eye, it curls up wherever there is sunlight.* The subject pronoun *it* refers to the cat Asheeb, introduced in the prior sentence: *… you might think that their cat Asheeb actually does [own the bodega].* The correct answer states that the possibly deleted sentence provides details that *describe the cat physically*. These details are given in the opening modifier: *Stark white and missing an eye.* In addition, the correct answer states that the sentence "explain[s] a previous statement about it [the cat]." This previous statement is that the cat seems to own the bodega; the sentence on the chopping block explains this point by stating that the cat *curls up wherever there is sunlight*, as if it owned the place.

The incorrect answers make erroneous claims about what the sentence in question does. The sentence does not explain why the narrator prefers to spend time at the bodega (in fact, the narrator is not even mentioned). The sentence does not suggest that the cat's behavior (curling up in the sunlight) is linked to its unusual characteristics (its whiteness and lack of an eye)—no connection is made between the two. Finally, the sentence does not contradict an earlier assertion of any kind. The correct answer is (G).

69.   **(D)** Should the writer make this addition here? No, because it distracts the reader from the main focus of this paragraph.

Rhetorical Skills   Writing Strategy   Additions

The sentence that could be added is this: "His name is not pronounced as you might guess from the spelling; it sounds like 'Ellie.'" This comment is almost completely irrelevant to the paragraph, which focuses on the people (and the local cat) within the environment of the bodega. If there were a conversation between Eli and the narrator, the proper pronunciation of Eli's name might be more relevant, but without such a context, the sentence is just a distraction. The correct answer is (D).

70.   **(G)** … he tells me about his hometown of Kairouan, the fourth holiest city in Islam.

Usage/Mechanics   Sentence Structure   Whole Sentences & Modifiers

The original sentence is a run-on, since inserting *it is* after *Kairouan* creates a new independent clause (*it is the fourth holiest city …*), one that is joined to the earlier independent clause (*he tells me …*) by just a comma. The right answer corrects the error by removing *it is*, allowing *the fourth holiest city …* to be an appositive phrase modifying the word *Kairouan*.

Kairouan must be followed by a comma, since this additional phrase is a nonessential modifier. Finally, the infinitive *to be* should not be used here; *he tells me about his hometown to be …* would mean that the subject *he* is trying *to be* something, but *he* is not actually trying *to be* the fourth holiest city in Islam. The correct answer is (G).

71.   **(C)** … in some tiny building in that city, a blind camel walks in an endless circle, pumping water from a sacred well …

Usage/Mechanics   Sentence Structure   Whole Sentences & Modifiers)

As in the previous problem, the original sentence is a run-on. *It pumps water …* is an independent clause, which is improperly joined to another independent clause (*a blind camel walks …*) by a comma.

The correct answer changes the second clause into a modifier by replacing *it pumps* with the *-ing* form *pumping*. This form tells you what the camel is doing as it walks, or what happens as a result of its walking.

Choice (B) uses the word *and*, but there is no parallel list (*while pumping* is not parallel to *walks*). Finally, choice (D) uses the present tense form *pumps*, which is parallel to *walks*, but there is no *and* here. A two-item list on the ACT requires an *and* in the middle: "a blind camel walks … and pumps … " The correct answer is (C).

72.   **(F)** He grew up …

Usage/Mechanics   Grammar & Usage   Verb Forms

The past tense of the verb *grow* is *grew*, not *growed*. The past participle *grown*, not the past tense *grew*, should follow *had* (or *have* or *has*, for that matter); *had grew* is always wrong. Conversely, *grown* is not a complete verb by itself and cannot run a sentence. You need a form of the verb *have* (or *be*) to make *grown* complete. The correct answer is (F).

73. **(C)** Least acceptable alternative: I am not <u>disputing</u> that I am an expert …

Rhetorical Skills   Style   Word Choice

The original *-ing* form is *stating*. The narrator is *not stating* that he or she is an expert. Equivalently, the narrator is not *claiming, asserting,* or *arguing* that this is true. However, if you write that you do not *dispute* that something is true, then you are not arguing *with* that statement—in other words, you are accepting the statement. The word *disputing* is not an acceptable substitute for *stating*, so this choice is the right answer.

"Joan argues that X is true" means that Joan argues *for* the claim. "Joan disputes that X is true" means that Joan argues *against* the claim. The verbs *dispute* and *argue* may seem to be synonyms, but they have very different meanings when followed by *that*. The correct answer is (C).

74. **(J)** The best placement for the underlined phrase would be after the phrase *"thank you"* (ending the sentence with a period).

Usage/Mechanics   Sentence Structure   Modifier Placement

The phrase in question is *expressed sincerely from the heart*. This modifier should immediately follow a noun that is intended to be expressed that way. The best option is the *"thank you"* at the end of the sentence.

In its current position, the modifier is next to the *"thank you,"* but a long modifying phrase (such as this one) has to be placed after whatever it's meant to modify. There is no appropriate noun to be modified at the very beginning of the sentence, nor is there one after the word *mean* (the phrase cannot modify a verb, such as *mean*). In theory, the phrase might be able to fit after *"shukran"* or *"gracias,"* but you are not given those options. The correct answer is (J).

75. **(C)** Fulfills goal of making a detailed comparison between a neighborhood bodega and a bigger grocery store? No, because it focuses almost exclusively on the features of the bodega.

Rhetorical Skills   Writing Strategy   Goal of essay

The essay barely mentions a "big grocery store" at all. At the end of the second paragraph, the text mentions that the bodega's prices *are only a little higher than at the big grocery store several blocks away*. That's not a very detailed comparison. Even with an added sentence to help the transition to the next paragraph, the essay gives barely any attention to comparing the bodega and its bigger competitor. Rather, the essay focuses its attention "almost exclusively" on the narrator's favorite bodega: how it functions as the neighborhood meeting place, how convenient it is, how interesting the people are who work there, etc. The correct answer is (C).

Chapter 11 *of*

5lb. Book of ACT® Practice Problems

Math:
Pre-Algebra

In This Chapter...

Pre-Algebra Problems & Solutions

Chapter 11
Math: Pre-Algebra

The Math problems in this chapter are drawn from pre-algebra—that is, all the math you did before algebra. The topics include the following:

1. Number Properties and Operations. Arithmetic operations, multiples and factors, odds and evens, and rounding.

2. Arithmetic Word Problems. Word problems that don't require algebra to solve.

3. Fractions, Decimals, and Percents. These ways of expressing part-to-whole relationships, plus digits.

4. Proportions and Ratios. These additional ways of expressing part-to-whole or part-to-part relationships, but not involving algebra.

5. Possibilities and Probability. Counting possible outcomes, calculating probabilities, etc.

6. Statistics. Average (arithmetic mean), median, interpretation of data tables and charts.

How should you use this chapter? Here are some recommendations, according to the level you've reached in ACT Math.

1. Fundamentals. Start slowly, with the easier problems at the beginning. Do at least some of these problems untimed. This way, you give yourself a chance to think deeply about the principles at work. Review the solutions closely, and articulate what you've learned. Redo problems as necessary.

2. Fixes. Do a few problems untimed, examine the results, learn your lessons, then test yourself with longer timed sets.

3. Tweaks. Confirm your mastery by doing longer sets of problems under timed conditions. Aim to improve the speed and ease of your solution process. Mix the problems up by jumping around in the chapter. Definitely push to the harder, higher-numbered problems.

Good luck on the problems!

1. Alexa drove $5\frac{2}{3}$ miles from home to school. Then, taking a different route, she drove $4\frac{3}{5}$ miles back home. What was the total distance, in miles, Alexa drove round-trip?

    A. $9\frac{2}{5}$

    B. $9\frac{5}{8}$

    C. $9\frac{11}{15}$

    D. $10\frac{4}{15}$

    E. $10\frac{2}{5}$

2. An unusual circular clock rotates at a constant rate to keep time. If it rotates 45° every 2 hours, how many degrees will it rotate in 24 hours?

    F. 180°

    G. 270°

    H. 360°

    J. 480°

    K. 540°

3. Alberto used $1\frac{1}{3}$ cups of milk in one recipe and $2\frac{1}{4}$ cups of milk in another recipe. How much milk, in cups, did Alberto use in the two recipes?

    A. $3\frac{1}{12}$

    B. $3\frac{1}{6}$

    C. $3\frac{2}{7}$

    D. $3\frac{5}{12}$

    E. $3\frac{7}{12}$

4. Umberto scored 14, 15, 19, and 13 points in four separate basketball games. How many points must he score in an upcoming fifth game to average 16 points for the five games this season?

    F. 16

    G. 17

    H. 19

    J. 22

    K. 25

5. Remi buys a package of 6 hot dogs for a cost of $4.50. What is the cost per hot dog?

    A. $0.25

    B. $0.50

    C. $0.75

    D. $1.25

    E. $1.50

6. John is a lamp salesman. He earned commissions of $24, $28, $21, and $30 on the lamps he has sold this week. If he sells one more this week, how much commission must he earn to average $25 in commissions on lamps sold this week?

    F. $22

    G. $24

    H. $26

    J. $28

    K. $30

7. Jennifer purchased a video game console plus an assortment of games for the console for a total cost of $700. The cost of the console, by itself, was $280. If games for the console cost $20 apiece, how many games did she purchase?

    A. 14

    B. 21

    C. 26

    D. 32

    E. 35

MANHATTAN PREP

8. A box of 36 candles costs $27.00. At that price per candle, how much would 5 candles cost?

F. $0.75

G. $1.50

H. $2.75

J. $3.75

K. $4.50

9. Triangle Construction pays Square Insurance $5,980 to insure a construction site for 92 days. To extend the insurance beyond the 92 days costs $97 per day. At the end of this period, if Triangle extends the insurance by 1 day, how much more does Triangle pay for that day than it paid per day during the first period of time?

A. $5

B. $32

C. $37

D. $65

E. $67

10. Andrea joined a movie club, in which members can purchase movies for $12 each, after paying the lifetime membership fee. Including the fee, her average cost per movie has been $16. If Andrea has purchased 24 movies, what is the cost of lifetime membership in the movie club?

F. $96

G. $120

H. $192

J. $288

K. $384

11. Farmer A sells 30 pounds of tomatoes for $27.60. Farmer B sells the same kind of tomato at a price of $45.00 for 50 pounds of tomatoes. Which farmer's price per pound of tomatoes is more expensive, and what is that price?

A. Farmer A, $0.90 per pound

B. Farmer A, $0.92 per pound

C. Farmer B, $0.90 per pound

D. Farmer B, $0.92 per pound

E. Farmer B, $0.93 per pound

12. Risha purchases 39 identical leather-bound notebooks for a total cost of $273. She then sells one of the notebooks for $13. If Risha allocates the total cost equally across all the notebooks, what is her profit on the sale of the notebook?

F. $6

G. $7

H. $8

J. $9

K. $10

13. On five 50-point quizzes, Samuel has earned the following scores: 35, 42, 48, 37, and 38. What score must Samuel earn on the sixth 50-point quiz to earn an average quiz grade of 41 out of 50 for the six quizzes?

A. 36

B. 39

C. 40

D. 46

E. 49

11

14. Andrew purchased 5 rakes for a leaf-cleaning project at a total cost of $95. Melanie also purchased rakes, buying 4 rakes for a total cost of $80. Which person spent less money per rake, and by how much?

   F. Andrew, $1 per rake

   G. Andrew, $2 per rake

   H. Andrew, $5 per rake

   K. Melanie, $1 per rake

   J. Melanie, $5 per rake

15. Janice participates in a 5-game bowling tournament. If she scores 180 in each of the first 3 games and scores 200 in each of the last 2 games, what is her average score for the tournament?

   A. 184

   B. 188

   C. 190

   D. 194

   E. 196

16. The only three people in a rowboat weigh 105 pounds, 122 pounds, and 133 pounds. If the average weight in the boat is to be no more than 125 pounds per person, what is the maximum weight, in pounds, of a fourth person getting into the boat?

   F. 90

   G. 105

   H. 120

   J. 130

   K. 140

17. At a supermarket, apples cost $0.85 each unless 12 or more are purchased, in which case the cost per apple (for all apples purchased) is $0.70. Morgan recently purchased 17 apples from the supermarket but was incorrectly charged $0.85 per apple. How much of a refund is he owed?

   A. $0.75

   B. $1.80

   C. $2.55

   D. $8.40

   E. $14.45

18. In thermodynamics, the efficiency of a combustion engine is calculated by dividing the useful work the engine performs by the heat absorbed by the engine from burning fuel, and then converting to a percent. If an engine performs 453 joules of useful work while absorbing 715 joules of heat from burning fuel, what is the efficiency of the engine, to the nearest percent?

   F. 58%

   G. 63%

   H. 67%

   J. 72%

   K. 76%

19. What is the value of $322 + 189 + 444$, rounded to the nearest ten?

   A. 930

   B. 940

   C. 950

   D. 960

   E. 970

11

20. The annual return of an investment account is found by dividing the interest, in dollars, that the account generates over a year by the initial amount of money invested into the account, assuming no further investments, and then converting to a percent. If $13 in interest is generated over a year by an account in which $434 was initially invested, and no further investments were made, what is the annual return of the account, to the nearest percent?

   F. 1%

   G. 2%

   H. 3%

   J. 4%

   K. 5%

21. From among the 8 members of an Olympic skiing team, one must be chosen to act as ambassador at the international competition. The ambassador CANNOT be one of the team's 3 captains, but the other members are equally likely to be chosen. If Miguel is a non-captain on the team, what is his probability of being chosen as ambassador?

   A. $\dfrac{1}{5}$

   B. $\dfrac{1}{8}$

   C. $\dfrac{1}{11}$

   D. $\dfrac{3}{8}$

   E. $\dfrac{3}{11}$

22. What is the value of 3(231) + 2(185), rounded to the nearest hundred?

   F. 800

   G. 900

   H. 1,000

   J. 1,100

   K. 1,200

23. A phone company charges a fee of $0.50 plus $0.10 per minute for all phone calls. If a single call costs $1.60, what was the total duration of the phone call, in minutes?

   A. 11

   B. 12

   C. 13

   D. 14

   E. 16

24. For which of the following values of x will $\dfrac{25}{x} = \dfrac{5}{25}$ be true?

   F. 125

   G. 25

   H. 10

   J. 5

   K. 1

25. When Pleasantville Apartments opened, they had 25 apartment units built. If they built an additional 5 units each week and there are now 135 units built, how many weeks have passed?

   A. 4.5

   B. 11

   C. 15.5

   D. 22

   E. 27

26. If $x \geq 52$ and $x \leq 65$, for how many integer values of x is the tens digit larger than the ones digit?

   F. 4

   G. 5

   H. 7

   J. 9

   K. 10

11

27. There are 14 freshmen, 14 sophomores, and 12 juniors on a camping trip. If one of the students is chosen at random, what is the probability that the person chosen will NOT be a sophomore?

A. $\dfrac{3}{5}$

B. $\dfrac{3}{10}$

C. $\dfrac{7}{10}$

D. $\dfrac{7}{20}$

E. $\dfrac{13}{20}$

28. The set S includes all of the integers from 401 to 413. For how many of the integers in set S is the hundreds digit less than or equal to the units digit?

F. 5

G. 6

H. 7

J. 10

K. 12

29. The cost, in dollars, of a certain metal alloy is directly proportional to its weight, in ounces. A piece of this metal alloy weighing 42 ounces has a cost of $280. What is the cost, in dollars, of a piece of this metal alloy with a weight of 18 ounces?

A. $120

B. $140

C. $256

D. $304

E. $560

30. A coin is randomly chosen from a bag of 60 coins. If the probability is 0.15 that the coin is a nickel, how many coins in the bag are NOT nickels?

F. 6

G. 9

H. 45

J. 51

K. 54

Use the following information to answer questions 31–32.

The following chart shows the expected attendance at an upcoming medical convention on infectious disease.

Presentation Title	Room	Time	Expected Attendance
Antibiotics	Avery	9–10am	34
	Brown	10–11am	38
	Carlyle	11am–12pm	33
Antivirals	Avery	10–11am	39
Antifungals	Brown	9–10am	31
	Carlyle	10–11am	30
Antiparasitics	Avery	11am–12 pm	37

31. What is the average number of expected attendees per Antibiotics session?

A. 33

B. 34

C. 35

D. 36

E. 38

MANHATTAN
PREP

32. The hotel where the convention is being held wants to manage the total number of chairs used at various times during the event. If one chair is needed for each expected attendee, the overall need for chairs will vary according to which of the following as the morning progresses?

    F. The need will first increase by 42 chairs and then decrease by 37 chairs.

    G. The need will first increase by 30 chairs and then decrease by 33 chairs.

    H. The need will first decrease by 41 chairs and then decrease again by 6 chairs.

    J. The need will first decrease by 28 chairs and then increase by 11 chairs.

    K. The need will first decrease by 38 chairs and then increase by 33 chairs.

33. Joan is riding her bicycle along a track at 15 miles per hour. Anthony, who is ahead of Joan on the same track, is riding his bicycle at 12 miles per hour. If it will take Joan 5 hours to catch Anthony at their current speeds, how many miles ahead of Joan on the track is Anthony?

    A. 3

    B. $\dfrac{5}{3}$

    C. $\dfrac{10}{3}$

    D. 12

    E. 15

34. If $2.438 \times 10^x = 0.002438$, what is the value of x?

    F. −6

    G. −3

    H. −2

    J. 3

    K. 6

35. The cost of renting a certain car from Ace Rentals is $30 for the 1st day or any part thereof, $20 for the 2nd day or any part thereof, and $15 for each additional day or any part thereof after the 2nd day. If Miranda rents a car at 11:45am on Tuesday and returns the car at 5:45pm on Saturday, how much is the total rental cost?

    A. $110.00

    B. $95.00

    C. $83.75

    D. $80.90

    E. $80.00

36. If $5.7 \times 10^k = 570{,}000$, what is the value of k?

    F. −6

    G. −5

    H. −4

    J. 5

    K. 6

37. Anthony must choose from among 35 different flavors of ice cream and 20 different toppings at his local ice cream store. If Anthony can select one of each for an ice cream cone, how many different combinations of ice cream flavors and toppings are possible?

    A. 15

    B. 35

    C. 55

    D. 70

    E. 700

11

38. A level building is built into the side of a steeply sloped hill. For every 100 feet of horizontal distance, the hill rises 12 feet. If the ground is 3 feet higher at the back of the building than at the front of the building, what is the *horizontal* depth of the building, in feet?

   F. 12

   G. 25

   H. 36

   J. 250

   K. 400

39. Pauline is looking into purchasing a new washer/dryer combination for her home. At the store, there are 20 different models available for the washer unit, and each is compatible with all of the 16 different models available for the dryer unit. How many different combinations of a washer and a dryer can Pauline potentially purchase?

   A. 4

   B. 20

   C. 36

   D. 320

   E. 480

40. Which of the following is true about any two odd numbers?

   F. Their quotient is even.

   G. Their quotient is odd.

   H. Their product is even.

   J. Their product is odd.

   K. Their sum is odd.

> Use the following information to answer questions 41–42.

A survey at a seminar for people interested in applying for membership at a fitness center asked the 25 respondents how many days in the past week they had exercised. The 25 responses are summarized in the following column chart:

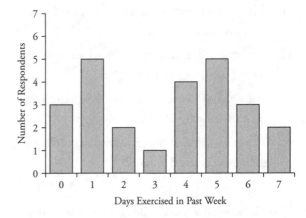

41. What percentage of the respondents exercised fewer than 4 days in the past week?

   A. 40%

   B. 44%

   C. 50%

   D. 56%

   E. 60%

42. What is the average (arithmetic mean) number of days in the past week that the 25 respondents exercised?

   F. 1.8

   G. 3.0

   H. 3.4

   J. 3.8

   K. 4.0

MANHATTAN PREP

43. If *a* is an even integer and *b* is an odd integer, which of the following must be true?

A. ab = odd

B. $a + b$ = even

C. $a - b$ = odd

D. $\dfrac{a}{b}$ = even

E. $\dfrac{b}{a}$ = odd

> **Use the following information to answer questions 44–46.**

At a conference on better eating, the speaker asked members of the audience to fill out a questionnaire regarding their eating habits. 25 audience members responded. The following column chart summarizes the number of times the audience members had eaten red meat in the past week. Note that "7+" indicates "7 or more times":

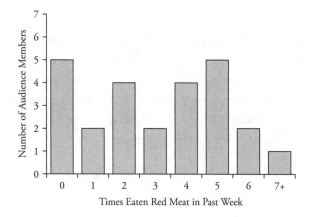

44. What is the average (arithmetic mean) number of times in the past week that the 25 responding audience members consumed red meat?

F. 2.8

G. 3.2

H. 3.5

J. 3.7

K. Cannot be determined from the given information.

45. What is the median number of times that the 25 responding audience members consumed red meat in the past week?

A. 2

B. 3

C. 4

D. 5

E. Cannot be determined from the given information.

46. What fraction of the audience members consumed red meat at least twice in the past week?

F. $\dfrac{7}{25}$

G. $\dfrac{3}{5}$

H. $\dfrac{7}{10}$

J. $\dfrac{18}{25}$

K. $\dfrac{4}{5}$

11

47. To build a certain house, it took 5 tons of wooden beams, 3 tons of stone, and 1 ton of miscellaneous materials. Each ton of wooden beams costs $6,500, each ton of stone costs $8,000, and each ton of miscellaneous materials costs $10,000. How many dollars did it cost, in materials alone, to build the house?

   A. $66,500

   B. $59,500

   C. $56,500

   D. $24,500

   E. $18,000

48. If p is any positive integer, then $15p - 6p$ is *always* divisible by which of the following?

   F. 6

   G. 9

   H. 11

   J. 15

   K. 90

49. During a severe drought, a reservoir contains only 100,000 gallons of water. Each gallon of water weighs 8.5 pounds. Which of the following is closest to the weight of the water in the reservoir during a severe drought, in pounds?

   A. 850,000

   B. 185,000

   C. 100,008

   D. 85,000

   E. 11,765

50. If q is any positive integer, then the sum of $2q$, $4q$, and $5q$ is always divisible by which of the following?

   F. 2

   G. 4

   H. 5

   J. 11

   K. 40

51. Jonathan is selling vintage albums to a rare music dealer. He earned $20 for each of the first 3 vintage albums that he sold; he then earned $32 per album for the next 5 vintage albums he sold. What was the average amount Jonathan earned on the 8 albums?

   A. $24.50

   B. $26.00

   C. $27.00

   D. $27.50

   E. $29.00

52. At a singing competition, 5 women and 6 men are participating. One women and one man are to be chosen to perform a duet to begin the competition. Among the competitors, there is exactly one brother–sister pair: Amy and Brian. What is the probability that the duet performers will be brother and sister?

   F. $\dfrac{1}{5}$

   G. $\dfrac{1}{6}$

   H. $\dfrac{1}{11}$

   J. $\dfrac{1}{30}$

   K. $\dfrac{11}{30}$

53. Students at a local high school are putting on a production of Shakespeare, hoping to raise at least $10,000 in ticket sales to fund the cost of a class field trip. Tickets for the event cost $15 each for mezzanine seats and $25 each for orchestra seats. If a total of 331 mezzanine tickets are sold, what is the *minimum* number of orchestra tickets that need to be sold in order for the class to achieve its goal?

A. 135

B. 167

C. 200

D. 202

E. 256

54. Tony is ordering balloons for a party from a party supplies distributor. The distributor only sells balloons in boxes of 20 bags, and the bags contain 60 balloons apiece. Tony needs at least 5,000 balloons, and the boxes may NOT be divided. What is the minimum number of boxes Tony must purchase?

F. 4

G. 5

H. 6

J. 10

K. 12

55. What is the least common multiple of 3, 4, 9, and 12?

A. 36

B. 48

C. 72

D. 180

E. 1,296

56. A ticket in a charity raffle costs $4.00. When Amelie buys 7 raffle tickets, she is given 2 additional tickets at no cost. What is the average cost per ticket to Amelie, in dollars, for 9 raffle tickets? Round your answer to the nearest penny.

F. $5.14

G. $4.00

H. $3.56

J. $3.25

K. $3.11

57. In evaluating the expression $\frac{a}{10} + \frac{b}{15} - \frac{c}{12}$, what is the least common denominator that can be chosen for the fractions?

A. 40

B. 50

C. 60

D. 80

E. 90

58. Johanna participates in a loyalty program at her favorite local coffee bar. In this program, she gets her 9th cappuccino for free after she buys the first 8 cappuccinos at regular price. If the total cost to Johanna of 9 cappuccinos is $36, what is the regular price of a cappuccino?

F. $3.60

G. $4.00

H. $4.11

J. $4.50

K. $5.20

59. A math teacher owns 10 pairs of pants, 2 pairs of shoes, and 6 shirts. Each outfit the teacher wears includes a combination of 1 shirt, 1 pair of shoes, and 1 pair of pants. How many possible outfits could the math teacher wear?

   A. 120

   B. 112

   C. 62

   D. 26

   E. 18

60. If $3\dfrac{1}{4} = y - 4\dfrac{2}{3}$, then what is y?

   F. $\dfrac{85}{12}$

   G. $\dfrac{32}{4}$

   H. $1\dfrac{5}{12}$

   J. $6\dfrac{1}{12}$

   K. $7\dfrac{11}{12}$

61. José regularly orders dinner at a restaurant that offers 6 appetizers, 5 entrées, and 3 desserts. If each day José orders a different combination of one of each, how many days in a row can he dine at this restaurant without repeating any combination?

   A. 30

   B. 60

   C. 90

   D. 120

   E. 180

62. In the equation $\left(1 \nabla 5\right)^{2} - \left(5 \nabla 1\right)^{2} = 0$, the symbol ∇ represents a basic arithmetic operation. Which of the following *could* be the arithmetic operation that ∇ represents?

   I. Multiplication

   II. Addition

   III. Subtraction

   F. I only

   G. II only

   H. I and II only

   J. II and III only

   K. I, II, and III

63. If $4\dfrac{1}{8} = a + 2\dfrac{3}{4}$, then what is a?

   A. $1\dfrac{3}{8}$

   B. $2\dfrac{5}{8}$

   C. $3\dfrac{5}{8}$

   D. $5\dfrac{3}{8}$

   E. $6\dfrac{7}{8}$

64. The cost of a new Z-phone was $380 the day it was released. Twenty weeks later, the price had dropped to $120. Assuming that the price dropped linearly over time, what was the price 8 weeks after the Z-phone was released?

   F. $289

   G. $276

   H. $263

   J. $180

   K. $104

MANHATTAN
PREP

65. In the equation $(2 \odot 4)^2 = (4 \odot 2)^2$ the symbol $\odot$ represents a basic arithmetic operation. Which of the following *could* be the arithmetic operation that $\odot$ represents?

   I. Multiplication

  II. Division

 III. Subtraction

  A. I only

  B. II only

  C. I and III only

  D. II and III only

  E. I, II, and III

66. Earvin plans to make an ice cream sundae with one kind of ice cream, one topping, and a cookie on the side. He has available 5 different kinds of ice cream, 4 different kinds of toppings, and 2 different kinds of cookies. How many distinct sundaes can Earvin make?

  F. 11

  G. 14

  H. 18

  J. 22

  K. 40

67. In 2000, the value of a new Model X car was $15,750. In 2005, five years later, the value of the same Model X car was $9,500. Assuming that the value decreased linearly over time, what was the value of the Model X car in 2003?

  A. $3,750

  B. $6,250

  C. $10,000

  D. $12,000

  E. $14,500

68. A solvent manufacturing company is producing toluene, and stocking it in two different vats with 10,000 gallons of capacity each. Vat A currently contains 450 gallons of toluene, and its contents are increasing at a rate of 40 gallons per minute. Vat B currently contains 1,250 gallons of toluene, and its contents are increasing at a rate of 15 gallons per minute. In how many minutes will the two vats contain equal amounts of toluene?

  F. 30

  G. 32

  H. 48

  J. 50

  K. 60

69. Tasha flips a coin and writes down "H" if the coin comes up heads and "T" if the coin comes up tails. She does this process four times, so that she has a string of four letters, in order, on her paper. How many distinct strings of letters are possible?

  A. 4

  B. 6

  C. 8

  D. 16

  E. 32

70. At a smelting plant, 9,000,000 pounds of low-grade bauxite ore are required to produce 1,200,000 pounds of aluminum. How many pounds of this ore are required to produce 400 pounds of aluminum?

  F. 3,000

  G. 3,600

  H. 16,000

  J. 27,000

  K. 30,000

11

MANHATTAN
PREP

71. Before Joseph paints his house, he puts blue paint into 2 buckets of different sizes. He notices that the volume of the larger bucket is 3 times the volume of the smaller bucket. At the end of the day, Joseph estimates that the larger bucket is $\frac{3}{4}$ full and the smaller bucket is $\frac{1}{3}$ full. He decides to pour all of the paint from the smaller bucket into the larger bucket. After that, how full is the larger bucket?

A.　$\frac{31}{36}$

B.　$\frac{4}{13}$

C.　$\frac{7}{9}$

D.　Overflowing

E.　100% full

72. In a pharmaceutical plant, the bark from 4,800 full-grown yew trees is needed to extract 16 kilograms of a cancer drug. The bark of how many yew trees would be needed to extract 500 kilograms of the drug?

F.　3,000

G.　15,000

H.　30,000

J.　150,000

K.　300,000

73. A train travels 720 miles in 8 hours of actual traveling time. How many hours can be saved from the train's trip if it travels 30 miles per hour faster?

A.　$\frac{3}{4}$

B.　$1\frac{1}{2}$

C.　$1\frac{2}{3}$

D.　2

E.　3

74. The graph below shows the number of copies of a particular book sold in 5 cities, to the nearest 500 copies. According to the graph, what fraction of the copies sold in all 5 cities were sold in either Alphaville or Echo Hill?

F.　$\frac{1}{10}$

G.　$\frac{7}{30}$

H.　$\frac{4}{15}$

J.　$\frac{1}{3}$

K.　$\frac{7}{15}$

75. Marcy travels the 420 miles from Cleveland to Philadelphia by bus. The trip takes 12 hours traveling at a constant speed. If Marcy wants her return trip to take only 10 hours, how much faster, in miles per hour, must the return bus travel than the original bus?

A.　5

B.　7

C.　8

D.　10

E.　12

MANHATTAN PREP

76. The median of a set of 5 different integers is equal to x. There are 2 new integers added to the set, both of which are greater than any integers originally in the set. Which of the following statements *must* be true of the new median?

    F. It is equal to the average (arithmetic mean) of the 2 new integers added.

    G. It is equal to the second largest integer in the original set of 5 integers.

    H. It is equal to the average (arithmetic mean) of all 7 integers in the set.

    J. It is less than the median of the original data set.

    K. It is less than the average (arithmetic mean) of the original set of 5 integers.

77. Over the past 10 years, the net exports of Country X have been $30 billion, $60 billion, $12 billion, −$8 billion, −$4 billion, −$16 billion, $4 billion, $15 billion, −$11 billion, and −$2 billion. What is the median of the county's net export figures over the past 10 years?

    A. −$4 billion

    B. −$3 billion

    C. −$2 billion

    D. −$1 billion

    E. $1 billion

78. In a set of 6 integers, the median of the integers in the set is equal to the average (arithmetic mean) of the integers in the set. If 2 new integers are added to the set, and the average (arithmetic mean) of the 2 new integers is equal to the average (arithmetic mean) of the 6 integers in the original set, which of the following statements is true?

    F. The median of the new set will be less than the median of the original set.

    G. The median of the new set will be greater than the median of the original set.

    H. The median of the new set will be equal to the median of the original set.

    J. The median of the new set will be greater than the average (arithmetic mean) of the 2 new integers.

    K. It cannot be determined how the median of the new set will compare with the median of the original set or the average (arithmetic mean) of the 2 new integers.

79. Yasmine has measured the number of phone calls her household has received over the past week. Those numbers, starting with Sunday and continuing through Saturday, were: 12, 3, 6, 2, 6, 11, and 9 phone calls, respectively. By how much did the average (arithmetic mean) number of calls per day exceed the median number of calls day?

    A. 0

    B. 0.5

    C. 1

    D. 2

    E. 2.5

11

80. The graph below shows the proposed expense budget for next year for Corporation XYZ:

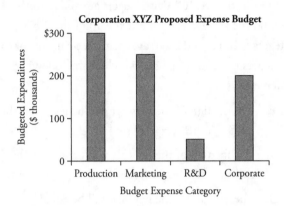

Corporation XYZ Proposed Expense Budget

In discussing the budget, management felt that not enough money was being spent to further important Research & Development (R&D) initiatives to support future growth in the business. If XYZ decides to triple the R&D expenditures proposed in the budget, approximately what percent of the overall budget will be for Corporate expenses?

F. 20%

G. 22%

H. 25%

J. 26%

K. 28%

81. $\dfrac{6 \times 10^{-3}}{2 \times 10^{4}}$ is equal to which of the following?

A. 3.3×10^{1}

B. 3×10^{-1}

C. 3×10^{12}

D. 3.3×10^{-12}

E. 3×10^{-7}

82. If n is an integer and $n^4 < 1,000$, what is the largest possible value for n?

F. 2

G. 3

H. 4

J. 5

K. 6

83. Of the 945 tiles that a certain store has in stock, $\dfrac{2}{7}$ are clay tiles, and $\dfrac{1}{3}$ of the clay tiles are glazed. How many glazed clay tiles does the store have in stock?

A. 30

B. 65

C. 90

D. 270

E. 315

84. If the least common multiple of a^2b and ab^2, where a and b are different prime numbers, is 36, then $ab = ?$

F. 2

G. 3

H. 6

J. 12

K. 18

85. Of the 432 different solid chemicals in a storeroom, $\dfrac{1}{3}$ are soluble in water, and $\dfrac{2}{3}$ of the solid chemicals soluble in water make clear solutions. If $\dfrac{1}{2}$ of the solid chemicals that both are soluble in water and make clear solutions are also weak bases, and there are no other weak bases in the storeroom, how many of the solid chemicals in the storeroom are weak bases?

A. 48

B. 96

C. 144

D. 216

E. 288

MANHATTAN
PREP

86. If 25% more than a number is 325, what is 20% less than the number?

   F. 52

   G. 165

   H. 180

   J. 208

   K. 260

87. A company's office has 8 conference rooms available, and each conference room will hold up to 6 chairs apiece. If the company has 25 chairs in the office and each conference room must have at least 1 chair in it at all times, what is the maximum number of conference rooms that could have 6 chairs in them at any given time?

   A. 0

   B. 1

   C. 2

   D. 3

   E. 4

88. If 12.5% of z is 880, then what number is 250% of z?

   F. 275

   G. 385

   H. 1,100

   J. 7,040

   K. 17,600

89. If a is an odd integer and b is an even integer, which of the following MUST be an odd integer?

   A. ab

   B. $2a + b$

   C. $a + ab$

   D. $a^2 b$

   E. $4(a - b)$

90. John spent an average of $12 on four items at the store. If the most expensive item was $21, what was the average price of the other three items?

   F. $14

   G. $12\dfrac{2}{3}$

   H. $9

   J. $6\dfrac{3}{4}$

   K. $4

91. If x is an odd integer, which of the following MUST be an even integer?

   A. $\dfrac{x}{2}$

   B. x^3

   C. x^2

   D. $x^2 + 4$

   E. $x^2 + 3x$

11

Use the following information to answer
questions 92–94.

The table below shows partial information on monthly
sales for a retail department store, by department (in
thousands of dollars). Unfortunately, not all of the data
is available yet because the accounting department is in
the process of revamping its sales database. The data that
has been included in this table, however, is accurate:

Department	Month			
	January	February	March	April
Women's Clothing	$115	$122	$108	
Women's Accessories	$100			
Men's Clothing	$75	$72		$81

92. Though the data has not been compiled yet (except for January), management feels that the Women's Accessories department may be in trouble. It estimates that sales fell 10% per month in each of the subsequent months displayed in the data table. If this is accurate, which of the following is closest to the sales amount for Women's Accessories in April, in thousands of dollars?

   F. $80

   G. $75

   H. $73

   J. $72

   K. $70

93. Approximately what percentage of the department store's sales in the month of January did Men's Clothing account for? (Assume that the department store only generates sales in the 3 departments listed.)

   A. 23%

   B. 26%

   C. 29%

   D. 31%

   E. 33%

94. The department store manager believes that the Women's Clothing department averaged $120,000 per month in sales over the 4-month period listed. If this is the case, how much were Women's Clothing sales in April, in thousands of dollars?

   F. $122

   G. $125

   H. $128

   J. $135

   K. $142

95. Samir had an average score of 92 on his last 8 tests. If he received an 85 on one of those tests, what was the average for the other 7 tests?

   A. $81\frac{3}{8}$

   B. $90\frac{2}{7}$

   C. 93

   D. $95\frac{2}{3}$

   E. 96

MANHATTAN
PREP

96. The ratio of *a* to *b* is 2 to 10, and the ratio of *c* to *b* is 3 to 1. What is the simplified ratio of *c* to *a*?

   F. 15 to 1

   G. 15 to 2

   H. 3 to 2

   J. 2 to 1

   K. 2 to 30

> Use the following information to answer questions 97–98.

Aaron, Bonnie, and Carl are members of a competitive bowling team. The 3-person team competed in a 4-game regional bowling tournament recently where it came in 2nd place out of 12 teams. The table below shows partial information from scores that Aaron wrote down during the course of the tournament. Unfortunately, he did not get a chance to write down all of the results, but those that he did record are accurate:

Team Member	Tournament Results			
	Game 1	Game 2	Game 3	Game 4
Aaron	208			
Bonnie	231	219	240	
Carl	165	180	188	201

97. By approximately what percent did Carl's score increase from Game 1 to Game 2?

   A. 6.1%

   B. 8.3%

   C. 9.1%

   D. 10.3%

   E. 15.0%

98. Bonnie mentions to Aaron that she's certain her average score for the 4 games was 235. If Bonnie is right, what was her score for Game 4?

   F. 260

   G. 257

   H. 255

   J. 252

   K. 250

99. In a pack of wolves, the 150 male wolves have an average weight of 50 kg. The 100 females have an average weight of 40 kg. What is the average weight of the entire population of the pack of wolves?

   A. 45 kg

   B. 46 kg

   C. 47 kg

   D. 48 kg

   E. 49 kg

100. The ratio of *a* to *c* is 2 to 8, and the ratio of *b* to *c* is 2 to 3. What is the simplified ratio of *b* to *a*?

   F. 12 to 1

   G. 8 to 3

   H. 3 to 8

   J. 1 to 6

   K. 1 to 12

101. The price of a stock increased by 40% in Year 1, then increased by 30% in Year 2. By what percent did the price of the stock increase over the 2-year period?

   A. 93%

   B. 82%

   C. 77%

   D. 70%

   E. 35%

11

102. On October 1, a watch sold by a department store was priced at $60. On November 1, the price of the watch increased by 20%. On December 1, the price of the watch was lowered by 25%. The next day, Janet purchased the watch. What percent of the original price was the watch's price when Janet purchased it?

    F. 5%

    G. 45%

    H. 72%

    J. 90%

    k. 95%

103. The profits of Corporation X increased by 30% from 2011 to 2012. Then, the profits fell by 30% from 2012 to 2013. By what percent did the profits of the company change from 2011 to 2013?

    A. −9%

    B. −3%

    C. −1%

    D. 0%

    E. 1%

104. $\dfrac{w}{3} + \dfrac{x}{4} + \dfrac{y}{5} + \dfrac{z}{6} =$

    F. $\dfrac{3w}{60} + \dfrac{4x}{60} + \dfrac{5y}{60} + \dfrac{6z}{60}$

    G. $\dfrac{20w}{60} + \dfrac{15x}{60} + \dfrac{12y}{60} + \dfrac{10z}{60}$

    H. $\dfrac{6w}{3} + \dfrac{12x}{5} + \dfrac{15y}{4} + \dfrac{20z}{6}$

    J. $\dfrac{10w}{60} + \dfrac{12x}{60} + \dfrac{15y}{60} + \dfrac{20z}{60}$

    K. $\dfrac{3w}{6} + \dfrac{4x}{5} + \dfrac{5y}{4} + \dfrac{6z}{3}$

105. Monica was using a calculator to do a math problem. She intended to multiply a number by 3 and then add 4 to the result, but instead accidentally divided the number by 3 and then added 4. What set of operations should she perform now to get the correct result that she originally desired?

    A. Divide by 4 then multiply by 3

    B. Subtract 4 then multiply by 3

    C. Multiply by 3 then subtract 4

    D. Multiply by 9 then subtract 32

    E. Multiply by 9 then add 32

106. A wooden rod of length $12\frac{2}{3}$ feet is cut into 3 pieces, with nothing left over (and with no loss of wood in the cuts themselves). If the lengths of two of the pieces are $6\frac{5}{9}$ feet and $3\frac{13}{18}$ feet, what is the length of the third piece, in feet?

    F. $2\dfrac{7}{18}$

    G. $2\dfrac{11}{18}$

    H. 3

    J. $3\dfrac{7}{18}$

    K. $3\dfrac{11}{18}$

107. If x is a positive integer such that x^3 is a 3-digit integer, how many possible values are there for x?

    A. 3

    B. 5

    C. 6

    D. 7

    E. 10

108. Lena and Daisy were hired to paint a total of $15\frac{1}{2}$ rooms. During their first week working on the job, Lena painted $5\frac{3}{4}$ rooms and Daisy painted $6\frac{5}{8}$ rooms. How many rooms were not painted in that first week?

    F. $4\frac{7}{8}$

    G. $4\frac{1}{8}$

    H. 3

    J. $3\frac{7}{8}$

    K. $3\frac{1}{8}$

109. If p and q are prime numbers, what is the smallest possible value of $p + q$ such that $pq \geq 100$?

    A. 20

    B. 22

    C. 24

    D. 28

    E. 31

110. If m is a perfect cube with exactly 4 digits, how many digits does $\sqrt[3]{m}$ have?

    F. 1

    G. 2

    H. 3

    J. 4

    K. Cannot be determined from the given information.

111. The fastest jet airplane can fly at a top speed of about 3,200 feet per second. Approximately how many miles can the jet travel in 15 hours, if it is traveling at top speed? (Note: There are 5,280 feet in one mile.)

    A. 1.7×10^8

    B. 2.9×10^6

    C. 3.3×10^4

    D. 1.1×10^4

    E. 5.5×10^2

112. If k is a positive integer, then for every value of k, the sum of the k smallest distinct odd positive integers is equal to which of the following?

    F. k

    G. $2k$

    H. $2k - 1$

    J. k^2

    K. $2k^2$

113. Lightning travels at a speed of 3,700 miles per second. In $\frac{1}{30}$ of a minute, approximately how far will a bolt of lightning have traveled, in feet? (Note: There are 5,280 feet in one mile.)

    A. 1.17×10^4

    B. 6.51×10^5

    C. 7.40×10^6

    D. 1.95×10^7

    E. 3.91×10^7

11

114. In a small town, the 200 adult males have an average height of 72 inches. The 100 adult females have an average height of 68 inches. The 100 children in the town have an average height of 48 inches. What is the average height, to the nearest inch, of the entire town's population?

   F.   63

   G. 64

   H. 65

   J.   66

   K. 67

115. In February, the price per barrel of oil rose by 20%. In March, the price per barrel of oil rose again by 15%. It ended the month of March at a price of $90 per barrel. What is the closest approximate dollar value of a barrel of oil before these price increases?

   A. $61

   B. $65

   C. $68

   D. $90

   E. $124

Answer Key

Write in whether you got each problem right or wrong (or left it blank). If your answer was correct, put a 1 in every blank to the right of that problem. Sum up each column and compare your total to the total possible "Out Of" points.

Problem	Correct Answer	Right/Wrong/Blank
1	D	
2	K	
3	E	
4	H	
5	C	
6	F	
7	B	
8	J	
9	B	
10	F	
11	B	
12	F	
13	D	
14	F	
15	B	
16	K	
17	C	
18	G	
19	D	
20	H	
21	A	
22	J	
23	A	
24	F	
25	D	
26	J	
27	E	
28	G	

Problem	Correct Answer	Right/Wrong/Blank
29	A	
30	J	
31	C	
32	F	
33	E	
34	G	
35	B	
36	J	
37	E	
38	G	
39	D	
40	J	
41	B	
42	H	
43	C	
44	K	
45	B	
46	J	
47	A	
48	G	
49	A	
50	J	
51	D	
52	J	
53	D	
54	G	
55	A	
56	K	

Problem	Correct Answer	Right/ Wrong/Blank
57	C	
58	J	
59	A	
60	K	
61	C	
62	K	
63	A	
64	G	
65	C	
66	K	
67	D	
68	G	
69	D	
70	F	
71	A	
72	J	
73	D	
74	J	
75	B	
76	G	
77	E	
78	H	
79	C	
80	G	
81	E	
82	J	
83	C	
84	H	
85	A	
86	J	
87	D	

Problem	Correct Answer	Right/ Wrong/Blank
88	K	
89	C	
90	H	
91	E	
92	H	
93	B	
94	J	
95	C	
96	F	
97	C	
98	K	
99	B	
100	G	
101	B	
102	J	
103	A	
104	G	
105	D	
106	F	
107	B	
108	K	
109	B	
110	G	
111	C	
112	J	
113	E	
114	H	
115	B	
Total		
Out Of		115

11

Pre-Algebra Solutions

1. **(D)** $10\dfrac{4}{15}$ Pre-Algebra   Fractions, Decimals, Percents

To add mixed numbers, add the fractions first, converting to a common denominator.

$$5\frac{2}{3}+4\frac{3}{5}=5+\frac{2}{3}+4+\frac{3}{5}$$

$$\frac{2}{3}=\frac{2\times5}{3\times5}=\frac{10}{15}$$

$$\frac{3}{5}=\frac{3\times3}{5\times3}=\frac{9}{15}$$

$$\frac{2}{3}+\frac{3}{5}=\frac{10}{15}+\frac{9}{15}=\frac{19}{15}=\frac{15+4}{15}=1\frac{4}{15}$$

$$5+\frac{2}{3}+4+\frac{3}{5}=5+4+1\frac{4}{15}=10\frac{4}{15}$$

The correct answer is (D).

2. **(K)** $540°$ Pre-Algebra   Arithmetic Word Problems

If the clock rotates 45° every 2 hours, it rotates 45° ÷ 2 = 22.5° every hour. In 24 hours, then, it will rotate 22.5° × 24 = 540°.

An alternative calculation is as follows: the clock rotates 45° every "time chunk," where in this case, a time chunk is 2 hours. There are 24 ÷ 2 = 12 such time chunks in a day (24 hours), so it will rotate 45° × 12 = 540° in a day. The correct answer is (K).

3. **(E)** $3\dfrac{7}{12}$ Pre-Algebra   Fractions, Decimals, Percents

To add mixed numbers, add the fractions first, converting to a common denominator.

$$1\frac{1}{3}+2\frac{1}{4}=1+\frac{1}{3}+2+\frac{1}{4}$$

$$\frac{1}{3}=\frac{1\times4}{3\times4}=\frac{4}{12}$$

$$\frac{1}{4}=\frac{1\times3}{4\times3}=\frac{3}{12}$$

$$\frac{1}{3}+\frac{1}{4}=\frac{4}{12}+\frac{3}{12}=\frac{4+3}{12}=\frac{7}{12}$$

$$1+\frac{1}{3}+2+\frac{1}{4}=1+2+\frac{7}{12}=3\frac{7}{12}$$

The correct answer is (E).

4.   (H) 19   Pre-Algebra   Statistics (Averages)

Let x be the unknown score. The sum of all scores is $14 + 15 + 19 + 13 + x$. The average of all scores is:

$$\frac{14+15+19+13+x}{5}$$

For the average to equal 16, that means:

$$\frac{14+15+19+13+x}{5} = 16$$

To solve for x, multiply both sides of the equation by 5 to get:

$$14+15+19+13+x = 80$$

Combine terms to get:

$$61+x = 80$$

Isolate the x variable by subtracting 61 from both sides: $x = 19$. The correct answer is (H).

5.   (C) $0.75   Pre-Algebra   Proportions and Ratios

If the package of 6 hot dogs costs $4.50, then the cost per hot dog is $4.50 ÷ 6:

$$\frac{\$4.50}{6} = \$0.75$$

The correct answer is (C).

6.   (F) $22   Pre-Algebra   Statistics (Averages)

Let x be the unknown commission for the fifth lamp. The sum of all commissions including x is given by $24 + $28 + $21 + $30 + x$. The average of all commissions is:

$$\frac{\$24+\$28+\$21+\$30+x}{5}$$

For the average to equal $25, that means:

$$\frac{\$24+\$28+\$21+\$30+x}{5} = \$25$$

To solve for x, multiply both sides of the equation by 5 to get:

$$\$24+\$28+\$21+\$30+x = \$125$$

Combine terms to get:

$$\$103+x = \$125$$

Isolate the x variable by subtracting $103 from both sides: $x = \$22$. The correct answer is (F).

7.   (B) 21   Pre-Algebra   Arithmetic Word Problems

In total, Jennifer spent $700 on the console plus the games. The console, by itself, cost $280, so she spent $700 – $280 = $420 on games for the console. Because the cost of the games was $20 each, she must have purchased $420 ÷ $20 = 21 games for the console. The correct answer is (B).

8.   (J) $3.75   Pre-Algebra   Proportions and Ratios

If the box of 36 candles costs $27.00, then the cost per candle is $27.00 ÷ 36:

$$\frac{\$27.00}{36} = \$0.75$$

Therefore, the cost of 5 candles is 5 × $0.75 = $3.75.

Alternatively, you could set this question up as a proportions/ratio question. Using C to represent the cost of 5 candles:

$$\frac{\$27.00}{36} = \frac{C}{5}$$
$$5(\$27.00) = 36C$$
$$C = \frac{5(\$27.00)}{36} = 5\left(\frac{\$27.00}{36}\right) = 5(\$0.75) = \$3.75$$

The correct answer is (J).

9.   (B) $32   Pre-Algebra   Arithmetic Word Problems

Triangle Construction pays Square Insurance $5,980 to insure a construction site for 92 days, so the cost per day is $5,980 ÷ 92 = $65 per day. Since the extended insurance costs $97 per day, Triangle pays $97 – $65 = $32 more for that extended day. The correct answer is (B).

10.   (F) $96   Pre-Algebra   Arithmetic Word Problems

Andrea has purchased a total of 24 movies. The cost for each of the movies by themselves is $12, so the standalone cost of these movies was 24 × $12 = $288. However, her average cost per movie including the membership fee was $16. Therefore, including this fee, she has spent 24 × $16 = $384. The difference between these amounts is $384 – $288 = $96, which must equal the cost of the membership fee. The correct answer is (F).

11.   (B) Farmer A, $0.92 per pound   Pre-Algebra   Proportions and Ratios

Farmer A sells 30 pounds of tomatoes for $27.60, or $\dfrac{\$27.60}{30}$ per pound, which is equal to $0.92 per pound.

Farmer B sells 50 pounds of tomatoes for $45.00, or $\dfrac{\$45.00}{50}$ per pound, which is equal to $0.90 per pound.

Farmer A's price per pound of tomatoes is more expensive than Farmer B's price per pound. The answer is Farmer A with $0.92 per pound. The correct answer is (B).

12. **(F)** $6   Pre-Algebra   Arithmetic Word Problems

Risha allocates the total cost of $273 equally across all 39 notebooks, so the cost per notebook is $273 ÷ 39 = $7 per notebook. Since she sells the notebook for $13, her profit (the difference between the money she receives and the cost) is $13 – $7 = $6. The correct answer is (F).

13. **(D)** 46   Pre-Algebra   Statistics (Averages)

Samuel wants an average quiz grade of 41 points. That average would be the total points earned, divided by the total number of quizzes (6), so the total points earned would have to be 41 × 6 = 246 points. So far, he has earned 35 + 42 + 48 + 37 + 36 = 200 points. Thus, he needs 246 – 200 = 46 more points from the sixth quiz to achieve his goal. The correct answer is (D).

14. **(F)** Andrew, $1 per rake   Pre-Algebra   Proportions and Ratios

Andrew purchased 5 rakes for $95, or $\frac{\$95}{5}$ per rake, which is equal to $19 per rake.

Melanie purchased 4 rakes for $80, or $\frac{\$80}{4}$ per rake, which is equal to $20 per rake.

The rakes Andrew bought were therefore $1 per rake less expensive than the ones Melanie bought. The correct answer is (F).

15. **(B)** 188   Pre-Algebra   Statistics (Averages)

Janice's total score from the 5 games in the tournament is 180 + 180 + 180 + 200 + 200 = 540 + 400 = 940. Her average score is therefore 940 ÷ 5 = 188. Note that because she scored 180 more frequently than 200, her average score must be closer to 180 than to 200 (in other words, it must be less than 190). This eliminates choices (C), (D), and (E) immediately. A common incorrect answer is (C). 190, which is the simple average of Janice's scores (180 and 200). The correct answer is (B).

16. **(K)** 140   Pre-Algebra   Statistics (Averages)

The average weight is to be no more than 125 pounds per person. If there are to be 4 people in the boat, then the total weight cannot be more than 125 × 4 = 500 pounds. The total weight of the first 3 people is 105 + 122 + 133 = 360 pounds. Therefore, the fourth person cannot weigh more than 500 – 360 = 140 pounds. The correct answer is (K).

17. **(C)** $2.55   Pre-Algebra   Arithmetic Word Problems

Morgan purchased 17 apples at a cost of $0.85 apiece. Therefore, he spent 17($0.85) = $14.45. However, because he purchased 12 or more apples, he should have paid only $0.70 apiece. This would have cost him only 17($0.70) = $11.90. Therefore, he overpaid by $14.45 – $11.90 = $2.55, and that is the amount of refund he is owed. Alternatively, you could simplify the arithmetic needed to solve this problem somewhat by inferring from the problem that Morgan overpaid by $0.85 – $0.70 = $0.15 *per apple*, and that therefore he is owed a refund of 17($0.15) = $2.55. The correct answer is (C).

18. **(G)** 63%   Pre-Algebra   Fractions, Decimals, Percents

The first sentence defines efficiency as work divided by heat (converted to a percent). The second sentence tells you that work = 453 joules, while heat = 715 joules. So the efficiency is $453 \div 715 = 0.633 \ldots \approx 0.63 \times 100\% = 63\%$. The correct answer is (G).

19. **(D)** 960   Pre-Algebra   Rounding

For rounding problems, only round the final answer to avoid rounding errors. The sum of the numbers is 322 + 189 + 444 = 955. To round to the nearest ten, use the units digit to determine whether you round up (5, 6, 7, 8, or 9) or round down (0, 1, 2, 3, or 4). Since the units digit is 5, round the tens digit up to get 960. The correct answer is (D).

20. **(H)** 3%   Pre-Algebra   Fractions, Decimals, Percents

In the first sentence, the annual return is defined as interest divided by initial investment (converted to a percent). Since the interest is \$13 and the initial investment is \$434, the annual return is $\$13 \div \$434 = 0.0299 \ldots \approx 0.03 \times 100\% = 3\%$. The correct answer is (H).

21. **(A)** $\dfrac{1}{5}$ Pre-Algebra   Possibilities and Probability

The general formula for probability is as follows, assuming that all outcomes are equally likely:

$$P(\text{success}) = \frac{\text{Number of possible successful outcomes}}{\text{Number of total possible outcomes}}$$

In this problem, there are 8 skiing team members, but 3 of them are ineligible because they are team captains. Therefore, there are 8 − 3 = 5 possible outcomes. The only successful outcome in this case is for Miguel to be chosen, so the correct probability is $\dfrac{1}{5}$. The correct answer is (A).

22. **(J)** 1,100   Pre-Algebra   Rounding

For rounding problems, only round the final answer to avoid rounding errors. First simplify the expression by multiplying and then adding:

$$3(231) + 2(185) = 693 + 370 = 1,063$$

To round to the nearest hundred, use the tens digit to determine whether you round up (5, 6, 7, 8, or 9) or round down (0, 1, 2, 3, or 4). Since the tens digit is a 6, round the hundreds digit up to get 1,100. The correct answer is (J).

23. **(A)** 11   Pre-Algebra   Arithmetic Word Problems

The total cost of the call, \$1.60, includes both the \$0.50 fee and the per-minute cost of \$0.10. Subtracting the \$0.50 fee leaves \$1.10 for the per-minute charge. To determine the total number of minutes divide the remaining balance by the cost per minute: $\dfrac{\$1.10}{\$0.10} = 11$ minutes. The correct answer is (A).

24. **(F)** 125   Pre-Algebra   Proportions and Ratios

To solve for x in this equation, first cross-multiply—that is, multiply by the denominators in the equation (x and 25):

$$\frac{25}{x} = \frac{5}{25}$$

$$(25)25 = 5(x)$$

Now divide by 5 and solve for x:

$$\frac{(25)25}{5} = x$$

$$x = \frac{625}{5} = 125$$

The correct answer is (F).

25. **(D)** 22   Pre-Algebra   Arithmetic Word Problems

The total number of units built, 135, includes both the 25 original units and the 5 units built each week. Subtracting the original 25 leaves 110 to be built. To determine the number of weeks, divide the remaining 110 units by the number of units built per week: $\frac{110}{5} = 22$ weeks. The correct answer is (D).

26. **(J)** 9   Pre-Algebra   Digits

Since $x \geq 52$ and $x \leq 65$, x can be any integer value between 52 and 65, inclusive. That means x could equal 52, 53, 54, 55, 56, 57, 58, 59, 60, 61, 62, 63, 64, or 65. Listing out these numbers makes it easier to see that the tens digit is larger than the units digit for 9 of these numbers: 52, 53, 54, 60, 61, 62, 63, 64, and 65. The correct answer is (J).

27. **(E)** $\frac{13}{20}$ Pre-Algebra   Possibilities and Probability

The probability, or chance, of success is the number of non-sophomores divided by the total number of people. The number of non-sophomores is 14 freshmen + 12 juniors = 26 non-sophomores. The total number of people is 14 + 14 + 12 = 40. So the probability of choosing a non-sophomore is $\frac{26}{40} = \frac{13}{20}$. The correct answer is (E).

28. **(G)** 6   Pre-Algebra   Digits

List out the integers in set S: 401, 402, 403, 404, 405, 406, 407, 408, 409, 410, 411, 412, and 413. The hundreds digit is less than the units digit in five cases: 405, 406, 407, 408, and 409. The hundreds digit is equal to the units digit in one case: 404. Therefore, the hundreds digit is less than or equal to the units digit in 5 + 1 = 6 cases. The correct answer is (G).

MANHATTAN
PREP

29. (A) $120   Pre-Algebra   Proportions and Ratios

"The cost, in dollars, of a certain metal alloy is directly proportional to its weight, in ounces" implies that the ratio $\dfrac{\text{cost, in dollars}}{\text{weight, in ounces}}$ must be equal for all instances of this specific metal alloy. Therefore, you can set the ratio $\dfrac{\$280}{42 \text{ ounces}}$ equal to the ratio $\dfrac{\$d}{18 \text{ ounces}}$ and solve:

$$\frac{\$280}{42 \text{ ounces}} = \frac{\$d}{18 \text{ ounces}}$$
$$280(18) = 42(d)$$
$$d = \frac{\$5,040}{42}$$
$$d = \$120$$

The correct answer is (A).

30. (J) 51   Pre-Algebra   Possibilities and Probability

The probability of choosing a nickel at random from the bag is the number of nickels divided by the total number of coins. Inserting 0.15 for the probability and 60 for the number of coins, you get the following:

$$0.15 = \frac{\text{Nickels}}{60}$$
$$(0.15)(60) = \text{Nickels}$$
$$9 = \text{Nickels}$$

Since you want the coins that are *not* nickels, subtract this number from the total: $60 - 9 = 51$ non-nickels. The correct answer is (J).

31. (C) 35   Pre-Algebra   Statistics (Averages)

According to the table, there are three Antibiotics sessions with expected attendances of 34, 38, and 33 people. Add these three numbers to get the total expected attendance: $34 + 38 + 33 = 105$. Finally, divide by 3 to get the average attendance: $105 \div 3 = 35$. According to the test directions, the term "average" indicates arithmetic mean (as calculated above) unless you are specifically told otherwise. The correct answer is (C).

32. (F) The need will first increase by 42 chairs and then decrease by 37 chairs.
Pre-Algebra   Statistics (Data Interpretation)

To track the overall need for chairs at different times, add up the expected attendance for each time slot. Note that the time slots are not grouped together in the table—you need to read the table carefully:

9–10am: $34 + 31 = 65$ chairs needed

10–11am: $38 + 39 + 30 = 107$ chairs needed

11am–12pm: $33 + 37 = 70$ chairs needed

Thus, the need for chairs increases from 65 to 107, then falls from 107 to 70. The initial increase is 107 − 65 = 42 chairs, while the decrease is 107 − 70 = 37 chairs. The correct answer is (F).

33. **(E)** 15   Pre-Algebra   Arithmetic Word Problems

Each hour, the distance between Joan and Anthony decreases, because he is ahead of her on the track but Joan is riding faster than Anthony. Because Anthony's lead is unknown, assign a variable (x) to represent that lead, and observe what happens in the first few hours:

	Now	+1 hour	+2 hours	+3 hours
Anthony	x miles	$x + 12$ miles	$x + 24$ miles	$x + 36$ miles
Joan	0 miles	15 miles	30 miles	45 miles
Difference	x miles	$x − 3$ miles	$x − 6$ miles	$x − 9$ miles

The lead Anthony has over Joan is getting smaller by 3 miles every hour. This makes sense, because the difference in the rates at which Joan and Anthony are riding their bicycles is (15 mph − 12 mph) = 3 miles per hour.

Since it takes Joan 5 hours to reach Anthony at a difference of 3 miles per hour, he must be 5 × 3 = 15 miles ahead of Joan at the start.

The correct answer is (E).

34. **(G)** −3   Pre-Algebra   Fractions, Decimals, Percents (Scientific Notation)

The value 2.438×10^x is shown in scientific notation form, $A \times 10^x$, where $1 \le A < 10$, and x is an integer. In order to move from 0.002438 to 2.438, you must move the decimal 3 places to the right (making the value larger). Therefore, the exponent on 10 must be made smaller by 3 to compensate, so $x = −3$. The correct answer is (G).

35. **(B)** $95.00   Pre-Algebra   Arithmetic Word Problems

Since the cost of the rental is for a day or any part thereof, all times will be rounded up to the nearest integer value of days. For example, if Miranda rented a car for 3 days and 5 hours, she would owe as though she had rented the car for 4 days. If Miranda rents a car from Ace Rentals on Tuesday at 11:45am and returns the car on Saturday at 5:45pm, she will have rented the car for 4 days and 6 hours, so she owes for 5 days. The 1st day costs $30, the 2nd day costs $20, and the 3rd, 4th, and 5th days each cost $15. The total owed for this rental would be $30 + $20 + 3($15) = $95.00. The correct answer is (B).

36. **(J)** 5   Pre-Algebra   Fractions, Decimals, Percents (Scientific Notation)

5.7×10^k is shown in scientific notation form, $A \times 10^k$, where $1 \le A < 10$, and k is an integer. In order to move from 570000.0 to 5.7, you must move the decimal 5 places to the left (making the value smaller). Therefore, the exponent on 10 must be made larger by 5 to compensate, so $x = 5$. The correct answer is (J).

11

MANHATTAN
PREP

37. **(E)** 700   Pre-Algebra   Possibilities and Probability

For *each* of the 35 different flavors of ice cream, Anthony can choose one of 20 different toppings. He has 35 choices for the first option, and for *each* of those, there are 20 choices for the second option. The number of combinations of ice cream flavors and toppings is therefore 35 × 20 = 700. The correct answer is (E).

38. **(G)** 25   Pre-Algebra   Proportions and Ratios

The figure below shows the gradation of the hill and the increase in ground height through the building:

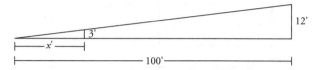

The slope of the hill is given as 12 feet per 100 feet of horizontal distance. Since the portion of the diagram representing the building and the whole diagram are similar triangles, the ratio of corresponding sides between the two triangles will always have the same ratio (i.e., they will always be in the same proportion). Therefore:

$$\frac{3}{x} = \frac{12}{100}$$
$$3 \cdot 100 = 12x$$
$$x = \frac{300}{12} = 25$$

The correct answer is (G).

39. **(D)** 320   Pre-Algebra   Possibilities and Probability

For *each* of the 20 different washer units available, Pauline can choose one of 16 different dryer units. She has 20 choices for the first option, and for *each* of those, there are 16 choices for the second option. The number of combinations of washer units and dryer units is therefore 20 × 16 = 320. The correct answer is (D).

40. **(J)** Their product is odd.   Pre-Algebra   Number Properties and Operations (Odds and Evens)

To solve this problem, work through the answer choices, eliminating any you know to be false. You can always test numbers, say 3 and 5, to verify more general principles:

   F. Eliminate because division does not even guarantee an integer result.

   G. Eliminate because division does not even guarantee an integer result.

   H. Eliminate because the product of two odd numbers is always odd, not even.

   J. **CORRECT.** The product of any two odd numbers is odd.

   K. Eliminate because the sum of two odd numbers is always even, not odd.

The correct answer is (J).

41. **(B)** 44%   Pre-Algebra   Fractions, Decimals, Percents

The histogram (in column chart format) lists the number of respondents who reported that they had exercised 0 days, 1 day, 2 days, etc., in the previous week. Perhaps the easiest thing to do is to go through each column and write down this information in table format; this will help solve any other questions related to this chart:

Days Exercised	# Respondents
0	3
1	5
2	2
3	1
4	4
5	5
6	3
7	2
Total	25

The first question asks what percentage of the respondents exercised fewer than 4 days in the past week. This is equal to the sum of the count of the respondents exercising 0 days, 1 day, 2 days, and 3 days, divided by the total number of respondents (25):

$$\frac{3+5+2+1}{25} = \frac{11}{25}$$

Now, multiply by 100% to convert the fraction to a percentage:

$$\left(\frac{11}{25}\right)100\% = 11 \cdot 4\% = 44\%$$

The correct answer is (B).

42. **(H)** 3.4   Pre-Algebra   Statistics (Averages)

To compute the average number of days exercised in the past week for the 25 respondents, you need the sum of the number of days exercised for each respondent. Then, you need to divide that sum by 25. Refer to the table version of the histogram data again:

Days Exercised	# Respondents
0	3
1	5
2	2
3	1
4	4
5	5
6	3
7	2
Total	25

One way you could compute this sum is to list out all 25 instances of a respondent's number of days exercised: 0 + 0 + 0 + 1 + 1 + 1 + 1 + 1 … However, this process will be somewhat laborious. Instead, take the sum of the *products of* the number of people in each group and the number of days each of those people exercised in the past week. This is called the "weighted sum"—you can then divide by 25:

$$\frac{(0 \cdot 3) + (1 \cdot 5) + (2 \cdot 2) + (3 \cdot 1) + (4 \cdot 4) + (5 \cdot 5) + (6 \cdot 3) + (7 \cdot 2)}{25}$$

$$= \frac{0 + 5 + 4 + 3 + 16 + 25 + 18 + 14}{25}$$

$$= \frac{85}{25} = \frac{17}{5} = 3.4$$

Thus, the average number of days the respondents exercised in the past week was 3.4. The correct answer is (H).

43. **(C)** $a - b =$ odd   Pre-Algebra   Number Properties and Operations (Odds and Evens)

To solve this problem, work through the answer choices, eliminating any you know to be false. You can always test numbers, such as 2 for a and 3 for b, to check the answer choices:

A. Eliminate because the product of an even number with anything is even, not odd.

B. Eliminate because the sum of an odd and an even number is odd, not even.

C. **CORRECT.** The sum of an odd and an even integer is always odd; therefore, the difference is always odd as well.

D. Eliminate because division does not even guarantee an integer result.

E. Eliminate because division does not even guarantee an integer result.

The correct answer is (C).

44. **(K)** It cannot be determined from the given information.   Pre-Algebra   Statistics (Averages)

To compute the average number of times in the past week that the 25 responding audience members ate red meat, you need the sum of the number of times they ate red meat for each respondent. Then, you need to divide by 25. However, there is a problem: one of the responding audience members ate red meat 7 *or more* times in the past week. With the information given, you do not know whether he or she ate red meat exactly 7 times, or 8 times, or 10 times, or 20 times! Therefore, you cannot compute the exact sum of the number of times responding audience members ate red meat in the previous week. Since you cannot calculate the sum, you cannot compute the average. The correct answer cannot be determined from the given information. The correct answer is (K).

45. **(B)** 3   Pre-Algebra   Statistics (Median)

In order to determine the median number of times the 25 responding audience members ate red meat in the past week, you need the "middle" number of the set. Perhaps the easiest thing to do is to go through each column and write down the information given in table format:

Times Eaten Red Meat	# Audience Members
0	5
1	2
2	4
3	2
4	4
5	5
6	2
7+	1
Total	25

The "middle" number of 25 data points will be the 13th-smallest data point. Why? Because there will be 12 numbers that are smaller than the 13th-smallest number (or equal to it) and 12 numbers that are larger than the 13th-smallest number (or equal to it). In this data set, 5 people did not eat red meat in the past week; these are the 5 smallest numbers in the set (all 0). Next, 2 people ate red meat 1 time in the past week—these are the 6th and 7th smallest numbers (all 1). 4 people ate red meat twice; these with be the 8th through 11th smallest numbers (all 2). Finally, 2 people ate red meat 3 times; these are the 12th and 13th smallest numbers. As you can see in the data table, there are 12 people who ate red meat more than 3 times, and 12 people who ate red meat less than (or equal to) 3 times. Therefore, 3 is the median number of times the responding audience members ate red meat in the previous week. The correct answer is (B).

46. **(J)** $\dfrac{18}{25}$ Pre-Algebra   Fractions

This question asks what fraction of the responding audience members ate red meat 2 or more times in the past week. Refer to the table version of the histogram data:

Times Eaten Red Meat	# Audience Members
0	5
1	2
2	4
3	2
4	4
5	5
6	2
7+	1
Total	25

The fraction of the responding audience members who ate red meat 2 or more times is equal to the sum of the count of the audience members eating red meat 2 times, 3 times, 4 times, 5 times, 6 times, and 7 or more times, divided by the total number of audience members who responded (25):

$$\frac{(4+2+4+5+2+1)}{25}=\frac{6+9+3}{25}=\frac{18}{25}$$

Therefore, the correct answer is $\dfrac{18}{25}$. The correct answer is (J).

47. **(A)** $66,500   Algebra   Arithmetic Word Problems

To find the cost of materials used in building the house, multiply the cost for each unit of a resource times the number of units of each resource that was used:

($6,500 × 5) + ($8,000 × 3) + ($10,000 × 1) = $32,500 + $24,000 + $10,000 = $66,500

The correct answer is (A).

48. **(G)** 9   Pre-Algebra   Number Properties and Operations (Multiples and Factors)

$15p - 6p = 9p$. This difference is a multiple of 9 and therefore divisible by 9. The correct answer is (G).

49. **(A)** 850,000   Pre-Algebra   Arithmetic Word Problems

If 1 gallon of water weighs 8.5 pounds, and the reservoir contains 100,000 gallons of water, then the weight of the water, in pounds, is (8.5)100,000 = 850,000. The correct answer is (A).

50. **(J)** 11　　　Pre-Algebra　　　Number Properties and Operations (Multiples and Factors)

$2q + 4q + 5q = 11q$. This sum is a multiple of 11 and therefore divisible by 11. The correct answer is (J).

51. **(D)** $27.50　　　Pre-Algebra　　　Statistics (Averages)

Jonathan's total proceeds from the 8 albums sold is $20 + $20 + $20 + $32 + $32 + $32 + $32 + $32 = $60 + $160 = $220. His average proceeds is therefore $220 ÷ 8 = $27.50. Note that because he sold more albums for $32 than for $20, his average proceeds must be closer to $32 than to $20 (in other words, it must be more than $26). This eliminates choices (A) and (B) immediately. A common incorrect answer is (B) $26.00, which is the simple average of the proceeds per album from the two groups ($20 and $32). The correct answer is (D).

52. **(J)** $\dfrac{1}{30}$　　　Pre-Algebra　　　Possibilities and Probability

The general formula for probability is as follows, assuming that all outcomes are equally likely:

$$P(\text{success}) = \frac{\text{Number of possible successful outcomes}}{\text{Number of total possible outcomes}}$$

In this problem, there are 5 women and 6 men. For each woman who is chosen, there are therefore 6 men who could be chosen as a duet partner, so there are $5 \times 6 = 30$ possible male–female combinations for the duet. Of these, there is only one combination that is brother and sister: Amy and Brian. Since that is the only successful outcome out of 30 possible outcomes, the correct ratio is $\dfrac{1}{30}$. The correct answer is (J).

53. **(D)** 202　　　Pre-Algebra　　　Arithmetic Word Problems

The student goal is to raise at least $10,000 for the cost of a field trip. The 331 mezzanine tickets sold will raise a total of $331 \times (\$15) = \$4,965$ towards that goal. Therefore, the students need to raise at least $10,000 − $4,965 = $5,035 from orchestra tickets.

Orchestra tickets cost $25 each, so the students must sell at least $5,035 ÷ $25 = 201\dfrac{10}{25} = 201.4$ tickets. However, because an integer number of tickets must be sold, round up: the students need to sell at least 202 orchestra tickets. The correct answer is (D).

54. **(G)** 5　　　Pre-Algebra　　　Arithmetic Word Problems

Tony must purchase at least 5,000 balloons and each box contains $20 \times 60 = 1,200$ balloons. Since $5,000 ÷ 1,200 = \dfrac{5,000}{1,200} = \dfrac{50}{12} = \dfrac{25}{6} = 4\dfrac{1}{6}$, if he purchases only 4 boxes, he would not have enough balloons (he would have 4,800 to be exact). Therefore, he must purchase 5 boxes. The correct answer is (G).

55. **(A)** 36　　　Pre-Algebra　　　Number Properties and Operations (Multiples and Factors)

The least common multiple of 12, 9, 4, and 3 is the smallest number that is divisible by all of these numbers. To solve for this number, express each number in prime-power form as $2^2 \cdot 3$, 3^2, 2^2, and 3. The least common multiple must include all of the prime factors that appear, and it must include those primes to the highest power that each appears in the list of prime-power expressions of the numbers in the list. To demonstrate: the prime factor 2 appears twice in the prime-power form of 12 ($2^2 \cdot 3$); the prime factor 3 appears twice in the prime-power form of 9 (3^2). Those are the only prime factors that appear, and 2 is the highest power to which each prime number appears in the prime-power expression of the list of numbers. Therefore, the least common multiple must consist of 2^2 and 3^2. Now form the product: $2^2 \cdot 3^2 = 36$. The correct answer is (A).

The number 36 is divisible by all of the numbers in the list: 3, 4, 9, and 12 (you can test each individually and verify this), and no smaller number is divisible by all of the numbers in this list. Therefore, 36 is the least common multiple. The correct answer is (A).

56. **(K)** $3.11   Pre-Algebra   Statistics (Averages)

Each raffle ticket that Amelie buys costs $4.00, so 7 raffle tickets will cost $28.00. However, this price includes the 2 free tickets Amelie receives.

Therefore, the average cost of each ticket is given by:

$$\frac{\$28.00}{9} \approx \$3.11$$

The correct answer is (K).

57. **(C)** 60   Pre-Algebra   Number Properties and Operations (Multiples and Factors)

In order to add and subtract these fractions, you need the least common multiple of the denominators 10, 15, and 12. The least common multiple is the smallest number that is divisible by all of these numbers. To solve for this number, express each number in prime-power form as $2 \cdot 5$, $3 \cdot 5$, and $3 \cdot 2^2$. The least common multiple must include all of the prime factors that appear, and it must include those primes to the highest power that each appears in the list of prime-power expressions of the numbers in the list. To demonstrate: the prime factor 2 appears twice in the prime-power form of 12 ($3 \cdot 2^2$); the prime factor 3 appears once in the prime-power form of 15 ($3 \cdot 5$) or 12 ($3 \cdot 2^2$); the prime factor 5 appears once in the prime-power form of 10 ($2 \cdot 5$) or 15 ($3 \cdot 5$). Those are the only prime factors that appear, taken to the highest power to which each prime number appears in the prime-power expression of the list of numbers. Therefore, the least common multiple must consist of 2^2, 3, and 5. Finally, $2^2 \cdot 3 \cdot 5 = 60$. The correct answer is (C).

58. **(J)** $4.50   Pre-Algebra   Statistics (Averages)

If Johanna buys 8 cappuccinos, she is given 1 for free. You know that she spends $36 on these 9 cappuccinos, so that cost comes from the first 8 cappuccinos (since the 9th cappuccino costs nothing). Therefore, the cost per cappuccino must be $\frac{\$36}{8} = \$4.50$. The correct answer is (J).

11

59. **(A)** 120   Pre-Algebra   Possibilities and Probability

For each of the 10 pairs of pants, the teacher can wear either of 2 pairs of shoes. The number of combinations of pants and shoes is represented by $10 \times 2 = 20$. For each of these 20 combinations of pants and shoes, the teacher can also wear any of the 6 shirts. The number of combinations of pants/shoes together with shirts is therefore represented by $20 \times 6 = 120$. The number of unique combinations of all three (pants, shoes, and shirts) is therefore 120. This can be calculated more directly simply by the product $10 \times 2 \times 6 = 120$. The correct answer is (A).

60. **(K)** $7\dfrac{11}{12}$ Pre-Algebra   Fractions, Decimals, Percents (Adding Mixed Fractions)

Add $4\dfrac{2}{3}$ to both sides of the equation to get $3\dfrac{1}{4} + 4\dfrac{2}{3} = y$.

To add mixed fractions, find the sum of the whole numbers: $3 + 4 = 7$. Next, find the sum of the fractions $\dfrac{1}{4}$ and $\dfrac{2}{3}$.
$\dfrac{1}{4} + \dfrac{2}{3} = \dfrac{3}{12} + \dfrac{8}{12} = \dfrac{11}{12}$.

Add the whole number sum to the sum of the fractions to get $7\dfrac{11}{12}$.

The correct answer is (K).

61. **(C)** 90   Pre-Algebra   Possibilities and Probability

With each of the 6 appetizers, José can order any of the 5 different entrées. The number of combinations of appetizers and entrées is represented by $6 \times 5 = 30$. For each of these 30 combinations of appetizers and entrées, José can also order any of the 3 desserts. The number of combinations of appetizers/entrées together with desserts is therefore represented by $30 \times 3 = 90$. The number of unique combinations of all three (appetizers, entrées, and desserts) is therefore 90, and José can eat at the restaurants 90 days in a row without eating the same combination. This can be calculated more directly by the product $6 \times 5 \times 3 = 90$. The correct answer is (C).

62. **(K)** I, II, and III   Pre-Algebra   Number Properties & Operations

Probably the easiest way to solve this problem is to substitute each of the basic mathematical operations in each of the Roman numerals for ∇ in the equation and see whether it holds:

Operation	Equation	Correct?
Multiplication	$(1 \times 5)^2 - (5 \times 1)^2 = 0$ $5^2 - 5^2 = 0$	YES
Addition	$(1 + 5)^2 - (5 + 1)^2 = 0$ $6^2 - 6^2 = 0$	YES
Subtraction	$(1 - 5)^2 - (5 - 1)^2 = 0$ $(-4)^2 - 4^2 = 0$	YES

As can be seen, the equation holds for each of the mathematical operations listed. Therefore, all the Roman numerals hold. The correct answer is (K).

63. **(A)** $1\frac{3}{8}$ Pre-Algebra   Fractions, Decimals, Percents (Adding Mixed Fractions)

To start, you need to isolate a. Subtract $2\frac{3}{4}$ from both sides of the equation to get $4\frac{1}{8} - 2\frac{3}{4} = a$.

To subtract mixed fractions, find the difference of the whole numbers, $4 - 2 = 2$. Next, find the difference of the fractions, $\frac{1}{8} - \frac{3}{4}$. $\frac{1}{8} - \frac{3}{4} = \frac{1}{8} - \frac{6}{8} = -\frac{5}{8}$.

Since the fraction is negative, you need to "borrow" 1 from the whole number and give it to the fraction to make it positive. Therefore, the whole number becomes $2 - 1 = 1$, and the fraction becomes $-\frac{5}{8} + 1 = -\frac{5}{8} + \frac{8}{8} = \frac{3}{8}$. Thus, $a = 1\frac{3}{8}$.

The correct answer is (A).

64. (G) $276   Pre-Algebra   Arithmetic Word Problems

Assuming that the price dropped linearly over time is the same as saying that the price dropped by the same amount each week. For that reason, you can calculate the constant weekly drop as the difference in starting and ending prices, divided by the total number of weeks:

$$\frac{\$380 - \$120}{20} = \frac{\$260}{20} = \$13.$$

The price after 8 weeks must have dropped by 8($13) = $104. Thus, the price at that time was $380 – $104 = $276. The correct answer is (G).

65. (C) I and III only   Pre-Algebra   Number Properties & Operations

Probably the easiest way to solve this problem is to substitute each of the basic mathematical operations in each of the Roman numerals for $\odot$ in the equation and see whether it holds:

Operation	Equation	Correct?
Multiplication	$(2 \times 4)^2 = (4 \times 2)^2$ $8^2 = 8^2$	YES
Division	$(2 \div 4)^2 = (4 \div 2)^2$ $\left(\frac{1}{2}\right)^2 = 2^2$	NO
Subtraction	$(2-4)^2 = (4-2)^2$ $(-2)^2 = 2^2$	YES

As can be seen, the equation holds for multiplication and subtraction, but not for division. Therefore, only Roman numerals I and III hold. The correct answer is (C).

66. (K) 40   Pre-Algebra   Possibilities and Probability

Consider just the ice cream and the topping choices. For each flavor of ice cream, Earvin has 4 options for the topping, so he has 5 × 4 = 20 ice cream topping combinations. Now, for each of those combinations, he has to select one of the 2 types of cookies to complete his sundae. In all, he can make 20 × 2 = 40 possible sundaes. The correct answer is (K).

67. **(D)** $12,000   Pre-Algebra   Arithmetic Word Problems

Assuming that the price dropped linearly over time is the same as saying that the price dropped by the same amount each year. For that reason, you can calculate the yearly drop in price as the difference in starting and ending prices divided by the total number of years: $\dfrac{\$15,750-\$9,500}{5}$, or $1,250 per year. Therefore, the value of the Model X car in 2003 (3 years after 2000) is:

$$\$15,750-(3\text{ years})(\$1,250\text{ per year})$$
$$= \$15,750-\$3,750 = \$12,000.$$

The correct answer is (D).

68. **(G)** 32   Pre-Algebra   Arithmetic Word Problems

Each minute, the amount of toluene in both vats increases. Observe what happens within the first few minutes:

	Now	+1 minute	+2 minutes	+3 minutes
Vat B	1,250 gallons	1,265 g	1,280 g	1,295 g
Vat A	450 gallons	490 g	530 g	570 g
Difference	800 gallons	775 g	750 g	725 g

The amounts of toluene in Vat A and Vat B are getting closer to each other, and each minute the difference decreases by 25 gallons. This makes sense, because the difference in the rates at which toluene is being added to them is $(40 - 15) = 25$ gallons per minute.

The vats originally started with a difference of $(1,250 - 450) = 800$ gallons of toluene. Therefore, it will take $800 \div 25 = 32$ minutes before the vats contain equal amounts of toluene. The correct answer is (G).

69. **(D)** 16   Pre-Algebra   Possibilities and Probability

To consider all the possible 4-letter strings, write out 4 slots:

$$\underline{\quad} \quad \underline{\quad} \quad \underline{\quad} \quad \underline{\quad}$$
$$\text{1}^{\text{st}}\text{ flip} \quad \text{2}^{\text{nd}}\text{ flip} \quad \text{3}^{\text{rd}}\text{ flip} \quad \text{4}^{\text{th}}\text{ flip}$$

Each flip has 2 possible results: H (heads) or T (tails). Put a 2 in each slot:

$$\underline{\ 2\ } \quad \underline{\ 2\ } \quad \underline{\ 2\ } \quad \underline{\ 2\ }$$
$$\text{1}^{\text{st}}\text{ flip} \quad \text{2}^{\text{nd}}\text{ flip} \quad \text{3}^{\text{rd}}\text{ flip} \quad \text{4}^{\text{th}}\text{ flip}$$

Finally, multiply the results. Here's why you multiply. Imagine just the first two flips. For the first flip you have two options, heads or tails. For each of those options, you can follow it with either of two options for the second flip, heads or tails. This is now 4 outcomes (HH, HT, TH, TT), or 2×2. When you add the third flip, you add another two options for *each* of the previous outcomes; now you're up to $8 = 2 \times 2 \times 2$. Finally the fourth flip brings two more options for *each* of the previous outcomes, and a total of 16 or $2 \times 2 \times 2 \times 2$ outcomes. You could write out all 16 possibilities (HHHH, HHHT, etc.), but that will take you a long time. The correct answer is (D).

11

70. **(F)** 3,000   Pre-Algebra   Proportions and Ratios

The ratio of ore used to aluminum produced must be constant (otherwise, the problem would not be solvable). In other words, you can scale the "recipe" up or down, so set up a proportion: an equation in which the first ratio equals the second ratio. Call the unknown number x and cross-multiply to solve. Always cancel factors when simplifying fractions:

$$\frac{9,000,000 \text{ pounds of ore}}{1,200,000 \text{ pounds of aluminum}} = \frac{x \text{ pounds of ore}}{400 \text{ pounds of aluminum}}$$

$$\frac{9,000,000 \times 400}{1,200,000} = x$$

$$\frac{9,0\cancel{00},\cancel{000} \times 400}{1,2\cancel{00},\cancel{000}} = \frac{90 \times 400}{12} = \frac{90 \times \cancel{4}00}{3 \times \cancel{4}}$$

$$= 3,000 = x$$

The correct answer is (F).

71. **(A)** $\dfrac{31}{36}$ Pre-Algebra   Fractions, Decimals, Percents (Word Problems with Fractions)

Let the volume of the larger bucket be X ounces. Because the larger bucket is three times larger than the smaller bucket, you can determine the smaller bucket's volume to be $\frac{1}{3}X$. At the end of the day, the large bucket contains $\frac{3}{4}X$ paint.

The smaller bucket contains $\frac{1}{3} \cdot \left(\frac{1}{3}X\right)$ paint. When the contents of the smaller bucket are poured into the larger bucket, the total paint in the larger bucket will be $\frac{3}{4}X + \frac{1}{9}X$, which is $\frac{31}{36}X$. This means the larger bucket is $\frac{31}{36}$ full.

Alternatively, you could pick numbers for the capacities of the buckets. Assume that the larger bucket has a capacity of 36 units. In that case, the smaller bucket has a capacity of 12 units, because it is one-third of the size of the larger bucket. The larger bucket contains $\frac{3}{4} \cdot 36 = 27$ units of paint, while the smaller bucket contains $\frac{1}{3} \cdot 12 = 4$ units of paint. Therefore, when the contents of the smaller bucket are poured into the larger bucket, the larger bucket will be $\frac{27+4}{36} = \frac{31}{36}$ full. The correct answer is (A).

MANHATTAN
PREP

72. **(J)** 150,000   Pre-Algebra   Proportions and Ratios

Set up a proportion relating the number of yew trees to the kilograms of the cancer drug. Units (such as "yew trees" or "kilograms of cancer drug") can help you put the numbers in the right places. Name the unknown quantity x, then solve for that variable. Always cancel factors when simplifying fractions.

$$\frac{4,800 \text{ yew trees}}{16 \text{ kilograms of cancer drug}} = \frac{x \text{ yew trees}}{500 \text{ kilograms of cancer drug}}$$

$$\frac{4,800 \times 500}{16} = x$$

$$\frac{48 \times 100 \times 500}{16} = 3 \times 100 \times 500 = 150,000 = x$$

The correct answer is (J).

73. **(D)** 2   Pre-Algebra   Arithmetic Word Problems

Because the train travels 720 miles in 8 hours, its average speed is $\frac{720}{8} = 90$ miles per hour. If the train's speed increases by 30 miles per hour, it would be traveling at 120 miles per hour. Traveling 720 miles at 120 miles per hour takes $\frac{720}{120} = 6$ hours. The time saved by traveling at 120 miles per hour is 8 hours – 6 hours = 2 hours. The correct answer is (D).

74. **(J)** $\frac{1}{3}$ Pre-Algebra   Statistics (Data Interpretation)

Each full "book" icon corresponds to 1,000 copies, according to the key below the graph, so the half-book in some rows corresponds to half of 1,000, or 500 copies. For each row, count up all the icons.

Alphaville: 1,000 + 500 = 1,500 copies

Bravotown: 3,000 + 500 = 3,500 copies

Charlie City: 2,000 + 500 = 2,500 copies

Deltaburg: 4,000 copies

Echo Hill: 3,500 copies

The total number of books sold in these 5 cities is the sum of these numbers (in fact, it may be easiest to count them directly on the graph, first adding whole books and then finishing with the pairs of half-books). 1,500 + 3,500 + 2,500 + 4,000 + 3,500 = 15,000 copies in all.

The problem asks for the fraction of books sold in *either* Alphaville or Echo Hill, so you must add the numbers for those two towns: 1,500 + 3,500 = 5,000 copies.

Finally, divide: $5,000 \div 15,000 = \frac{1}{3}$.

The correct answer is (J).

11

75. **(B)** 7   Pre-Algebra   Arithmetic Word Problems

Because the original bus traveled 420 miles in 12 hours, its average speed was $\frac{420}{12} = 35$ miles per hour. If the return bus is to complete the trip in 10 hours, it must travel at a rate of $\frac{420}{10} = 42$ miles per hour. This represents an increased speed of 42 miles per hour – 35 miles per hour = 7 miles per hour. The correct answer is (B).

76. **(G)** It is equal to the second largest integer in the original set of 5 integers.   Pre-Algebra   Statistics (Median)

The problem states that the original set consists of 5 different integers. Call these integers v, w, x, y, and z, listed in order from least to greatest:

$\{v, w, \underline{x}, y, z\}$

The median of this set is c, because it is the "middle" number in the set.

Next, two additional integers are added—and both new integers are larger than any integer in the original set. Call these new integers p and q. (If one of the two new integers is smaller than the other, assign it to f rather than to g.) Because they are larger than any integers in the original set, the following set must also be in order from least to greatest:

$\{v, w, x, \underline{y}, z, p, q\}$

In this set, the median is d, because it is the "middle" number in the set. This is the second largest integer in the original set, so the correct answer must be (G).

Note that you can verify that this is the correct answer by choosing numbers that fit the information in the problem. Assume that the original set of numbers is:

$\{1, 2, 3, 4, 5\}$

The median of this set is 3. If the numbers 6 and 7 are added, the median will become 4, which is the second largest integer in the original set. This will hold for any set of numbers chosen that conforms to the information given in the problem. The correct answer is (G).

77. **(E)** $1 billion   Pre-Algebra   Statistics (Median)

The median of 10 different numbers is equal to the average of the two "middle" numbers in the set—in this case, the 5th and 6th largest observations. To determine which numbers are the "middle" numbers, it helps to list them in order from least to greatest ($ billions):

$\{-16, -11, -8, -4, \underline{-2, 4}, 12, 15, 30, 60\}$

The median of this set $(-2 + 4) \div 2 = 1$. Therefore, the correct answer is $1 billion; (E).

78. **(H)** The median of the new set will be equal to the median of the original set.   Pre-Algebra   Statistics (Median)

The problem states that the original set consists of 6 integers, and the median of these integers is equal to the average. Call these integers a, b, c, d, e, and f, listed in order from least to greatest:

$\{a, b, \underline{c, d}, e, f\}$

The median of this set is the average of c and d, that is, $(c + d) \div 2$, because when a set of numbers has an even number of elements, the median is the average of the two "middle" numbers in the set. Furthermore, the average of c and d is equal to the average of all of the numbers in the set, that is, $(c + d) \div 2 = (a + b + c + d + e + f) \div 6$.

Next, two additional integers are added. Call these new integers g and h. (Assume that if one of the two new integers is smaller than the other, assign it to g rather than to h.) It is given in the problem that the average of the two new integers is equal to the average of the integers in the original set. Therefore, $(g + h) \div 2 = (a + b + c + d + e + f) \div 6$. From above, you can determine that $(g + h) \div 2 = (c + d) \div 2$. In other words, $g + h = c + d$. If g (the smaller of the two integers, by construction) is less than c, then h must be greater than d. If g is equal to c, then h must be equal to d. Either way, c and d will remain "in the middle" of the set, when ordering the set from least to greatest:

Therefore, the correct answer must be (H).

Note that you can verify that this is the correct answer by choosing numbers that fit the information in the problem. Assume that the original set of numbers is:

$\{1, 2, \underline{3, 4}, 5, 6\}$

The median of this set is equal to the average of 3.5. If the numbers 0 and 7 are added, the median will still be 3.5, because 3 and 4 will continue to be the middle numbers: $\{0, 1, 2, \underline{3, 4}, 5, 6, 7\}$. Likewise, if 3 and 4 are added, 3 and 4 will continue to be the middle numbers: $\{1, 2, 3, \underline{3, 4}, 4, 5, 6\}$. This will hold for any set of numbers chosen that conforms to the information given in the problem.

79. **(C)** 1   Pre-Algebra   Statistics (Median)

To solve this problem, you need to determine both the average (arithmetic mean) and median numbers in the set. Start with the median.

The median of 7 different numbers is equal to the "middle" number in the set. In this case, the "middle" number is the 4th largest observation. To determine which number is the "middle" number, it helps to list them in order from least to greatest:

$\{2, 3, 6, \underline{6}, 9, 11, 12\}$

You can see, the "middle" number in this set (hence the median) is 6.

Next, you need to find the average of the numbers. This can be done by taking the sum of the numbers in the set and dividing by the number of items in the set (7):

$$\frac{2+3+6+6+9+11+12}{7} = \frac{5+12+20+12}{7} = \frac{49}{7} = 7$$

Therefore, the average number in the set is 7. The question asks for the difference between the average number of phone calls and median number of phone calls, so the correct answer is $7 - 6 = 1$. The correct answer is (C).

80. **(G)** 22%   Pre-Algebra   Percents

To solve this problem, first analyze the graph to determine the amount of money (in thousands) that the budget projects to spend on each category:

Category	Expense Amount (thousands)
Production	$300
Marketing	$250
R&D	$50
Corporate	$200

Therefore, the overall budget calls for $(300 + 250 + 50 + 200) = \$800$ in expenditures. If R&D expenses are tripled (that is, multiplied by 3), this number will increase from $50 to $150, increasing the overall budget from $800 to $900 (all in thousands). In this scenario, the Corporate category will account for approximately 22% of the overall budget:

$$\frac{\$200}{(\$300+\$250+\$150+200)} = \frac{\$200}{\$900}$$
$$= 22.222\ldots\%$$
$$\approx 22\%$$

The correct answer is (G).

81. **(E)** 3×10^{-7} Pre-Algebra   Fractions, Decimals, Percents (Scientific Notation)

Note that when you are working with scientific notation, it is best to separate the digit terms (in this case, 6 and 2) from the exponential terms (in other words, the powers of 10). Then, work on each piece separately and bring the results together at the end:

$$\frac{6 \times 10^{-3}}{2 \times 10^4} = \frac{6}{2} \times \frac{10^{-3}}{10^4} = 3 \times 10^{-3-4} = 3 \times 10^{-7}$$

In the final step, don't forget the exponent rule that $\frac{a^b}{a^c} = a^{b-c}$, not a^{bc}, a^{b+c}, or a^{-bc}. The correct answer is (E).

82.   **(J)** 5   Pre-Algebra   Fractions, Decimals, Percents (Digits)

You can determine the correct answer by taking each choice to the 4th power and determining which result is the largest number that is less than 1,000:

$2^4 = 16$ INCORRECT: the next choice is less than 1,000

$3^4 = 81$ INCORRECT: the next choice is less than 1,000

$4^4 = 256$ INCORRECT: the next choice is less than 1,000

$5^4 = 625$ CORRECT: this result is less than 1,000 and the next result is greater than 1,000

$6^4 = 1,296$ INCORRECT: 6^4 is greater than 1,000

Strategically, it might make sense to start with the largest choice (6) and work backwards; as soon as a number smaller that 1,000 is obtained, the correct answer will be known.

Alternatively, you can calculate the value of $\sqrt[4]{1,000}$ by taking the square root twice of 1,000 (your calculator should be able to take a square root). You will get approximately 5.623. The correct answer is (J).

83.   **(C)** 90   Pre-Algebra   Fractions, Decimals, Percents

First, multiply 945 (total tiles) by $\dfrac{2}{7}$ (the fraction of all tiles that are clay) to get $945 \times \dfrac{2}{7} = \dfrac{945 \times 2}{7} = \dfrac{1,890}{7} = 270$.

This is the number of clay tiles. Now multiply that result by $\dfrac{1}{3}$ (the fraction of *clay* tiles that are glazed) to get

$270 \times \dfrac{1}{3} = \dfrac{270}{3} = 90$ glazed clay tiles. The correct answer is (C).

84.   **(H)** 6   Pre-Algebra   Number Properties and Operations (Multiples and Factors)

Given that a and b are different prime numbers, the least common multiple of a^2b and ab^2 has to have the highest power of a that you see (that is, a^2), as well as the highest power of b that you see (that is, b^2). So the least common multiple is a^2b^2, which is divisible by both a^2b and ab^2, but it has no "extra" factors in it. Now set a^2b^2 equal to 36 and solve for ab:

$a^2b^2 = 36$ ➔ $(ab)^2 = 36$ ➔ $ab = 6$

Because both a and b are prime numbers (prime numbers are all integers greater than 0), –6 isn't an option.

Alternatively, you can pick numbers for a and b, using for inspiration both the question text and the answer choices, until you match the condition that the least common multiple of a^2b and ab^2 is 36. Whatever values of a and b work must generate the right value for ab (otherwise the question would have more than one right answer). The possibilities are $a = 2$ and $b = 3$, or vice versa. Either way, the pair multiplies to 6. The correct answer is (H).

85. (A) 48   Pre-Algebra   Fractions, Decimals, Percents

It may be safest to calculate intermediate subtotals as you go, as long as you don't mistake those numbers for the final result. The number of solid chemicals that are soluble in water is $432 \times \dfrac{1}{3} = \dfrac{432}{3} = 144$. Next, since $\dfrac{2}{3}$ of those chemicals make clear solutions, the number of such chemicals is $144 \times \dfrac{2}{3} = \dfrac{144 \times 2}{3} = \dfrac{288}{3} = 96$. Finally, since $\dfrac{1}{2}$ of *these* chemicals are weak bases (and there are no other weak bases), you can calculate that there are $96 \times \dfrac{1}{2} = \dfrac{96}{2} = 48$ weak bases in the storeroom. The correct answer is (A).

86. (J) 208   Pre-Algebra   Fractions, Decimals, Percents

25% more than a number is equal to that number plus 25% of that number. Call the number x. Then 25% more than x is $x + 0.25x = 1.25x$. (In other words, 25% more than x is 125% of x.)

So you have $1.25x = 325$. Solve for x by dividing 325 by 1.25 in your calculator: $x = \dfrac{325}{1.25} = 260$

Don't stop here. Now you need to take 20% off. You can calculate 20% of 260, then subtract it from 260. Alternatively, since $x - 0.20x = 0.80x$, you can just compute 80% of 260 to get $0.8 \times 260 = 208$. The correct answer is (J).

87. (D) 3   Pre-Algebra   Arithmetic Word Problems (Maximizing/Minimizing)

The best way to solve this problem is to assign 1 chair to each conference room, keeping track of the remaining chairs:

CR#1	CR#2	CR#3	CR#4
1 chair	1 chair	1 chair	1 chair

CR#5	CR#6	CR#7	CR#8
1 chair	1 chair	1 chair	1 chair

Remaining Chairs: 25 − 8 = 17

In order for a conference room to have 6 chairs, 5 of the remaining chairs must be added to it. Therefore, you can add 5 chairs to CR #1 to fill it up. Now there are 17 − 5 = 12 chairs remaining. Similarly, 5 chairs can be added to CR #2 and CR #3. After this, there will be only 12 − 2(5) = 2 chairs remaining, which is not enough to fill up any more conference rooms; they must be put into one of the conference rooms. It does not make any difference which, so they might as well all be placed in CR #4:

CR#1	CR#2	CR#3	CR#4
6 chair	6 chair	6 chair	3 chair

CR#5	CR#6	CR#7	CR#8
1 chair	1 chair	1 chair	1 chair

Remaining Chairs: 0

MANHATTAN
PREP

As a final check, there are $6 + 6 + 6 + 3 + 1 + 1 + 1 + 1 = 25$ chairs allocated to the 8 conference rooms, and it is thus impossible for more than 3 of the rooms to have 6 chairs if each room must have at least 1 chair. The correct answer is (D).

88. **(K)** 17,600   Pre-Algebra   Fractions, Decimals, Percents

To write the given fact as an equation, convert 12.5% to its decimal equivalent and multiply it by z, since "of" means "times": $0.125z = 880$.

Solve for z by dividing 880 by 0.125 in your calculator: $z = \dfrac{880}{0.125} = 7{,}040$.

Then multiply the result by 2.5, the decimal equivalent of 250%, to get $2.5 \times 7{,}040 = 17{,}600$. The correct answer is (K).

89. **(C)** $a + ab$ Pre-Algebra   Number Properties and Operations (Odds and Evens)

You can solve this problem using the Odd/Even properties for the required operations in the problem: addition, subtraction, and multiplication. For further verification, you can also choose smart numbers to test each answer choice. For example, you could choose $a = 7$ and $b = 2$:

Expression	Odd/Even Rules	Example Numbers
ab	Odd × Even = Even	$(7)(2) = 14$
$2a + b$	Even × Odd + Even = Even + Even = Even	$2(7) + (2) = 14$
$a + ab$	**Odd + Odd × Even = Odd + Even = Odd**	**$(7) + (7)(2) = 21$**
a^2b	$(\text{Odd})^2$ × Even = Odd × Even = Even	$(7)^2(2) = 98$
$4(a - b)$	Even × (Odd − Even) = Even × Odd = Even	$4(7 - 2) = 20$

Using either method, you can see that the correct answer must be $a + ab$. The correct answer is (C).

90. **(H)** \$9   Pre-Algebra   Statistics (Averages)

If the average of 4 items is \$12, then the total John spent was $4 \times \$12 = \$48$. If one item was \$21, the other items cost a total of $\$48 - \$21 = \$27$. The average price of those 3 items is $\$27 \div 3 = \$9$. The correct answer is (H).

91. **(E)** $x^2 + 3x$ Pre-Algebra   Number Properties and Operations (Odds and Evens)

You can solve this problem using the Odd/Even properties for the required operations in the problem: addition, multiplication, and division. For further verification, you can also choose a smart number to test each answer choice. For example, you could choose $x = 7$:

Expression	Odd/Even Rules	Example Numbers
$\dfrac{x}{2}$	Odd ÷ Even = non-integer	$\dfrac{7}{2} = 3\dfrac{1}{2}$
x^3	Odd × Odd × Odd = Odd	$(7)^3 = 343$
x^2	Odd × Odd = Odd	$(7)^2 = 49$
$x^2 + 4$	(Odd)² + Even = Odd + Even = Odd	$(7)^2 + 4 = 53$
$x^2 + 3x$	**(Odd)² + Odd × Odd = Odd + Odd = Even**	**$(7)^2 + 3(7) = 70$**

Using either method, you can see that the correct answer must be $x^2 + 3x$. The correct answer is (E).

92. **(H)** $73   Pre-Algebra   Fractions, Decimals, Percents (Percent Change)

The sales for Women's Accessories (in thousands) was $100 in January. You are told that management believes sales declined by 10% each month relative to the previous month in February, March, and April. If decreased by 10% in February, it will have decreased by 10% × $100 = $10, to $90. Then, in March, if it decreased another 10%, it will have decreased by 10% × $90 = $9, to $81. Finally, in April, if it decreased another 10%, it will have decreased by 10% × $81 = $8.10, to $81 − $8.10 = $72.90. Therefore, the answer is $73, which is only $0.10 away from the exact amount (assuming management's estimates are exactly correct).

Often, for percentage change problems, you can use a multiple to represent the percentage change. For example, a 10% decrease is equal to multiplying the original number by $\dfrac{90}{100}$, which is equal to 0.9 in decimal form; doing this for 3 months in a row would yield $(0.9)^3 = 0.729$. For this problem, $100 × 0.729 = $72.90, which again is very close to the correct answer of $73. The correct answer is (H).

93. **(B)** 26%   Pre-Algebra   Fractions, Decimals, Percents

This question asks approximately what percentage of the January sales were from the Men's Clothing department. This is equal to January Men's Clothing sales ($75), divided by the total sales in January for the 3 departments ($115 + $70 + $75):

$$\frac{\$75}{\$115 + \$100 + \$75} = \frac{\$75}{\$290} = \frac{\$15}{\$58}$$

Notice that this fraction is just barely greater than $\dfrac{\$15}{\$60}$, which is equal to 0.25, because the denominator is only slightly smaller. (The exact ratio, rounded to 4 decimal places, is 0.2586.)

Now multiply by 100% to convert the decimal to a percentage:

$(0.2586)(100\%) = 25.86\%$

The closest answer choice is 26%. The correct answer is (B).

94. **(J)** $135   Pre-Algebra   Statistics (Averages)

The data table lists some of the monthly sales figures (in thousands of dollars) for each of the three departments of a department store for the months of January through April:

Department	Month			
	January	**February**	**March**	**April**
Women's Clothing	$115	$122	$108	
Women's Accessories	$100			
Men's Clothing	$75	$72		$81

The problem tells you that management estimates average monthly sales in Women's Clothing (in thousands) to be $120. Let x be the April sales amount for Women's Clothing. The sum of all sales amounts is $115 + $122 + $108 + x. The average of all sales amounts is:

$$\frac{\$115 + \$122 + \$108 + x}{4}$$

For the average to equal $120, that means:

$$\frac{\$115 + \$122 + \$108 + x}{4} = \$120$$

To solve for x, multiply both sides of the equation by 4 to get:

$$\$115 + \$122 + \$108 + x = \$120 \cdot 4$$

Simplify and combine terms to get:

$$\$345 + x = \$480$$
$$x = \$135$$

The correct answer is (J).

95. **(C)** 93   Pre-Algebra   Statistics (Averages)

If the average of 8 tests is 92, then the total of all of Samir's scores was $8 \times 92 = 736$. If he received an 85 on one test, the sum of the remaining 7 tests was $736 - 85 = 651$. The average score on those 7 tests is $651 \div 7 = 93$. The correct answer is (C).

96. **(F)** 15 to 1   Pre-Algebra   Proportions and Ratios

It is given in the problem that the ratio $\dfrac{a}{b} = \dfrac{2}{10}$, and the ratio $\dfrac{c}{b} = \dfrac{3}{1}$. You need the ratio $\dfrac{c}{a}$. This ratio can be

written as $\dfrac{c}{a} = \left(\dfrac{c}{b}\right)\left(\dfrac{b}{a}\right)$. By substituting in values for a, b, and c in the ratios above, you get $\dfrac{c}{a} = \left(\dfrac{3}{1}\right)\left(\dfrac{10}{2}\right) = \dfrac{30}{2} = \dfrac{15}{1}$,

or 15 to 1. The correct answer is (F).

97. **(C)** 9.1%   Pre-Algebra   Fractions, Decimals, Percents (Percent Change)

The definition of a percentage increase for a number is the change in the number, divided by the original number. According to the data table, Carl scored 180 in Game 2 and 165 in Game 1. Therefore, the change in the number is $180 - 165 = 15$, and the original number is his *first* score, not his second. Therefore, the percentage change is given by the following equation:

$$\frac{180-165}{165} = \frac{15}{165} = \frac{1}{11}$$

Now multiply by 100% to convert the fraction to a percentage:

$$\frac{1}{11}(100\%) = \frac{100\%}{11} = 9\frac{1}{11}\% = 9.0909...\%$$

The closest answer choice is therefore 9.1%. The correct answer is (C).

98. **(K)** 250   Pre-Algebra   Statistics (Averages)

The data table lists some of the game score results for each of the three members of a competitive bowling team in a 4-game tournament:

Team Member	Tournament Results			
	Game 1	Game 2	Game 3	Game 4
Aaron	208			
Bonnie	231	219	240	
Carl	165	180	188	201

The problem tells you that Bonnie believes she averaged a score of 235 for the 4 games. Let x be her Game 4 score. The sum of all scores for Bonnie is $231 + 219 + 240 + x$. The average of all of her scores is:

$$\frac{231+219+240+x}{4}$$

For the average to equal 235, set the equation equal to 235:

$$\frac{231+219+240+x}{4} = 235$$

To solve for x, multiply both sides of the equation by 4:

$$231+219+240+x = 235 \cdot 4$$

MANHATTAN
PREP

Next, simplify and combine terms:

$$690 + x = 940$$
$$x = 250$$

The correct answer is (K).

99. **(B)** 46 kg   Pre-Algebra   Statistics (Averages)

In this problem, you must take the average of two averages. However, it is given in the problem that some of the observations occur more frequently in the population whose average you are measuring; such problems involving averages are called "weighted averages," because you must weight the numbers you are averaging by the relative frequency with which they occur. By multiplying the average observations for each group by the number of items in that group, you arrive at the sum of the values contributed to the overall average by each group; divide by the sum of the weights to arrive at the overall, "weighted" average.

This process can be expressed mathematically as:

$$\frac{\sum \left(\text{Weights for each group}\right) \times \left(\text{Average value in each group}\right)}{\sum \left(\text{Weights for each group}\right)}$$

To illustrate: there are 150 male wolves that have an average weight of 50 kg. Since the sum of the weights of all of the male wolves must equal $150 \times 50 = 7{,}500$ kg, use that weighted sum in your calculation. Similarly, the 100 female wolves have an average weight of 40 kg. The total combined weight of the female wolves is therefore $100 \times 40 = 4{,}000$ kg. Find the average weight of the entire pack of wolves by summing the combined weights, and dividing by the number of wolves:

$$\frac{7{,}500 + 4{,}000}{150 + 100} = \frac{11{,}500}{250} = 46$$

Therefore, the weighted average weight (i.e., the average weight) of the pack of wolves is 46 kg.

100. **(G)** 8 to 3   Pre-Algebra   Ratios

It is given in the problem that the ratio $\frac{a}{c} = \frac{2}{8}$, and the ratio $\frac{b}{c} = \frac{2}{3}$. Find the ratio $\frac{b}{a}$. This ratio can be written as $\frac{b}{a} = \left(\frac{b}{c}\right)\left(\frac{c}{a}\right)$. (Note that the last ratio is the reciprocal of the first ratio given in the problem.) By substituting in values for a, b, and c in the ratios above, you get $\frac{b}{a} = \left(\frac{2}{3}\right)\left(\frac{8}{2}\right) = \frac{16}{6} = \frac{8}{3}$, or 8 to 3.

101. **(B)** 82%   Pre-Algebra   Fractions, Decimals, Percents (Percentage Change)

Let the price of the stock be $100 at the beginning of Year 1. If the price increased by 40% in Year 1, it will have increased by $40\% \times \$100 = \$40$, to $140. Then, in Year 2, if it increases another 30%, it will increase by $30\% \times \$140 = \$42$, to $182. The total percent increase is given by:

$$\frac{\$182 - \$100}{\$100} = \frac{\$82}{\$100} = 82\%$$

Typically, percentage change problems can be solved more easily if 100 can be chosen as a number to help solve the problem. In other cases, you can use a multiple to represent the percentage change. For example, a 40% increase is equal to multiplying the original number by $1\frac{40}{100} = 1.4$; similarly, a 30% increase is equal to multiplying a number by 1.3. When a problem includes successive percent changes, these multiples can be multiplied together; (1.4)(1.3) = 1.82, which signifies an 82% increase. The correct answer is (B).

102. **(J)** 90%   Pre-Algebra   Percents (Percentage Change)

To find the price of the watch when Janet made her purchase, increase the watch's original price by 20%, then decrease the resulting price by 25%. Do this by twice taking the initial price, then adding/subtracting a percentage of that price to find a new price.

You are told that the price increased by 20% on November 1. Thus the price increased by 20% × $60 = $12, to $72. Then, on December 1, the price decreased by 25%, so it decreased by 25% × $72 = $18, to $54. The total percentage change is given by:

$$\frac{\$54 - \$60}{\$60} = \frac{-\$6}{\$60} = -10\%$$

Thus overall the price of the watch decreased by 10%, so the new price of the watch is 100% − 10% = 90% of the original price.

For percentage change problems, use a multiple to represent the percentage change. For example, a 20% increase is equal to multiplying the original number by $1\frac{20}{100} = 1.2$. Similarly, a 25% decrease is equal to multiplying the number by 0.75. When a problem includes successive percent changes, these multiples can be multiplied together: (1.2)(0.75) = 0.9, which signifies 90% of the original price. The correct answer is therefore (J).

103. **(A)** −9%   Pre-Algebra   Fractions, Decimals, Percents (Percentage Change)

Let the profits of Corporation X be $100 in 2011. If the profits increased by 30% in 2012, it will have increased by 30% × ($100) = $30, to $130. Then, in 2013, profits decreased by 30%, so they will have decreased by 30% × ($130) = $39, to $130 − $39 = $91. The total percentage change is given by:

$$\frac{\$91 - \$100}{\$100} = \frac{-\$9}{\$100} = -9\%$$

The key to solving this problem is to apply the percentage changes and not assume that because the profits increased then decreased by the same percentage, they ended up where they started.

Typically, percentage change problems can be solved more easily if 100 can be chosen as a number to help solve the problem. In other cases, use a multiple to represent the percentage change. For example, a 30% increase is equal to multiplying the original number by $1\frac{30}{100} = 1.3$; similarly, a 30% decrease is equal to multiplying a number by 0.7. When a

MANHATTAN
PREP

problem includes successive percent changes, these multiples can be multiplied together: $(1.3)(0.7) = 0.91$, which signifies a 9% decrease. The correct answer is (A).

104. **(G)** $\dfrac{20w}{60} + \dfrac{15x}{60} + \dfrac{12y}{60} + \dfrac{10z}{60}$ Pre-Algebra   Number Properties and Operations (Multiples and Factors)

In order to add these fractions, you need to find the least common multiple of the denominators (3, 4, 5, and 6). The least common multiple is the smallest number that is divisible by all of these numbers. To solve for this number, express each number in prime-power form as 3, 2^2, 5, and 3×2. The least common multiple must include all of the prime factors that appear, and it must include those primes to the highest power that each appears in the list of prime-power expressions of the numbers in the list.

To demonstrate: the prime factor 2 appears twice in the prime-power form of 4 (2^2); the prime factor 3 appears once in the prime-power form of 3 (3) or 6 (= 3×2); the prime factor 5 appears once in the prime-power form of 5 (5). Those are the only prime factors that appear, taken to the highest power to which each prime number appears in the prime-power expression of the list of numbers. Therefore, the least common multiple must consist of 2^2, 3, and 5. Finally, $2^2 \times 3 \times 5 = 60$.

Next, determine the amount by which to multiply each numerator and denominator so that each denominator is equal to the least common denominator. For example:

In $\dfrac{w}{3}$, $\dfrac{60}{3} = 20$, so $\dfrac{(20)w}{(20)3} = \dfrac{20w}{60}$.

In $\dfrac{x}{4}$, $\dfrac{60}{4} = 15$, so $\dfrac{(15)x}{(15)4} = \dfrac{15x}{60}$.

In $\dfrac{y}{5}$, $\dfrac{60}{5} = 12$, so $\dfrac{(12)y}{(12)5} = \dfrac{12y}{60}$.

In $\dfrac{z}{6}$, $\dfrac{60}{6} = 10$, so $\dfrac{(10)z}{(10)6} = \dfrac{10z}{60}$.

The correct final expression is $\dfrac{20w}{60} + \dfrac{15x}{60} + \dfrac{12y}{60} + \dfrac{10z}{60}$. The correct answer is (G).

105. **(D)** Multiply by 9 then subtract 32   Pre-Algebra   Arithmetic Word Problems

Assume that before Monica made the error, the calculator displayed 12. The correct procedure would have yielded 36 after multiplying by 3; after that, adding 4 would have yielded 40. Instead, she divided by 3 first, which would yield a result of 4; then, after adding 4, her result would be 8. Now test each answer choice to determine which will result in the correct result of 40:

A.	Divide by 4 then multiply by 3	NO; yields a result of $(8 \div 4)3 = 6$
B.	Subtract 4 then multiply by 3	NO; yields a result of $(8 - 4)3 = 12$
C.	Multiply by 3 then subtract 4	NO; yields a result of $8(3) - 4 = 20$
D.	**Multiply by 9 then subtract 32**	**YES; yields a result of $8(9) - 32 = 40$**
E.	Multiply by 9 then add 32	NO; yields a result of $8(9) + 32 = 104$

Using these example numbers, you can see that choice (D) must be correct.

The correct result can also be found algebraically. Assume that the original number shown on the calculator was x. Then the correct result should be $3x + 4$. Call this result y. However, the actual result displayed will be $(x \div 3) + 4$. Call this result z. Now solve for y in terms of z to determine what operations to perform on z to get the correct result:

$$3x + 4 = y$$
$$\frac{x}{3} + 4 = z$$
$$x + 4(3) = 3z$$
$$x = 3z - 12$$
$$3(3z - 12) + 4 = y$$
$$9z - 36 + 4 = y$$
$$9z - 32 = y$$

Therefore, Monica needs to take the incorrect result, multiply by 9, and subtract 32. The correct answer is (D).

106. **(F)** $2\frac{7}{18}$　　　Pre-Algebra　　　Fractions, Decimals, Percents

Let the length of the unknown piece be x. Because the lengths of the three pieces of wood must equal the length of the original wooden rod, set up the following equation:

$$6\frac{5}{9} + 3\frac{13}{18} + x = 12\frac{2}{3}$$
$$\frac{59}{9} + \frac{67}{18} + x = \frac{38}{3}$$
$$x = \frac{38}{3} - \frac{59}{9} - \frac{67}{18}$$
$$x = \frac{228}{18} - \frac{118}{18} - \frac{67}{18}$$
$$x = \frac{43}{18}$$
$$x = 2\frac{7}{18}$$

The correct answer is (F).

107. **(B)** 5　　　Pre-Algebra　　　Fractions, Decimals, Percents (Digits)

One way to approach this problem is to enumerate the third power of all integers, starting with 1, until a 4-digit integer is obtained, and then count how many results have 3 digits:

$1^3 = 1$	$2^3 = 8$	$3^3 = 27$
$4^3 = 64$	$\underline{5^3 = 125}$	$\underline{6^3 = 216}$
$\underline{7^3 = 343}$	$\underline{8^3 = 512}$	$\underline{9^3 = 729}$
$10^3 = 1{,}000$	(STOP)	

Since 10^3 has 4 digits, you can stop; any larger integer will produce at least 4 digits when taken to the third power. The underlined results have 3 digits, and since there are 5 of them, the correct answer is 5.

Alternatively, you could attempt to compute the answer algebraically. If x^3 has 3 digits, then it must be the case that $100 \leq x^3 < 1,000$. You can simplify this inequality:

$$100 \leq x^3 < 1,000$$
$$\sqrt[3]{100} \leq x < \sqrt[3]{1,000}$$
$$\sqrt[3]{100} \leq x < \sqrt[3]{(10)(10)(10)}$$
$$\sqrt[3]{100} \leq x < 10$$

Unfortunately, the leftmost term in this inequality is difficult to estimate (it is approximately 4.642). Through trial and error, it can be estimated to be somewhere between 4 and 5. (Of course, if your calculator can take cube roots and you know how to make it do so, you can compute the number to many decimal points.) Knowing that the cube root is between 4 and 5, you can determine that the integers that would produce a 3-digit integer when taken to the third power are 5, 6, 7, 8, and 9. The correct answer is (B).

108. **(K)** $\dfrac{1}{3x^2}$ Pre-Algebra   Fractions, Decimals, Percents

Let x be the number of rooms not painted in that first week. The total number of rooms they were hired to paint is the sum of Lena's work, Daisy's work, and the work left undone. You can set up and solve the following equation:

$$5\frac{3}{4} + 6\frac{5}{8} + x = 15\frac{1}{2}$$
$$\frac{23}{4} + \frac{53}{8} + x = \frac{31}{2}$$
$$x = \frac{31}{2} - \frac{23}{4} - \frac{53}{8}$$
$$x = \frac{124}{8} - \frac{46}{8} - \frac{53}{8}$$
$$x = \frac{25}{8}$$
$$x = 3\frac{1}{8}$$

The correct answer is (K).

109. **(B)** 22   Pre-Algebra   Number Properties & Operations (Multiples and Factors (Prime Numbers))

Perhaps the best way to approach this problem is to begin by listing some of the prime numbers, starting with the smallest prime number (2), and then experimenting with different combinations of them that, when multiplied together, yield at least 100, but add up to a relatively small sum. The smallest prime numbers are:

2, 3, 5, 7, 11, 13, 17, 19, 23 …

A very small prime number, such as 2 or 3, is going to need to be multiplied by a relatively large prime number in order to yield a product of at least 100. Therefore, it probably makes sense to try numbers that are fairly close together, such as $7 \times 19 = 133$, which has a sum of 26. Can you do better than this? Yes, because $7 \times 17 = 119$, which sums to 24. Additionally, $11 \times 13 = 143$, and $11 + 13$ also equals 24.

The key to solving this problem is to recognize that p and q do not need to be *different* prime numbers—in fact, the best answer is $11 \times 11 = 121$, which sums to $11 + 11 = 22$.

By way of verification, the following table lists the product and sum of the smallest prime numbers (excluding 2). Grey boxes indicate that the product is smaller than 100 and can therefore be ignored. As can be seen, the optimal answer is $p = 11$ and $q = 11$:

Product/Sum	3	5	7	11	13	17	19	23
3	9	15	21	33	39	51	57	69
	6	8	10	14	16	20	22	26
5	–	25	35	55	65	85	95	115
	–	10	12	16	18	22	24	28
7	–	–	49	77	91	119	133	161
	–	–	14	18	20	24	26	30
11	–	–	–	*121*	143	187	209	253
	–	–	–	*22*	24	28	30	34
13	–	–	–	–	169	221	247	299
	–	–	–	–	26	30	32	36
17	–	–	–	–	–	289	323	391
	–	–	–	–	–	34	36	40
19	–	–	–	–	–	–	361	437
	–	–	–	–	–	–	38	42
23	–	–	–	–	–	–	–	529
	–	–	–	–	–	–	–	46

The correct answer is (B).

110. (G) 2   Pre-Algebra   Fractions, Decimals, Percents (Digits)

One way to approach this problem is to enumerate the 3rd power of all integers, starting with 1, until a 4-digit integer is obtained, and then determine the pattern thereafter:

$1^3 = 1$	$2^3 = 8$	$3^3 = 27$
$4^3 = 64$	$5^3 = 125$	$6^3 = 216$
$7^3 = 343$	$8^3 = 512$	$9^3 = 729$
$10^3 = 1,000$	(STOP)	

Since 10^3 has 4 digits, you can stop. The number 10 is a 2-digit integer; no 1-digit integers have a cube of 4 digits. Any integer larger than 10 will produce at least 4 digits. And since the smallest number that is more than 2 digits is 100, and $100^3 = 1,000,000$ (7 digits), you know that any perfect cube of 4 digits must have a cube root that is 2 digits.

Alternatively, you could attempt to compute the answer algebraically. If m has 4 digits, then it must be the case that $1,000 \leq m < 10,000$. Simplify this inequality:

$$1,000 \leq m < 10,000$$
$$\sqrt[3]{1,000} \leq \sqrt[3]{m} < \sqrt[3]{10,000}$$
$$\sqrt[3]{(10)(10)(10)} \leq \sqrt[3]{m} < \sqrt[3]{(10)(10)(10)(10)}$$
$$10 \leq \sqrt[3]{m} < 10 \cdot \sqrt[3]{10}$$

Therefore, $\sqrt[3]{m}$ must have at least 2 digits and, since $\sqrt[3]{10} < 10$, it can have *at most* 2 digits. (Note: $\sqrt[3]{10} \approx 2.154$.) The correct answer is (G).

111. (C) 3.3×10^4 Pre-Algebra   Arithmetic Word Problems (Converting/Canceling Units)

You need to carefully convert 3,200 feet per second into an unknown quantity of miles by setting up an expression and canceling units. To do this, set up the following expression, making sure that all units not desired in the result will be canceled out (i.e., all units *except* for miles):

$$\frac{3,200 \text{ feet}}{1 \text{ second}} \times \frac{60 \text{ seconds}}{1 \text{ minute}} \times \frac{60 \text{ minutes}}{1 \text{ hour}} \times \frac{15 \text{ hours}}{1} \times \frac{1 \text{ mile}}{5,280 \text{ feet}}$$

Notice that every unit that appears in the numerator also appears in the denominator (and vice versa), *except* for miles, which is the unit in which the result is desired to be. Now cancel units and simplify the math, estimating if necessary at the end:

$$\frac{3,200 \cancel{\text{ feet}}}{1 \cancel{\text{ second}}} \times \frac{60 \cancel{\text{ seconds}}}{1 \cancel{\text{ minute}}} \times \frac{60 \cancel{\text{ minutes}}}{1 \cancel{\text{ hour}}} \times \frac{15 \cancel{\text{ hours}}}{1} \times \frac{1 \text{ mile}}{5,280 \cancel{\text{ feet}}}$$

$$\frac{3,200 \cdot 60 \cdot 60 \cdot 15}{5,280} \text{ miles} = \left(\frac{48,000}{5,280} \right) (3,600) \text{ miles}$$

The fraction in this expression is a little bit less than 10, so the correct answer should be slightly less than 36,000, or slightly less than 3.6×10^4. Therefore, the correct answer must be 3.3×10^4. You can also crunch these computations in your calculator. The correct answer is (C).

112. **(J)** k^2 Pre-Algebra   Number Properties and Operations (Odds and Evens)

When a problem is hard to read and interpret, as this one is, try plugging in actual numbers. "… k is a positive integer" means that k is 1, or 2, or 3, etc. "The sum of the k smallest distinct odd positive integers" is a rough phrase. Start from the end:

"odd positive integers" = 1, 3, 5, etc.

"distinct odd positive integers" = you can't double-count 1, or 3, etc.

"smallest distinct odd positive integers" = 1, 3, 5, etc. but not skipping any.

"k smallest distinct odd positive integers": Say $k = 2$. Then you want the 2 "smallest distinct odd positive integers," in other words, 1 and 3.

"The sum of the k smallest …": If $k = 2$, then you take the 2 smallest odds and you add them: $1 + 3 = 4$. So try a few different values of k, and look for the pattern:

$k = 1$ →   Take the sum of the 1 smallest distinct odd positive integer = Take the smallest = 1.

$k = 2$ →   Take the sum of the 2 smallest … = $1 + 3 = 4$.

$k = 3$ →   Take the sum of the 3 smallest … = $1 + 3 + 5 = 9$.

If you don't already notice the squares, test the results against the answers. The only answer that fits is k^2. This cool pattern is evident in a square array of dots, which can always be regrouped into a sequence of the smallest positive odd numbers:

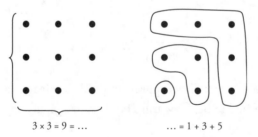

$3 \times 3 = 9 = \ldots$ $\ldots = 1 + 3 + 5$

The correct answer is (J).

113. **(E)** 3.91×10^7 Pre-Algebra   Arithmetic Word Problems (Converting/Canceling Units)

You need to carefully convert 3,700 miles per second into an unknown quantity of feet by setting up an expression and canceling units. To do this, set up the following expression, making sure that all units not desired in the result will be canceled out (i.e., all units *except* for feet):

MANHATTAN
PREP

$$\frac{3,700 \text{ miles}}{1 \text{ second}} \times \frac{60 \text{ seconds}}{1 \text{ minute}} \times \frac{1 \text{ minute}}{30} \times \frac{5,280 \text{ feet}}{1 \text{ mile}}$$

Notice that every unit that appears in the numerator also appears in the denominator (and vice versa), *except* for feet, which is the unit in which the result is desired to be. Now cancel units and simplify the math, estimating if necessary at the end:

$$\frac{3,700 \,\cancel{\text{miles}}}{1 \,\cancel{\text{second}}} \times \frac{60 \,\cancel{\text{seconds}}}{1 \,\cancel{\text{minute}}} \times \frac{1 \,\cancel{\text{minute}}}{30} \times \frac{5,280 \text{ feet}}{1 \text{ mile}}$$

$$\frac{3,700 \cdot 60 \cdot 5,280}{30} \text{ feet} = (2)(3,700)(5,280) \text{ feet}$$

In order to maintain accuracy of the number of decimal places, multiply the first two numbers together, convert to scientific notation, and estimate:

$$(2)(3,700)(5,280) \text{ feet} = 7,400 \times 5,280$$
$$\approx \left(7.4 \times 10^3\right) \times \left(5.3 \times 10^3\right)$$
$$\approx 38 \times 10^6$$
$$\approx 3.8 \times 10^7 \text{ feet}$$

Thus, the correct answer must be 3.91×10^7. You can also crunch these numbers in your calculator. The correct answer is (E).

114. **(H)** 65   Pre-Algebra   Statistics (Averages)

In this problem, you must take the average of three averages. However, it is given in the problem that some of the observations occur more frequently in the population whose average you are measuring; such problems involving averages are called "weighted averages," because you must weight the numbers you are averaging by the relative frequency with which they occur. By multiplying the average observations for each group by the number of items in that group, you arrive at the sum of the values contributed to the overall average by each group; divide by the sum of the weights to arrive at the overall, "weighted" average.

This process can be expressed mathematically as:

$$\frac{\sum \Big(\text{Weights for each group}\Big) \times \Big(\text{Average value in each group}\Big)}{\sum \Big(\text{Weights for each group}\Big)}$$

To illustrate: there are 200 adult males that have an average height of 72 inches. Since the sum of the heights of all of the adult males must equal $200 \times 72 = 14{,}400$ inches, use that weighted sum in your calculation. Similarly, the 100 adult females have an average height of 68 inches. The total combined height of the adult females is therefore $100 \times 68 = 6{,}800$ inches. Finally, the 100 children in the town have an average height of 48 inches. The total combined height of the children is therefore $48(100) = 4{,}800$ inches. Find the average height of the entire population of the town by summing the combined heights, and dividing by the sum of the weights (i.e., dividing by the number of people in the town):

MANHATTAN
PREP   465

$$\frac{14,400 + 6,800 + 4,800}{200 + 100 + 100} = \frac{26,000}{400} = 65$$

Therefore, the weighted average height (i.e., the average height) of the people in the town is 65 inches. The correct answer is (H).

115. **(B)** $65   Pre-Algebra   Percents (Percentage Change)

In this percentage change problem, you are given the resulting amount, rather than the original amount. In such cases it is often best to assign a variable to the original amount (say, x) and solve for it.

For percentage change problems, use a multiple to represent the percentage change. For example, a 20% increase is equal to multiplying the original number by $1\frac{20}{100} = 1.2$. Similarly, a 15% increase is equal to multiplying the number by 1.15. When a problem includes successive percent changes, these multiples can be multiplied together: $(1.2)(1.15) = 1.38$, which signifies a total increase of 38%.

Since increasing x by 38% yields 90, set up an equation to solve for x:

$$x + (38\%)x = \$90$$
$$1.38x = \$90$$
$$x = \frac{\$90}{1.38}$$

This number can be computed exactly with a calculator ($65.22, to the nearest penny), or it can be estimated: $90 ÷ 1.35 is $66\frac{2}{3}$, and $90 ÷ 1.4 is about $64.3. Thus, the correct answer should be around $65, and that is indeed one of the answer choices (no other answer choice is between $64 and 66\frac{2}{3}$). The correct answer is therefore (B).

MANHATTAN
PREP

Chapter *of* 12

5lb. Book of ACT® Practice Problems

Math:
Elementary Algebra

In This Chapter...

Elementary Algebra Problems & Solutions

Chapter 12

Math: Elementary Algebra

The Math problems in this chapter are drawn from elementary algebra—think Algebra 1 class. The topics include the following:

1. Expressing Relationships. Writing down mathematical relationships using algebra.

2. Linear Equations. Solving or otherwise working with this kind of equation.

3. Evaluate or Simplify. Simplifying expressions, distributing and factoring, substituting variables, solving systems of equations.

4. Polynomials and Exponents. Dealing with these expressions at an Algebra 1 level.

5. Simple Quadratics. Factoring or otherwise dealing with simple quadratic equations.

6. Other Elementary Algebra. Inequalities, statistics that require algebra, and proportions that require algebra.

How should you use this chapter? Here are some recommendations, according to the level you've reached in ACT Math.

1. Fundamentals. Start slowly with the easier problems at the beginning. Do at least some of these problems untimed. This way, you give yourself a chance to think deeply about the principles at work. Review the solutions closely, and articulate what you've learned. Redo problems as necessary.

2. Fixes. Do a few problems untimed, examine the results, learn your lessons, then test yourself with longer timed sets.

3. Tweaks. Confirm your mastery by doing longer sets of problems under timed conditions. Aim to improve the speed and ease of your solution process. Mix the problems up by jumping around in the chapter. Definitely push to the harder, higher-numbered problems.

Good luck on the problems!

1. If $15 - \dfrac{6}{3b} = 10$, then $b = ?$

    A. $-\dfrac{10}{3}$

    B. $-\dfrac{3}{5}$

    C. $-\dfrac{2}{25}$

    D. $\dfrac{3}{10}$

    E. $\dfrac{2}{5}$

2. The expression $3p^3 \cdot \left(2p^2\right)^2$ is equivalent to which of the expressions below?

    F. $12p^6$

    G. $6p^7$

    H. $12p^7$

    J. $6p^{12}$

    K. $7p^{12}$

3. If $\dfrac{2z}{3} + 6 = \dfrac{3}{2}$, then what is the value of z?

    A. $-\dfrac{27}{4}$

    B. $-\dfrac{3}{4}$

    C. $\dfrac{8}{3}$

    D. $\dfrac{27}{4}$

    E. 9

4. If $y = -4$, what is $\dfrac{(y-4)^2}{y}$?

    F. 0

    G. -16

    H. -4

    J. 4

    K. 16

5. Assuming that $z \neq 0$, the expression $\dfrac{9z^6}{6z^2}$ is equivalent to which of the expressions below?

    A. $\dfrac{3z^3}{2}$

    B. $\dfrac{3z^4}{2}$

    C. $\dfrac{z^4}{3}$

    D. $3z^3$

    E. $2z^8$

6. The expression $[w - (x + y)]z$ is equivalent to which of the following?

    F. $wz - xz + yz$

    G. $wz - xz - yz$

    H. $w - xz + yz$

    J. $w - x + yz$

    K. $w - x - yz$

7. If $z = 6$, what is $\dfrac{4 - z^2}{2 - z}$?

    A. 10

    B. 8

    C. 6

    D. -1

    E. -4

12

MANHATTAN
PREP

8. The equation $3z - \left(\dfrac{z}{2} + 5\right) = 10$ is true when z equals which of the following values?

   F. 2

   G. $\dfrac{5}{2}$

   H. 3

   J. 6

   K. 15

9. If $5z + 7 = 12z - 2$, then $z = ?$

   A. $\dfrac{9}{7}$

   B. $\dfrac{7}{9}$

   C. $\dfrac{5}{7}$

   D. $\dfrac{7}{15}$

   E. $\dfrac{9}{17}$

10. $4(p - 2) = 17 - p$

The equation above is true for what value of p?

   F. $\dfrac{3}{5}$

   G. $\dfrac{9}{5}$

   H. 3

   J. 5

   K. $\dfrac{25}{3}$

11. A spring that is stretched x centimeters from its normal position stores energy, E, in joules, according to the equation $E = (2.4)x^2$. By how many centimeters, approximately, must the spring be stretched from its normal position for it to store 0.53 joules of energy?

   A. 0.22

   B. 0.47

   C. 0.67

   D. 0.98

   E. 1.13

12. The relationship between temperature in degrees Fahrenheit, F, and units kelvin, K, is given by the formula $K = \dfrac{5}{9}(F - 32°) + 273.15$. Which of the following readings, in kelvins, is equivalent to a Fahrenheit reading of 77° (rounded to the nearest hundredth decimal place)?

   F. −273.15

   G. 273.15

   H. 298.15

   J. 315.93

   K. 350.15

13. If $11y - 13 = 17y + 3$, then $y = ?$

   A. $-\dfrac{2}{3}$

   B. $-\dfrac{5}{3}$

   C. $-\dfrac{8}{3}$

   D. $-\dfrac{11}{3}$

   E. $-\dfrac{14}{3}$

12

14. If $abc > 0$, $\dfrac{a}{b} = \dfrac{1}{2}$, $\dfrac{b}{c} = 8$, and $c = 4$, what is the value of a?

   F. 2

   G. 8

   H. 16

   J. 32

   K. 64

15. If $6(14 - y) = 8$, what is the value of y?

   A. 12

   B. $\dfrac{38}{3}$

   C. $\dfrac{46}{3}$

   D. 16

   E. 34

16. Variables x, y, and z are integers such that $xyz > 0$. If $xy = 30$, $\dfrac{x}{z} = \dfrac{2}{3}$, and $z = 9$, what is the value of y?

   F. $\dfrac{10}{3}$

   G. 5

   H. 6

   J. 20

   K. 180

17. The All Stars earned an average of 42 points during their last 5 games. What must they score in their next game in order for the average of all 6 games to be 45 points?

   A. 10

   B. 15

   C. 48

   D. 52

   E. 60

18. If $5(3 - z) = 4 - z$, what is the value of z?

   F. $-1\dfrac{1}{4}$

   G. $-4\dfrac{1}{3}$

   H. $5\dfrac{1}{2}$

   J. $4\dfrac{1}{3}$

   K. $2\dfrac{3}{4}$

19. The time it takes to complete a certain job is directly proportional to the number of units produced. If it takes 22 minutes to produce 18 units, how many units are produced in 33 minutes?

   A. 12

   B. 27

   C. 29

   D. 40

   E. 54

20. We-Haul trucking company has 6 trucks that have an average towing capacity of 2 tons, as well as 3 trucks that have an average towing capacity of t tons. Solving which of the following equations for t gives the average towing capacity of 2.8 tons for all 9 trucks?

   F. $2 + t = \dfrac{2.8}{9}$

   G. $\dfrac{2 + t}{9} = 2.8$

   H. $6(2) + 3(t) = \dfrac{2.8}{9}$

   J. $\dfrac{6(2) + 3(t)}{9} = 2.8$

   K. $\dfrac{2}{6} + \dfrac{t}{3} = 2.8$

21. If $3y = -9(8 - y)$, what is the value of y?

    A. -4

    B. -2

    C. 0

    D. 4

    E. 12

22. For any value of z, $(5z - 1)^2$ is equal to which of the following?

    F. $10z^2 - 2z + 1$

    G. $25z^2 - 10z + 1$

    H. $25z^2 - 5z + 5$

    J. $10z - 2$

    K. $25z - 5z$

23. What is the value of a if $-2(a - 4) = -3a + 3$?

    A. -5

    B. -1

    C. 2

    D. 3

    E. 4

24. $\dfrac{8(x + 2) + 9}{9(x + 2) + 5}$

The expression given above is equivalent to which of the following expressions?

    F. $\dfrac{25}{23}$

    G. $\dfrac{17}{14}$

    H. $\dfrac{8}{5}$

    J. $\dfrac{8x + 25}{9x + 23}$

    K. $\dfrac{17x + 16}{14x + 18}$

25. $(2s + 3)(2s - 3)$ is equivalent to

    A. $4s - 2s + 6$

    B. $4s^2 - 2s + 6$

    C. $4s^2 - 9$

    D. $2s - 9$

    E. $2s^2 - 6s - 9$

26. The value of x is directly proportional to the value of y. When $x = 9$, $y = 12$. What is x when $y = 16$?

    F. $\dfrac{1}{12}$

    G. $\dfrac{64}{3}$

    H. 5

    J. 12

    K. 13

27. Which of the following expressions is equivalent to the one given below?

$$\frac{5(z + 2) - 4}{18 - 4(z + 2)}$$

    A. $\dfrac{5z + 14}{26 - 4z}$

    B. $\dfrac{5z + 6}{10 - 4z}$

    C. $\dfrac{z + 2}{14z + 28}$

    D. $\dfrac{5}{18}$

    E. $\dfrac{1}{14}$

12

28. What are the values for x that satisfy the equation $(2x + a)(x - b) = 0$?

    F. $\dfrac{-a}{2}$ and b

    G. $2a$ and $-b$

    H. $-2a$ and b

    J. $\dfrac{-ab}{2}$

    K. $\dfrac{a}{2}$ and $-b$

29. The value of s is directly proportional to the value of t. When $s = 9$, $t = 36$. What is s when $t = 30$?

    A. $\dfrac{1}{5}$

    B. $\dfrac{15}{2}$

    C. 3

    D. 5

    E. 15

30. $7(4 + 2y) - 3(4 - 2y) =$

    F. $8y + 16$

    G. $20y + 16$

    H. $20y + 40$

    J. $26y + 28$

    K. $26y + 40$

31. If $(y + m)(y - n) = 0$, and m and n are distinct numbers, then which of the following MUST be true?

    A. Either $y = m$ or $y = n$

    B. Either $y = -m$ or $y = n$

    C. Either $y = m$ or $y = -n$

    D. $y = m - n$

    E. $y = -mn$

32. Two friends, Bill and Todd, have finished having dinner together and are trying to figure out how to split the check. If the total cost of the check is $52, and Bill ordered items costing $14 more than what Todd ordered, how much does Bill owe for the check? (Ignore all tax and tip considerations.)

    F. $19

    G. $26

    H. $33

    J. $36

    K. $40

33. The expression $-3(z + 1) + 5(3 + 2z)$ is equivalent to which of the following, for all real number values of z?

    A. $7z + 12$

    B. $7z + 18$

    C. $8z + 16$

    D. $10z + 14$

    E. $10z + 18$

34. If the quadratic expression $(4z - 1)^2$ is written in the form $az^2 + bz + c$, where a, b, and c are integers, what is the value of the product abc?

    F. 16

    G. 32

    H. -16

    J. -64

    K. -128

35. If $a + 2b = 14$ and $a - 2b = 42$, what is the value of b?

    A. 14

    B. 7

    C. 0

    D. -7

    E. -14

36. Which of the following is the equation $7(a - b) = 4$ solved for b?

   F. $b = \dfrac{4}{7}a$

   G. $b = \dfrac{4}{7} - a$

   H. $b = a - \dfrac{4}{7}$

   J. $b = 28 - a$

   K. $b = a - 28$

37. What number can be subtracted from both the numerator and denominator of $\dfrac{7}{10}$ to get $\dfrac{2}{5}$?

   A. -5

   B. $\dfrac{4}{7}$

   C. 1

   D. $4\dfrac{1}{2}$

   E. 5

38. Which of the following is the equation $6(p - q) = 3$ solved for q?

   F. $q = 18 - p$

   G. $q = p - 18$

   H. $q = \dfrac{1}{2}p$

   J. $q = p - \dfrac{1}{2}$

   K. $q = \dfrac{1}{2} - p$

39. At work this week, David was able to edit over 25% of the documents his boss delivered to him. If there were 140 documents in total, which of the following expressions is true about E, the minimum number of documents that David was able to edit?

   A. $E > 36$

   B. $E < 36$

   C. $E > 35$

   D. $E = 35$

   E. $E < 35$

40. In a recent shipment, fewer than 30% of the items arrived were damaged. If there were 270 items in the shipment, which of the following expressions is true about d, the maximum number of items damaged in the shipment?

   F. $d > 80$

   G. $d < 80$

   H. $d > 81$

   J. $d = 81$

   K. $d < 81$

41. Which of the following is equivalent to the expression $(-n^2 + 2n + 1) - 2(n^2 + 4n - 1)$?

   A. $n^2 + 10n - 1$

   B. $n^2 + 6n - 3$

   C. $-3n^2 + 10n + 1$

   D. $-3n^2 - 6n + 1$

   E. $-3n^2 - 6n + 3$

12

42. What is the value of the expression $(z-1) \cdot 3(z-2)^2$ for $z = 3$?

   F. 2

   G. 3

   H. 5

   J. 6

   K. 9

43. A company that rents gas-powered scooters charges customers $15 per day to rent the scooter, plus an additional $0.15 for each mile the scooter is driven. If Charlie rents a scooter for x days and drives it y miles each day, what will be the total cost of her rental in terms of x and y?

   A. $15x + \$0.15xy$

   B. $15y + \$0.15x$

   C. $15x + \$0.15y$

   D. $15x + y$

   E. $15.15xy$

44. What is the value of the expression $h^2 \cdot (5-h)$ when $h = -4$?

   F. −80

   G. −16

   H. 16

   J. 80

   K. 144

45. A mobile phone provider offers a plan that costs $60.00 for unlimited calls and $0.20 for every 10 text messages sent. Which of the following expressions represents a customer's monthly phone bill, in dollars, for the use of $10t$ text messages sent and unlimited calls? Assume that t is an integer.

   A. $60.20

   B. $60.00t + \$0.20$

   C. $60.00 + \$0.20 + \$t$

   D. $60.00 + \$0.20t$

   E. $60.00 + \$2.00t$

46. What is the value of x that satisfies the equation $4(x-3) = x + 6 \cdot 2^2$?

   F. 3

   G. 4

   H. 9

   J. 12

   K. 15

47. North Star Electric Company charges customers $18.00 per month for electric service. In addition, customers are charged $0.16 per kilowatt-hour (kWh) used in excess of 30 kWh (the first 30 kWh are included in the monthly account charge). Which of the following expressions represents a customer's monthly electric cost, in dollars, for the use of s kWh, assuming that $s > 30$?

   A. $18.00 + \$0.16s$

   B. $16.00 + \$0.18s$

   C. $16.00 + \$0.18s - 30s$

   D. $18.00 + \$0.16s - 30$

   E. $13.20 + \$0.16s$

12

MANHATTAN
PREP

48. Given that $x - y = 4$, what is the value of $2x - 2y - \dfrac{y-x}{2} + (y-x)^2$?

F. 6

G. 8

H. 14

J. 22

K. 26

49. What is the value of z that satisfies the equation $-4z + 5 = 2(z - 3)$?

A. $\dfrac{11}{6}$

B. $\dfrac{11}{3}$

C. $2\dfrac{1}{3}$

D. 2

E. 3

50. Which of the following expressions is equivalent to $-4y^2(x^3y^2 - 3x^2y^8)$?

F. $3x^2y^{10} - 4x^3y^4$

G. $4x^3y^4 + 12x^2y^{10}$

H. $12x^2y^{10} - 4x^3y^4$

J. $12x^5y^{10} - 4x^5y^4$

K. $8x^{-1}y^6$

51. The combined weight of 2 objects is 48 pounds. If the heavier object weighs 6 pounds more than twice the weight of the lighter object, what is the weight of the heavier object?

A. 14 pounds

B. 24 pounds

C. 28 pounds

D. 30 pounds

E. 34 pounds

52. For all values of a and b, $4ab(a^2 - 2ab^2)$ will always be equal to which of the following?

F. $4a^3b - 8a^2b^3$

G. $4a^2b - 8a^2b^2$

H. $8ab^3 - 4a^2b^2$

J. $8a^2b^3 - 4a^2b$

K. $8a^3b - 4a^2b^3$

53. If $x^2 = 36$ and $y^2 = 64$, which of the following CANNOT be a possible value of $x + y$?

A. -14

B. -2

C. 0

D. 2

E. 14

54. In the table below, a, b, and c represent different integers. Which of the following expressions could be the sum of the empty cells, in order that the sums of each row and each column, but not of the diagonals, are equal for all values of a, b, and c?

a	b	
	c	b

F. $a + b + c$

G. $2a + 2b + c$

H. $a + 2b + 2c$

J. $2a + b + 2c$

K. $2a + 2b + 2c$

55. The integer x is subtracted from 6 and this result is then multiplied by 5. Then, the result is added to 4. Which of the following is equivalent to this expression?

   A. $x - 34$

   B. $x + 26$

   C. $5x - 26$

   D. $34 - 5x$

   E. $26 - 5x$

56. 4 is subtracted from the integer y, and the result is divided by 8. This expression is equal to 7 more than half of y. What is the value of y?

   F. -20

   G. -10

   H. -4

   J. 12

   K. 20

57. Which of the following is a solution to the equation $h^2 + 3h = 88$?

   A. -11

   B. -8

   C. -3

   D. 3

   E. 11

58. Jeremy and Andrew collect baseball cards of their favorite professional players. Jeremy currently collects x playing cards per month, and Andrew currently collects y playing cards per month. Jeremy currently has 150 baseball cards and Andrew has 190. If Jeremy's collection will have as many baseball cards as Andrew's in 5 months, what is $x - y$?

   F. 45

   G. 35

   H. 12

   J. 10

   K. 8

59. Which of the following is a solution to the equation $y^2 = 16y$?

   A. 32

   B. 16

   C. 8

   D. 4

   E. 2

60. Luis is a photographer who currently earns \$50,000 per year. Luis's wife is a dentist, and she earns \$74,000 per year. Luis expects that his business will continue to expand and that his income will increase \$4,000 each year for the foreseeable future. Meanwhile, Luis's wife expects her annual income to increase only \$1,000 each year. If z represents the number of years it will take for Luis's income to be equal to that of his wife, which of the following equations could be solved to find the value of z?

   F. $\$50{,}000 + \$4{,}000z = \$74{,}000 + \$1{,}000z$

   G. $\$50{,}000 - \$4{,}000z = \$74{,}000 - \$1{,}000z$

   H. $\$50{,}000 - \$3{,}000z = \$74{,}000 + \$3{,}000z$

   J. $\$50{,}000 + \$74{,}000 = -\$4{,}000z - \$1{,}000z$

   K. $\$50{,}000 - \$74{,}000 = \$3{,}000z + \$3{,}000z$

61. Let $3a + 2b = 3$ and $4a + 5b = 11$. What is the value of $5a + 8b$?

   A. -19

   B. -8

   C. -1

   D. 3

   E. 19

MANHATTAN
PREP

62. Which of the following is a solution to the equation $x^3 - 64x = 0$?

   F. −2

   G. 4

   H. −8

   J. 16

   K. −32

63. Let $2x - 5y = 16$ and $5x + 3y = 9$. What is the value of $12x + y$?

   A. −34

   B. −3

   C. −2

   D. 3

   E. 34

64. What number can be added to both the numerator and denominator of $\frac{2}{7}$ to get $\frac{3}{4}$?

   F. $\frac{6}{7}$

   G. 13

   H. −5

   J. $\frac{21}{8}$

   K. 28

65. What is the product of the 2 solutions for a in the quadratic equation $a^2 + 8a - 33 = 0$?

   A. −33

   B. −11

   C. −8

   D. 8

   E. 14

66. What is the sum of the 2 solutions for x in the quadratic equation $x^2 + x - 56 = 0$?

   F. 15

   G. 13

   H. −1

   J. 1

   K. 7

67. For all pairs of real numbers q and h where $q = 11h - 13$, $h = ?$

   A. $11q + 13$

   B. $\frac{q}{11} - 13$

   C. $\frac{q}{11} + 13$

   D. $\frac{q - 13}{11}$

   E. $\frac{q + 13}{11}$

12

Use the following information to answer question 68.

The parabola $y = -0.04x^2 + 100$ and the line segments from A (–50, 0) to B (0, 100) and from B to C (50, 0) are displayed in the standard (x, y) coordinate plane below.

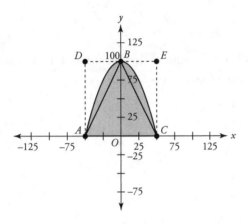

68. What is the y-coordinate on the parabola when $x = -40$?

   F. –40

   G. 20

   H. 36

   J. 100

   K. 164

69. How many distinct, real-number solutions does the equation $v^2 - 14v + 49 = 0$ have?

   A. 0

   B. 1

   C. 2

   D. 3

   E. Cannot be determined from the given information

70. If $y = x - 3$, then $(y - x)^{(x-y)} = ?$

   F. –27

   G. –9

   H. 9

   J. 18

   K. 27

71. The smaller of two numbers is 3 less than half the larger number. The sum of twice the larger and 4 times the smaller number is 36. If b is the larger number, which equation below determines the correct value of b?

   A. $2b + (2b - 3) = 36$

   B. $2b + 4\left(\dfrac{1}{2}b + 3\right) = 36$

   C. $2b + 4\left(\dfrac{1}{2}b - 3\right) = 36$

   D. $4b + 2(2b - 3) = 36$

   E. $4b + 2\left(\dfrac{1}{2}b + 3\right) = 36$

72. Which of the following expressions is equivalent to $\left(a + \dfrac{2}{b}\right)^2$?

   F. $2a + 2 \cdot \dfrac{4}{b}$

   G. $2a + \dfrac{4}{b} + \dfrac{4}{b^2}$

   H. $a^2 + 4ab + 4b^2$

   J. $a^2 + \dfrac{4a}{b} + 4b^2$

   K. $a^2 + \dfrac{4a}{b} + \dfrac{4}{b^2}$

12

MANHATTAN
PREP

73. The difference between two numbers is 6. Three times the larger number exceeds 4 times the smaller number by 2. If x is the smaller number and y is the larger number, which of the following systems of equations determines the correct values of x and y ?

- **A.** $y - x = 6$ and $3y = 4x + 2$
- **B.** $x - y = 6$ and $3y = 4x - 2$
- **C.** $y - x = 6$ and $3x = 4y + 2$
- **D.** $x - y = 6$ and $3y = 2x - 4$
- **E.** $y - x = 6$ and $3x = 2y + 4$

74. Todd is playing a carnival game in which a ball of 1 of 3 colors (red, green, or purple) comes out of the machine whenever he puts money into it. Red balls are worth 1 point; green balls are worth 5 points; purple balls are worth 10 points. He has 5 times as many red balls as green ones, and he has 1 more purple ball than he has green balls. Currently, he has a total of 150 points. How many purple balls does he have?

- **F.** 7
- **G.** 8
- **H.** 12
- **J.** 18
- **K.** 35

75. Which of the following equations has the solutions $x = 2y^2$ and $x = -3z$?

- **A.** $x^2 - 2x(3z + y^2) - 6yz = 0$
- **B.** $x^2 + 3xz - 2y^2(3z + x) = 0$
- **C.** $x^2 - 3xz + 2y^2(3z + x) = 0$
- **D.** $x^2 + 6xz^2 + 2y^2(z - 3x) = 0$
- **E.** $x^2 - 6y^2z + 2x(z + 3y) = 0$

76. If $x = 3b - 2c + 7$, how does the value of x change when b is increased by 2 and c is decreased by 1?

- **F.** x is unchanged
- **G.** x decreases by 1
- **H.** x increases by 4
- **J.** x increases by 8
- **K.** x increases by 10

77. If $y = a^2$ and $x = a + 2$, which of the following equations correctly expresses y in terms of x?

- **A.** $y = x^2 - 4$
- **B.** $y = x^2 - 2$
- **C.** $y = x^2 + 2$
- **D.** $y = (x + 2)^2$
- **E.** $y = (x - 2)^2$

78. If $x = 5s + 3r - 6$, how does the value of x change when r is increased by 3 and s is decreased by 1?

- **F.** x decreases by 2
- **G.** x is unchanged
- **H.** x increases by 1
- **J.** x increases by 2
- **K.** x increases by 4

79. At a Mexican restaurant, Sally bought 3 tacos and a burrito for a cost of $7.40. The next day, she bought a taco and 2 burritos for a cost of $7.30. Assuming the prices for each item are unchanged each day, what is the cost of one taco and one burrito?

- **A.** $2.90
- **B.** $4.40
- **C.** $5.10
- **D.** $5.40
- **E.** $6.10

12

80. A sample of bacteria has a population that is expected to grow and then decay. It is modeled by the equation $p(t) = -4t(t - 25)$, where t is time measured in hours. At which of the following values of t is the population expected to equal 400?

   F. 10

   G. 12

   H. 15

   J. 20

   K. 24

81. Tammy is an avid golfer and mathematics enthusiast. One day, while preparing to hit a bucket of golf balls at a driving range, she observed, "The number of balls I have in this bucket squared, minus 37 times the number of balls in the bucket, is equal to 120!" How many golf balls were in the bucket Tammy had?

   A. 40

   B. 37

   C. 19

   D. 16

   E. 3

> **Use the following information to answer question 82.**

A portion of the circle $y^2 + (x - 3)^2 = 9$ is displayed in the standard (x, y) coordinate plane below. The circle is centered at $(3, 0)$. In addition, the line segments from A $(0, 0)$ to B $(0, -3)$, B to C $(6, -3)$, C to D $(6, 0)$, and D to A are shown.

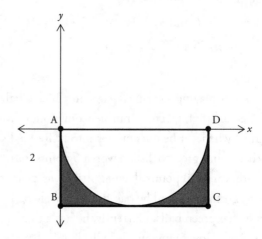

82. What is the y-coordinate for the point on the portion of the circle shown with an x-coordinate of 1?

   F. $-\sqrt{5}$

   G. $\sqrt{5}$

   H. 2

   J. -2

   K. -8

83. Assume that $(x - 4)$ is a factor of $2x^2 - 4x - z$. What is the value of z?

   A. 2

   B. 4

   C. 8

   D. 14

   E. 16

84. Which of the following are solutions for the equation $x^2 + x(5s - 4r^2) - 20r^2s = 0$?

   F. $x = -4r^2$ and $x = s^2$

   G. $x = -5r^2$ and $x = 4s$

   H. $x = 5r^2$ and $x = -4s$

   J. $x = -4r^2$ and $x = 5s$

   K. $x = 4r^2$ and $x = -5s$

85. If $y = t + 5$ and $x = 3t + 2$, which of the following equations correctly expresses y in terms of x?

   A. $y = \dfrac{x + 13}{3}$

   B. $y = \dfrac{x - 13}{3}$

   C. $y = \dfrac{x - 17}{3}$

   D. $y = 3x - 13$

   E. $y = 3x + 13$

12

MANHATTAN
PREP

Answer Key

Write in whether you got each problem right or wrong (or left it blank). If your answer was correct, put a 1 in every blank to the right of that problem. Sum up each column and compare your total to the total possible "Out Of" points.

Problem	Correct Answer	Right/Wrong/Blank	Problem	Correct Answer	Right/Wrong/Blank
1	E		29	B	
2	H		30	G	
3	A		31	B	
4	G		32	H	
5	B		33	A	
6	G		34	K	
7	B		35	D	
8	J		36	H	
9	A		37	E	
10	J		38	J	
11	B		39	C	
12	H		40	K	
13	C		41	E	
14	H		42	J	
15	B		43	A	
16	G		44	K	
17	E		45	D	
18	K		46	J	
19	B		47	E	
20	J		48	K	
21	E		49	A	
22	G		50	H	
23	A		51	E	
24	J		52	F	
25	C		53	C	
26	J		54	J	
27	B		55	D	
28	F		56	F	

12

Problem	Correct Answer	Right/ Wrong/Blank
57	A	
58	K	
59	B	
60	F	
61	E	
62	H	
63	E	
64	G	
65	A	
66	H	
67	E	
68	H	
69	B	
70	F	
71	C	
72	K	
73	A	
74	G	
75	B	
76	J	
77	E	
78	K	
79	B	
80	J	
81	A	
82	F	

Problem	Correct Answer	Right/ Wrong/Blank
83	E	
84	K	
85	A	
Total		
Out Of		85

Elementary Algebra Solutions

1. **(E)** $\dfrac{2}{5}$ Elementary Algebra   Linear Equations

Combine like terms by subtracting 15 from both sides of the equation. Multiply both sides by $-3b$, divide by 15, and reduce:

$$15-\frac{6}{3b}=10$$

$$-\frac{6}{3b}=-5$$

$$6=15b$$

$$\frac{6}{15}=b$$

$$\frac{2}{5}=b$$

The correct answer is (E).

2. **(H)** $12p^7$ Elementary Algebra   Exponents

When you raise an expression $(2p^2)$ to a power, you apply that power to every term inside the parentheses, $2^2\left(p^2\right)^2$, and when you raise base to a power and then to a power again, you multiply the exponents. Since the dot means multiply, when you multiply expressions such as p^3 and p^4 with the same base (p), add the exponents:

$$3p^3\cdot\left(2p^2\right)^2=3p^3\cdot2^2\left(p^2\right)^2=3p^3\cdot2^2\,p^4$$

$$=(3\cdot4)\cdot\left(p^3\cdot p^4\right)=12p^7$$

The correct answer is (H).

3. **(A)** $-\dfrac{27}{4}$ Elementary Algebra   Linear Equations

Combine like terms by subtracting 6 from both sides and finding a common denominator. Cross-multiply to get rid of the denominators and then divide by 4:

$$\frac{2z}{3}+6=\frac{3}{2}$$

$$\frac{2z}{3}=\frac{3}{2}-6$$

$$\frac{2z}{3}=\frac{3}{2}-\frac{12}{2}$$

$$\frac{2z}{3}=-\frac{9}{2}$$

$$4z=-27$$

$$z=-\frac{27}{4}$$

The correct answer is (A).

12

MANHATTAN
PREP

4.   **(G)** –16   Elementary Algebra   Evaluate or Simplify

Substitute –4 for every instance of y in the expression $\dfrac{(y-4)^2}{y}$ to get:

$$\dfrac{(-4-4)^2}{-4}$$

Simplify using the standard order of operations (often called PEMDAS) to get:

$$\dfrac{(-8)^2}{-4} = \dfrac{64}{-4} = -16$$

The correct answer is (G).

5.   **(B)** $\dfrac{3z^4}{2}$ Elementary Algebra   Exponents

When you divide expressions such as z^6 and z^2 with the same base (z), subtract the exponents:

$$\dfrac{9z^6}{6z^2} = \left(\dfrac{9}{6}\right)\left(\dfrac{z^6}{z^2}\right) = \dfrac{3}{2} \cdot z^4 = \dfrac{3z^4}{2}$$

The correct answer is (B).

6.   **(G)** $wz - xz - yz$ Elementary Algebra   Evaluate or Simplify

One way to approach this problem is from the inside out. First, simplify the expression within the square brackets:

$w - (x + y) = w - x - y$ Notice that the minus sign must be distributed to the y.

Finally, since the whole expression in the square brackets is being multiplied by z, distribute a z to each of those terms:

$[w - x - y]z = wz - xz - yz$

The correct answer is (G).

7.   **(B)** 8   Elementary Algebra   Evaluate or Simplify

Substitute 6 for every instance of z in the expression $\dfrac{4 - z^2}{2 - z}$ to get:

$$\dfrac{4 - 6^2}{2 - 6}$$

Simplify using the standard order of operations (abbreviated as PEMDAS) to get:

$$\dfrac{4 - 36}{2 - 6} = \dfrac{-32}{-4} = 8$$

The correct answer is (B).

8. **(J)** 6   Elementary Algebra   Linear Equations

An equation is true when the two sides are equal. To determine the value of z, solve the equation by isolating z. Start by distributing the negative and then combine like terms and simplify:

$$3z - \left(\frac{z}{2} + 5\right) = 10$$
$$3z - \frac{z}{2} - 5 = 10$$
$$\frac{6z}{2} - \frac{z}{2} = 15$$
$$\frac{5z}{2} = 15$$
$$5z = 30$$
$$z = 6$$

The correct answer is (J).

9. **(A)** $\frac{9}{7}$ Elementary Algebra   Linear Equations

Combine like terms, subtracting $5z$ from both sides and adding 2 to both sides. Finally, divide both sides by 7 to isolate z.

$$5z + 7 = 12z - 2$$
$$7 = 7z - 2$$
$$9 = 7z$$
$$\frac{9}{7} = z$$

The correct answer is (A).

10. **(J)** 5   Elementary Algebra   Linear Equations

An equation is true when the two sides are equal. To determine the value of p, solve the equation by isolating p. Start by distributing the 4 and then combine like terms and simplify:

$$4(p - 2) = 17 - p$$
$$4p - 8 = 17 - p$$
$$5p = 25$$
$$p = 5$$

The correct answer is (J).

11. **(B)** 0.47   Elementary Algebra   Simple Quadratics

You are given an equation for the energy, E, stored in a particular stretched spring: $E = (2.4)x^2$, where x is the distance the spring is stretched. The units of distance (centimeters) and energy (joules) are consistent throughout the problem, so you can ignore them. Note that you have to solve for the x that results in a given E (= 0.53), so don't plug in 0.53 for x. Plug it in for E and solve, using your calculator for computations:

$$E = (2.4)\, x^2 \;\rightarrow\; 0.53 = (2.4)\, x^2 \;\rightarrow\; 0.221 = x^2 \;\rightarrow\; x = 0.47$$

The correct answer is (B).

12. **(H)** 298.15   Elementary Algebra   Evaluate or Simplify

You are told that kelvins and degrees Fahrenheit are related to each other by the following equation:

$$K = \frac{5}{9}(F - 32°) + 273.15$$

By substituting 77° for F, you can solve for K as follows:

$$K = \frac{5}{9}(77° - 32°) + 273.15$$

$$K = \frac{5}{9}(45°) + 273.15$$

$$K = 25 + 273.15 = 298.15$$

The correct answer is (H).

13. **(C)** $-\dfrac{8}{3}$ Elementary Algebra   Linear Equations

Combine like terms, subtracting $11y$ from both sides and subtracting 3 from both sides. Notice that you wind up with -16 on the left side. Next, divide both sides by 6, then reduce the resulting fraction by taking a 2 out from top and bottom:

$$11y - 13 = 17y + 3$$
$$-13 = 6y + 3$$
$$-16 = 6y$$
$$\frac{-16}{6} = y$$
$$-\frac{8}{3} = y$$

The correct answer is (C).

14. **(H)** 16   Elementary Algebra   System of Equations

To solve this system of equations, start by substituting the value of 4 in for c in the second equation: $\frac{b}{4} = 8 \rightarrow b = 32$.

Now plug the value of 32 in for b in the first equation: $\frac{a}{32} = \frac{1}{2} \rightarrow a = \frac{32}{2} = 16$. The correct answer is (H).

15. **(B)** $\frac{38}{3}$ Elementary Algebra   Linear Equations (Solving for 1 Variable)

In order to solve for y, isolate it on one side of the equation. First divide by 6, then add y to both sides of the equation:

$$6(14 - y) = 8$$
$$14 - y = \frac{8}{6} = \frac{4}{3}$$
$$14 = \frac{4}{3} + y$$

Now subtract $\frac{4}{3}$ from both sides of the equation and simplify:

$$14 - \frac{4}{3} = y$$
$$\frac{14(3) - 4}{3} = y$$
$$\frac{38}{3} = y$$

The correct answer is (B).

16. **(G)** 5   Elementary Algebra   System of Equations

To solve this system of equations, start by substituting the value of 9 in for z in the second equation: $\frac{x}{9} = \frac{2}{3} \rightarrow x = \frac{18}{3} = 6$.

Next, plug the value of 6 in for x in the first equation: $(6)y = 30 \rightarrow y = \frac{30}{6} = 5$. The correct answer is (G).

17. **(E)** 60   Elementary Algebra   Statistics (Averages)

To compute an average, use the formula, $\text{Average} = \frac{\text{Sum of terms}}{\text{\# of terms}}$. You can compute the sum of the first 5 games using this formula:

$$42 = \frac{\text{Sum of Terms}}{5} \rightarrow \text{Sum} = 42(5) = 210$$

Now you can compute the new average as the sum of the first 5 games plus a variable (x) for the unknown score for the 6th game. Divided by 6 (since there are now 6 total games), this number will result in an average of 45 points. Solve for x:

$$45 = \frac{210 + x}{6}$$
$$6(45) = 210 + x$$
$$270 = 210 + x$$
$$60 = x$$

The correct answer is (E).

18.　**(K)** $2\frac{3}{4}$　　　Elementary Algebra　　　Linear Equations (Solving for 1 Variable)

In order to solve for z, isolate it on one side of the equation. First distribute the term on the left side of the equation, then add $5z$ to both sides of the equation:

$$5(3 - z) = 4 - z$$
$$15 - 5z = 4 - z$$
$$15 = 4 + 4z$$

Now subtract 4 from both sides of the equation, divide by 4, and simplify:

$$15 - 4 = 4z$$
$$\frac{15 - 4}{4} = z$$
$$z = \frac{11}{4} = 2\frac{3}{4}$$

The correct answer is (K).

19.　**(B)** 27　　　Elementary Algebra　　　Proportions

"The time it takes to complete a certain job is directly proportional to the number of units produced" implies that the ratio $\dfrac{\text{time to complete the job, in minutes}}{\text{units produced}}$ must be equal for all instances of the job. Therefore, you can set the ratio $\dfrac{22 \text{ minutes}}{18 \text{ units}}$ equal to the ratio $\dfrac{33 \text{ minutes}}{u \text{ units}}$ and solve:

$$\frac{22 \text{ minutes}}{18 \text{ units}} = \frac{33 \text{ minutes}}{u \text{ units}}$$
$$22u = 33(18)$$
$$u = \frac{594}{22}$$
$$u = 27$$

The correct answer is (B).

20. **(J)** $\dfrac{6(2)+3(t)}{9}=2.8$ Elementary Algebra   Statistics (Averages)

To find the average of all 9 trucks, you need to use the average formula: $\text{Average}=\dfrac{\text{Sum of terms}}{\text{\# of terms}}$. Since there are 6 trucks with an average towing capacity of 2, the sum for these terms can be computed by the following:

$2=\dfrac{\text{Sum of terms}}{6}\rightarrow\text{Sum}=6(2)$. The sum for the 3 trucks with a capacity of t tons can be computed by the following: $t=\dfrac{\text{Sum of terms}}{3}\rightarrow\text{Sum}=3(t)$.

Therefore, the sum of all 9 trucks is $6(2)+3(t)$, and after you divide by 9 and set the result equal to the average, the correct formula is $\dfrac{6(2)+3(t)}{9}=2.8$. The correct answer is (J).

21. **(E)** 12   Elementary Algebra   Linear Equations (Solving for 1 Variable)

First, distribute the expression on the right-hand side of the equation:

$3y=-9(8-y)$
$3y=-72+9y$ (Don't forget to turn the double negative into a positive.)

Next, subtract $9y$ from both sides of the equation and divide by -6:

$-6y=-72$
$y=12$

The correct answer is (E).

22. **(G)** $25z^2-10z+1$ Elementary Algebra   Simple Quadratics

$(5z-1)^2$ can be rewritten as $(5z-1)(5z-1)$. To expand this quadratic expression, use the FOIL method (first, outer, inner, last) to get:

$5z\times5z-5z-5z+(-1)(-1)=25z^2-10z+1$

The correct answer is (G).

23. **(A)** -5 Elementary Algebra   Linear Equations (Solving for 1 Variable)

First, distribute the expression on the left-hand side of the equation:

$-2(a-4)=-3a+3$
$-2a+8=-3a+3$ (Don't forget to turn the double negative into a positive.)

MANHATTAN
PREP

Next, add $3a$ to, and subtract 8 from, both sides of the equation:

$$-2a + 8 = -3a + 3$$
$$a + 8 = 3$$
$$a = -5$$

The correct answer is (A).

24. **(J)** $\dfrac{8x + 25}{9x + 23}$ Elementary Algebra   Simplifying Expressions

To simplify the given expression, distribute the 8 and the 9, then combine like terms:

$$\frac{8(x+2)+9}{9(x+2)+5} = \frac{8x+16+9}{9x+18+5} = \frac{8x+25}{9x+23}$$

The correct answer is (J).

25. **(C)** $4s^2 - 9$ Elementary Algebra   Simple Quadratics

To expand this quadratic expression, use the FOIL method (first, outer, inner, last) to get:

$$4s^2 - 6s + 6s - 9 = 4s^2 - 9.$$

Notice that for any quadratic expression of the form $(x + y)(x - y)$, the outer and inner terms will cancel, and the result will be $x^2 - y^2$. The correct answer is (C).

26. **(J)** 12   Elementary Algebra   Other Elementary Algebra (Direct Proportions)

"The value of x is directly proportional to the value of y" implies that the ratio $\dfrac{x}{y}$ must be equal for all instances of x and y. Therefore, set the ratio $\dfrac{9}{12}$ equal to the ratio $\dfrac{x}{16}$ and solve:

$$\frac{9}{12} = \frac{x}{16}$$
$$12x = 144$$
$$x = \frac{144}{12}$$
$$x = 12$$

The correct answer is (J).

27. **(B)** $\dfrac{5z+6}{10-4z}$ Elementary Algebra   Evaluate or Simplify

To simplify the given expression, distribute the 5 and the 4, then combine like terms:

$$\frac{5(z+2)-4}{18-4(z+2)} = \frac{5z+10-4}{18-4z-8} = \frac{5z+6}{10-4z}$$

The correct answer is (B).

28. **(F)** $\dfrac{-a}{2}$ and b Elementary Algebra   Simple Quadratics

The question is asking for the values of x such that the two expressions multiplied together equal 0. That will be true when either expression equals 0. Therefore, separate each factor in the expression and set it equal to 0, and then solve for x:

$$(2x+a)(x-b)=0$$

$2x+a=0$
$2x=-a$
$\dfrac{2x}{2}=\dfrac{-a}{2}$ $x-b=0$
                                      $x=b$
$x=\dfrac{-a}{2}$

The two possible solutions to this problem are therefore $x=\dfrac{-a}{2}$ and $x=b$. The correct answer is (F).

29. **(B)** $\dfrac{15}{2}$ Elementary Algebra   Other Elementary Algebra (Proportions)

"The value of s is directly proportional to the value of t" implies that the ratio $\dfrac{s}{t}$ must be equal for all instances of s and t. Therefore, you can set the ratio $\dfrac{9}{36}$ equal to the ratio $\dfrac{s}{30}$ and solve:

$\dfrac{9}{36}=\dfrac{s}{30}$
$36s=270$
$s=\dfrac{270}{36}$
$s=\dfrac{15}{2}$

The correct answer is (B).

MANHATTAN
PREP

30. **(G)** $20y + 16$ Elementary Algebra   Polynomials and Exponents

Distribute each factored expression and combine like terms:

$7(4 + 2y) - 3(4 - 2y) = 7(4) + 7(2y) - 3(4) - 3(-2y) = 28 - 12 + 14y + 6y = 20y + 16$

Remember to distribute the negative sign from –3 to *both* of the terms inside the parentheses. A very common mistake is to forget to turn the double negative into a positive. The correct answer is (G).

31. **(B)** Either $y = -m$ or $y = n$ Elementary Algebra   Simple Quadratics

In order for it to be the case that $(y + m)(y - n) = 0$, then either $(y + m) = 0$ or $(y - n) = 0$. In the former case, $y + m = 0$, by subtracting m from both sides of the equation, you get $y = -m$. In the latter case, $y - n = 0$, by adding n to both sides of the equation, you get $y = n$. Therefore, either $y = -m$ or $y = n$. The correct answer is (B).

32. **(H)** $33   Elementary Algebra   Linear Equations (Solving for 2 Variables)

You can solve this problem algebraically by assigning variables to Bill's amount (B) and Todd's amount (T) and creating equations based on the information given in the question. The combined amount owed is $52, so $B + T = \$52$. Additionally, Bill owes $14 more than Todd does, so $B - T = \$14$. Solve for T in the second equation ($T = B - \$14$), and then substitute this expression for T in the first equation to solve for B:

$$T = B - \$14$$
$$B + (B - \$14) = \$52$$
$$2B - \$14 = \$52$$
$$2B = \$66$$
$$B = \$33$$

Alternatively, you could use elimination to solve for B by adding the two original equations together:

$$B + T = \$52$$
$$\underline{B - T = \$14}$$
$$2B = \$66$$
$$B = \$33$$

The correct answer is (H).

33. **(A)** $7z + 12$ Elementary Algebra   Polynomials and Exponents

Distribute each factored expression and combine like terms:

$-3(z + 1) + 5(3 + 2z) = -3(z) + -3(1) + 5(3) + 5(2z) = -3z - 3 + 15 + 10z = 7z + 12$

Remember to distribute the negative sign from –3 to *both* of the terms inside the parentheses. A very common mistake is to forget to turn the second term negative. The correct answer is (A).

12

34. **(K)** –128   Elementary Algebra   Simple Quadratics

In order to express $(4z - 1)^2$ in the form $az^2 + bz + c$, expand and distribute the quadratic equation. First, rewrite it as $(4z - 1)(4z - 1)$. Next, use the FOIL method (first, outer, inner, last). Use the distributive property to expand the expression and group common terms to get:

$$(4z-1)(4z-1) = (4z)(4z) + (4z)(-1) + (-1)(4z) + (-1)^2$$
$$= 16z^2 - 4z - 4z + 1$$
$$= 16z^2 - 8z + 1$$

The question asks for the product of the coefficients abc when the quadratic expression is written in this form. In this case, $a = 16$, $b = -8$, and $c = 1$. Therefore, $abc = (16)(-8)(1) = -128$. The correct answer is (K).

35. **(D)** –7   Elementary Algebra   Linear Equations (Solving for 2 Variables)

You can solve for a in the second equation and then substitute this expression for a in the first equation to solve for b:

$$a - 2b = 42$$
$$a = 42 + 2b$$
$$(42 + 2b) + 2b = 14$$
$$4b = -28$$
$$b = -7$$

Alternatively, you could use elimination to solve for b, by subtracting the second equation from the first:

$$a + 2b = 14$$
$$\underline{-(a - 2b = 42)}$$
$$4b = -28$$
$$b = -7$$

The correct answer is (D).

36. **(H)** $b = a - \dfrac{4}{7}$ Elementary Algebra   Linear Equations (Solving for 2 Variables)

To solve this expression for b, you must isolate b. First divide both sides by 7, subtract a, and then multiply through by a negative:

$$7(a - b) = 4$$
$$a - b = \frac{4}{7}$$
$$-b = \frac{4}{7} - a$$
$$b = -\frac{4}{7} + a$$
$$b = a - \frac{4}{7}$$

The correct answer is (H).

37. **(E)** 5   Elementary Algebra   Linear Equations (Solving for 1 Variable)

Let x be the number that is subtracted from the numerator and the denominator of $\frac{7}{10}$. Now, find the value of x that satisfies the equation $\frac{7-x}{10-x} = \frac{2}{5}$. Cross-multiply to get $5(7-x) = 2(10-x)$, which is equivalent to $35 - 5x = 20 - 2x$. Isolate the x variable to get $3x = 35 - 20 = \frac{15}{3}$. Reduce the fraction to get $x = 5$. Note that choice (A) is incorrect; if -5 were subtracted from the numerator and denominator, it would be the same as adding 5 to each, not subtracting 5 from each.

To confirm the correct answer, subtract 5 from the numerator and denominator of $\frac{7}{10}$ to get $\frac{7-5}{10-5} = \frac{2}{5}$. The correct answer is (E).

38. **(J)** $q = p - \frac{1}{2}$ Elementary Algebra   Linear Equations (Solving for 2 Variables)

To solve this expression for q, you must isolate q. First divide both sides by 6, subtract p, and then multiply through by a negative:

$$6(p-q) = 3$$
$$p - q = \frac{3}{6}$$
$$-q = \frac{1}{2} - p$$
$$q = -\frac{1}{2} + p$$
$$q = p - \frac{1}{2}$$

The correct answer is (J).

39. **(C)** $E > 35$ Elementary Algebra   Other Elementary Algebra (Inequalities)

Because David was able to edit *more* than 25% of the 140 documents, the minimum number he edited, E, is greater than 25% of 140, as the following inequality expresses:

$E > 25\%(140)$
$E > 0.25(140)$
$E > 35$

The correct answer is (C).

40. **(K)** $d < 81$ Elementary Algebra   Other Elementary Algebra (Inequalities)

Because *fewer* than 30% of the 270 items were damaged, the value of d is less than 30% of 270, as the following inequality expresses:

$d < 30\%(270)$
$d < 0.3(270)$
$d < 81$

The correct answer is (K).

41. **(E)** $-3n^2 - 6n + 3$ Elementary Algebra   Polynomials and Exponents

Distribute the expression and combine like terms:

$(-n^2 + 2n + 1) - 2(n^2 + 4n - 1) = -n^2 + 2n + 1 - 2n^2 - 8n + 2 = -3n^2 - 6n + 3.$

Remember to distribute both the 2 and the negative sign to each term inside the parentheses in the second part of the expression. A very common mistake is to forget to carry the negative sign or the 2 to the second term ($+4n$), or to forget to turn the double negative into a positive on the third term (-1). The correct answer is (E).

42. **(J)** 6   Elementary Algebra   Evaluate or Simplify

Substitute 3 for every instance of z in the expression $(z-1) \cdot 3(z-2)^2$ to get:

$(3-1) \cdot 3(3-2)^2$

Simplify using the standard order of operations (often abbreviated as PEMDAS) to get:

$(2) \cdot 3(1)^2 = 2 \times 3 = 6$

The correct answer is (J).

43. **(A)** $\$15x + \$0.15xy$ Elementary Algebra   Expressing Relationships

If Charlie rents a scooter for x days, the daily charge for the rental will be $\$15x$. The more challenging part of the problem involves correctly accounting for mileage.

According to the problem, Charlie rents the scooter for x days and drives it y miles each day. Thus, the total number of miles she drives is given by xy. Since there is a charge of $\$0.15$ per mile driven, Charlie's total mileage charge will be $\$0.15xy$.

The correct answer is therefore $\$15x + \$0.15xy$. The correct answer is (A).

44. **(K)** 144   Elementary Algebra   Evaluate or Simplify

Substitute −4 for every instance of h in the expression $h^2 \cdot (5 - h)$ to get:

$$(-4)^2 \cdot \left(5 - (-4)\right)$$

Simplify using the standard order of operations (often abbreviated as PEMDAS) to get:

$$(-4)^2 \cdot (5 + 4) = 16 \times 9 = 144$$

The correct answer is (K).

45. **(D)** $60.00 + $0.20t   Elementary Algebra   Expressing Relationships

Every 10 text messages cost times $0.20, so t of these groups of 10 text messages cost t times $0.20, or $0.20t. In addition, each month a $60.00 fee is charged.

The resulting expression for both costs is $60.00 + $0.20t. The correct answer is (D).

46. **(J)** 12   Pre-Algebra   Linear Equations (Solving for 1 Variable)

The left side of the equation can be simplified to $4x - 12$. The right side of the equation can be simplified to $x + 24$ (using the standard order of operations: $6 \times 2^2 = 6 \times 4 = 24$). Set each side equal to one another to get $4x - 12 = x + 24$.

You need to isolate the variable x. Subtract x from both sides to get $3x - 12 = 24$. Add 12 to both sides to get $3x = 36$. Divide both sides of the equation by 3 to get $x = 12$. The correct answer is (J).

47. **(E)** $13.20 + $0.16s   Elementary Algebra   Expressing Relationships

Every kWh beyond 30 kWh costs $0.16 apiece. Therefore, assuming $s > 30$, the expression $0.16s will include $0.16 for every kWh of electricity above 30 used, but will also include a cost of $0.16 \times 30 = $4.80 for the first 30 kWh used. The customer will not need to pay this $4.80 cost. Therefore, this $4.80 amount must be subtracted out: the variable portion of the customer's electric bill will be $0.16s − $4.80 (provided, of course, that the customer uses at least 30 kWh of electricity).

When the $18.00 monthly account charge is added, the total cost of electricity for the customer will be $18.00 + $0.16s − $4.80 = $13.20 + $0.16s. The correct answer is (E).

48. **(K)** 26   Elementary Algebra   Evaluate or Simplify

In order to substitute the value 4 for $x - y$ in the expression below, factor the first two terms:

$$2x - 2y - \frac{y-x}{2} + (y-x)^2 = 2(x-y) - \frac{y-x}{2} + (y-x)^2$$

Additionally, notice that several terms include the expression $y - x$. This is the additive inverse of $x - y$. In other words, if $x - y = 4$, then $y - x = -4$. Now substitute:

$$2(x-y) - \frac{y-x}{2} + (y-x)^2$$

$$2(4) - \frac{-4}{2} + (-4)^2$$

Simplify using the normal order of operations (often abbreviated as PEMDAS) to get:

$$2(4) - \frac{-4}{2} + (-4)^2 = 8 - (-2) + 16 = 8 + 2 + 16 = 26$$

The correct answer is (K).

49. **(A)** $\dfrac{11}{6}$ Pre-Algebra   Linear Equations (Solving for 1 Variable)

The right side of the equation can be distributed, resulting in $2z - 6$. You need to isolate the variable z. Add 6 to both sides of the equation, then add $4z$ to both sides of the equation, and finally divide:

$$-4z + 5 = 2(z - 3)$$
$$-4z + 5 = 2z - 6$$
$$-4z + 11 = 2z$$
$$11 = 6z$$
$$\frac{11}{6} = z$$

The correct answer is (A).

50. **(H)** $12x^2y^{10} - 4x^3y^4$ Elementary Algebra   Polynomials and Exponents

Distribute the expression and combine exponents of the same base by adding the exponents:

$$-4y^2(x^3y^2 - 3x^2y^8) = -4x^3y^{2+2} - (-4)x^2y^{2+8} = 12x^2y^{10} - 4x^3y^4.$$

Remember to distribute the negative sign on $-4y^2$ to both of the terms inside the parentheses. A very common mistake is to forget to turn the double negative into a positive. The correct answer is (H).

51. **(E)** 34 pounds   Elementary Algebra   Linear Equations (Solving for 2 Variables)

Represent the weight of the heavier object with the variable H and the weight of the lighter object with the variable L. According to the problem:

$$H + L = 48$$
$$H = 2L + 6$$

There are many different ways to solve for the values of 2 variables in a system of 2 equations. Perhaps the easiest in this example is to substitute the expression for H in the second equation into the first equation and solve for L:

$$(2L + 6) + L = 48$$
$$3L + 6 = 48$$
$$3L = 42$$
$$L = 14$$

Since $H + L = 48$, $H = 48 - 14 = 34$ pounds. The correct answer is (E).

52. **(F)** $4a^3b - 8a^2b^3$ Elementary Algebra   Polynomials and Exponents

Distribute the expression and combine exponents of the same base by adding the exponents:

$$4ab\left(a^2 - 2ab^2\right) = 4a^{1+2}b^1 - 2 \cdot 4a^{1+1}b^{1+2} = 4a^3b - 8a^2b^3 \,.$$

The correct answer is (F).

53. **(C)** 0   Elementary Algebra   Simple Quadratics

The only numbers that satisfy the equation $x^2 = 36$ are 6 and -6. The only numbers that satisfy the equation $y^2 = 64$ are 8 and -8. All the possible sums of either 6 or -6 and either 8 or -8 cannot result in 0. To demonstrate:

$$6 + 8 = 14$$
$$6 + (-8) = -2$$
$$(-6) + 8 = 2$$
$$(-6) + (-8) = 14$$

Therefore, 0 cannot be a possible value. The correct answer is (C).

54. **(J)** $2a + b + 2c$ Elementary Algebra   Linear Equations

First, try to make the first two rows equivalent, because you have the most letters filled in. The natural thing to do is to put in the "missing" letter out of the group of *a, b,* and *c.*

a	b	c
a	c	b

This way, the two rows both add up to $a + b + c$. This is now the target sum for each row and each column.

What should you do now with the first column, with its two a's? Well, skip that one for a moment and complete the other two columns so that each one adds up to $a + b + c$.

a	b	c
a	c	b
	a	a

Now you have to deal with the first column (and last row). You need the first column to add up to $a + b + c$ again, and you have two a's. Call the missing cell x and write an equation:

$$a + b + c = a + a + x \longrightarrow b + c - a = x$$

That last cell contains more than just a single letter, but that's okay.

a	b	c
a	c	b
$b + c - a$	a	a

Finally, the sum of the previously blank cells is $a + (b + c - a) + a + a + c = 2a + b + 2c$. There are other possibilities (it turns out that you can add any constant you want to this expression), but none of the other answers work for all possible values of the variables.

Alternatively, you might have noticed that there were 5 empty cells. With 9 cells in all, you need a total of 3 a's, 3 b's, and 3 c's. You already have 1 a, 2 b's, and 1 c. So you need 2 more a's, 1 more b, and 2 more c's: in other words, $2a + b + 2c$. The correct answer is (J).

55. **(D)** $34 - 5x$ Elementary Algebra   Expressing Relationships

The phrase "x is subtracted from 6" is represented as $6 - x$ (note that this is NOT $x - 6$); multiplying this expression by 5 yields $5(6 - x) = 30 - 5x$. When 4 is then added to the expression, it becomes $30 - 5x + 4$ which is equal to $34 - 5x$. The correct answer is (D).

56. (F) −20   Elementary Algebra   Expressing Relationships

The phrase "4 is subtracted from y" is represented as $y − 4$; dividing this expression by 8 yields $\frac{y-4}{8}$. On the other side of the equation, "7 more than half of y" is represented by the expression $\frac{1}{2}y + 7$. Set these expressions equal to each other, multiply both sides of the equation by 8, and simplify to solve for y:

$$\frac{y-4}{8} = \frac{1}{2}y + 7$$
$$y - 4 = 4y + 56$$
$$-60 = 3y$$
$$y = -20$$

The correct answer is (F).

57. (A) −11   Elementary Algebra   Simple Quadratics

The question asks for a solution to the quadratic equation $h^2 + 3h = 88$. This can be determined by factoring and solving for h:

$$h^2 + 3h = 88$$
$$h^2 + 3h - 88 = 0$$
$$(h+11)(h-8) = 0$$

Therefore, the solution to the quadratic equation is $h = -11$ or $h = 8$. Since 8 is not a choice, the correct answer is −11. The correct answer is (A).

58. (K) 8   Elementary Algebra   Expressing Relationships

Each month, the difference between Jeremy's and Andrew's collection size decreases, because you know that in 5 months, Jeremy's collection size will catch up to that of Andrew. Observe what happens in the first few months:

	Now	+1 months	+2 months	+3 months
Andrew	190 cards	$190 + y$ cards	$190 + 2y$ cards	$190 + 3y$ cards
Jeremy	150 cards	$150 + x$ cards	$150 + 2x$ cards	$150 + 3x$ cards
Difference	40 cards	$40 + y - x$ cards	$40 + 2y - 2x$ cards	$40 + 3y - 3x$ cards

As you can see, in 5 months the difference will be $40 + 5y − 5x$ cards, and you are told in the problem that this difference will equal 0. Now solve for $x − y$:

$$40 + 5y - 5x = 0$$
$$40 + 5(y - x) = 0$$
$$5(y - x) = -40$$
$$y - x = -8$$
$$x - y = 8$$

Alternatively, you could note that the original difference is 40 and Jeremy will catch up to Andrew in 5 months. Thus, $x - y$, which is the difference in the rates at which they obtain new baseball cards, must equal $40 \div 5 = 8$. The correct answer is (K).

59. **(B)** 16   Elementary Algebra   Simple Quadratics

Although you might be tempted to just divide both sides of the equation by y, it's dangerous in general to do so, because you are eliminating the possibility that $y = 0$. The proper way to solve the given equation is to rearrange the equation to make one side equal to 0, then factor.

$$y^2 = 16y$$
$$y^2 - 16y = 0$$
$$y(y - 16) = 0$$

This equation means that either $y = 0$ or $y - 16 = 0$, that is, $y = 16$. Since $y = 0$ is not an available choice, you must choose $y = 16$. The correct answer is (B).

60. **(F)** $\$50,000 + \$4,000z = \$74,000 + \$1,000z$ Elementary Algebra   Expressing Relationships

Each year, Luis's income is expected to increase by \$4,000, and his wife's income is expected to increase by \$1,000. Thus, in 1 year, Luis expects to earn $\$50,000 + \$4,000$ and his wife, $\$74,000 + \$1,000$. Likewise, in 2 years, Luis expects to earn $\$50,000 + \$4,000(2)$ and his wife $\$74,000 + \$1,000(2)$. This can be generalized to the expressions $\$50,000 + \$4,000z$ and $\$74,000 + \$1,000z$, respectively, for Luis's income and his wife's income in z years.

In order to determine the number of years until their incomes are equal, set the expressions equal to each other. Therefore, the correct answer is $\$50,000 + \$4,000z = \$74,000 + \$1,000z$. The correct answer is (F).

61. **(E)** 19   Elementary Algebra   Linear Equations (Solving for 2 Variables)

To solve this system of equations, solve the first equation for a and then substitute that into the second equation:

$$3a + 2b = 3$$
$$3a = 3 - 2b$$
$$a = 1 - \frac{2}{3}b$$

$$4\left(1 - \frac{2}{3}b\right) + 5b = 11$$
$$4 - \frac{8}{3}b + 5b = 11$$
$$-\frac{8}{3}b + \frac{15}{3}b = 7$$
$$\frac{7}{3}b = 7$$
$$b = 3$$

$$a = 1 - \frac{2}{3}(3)$$

$$a = 1 - 2$$

$$a = -1$$

$$5(-1) + 8(3) = -5 + 24 = 19$$

Alternatively, you can recognize that twice the second equation ($8a + 10b = 22$) minus the first equation ($3a + 2b = 3$) results in the expression $5a + 8b$:

$$8a + 10b = 22$$
$$\underline{- (3a + 2b = 3)}$$
$$5a + 8b = 19$$

The correct answer is (E).

62. **(H)** –8   Elementary Algebra   Simple Quadratics

Although the given equation is not technically a quadratic, you can quickly pull out a common factor of x. You are left with ($x^2 - 64$), which can be factored to ($x + 8$)($x - 8$). Be ready to factor a difference of squares such as $x^2 - 64$ in this way.

$$x^3 - 64x = 0$$

$$x(x^2 - 64) = 0$$

$$x(x + 8)(x - 8) = 0$$

Thus, there are three possible values of x: 0, –8, and 8. The only available answer is –8. The correct answer is (H).

63. **(E)** 34   Elementary Algebra   Linear Equations (Solving for 2 Variables)

To solve this system of equations, solve the first equation for a and then substitute that into the second equation:

$$2x = 16 + 5y$$

$$x = 8 + \frac{5}{2}y$$

$$5\left(8 + \frac{5}{2}y\right) + 3y = 9$$

$$40 + 12.5y + 3y = 9$$

$$15.5y = -3$$

$$y = -2$$

$$x = 8 + \frac{5}{2}(-2)$$

$$x = 8 - 5$$

$$x = 3$$

$$12(3) + (-2) = 36 - 2 = 34.$$

Alternatively, you can recognize that twice the second equation ($10x + 6y = 18$) plus the first equation ($2x - 5y = 16$) results in the expression $12x + y$:

$$10x + 6y = 18$$
$$+ \ 2x - 5y = 16$$
$$\overline{12x + y = 34}$$

The correct answer is (E).

64. **(G)** 13   Elementary Algebra   Linear Equations (Solving for 1 Variable)

Let x be the number that is added to the numerator and the denominator of $\dfrac{2}{7}$. Now, find the value of x that satisfies the equation $\dfrac{2+x}{7+x} = \dfrac{3}{4}$. Cross-multiply to get $4(2 + x) = 3(7 + x)$, which is equivalent to $8 + 4x = 21 + 3x$. Isolate the x variable to get $x = 21 - 8 = 13$.

To confirm this answer, add 13 to the numerator and denominator of $\dfrac{2}{7}$ to get $\dfrac{2+13}{7+13} = \dfrac{15}{20}$, then reduce to get $\dfrac{3}{4}$. The correct answer is (G).

65. **(A)** –33   Elementary Algebra   Simple Quadratics

The question requires you to find the solutions to the quadratic equation $a^2 + 8a - 33 = 0$ and take their product. This can be determined by factoring and solving for a:

$$a^2 + 8h - 33 = 0$$
$$(a + 11)(a - 3) = 0$$

Therefore, the solution to the quadratic equation is $a = -11$ or 3. The product of these solutions is $(-11)(3) = -33$. The correct answer is (A).

66. **(H)** –1   Elementary Algebra   Simple Quadratics

The question requires you to find the solutions to the quadratic equation $x^2 + x - 56 = 0$ and take their sum. This can be determined by factoring and solving for x:

$$x^2 + x - 56 = 0$$
$$(x + 8)(x - 7) = 0$$

Therefore, the solution to the quadratic equation is $x = -8$ or 7. The sum of these solutions is $-8 + 7 = -1$. The correct answer is (H).

67. **(E)** $\dfrac{q+13}{11}$ Elementary Algebra   Linear Equations

Don't be distracted by the fact that the letters for these variables are unusual. Take the given equation and rearrange it to solve for h. This process is the entire problem, so execute each step carefully. First, add 13 to both sides, then divide both sides by 11. Rewrite the left side as a fraction so that you can divide that entire side by 11.

$$q = 11h - 13$$
$$q + 13 = 11h$$
$$\frac{q+13}{11} = h$$

The correct answer is (E).

68. **(H)** 36   Elementary Algebra   Evaluate or Simplify

Substitute -40 for x in the given equation for the parabola ($y = -0.04x^2 + 100$) and solve:

$$y = -0.04(-40)^2 + 100$$
$$y = -0.04(1{,}600) + 100$$
$$y = -64 + 100 = 36$$

The correct answer is (H).

69. **(B)** 1   Elementary Algebra   Simple Quadratics

The question requires you to find the solutions to the quadratic equation $v^2 - 14v + 49 = 0$ and determine how many unique, real-number solutions there are. A quadratic equation can never have more than 2 solutions, so this rules out choice (D). Additionally, all quadratic equations have solutions that can be determined, even if they are complex numbers. This elminates choice (E).

Factor the equation and solve for v:

$$v^2 - 14v + 49 = 0$$
$$(v - 7)(v - 7) = 0$$

Therefore, the solution to the quadratic equation is $v = 7$ or 7. Since these numbers are the same, there is only one distinct solution. The correct answer is (B).

70. **(F)** -27 Elementary Algebra   Polynomials and Exponents

You are only given one equation, so you cannot solve for x or for y independently. You must be able to get a numeric answer, however, without any variables (since the answer choices are all numbers). One approach is to substitute in $x - 3$ for y and simplify. Another approach is to rearrange the given equation to get the "combos" or chunks that you need within the target expression: $y - x$ and $x - y$.

$$y = x - 3 \quad \rightarrow \quad y - x = -3$$
$$y = x - 3 \quad \rightarrow \quad 0 = x - y - 3 \quad \rightarrow \quad 3 = x - y$$

You could also notice that $y - x$ and $x - y$ are opposites of each other, so once you know that $y - x = -3$, then you also know that $x - y = 3$.

Now substitute into the target expression for each of these combos:

$$(y - x)^{(x - y)} = (-3)^{(3)} = (-3) \times (-3) \times (-3) = -27$$

The correct answer is (F).

71.   **(C)** $2b + 4\left(\dfrac{1}{2}b - 3\right) = 36$ Elementary Algebra   Expressing Relationships

Translate one sentence at a time, using b for the larger number (as given) and a for the smaller number, as a temporary placeholder. "The smaller of two numbers is 3 less than half the larger number" becomes $a = \dfrac{1}{2}b - 3$. Likewise, "The sum of twice the larger and 4 times the smaller number is 36" becomes $2b + 4a = 36$. Now substitute into the second equation to get rid of a:

$$2b + 4a = 36 \quad \rightarrow \quad 2b + 4\left(\dfrac{1}{2}b - 3\right) = 36$$

There is no need to actually figure out the value of b; don't waste your time doing unnecessary work. The correct answer is (C).

72.   **(K)** $a^2 + \dfrac{4a}{b} + \dfrac{4}{b^2}$ Elementary Algebra   Simple Quadratics

$\left(a + \dfrac{2}{b}\right)^2$ can be rewritten as $\left(a + \dfrac{2}{b}\right)\left(a + \dfrac{2}{b}\right)$. To expand this quadratic expression, use the FOIL method (first, outer, inner, last). Use the distributive property to expand the expression and group common terms to get:

$$\left(a + \dfrac{2}{b}\right)\left(a + \dfrac{2}{b}\right) = (a)(a) + a \cdot \dfrac{2}{b} + a \cdot \dfrac{2}{b} + \left(\dfrac{2}{b}\right)^2$$

$$= a^2 + 2\left(a \cdot \dfrac{2}{b}\right) + \dfrac{4}{b^2}$$

$$= a^2 + \dfrac{4a}{b} + \dfrac{4}{b^2}$$

The correct answer is (K).

73.   **(A)** $y - x = 6$ and $3y = 4x + 2$ Elementary Algebra   Expressing Relationships

Using x to indicate the smaller number and y to indicate the larger number, translate each relationship from words to algebra. "The difference between two numbers is 6" is a little tricky. A difference is subtraction, but which way? Since the difference is 6, a positive number, the difference must be taken as the larger number minus the smaller number. Thus, you get $y - x = 6$.

"Three times the larger number" is $3y$, while "4 times the smaller number" is $4x$. "Three times the larger number exceeds 4 times the smaller number by 2" means that $3y$ is 2 bigger than $4x$, or $3y = 4x + 2$. The correct answer is (A).

74. (G) 8   Elementary Algebra   Linear Equations (Solving for 3 Variables)

In this problem, there are 3 unknown quantities: the number of red balls, the number of green balls, and the number of purple balls. You are also given 3 pieces of information about these quantities, so you should be able to solve for the values of all 3 of them. You can represent the unknown quantities as r, g, and p.

The problem states that red balls are worth 1 point, green balls are worth 5 points, and purple balls are worth 10 points. You are also told that the total number of points Todd has is 150. These facts can be represented by this equation:

$$1r + 5g + 10p = 150$$

You are also told that there are 5 times as many red balls as green balls:

$$r = 5g, \text{ or } g = \frac{1}{5}r$$

Finally, you are told that Todd has 1 more purple ball than green balls:

$$p = g + 1$$

Since all 3 of these equations give information with respect to g, the easiest way to solve the problem is to substitute these expressions in terms of g into the first equation for p and r, and solve for the value of g. You can then solve for the other variables:

$$1r + 5g + 10p = 150$$
$$1(5g) + 5g + 10(g + 1) = 150$$
$$5g + 5g + 10g + 10 = 150$$
$$20g = 140$$
$$g = 7$$

Therefore, $p = (7 + 1) = 8$ and $r = 5(7) = 35$. The question asks for the number of purple balls, so the correct answer is 8. (Note that as a check, you can substitute these values into the first equation and see that they fit: $1(35) + 5(7) + 10(8) = 35 + 35 + 80 = 150$.) The correct answer is (G).

75. (B) $x^2 + 3xz - 2y^2(3z + x) = 0$ Elementary Algebra   Simple Quadratics

A quadratic equation that has the solutions $x = 2y^2$ and $x = -3z$ will be equal to the equation $(x - 2y^2)(x + 3z) = 0$. Therefore, you can start with this equation, distribute it using the FOIL method, and manipulate the expressions to look like one of the choices:

$$(x - 2y^2)(x + 3z) = 0$$
$$x^2 + 3xz - 2y^2x - 6y^2z = 0$$

Already you can see that the correct equation will have the terms $+x^2$ and $+3xz$ in it. This eliminates all choices except for G. However, you can confirm that this is the correct answer by factoring out a $-2y^2$ from the last two terms:

$$x^2 + 3xz + (-2y^2)x + 3(-2y^2)z = 0$$
$$x^2 + 3xz + (-2y^2)(x + 3z) = 0$$
$$x^2 + 3xz - 2y^2(3z + x) = 0$$

The correct answer is (B).

76. **(J)** x increases by 8   Elementary Algebra   Variable Evaluate or Simplify

The new value of b is $(b + 2)$ and the new value of c is $(c - 1)$. Substitute the new values of b and c into the original equation:

$$x = 3(b + 2) - 2(c - 1) + 7$$
$$x = 3b + 6 - 2c + 2 + 7$$
$$x = 3b - 2c + 15$$

Compare the new equation $x = 3b - 2c + 15$ with the original equation $x = 3b - 2c + 7$. Note that the new equation's constant term (15) is 8 more than that of the original equation (7). For any values of b and c, the new equation will always be 8 greater than the original equation. The correct answer is (J).

77. **(E)** $y = (x - 2)^2$ Elementary Algebra   Expressing Relationships

The direct relationship between x and y can be found if one of those equations ($x = a + 2$) is first solved for the parameter a in terms of x, and then that expression is substituted into the other equation for a:

$$x = a + 2$$
$$a = x - 2$$
$$y = a^2$$
$$y = (x - 2)^2$$

The correct answer is (E).

78. **(K)** x increases by 4   Elementary Algebra   Variable Substitution

The new value of s is $(s - 1)$, and the new value of r is $(r + 3)$. Substitute these new expressions for r and s into the original equation:

$$x = 5(s - 1) + 3(r + 3) - 6$$
$$x = 5s - 5 + 3r + 9 - 6$$
$$x = 5s + 3r - 2$$

Compare the new equation $x = 5s + 3r - 2$ with the original equation $x = 5r + 3s - 6$. Note that the new equation's constant term (-2) is 4 more than that of the original equation (-6). For any values of r and s, the new equation will always be 4 greater than the original equation. The correct answer is (K).

MANHATTAN
PREP

79. **(B)** $4.40   Elementary Algebra   Linear Equations (Solving for 2 Variables)

Represent the cost of a taco with the variable T and the cost of a burrito with the variable B. According to the problem:

$$3T + B = \$7.40$$
$$T + 2B = \$7.30$$

There are many different ways to solve for the values of 2 variables in a system of 2 equations. Perhaps the easiest in this example is to solve for the value of T in the second equation, and substitute the resulting expression into the first equation:

$$T + 2B = \$7.30$$
$$T = \$7.30 - 2B$$
$$3(\$7.30 - 2B) + B = \$7.40$$

You can use this resulting equation to solve for the value of B:

$$3(\$7.30 - 2B) + B = \$7.40$$
$$\$21.90 - 6B + B = \$7.40$$
$$-6B + B = \$7.40 - \$21.90$$
$$-5B = -\$14.50$$
$$B = \$2.90$$

Then substitute that value back into the second equation to solve for T:

$$T + 2B = \$7.30$$
$$T + 2(\$2.90) = \$7.30$$
$$T + \$5.80 = \$7.30$$
$$T = \$7.30 - \$5.80$$
$$T = \$1.50$$

The question asks for the value of $T + B$, which is $1.50 + $2.90 = $4.40. The correct answer is (B).

80. **(J)** 20   Elementary Algebra   Simple Quadratics

The population function specified in the problem is a quadratic function. If $p(t) = -4t(t - 25)$, then $p(t) = -4t^2 + 100t$. The question asks which value of t (among the choices) will result in a sample bacteria population of 400, according to the model. This can be determined by setting the function equal to 400 and solving for t:

$$p(t) = -4t^2 + 100t$$
$$400 = -4t^2 + 100t$$
$$4t^2 - 100t + 400 = 0$$
$$t^2 - 25t + 100 = 0$$
$$(t - 5)(t - 20) = 0$$

Thus, when $t = 5$ and when $t = 20$, the population of the bacteria sample is expected to equal 400. Since only 20 is one of the choices, it must be the correct answer.

Note that this can be verified by substituting 20 for t in the original function and checking to see whether 400 is the result:

$$p(t) = -4t(t - 25)$$
$$p(t) = -4(20)(20 - 25)$$
$$p(t) = -4(20)(-5) = 400$$

The correct answer is (J).

81. **(A)** 40   Elementary Algebra   Expressing Relationships

To solve this problem, you must translate Tammy's statement into algebra and then solve. Let g represent the number of golf balls in the bucket that she has. "The number of balls I have in this bucket squared" translates to g^2; "minus 37 times the number of balls in the bucket" translates to $-37g$; and "is equal to 120!" translates to $= 120$. Therefore, the entire equation representing Tammy's statement is:

$$g^2 - 37g = 120$$

Now find the solutions for g in this quadratic equation by factoring:

$$g^2 - 37g = 120$$
$$g^2 - 37g - 120 = 0$$
$$(g - 40)(g + 3) = 0$$

Therefore, the solution to the quadratic equation is $g = -3$ or 40. Obviously, Tammy cannot have a negative number of golf balls, so the correct answer must be 40. The correct answer is (A).

82. **(F)** $-\sqrt{5}$ Elementary Algebra   Evaluate or Simplify

Substitute 1 for x in the equation for the circle $(y^2 + (x - 3)^2 = 9)$ and solve:

$$y^2 + (1 - 3)^2 = 9$$
$$y^2 + 4 = 9$$
$$y = \pm\sqrt{5}$$

The portion of the curve displayed is in the fourth quadrant, that is, $x \geq 0$ and $y \leq 0$. Therefore, it must be the case that $y = -\sqrt{5}$. The correct answer is (F).

MANHATTAN
PREP

83. **(E)** 16   Elementary Algebra   Simple Quadratics

It is given in the problem that one factor of $2x^2 - 4x - z$ is $(x - 4)$. Because the first term in the quadratic is $2x^2$, you know that the other factor must be of the form $(2x + k)$, where k is a placeholder variable for a constant value. Therefore, the factored quadratic will be of the form $(x - 4)(2x + k)$. When this is distributed, it will equal:

$2x^2 - 8x + kx - 4(k)$

The middle term of the quadratic expression is $-4x$, so you can set up the following equation based off of like terms in the above expression to solve for k:

$-4x = -8x + kx$
$4x = kx$
$4 = k$

Now substitute 4 for k in the second factor to get $(2x + 4)$. Finally, distribute the quadratic $(x - 4)(2x + 4)$ to get $2x^2 - 4x - 16$. The last term, 16, corresponds to the value of the variable z. The correct answer is (E).

84. **(K)** $x = 4r^2$ and $x = -5s$ Elementary Algebra   Simple Quadratics

The quadratic equation given in the problem has an x^2 term, two terms multiplied by x ($5s$ and $-4r^2$), and a fourth term that is the product of the two terms that are multiplied by x ($5s \cdot (-4r^2) = -20r^2s$). By thinking about the FOIL process in reverse, you can see that these two terms (that are multiplied by x) must be the two additional terms added to x in the factored quadratic. In other words, the factored equation must be $(x - 4r^2)(x + 5s) = 0$. Therefore, the solutions to the equation must be $x = 4r^2$ and $x = -5s$.

Alternatively, you could attempt to substitute the solutions given in each choice into the original equation for x, and see which set of solutions fits. This will be a cumbersome process, but substituting $4r^2$ and $x = -5s$ into the given equation will work:

$$x^2 + x(5s - 4r^2) - 20r^2s = 0$$
$$(4r^2)^2 + (4r^2)(5s - 4r^2) - 20r^2s = 0$$
$$16r^4 + 4r^2(5s) - 4r^2(4r^2) - 20r^2s = 0$$
$$16r^4 + 20r^2s - 16r^4 - 20r^2s = 0$$
$$0 = 0$$

and:

$$x^2 + x\left(5s - 4r^2\right) - 20r^2s = 0$$

$$(-5s)^2 + (-5s)\left(5s - 4r^2\right) - 20r^2s = 0$$

$$25s^2 + 5s(-5s) + 5s\left(4r^2\right) - 20r^2s = 0$$

$$25s^2 - 25s^2 + 20sr^2 - 20r^2s = 0$$

$$0 = 0$$

The correct answer is (K).

85. **(A)** $y = \dfrac{x+13}{3}$ Elementary Algebra   Expressing Relationships

The direct relationship between x and y can be found if both equations are first solved directly for the parameter t and then set equal to each other:

$$y = t + 5 \qquad x = 3t + 2$$
$$t = y - 5 \qquad 3t = x - 2$$
$$t = \frac{x-2}{3}$$

$$y - 5 = \frac{x-2}{3}$$

$$y = \frac{x-2}{3} + 5$$

$$y = \frac{x-2}{3} + \frac{15}{3}$$

$$y = \frac{x+13}{3}$$

The correct answer is (A).

Chapter *of* 13

5lb. Book of ACT® Practice Problems

Math:

Intermediate Algebra

In This Chapter...

Intermediate Algebra Problems & Solutions

Chapter 13
Math: Intermediate Algebra

The Math problems in this chapter are drawn from intermediate algebra—think Algebra 2 class. The topics include the following:

1. Quadratics. Algebra 2 problems involving quadratic expressions, including inequalities; quadratic formula.

2. Exponents, Radicals, and Rationals. Rules of exponents and roots, radical expressions, rational expressions.

3. Inequalities and Absolute Value. Algebra 2 problems involving these concepts.

4. Formulas, Functions, and Sequences. Dealing with these expressions at an Algebra 2 level.

5. Logarithms. Rules of logarithms, solving problems involving logs.

6. Other Intermediate Algebra. Matrices, complex numbers, and overlapping sets.

How should you use this chapter? Here are some recommendations, according to the level you've reached in ACT Math.

1. Fundamentals. Start slowly with the easier problems at the beginning. Do at least some of these problems untimed. This way, you give yourself a chance to think deeply about the principles at work. Review the solutions closely, and articulate what you've learned. Redo problems as necessary.

2. Fixes. Do a few problems untimed, examine the results, learn your lessons, then test yourself with longer timed sets.

3. Tweaks. Confirm your mastery by doing longer sets of problems under timed conditions. Aim to improve the speed and ease of your solution process. Mix the problems up by jumping around in the chapter. Definitely push to the harder, higher-numbered problems.

Good luck on the problems!

1. $3a^2 \cdot 2a^3b \cdot 2b$ is equivalent to which of the following?

  A. $7a^5b$

  B. $7a^6b^2$

  C. $12a^5b^2$

  D. $12a^6b$

  E. $12a^6b^2$

2. If $g(x) = \dfrac{x+3}{x^2-9}$ for all $x \neq 3$, what is the value of $g(5)$?

  F. -2

  G. $-\dfrac{1}{2}$

  H. $\dfrac{1}{2}$

  J. $\dfrac{4}{7}$

  K. 2

3. $4w \cdot 2w^2z \cdot 2w^3z^2 \cdot w^4$ is equivalent to which of the following?

  A. $8w^{10}z^2$

  B. $8w^{24}z^2$

  C. $8w^{24}z^3$

  D. $16w^{10}z^3$

  E. $16w^{24}z^2$

4. If three numbers are placed in the blanks below so that the difference between consecutive numbers is the same, then the second-to-last number in the sequence is:

  11, _____ , _____ , _____ , 35

  F. 25

  G. 26

  H. 27

  J. 28

  K. 29

5. If $f(y) = \dfrac{32}{y^2} + y - 9$ for all $y \neq 0$, what is the value of $f(4)$?

  A. -3

  B. 3

  C. 9

  D. 16

  E. 23

6. The formula for the volume V of a right cylinder with radius r and height h is $V = \pi r^2 h$. If the radius of a wooden cylinder is $1\dfrac{1}{3}$ centimeters and its height is 2 centimeters, what is its volume to the nearest cubic centimeter?

  F. 6

  G. 7

  H. 8

  J. 11

  K. 15

7. If a is a real number such that $a^3 = 8$, then $2^a + a^2 = ?$

  A. 2

  B. 4

  C. 6

  D. 8

  E. 16

8. If $g(y) = -44 - 8y + 3y^2$, what is $g(-4)$?

  F. -124

  G. -60

  H. -28

  J. 36

  K. 80

MANHATTAN PREP

13

9. The formula for the volume V of a sphere with radius r is $V = \frac{4}{3}\pi r^3$. If a steel sphere has a volume of 115 cubic inches, what is its radius to the nearest inch?

A. 2

B. 3

C. 4

D. 5

E. 6

10. The number of trees in a certain park can be shown by the following matrix.

$$\begin{array}{cccc} \text{Oak} & \text{Elm} & \text{Pine} & \text{Birch} \\ [\,70 & 30 & 40 & 50\,] \end{array}$$

A park ranger estimates the ratio of the number of healthy trees to the total number of trees of each kind and constructs the following matrix with those ratios.

$$\begin{array}{c} \text{Oak} \\ \text{Elm} \\ \text{Pine} \\ \text{Birch} \end{array} \begin{pmatrix} 0.4 \\ 0.6 \\ 0.8 \\ 0.7 \end{pmatrix}$$

Given these matrices, what is the park ranger's estimate for the number of healthy trees in the park?

F. 113

G. 115

H. 117

J. 118

K. 119

11. If $f(z) = (z-1)^2 + 3z - \frac{4}{z}$ what is $f(-2)$?

A. 1

B. 5

C. 13

D. 15

E. 17

12. If $f(z) = \sqrt{3z+1}$ and $g(z) = z^2 + 3$, what is the value of $\frac{f(5)}{g(5)}$?

F. $\frac{4}{7}$

G. $\frac{4}{5}$

H. $\frac{1}{7}$

J. $\frac{1}{5}$

K. $\frac{5}{28}$

13. Before she leaves her house, Gertrude spends 90 minutes bathing, getting dressed, eating breakfast, getting into her car, and driving to work. Because she carpools, she sometimes has to travel out of her way to pick up coworkers during her commute. The equation $t = 5c + 90$ models the time, in t minutes, Gertrude budgets to get to work while picking up c carpoolers. Which of the following statements is necessarily true according to this model?

A. She budgets 90 minutes for each carpooler she picks up on her way to work.

B. She budgets 90 minutes for days without traffic, and 95 minutes for days with light traffic.

C. She budgets 5 minutes for each traffic light on her way to work.

D. She budgets 95 minutes for her daily commute to work.

E. She budgets 5 minutes for each carpooler she picks up on her way to work.

13

14. When a photon, or particle of light, strikes a particular material, an electron may be ejected. The maximum energy, K, in electron-volts of the ejected electron is given by the equation $K = \dfrac{1,240}{L} - 2.1$, where L is the photon's wavelength in nanometers. What must a photon's wavelength in nanometers be, approximately, for the maximum energy of an electron ejected by that photon to be 0.24 electron-volts?

   F. 297

   G. 530

   H. 1,158

   J. 2,660

   K. 5,172

15. In her district, Marion employs an 8-member sales team. The team made exactly 80 sales during the month of July and brought in a maximum of $3,200 for all of those sales combined. If the average value of an individual sale value during the month of July was s dollars, which of the following best describes all possible values of s?

   A. $s \geq \$240$

   B. $s \geq \$40$

   C. $s \leq \$40$

   D. $s \geq \$5$

   E. $s \leq \$5$

16. Takeshi earns $7.00 allowance each week for walking the family dog, helping his sister with homework, taking out the garbage, and keeping his room clean. The equation $d = \$3.00m + \$7.00$ represents the amount, in d dollars, Takeshi can earn each week for completing his family chores in addition to mowing lawns in his neighborhood, assuming m lawns mowed. Which of the following statements is necessarily true according to Takeshi's model?

   F. Takeshi earns $3.00 for each neighborhood lawn he mows.

   G. Takeshi earns $10.00 each week for completing all his chores.

   H. Takeshi earns $7.00 for each neighborhood lawn he mows.

   J. Takeshi earns $7.00 for difficult chores and $3.00 for easy chores.

   K. Takeshi earns $3.00 for each chore he completes for a neighbor.

17. For all positive integers a, b, and c, which of the following expressions is equivalent to $\dfrac{a^2}{bc}$?

   A. $\dfrac{a^2 b}{bc^2}$

   B. $\dfrac{a^2 b}{b^2 c}$

   C. $\dfrac{ab^2}{bc^2}$

   D. $\dfrac{a^2 + b}{bc + b}$

   E. $\dfrac{a^2 - c}{bc - c}$

18. Frank worked 70 hours over the last 7-day pay period and his paycheck was a minimum of $1,470. Frank's average hourly wage, h, over the 7-day period is best expressed by which of the following inequalities?

F. $h \leq \$3$

G. $h \geq \$3$

H. $h \leq \$21$

J. $h \geq \$21$

K. $h \geq \$147$

19. By definition, the determinant of the 2×2 matrix $\begin{bmatrix} w & y \\ x & z \end{bmatrix}$ equals $wz - yx$. What is the value of the determinant of $\begin{bmatrix} 2a & 8b \\ 4b & 3a \end{bmatrix}$ when $a = 2$ and $b = -1$?

A. -8

B. -26

C. -32

D. 12

E. 26

20. For non-zero numbers j, k, m, and n, which of the following expressions is equivalent to $\dfrac{j \cdot k}{m}$?

F. $\dfrac{j \cdot k \cdot m}{m \cdot n}$

G. $\dfrac{j \cdot k \cdot m \cdot n}{j \cdot n}$

H. $\dfrac{j \cdot k \cdot j}{m \cdot j}$

J. $\dfrac{j \cdot k \cdot k}{m \cdot n \cdot k}$

K. $\dfrac{j \cdot j \cdot k}{j \cdot n}$

21. If $f(y) = 3y + y^2$ and $g(y) = 6y - 2$, for which of the following values of y does $f(y) = g(y)$?

A. $\dfrac{2}{3}$

B. 1

C. 3

D. $\dfrac{9}{2}$

E. 6

22. By definition, the dot product of two vectors $\begin{bmatrix} a_1 \\ a_2 \\ \ldots \\ a_n \end{bmatrix}$ and $\begin{bmatrix} b_1 \\ b_2 \\ \ldots \\ b_n \end{bmatrix}$ equals $a_1 \cdot b_1 + a_2 \cdot b_2 + \ldots + a_n \cdot b_n$.

What is the dot product of $\begin{bmatrix} x \\ y \\ z \end{bmatrix}$ and $\begin{bmatrix} z \\ y \\ x \end{bmatrix}$ when $x = 2$, $y = -3$ and $z = 4$?

F. -24

G. -12

H. 25

J. 36

K. 48

13

23. In the standard (x, y) coordinate plane, a line is drawn. If the following table correctly summarizes points located on that line, what is the y-coordinate of the point on the line when $x = 3$?

x	$y = f(x)$
−1	4.4
0	3.8
1	
2	
3	
4	
5	0.8

- **A.** 5.6
- **B.** 3.2
- **C.** 2.6
- **D.** 2.3
- **E.** 2.0

24. Which of the following integers does NOT satisfy the inequality $|2x - 1| \le 40$?

- **F.** −20
- **G.** −18
- **H.** −15
- **J.** 0
- **K.** 20

25. If $9 - 3(y - 3) \le 0$, which of the following correctly characterizes the range of possible values for y?

- **A.** $y = 3$ only
- **B.** All $y \le -6$
- **C.** All $y \ge -6$
- **D.** All $y \le 3$
- **E.** All $y \ge 6$

26. If $|x| < |y|$, then which of the following *must* be true?

- **F.** $x < 0$
- **G.** $x < y$
- **H.** $x > y$
- **J.** $x^2 < y^2$
- **K.** $x^2 > y^2$

27. If 4 times a number x is subtracted from 16, the result will be less than −20. Which of the following correctly characterizes the range of possible values for x?

- **A.** All $x > 9$
- **B.** All $x > -9$
- **C.** $x = 9$ only
- **D.** $x = -16$ only
- **E.** All $x < 20$

28. Which of the following is a value of a that satisfies $\log_a 64 = 3$?

- **F.** 2
- **G.** 4
- **H.** 6
- **J.** 8
- **K.** $\dfrac{64}{3}$

29. Which of the following expressions is equivalent to $(3x^3 \cdot y^5 \cdot 2z^4)^2$?

- **A.** $6x^6y^{10}z^8$
- **B.** $6x^5y^7z^6$
- **C.** $9x^5y^7z^6$
- **D.** $36x^6y^{10}z^8$
- **E.** $36x^9y^{25}z^{16}$

13

MANHATTAN
PREP

30. Which of the following is a value of x that satisfies $\log_x\left(\dfrac{1}{16}\right) = 2$?

   F. $\dfrac{1}{8}$

   G. $\dfrac{1}{6}$

   H. $\dfrac{1}{4}$

   J. 4

   K. 8

31. If G and L are both positive numbers that satisfy the equation $G = 4L^2 - 7$, then $L = $?

   A. $2\sqrt{G} + 7$

   B. $\sqrt{\dfrac{G+7}{4}}$

   C. $\sqrt{\dfrac{G-7}{4}}$

   D. $\sqrt{\dfrac{G}{4}} + 7$

   E. $\dfrac{\sqrt{G-7}}{4}$

32. Which of the following expressions is equivalent to $\left(6x^2 \cdot \sqrt{2}y^3\right)^2$?

   F. $72x^4y^6$

   G. $72x^4y^5$

   H. $12x^4y^3$

   J. $36\sqrt{2}x^4y^6$

   K. $36\sqrt{2}x^2y^5$

33. Which of the following is the correct fifth term in the following geometric sequence?

4, 12, 36, …

   A. 76

   B. 132

   C. 108

   D. 216

   E. 324

34. If $y = 3x^2 + 6$ and $xy < 0$, then $x = $?

   F. $\sqrt{\dfrac{y-6}{3}}$

   G. $\sqrt{\dfrac{6-y}{3}}$

   H. $-\sqrt{\dfrac{y-6}{3}}$

   J. $-\sqrt{\dfrac{y}{3}-6}$

   K. $\sqrt{y-2}$

35. Which of the following inequalities correctly represents the set of possible values for x in the inequality $15 - 3x \geq 48$?

   A. $x \geq -16$

   B. $x \geq -11$

   C. $x \leq -11$

   D. $x \leq \dfrac{16}{5}$

   E. $x \geq -\dfrac{16}{5}$

13

36. If $2j = 4k + 8$ and $i^2 = -1$, then $\sqrt{-(2k-j)} = ?$

   F. $2i$

   G. $4i$

   H. $8i$

   J. 2

   K. 4

37. Assuming that $ab \neq 0$, the expression $\dfrac{4a+3b}{24ab}$ is equivalent to:

   A. $\dfrac{1}{2}$

   B. $\dfrac{2}{ab}$

   C. $\dfrac{1}{2ab}$

   D. $\dfrac{1}{6b} + \dfrac{1}{8a}$

   E. $\dfrac{a+b}{2ab}$

38. The growth of a population of rabbits in a forest, R, can be modeled by the equation $R = \dfrac{e^t}{h} \times 2{,}000$, where t is the time measured in months, such that $t > 0$. The variable h represents a growth coefficient, such that $0 < h \leq 10$. With ample food and few natural predators, $h = 2$. e is a natural constant that has a value of approximately 2.718. After 3 months, approximately how large is the population of rabbits in an environment with ample food and few predators?

   F. 7.3×10^3

   G. 2.0×10^4

   H. 7.3×10^4

   J. 2.0×10^5

   K. 7.3×10^5

39. Assuming $x \neq 0$, the expression $\dfrac{5x^2 - 3x}{30x^2}$ is equivalent to:

   A. $\dfrac{1}{6} - \dfrac{1}{10x}$

   B. $\dfrac{x-1}{2x}$

   C. $\dfrac{1}{3x^2}$

   D. $\dfrac{1}{15x}$

   E. $\dfrac{1}{2}$

40. The solution set of $\sqrt{2x+6} \leq 8$ is the set of all real numbers x such that:

   F. $-3 \leq x \leq 1$

   G. $-3 \leq x \leq -1$

   H. $-3 \leq x \leq 32$

   J. $-3 \leq x \leq 29$

   K. $-3 \leq x \leq 36$

41. Given that $a > 10$, which of the following expressions is equivalent to $\dfrac{(a^2 + 3a + 2)(a-3)}{(a^2 - 4a + 3)(a+2)}$?

   A. -1

   B. $a - 1$

   C. $\dfrac{a-3}{a+3}$

   D. $\dfrac{2a-1}{a+2}$

   E. $\dfrac{a+1}{a-1}$

42. The solution set of $\sqrt{x^2 - 7} \le \sqrt{93}$ is the set of all real numbers x such that:

    F. $0 \le x \le 100$

    G. $0 \le x \le 10$

    H. $-1 \le x \le 1$

    J. $-10 \le x \le -1$

    K. $\sqrt{7} \le |x| \le 10$

43. Which of the following statements is true about the arithmetic sequence $-11, -8, -5, -2, \ldots$?

    A. None of the terms in the sequence is positive.

    B. The sum of the first 10 terms is negative.

    C. The sixth term in the sequence is 4.

    D. 8 is a term in the sequence.

    E. The common difference of consecutive terms is 4.

44. If the complex number i, defined as the square root of -1, is raised to a positive integer power, which of the following is NOT a possible result?

    F. 0

    G. 1

    H. -1

    J. i

    K. $-i$

45. Which of the following is the matrix result of the product $\begin{bmatrix} 3b \\ -2a \end{bmatrix} \begin{bmatrix} x & -y \end{bmatrix}$?

    A. $\begin{bmatrix} 3bx - 2ay \end{bmatrix}$

    B. $\begin{bmatrix} 3bx + 2ay \end{bmatrix}$

    C. $\begin{bmatrix} 3bx \\ 2ay \end{bmatrix}$

    D. $\begin{bmatrix} 3bx & 0 \\ 2ay & -2ax \end{bmatrix}$

    E. $\begin{bmatrix} 3bx & -3by \\ -2ax & 2ay \end{bmatrix}$

46. For the complex number i, defined as the square root of -1, which of the following is equal to $-i$?

    F. i

    G. i^2

    H. i^3

    J. i^4

    K. i^5

47. Consider the quadratic equation $a = (b - 4)^2 + 12$. Which of the following values for b will provide the lowest possible value for a?

    A. 0

    B. 1

    C. 2

    D. 3

    E. 4

13

48. Which of the following is the matrix result of the

product $\begin{bmatrix} 6 & 7 & 8 \end{bmatrix} \begin{bmatrix} x \\ 0 \\ -z \end{bmatrix}$?

  F. $\begin{bmatrix} -2xz \end{bmatrix}$

  G. $\begin{bmatrix} 6x - 8z \end{bmatrix}$

  H. $\begin{bmatrix} 6x \\ 0 \\ -8z \end{bmatrix}$

  J. $\begin{bmatrix} 6x & -7z & 8 \end{bmatrix}$

  K. $\begin{bmatrix} 6x & 0 & -6z \\ 7x & 0 & -7z \\ 8x & 0 & -8z \end{bmatrix}$

Use the following information to answer question 49.

Aaron, Bonnie and Carl are members of a competitive bowling team. The 3-person team competed in a 4-game regional bowling tournament recently, where it came in 2nd place out of 12 teams. The table below shows partial information from scores that Aaron wrote down during the course of the tournament. Unfortunately, he did not get a chance to write down all of the results, but those that he did record are accurate:

Team	Tournament Results			
Member	Game 1	Game 2	Game 3	Game 4
Aaron	208			
Bonnie	231	219	240	
Carl	165	180	188	201

49. Carl then said to Aaron that "it's a good thing all of your scores were so easy to remember! Each of your scores after Game 1 was 7 higher than your previous score." If Carl's memory is accurate, what was the total score achieved by Aaron over the course of the 4 games?

  A. 832

  B. 853

  C. 860

  D. 874

  E. 886

50. Consider the equation $y = x^2 - 3$. Which of the following values for x will produce the highest value for y?

  F. –3

  G. –2

  H. –1

  J. 0

  K. 1

51. If $\log_2 16^2 = x$, what is the value of x?

  A. –8

  B. –6

  C. 6

  D. 8

  E. 16

52. Which real number value for b satisfies the equation $3^b (9) = 3^9$?

  F. 1

  G. 3

  H. 5

  J. 7

  K. 9

MANHATTAN
PREP

53. The expression $\log_5 \dfrac{5^x}{5^y}$ is equivalent to which of the following?

   A. $x - y$

   B. $x + y$

   C. $\dfrac{x}{y}$

   D. $\dfrac{y}{x}$

   E. xy

54. What is the largest value of x such that $x^2 - 2x \leq 80$?

   F. 6

   G. 7

   H. 8

   J. 9

   K. 10

55. $3^3 - 3^4 + 3^5 =$

   A. 81

   B. 121

   C. 189

   D. 211

   E. 243

56. The number of defective springs in a batch produced by a manufacturer is known to satisfy the inequality $\left| \dfrac{50d}{b} - 4 \right| \leq 1$, where d is the number of defective springs and b is the batch size. If the company manufactures a batch of 400 springs, which of the following is a possible number of defective springs in the batch that satisfies the inequality?

   F. 12

   G. 16

   H. 18

   J. 20

   K. 24

57. The formula for the rate of transfer of heat via radiation from a warm object to its cooler surroundings is given by the formula $H(T) = T^4 k$, where T is the temperature differential between the object and its surroundings and k is a constant. Suppose that two identical objects at the same high temperature are placed in two different rooms with cooler surrounding air at lower, but different, temperatures. If the object in the cooler room transfers heat to its surroundings at a rate 20 times that of the other object (in the warmer room), approximately what is the ratio of the temperature differential between the object and the surrounding air in the cooler room to the temperature differential between the object and the surrounding air in the warmer room?

   A. Between $\dfrac{1}{4}$ and $\dfrac{1}{2}$

   B. Between $\dfrac{1}{2}$ and 1

   C. Between 1 and 2

   D. Between 2 and 3

   E. Greater than 3

58. Alexa is writing a novel and has decided that in order to complete the novel on time, she will need to write a few pages each day. On the first day, she writes 2 pages, and on each day thereafter she writes 2 more pages than she did the day before. Therefore, Alexa writes 4 pages on the second day, 6 pages on the third day, and so on. If it took Alexa 20 days to finish her novel, and she wrote 40 pages on the last day, how many pages did she write in total?

   F. 78

   G. 208

   H. 418

   J. 420

   K. 432

13

59. What is the correct expression for the missing (third) term in the geometric sequence given below?

$(a + b)$; $(a + b)a^2c$; _____; $(a + b)a^6c^3$; $(a + b)a^8c^4$ ...

    A. $(a + b)ac^3$

    B. $(a + b)a^3c^3$

    C. $(a + b)a^4c^2$

    D. $(a + b)a^{10}c^5$

    E. $(a - b)a^5c^2$

60. Leslie is trying to save money to buy a car and has a jar on her counter to save her change each day. On the first day, she put $1 in the jar, and on each day thereafter she put $1 more in the jar than she did the day before. Therefore, Leslie put $2 in on the second day, $3 in on the third day, and so on. If Leslie continues in this way for a total of 26 days, how much money will she have in the jar?

    F. $1,378

    G. $1,326

    H. $689

    J. $406

    K. $351

61. Which of the following equations correctly expresses x in terms of z for all positive values of x, y, and z if $z = y^2$ and $y = x^3$?

    A. $x = z^6$

    B. $x = z^5$

    C. $x = 2z^{\frac{1}{3}}$

    D. $x = z^{\frac{1}{5}}$

    E. $x = z^{\frac{1}{6}}$

62. Which of the following expressions CANNOT yield a rational number, assuming that x and y are non-negative integers that are not perfect squares?

    F. $\sqrt{xy}$

    G. $\dfrac{\sqrt{x}}{\sqrt{y}}$

    H. $\sqrt{x + y}$

    J. $\sqrt{x} - \sqrt{y}$

    K. $\sqrt{x} + \sqrt{y}$

63. Which of the following equations correctly expresses r in terms of s for all positive values of r, s, and t given that $r = t^3$ and $t = s^4$?

    A. $r = s^{12}$

    B. $r = s^7$

    C. $r = 4s^3$

    D. $r = s^{\frac{2}{7}}$

    E. $r = s^{\frac{1}{12}}$

64. The sum of 4 consecutive odd integers is m. In terms of m, what is the sum of the largest and smallest of these integers?

    F. $m + 3$

    G. $\dfrac{1}{4}m - 3$

    H. $\dfrac{1}{4}m + 3$

    J. $\dfrac{1}{2}m - 6$

    K. $\dfrac{1}{2}m$

65. In the complex numbers, where $i^2 = -1$, the product $(2 + 3i)(2 - 3i) = ?$

  A. $4 + 6i$

  B. $-5 + 6i$

  C. $-5 + 12i$

  D. 9

  E. 13

66. The sum of 3 consecutive even integers is p. In terms of p, what is the value of the largest of these integers?

  F. $\dfrac{p}{3} - 6$

  G. $\dfrac{p}{3} - 2$

  H. $\dfrac{p}{3} + 2$

  J. $\dfrac{2p}{3} - 6$

  K. $\dfrac{2p}{3}$

67. Which of the following expressions are always equal to 1 for all non-zero values of z?

  I. $\dfrac{\sqrt{z^2}}{z}$

  II. $\left|\dfrac{|z|}{z}\right|$

  III. $\dfrac{\sqrt{z^2}}{|z|}$

  A. II only

  B. III only

  C. I and II only

  D. II and III only

  E. I, II, and III

68. In the complex numbers, where $i = \sqrt{-1}$,

$$\frac{i+1}{1-i} \cdot \frac{2}{i} = ?$$

  F. $\dfrac{2 + 2i}{1 - i}$

  G. $\dfrac{2 - 2i}{1 + i}$

  H. 2

  J. $2i$

  K. $1 + i$

69. What is the value of $\log_{10}\left(1{,}000^{\frac{3}{2}}\right)$?

  A. 4

  B. 4.5

  C. 6

  D. 9

  E. 18

70. Which of the following expressions, if any, are always equivalent to $|x|$ for any non-zero value of x?

  I. $\sqrt{|x|} \cdot \sqrt{|x|}$

  II. $\dfrac{x^2}{x}$

  III. $|-x|$

  F. I only

  G. II only

  H. I and III only

  J. II and III only

  K. None of the expressions are equivalent to $|x|$.

13

71. Out of a group of 19 people, 15 like basketball, and 14 like soccer. What is the minimum number of people who like exactly one of these two sports?

    A. 0

    B. 1

    C. 2

    D. 3

    E. 4

72. If x and y are positive and $\log_x 16 = 2$ and $\log_y 81 = 4$, what is $x + y$?

    F. 7

    G. 6

    H. 5

    J. 4

    K. 3

73. Let $x^{y^2+9} = x^{6y}$. What is the set of all real values of y that satisfy that equation for all values of x that do not equal 0 or 1?

    A. {-3}

    B. {2}

    C. {3}

    D. {-2, 2}

    E. {-3, 3}

74. Umberto is a newspaper delivery boy. He delivers newspapers every day of the week. On Sunday, his first day on the job, he delivered newspapers to 18 houses in his neighborhood. Each day afterward, his delivery route included 7 more houses than it did the previous day. How many total newspapers did Umberto deliver in his first 2 weeks on the job?

    F. 252

    G. 343

    H. 637

    J. 889

    K. 1,260

75. If $3^{10+3x-x^2} = 1$, then which of the following is the set of all real solutions for x?

    A. {−2}

    B. {5}

    C. {−2, −5}

    D. {−2, 5}

    E. {2, 5}

76. Which of the following graphs represents the solution set for the inequality $|2x| \geq 6$?

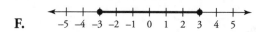

77. What is the sum of all the even integers between 1 and 101?

    A. 1,250

    B. 2,550

    C. 5,000

    D. 5,100

    E. 10,000

78. If $|x^2 - 20| = 16$, how many possible values are there for x?

    F. 4

    G. 3

    H. 2

    J. 1

    K. 0

MANHATTAN
PREP

79. Which of the following graphs represents the solution set of the inequality $|2x - 3| \geq 5$?

A.
$-6\ -5\ -4\ -3\ -2\ -1\ \ 0\ \ 1\ \ 2\ \ 3\ \ 4\ \ 5\ \ 6$

B.
$-6\ -5\ -4\ -3\ -2\ -1\ \ 0\ \ 1\ \ 2\ \ 3\ \ 4\ \ 5\ \ 6$

C.
$-6\ -5\ -4\ -3\ -2\ -1\ \ 0\ \ 1\ \ 2\ \ 3\ \ 4\ \ 5\ \ 6$

D.
$-6\ -5\ -4\ -3\ -2\ -1\ \ 0\ \ 1\ \ 2\ \ 3\ \ 4\ \ 5\ \ 6$

E.
$-6\ -5\ -4\ -3\ -2\ -1\ \ 0\ \ 1\ \ 2\ \ 3\ \ 4\ \ 5\ \ 6$

80. Which of the following is NOT a solution to the equation $|b^2 - 14| = 11$?

F. -5

G. $-\sqrt{3}$

H. $\sqrt{3}$

J. $\sqrt{5}$

K. 5

81. If $g(x) = x^2 + x + 1$, which of the following is equal to $g(a + b)$?

A. $a^2 + b^2 + 1$

B. $a^2 + b^2 + a + b + 1$

C. $a^2 + b^2 + 2a + 2b + 1$

D. $a^2 + b^2 + a + b + 2ab + 1$

E. $a^2 + b^2 + a + b + 2ab + 2$

82. The electrical resistance, measured in ohms, of a solid aluminum wire m meters long is approximately $\dfrac{m \times 2.65 \times 10^{-4}}{A}$, where A is the cross-sectional area of the wire in square centimeters. Because the cross-section of a wire is circular, $A = \pi r^2$, where r is the radius of the wire cross-section in centimeters. Patricia is replacing aluminum wiring in a home and will be using aluminum wire that is twice as long, but with a radius that is triple that of the existing wire. By what factor will the resistance of the wiring change after this replacement?

F. $\dfrac{9}{4}$

G. $\dfrac{9}{2}$

H. $\dfrac{4}{3}$

J. $\dfrac{4}{9}$

K. $\dfrac{2}{9}$

83. The quadratic equation $x^2 + 10x + 2 = 0$ has how many irrational solutions?

A. 4

B. 3

C. 2

D. 1

E. 0

84. If $\log_x z = r$ and $\log_x y = s$, what is the value of $\log_x \dfrac{z^2}{y}$, in terms of r and s?

F. 1

G. $\dfrac{2r}{s}$

H. $\dfrac{r^2}{s}$

J. $2r - s$

K. $2r + s$

13

85. Consider all pairs of positive integers a and b such that $9^a = x$ and $x^b = 3^{16}$. What is the smallest possible value for $a + b$?

    A. 4

    B. 5

    C. 6

    D. 8

    E. 9

86. If $\log_b x^c = a$, what is the value of x in terms of a, b, and c?

    F. $b(a-c)$

    G. $b \cdot a^c$

    H. $\dfrac{ab}{c}$

    J. b^{a-c}

    K. $b^{\frac{a}{c}}$

87. Let the function $f(x, y)$ be defined as $f(x,\ y) = \dfrac{x-y}{2}$. For all a and b, $f\left((b^2 - a^2), (a^2 - b^2)\right) = ?$

    A. $-a^2$

    B. $\dfrac{-a^2}{2}$

    C. $b^2 - a^2$

    D. $\dfrac{b^2 - a^2}{2}$

    E. $\dfrac{a^2 + b^2}{2}$

88. Consider all pairs of positive integers r and s such that $8^r = t$ and $t^s = 4^{12}$. How many possible values are there for r?

    F. 0

    G. 1

    H. 2

    J. 3

    K. 4

89. Let the function $f(x, y)$ be defined as $f(x, y) = \dfrac{x}{y}$. For all m and n that do not equal each other,

$$f((m+n), (m^2 - n^2)) = ?$$

    A. $m - n$

    B. $m + n$

    C. $\dfrac{1}{m-n}$

    D. $\dfrac{1}{m+n}$

    E. $m^2 - n^2$

Answer Key

Write in whether you got each problem right or wrong (or left it blank). If your answer was correct, put a 1 in every blank to the right of that problem. Sum up each column and compare your total to the total possible "Out Of" points.

Problem	Correct Answer	Right/Wrong/Blank
1	C	
2	H	
3	D	
4	K	
5	A	
6	J	
7	D	
8	J	
9	B	
10	F	
11	B	
12	H	
13	E	
14	G	
15	C	
16	F	
17	B	
18	J	
19	A	
20	H	
21	B	
22	H	
23	E	
24	F	
25	E	
26	J	
27	A	
28	G	

Problem	Correct Answer	Right/Wrong/Blank
29	D	
30	H	
31	B	
32	F	
33	E	
34	H	
35	C	
36	J	
37	D	
38	G	
39	A	
40	J	
41	E	
42	K	
43	C	
44	F	
45	E	
46	H	
47	E	
48	G	
49	D	
50	F	
51	D	
52	J	
53	A	
54	K	
55	C	
56	K	

13

Problem	Correct Answer	Right/ Wrong/Blank
57	D	
58	J	
59	C	
60	K	
61	E	
62	K	
63	A	
64	K	
65	E	
66	H	
67	D	
68	H	
69	B	
70	H	
71	B	
72	F	
73	C	
74	J	
75	D	
76	K	
77	B	
78	F	
79	D	
80	J	
81	D	
82	K	
83	C	
84	J	
85	C	
86	K	

Problem	Correct Answer	Right/ Wrong/Blank
87	C	
88	K	
89	C	
Total		
Out Of		89

13

MANHATTAN
PREP

Intermediate Algebra Solutions

1. **(C)** $12a^5b^2$ Intermediate Algebra   Exponents, Radicals, Rationals

The dot means multiply. When you multiply expressions such as a^2 and a^3 with the same base (a), add the exponents to get $a^{2+3} = a^5$. The operation $b \cdot b$ gives you b^2.

$$3a^2 \cdot 2a^3b \cdot 2b = (3 \cdot 2 \cdot 2)\, a^2 \cdot a^3 \cdot b \cdot b = 12a^5b^2$$

The correct answer is (C).

2. **(H)** $\dfrac{1}{2}$ Intermediate Algebra   Functions

To find a specific value for the function $g(x)$, you need to replace all instances of x with the given value (5) and simplify.

$$g(5) = \frac{(5)+3}{(5)^2 - 9} = \frac{8}{25-9} = \frac{8}{16} = \frac{1}{2}$$

The correct answer is (H).

3. **(D)** $16w^{10}z^3$ Intermediate Algebra   Exponents, Radicals, Rationals

The dot means multiply. When you multiply expressions such as w, w^2, w^3, and w^4 with the same base (w), add the exponents. Don't forget that w by itself has an exponent of 1. The same process holds true for z.

$$4w \cdot 2w^2z \cdot 2w^3z^2 \cdot w^4 = (4 \cdot 2 \cdot 2)\, w \cdot w^2 \cdot w^3 \cdot w^4 \cdot z \cdot z^2$$
$$= 16w^{1+2+3+4}z^{1+2} = 16w^{10}z^3$$

The correct answer is (D).

4. **(K)** 29   Intermediate Algebra   Formulas, Functions, Sequences

Rather than use trial and error, try applying theory. If the difference between consecutive numbers is the same, call that difference x and notice that the difference between 11 and 35 is 4 intervals, or $4x$:

The difference between 11 and 35 is $35 - 11 = 24$, so $24 = 4x$, or $x = 6$. That's the size of each interval. Finally, you can count up 3 intervals from 11 or down 1 interval from 35 to get the answer as 29.

The correct answer is (K).

5.   **(A)** −3   Intermediate Algebra   Functions

To find a specific value for the function $f(y)$, you need to replace all instances of y with the given value (4) and simplify:

$$f(4) = \frac{32}{(4)^2} + (4) - 9 = \frac{32}{16} - 5 = 2 - 5 = -3$$

The correct answer is (A).

6.   **(J)** 11   Intermediate Algebra   Formulas, Functions, Sequences

The problem provides the radius r and the height h, while asking for the volume. You don't need to rearrange the given formula, because it already has volume by itself on one side of the equation: $V = \pi r^2 h$. First, you need to convert the mixed number $1\frac{1}{3}$ to a fraction: $1\frac{1}{3} = 1 + \frac{1}{3} = \frac{3}{3} + \frac{1}{3} = \frac{4}{3}$.

No,w plug into the formula and calculate V, using 3.14 as an approximation for pi. Feel free to round after a couple of decimal places, as you use your calculator:

$$V = \pi r^2 h = \pi \left(\frac{4}{3}\right)^2 (2) \approx (3.14)(1.33)^2 (2) \approx 11.1 \approx 11$$

The correct answer is (J).

7.   **(D)** 8   Intermediate Algebra   Exponents, Radicals, Rationals

If $a^3 = 8$, then a must be 2, since $2^3 = 8$. This fact can also be expressed as $\sqrt[3]{8} = 2$. Next, plug this value of a into the expression you are asked about:

$$2^a + a^2 = 2^2 + 2^2 = 4 + 4 = 8$$

The correct answer is (D).

8.   **(J)** 36   Intermediate Algebra   Formulas, Functions, Sequences

Calculate the values of each term in the function by substituting −4 for y, then simplify, making sure to use the correct order of operations (often called PEMDAS):

$$g(-4) = -44 - 8(-4) + 3(-4)^2$$
$$g(-4) = -44 - (-32) + 3(16)$$
$$g(-4) = -44 + 32 + 48 = 36$$

The correct answer is (J).

MANHATTAN
PREP

9.   **(B)** 3   Intermediate Algebra   Formulas, Functions, Sequences

The formula gives you the volume when you plug in the radius, but you want the radius for a given volume. So you can either rearrange the formula to isolate the radius or try the answer choices in the original formula. Start by isolating the radius:

$$V = \frac{4}{3}\pi r^3$$

$$\frac{3}{4}V = \pi r^3$$

$$\frac{3V}{4\pi} = r^3$$

$$\sqrt[3]{\frac{3V}{4\pi}} = r$$

Now, plug in the volume V:

$$\sqrt[3]{\frac{3V}{4\pi}} = r$$

$$\sqrt[3]{\frac{3(115)}{4\pi}} \approx 3.02 \approx 3$$

Alternatively, plug each answer choice in for r and see which one gets you the closest to 115, using 3.14 as an approximation for pi. The value of 3 gets you a volume of approximately 113; none of the other choices are even close to 115. The correct answer is (B).

10.   **(F)** 113   Intermediate Algebra   Other Intermediate Algebra (Matrices)

If you're not familiar with matrices, just think of them as fancy tables. The fact that one of the matrices is horizontal, while the other one is vertical, is not truly important. Focus on one type of tree at a time. Oak: There are 70 oak trees total, and the ratio of healthy oak trees to total oak trees is 0.4. This means that the number of healthy oak trees is $0.4 \times 70 = 28$. (Check the result if you need to: 28 healthy oaks ÷ 70 oaks = 0.4, the right ratio.)

Now repeat the calculation for the other types of trees. Healthy elms: $0.6 \times 30 = 18$. Healthy pines: $0.8 \times 40 = 32$. Healthy birches: $0.7 \times 50 = 35$. Finally, sum all these healthy trees up: $28 + 18 + 32 + 35 = 113$.

If you know how to do matrix multiplication, the calculations are identical. The correct answer is (F).

13

11. **(B)** 5   Intermediate Algebra   Formulas, Functions, Sequences

Calculate the values of each term in the function by substituting -2 for z, then simplify, making sure to use the correct order of operations (abbreviated as PEMDAS):

$$f(-2) = \left[(-2) - 1\right]^2 + 3(-2) - \frac{4}{-2}$$
$$f(-2) = (-3)^2 + (-6) - (-2)$$
$$f(-2) = 9 - 6 + 2 = 5$$

The correct answer is (B).

12. **(H)** $\dfrac{1}{7}$ Intermediate Algebra   Formulas, Functions, Sequences

Calculate the values of each function by substituting 5 for z in each expression:

$$f(z) = \sqrt{3z + 1} \qquad g(z) = z^2 + 3$$
$$f(5) = \sqrt{3 \cdot 5 + 1} \qquad g(5) = 5^2 + 3$$
$$f(5) = \sqrt{16} = 4 \qquad g(5) = 28$$

Therefore, $\dfrac{f(5)}{g(5)} = \dfrac{4}{28} = \dfrac{1}{7}$. The correct answer is (H).

13. **(E)** She budgets 5 minutes for each carpooler she picks up on her way to work.

          Intermediate Algebra   Formulas, Functions, Sequences

In the equation provided, $t = 5c + 90$, the 5 represents the number of minutes that the length of time of Gertrude's commute changes when the number of carpoolers increases by 1 (thus 5 represents the slope of the linear equation). Therefore, Gertrude is budgeting 5 minutes for each carpooler she picks up on her way to work, in addition to the 90 minutes it takes to get to work without any carpoolers. The correct answer is (E).

13

MANHATTAN
PREP

14. **(G)** 530   Intermediate Algebra   Exponents, Radicals, Rationals

There's a lot of scientific jargon in this problem, but don't let it throw you. You only care about two quantities, K and L, which are related by the given equation. You are given a value of K and asked which value of L corresponds to that K. So you plug in this value of K and solve for L. Notice that you have to multiply both sides by L partway through in order to get L out of the denominator of the term it's in:

$$K = \frac{1,240}{L} - 2.1$$

$$0.24 = \frac{1,240}{L} - 2.1$$

$$2.34 = \frac{1,240}{L}$$

$$2.34L = 1,240$$

$$L = \frac{1,240}{2.34} = 530$$

The correct answer is (G).

15. **(C)** $s \le \$40$ Intermediate Algebra   Inequalities and Absolute Value

The number of sales times the average value per sale ($80 \times \$s$) is the total value of the combined sales over the month-long period. Since \$3,200 is the maximum value of the combined sales, $80s \le \$3,200$ or $s \le \$40$. The correct answer is (C).

16. **(F)** Takeshi earns \$3.00 for each neighborhood lawn he mows.

        Intermediate Algebra   Formulas, Functions, Sequences

In the equation provided, $d = \$3.00m + \$7.00$, the \$3.00 represents the number of dollars Takeshi can add to his weekly earnings by mowing 1 additional neighborhood lawn (with \$3.00 representing the slope of a linear equation). Therefore, Takeshi earns \$3.00 for each neighborhood lawn he mows. The correct answer is (F).

17. **(B)** $\dfrac{a^2 b}{b^2 c}$ Intermediate Algebra   Exponents, Radicals, Rationals

The target expression $\dfrac{a^2}{bc}$ is already as simplified as it can be. You'll have to work backwards from the answer choices, simplifying these expressions as efficiently you can. Choices (D) and (E) can be eliminated quickly, because there's no way to factor the numerators $a^2 + b$ or $a^2 - c$ and simplify the fractions by canceling. The remaining choices only contain multiplication and division, so they can be reduced by canceling common factors:

Choice (A): $\dfrac{a^2 b}{bc^2} = \dfrac{a^2 \cancel{b}}{\cancel{b}c^2} = \dfrac{a^2}{c^2}$ Doesn't match

Choice (B): $\dfrac{a^2 b}{b^2 c} = \dfrac{a^2 \cancel{b}}{b^{\cancel{2}} c} = \dfrac{a^2}{bc}$ Match!

Stop as soon as you are confident that you've found a match, but for the sake of completeness, here is the remaining choice:

Choice (C): $\dfrac{ab^2}{bc^2} = \dfrac{ab^{\cancel{2}}}{\cancel{b}c^2} = \dfrac{ab}{c^2}$ Doesn't match

The correct answer is (B).

18. **(J)** $h \geq \$21$ Intermediate Algebra   Inequalities and Absolute Value

The number of hours worked times the average hourly wage $(70 \times \$h)$ is Frank's total paycheck. Since $\$1,470$ is the minimum paycheck, $70h \geq \$1,470$, or $h \geq \$21$. The correct answer is (J).

19. **(A)** -8 Intermediate Algebra   Other Intermediate Algebra (Matrices)

The determinant of $\begin{bmatrix} 2a & 8b \\ 4b & 3a \end{bmatrix}$ has the value $(2a)(3a) - (4b)(8b) = 6a^2 - 32b^2$. Substituting $a = 2$ and $b = -1$, this expression becomes $6(2)^2 - 32(-1)^2 = 24 - 32 = -8$. The correct answer is (A).

20. **(H)** $\dfrac{j \cdot k \cdot j}{m \cdot j}$ Intermediate Algebra   Exponents, Radicals, Rationals

The target expression $\dfrac{j \cdot k}{m}$ is already as simplified as it can be. You'll have to work backwards from the answer choices, simplifying these expressions as efficiently you can. Since every operation is multiplication (the dots) or division, you can cancel factors:

Choice (F): $\dfrac{j \cdot k \cdot m}{m \cdot n} = \dfrac{j \cdot k \cdot \cancel{m}}{\cancel{m} \cdot n} = \dfrac{j \cdot k}{n}$ Close, but doesn't match

Choice (G): $\dfrac{j \cdot k \cdot m \cdot n}{j \cdot n} = \dfrac{\cancel{j} \cdot k \cdot m \cdot \cancel{n}}{\cancel{j} \cdot \cancel{n}} = k \cdot m$ Doesn't match

Choice (H): $\dfrac{j \cdot k \cdot j}{m \cdot j} = \dfrac{j \cdot k \cdot \cancel{j}}{m \cdot \cancel{j}} = \dfrac{j \cdot k}{m}$ Match!

Stop as soon as you are confident that you've found a match, but for the sake of completeness, here are the remaining choices.

Choice (J): $\dfrac{j \cdot k \cdot k}{m \cdot n \cdot k} = \dfrac{j \cdot k}{m \cdot n}$

Choice (K): $\dfrac{j \cdot j \cdot k}{j \cdot n} = \dfrac{\cancel{j} \cdot j \cdot k}{\cancel{j} \cdot n} = \dfrac{j \cdot k}{n}$ Close again, but doesn't match

The correct answer is (H).

21. **(B)** 1   Intermediate Algebra   Formulas, Functions, Sequences

To determine what values of y make $f(y)$ and $g(y)$ equal to each other, set the expressions in each function equal to each other and solve for y:

$$3y + y^2 = 6y - 2$$
$$y^2 - 3y + 2 = 0$$
$$(y - 2)(y - 1) = 0$$

Therefore, $f(y)$ and $g(y)$ will be equal to each other whenever $y = 1$ or 2. Since 2 is not a choice, the correct answer is 1. You can verify that this is the correct answer by substituting 1 into the expression for each function and determining that the results are equal:

$$f(1) = 3 \cdot 1 + 1^2 = 4$$
$$g(1) = 6 \cdot 1 - 2 = 4$$

The correct answer is (B).

22. **(H)** 25   Intermediate Algebra   Other Intermediate Algebra (Matrices)

The dot product has the value $xz + y^2 + zx = 2xz + y^2$. Substituting $x = 2$, $y = -3$ and $z = 4$, this expression becomes $2(2)(4) + (-3)^2$, which simplifies to $16 + 9 = 25$. The correct answer is (H).

23. **(E)** 2.0   Intermediate Algebra   Formulas, Functions, Sequences

The value of y is defined by $f(x)$, that is, as a function of the value of x. It is given in the problem that the function takes the form of a line in the standard (x, y) coordinate plane. Therefore, for every amount of change in x, there will be a constant change in y.

The function will take the form $f(x) = y = mx + b$, where m is the slope of the line (defined as the change in y divided by the change in x), and b is a constant. You can solve for m and b using any two points in the chart. First solve for m by using the points for $x = -1$ and $x = 0$:

$$m = \frac{(\text{change in } y)}{(\text{change in } x)} = \frac{(4.4 - 3.8)}{(-1 - 0)} = \frac{0.6}{-1} = -0.6$$

Thus, the slope of the line is -0.6. In other words, every time x increases 1 unit, y decreases by 0.6 units. Use this information to fill in the entire table given:

x	$y = f(x)$
−1	4.4
0	3.8
1	*3.2*
2	*2.6*
3	**2.0**
4	*1.4*
5	0.8

The question asks for the y-coordinate when $x = 3$, so the correct answer is 2.0.

Alternatively, you could continue to use the slope-intercept equation to solve for this y-coordinate. Once you know that $m = -0.6$, you can substitute any known point on the line into the equation to solve for b. Using (0, 3.8) you get the following:

$$y = -0.6x + b$$
$$3.8 = -0.6(0) + b$$
$$b = 3.8$$

The complete equation for the line is therefore $y = -0.6x + 3.8$. Now substitute 3 for x into this equation to determine the y-coordinate at $x = 3$:

$$y = -0.6(3) + 3.8 = -1.8 + 3.8 = 2.0$$

The correct answer is (E).

24.   **(F)** –20   Intermediate Algebra   Inequalities and Absolute Value

One method to solve this problem is to test all the choices:

$|2(-20)-1| = 41$ **NOT less than or equal to 40**

$|2(-18)-1| = 37$ Less than or equal to 40

$|2(-15)-1| = 31$ Less than or equal to 40

$|2(0)-1| = 1$ Less than or equal to 40

$|2(20)-1| = 39$ Less than or equal to 40

This approach yields the correct answer, –20.

Another interpretation of the problem is to think about the absolute value expression as measuring distance: $|a - b|$ measures the distance between a and b on the number line. In this case, $|2x - 1|$ corresponds to the distance between $2x$ and 1.

For which of these values is the distance between $2x$ and 1 greater than 40? It is when $x = -20$, because $2x$ is -40 and this is more than 40 units away from 1 on the number line. By contrast, when $x = 20$, $2x$ is 40, which is just less than 40 units away from 1 on the number line (39 to be exact). The correct answer is (F).

MANHATTAN
PREP

25.   **(E)** All $y \geq 6$ Intermediate Algebra   Inequalities and Absolute Value

You can determine the appropriate range for y algebraically as follows:

$9 - 3(y - 3) \leq 0$	Original inequality
$9 \leq 3(y - 3)$	Add $3(y - 3)$ to both sides
$3 \leq (y - 3)$	Divide both sides by 3
$6 \leq y$	Add 3 to both sides
$y \geq 6$	Reverse the direction of the inequality

In the final step, you can say that "if 6 must be less than or equal to y, then y must be greater than or equal to 6." The correct answer is that all values equal to or greater than 6 for y will satisfy the inequality. The correct answer is (E).

26.   **(J)** $x^2 < y^2$ Intermediate Algebra   Inequalities and Absolute Value

To solve this problem, pick numbers to eliminate incorrect answer choices. For example, if $x = 2$ and $y = 3$, then $|x| < |y|$, so you can eliminate choices (F) and (H). If $x = 5$ and $y = -10$, $|x| < |y|$, but $x > y$ and $x^2 < y^2$, so you can eliminate choices (G) and (K). These two examples leave only choice (J) remaining.

Alternatively, you can think of the absolute value expression as measuring distance: $|x|$ is the distance between x and 0 on the number line, just as $|y|$ is the distance between y and 0. According to the problem, then, x is closer to 0 than y is. The only choice that will be necessarily true in that case is (J), $x^2 < y^2$, because by squaring the numbers you are squaring their distance from 0 (positive/negative signs can be ignored). If x is closer to 0 than y, then the square of its distance from 0 will be smaller than the square of the distance between y and 0. The correct answer is (J).

27.   **(A)** All $x > 9$ Intermediate Algebra   Inequalities and Absolute Value

The phrase "4 times a number x" is represented as $4x$; subtracting this quantity from 16 yields $16 - 4x$. If this result must be less than -20, then $16 - 4x < -20$.

You can determine the appropriate range for x algebraically as follows:

$16 - 4x < -20$	Original inequality
$16 < 4x - 20$	Add $4x$ to both sides
$4 \leq x - 5$	Divide both sides by 5
$9 < x$	Add 5 to both sides
$x > 9$	Reverse the direction of the inequality

In the final step, you can say that "if 9 must be less than x, then x must be greater than 9." The correct answer is that all values larger than 9 for x will satisfy the inequality. The correct answer is (A).

28.   **(G)** 4   Intermediate Algebra   Logarithms

By the definition of a logarithm, $\log_a 64$ means that a is raised to a certain power and the result is 64. If $\log_a 64 = 3$, you can restate the equation as $a^3 = 64$. The value $a = 4$ satisfies this equation. The correct answer is (G).

13

29. **(D)** $36x^6y^{10}z^8$ Intermediate Algebra   Exponents, Radicals, Rationals

$(3x^3 \cdot y^5 \cdot 2z^4)^2 = 3^2(x^3)^2 \cdot (y^5)^2 \cdot 2^2(z^4)^2 = 9x^6 \cdot y^{10} \cdot 4z^8 = 36x^6y^{10}z^8$. Don't forget the exponent rule that $(x^a)^b = x^{ab}$, not x^{a+b}. The correct answer is (D).

30. **(H)** $\dfrac{1}{4}$ Intermediate Algebra   Logarithms

By the definition of a logarithm, $\log_x \dfrac{1}{16}$ means that x is raised to a certain power and the result is $\dfrac{1}{16}$. If $\log_x \dfrac{1}{16} = 2$,

you can restate the equation as $x^2 = \dfrac{1}{16}$. The value $x = \dfrac{1}{4}$ satisfies this equation, because $\left(\dfrac{1}{4}\right)^2 = \dfrac{1 \cdot 1}{4 \cdot 4} = \dfrac{1}{16}$. The correct

answer is (H).

31. **(B)** $\sqrt{\dfrac{G+7}{4}}$ Intermediate Algebra   Exponents, Radicals, Rationals

The given equation expresses G in terms of L. Rearrange this equation to solve for L in terms of G.

$$G = 4L^2 - 7$$
$$G + 7 = 4L^2$$
$$\dfrac{G+7}{4} = L^2$$
$$\sqrt{\dfrac{G+7}{4}} = L$$

Notice that in the last step, you put the square root symbol (the radical) around the entire left side. Because you are told that both numbers are positive, you don't have to worry about the possibility of negative roots. The correct answer is (B).

32. **(F)** $72x^4y^6$ Intermediate Algebra   Exponents, Radicals, Rationals

$\left(6x^2 \cdot \sqrt{2}y^3\right)^2 = 6^2(x^2)^2 \cdot (\sqrt{2})^2(y^3)^2 = 36x^4 \cdot 2y^6 = 72x^4y^6$. Don't forget the exponent rule that $(a^x)^y = a^{xy}$, not a^{x+y}. The correct answer is (F).

33. **(E)** 324   Intermediate Algebra   Sequences

By definition, the items in a geometric sequence are multiplied by some constant term from one item in the sequence to the next. In this question, the first numbers given in the sequence are 4, 12, and 36. Since $12 \div 4 = 3$ and $36 \div 12 = 3$, therefore, the common ratio for the geometric sequence is 3.

13

The first 5 terms in the sequence, are thus as follows:

Term 1:   4

Term 2: $4 \times 3 = 12$

Term 3: $12 \times 3 = 36$

Term 4: $36 \times 3 = 108$

Term 5: $108 \times 3 = \mathbf{324}$

The question asks for the 5th term in the sequence, so the correct answer is 324. The correct answer is (E).

34.   **(H)** $-\sqrt{\dfrac{y-6}{3}}$ Intermediate Algebra   Exponents, Radicals, Rationals

You will take the given equation ($y = 3x^2 + 6$) and solve for x in terms of y. However, before you dive in, take a look at the other fact you're given: $xy < 0$. This is code for the fact that the values of x and y under consideration must have opposite signs. One of the values is positive, while the other is negative. Moreover, since $y = 3x^2 + 6$, the value of y must be positive: it is a square (x^2), which for real numbers can never be less than 0, times 3, plus 6. In fact, the lowest value of y is 6, so it is quite safely positive for any corresponding value of x. Because the two variables have opposite signs according to the given condition, the value of x must therefore be negative.

Go ahead and rearrange the equation to isolate x.

$$y = 3x^2 + 6$$
$$y - 6 = 3x^2$$
$$\frac{y-6}{3} = x^2$$

The final step is to "unsquare" both sides of the equation—that is, take the square root. However, when you take the square root of both sides of an equation, you must consider both the positive and the negative possibilities. For instance, if $x^2 = 4$, then x could be 2 or –2. In other words, x could be $\sqrt{4}$ or $-\sqrt{4}$. Notice that the square root symbol (the radical) always means "take the positive root," so if you want the negative square root, you must place a negative sign outside the radical.

Since x must have a negative value, take the square root and place a minus sign in front.

$$\frac{y-6}{3} = x^2$$
$$-\sqrt{\frac{y-6}{3}} = x$$

The correct answer is (H).

35.   **(C)** $x \le -11$ Intermediate Algebra   Inequalities and Absolute Value

To find the set of solutions for this inequality, subtract 15 from both sides of the inequality $15 - 3x \ge 48$ to get $-3x \ge 48 - 15$, or $-3x \ge 33$. You can then isolate x by dividing both sides by -3 to get $x \le -11$. (Note that when you divide or multiply both sides of an inequality by a negative number, the inequality sign must be reversed.) The correct answer is (C).

36. **(J)** 2   Intermediate Algebra   Exponents, Radicals, Rationals

Rearrange the given equation to make one side equal to $2k - j$.

$$2j = 4k + 8 \quad \rightarrow \quad j = 2k + 4 \quad \rightarrow \quad 0 = 2k + 4 - j \quad \rightarrow \quad -4 = 2k - j$$

Now substitute into the target expression.

$$\sqrt{-(2k - j)} = \sqrt{-(-4)} = \sqrt{4} = 2$$

This problem raises the specter of complex numbers (the imaginary number i is surfaced in the question). This allows for a "complex" answer, if you had to take the square root of a negative number. However, in the end, the answer is completely real in the mathematical sense: there's no imaginary part. The correct answer is (J).

37. **(D)** $\dfrac{1}{6b} + \dfrac{1}{8a}$ Intermediate Algebra   Exponents, Radicals, Rationals

When adding two fractions with the same base, you add the numerators and keep the common denominator. You can also work backwards. If there is a sum or a difference in the numerator, you can split that numerator up over the common base and then cancel any common factors:

$$\frac{4a + 3b}{24ab} = \frac{4a}{24ab} + \frac{3b}{24ab} = \frac{1}{6b} + \frac{1}{8a}$$

The correct answer is (D).

38. **(G)** 2.0×10^4 Intermediate Algebra   Formulas, Functions, Sequences

h is given to be 2, and e is given to be 2.718. Because the time interval expressed in the question prompt is three months, the resulting equation is $R = \dfrac{2.718^3}{2} \times 2{,}000 = 1{,}000(2.718)^3$. You know that $2^3 = 8$ and $3^3 = 27$, so $(2.718)^3$ must be between 8 and 27 (and probably closer to 27—in fact, 2.718^3 is approximately 20). Therefore, the entire expression is between 8,000 (8.0×10^3) and 27,000 (2.7×10^4), so only choice (G), 2.0×10^4, can be correct. You can also do these calculations in your calculator. The correct answer is (G).

39. **(A)** $\dfrac{1}{6} - \dfrac{1}{10x}$ Intermediate Algebra   Exponents, Radicals, Rationals

When adding two fractions with the same base, you add the numerators and keep the common denominator. You can also work backwards. If there is a sum or a difference in the numerator, you can split that numerator up over the common base and then cancel any common factors:

$$\frac{5x^2 - 3x}{30x^2} = \frac{5x^2}{30x^2} - \frac{3x}{30x^2} = \frac{1}{6} - \frac{1}{10x}$$

The correct answer is (A).

MANHATTAN
PREP

40. **(J)** $-3 \leq x \leq 29$ Intermediate Algebra   Inequalities and Absolute Value

You must find all the possible x values that satisfy the inequality $\sqrt{2x+6} \leq 8$. To do so, isolate x within the inequality:

$$\sqrt{2x+6} \leq 8$$
$$\left(\sqrt{2x+6}\right)^2 \leq 8^2$$
$$2x+6 \leq 64$$
$$2x \leq 58$$
$$x \leq 29$$

Now add the requirement that $x \geq -3$, because otherwise, the value under the radical would be negative and the expression would not be a real number. Thus, $-3 \leq x \leq 29$.

If you substitute any number between 29 and -3 into the original inequality, you'll see that the inequality is validated. The correct answer is (J).

41. **(E)** $\dfrac{a+1}{a-1}$ Intermediate Algebra   Quadratics

To simplify this expression, factor the quadratic expressions in both the numerator and the denominator:

$$\frac{\left(a^2+3a+2\right)(a-3)}{\left(a^2-4a+3\right)(a+2)} = \frac{(a+2)(a+1)(a-3)}{(a-3)(a-1)(a+2)}$$

Notice that both the numerator and denominator contain the factors $(a+2)$ and $(a-3)$. It is given in the problem that a must be greater than 10; therefore, these terms cannot equal 0 and will cancel each other out, leaving only one factor each in the numerator and denominator:

$$\frac{\cancel{(a+2)}(a+1)\cancel{(a-3)}}{\cancel{(a-3)}(a-1)\cancel{(a+2)}} =$$

$$\frac{(a+1)}{(a-1)}$$

The correct answer is (E).

42. **(K)** $\sqrt{7} \leq |x| \leq 10$ Intermediate Algebra   Inequalities and Absolute Value

You must find all the possible x values that satisfy the inequality $\sqrt{x^2-7} \leq \sqrt{93}$. To do so, isolate x within the inequality:

$$\sqrt{x^2-7} \leq \sqrt{93}$$
$$\left(\sqrt{x^2-7}\right)^2 \leq \left(\sqrt{93}\right)^2$$
$$x^2 \leq 100$$
$$\sqrt{x^2} \leq \sqrt{100}$$

13

By definition, $\sqrt{x^2} = |x|$. Therefore, the final inequality translates to $|x| \le 10$. In order for the absolute value of x to be less than or equal to 10, it must be no more than 10 units away from 0 on the number line. That will be the case whenever $-10 \le x \le 10$. However, a final correction must be added: $\sqrt{x^2 - 7}$ is undefined whenever the expression inside the radical is less than 0. In other words, x^2 must be greater than or equal to 7. This condition is achieved when $|x|$ is greater than or equal to $\sqrt{7}$. Adding this condition to the range $-10 \le x \le 10$ yields, in a compact form, $\sqrt{7} \le |x| \le 10$. The correct answer is (K).

43. **(C)** The sixth term in the sequence is 4.   Intermediate Algebra   Formulas, Functions, Sequences

An arithmetic sequence is defined as a series of numbers, each of which is a constant amount greater (or less) than the term before it. In this case, $-8 - (-11) = -8 + 11 = 3$; $-5 - (-8) = -5 + 8 = 3$; $-2 - (-5) = -2 + 5 = 3$; and so on. The common difference of consecutive terms is 3. That is, you just add 3 to get to the next term. You can extend the sequence a bit further:

   $-11, -8, -5, -2, 1, 4, 7, 10, 13, 16, \dots$

Using this extended version of the sequence, it will be straightforward to evaluate each of the choices:

None of the terms in the sequence is positive.   INCORRECT. All terms after and including the fifth term are positive.

The sum of the first 10 terms is negative.   INCORRECT. Grouping the first 10 terms from the inside-out, you have $(-11 + 16) = 5$, $(-8 + 13) = 5$, $(-5 + 10) = 5$, $(-2 + 7) = 5$, and $(1 + 4) = 5$. $5 + 5 + 5 + 5 + 5 = 25$.

The sixth term in the sequence is 4.   CORRECT. The sequence is $-11, -8, -5, -2, 1, \underline{4}, \dots$

8 is a term in the sequence.   INCORRECT. The seventh term in the sequence is 7, and the eighth term in the sequence is 10. Because the sequence is always increasing after that, 8 cannot be a term in the sequence.

The common difference of consecutive terms is 4.   INCORRECT. As demonstrated above, the common difference of consecutive terms is 3.

The correct answer is therefore that the sixth term in the sequence is 4. The correct answer is (C).

44. **(F)** 0   Intermediate Algebra   Other Intermediate Algebra (Complex Numbers)

The definition of the complex number i is $i = \sqrt{-1}$. You can determine the next several powers of i by multiplying i by itself and carrying the product forward:

Expression	Calculation	Result
$i^1 = i$	$\sqrt{-1}$	$\sqrt{-1} = i$
i^2	$(\sqrt{-1})(\sqrt{-1})$	-1
i^3	$-1(\sqrt{-1})$	$-\sqrt{-1} = -i$
i^4	$(-\sqrt{-1})(\sqrt{-1})$	$-(-1) = 1$
i^5	$1(\sqrt{-1})$	$\sqrt{-1} = i$

As you can see, a pattern emerges: $i^5 = i^1 = \sqrt{-1}$, and all of the values going forward for higher powers of i will repeat this pattern: i, -1, $-i$, 1, i, etc. Therefore, the only choice in the problem that cannot be the result of i to an integer power is 0. The correct answer is (F).

45. **(E)** $\begin{bmatrix} 3bx & -3by \\ -2ax & 2ay \end{bmatrix}$ Intermediate Algebra   Other Intermediate Algebra (Matrices)

When calculating a matrix product, it is important to remember the following rules:

- The number of rows in the product will equal the number of rows in the *leftmost* matrix or vector being multiplied.
- The number of columns in the product will equal the number of columns in the *rightmost* matrix or vector being multiplied.

In the matrix product displayed in the problem, the leftmost matrix contains 2 rows and the rightmost matrix contains 2 columns. Therefore, the result will be a 2-by-2 matrix, which eliminates choices (A), (B), and (C):

$$\begin{bmatrix} ? & ? \\ ? & ? \end{bmatrix}$$

The entries in the resulting matrix are calculated as follows: the entry in (row i, column j) of the product is equal to the sum of the products of (the elements of row i of the leftmost matrix) and (the elements of column j of the rightmost matrix). Since each row in the leftmost matrix and each column in the rightmost matrix only contain one element, the value in each element of the result will be the product of those two elements.

For example, the element of row 1, column 1 of the matrix product equals row 1 of the leftmost matrix ($3b$) times column 1 of the rightmost matrix (x). Therefore, that element is $3bx$. Each of the other elements in the product are calculated in the same manner:

$$\begin{bmatrix} (3b)(x) & (3b)(-y) \\ (-2a)(x) & (-2a)(-y) \end{bmatrix} = \begin{bmatrix} 3bx & -3by \\ -2ax & 2ay \end{bmatrix}$$

The correct answer is (E).

46. **(H)** i^3 Intermediate Algebra   Other Intermediate Algebra (Complex Numbers)

The definition of the complex number i is $i = \sqrt{-1}$. You can determine the next several powers of i by multiplying i by itself and carrying the product forward:

Expression	Calculation	Result
$i^1 = i$	$\sqrt{-1}$	$\sqrt{-1} = i$
i^2	$\left(\sqrt{-1}\right)\left(\sqrt{-1}\right)$	-1
i^3	$-1\left(\sqrt{-1}\right)$	$-\sqrt{-1} = -i$
i^4	$\left(-\sqrt{-1}\right)\left(\sqrt{-1}\right)$	$-(-1) = 1$
i^5	$1\left(\sqrt{-1}\right)$	$\sqrt{-1} = i$

As you can see, a pattern emerges: $i^5 = i^1 = \sqrt{-1}$, and all of the values going forward for higher powers of i will repeat this pattern: i, -1, $-i$, 1, i, etc. This question asks which power of i produces the result $-i$. The correct answer is (H).

47. **(E)** 4   Intermediate Algebra   Quadratics (Maximization/Minimization)

Perhaps the easiest way to solve this problem is to test the choices and see which value, when substituted for b, produces the lowest value for a:

$(0 - 4)^2 + 12 = (-4)^2 + 12 = 16 + 12 = 28$
$(1 - 4)^2 + 12 = (-3)^2 + 12 = 9 + 12 = 21$
$(2 - 4)^2 + 12 = (-2)^2 + 12 = 4 + 12 = 16$
$(3 - 4)^2 + 12 = (-1)^2 + 12 = 1 + 12 = 13$
$\mathbf{(4 - 4)^2 + 12 = (0)^2 + 12 = 0 + 12 = 12}$

Among the choices, the lowest possible value for a is 12, achieved when $b = 4$, so choice (E) is correct.

Alternatively, you could observe that the squared term in the quadratic expression is $(b - 4)^2$. This value will always be non-negative, because squared numbers cannot be negative. Therefore, to make a as small as possible, try to make the squared term as small as possible. The smallest it can be is 0, and that will occur when $b = 4$, because $(4 - 4)^2 = 0$. The correct answer is (E).

48. **(G)** $[6x - 8z]$ Intermediate Algebra   Other Intermediate Algebra (Matrices (Matrix Multiplication))

When calculating a matrix product, it is important to remember the following rules:

- The number of rows in the product will equal the number of rows in the *leftmost* matrix or vector being multiplied.
- The number of columns in the product will equal the number of columns in the *rightmost* matrix or vector being multiplied.

In the matrix product displayed in the problem, the leftmost matrix contains 1 row and the rightmost matrix contains 1 column. Therefore, the result will be a 1-by-1 matrix (or alternatively, a simple expression, depending on the context), which eliminates choices (H), (J), and (K). The correct answer will look like:

[?]   or   ?

The entries in the resulting matrix are calculated as follows: the entry in (row i, column j) of the product is equal to the sum of the products of (the elements of row i of the leftmost matrix) and (the elements of column j of the rightmost matrix). In this case, there is only 1 row in the leftmost matrix and only 1 column in the rightmost matrix. Therefore, the result will be the sum of the products of the 3 elements of each matrix (going left-to-right and top-to-bottom, respectively):

$$[(6)(x)+(7)(0)+(8)(-z)] = [6x - 8z]$$

The correct answer is (G).

49. **(D)** 874   Intermediate Algebra   Formulas, Functions, Sequences

According to Carl, Aaron's scores for the 4 games constitute an arithmetic sequence. An arithmetic sequence is defined as a series of numbers, each of which is a constant amount greater (or less) than the term before it. This constant amount is called the "common difference." The common difference in this case is given as 7. You can extend the sequence to all 4 games:

208, 215, 222, 229

Notice that the sum of the first and last terms is $208 + 229 = 437$, and the sum of the middle two terms is $215 + 222 = 437$. (This will always work for an arithmetic sequence, and can make the process of summing the numbers in the sequence easier.)

Thus, Aaron's total score for the tournament is $437 \times 2 = 874$. The correct answer is (D).

50. **(F)** –3   Intermediate Algebra   Quadratics (Maximization/Minimization)

Perhaps the easiest way to solve this problem is to test the choices and see which value, when substituted for x, produces the highest value for y:

$(-3)^2 - 3 = 9 - 3 = 6$
$(-2)^2 - 3 = 4 - 3 = 1$
$(-1)^2 - 3 = 1 - 3 = -2$
$(0)^2 - 3 = 0 - 3 = -3$
$(1)^2 - 3 = 1 - 3 = -2$

Among the choices, the highest possible value for y is 6, achieved when $x = -3$, so choice (F) is correct.

Alternatively, you could observe that the squared term in the quadratic expression is x^2. This value will always be non-negative, because squared numbers cannot be negative. Furthermore, it will get larger the farther away from 0 that x gets on the number line. Among the choices, the farthest value from 0 is choice (F), –3, even though it is the smallest number among the choices. The correct answer is (F).

13

51. **(D)** 8   Intermediate Algebra   Logarithms

To solve this logarithm problem, you can recognize the following:

$$\log_b a = c \quad \rightarrow \quad b^c = a$$

Transform the logarithm function: $2^x = 16^2$.

Using exponent rules, you can write 16^2 as $(2^4)^2$ or 2^8.

Therefore, $2^x = 2^8$ or $x = 8$. The correct answer is (D).

52. **(J)** 7   Intermediate Algebra   Exponents, Radicals, Rationals

The equation can be restated as:

$$3^b(9) = 3^9$$
$$3^b(3^2) = 3^9$$
$$3^{b+2} = 3^9$$

If the two exponent bases are the same, the exponents on the left and right side of the equation must be equal:

$$3^{b+2} = 3^9$$
$$b + 2 = 9$$
$$b = 7$$

The correct answer is (J).

53. **(A)** $x - y$ Intermediate Algebra   Logarithms

To solve this logarithm problem, you can recognize the following:

$$\log_b a = c \quad \rightarrow \quad b^c = a$$

As a special case, if a is already written as a power of the base b, then the logarithm of a equals that power.

Back to the given problem. First, use exponent rules to simplify the term $\dfrac{5^x}{5^y} = 5^{x-y}$.

By the special case described above, $\log_5 5^{x-y}$ is $x - y$. The correct answer is (A).

54. **(K)** 10   Intermediate Algebra   Quadratic

The question asks for the largest value of x such that the quadratic expression $x^2 - 2x$ is less than 80. In order to solve this problem, first manipulate the inequality so that all terms are on one side:

$$x^2 - 2x \le 80$$
$$x^2 - 2x - 80 \le 0$$

MANHATTAN
PREP

Next, solve for the solutions to the equivalent equation to determine the values for which the quadratic expression equals 0:

$x^2 - 2x - 80 = 0$
$(x - 10)(x + 8) = 0$

Therefore, the solution to the equivalent equation is $x = -8$ or $x = 10$. These will be the points at which the "greater than or equal to" relation in the inequality will just hold—that is, the left hand side of the inequality will equal 0 (or, in the original inequality in the problem, the left hand side will equal 80).

You can segment the possibilities for x according to these points and evaluate the inequality in the ranges above and below them, keeping in mind that the left-hand side must be negative or 0:

$x^2 - 2x - 80 \leq 0$
$(x - 10)(x + 8) \leq 0$

	$x < -8$	$-8 < x < 10$	$x > 10$
$(x - 10)$	Negative	*Negative*	Positive
$(x + 8)$	Negative	*Positive*	Positive
$(x - 10)(x + 8)$	Positive	*Negative*	Positive

The only range over which $(x - 10)(x + 8)$ is negative is when $-8 < x < 10$. Since $(x - 10)(x + 8)$ equals 0 when $x = 10$, 10 is the largest possible value for which the inequality holds. The correct answer is (K).

55. **(C)** 189   Intermediate Algebra   Exponents, Radicals, Rationals

One way to simplify the calculation of this expression is to notice that each term has the common factor, 3^3. This can be factored out:

$3^3 - 3^4 + 3^5 =$
$3^3(1 - 3^1 + 3^2) =$
$3^3(1 - 3 + 9) = 3^3(7)$

Since $3^3 = 27$, the expression equals $27 \times 7 = 189$. You can also crunch the whole calculation in your calculator. The correct answer is (C).

56. **(K)** 24   Intermediate Algebra   Inequalities and Absolute Value

One method to solve this problem is to test all the choices:

$\left| \dfrac{50(12)}{(400)} - 4 \right| = |1.5 - 4|$ NOT less than or equal to 1

$\left| \dfrac{50(16)}{(400)} - 4 \right| = |2 - 4|$ NOT less than or equal to 1

$$\left|\frac{50(18)}{(400)} - 4\right| = |2.25 - 4|$$ NOT less than or equal to 1

$$\left|\frac{50(20)}{(400)} - 4\right| = |2.5 - 4|$$ NOT less than or equal to 1

$$\left|\frac{50(24)}{(400)} - 4\right| = |3 - 4|$$ **Less than or equal to 1**

This approach yields the correct answer, 24.

Another interpretation of the problem is to think about the absolute value expression as measuring distance. First, substitute 400 for b into the inequality and simplify it for further analysis:

$$\left|\frac{50d}{b} - 4\right| \leq 1$$

$$\left|\frac{50d}{400} - 4\right| \leq 1$$

$$\left|\frac{1}{8}d - 4\right| \leq 1$$

$$|d - 32| \leq 8$$

$|a - b|$ measures the distance between a and b on the number line. In this case, $|d - 32| \leq 8$ corresponds to the distance between d and 32. Since d and 32 have to be no more than 8 units apart on the number line, d must be between 24 and 40, inclusive.

The answer choice which fulfills this criterion is (K), 24.

57.   **(D)** between 2 and 3   Intermediate Algebra   Formulas, Functions, Sequences

It is given in the problem that the rate of heat transfer is given by the equation $H(T) = T^4 k$, where T is the temperature differential between the object and its surroundings and k is a constant. Therefore, the higher the temperature differential, the higher the heat transfer; since the objects are of the same temperature, the colder room will have the higher temperature differential. The question asks for the ratio of the temperature differential involving the colder room to the temperature differential involving the warmer room, so the ratio will be greater than 1. This eliminates choices (A) and (B).

In Room 1, the rate of heat transfer from the object is 20 times that from the object in Room 2. The objective is to determine the ratio of the temperature differential in Room 1 to the temperature differential in Room 2. For the sake of simplicity, call those temperature differentials T_1 and T_2, respectively:

$$\frac{H(T_1)}{H(T_2)} = \frac{k \cdot (T_1)^4}{k \cdot (T_2)^4} = \frac{(T_1)^4}{(T_2)^4} = \left(\frac{T_1}{T_2}\right)^4 = 20$$

$$\frac{T_1}{T_2} = \sqrt[4]{20}$$

By simplifying, you can see that the ratio of the heat transfers in the 2 rooms (20) is equal to the ratio of the temperature differentials, taken to the 4th power. Therefore, you need to estimate the 4th root of 20 to estimate the temperature differentials. Because $1^4 = 1$, $2^4 = 16$, and $3^4 = 81$, the 4th root of 20 must be between 2 and 3, and likely much closer to 2 (indeed, if you take the square root of 20 twice in your calculator, you'll find that $\sqrt[4]{20} \approx 2.115$, as you can see if you take the square root of 20 twice). Therefore, the correct answer must be (D).

Alternatively, you can think through the choices listed to determine which will produce the correct heat transfer ratio. In choice (D), the ratio of the temperature differentials is between 2 and 3 (in other words, the larger temperature differential is 2 to 3 times the smaller temperature differential). If this is the case, it will result in the higher-differential object exhibiting a heat transfer rate of between $2^4 = 16$ and $3^4 = 81$ times that of the lower-differential object. Since 20 is between 16 and 81, then once again the ratio of temperature differentials must be between 2 and 3.

58. **(J)** 420   Intermediate Algebra   Formulas, Functions, Sequences

The series of all even integers from 2 to 40 constitutes an arithmetic sequence. Unfortunately, because there are so many items in this sequence, it is going to be cumbersome, if not impossible, to compute this sum in a timely, accurate fashion:

$2 + 4 + 6 + 8 + \ldots + 38 + 40$

Perhaps the best way to compute the total is to factor the sum, because all integers in the sequence are divisible by 2:

$(2 + 4 + 6 + 8 + \ldots + 38 + 40) =$
$2(1 + 2 + 3 + 4 + \ldots + 19 + 20)$

A useful formula to remember for the sum of consecutive integers from A to B is as follows:

$$(B - A + 1)\left(\frac{B+A}{2}\right)$$

In this product, the leftmost expression equals the number of items in the set of consecutive integers. Here, $B - A + 1 = 20 - 1 + 1 = 20$. The rightmost expression equals the average value of the items in the set of consecutive integers. Here, $\left(\frac{B+A}{2}\right) = \left(\frac{20+1}{2}\right) = 10.5$. Therefore, the sum of the consecutive integers from 1 to 20 is equal to $20 \times 10.5 = 10 \times 21 = 210$. Now you can compute the entire sum:

Sum of even integers from 2 to 40 $= 2 \cdot 210 = 420$

The correct answer is (J).

59. **(C)** $(a + b)a^4c^2$ Intermediate Algebra   Formulas, Functions, Sequences

By definition, the items in a geometric sequence are multiplied by some constant term from one item in the sequence to the next. In this question, the first numbers given in the sequence are $(a + b)$ and $(a + b)a^2c$; $(a + b)a^2c \div (a + b)$ is equal to a^2c. This is the common ratio for the geometric sequence. To confirm this, you can also look at the 4th and 5th terms in the sequence: $(a + b)a^6c^3$ and $(a + b)a^8c^4$. Once again, $(a + b)a^8c^4 \div (a + b)a^6c^3 = a^2c$.

The first five terms in the sequence, therefore, are as follows:

Term 1: $(a + b)$

Term 2: $(a + b) \times a^2c = (a + b)a^2c$

Term 4: $(a + b)a^2c \times a^2c = \boldsymbol{(a + b)a^4c^2}$

Term 4: $(a + b)a^4c^2 \times a^2c = (a + b)a^6c^3$

Term 5: $(a + b)a^6c^3 \times a^2c = (a + b)a^8c^4$

The question asks for the 3rd term in the sequence, so the correct answer is $(a + b)a^4c^2$. The correct answer is (C).

60. **(K)** $351   Intermediate Algebra   Formulas, Functions, Sequences

The series of all integers from 1 to 26 constitutes an arithmetic sequence—specifically, a sequence of consecutive integers. Unfortunately, because there are so many items in this sequence, it is going to be cumbersome, if not impossible, to compute this sum in a timely, accurate fashion:

$$\$1 + \$2 + \$3 + \$4 + \ldots + \$25 + \$26$$

A useful formula to remember for the sum of consecutive integers from A to B is as follows:

$$(B - A + 1)\left(\frac{B+A}{2}\right)$$

In this product, the leftmost expression equals the number of items in the set of consecutive integers. Here, $B - A + 1 = 26 - 1 + 1 = 26$. The rightmost expression equals the average value of the items in the set of consecutive integers. Here,

$$\left(\frac{B+A}{2}\right) = \left(\frac{26+1}{2}\right) = \$13.5.$$

Therefore, the sum of the consecutive integers from 1 to 26 is equal to $26 \times \$13.5 = 13 \times \$27 = \$351$. The correct answer is (K).

13

61. **(E)** $x = z^{\frac{1}{6}}$ Intermediate Algebra   Exponents, Radicals, Rationals

It is given in the problem that $z = y^2$ and $y = x^3$. First, connect x with z directly by substituting x^3 into the first equation for y:

$$z = (x^3)^2 = x^6 \qquad \text{(Don't forget the exponent rule that } (a^b)^c = a^{bc}, \text{ not } a^{b+c}.)$$

The question asks you to solve for x in terms of z. Therefore, find the 6th root of both sides of the equation:

$$z = x^6$$
$$x^6 = z$$
$$\sqrt[6]{x^6} = \sqrt[6]{z}$$
$$x = \sqrt[6]{z} = z^{\frac{1}{6}}$$

The correct answer is $x = z^{\frac{1}{6}}$. You can test this using numbers. Assume that $z = 64$. Then $64 = y^2$, so $y = 8$ (you are told that the variables are positive, so you can ignore the negative root), and thus $x^3 = 8$. This results in $x = 2$ (again ignoring the negative root), thus $x = z^{\frac{1}{6}}$, because $\sqrt[6]{64} = 2$. The correct answer is (E).

62. **(K)** $\sqrt{x} + \sqrt{y}$ Intermediate Algebra   Exponents, Radicals, Rationals

For this problem, you must determine which answer choice cannot be rational if x and y are integers but not perfect squares. Perhaps the easiest way to approach this question is to test each choice with numbers, trying to come up with a combination of values for x and y that make the result rational:

$\sqrt{xy}$ INCORRECT. If $x = y$, then $\sqrt{xy} = \sqrt{x^2} = x$. For example, if $x = 3$ and $y = 3$, then $\sqrt{xy} = 3$.

$\dfrac{\sqrt{x}}{\sqrt{y}}$ INCORRECT. If $x = y^3$, then $\dfrac{\sqrt{x}}{\sqrt{y}} = y$. For example, if $x = 27$ and $y = 3$, then $\dfrac{\sqrt{x}}{\sqrt{y}} = 3$.

$\sqrt{x+y}$ INCORRECT. Many non-squares sum to a square. For example, if $x = 2$ and $y = 14$, then $\sqrt{x+y} = 4$.

$\sqrt{x} - \sqrt{y}$ INCORRECT. If $x = y$, then $\sqrt{x} - \sqrt{y} = 0$. For example, if $x = 5$ and $y = 5$, then
$\sqrt{x} - \sqrt{y} = \sqrt{5} - \sqrt{5} = 0$.

$\sqrt{x} + \sqrt{y}$ **CORRECT.** There is no combination of values for x and y such that $\sqrt{x} + \sqrt{y}$ will be rational. For example, if $x = 5$ and $y = 5$, then $\sqrt{x} + \sqrt{y} = \sqrt{5} + \sqrt{5} = 2\sqrt{5}$, which is still irrational. If x and y do not share a common radical, then the result will simply be two radical expressions, which is still irrational. Finally, $\sqrt{x} + \sqrt{y} \neq 0$, because that would only be possible if $x = 0$ and $y = 0$; however, 0 is a perfect square, so this cannot be the case.

Here is a proof by contradiction: assume for a moment that $\sqrt{x} + \sqrt{y}$ is indeed rational. x and y are integers, so $x - y$ is an integer. Additionally, if $\sqrt{x} + \sqrt{y}$ is rational, then $\sqrt{x} - \sqrt{y}$ must also be rational, because

$\sqrt{x} - \sqrt{y} = \left(\sqrt{x} - \sqrt{y}\right)\dfrac{\left(\sqrt{x} + \sqrt{y}\right)}{\left(\sqrt{x} + \sqrt{y}\right)} = \dfrac{x - y}{\sqrt{x} + \sqrt{y}}$, and the ratio of two rational numbers is always rational. Then the sum

$\left(\sqrt{x} + \sqrt{y}\right) + \left(\sqrt{x} - \sqrt{y}\right) = 2\sqrt{x}$ must be rational and the difference $\left(\sqrt{x} + \sqrt{y}\right) - \left(\sqrt{x} - \sqrt{y}\right) = 2\sqrt{y}$ must be rational, because the sum and difference of rational numbers is always rational.

This is impossible because the problem stipulates that both x and y are not perfect squares, so their square roots will be irrational. Therefore, it cannot be the case that $\sqrt{x} + \sqrt{y}$ is rational.

The correct answer is (K).

13

63. **(A)** $r = s^{12}$ Intermediate Algebra   Exponents, Radicals, Rationals

It is given in the problem that $r = t^3$ and $t = s^4$. First, connect r with s directly by substituting s^4 into the first equation for t:

$r = (s^4)^3 = s^{12}$ (Don't forget the exponent rule that $(a^b)^c = a^{bc}$, not a^{b+c}.)

Therefore, the correct answer is $r = s^{12}$. You can test this using numbers. Assume that $s = 2$. Then, $t = 2^4$, so $t = 16$, and $r = 16^3$, which equals $16 \times 16 \times 16 = 256 \times 16 = 4{,}096$. This is equal to 2^{12}, so $r = s^{12}$. The correct answer is (A).

64. **(K)** $\frac{1}{2}m$ Intermediate Algebra   Formulas, Functions, Sequences

Let x represent the first of the consecutive terms. Then the next odd integer will be given by $x + 2$, the third by $x + 4$, and the fourth by $x + 6$. The sum, m, is equal to $x + x + 2 + x + 4 + x + 6 = 4x + 12$. Solve for x in terms of m:

$4x + 12 = m$

$4x = m - 12$

$x = \frac{1}{4}m - 3$

The sum of the largest and smallest is $x + 6 + x = 2x + 6$:

$x = 2\left(\frac{1}{4}m - 3\right) + 6 = \frac{1}{2}m - 6 + 6 = \frac{1}{2}m$

The correct answer is (K).

65. **(E)** 13   Intermediate Algebra   Other Intermediate Algebra (Complex Numbers)

The key here is to treat i like any other letter in algebra: pretend it's a variable, do the math, and at the end replace any i^2 that you see with -1.

You can FOIL out the product here: $(2 + 3i)(2 - 3i) = 4 + 6i - 6i - 9i^2 = 4 - 9i^2 = 4 - 9(-1) = 4 + 9 = 13$

Notice that the cross-products ($6i$ and $-6i$) cancel out. That always happens when you multiply $(a + b)$ by $(a - b)$, whether you're dealing with complex numbers or not. The correct answer is (E).

66. **(H)** $\frac{p}{3} + 2$ Intermediate Algebra   Formulas, Functions, Sequences

Let x represent the first of the consecutive terms. Then the next even integer will be given by $x + 2$, the third by $x + 4$. The sum, m, is equal to $x + x + 2 + x + 4 = 3x + 6$. Solve for x in terms of p:

$3x + 6 = p$

$3x = p - 6$

$x = \frac{p}{3} - 2$

13

The largest of these integers is given by $x + 4$:

$$x + 4 = \left(\frac{p}{3} - 2\right) + 4 = \frac{p}{3} + 2$$

The correct answer is (H).

67. **(D)** II and III only   Intermediate Algebra   Inequalities and Absolute Value

The question asks you to determine which of the given expressions in the Roman numerals is equivalent to 1 for all values of z (except 0, because z constitutes a denominator in all of the expressions given). Evaluate each statement in turn:

    I. NO. By definition, $\sqrt{z^2} = |z|$, because in each case, the result will be the positive value of z, whether z was originally negative or not. Therefore, $\dfrac{\sqrt{z^2}}{z}$ will equal 1 if and only if z is positive (provided that z is not equal to 0); otherwise it will equal -1.

    II. YES. The inner expression, $\dfrac{|z|}{z}$, will equal 1 whenever z is positive and -1 whenever z is negative. Therefore, the entire expression will evaluate to $|-1|$ or $|1|$, depending on the sign of z (provided that z is not equal to 0). Either way, the result will be 1.

    III. YES. As noted above, $\sqrt{z^2} = |z|$ in all cases. Therefore, this expression evaluates to $\dfrac{|z|}{|z|}$, which will always equal 1 (provided that z is not equal to 0).

The correct answer is (D).

68. **(H)** 2   Intermediate Algebra   Other Intermediate Algebra (Complex Numbers)

Multiply the two fractions together as you would any two other fractions. Add in parentheses to ensure that you distribute the 2 and the i correctly:

$$\frac{i+1}{1-i} \cdot \frac{2}{i} = \frac{(i+1) \times 2}{(1-i) \times i} = \frac{2i+2}{i-i^2}$$

The fact that $i = \sqrt{-1}$ can also be expressed as $i^2 = -1$. So replace the i^2 in the denominator with -1:

$$\frac{2i+2}{i-i^2} = \frac{2i+2}{i-(-1)} = \frac{2i+2}{i+1}$$

Finally, factor the 2 back out of the numerator, so that you can cancel the $(i + 1)$ on top and bottom:

$$\frac{2i+2}{i+1} = \frac{2(i+1)}{i+1} = 2$$

The correct answer is (H).

69. (B) 4.5   Intermediate Algebra   Logarithms

By the definition of a logarithm, $\log_x z$ means that x is raised to a certain power and the result is z. Define a variable y such that $\log_{10}\left(1{,}000^{\frac{3}{2}}\right) = y$. Then, $10^y = (1{,}000)^{\frac{3}{2}}$. You can now write $(1{,}000)^{\frac{3}{2}}$ as $\left((10)^3\right)^{\frac{3}{2}}$ and solve for y by setting the bases equal to each other and solving for the exponent:

$$\left((10)^3\right)^{\frac{3}{2}} = 10^y$$

$$10^{3 \times \frac{3}{2}} = 10^y$$

$$3 \times \frac{3}{2} = y$$

$$y = \frac{9}{2} = 4.5$$

Therefore, the correct answer is 4.5. (Don't forget the exponent rule that $(a^b)^c = a^{bc}$, not a^{b+c}.) The correct answer is (B).

70. (H) I and III only   Intermediate Algebra   Inequalities and Absolute Value

The question asks you to determine which of the given expressions in the Roman numerals is equivalent to $|x|$ for all values of x (except possibly 0, because x constitutes the denominator of one of the expressions given). Evaluate each statement in turn:

I. YES. $\sqrt{|x|} \cdot \sqrt{|x|} = |x|$, because the square root of any expression (as long as that expression is non-negative, as $|x|$ is) times itself equals that expression.

II. NO. Unless $x = 0$, $\dfrac{x^2}{x} = x$ for any real number value of x. Therefore, $\dfrac{x^2}{x}$ will equal $|x|$ if and only if x is positive. If it is negative, then $\dfrac{x^2}{x}$ will be negative, and absolute value by definition can never be negative.

III. YES. $|-x| = |(-1) \cdot x| = |-1| \cdot |x| = 1|x| = |x|$.

The correct answer is I and III only. The correct answer is (H).

71. (B) 1   Intermediate Algebra   Other Intermediate Algebra (Overlapping Sets)

If you want to minimize the number of people who like exactly one sport, then you should maximize the people who like either *both* sports or *neither* sport. To maximize the number who like both sports, imagine that all 14 people who like soccer are included in the 15 people who like basketball. Then 15 – 14 = 1 person likes only basketball. No one likes only soccer: 1 + 0 = 1. The other 19 – 15 = 4 people don't like either sport.

You can visualize this situation in a table that adds across and down:

MANHATTAN
PREP

	Soccer	Not Soccer	Total
Basketball	14	1	15
Not Basketball	0	4	4
Total	14	5	19

The correct answer is (B).

72. **(F)** 7   Intermediate Algebra   Logarithms

By the definition of a logarithm, $\log_a b$ means that a is raised to a certain power and the result is b. Therefore, if $\log_x 16 = 2$ and $\log_y 81 = 4$, then $x^2 = 16$ and $y^4 = 81$. Now solve for x and y by setting the exponents equal to each other and solving for the base:

$$x^2 = 16 \qquad y^4 = 81$$
$$x^2 = 4^2 \qquad y^4 = 3^4$$
$$x = 4 \qquad y = 3$$

Therefore, the correct answer is $4 + 3 = 7$. (Note that x and y must be positive, because you are told so in the problem.). The correct answer is (F).

73. **(C)** {3}   Intermediate Algebra   Exponents, Radicals, Rationals

To find the values of y that satisfy this equation, use the fact that when the bases are equal, then the exponents must also be equal. (The only exceptions to this rule occur when the base is 0 or 1, but these cases are specifically excluded from the problem.) Here, the general rule indicates the following:

$$x^{y^2+9} = x^{6y}$$
$$y^2 + 9 = 6y$$
$$y^2 - 6y + 9 = 0$$
$$(y - 3)(y - 3) = 0$$
$$y = 3$$

The correct answer is (C).

74. **(J)** 889   Intermediate Algebra   Formulas, Functions, Sequences

Umberto delivers 18 newspapers on Day 1, and this number increases by 7 each day through Day 14. Therefore, the number of newspapers delivered each day is an arithmetic sequence. The number of newspapers delivered each day can be tabulated as follows:

13

Day #	1	2	3	4	5	6	7
Newspapers	18	25	32	39	46	53	60

Day #	8	9	10	11	12	13	14
Newspapers	67	74	81	88	95	102	109

To compute the sum, you could just add all 14 numbers together. However, such a calculation would be time consuming and could be error-prone. Instead, perhaps the best way to compute the total is by separating the arithmetic sequence into two pieces and computing each sum separately: the base number of newspapers each day, plus the growth in the number of newspapers.

The base number of newspapers each day is 18, so for 14 days that total will equal $18 \times 14 = 252$. The growth in newspapers each day will be 0 on Day 1, 7 on Day 2, 14 on Day 3, etc. Since all of these numbers are multiples of 7, you can factor the sum as follows:

$$(0 + 7 + 14 + \ldots + 91) =$$
$$7(0 + 1 + 2 + \ldots + 13)$$

A useful formula to remember for the sum of consecutive integers from A to B is as follows:

$$(B - A + 1)\left(\frac{B + A}{2}\right)$$

In this product, the leftmost expression equals the number of items in the set of consecutive integers. Here, $B - A + 1 = 13 - 0 + 1 = 14$. The rightmost expression equals the average value of the items in the set of consecutive integers. Here, $\left(\frac{B + A}{2}\right) = \left(\frac{13 + 0}{2}\right) = 6.5$. Therefore, the sum of the consecutive integers from 0 to $13 = 14 \times 6.5 = 7 \times 13 = 91$. Now you can compute the entire sum:

Number of newspapers $= 18 \times 14 + 7 \times 91 = 252 + 637 = 889$

The correct answer is (J).

75. **(D)** {–2, 5}   Intermediate Algebra   Exponents, Radicals, Rationals

To find the values of x that satisfy this equation, use the fact that when the bases are equal, then the exponents must also be equal. (The exceptions to this general rule occur when the base is 0 or 1, but here, the base is 3.) Note also that 1 is equivalent to any non-zero base to a power of 0. Therefore, you have the following:

$$3^{10+3x-x^2} = 1$$
$$3^{10+3x-x^2} = 3^0$$
$$10 + 3x - x^2 = 0$$
$$(5 - x)(2 + x) = 0$$
$$x = 5, x = -2$$

The correct answer is (D).

MANHATTAN
PREP

76. **(K)**   Intermediate Algebra   Inequalities and Absolute Value

The number line interpretation of $|x|$ is the (positive) distance between x and 0. You need to find a number line graph in which all values of x are at least 3 units from 0, and this is represented by choice (K).

You can also solve the inequality to find the solution sets for x, and then graph them on a number line. For absolute value, there are two scenarios: the expression inside the absolute value bars is positive and the expression inside the absolute value bars is negative. Evaluate these scenarios separately:

$2x$ is Positive	or	**$2x$ is Negative**
$2x \geq 6$		$(-2x) \geq 6$
$x \geq 3$		$-2x \geq 6$
		$x \leq -3$

(Don't forget that when an inequality is multiplied or divided by a negative number, the sign must be reversed).

Therefore, the correct range for the inequality is $x \geq 3$ or $x \leq -3$. The correct answer is (K).

77. **(B)** 2,550   Intermediate Algebra   Formulas, Functions, Sequences

The series of all even integers between 1 and 101 constitutes an arithmetic sequence. The smallest such integer is 2, and the largest is 100. Unfortunately, because there are so many items in this sequence, it is going to be cumbersome if not impossible to compute this sum in a timely, accurate fashion:

$$2 + 4 + 6 + 8 + \ldots + 98 + 100$$

Perhaps the best way to compute the total is to factor the sum, because all integers in the sequence are divisible by 2:

$$(2 + 4 + 6 + 8 + \ldots + 98 + 100) =$$
$$2(1 + 2 + 3 + 4 + \ldots + 49 + 50)$$

A useful formula to remember for the sum of consecutive integers from A to B is as follows:

$$(B - A + 1)\left(\frac{B + A}{2}\right)$$

In this product, the leftmost expression equals the number of items in the set of consecutive integers. Here, $B - A + 1 = 50 - 1 + 1 = 50$. The rightmost expression equals the average value of the items in the set of consecutive integers. Here, $\left(\frac{B + A}{2}\right) = \left(\frac{50 + 1}{2}\right) = 25.5$. Therefore, the sum of the consecutive integers from 1 to 50 is equal to $50 \times 25.5 = 1,275$. Now compute the entire sum:

Sum of even integers from 2 to 100 = $2 \times 1,275 = 2,550$

The correct answer is (B).

78. **(F)** 4   Intermediate Algebra   Inequalities and Absolute Value

The problem asks for the number of solutions to the equation $|x^2 - 20| = 16$. It is helpful to recognize that the absolute value of any expression is equal to the square root of the square of the expression, for any real number a. In other words, $|a| = \sqrt{a^2}$. Therefore, you can rewrite the equation:

$$|x^2 - 20| = 16$$

$$\sqrt{(x^2 - 20)^2} = 16$$

Now square both sides, distribute using the FOIL method, and re-factor the quadratic:

$$\sqrt{(x^2 - 20)^2} = 16$$

$$(x^2 - 20)^2 = 256$$

$$x^4 - 20x^2 - 20x^2 + 400 = 256$$

$$x^4 - 40x^2 + 144 = 0$$

$$(x^2 - 36)(x^2 - 4) = 0$$

Therefore, the equation will hold whenever $x^2 = 36$ or $x^2 = 4$. In other words, it will hold whenever $x = 6, -6, 2,$ or -2. Check this result by substituting all 4 values back into the original equation:

$$|(6)^2 - 20| = 16 \qquad |(-6)^2 - 20| = 16$$

$$|36 - 20| = 16 \qquad |36 - 20| = 16$$

$$|16| = 16 \qquad |16| = 16$$

$$|(2)^2 - 20| = 16 \qquad |(-2)^2 - 20| = 16$$

$$|4 - 20| = 16 \qquad |4 - 20| = 16$$

$$|-16| = 16 \qquad |-16| = 16$$

There are therefore 4 possible values for x. The correct answer is (F).

79. **(D)**   Intermediate Algebra   Absolute Value

The number line interpretation of $|2x - 3|$ is the (positive) distance between $2x$ and 3. Find a number line graph in which all values of $2x$ and 3 are at least 5 units apart on the number line. Since they must be *at least* 5 units apart, this will result in a 2-part range rather than a 1-part range. This eliminates choices (A), (B) and (C).

Solve the inequality to find the solution sets for x, and then graph them on a number line. For absolute value, there are two scenarios: the expression inside the absolute value bars is positive, or the expression inside the absolute value bars is negative. Evaluate these scenarios separately:

2x − 3 is Positive	or	**2x − 3 is Negative**
$2x - 3 \geq 5$		$(-2x + 3) \geq 5$
$x \geq 4$		$-2x \geq 2$
		$x \leq -1$

(Don't forget that when an inequality is multiplied or divided by a negative number, the sign must be reversed.)

Therefore, the correct range for the inequality is $x \geq 4$ or $x \leq -1$, and this is correctly represented in the number line graph in choice (D).

80. **(J)** $\sqrt{5}$ Intermediate Algebra   Inequalities and Absolute Value

To solve this problem, you can test the choices to see which answer does not fit the equation or you can solve the equation to determine the solutions to it. First try solving the equation: $\left|b^2 - 14\right| = 11$. It is helpful to recognize that the absolute value of any expression is equal to the square root of the square of the expression, for any real number a. In other words, $|a| = \sqrt{a^2}$. Therefore, you can rewrite the equation as:

$$\left|b^2 - 14\right| = 11$$

$$\sqrt{\left(b^2 - 14\right)^2} = 11$$

Now square both sides, distribute using the FOIL (first, outer, inner, last) method, and re factor the quadratic:

$$\sqrt{\left(b^2 - 14\right)^2} = 11$$

$$\left(b^2 - 14\right)^2 = 121$$

$$b^4 - 14b^2 - 14b^2 + 196 = 121$$

$$b^4 - 28b^2 + 75 = 0$$

$$\left(b^2 - 25\right)\left(b^2 - 3\right) = 0$$

Therefore, the equation will hold whenever $b^2 = 25$ or $b^2 = 3$. In other words, whenever $b = 5, -5, \sqrt{3}$, or $-\sqrt{3}$. Thus, only $\sqrt{5}$ does not fit, and therefore must be the correct answer.

Test the choices to confirm this result:

$$\left|(-5)^2 - 14\right| = 11 \qquad \left|\left(-\sqrt{3}\right)^2 - 14\right| = 11 \qquad \left|\left(\sqrt{3}\right)^2 - 14\right| = 11$$

$$\left|25 - 14\right| = 11 \qquad\qquad \left|3 - 14\right| = 11 \qquad\qquad \left|3 - 14\right| = 11$$

$$\left|11\right| = 11 \qquad\qquad\qquad \left|-11\right| = 11 \qquad\qquad \left|-11\right| = 11$$

$$\left|\left(\sqrt{5}\right)^2 - 14\right| \neq 11 \qquad \left|(5)^2 - 14\right| = 11$$

$$\left|5 - 14\right| \neq 11 \qquad\qquad \left|25 - 14\right| = 11$$

$$\left|-9\right| \neq 11 \qquad\qquad\qquad \left|11\right| = 11$$

Once again, $\sqrt{5}$ is the correct answer. The correct answer is (J).

13

81. **(D)** $a^2 + b^2 + a + b + 2ab + 1$ Intermediate Algebra   Formulas & Functions

The g function is defined as $g(x) = x^2 + x + 1$, meaning that anything that is put inside the parentheses of the g function is substituted in place of every x. For example, $g(3) = 3^2 + 3 + 1 = 13$.

In the case of $g(a+b)$, the entire "$a + b$" expression is substituted in for every x in the g function. Therefore, you can substitute $a + b$ into the definition of the function, distribute, and match to the answer choices:

$$g(a+b) = (a+b)^2 + (a+b) + 1$$
$$= a^2 + 2ab + b^2 + a + b + 1$$
$$= a^2 + b^2 + a + b + 2ab + 1$$

The correct answer is (D).

82. **(K)** $\dfrac{2}{9}$ Intermediate Algebra   Formulas, Functions, Sequences

Because the area of the cross-section of the wire is given by $A = \pi r^2$, you can substitute this expression for A in the original equation:

$$\frac{m \times 2.65 \times 10^{-4}}{A} = \frac{m \times 2.65 \times 10^{-4}}{\pi r^2}$$

According to the information given in the problem, relative to the original wire, m will be doubling and r will be tripling. Because ohms is directly related to m, doubling m will double the number of ohms (i.e., increase it by a factor of 2). Because ohms is directly related to $\dfrac{1}{r^2}$, tripling r (that is, multiplying r by 3) will cause ohms to change by a factor of $\left(\dfrac{1}{3}\right)^2 = \dfrac{1}{9}$. Therefore, the combined effect will be to multiply the resistance of the aluminum wire (in ohms) by a factor of $2 \times \dfrac{1}{9} = \dfrac{2}{9}$. The correct answer is (K).

83. **(C)** 2   Intermediate Algebra   Quadratics (Quadratic Formula)

To solve this problem, you can try to factor the original equation:

$$x^2 + 10x + 2 = 0$$

However, this equation cannot be factored into integer components. (This should alert you to the fact that the solutions to the equation are most likely either irrational or complex numbers.)

Therefore, you should use another method, such as completing the square or the quadratic formula, to find the solutions to the problem.

First, try the quadratic formula. For any quadratic equation in the standard form $ax^2 + bx + c = 0$, the solution to the equation is given by the following:

$$x = \frac{-b \pm \sqrt{b^2 - 4ac}}{2a}$$

The portion under the radical, $\sqrt{b^2 - 4ac}$, is called the discriminant of the polynomial. If $b^2 - 4ac$ is a positive perfect square, the equation will have two real, rational solutions. If it is positive but not a perfect square, the equation will have two real, irrational solutions. If it is equal to 0, it will have exactly one real, rational solution. Finally, if it is negative, the equation will have two imaginary (complex) solutions.

For this equation, the discriminant $b^2 - 4ac = (10)^2 - 4(1)(2) = 92$, which is positive but not a perfect square. Therefore, the equation will have 2 irrational solutions.

You can prove this result by substituting the values into the quadratic formula and solving:

$$x = \frac{-b \pm \sqrt{b^2 - 4ac}}{2a}$$

$$x = \frac{-10 \pm \sqrt{10^2 - 4(1)(2)}}{2(1)}$$

$$x = -\frac{10}{2} \pm \frac{\sqrt{92}}{2}$$

$$x = -5 \pm \frac{2\sqrt{23}}{2}$$

$$x = -5 + \sqrt{23} \qquad x = -5 - \sqrt{23}$$

The correct answer is (C).

84. **(J)** $2r - s$ Intermediate Algebra   Logarithms

By the definition of a logarithm, $\log_x z$ means that x is raised to a certain power and the result is z. Since $\log_x z = r$, $x^r = z$.

Similarly, since $\log_x y = s$, $x^s = y$. The question asks you to determine the value of $\log_x \dfrac{z^2}{y}$, in terms of r and s. In other words:

$$x^? = \frac{z^2}{y}$$

First, you know that $x^r = z$. Therefore, in order to get z^2, square both sides: $\left(x^r\right)^2 = x^{2r} = z^2$. Furthermore, because $x^s = y$, in order to get $\dfrac{1}{y}$, you need to take the reciprocal of each side: $\dfrac{1}{x^s} = x^{-s} = \dfrac{1}{y}$. By multiplying these expressions together, you get:

$$\left(x^{2r}\right)\left(x^{-s}\right) = x^{2r-s} = \left(z^2\right)\left(\frac{1}{y}\right) = \frac{z^2}{y}$$

Therefore, to get $\dfrac{z^2}{y}$, you have to raise x to the $2r - s$ power. Thus, $2r - s$ is the correct answer. The correct answer is (J).

85. **(C)** 6   Intermediate Algebra   Exponents, Radicals, Rationals

It is given in the problem that $9^a = x$ and $x^b = 3^{16}$. Substituting for x in the second equation, you get $(9^a)^b = 3^{16}$. You can now simplify the equation relating a and b by writing 9 in prime-power form, setting the bases equal to each other, and solving for the exponent:

$$\left(9^a\right)^b = 3^{16}$$
$$9^{ab} = 3^{16}$$
$$\left(3^2\right)^{ab} = (3)^{16}$$
$$3^{2ab} = 3^{16}$$
$$2ab = 16$$
$$ab = 8$$

(Don't forget the exponent rule that $(x^y)^z = x^{yz}$, not x^{y+z}.)

It is given in the problem that a and b much be positive integers. Therefore, a and b must be factors of the number 8. The only factors of 8 are 1, 2, 4, and 8, so the combinations are:

$a = 1, b = 8; a + b = 9$
$a = 2, b = 4; a + b = 6$
$a = 4, b = 2; a + b = 6$
$a = 8, b = 1; a + b = 9$

As can be seen above, two of the solutions yield a value of 6 for the sum $a + b$. The correct answer is (C).

86. **(K)** $b^{\frac{a}{c}}$ Intermediate Algebra   Logarithms

By the definition of a logarithm, $\log_b x^c$ means that b is raised to a certain power and the result is x^c. Since $\log_b x^c = a$, $b^a = x^c$. The question asks you to determine the value of x, in terms of a, b, and c. In other words, $b^? = x$.

Since you know that $b^a = x^c$, take the cth root of both sides of the equation to solve for x:

$$b^a = x^c$$
$$\sqrt[c]{b^a} = \sqrt[c]{x^c} = x$$
$$x = \sqrt[c]{b^a} = b^{\frac{a}{c}}$$

(Don't forget the exponent rule that $\sqrt[z]{x^y} = x^{\frac{y}{z}}$, not x^{y-z}.)

Therefore, to solve for x, you need to raise b to the $\frac{a}{c}$ power. The correct answer is (K).

87. **(C)** $b^2 - a^2$ Intermediate Algebra   Formulas, Functions, Sequences

To solve this complicated function problem, carefully plug each term into the original function. Here, $x = b^2 - a^2$ and $y = a^2 - b^2$, so you can set up and solve:

MANHATTAN
PREP

$$f(x, y) = \frac{x - y}{2} = \frac{(b^2 - a^2) - (a^2 - b^2)}{2} = \frac{b^2 - a^2 - a^2 + b^2}{2}$$

$$= \frac{2b^2 - 2a^2}{2} = b^2 - a^2$$

The correct answer is (C).

88. **(K)** 4   Intermediate Algebra   Exponents, Radicals, Rationals

It is given in the problem that $8^r = t$ and $t^s = 4^{12}$. Substituting for t in the second equation, you get $(8^r)^s = 4^{12}$. You can now simplify the equation relating r and s by writing 8 and 4 in prime-power form, setting the bases equal to each other, and solving for the exponent:

$$\left(8^r\right)^s = 4^{12}$$

$$8^{rs} = 4^{12}$$

$$\left(2^3\right)^{rs} = \left(2^2\right)^{12}$$

$$2^{3rs} = 2^{24}$$

$$3rs = 24$$

$$rs = 8$$

(Don't forget the exponent rule that $(a^b)^c = a^{bc}$, not a^{b+c}.)

It is given in the problem that r and s must be positive integers. Therefore, r and s must be factors of the number 8. The only factors of 8 are 1, 2, 4, and 8, so the combinations are:

$r = 1, s = 8$
$r = 2, s = 4$
$r = 4, s = 2$
$r = 8, s = 1$

There are therefore 4 possible values for r. The correct answer is (K).

13

89. **(C)** $\dfrac{1}{m - n}$ Intermediate Algebra   Formulas, Functions, Sequences

To solve this complicated function problem, carefully plug each term into the original function. Here, $x = (m + n)$ and $y = m^2 - n^2$, so you can set up and solve:

$$f(x, y) = \frac{x}{y} = \frac{m + n}{m^2 - n^2} = \frac{m + n}{(m + n)(m - n)} = \frac{1}{m - n}$$

There is no possibility of dividing by 0, because you are told that m and n are not equal to each other (so their difference is not 0). The correct answer is (C).

Chapter *of* 14

5lb. Book of ACT® Practice Problems

Math:
Coordinate Geometry

In This Chapter...

Coordinate Geometry Problems & Solutions

Chapter 14
Math: Coordinate Geometry

The Math problems in this chapter are drawn from coordinate geometry—all that happens in an (x, y) plane. The topics include the following:

1. Properties of the Plane. Properties of the coordinate plane, interpreting the plane, and rotations and transformations.

2. Equations of Lines. Dealing with line graphs and their corresponding equations.

3. Midpoints. Finding midpoints of line segments.

4. Distance and Area. Computing distance and area in the plane; properties of the number line.

5. Graphs in the Plane. Graphs of functions, circles, and polynomial equations; finding intercepts; interpreting graphs.

How should you use this chapter? Here are some recommendations, according to the level you've reached in ACT Math.

1. Fundamentals. Start slowly with the easier problems at the beginning. Do at least some of these problems untimed. This way, you give yourself a chance to think deeply about the principles at work. Review the solutions closely, and articulate what you've learned. Redo problems as necessary.

2. Fixes. Do a few problems untimed, examine the results, learn your lessons, then test yourself with longer timed sets.

3. Tweaks. Confirm your mastery by doing longer sets of problems under timed conditions. Aim to improve the speed and ease of your solution process. Mix the problems up by jumping around in the chapter. Definitely push to the harder, higher-numbered problems.

Good luck on the problems!

1. The graph and chart below show the pricing plans for a single long-distance phone call. The pricing tier is a function of the duration of the call, and each pricing tier is associated with a cost per minute. What is the total cost for a long-distance call that has a duration of 15 minutes?

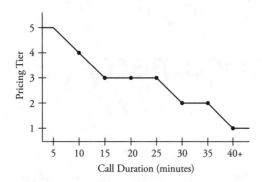

Pricing Tier	Price per Min
1	$0.15
2	$0.18
3	$0.20
4	$0.22
5	$0.30

A. $0.20

B. $0.60

C. $2.20

D. $3.00

E. $4.20

2. In the standard (x, y) coordinate plane, an equation of a parabola is given as $y = x^2 - 2x - 15$. At what points does the parabola intersect the x-axis?

F. (0, 5) and (0, 3)

G. (0, –5) and (0, 3)

H. (0, 5) and (0, –3)

J. (–5, 0) and (3, 0)

K. (5, 0) and (–3, 0)

3. On the real number line, what is the midpoint of 17 and 33?

A. 16

B. 23

C. 25

D. 27.5

E. 50

4. In the standard (x, y) coordinate plane, an equation of an ellipse is given as $16x^2 + 25y^2 = 400$. At what points does the ellipse intersect the x-axis?

F. (4, 0) and (–4, 0)

G. (5, 0) and (–5, 0)

H. (16, 0) and (–16, 0)

J. (20, 0) and (–20, 0)

K. (25, 0) and (–25, 0)

14

MANHATTAN
PREP

5. A linear relationship is drawn in the standard (x, y) coordinate graph below. Which of the following equations correctly reflects that relationship?

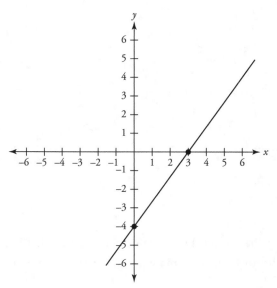

A. $y = \dfrac{4}{3}x - 4$

B. $y = \dfrac{4}{3}x + 4$

C. $y = \dfrac{3}{4}x - 4$

D. $y = -\dfrac{3}{4}x - 4$

E. $y = -\dfrac{3}{4}x + 4$

6. In the standard (x, y) coordinate plane, which of the following lines do NOT intersect the y-axis?

F. $y = 3$

G. $y = 2x$

H. $x = 4$

J. $x = y + 2$

K. $y = x + 2$

7. One of the equations below matches the linear relationship displayed in the following standard (x, y) coordinate graph. Which is the correct equation?

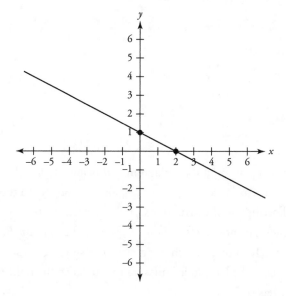

A. $y = 2x - 1$

B. $y = 2x + 1$

C. $y = -2x - 1$

D. $y = -\dfrac{1}{2}x - 1$

E. $y = -\dfrac{1}{2}x + 1$

8. What is the slope of the line $1 + 2x + 3y = 0$ in the standard (x, y) coordinate plane?

F. $-\dfrac{3}{2}$

G. $-\dfrac{2}{3}$

H. 1

J. $\dfrac{2}{3}$

K. 2

14

MANHATTAN
PREP   575

9. In the standard (x, y) coordinate plane, which of the following equations is perpendicular to the line $y = 3x - 2$?

    A. $y = 3x + 2$

    B. $y = -3x + 2$

    C. $y = 2x - 3$

    D. $y = -\dfrac{1}{3}x - 2$

    E. $y = \dfrac{1}{3}x + 2$

10. On a straight road diagrammed below, with mile markers as labeled, a police car moves according to the following set of instructions: starting at point A, the police car moves left to point C, then right to point B, then left to point D, then right until it stops at point C. What is the length, in miles, of the distance the police car has traveled?

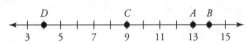

    F. 31

    G. 28

    H. 24

    J. 21

    K. 12

11. What is the slope of any line perpendicular to $4x + 3y = 6$ in the standard (x, y) coordinate plane?

    A. -4

    B. -2

    C. $-\dfrac{4}{3}$

    D. $\dfrac{3}{4}$

    E. $\dfrac{3}{2}$

12. What is the slope of the line that corresponds to the equation $6x - 5y = 4$ in the standard (x, y) coordinate plane?

    F. $\dfrac{2}{3}$

    G. $-\dfrac{5}{6}$

    H. $\dfrac{5}{6}$

    J. $-\dfrac{6}{5}$

    K. $\dfrac{6}{5}$

13. In the standard (x, y) coordinate plane, what is the distance, in coordinate units, between $(7, -3)$ and $(-2, 5)$?

    A. 7

    B. 17

    C. $\sqrt{17}$

    D. $\sqrt{29}$

    E. $\sqrt{145}$

14. What is the y-intercept of the linear equation $3(x + 2) - 2y = 0$ when graphed in the standard (x, y) coordinate plane?

    F. 6

    G. 3

    H. 0

    J. -2

    K. -6

14

MANHATTAN
PREP

15. What is the slope of the line in the standard (x, y) coordinate plane for the equation $10x + 2y - 20 = 0$?

   A. -5

   B. $-\dfrac{1}{5}$

   C. $\dfrac{1}{5}$

   D. $\dfrac{5}{2}$

   E. 5

16. Which of the following equations represents the line in the standard (x, y) coordinate plane that passes through the points $(2, -5)$ and $(-1, 4)$?

   F. $y = -3x + 1$

   G. $y = 3x - 11$

   H. $y = 3x + 7$

   J. $y = -\dfrac{1}{3}x + \dfrac{11}{3}$

   K. $y = \dfrac{1}{3}x - \dfrac{17}{3}$

17. What is the midpoint of the line segment in the standard (x, y) coordinate plane that begins at $(-2, -4)$ and ends at $(1, 2)$?

   A. $\left(-\dfrac{1}{2}, -1\right)$

   B. $\left(-\dfrac{1}{2}, 1\right)$

   C. $\left(\dfrac{1}{2}, -2\right)$

   D. $\left(\dfrac{1}{2}, -1\right)$

   E. $\left(\dfrac{1}{2}, 1\right)$

18. What is the slope of the line given by the equation $-13x - 26y = -18$?

   F. $-\dfrac{9}{13}$

   G. $-\dfrac{1}{2}$

   H. $\dfrac{1}{2}$

   J. $\dfrac{18}{13}$

   K. 2

19. The coordinates of the endpoints of $\overline{AB}$ in the standard (x, y) coordinate plane are $(9, -2)$ and $(-5, 8)$. What is the x-coordinate of the midpoint of $\overline{AB}$?

   A. -2

   B. 2

   C. 3

   D. 4

   E. 7

20. What is the y-coordinate of the midpoint of the line segment in the standard (x, y) coordinate plane that runs from the point $(0, 5)$ to the point $(3, -1)$?

   F. 3

   G. 2

   H. $1\dfrac{1}{2}$

   J. -1

   K. -2

14

21. Circle O (not shown) passes through point $(-3, -2)$ and has its center at point $(-3, 0)$. When the circle is graphed in the standard (x, y) coordinate plane, what percent of the total area of the circle lies in Quadrant II?

    A. 25%

    B. 40.5%

    C. 50%

    D. 55%

    E. 75%

22. The coordinates of the endpoints of $\overline{PQ}$ in the standard (x, y) coordinate plane are $(3, 6)$ and $(-11, -18)$. What is the y-coordinate of the midpoint of $\overline{PQ}$?

    F. 24

    G. 6

    H. -4

    J. -6

    K. -12

23. What is the x-intercept of the line in the standard (x, y) coordinate plane that goes through the points $(-1, 2)$ and $(5, -2)$?

    A. -2

    B. 0

    C. 1

    D. 1.5

    E. 2

24. The vertices of a triangle are $(-3, -2)$, $(2, 2)$, and $(2, -2)$ in the standard (x, y) coordinate plane. What percent of the total area of the triangle lies in Quadrant IV?

    F. 40%

    G. 30%

    H. 25%

    J. 20%

    K. 10%

25. In which of the following quadrants, not including the axes, of the standard (x, y) coordinate plane shown below will the product of the x-coordinate and the y-coordinate of every point be positive?

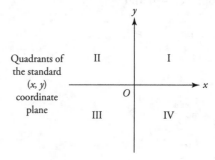

    A. Quadrant I only

    B. Quadrant II only

    C. Quadrants I and III only

    D. Quadrants II and III only

    E. Quadrants II and IV only

26. If the x-intercept of a line in the standard (x, y) coordinate plane is 2 and the line goes through the point $(3, 3)$, what is the y-intercept of the line?

    F. -6

    G. -5

    H. -3

    J. 0

    K. 4

14

MANHATTAN
PREP

27. Observe these two equations:

$$y = -\frac{1}{3}x + 4$$
$$y = 3x + 4$$

Which of the following correctly describes the graph of these equations in the standard (x, y) coordinate plane?

   A. Two perpendicular lines

   B. A single line with negative slope

   C. A single line with positive slope

   D. Two parallel lines with positive slope

   E. Two parallel lines with negative slope

28. In which of the following quadrants, not including the axes, of the standard (x, y) coordinate plane shown below can the sum of the x-coordinate and the y-coordinate of a point be negative?

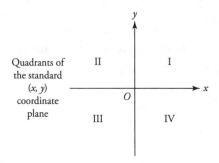

   F. Quadrant II only

   G. Quadrant III only

   H. Quadrants II and IV only

   J. Quadrants III and IV only

   K. Quadrants II, III, and IV only

29. The graph shown in the standard (x, y) coordinate plane below is to be rotated in the plane 180° around the origin.

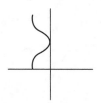

Which of the following graphs is the result of this rotation?

  A.   **B.**

  C.   **D.**

  E.

30. In the standard (x, y) coordinate plane, what is the distance between the point (–52, 39) and the origin at (0, 0)?

   F. 13

   G. 26

   H. 65

   J. 91

   K. 130

14

31. What is the slope-intercept form of $-5x - y = 3$?

   A. $y = 5x + 3$

   B. $y = 5x - 3$

   C. $y = -5x + 3$

   D. $y = -5x - 3$

   E. $y = -3x + 5$

32. What is the x-coordinate of the point in the standard (x, y) coordinate plane at which the two lines $2y - 3x + 9 = 0$ and $y = 6$ intersect?

   F. 1

   G. 3

   H. 4

   J. 6

   K. 7

33. What is the slope of the line formed by $4x - 5y + 10 = 0$?

   A. $\dfrac{4}{5}$

   B. $\dfrac{5}{4}$

   C. $-\dfrac{4}{5}$

   D. $-\dfrac{2}{5}$

   E. -2

34. What is the y-coordinate of the point of intersection of the two lines $y = -x + 3$ and $y = 4x - 12$, in the standard (x, y) coordinate plane?

   F. 0

   G. 1

   H. 3

   J. 5

   K. 6

> Use the following information to answer questions 35–36.

A portion of the circle $y^2 + (x - 3)^2 = 9$ is displayed in the standard (x, y) coordinate plane below. The circle is centered at $(3, 0)$. In addition, the line segments from A $(0, 0)$ to B $(0, -3)$, B to C $(6, -3)$, C to D $(6, 0)$, and D to A are shown.

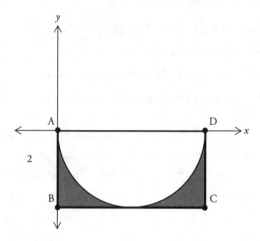

35. What is the distance between points A and C in the diagram (line segment not displayed)?

   A. $3\sqrt{5}$

   B. $6\sqrt{2}$

   C. 3

   D. 6

   E. 12

36. What is the area of the shaded region in the diagram?

   F. $\dfrac{9}{2}\pi$

   G. 9π

   H. $18 - 12\pi$

   J. $36 - 9\pi$

   K. $18 - \dfrac{9}{2}\pi$

MANHATTAN
PREP

37. Kelvin cuts a flat piece of wood in the shape and dimensions in inches given below, with right angles at every corner. Halfway between point A and point C, he wishes to drill a small hole. In relation to point D, which of the following should be the location of the hole?

(Note: The sides of the piece of wood run up–down or right–left, as oriented below.)

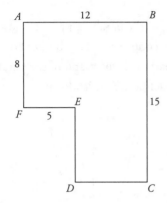

A. $\dfrac{1}{2}$ inch to the right and 6 inches up

B. $\dfrac{1}{2}$ inch to the right and $6\dfrac{1}{2}$ inches up

C. $\dfrac{1}{2}$ inch to the right and $7\dfrac{1}{2}$ inches up

D. 1 inch to the right and $6\dfrac{1}{2}$ inches up

E. 1 inch to the right and $7\dfrac{1}{2}$ inches up

38. What is the distance, in coordinate units, between points $(-10, -13)$ and $(6, -1)$ in the standard (x, y) coordinate plane?

F. $\sqrt{56}$

G. $\sqrt{28}$

H. $\sqrt{20}$

J. 28

K. 20

39. In the standard (x, y) coordinate plane, what is the distance between the points $(0,2)$ and $(-3,0)$?

A. 1

B. $\sqrt{5}$

C. 3

D. $\sqrt{13}$

E. 5

40. What is the distance, in coordinate units, between points $(-5, -13)$ and $(15, 2)$ in the standard (x, y) coordinate plane?

F. $2\sqrt{5}$

G. $4\sqrt{61}$

H. 16

J. 20

K. 25

41. What is the distance in the standard (x, y) coordinate plane between the points $(1, 2)$ and $(3, 4)$?

A. $\sqrt{2}$

B. 2

C. $\sqrt{8}$

D. 4

E. $\sqrt{32}$

42. In the standard (x, y) coordinate plane, what is the circumference of the circle defined by the equation $x^2 + y^2 = 36$?

F. 36π

G. 36

H. 12π

J. 12

K. 6π

14

43. A circle in the standard (x, y) coordinate plane is centered at the point $(0,0)$ and passes through the point $(2,4)$. What is the radius of the circle?

A. $\sqrt{5}$

B. $2\sqrt{5}$

C. $3\sqrt{5}$

D. $4\sqrt{5}$

E. $5\sqrt{5}$

44. A car departs from one location, heading to a second location. The driver of the car hears on the radio that there could be heavy traffic near his terminal location. The graph below shows the speed of the car as a function of the length of time that the car has been driving.

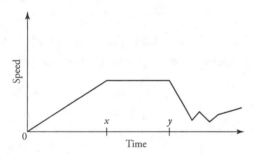

Based on the graph above, which of the following conclusions *could* be true about the car's trip from one location to the other?

  I.   At time x, the car decreased its speed.

  II. At time y, the car started encountering heavy traffic.

  III. From time x to time y, the speed of the car did not change.

F. I only

G. II only

H. III only

J. I and II only

K. II and III only

45. In the standard (x, y) coordinate plane, a circle defined by the equation $(x + 2)^2 + (y - 1)^2 = 49$ is drawn. What is the area of the circle, in square units?

A. 49π

B. 49

C. 28π

D. 14π

E. 14

46. The graph of the parabola $y = x^2$ is shown in the standard (x, y) coordinate plane below. For which of the following equations is the graph of the parabola shifted 2 units to the left and 3 units down?

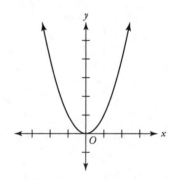

F. $y = (x - 2)^2 - 3$

G. $y = (x - 2)^2 + 3$

H. $y = (x + 2)^2 - 3$

J. $y = (x + 2)^2 + 3$

K. $y = (x + 3)^2 - 2$

MANHATTAN
PREP

47. A driver in a car departs from one location, heading to a second location. The graph below shows the volume of gasoline in the car's gas tank as a function of time:

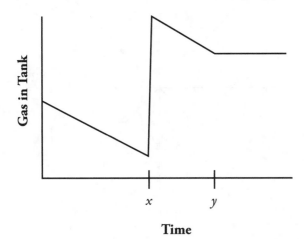

Based on the graph above, which of the following statements is(are) *likely* true about the car and driver's trip from one destination to the other?

   I.   At time x, the driver filled the gas tank.

   II. Between time x and time y, the car was accelerating and decelerating abruptly.

   III. At time y, the ignition of the car was turned off.

A. I only

B. II only

C. I and II only

D. I and III only

E. II and III only

48. The graph of the equation $y = 2.2 - 0.2x$ is shown below for values of x such that $1 \le x < 6$. Which of the statements that follow must be true?

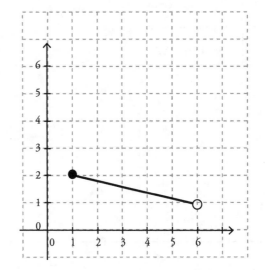

   I.   The graph has a constant slope of $-\dfrac{1}{5}$.

   II. The x-intercept of the polynomial $2.2 - 0.2x$ lies at point $(11, 0)$.

   III. The range of the graph contains all values of y such that $1 < y \le 2$.

F. I only

G. II only

H. I and II only

J. II and III only

K. I, II, and III

14

49. Which of the following choices is the correct graph in the standard (x, y) coordinate plane for:

$$y = \begin{cases} x \text{ when } x \le -2 \\ |x| \text{ when } -2 < x < 2 \\ -x \text{ when } x \ge 2 \end{cases}$$

C.

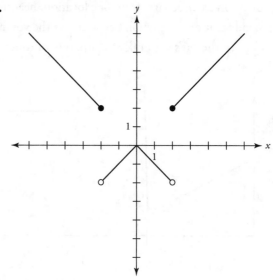

A.

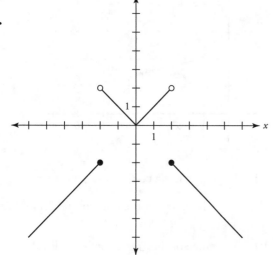

D.

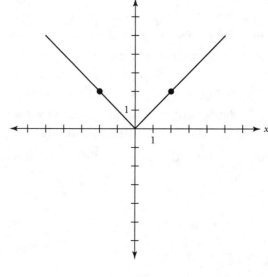

B.

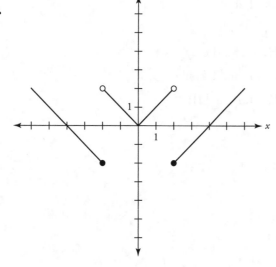

E.

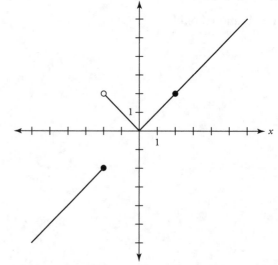

50. The graph of the parabola $y = x^2$ is shown in the standard (x, y) coordinate plane below. For which of the following equations is the graph of the parabola shifted 4 units to the right and 5 units up?

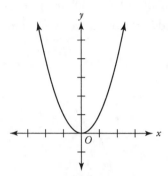

   F. $y = (x - 5)^2 - 5$

   G. $y = (x - 4)^2 - 5$

   H. $y = (x - 4)^2 + 5$

   J. $y = (x + 4)^2 - 5$

   K. $y = (x + 4)^2 + 5$

51. If a line through the points $(6, 5)$ and $(x, -5)$ has a slope of 2, what is the value of x?

   A. -6

   B. $-\dfrac{2}{7}$

   C. $-\dfrac{1}{2}$

   D. 1

   E. 28

52. A line passes through points $(-3, 17)$ and $(2, 2)$ in the (x, y) coordinate plane. What is the value of b if the point $(7, b)$ is also on the line?

   F. -21

   G. -13

   H. -3

   J. 8

   K. 17

53. Beth has errands to run on her bike along a straight road that runs East–West. Her house is also located on that road. The graph below shows Beth's distance from her house over the course of the 6-hour trip. Which of the following statements about Beth's trip MUST be true?

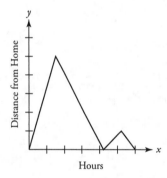

   I.   Beth was traveling at her fastest speed between hours 5 and 6.

   II. Between hours 1 and 2, Beth changed direction.

   III. Between hours 4 and 5, Beth changed direction.

   A. I only

   B. II only

   C. III only

   D. I and II only

   E. I and III only

14

54. A circle with the equation $(x - 1)^2 + (y - 2)^2 = 16$ is drawn in the standard (x, y) coordinate plane. The circle is inscribed inside a square. What are the coordinates of point A?

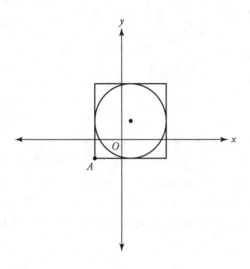

F. (2, 3)

G. (–2, –3)

H. (–3, –2)

J. (–4, 1)

K. (–4, –1)

> Use the following information to answer questions 55–56.

The parabola $y = -0.04x^2 + 100$ and the line segments from A (–50, 0) to B (0, 100) and from B to C (50, 0) are displayed in the standard (x, y) coordinate plane below.

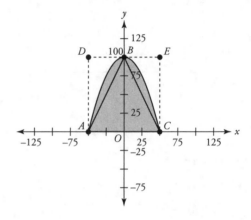

55. The length of the curve displayed can be estimated by finding the sum of the lengths of $\overline{AB}$ and $\overline{BC}$. What is the sum of the lengths of $\overline{AB}$ and $\overline{BC}$, and is the curve longer or shorter than this sum?

A. $100\sqrt{5}$, shorter

B. $100\sqrt{5}$, longer

C. $200\sqrt{3}$, shorter

D. $200\sqrt{3}$, longer

E. 300, longer

MANHATTAN
PREP

56. An estimate of the area of shaded region is the area of triangle $\triangle ABC$. The base and height of $\triangle ABC$ are both 100, so the area of the triangle is $\frac{1}{2}bh = \frac{1}{2}(100)(100)$ = 5,000. Which of the following statements about the area of the shaded region is true?

- **F.** The area of the shaded region is less than 5,000 square units.
- **G.** The area of the shaded region is equal to 5,000 square units.
- **H.** The area of the shaded region is greater than 5,000 square units but less than 10,000 square units.
- **J.** The area of the shaded region is equal to 10,000 square units.
- **K.** The area of the shaded region is greater than 10,000 square units.

57. In the standard (x, y) coordinate plane, a parallelogram is drawn with vertices at $(0, 0)$, $(-7, 0)$, $(-11, -10)$, and $(-4, -10)$. What is the area of the parallelogram, in square units?

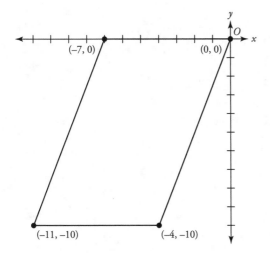

- **A.** 110
- **B.** 77
- **C.** 70
- **D.** 44
- **E.** 40

58. Lawrence County is a geographically square county, measuring 70 miles from the northernmost edge to the southernmost edge. Carmen is carrying a scaled map of the county that measures 10 inches-by-10 inches. Each inch is demarcated with coordinate points, starting at the bottom-left at point $(0, 0)$ and running to the top-right at point $(10, 10)$. If the city of Greenville is located at $(2, 1)$ on the map and the city of Brownville is located at $(3, 8)$, what is the distance between the two towns, in miles?

- **F.** 56
- **G.** $14\sqrt{5}$
- **H.** $14\sqrt{10}$
- **J.** $35\sqrt{2}$
- **K.** $70\sqrt{2}$

59. In the standard (x, y) coordinate plane, a right triangle is drawn with vertices at $(5, 0)$, $(9, 3)$, and $(-1, 8)$. What is the area of the triangle, in square units?

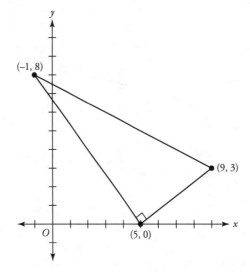

- **A.** 50
- **B.** $10\sqrt{10}$
- **C.** 30
- **D.** 25
- **E.** $5\sqrt{5}$

14

60. A circle in the standard (x,y) coordinate plane is tangent both to the x-axis and to the line $y = 6$. Which of the following could be an equation of the circle?

   F. $x^2 + y^2 = 36$

   G. $x^2 + (y - 3)^2 = 36$

   H. $(x - 3)^2 + y^2 = 36$

   J. $(x - 3)^2 + (y + 3)^2 = 9$

   K. $(x + 3)^2 + (y - 3)^2 = 9$

61. In the standard (x, y) coordinate plane shown below, a rectangle is located on the x-axis. The upper-left vertex of the rectangle touches the graph of the function $y = \sqrt{x} + 2$. Let r represent the value of x that corresponds to the left-hand side of the rectangle, such that $0 < r < 5$. The right-hand side of the rectangle occurs at $x = 5$. Which of the following expressions accurately measures the area, in square coordinate units, of the rectangle in terms of r?

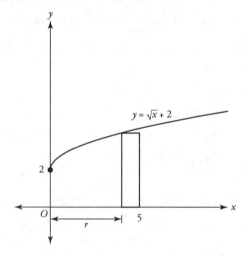

   A. $10 - 2r + (5 - r)\sqrt{r}$

   B. $5 + 2r - (10 - r)\sqrt{r}$

   C. $5 - 2r + (10 + r)\sqrt{r}$

   D. $5r + (2 - r)\sqrt{r}$

   E. $5r + (2 + r)\sqrt{r}$

62. Three functions are graphed below in the standard (x, y) coordinate plane. Which of the following could be a general equation that defines these three functions, for all $1 \le n \le 3$?

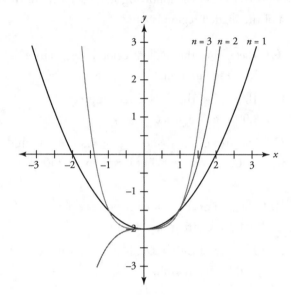

   F. $y = \dfrac{1}{2}x^{n+1} + 2$

   G. $y = \dfrac{1}{2}x^{n+1} - 2$

   H. $y = -\dfrac{1}{2}x^2 + n$

   J. $y = \dfrac{1}{2}x^n + 2$

   K. $y = -x^{n+1} + 2$

14

63. Which of the following choices is the correct graph in the standard (x, y) coordinate plane for:

$$y = \begin{cases} -x^2 + 12 \text{ when } x > 3 \\ |2 - x| \text{ when } -1 \le x \le 3 \\ x + 3 \text{ when } x < -1 \end{cases}$$

A.

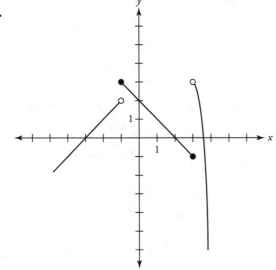

B.

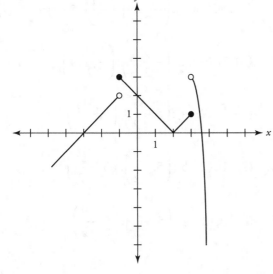

C.

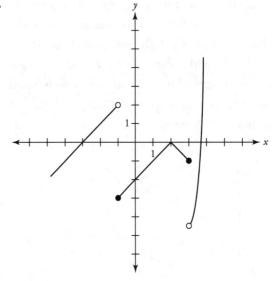

D.

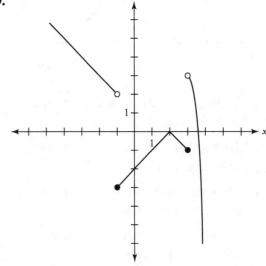

E.

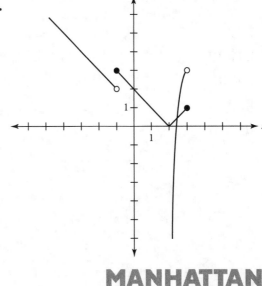

64. Andy is looking for buried treasure on a beach for 10 minutes. He is using a metal detector, which tells him his distance from the buried treasure, but does not tell him in which direction the treasure is located. During the course of these 10 minutes, which 3 of the following actions, in order, could Andy undertake that would best fit this graph?

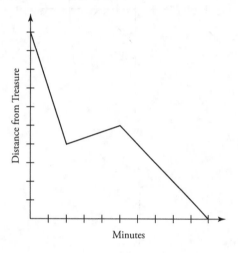

Minutes

I.   He walks towards the treasure at a rate of 90 feet per minute.

II. He walks towards the treasure at a rate of 60 feet per minute.

III. He walks towards the treasure at a rate of 30 feet per minute.

IV. He walks away from the treasure at a rate of 30 feet per minute.

V.   He walks away from the treasure at a rate of 10 feet per minute.

F. I, IV, II

G. I, IV, III

H. I, V, III

J. II, IV, III

K. II, V, III

65. A parallelogram, drawn below in the standard (x, y) coordinate plane, uses the lines represented by the equations $y = 2x$ and $y = 5$ as two of the sides. The additional lines used to complete the parallelogram are also presented. If this parallelogram is reflected across the y-axis, which of the following lists of coordinate points will correspond to the vertices of the new parallelogram?

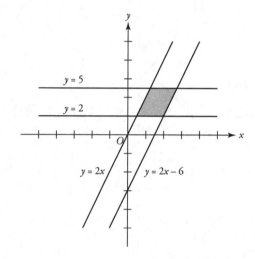

A. $(-1, 2); (-4, 2); \left(-\dfrac{5}{2}, 5\right); \left(-\dfrac{11}{2}, 5\right)$

B. $(-1, 2); (-2, 4); \left(-\dfrac{5}{2}, 2\right); \left(-\dfrac{11}{2}, 4\right)$

C. $(2, -1); (2, -4); \left(5, -\dfrac{5}{2}\right); \left(5, -\dfrac{11}{2}\right)$

D. $(2, -1); (2, -5); \left(5, -\dfrac{7}{2}\right); \left(5, -\dfrac{11}{2}\right)$

E. $(1, -2); (2, -4); \left(5, -\dfrac{7}{2}\right); \left(5, -\dfrac{9}{2}\right)$

66.

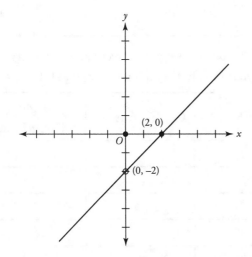

Which of the following is the correct equation of the graph above?

F. $y = x - 2$

G. $y = \dfrac{x - 2}{x}$

H. $y = \dfrac{x^2 - 2x}{x}$

J. $y = \dfrac{x + 2}{x}$

K. $y = \dfrac{x^2 + 2x}{x}$

67. Two triangles, $\triangle ABC$ and $\triangle BCD$, are drawn in the standard (x, y) coordinate plane below. The vertices of $\triangle ABC$ are A (-3, 1), B (0, -2), and C (4, 1). $\triangle BCD$ shares points B and C, but its third vertex is point D (5, 7). What is the absolute difference between the area of $\triangle ABC$ and the area of $\triangle BCD$?

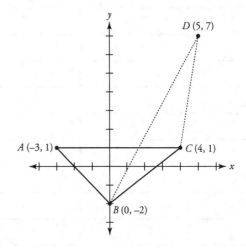

A. 0

B. $1\dfrac{3}{4}$

C. $2\dfrac{1}{3}$

D. $3\dfrac{1}{2}$

E. 7

14

Answer Key

Write in whether you got each problem right or wrong (or left it blank). If your answer was correct, put a 1 in every blank to the right of that problem. Sum up each column and compare your total to the total possible "Out Of" points.

Problem	Correct Answer	Right/Wrong/Blank
1	D	
2	K	
3	C	
4	G	
5	A	
6	H	
7	E	
8	G	
9	D	
10	H	
11	D	
12	K	
13	E	
14	G	
15	A	
16	F	
17	A	
18	G	
19	B	
20	G	
21	C	
22	J	
23	E	
24	F	
25	C	
26	F	
27	A	
28	K	

Problem	Correct Answer	Right/Wrong/Blank
29	D	
30	H	
31	D	
32	K	
33	A	
34	F	
35	A	
36	K	
37	E	
38	K	
39	D	
40	K	
41	C	
42	H	
43	B	
44	K	
45	A	
46	H	
47	D	
48	K	
49	A	
50	H	
51	D	
52	G	
53	B	
54	H	
55	B	
56	H	

14

MANHATTAN
PREP

Problem	Correct Answer	Right/ Wrong/Blank
57	C	
58	J	
59	D	
60	K	
61	A	
62	G	
63	B	
64	H	
65	A	
66	H	
67	A	
Total		
Out Of		67

14

Coordinate Geometry Solutions

1.   **(D)** $3.00   Coordinate Geometry   Interpreting Graphs

To solve this problem, use the graph to identify the corresponding Pricing Tier for a call with a duration of 15 minutes. Reading off the graph, you can see the appropriate Tier is 3. Look up the per-minute pricing for Tier 3 in the chart: $0.20 per minute. Since the call is 15 minutes at $0.20 per minute, multiply to find the total cost: 15 × ($0.20) = $3.00. The correct answer is (D).

2.   **(K)** (5, 0) and (−3, 0)   Coordinate Geometry   Finding Intercepts

The x-intercepts of an equation are the values where $y = 0$. Therefore, find these intercepts by setting y equal to 0, factoring the quadratic, setting each factor equal to 0, and solving for the values of x:

$$0 = x^2 - 2x - 15$$
$$0 = (x - 5)(x + 3)$$
$$0 = (x - 5) \text{ or } 0 = (x + 3)$$
$$x = 5 \text{ or } x = -3$$

The (x, y) coordinates are therefore (5, 0) and (−3, 0). The correct answer is (K).

3.   **(C)** 25   Coordinate Geometry   Midpoints

The distance between points 17 and 33 is 16. To find half the distance between 17 and 33, divide 16 by 2, and add the result to 17, the smaller number, $\dfrac{16}{2} + 17 = 8 + 17 = 25$. One way to check this result is that the difference between the midpoint (25) and 17 is 8, and the difference between 33 and the midpoint (25) is also 8. Therefore, 25 is the midpoint of 17 and 33. The correct answer is (C).

4.   **(G)** (5, 0) and (−5, 0)   Coordinate Geometry   Finding Intercepts

The x-intercepts of an equation are the values where $y = 0$. Therefore, find these intercepts by setting y equal to 0, dividing both sides by 16, and taking the square root:

$$16x^2 + 25(0)^2 = 400$$
$$16x^2 = 400$$
$$x^2 = 25$$
$$x = \pm 5$$

The (x, y) coordinates are therefore (5, 0) and (−5, 0). The correct answer is (G).

5.　**(A)** $y = \dfrac{4}{3}x - 4$　　　Coordinate Geometry　　　Equations of Lines

As can be seen in the diagram, the line drawn passes through the points (3, 0) and (0, –4). Recall that a line is defined by the equation $y = mx + b$, where m is the slope and b is the y-intercept. The slope of the line is the change in y divided by the change in x:

$$\frac{\left(0 - (-4)\right)}{(3 - 0)} = \frac{4}{3}$$

You can solve for b by plugging one of the coordinate points on the line into the equation with a slope of $\dfrac{4}{3}$. Using the point (3, 0) you get the following:

$$y = \frac{4}{3}x + b$$

$$-0 = \frac{4}{3}(3) + b$$

$$b = -\frac{4}{3}(3) = -4 \quad \text{(or you can read this off the } y\text{-axis where the line crosses)}$$

Therefore, the correct equation for the line is $y = \dfrac{4}{3}x - 4$. The correct answer is (A).

6.　**(H)** $x = 4$　　　Coordinate Geometry　　　Graphs in the Plane

By definition, a line crosses the y-axis when $x = 0$. If a line does not cross the y-axis, it is because it is not possible for x to equal 0. Inspect the equations in each of the choices to determine whether (and when) the line will intersect the y-axis:

$y = 3$　　　y always equals 3; line crosses y-axis at (0, 3).

$y = 2x$　　　substituting 0 for x, line crosses y-axis at (0, 0).

$x = 4$　　　Since x always equals 4, line never intercepts y-axis.

$x = y + 2$　　standard form is $y = x - 2$; substituting 0 for x, line crosses y-axis at (0, –2).

$y = x + 2$　　substituting 0 for x, line crosses y-axis at (0, 2).

The correct answer is $x = 4$. The correct answer is (H).

7.　**(E)** $y = -\dfrac{1}{2}x + 1$　　　Coordinate Geometry　　　Equations of Lines

As can be seen in the diagram, the line drawn passes through the points (0, 1) and (2, 0). Recall that a line is defined by the equation $y = mx + b$, where m is the slope and b is the y-intercept. The slope of the line is the change in y divided by the change in x:

$$\frac{(1 - 0)}{(0 - 2)} = \frac{1}{-2} = -\frac{1}{2}$$

You can solve for b by plugging one of the coordinate points on the line into the equation with a slope of $-\dfrac{1}{2}$. Using the point (0, 1) you get the following:

$$y = -\frac{1}{2}x + b$$

$$1 = -\frac{1}{2}(0) + b$$

$$b = 1 \qquad \text{(or you can read this off the } y\text{-axis where the line crosses)}$$

Therefore, the correct equation for the line is $y = -\frac{1}{2}x + 1$. The correct answer is (E).

8.   **(G)** $-\frac{2}{3}$ Coordinate Geometry   Equations of Lines (Slope)

The slope of any line in the coordinate plane is represented by m in the standard notation $y = mx + b$. Therefore, to find the slope, first solve for y and note the coefficient on the x term:

$$1 + 2x + 3y = 0$$

$$3y = -2x - 1$$

$$y = -\frac{2}{3}x - \frac{1}{3}$$

The slope of the line is therefore $-\frac{2}{3}$. The correct answer is (G).

9.   **(D)** $y = -\frac{1}{3}x - 2$ Coordinate Geometry   Equations of Lines

By definition, two lines are perpendicular if, in standard form, the slopes are negative reciprocals of one another. In other words, the product of the slopes must equal −1. Inspect the equations in each of the choices to determine whether the slope is a negative reciprocal of the slope of the original line (3):

$y = 3x + 2$ Product of the slopes is $3 \times 3 = 9$.

$y = -3x + 2$ Product of the slopes is $3 \times (-3) = -9$.

$y = 2x - 3$ Product of the slopes is $3 \times 2 = 6$

$y = -\frac{1}{3}x - 2$ **Product of the slopes is** $3 \times \left(-\frac{1}{3}\right) = -1$.

$y = \frac{1}{3}x + 2$ Product of the slopes is $3 \times \left(\frac{1}{3}\right) = 1$.

The correct answer is $y = -\frac{1}{3}x - 2$. The correct answer is (D).

MANHATTAN
PREP

10. **(H)** 24   Coordinate Geometry   Distance & Area

To find the total distance the police car has traveled, count and record each individual movement made by the police car from point to point. The police car moves 4 miles to the left, 5 miles to the right, 10 miles to the left, and 5 miles to the right. The sum of the distances is $4 + 5 + 10 + 5 = 24$ miles.

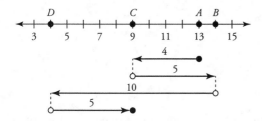

The correct answer is (H).

11. **(D)** $\dfrac{3}{4}$ Coordinate Geometry   Equations of Lines (Slope)

The slope of any line in the coordinate plane is represented by m in the standard notation $y = mx + b$. Therefore, to solve for the slope, first solve for y and note the coefficient on the x term:

$$4x + 3y = 6$$
$$3y = -4x + 6$$
$$y = -\frac{4}{3}x + 2$$

The slope of the line is therefore $-\dfrac{4}{3}$. By definition, two lines are perpendicular if, in standard form, the slopes are negative reciprocals of one another. In other words, the product of the slopes must equal –1. Therefore, the slope of a line perpendicular to the line given in the problem is:

$$-\frac{1}{-\dfrac{4}{3}} = \frac{3}{4}$$

The correct answer is (D).

14

12. **(K)** $\dfrac{6}{5}$ Coordinate Geometry   Equations of Lines (Slope)

Put the given equation into standard slope-intercept form ($y = mx + b$) by solving for y:

$6x - 5y = 4$

$\quad -5y = -6x + 4$

$\quad \dfrac{-5}{-5}y = \dfrac{-6}{-5}x + \dfrac{4}{-5}$

$\quad\quad y = \dfrac{6}{5}x - \dfrac{4}{5}$

In standard slope-intercept form, m represents the slope of the line. Therefore, the slope of this line is $\dfrac{6}{5}$. The correct answer is (K).

13. **(E)** $\sqrt{145}$ Coordinate Geometry   Distance & Area

To find the distance, you can use the distance formula:

$$d = \sqrt{\left(x_2 - x_1\right)^2 + \left(y_2 - y_1\right)^2} = \sqrt{\left(-2 - 7\right)^2 + \left(5 - (-3)\right)^2}$$
$$= \sqrt{\left(-9\right)^2 + \left(8\right)^2} = \sqrt{81 + 64} = \sqrt{145}$$

Alternatively, you can graph the points and use the Pythagorean theorem, from which the distance formula is derived.

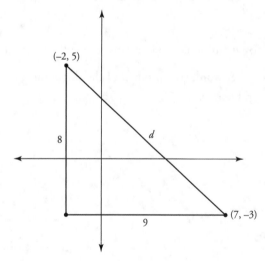

$d^2 = \left(9\right)^2 + \left(8\right)^2 = 145$, so $d = \sqrt{145}$

The correct answer is (E).

MANHATTAN
PREP

14. **(G)** 3   Coordinate Geometry   Equations of Lines (*y*-Intercept)

Put the given equation into standard slope-intercept form ($y = mx + b$) by solving for y:

$$3(x + 2) - 2y = 0$$
$$-2y = -3x - 6$$
$$\frac{-2}{-2}y = \frac{-3}{-2}x + \frac{-6}{-2}$$
$$y = \frac{3}{2}x + 3$$

In standard slope-intercept form, b represents the y-intercept of the line. In other words, b is the value of y when $x = 0$. Therefore, the y-intercept of this line is 3. The correct answer is (G).

15. **(A)** –5   Coordinate Geometry   Equations of Lines (Slope)

Put the given equation into standard slope-intercept form ($y = mx + b$) by solving for y:

$$10x + 2y - 20 = 0$$
$$2y = -10x + 20$$
$$\frac{2}{2}y = \frac{-10}{2}x + \frac{20}{2}$$
$$y = -5x + 10$$

In standard slope-intercept form, m represents the slope of the line. Therefore, the slope of this line is –5. The correct answer is (A).

16. **(F)** $y = -3x + 1$ Coordinate Geometry   Equations of Lines

The equation for a line in the (x, y) coordinate plane will take the form $y = mx + b$, where m is the slope of the line (defined as the change in y divided by the change in x) and b is a constant. You can solve for m and b using the two coordinate points given. First solve for m:

$$m = \frac{\left(\text{change in } y\right)}{\left(\text{change in } x\right)} = \frac{(-5-4)}{(2-(-1))} = \frac{-9}{3} = -3$$

Thus, the slope of the line is –3.

Next, solve for b by substituting one of the known points on the line into the equation. Using (2, –5), you get the following:

$$y = -3x + b$$
$$-5 = -3(2) + b$$
$$b = 6 - 5 = 1$$

The complete equation for the line is therefore $y = -3x + 1$. The correct answer is (F).

14

17.   **(A)** $\left(-\dfrac{1}{2},-1\right)$ Coordinate Geometry   Midpoints

As with most Coordinate Geometry problems, it is helpful to visualize the problem by drawing a picture:

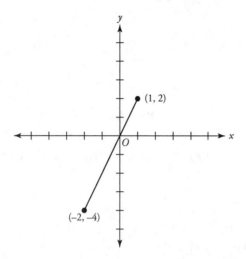

By drawing the diagram neatly, you can see that the midpoint of the line segment is probably in the 3rd quadrant (i.e., both the *x*-coordinate and the *y*-coordinate are negative). If this is accurate, then choice (A) must be correct, because it is the only choice in which both coordinates are negative.

You can use the midpoint formula to prove this. The midpoint for any line segment in the (*x*, *y*) coordinate plane is the average of the *x*-coordinates and *y*-coordinates of the beginning and ending points of the line segment. In other words:

$$\text{Midpoint} = \left(\frac{x_1 + x_2}{2}, \frac{y_1 + y_2}{2}\right)$$

In this formula, the beginning point of the line segment is (x_1, y_1) and the ending point of the line segment is (x_2, y_2). Substitute the coordinates (–2, –4) and (1, 2) to solve for the midpoint:

$$\left(\frac{x_1 + x_2}{2}, \frac{y_1 + y_2}{2}\right) = \left(\frac{-2+1}{2}, \frac{-4+2}{2}\right) = \left(-\frac{1}{2}, -1\right)$$

Therefore, the midpoint of the line segment is $\left(-\dfrac{1}{2}, -1\right)$. The correct answer is (A).

14

MANHATTAN
PREP

18. **(G)** $-\dfrac{1}{2}$ Coordinate Geometry   Equations of Lines (Slope)

Put the given equation into standard slope-intercept form ($y = mx + b$) by solving for y:

$$-13x - 26y = -18$$
$$-26y = 13x - 18$$

$$\frac{-26}{-26}y = \frac{13}{-26}x - \frac{-18}{-26}$$

$$y = -\frac{1}{2}x - \frac{9}{13}$$

In standard slope-intercept form, m represents the slope of the line. Therefore, the slope of this line is $-\dfrac{1}{2}$. The correct answer is (G).

19. **(B)** 2   Coordinate Geometry   Midpoints

The midpoint of a segment with endpoints (x_1, y_1) and (x_2, y_2) is given by the formula: $\left(\dfrac{x_1 + x_2}{2}, \dfrac{y_1 + y_2}{2}\right)$.

The x-coordinate is therefore $\dfrac{9 + (-5)}{2} = \dfrac{4}{2} = 2$. The correct answer is (B).

20. **(G)** 2   Coordinate Geometry   Midpoints

As with most Coordinate Geometry problems, it is helpful to visualize the problem by drawing a picture:

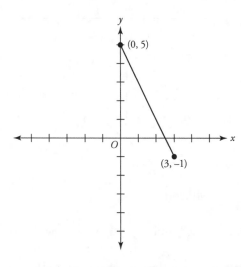

By drawing the diagram neatly, you can see that the midpoint of the line segment is in the 1st quadrant (i.e., both the x-coordinate and the y-coordinate are positive). If this is accurate, then choices (J) and (K) must be incorrect, because they are negative numbers. However, the other choices are fairly close together, so you cannot be certain which choice is correct based on the diagram alone.

You can use the midpoint formula to calculate the exact answer. The midpoint for any line segment in the (x, y) coordinate plane is the average of the x-coordinates and y-coordinates of the beginning and ending points of the line segment. In other words:

$$\text{Midpoint} = \left(\frac{x_1 + x_2}{2}, \frac{y_1 + y_2}{2} \right)$$

In this formula, the beginning point of the line segment is (x_1, y_1) and the ending point of the line segment is (x_2, y_2). Substitute the coordinates $(0, 5)$ and $(3, -1)$ to solve for the midpoint:

$$\left(\frac{x_1 + x_2}{2}, \frac{y_1 + y_2}{2} \right) = \left(\frac{0 + 3}{2}, \frac{5 - 1}{2} \right) = \left(1\frac{1}{2}, 2 \right)$$

The question asks for the y-coordinate of the midpoint, so the correct answer is 2. The correct answer is (G).

21. **(C)** 50%   Coordinate Geometry   Graphs in the Plane

As shown in the figure below, the circle given is centered on the x-axis with a radius of 2. This means that the entire circle is contained in Quadrants II and III, and the x-axis divides the circle in half. This means that 50% of the total area of the circle lies in Quadrant II:

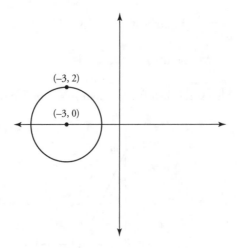

The correct answer is (C).

22. **(J)** −6   Coordinate Geometry   Midpoints

The midpoint of a segment with endpoints (x_1, y_1), and (x_2, y_2) is given by the formula: $\left(\frac{x_1 + x_2}{2}, \frac{y_1 + y_2}{2} \right)$.

The y-coordinate is therefore $\frac{6 + (-18)}{2} = \frac{-12}{2} = -6$. The correct answer is (J).

MANHATTAN
PREP

23. **(E)** 2   Coordinate Geometry   Graphs in the Plane

As with most Coordinate Geometry problems, it is helpful to visualize the problem by drawing a picture:

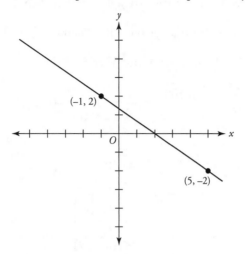

By drawing the diagram neatly, you can see that the line probably intersects the x-axis at $(2, 0)$. However, you can prove that this is the case algebraically. First, recall that a line is defined by the equation $y = mx + b$, where m is the slope and b is the y-intercept. The slope of the line is the change in y divided by the change in x:

$$\frac{(2-(-2))}{(-1-5)} = \frac{4}{-6} = -\frac{2}{3}$$

You can solve for b by plugging one of the coordinate points on the line into the equation with a slope of $-\frac{2}{3}$. Using the point $(-1, 2)$:

$$y = -\frac{2}{3}x + b$$

$$2 = -\frac{2}{3}(-1) + b$$

$$b = 2 - \frac{2}{3} = \frac{4}{3}$$

$$y = -\frac{2}{3}x + \frac{4}{3}$$

The x-intercept of the line is the point at which the line crosses the x-axis. This occurs when $y = 0$. Substitute 0 for y into the above equation and solve for x:

$$y = -\frac{2}{3}x + \frac{4}{3}$$

$$0 = -\frac{2}{3}x + \frac{4}{3}$$

$$-\frac{4}{3} = -\frac{2}{3}x$$

$$x = \left(-\frac{4}{3}\right)\left(-\frac{3}{2}\right) = 2$$

The x-intercept of the line that goes through both points is therefore 2. The correct answer is (E).

14

24. **(F)** 40%　　　Coordinate Geometry　　　Distance & Area

As shown in the figure below, the given vertices form a triangle with base 5 and height 4, which has an area of $\frac{1}{2}(5)(4) = 10$ square units. The portion of that triangle lying in Quadrant IV is shown in the figure as the 2-unit-by-2-unit shaded square, which has an area of $2 \times 2 = 4$ square units. Therefore, the percent of the total area of the triangle lying in

Quadrant IV $= \dfrac{\text{the area of the shaded square}}{\text{area of the triangle}} \times 100\% = \dfrac{4}{10} \times 100\% = 40\%$.

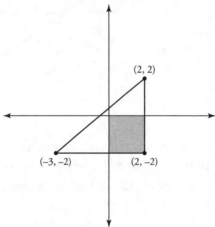

The correct answer is (F).

25. **(C)** Quadrants I and III only　　　Coordinate Geometry　　　Properties of Plane

In Quadrant I, both the x-coordinate and the y-coordinate are positive, so the product of the points must be positive. In Quadrant III, both the x-coordinate and the y-coordinate are negative, so the product of the points must be positive (since a negative times a negative is always positive). In the other two quadrants (II and IV), the signs of the coordinates are opposite to each other, so the product of the coordinates would be negative. The correct answer is (C).

26. **(F)** –6   Coordinate Geometry   Graphs in the Plane

As with most Coordinate Geometry problems, it is helpful to visualize the problem by drawing a picture. Note that since the *x*-intercept of the line is 2, the line crosses through the point (2, 0):

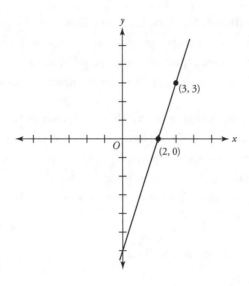

By drawing the diagram neatly, you can see that the line probably intersects the *y*-axis at (0, –6). However, you can prove that this is the case algebraically. First, recall that a line is defined by the equation $y = mx + b$, where *m* is the slope and *b* is the *y*-intercept. The slope of the line is the change in *y* divided by the change in *x*:

$$\frac{(3-0)}{(3-2)} = \frac{3}{1} = 3$$

You can solve for *b* by plugging one of the coordinate points on the line into the equation with a slope of 3. Using the point (3, 3):

$$y = 3x + b$$
$$3 = 3(3) + b$$
$$b = 3 - 3(3) = -6$$

b is defined as the *y*-intercept of the line, so the correct answer is –6. The correct answer is (F).

27. **(A)** Two perpendicular lines   Coordinate Geometry   Equations of Lines

The slope of the first line is $-\frac{1}{3}$. The slope of the second line is 3, the negative reciprocal of the slope of the first line, since $-\frac{1}{3} \times 3 = -1$. Lines whose slopes are negative reciprocals of each other are always perpendicular. The correct answer is (A).

28. **(K)** Quadrants II, III, and IV only   Coordinate Geometry   Properties of Plane

Pay close attention to the language of the question: you don't need the sum of the coordinates to be negative for *every* point in the quadrant. You just need it to be possible for *at least one* point in the quadrant.

The clearest case is probably Quadrant III, in which both the *x*-coordinate and the *y*-coordinate are negative. The sum of two negative numbers is always negative, so in fact the condition will be true for every point in Quadrant III. Conversely, in Quadrant I, both coordinates are positive, so the sum will always be positive, and no point will satisfy the condition. At this stage, you know that the answer must contain Quadrant III and not Quadrant I, so you can eliminate choices (F) and (H).

How about Quadrant II? The *x*-coordinate there is negative, while the *y*-coordinate is positive. The sum of a negative and a positive is sometimes positive (e.g., $-3 + 5 = 2$) and sometimes negative (e.g., $-5 + 3 = -2$). So there are some points in Quadrant II for which the sum of the coordinates is negative: for instance, point $(-5, 3)$. Similar reasoning holds for Quadrant IV: for example, for point $(7, -10)$, the sum of the coordinates is $7 + (-10) = -3$. So the condition is true for at least some points in Quadrant II and IV. All together, three of the four quadrants (II, III, and IV) match the condition in the question. The correct answer is (K).

29. **(D)**   Coordinate Geometry   Properties of Plane

To rotate the graph 180° around the origin, turn it halfway around a circle centered at the origin, as follows:

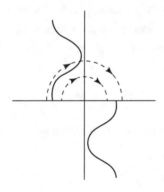

The correct answer is (D).

30. **(H)** 65   Coordinate Geometry   Distance & Area

Draw a picture of the coordinate plane and place the point (–52, 39).

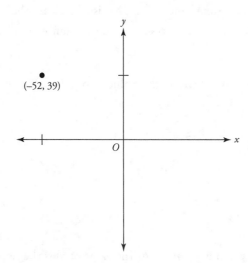

The distance between the point and the origin is the hypotenuse of the following triangle:

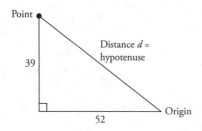

Now apply the Pythagorean theorem:

$39^2 + 52^2 = d^2$ → $1{,}521 + 2{,}704 = d^2$ → $d^2 = 4{,}225$ → $d = 65$

The correct answer is (H).

31. **(D)** $y = -5x - 3$ Coordinate Geometry   Equations of Lines

Rearrange the given equation to isolate y on one side of the equals sign. Pay close attention to signs, because most of the answer choices differ only by plus and minus signs.

Here is one path: add y to both sides, then subtract 3 from both sides:

$-5x - y = 3$
$\quad -5x = 3 + y$
$-5x - 3 = y$

The correct answer is (D).

32. **(K)** 7   Coordinate Geometry   Equations of Lines

Although this is a coordinate geometry problem, the fast way to solve this problem (or any other problem involving the intersection of two graphs such as lines) is to make the equations into one "system" and solve. That is, the x's are the same as each other in each equation, and the y's are the same as each other in each equation, so you can combine, substitute, eliminate, etc.

Here, there is no x in the second equation, which is very simple: $y = 6$. Simply substitute this value into the first equation and solve for x.

$$2y - 3x + 9 = 0 \quad \rightarrow \quad 2(6) - 3x + 9 = 0 \quad \rightarrow \quad 12 - 3x + 9 = 0 \rightarrow \quad 21 = 3x \quad \rightarrow \quad x = 7$$

The correct answer is (K).

33. **(A)** $\dfrac{4}{5}$ Coordinate Geometry   Equations of Lines

To find the slope of the line, put the equation into slope-intercept form, which is $y = mx + b$. The value of m is the slope.

Isolate the y term on one side of the equation, then divide away its coefficient. Pay attention to signs, as always:

$$4x - 5y + 10 = 0$$
$$4x + 10 = 5y$$
$$\frac{4}{5}x + \frac{10}{5} = y$$
$$\frac{4}{5}x + 2 = y$$

The coefficient of the x term is $\dfrac{4}{5}$, so this is the slope of the line. The correct answer is (A).

34. **(F)** 0   Coordinate Geometry   Equations of Lines

Rather than graph these lines and manually find their intersection point, set the two equations for y equal to each other and solve for x (which must also be the same value in both equations, as is always true by definition at an intersection point).

$$y = -x + 3 \text{ and } y = 4x - 12 \quad \rightarrow \quad -x + 3 = 4x - 12 \quad \rightarrow \quad 15 = 5x \quad \rightarrow \quad x = 3$$

Careful! This value is not what the problem is asking for, which is the y-coordinate. To find this coordinate, plug back into either equation (it doesn't matter which, because they both must give you the same y—that's the reason you set them equal to each other).

$$y = -x + 3 \quad \rightarrow \quad y = -3 + 3 \quad \rightarrow \quad y = 0$$

The correct answer is (F).

35. **(A)** $3\sqrt{5}$ Coordinate Geometry   Distance & Area

Distance (or length) in the standard (x, y) coordinate plane can be determined using the distance formula, which is based upon the Pythagorean theorem:

$$\text{Distance} = \sqrt{(x_1 - x_2)^2 + (y_1 - y_2)^2}$$

$$\text{Distance from } A \text{ to } C = \sqrt{(0-6)^2 + (0-(-3))^2}$$

$$= \sqrt{(6)^2 + (3)^2}$$

$$= \sqrt{36+9}$$

$$= \sqrt{45} = \sqrt{(3)(3)(5)} = 3\sqrt{5}$$

Therefore, the distance between A and C is $3\sqrt{5}$. The correct answer is (A).

36. **(K)** $18 - \dfrac{9}{2}\pi$ Coordinate Geometry   Distance & Area

The shaded region in the diagram corresponds to half of the difference between the area of a square and the area of a circle inscribed in the square, both centered at (3, 0). The shapes both span from $x = 0$ to $x = 6$ on the x-axis, so the dimensions of the full shapes can be drawn thusly:

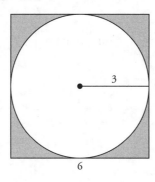

The formula for the area of a circle is $A = \pi r^2$. In this case, $A = \pi(3)^2 = 9\pi$.

The formula for the area of a square is $A = s^2$. In this case, $A = (6)^2 = 36$.

Therefore, the difference in area between the full square and the full circle is $36 - 9\pi$. In the original diagram, the difference is only half of that, because the original diagram contains only half of each shape: $\dfrac{36-9\pi}{2} = \dfrac{36}{2} - \dfrac{9\pi}{2} = 18 - \dfrac{9}{2}\pi$. The correct answer is (K).

14

37. **(E)** 1 inch to the right and $7\frac{1}{2}$ inches up   Coordinate Geometry   Distance & Area

Although this problem does not give you an (x, y) plane, one way to tackle this problem is to overlay a pair of axes centered on point D (because you want the coordinates of the hole *relative* to that point. Compute the coordinates of every other labeled point by adding or subtracting side lengths. The length of $\overline{ED}$ is $15 - 8 = 7$ and the length of $\overline{DC}$ is $12 - 5 = 7$ as well.

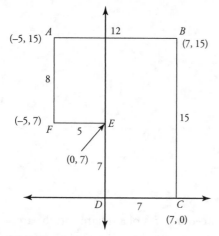

Kelvin will drill a hole at the midpoint of a line segment between point A and point C. The x-coordinate of that midpoint is just the average of the x-coordinates of the two endpoints: $\frac{-5+7}{2} = \frac{2}{2} = 1$. The y-coordinate is the same sort of average: $\frac{15+0}{2} = \frac{15}{2} = 7\frac{1}{2}$. Thus, the coordinates of the midpoint are $\left(1, 7\frac{1}{2}\right)$. That is, relative to point D, the desired position is 1 inch to the right and $7\frac{1}{2}$ inches up.

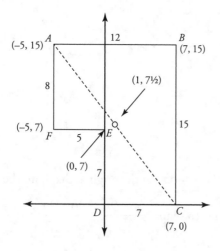

The correct answer is (E).

MANHATTAN
PREP

38. **(K)** 20   Coordinate Geometry   Distance & Area

You can find the solution by using the distance formula, $D = \sqrt{\left(x_1 - x_2\right)^2 + \left(y_1 - y_2\right)^2}$, or by using the Pythagorean theorem. Either technique will produce the same result.

To use the Pythagorean theorem, construct a triangle with an unknown hypotenuse length, but with legs equal to the x distance between -10 and 6 and the y distance between -13 and -1 in the (x, y) coordinate plane, respectively.

The x distance between -10 and 6 is 16. The y distance between -13 and -1 is 12. Using 16 and 12 as the lengths of the legs of the triangle, you can find the hypotenuse length by using the Pythagorean theorem:

$$c^2 = 12^2 + 16^2$$
$$c = \sqrt{12^2 + 16^2}$$
$$c = \sqrt{144 + 256} = \sqrt{400} = 20$$

The correct answer is (K).

39. **(D)** $\sqrt{13}$ Coordinate Geometry   Distance & Area

You can calculate the distance between these two points by using the Pythagorean theorem.

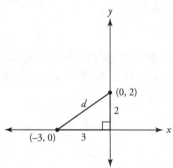

The legs of the right triangle have lengths 2 and 3, because the point $(0, 2)$ is 2 units away from the origin at $(0, 0)$, while the point $(-3, 0)$ is 3 units away from the origin. The hypotenuse (here labeled d) is the distance you want. Now solve:

$$2^2 + 3^2 = d^2 \quad \rightarrow \quad 4 + 9 = 13 = d^2 \quad \rightarrow \quad d = \sqrt{13}$$

The correct answer is (D).

40. **(K)** 25   Coordinate Geometry   Distance & Area

You can find the solution by using the distance formula, $D = \sqrt{\left(x_1 - x_2\right)^2 + \left(y_1 - y_2\right)^2}$, or by using the Pythagorean theorem. Either technique will produce the same result.

To use the Pythagorean theorem, construct a triangle with an unknown hypotenuse length, but with legs equal to the x distance between -5 and 15 and the y distance between -13 and 2 in the (x, y) coordinate plane, respectively.

The x distance between −5 and 15 is 20. The y distance between −13 and 2 is 15. Using 20 and 15 as the lengths of the legs of a triangle, you can find the hypotenuse length by using the Pythagorean theorem:

$$c^2 = 20^2 + 15^2$$
$$c = \sqrt{20^2 + 15^2}$$
$$c = \sqrt{400 + 225} = \sqrt{625} = 25$$

The correct answer is (K).

41. **(C)** $\sqrt{8}$ Coordinate Geometry   Distance & Area

The formula to compute the distance between two points in the plane is derived from the Pythagorean theorem, which is probably easier to remember.

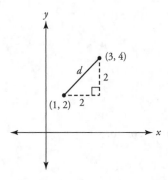

The difference between the x-coordinates is $3 − 1 = 2$, so the horizontal leg of the right triangle shown has length 2. Likewise, the difference between the y-coordinates is $4 − 2 = 2$, so the vertical leg also has length 2. Thus, the hypotenuse (which is the distance d between the points as well) can be computed as follows.

$$2^2 + 2^2 = d^2 \quad \rightarrow \quad 4 + 4 = 8 = d^2 \quad \rightarrow \quad d = \sqrt{8}$$

The correct answer is (C).

42. **(H)** 12π Coordinate Geometry   Graphs in the Plane (Circumference)

The equation for the circle given in the problem is $x^2 + y^2 = 36$. This is equivalent to $(x − 0)^2 + (y − 0)^2 = 36$. Therefore, the circle will be centered at $x = −(0) = 0$ and $y = −(0) = 0$. The radius of the circle is $\sqrt{36} = 6$. Finally, the circumference of any circle is defined as $2\pi r$, where r is the radius of the circle. Therefore, the circumference of the circle is equal to $2\pi(6) = 12\pi$. The correct answer is (H).

43. **(B)** $2\sqrt{5}$ Coordinate Geometry   Distance & Area

The radius of the circle is the distance between the center at $(0, 0)$ and any point on the circle itself. You know the coordinates of one of those points: $(2, 4)$. Now, the distance d between any two points in the coordinate plane obeys the Pythagorean theorem. The distance is the hypotenuse of a right triangle; the lengths of the legs of that triangle are the differences in the coordinates. The typical $a^2 + b^2 = c^2$ becomes (difference in x-coordinates)^2 + (difference in y-coordinates)$^2 = d^2$.

MANHATTAN
PREP

Here, since one of the points is (0, 0), these differences are just the coordinates of the other point. So you have this equation:

$$2^2 + 4^2 = d^2 \quad \rightarrow \quad 4 + 16 = 20 = d^2 \quad \rightarrow \quad d = \sqrt{20}$$

That result doesn't match any of the answer choices exactly. So you must simplify by taking out a square:

$$d = \sqrt{20} = \sqrt{4 \times 5} = \sqrt{4} \times \sqrt{5} = 2 \times \sqrt{5} = 2\sqrt{5}$$

The correct answer is (B).

44. **(K)** II and III only   Coordinate Geometry   Graphs in the Plane

You can see from the graph that from the period of time x to time y, the car's speed remains constant. This fact supports conclusion III, and invalidates conclusion I.

In addition, the question prompt mentions heavy traffic during a commute. During a traffic jam, a car's speed is greatly decreased, even though it might range between very low and moderate speeds at different times. At time y, therefore, you can conclude the car possibly encountered heavy traffic, which makes conclusion II possible. Note that it does not prove this conclusion, but you are only asked what *could* be true. The correct answer is (K).

45. **(A)** 49π Coordinate Geometry   Graphs in the Plane (Area)

The equation for the circle given in the problem is $(x + 2)^2 + (y - 1)^2 = 49$. Therefore, the circle will be centered at $x = -(2) = -2$ and $y = -(-1) = 1$. The radius of the circle is $\sqrt{49} = 7$. Finally, the area of any circle is defined as πr^2, where r is the radius of the circle. Therefore, the area of the circle is equal to $\pi(7)^2 = 49\pi$. (Note that for an equation for a circle in the standard form given in the problem, a shortcut for finding the area is to take the constant on the right-hand side of the equation and multiply by π.) The correct answer is (A).

46. **(H)** $y = (x + 2)^2 - 3$ Coordinate Geometry   Graphs in the Plane

It is easiest to think of parabola shifts when the parabola is expressed in its vertex form, $y = (x - h)^2 + k$. In this form, the h controls left and right shifts from the origin; $h > 0$ represents a shift to the right and $h < 0$ represents a shift to the left. The k term controls shifts up and down; $k > 0$ represents a shift up and $k < 0$ represents a shift down. The up–down shifts may be more intuitive, because the formula contains a plus sign. For the right–left shifts, the minus sign can be confusing. Remember that if you are subtracting within the parentheses, you are shifting to the *right*. If you are adding within the parentheses, you are shifting to the *left*.

Therefore, to shift a parabola left 2 units and down 3 units, the correct vertex form is $y = (x + 2)^2 - 3$. The correct answer is (H).

47. **(D)** I and III only   Coordinate Geometry   Interpreting Graphs

Notice from the graph that at time x, the amount of gas in the gas tank increased dramatically over the course of virtually no time at all. Assume that gas is being added to the tank at time x, which supports statement I.

Starting at time y, notice that gas is neither being added to nor removed from the gas tank. This must mean that the car is not using gas, which means that the car ignition is most likely off during this time. This supports statement III, and answer choice (D) (I and III only).

While statement II might seem correct at first glance, take care: the graph only represents the amount of gas in the gas tank over time, not the driver's speed or acceleration. For example, it is possible that the car was running but parked between time x and time y. However, it is very unlikely that the car was accelerating and decelerating abruptly during this time, because the change in gasoline per unit of time over the period appears to be constant. If the car were accelerating and decelerating abruptly during this time, the change in gas over time would almost certainly not be constant. The correct answer is (D).

48.   **(K)** I, II, and III   Coordinate Geometry   Equations of Lines

From examining both the graph and the linear equation $y = -0.2x + 2.2$ (written here in $y = mx + b$ form), notice that the slope of the line is -0.2. Written as an improper fraction, $-0.2 = -\frac{1}{5}$, which proves statement I. By setting the equation's y value equal to 0, solve for the value of x, which will give you the x-intercept. The x-intercept is located at $(11, 0)$; this proves statement II.

Statement III is also correct. The range of the equation (for domain $1 \le x < 6$) is $1 < y \le 2$, which means it excludes the value of 1 but includes the value of 2. Note the solid dot at point $(1, 2)$ and the open dot at point $(6, 1)$. Because all three statements are true, the correct answer is (K).

49.   **(A)**   Coordinate Geometry   Graphs in the Plane

The best way to approach this problem is to use known properties of the function described to eliminate choices whenever the graph doesn't match what is known about the function given.

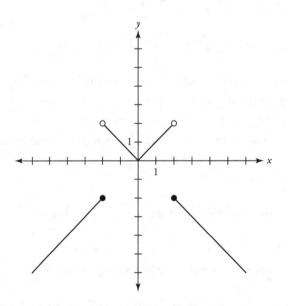

The function described in the question has three main parts. The first part, for all $x \leq -2$, is the graph of $y = x$. This line will have a slope of 1 and will terminate at point $(-2, -2)$. This component alone eliminates choices (B) (wrong slope), (C) (wrong slope and wrong terminal point), and (D) (wrong slope and wrong terminal point).

Next, evaluate the middle component, $y = |x|$, for $-2 < x < 2$. This function will evaluate to $-x$ whenever x is negative, and x whenever x is zero or positive. Therefore, the graph of this function will form a "V" shape, with the bottom of the "V" touching point $(0, 0)$. This also eliminates choice (C).

Finally, evaluate the last component, $y = -x$, for $x \geq 2$. This will have a slope of -1, and will begin at the point $(2, -2)$. This eliminates all choices except for choice (A).

The correct answer is (A).

50.   **(H)** $y = (x - 4)^2 + 5$ Coordinate Geometry   Graphs in the Plane

It is easiest to think of parabola shifts when the parabola is expressed in its vertex form, $y = (x - h)^2 + k$. In this form, the h controls left and right shifts from the origin; $h > 0$ represents a shift to the right and $h < 0$ represents a shift to the left. The k term controls shifts up and down; $k > 0$ represents a shift up and $k < 0$ represents a shift down. The up–down shifts may be more intuitive, because the formula contains a plus sign. For the right–left shifts, the minus sign can be confusing. Remember that if you are subtracting within the parentheses, you are shifting to the *right*. If you are adding within the parentheses, you are shifting to the *left*.

Therefore, to shift a parabola right 4 units and up 5 units, the correct vertex form is $y = (x - 4)^2 + 5$. The correct answer is (H).

51.   **(D)** 1   Coordinate Geometry   Equations of Lines (Slope)

To solve this problem, you can plug the first point and the slope into the slope-intercept form of a line ($y = mx + b$) and solve for the y-intercept, which is b. Then use the completed slope-intercept form with the other point on the line to solve for the missing x:

$5 = 2(6) + b$
$b = -7$

$-5 = 2(x) - 7$
$2 = 2(x)$
$x = 1$

14

Alternatively, you can use the formula for slope, rise over run, to solve for x:

$$Slope = \frac{Rise}{Run} = \frac{y_2 - y_1}{x_2 - x_1}$$

$$2 = \frac{-5 - 5}{x - 6}$$
$$2x - 12 = -10$$
$$2x = 2$$
$$x = 1$$

The correct answer is (D).

52.   **(G)** -13 Coordinate Geometry   Equations of Lines (Slope)

To solve this problem, you can use the given points to solve for the slope-intercept form of the line, $y = mx + b$, where m is the slope and b is the y-intercept:

$(-3, 17)$ → $17 = m(-3) + b$ → $b = 17 + 3m$

$(2, 2)$ → $2 = m(2) + b$

Plug the first into the second:

$2 = 2m + (17 + 3m)$
$2 = 2m + 17 + 3m$
$-15 = 5m$
$m = -3$

Now plug back in to solve for b:
$b = 17 + 3(-3) = 17 - 9 = 8$

Now use the slope-intercept form to find the missing y-coordinate:

$y = -3x + 8$
$y = -3(7) + 8$
$y = -21 + 8$
$y = -13$

The correct answer is (G).

53.   **(B)** II only   Coordinate Geometry   Graphs in the Plane

You can see from the graph that the slope of the line from hour 0 to sometime between hour 1 and hour 2 is the steepest slope in the graph (either positive or negative). Therefore, that was the fastest speed that Beth was traveling. This invalidates conclusion I.

MANHATTAN
PREP

Conclusion II must be true, because Beth reached her farthest point from home between hour 1 and hour 2, and then started getting closer to home. The only way that is possible is if Beth switched direction by going towards home instead of away from it.

Conclusion III, however, does not need to be true, even though it might appear so at first glance. Sometime between hours 4 and 5, Beth is a distance of 0 from home, and then her distance from home starts increasing again. This could be because she stopped at home and returned to where she was coming from, or because she got to home and kept riding past home in the *same* direction. Either is possible, and this invalidates conclusion III.

Therefore, conclusion II is the only statement that MUST be true. The correct answer is (B).

54. **(H)** (–3, –2)   Coordinate Geometry   Graphs in the Plane

The equation for the circle in the diagram is $(x-1)^2 + (y-2)^2 = 16$. Therefore, the circle will be centered at $x = -(-1) = 1$ and $y = -(-2) = 2$. The radius of the circle is $\sqrt{16} = 4$. Therefore, the circle will span from $x = (1-4) = -3$ to $x = (1+4) = 5$, and from $y = (2-4) = -2$ to $y = (2+4) = 6$.

Because the circle is inscribed inside the square in the diagram, the square will also span the same x-coordinates and y-coordinates. The corners of the square will be located at (–3, 6), (–3, –2), (5, –2), and (5, 6). Point A is in the lower left corner, so its coordinates must be (–3, –2). The correct answer is (H).

55. **(B)** $100\sqrt{5}$, longer   Coordinate Geometry   Distance & Area

Distance (or length) in the standard (x, y) coordinate plane can be determined using the distance formula, which is based upon the Pythagorean theorem:

$$\text{Distance} = \sqrt{\left(x_1 - x_2\right)^2 + \left(y_1 - y_2\right)^2}$$

$$\overline{AB} = \sqrt{\left(-50-0\right)^2 + \left(0-100\right)^2} \qquad \overline{BC} = \sqrt{\left(0-50\right)^2 + \left(100-0\right)^2}$$
$$= \sqrt{\left(-50\right)^2 + \left(-100\right)^2} \qquad\qquad = \sqrt{\left(-50\right)^2 + \left(100\right)^2}$$
$$= \sqrt{2,500 + 10,000} \qquad\qquad\quad = \sqrt{2,500 + 10,000}$$
$$= \sqrt{12,500} \qquad\qquad\qquad\qquad = \sqrt{12,500}$$
$$= \sqrt{125} \cdot \sqrt{100} \qquad\qquad\qquad = \sqrt{125} \cdot \sqrt{100}$$
$$= 5\sqrt{5} \cdot 10 = 50\sqrt{5} \qquad\qquad = 5\sqrt{5} \cdot 10 = 50\sqrt{5}$$

14

Therefore, $\overline{AB} + \overline{BC} = 50\sqrt{5} + 50\sqrt{5} = 100\sqrt{5}$. The curve must be longer than that, because going left to right, the curve traverses points A and B and then points B and C, but does not follow a straight line. The shortest distance between two points is a straight line, so the curve ABC must be longer than the sum of the line segments $\overline{AB}$ and $\overline{BC}$. The correct answer is (B).

56. **(H)** The area of the shaded region is greater than 5,000 square units but less than 10,000 square units.

Coordinate Geometry   Distance & Area

Triangle $\triangle ABC$ is entirely contained within the shaded region under the parabola. This eliminates choices (F) and (G): the area of triangle $\triangle ABC$ must be less than the area of the shaded region, so the area of the shaded region must be greater than 5,000 square units. However the remaining choices require you to decide whether the shaded region is less than, equal to, or greater than 10,000.

Returning to the original diagram, you can add points D and E at (– 50, 100) and (50, 100), respectively. By drawing lines to connect A to D, D to E, and E to C, you have drawn a square with sides of length 100. The area of this square is therefore (100)(100) = 10,000 square units. As can be seen from the diagram below, square $ACED$ contains all of the shaded region, so the shaded region is less than the area of the square. The correct answer is that the area of the shaded region is greater than 5,000 square units but less than 10,000 square units:

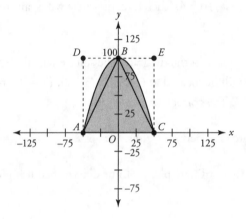

The correct answer is (H).

57. **(C)** 70   Coordinate Geometry   Distance & Area

The area of a parallelogram is given by the formula $A = bh$, where b is the base and h is the height. The base and height must be perpendicular to each other, so the easiest way to assign the base and height in this example is to set the base equal to the horizontal line at the top of the parallelogram (or bottom), and set the height equal to the distance between the top and the bottom of the parallelogram:

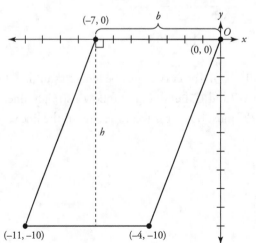

MANHATTAN
PREP

Because the base is parallel to the *x*-axis and the height is parallel to the *y*-axis, it is fairly easy to compute their lengths. The base is the difference between the *x*-coordinates of the two points that the base spans: (–7, 0) and (0, 0). Therefore, base = (0 – (–7)) = 7. The height is the difference between the *y*-coordinates of a point on the top of the parallelogram and a point on the bottom: (0, 0) and (–4, –10). Thus, height = (0 – (10)) = 10. The area of the parallelogram is therefore 7 × 10 = 70.

Notice in the diagram above that if the right triangle formed to the left of the dotted line were removed and placed to the right of the remaining figure, the new shape would be a 7-by-10 rectangle. This provides good visual confirmation that the area of the parallelogram is indeed 7 × 10 = 70. The correct answer is (C).

58. **(J)** $35\sqrt{2}$ Coordinate Geometry   Distance & Area

In this problem, the locations of two towns are given from a map on which every inch represents 70 ÷ 10 = 7 miles. Simulate the map using the (*x*, *y*) coordinate plane:

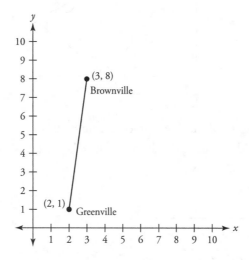

Distance (or length) in the standard (*x*, *y*) coordinate plane can be determined using the distance formula, which is based upon the Pythagorean theorem:

$$\text{Distance} = \sqrt{(x_1 - x_2)^2 + (y_1 - y_2)^2}$$

$$\text{Distance} = \sqrt{(2-3)^2 + (1-8)^2}$$
$$= \sqrt{(-1)^2 + (-7)^2}$$
$$= \sqrt{1 + 49}$$
$$= \sqrt{50}$$
$$= \sqrt{2} \cdot \sqrt{25}$$
$$= 5\sqrt{2}$$

Therefore, the distance on the map between Greenville and Brownville is $5\sqrt{2}$ inches. However, every inch on the map represents 7 miles, so the distance between Greenville and Brownville is $7 \cdot 5\sqrt{2} = 35\sqrt{2}$ miles. The correct answer is (J).

59. **(D)** 25   Coordinate Geometry   Distance & Area

The area of a triangle is given by the formula $A = \dfrac{1}{2} bh$. It is given in the problem that the vertices of the triangle are at (5, 0), (9, 3), and (–1, 8). It is also shown in the diagram that the angle formed at (5, 0) is a right angle, and a right angle in a triangle will form the intersection of the base and the height:

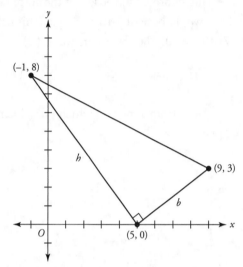

Thus, you need to calculate the lengths of the line segments from (5, 0) to (9, 3) (this is the base), and from (5, 0) to (–1, 8) (this is the height). You can do so using the distance formula, which is based upon the Pythagorean theorem:

$$\text{Distance} = \sqrt{\left(x_1 - x_2\right)^2 + \left(y_1 - y_2\right)^2}$$

$$
\begin{aligned}
b &= \sqrt{(9-5)^2 + (3-0)^2} \\
&= \sqrt{(4)^2 + (3)^2} \\
&= \sqrt{16+9} \\
&= \sqrt{25} \\
&= 5
\end{aligned}
\qquad
\begin{aligned}
h &= \sqrt{(5-(-1))^2 + (0-8)^2} \\
&= \sqrt{(6)^2 + (-8)^2} \\
&= \sqrt{36+64} \\
&= \sqrt{100} \\
&= 10
\end{aligned}
$$

Therefore, the base of the triangle has length 5 and the height has length 10. The area of the triangle is therefore equal to $\dfrac{1}{2}(5)(10) = 25$. The correct answer is (D).

14

MANHATTAN
PREP

60. **(K)** $(x+3)^2 + (y-3)^2 = 9$ Coordinate Geometry   Graphs in the Plane (Circles)

Draw both the x-axis and the line $y = 6$ in the coordinate plane, so that you can visualize the constraints.

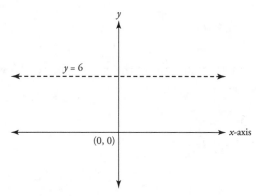

If you want a circle to be tangent to—that is, just touching—the two lines mentioned, then you have to wedge the circle in between, so that it just fits. The right-left position doesn't matter, but the circle has to be the right size, and it has to be centered exactly between the two lines. Here's an example:

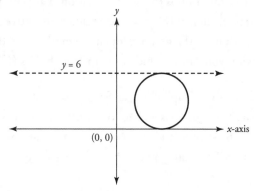

The center of the circle has to have a y-coordinate of 3, halfway between 6 and 0, so the form of the equation of the circle must include $(y-3)^2$. The reason is that in general, the equation of a circle with center (h, k) and radius r is $(x-h)^2 + (y-k)^2 = r^2$. Here, k is 3, but h doesn't matter as long as the x-term is some form of $(x-h)^2$. The other thing to notice about the circle is that it must "just" fit between the two lines, so the diameter is 6. Thus, the radius is 3, and r^2 is 9.

The equation of the circle must fit this form: $(x-h)^2 + (y-3)^2 = 9$. The only answer choice that fits is $(x+3)^2 + (y-3)^2 = 9$. The correct answer is (K).

14

61. **(A)** $10 - 2r + (5-r)\sqrt{r}$ Coordinate Geometry   Graphs in the Plane

The problem states that the x-coordinates of the rectangle span from r to 5, and that bottom of the rectangle is located on the x-axis. The problem also states that the upper-left vertex of the rectangle touches the graph of the function $y = \sqrt{x} + 2$, which implies that the rectangle's y-coordinates span from 0 to $\sqrt{r} + 2$.

The area of a rectangle is given by the formula $A = lw$, where l is the length of the rectangle and w is the width. The length of the rectangle is the difference between the y-coordinates: $(\sqrt{r} + 2) - (0) = \sqrt{r} + 2$. The width is given by the difference between the x-coordinates: $5 - r$. (Remember that the width must be a positive number, and that $r < 5$.)

Therefore, you can calculate the area of the rectangle in terms of r as follows, using the FOIL method:

$$A = lw = \left(y_2 - y_1\right)\left(x_2 - x_1\right)$$
$$= \left(\sqrt{r} + 2\right)\left(5 - r\right)$$
$$= 5\sqrt{r} - r\sqrt{r} + 10 - 2r$$

Note that this expression does not exactly match any of the answer choices. However, as a final step, you can rearrange the terms and factor two of the like terms that contain $\sqrt{r}$:

$$5\sqrt{r} - r\sqrt{r} + 10 - 2r = 10 - 2r + 5\sqrt{r} - r\sqrt{r}$$
$$= 10 - 2r + (5 - r)\sqrt{r}$$

The correct answer is (A).

62. **(G)** $y = \dfrac{1}{2}x^{n+1} - 2$ Coordinate Geometry   Graphs in the Plane

Perhaps the best way to approach this question is to use information that is known about the graphs of the functions to eliminate answer choices. For example, choices (H) and (K) include a negative sign in front of the independent variable x, which would force the three functions in the graph to open downwards or "flip" in the case of a cube function. Since the graphs do not show this behavior, you can conclude that answer choices (H) and (K) are incorrect.

As n increases from 1 to 3, the curve of the graph changes from a parabola (y is a function of x^2) to a cube function (y is a function of x^3) to a 4th power function (y is a function of x^4). In each case, the exponent above the base of x increases by 1 for each successive increase of n, and starts at $n + 1$. You can restate this progression by saying that y is a function of x^{n+1}, for n values of 1 to 3. Thus far, you can conclude that the general equation is equal to $y = ax^{n+1} + b$, where a and b are constants.

You can also observe from the graph that the y-intercept for all functions is –2 and that the scaling factor for each answer response is $\dfrac{1}{2}$, so the general equation for this family of functions is $y = \dfrac{1}{2}x^{n+1} - 2$. The correct answer is (G).

14

63. **(B)**   Coordinate Geometry   Graphs in the Plane

The best way to approach this problem is to use known properties of the function described to eliminate choices whenever the graph doesn't match what is known about the function given.

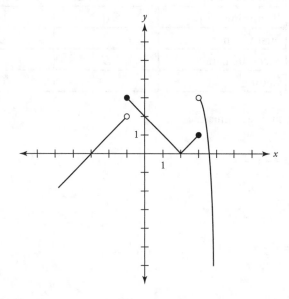

The function described in the question has three main parts. The first part, for all $x > 3$, is the graph of a parabola. This parabola will point upward because the sign on the x term is negative. The parabola will cross through the points (3, 3) and (4, –4). This component eliminates choices (C) (the parabola does not cross through the correct points and is upward-sloping) and (E) (the parabolic portion of the graph is for $x < 3$, not $x > 3$, and is in the wrong location).

Next, evaluate the middle component, $y = |2 - x|$, for $-1 \le x < 3$. The absolute value of $2 - x$ is equal to the positive distance between 2 and x on the number line. In other words, the graph will evaluate to $2 - x$ whenever x is less than 2, and $x - 2$ whenever x is greater than or equal to 2. Therefore, the graph of this function should form a "V" shape, with the bottom of the "V" touching point (2, 0). This eliminates choices (A) (not V-shaped and y goes below 0), (C) (is negative instead of positive) and (D) (same reason). Therefore, at this point, you have already eliminated all choices except for (B), which is the correct answer.

Finally, just as a double-check, evaluate the last component, $y = x + 3$, for $x < -1$. This will have a slope of 1, and will terminate at the point (–1, 2). This eliminates choices (D) and (E) (both have the wrong slope).

The correct answer is (B).

64. **(H)** I, V, III   Coordinate Geometry   Graphs in the Plane

You can see from the graph that Andy is first walking toward the treasure, then walking away from it, then walking towards it. You need to decide which combination of rates would fit the speeds implied by the slopes of the 3 piecewise line segments.

14

Perhaps the easiest way to determine these implied speeds is by calculating the slope of each line segment. The slope of the line is the change in y divided by the change in x. Set up a table of the beginning and ending points of each line segment:

Point on Graph	x-Coordinate	y-Coordinate
Beginning	0	10
First Change	2	4
Second Change	5	5
Ending	10	0

Now calculate the slopes of each line segment:

$$\text{Line segment } 1: \frac{(10-4)}{(0-2)} = \frac{6}{-2} = -3$$

$$\text{Line segment } 2: \frac{(4-5)}{(2-5)} = \frac{-1}{-3} = \frac{1}{3}$$

$$\text{Line segment } 3: \frac{(5-0)}{(5-10)} = \frac{5}{-5} = -1$$

The slopes of the 3 line segments are -3, $\frac{1}{3}$, and -1, so the speeds for each line segment must be in the same proportion. (Notice that a negative line slope implies that Andy was walking toward the treasure and a positive one implies that he was walking away from it.) Multiply these slopes by 3 to get -9, 1, and -3 as the relative speeds for each leg of Andy's search for the treasure.

Among the statements, the highest speed is 90 feet per minute (towards the treasure) and the lowest speed is 10 feet per minute (away from the treasure), and the ratio of these speeds is $9:1$. Therefore, the only combination that will fit the $-9:1:-3$ ratio is 90 feet per minute (towards), 10 feet per minute (away), and 30 feet per minute (towards). The correct answer is (H).

65. **(A)** $(-1,2)$; $(-4,2)$; $\left(-\dfrac{5}{2},5\right)$; $\left(-\dfrac{11}{2},5\right)$ Coordinate Geometry   Rotations and Transformations

You can solve for the coordinates of the vertices of original parallelogram by finding the points at which the lines intersect. For example, the lines $y = 2$ and $y = 2x$ will intersect when $2 = 2x$, or $x = 1$ and $y = 2$. The four coordinate points found by solving in this manner are as follows:

Coordinate Point	Equations	x-Coordinate	y-Coordinate
Lower-left	$y = 2$; $y = 2x$	1	2
Lower-right	$y = 2$; $y = 2x - 6$	4	2
Upper-left	$y = 5$; $y = 2x$	$\dfrac{5}{2}$	5
Upper-right	$y = 5$; $y = 2x - 6$	$\dfrac{11}{2}$	5

By reflecting the parallelogram about the y-axis, the graph will look like this:

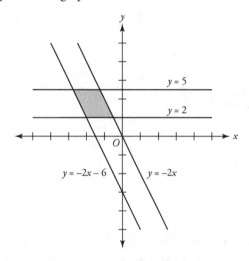

Put simply, by reflecting the graph across the y-axis, all of the y-values stay the same, but the values of the x-coordinates become the negative of the values in the original graph (i.e., you put a minus sign in front of them).

14

Therefore, for the reflected parallelogram, the coordinate points of the vertices of the parallelogram are:

Coordinate Point	Equations	x-Coordinate	y-Coordinate
Lower-left	$y = 2;$ $y = -2x$	-1	2
Lower-right	$y = 2;$ $y = -2x - 6$	-4	2
Upper-left	$y = 5;$ $y = -2x$	$-\dfrac{5}{2}$	5
Upper-right	$y = 5;$ $y = -2x - 6$	$-\dfrac{11}{2}$	5

The correct answer is (A).

66. **(H)** $y = \dfrac{x^2 - 2x}{x}$ Coordinate Geometry   Graphs of Functions

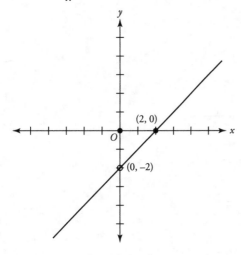

The graph above is of a line that has a missing point at $(0, -2)$. That is, there is a restriction to its domain such that $x \neq 0$. The equation that you are looking for should largely be in the form of $y = mx + b$, but must take in to account the domain restriction. A domain restriction of $x \neq 0$ happens when there is an x in the denominator, because that would mean that x cannot be 0 (it is illegal to divide by 0).

It is easiest to work backwards in this question, considering the answer choices. You can start by looking at answer choices (G), (H), (J) and (K), because choice (F) would not have any domain restrictions.

Remember, the equation also must be that of a line. What you want is a numerator that *also* has an extra x as a factor that will cancel with the x needed in the denominator for the domain restriction.

MANHATTAN
PREP

This leaves two possible answers:

(H) $y = \dfrac{x^2 - 2x}{x} = \dfrac{x(x-2)}{x} = x - 2$ (Whenever $x \neq 0$)

(J) $y = \dfrac{x^2 + 2x}{x} = \dfrac{x(x+2)}{x} = x + 2$ (Whenever $x \neq 0$)

The first, (H), gives you the equation of the line $y = x - 2$; this line has a y-intercept of $(0, -2)$ as in the graph. The correct answer is (H).

67. **(A)** 0   Coordinate Geometry   Area in the (x, y) Plane

If the lengths of all 3 sides are known, the area of any triangle can be computed, using a complicated procedure known as Heron's Formula (which you do not need to know for the ACT!). However, you can demonstrate that the two triangles, $\triangle ABC$ and $\triangle BCD$, displayed in the diagram are of equal area (and therefore the difference between the areas is 0) by taking a different approach.

For any given triangle, the area is given by $\dfrac{1}{2}bh$, where b is the base and h is the height. The base and the height must be perpendicular to each other and must stretch from one end of the triangle to the next.

In this problem, triangles $\triangle ABC$ and $\triangle BCD$ share a common base: $\overline{BC}$.

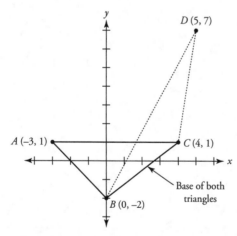

Now determine their relative height. For $\triangle ABC$, the height must connect the line segment $\overline{BC}$ (extended, if need be, for a triangle with an angle greater than 90°) with point A. Likewise, for $\triangle BCD$, the height must connect the line segment $\overline{BC}$ with point D.

However, first, notice the slope of the line segment $\overline{BC}$ as well as the line segment (not drawn) connecting points A and D. Slope is defined as the change in the y-coordinates divided by the change in the x-coordinates:

Slope of $\overline{BC} = \dfrac{(-2-1)}{(0-4)} = \dfrac{-3}{-4} = \dfrac{3}{4}$

Slope of $\overline{AD} = \dfrac{(1-7)}{(-3-5)} = \dfrac{-6}{-8} = \dfrac{3}{4}$

14

The slope of the two line segments is the same, which means that they are parallel! If that is the case, any line segment perpendicular to $\overline{BC}$ and $\overline{AD}$ that connects the two line segments (or any line extending from them) must be of the same length. In other words, the two triangles have the same height:

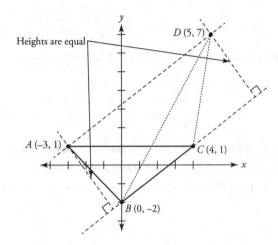

While the heights of the two triangles can be calculated, there is no need to do so: you have demonstrated that $\triangle ABC$ and $\triangle BCD$ have the same base and the same height, and must therefore have the same area. The correct answer is 0. The correct answer is (A).

14

Chapter 15
of

5lb. Book of ACT® Practice Problems

Math:
Plane Geometry

In This Chapter...

Plane Geometry Problems & Solutions

Chapter 15
Math: Plane Geometry

The Math problems in this chapter are drawn from plane geometry—most of what you do in Geometry class. The topics include the following:

1. Lines and Angles. Lines, angles, distance on a line, and degrees vs. radians.

2. Triangles. Rules and properties of triangles, by themselves or formed by diagonals inside other figures.

3. Polygons. Rules and properties of quadrilaterals and of other polygons.

4. Circles. Rules and properties of circles.

5. Other Plane Geometry. Visualizing in one, two, and three dimensions; working with solid figures; drawing logical conclusions.

How should you use this chapter? Here are some recommendations, according to the level you've reached in ACT Math.

1. Fundamentals. Start slowly with the easier problems at the beginning. Do at least some of these problems untimed. This way, you give yourself a chance to think deeply about the principles at work. Review the solutions closely, and articulate what you've learned. Redo problems as necessary.

2. Fixes. Do a few problems untimed, examine the results, learn your lessons, then test yourself with longer timed sets.

3. Tweaks. Confirm your mastery by doing longer sets of problems under timed conditions. Aim to improve the speed and ease of your solution process. Mix the problems up by jumping around in the chapter. Definitely push to the harder, higher-numbered problems.

Good luck on the problems!

1. In the figure below, *ABCD* and *EFGH* are similar rectangles with the given side lengths in feet. What is the value of *x*?

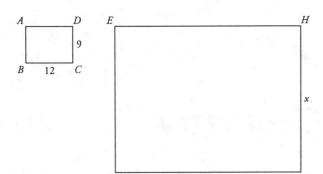

A. 27

B. 36

C. 54

D. 60

E. 72

2. A rectangle measures 2.5 meters by 3.0 meters. What is the perimeter, in meters, of the rectangle?

F. 5.0

G. 5.5

H. 6.0

J. 7.5

K. 11.0

3. A rectangular swimming pool measures 12 feet in width by 20 feet in length. Brett decides that he wants to build a similar swimming pool at his home, only much larger. If Brett plans to make his swimming pool 120 feet in length, what should the width of his new pool be?

A. 60 feet

B. 72 feet

C. 112 feet

D. 144 feet

E. 200 feet

4. In the figure of quadrilateral *ABCD* below, what is the measure of angle *A*?

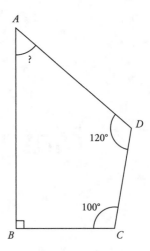

F. 50°

G. 60°

H. 70°

J. 90°

K. 105°

5. The perimeter of a rectangular plot of land is 280 feet. If one of the sides of the rectangular plot is 50 feet in length, what is the length, in feet, of each of the longer sides of the plot?

A. 90

B. 115

C. 140

D. 180

E. 230

6. What is the perimeter of a rectangle with a width of 11 and a length of 13?

F. 24

G. 26

H. 48

J. 62

K. 143

MANHATTAN
PREP

7. In the following diagram of △*ABC*, what is *y*?

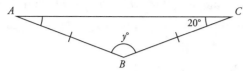

- **A.** 20°
- **B.** 40°
- **C.** 100°
- **D.** 140°
- **E.** 160°

8. In the figure below, *ABCD* and *EFGH* are similar rectangles with the given side lengths in inches. If the area of *ABCD* is 60 square inches, what is the perimeter of *EFGH*, in inches?

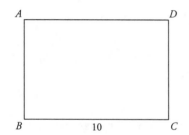 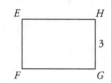

- **F.** 16
- **G.** 18
- **H.** 20
- **J.** 22
- **K.** 30

9. Six points are shown on the line in the figure below. Which of the following rays contains point *C* but not point *E*?

- **A.** $\overrightarrow{DF}$
- **B.** $\overrightarrow{DB}$
- **C.** $\overrightarrow{BD}$
- **D.** $\overrightarrow{BA}$
- **E.** $\overrightarrow{AF}$

10. In the figure below, △*ABC* and △*DEF* are similar triangles with the given side lengths in meters. What is the perimeter of △*DEF*, in meters?

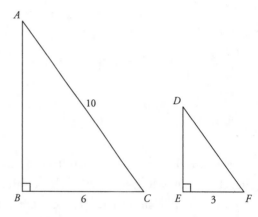

- **F.** 8
- **G.** 11
- **H.** 12
- **J.** 14
- **K.** 15

11. In the figure below, point *F* is on $\overleftrightarrow{EG}$, and points *B* and *C* are on $\overleftrightarrow{AD}$. $\overleftrightarrow{AD}$ is parallel to $\overleftrightarrow{EG}$. What is the measure of ∠*ABF*?

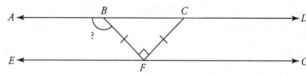

- **A.** 30°
- **B.** 45°
- **C.** 90°
- **D.** 120°
- **E.** 135°

15

12. Nine points are shown on the line in the figure below. Which of the following rays contains point U?

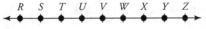

    F. $\overrightarrow{SR}$

    G. $\overrightarrow{TR}$

    H. $\overrightarrow{VZ}$

    J. $\overrightarrow{WY}$

    K. $\overrightarrow{XV}$

13. Nick is refurbishing the rectangular floor of a ballroom, which measures 40 feet by 12 feet, by installing new tile on the floor. Each tile Nick lays measures 2 feet by 3 feet. What is the minimum number of tiles that Nick will need to lay to complete the refurbished flooring of the entire ballroom?

    A. 12

    B. 20

    C. 40

    D. 60

    E. 80

14. A rectangle has an area of 77 square inches. If the lengths of each of the sides of the rectangle are prime numbers, what is the perimeter of the rectangle, in inches?

    F. 28

    G. 36

    H. 40

    J. 42

    K. 44

15. Each of the following lists 2 out of the 3 interior angle measurements for a triangle. For which list do the angle measurements constitute 2 out of the 3 angles in an isosceles triangle?

    A. 30° and 90°

    B. 40° and 80°

    C. 50° and 70°

    D. 50° and 80°

    E. 60° and 70°

16. A certain rectangular painted canvas has an area of 120 square inches and a perimeter of 58 inches. What are the dimensions of the painted canvas?

    F. 4-by-30 inches

    G. 5-by-24 inches

    H. 8-by-21 inches

    J. 11-by-18 inches

    K. 12-by-10 inches

17. A triangle has a perimeter of 70 meters and its longest side measures 28 meters. If the lengths of the two other sides of the triangle have a ratio of $3:4$, what is the length of the *shortest* side of the triangle, in meters?

    A. 18

    B. 20

    C. 24

    D. 28

    E. 30

18. Point Z lies on $\overleftrightarrow{XY}$ between X and Y. Point W is a point not on $\overleftrightarrow{XY}$ such that the measure of $\angle YZW$ is 62°. What is the measure of $\angle XZW$?

    F. 128°

    G. 118°

    H. 87°

    J. 62°

    K. 28°

19. A hotel chain has decided to install a rectangular pool in each of its newest locations in order to attract more guests. Each pool must have a top surface area of 150 square meters and a perimeter of 62 meters. What must be the dimensions of the each pool, in meters?

A. 5×30

B. 6×25

C. 10×15

D. 12×19

E. 15×16

20. One side of a triangle is 19 millimeters long and another side is 12 millimeters long. Which of the following is a possible length, in millimeters, for the third side?

F. 7

G. 23

H. 31

J. 33

K. 45

21. As shown in the figure below, $\overrightarrow{AB}$ is perpendicular to $\overrightarrow{CD}$. The two lines intersect at point X. If point Z is a point neither on $\overrightarrow{AB}$ nor on $\overrightarrow{CD}$ such that $\angle CXZ$ (not shown) is 28°, what is the measure of $\angle ZXB$ (not shown)?

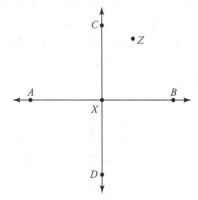

A. 56°

B. 62°

C. 76°

D. 118°

E. 152°

22. Points Y and Z lie on the circle below, where the central angle $\angle YXZ$ measures 95°. What is the measure of $\angle XZY$?

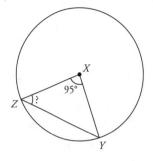

F. 37.5°

G. 40°

H. 42.5°

J. 54°

K. Cannot be determined from the given information

23. One side of a triangle is 10 inches long and another side is 34 inches long. Which of the following is a possible length, in inches, for the third side?

A. 4

B. 10

C. 24

D. 30

E. 45

24. What is the positive difference between the degree measures of $\angle ABD$ and $\angle CBD$ in the diagram below?

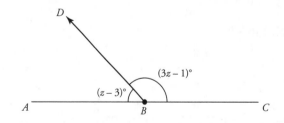

F. 46°

G. 77°

H. 94°

J. 103°

K. 137°

15

25. Points *M* and *N* lie on the circle below, where the angle ∠*NMO* measures 70°. What is the measure of central angle ∠*NOM* ?

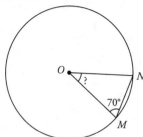

   A. 30°

   B. 40°

   C. 55°

   D. 70°

   E. Cannot be determined from the given information

26. What percent of the sum of the interior angles of △*ABC* does ∠*ABC* represent?

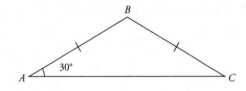

   F. $66\frac{2}{3}\%$

   G. 50%

   H. $33\frac{1}{3}\%$

   J. 20%

   K. $16\frac{2}{3}\%$

27. What is the degree measure of the smallest interior angle of △*DEF* below?

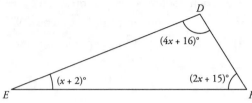

   A. 21°

   B. 23°

   C. 42°

   D. 44°

   E. 57°

28. A triangular park is 500 meters long on its eastern border and 200 meters long on its southern border. If a city planner is building a scale model of the park, and the scale model has a southern border that is 5 feet long, how many feet long should the eastern border of the scale model be?

   F. 2

   G. 4

   H. 10

   J. 12.5

   K. 25

29. A cable of unknown length stretches from the ground to the top of a pole in a straight line. The pole is 12 feet tall and the distance from the base of the pole to the base of the cable measures 9 feet. How many feet, in length, is the cable?

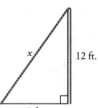

   A. 5

   B. 15

   C. 18

   D. $\sqrt{30}$

   E. $10\sqrt{3}$

30. What is the perimeter of a 45°–45°–90° triangle that has an area of 16?

F. $8\sqrt{2}$

G. 16

H. $16\sqrt{2}$

J. $4+16\sqrt{2}$

K. $8+8\sqrt{2}$

31. Reshma needs to purchase fence to enclose a triangular garden in her yard (see diagram). If the longest side of her garden is 13 feet long, and the next longest side of the garden is 12 feet long, how many feet of fence must she purchase to enclose the entire garden?

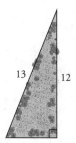

A. 5

B. 12

C. 15

D. 30

E. 36

32. In the following diagram, the marked line segments are of equal length, and the marked angle measures 10°. What is the value of z?

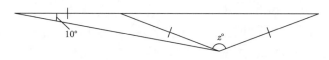

F. 180

G. 170

H. 160

J. 150

K. 140

33. In the diagram below, a smaller (inside) square is contained within a larger (outside) square. The non-overlapping portion of the two squares can be subdivided into 16 smaller squares that are each 9 square feet in area. What is the perimeter, in feet, of the larger (outside) square?

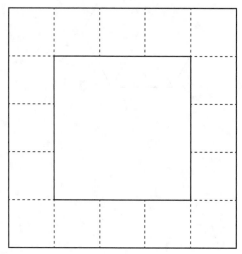

A. 36

B. 48

C. 60

D. 108

E. 144

34. In the diagram below, $x \geq 2y$. What is the minimum possible value for x?

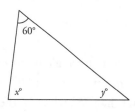

F. 40

G. 50

H. 60

J. 70

K. 80

35. In the diagram below, a regular hexagon can be subdivided into 6 identical equilateral triangles. If the perimeter of each of these triangles is 15 centimeters, what is the perimeter of the hexagon, in centimeters?

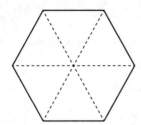

   A. 15

   B. 30

   C. $\dfrac{75\sqrt{3}}{4}$

   D. $20\sqrt{3}$

   E. $15\sqrt{5}$

36. Five towns, A, B, C, D, and E, are located such that Town D is 1 mile directly east of Town E, Town D is exactly 2 miles north of Town B, and Town A is exactly 4 miles south of Town C and 3 miles east of Town B. Which city is the furthest north?

   F. Town A

   G. Town B

   H. Town C

   J. Town D

   K. Town E

37. In a triangle, the interior angle measures are $\angle D$, $\angle E$, and $\angle F$. If $\angle E$ measures at least 50° and the measure of $\angle F$ is greater than 75°, which of the following accurately describes the range of possible angle measures for $\angle D$?

   A. $0° < \angle D < 55°$

   B. $0° < \angle D < 75°$

   C. $-55° < \angle D < 75°$

   D. $45° < \angle D < 55°$

   E. $65° < \angle D < 75°$

38. In the figure below, lines m and n intersect one another to form an angle of 25°, and both lines intersect line s to form two other marked angles. If one of these angles measures 80°, what is the value of z?

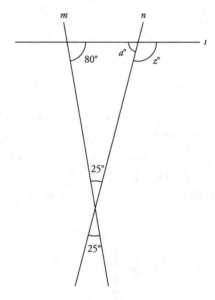

   F. 115°

   G. 105°

   H. 100°

   J. 90°

   K. 80°

39. Four points, W, X, Y, and Z, are located on a horizontal line. W is 4 units to the left of Y. W is 3 units to the right of X. Y is 6 units to the right of Z. Which of the following is the order of points from left to right?

   A. W, X, Y, Z

   B. X, W, Z, Y

   C. X, Z, W, Y

   D. Y, W, Z, X

   E. Z, X, W, Y

40. If a rectangle measures 35 inches by w inches, and the diagonal of the rectangle is 91 inches, then $w = ?$

 F. 56

 G. 84

 H. 97

 J. 126

 K. 182

41. In the diagram below, a wheelchair ramp is positioned to allow entry to a door that is 9 feet above the ground. If the length of the wheelchair ramp is 41 feet, what is the *horizontal* distance covered by the ramp, in feet?

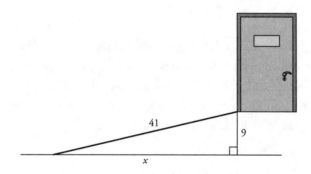

 A. $\dfrac{41}{9}$

 B. 27

 C. 32

 D. 40

 E. 41

42. Assuming that all interior angles of the figure below are either right angles or 270° angles, what is the area of the figure, in square units?

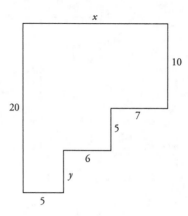

 F. 360

 G. 260

 H. 200

 J. 180

 K. 80

43. A chord is 9 centimeters from the center of a circle of radius 15 centimeters, shown below. What is the length of the chord d, to the nearest tenth of a centimeter?

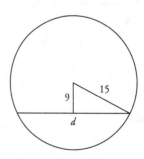

 A. 7.5

 B. 12.0

 C. 18.5

 D. 21.0

 E. 24.0

15

44. If the given dimensions of the trapezoid in the figure below are in meters, what is the area of the trapezoid, in square meters?

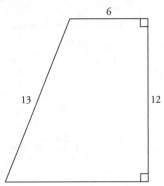

    F. 102

    G. 84

    H. 78

    J. 72

    K. 36

45. 35,000 cubic feet of water flooded an empty rectangular warehouse, with dimensions shown below, creating a pool of water of uniform depth. If no water leaked out, about how many feet deep was the pool of water?

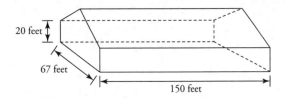

    A. 0.17

    B. 0.35

    C. 2.3

    D. 3.5

    E. 5.2

46. If $\overline{AC}$ is a diameter of the circle, as shown below, passing through center O, then $r = ?$

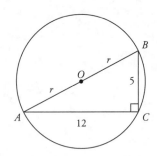

    F. 5.5

    G. 6.0

    H. 6.5

    J. 10.5

    K. 13.0

47. To sterilize an insect-infected building, 2,700 cubic feet of chlorine gas, which is heavier than air, is pumped inside. If the chlorine gas forms a layer along the floor that is uniformly 0.4 feet thick, about how many square feet of floor space are inside the building?

    A. Less than 1,000

    B. Between 1,000 and 2,000

    C. Between 2,000 and 3,000

    D. Between 3,000 and 4,000

    E. More than 4,000

48. Rectangle *ABCD* and rectangle *EFGH* are similar rectangles. *ABCD* has a height of 7 inches and a width of 12 inches. *EFGH* has a perimeter that is 3 times that of *ABCD*. What is the area of the larger rectangle?

    F. 84

    G. 252

    H. 432

    J. 756

    K. 864

49. Points L and M lie on $\overline{KN}$ as shown below. Point L is halfway between points K and M. The length of $\overline{KM}$ is 12 inches, while $\overline{LN}$ is 18 inches long. How many inches long, if it can be determined, is $\overline{KN}$?

A. 21

B. 24

C. 27

D. 30

E. Cannot be determined from the given information.

50. Two similar right triangles have side lengths in the ratio of 7 : 10. The larger right triangle has legs (i.e., not the hypotenuse) of length 5 and 12. What is the perimeter of the smaller triangle?

F. $15\sqrt{2}$

G. $10\sqrt{3}$

H. 21

J. 30

K. $42\dfrac{6}{7}$

51. The lateral surface area of a right circular cylinder with a radius of 9 inches is 180π square inches. What is the volume, in cubic inches, of this cylinder?

(Note: For a right circular cylinder with radius r and height h, the volume is $\pi r^2 h$, and the lateral surface area is $2\pi rh$.)

A. 405π

B. 480π

C. 640π

D. 810π

E. $1,620\pi$

52. A man standing near a streetlight casts a shadow that is 10 feet long. If the streetlight is 35 feet tall and the man is 6 feet tall, which of the following is the closest to the horizontal distance, x feet, between the man and the streetlight?

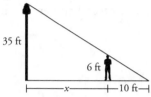

F. 29

G. 39

H. 48

J. 49

K. 58

53. In the diagram below, point A on square $ABCD$ is at the center of the larger square $EFCG$. If $\overline{DG} = 8$ inches, what is the area of the shaded region, in square inches?

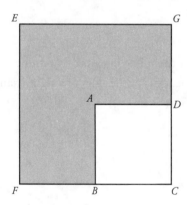

A. 64

B. 128

C. 192

D. 224

E. 256

MANHATTAN

15

54. A fire truck is parked near a 200-foot-tall building, with its ladder extended diagonally to the top. Part of the way up the ladder, a first responder has dropped 60 feet of hose to the ground. If the hose is 70 feet away from the building, which of the following is the horizontal distance, x feet, between the fire truck and the building?

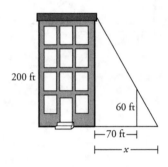

F. 30

G. 60

H. 70

J. 100

K. 140

55. Which of the following sets of 3 numbers could be equal to the lengths of the sides of a right triangle?

A. $1, \sqrt{2}, 3$

B. $2, 3, \sqrt{5}$

C. $3, 5, \sqrt{7}$

D. $4, 5, 6$

E. $5, 6, 8$

56. Two circles have diameters that are in a 2 : 1 ratio. If the area of the smaller circle is equal to 36π, how much *larger* is the area of the larger circle than that of the smaller circle?

F. 144

G. 36

H. 144π

J. 108π

K. 36π

Use the following diagram to answer questions 57–58.

Parallelogram *WXYZ*, with dimensions in feet, is shown in the diagram below.

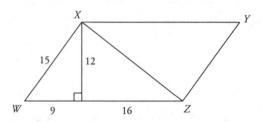

57. What is the length of $\overline{XZ}$, in feet?

A. 20

B. 22

C. 24

D. 25

E. 28

58. What is the area of the parallelogram?

F. 180

G. 192

H. 300

J. 375

K. 450

MANHATTAN
PREP

Use the following information to answer question 59.

A survey at a seminar for people interested in applying for membership at a fitness center asked the 25 respondents how many days in the past week they had exercised. The 25 responses are summarized in the following column chart:

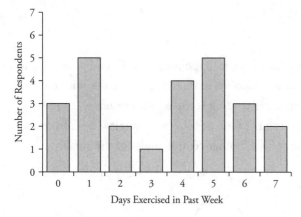

59. Assume that, rather than being presented as a column chart, the data was presented in the form of a circle chart (i.e., a pie chart). What would be the central angle measure for the sector of the chart that represents the people who exercised 5 days in the past week?

A. 5°

B. 14.4°

C. 36°

D. 72°

E. 90°

Use the following information to answer questions 60–62.

A machine assembly consists of a solid metal disc that is 9 inches in diameter and is 4 inches thick. The disc rests upon a square metal sheet, as shown in the diagram below. The disc is designed to rotate on top of the metal sheet; a tracking marker is included on the top and side of the disc. When the machine is off, the tracking marker should line up with the matching marker on the metal sheet, as shown in the diagram.

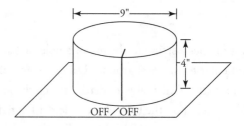

60. If a cubic inch of the metal used to make the solid disc weighs 0.3 pounds, what is the approximate weight of the metal disc, in pounds?

F. 38

G. 45

H. 76

J. 94

K. 124

61. When the machine is operating at full speed, the solid disc on top of the metal sheet rotates once every 2 seconds. How far will a point on the edge of the disc travel in 1 minute when the machine is operating at full speed, in inches?

A. 270π

B. 360π

C. 450π

D. 540π

E. 1,080π

62. If one edge of the metal sheet is 15 inches in length, what is the area of the metal sheet that is exposed (i.e., not covered by the solid disc), in square inches?

F. $225 - \dfrac{9}{2}\pi$

G. $225 - \dfrac{81}{4}\pi$

H. $225 - \dfrac{81}{2}\pi$

J. $225 - 81\pi$

K. $225 - 162\pi$

63. Monroe ties a string to the top of a pole that stands perpendicular to the level ground. Using the end of the 25-foot string, he is able to mark off a circle on the ground, centered on the base of the pole, with a radius of 12 feet. To the nearest foot, how tall is the pole?

A. 13

B. 17

C. 22

D. 27

E. 37

64. Katya is 41 feet above sea level at the top of a straight water slide. She then slides 90 feet down the slide to sea level. To the nearest foot, how far horizontally has Katya traveled?

F. 49

G. 54

H. 64

J. 74

K. 80

65. What is the surface area of a right circular cylinder with radius 4 centimeters and height 10 centimeters, in square centimeters?

A. 16π

B. 32π

C. 40π

D. 80π

E. 112π

66. Points E and B, points F and C, and points A and D are the endpoints of diameters of a circle with center P, respectively. What is the result, in *radians*, from subtracting the measure of central angle $\angle BPC$ from the sum of the 5 other central angles of the circle?

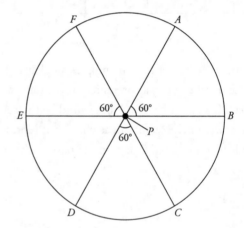

F. $\dfrac{4}{3}\pi$

G. $\dfrac{5}{3}\pi$

H. π

J. 2π

K. 4π

67. A square is circumscribed around a circle, as shown below. If the area of the square is 144 square centimeters, what is the area of the circle, in square centimeters?

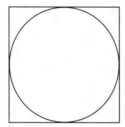

A. 12π

B. 24π

C. 32π

D. 36π

E. 48π

68. The ratio of side lengths for a triangle is 3 : 4 : 6. In a second triangle similar to the first, the median length of a side is 10 centimeters. To the nearest tenth of a centimeter, what is the length of the shortest side of the second triangle?

F.   5.0

G.   7.5

H.   8.0

J.   8.5

K.   9.0

69. Two circles, tangent to each other and with equal radii, are drawn within a rectangle such that the circles each touch the rectangle in exactly three places, as shown below. If the radius of each circle is 5 feet, what is the area of the rectangle, in square feet?

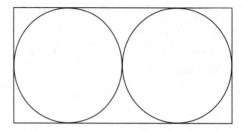

A.   50

B.   100

C.   125

D. 50π

E.   200

70. As shown below with dimensions in inches, $\triangle ABC$ and $\triangle ADE$ are similar to each other. What is the perimeter, in inches, of $\triangle ADE$?

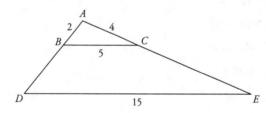

F.   26

G.   32

H.   33

J.   36

K.   Cannot be determined from the given information

> **Use the following information to answer questions 71–72.**

The cross-section of a house is shown in the figure below. From floor to ceiling (which is at the bottom of the triangular roof), the house is 15 feet tall. The distance between the highest point of the triangular roof and the floor is 25 feet. The house is 100 feet deep (into the page), as is the roof, with exactly the same cross-section.

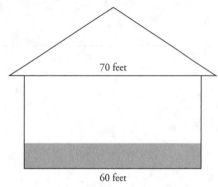

70 feet

60 feet

71. What is the total volume of the structure, in cubic feet?

   A.   90,000

   B. 120,000

   C. 125,000

   D. 160,000

   E. 225,000

72. During a severe wind and rainstorm, the house's roof is blown off the structure. In addition, the house floods with water, as represented by the shaded area in the diagram. The water depth reaches 4 feet. Approximately what percentage of the house's new volume (after the roof structure has been removed) does the volume of the floodwater represent?

   F.   4%

   G.   6%

   H. 16%

   J.   20%

   K. 27%

73. The ratio of side lengths in a triangle is 5 : 6 : 7. The perimeter of the triangle is 108 feet. What is the length of the longest side of the triangle, in feet?

   A. 30

   B. 36

   C. 42

   D. 49

   E. 56

74. In the figure below, all angles between adjoining straight sides are right, and all lengths are in centimeters. What is the average length, in centimeters, of a side of the figure?

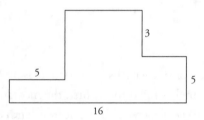

   F.   4

   G.   6

   H.   8

   J. 10

   K. 12

75. In the figure below, $WXYZ$ is a trapezoid, and angle measures are as marked. If V lies on $\overleftrightarrow{WX}$, what is the measure of $\angle VWZ$?

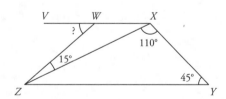

   A. 25°

   B. 30°

   C. 35°

   D. 40°

   E. 45°

MANHATTAN
PREP

15

76. The figure below illustrates a right pyramid with a square base. The length of each side of the square is 6, while the slant height (from the center of a side to the top) is 10. What is the combined surface area of the faces of the right pyramid below, *excluding* the base?

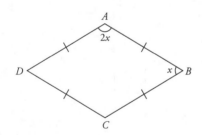

F. 360

G. 240

H. 180

J. 120

K. 108

77. What percent of the sum of the interior angles of quadrilateral *ABCD* does angle $\angle DCB$ constitute?

A. 75%

B. $66\frac{2}{3}$%

C. $33\frac{1}{3}$%

D. 25%

E. $16\frac{2}{3}$%

78. The length and radius of a horizontal right circular cylinder is given in feet in the figure below. What is the volume of the cylinder, in cubic feet?

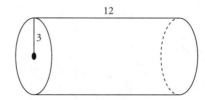

F. 36π

G. 108π

H. 324π

J. 432π

K. $1,296\pi$

Use the following information to answer questions 79–81.

In the figure below, *ABCD* is a parallelogram with sides of length *b* and *c* and height *a*. The triangles $\triangle ABF$, $\triangle BCG$, $\triangle CDH$, and $\triangle ADE$ are all equilateral triangles. The area of an equilateral triangle with sides that are each *x* units long is $\frac{\sqrt{3}}{4}x^2$ square units.

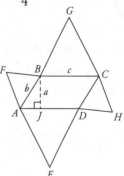

79. Which of the following expressions gives the correct perimeter for the entire figure?

A. $2a + 2b + 2c$

B. $3a + 3b + 3c$

C. $4a + 4b$

D. $4a + 4c$

E. $4b + 4c$

15

80. Which of the following expressions gives the correct length of the line segment $\overline{AJ}$?

   F. $\sqrt{b^2 - a^2}$

   G. $\sqrt{b^2 - c^2}$

   H. $\sqrt{c^2 - a^2}$

   J. $\sqrt{c^2 - b^2}$

   K. $\sqrt{a^2 - b^2}$

81. Which of the following expressions gives the correct area for the entire figure, in square units?

   A. $ac + \dfrac{\sqrt{3}}{2}(b^2 + c^2)$

   B. $ac + \dfrac{\sqrt{3}}{4}(b^2 + c^2)$

   C. $bc + \dfrac{\sqrt{3}}{2}(b^2 + c^2)$

   D. $bc + \dfrac{\sqrt{3}}{4}(b^2 + c^2)$

   E. $bc + \dfrac{\sqrt{3}}{8}(b^2 + c^2)$

82. The trapezoid below can be divided into two right triangles and a rectangle. What is the area of the trapezoid, in square units?

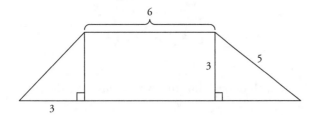

   F.   28.5

   G.   30

   H.   33

   J.   36.5

   K.   39

83. If the statement "If it is raining, then the humidity is above 64%" were true, which of the following statements would also have to be true?

   A.   "If it is not raining, then the humidity is not above 64%."

   B.   "If it is not raining, then the humidity is above 64%."

   C.   "If the humidity is above 64%, then it is raining."

   D.   "If the humidity is above 64%, then it is not raining."

   E.   "If the humidity is not above 64%, then it is not raining."

84. In the following diagram of an object, all adjacent line segments are perpendicular to one another. The dimensions given are in feet. What is the perimeter of the object, in feet?

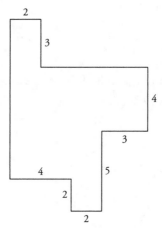

   F.   27

   G.   36

   H.   39

   J.   40

   K.   42

85. If the statement "If today is a vacation day, then I sleep until noon" were true, which of the following statements would also have to be true?

   A. "If I sleep until noon, then today is a vacation day."

   B. "If today is not a vacation day, then I sleep until noon."

   C. "If today is not a vacation day, then I do not sleep until noon."

   D. "If I do not sleep until noon, then today is not a vacation day."

   E. "If I do not sleep until noon, then today is a vacation day."

86. A 12-feet-by-5-feet rectangle is inscribed in a circle as shown below. What is the circumference of the circle, in feet?

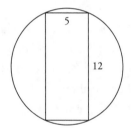

   F. 13π

   G. 17π

   H. 26π

   J. 34π

   K. 48π

87. A large cube has edges that are four times as long as those of a smaller cube. The volume of the larger cube is how many times that of the smaller cube?

   A. 64

   B. 16

   C. 12

   D. 4

   E. 3

88. As shown in the figure below, a circular analog clock advances time from 2:00pm to the current time. If the tip of the minute hand is 8 inches from the center of the clock, and since 2:00pm the tip of the minute hand has moved 52π inches, what is the current time?

   F. 5:15pm

   G. 6:00pm

   H. 6:20pm

   J. 7:40pm

   K. 8:30pm

89. In the diagram below, a sphere with a radius of 4 inches is inscribed inside of a cube, so that the sphere touches all 6 faces of the cube. What is the volume of the cube, in cubic inches?

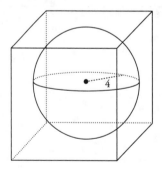

   A. 64

   B. 256

   C. 512

   D. 128π

   E. 256π

90. Consider the following 3 statements to be true:

All animals that eat dog food are dogs.

Animal E is not a dog.

Animal F eats dog food.

Which of the following statements is necessarily true?

   F. Animal E is a dog and does not eat dog food.

   G. Animal E eats dog food.

   H. Animal F eats cat food.

   J. Animal F is not a dog.

   K. Animal E does not eat dog food.

91. In the following diagram, points B, C, D, E, and F all lie along the same line. The same is true of points A, E, and G. Additionally, the length of $\overline{AC}$ is equal to the length of both $\overline{AD}$ and $\overline{DE}$, and $\angle FEG = 35°$. What is the ratio of y to x?

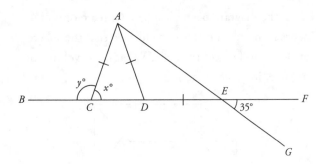

   A. $\dfrac{7}{2}$

   B. $\dfrac{13}{5}$

   C. $\dfrac{11}{7}$

   D. 2

   E. 3

92. In triangle $\triangle ACE$, D, F, and B are points on $\overline{EC}$, $\overline{EA}$, and $\overline{AC}$, respectively. $\overline{FA}$ is equal to $\overline{BA}$. What is the value of $r + s$?

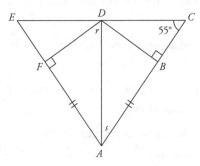

   F. 35°

   G. 50°

   H. 65°

   J. 90°

   K. 110°

93. The points W, X, Y, and Z are located on the number line. Point X is between points W and Y. Point Y is between points X and Z. Which of the following inequalities *must* be true about the lengths of line segments connecting these points?

   A. $\overline{YZ} < \overline{WX}$

   B. $\overline{XY} < \overline{WX}$

   C. $\overline{WY} < \overline{XZ}$

   D. $\overline{WX} < \overline{YZ}$

   E. $\overline{YZ} < \overline{XZ}$

94. In the figure below, points H, D, and G are all located on line $\overleftrightarrow{AB}$; points C, D, and E are collinear; and $\overleftrightarrow{AB}$ bisects $\angle FHC$. Known angle measures are marked. What is the measure of $\angle HCD$?

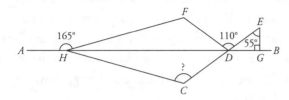

F. 110°

G. 115°

H. 130°

J. 140°

K. 145°

95. A line contains the points E, F, G, and H. Point H is between points E and G. Point F lies to the right of points E and G. Which of the following inequalities *must* be true about the lengths of different segments of this line?

A. $\overline{EH} < \overline{EG}$

B. $\overline{FG} < \overline{FH}$

C. $\overline{EG} < \overline{FH}$

D. $\overline{EG} < \overline{GH}$

E. $\overline{GH} < \overline{FG}$

> Use the following information to answer questions 96–97.

A birds-eye view of a square castle surrounded by a moat is shown in the figure below. The distance from the center of the castle to the near side of the moat is 80 feet. The distance from the center of the castle to the far side of the moat is 100 feet. The shaded area represents the water in the moat, which is 10 feet deep.

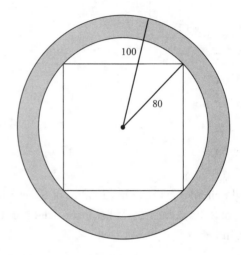

96. Which of the following is closest to the volume of the moat, in cubic feet?

F. 36,000

G. 115,000

H. 220,000

J. 314,000

K. 520,000

97. Each corner of the square castle is tangent to the moat. What is the length, in feet, of one of the castle's walls?

A. $80\sqrt{2}$

B. $100\sqrt{2}$

C. $160\sqrt{2}$

D. 80

E. 360

15

98. Ripley is wrapping a gift in a cylindrical box, shown below. The radius of the top surface is 8 inches. What is the minimum amount of wrapping paper she will need, in square inches, to wrap the entire package?

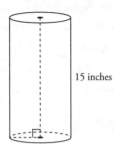

15 inches

   F. 368π

   G. 320π

   H. 304π

   J. 120π

   K. 96π

99. A right circular cylinder has a radius of 6 feet and a volume of 270π cubic feet. What is the height of the cylinder, in feet?

   A.   7.5

   B.   12.5

   C.   16

   D.   22.5

   E.   45

> **Use the following information to answer questions 100-101.**

In the figure below, *ABCD* is a square with a circle centered at *E* inscribed inside of it. A right triangle is inscribed inside of the circle; its hypotenuse forms a diameter of the circle of length $c + d$. The lengths of the legs of the right triangle are *a* and *b*, where $0 < b < a$. The line segment connecting *E* and the right angle of the right triangle is of length *e*.

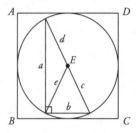

100. Which of the following expressions correctly expresses the ratio of the area of the square to the area of the right triangle?

   F. $\dfrac{4(c+d)^2}{ab}$

   G. $\dfrac{4(a+b)^2}{cd}$

   H. $\dfrac{2(c+d)^2}{ab}$

   J. $\dfrac{2(c+d)^2}{ae}$

   K. $\dfrac{2(a+b)^2}{cd}$

101. Which of the following expressions gives the correct circumference for the circle?

   A. πa^2

   B. πc^2

   C. $2\pi a$

   D. $2\pi b$

   E. $2\pi e$

MANHATTAN
PREP

102. Triangles $\triangle ABC$, $\triangle DEF$, and $\triangle GHJ$ in the diagram below are similar right triangles. The ratio of the perimeter of $\triangle ABC$ to the perimeter of $\triangle GHJ$ is $1:5$. The ratio of the perimeter of $\triangle DEF$ to the perimeter of $\triangle GHJ$ is $2:3$. If $\overline{DF}$ is 4 meters long, what is the length of $\overline{AC}$, in meters?

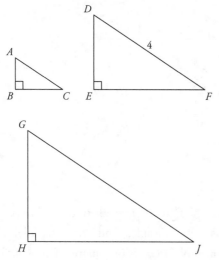

F. $\dfrac{8}{15}$

G. $\dfrac{6}{5}$

H. $\dfrac{12}{5}$

J. $\dfrac{8}{3}$

K. $\dfrac{40}{3}$

103. Rectangles $ABCD$, $AEFG$, and $AHJK$ in the diagram below are similar rectangles. The ratio of the area of $ABCD$ to the area of $AEFG$ is $1:4$. The ratio of the area of $AEFG$ to the area of $AHJK$ is $9:25$. If $\overline{AD}$ is 6 centimeters long, what is the length of $\overline{AK}$, in centimeters?

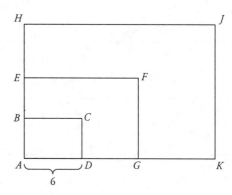

A. $\dfrac{9}{5}$

B. $16\dfrac{2}{3}$

C. 20

D. $66\dfrac{2}{3}$

E. 200

104. Jared is creating a tessellated mosaic, which has an area of 20 inches by 15 inches, by covering it with small right triangular tiles. Each triangular tile's sides are 3 inches, 4 inches, and 5 inches, respectively, and the triangular tiles will be laid in an alternating top-to-bottom fashion to form rectangles. Each tile is half an inch thick, and its top and bottom surfaces are painted. What is the number of tiles he will need to fully cover the mosaic?

F. 5

G. 25

H. 30

J. 50

K. 60

15

105. In the diagram below, lines $\overleftrightarrow{GJ}$, $\overleftrightarrow{DF}$, and $\overleftrightarrow{AC}$ are parallel to each other. Point B lies on $\overleftrightarrow{AC}$, point E lies on $\overleftrightarrow{DF}$, and point H lies on $\overleftrightarrow{GJ}$. Points A, D, and G are collinear. If the length of $\overline{AB}$ is 20 and all other line segments and angle measures are as marked, what is the length of $\overline{GH}$?

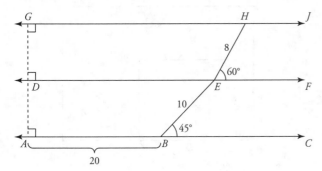

A. $24+5\sqrt{2}$

B. $25+4\sqrt{3}$

C. $20+5\sqrt{2}+4\sqrt{3}$

D. $20+2\sqrt{5}+8\sqrt{2}$

E. 36

106. The ratio of the diagonals of two squares is 3:5. What is the ratio of their perimeters?

F. $\sqrt{3}:\sqrt{5}$

G. $3:5$

H. $3\sqrt{3}:5\sqrt{5}$

J. $9:16$

K. $9:25$

107. The ratio of the area of two circles is 9 : 16. What is the ratio of their diameters?

A. $3:4$

B. $3:5$

C. $9:16$

D. $9:25$

E. Cannot be determined from the given information.

108. Parallelogram $ABCD$ is drawn below. If $\triangle ABE$ is a right triangle, what is the area of the shaded region $AECD$?

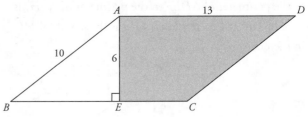

F. 24

G. 48

H. 54

J. 78

K. 130

109. In the figure below, all triangles are equivalent $45°$–$45°$–$90°$ triangles, and $\overline{AB}$ is parallel to $\overline{CD}$. If the area of $EFGH$ is 64 square units, what is the perimeter of $ABCD$?

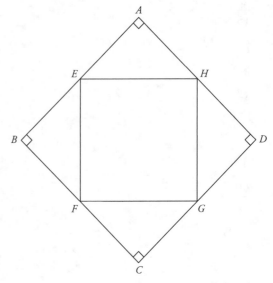

A. $16\sqrt{2}$

B. $16\sqrt{3}$

C. 32

D. $32\sqrt{2}$

E. 64

110. In the following diagram, points *A*, *B*, *C*, and *D* are collinear; points *B* and *F* are collinear; and points *G*, *C*, and *E* are collinear. Additionally, $\overline{BF}$ is parallel to $\overline{GE}$, and angles ∠*BFC*, ∠*BGC*, and ∠*CED* are right angles, as marked. Which of the following statements need NOT necessarily be true based on the information given?

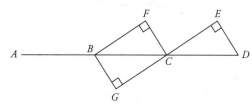

  F. The area of Δ*BCF* is equal to the area of Δ*BCG*.

  G. Δ*CED* is similar to Δ*BCF*.

  H. $\overline{BG}$ is congruent to $\overline{CF}$.

  J. $\overline{CF}$ is perpendicular to $\overline{GE}$.

  K. $\overline{CE}$ is congruent to $\overline{BF}$.

111. In the following diagram of an object, all of the line segments drawn are either vertical or horizontal. What is the ratio of the area of the shaded region to the area of the unshaded region, both in square units?

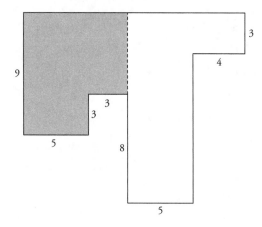

  A. $\dfrac{63}{82}$

  B. $\dfrac{3}{4}$

  C. $\dfrac{31}{41}$

  D. $\dfrac{9}{13}$

  E. $\dfrac{7}{12}$

112. Gus is at a carnival playing a game. Gus will win a prize if the results of three spins on a wheel sum to 80 or more. The result of each spin is random. The central angle for the 5-point sector is 135°. The central angle for each 10-point sector is 45°. The central angle for each 20-point sector is 30°. The central angle for each equivalent 50-point sector is unknown. If Gus's first two spins were 20 and 10, what is the percent chance that Gus will win a prize on his final spin?

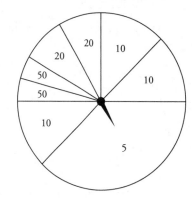

  F. $4\dfrac{1}{6}\%$

  G. $8\dfrac{1}{3}\%$

  H. $12\dfrac{1}{2}\%$

  J. 25%

  K. $33\dfrac{1}{3}\%$

15

113. A hexagon has 9 diagonals that connect corners that are not next to each other on the hexagon, as illustrated below.

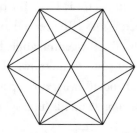

How many diagonals does the decagon (10-sided polygon) below have?

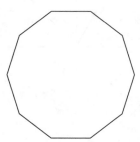

   A. 15

   B. 20

   C. 25

   D. 30

   E. 35

114. A large cube has edges that are three times as long as those of a smaller cube. The surface area of the larger cube is how many times the surface area of the smaller cube?

   F. 27

   G. 9

   H. 6

   J. 3

   K. 2

115. The center of the unit circle shown below is O. $\overline{WZ}$ forms a diameter of circle O. The measure of $\angle b$ is twice the measure of $\angle a$. The measure of $\angle c$ is three times the measure of $\angle a$. The measure of $\angle d$ is twice the measure of $\angle b$. What is the measure of $\angle b + \angle d - \angle a$, in radians?

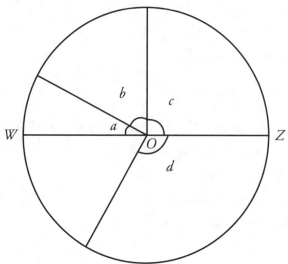

   A. $\dfrac{5\pi}{6}$

   B. $\dfrac{\pi}{6}$

   C. $\dfrac{4\pi}{3}$

   D. $\dfrac{\pi}{3}$

   E. π

MANHATTAN
PREP

Answer Key

Write in whether you got each problem right or wrong (or left it blank). If your answer was correct, put a 1 in every blank to the right of that problem. Sum up each column and compare your total to the total possible "Out Of" points.

Problem	Correct Answer	Right/Wrong/Blank
1	B	
2	K	
3	B	
4	F	
5	A	
6	H	
7	D	
8	F	
9	B	
10	H	
11	E	
12	K	
13	E	
14	G	
15	D	
16	G	
17	A	
18	G	
19	B	
20	G	
21	B	
22	H	
23	D	
24	H	
25	B	
26	F	
27	B	
28	J	

Problem	Correct Answer	Right/Wrong/Blank
29	B	
30	K	
31	D	
32	K	
33	C	
34	K	
35	B	
36	H	
37	A	
38	G	
39	C	
40	G	
41	D	
42	G	
43	E	
44	F	
45	D	
46	H	
47	E	
48	J	
49	B	
50	H	
51	D	
52	H	
53	C	
54	J	
55	B	
56	J	

MANHATTAN
PREP

Problem	Correct Answer	Right/Wrong/Blank
57	A	
58	H	
59	D	
60	H	
61	A	
62	G	
63	C	
64	K	
65	E	
66	F	
67	D	
68	G	
69	E	
70	H	
71	C	
72	K	
73	C	
74	G	
75	D	
76	J	
77	C	
78	G	
79	E	
80	F	
81	A	
82	F	
83	E	
84	K	
85	D	
86	F	
87	A	
88	F	

Problem	Correct Answer	Right/Wrong/Blank
89	C	
90	K	
91	C	
92	J	
93	E	
94	H	
95	A	
96	G	
97	A	
98	F	
99	A	
100	H	
101	E	
102	G	
103	C	
104	J	
105	A	
106	G	
107	A	
108	H	
109	D	
110	K	
111	A	
112	G	
113	E	
114	G	
115	A	
Total		
Out Of		115

MANHATTAN
PREP

Plane Geometry Solutions

1. **(B)** 36   Plane Geometry   Polygons (Rectangles)

Because *ABCD* and *EFGH* are similar rectangles, the ratio of corresponding sides between the two rectangles will always be the same (i.e., the sides will always be in the same proportion). Therefore:

$$\boxed{\frac{\overline{AB}}{\overline{EF}} = \frac{\overline{BC}}{\overline{FG}} = \frac{\overline{CD}}{\overline{GH}} = \frac{\overline{AD}}{\overline{EH}}}$$

In this problem, you are given the values of $\overline{BC}, \overline{CD}$, and $\overline{FG}$ and must solve for the value of $\overline{GH}$:

$$\frac{\overline{BC}}{\overline{FG}} = \frac{\overline{CD}}{\overline{GH}}$$

$$\frac{12}{48} = \frac{9}{x}$$

$$12x = 48 \times 9$$

$$x = \frac{48 \times 9}{12} = 4 \times 9 = 36$$

The correct answer is (B).

2. **(K)** 11.0   Plane Geometry   Polygons

The perimeter of a rectangle is the distance around the entire rectangle, which is the same as twice the width plus twice the height. In this case, then, the perimeter is $2 \times 2.5 + 2 \times 3.0 = 5.0 + 6.0 = 11.0$ meters. The correct answer is (K).

3. **(B)** 72 feet   Plane Geometry   Polygons (Rectangles)

Brett plans to build a rectangular swimming pool that is similar to the swimming pool that is 12 feet in width by 20 feet in length. Because these rectangles are similar, the ratio of corresponding sides between the two rectangles will always have the same ratio (i.e., they will always be in the same proportion). You can draw this as follows:

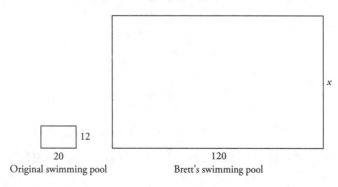

Original swimming pool   Brett's swimming pool

Note that *x* represents the width of Brett's swimming pool. Corresponding sides of the swimming pools must be in the same ratio. Therefore:

$$\frac{12}{20} = \frac{x}{120}$$

$$12 \times 120 = 20x$$

$$x = \frac{12 \times 120}{20} = 12 \times 6 = 72$$

The correct answer is (B).

4.   **(F)** 50°   Plane Geometry   Polygons (Lines and Angles)

The sum of the interior angles of any quadrilateral (any 4-sided shape) must equal 360°. Therefore, $\angle A + \angle B + \angle C + \angle D = 360°$. Additionally angle B equals 90°, as determined by the right-angle box drawn into it. Because you are given the values of angles C and D, you can substitute these values into the equation and solve for angle A:

$$\angle A + \angle B + \angle C + \angle D = 360°$$

$$\angle A + 90° + 100° + 120° = 360°$$

$$\angle A = 360° - 90° - 100° - 120° = 50°$$

The correct answer is (F).

5.   **(A)** 90   Plane Geometry   Polygons

The perimeter of a rectangular plot of land is the distance around the plot (counting all four sides). If one side of the plot is 50 feet, then the side opposite is also 50 feet. Together, these sides account for $50 + 50 = 100$ feet of the perimeter, leaving $280 - 100 = 180$ feet for the other two sides. Since those sides are equal in length, they are each $180 \div 2 = 90$ feet long. Because 90 is greater than 50, these two sides are the longer sides of the rectangle. The correct answer is (A).

6.   **(H)** 48   Plane Geometry   Polygons (Perimeter)

The formula for the perimeter of a rectangle is $2L + 2W$, where L is the length of the rectangle and W is the width of the rectangle:

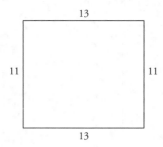

The perimeter of the rectangle is $2(13) + 2(11) = 26 + 22 = 48$. The correct answer is (H).

7.   **(D)** 140°   Plane Geometry   Triangles (Lines and Angles)

The sum of the interior angles of any triangle must equal 180°. Therefore, $\angle A + \angle B + \angle C = 180°$. Additionally it is given that angle C equals 20°, and that $\overline{AB} = \overline{BC}$. Whenever 2 of the 3 sides of a triangle are equal, the triangle is an

MANHATTAN
PREP

isosceles triangle. Angles opposite sides of equal length in an isosceles triangle are equal to each other. Therefore, you can solve for y:

$$\angle A + \angle B + \angle C = 180°$$
$$20° + y° + 20° = 180°$$
$$y° = 180° - 20° - 20° = 140°$$

The correct answer is (D).

8.   **(F)** 16   Plane Geometry   Polygons (Perimeter)

You are told in the problem that the area of *ABCD* is 60 square inches. Area = length × width, so the width of *ABCD* (denoted by $\overline{CD}$) must equal 60 ÷ 10 = 6 inches.

Because *ABCD* and *EFGH* are similar rectangles, the ratio of corresponding sides between the two rectangles will always have the same ratio (i.e., they will always be in the same proportion). Therefore:

$$\frac{\overline{BC}}{\overline{FG}} = \frac{\overline{CD}}{\overline{GH}}$$
$$\frac{10}{\overline{FG}} = \frac{6}{3}$$
$$6\overline{FG} = 3 \times 10$$
$$\overline{FG} = \frac{3 \times 10}{6} = 5$$

The perimeter of *EFGH* is given by the sum of all sides of the rectangle. Because it is a rectangle, opposite sides of the rectangle are equal. Therefore, $\overline{EF} = \overline{GH} = 3$ and $\overline{EH} = \overline{FG} = 5$. The sum of all sides is therefore 3 + 3 + 5 + 5 = 16. The correct answer is (F).

9.   **(B)** $\overrightarrow{DB}$ Plane Geometry   Lines and Angles

In ray notation, the first letter represents the endpoint of the ray, and the second letter represents a second point through which the ray extends. For example, ray $\overrightarrow{EF}$ is a ray that starts at point *A*, continues through point *F*, and extends infinitely to the right.

To find the ray that contains point *C* but does **not** contain point *E*, sketch out each of the rays given.

A. $\overrightarrow{DF}$ does not include point *C*.

B. Correct. $\overrightarrow{DB}$ contains point *C* but does **not** contain point *E*.

C. $\overrightarrow{BD}$ contains point C; however, it also contains point E.

D. $\overrightarrow{BA}$ does not contain point C.

E. $\overrightarrow{AF}$ contains point C; however, it also contains point E.

The correct answer is (B).

10. **(H)** 12   Plane Geometry   Triangles (Perimeter)

Because $\triangle ABC$ and $\triangle DEF$ are similar triangles, the ratio of corresponding sides between the two triangles will always have the same ratio (i.e., they will always be in the same proportion). Therefore:

$$\frac{\overline{BC}}{\overline{EF}} = \frac{\overline{AC}}{\overline{DF}}$$

$$\frac{6}{3} = \frac{10}{\overline{DF}}$$

$$6\overline{DF} = 3 \times 10$$

$$\overline{DF} = \frac{3 \times 10}{6} = 5$$

Now you know the length of two sides of $\triangle DEF$:

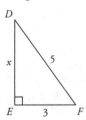

What about the third side? Because $\triangle DEF$ is a right triangle, you can use the Pythagorean theorem, $a^2 + b^2 = c^2$, to get $3^2 + x^2 = 5^2$. Simplify the equation to get $9 + x^2 = 25$. Isolate x by subtracting 9 from both sides: $x^2 = 25 - 9 = 16$. Take the square root of both sides to solve for x:

$$\sqrt{x^2} = \sqrt{16}$$

$$x = 4$$

The perimeter of $\triangle DEF$ is therefore $3 + 4 + 5 = 12$ meters.

Alternatively, for this final step you could recognize that the lengths 3 and 5 are two parts of a $3:4:5$ right triangle. Therefore, the perimeter of the triangle must be $3 + 4 + 5 = 12$. The correct answer is (H).

11. **(E)** 135°   Plane Geometry   Lines & Angles (Triangles)

To determine the angle measure of ∠ABF , first find the interior angles of △BCF . ∠BCF is 90°. Because two sides of △BCF are congruent, you can prove that this triangle is an isosceles triangle.

Because one angle of the isosceles triangle is 90°, the other two angle measures must be 45° (because 180° = 90° + 2x). If ∠CBF is 45°, its supplement (to make a straight line) is 180° − 45° = 135°. The supplement of ∠CBF is ∠ABF , so ∠ABF = 135°. The correct answer is (E).

12. **(K)** $\overrightarrow{XV}$ Plane Geometry   Lines & Angles

In ray notation, the first letter represents the endpoint of the ray, and the second letter represents a second point through which the ray extends. For example, ray $\overrightarrow{UV}$ is a ray that starts at point U, continues through point V, and extends infinitely to the right. Notice that the ray does not stop at point V.

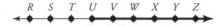

To find the ray that contains point U, sketch out each of the rays given.

  F. $\overrightarrow{SR}$ does not contain point U.

  G. $\overrightarrow{TR}$ does not contain point U.

  H. $\overrightarrow{VZ}$ does not contain point U.

  J. $\overrightarrow{WY}$ does not contain point U.

  K. **Correct.** $\overrightarrow{XV}$ contains point U.

Remember, the ray does not stop at point V, but continues to the left from point X infinitely far, so the ray will pass through point U (as well as through points T, S, and R). The correct answer is (K).

13. **(E)** 80   Plane Geometry   Polygons (Rectangles)

In order to lay the minimum number of tiles in the ballroom, Nick should lay the tiles such that the number of feet in each dimension of the ballroom is divisible by the number of feet in each dimension of the tile. In this case, 40' is divisible by 2' and 12' is divisible by 3', so the tile should be laid sideways as follows:

Each tile will fit 12' ÷ 3' = 4 times widthwise, and 40' ÷ 2' = 20 times lengthwise. Therefore, the minimum number of tiles to lay is 4 × 20 = 80.

Alternatively, you could calculate that the ballroom is 40' × 12' = 480 square feet, and that each tile is 2' × 3' = 6 square feet. Therefore, the floor should require 480 ÷ 6 = 80 tiles to be covered fully. This assumes, of course, that the dimensions of the floor are perfectly divisible by the dimensions of the tile. In this case, this assumption holds. The correct answer is (E).

14. **(G)** 36 Plane Geometry Polygons (Perimeter)

For a rectangle, area = length × width. In the problem it is stated that both length and width are prime numbers. Since the prime factorization of 77 is 7 × 11, either the length equals 7 and the width equals 11, or vice versa.

Either way, the perimeter of a rectangle is equal to the sum of all of the sides of the rectangle. Since the two width line segments of the rectangle are equal to each other, and the two length line segments are equal to each other, you can calculate the perimeter as $2(W + L) = 2(7 + 11) = 36$. The correct answer is (G).

15. **(D)** 50° and 80° Plane Geometry Triangles (Isosceles Triangles)

For a triangle to be an isosceles triangle, 2 out of the 3 interior angles (and sides) of the triangle must equal each other. In order to determine which list is the correct answer, calculate the implied third angle measurement based on the values of the 2 angles given. Since $\angle A + \angle B + \angle C = 180°$ for any triangle $\triangle ABC$, you can assume the given angles are $\angle A$ and $\angle B$ and subtract the two angles given in each list from 180° to derive $\angle C$. You can then determine whether the triangle is isosceles if $\angle C$ matches either $\angle A$ or $\angle B$:

180° – 30° – 90° = 60° Does not match either angle.

180° – 40° – 80° = 60° Does not match either angle.

180° – 50° – 70° = 60° Does not match either angle.

180° – 50° – 80° = 50° Matches 50°.

180° – 60° – 70° = 50° Does not match either angle.

Therefore, the correct answer is 50° and 80°. The correct answer is (D).

16. **(G)** 5-by-24 inches Plane Geometry Polygons (Rectangles)

The "dimensions" of the rectangular painting ("something-by-something") are the length and width of the rectangle. You can solve this problem by setting up the algebraic equations for the area and perimeter of a rectangle: $wl = 120$ and $2w + 2l = 58$. However, the quadratic involved might be tricky to solve. In fact, if you try to factor the quadratic, you will need to find two numbers that multiply to 120 and add to 29 (half of 58). That is essentially the task you are already faced with!

An easier method is to work backwards from the answer choices. It does not matter which dimension is the length and which is the width of the rectangle:

   F. The area $(4 \times 30) = 120$, but the perimeter $= 2(4) + 2(30) = 78$

   G. **CORRECT.** The area $(5 \times 24) = 120$, and the perimeter $= 2(5) + 2(24) = 58$

   H. The area $(8 \times 21) = 168$

   J. The area $(11 \times 18) = 198$

   K. The area $(12 \times 10) = 120$, but the perimeter $= 2(12) + 2(10) = 44$

The correct answer is (G).

17. **(A)** 18   Plane Geometry   Triangles (Perimeter)

For a triangle, the perimeter is equal to the sum of all sides of the triangle. In the problem, it is stated that the perimeter of the triangle in question is 70 and its longest side is 28. Therefore, the combined length of the two other sides is $70 - 28 = 42$.

Additionally, the problem states that the ratio of the lengths of the two unknown sides is $3:4$. You can solve for the other sides algebraically. Assign x and y to the lengths of the two other sides. Using the two pieces of information given in the problem, you get the following:

$$x + y = 42$$
$$\frac{x}{y} = \frac{3}{4}$$
$$4x = 3y$$
$$x = \frac{3}{4}y$$

Substitute this expression for x into the first equation to solve for the value of y:

$$\left(\frac{3}{4}y\right) + y = 42$$
$$\frac{7}{4}y = 42$$
$$y = \frac{42 \times 4}{7} = 6 \times 4 = 24$$

Plugging back into the first equation, you get $x + 24 = 42$, so $x = 42 - 24 = 18$. The lengths of the three sides of the triangle are 18, 24, and 28, so the correct answer is 18. The correct answer is (A).

18. **(G)** 118°   Plane Geometry   Lines & Angles

As shown in the figure below, $\angle YZW$ and $\angle XZW$ form a line and are therefore supplementary angles. The sum of $a°$ and $62°$ must equal $180°$:

$a° + 62° = 180°$

$a° = 118°$

The correct answer is (G).

19. **(B)** 6×25 Plane Geometry   Polygons (Rectangles)

You are asked for the dimensions (length and width) of a rectangle, given its area and perimeter. You can solve this problem by setting up the algebraic equations for the area and perimeter of a rectangle: $wl = 150$ and $2w + 2l = 62$. However, the quadratic involved might be tricky to solve. In fact, if you try to factor the quadratic, you will need to find two numbers that multiply to 150 and add to 31 (half of 62). That is essentially the task you are already faced with!

An easier method is to work backwards from the answer choices, trying to match the given area and perimeter.

    A.   The area $(5 \times 30) = 150$, but the perimeter $= 2(5) + 2(30) = 70$

    B.   **CORRECT.** The area $(6 \times 25) = 150$, and the perimeter $= 2(6) + 2(25) = 62$

    C.   The area $(10 \times 15) = 150$, but the perimeter $= 2(10) + 2(15) = 50$

    D.   The area $(12 \times 19) = 228$

    E.   The area $(15 \times 16) = 240$

The correct answer is (B).

20. **(G)** 23   Plane Geometry   Triangles

Because the shortest distance between two points is a line, any side of a triangle must be shorter than the sum of the remaining two sides. For example, if the third side of the given triangle were 7 millimeters, the sum of the sides (7 mm + 12 mm) would be exactly equal to the third side, 19 millimeters, and the triangle would collapse to a line.

Rather than test every answer choice, the shortcut is to recognize that the missing size must be longer than the difference of the two given sides (19 mm − 12 mm = 7 mm) and must also be shorter than the sum of the two given sides (19 mm + 12 mm = 31 mm). The only answer that fits in that range is 23. The correct answer is (G).

21. **(B)** $62°$ Plane Geometry   Lines & Angles

As shown in the figure below, $\angle CXZ$ and $\angle ZXB$ form a right angle and are therefore complementary angles. The sum of 28° and P° must equal 90°:

$28° + P° = 90°$

$P° = 62°$

MANHATTAN
PREP

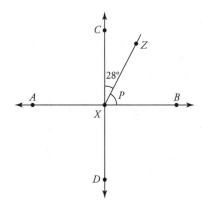

The correct answer is (B).

22. **(H)** 42.5°   Plane Geometry   Circles (Lines & Angles)

Notice that two sides, *XZ* and *XY*, of the given triangle are radii of the circle. So they must have the same length, and triangle *XYZ* is isosceles. The angles across from congruent sides must also be congruent, so angles *Z* and *Y* are equal. Letting *a* equal the measure of either of those angles, the sum of all three angles in the triangle must be 180°. Solve for *a*:

$a + a + 95° = 180°$

$2a = 85°$
$a = 42.5°$

The correct answer is (H).

23. **(D)** 30   Plane Geometry   Triangles

Because the shortest distance between two points is a line, any side of a triangle must be shorter than the sum of the remaining two sides. For example, if the third side of the given triangle were 4 inches, the sum of the sides (4 in + 10 in) would be shorter than the third side, 34 inches, an impossible situation.

Rather than test every answer choice, the shortcut is to recognize that the missing size must be longer than the positive difference of the two given sides (34 in − 10 in = 24 in) and must also be shorter than the sum of the two given sides (34 in + 10 in = 44 in). The only answer that fits in that range is 30. The correct answer is (D).

24. **(H)** 94°   Plane Geometry   Lines & Angles

Point *B* lies on $\overline{AC}$, which is a straight line. Therefore, $\angle ABD$ and $\angle CBD$ are supplementary angles, and must sum to 180°. Set up an equation to solve for *z*:

$\angle ABD + \angle CBD = 180°$
$(z - 3)° + (3z - 1)° = 180°$
$z - 3 + 3z - 1 = 180$
$4z = 184$
$z = 46$

Now that you have solved for z, you can determine that $\angle ABD = (46 - 3)° = 43°$ and $\angle CBD = (3 \cdot 46 - 1)° = 137°$. The positive difference between the larger and smaller angles is therefore $|137° - 43°| = 94°$. The correct answer is (H).

25. **(B)** 40°   Plane Geometry   Circles (Lines & Angles)

Notice that two sides, *NO* and *MO,* of the given triangle are radii of the circle, so they must have the same length, and triangle *NOM* is isosceles. The angles across from congruent sides must also be congruent, so angles *M* and *N* are equal. If you let *a* equal the measure of the missing angle, the sum of all three angles in the triangle must be 180°. Solve for *a*:

$a + 70° + 70° = 180°$
$a + 140° = 180°$
$a = 40°$

The correct answer is (B).

26. **(F)** $66\frac{2}{3}$%   Plane Geometry   Triangles (Lines and Angles)

Because $\overline{AB} \cong \overline{BC}$, you know that $\triangle ABC$ is isosceles. The two base angles each measure 30°, so the vertex $\angle ABC = 180° - 30° - 30° = 120°$. The problem then asks for the percent 120° is of 180°. $\frac{120°}{180°}(100\%) = \frac{2}{3}(100\%) = 66\frac{2}{3}\%$. The correct answer is (F).

27. **(B)** 23°   Plane Geometry   Triangles (Lines and Angles)

The 3 interior angles of a triangle must sum to 180°. Set up an equation to solve for x:

$(x + 2)° + (2x + 15)° + (4x + 16)° = 180°$
$x + 2 + 2x + 15 + 4x + 16 = 180$
$7x = 147$
$x = 21$

Now that you have solved for x, you can determine that the interior angles of $\triangle DEF$ measure $(21 + 2)° = 23°$, $(2 \times 21 + 15)° = 57°$, and $(4 \times 21 + 16)° = 100°$. The smallest interior angle is therefore 23°. The correct answer is (B).

28. **(J)** 12.5   Plane Geometry   Triangles (Right Triangles)

By definition, the scale model should replicate the dimensions of the park. In other words, the scale model and the park itself should be similar triangles. In this case, the ratio of corresponding sides between the two sides will always have the same ratio (i.e., they will always be in the same proportion). Therefore, assign *x* to the value of the eastern border of the scale model and set up an equation:

$$\frac{5 \text{ feet}}{x \text{ feet}} = \frac{200 \text{ meters}}{500 \text{ meters}}$$

$$5 \cdot 500 = 200x$$

$$x = \frac{2,500}{200} = \frac{25}{2} = 12.5$$

The correct answer is (J).

29. **(B)** 15   Plane Geometry   Triangles (Right Triangles)

Redraw the triangle and label the unknown side.

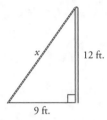

Substitute the triangle's sides into the Pythagorean theorem, $a^2 + b^2 = c^2$, to get $12^2 + 9^2 = x^2$. Simplify the equation to get $225 = x^2$. Take the square root of both sides to solve for x:

$$\sqrt{225} = \sqrt{x^2}$$

$$15 = x$$

Alternatively, recognize the lengths 9 and 12 as being two parts of a $3:4:5$ right triangle. The multiplier to use is 3, since $\frac{9}{3} = 3$ and $\frac{12}{4} = 3$. Thus, the third side must equal $3 \times 5 = 15$. The correct answer is (B).

30. **(K)** $8 + 8\sqrt{2}$ Plane Geometry   Triangles (Perimeter)

The formula for the perimeter of a triangle is the sum of all of its sides. The formula for the area of a triangle is $\frac{1}{2}bh$, where b is the base of the triangle and h is the height of the triangle. Because the triangle is a 45°–45°–90° triangle, the base and height will be equal, and the 90° angle will be opposite the hypotenuse:

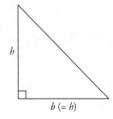

The area of the triangle is 16, so $\frac{1}{2}bh = 16$, and you can substitute b for h (or vice versa):

$$\frac{1}{2}bh = 16$$

$$\frac{1}{2}(b)^2 = 16$$

$$b^2 = 32$$

$$b = \sqrt{32} = \sqrt{2 \cdot 2 \cdot 2 \cdot 2 \cdot 2} = 4\sqrt{2}$$

b and h are equal, so b also equals $4\sqrt{2}$. The length of the hypotenuse can be found using the Pythagorean theorem, which states that $a^2 + b^2 = c^2$ for any right triangle:

$$a^2 + b^2 = c^2$$

$$c^2 = 2\left(4\sqrt{2}\right)^2 = 2(32) = 64$$

$$c = 8$$

The perimeter of the triangle is therefore $8 + 2\left(4\sqrt{2}\right) = 8 + 8\sqrt{2}$. The correct answer is (K).

31. **(D)** 30   Plane Geometry   Triangles (Right Triangles)

Redraw the triangle and label the unknown side.

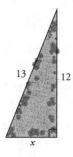

Substitute the triangle's sides into the Pythagorean theorem, $a^2 + b^2 = c^2$, to get $12^2 + x^2 = 13^2$. Simplify the equation to get $144 + x^2 = 169$. Isolate x by subtracting 144 from both sides: $x^2 = 169 - 144 = 25$. Take the square root of both sides to solve for x:

$$\sqrt{x^2} = \sqrt{25}$$

$$x = 5$$

The perimeter of the garden is therefore $5 + 12 + 13 = 30$ feet in length.

Alternatively, recognize that the lengths 12 and 13 are two parts of a $5 : 12 : 13$ right triangle. Therefore, the perimeter of the garden must be $5 + 12 + 13$. The correct answer is (D).

32. **(K)** 140   Plane Geometry   Triangles (Lines and Angles)

To find z, use the properties of plane geometry to solve for the values of other pieces of information in the diagram:

MANHATTAN
PREP

The marked angle is part of an isosceles triangle (the leftmost triangle), and because the side opposite it is equal in length to the line segment at the top left, the angle opposite that line segment also measures 10° (the angle in the lower right of the leftmost triangle). All interior angles of a triangle must sum to 180°, so the angle in the top-middle of the leftmost triangle must equal 180° − 10° − 10° = 160°. The updated diagram appears as follows:

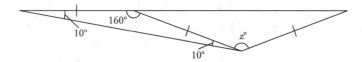

Next, focus on components of the rightmost triangle. The angle opposite the one measuring 160° must measure 180° − 160° = 20°, because supplementary angles must sum to 180°. Additionally, the side opposite that angle is equal in length to the left side of the rightmost triangle (i.e., the side of the rightmost triangle that is shared with a side of the leftmost triangle). Therefore, the rightmost triangle is also isosceles, which means that the rightmost angle in that triangle also measures 20°:

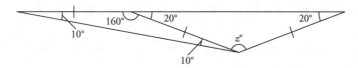

Because $z°$ is the third angle in a triangle that contains angle measures of 20° and 20°, $z° = 180° − 20° − 20° = 140°$. The correct answer is (K).

33. **(C)** 60   Plane Geometry   Polygons (Perimeter)

Each of the small squares that subdivide the non-overlapping space between the two squares is 9 square feet in area. Therefore, each side of these squares is $\sqrt{9} = 3$ feet in length. Because there are 5 such squares along each dimension of the larger (outside) square, that square has sides that are $3 \times 5 = 15$ feet in length. The formula for the perimeter of a square is $P = 4s$, where s is the length of one of the sides. Therefore, the perimeter of the square is $4 \times 15 = 60$ feet. The correct answer is (C).

34. **(K)** 80   Plane Geometry   Triangles (Lines and Angles)

It is given in the problem that $x \geq 2y$. It is also given in the diagram that x and y constitute the degree measures of 2 angles in a triangle, and the third angle has a measure of 60°. Therefore, $x° + y° + 60° = 180°$, so $x + y = 120$. Solve this equation for y and substitute it into the inequality given in the problem:

$$x + y = 120$$
$$y = 120 − x$$
$$x \geq 2(120 − x)$$
$$x \geq 240 − 2x$$
$$3x \geq 240$$
$$x \geq 80$$

Therefore, x must be at least 80. The correct answer is (K).

35. **(B)** 30   Plane Geometry   Polygons (Perimeter)

Each of the small triangles that subdivide the hexagon has a perimeter of 15 centimeters (cm). Because all 3 sides of an equilateral triangle are of equal length, each side of the small triangles is $15 \div 3 = 5$ cm in length. There are 6 such sides that comprise the perimeter of the hexagon, so the hexagon's perimeter is $5 \times 6 = 30$ cm. The correct answer is (B).

36. **(H)** Town C Plane Geometry   Other Plane Geometry (Visualization)

You can approach this problem by drawing a series of sketches that represent the locations of the 5 cities relative to one another.

Since "Town D is 1 mile directly east of Town E", draw E 1 unit space to the left of D. (See Figure 1 below.)

Since "Town D is exactly 2 miles north of Town B", draw a new point, B, 2 units below D. (See Figure 2 below.)

Since "Town A is exactly 4 miles south of Town C and 3 miles east of Town B", draw a new point A that is 3 units to the right of B, and then draw a new point C that is 4 units above A. (See Figure 3 below).

Figure 3 shows the final arrangement of towns, and Town C is the furthest north:

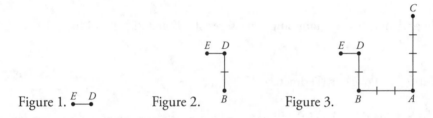

Figure 1.   Figure 2.   Figure 3.

The correct answer is (H).

37. **(A)** $0° < \angle D < 55°$ Plane Geometry   Triangles (Lines and Angles)

It is given in the problem that $\angle D$, $\angle E$, and $\angle F$ are three interior angle measurements in a triangle, and that $\angle E \geq 50°$ and $\angle F > 75°$. Combining these two inequalities, you have:

$$\angle E + \angle F > 50° + 75° = 125°$$

Because the 3 angles are the interior angles of a triangle, they must sum to 180°. Hence, $\angle D + \angle E + \angle F = 180°$. Subtract this equation from the inequality to solve for $\angle D$:

$$\angle E + \angle F > 125°$$
$$-(\angle D + \angle E + \angle F) = -180°$$
$$-\angle D > -55°$$
$$\angle D < 55°$$

(Don't forget that when you multiply or divide both sides of an inequality by a negative number, you must reverse the inequality sign.)

Therefore, the upper bound on $\angle D$ is 55°. The only other requirement of an angle in a triangle is that is have a positive value, so $0° < \angle D < 55°$. The correct answer is (A).

MANHATTAN
PREP

15

38. **(G)** 105°   Plane Geometry   Lines & Angles

In order to help solve this problem, it is helpful to mark the angle adjacent to $z°$, as well as the angle opposite 25°, as follows:

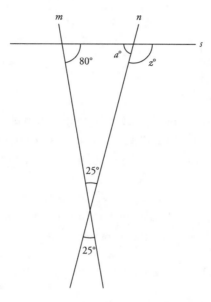

In the figure above, the vertical angles at the bottom are equal (25°) and the angles 80°, 25°, and $a°$ form the interior angles of a triangle. Therefore, $80° + 25° + a° = 180°$, so $a = 75°$.

Since a and z form a straight line, $a° + z° = 180°$. Substituting and solving, $75° + z° = 180°$, so $z = 105°$. The correct answer is (G).

39. **(C)** X, Z, W, Y Plane Geometry   Other Plane Geometry (Visualization)

You can approach this problem by drawing a series of sketches that represent the locations of the 4 points relative to one another.

Since "W is 4 units to the left of Y," draw a line with W on the left and Y on the right with 4 spaces between them:

Since "W is 3 units to the right of X," draw a new point X that is 3 units to the left of W:

Since, "Y is 6 units to the right of Z," draw a new point Z that is 6 units left of Y:

This figure shows the final arrangement of points, and the correct order from left to right is X, Z, W, Y. The correct answer is (C).

40. (G) 84　　　Plane Geometry　　　Triangles

It's worth drawing a picture, to ensure that you are processing the given information correctly.

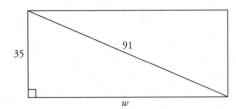

At this point, you might notice that since the diagonal has to be longer than either side of the rectangle, w must be less than 91. This eliminates all but answer choices (F) and (G). Moreover, since the two sides together must be longer than the diagonal, the missing side must be longer than $91 - 35 = 56$. It cannot actually equal 56, so (F) is impossible, leaving only (G) as the right answer.

Here's how to calculate the number exactly. The Pythagorean theorem relates the two legs of the right triangle (the sides of the rectangle) and the hypotenuse (the diagonal of the rectangle). Use your calculator to perform the calculations.

$$35^2 + w^2 = 91^2 \quad \rightarrow \quad 1{,}225 + w^2 = 8{,}281 \quad \rightarrow \quad w^2 = 7{,}056 \quad \rightarrow \quad w = 84$$

The correct answer is (G).

41. (D) 40　　　Plane Geometry　　　Triangles (Right Triangles)

Because the wheelchair ramp forms a right triangle, you can use the Pythagorean theorem, $a^2 + b^2 = c^2$, to determine the horizontal distance covered by the ramp. Call that distance x:

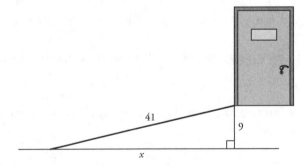

$$9^2 + x^2 = 41^2$$
$$x^2 = 41^2 - 9^2$$
$$x^2 = 1{,}600$$
$$x = 40$$

The horizontal distance covered by the ramp is therefore 40 feet. The correct answer is (D).

42. (G) 260　　　Plane Geometry　　　Polygons (Area)

The question asks you to determine the area of this 8-sided object based on an incomplete listing of the lengths of all of the sides of the object. However, it is given in the problem that all of the interior angles are either right angles (90°)

MANHATTAN
PREP

or 270° angles. Therefore, all of the line segments are perpendicular to one another, and the sum of the lengths of the horizontal line segments at the top must equal the sum of the horizontal line segments at the bottom. Similarly, the sum of the lengths of the vertical line segments at the left must equal the sum of the vertical line segments at the right. Assign x and y to the lengths of the unknown sides:

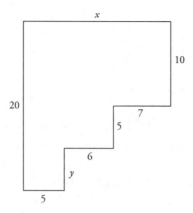

It must be the case that $x = 5 + 6 + 7 = 18$. Furthermore, $y + 10 + 5 = 20$, so $y = 5$. Now calculate the area of each component of the diagram. Separate the figure into three rectangles:

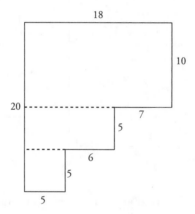

The top rectangle has a width of 18 and a height of 10. Therefore, its area is $18 \times 10 = 180$. The middle rectangle has a width of $(6 + 5) = 11$ and a height of 5. Therefore, its area is $11 \times 5 = 55$. Finally, the bottom rectangle is actually a 5-by-5 square, and thus has an area of $5 \times 5 = 25$.

The area of the figure is therefore the sum of the area of these three polygons: $180 + 55 + 25 = 260$ square units. The correct answer is (G).

43. **(E)** 24.0   Plane Geometry   Circles (and Right Triangles)

The important thing to recognize about the triangle shown is that it doesn't just look like a right triangle; it *is* a right triangle, because the distance between a line (or a line segment or a chord) and a point (say, the center of this circle) is always the perpendicular, or right-angle, distance.

So focus on the triangle alone, and solve for the unknown side (which is half of the chord). Call that length x, and apply the Pythagorean theorem:

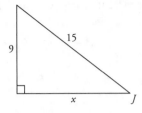

$$9^2 + x^2 = 15^2 \quad \rightarrow \quad 81 + x^2 = 225 \quad \rightarrow \quad x^2 = 144 \quad \rightarrow \quad x = 12$$

Careful—this isn't the answer yet. You have to double the 12, because the side you found is only half of the chord. Thus, the answer is $12 \times 2 = 24$, or 24.0 expressed to tenths. The correct answer is (E).

44. **(F)** 102   Plane Geometry   Polygons (Area of a Trapezoid)

The area of the trapezoid can be taken as the sum of 2 parts: the right triangle at the left, and the rectangle at the right:

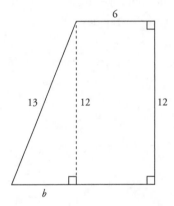

First, the triangle at left: The formula for the area of a triangle is $A = \dfrac{1}{2}\,bh$. The lengths of the hypotenuse (13) and the height (12) are known, so you can use them to solve for the length of the base b using the Pythagorean theorem:

$$12^2 + b^2 = 13^2$$
$$b^2 = 13^2 - 12^2$$
$$b = \sqrt{169 - 144} = \sqrt{25} = 5$$

Therefore, the area of the triangle at left is:

$$\frac{1}{2}(5)(12) = 30$$

The formula for the area of the rectangle at right is $A = bh$, where b is the base and h is the height. The base and height are given in the diagram as 6 and 12, respectively. Therefore, the area of the rectangle is $6 \times 12 = 72$.

The area of the entire trapezoid is thus $30 + 72 = 102$ square meters. The correct answer is (F).

MANHATTAN
PREP

45. **(D)** 3.5   Plane Geometry   Other Plane Geometry (Solid Figures)

The water forms a solid rectangular box inside the warehouse.

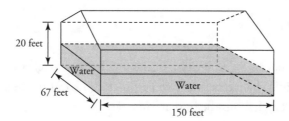

The volume of the box is 35,000 cubic feet. In general, the volume, V, of a rectangular solid is given by the equation $V = L \times W \times H$, or length times width times height. The length and width of the box are the same as the equivalent dimensions of the warehouse; what is not known is the height of the box (the depth of the water). Plug in to the equation and solve for H:

$$V = L \times W \times H \quad \rightarrow \quad 35,000 = 150 \times 67 \times H \quad \rightarrow \quad H = 35,000 \div (150 \times 67) \quad \rightarrow \quad H \approx 3.5$$

Notice that the height *of the warehouse* is irrelevant (except for the fact that this height, 20 feet, needs to be bigger than your answer). The correct answer is (D).

46. **(H)** 6.5   Plane Geometry   Circles (and Right Triangles)

Examine the triangle inside the circle. The triangle is right, so it obeys the Pythagorean theorem. You know the lengths of the two legs, and from that information you can find the hypotenuse. If you know the 5–12–13 triple, then you can leap to the hypotenuse right away, or you can apply Pythagoras:

$$5^2 + 12^2 = c^2 \quad \rightarrow \quad 25 + 144 = c^2 \quad \rightarrow \quad 169 = c^2 \quad \rightarrow \quad 13 = c$$

This is *not* the final answer. The value you just found, 13, is the diameter of the circle, but the radius is half that much. So the radius is equal to $13 \div 2 = 6.5$. The correct answer is (H).

47. **(E)** More than 4,000   Plane Geometry   Other Plane Geometry (Solid Figures)

2,700 cubic feet (a volume) of chlorine gas form a layer of gas that is uniformly 0.4 feet thick. This layer can be assumed for now to be a rectangular solid. The formula for the volume of a rectangular solid is $V = L \times W \times H$, or length times width times height. You know the height (or thickness of the layer) and you know the volume. Plug in and see what you get:

$$V = L \times W \times H \quad \rightarrow \quad 2,700 = L \times W \times 0.4 \quad \rightarrow \quad L \times W = 2,700 \div 0.4 = 6,750$$

You can't solve for the length or width of the floor independently, but you know that their product is 6,750—and, in fact, this product is exactly the area you are looking for. The result is more than 4,000, as the correct answer choice states.

The floor does not actually have to be rectangular. The volume of any right solid (e.g., a box or cylinder) that has a constant horizontal cross-section is the area of the "floor" times the height: $V = A \times H$. This equation doesn't hold for a pyramid or cone, because the cross-section shrinks as you move upward. The correct answer is (E).

15

48. (J) 756   Plane Geometry   Polygons (Rectangles)

Because *ABCD* and *EFGH* are similar rectangles, the ratio of corresponding sides between the two rectangles will always have the same ratio (i.e., they will always be in the same proportion). Therefore:

$$\frac{\overline{EF}}{\overline{AB}} = \frac{\overline{FG}}{\overline{BC}} = \frac{\overline{GH}}{\overline{CD}} = \frac{\overline{EH}}{\overline{AD}}$$

In this problem, you are given the values of $\overline{BC}$ (the width of the smaller rectangle) = 12 and $\overline{AB}$ (the height of the smaller rectangle) = 7; you are also given the ratio of the two perimeters (3 : 1). If the perimeters are in a 3 : 1 ratio, then all corresponding sides of the two rectangles must be in that same ratio:

$$\frac{\overline{EF}}{\overline{AB}} = \frac{\overline{FG}}{\overline{BC}} = \frac{\overline{GH}}{\overline{CD}} = \frac{\overline{EH}}{\overline{AD}} = 3$$

You can now solve for the height and width of rectangle *EFGH*:

$$\frac{\overline{EF}}{\overline{AB}} = 3 \qquad \frac{\overline{FG}}{\overline{BC}} = 3$$

$$\frac{\overline{EF}}{7} = 3 \qquad \frac{\overline{FG}}{12} = 3$$

$$\overline{EF} = 3 \cdot 7 = 21 \qquad \overline{FG} = 3 \cdot 12 = 36$$

The area of rectangle *EFGH* is equal to the height times the width, or 21 × 36 = 756. The correct answer is (J).

49. (B) 24   Plane Geometry   Lines & Angles

Add facts to the diagram and draw conclusions. First, add the distances, since those are actual numbers. All units are inches, so you can leave them out of your computations.

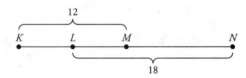

Since *L* is halfway between *K* and *M*, it splits the distance of 12 in two. Thus, the distance from *K* to *L* is 6, as is the distance from *L* to *M*.

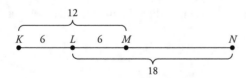

MANHATTAN
PREP

Next, if the whole distance from L to N is 18 and the distance partway there (as far as M) is 6, then the rest of the distance (from M to N) is $18 - 6 = 12$.

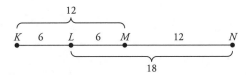

Finally, add up the lengths of all the short line segments. $6 + 6 + 12 = 24$. The correct answer is (B).

50. **(H)** 21   Plane Geometry   Triangles (Area)

Because the triangles are similar triangles, the ratio of corresponding sides between the two triangles will always have the same ratio (i.e., they will always be in the same proportion). It is given in the problem that this ratio is $7 : 10$. Therefore:

$$\frac{\text{side 1 small}}{\text{side 1 large}} = \frac{\text{side 2 small}}{\text{side 2 large}} = \frac{\text{side 3 small}}{\text{side 3 large}} = \frac{7}{10}$$

You know the lengths of the two legs of the large triangle. What about the third side? Because it is a right triangle, you can use the Pythagorean theorem, $a^2 + b^2 = c^2$, to get $5^2 + 12^2 = c^2$. Simplify the equation to get $c^2 = 25 + 144 = 169$. Therefore, the hypotenuse c is equal to $\sqrt{169} = 13$.

You could use the ratio above to calculate the length of each of the sides of the smaller triangle (they are 3.5, 8.4, and 9.1, respectively). However, in this case it is easier to calculate the perimeter of the large triangle ($5 + 12 + 13 = 30$) and multiply by the ratio $7 : 10$:

$$\left(5 + 12 + 13\right)\left(\frac{7}{10}\right) = \frac{30 \times 7}{10} = \frac{210}{10} = 21$$

Therefore, the perimeter of the smaller triangle equals 21. The correct answer is (H).

51. **(D)** 810π Plane Geometry   Circles (Cylinders)

Since the problem provides the formulas, you can substitute and solve:

Lateral Surface Area $= 2\pi rh$
$180\pi = 2\pi(9)(h)$
$h = 10$

Volume $= \pi r^2 h = \pi(9)^2(10) = 810\pi$

The correct answer is (D).

15

52. **(H)** 48   Plane Geometry   Triangles

The two figures below show two separate triangles—one for the streetlight and one for the man.

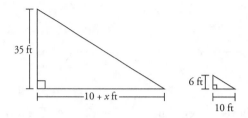

The two triangles are geometrically similar because two of the angles (and therefore the third) are the same in both triangles. Therefore, the ratios of the corresponding sides must be equal. Solve the following proportion for x:

$$\frac{35}{10+x} = \frac{6}{10}$$
$$350 = 60 + 6x$$
$$290 = 6x$$
$$x = 48.\overline{3}$$

This result closest to 48 feet. The correct answer is (H).

53. **(C)** 192   Plane Geometry   Polygons (Area)

The problem states that A is at the center of the larger square. Therefore, $\overline{DG}$ must be equal to half of the length of $\overline{CG}$. Since $ABCD$ and $EFCG$ are both squares, all sides of these shapes must be equal:

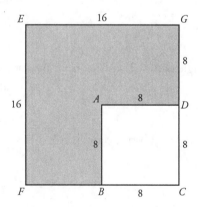

Since $\overline{EF} = \overline{EG} = 16$ and $\overline{AB} = \overline{AD} = 8$, calculate the area of the two squares as follows:

Area of $EFCG = 16 \times 916 = 256$
Area of $ABCD = 8 \times 98 = 64$

The area of the shaded region is the difference in area of these two squares, or $256 - 64 = 192$. The correct answer is (C).

54. (J) 100   Plane Geometry   Triangles

The two figures below show two separate triangles—one for the building to the fire truck and one for the hose to the fire truck. The two triangles are geometrically similar by the because two of the angles (and therefore the third) are the same in both triangles. Therefore, the ratios of the corresponding sides must be equal. Solve the following proportion for x:

$$\frac{200}{x} = \frac{60}{x-70}$$
$$200x - 14{,}000 = 60x$$
$$140x = 14{,}000$$
$$x = 100$$

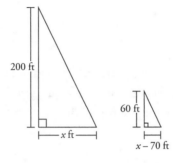

The correct answer is (J).

55. (B) 2, 3, $\sqrt{5}$ Plane Geometry   Triangles (Right Triangles)

If a triangle is a right triangle, then according to the Pythagorean theorem, the sum of the squares of the two shorter sides will be equal to the square of the longest side. You can test each answer choice to see whether this the case for the numbers given in the set:

$1^2 = 1; \left(\sqrt{2}\right)^2 = 2; 3^2 = 9$ NO: $1 + 2 \neq 9$

$\mathbf{2^2 = 4; 3^2 = 9; \left(\sqrt{5}\right)^2 = 5}$ **YES: $4 + 5 = 9$**

$3^2 = 9; 5^2 = 25; \left(\sqrt{7}\right)^2 = 7$ NO: $9 + 7 \neq 25$

$4^2 = 16; 5^2 = 25; 6^2 = 36$ NO: $16 + 25 \neq 36$

$5^2 = 25; 6^2 = 36; 8^2 = 64$ NO: $25 + 36 \neq 64$

The correct answer is therefore 2, 3, and $\sqrt{5}$. The correct answer is (B).

56. (J) 108π Plane Geometry   Circles (Area)

The area of a circle is given by the formula $A = \pi r^2$. You are told in the problem that the smaller circle has an area of 36π, so for the smaller circle, $36\pi = \pi r^2$. Canceling π from both sides, you get $r^2 = 36$, so $r = 6$. The diameter of a circle is twice the radius, so the diameter of the smaller circle is $2 \times 6 = 12$.

MANHATTAN
PREP   681

The problem states that the diameters of the circles are in a $2:1$ ratio, so the diameter of the larger circle is twice that of the smaller circle, or 24. The radius of the larger circle is $24 \div 2 = 12$, making the area of the larger circle $\pi(12)^2 = 144\pi$.

The larger circle is therefore $144\pi - 36\pi = 108\pi$ larger in area than the smaller circle. The correct answer is (J).

57. **(A)** 20   Plane Geometry   Triangles

Notice that the line segment in question, $\overline{XZ}$, is the hypotenuse of a right triangle with legs of length 12 and 16. You can apply the Pythagorean theorem to solve for the unknown length:

$$12^2 + 16^2 = (XZ)^2$$
$$144 + 256 = (XZ)^2$$
$$400 = (XZ)^2$$
$$20 = XZ$$

Alternatively, you might have recognized that this right triangle has legs in the ratio of $12:16$, or $3:4$. Thus, you have a $3:4:5$ right triangle. To figure out the missing length, you can scale up $3:4:5$ to match $12:16:h$, where h is the hypotenuse. You would need to multiply $3:4:5$ by 4 to match the first part of the ratio $12:16:h$, so $h = 4 \times 5 = 20$. The correct answer is (A).

58. **(H)** 300   Plane Geometry   Polygons

To find the area of the parallelogram, multiply the base by the height. The base is $9 + 16 = 25$. The height from that base to the other base (the "ceiling") is 12. So the area is $25 \times 12 = 300$. The correct answer is (H).

59. **(D)** 72°   Plane Geometry   Circles (Lines and Angles)

This question asks how many degrees the central angle would span for the sector representing the respondents who exercised 5 days in the past week. The sum of the central angles of a circle is 360°; therefore, you should take the ratio of the number of respondents in this sector to the total number of respondents. There were 5 respondents who exercised 5 days in the previous week, out of 25 respondents. Therefore:

$$\frac{5}{25} \cdot 360° = \frac{1}{5} \cdot 360° = 72°$$

The central angle for the sector representing the respondents who exercised 5 days in the past week is therefore 72°, or $\frac{1}{5}$ of the circle. The correct answer is (D).

60. **(H)** 76   Plane Geometry   Circles (Cylinders)

To answer this question, calculate the volume of the disc (which is just a cylinder with a relatively short height), in cubic inches, and multiply it by the weight of a cubic inch of the metal (given as 0.3 pounds). The formula for the volume of a cylinder is $V = \pi r^2 h$, where r is the radius of the circular end of the cylinder and h is the height. Remember, you are given the diameter of the cylinder (9 inches), so to get the radius, divide by 2. Thus, the calculation is as follows:

Weight of disc = (Volume of disc) × (Weight per cubic inch)

$$= \pi r^2 h(0.3)$$

$$= \pi \left(\frac{9}{2}\right)^2 (4)(0.3)$$

$$= \pi \left(\frac{81}{4}\right)(4)(0.3)$$

$$= 81(0.3)\pi$$

Note that a reasonable estimate for π is 3.14, so $\pi \times (0.3)$ will be just smaller than 1 (the exact amount with this approximation is 0.942). Therefore, the correct answer should be slightly smaller than 81, and indeed 76 is the only close choice, so it must be correct. The exact answer, rounded to 3 decimal places, is 76.341 pounds. The correct answer is (H).

61. **(A)** 270π Plane Geometry   Circles (Circumference)

If the disc rotates once every 2 seconds, it will rotate $60 \div 2 = 30$ times in 1 minute. Therefore, multiply the circumference of the circle by 30 to answer this question.

Circumference is given by the formula $C = 2\pi r = \pi d$. In this problem, you are given the diameter (9 inches) rather than the radius of the circle, so it is easiest to use d for the calculation. The circumference is thus 9π, and the distance traveled by any point on the edge of the disc in 1 minute will be $30 \times 9\pi = 270\pi$ inches. The correct answer is (A).

62. **(G)** $225 - \frac{81}{4}\pi$ Plane Geometry   Polygons (Area)

To solve this problem, subtract the area of the solid disc from the area of the metal sheet. The area of the square metal sheet is given by $A = s^2$, where s is the length of one of the sides of the square. Therefore, the metal sheet has an area of $(15)^2 = 225$ square inches.

Meanwhile, the area covered by the disc is equal to the area of the circular top (or bottom) surface of the disc. The formula for the area of a circle is given by $A = \pi r^2$, where r is the radius of the circle. The radius is half the length of the diameter, which is given as 9 inches in the problem. Therefore, the area covered by the disc is $\pi \left(\frac{9}{2}\right)^2 = \frac{81}{4}\pi$. The difference is $225 - \frac{81}{4}\pi$ square inches. The correct answer is (G).

63. **(C)** 22   Plane Geometry   Triangles

It's a good idea to draw a picture, so that you visualize the situation correctly.

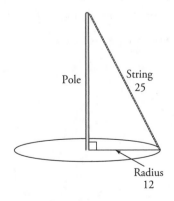

The pole, the radius, and the string form a right triangle. Since you know two of the sides, you can find the third by the Pythagorean theorem, calling the height of the pole h.

$$h^2 + 12^2 = 25^2 \quad \rightarrow \quad h^2 + 144 = 625 \quad \rightarrow \quad h^2 = 481 \quad \rightarrow \quad h \approx 21.93 \approx 22$$

The correct answer is (C).

64. **(K)** 80   Plane Geometry   Triangles

Draw a quick diagram of the water slide, adding in the given information.

Now apply the Pythagorean theorem to find the unknown horizontal distance d.

$$41^2 + d^2 = 90^2 \quad \rightarrow \quad 1{,}681 + d^2 = 8{,}100 \quad \rightarrow \quad d^2 = 6{,}419 \quad \rightarrow \quad d \approx 80.12 \approx 80$$

The correct answer is (K).

65. **(E)** 112π Plane Geometry   Circles (Cylinders)

The surface area for a right circular cylinder is the lateral surface area = $2\pi rh$, plus the areas of the two circular ends = $2\pi r^2$:

$$\text{Surface Area} = 2\pi rh + 2\pi r^2 = 2\pi(4)(10) + 2\pi(4)^2 = 80\pi + 32\pi = 112\pi$$

The correct answer is (E).

66. **(F)** $\dfrac{4}{3}\pi$ Plane Geometry   Lines & Angles (Degrees & Radians)

In order to solve this problem, remember that π radians equates to 180°. Therefore, the conversion from degrees to radians requires you to multiply by $\dfrac{\pi}{180°}$.

The circle with center P is divided into 6 equal parts or slices, the angles of which all measure 60° (remember that vertical angles are equal, so $\angle EPF = \angle BPC = 60°$, for example). Therefore, each central angle is equal to $60° \times \dfrac{\pi}{180°} = \dfrac{\pi}{3}$ radians.

The question asks you to find the difference between $\angle BPC$ and the sum of the 5 other central angles of the circle (in radians). Since each slice of the circle measures $\dfrac{\pi}{3}$ radians, you can calculate the answer as follows:

$$\left(5 \text{ other angles}\right) - \left(\angle BPC\right) = 5\left(\dfrac{\pi}{3}\right) - \left(\dfrac{\pi}{3}\right) = 4\left(\dfrac{\pi}{3}\right) = \dfrac{4}{3}\pi$$

The correct answer is (F).

MANHATTAN
PREP

67. **(D)** 36π Plane Geometry   Circles (and Polygons)

Add labels to the figure. If the area of the square is 144 square centimeters, then the sides of the square are each $\sqrt{144}$ = 12 centimeters long. That means the diameter of the circle is also 12 centimeters long, because the circle fits exactly within the square:

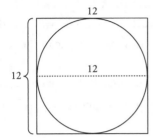

Since the radius is half the diameter, $r = 12 \div 2 = 6$ centimeters, then the area of the circle is $\pi r^2 = \pi 6^2 = 36\pi$.

In a pinch, you could estimate π as 3.14, compute the answer choices, then eliminate unreasonably large answers (> 144, since the circle is smaller than the square) and unreasonably small answers (since the circle takes up most of the square). It would be difficult, however, to distinguish between 32π ($\approx$ 101) and 36π ($\approx$ 113). The correct answer is (D).

68. **(G)** 7.5   Plane Geometry   Triangles

Recall that *median* means "middle"; the median length of three lengths is the one in the middle, neither the shortest nor the longest. In the first triangle, the ratio of the shortest side to the middle-length side is 3 : 4. In the second triangle, if you represent the unknown short side as *x*, that same ratio is x : 10, since you know that the median length is 10 centimeters.

Because the two triangles are similar to each other, these two ratios must equal each other. Now you can set up a proportion and solve for *x*:

$$\frac{3}{4} = \frac{x}{10}$$
$$\frac{3 \times 10}{4} = x$$
$$7.5 = x$$

The correct answer is (G).

69. **(E)** 200   Plane Geometry   Circles (and Polygons)

Draw in and label radii, so that you can see how the dimensions of the circles give you the dimensions of the rectangle:

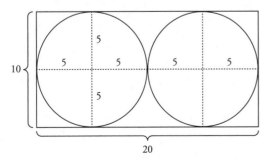

The length of the rectangle is 4 radii, or 20 feet, and the height of the rectangle is 2 radii, or 10 feet. Thus, the area of the rectangle is 20 × 10 = 200 square feet. The correct answer is (E).

70.   **(H)** 33   Plane Geometry   Triangles

Since the two triangles are similar, the ratio of corresponding sides must be equal. In this case, $\overline{BC}$ and $\overline{DE}$ are corresponding sides. The ratio of their lengths is 5 : 15, or 1 : 3. Therefore, the ratio for each of the other two pairs of sides must also be 1 : 3. In other words, each side in the big triangle is 3 times as long as the corresponding side in the small triangle.

Apply this insight to compute the unknown sides of ΔADE. Side $\overline{AB}$ in the small triangle is 2 inches long, so side $\overline{AD}$ in the big triangle is 2 × 3 = 6 inches long. Likewise, side $\overline{AC}$ in the small triangle is 4 inches long, so side $\overline{AE}$ in the big triangle is 4 × 3 = 12 inches long.

Finally, to get the perimeter, add up all the sides of the big triangle: 6 + 12 + 15 = 33 inches.

Alternatively, you could compute the perimeter of the small triangle: 2 + 4 + 5 = 11 inches. Then multiply by the scaling factor of 3 to get 33 inches as the perimeter of the big triangle. Every corresponding distance that you would measure in inches obeys the same scaling ratio of 1 : 3 here. The correct answer is (H).

71.   **(C)** 125,000   Plane Geometry   Triangles (3D Objects)

The roof of the house forms a triangular prism, which has a formula for volume equal to:

$$\frac{1}{2}(\text{base})(\text{height})(\text{depth “into the page”})$$

The roof's height can be found by finding the difference between the floor-to-ceiling height and the floor-to-apex height: 25 − 15 = 10. By substituting in values provided by the diagram and the question, you can find that the volume of the roof is $\frac{1}{2}(70)(10)(100) = 35,000$ cubic feet.

The lower portion of the house forms a rectangular box, which has a formula for volume equal to (width)(height)(depth). By substituting in the given values, you can find that the volume of the lower part of the house is (60)(15)(100) = 90,000.

The total volume of the house is the sum of these two components: 35,000 + 90,000 = 125,000 cubic feet (since all the distances are in feet). The correct answer is (C).

72.   **(K)** 27%   Plane Geometry   Polygons (3D Objects)

Because the roof of the house has been blown off the structure, you should not include its volume. To find the percentage of the new house's volume that is now flooded, as a percentage of total volume, you must find the volume of both the flooded area and the house:

Volume Flooded = $(w)(h)(d) = (60)(4)(100) = 24,000$ cubic feet

Volume of House = $(w)(h)(d) = (60)(15)(100) = 90,000$ cubic feet

To find the percentage of the house that's flooded, divide 24,000 by 90,000 and multiply the result by 100% to convert to percentages:

$$\frac{24,000}{90,000} = \frac{24}{90} = \frac{4}{15} = \frac{400}{15}\% = \frac{80}{3}\% = 26\frac{2}{3}\%$$

The best answer is therefore 27%. The correct answer is (K).

73. (C) 42   Plane Geometry   Triangles

The ratio of the side lengths in this triangle may be 5 : 6 : 7, but that does not mean that the actual measurements of the sides are 5 feet, 6 feet, and 7 feet. After all, those lengths would only give you a perimeter of 5 + 6 + 7 = 18 feet. The perimeter you need is much bigger: 108 feet.

At this point, though, you are close. Figure out how much you need to "scale up" this small triangle with perimeter 18 feet to get 108 feet instead. Since 108 ÷ 18 = 6, the desired triangle is 6 times as big as this small triangle. Now multiply every side length in the small triangle by a factor of 6 to get these sides:

   5 × 6 = 30 feet   6 × 6 = 36 feet   7 × 6 = 42 feet

A quick double-check confirms that 30 + 36 + 42 = 108, the desired perimeter. Thus, the longest side in the actual triangle is 42 feet.

The method of "the unknown multiplier" is essentially the method above in an algebraic costume. Express the unknown multiplier (or scaling factor) as x. The sides are in a ratio of 5 : 6 : 7, so each side really measures $5x$, $6x$, and $7x$ feet. The perimeter of the triangle is $5x + 6x + 7x = 18x = 108$. Solving for x, you find that $x = 6$ (the same factor as you found before), and the side lengths are 30, 36, and 42 feet. The correct answer is (C).

74. (G) 6   Plane Geometry   Polygons

There are 8 sides of the figure, as you can count: 4 horizontal sides (3 on top and 1 on bottom) and 4 vertical sides (2 on the left and 2 on the right). To get the average side length, you need the total length of all the sides—that is, the perimeter—then divide by 8 sides.

There seem to be too many unknowns: 4 side lengths are unlabeled. However, since every side is either perfectly horizontal or perfectly vertical, you can figure out the sums of certain sides. For instance, to get from the left side of the figure to the right side, ignoring up and down motion, you can either go straight along the bottom (16 centimeters) or take the upper route. The three horizontal line segments on top (one 5-cm length and two unlabeled) must *also* sum to 16 centimeters. By a similar argument, the height of the figure is 8 centimeters (3 + 5, the vertical sides on the right), so the two vertical sides on the left must sum to 8 as well.

So the perimeter of the figure is 8 (left vertical sides) + 8 (right vertical sides) + 16 (top horizontal sides) + 16 (bottom horizontal sides) = 48 centimeters. Finally, divide by 8 sides to get an average side length of 6 centimeters. The correct answer is (G).

75. **(D)** 40°   Plane Geometry   Triangles

A good first move is to look for triangles with two known angles: you can apply the 180° rule to figure out the third angle. Triangle *XYZ* fits the bill: 180 − (110 + 45) = 180 − 155 = 25°. Add this angle to the diagram.

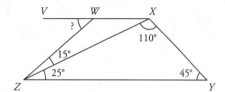

The two angles at *Z* add up to 15 + 25 = 40°. Now, since *WXYZ* is a trapezoid, you know that exactly two sides must be parallel. By inspecting the diagram, you can be sure that the two parallel sides are $\overline{WX}$ and $\overline{ZY}$. The line segment $\overline{WZ}$ is a transversal, cutting across those two parallel sides. Here's what the diagram would look like, if you could highlight just the important facts at this point.

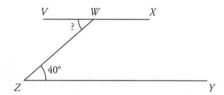

It may now be more obvious that the angle you're looking for is also 40°. Transversals cutting across parallel lines create sets of equal angles: all the acute angles (< 90°) will be equal to each other and all the obtuse angles (> 90°) will also be equal to each other. The correct answer is (D).

76. **(J)** 120   Plane Geometry   Triangles and Diagonals (3D Objects)

The formula for surface area of a right pyramid $= \dfrac{1}{2} \times$ (base perimeter) × (slant height) + (base area). Because you were asked to find the surface area of only the four lateral faces of the pyramid, the amended formula is $\dfrac{1}{2} \times$ (base perimeter) × (slant height). By substituting values given in the diagram, you get $\dfrac{1}{2}(6 + 6 + 6 + 6)(10) = 120$.

Alternatively, you can find the area of one lateral face and multiply it by 4: $\dfrac{1}{2}(6)(10)(4) = 120$. The correct answer is (J).

77. **(C)** $33\dfrac{1}{3}$%   Plane Geometry   Polygons (Lines and Angles)

Because quadrilateral *ABCD* has 4 sides, the sum of its interior angles is 360°. Because all 4 sides of the quadrilateral are equal, opposite interior angles must be equal. Therefore, ∠*DCB* = ∠*DAB* = 2*x* and ∠*ADC* = ∠*ABC* = *x*. To find *x*, use the following equation: 4*x* + 2*x* = 360°. Therefore, 6*x* = 360°, and *x* = 60°.

This implies that ∠*DAB* = 2(60°) = 120°, so its opposite angle, ∠*DCB*, must equal 120°. To find the percentage of the sum of the interior angles of quadrilateral *ABCD* that ∠*DCB* comprises, divide the measure of ∠*DCB* by 360°: $\dfrac{120°}{360°} = \dfrac{1}{3} = 33\dfrac{1}{3}$%. The correct answer is (C).

15

78. **(G)** 108π Plane Geometry   Circles (Cylinders)

The formula for the volume of a right circular cylinder is given by the formula $V = hr^2\pi$, where h is the height of the cylinder and r is the radius of the circle on the base or top. In this case, the cylinder is turned on its side, so you can think of h as being l (length) in this case and r as being the radius of the circle on either end.

Because you are given the values of l and r in the diagram in the problem, you can substitute the values into the equation for volume and simplify:

$$V = lr^2\pi$$
$$V = (12)(3)^2\pi = 12 \cdot 9\pi = 108\pi$$

Therefore, the volume of the cylinder is 108π cubic feet. The correct answer is (G).

79. **(E)** $4b + 4c$ Plane Geometry   Polygons (Perimeter)

In the diagram shown, the perimeter of the entire figure is comprised of 8 sides. All 8 sides coincide with sides of equilateral triangles, all of which have sides of length b or c. Starting with point A and tracing clockwise, there are 2 line segments of length b, followed by 2 line segments of length c, followed by another 2 line segments of length b, followed by another 2 line segments of length c. Therefore, the perimeter consists of 4 sides of length b and 4 sides of length c, so the correct expression is $4b + 4c$. The correct answer is (E).

80. **(F)** $\sqrt{b^2 - a^2}$ Plane Geometry   Triangles and Diagonals

The line segments connecting points A, B, and J make up the right triangle $\triangle ABJ$, and you are asked for an expression for the length of $\overline{AJ}$. The lengths of the two other sides are a (the longer leg of the triangle) and b (the hypotenuse). Therefore, you can solve for an expression for the value of $\overline{AJ}$ by using the Pythagorean theorem:

$$\left(\overline{AJ}\right)^2 + a^2 = b^2$$
$$\left(\overline{AJ}\right)^2 = b^2 - a^2$$
$$\overline{AJ} = \sqrt{b^2 - a^2}$$

The correct answer is (F).

81. **(A)** $ac + \dfrac{\sqrt{3}}{2}\left(b^2 + c^2\right)$ Plane Geometry   Polygons (Area)

The area of the diagram can be broken down into its component parts:

- A parallelogram in the center, with length c and height a
- Two smaller equilateral triangles, each with sides of length b
- Two larger equilateral triangles, each with sides of length c

15

It is given in the problem that the area of an equilateral triangle with sides x units long is $\frac{\sqrt{3}}{4}x^2$ square units. Therefore, the smaller equilateral triangles have an area of $\frac{\sqrt{3}}{4}b^2$, and the larger equilateral triangles have an area of $\frac{\sqrt{3}}{4}c^2$. Meanwhile, the formula for the area of a parallelogram is (height) × (length), or ac.

You can now solve for the area of the entire figure by adding together the component parts, making sure to remember that there are 2 of each size of triangle:

$$\text{Area} = ac + 2\left(\frac{\sqrt{3}}{4}\right)b^2 + 2\left(\frac{\sqrt{3}}{4}\right)c^2$$

$$= ac + \left(\frac{\sqrt{3}}{2}\right)b^2 + \left(\frac{\sqrt{3}}{2}\right)c^2$$

$$= ac + \frac{\sqrt{3}}{2}\left(b^2 + c^2\right)$$

Therefore, the correct answer is (A).

82. **(F)** 28.5   Plane Geometry   Polygons (Area of a Trapezoid)

The area of the trapezoid can be taken as the sum of 3 parts: the leftmost right triangle, the rectangle in the middle, and the rightmost triangle.

First, the leftmost triangle: The formula for the area of a triangle is $A = \frac{1}{2}bh$. The base is given as 3 and the height must be equal to the height of the rightmost triangle (3), because the top and bottom lines of the trapezoid are parallel. Therefore, the area of the leftmost triangle is:

$$\frac{1}{2}(3)(3) = 4.5$$

The formula for the area of the middle rectangle is $A = bh$, where b is the base and h is the height. The base and height are given in the diagram as 6 and 3, respectively. Therefore, the area of the rectangle is $6 \times 3 = 18$.

Finally, add the area of the rightmost triangle to the area of the other 2 pieces of the trapezoid. The lengths of the hypotenuse (5) and the height (3) are known, so you can use them to solve for the length of the base using the Pythagorean theorem:

$$3^2 + (\text{base})^2 = 5^2$$

$$(\text{base})^2 = 5^2 - 3^2$$

$$\text{base} = \sqrt{25-9} = \sqrt{16} = 4$$

Therefore, the area of the rightmost triangle is $\frac{1}{2}(3)(4) = 6$, and the area of the entire trapezoid is $4.5 + 18 + 6 = 28.5$. The correct answer is (F).

MANHATTAN
PREP

15

83. **(E)** "If the humidity is not above 64%, then it is not raining."   Plane Geometry   Other Plane Geometry
                                                                                                      (Logical Conclusions)

The statement given in the question is a conditional statement, "If P, then Q," where P is the statement "it is raining"
and Q is the statement "the humidity is above 64%." A conditional statement and its contrapositive—"If not Q, then not
P"—are logically equivalent. Therefore, if the statement is true, its contrapositive must also be true.

"If not Q, then not P" → "If the humidity is not above 64%, then it is not raining." The correct answer is (E).

84. **(K)** 42   Plane Geometry   Polygons (Perimeter)

The question asks you to determine the perimeter based on an incomplete listing of the lengths of all of the sides of the
10-sided object. However, it is given in the problem that all of the line segments are perpendicular to one another. Therefore, all of the line segments are either horizontal or vertical, and the sum of the lengths of the horizontal line segments at
the top must equal the sum of the horizontal line segments at the bottom. Similarly, the sum of the lengths of the vertical
line segments at the left must equal the sum of the vertical line segments at the right. Assign x and y to the lengths of the
unknown sides:

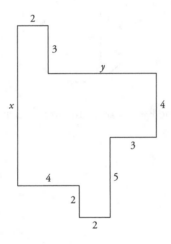

It must be the case that $x + 2 = 5 + 4 + 3$. Furthermore, $y + 2 = 4 + 2 + 3$. Therefore, $x = 10$ and $y = 7$.

Now add up the lengths of the 10 sides of the object, starting at the top left and tracing the sides of the object in a
clockwise manner, as follows:

$2 + 3 + 7 + 4 + 3 + 5 + 2 + 2 + 4 + 10 =$
$12 + 12 + 8 + 10 =$
$24 + 18 = 42$

The correct answer is therefore 42.

Also notice that since the sum of the vertical sides on the right side of the diagram sum to 12, and the sum of the horizontal side of the diagram sum to 9, the perimeter must be $(12 + 9) \times 2 = 21 \times 2 = 42$. The correct answer is (K).

15

85. **(D)** "If I do not sleep until noon, then today is not a vacation day."

Plane Geometry   Other Plane Geometry (Logical Conclusions)

The statement given in the question is a conditional statement, "If P, then Q," where P is the statement "today is a vacation day" and Q is the statement "I sleep until noon." A conditional statement and its contrapositive—"If not Q, then not P"—are logically equivalent. Therefore, if the statement is true, its contrapositive must also be true.

"If not Q, then not P" → "If I do not sleep until noon, then today is not a vacation day." The correct answer is (D).

86. **(F)** 13π Plane Geometry   Circles (Circumference)

To find the circumference of the circle, you need to determine the radius (or diameter) of the circle, because circumference $= 2\pi r = \pi d$. The lengths of the sides of the rectangle will not give you the radius directly. However, you can draw a diagonal through the rectangle, and it will cross through the center of the circle, because the rectangle is inscribed inside of the circle. This diagonal will then be a diameter of the circle:

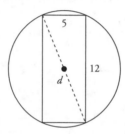

The length of the diagonal can be found using the Pythagorean theorem, because it cuts the rectangle into two right triangles:

$$5^2 + 12^2 = d^2$$
$$25 + 144 = d^2$$
$$169 = d^2$$
$$d = 13$$

Therefore, the circumference of the circle $= 13\pi$.

Alternatively, you could have observed that the sides of the rectangle (5 and 12) constituted two parts of a $5:12:13$ right triangle, and thereby avoided using the Pythagorean theorem. The correct answer is (F).

87. **(A)** 64   Plane Geometry Polygons (3D Objects)

The large cube's dimensions are 4 times larger than those of the smaller cube. For any side length, the ratio of the larger cube's edge to the smaller cube's edge will be $4:1$. If you assume that the edge length of the smaller cube is s, then the larger cube's edge length will be $4s$.

The volume of the smaller cube is the cube of its sides: $s \times s \times s = s^3$. The volume of the larger cube is the cube of its sides: $4s \times 4s \times 4s = 4^3 s^3 = 64s^3$. By comparing the larger cube's volume to that of the smaller cube, notice that $64s^3$ is 64 times larger than s^3. The correct answer is (A).

88. **(F)** 5:15pm   Plane Geometry   Circles (Lines and Angles)

For the clock shown, the minute hand in 1 hour will trace a circle with a radius of 8 inches. The circumference of that circle equals $2\pi r = 2\pi(8) = 16\pi$ inches.

Therefore, if the tip of the minute hand travels 52π inches, it will take $52\pi \div 16\pi = 3\frac{1}{4}$ hours to do so. Three hours after 2:00pm is 5:00pm, and $\frac{1}{4}$ hour after that is 5:15pm. The correct answer is (F).

89. **(C)** 512   Plane Geometry   Polygons (3D Objects)

The sphere is inscribed inside of the cube, so the sphere touches each of the 6 faces of the cube at the center point of those faces. Connecting any 2 such points on opposite sides of the sphere will yield a diameter of the sphere, and since $d = 2r$, the diameter will equal $4 \times 2 = 8$.

This diameter is equal in length to any of the edges on the cube itself. Therefore, the cube's dimensions are $8 \times 8 \times 8$ inches. The volume of a cube is given by the formula $V = s^3$, where s is the length of one of the sides of the cube.

Thus, the correct answer is $8^3 = 512$ cubic inches. The correct answer is (C).

90. **(K)** Animal E does not eat dog food   Plane Geometry   Other Plane Geometry (Logical Conclusions)

The first statement is that "All animals that eat dog food are dogs." You can deduce that if an animal eats dog food, it must be a dog. The contrapositive of this premise is "If an animal is not a dog, it does not eat dog food."

You can also deduce that if Animal F eats dog food, it must be a dog.

Examine each answer response, and see whether it satisfies the logical rules stated above.

Choices (F), (G), (H), and (K) all violate the logical rules established in the three premise statements. Choice (K) satisfies all three premise statements. The correct answer is (K).

91. **(C)** $\frac{11}{7}$ Plane Geometry   Lines & Angles (Triangles)

To find the ratio of y to x, use the properties of plane geometry to solve for the value of other pieces of information in the diagram:

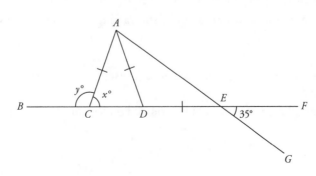

15

Vertical angles are equal, so $\angle AED = \angle FEG = 35°$. Additionally, $\overline{AD} = \overline{DE}$, so ΔADE is an isosceles triangle. Angles opposite equal sides of an isosceles triangle are equal, so $\angle EAD = \angle AED = 35°$. $\angle ADE$ is the third angle of this triangle, and all interior angles of a triangle must sum to 180°, so $\angle ADE = 180° - 35° - 35° = 110°$.

Next, focus on components of ΔACD. In the diagram, $\angle ADC$ and $\angle ADE$ form supplementary angles, which means they must sum to 180°. Therefore, $\angle ADC = 180° - 110° = 70°$. Additionally, $\overline{AC} = \overline{AD}$, so ΔACD is an isosceles triangle. Angles opposite equal sides of an isosceles triangle are equal, so $x° = \angle ADC = 70°$. $x°$ and $y°$ form supplementary angles, so $y° = 180 - x° = 180° - 70° = 110°$. In the diagram all of this information appears as follows:

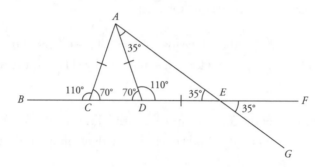

The correct ratio of y to x is $\dfrac{110}{70} = \dfrac{11}{7}$. The correct answer is (C).

92. **(J)** 90°   Plane Geometry   Triangles (Proofs)

In the diagram, ΔABD and ΔAFD share a number of common elements and are in fact congruent. In order to prove this to be the case, you need to prove that all three sides of both triangles are congruent. You can do so using the side–side–side congruence postulate.

To use side–side–side congruence, you need to know that all three sides of both triangles are congruent, or equal in length. It is given that $\overline{FA} \cong \overline{BA}$. The two triangles also share a common side, $\overline{DA}$, so $\overline{DA} \cong \overline{DA}$. Because ΔABD and ΔAFD are both right triangles and two of the sides in each triangle are equal (one of which is the hypotenuse in each case), by the Pythagorean theorem, the third sides of the two triangles must be equal. As a result, $\overline{DF} \cong \overline{DB}$. Therefore, each of the three sides of one triangle are congruent with a side of the other triangle, so ΔABD and ΔAFD must be congruent.

Because ΔABD and ΔAFD are congruent, you know their interior angles must also be congruent. Thus, the interior angles of ΔABD consist of a 90° angle, $\angle s$, and another angle congruent to (equal to) $\angle r$. The interior angles of any triangle sum to 180°, so algebraically, you can express this fact as $180° = 90° + \angle s + \angle r$. Because you are concerned with the sum $\angle s + \angle r$, isolate the sum of those two variables by subtracting 90° from both sides. $\angle s + \angle r = 180° - 90° = 90°$. The correct answer is (J).

93. **(E)** $\overline{YZ} < \overline{XZ}$ Plane Geometry   Lines & Angles (Distance on a Line)

Here are some examples of how all four points could be oriented on the number line, given the information available in the problem:

MANHATTAN
PREP

15

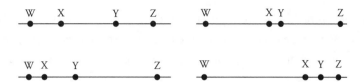

Because point *X* is between points *W* and *Y*, distances $\overline{WX}$ and $\overline{XY}$ will always be shorter than $\overline{WY}$. Because point *Y* is between *X* and *Z*, distances $\overline{XY}$ and $\overline{YZ}$ will always be shorter than $\overline{XZ}$. However, you can't tell anything for certain about the relative lengths of $\overline{WX}$, $\overline{XY}$, and $\overline{YZ}$. Similarly, you cannot tell anything about the relative lengths of $\overline{WY}$ and $\overline{XZ}$.

As a result, while any of the answer choices *could* be true, only choice (E) *must* be true, no matter what the distance between the points is, because point *Y* is *between* points *X* and *Z*. The correct answer is (E).

94. (H) 130°   Plane Geometry   Triangles (Proofs)

The interior angles of a triangle must sum to 180°, so you can find the measure of ∠*EDG* by subtracting 180° − 55° − 90° = 35°. ∠*EDG* and ∠*CDH* are vertical angles, so ∠*CDH* = ∠*EDG* = 35°. Therefore, ∠*CDH* measures 35.

Because $\overrightarrow{AB}$ bisects ∠*FHC*, the measure of ∠*FHC* is divided into two congruent angles (∠*FHD* and ∠*CHD*). The measure of ∠*FHD* is found by subtracting supplementary angle ∠*FHA* from 180°: 180° − 165° = 15°. Therefore, ∠*FHD* = 15°, which implies that ∠*CHD* also equals 15° (both ∠*FHD* and ∠*CHD* are bisections of ∠*FHC*, so they must be equal).

You have now proven that ∠*CHD* = 15° and ∠*CDH* = 35°. Since ∠*CHD* and ∠*CDH* form two of the interior angles of Δ*HCD*, you can find the measure of the third interior angle, ∠*HCD*, by subtracting 180° − 15° − 35° = 130°. The correct answer is (H).

95. (A) $\overline{EH} < \overline{EG}$ Plane Geometry   Lines & Angles (Distance on a Line)

Here are some examples of how all four points could be oriented on the number line, given the information available in the problem:

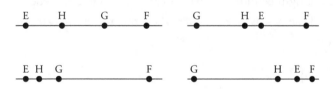

Because point *F* is to the right of points *E* and *G*, whichever point (*E* or *G*) is closest to *F* will have shorter distances from *F* than will the other points. However, based on the information given in the problem, it is impossible to tell which point is closest to *F*. Therefore, any choices that involve point *F* will be incorrect—nothing can be told for certain about the relative distances involving the point *F*. As a result, choices (B), (C) and (E) can all be eliminated.

Also given in the problem is that point H is between points E and G. As a result, distances $\overline{EH}$ and $\overline{GH}$ will always be shorter than $\overline{EG}$. Thus choice (A) *must* be true, no matter the distance between the points, because point H is *between* points E and G. For a similar reason, choice (D) *must be false*, because $\overline{GH}$ must be a shorter distance than $\overline{EH}$. The correct answer is (A).

96. **(G)** 115,000   Plane Geometry   Circles (Cylinders)

To find the volume of the moat, the shaded region in the diagram, you must first find the surface area of the moat. To do this, subtract the area of the smaller circle with radius 80 from that of thte larger circle with radius 100. The difference is $\pi(100)^2 - \pi(80)^2 = (10,000 - 6,400)\pi = 3,600\pi$.

Now that you have the area of the shaded region, multiply by the depth of the water (10) to get a volume of $36,000\pi$. In order to estimate this amount, recall that π is approximately equal to 3.14, or slightly larger than 3. Next, $36,000 \times 3 = 108,000$, so the correct answer should be slightly larger than 108,000. The best answer is therefore 115,000 (the exact answer, with rounding, is 113,097.3). The correct answer is (G).

97. **(A)** $80\sqrt{2}$ Geometry   Triangles and Diagonals (Right Triangles)

The distance from the castle's center to the moat is the same as the distance from the center of the castle to any of its corners. Therefore, the distance between the center of the castle and any corner of the castle is equal to 80 feet. Furthermore, because the castle is square in shape, lines connecting adjacent corners of the castle to the center of the castle will form a right triangle, with the castle wall c in between them as the hypotenuse. Use the Pythagorean theorem to find the length of c:

$$80^2 + 80^2 = c^2$$
$$\sqrt{2(80)^2} = c$$
$$80\sqrt{2} = c$$

The correct answer is (A).

98. **(F)** 368π Plane Geometry   Circles (Cylinders)

The formula for surface area of a right cylinder = 2(base area) + (base circumference)(height). The base area is given by πr^2, and the circumference of the base is given by $2\pi r$. Therefore, the entire expression for the surface area of a cylinder can be expressed as follows:

$$SA = 2\pi r^2 + 2\pi rh = 2\pi r(r+h)$$

By substituting in the given values, you get the following for the surface area of the cylinder:

$$SA = 2\pi(8)(8+15)$$
$$= 16\pi(23)$$
$$= 368\pi$$

The correct answer is (F).

99. **(A)** 7.5   Plane Geometry   Circles (Cylinders)

The formula for the volume of a right circular cylinder is given by the formula $V = hr^2\pi$, where h is the height of the cylinder and r is the radius of the circle on the base or top. In this problem, you are given the values of the volume and the radius, and must solve for the height, in feet:

$$V = hr^2\pi$$
$$(270\pi) = h(6)^2\pi$$
$$h = \frac{270\pi}{6^2\pi} = \frac{270}{36} = \frac{30}{4} = 7.5$$

Thus, the height of the cylinder is 7.5 feet. The correct answer is (A).

100. **(H)** $\dfrac{2(c+d)^2}{ab}$ Plane Geometry   Polygons (Area)

To solve this problem, divide the area of the square by the area of the right triangle. The area of the square is given by $A = s^2$, where s is the length of one of the sides of the square. Recall in the problem description that the circle is inscribed inside the square, which means that the circle touches each side of the square in the middle of that side. Therefore, the diameter of the circle is equal to the length of the sides of the square. It is also given in the problem that the hypotenuse of the triangle, $c + d$, is a diameter of the circle. Therefore, the hypotenuse length is also equal to the lengths of the sides of the square. The square has an area of $(c + d)^2$ square units.

Meanwhile, the area for a triangle is given by the formula $\dfrac{1}{2}bh$, where b is the base of the triangle and h is the height. In a right triangle, the legs (a and b in this case) always constitute the base and the height of the triangle. Therefore, the area of the triangle is $\dfrac{ab}{2}$. You can now express these areas as a ratio:

$$\frac{\text{Area of square}}{\text{Area of triangle}} = \frac{(c+d)^2}{\dfrac{ab}{2}} = \frac{2(c+d)^2}{ab}$$

The correct answer is (H).

101. **(E)** $2\pi e$ Plane Geometry   Circles (Circumference)

The formula for the circumference of a circle is given by the formula $2\pi r = \pi d$, where r is the radius of the circle and d is the diameter of the circle. In this problem, you are not given any variables that represent the diameter of the circle directly, but there are no fewer than 3 different variables that represent the radius: all of c, d, and e represent the lengths of line segments that connect the center of the circle to its edge. Therefore, by definition, all 3 measures are radii, and the correct answer could be $2\pi c$, $2\pi d$, or $2\pi e$. Only $2\pi e$ is available. The correct answer is (E).

102. **(G)** $\dfrac{6}{5}$ Plane Geometry   Triangles (Perimeter)

Because $\triangle ABC$, $\triangle DEF$, and $\triangle GHJ$ are all similar triangles, the corresponding sides among the three triangles will always have the same ratio (i.e., they will always be in the same proportion). Because the perimeter of a triangle is the sum of its sides, the ratio of the perimeters of the triangles will equal the ratio of the corresponding side lengths of the triangles.

15

In this case, $\overline{AC}$, $\overline{DF}$, and $\overline{GJ}$ are all the hypotenuses of their respective triangles. Therefore:

$$\frac{\text{Perimeter of } \triangle ABC}{\text{Perimeter of } \triangle GHJ} = \frac{\overline{AC}}{\overline{GJ}} = \frac{1}{5}$$

$$\frac{\text{Perimeter of } \triangle DEF}{\text{Perimeter of } \triangle GHJ} = \frac{\overline{DF}}{\overline{GJ}} = \frac{2}{3}$$

You are given the length of $\overline{DF}$ and must first solve for $\overline{GJ}$ on the way to solving for $\overline{AC}$:

$$\frac{\overline{DF}}{\overline{GJ}} = \frac{2}{3} \qquad\qquad \frac{\overline{AC}}{\overline{GJ}} = \frac{1}{5}$$

$$\frac{4}{\overline{GJ}} = \frac{2}{3} \qquad\qquad \frac{\overline{AC}}{6} = \frac{1}{5}$$

$$\overline{GJ} = \frac{3 \cdot 4}{2} = 6 \qquad\qquad \overline{AC} = \frac{6 \cdot 1}{5} = \frac{6}{5}$$

Thus, the length of $\overline{AC}$ is $\frac{6}{5}$ meters. The correct answer is (G).

103. **(C)** 20   Plane Geometry   Polygons (Area)

Because $ABCD$, $AEFG$ and $AHJK$ are all similar rectangles, the corresponding sides among the three rectangles will always have the same ratio (i.e., they will always be in the same proportion). Because the area of a rectangle is the product of the length and the width of the rectangle, the areas with be in a ratio that is the square of the ratio of the corresponding sides. For example, if one rectangle has sides that are all double the length of that of another, similar rectangle, it will have 4 times the area of the other rectangle. Similarly, if one rectangle has sides that are all triple the length of that of another, similar rectangle, it will have 9 times the area of the other rectangle. And so on.

In this case, $\overline{AD}$, $\overline{AG}$, and $\overline{AK}$ are all widths of their respective rectangles. Therefore:

$$\frac{\text{Area of } ABCD}{\text{Area of } AEFG} = \left(\frac{\overline{AD}}{\overline{AG}}\right)\left(\frac{\overline{AB}}{\overline{AE}}\right) = \left(\frac{\overline{AD}}{\overline{AG}}\right)^2 = \frac{1}{4}$$

$$\frac{\overline{AD}}{\overline{AG}} = \sqrt{\frac{1}{4}} = \frac{1}{2}$$

$$\frac{\text{Area of } AEFG}{\text{Area of } AHJK} = \left(\frac{\overline{AG}}{\overline{AK}}\right)\left(\frac{\overline{AE}}{\overline{AH}}\right) = \left(\frac{\overline{AG}}{\overline{AK}}\right)^2 = \frac{9}{25}$$

$$\frac{\overline{AG}}{\overline{AK}} = \sqrt{\frac{9}{25}} = \frac{3}{5}$$

You are given the length of $\overline{AD}$ and must first solve for $\overline{AG}$ on the way to solving for $\overline{AK}$:

$$\frac{\overline{AD}}{\overline{AG}} = \frac{1}{2} \qquad\qquad \frac{\overline{AG}}{\overline{AK}} = \frac{3}{5}$$

$$\frac{6}{\overline{AG}} = \frac{1}{2} \qquad\qquad \frac{12}{\overline{AK}} = \frac{3}{5}$$

$$\overline{AG} = \frac{6 \cdot 2}{1} = 12 \qquad \overline{AK} = \frac{12 \cdot 5}{3} = 20$$

Thus, the length of $\overline{AK}$ is 20 meters. The correct answer is (C).

104. **(J)** 50   Plane Geometry   Triangles (Area)

The mosaic dimensions are 20 inches by 15 inches. Two triangular tiles must be arranged top to bottom to form a double-tile rectangle with dimensions 4 inches by 3 inches:

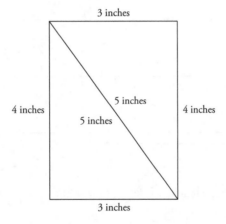

When double-tile rectangles are laid vertically, 5 of them can fit top to bottom along the length of the mosaic, because 20 inches ÷ 4 inches = 5. Similarly, 5 double-tile rectangles can fit side-to-side along the width of the mosaic, because 15 inches ÷ 3 inches = 5.

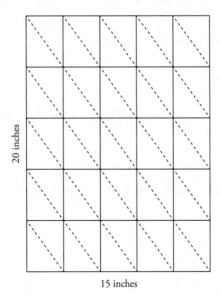

Therefore, 5 × 5 = 25 double-tile rectangles can fit within the 20 inch-by-15 inch dimensions of the mosaic. Because each double-tile rectangle consists of 2 tiles, (25)(2) = 50 tiles will be required.

Alternatively, you could calculate that the mosaic is 20" × 15" = 300 square inches, and that each tile is $\frac{1}{2} \times 3" \times 4" =$ 6 square inches. Therefore, the mosaic should require 300 ÷ 6 = 50 tiles to be covered fully. This assumes, of course, that the dimensions of the mosaic are perfectly divisible by the dimensions of the tile. In this case this assumption holds. The correct answer is (J).

105. (A) $24 + 5\sqrt{2}$ Plane Geometry   Triangles (Lines and Angles)

It is given in the problem that $\overline{GJ} \parallel \overline{DF} \parallel \overline{AC}$ and that $\overline{AG}$ is perpendicular to all 3 lines. Therefore, you can draw two more lines parallel to $\overline{AG}$ (that is, perpendicular to $\overline{GJ}$, $\overline{DF}$, and $\overline{AC}$) at points B and E. By doing so, you can create 2 right triangles to work with and dissect the length of $\overline{GH}$ into 3 pieces to add up:

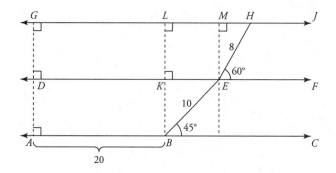

Note that new points K, L, and M have been labeled. Use the new points to solve for the length of $\overline{GH}$ by decomposing it into three pieces:

$$\overline{GH} = \overline{GL} + \overline{LM} + \overline{MH}$$

Also note that by adding these perpendicular lines, two right triangles ($\triangle BEK$ and $\triangle EHM$) and a rectangle ($EMLK$) have been added. Since $EMLK$ is a rectangle, $\overline{LM} = \overline{KE}$. Also note that $ABKD$ and $DKLG$ are newly formed rectangles. Therefore, $\overline{GL} = \overline{DK} = \overline{AB} = 20$. Now express $\overline{GH}$ as follows:

$$\overline{GH} = \overline{AB} + \overline{KE} + \overline{MH} = 20 + \overline{KE} + \overline{MH}$$

Now analyze the right triangles. $\angle KBC$ is a right angle because the lines are perpendicular by construction. Therefore, $\angle KBE = \angle KBC - \angle EBC = 90° - 45° = 45°$. $\angle EKB$ is also a right angle by construction, so $\angle KEB = 180° - 90° - 45° = 45°$.

$\triangle BEK$ is therefore a 45°–45°–90° triangle, and 45°–45°–90° triangles always have side lengths in the ratio $1 : 1 : \sqrt{2}$. As a result, $\overline{KE} = 10 \div \sqrt{2} = 5\sqrt{2}$.

Now express $\overline{GH}$ as follows:

$$\overline{GH} = \overline{AB} + \overline{KE} + \overline{MH} = 20 + 5\sqrt{2} + \overline{MH}$$

15

Finally, analyze right triangle $\triangle EHM$. $\angle MEF$ is a right angle, because the lines are perpendicular by construction. Therefore, $\angle MEH = \angle MEF - \angle HEF = 90° - 60° = 30°$. $\angle HME$ is also a right angle by construction, so $\angle MHE = 180° - 90° - 30° = 60°$.

$\triangle EHM$ is therefore a $30°$–$60°$–$90°$ triangle, and $30°$–$60°$–$90°$ triangles always have side lengths in the ratio $1 : \sqrt{3} : 2$. As a result, $\overline{MH} = 8 \div 2 = 4$. (Note that $\overline{MH}$ corresponds to the "1" portion of the 3-part ratio, not the "$\sqrt{3}$" portion!)

You can finally express $\overline{GH}$ as follows, and simplify:

$$\overline{GH} = \overline{AB} + \overline{KE} + \overline{MH} = 20 + 5\sqrt{2} + 4 = 24 + 5\sqrt{2}$$

The correct answer is (D).

106. **(G)** $3:5$ Plane Geometry   Polygons

Every square is similar to every other square: they may have different sizes, but they all have the same shape. As a result, if Square A has sides that are twice as long as Square B's sides, then Square A also has a diagonal that's twice as long and a perimeter that's twice as long. (If the side of a square is s, then the diagonal is always $s\sqrt{2}$, and the perimeter is always $4s$. These formulas never vary, because all squares have the same shape.) Anything about Squares A and B measured in units of length would have a ratio of $2:1$, and the areas of the squares would just have a ratio of $2^2 : 1^2$, or $4:1$. This sort of relationship holds for any two figures that are similar.

In the specific case of the problem, since the ratio of the diagonals is $3:5$, then the ratio of the sides will also be $3:5$, and so will the ratio of the perimeters.

If you want to see the proof, here you go. Since the ratio of the diagonals is $3:5$, you can actually say that the diagonal of Square A is 3 units of some kind, and the diagonal of Square B must be 5 units of the same kind. Then each side of Square A is $\dfrac{3}{\sqrt{2}}$ units long, while each side of Square B is $\dfrac{5}{\sqrt{2}}$ units long. (Notice that the sides will still have a ratio of $3:5$.) Finally, the perimeter of Square A is $4 \times \dfrac{3}{\sqrt{2}} = \dfrac{12}{\sqrt{2}}$ units, while the perimeter of Square B is $4 \times \dfrac{5}{\sqrt{2}} = \dfrac{20}{\sqrt{2}}$ units.

The ratio of the perimeters is thus $\dfrac{12}{\sqrt{2}} : \dfrac{20}{\sqrt{2}} = 12:20 = 3:5$. Avoid doing this derivation on the ACT itself, of course, if you can help it. The correct answer is (G).

107. **(A)** $3:4$ Plane Geometry   Circles

If the ratio of the areas of two circles is $9:16$, then the ratio of any "linear measures" (radius, diameter, or circumference) of the circles will be $\sqrt{9} : \sqrt{16}$, or $3:4$. Here's why. As a starting point, imagine that one circle has radius 3. Then the area of that circle will be $\pi r^2 = 9\pi$. If you want the ratio of the areas to be $9:16$, then the other circle has to have area 16π, meaning that its radius is 4. The radii are then in a ratio of $3:4$. A diameter is double the radius, so the diameters will be in a ratio of $6:8$, which reduces to $3:4$ again. (By the way, the circumferences will be in a ratio of $6\pi : 8\pi$, which also reduces to $3:4$.)

15

Therefore, if the areas of two similar figures (such as circles, squares, equilateral triangles, etc.) are in a ratio of $a:b$, then any linear measure—a radius, a side, a diagonal, anything you would measure in units of length, not area—will be in a ratio of $\sqrt{a}:\sqrt{b}$. The correct answer is (A).

108. (H) 54   Plane Geometry   Polygons (Area of a Parallelogram)

The area of a parallelogram is given by the formula $A = bh$, where b is the base and h is the height. The base and height must be perpendicular to each other, so the easiest way to assign the base and height in this example is to set the base equal to $\overline{AD} = 13$. Because $ABCD$ is a parallelogram, $\overline{AD}$ is parallel to $\overline{BC}$, and since $\overline{AE}$ is perpendicular to $\overline{BC}$, it must also be perpendicular to $\overline{AD}$. Therefore, the height = $\overline{AD}$ = 6. This makes the area of the entire parallelogram $13 \times 6 = 78$.

In order to compute the area of $AECD$, subtract the area of the right triangle $\triangle ABE$ from the area of the parallelogram. The formula for the area of a triangle is $A = \frac{1}{2}bh$. The lengths of $\overline{AB}$ (the hypotenuse) and $\overline{AE}$ (the height) are known, so you can use them to solve for $\overline{BE}$ (the base) using the Pythagorean theorem:

$$\left(\overline{AE}\right)^2 + \left(\overline{BE}\right)^2 = \left(\overline{AB}\right)^2$$
$$6^2 + \left(\overline{BE}\right)^2 = 10^2$$
$$\left(\overline{BE}\right)^2 = 10^2 - 6^2$$
$$\overline{BE} = \sqrt{100 - 36} = \sqrt{64} = 8$$

Therefore, the area of the triangle $\triangle ABE$ is $\frac{1}{2}(8)(6) = 24$, and the area of $AECD = 78 - 24 = 54$. The correct answer is (H).

109. (D) $32\sqrt{2}$ Plane Geometry   Polygons (Area)

It is given in the problem that $\triangle AEH$, $\triangle BEF$, $\triangle CFG$, and $\triangle DGH$ are all equal 45°–45°–90° triangles. Mark the diagram accordingly:

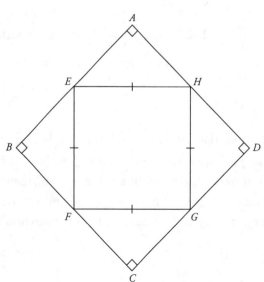

Furthermore, it is given that the area of *EFGH* is 64. Since all sides of *EFGH* are equal, it is a square, and each side is $\sqrt{64} = 8$ units in length. These sides all correspond to the hypotenuses of the 45°–45°–90° triangles.

You can therefore solve for the lengths of all of the legs of the 45°–45°–90° triangles. Since they are isosceles, all of the legs must be of equal length. Assigning the variable *x* to the length of any of the legs of the 45°–45°–90° triangles and using the Pythagorean theorem for any one such triangle, you have:

$$x^2 + x^2 = 8^2$$
$$2x^2 = 64$$
$$x^2 = 32$$
$$x = \sqrt{32} = \sqrt{2 \cdot 2 \cdot 2 \cdot 2 \cdot 2} = 4\sqrt{2}$$

Each of the legs of the right triangles is therefore $4\sqrt{2}$ in length. Since the perimeter of *ABCD* is comprised of 8 such legs, the perimeter of the *ABCD* is $(8)4\sqrt{2} = 32\sqrt{2}$. The correct answer is (D).

110. **(K)** $\overline{CE}$ is congruent to $\overline{BF}$.   Plane Geometry   Triangles (Proofs)

The question asks you to determine which of the choices does not necessarily have to be true given the information in the problem description and the diagram. The best way to answer the question is to try to prove (or disprove) each of the choices:

F. *The area of △BCF is equal to the area of △BCG.* This must be true. $\overline{BF} \parallel \overline{GE}$, so $\overline{AD}$ is a transversal of $\overline{BF}$ and $\overline{GE}$, as are $\overline{BG}$ and $\overline{FC}$. Alternating angles in a transversal are equal to each other, so you can conclude the following:

$$\angle FBG = \angle BGC = 90°$$
$$\angle BFC = \angle FCG = 90°$$
$$\angle ECD = \angle BCG = \angle CBF$$

As a result, you know that $\angle BGC = \angle BFC = 90°$ and $\angle BCG = \angle CBF$. Since all angles of a triangle must add up to 180°, you have the following:

$$\angle BGC + \angle CBG + \angle BCG = 180°$$
$$\angle BFC + \angle BCF + \angle CBF = 180°$$

Substituting, you get the following:

$$\angle BGC + \angle CBG + \angle BCG = \angle BFC + \angle BCF + \angle CBF$$
$$\angle BFC + \angle CBG + \angle CBF = \angle BFC + \angle BCF + \angle CBF$$
$$\angle CBG = \angle BCF$$

You have now demonstrated that △*BCF* and △*BCG* are similar triangles, because the 3 angle measures in one triangle are equal to the corresponding angle measures in the other triangle. Furthermore, the two triangles are right triangles that share a hypotenuse ($\overline{BC}$), so all of the sides of the two triangles must be equal. They are identical triangles and thus have the same area.

G. **ΔCED is similar to ΔBCF.** This also must be true. As demonstrated above, ∠ECD = ∠CBF, and both ∠BFC and ∠CED are 90° angles. Therefore, you can undergo a similar exercise to that above to demonstrate that ΔCED is similar to ΔBCF, because the 3 angle measures in one triangle are equal to the corresponding angle measures in the other triangle.

H. $\overline{BG}$ *is congruent to* $\overline{CF}$. This also must be true. As demonstrated above, ∠BFC = ∠FBG = ∠BGC = ∠FCG = 90°. Therefore, BGCF is a rectangle and opposite sides of a rectangle are equal.

J. $\overline{CF}$ *is perpendicular to* $\overline{GE}$. This also must be true. As stated above, ∠BFC = ∠FBG = ∠BGC = ∠FCG = 90°, so BGCF is a rectangle. Adjacent sides of a rectangle are perpendicular.

K. **$\overline{CE}$ is congruent to $\overline{BF}$.** This is not necessarily true. It has been demonstrated above that ΔCED is similar to ΔBCF. However, you have no evidence that corresponding sides of the triangles are of equal length. For example, none of the given information precludes the diagram from looking like the one below, and all other choices can be proven to be true, so this choice must be the correct answer:

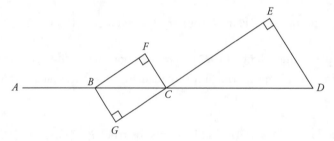

The correct answer is (K).

111. **(A)** $\dfrac{63}{82}$ Plane Geometry   Polygons (Area)

The question asks you to determine the ratio of the areas of the shaded and unshaded regions based on an incomplete listing of the lengths of all of the sides of the 10-sided object. However, it is given in the problem that all of the line segments are either vertical or horizontal. Therefore, all of the line segments are perpendicular to one another, and the sum of the lengths of the horizontal line segments at the top must equal the sum of the horizontal line segments at the bottom. Similarly, the sum of the lengths of the vertical line segments at the left must equal the sum of the vertical line segments at the right. Assign x and y to the lengths of the unknown sides:

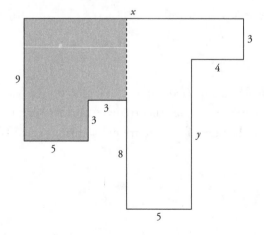

It must be the case that $x = 5 + 3 + 5 + 4 = 17$. Furthermore, $y + 3 = 9 + 8 - 3$, so $y = 11$. Now calculate the area of each component of the diagram.

The shaded region is a rectangle, minus a 3-by-3 square. The dimensions of the rectangle are 9 by $5 + 3 = 8$. Therefore, the area of the rectangle is $9 \times 8 = 72$ and the area of the shaded region is $72 - 3 \times 3 = 72 - 9 = 63$.

The unshaded region is also a rectangle minus another shape. In this case, the larger rectangle is $11 + 3 = 14$ by $5 + 4 = 9$. Therefore, its area is $14 \times 9 = 126$. The missing piece of the region is 11 by 4, so its area is $11 \times 3 = 44$. Therefore, the area of the unshaded region is $126 - 44 = 82$.

Alternatively, you can add two rectangles together to get the unshaded region: the left portion of the unshaded region is a 14-by-5 rectangle, so its area is $14 \times 5 = 70$, and the right portion is a 4-by-3 rectangle, so its area is $4 \times 3 = 12$. Finally, $70 + 12 = 82$.

Therefore, the ratio of the areas of the shaded region and the unshaded region is $\dfrac{63}{82}$. The correct answer is (A).

112. **(G)** $8\dfrac{1}{3}$%   Geometry   Circles (Lines and Angles)

In order for Gus to win the game, the result of his spin must land on one of two 50-point sectors. To find the central angle measure for each 50-point sector, subtract the other central angle measures from 360° and divide by 2:

$$2x = 360° - 1(135°) - 3(45°) - 2(30°)$$
$$= 360° - 135° - 135° - 60° = 30°$$
$$2x = 30°$$
$$x = 15°$$

You must now find what percent of the board the two 50-point sectors constitute. To do this, take the ratio of the sum of their central angle measures to 360°:

$$\frac{15° + 15°}{360°} = \frac{30°}{360°} = \frac{1}{12} = 8.3\overline{3}\% = 8\frac{1}{3}\%.$$

The correct answer is (G).

113. **(E)** 35   Geometry   Polygons

If you like formulas, the formula for the number of diagonals in an n-sided polygon is: $\dfrac{n(n-3)}{2}$.

According to this formula, the given hexagon would in fact have $\dfrac{6(3)}{2} = 9$ diagonals.

The decagon, or 10-sided polygon, would have $\dfrac{10(7)}{2} = 35$ diagonals.

However, if (like most people) you didn't know the formula for the number of diagonals, it is difficult to draw the diagonals of a decagon and count them. You could use some reasoning instead. Each vertex of the decagon is connected to each of 7 other vertices with a diagonal (7 since there are 10 vertices overall and you don't count the vertex itself or its two closest neighbors, which are already connected to the vertex by a side). However, you can't just multiply each of the 10 vertices by 7. That double-counts the diagonals.

Start with vertex A somewhere, and draw 7 diagonals from it. Do the same thing for every other one of the 10 vertices (B, C, etc.), always drawing 7 diagonals. Redraw if necessary. What you'll see is that you'll draw each diagonal exactly twice. For instance, you first draw a diagonal from A to C as you draw all the diagonals radiating from A. Then, while you're drawing all the diagonals radiating from C, you'll redraw that one from C to A. Every pair of points that share a diagonal would be counted twice if you multiply 10 vertices by 7 diagonals each. So you divide 70 by 2 to get 35. The correct answer is (E).

114. (G) 9   Plane Geometry   Polygons (3D Objects)

The large cube's dimensions are 3 times larger than those of the smaller cube. For any side length, the ratio of the larger cube's edge to the smaller cube's edge will be $3:1$. If you assume that the edge length of the smaller cube is s, then the larger cube's edge length will be $3s$.

The surface area of the smaller cube is the sum of the area of each of the cube's 6 faces: $6s^2$. The surface area of the larger cube is the sum of the area of each of that cube's 6 faces: $6(3s)^2 = 6(9s^2) = 54s^2$. By comparing the larger cube's surface area to that of the smaller cube, you can see that $54s^2$ is exactly 9 times larger than $6s^2$. The correct answer is (G).

115. (A) $\dfrac{5\pi}{6}$ Plane Geometry   Circles (Lines and Angles)

You are told that $\overline{WZ}$ forms a diameter of circle O, so you know that the angles on either side of $\overline{WZ}$ sum to 180°. (It is often easier to do angle computations in degrees first, then switch to radians at the end.) You are also told that $\angle b = 2(\angle a)$, and that $\angle c = 3(\angle a)$. These three angles constitute 180° of the circle. Now solve for $\angle a$ by substituting:

$$\angle a + \angle b + \angle c = 180$$
$$\angle a + 2\angle a + 3\angle a = 180$$
$$6\angle a = 180$$
$$\angle a = 30°$$

Therefore $\angle b = 2(30°) = 60°$, and $\angle c = 3(30°) = 90°$. It is given in the problem that $\angle d = 2(\angle b)$, so $\angle d = 2(60°) = 120°$. Now that you have assigned degree measures for all of the unknown angles, solve for $\angle b + \angle d - \angle a = 60° + 120° - 30° = 150°$.

Finally, convert 150° into radians by multiplying the degree value by $\dfrac{\pi}{180°}$:

$$150° \times \frac{\pi}{180°} = \frac{5\pi}{6}$$

The correct answer is (A).

Chapter 16

of

5lb. Book of ACT® Practice Problems

Math:

Trigonometry

In This Chapter...

Trigonometry Problems & Solutions

Chapter 16
Math: Trigonometry

The Math problems in this chapter are drawn from trigonometry. The topics include the following:

1. Triangle Ratios. Working with trigonometric quantities as ratios of the sides of a triangle.

2. Trig Functions. Trigonometric functions and their graphs.

3. Trig Laws. Law of sines and law of cosines.

How should you use this chapter? Here are some recommendations, according to the level you've reached in ACT Math.

1. Fundamentals. Start slowly with the easier problems at the beginning. Do at least some of these problems untimed. This way, you give yourself a chance to think deeply about the principles at work. Review the solutions closely, and articulate what you've learned. Redo problems as necessary.

2. Fixes. Do a few problems untimed, examine the results, learn your lessons, then test yourself with longer timed sets.

3. Tweaks. Confirm your mastery by doing longer sets of problems under timed conditions. Aim to improve the speed and ease of your solution process. Mix the problems up by jumping around in the chapter.

Good luck on the problems!

1. In right triangle $\triangle DEF$ shown below, which of the following statements is true for $\angle D$?

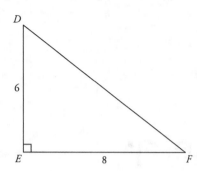

A. $\cos D = \dfrac{3}{4}$

B. $\sin D = \dfrac{3}{4}$

C. $\cos D = \dfrac{4}{3}$

D. $\tan D = \dfrac{4}{5}$

E. $\tan D = \dfrac{4}{3}$

2. For right triangle $\triangle JKM$ shown below, which of the following expressions is equal to $\dfrac{1}{\tan J}$?

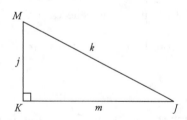

F. $\dfrac{m}{j}$

G. $\dfrac{j}{k}$

H. $\dfrac{j}{m}$

J. $\dfrac{m}{k}$

K. $\dfrac{k}{j}$

3. For right triangle $\triangle ABC$ shown below, which of the following trigonometric measures is greater than 1?

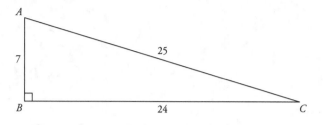

A. $\sin A$

B. $\cos A$

C. $\tan A$

D. $\sin C$

E. $\tan C$

4. In the following diagram, which of the following expressions gives the correct length of $\overline{AC}$ in triangle $\triangle ABC$?

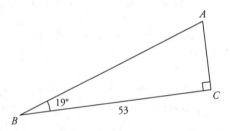

F. $\dfrac{53}{\cos 71°}$

G. $\dfrac{53}{\tan 19°}$

H. $53 \tan 19°$

J. $53 \cos 19°$

K. $53 \cos 71°$

16

5. The diagram of a pool is below. The builder included the length of the pool in meters, but forgot to include the width, $\overline{CD}$. Which of the following expressions gives the length, in meters, of $\overrightarrow{CD}$?

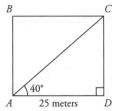

A. $\dfrac{25}{\cos 40°}$

B. $\dfrac{25}{\tan 40°}$

C. $25 \sin 40°$

D. $25 \cos 40°$

E. $25 \tan 40°$

6. In triangle $\triangle DEF$ below, the lengths of the sides are given in inches, with $0 < x < 3$. What is the cotangent of $\angle E$, in terms of x?

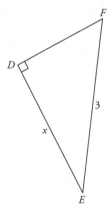

F. $\dfrac{3}{x}$

G. $\dfrac{x}{3}$

H. $1 - \dfrac{3}{x}$

J. $\dfrac{x}{\sqrt{9 - x^2}}$

K. $\dfrac{\sqrt{9 - x^2}}{x}$

7. A ramp must be built to reach a height of 5 feet, with an incline of 18°. What is the length of the ramp, $\overline{AB}$ in feet?

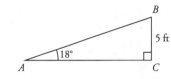

A. $\dfrac{5}{\sin 18°}$

B. $\dfrac{5}{\cos 18°}$

C. $5 \sin 18°$

D. $5 \cos 18°$

E. $5 \tan 18°$

> Use the following information to answer question 8.

In the figure below, $ABCD$ is a square with a circle centered at E inscribed inside of it. A right triangle is inscribed inside of the circle; its hypotenuse forms a diameter of the circle of length $c + d$. The lengths of the legs of the right triangle are a and b, where $0 < b < a$. The line segment connecting E and the right angle of the right triangle is of length e.

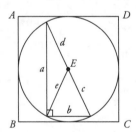

8. Which of the following statements correctly relates the length of a, c, d, and e?

F. $a < c < d < e$

G. $a > c > d > e$

H. $a = c = d < e$

J. $a > c = d = e$

K. $a > c = d > e$

16

9. Right triangle $\triangle XYZ$ has side lengths measured in feet, as drawn below. For triangle $\triangle XYZ$, $(\sin X)(\cos Y)$ is equivalent to:

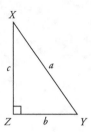

A. $\dfrac{b}{a}$

B. $\dfrac{c}{a}$

C. $\dfrac{b^2}{a^2}$

D. $\dfrac{c^2}{a^2}$

E. $\dfrac{bc}{a^2}$

10. Which of the following trigonometric functions is equivalent to the function $f(x) = \dfrac{\sin x}{\cos x}$?

F. $g(x) = \sin x$

G. $g(x) = \cos x$

H. $g(x) = \tan x$

J. $g(x) = \cot x$

K. $g(x) = \csc x$

11. Right triangle $\triangle XYZ$ has side lengths measured in meters, as drawn below. For triangle $\triangle XYZ$, $(\cos X)(\tan X)$ is equivalent to:

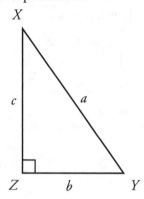

A. $\dfrac{b}{a}$

B. $\dfrac{c}{a}$

C. $\dfrac{b^2}{a^2}$

D. $\dfrac{c^2}{ab}$

E. $\dfrac{bc}{a^2}$

12. For the trigonometric function graphed below, the *x*-axis can be partitioned into intervals, each of length *d* radians, such that the curve over any one interval of length *d* is an exact repetition of the curve over each of the other intervals of length *d*. What is the least possible value for *d* for this function?

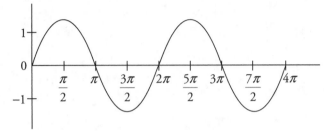

F. 3π

G. 2π

H. $\dfrac{3\pi}{2}$

J. π

K. $\dfrac{\pi}{2}$

13. A trigonometric function is graphed below in the standard (*x*, *y*) coordinate plane. The equation of the function is of the form $f(x) = y = a\cos(bx + c)$, where *a*, *b*, and *c* are constants. The graph regularly repeats itself. The period of the function is defined as the smallest positive number *r* such that $f(x + r) = f(x)$. Which of the following is the period of the function graphed below?

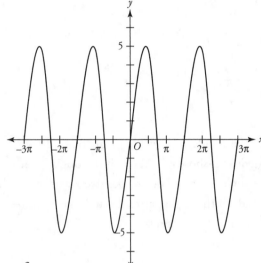

A. $\dfrac{3\pi}{4}$

B. $\dfrac{3\pi}{2}$

C. $\dfrac{\pi}{2}$

D. 3π

E. 6π

16

14. The value of tan θ is equal to -6.4 (rounded to the nearest tenth). Which of the following correctly indicates a range in which θ could fall?

F. $\dfrac{\pi}{4} < \theta < \dfrac{\pi}{3}$

G. $\dfrac{\pi}{3} < \theta < \dfrac{\pi}{2}$

H. $\dfrac{\pi}{2} < \theta < \dfrac{3\pi}{4}$

J. $\dfrac{3\pi}{4} < \theta < \dfrac{4\pi}{5}$

K. $\dfrac{4\pi}{5} < \theta < \pi$

15. In the standard (x, y) coordinate plane drawn below, the angle ψ is shown; its vertex is the origin. One side of the angle is located on the positive x-axis, while the other side of the angle passes through the point $(-7, 24)$. What is the value of sin ψ?

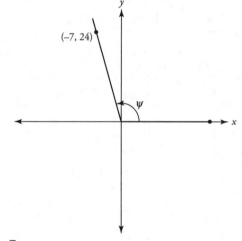

A. $-\dfrac{7}{24}$

B. $-\dfrac{7}{25}$

C. $-\dfrac{24}{25}$

D. $\dfrac{7}{25}$

E. $\dfrac{24}{25}$

16. If the value of sin $\theta = 1$, which of the following could be the value of θ?

F. $\dfrac{\pi}{2}$

G. $\dfrac{\pi}{4}$

H. $\dfrac{3\pi}{2}$

J. π

K. 2π

17. Which of the following expressions correctly represents the length of $\overline{DE}$ in triangle ΔDEF in the diagram below?

(Note: The law of cosines states that for any triangle with vertices A, B, and C and sides opposite those vertices with lengths a, b, and c, respectively, $c^2 = a^2 + b^2 - 2ab \cdot \cos C$.)

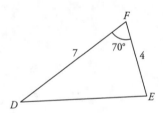

A. $\sqrt{49 + 16 - 2 \cdot 28 \cdot \cos 55°}$

B. $\sqrt{49 - 4 - 28 \cdot \cos 55°}$

C. $\sqrt{49 + 4 - 28 \cdot \cos 110°}$

D. $\sqrt{49 - 16 + 28 \cdot \cos 70°}$

E. $\sqrt{49 + 16 - 2 \cdot 28 \cdot \cos 70°}$

MANHATTAN
PREP

18. In the following diagram, which of the following expressions gives the correct length of $\overline{DF}$ in triangle $\triangle DEF$?

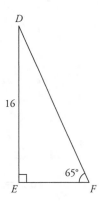

F. $\dfrac{16}{\sin 65°}$

G. $\dfrac{16}{\cos 65°}$

H. $\dfrac{16}{\tan 65°}$

J. $16 \sin 65°$

K. $16 \tan 65°$

19. Which of the following expressions correctly represents the length of $\overline{AB}$ in triangle $\triangle ABC$ in the diagram below?

(Note: The law of sines states that for any triangle with vertices X, Y, and Z and sides opposite those vertices with lengths x, y, and z, respectively,

$$\frac{\sin X}{x} = \frac{\sin Y}{y} = \frac{\sin Z}{z}.)$$

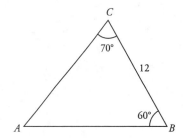

A. $\dfrac{\sin 60°}{12 \cdot \sin 70°}$

B. $12\left(\dfrac{\sin 60°}{\sin 70°}\right)$

C. $12\left(\dfrac{\sin 70°}{\sin 50°}\right)$

D. $12\left(\dfrac{\sin 60°}{\sin 50°}\right)$

E. $\dfrac{\sin 70°}{12 \cdot \sin 50°}$

16

20. In triangle $\triangle DEF$ below, the lengths of the sides are given in meters, with $x > y > 0$. What is the tangent of $\angle D$, in terms of x and y?

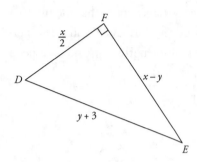

F. $2 - \dfrac{2y}{x}$

G. $x - \dfrac{2x}{y}$

H. $\dfrac{x-y}{2x}$

J. $\dfrac{x}{2x-2y}$

K. $\dfrac{x}{2x+y}$

21. If $\cos A = \dfrac{x}{z}$, $x > 0$, $z > 0$, and $0 < A < 90°$, what is $\tan A$ in terms of x and z?

A. $\dfrac{\sqrt{z^2 - x^2}}{x}$

B. $\dfrac{x}{\sqrt{z^2 - x^2}}$

C. $\dfrac{\sqrt{z^2 - x^2}}{\sqrt{x^2 - z^2}}$

D. $\dfrac{z}{x}$

E. $\dfrac{z^2 - x}{x}$

22. Which of the following trigonometric functions is equivalent to the function $f(x) = \cos x \csc x$?

(Note: $\csc x = \dfrac{1}{\sin x}$)

    F. $g(x) = \sin x$

    G. $g(x) = \cos x$

    H. $g(x) = \tan x$

    J. $g(x) = \cot x$

    K. $g(x) = \csc x$

23. In right triangle $\triangle ABC$ below, $\tan B = 1\dfrac{1}{3}$. What is the unit length of $\overline{BC}$?

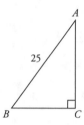

    A. 3

    B. 5

    C. 12.5

    D. 15

    E. 20

MANHATTAN
PREP

24. In the standard (x, y) coordinate plane drawn below, the angle ζ is shown; its vertex is the origin. One side of the angle is located on the positive x-axis, while the other side of the angle consists of a line segment 18 units long that ends 12 units below the x-axis. What is the value of $\tan \zeta$?

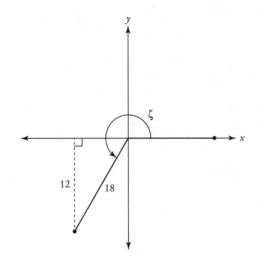

F. $-\dfrac{2\sqrt{5}}{3}$

G. $-\dfrac{2\sqrt{10}}{3}$

H. $\dfrac{2\sqrt{5}}{5}$

J. $\dfrac{2\sqrt{5}}{3}$

K. $\dfrac{2\sqrt{3}}{3}$

25. In the right triangle given below, x is the measure of the marked angle and y is the length of the hypotenuse. If $\sin x = \dfrac{\sqrt{3}}{2}$, what is y?

A. $15\sqrt{2}$

B. $10\sqrt{3}$

C. $\dfrac{10\sqrt{3}}{3}$

D. 30

E. 20

26. For the angle ϕ, which of the following could be the value of $\tan \phi$ if $180° < \phi < 225°$?

F. -12

G. $-\dfrac{3}{4}$

H. 12

J. $\dfrac{4}{3}$

K. $\dfrac{3}{4}$

27. For the angle Υ, where $135° < \Upsilon < 180°$, $\sin \Upsilon = \dfrac{3}{5}$. What is the value of $\cos \Upsilon$?

A. $-\dfrac{4}{5}$

B. $-\dfrac{3}{4}$

C. $-\dfrac{3}{5}$

D. $\dfrac{3}{4}$

E. $\dfrac{4}{5}$

28. The hypotenuse of the right triangle $\triangle XYZ$ shown below is 31 meters long. The cosine of $\angle X$ is $\dfrac{5}{13}$. About how many meters long is $\overline{XY}$?

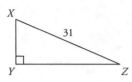

F.   11.9

G.   15.5

H.   18.6

J.   23.8

K.   28.6

29. In the right triangle $\triangle ABC$ shown below, $\overline{BC}$ is 67 feet long. If the tangent of $\angle A$ is 1.5, approximately how many feet long is $\overline{AB}$?

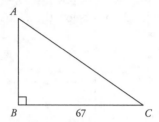

A.   33.5

B.   44.7

C.   51.8

D.   100.5

E.   116.0

Answer Key

Write in whether you got each problem right or wrong (or left it blank). If your answer was correct, put a 1 in every blank to the right of that problem. Sum up each column and compare your total to the total possible "Out Of" points.

Problem	Correct Answer	Right/Wrong/Blank
1	E	
2	F	
3	C	
4	H	
5	E	
6	J	
7	A	
8	J	
9	C	
10	H	
11	A	
12	G	
13	B	
14	H	
15	E	
16	F	
17	E	
18	F	
19	C	
20	F	
21	A	
22	J	
23	D	
24	H	
25	E	
26	K	

Problem	Correct Answer	Right/Wrong/Blank
27	A	
28	F	
29	B	
Total		
Out Of		29

16

Trigonometry Solutions

1. **(E)** $\tan D = \dfrac{4}{3}$ Trigonometry   Triangle Ratios

The trigonometric functions for an angle in a right triangle are defined as follows:

$$\cos D = \frac{\text{adjacent}}{\text{hypotenuse}}$$

$$\sin D = \frac{\text{opposite}}{\text{hypotenuse}}$$

$$\tan D = \frac{\text{opposite}}{\text{adjacent}}$$

The hypotenuse of any right triangle can be calculated using the Pythagorean theorem, i.e., $a^2 + b^2 = c^2$. In this case, $6^2 + 8^2 = c^2$, so $c^2 = 100$ and $c = 10$. The values of the trigonometric functions for $\angle D$ are as follows:

$$\cos D = \frac{6}{10} = \frac{3}{5}$$

$$\sin D = \frac{8}{10} = \frac{4}{5}$$

$$\tan D = \frac{8}{6} = \frac{4}{3}$$

The correct answer is $\tan D = \dfrac{4}{3}$. The correct answer is (E).

2. **(F)** $\dfrac{m}{j}$ Trigonometry   Triangle Ratios

The tangent of an angle in a right triangle is the opposite side over the adjacent side, or $\dfrac{\text{Opposite}}{\text{Adjacent}}$. Therefore, the reciprocal of the tangent of an angle, such as $\dfrac{1}{\tan J}$, is that fraction flipped, or $\dfrac{\text{Adjacent}}{\text{Opposite}}$.

For angle J, the adjacent side is m, while the opposite side is j. Thus, $\dfrac{1}{\tan J} = \dfrac{\text{Adjacent}}{\text{Opposite}} = \dfrac{m}{j}$.

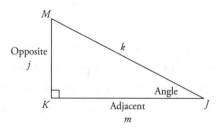

The correct answer is (F).

16

3.   **(C)** tan *A*   Trigonometry   Triangle Ratios

The trigonometric functions for an angle in a right triangle are defined as follows:

$$\cos A = \frac{\text{adjacent}}{\text{hypotenuse}}$$

$$\sin A = \frac{\text{opposite}}{\text{hypotenuse}}$$

$$\tan A = \frac{\text{opposite}}{\text{adjacent}}$$

The values of the trigonometric functions for $\angle A$ and $\angle C$ in $\triangle ABC$ are as follows:

$$\sin A = \frac{24}{25} \qquad\qquad \sin C = \frac{7}{25}$$

$$\cos A = \frac{7}{25} \qquad\qquad \cos C = \frac{24}{25}$$

$$\tan A = \frac{24}{7} \qquad\qquad \tan C = \frac{7}{24}$$

Only tan *A* is larger than 1.

Note that choices (A), (B), and (D) can be eliminated immediately, because sin and cos can never be larger than 1; the opposite and adjacent sides of an angle in a right triangle will always be smaller than the hypotenuse. The correct answer is (C).

4.   **(H)** 53 tan 19°   Trigonometry   Triangle Ratios

The trigonometric functions for an angle in a right triangle are defined as follows:

$$\cos A = \frac{\text{adjacent}}{\text{hypotenuse}}$$

$$\sin A = \frac{\text{opposite}}{\text{hypotenuse}}$$

$$\tan A = \frac{\text{opposite}}{\text{adjacent}}$$

In the diagram, you are given the measure of $\angle B$ as well as the length of $\overline{BC}$ which is the side adjacent to the angle. The question asks for the expression for the length of $\overline{AC}$ the side opposite $\angle B$. The tangent is the trigonometric function that relates the opposite and adjacent sides. Therefore, you can restate the above formula for the tangent of an angle as follows and solve for $\overline{AC}$:

$$\tan \angle B = \frac{\text{opposite}}{\text{adjacent}} = \frac{\overline{AC}}{\overline{BC}}$$

$$\tan 19° = \frac{\overline{AC}}{53}$$

$$\overline{AC} = 53 \tan 19°$$

The correct answer is (H).

5.   **(E)** $25 \tan 40°$ Trigonometry   Triangle Ratios

Because the question wants you to relate the side opposite the given angle with the side adjacent the given angle, you can use the tangent ratio:

$$\tan \angle A = \frac{\text{opposite}}{\text{adjacent}}$$

$$\tan 40° = \frac{x}{25}$$

$$25 \tan 40° = x$$

The correct answer is (E).

6.   **(J)** $\dfrac{x}{\sqrt{9-x^2}}$ Trigonometry   Triangle Ratios

The cotangent function for an angle in a right triangle is defined as follows:

$$\cot A = \frac{\text{side adjacent to angle } A}{\text{side opposite angle } A}$$

The lengths of the hypotenuse and adjacent side for $\angle E$ are labeled, but the length of opposite side, $\overline{DF}$, is not. Therefore, calculate the expression for the length of $\overline{DF}$ in terms of x and 3. Using the Pythagorean theorem:

$$a^2 + b^2 = c^2$$

$$\left(\overline{DF}\right)^2 + x^2 = 3^2$$

$$\left(\overline{DF}\right)^2 = 9 - x^2$$

$$\overline{DF} = \sqrt{9 - x^2}$$

Now you can calculate the answer by substituting:

$$\cot \angle E = \frac{\text{side adjacent to } \angle E}{\text{side opposite } \angle E}$$

$$= \frac{x}{\sqrt{9 - x^2}}$$

The correct answer is (J).

16

7. **(A)** $\dfrac{5}{\sin 18°}$ Trigonometry   Triangle Ratios

Because the question wants you to relate the side opposite the given angle with the hypotenuse, you can use the sine ratio:

$$\sin \angle A = \frac{\text{opposite}}{\text{hypotenuse}}$$

$$\sin 18° = \frac{5}{x}$$

$$x \sin 18° = 5$$

$$x = \frac{5}{\sin 18°}$$

The correct answer is (A).

8. **(J)** $a > c = d = e$ Plane Geometry   Triangles and Diagonals

It is noted in the problem that $a > b$ and a and b make up the lengths of a right triangle inscribed inside a circle. The hypotenuse of the inscribed triangle constitutes a diameter of the circle (in this problem, the length of the hypotenuse is represented by the expression $c + d$, where c and d are radii of the circle, because they connect the center of the circle to the edge of the circle).

Because the hypotenuse represents a straight line through the circle while a and b connect to the same points but NOT in a straight line, it must be the case that $a + b > c + d$. Since a is larger than b and c is equal to d (both are radii), it must be the case that $a > c$, $a > d$, and $c = d$. Therefore, $a > c = d$. (Note: you cannot tell for certain whether b is smaller than or larger than c and d.)

Finally, note that e also represents the length of a radius of the circle, because it connects the center of the circle to the edge of the circle. Therefore, it is the same length as c and d, and $a > c = d = e$. The correct answer is (J).

9. **(C)** $\dfrac{b^2}{a^2}$ Trigonometry   Triangle Ratios

For $\triangle XYZ$, $\sin X = \dfrac{\text{side opposite angle } X}{\text{hypotenuse}} = \dfrac{b}{a}$. Similarly, $\cos Y = \dfrac{\text{side adjacent to angle } Y}{\text{hypotenuse}} = \dfrac{b}{a}$. By taking the product of $\sin X$ and $\cos Y$, you get $\left(\dfrac{b}{a}\right)\left(\dfrac{b}{a}\right) = \dfrac{b^2}{a^2}$.

The correct answer is (C).

16

10. **(H)** $g(x) = \tan x$ Trigonometry   Trig Functions

Trigonometric identities tell you that the ratio of sin x to cos x is equal to tan x. In fact, this is the definition of the tangent function. The correct answer is (H).

11. **(A)** $\dfrac{b}{a}$ Trigonometry   Triangle Ratios

For $\triangle XYZ$, cos $X = \dfrac{\text{side adjacent to angle } X}{\text{hypotenuse}} = \dfrac{c}{a}$. Similarly, tan $X = \dfrac{\text{side opposite angle } X}{\text{side adjacent to angle } X} = \dfrac{b}{c}$. By taking the

product of cos X and tan X, you get $\left(\dfrac{c}{a}\right)\left(\dfrac{b}{c}\right) = \dfrac{b}{a}$. The correct answer is (A).

12. **(G)** 2π Trigonometry   Trigonometric Function Graphs

This problem indirectly asks you to find the period for this function. The period of a trigonometric function is the distance along the x-axis, in radians, that it takes for the graph to begin to repeat itself in shape and value. In other words, the period is the width of the shortest repeating vertical "slice" of the function.

The figure below divides the x-axis into intervals of length 2π units. Notice that the function in one interval is identical to the function in any other interval of length 2π units:

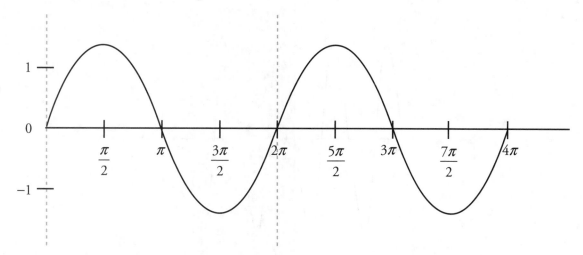

Note also that it does not matter where the period interval begins. If the period started at $\dfrac{\pi}{2}$, for example, the graph would begin to repeat itself at $\dfrac{5\pi}{2}$, which is 2π more than $\dfrac{\pi}{2}$:

16

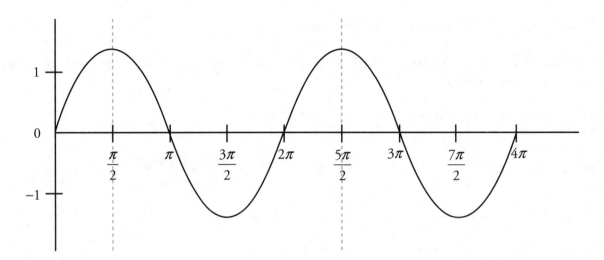

The period of the graph is therefore 2π, and the correct answer is (G).

13. **(B)** $\dfrac{3\pi}{2}$ Trigonometry   Trig Functions

As mentioned in the problem, the graph of any trigonometric function repeats itself regularly. In other words, every repetition of the graph covers equal length along the x-axis. The task is to determine how long that length is:

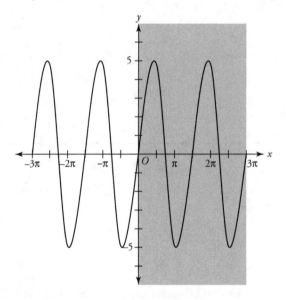

As can be seen in the highlighted version of the graph above, between 0 and 3π, the graph repeats twice: it starts at 0 sloping upwards, and ends at 0 sloping upwards. Therefore, the period of the graph is $3\pi \div 2 = \dfrac{3\pi}{2}$. The correct answer is (B).

16

14. **(H)** $\frac{\pi}{2} < \theta < \frac{3\pi}{4}$ Trigonometry   Triangle Ratios

The tangent function is negative whenever the angle is between 90° and 180° (i.e., in Quadrant II) and between 270° and 360° (i.e., Quadrant IV). This is because in those quadrants only one of the adjacent side and the opposite side will be negative—not both. To convert these angle measures to radians, multiply by $\frac{\pi}{180°}$: $\frac{\pi}{180°}(90°) = \frac{\pi}{2}$, and $\frac{\pi}{180°}(180°) = \pi$. Ignore the 270° to 360° ranges, because none of the ranges in the choices is that large. Therefore, $\frac{\pi}{2} < \theta < \pi$. This eliminates choices (F) and (G).

Next, remember that the formula for the tangent of an angle in a right triangle is defined as follows:

$$\tan A = \frac{\text{side opposite angle } A}{\text{side adjacent to angle } A}$$

In the (x, y) coordinate plane, the tangent of an angle is the ratio of the y-coordinate of a point on the line emanating from the angle to the x-coordinate of that point. Because the graph of this function must be in Quadrant II, the "opposite" side will be positive and the "adjacent" side will be negative. Additionally, the ratio is large in absolute terms: the y-coordinate must be more than 6 times as long as the x-coordinate. Therefore, the graph will look something like this:

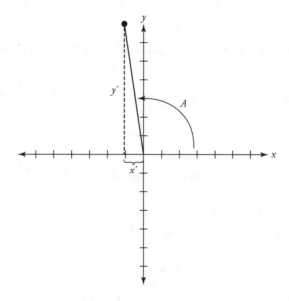

The tangent of $\angle A$ is equal to $\frac{y'}{x'}$ in this drawing, which equals −6.4. Therefore, the angle is only very slightly larger than 90°, or $\frac{\pi}{2}$. The correct answer must be $\frac{\pi}{2} < \theta < \frac{3\pi}{4}$. (In fact, a very close approximation for θ is 98.9°, or 0.55π.). The correct answer is (H).

15. **(E)** $\frac{24}{25}$ Trigonometry   Triangle Ratios

The sine function is positive whenever the angle is between 0° and 180° (i.e., in Quadrant I or Quadrant II), because in those quadrants the opposite side is positive while the hypotenuse is always positive. Therefore, since $90° < \psi < 180°$, Choices (A), (B) and (C) can be eliminated, because the sine must be positive.

16

Remember that the formula for the sine of an angle in a right triangle is defined as follows:

$$\sin A = \frac{\text{side opposite angle } A}{\text{hypotenuse}}$$

In the (x, y) coordinate plane, the sine of an angle is the ratio of the y-coordinate of a point on the line emanating from the angle (in this case, 24) to the hypotenuse:

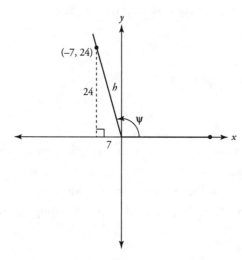

Because the triangle formed above is a right triangle, you can solve for the hypotenuse using the Pythagorean theorem:

$$24^2 + 7^2 = h^2$$
$$h^2 = 576 + 49 = 625$$
$$h = 25$$

Therefore, the opposite side is 24, the hypotenuse is 25, and the sine of ψ is $\frac{24}{25}$.

(Alternatively, you could recognize that the short leg of the right triangle and the long leg of the triangle constitute 2 parts of a 7–24–25 right triangle.) The correct answer is (E).

16. **(F)** $\frac{\pi}{2}$ Trigonometry   Triangle Ratios

The sine function varies between −1 and 1 for all values of θ. It is defined for the angle in a right triangle as follows:

$$\sin A = \frac{\text{side opposite angle } A}{\text{hypotenuse}}$$

In the (x, y) coordinate plane, the sine of an angle is the ratio of the y-coordinate of a point on a line segment emanating from the angle to the length of that line segment. In other words, the y-coordinate must be equal to the length of the line segment. The only way that this is possible is if the x-coordinate equals 0. This will happen whenever the angle is 90° or 270°. However, in the case of 270°, the y-coordinate will be negative and the sine function will equal −1.

Therefore, the angle must equal 90°. To convert degrees to radians, multiply by $\frac{\pi}{180°}$: $\frac{\pi}{180°}(90°) = \frac{\pi}{2}$. The correct answer is (F).

MANHATTAN
PREP

17.   **(E)** $\sqrt{49+16-2\cdot 28\cdot \cos 70°}$ Trigonometry   Trig Laws

The law of cosines states that for any triangle, the square of the length of a side is equal to the sum of the squares of the two other sides, minus a term that incorporates the other two sides and the cosine of the angle opposite the side in question:

$$c^2 = a^2 + b^2 - 2ab\cdot \cos C$$

In this case, the side you are concerned with is $\overline{DE}$, and the other sides are 7 and 4. The size of the angle opposite $\overline{DE}$ is 70°. Therefore:

$$\left(\overline{DE}\right)^2 = 7^2 + 4^2 - 2\cdot 7\cdot 4\cdot \cos 70°$$

Now, manipulate this expression to get it match one of the choices:

$$\left(\overline{DE}\right)^2 = 49+16-2\cdot 28\cdot \cos 70°$$
$$\overline{DE} = \sqrt{49+16-2\cdot 28\cdot \cos 70°}$$

This expression matches that found in choice (E), which is the correct answer.

18.   **(F)** $\dfrac{16}{\sin 65°}$ Trigonometry   Triangle Ratios

The trigonometric functions for an angle in a right triangle are defined as follows:

$$\cos A = \frac{\text{adjacent}}{\text{hypotenuse}}$$

$$\sin A = \frac{\text{opposite}}{\text{hypotenuse}}$$

$$\tan A = \frac{\text{opposite}}{\text{adjacent}}$$

In the diagram, you are given the measure of $\angle F$ as well as the length of $\overline{DE}$, which is the side opposite the angle. The question asks for the expression for the length of $\overline{DF}$, which is the hypotenuse of the triangle. The sine is the trigonometric function that relates the opposite side to the hypotenuse. Therefore, you can restate the above formula for the sine of an angle as follows and solve for $\overline{DF}$:

$$\sin \angle F = \frac{\text{opposite}}{\text{hypotenuse}} = \frac{\overline{DE}}{\overline{DF}}$$

$$\sin 65° = \frac{16}{\overline{DF}}$$

$$\overline{DF} = \frac{16}{\sin 65°}$$

The correct answer is (F).

16

19. **(C)** $12\left(\dfrac{\sin 70°}{\sin 50°}\right)$ Trigonometry   Trig Laws

The law of sines states that for any triangle, the ratio of the sine of a vertex (angle) to the length of the side opposite the angle is the same for all three pairs of vertices and sides. Add a notation for the third angle, because it is opposite the side of known length:

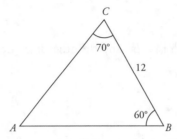

Because the 3 interior angles of a triangle must sum to 180°, you can solve for x: $x + 70° + 60° = 180°$, so $x = 180° - 70° - 60° = 50°$. Using the law of sines, write:

$$\frac{\sin X}{x} = \frac{\sin Y}{y} = \frac{\sin Z}{z}$$

$$\frac{\sin 50°}{12} = \frac{\sin 70°}{\overline{AB}} = \frac{\sin 60°}{\overline{AC}}$$

The question asks about the length of $\overline{AB}$, so you can ignore the third term in the above equation and solve for $\overline{AB}$:

$$\frac{\sin 50°}{12} = \frac{\sin 70°}{\overline{AB}}$$

$$\overline{AB}(\sin 50°) = 12(\sin 70°)$$

$$\overline{AB} = \frac{12(\sin 70°)}{\sin 50°} = 12\left(\frac{\sin 70°}{\sin 50°}\right)$$

Therefore, the correct answer is $12\left(\dfrac{\sin 70°}{\sin 50°}\right)$. The correct answer is (C).

16

MANHATTAN
PREP

20. **(F)** $2 - \dfrac{2y}{x}$ Trigonometry   Triangle Ratios

The tangent function for an angle in a right triangle is defined as follows:

$$\tan A = \frac{\text{side opposite angle } A}{\text{side adjacent to angle } A}$$

Because the question asks about the tangent of $\angle D$, you can calculate the answer as follows:

$$\tan D = \frac{x-y}{\dfrac{x}{2}} = 2\left(\frac{x-y}{x}\right)$$

However, none of the choices matches this expression exactly, so manipulate the expression to get it to match one of the choices:

$$2\left(\frac{x-y}{x}\right) = 2\left(\frac{x}{x} - \frac{y}{x}\right)$$
$$= 2\left(1 - \frac{y}{x}\right)$$
$$= 2 - \frac{2y}{x}$$

The correct answer is (F).

21. **(A)** $\dfrac{\sqrt{z^2 - x^2}}{x}$ Trigonometry   Triangle Ratios

It's worth drawing a triangle and assigning labeling to its sides in order to discern side lengths, and therefore the trigonometric ratios, of the triangle. Using the given expression for cos A, illustrate the triangle below:

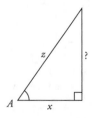

You are asked to find tan A, which equals $\dfrac{\text{side opposite of angle } A}{\text{side adjacent to angle } A}$, or $\dfrac{?}{x}$. You have to solve for the missing side. The hypotenuse = z, and the leg of the triangle opposite $A = x$. Use the Pythagorean theorem to find the missing side in terms of the variables z and x:

$$x^2 + \text{side}^2 = z^2$$
$$\text{side}^2 = z^2 - x^2$$
$$\text{side} = \sqrt{z^2 - x^2}$$

$$\tan A = \frac{\text{side opposite of angle } A}{\text{side adjacent to angle } A} = \frac{\sqrt{z^2 - x^2}}{x}$$

The correct answer is (A).

22. **(J)** $g(x) = \cot x$ Trigonometry   Trig Functions

This question gives you the identity that $\csc x = \dfrac{1}{\sin x}$, so substitute in:

$$\cos x \left(\frac{1}{\sin x} \right) = \frac{\cos x}{\sin x} = \cot x$$

Note that $\cot x$ is the reciprocal of $\tan x$. Keep these two functions straight. The correct answer is (J).

23. **(D)** 15   Trigonometry   Triangle Ratios

It is given in the problem that the length of the hypotenuse of $\triangle ABC$ is 25 and that the tangent of $\angle B = 1\frac{1}{3} = \frac{4}{3}$. The trigonometric functions for an angle in a right triangle are defined as:

$$\cos A = \frac{\text{adjacent}}{\text{hypotenuse}}$$

$$\sin A = \frac{\text{opposite}}{\text{hypotenuse}}$$

$$\tan A = \frac{\text{opposite}}{\text{adjacent}}$$

Therefore, you can create a variable, x, to represent $\overline{BC}$ and label $\overline{AC}$ and $\overline{BC}$ as follows:

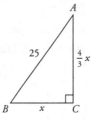

Furthermore, by the Pythagorean theorem, $x^2 + \left(\frac{4}{3}x \right)^2 = 25^2$. Now solve for x:

$$x^2 + \left(\frac{4}{3}x \right)^2 = 25^2$$

$$x^2 + \frac{16}{9} \cdot x^2 = 25^2$$

$$\frac{25}{9} x^2 = 25^2$$

$$x^2 = \frac{9 \cdot 25^2}{25} = 9 \cdot 25$$

$$x = \sqrt{9 \cdot 25} = 3 \cdot 5 = 15$$

MANHATTAN
PREP

16

Therefore, the length of $\overline{BC}$ is 15. Check the accuracy of this calculation by noting that this implies that $\overline{AC} = \left(\frac{4}{3}\right)15 = 20$, and $15:20:25$ is a multiple of the common $3:4:5$ right triangle. The correct answer is (D).

24. **(H)** $\dfrac{2\sqrt{5}}{5}$ Trigonometry   Triangle Ratios

The tangent function is positive whenever the angle is between $0°$ and $90°$ (i.e., in Quadrant I) and between $180°$ and $270°$ (i.e., Quadrant III). This is because in those quadrants the adjacent side and the opposite side will have the same sign—positive in Quadrant I and negative in Quadrant III. Therefore, choices (F) and (G) can be eliminated.

Next, remember that the formula for the tangent of an angle in a right triangle is defined as follows:

$$\tan A = \frac{\text{side opposite angle } A}{\text{side adjacent to angle } A}$$

In the (x, y) coordinate plane, the tangent of an angle is the ratio of the y-coordinate of a point on the line emanating from the angle to the x-coordinate of that point. You are given the length of the hypotenuse and the length of the opposite side in the problem (thereby giving you the y-coordinate), and you can use the Pythagorean theorem to solve for the adjacent side length (and thereby the x-coordinate):

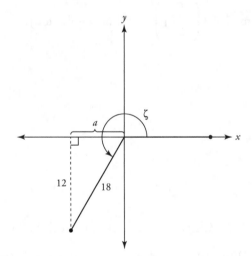

$$12^2 + a^2 = 18^2$$
$$a^2 = 18^2 - 12^2 = 324 - 144 = 180$$
$$a = \sqrt{180} = \sqrt{2 \cdot 2 \cdot 3 \cdot 3 \cdot 5} = 6\sqrt{5}$$

Therefore, the opposite side is 12, the adjacent side is $6\sqrt{5}$, and the tangent of $\zeta = \dfrac{12}{6\sqrt{5}} = \dfrac{2}{\sqrt{5}}\left(\dfrac{\sqrt{5}}{\sqrt{5}}\right) = \dfrac{2\sqrt{5}}{5}$. The correct answer is (H).

25. (E) 20   Trigonometry   Triangle Ratios

It is given in the problem that the length of the small leg of the triangle is 10 and that $\sin x = \dfrac{\sqrt{3}}{2}$. The trigonometric functions for an angle in a right triangle are defined as:

$$\cos A = \frac{\text{adjacent}}{\text{hypotenuse}}$$

$$\sin A = \frac{\text{opposite}}{\text{hypotenuse}}$$

$$\tan A = \frac{\text{opposite}}{\text{adjacent}}$$

Therefore, you can express the long leg of the triangle in terms of y as follows:

Furthermore, by the Pythagorean theorem, $10^2 + \left(\dfrac{\sqrt{3}}{2} y\right)^2 = y^2$. Now solve for y:

$$10^2 + \left(\frac{\sqrt{3}}{2} y\right)^2 = y^2$$

$$10^2 + \frac{3}{4} \cdot y^2 = y^2$$

$$10^2 = \frac{y^2}{4}$$

$$y = \sqrt{4 \cdot 100} = 20$$

Therefore, the length of y, the hypotenuse, is 20. Check the accuracy of this calculation by noting that this implies that the long leg of the triangle is equal to $\dfrac{\sqrt{3}}{2} (20) = 10\sqrt{3}$, and $10 : 10\sqrt{3} : 20$ is a multiple of the common $1 : \sqrt{3} : 2$ right triangle. The correct answer is (E).

26. (K) $\dfrac{3}{4}$ Trigonometry   Triangle Ratios

The tangent function is positive whenever the angle is between 0° and 90° (i.e., in Quadrant I) and between 180° and 270° (i.e., Quadrant III). This is because in those quadrants the adjacent side and the opposite side will have the same sign—positive in Quadrant I and negative in Quadrant III. Therefore, choices (F) and (G) can be eliminated.

Next, remember that the formula for the tangent of an angle in a right triangle is defined as follows:

$$\tan A = \frac{\text{Side opposite angle } A}{\text{Side adjacent to angle } A}$$

In the (x, y) coordinate plane, the tangent of an angle is the ratio of the y-coordinate of a point on the line emanating from the angle to the x-coordinate of that point. The possible range of angles for ϕ is demonstrated in this graph, with an example drawn in the range:

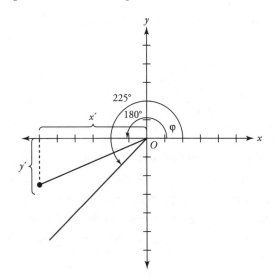

For the point chosen in the graph, the tangent of ϕ is equal to $\dfrac{y'}{x'}$, and y is obviously a smaller length than x. Therefore, the tangent must be between 0 and 1. The correct answer thus must be $\dfrac{3}{4}$, because it is the only positive number among the choices that is between 0 and 1. (In fact, for $\tan \phi = \dfrac{3}{4}$, a very close approximation for ϕ is 217°.) The correct answer is (K).

27. **(A)** $-\dfrac{4}{5}$ Trigonometry   Triangle Ratios

The sine function is positive whenever the angle is between 0° and 180° (i.e., in Quadrant I or Quadrant II), because in those quadrants the opposite side is positive while the hypotenuse is always positive. However, the cosine is positive whenever the angle is between 0° and 90° (i.e., in Quadrant I), but negative whenever the angle is between 90° and 180° (i.e., in Quadrant II), because the adjacent side is positive in Quadrant I and negative in Quadrant 2. Therefore, since $135° < \Upsilon < 180°$, Choices (D) and (E) can be eliminated because the cosine must be negative.

If you are familiar with the Pythagorean identities for trigonometric functions, this question can be solved using that method. Using the rule that $\sin^2 x + \cos^2 x = 1$:

$$\sin^2 \Upsilon + \cos^2 \Upsilon = 1$$

$$\left(\frac{3}{5}\right)^2 + \cos^2 \Upsilon = 1$$

$$\cos^2 \Upsilon = 1 - \frac{9}{25}$$

$$\cos^2 \Upsilon = \frac{16}{25}$$

$$\cos \Upsilon = -\frac{4}{5}$$

16

Choose the negative solution because, as stated above, the cosine must be negative.

However, even without knowing the identity, you can solve it using standard triangle analysis.

Remember that the formulas for the sine and cosine of an angle in a right triangle are defined as follows:

$$\sin A = \frac{\text{Side opposite angle } A}{\text{hypotenuse}}$$

$$\cos A = \frac{\text{Side adjacent to angle } A}{\text{hypotenuse}}$$

In the (x, y) coordinate plane, you can figure out the sine and cosine of an angle formed with the positive x-axis by picking a point "on" the angle (on the ray that forms the angle with the positive x-axis). Take the coordinates of that point and also figure out the distance from that point to the origin (the hypotenuse of the triangle). The sine of the angle is the y-coordinate of the point divided by that distance. The cosine of the angle is the x-coordinate divided by that distance. The possible range of angles for Υ is demonstrated in this graph, with the appropriate line segment for $\sin \Upsilon = \frac{3}{5}$ drawn in:

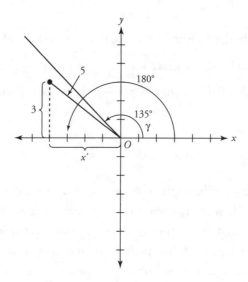

For the line segment in the graph, the sine of Υ is equal to $\frac{3}{5}$. x' can be solved using the Pythagorean theorem:

$$3^2 + \left(x'\right)^2 = 5^2$$
$$\left(x'\right)^2 = 25 - 9 = 16$$
$$x' = -4$$

(Remember, choose the negative solution because the cosine must be negative.)

Therefore, the cosine of Υ is $-\frac{4}{5}$.

**MANHATTAN
PREP**

Alternatively, you could recognize that the short leg of the right triangle and the hypotenuse of the right triangle constitute 2 parts of a $3:4:5$ triangle. The correct answer is (A).

28. **(F)** 11.9   Trigonometry   Triangle Ratios

The cosine of an angle in a right triangle is the adjacent (or touching) side, divided by the hypotenuse (the longest side). The adjacent side to angle X is the $\overline{XY}$. The length of this side is the unknown quantity you're looking for (call it z, since it's opposite angle Z). The hypotenuse is 31. You also are given a value of the cosine of angle X: $\dfrac{5}{13}$. Plug the given values into the formula for cosine, and solve for z:

$$\cos X = \frac{\text{Adjacent}}{\text{Hypotenuse}}$$

$$\frac{5}{13} = \frac{z}{31}$$

$$\frac{5 \times 31}{13} = z$$

$$11.9 \approx z$$

The correct answer is (F).

29. **(B)** 44.7   Trigonometry   Triangle Ratios

The tangent of an angle in a right triangle is the opposite side over the adjacent side, or $\dfrac{\text{Opposite}}{\text{Adjacent}}$.

Thus, the tangent of angle A is the length of $\overline{BC}$, or 67, divided by the length of $\overline{AB}$, which is what the problem is asking for. Call that length c. The tangent of the angle is given as 1.5. Plug into the formula for tangent and solve for c.

$$\tan A = \frac{\text{Opposite}}{\text{Adjacent}}$$

$$1.5 = \frac{67}{c}$$

$$(1.5)c = 67$$

$$c = \frac{67}{1.5} \approx 44.7$$

The correct answer is (B).

16

Chapter *of* 17

5lb. Book of ACT® Practice Problems

Reading:

Literary Narrative

In This Chapter...

Literary Narrative Passages & Solutions

Chapter 17
Reading: Literary Narrative

The Reading passages in this chapter are literary narratives—that is, extracts from fictional short stories and novels, as well as from memoirs and other literary nonfiction. A small amount of context is given at the start, but each passage is self-contained.

Various kinds of questions are asked about these passages, including the following:

1. Main Ideas/Author's Approach. Main idea or ideas of the passage (or a part of it); the approach, voice, point of view, method, or purpose of the author.

2. Details. Specific details mentioned in the passage.

3. Relationships. Comparisons, sequences of events, cause-effect relationships, or other relationships that are described or implied in the passage.

4. Meanings of Words. The meaning of a word or phrase, in its context, in the passage.

5. Generalizations. Conclusions, broad observations, or other generalizations that can be drawn from the passage.

How should you use this chapter? Here are some recommendations, according to the level you've reached in ACT Reading.

1. Fundamentals. Do a passage or two untimed to begin with. As you become more comfortable, put the clock on. In all cases, review the solutions closely, and articulate what you've learned. Reread the passage again to ensure that you fully understand it, and redo problems as necessary.

2. Fixes. Do one passage at a time under timed conditions. Examine the results, learn your lessons, then test yourself with more passages (one from each Reading chapter) at once.

3. Tweaks. Confirm your mastery by doing a few passages (one from each Reading chapter) at once under timed conditions. A full set of four is the ultimate goal. Aim to improve the speed and ease of your reading and solution process.

Good luck on the problems!

PASSAGE 1

LITERARY NARRATIVE: This passage is adapted from a short story that takes place in the late 1990s in Midwestern America.

The new neighbors were not like us. They yelled, even when they were just talking, the father especially. It wasn't angry yelling but matter-of-fact yelling, like words were simply meant to be spoken at high volume, 5 or you might not be heard. The daughters were loud in a different way—shrill, incessant. They sat on the front porch for hours in the evening jabbering about things I didn't know about. I was eleven and an only child. I didn't understand girls yet, especially older ones.

10 So when I first spotted Ilan, I was startled; I hadn't known there was another child in that large, boisterous house that was twice the size of ours. It was summer when they moved in, so school had not yet started; had it been fall, we would have shared the bus stop as he looked 15 about my age. But still, I was surprised I had not seen him playing outdoors, or even sitting out with his sisters.

I saw him through his kitchen window, which faced our trash cans. I was cleaning up the mess made by the raccoons during the night when I heard a crash and turned. 20 He had shut the window and was staring at me from the other side of it. I waved. He hesitated before waving back. He looked as curious about me as I was about him. I resumed cleaning, aware of his eyes on me as I, embarrassed for my dad, shoveled the empty milk cartons and macaroni boxes 25 and cans upon cans of Dr. Pepper into the bag. I wondered if his dad drank as much Dr. Pepper as mine.

The next day, I went over to his house and knocked on the door. It was a bright afternoon, and I wondered if he wanted to play tag or see my fort. He opened the door 30 slowly, even after he saw it was me, like he wasn't sure it was a good idea.

"Hi," I said and told him my name, Sergio. He told me his name was Ilan. I had never met anyone with that name, but didn't say so in case it was rude. I asked if he wanted to 35 play. He nodded and went back inside for a moment while I waited. I assumed he was telling his mom. A few seconds later he returned and followed me back over to my yard, where I asked if he wanted to play tag or something else. He was fine with tag. I don't remember what else we did 40 that first afternoon, but he stayed until his father hollered for him to come home for dinner. Watching him go, I was filled with sadness and joy at once—delight at the friend I had made, and already lonely under the great weight of time until I would see him again.

45 I didn't have many friends outside of school, because we lived too far outside of town. Mom worked, and we only had one car, so dad and I stayed home during the summer. It was lonely with only the two of us there all day, every day. He watched TV shows I thought 50 were boring, and I wasn't allowed to go farther than the block, so I spent hours drifting between the front and back yards, talking to myself. I was never good at having imaginary friends. I couldn't forget they were fake.

Ilan and I began playing every day for as long as 55 our parents would allow. We made the fort better—added wood slats from the back of his house that his dad let us bring over to the wall of sticks I'd made. We brought in a tire for steering when it became a ship. Over the late weeks of August, we made a whole civilization with villains. I 60 forgot that there were any adults around. I stopped hearing his sister's banter. I'm not sure he ever heard it.

One day, we were sitting in the fort with its fresh, thicker wall shielding us from the sun and the world of grown ups when Ilan confessed he'd forgotten my name.

65 "I just didn't know how to pronounce it," he said. "So I forgot it." I told him the correct pronunciation— SER-heeo. After that, he said it all the time. I think he liked knowing a Sergio.

As the first day of school loomed closer, I hoped 70 Ilan and I would be able to keep up the summer's fun, our game and our afternoons in the fort, but I wondered. School was different. There would be more people there for him to befriend; there would be my old friends, too. How would it change us?

75 The day the bus pulled up for the first time since May, Ilan kissed his mom goodbye and we climbed in and took a seat in the middle, on the same seat, even though there weren't any other kids on it, as our stop was the farthest out. His mom hollered after us, so I could 80 hear even through the windows and over the motor as we drove away, "Be good!" Ilan rolled his eyes. I hadn't seen him do that before.

"She drives me crazy," he said. I hadn't known that. We hadn't discussed family before, I realized. We had 85 just played.

"Yeah," I said. I didn't think my mom would drive me crazy if she was home more. I began to feel something was different now, and I didn't understand.

So much was new already, and we weren't even 90 there, yet.

17

1. At the time of the events in the story, the narrator is:

   A. a teenager with older siblings.
   B. a boy with no siblings.
   C. an adult reflecting on his childhood.
   D. a boy who has no friends at school.

2. It can reasonably be inferred that the narrator initially views the new boy next door as:

   F. a curiosity to regard from a distance.
   G. a potential opportunity for friendship.
   H. a means to meet the boy's older sisters.
   J. a threat to his way of life.

3. It can reasonably be inferred from the passage that the new neighbors:

   A. have a different dynamic than the narrator's family.
   B. are wealthier than the narrator's family.
   C. practice a different religion than the narrator's family.
   D. are closer to each other than the narrator's family.

4. The passage states that the narrator regards summer as all of the following EXCEPT:

   F. a period of time that he found especially lonely given his mother's absence for work, lack of friends in his neighborhood, and father's habits.
   G. a period of time that he filled largely by entertaining himself outdoors.
   H. a period of time in which there was no car available for his father to drive them anywhere during the day.
   J. a period of time in which he dreaded returning to school in the fall because he feared that his friends would no longer be his friends.

5. It can reasonably be inferred that the narrator views his father's daily habits with a mixture of:

   A. disdain and disinterest.
   B. amusement and embarrassment.
   C. anger and bitterness.
   D. curiosity and desire.

6. The passage states that the narrator became aware of a shift beginning between himself and Ilan as a result of:

   F. Ilan's complimentary remark regarding the narrator's mother after the two of them had boarded the bus.
   G. Ilan's negative remark regarding his own mother after the two of them had boarded the bus.
   H. the kiss given to Ilan by his own mother on the first day of school, and the absence of the narrator's mother to see him off.
   J. Ilan's having forgotten the narrator's name after they had already become friends.

7. The narrator states that the other children at his school:

   A. would be unlikely to befriend Ilan, because they already had each other as friends.
   B. are friends of his during the school year.
   C. did not ride the bus like him and Ilan.
   D. would not welcome the narrator back into their social group when school resumed.

8. Which of the following statements best describes the way the second-to-last paragraph (lines 86–88) functions in the passage as a whole?

   F. It reveals that the narrator's interest in a friendship with Ilan has been more about envy than about enjoying their time together.
   G. It provides an example of a theme introduced in the first paragraph of the passage.
   H. It reveals that the newfound distance between the narrator and his friend is not solely about the friendships they will or will not develop with other children at school.
   J. It shows that the narrator is able to empathize with Ilan in a way that he would not have been able to in the early days of their friendship.

9. The statement "I was filled with sadness and joy at once" (lines 41–42) functions in the passage to support the idea that the narrator regarded his new friendship as:

   A. precious and delightful.
   B. necessary and urgent.
   C. long-awaited and expected.
   D. bittersweet and ironic.

10. The narrator refers to the neighbors' loudness as behavior he views as:

    F. upsetting.
    G. soothing.
    H. foreign.
    J. threatening.

17

PASSAGE 2

LITERARY NARRATIVE: This passage is adapted from a short story set in the late 1980s in the southeastern United States.

The morning I planned to run away, I packed my small, lavender suitcase only with items without which I knew I could not survive the several days I planned to be gone—my favorite Cabbage Patch doll, Sheila, a book of
5   Grimm's fairy tales, and two apples.

"I'll be in the backyard!" I hollered toward my parents' room, where I knew my mother would be lying on their oversized bed that sunk low in the center, such that when we crawled into it with her in the mornings,
10 she would shove us close to the edge and wrap her arms around us there, all three of us layered, teetering, like spoons on a precipice as father snored slow and distant on the other side of no man's land.

When she didn't answer, I knew it would not be
15 long before her medicine kicked in fully and she herself would be asleep, her breath audible and even, but not quite loud enough to be called snoring.

In the entryway that contained the pantry and the washing machine, I reached over the drying rack to
20 fetch one of the several umbrellas hanging off the wall hooks my father had installed before he had the job that required him to catch the 6 a.m. before even Janie woke up. I took the longest umbrella, the one that came to my chest, because it was the biggest. I had to hold it
25 by its middle rather than by its handle so that it wouldn't drag.

I stepped outside and closed the door behind me. I took the two steps down onto the patio and unlatched the gate on the left, taking care to replace the latch
30 properly. I walked around the side of the house to where our side-yard met the street and began to make my way up the long hill at the top of which sat the Ortizes' house. In the setting sun, a golden halo crowned its chimney, and the windows were as shiny as the silver fish in the
35 stream in late August.

It would take me a little while to reach the stream and to settle under the bridge where I planned to live until I could find somewhere else. I would have apples for dinner. I wouldn't have been able to catch any fish, anyway, because
40 it was already November and there weren't as many to be caught, but regardless, I hadn't brought my fishing supplies.

As I approached the peak of the hill, I thought about Janie. She would be home from speech therapy soon and would wonder where I was. She would search
45 for me around the house and, unable to find me, would wake up mom. Well, she'd try to wake up mom. It was rare that mom was able to rise if she took her medicine so late in the day. I would search in the fridge for something for Janie and me to eat for supper. Usually string cheese
50 and a little cup of apple sauce and maybe some ham rolled around carrots, which my mom called pencils when she made them for lunch.

I slowed. My arm was getting a little tired from carrying the suitcase. The Ortizes' lab began to bark
55 at me, and I hurried past so Margaret Ortiz would not look out her window and see me running away. I was breathing hard. I could see the stream up ahead, just around the curve where the Reece children rode bikes.

I wondered when they would realize I was gone.
60 When my dad returned, probably. It would be late, very dark by then—chilly. I wished I had brought a blanket, or something. I shivered at the thought of sitting under the bridge in the late October night air without a blanket or even a sweatshirt.

65 I switched arms, putting the suitcase in my right and the umbrella in my left, and took a deep breath. I had thought long and hard about this, ever since we knew my mom would probably not be with us by Halloween. That morning when I had woken up, I knew that I did
70 not want to be around, either. I decided that by night, I would be gone, and now, I was going.

For a flicker of a second, I wondered, *but what if she isn't?* Of course she would be, though; I had heard the doctor say as much on the phone when I picked it
75 up during their call last Tuesday, which used to be my favorite day, until last week. He said before the end of the month. *But the end of the month is Halloween*, had been my first thought. Then I had hung up without trying to be quiet, and she came in to ask if I had been listening,
80 then cried while telling me not to cry.

The Reeces' garage was open and their bikes were gone. They must have gone out riding somewhere else. The street was unusually quiet, and I started to feel lonely.

When I reached the bridge, I looked down at the
85 left bank, wondering if it would be better to set up there or on the other side. I looked at my watch. It had only been 10 minutes since I left home. Janie's bus wouldn't arrive for at least 30. If I hurried, I could make it before she ever knew I was gone. I turned and began to run. My
90 sister would need dinner.

11. The passage best supports which of the following conclusions about the protagonist?

   A. She loves her family, but feels overwhelmed by the pressures and sadness brought on by her mom's illness.

   B. She feels fed up by her younger sister's neediness.

   C. She values independence and wants to run away in order to free herself from her family's influence.

   D. She is a solitary child who prefers to spend her time alone.

12. It can reasonably be inferred from the passage that the narrator lives:

   F. in a highly rural area near a stream.

   G. in a dense city with a bridge.

   H. in a neighborhood near other families.

   J. in an apartment building near other apartment buildings.

13. Which of the following details is offered by the passage to give a sense of the mom's feelings toward her daughters?

   A. The mom tries to comfort her daughter about her illness while crying herself.

   B. The mom requires speech therapy.

   C. The mom sleeps a lot, and has a hard time waking up.

   D. The mom does not make dinner for her daughters.

14. What does the narrator plan to eat after running away?

   F. Applesauce

   G. Carrots wrapped in ham

   H. Fish

   J. Apples

15. The main purpose of the seventh paragraph (lines 42–52) is to:

   A. describe the narrator's journey toward the stream.

   B. introduce the narrator's sister and give a sense of their relationship.

   C. explain why the narrator is running away.

   D. introduce a character whom the narrator strongly dislikes.

16. It can be reasonably inferred from the passage that the narrator's relationship with her sister is characterized by:

   F. caretaking.

   G. petty fighting.

   H. jealousy.

   J. reciprocal chore-sharing.

17. According to the passage, which one of the following is true of the narrator's father?

   A. He feels alienated from his daughters.

   B. He does not like cooking dinner.

   C. He returns home late at night.

   D. He did not have a job until recently.

18. Which of the following items does the narrator NOT take with her when she runs away?

   F. An umbrella

   G. A book

   H. A doll

   J. Fishing supplies

19. According to the passage, the narrator runs home because:

   A. she does not want to run into the Reece children.

   B. she wants to get home before her sister knows she is gone.

   C. she is starting to feel cold.

   D. she does not want to anger her father.

20. The story strongly implies that the narrator is:

   F. a young adult who has moved back home to help take care of her little sister.

   G. the middle child in a family.

   H. a child with one sibling.

   J. a teenager with a job.

17

MANHATTAN
PREP   745

PASSAGE 3

LITERARY NARRATIVE: This passage is adapted from a short story set in the early 1990s in New Orleans.

I do not recall the moment when the shift took place, but like a hill rising, at some point I knew I was no longer on flat terrain without being able to pinpoint, precisely, the incline's origin. I was sixteen and had just
5 met my mother for the first time. That's what it felt like, at least.

"MyKhanh," she greeted me by using my Vietnamese name, and I instinctively looked around the McDonald's for anyone from my high school; they knew me as Anna,
10 and I preferred it that way.

Then, she spoke to me in Vietnamese. *You are very pretty*, she said. While I was surprised how well I understood, I still answered her questions in broken English, not because mine was broken, but because I
15 thought maybe she would better understand that way. I skipped over the unnecessary words, sticking with only the basics: "Yes," "No," "Not sick," "Good grades," "Run in circles." I did not know how to explain track to my mother. We spent several minutes laughing over
20 my gestures of a loop and running, followed by tapping my chest, "Me, me." As she continued to speak in rapid Vietnamese, not questioning my understanding in the same way I was hers, it was clear to me how delighted she was to see me after so many years—like she had been
25 waiting the whole time. It broke my heart.

I came to the United States when I was three. My parents sent me here to keep me safe, and I was adopted by a family in New Orleans who taught me English and some Cajun and fed me creole and let me learn jazz piano
30 and did not argue with me when, in fifth grade, I decided to go by an American name, which I chose for myself—Anna. Anna, after "Anne of Green Gables," which my American mother read to me as a girl and which I heard as "Anna Green Gables," like it was her full name, last
35 name Gables, and which I foolishly believed was the title even after I'd listened to the whole story, lying in my American mom's lap at night, falling asleep to her low, soothing voice.

"My American mom" did not always roll off my
40 tongue as it does now. I called her mom for thirteen years because she *was* my mom, the only mom I knew. I had no memory of any mom but her. But when my biological mom entered my life, suddenly my mom needed a qualification to distinguish her from the other.
45 She became half a mom, demoted from full parent to adoptive parent by moniker in a single day. And I became fragmented, as well. I was both Anna and MyKhanh; daughter of Nguyet and daughter of Jane; born at birth, born again at three-years-old and then, born a third time
50 at sixteen. I was given back the first three years of life as scattered memories, delivered in haphazard fashion and translated over years and oceans and, of course, languages. My first word. My first step. The origin of the scar on my forehead (toppled off a chair while standing
55 on it)—not unlike the one I invented then stuck with for all those years as my answers to the question, "What happened?" (I fell off my bike.)

I continued to call her mom to her face, of course, but with increasing frequency, to others I added the
60 additional "my" and "American," as I began to spend more and more time with my actual mother, the woman who shared my genes—visiting her in her small apartment in Village de L'Est at the end of Alcee Fortier Boulevard, and helping her out at the farmer's market on Saturdays.
65 I called her "Ma" from the beginning. She called herself it, and I never thought to call her otherwise.

My American mom and my ma are kind, respectful to one another—they seem to appreciate that without the other, I would not be here, would not be who I am. And
70 yet, while I have never sensed envy or disappointment on the part of either, there are moments when I think I detect sadness in my American mom's eyes as I describe a day with my other family. I have trained myself not to say, "It is hard to explain," because I can't bear to see the
75 expression on her face that I read to mean, "There is a part of my daughter I will never understand."

And yet, it is undeniable that at some point, my second mom, the mom who raised me from ages three through eighteen, when I left home for college,
80 became not only in name but in my own head, my own understanding, just that: my second mom. I love her no less, of course. But my discomfort at ceasing to think of her as plain "mom" has ceased, and her new moniker has settled into my identity and become a part of who I am,
85 without hesitation or doubt—a Vietnamese-American with two mothers, two identities, two homes in the same city, only several miles apart but different in a million indescribable ways.

21. The narrator would most likely agree with which of the following statements?

   A. She feels unable to connect to her biological mother.

   B. She detects resentment on the part of her adoptive mother.

   C. She loves and appreciates both of her mothers in different ways.

   D. She feels closer to her biological mother than to her adopted mother.

22. The narrator's biological mother can be best described as:

   F. introverted and stubborn.

   G. friendly but withdrawn.

   H. loving and joyful.

   J. caring but embittered.

23. Which of the following statements does NOT describe the narrator's reaction to her biological mother moving to the United States?

   A. She imagines what the intervening years have been like for her mother.

   B. She is willing to allow her biological mother into her life.

   C. She is attentive to the feelings of her adoptive mother.

   D. She is passionate about adopting her Vietnamese identity and rejoining her biological family.

24. The story the narrator tells in lines 32–38 about her mother reading to her primarily serves to:

   F. convey the intimacy of their relationship.

   G. illustrate the mistake that the narrator made in choosing her name.

   H. suggest that the narrator is conflicted about her biological mother's arrival.

   J. reveal hesitation on the narrator's part to identify as Vietnamese.

25. The main point of the last paragraph is that:

   A. the narrator's adoptive mom is now less important to her than before.

   B. the narrator's identity has shifted since her mother arrived from Vietnam.

   C. the narrator is considering changing how she views her mothers.

   D. the narrator wishes she could view her adoptive mom differently.

26. According to the passage, when MyKhanh/Anna initially speaks to her biological mother at sixteen, the narrator speaks in:

   F. fluent Vietnamese.

   G. basic Vietnamese.

   H. primarily gestures.

   J. basic English.

27. Which of the following statements most accurately expresses the narrator when she describes "a day with my other family" (line 73)?

   A. She notices and empathizes with the hurt experienced by her adoptive mother.

   B. She is fearful of upsetting her overly sensitive adoptive mother.

   C. She prefers not to share in order to keep the families separate.

   D. She finds herself growing more shy and timid around her adoptive mother.

28. It can logically be inferred from the passage that:

   F. the narrator is glad to have formed a relationship with her biological mother.

   G. the narrator is relieved to have discovered a newfound identity.

   H. the narrator wishes to have more of a singular identity.

   J. the narrator is regretful about the way she has acted toward her adoptive mother.

29. The scar on the narrator's forehead mentioned in line 54 is actually from:

   A. falling off her bike.

   B. falling off of a chair.

   C. unknown causes.

   D. her first step.

30. According to the passage, the reason the narrator spent thirteen years in the United States while her mother was back in Vietnam is because:

   F. her interest in learning English brought her to America.

   G. her adoptive mother sought her through an adoption agency.

   H. her biological mother was unable to provide for her.

   J. her biological mother was fearful for her safety.

17

PASSAGE 4

LITERARY NARRATIVE: This passage is an excerpt of a short story that takes place in the contemporary rural south.

The new restaurant wasn't far from the diner, just two blocks down South Street and four shorter ones on Eleventh, past the dry cleaner's. It used to be the Quicky Mart. Since the Quicky Mart closed, the church ladies
5 had taken it over, hosting Tuesday and Thursday morning Bible study in the big, sunny room because it was more pleasant than the church basement and Stu, the owner, didn't mind. Wayne imagined the ladies weren't happy when a young gal who grew up in town then went off
10 to college came back and bought the joint from Stu. She had it repainted bright red and put up some fluorescent sign you had to squint to read because it's in cursive. Now, she was hosting an "open mic."

No one knew what to make of it when Mike A.
15 came into the diner and announced the event two weeks earlier.

"New restaurant down the street says people can come sing if they want," he said, and then sat on his usual stool opposite Lars the German.

20   Wayne slowly moved to pour Mike a cup of coffee and waited to hear more.

"Sing what?" Wayne asked, setting down Mike A's coffee in front of him.

"Anything you want," Mike A. said, and Mike T.
25 chuckled from the corner booth where he was reading his newspaper. He sat there so he could see the TV better and not have to talk to Lars the German, who would talk your ear off about the color of dirt if you let him. "I hear the church ladies are going to be there
30 to perform a hymn, throw some religion in the mix," Mike A. continued.

"You go and sing some songs for those ladies, Mike!" the other Mike hollered.

"How much will you pay me?" Mike A. hollered back.

35   Wayne listened the rest of the afternoon as the two Mikes and Lars the German bantered, moving on fairly quickly to their usual topics—football, the president's ineptitude, and Wayne's decade-long crush on Matilda Waters, a crush that was partly a joke and partly the truth.

40   "You got to say something to her, Wayne," Lars the German shook his head. "Nothing to lose at this point."

"You know, I bet she'll be there tonight," said one of the Mikes, Wayne wasn't sure which one, because he was thinking about his idea. It was just after five, when
45 the evening staff got in and the day staff got off, unless you were working a double. Wayne wished he weren't—if only he could go …

But no, it was foolish, anyway.

The boys all left and Denise showed up and started
50 refilling napkin holders and wiping down menus. Wayne mopped the floor and dried the dishes.

Around seven, when the one table that had come in for dinner had paid and left, he went for it.

"Think you can handle it if I head out?" he said to
55 Denise, "being a slow night and all." He didn't want to say why he wanted to leave and hoped she didn't ask.

"Sure," Denise shrugged. "Feeling okay?"

"I could just use a night off. Been working a lot of doubles lately."

60   The Dive was lit in that way that you can see everything, but not too much of anything. A young fellow Wayne didn't recognize stood on stage slumped over a guitar. He strummed the guitar only once every sentence or so, and his voice shook. He finished his song
65 and shuffled off the stage to some sparse clapping. Wayne spotted Lars in the back. The Mikes were nowhere to be seen. They must have gone home. Wayne was glad. He'd pay for this tomorrow.

"Wayne Dewey!" Lars howled. "Get up there! I've
70 heard you sing! Get up there!" He swung his glass high.

"What you want me to sing, Lars?" Wayne yelled back. People seated at the small round tables turned to follow their conversation. There was Matilda, among them. Her hair was in a braid, like usual. It was the color
75 of dark chocolate, but with one grey streak in the front, like God had put it there on purpose to make sure people knew she was different. He didn't usually see her outside of the bank. Sometimes he waited a full day to cash a paycheck to make sure he did, though. Her schedule was
80 mornings, but she took off Tuesdays and Wednesdays to teach accounting at the high school.

She was looking at him. He smiled. Behind the bar, the ice machine rumbled.

"Sweet Home Alabama!" Lars yelled, and a woman
85 at one of the small tables let out a supportive "Whoop!"

"You can be more creative than that," Wayne said. "How about I sing one I wrote?"

"Even better," Lars said.

"Hey kid, can I borrow that?" Wayne asked the boy
90 with the guitar. The boy nodded and held it out for him. Wayne took it and climbed onto the platform, into the soft, reddish spotlight that lit the stage only a tad brighter than the rest of the room. He adjusted the microphone, pulling it higher, positioning it expertly.

95   "This is about a woman," he said, "named Matilda."

31. According to the passage, Wayne attributes which one of the following characteristics to Lars?

A. He is talkative.
B. He loves dirt.
C. He is an immigrant.
D. He is unemployed.

32. Which of the following is NOT an accurate description of the passage?

    F. The story of a man whose friendships with regular clients at the diner where he works lead him to make an uncharacteristically bold choice for him.

    G. A glimpse inside the social happenings of a small town undergoing a small but, for the narrator, consequential transition.

    H. A look at how one character summoned his bravery to make a choice that recent circumstances enabled.

    J. A portrait of a socially awkward adult man who has been driven into solitude and bitterness by his unrequited romantic inclinations.

33. In both the tenth and eleventh paragraphs (lines 40–47) "'You got to say …' if only he could go …", the two characters who speak are:

    A. projecting their own desires onto one another.

    B. expressing thoughts with the interests of a third character in mind.

    C. generally sympathetic to the decision of their friend to keep his feelings private.

    D. discovering that the reality of a situation is different from what they previously thought.

34. It can most reasonably be inferred that, as it is used in line 68, the phrase "pay for this tomorrow" refers to all of the following EXCEPT the possibility that:

    F. Wayne's clients at the diner would not fail to bring up what was about to happen in conversation.

    G. Wayne would likely be ridiculed by his friends at the diner.

    H. Wayne would owe his friends payment on a bet they had made.

    J. Wayne would feel embarrassed talking to his friends about the open mic.

35. Which of the following best describes the difference between Wayne at the beginning of the story and Wayne at the end of the story?

    A. At the beginning of the story, Wayne regards the new restaurant and its owner with skepticism. At the end of the story, Wayne is more trusting of her.

    B. At the beginning of the story, Wayne is dubious about the open mic. At the end of the story, Wayne has decided it is his opportunity to become famous.

    C. At the beginning of the story, Wayne harbors a secret crush on Matilda, a banker in town. At the end of the story, he has made the decision to make his feelings public.

    D. At the beginning of the story, Wayne hopes that his friends will invite him to the open mic with them. At the end of the story, he has decided to go to it on his own.

36. The passage indicates that the town in which the story takes place is one where:

    F. most residents know most other residents.

    G. everyone gets along without any conflict.

    H. there are great disparities in standards of living among the population.

    J. few children who grow up in the town move away when they reach adulthood.

37. The passage indicates that Wayne was not surprised by Matilda's presence at the open mic because:

    A. he had spoken with her earlier and knew that she would be there.

    B. he suspected she would be there given her work and volunteering schedule, which he knew by heart.

    C. the conversation in the diner earlier in the day led him to expect it.

    D. he prayed about it during his shift.

38. Which of the following best describes the way the final paragraph ("This is about a woman …") functions in the passage?

    F. It reinforces the revelation several paragraphs earlier that tonight will be the night that Wayne expresses his feelings for Matilda.

    G. It contradicts an earlier suggestion that Wayne would attend the event but would not be participating.

    H. It lends support to the suggestion that Wayne chose to perform in order to make the boy who had just stepped off the stage feel more comfortable.

    J. It confirms that Wayne's interest in performing at the open mic had to do with a shift in his approach to his long-held dilemma.

39. The passage establishes that Mike T. and Mike A. have all of the following traits in common EXCEPT:

    A. an interest in teasing one another.

    B. a friendly and well-worn friendship with the narrator.

    C. regular patronage of the diner where the narrator works.

    D. equal distaste for engaging in conversation with Lars the German.

40. Wayne feels that in relation to the rest of the town, the new restaurant:

    F. is unpopular.

    G. is different.

    H. has been around for generations.

    J. is unlikely to succeed.

17

PASSAGE 5

LITERARY NARRATIVE: This passage is adapted from a short story published in the early 2000s.

In August the fireflies are abundant. When we were kids, we would run around the backyard catching them in jars and leaving the jars by our bedsides overnight. In the morning, they would all be dead.

5   One year, dad showed us how to punch holes in the top of the jar so they would live longer, but the next morning they were still like always, and when I shook the jar, they didn't wake up.

The summer also meant the start of assembling 10 season. Mom would come home with the giant bags of dried lavender, and my sister Lou and I would shred it in between our palms and pack it into the sacks of brightly colored cloth, orange and purple and blue, then tie it up with twine. When Lou got old enough, she moved 15 over to the sewing machine to make the pillows. I stayed on sachet team my whole life, pretty much, because everyone, especially mom, knew I wasn't careful enough to handle such a delicate task as stitching.

The house was bustling and alive as people came 20 and went, carrying full boxes inside and empty ones out, or empty ones in and full ones out. The market wasn't the only destination for mom's goods. We shipped them, too. In bulk to wholesalers on the outskirts of the state, and in smaller packages to friends and family around the 25 country to remind them that mom was still around, and still making beautiful things.

"I don't want them to forget me!" she'd say and laugh like she was kidding, but we all knew she wasn't.

When I was a kid, I would make bracelets and 30 anklets out of the twine, braiding it into bands. I passed them out to kids at school, hoping they, like mom's family and friends far away whom I'd never met, would not forget me. I preferred sitting and working at recess on the sidelines as the game of four square became more and 35 more advanced. There were new rules, new complexities as we all climbed the measurement walls at our respective houses. My own marks were always just behind Lou's for the same age—her "Age 5" mark was an inch above my "Age 5" mark, her nine at least two inches, maybe three. 40 Her fifteen was nearly a foot.

When assembling season ended, market began. Every weekend, dad would awake us at four by calling our names quietly from the door, "Lou. Mara." But we were already up—we'd been up since the truck's engine 45 rumbled on around two, and the long tables and metal piping for scaffolding and thick drapes and finally, the product itself, had been loaded into the back. Lou and I were the last to be loaded in. We'd brush our teeth, pull back our hair, and put on the plain white t-shirts 50 and jeans that were our uniform underneath our LINDA'S LOVELIES aprons. We would climb into the front seat next to them both, mashed all together, a family packed into its weekend life. When she was old enough, Lou brought along her green plastic travel mug 55 of coffee. I tried it a couple of times but couldn't learn to like it.

We would arrive before sunrise and set up the booth. My job was arranging product. Until it was time for that, Lou and I mostly watched if it was warm, or on 60 the chillier mornings when the air nipped at our ears and burned our eyes, we'd wait in the truck, fiddling with the radio so that there was always a song we could sing along to until the light came and warmed the outside enough for us to join mom and dad.

65   Dad would keep lookout for the first signs of customers. "Here comes one," he'd say, "Look alive." I would smile to look alive. Lou usually sat up a little straighter, if anything. Dad smiled, too—people always recognized me as his daughter, and I wondered if it was 70 because we were the two smiling, but then, we are both the shorter ones with bushier eyebrows and thick hands. Lou and mom are tall with bigger nostrils and freckles.

Those days were fun, and special to me now even as I look back and realize how naïve I was, not to realize 75 it was all for me and Lou—so we could go to college. I didn't realize it until Lou chose not to go, and I saw it in mom's eyes. Lou wasn't holding up her end of the bargain.

Everything slowed down a bit after that. We 80 didn't need as much as quickly if Lou was going to stay home and keep working, and we still had three years before it would be my turn to choose where I'd go after graduation. Unlike my sister, it never crossed my mind not to go to university, so when mom asked, 85 "What about you, Mara? Are you going to do like Lou and settle for sticking around here?" I didn't hesitate to say, "Nope!" I loved the summers and falls of packing and tying and smiling at strangers, but I knew it wasn't my destiny. Mom did not have to fear that I would 90 breach the tacit agreement—her dreams for me were mine, too.

17

41. The main point of the second-to-last paragraph (lines 73–78) is that:

   A. Mara feels ashamed that she did not know her parents were saving money for college.
   B. Mara realized as she grew older that her parents were trying to help her and her sister get ahead by selling lavender.
   C. Lou breached a formal contract.
   D. Mara feels nostalgic thinking about the fun she had selling lavender as a child.

42. According to the passage, Mara and Lou's mom sends homemade goods to family and friends because:

   F. their mom wants to save money for her children's college educations.
   G. their mom's favorite pastime is making pillows.
   H. their mom wants to sell in bulk to wholesalers.
   J. their mom wants to remind her loved ones that she exists.

43. The father can be best described as:

   A. emotionally distant but hardworking.
   B. quiet and cold.
   C. kind and involved in his children's lives.
   D. friendly but unpredictable.

44. Which one of the following is NOT true of the family's business?

   F. The family creates sachets of brightly-colored fabric.
   G. Each family member helps to sew the pillows.
   H. The family creates some sachets and pillows that they do not sell for money.
   J. Most of the sachets and pillows are put together in the summertime.

45. It can be logically inferred from the passage that:

   A. Mara shares values with her mother.
   B. Mara feels angry at her sister for not going to college.
   C. Mara did not enjoy waking up at 4am to sell product.
   D. Mara sold bracelets at her family's market stand.

46. According to the passage, which one of the following is true about Lou in relation to Mara?

   F. Lou is taller than Mara.
   G. Lou is worse at school than Mara.
   H. Lou does not love her parents as much as Mara does.
   J. Lou enjoys selling at the market more than Mara does.

47. The narrator can be best described as:

   A. a child describing her family life.
   B. an objective observer of a family.
   C. an adult reminiscing about a specific aspect of her childhood.
   D. an adult offering a clinical account of a series of events.

48. Which one of the following best describes the function of the second-to-last paragraph (lines 73–78)?

   F. It serves to explain why Lou did not go to college.
   G. It sums up the previous paragraphs' descriptions of the market.
   H. It brings the story back to the introductory themes of fireflies and summertime.
   J. It offers a transition to and contrast between two different times in the narrator's life.

49. Which of the following best describes the function of the third paragraph (lines 9–18) in relation to the story as a whole?

   A. It describes all the activities the narrator did during the summer.
   B. It introduces the main topic and two of the main characters of the story.
   C. It relates key information about the narrator's carelessness.
   D. It distracts from the children's cruelty to fireflies.

50. According to the passage, Mara believes her mom's reaction to Lou's decision not to go to college was:

   F. anger at her daughter's laziness.
   G. sadness at her own failures as a parent.
   H. happiness about her daughter's independent thinking.
   J. disappointment that her daughter was not holding up an unspoken agreement.

17

PASSAGE 6

LITERARY NARRATIVE: This passage is adapted from a short story titled "The Doorman" that takes place in New York City in the early 2000s.

Wallace's grandchildren liked it when his hand shook. They'd grab at it, a twin on each knee, racing to stop the old man convulsion. "Me!" Fiona would squeal when she won. "You!" Henry would squeal along with her.
5 Wallace wondered how the submissive boy had come out so unlike his father. Then again, Simon himself was so unlike Wallace. Was there a gene that coded for an unfamiliar son?

"You can tell them to stop, dad," Simon would offer, but why would Wallace do that?

10 "Dad," Simon would sigh, "just retire," meaning Simon would take care of Wallace's rent and bologna and Listerine. But of course Wallace couldn't abandon the residents of the building where he was doorman. His son didn't think he was of any use anymore, but he was
15 wrong. The new girl in 33A, for example—who would she talk to after midnight, when she got her rumblings? And Simon clearly did not recall the time Wallace helped get that delivery man arrested, the one who swiped Mr. Harrington's wallet straight from his back pocket. Every
20 Veterans Day since, Mr. Harrington gave Wallace a crisp hundred.

"It has to bother people that you can't carry anything," Simon insisted a few days before the incident.

"They don't mind," Wallace plunged his right hand
25 into the pocket of his slacks to hide its quaking, which just made his whole pant leg tremble from top to bottom.

"Doesn't it bother you, then?"

Wallace didn't answer. He didn't say to his son, *I'm not a dog or a mule. My job isn't about how fast I can fetch or*
30 *how much weight my old back can take. I am respected, too.*

Simon didn't get that intangibles was the thing. Performance always mattered too much to him, even as a kid but being a lawyer had made him more that way.

The day after Simon had the heart attack, when
35 he was still hospitalized but stable, Wallace headed to work. The 7 train wasn't running from Queens, and the R held a new crowd—two dozen or so teenagers armed with band instruments.

Stiff knapsacks pressed in on him as Wallace made
40 his way through flutes and trumpets and clarinets and one tuba. His hearing aid amplified their squeals into shrieks, and he covered his ears as he charted a squiggly path to the open tip of a bench next to a slumbering woman in nurse shoes. How anyone could sleep in such
45 a circus he didn't know. He lowered himself next to her.

Wallace didn't mind the kids on the train. That was another difference between him and Simon—he could appreciate people, generally speaking. Once, Simon said, "Dad, why have you never said you were proud of me?
50 Not once?"

"That's foolish," Wallace had said. "I'm sure I have," but he couldn't remember if he had or not.

The boy had started going to see a psychologist because he had anxieties, and the doctor had told his son
55 that the reason he was anxious is because he felt he didn't deserve abundance.

"Let me get this straight," Wallace had teased, "I screwed you up because I taught you to be happy with less?" Simon had said no, he wasn't suggesting Wallace
60 had messed up, just that maybe the reason why Simon had a hard time accepting affluence is because he didn't grow up with it, himself.

"I did the best I could," Wallace had said.

"Do you look down on us for the way we live now?"
65 asked Simon. He had always been a serious person, even as a child, but law had made him more that way. The gulf between them held more than just seriousness, though. His wife wore the kind of jewelry that attracts scamming thieves. Handsome fellows in suits catered Thanksgiving
70 at their condo. Their children, who already had passports, ate baby food from a farm.

Of course not, Wallace thought. But instead, he said, "I wish I'd been able to afford to buy you more things," because Simon seemed hungry for him to express some
75 kind of regret.

Simon was a good person, a good son. Wallace just hadn't known how to relate to him lately. He hoped he had another chance to try.

Across the car, two boys holding trumpets were
80 wailing some tuneless song. Wallace studied them. How much fun they seemed to be having. As he watched, a familiar face peeked through the sliver between their lurching bodies. It took Wallace a few seconds to place the profile, and when he did, he was delighted. Frank
85 Harrington, son of Mr. Harrington, in 37D! Of course,

he must be on his way to the building. The second Saturday of the month meant breakfast with his dad.

Good boy, that Frank Harrington.

90 Suddenly, Wallace's right hand began to tremor. He slid the volatile arm into its refuge, his pants pocket, and clung to his lunch with the other, reliable left. The left hand still knew its way, knew how to be in the world.

51. The passage can be best described as about a man who:

   A. is hopeful that his adult son will survive through a present crisis but conflicted about their ability to communicate.

   B. is outraged at his adult son, whose demeanor and life choices conflict with those of the father.

   C. is on his commute to his job as a doorman, which he plans to quit soon.

   D. is a grandfather whose relationship to his grandkids is the most important thing to him.

52. The passage most strongly suggests that Wallace's son's family is:

   F. wealthier than Wallace.

   G. arrogant and entitled.

   H. more willing to be confrontational than Wallace.

   J. more religious than Wallace.

53. The passage does NOT mention which of the following as an attribute of Wallace?

   A. He uses Listerine.

   B. He cares about the residents of the building where he works.

   C. He is uncomfortable with abundance.

   D. He is unlike his son in several key ways.

54. Wallace views Simon as all of the following EXCEPT as:

   F. a serious child.

   G. a serious adult.

   H. a person with anxiety.

   J. a person with fear.

55. The "familiar face" mentioned in line 82 is:

   A. the son of Frank Harrington, who is a tenant in the building where Wallace works.

   B. Frank Harrington, a relative of someone who lives in the building where Wallace works.

   C. a metaphor for Wallace's own son, who has been hospitalized after having a heart attack.

   D. one of the boys holding a trumpet, who is related to one of the residents of the building where Wallace works.

56. The final sentence of the passage (lines 91–92) most likely is intended to emphasize which of the following characteristics of Wallace?

   F. His increasing unease at functioning in the world in the way that he was able to as a younger man

   G. His anger at his son, which is being manifest in his physical body in an involuntary way

   H. That he has Parkinson's disease but is unaware of it

   J. That he is delusional about his ability to continue performing his job adequately and that he should take his son's advice and retire

57. As it is used in line 31, the word "intangibles" most nearly means:

   A. things that Simon should want for himself.

   B. things that Wallace is incapable of providing.

   C. things with less value than tangible things.

   D. things with value that is difficult to quantify.

58. Which of the following is NOT on the train?

   F. A nurse

   G. A tuba

   H. A resident of the building where Wallace works

   J. A person Wallace knows

59. As it is used both times in line 76, the word "good" can reasonably be said to mean all of the following EXCEPT:

   A. ethical.

   B. caretaking.

   C. sincere.

   D. optimistic.

60. When Wallace recalls assisting a resident recover a stolen wallet, his feeling about the incident can be described as:

   F. regret.

   G. pride.

   H. elation.

   J. envy.

PASSAGE 7

LITERARY NARRATIVE: This passage takes place in Portland, Oregon in 2013. The narrator is a woman just out of college.

It starts with a bunch of boxes. We are to check one for each question. Nationality? Race? Religion? Gender? There is no "other" box, but a blank line on which to write our particular brand of otherness. But even the line
5 doesn't fit me.

Nationality: My mother is Chinese and Canadian. My father is missing. My step-father is Canadian and American. I have American and British citizenship but grew up in Beijing and London and Seattle and, for a
10 few pivotal weeks, in New York City. That was when my mother, always a nervous woman but suddenly so nervous she could not bathe and forgot to make meals and scratched at her knuckles until they bled, started telling me that a man was coming from the government
15 to lock us up. We sat up late into the night wielding kitchen knives behind the large chair in the apartment provided by the university where she was teaching for the fall semester. She forgot to teach her classes. My step-father was on another coast. I called him and told
20 him I thought something was wrong. I was right. I was eight. Her schizophrenic break eventually took her back to China to live with her own parents; I went to live with my step-father, also an academic. We moved a lot. By my eighteenth birthday, I had four driver's licenses in four
25 different states.

Race: I am half-Chinese and half-something-I-don't-know. At various times, back when she was well, my mother claimed various lineages—my father was Jewish once, Indian another time, Persian yet another. But was
30 she ever well if my father's background changed so often? After the few bad weeks in New York, I was raised by a Caucasian man with blonde hair and green eyes who looks nothing like me. "You're more white than black," a girl told me once in seventh grade when I tried to sit
35 with her and her friends in the cafeteria. But the white kids didn't seem to think so. I was in-between. I call my step-father Harry, because I always called him Harry, but I think of him as dad. His mother, I call grandmother. His sisters I call my aunts. They are all white. Am I not
40 in their family, too?

Religion: I went to mass every Sunday with Harry no matter where we were living. In every city, there is a church. But until I was eight, Harry went alone, when he was in the same city as us—my mother was

45 Buddhist and I learned about Buddhism from her. As an adult, I consider myself an atheist, although there are whole months at a time when I feel more agnostic than anything—certain only of my own uncertainty. When I am visiting home (which is now Montreal, where Harry
50 has settled in retirement, near my grandmother), I go to mass with them. While I am there, I sometimes feel a divine presence, a calmness. It feels real, and distinct, and powerful. But then I come back to Portland, to my small studio with the yellow orchid in the window, and
55 my new job writing code for this education start-up, and the feeling is gone, and I don't believe anything again, or I don't know what I believe.

Gender: This one is not hard for me to answer. I am a woman. I am the daughter of my mother, and the
60 adopted daughter of Harry. I am 22 years old. I am not dating anyone. I live alone. I like living alone—it makes me feel like an adult. But even though I am a woman, I don't think I will have children of my own. I just don't have any interest. I haven't seen my own mother in four
65 years. The last time, she had gained 100 pounds and her teeth were rotted all in front. Her apartment in Beijing smelled like millions of cigarettes. Harry held my hand while she ran hers along the thick, dark window—it was winter, and after sunset—talking to the cartoon decals
70 she had plastered there. Bugs. Tweety. Minnie Mouse. When we told her it was time to go to dinner, she put on a tutu. I hated her own mother—my real grandmother, I suppose, though I don't remember her at all—for buying it for her, for allowing her to take it out of some store
75 somewhere. It wasn't something a grown woman should wear. It was for a little girl. I would also never wear something like that.

"Is everyone finished?" the human resources officer asks. He wears a bow tie with black polka dots. His lips
80 are thin. We all nod.

"Please pass them to the front." As we do, he explains the point of the exercise. "I will tally the results," he takes the stack over to a white board, where he picks up a marker and uncaps it. "We will see just how diverse
85 we are as a company."

I raise my hand and wait for him to turn back around.

"Ting has a question," Danny, from Accounting, says. Danny and I met on smoke breaks. The bow-tied
90 man turns, raises his eyebrows at me.

"I wasn't able to complete mine," I say.

61. The point of view from which the passage is told can be described as a young woman who:

    A. is irate at the form she has been asked to complete because she considers her identity to be in constant fluctuation.

    B. declines to complete the form because she feels that it is too restrictive to others with different backgrounds than her.

    C. does not complete the form because she feels that it doesn't offer her identities as options.

    D. fluctuates between identities as a matter of choice.

62. The passage most strongly suggests that the narrator and her step-father moved around frequently because of:

    F. his academic posts at various universities.

    G. her mother's diagnosis.

    H. her grandmother.

    J. her special needs as a person with dual citizenship.

63. The narrator describes herself as "half-something-I-don't-know" in lines 26–27 because:

    A. her father had a combination of ethic backgrounds, but she is unsure of what particular combination.

    B. her father was unknown to her mother and to the narrator.

    C. her mother's descriptions of her father's ethnic heritage left her uncertain of it.

    D. her mother was not certain about her own ethnic heritage, and her father was Chinese.

64. The narrator describes her mother as all of the following EXCEPT as:

    F. childlike.

    G. paranoid.

    H. a Mandarin speaker.

    J. a teacher.

65. Which of the following is NOT a way in which the narrator distinguishes herself from other people, according to the passage?

    A. She distinguishes herself from her mother, as a grown woman.

    B. She distinguishes herself from her Catholic step-father with regard to her personal religious views.

    C. She distinguishes herself from the children in her seventh grade glass, ethnically.

    D. She distinguishes herself from her Canadian grandmother with regard to her national identity.

66. By "certain only of my own uncertainty" in line 48, the narrator is most precisely referring to:

    F. belief in a divine power.

    G. belief in the purpose of religion.

    H. adherence to the tenets of Catholicism.

    J. adherence to the tenets of Buddhism.

67. The narrator indicates that she thinks of Harry as all of the following EXCEPT as:

    A. her step-father.

    B. Caucasian.

    C. Canadian-American.

    D. her biological father.

68. When the narrator asks, "Am I not in their family, too?" at the end of the third paragraph (lines 39–40), she is using the rhetorical question to emphasize her feeling of:

    F. ambivalence over whether or not she should be considered a member of the family.

    G. disgust that she would ever be viewed as anything other than a full member of the family.

    H. frustration with the terms by which race is defined, which in her case conflict with her family history.

    J. interest in being taken more seriously by her family members as a person.

69. The hatred the narrator expresses for her biological grandmother in line 72 is a result of:

    A. her dislike of most of her grandmother's parenting choices.

    B. feeling that her grandmother should not have allowed her mother to make such a childlike purchase.

    C. a difference in opinion between her and her grandmother regarding what constitutes womanhood.

    D. loyalty to her non-biological grandmother.

70. The narrator's attitude toward the form can be described, overall, as:

    F. accepting.

    G. critical.

    H. magnanimous.

    J. repulsed.

17

PASSAGE 8

LITERARY NARRATIVE: This passage is adapted from a short story set in Miami in the year 2009. The narrator is a male teenager.

My mother's cancer was wild. It spread throughout her body, metastasizing in large solid chunks. The tumors crept around her organs, scurrying through her with nothing to check them. The day after hearing her diagnosis, my mother
5 *had cried all day. "What can we do?" she had sobbed.*

Louisa and I had been dating for seven months when I finally told her about my mother's cancer. "I'll pray for her," she said. "You can pray with me if you'd like." This was how I began to learn about Santería. It
10 was new to me; I had never been very religious, and before meeting Louisa, I had never known someone who practiced Santería.

I was eager to learn, and I often asked Louisa to tell me more about her beliefs. I learned that Santería is a
15 syncretic religion—a combination of Roman Catholicism and Afro-Caribbean Yoruba religions. When Catholic explorers came to the Caribbean, they brought with them a new culture that clashed with the local beliefs. Syncretism, the act of combining very different beliefs, was vital to the
20 conflicted faithful locals. One religion's ideas were laid on top of the other's to form a new faith. Santería allowed Yoruba beliefs to meld with Catholic dogma despite the evident contradictions. "When confronted with a spiritual dead end, what else could they do?" Louisa asked.

25 Santería is a very measured, orderly religion. The world is divided up into realms, and each realm is controlled by a saint known as an Orisha. There are Orishas for fire, violence, earth, human effort, illness, water, and more. A plethora of concepts can all be split
30 up into the realms of one Orisha or another. In the face of my mother's wild disease, this order comforted me.

After some time, I asked Louisa if we could perform a Santería ritual for my mother. "Of course," she replied.

We traveled across town to a *botanica*, where we
35 bought supplies. The store was part homeopathic hub and part religious trinket superstore. Waist-high buckets of dried herbs were cast about the floor. Candles and various clay statuettes lined the shelves along the walls. Louisa filled a dark plastic bag with rice and dried
40 chickpeas, then she picked out two slim purple candles and took them to the counter.

We returned to her house, where Louisa prepared the altar, first stretching a white lace cloth across a small mahogany table. Purple wax deposits caked the cloth, the
45 layers of different shades revealing the many candles that had melted away into little mounds. Fruit, feathers, and candles were next placed on top. Amid the wax stood a small statue of a slender man dressed in rags and strips of burlap. Across his head, he wore a yellow veil.

50 The man with the veil—although now it seemed like a wig of brilliant straw, or even perhaps natural golden hair—was Babalu Aye, the Orisha to whom we were praying. This particular Orisha, the saint of illnesses, was also known as Saint Lazarus.

55 Louisa tied a gnarled chicken foot to his thin ceramic arm. "We're ready now."

I placed a ceramic bowl at the feet of Babalu Aye. Louisa filled the bowl with a dark liquid. I wondered if it might be blood. I sprinkled in chickpeas and rice and a
60 small dried stone meant to represent my mother's tumors.

When this was done, we bowed our heads and said a short prayer. Then Louisa took my hand and led me out to the yard.

The final stage of the ritual was a *bembe*. We would
65 dance in Louisa's yard and invite Babalu Aye to join us. Orishas were said to appear at these rituals to answer prayers in person.

"He will seize one of us and make his presence known," Louisa explained.

70 We lit a small fire in the center of the yard and sat before it. Louisa gestured toward a small drum and told me to beat it when I felt the time was right. The taut leather drumhead seemed to quiver in anticipation, waiting for me to begin.

75 "Once the flames grow a bit, we can start the ritual," she said. I clutched her hands. Her grip suddenly felt so strong. As we both stared into the fire, I sensed a lightness grow inside of me, as if I had taken a deep breath of clean air.

80 We stayed by the fire long into the night. Periodically we would dance frenzied circles across the yard. The flames crackled as embers leaped into the air and fizzled moments before they touched the ground. At one point, Louisa danced over to the other side of the
85 fire. I didn't know if the Orisha had seized her; I didn't know what to look for. I simply pounded the drum.

From my seat, I watched Louisa as she twirled across the yard, in another world.

71. The narrator implies that Santería appeals to him in his current situation because:

    A. it was a religion that was new to him.
    B. Louisa, whom he respected and admired, practiced the religion.
    C. it is a very measured, orderly religion.
    D. it had the possibility of curing his mother's cancer through faith.

72. In the final paragraph (lines 87–88), the narrator describes Louisa as "across the yard, in another world" most likely to convey the idea that:

    F. she was separated from the narrator by the fire.
    G. she was seized by the Orisha while in the yard.
    H. she was physically in the yard, but her spirit was devoted to the ceremony.
    J. she was on the opposite side of a circle from the narrator.

73. The *purple wax deposits* mentioned in line 44 allow the reader to infer that:

    A. purple candles are exclusively used for Santería ceremonies.
    B. the cloth has been used several times for ceremonies in the past.
    C. the cloth is the only one used for Santería ceremonies.
    D. fruit, feathers, and candles are all used for ceremonies.

74. Each of the following was described as placed in the ceramic bowl at the feet of Babalu Aye EXCEPT:

    F. a dark liquid.
    G. a gnarled chicken foot.
    H. rice.
    J. a stone.

75. Where does the passage imply that Santería was formed?

    A. The Caribbean
    B. Africa
    C. Rome
    D. Spain

76. The passage provides evidence that before meeting Louisa, the narrator most likely:

    F. had never heard of Santería.
    G. did not believe in a higher power.
    H. did not know that Santería was a syncretic religion.
    J. had never participated in a religious ceremony.

77. The word *plethora* (line 29) as used in the passage most nearly means:

    A. excess.
    B. embarrassment.
    C. narrow range.
    D. large number.

78. The passage indicates that the narrator is unsure if Orisha had seized Louisa (lines 85–86) because:

    F. he wasn't confident that such a thing was possible.
    G. he didn't know which of the two would be seized.
    H. he was focused on pounding the drum.
    J. he didn't know what to look for.

79. Which of the following best describes the way the fourth paragraph (lines 25–31) functions in the passage?

    A. It explains why the narrator is drawn to the religion of Santería.
    B. It provides details about Santería.
    C. It is used to explain why the ceremony described at the end of the passage is performed.
    D. It is used to compare Santería with Catholicism.

80. It can most reasonably be inferred that, as used in line 15, the term *syncretic* refers to:

    F. a melding of different beliefs.
    G. a combination only of Roman-Catholic and Afro-Caribbean religions.
    H. a religion that involves Orishas.
    J. any combination of two separate ideas.

17

Answer Keys

Write in whether you got each problem right or wrong (or left it blank). If your answer was correct, put a 1 in every blank to the right of that problem. Sum up each column and compare your total to the total possible "Out Of" points in each column.

Passage 1

Problem	Correct Answer	Right/ Wrong/Blank	Main Ideas/ Author's Approach	Details	Relationships	Meanings of Words	Generalizations
1	B			—			
2	G			—			
3	A				—		
4	J			—			
5	A				—		
6	G				—		
7	B			—			
8	H						—
9	A					—	
10	H			—			
Total							
Out Of	10		0	5	3	1	1

Passage 2

Problem	Correct Answer	Right/ Wrong/Blank	Main Ideas/ Author's Approach	Details	Relationships	Meanings of Words	Generalizations
11	A						—
12	H						—
13	A			—			
14	J			—			
15	B		—				
16	F				—		
17	C			—			
18	J			—			
19	B				—		
20	H						—
Total							
Out Of	10		1	4	2	0	3

Passage 3

Problem	Correct Answer	Right/ Wrong/Blank	Main Ideas/ Author's Approach	Details	Relationships	Meanings of Words	Generalizations
21	C						—
22	H						—
23	D						—
24	F		—				
25	B		—				
26	J			—			
27	A				—		
28	F						—
29	B			—			
30	J			—			
Total							
Out Of		10	2	3	1	0	4

Passage 4

Problem	Correct Answer	Right/ Wrong/Blank	Main Ideas/ Author's Approach	Details	Relationships	Meanings of Words	Generalizations
31	A			—			
32	J		—				
33	B				—		
34	H					—	
35	C				—		
36	F			—			
37	C			—			
38	J		—				
39	D				—		
40	G				—		
Total							
Out Of		10	2	3	4	1	0

MANHATTAN
PREP

Passage 5

Problem	Correct Answer	Right/ Wrong/Blank	Main Ideas/ Author's Approach	Details	Relationships	Meanings of Words	Generalizations
41	B		—				
42	J				—		
43	C						—
44	G			—			
45	A				—		
46	F			—			
47	C						—
48	J		—				
49	B		—				
50	J				—		
Total							
Out Of		10	3	2	3	0	2

Passage 6

Problem	Correct Answer	Right/ Wrong/Blank	Main Ideas/ Author's Approach	Details	Relationships	Meanings of Words	Generalizations
51	A						—
52	F				—		
53	C			—			
54	J			—			
55	B			—			
56	F		—				
57	D					—	
58	H			—			
59	D					—	
60	G		—				
Total							
Out Of		10	2	4	1	2	1

17

Passage 7

Problem	Correct Answer	Right/ Wrong/Blank	Main Ideas/ Author's Approach	Details	Relationships	Meanings of Words	Generalizations
61	C		—				
62	F			—			
63	C		—				
64	H			—			
65	D			—			
66	F					—	
67	D			—			
68	H		—				
69	B				—		
70	G						—
Total							
Out Of		10	3	4	1	1	1

Passage 8

Problem	Correct Answer	Right/ Wrong/Blank	Main Ideas/ Author's Approach	Details	Relationships	Meanings of Words	Generalizations
71	C				—		
72	H		—				
73	B						—
74	G			—			
75	A			—			
76	H						—
77	D					—	
78	J			—			
79	A		—				
80	F					—	
Total							
Out Of		10	2	3	1	2	2

MANHATTAN
PREP

Literary Narrative Solutions

Passage 1 Solutions

1.   **(B)** a boy with no siblings.

Details

The narrator states, "I was eleven and an only child" (line 8). Choice (A) is incorrect because he is not a teenager and doesn't have siblings. Choice (C) is incorrect because the question wants the narrator's age at the time of the events, not at the time he is writing or telling this story. Choice (D) is incorrect because, in line 73, the narrator states that "there would be my old friends, too," meaning at school.

2.   **(G)** a potential opportunity for friendship.

Details

In lines 28–29, the narrator says, "I wondered if he wanted to play tag or see my fort." This is how you know (G) is correct—he visits his neighbor's home in order to initiate a friendship. Choice (F) is incorrect because of this same fact. If the narrator wanted to remain at a distance, he wouldn't have visited Ilan's home. Choices (H) and (J) aren't supported by anything in the passage.

3.   **(A)** have a different dynamic than the narrator's family.

Relationships (Comparisons)

In lines 1–2, the narrator writes, "The new neighbors were not like us. They yelled, even when they were just talking." This is different from his family, where his father watches TV alone in the house, and he talks to himself (line 52). There is no mention of the neighbors' wealth or religion, so (B) and (C) are unsupported. Choice (D) is also not supported by the facts in the passage. You don't actually know how close the family is; the fact that they talk more doesn't make them close, and it's possible the narrator might be very close to his mother, but since she is absent, it is unknown.

4.   **(J)** a period of time in which he dreaded returning to school in the fall because he feared that his friends would no longer be his friends.

Details

In the sixth paragraph, lines 45–53, the narrator writes that he "didn't have many friends outside of school … Mom worked … It was lonely with only the two of us there all day, every day." These revelations support (F). In the same paragraph, he writes that he would spend time outdoors "talking to myself" and that there was "no car," and so (G) and (H) are also true. Choice (J), however, is contradicted by the statement in line 73, "there would be my old friends, too," which indicates that the narrator assumes his old school friends *will* still be his friends.

17

5.   **(A)** disdain and disinterest.

Relationships

In lines 23–25, the narrator writes, "I, embarrassed for my dad, shoveled … cans of Dr. Pepper into the bag," and in lines 49–50, the narrator says, "He watched TV shows I thought were boring." Together, these statements support (A), that he to some extent disdained, or looked down upon, his father's habits of drinking so much Dr. Pepper, and that he was not interested in his father's habit of watching certain TV shows. (B) is incorrect because there isn't any indication that he is amused by his father. (C) is too extreme; the narrator doesn't express anger at his father. (D) is wrong because he is not curious about his father, nor does he seem to express clear desire for his father to behave differently.

6.   **(G)** Ilan's negative remark regarding his own mother after the two of them had boarded the bus.

Relationships (Cause–Effect)

In line 83, Ilan remarks, "She drives me crazy," referring to his mother. The narrator expresses surprise, writing in lines 87–90, "I began to feel something was different now … So much was new already, and we weren't even there, yet." What is "new" has been made clear to the narrator through Ilan's comment, so (G) is correct. (F) is incorrect because Ilan is talking about his own mother, not the narrator's. (H) is incorrect because it occurs *before* the narrator realizes there has been a change in dynamic. (J) references a moment that occurs long before anything changes between the two boys.

7.   **(B)** are friends of his during the school year.

Details

The narrator says in line 45, "I didn't have many friends outside of school," indicating that he *does* have friends at school. Also, in line 73, he mentions that when he returns, he'll see his old friends. (A) is contradicted by lines 72–73: "There would be more people there for him to befriend." (C) is not supported by anything in the passage, which states that while Ilan and the narrator live farthest out on the bus route, other children *do* ride it. And (D) is contradicted by line 73.

8.   **(H)** It reveals that the newfound distance between the narrator and his friend is not solely about the friendships they will or will not develop with other children at school.

Generalizations

The question is asking about lines 86–88: "'Yeah,' I said. I didn't think my mom would drive me crazy if she was home more. I began to feel something was different now, and I didn't understand." This is a moment in which the narrator is discovering a new distance growing between him and his summer friend. He had expected the distance would come, but he thought it would have to do with returning to school and the friends they had/that Ilan would make there. This paragraph, however, indicates that there was an additional piece to the growing distance—the different attitudes the two boys hold toward their mothers. (H) is supported. (F) is too extreme and isn't true. The narrator has enjoyed Ilan's friendship and has expressed no envy. (G) is incorrect because the first paragraph doesn't raise the theme of the narrator's relationship to his mother. (J) is contradicted by what the narrator is thinking. The narrator *doesn't* relate to Ilan in this moment, not the other way around.

9.   **(A)** precious and delightful.

Meaning of Words

The narrator feels sadness and joy at once because, as he writes in lines 42–44, it was "delight at the friend I had made, and already lonely under the great weight of time until I would see him again." Choice (A) is the closest match to this description. (B) is too extreme. (C) is incorrect because while "long-awaited" is true, "expected" is not. (D) is incorrect because the narrator does not take note of or suggest any irony in that moment.

10.   **(H)** foreign.

Details

In line 1, the narrator writes, "The new neighbors were not like us." The words in the incorrect choices—upsetting, soothing, and threatening—are all too extreme for how he feels about the neighbors, which is curious about them, and hopeful that the neighbor boy will become his friend.

Passage 2 Solutions

11.   **(A)** She loves her family, but feels overwhelmed by the pressures and sadness brought on by her mom's illness.

Generalizations

The best answer is (A) because the narrator decides to run away "since we knew my mom would probably not be with us by Halloween" (lines 67–68). Her mom's illness, then, is a precipitating event. At the same time, in lines 88–90, the narrator expresses care and worry about her family, deciding "If I hurried, I could make it before [my sister Janie] ever knew I was gone. I turned and began to run. My sister would need dinner." Choice (B) is incorrect because the narrator imagines Janie coming home and looking for her in a way that expresses concern rather than feelings of being "fed up." As for (C) and (D), the narrator never mentions anything like independence or solitude as motivations for running away.

12.   **(H)** in a neighborhood near other families.

Generalizations

The best answer is (H) because the narrator describes walking "around the side of the house" (line 30) through the yard to the street, where she passes by other families' houses (the Ortizes and the Reeces). While the narrator lives near a stream, the answer is not (F) because there is no evidence that she lives in a "highly rural area." The answer is not (G) because the narrator lives in a neighborhood with yards and a stream, and none of these details suggest a dense city. Finally, (J) is incorrect because the narrator lives in a house, not an apartment building.

13.   **(A)** The mom tries to comfort her daughter about her illness while crying herself.

Details

The narrator writes, "she came in to ask if I had been listening, then cried while telling me not to cry." This detail, offered in lines 79–80, demonstrates how the mom's love and care for her daughter persists even as she suffers.

17

Choice (B) is incorrect because Janie, the sister, requires speech therapy, not the mom. As for (C) and (D), while the mom sleeps a lot because of her medication and cannot make dinner because of her illness, these behaviors don't demonstrate her feelings toward her daughters.

14.   **(J)** Apples

Details

The narrator states, "I would have apples for dinner" in line 38.

15.   **(B)** introduce the narrator's sister and give a sense of their relationship.

Author's Voice and Method

This paragraph introduces Janie, the narrator's sister, and offers details that describe the protagonist's caretaking role in relation to her sister. The answer is not (A) because the paragraph is not describing the narrator's journey, not (C) because the narrator's relationship to her sister is not why she is running away, and not (D) because the narrator expresses no animosity towards her sister.

16.   **(F)** caretaking.

Relationships

According to lines 43–49, the narrator is responsible for greeting Janie when the latter gets home from speech therapy and for making her dinner.

17.   **(C)** He returns home late at night.

Details

The narrator states in lines 59–61, "I wondered when they would realize I was gone. When dad returned, probably. It would be late, very dark by then." None of the other possible answer choices are supported in the passage.

18.   **(J)** Fishing supplies

Details

The best answer is (J) because the narrator says, "I hadn't brought my fishing supplies" in line 41. As for (F), (G) and (H), the narrator describes packing all three of these items in the first and fourth paragraphs.

19.   **(B)** she wants to get home before her sister knows she is gone.

Relationships (Cause–Effect)

The narrator states in lines 88–90, "If I hurried, I could make it before [Janie] ever knew I was gone. I turned and began to run. My sister would need dinner." The answer is not (A) because the narrator observes that the Reece children are biking, but does not express anxiety about running into them, not (C) because the narrator anticipates getting cold under the bridge, but does not yet feel cold, and not (D) because the story never describes the father as angry.

20. **(H)** a child with one sibling.

Generalizations

The narrator seems like a child because of her choice to run away to a bridge with just fairy tales, a doll, and apples; this behavior is quite childlike. The narrator also describes her sister Janie, her mother, and her father. She describes no other family members.

Passage 3 Solutions

21. **(C)** She loves and appreciates both of her mothers in different ways.

Generalizations

The narrator expresses love and appreciation for both of her mothers throughout the passage. While she is reflective about the degree to which her own identity has changed and somewhat melancholy about it in places, at no point does she *detect resentment* in either mother or *express inability* to connect to her biological mother. She struggles to *communicate* with her biological mother initially, but this is different than being unable to connect.

22. **(H)** loving and joyful.

Generalizations

In lines 23–24, the passage states, " … it was clear to me how delighted she was to see me after so many years." Additionally, the biological mother sent the narrator to the United States to "keep [her] safe" (line 27). Choice (H) is best.

23. **(D)** She is passionate about adopting her Vietnamese identity and rejoining her biological family.

Generalizations

The tone of the narrator's feelings in the passage cannot accurately be described as *passionate*, which is too strong. While the narrator is pleased to reconnect with her biological mother and does pursue that relationship, it would be too extreme to describe this motivation as *passion*. She is happy to be a part of both families. Therefore, choice (D) is the correct answer to this EXCEPT question. The other choices are much less extreme and are supported by the text.

24. **(F)** convey the intimacy of their relationship.

Author's Voice and Method

The purpose of telling this story is to reveal that the narrator is, or at least was, very close to her American mother. While it is true that the story is told in the context of her describing how she, as a child, sought to Americanize her name and did so in a slightly mistaken way, the point of sharing this particular anecdote is not to emphasize the mistake. Choice (F) is best.

17

25. **(B)** the narrator's identity has shifted since her mother arrived from Vietnam.

Main Ideas

In lines 84–87, the narrator says, " … who I am, without hesitation or doubt—a Vietnamese-American with two mothers, two identities, two homes in the same city." This language clearly supports (B), that her identity has shifted since the arrival of her biological mother in America.

26. **(J)** basic English.

Details

In lines 13–14, the narrator says that she "answered her questions in broken English."

27. **(A)** She notices and empathizes with the hurt experienced by her adoptive mother.

Relationships

In lines 74–76, the narrator explains, "I can't bear to see the expression on her face that I read to mean, 'There is a part of my daughter I will never understand.'" Choice (A) is best.

28. **(F)** the narrator is glad to have formed a relationship with her biological mother.

Generalizations

Over the course of the passage, the narrator not only makes an effort to get to know her biological mother—visiting her, helping her at the farmer's market on Saturdays—she also continues to *call* her "ma." You can infer that her feelings about this relationship are positive.

29. **(B)** falling off of a chair.

Details

In lines 53–55, the narrator says, "The origin of the scar on my forehead (toppled off a chair while standing on it)." Falling off of her bike is the story that she invented as a child and not what actually happened to her.

30. **(J)** her biological mother was fearful for her safety.

Details

In lines 26–27, the narrator says, "I came to the United States when I was three. My parents sent me here to keep me safe." This text supports choice (J).

Passage 4 Solutions

31.   **(A)**   He is talkative.

Details

"Lars the German, who would talk your ear off about the color of dirt if you let him," is the introduction to this character in lines 27–29.

32.   **(J)**   A portrait of a socially awkward adult man who has been driven into solitude and bitterness by his unrequited romantic inclinations.

Main Idea

Wayne chooses to go to the open mic to sing a song he wrote about Matilda (line 96) after having a crush on her for a long time that he's never told her about (lines 38–41—" … Nothing to lose at this point"). Choice (F), then, is supported. So is (G), because there is a new restaurant in town. (H) is another way of saying what (F) says, but (J) is incorrect. Wayne isn't bitter, nor is he, as far as we know, socially awkward. He has friends and comes across as relatively content.

33.   **(B)**   expressing thoughts with the interests of a third character in mind.

Relationships

Lars the German and one of the Mikes are expressing their shared opinion that Wayne (the third character) should tell Matilda his feelings. Choice (B) is correct. (C) is the opposite of what you want—they *don't* want Wayne to keep his feelings private, and (A) and (D) are inaccurate descriptions of their motivations in this scene.

34.   **(H)**   Wayne would owe his friends payment on a bet they had made.

Meaning of Words

Just prior to the quoted text, Wayne arrives at the new restaurant and spots Lars in the back. In lines 66–67, he notes, "The Mikes were nowhere to be seen. They must have gone home. Wayne was glad." This description of Wayne's state of mind plus the earlier dynamic in the diner with the guys suggest that Wayne predicts he will be ridiculed the next day for the song he's about to sing. All of the answer choices are supported except (H), as there's no indication in the passage that they've made an actual *bet*.

35.   **(C)**   At the beginning of the story, Wayne harbors a secret crush on Matilda, a banker in town. At the end of the story, he has made the decision to make his feelings public.

Relationships (Comparisons)

Answer choice (C) correctly describes the emotional transition that Wayne makes over the course of the story. (A) is incorrect because there is no indication of Wayne's feelings toward the *owner* at the end of the story. Just because he goes to the open mic doesn't mean he is *trusting* (or, in fact, that he was ever *distrusting*). (B) is incorrect because there's no mention or suggestion of *fame* as Wayne's goal. (D) is incorrect because the passage never suggests that Wayne is hoping his friends will invite him to the open mic. On the contrary, he is scheduled to work and only decides later, when things are slow, to ask to take the night off.

17

36.　**(F)** most residents know most other residents.

Details

Both the first paragraph—the description of the town as a small and close-knit community—and lines 61–62 in which Wayne notes that he doesn't recognize the kid singing on stage (as if that is something strange) support (F). Choice (G) is too extreme; you'd need a great deal of support in the passage for the claim that everyone gets along without any conflict. (H) is not a fact for which you're given any evidence; you know little to nothing about the differences in how people live or their varying economic positions. (J) is also too extreme; you know that *one* person moved away (the owner of the new restaurant), but you don't know whether this behavior is unusual.

37.　**(C)** the conversation in the diner earlier in the day led him to expect it.

Details

"You know, I bet she'll be there tonight," says one of the Mikes in line 42. Thus, Wayne is led to expect Matilda's presence at the open mic. While Wayne does know Matilda's schedule, this isn't linked to his predicting her presence at the open mic, so (B) cannot be supported. Choices (A) and (D) are not mentioned at all.

38.　**(J)** It confirms that Wayne's interest in performing at the open mic had to do with a shift in his approach to his long-held dilemma.

Author's voice and method

The final paragraph is meant to reveal that Wayne has chosen to express his feelings for Matilda *to* Matilda by performing a song he wrote about her. Choice (J) confirms that the earlier discussion in the diner with his buddies led to this moment. (G) is incorrect because there was never a suggestion that Wayne would *attend* the open mic but not perform at it. (H) is unsupported because he doesn't perform to make the boy feel better. (F) is incorrect because, while there is foreshadowing that he may profess his feelings for Matilda, it is not *revealed* that he plans to until the final paragraph of the passage.

39.　**(D)** equal distaste for engaging in conversation with Lars the German.

Relationships (Comparisons)

In lines 32–34, the Mikes tease one another. Line 37 mentions their *usual topics*. Answer choices (A), (B), and (C) are all supported. Answer choice (D), however, is not. While Mike A. sits on his "usual stool opposite Lars the German" (line 19), Mike T. sits in a corner booth "so he could see the TV better and not have to talk to Lars the German," (lines 26–27). (D) is the answer.

40.　**(G)** is different.

Relationships (Comparisons)

Lines 10–12 describe how Wayne views the new restaurant: "She had it repainted bright red and put up some fluorescent sign you had to squint to read because it's in cursive." The tone of the sentence suggests that the façade of the new place is not familiar to Wayne; it is different in style than what he is used to seeing in the town. That's all you can really conclude about Wayne's thoughts or feelings about the new restaurant. Choices (F) and (J) aren't topics covered or alluded to in the passage. (H) is contradicted by it.

Passage 5 Solutions

41. **(B)** Mara realized as she grew older that her parents were trying to help her and her sister get ahead by selling lavender.

Main Idea

The best answer is (B) because as she got older, the main character (Mara) realized that her parents were saving money for her college education. The best answer is not (A) because, while Mara sees her childhood innocence as "naïve" in line 74, she does not express shame. (C) is wrong because, while Lou didn't hold up her end of the unspoken bargain between her and their mother, she did not breach an actual, formal contract. (D) is wrong because Mara expresses an important realization in this paragraph, not merely nostalgia.

42. **(J)** their mom wants to remind her loved ones that she exists.

Relationships (Cause–Effect)

In lines 22–25, the narrator says, "We shipped them … to friends and family around the country to remind them that mom was still around." This matches answer choice (J).

43. **(C)** kind and involved in his children's lives.

Generalizations

Mara describes her father as a smiling presence who helps his children save fireflies and sell lavender sachets. There is no evidence of emotional distance, and the father seems reliable rather than unpredictable.

44. **(G)** Each family member helps to sew the pillows.

Details

According to lines 15–19, Mara "stayed on sachet team my whole life, pretty much, because everyone … knew I wasn't careful enough to handle such a delicate task as stitching." Therefore, you know she never sewed the pillows. Thus, it is NOT true of the family's business that each family member helps to sew the pillows.

Choice (F) is incorrect because Mara describes making sachets of "brightly colored cloth, orange and purple and blue" (lines 12–13). (H) is wrong because the passage describes the family shipping small packages to family and friends to remind them that "mom was still around" (line 25). And (J) is incorrect because the passage states that "the summer also meant the start of assembling season" (lines 9–10).

45. **(A)** Mara shares values with her mother.

Relationships (Comparisons)

The narrator says, "[my mother's] dreams for me were mine, too" in lines 90–91. According to lines 30–33, Mara also gives bracelets to kids at school, an act that she describes as similar to the way her mom sends packages to far-flung loved ones.

46.   **(F)** Lou is taller than Mara.

Details

Answer choice (F) is correct because lines 36–40 state ". . . we all climbed the measurement walls at our respective houses. My own marks were always just behind Lou's for the same age—her 'Age 5' mark was an inch above my 'Age 5' mark, her nine at least two inches, maybe three. Her fifteen was nearly a foot." Choice (G) may be tempting, but although Lou chose not to go to college, the passage does not address how good at school Lou and Mara are.

47.   **(C)** an adult reminiscing about a specific aspect of her childhood.

Generalizations

The best answer is (C) because the main character is recollecting her childhood through the lens of passed time. For instance, in lines 15–16 she says that she "stayed on sachet team my whole life." The only way she could know this is after the fact. The narrator is no longer a child, nor is she an "objective observer." She also offers a subjective rather than a clinical take on her childhood. That is, she writes about her personal perspectives, feelings, and emotions; a "clinical" take would specifically remove any such descriptions.

48.   **(J)** It offers a transition to and contrast between two different times in the narrator's life.

Main Idea

This paragraph zooms from one time in the narrator's childhood (the assembling and the market) to a later time, having to do with going to college (or not). This paragraph does not explain why Lou did not go to college; it simply states this fact. The paragraph also does not really sum up the descriptions of the market. Lines 73–75, "Those days were fun, and special to me . . . ", do offer a summary perspective on that whole time period, but the paragraph quickly moves on to reveal the economic purpose of the assembling and the market: to send the girls to college. This issue is much more central to this paragraph. Finally, the paragraph never brings the story back to any introductory themes.

49.   **(B)** It introduces the main topic and two of the main characters of the story.

Main Idea

The best answer is (B) because this paragraph introduces the family business (the main topic of the story), as well as mom and Lou.

The third paragraph does not list all the activities that the narrator participated in during her summers. The information about the narrator's lack of carefulness is a detail rather than a main point. Finally, although the children may have been cruel to fireflies in the first two paragraphs, the function of the third paragraph is not to distract from any such cruelty, but to advance the story to a more central topic: the family business.

50. **(J)** disappointment that her daughter was not holding up an unspoken agreement.

Relationships

Mara states in lines 76–78, "I saw it mom's eyes. Lou wasn't holding up her end of the bargain." The mother's emotion here is best characterized as disappointment in Lou. Her mother doesn't express anger at the situation, however, and Mara offers no hint that her mother feels like a failure. Of course, the mother is not feeling happiness at this point either.

Passage 6 Solutions

51. **(A)** is hopeful that his adult son will survive through a present crisis but conflicted about their ability to communicate.

Generalizations

Line 34 tells you that "the day after Simon had the heart attack" is when Wallace, his father, is on the train. Lines 76–78 tell you, "Wallace just hadn't known how to relate to him lately. He hoped he had another chance to try." Choice (A) is supported by these portions of the passage. (B) is too extreme; Wallace isn't *outraged* at anyone. (C) is incorrect because there is no indication that Wallace plans to quit anytime soon. On the contrary, he plans *not* to quit. (D) isn't supported because while you know Wallace plays with his grandkids (from the paragraph), there isn't anything that suggests they're the most important thing to him. If anything, his job as a doorman and the residents in the building seem more important to him.

52. **(F)** wealthier than Wallace.

Relationships (Comparisons)

In lines 60–62, you learn that Simon was having a hard time "accepting affluence" because he "didn't grow up with it, himself." Two paragraphs later, in lines 68–71, you are given a list of features about Simon's family that demonstrate their affluence: His wife wears "the kind of jewelry that attracts scamming thieves," and "handsome fellows in suits" cater their Thanksgiving. All of this supports (F), that Wallace's son is wealthier than he is. Choice (G) is too extreme; Simon does not act arrogant or entitled in the passage. (H) isn't something you have any evidence for. In fact, Wallace confronted a robber in his building. (J) is incorrect because Simon's religion isn't mentioned at all.

53. **(C)** He is uncomfortable with abundance.

Details

In line 12, you learn Wallace uses Listerine, so (A) is out. In the following sentence, you are told that Wallace feels he "couldn't abandon the residents," so (B) is out. Choice (D) is true, as well: the end of the first paragraph, lines 5–6, read, "the submissive boy had come out so unlike his father." Choice (C), however, is not something you know. While *Simon* is uncomfortable with abundance, there isn't any suggestion that Wallace is, too.

17

54. (J) a person with fear.

Details

In lines 65–66, the passage states that Simon "had always been a serious person, even as a child, but law had made him more that way." Choices (F) and (G) are out as a result. Line 54 describes him as having "anxieties," eliminating (H). However, Simon is never described as being fearful in Wallace's eyes. Therefore, choice (J) is correct.

55. (B) Frank Harrington, a relative of someone who lives in the building where Wallace works.

Details

Later in the same paragraph, lines 84–85 read, "Frank Harrington, son of Mr. Harrington, in 37D!" He is the "familiar face." This supports choice (B).

56. (F) His increasing unease at functioning in the world in the way that he was able to as a younger man

Author's Voice and Method

Wallace's hand is trembling, which makes him self-conscious and harkens back to the conversation he had with his son in the first paragraph about how he should retire, which he doesn't want to do. Choice (F) captures this feeling. Choice (G) is too extreme—he doesn't have anger at Simon. Choice (H) may be true, but you don't actually know whether Wallace has this disease, and so there can be no way that the purpose of the sentence is to "emphasize" this point. Finally, (J) makes a judgment about what action Wallace should take; however, this judgment isn't supported by the passage. Therefore, (F) is correct.

57. (D) things with value that is difficult to quantify.

Meaning of Words

Line 31 reads, "Simon didn't get that intangibles was the thing." This paragraph follows a discussion between Wallace and Simon about how Wallace should retire because he can't do things he used to be able to do, such as lift heavy things and move quickly. Wallace, in his mind, thought of the things he *does* offer residents, like companionship. These are the "intangibles" the question is asking about, and (D) describes them: things that Wallace sees as having value but that are *difficult to quantify* or measure. Choices (A) and (C) aren't supported by anything in the passage, and (B) is the opposite of what Wallace thinks. He sees himself as *having* these intangible qualities that Simon fails to see. Therefore, (D) is correct.

58. (H) A resident of the building where Wallace works

Details

Although the *son* of one of the residents of the building where Wallace works is on the train, Frank Harrington (line 92), you don't know that Frank is a resident himself. In fact, it is likely that he is *not* a resident, since he is "on his way to the building" in order to have "breakfast with his dad" (lines 86–87). There is, however, a nurse (line 44), a tuba (line 41), and a person Wallace knows (Frank Harrington), which covers choices (F), (G), and (J). Therefore, choice (H) is the correct answer to this EXCEPT question.

59. **(D)** optimistic.

Meaning of Words

A "good" person is reasonably interpreted to mean "ethical," and a "good" son in this case can be interpreted to mean "caretaking" because at the beginning of the third paragraph (lines 10–15), you learn that Simon wants his dad to retire and "would take care of Wallace's rent ..." Choice (C), "sincere," is supportable because Simon does come across as sincere throughout the story. However, choice (D), "optimistic," is not something you're given evidence for with Simon. If anything, he seems to have a pessimistic outlook on life. Choice (D) is therefore correct.

60. **(G)** pride.

Author's Voice and Method

Wallace "helped get that delivery man arrested" and "every Veteran's Day since, Mr. Harrington gave Wallace a crisp hundred" (lines 17–21). In the same paragraph, you are told how Wallace is still helpful and important to the residents at the building where he works. Choice (G) is supported—he feels pride that he helped Mr. Harrington in this way. (F) and (J) are the opposite of what he feels; he has positive feelings toward the memory, not negative ones. (H) is extreme. While Wallace does feel positively about the recollection, it's a stretch to describe him as "elated," or overjoyed.

Passage 7 Solutions

61. **(C)** does not complete the form because she feels that it doesn't offer her identities as options.

Author's Voice and Method

Lines 3–4 introduce the idea that she cannot complete the form because it doesn't fit her, and the passage is devoted to exploring why she feels this way. Choice (A) is too extreme—*irate* (very angry) is not an accurate description of her state of mind. Choice (B) misconstrues the focus of the passage. The narrator is writing about herself, not others, feeling restricted by the form. Choice (D) may be tempting, but it's a mischaracterization of her fluid identities. She isn't saying she fluctuates between identities as a matter of *choice* but because she has *no* choice—she is who she is because of her life circumstances.

62. **(F)** his academic posts at various universities.

Details

Lines 22–23 read, "I went to live with my step-father, also an academic. We moved a lot," which supports answer choice (F). They moved because of his posts at universities. Choice (G) is incorrect because her mother moves back to China. Choice (H) is incorrect because her grandmother lives in Canada. Choice (J) is incorrect because she's never discussed as having special needs.

63. **(C)** her mother's descriptions of her father's ethnic heritage left her uncertain of it.

Author's Voice and Method

In the rest of the third paragraph, after the quoted text in lines 26–27, the narrator explains that her mother told her various ethnic identities of her biological father at various times. She is left uncertain of *what* her father's ethnic background actually was, which is stated in choice (C). Choice (A) is incorrect because she doesn't even know whether her biological father had a combination of ethnic backgrounds or not. Choice (B) is incorrect because presumably the narrator's mother knew the father. If not, we don't know. Choice (D) is incorrect because the mother is Chinese.

64. **(H)** a Mandarin speaker.

Details

The narrator never indicates what language her mother speaks. While you know her mother's nationality is Chinese, you are never told explicitly that she speaks Mandarin. She could speak other Chinese dialects, such as Cantonese. Thus, (H) is the correct answer, because it is *not* supported in the text. The narrator writes that her mother became "suddenly so nervous she could not bathe and forgot to make meals" (lines 11–12), then goes on to describe other manifestations of her schizophrenic mother's paranoia, so (G) is supported. The narrator refers to "the university where she was teaching" (line 17), supporting (J). And at the end of the passage, when she describes the visit to see her mother and writes of her mother's outfit, "It wasn't something a grown woman should wear. It was for a little girl" (lines 75–76), she is describing a woman who is *childlike*, which supports (F). Therefore, (H) is the correct answer to this EXCEPT question.

65. **(D)** She distinguishes herself from her Canadian grandmother with regard to her national identity.

Details

The narrator writes, "It wasn't something a grown woman should wear. It was for a little girl. I would also never wear something like that" (lines 75–77), which makes (A) incorrect. The narrator's step-father, Harry, is Catholic, but she says that "as an adult, I consider myself an atheist" (lines 45–46), so you can rule out (B). In lines 33–36, the narrator writes, "'You're more white than black,' a girl told me once in seventh grade when I tried to sit with her and her friends in the cafeteria. But the white kids didn't seem to think so. *I was in-between.*" Choice (D), however, is not something the narrator ever does explicitly. In the second paragraph, which covers the narrator's sense of her nationality, she never mentions her grandmother. Choice (D) is the correct answer.

66. **(F)** belief in a divine power.

Meaning of Words

In lines 51–56, the narrator discusses her religious views: "I sometimes feel a divine presence, a calmness ... But then ... the feeling is gone, and I don't believe anything again, or I don't know what I believe." She is referring to (F), a belief in a divine power. Choice (G) is incorrect because it isn't a discussion about the *point* of religion. (H) and (J) are too narrow; the narrator is talking about divinity more broadly, not just one of the religions that is or could be in her heritage (Catholicism is not mentioned explicitly). Therefore, (F) is correct.

67.   **(D)** her biological father.

Details

In lines 36–37, you learn that the narrator "calls [her] step-father Harry." Thus, (A) is supported in the text (and is therefore *not* right). Likewise, in lines 7–8, the narrator describes Harry as "Canadian and American," while in line 32, she describes him as "a Caucasian man." So (B) and (C) are out as well. Choice (D) is correct because "biological" is *not* how she sees Harry as a father. Her biological father is of unknown ethnic background to her.

68.   **(H)** frustration with the terms by which race is defined, which in her case conflict with her family history.

Author's Voice and Method

The quoted text immediately follows this sentence in line 39: "They are all white," in which the narrator is referring to her family. She is using the rhetorical question to suggest that there are illogical elements to her identifying as a different race than her family, even though technically, her ethnic heritage differs from theirs. Choice (H) is the best answer. Choice (F) is incorrect because she isn't questioning her status as a member of her own family. That literal interpretation of the question is not what she means; rather, she is challenging anyone who would *question* her status within her family. Choice (G) is too extreme because of "disgust." Choice (J) is incorrect because she isn't targeting her family's behavior here. She is criticizing the form.

69.   **(B)** feeling that her grandmother should not have allowed her mother to make such a childlike purchase.

Relationships (Cause–Effect)

In lines 72–74, the narrator writes, "I hated her own mother—my real grandmother, I suppose, though I don't remember her at all—for buying it for her," referring to a tutu that "was for a little girl." As (B) states, the narrator is upset with her grandmother's allowing her mother to make such a purchase. Choice (A) is too broad because of "most." You do not know anything about other parenting choices that the grandmother may or may not have made. Choice (C) misses the point; you don't know what her grandmother's vision of "womanhood" is. Choice (D) likewise misses the point. Her non-biological grandmother is not mentioned or invoked in this part of the passage. Therefore, (B) is correct.

70.   **(G)** critical.

Generalizations

The narrator's purpose in the passage is to identify the reasons why she is "critical," which matches choice (G), of the form and its parameters. Choice (F) is wrong: the narrator is *not* "accepting" of the form. Choice (J), "repulsed," is too extreme. Choice (H), "magnanimous" (which means "generous of spirit, open-hearted"), is out of scope.

Passage 8 Solutions

71. **(C)** it is a very measured, orderly religion.

Relationships (Cause–Effect)

The narrator introduces aspects of the religion with which he was previously unfamiliar. In lines 30–31, he writes "In the face of my mother's wild disease, this order comforted me." The order that he is referring to is discussed in line 25: "Santería is a very measured, orderly religion." The correct answer is (C).

72. **(H)** she was physically in the yard, but her spirit was devoted to the ceremony.

Author's Voice and Method

The statement used seems to contradict itself; how can someone be both across the yard and in another world at the same time? The narrator is using this terminology to show that Louisa's body is one place, but her spirit is in another. The narrator implies that she may even be seized by the Orisha. The reference of her being "in another world" is illustrating her immersion in the experience. The correct answer is (H).

73. **(B)** the cloth has been used several times for ceremonies in the past.

Generalizations

The narrator is using these deposits to describe the mounds of wax present on the cloth used for the ceremony. He mentions that there are different shades, which implies there were many candles used. You can conclude the cloth has been used in the past for other ceremonies. The other answer choices are too extreme or not supported. The correct answer is (B).

74. **(G)** a gnarled chicken foot.

Details

A gnarled chicken foot is described as being tied to the statue's arm (lines 55–56), but never placed in the ceramic bowl. The other items are all put inside the bowl in lines 58–60. The correct answer is (G).

75. **(A)** The Caribbean

Details

The narrator states, "When Catholic explorers came to the Caribbean … Syncretism, the act of combining very different beliefs, was vital to the conflicted faithful locals" (lines 16–20). The new religion of Santería was created as a result. The correct answer is (A).

MANHATTAN
PREP

76.   **(H)** did not know that Santería was a syncretic religion.

Generalization

Among the features of Santeria that the narrator lists as having "learned" from Louisa is that it is a syncretic religion (lines 14–15). The implication is that he did not know this fact previously. The correct answer is (H).

77.   **(D)** large number.

Meaning of Words

The narrator discusses the range of ideas that can be covered by one Orisha or another. He goes on to say that such order is a comfort to him. The idea he is trying to convey is that Orishas can cover a large number of concepts. The correct answer is (D).

78.   **(J)**   he didn't know what to look for.

Details

There is definitely a moment when the narrator observes a change in Louisa. He never concludes, however, that she has been seized by an Orisha because, in his words, "I didn't know what to look for" (lines 85–86). Even though the word "because" or "since" is not used, these words are connected to the prior thought by a semicolon, indicating the close logical connection. The fact that he "simply pounded the drum" in line 85 is stated as an additional fact. It is not the cause of his lack of knowledge; rather, it is probably the result (he didn't know whether Louisa had been seized, so he simply pounded the drum). The correct answer is (J).

79.   **(A)**   It explains why the narrator is drawn to the religion of Santería.

Main Idea

Though the narrator provides several details about Santería in the fourth paragraph, the purpose of this paragraph is to explain what draws the narrator to the religion. Likewise, the passage overall is not concerned with the details of the religion, but with the narrator's experience of it. The correct answer is (A).

80.   **(F)**   a melding of different beliefs.

Meaning of Words

The syncretic religion discussed in this passage is Santería, but the narrator never claims that it is the only syncretic religion. Instead, he defines syncretism as "the act of combining very different beliefs" (line 19). Syncretic refers to something that has gone through this process. The correct answer is (F).

Chapter *of* 18

5lb. Book of ACT® Practice Problems

Reading:
Social Studies

In This Chapter...

Social Studies Passages & Solutions

Chapter 18
Reading: Social Studies

The Reading passages in this chapter are classified within social studies, which include history, biography, psychology, anthropology, archaeology, economics, and other sciences that focus on human actions and interactions. A small amount of context is given at the start, but each passage is self-contained.

Various kinds of questions are asked about these passages, including the following:

1. Main Ideas/Author's Approach. Main idea or ideas of the passage (or a part of it); the approach, voice, point of view, method, or purpose of the author.

2. Details. Specific details mentioned in the passage.

3. Relationships. Comparisons, sequences of events, cause-effect relationships, or other relationships that are described or implied in the passage.

4. Meanings of Words. The meaning of a word or phrase, in its context, in the passage.

5. Generalizations. Conclusions, broad observations, or other generalizations that can be drawn from the passage.

How should you use this chapter? Here are some recommendations, according to the level you've reached in ACT Reading.

1. Fundamentals. Do a passage or two untimed to begin with. As you become more comfortable, put the clock on. In all cases, review the solutions closely, and articulate what you've learned. Reread the passage again to ensure that you fully understand it, and redo problems as necessary.

2. Fixes. Do one passage at a time under timed conditions. Examine the results, learn your lessons, then test yourself with more passages (one from each Reading chapter) at once.

3. Tweaks. Confirm your mastery by doing a few passages (one from each Reading chapter) at once under timed conditions. A full set of four is the ultimate goal. Aim to improve the speed and ease of your reading and solution process.

Good luck on the problems!

PASSAGE 1

SOCIAL STUDIES: This passage is adapted from an article about architecture and democracy.

In her article "Architects of Justice," scholar Linda Mulcahy writes about how the physical arrangement of the courtroom is a far cry from the apolitical, public-spirited space it was once idealized to be.

5   Imagine walking into a courtroom. In most court-rooms, officers of the court flank the entrance in the back and stand at the front as well, monitoring the room for rule violations. Invariably, the proceedings are separated from the viewing area by a low wall or divider. The topography

10 of the space—the judge seated on a raised platform, for example—allows the judge to observe the room's activity from an elevated position, clearly a calculated architectural choice. It often feels more like a theater than anything else—a performance rather than a truth-seeking

15 enterprise.

These architectural features, coupled with the "legalese" used by lawyers (unfamiliar to many lay people), the adversarial (typically hostile) nature of the litigation process, and the general attitude of resentment and

20 reluctance that pervades juries, leave little question why the public would find courtrooms less than welcoming.

In 2003, Bexar County, Texas took on the challenge of changing all this. In an innovative, pioneering project aimed at meeting the special needs of children in child

25 abuse and neglect cases, the county created a court complex to enable children to testify in the courtroom in a non-threatening and comforting environment. It was a radical departure from the traditional approach to courtroom design and renovation, and it sprang from

30 consensus in the county that a special courtroom to accommodate the high number of abused children was critical.

A design team was formed that included archi-tectural, electrical and mechanical engineers, a child psy-

35 chologist, and the local Deputy Director of the Center for Legal and Court Technology. The design team, work-ing with county officials, determined that two court-rooms were needed, along with two hearing rooms and two interview rooms.

40   The creation of dual rooms made clear the significant role that technology would play. According to the Center for Legal and Court Technology, "Each courtroom would need all technological tools available to present a case. The extensive use of video would be

45 expected to allow a participant in any location within the complex to communicate with another participant anywhere else. For example, a judge might need to interview a child in chambers with other participants viewing from the hearing room or courtroom. If a parent

50 became unruly, he/she would be removed to a holding area

to end disruption in the courtroom but could still listen to or testify at the proceedings. Remote communication was also designed into the system so parents who were incarcerated could participate from prison rather than

55 being transported to the courthouse."

The complex even included a special waiting room, designed for the protection and entertainment of children.

But endeavors like this remain rare and are, as in the

60 case of Bexar County, typically restricted to individuals with special needs, such as children.

Will the design of standard courtrooms ever follow suit in the future? Should they?

It is unlikely. Law is a highly traditional profession

65 that pays, by its nature, great respect to authority. Judges, statutes, and sacred, guiding documents, such as both state and federal constitutions, are given the utmost respect, and violations of them are taken seriously, involving law enforcement if necessary. Architecture

70 has reflected that somber, inherently hierarchical model. Consider not only the structure of a courtroom but that judges typically wear robes, as well—apparel that signifies prestige, distinction.

Perhaps the most striking example of hierarchical

75 American courthouse architecture is the Supreme Court itself. Forty-four steps rise up to meet its entrance; massive red curtains adorn the front of the courtroom; the elevation of the justices is striking; spectators are cabined by rank and admission standards. Considering the high-

80 stakes decisions made in the walls of the building, one might think these features are not only expected but also appropriate.

Yet law can be respected while still being made accessible, understandable and, in courtrooms, comfortable

85 enough for witnesses to be honest. For if trial participants are too intimidated to tell the truth, how can the courtroom achieve its fundamental purpose?

1.   Which one of the following best characterizes the author's attitude towards the new courtrooms in Bexar County, Texas?

    A. She welcomes them as appropriate for children, but is skeptical as to whether they are relevant to standard courtrooms.

    B. She is skeptical of them because they do not appropriately respect authority.

    C. She sees the redesign as a positive step towards making courtrooms more accessible and comfortable, but is skeptical as to whether other courtrooms will follow suit.

    D. She questions whether the redesign is sufficiently public-spirited and apolitical.

2. According to the passage, most standard courtrooms today are characterized by:

   F. a raised platform for the judge and a waiting room for children.
   G. forty-four steps in front of the entrance and red curtains in the front of the courtroom.
   H. a waiting room for children and red curtains in the front of the courtroom.
   J. a raised platform for the judge and a divider separating the viewing area from the proceedings.

3. According to the passage, the new courtrooms in Bexar County, Texas use video in order to:

   A. allow participants to view and testify at proceedings while in physically separate places.
   B. allow for a special waiting room for children's protection and entertainment.
   C. allow incarcerated parents to be transported to the courthouse.
   D. allow the judge to observe proceedings.

4. The author describes the architecture of the Supreme Court in order to support her point that:

   F. the law must always be given the utmost respect.
   G. the Supreme Court is designed to look like the most prestigious court in the United States.
   H. a hierarchical style of architecture in courtrooms is strongly ingrained in the United States.
   J. the elevation of the Supreme Court Justices is extreme and striking, even by American standards.

5. Which of the following is most probably what the author believes to be "unlikely" (line 64)?

   A. Standard courtrooms will adopt a less hierarchical style.
   B. Standard courtrooms should adopt a less hierarchical style.
   C. The law will become more traditional as a profession.
   D. Residents of Bexar Country, Texas will like their new courtrooms.

6. It can be most reasonably inferred from the passage that legal jargon:

   F. functions to praise authority and tradition in the courtroom.
   G. alienates and confuses many members of the general public.
   H. makes prospective jurors angry and resentful.
   J. includes many architectural terms.

7. It can be most reasonably inferred that the author holds which of the following views of Linda Mulcahy's scholarship?

   A. The scholarship is good because courtrooms should be centers of spirited debate.
   B. The scholarship is dangerous because courtroom architecture should reflect an appropriate respect for authority.
   C. The scholarship is valuable because we should examine how courtroom architecture reflects our values and facilitates justice.
   D. The scholarship is smart because no one had pointed out the discrepancy between American legal ideals and the realities of courtrooms before.

8. According to the passage, Bexar County, Texas undertook the challenge of redesigning a local courtroom because:

   F. local residents felt too intimidated by the previous courtroom architecture.
   G. local residents wanted to take on an innovative project.
   H. the number of incarcerated parents made child abuse cases difficult to prosecute.
   J. local residents believed that a special courtroom for childhood abuse cases was needed.

9. As described in lines 72–73, the wearing of robes by judges most reflects which one of the following attitudes about the law?

   A. "Law can be respected while still being made accessible" (lines 83–84).
   B. "It often feels more like a theater than anything else—a performance rather than a truth-seeking enterprise" (lines 13–15).
   C. "Judges, statutes, and sacred, guiding documents, such as both state and federal constitutions, are given the utmost respect" (lines 65–68).
   D. "Remote communication was also designed into the system so parents who were incarcerated could participate" (lines 52–54).

10. The author compares the courtroom to a "theater" (line 13) in order to:

   F. point out that legal proceedings are often scripted.
   G. provide an example of an alternative courtroom design.
   H. underscore the point that courtrooms are not the open, democratic spaces people once dreamed them to be.
   J. emphasize how judges must consider viewers in the way they conduct legal proceedings.

18

PASSAGE 2

SOCIAL STUDIES: This passage is adapted from a biography of Theodore Roosevelt.

A dinosaur looms in the entryway of the American Museum of Natural History. Spindly bones are arranged into a fierce, wild creature. The entryway's walls are made of shiny marble and are engraved with quotes.
5 The quotes' headings proclaim "NATURE" "YOUTH" "MANHOOD" and "THE STATE."

This hallway is a memorial to the United States' 26th president, Theodore "TR" Roosevelt. Like few presidents before or since, TR remains a mammoth. He is an icon of
10 passion, of masculinity, and of ferocious political instinct. An oft-repeated—and true—story tells of a presidential campaign stop in Wisconsin. An onlooker shot TR in the chest. Undeterred, TR began his speech.

"Friends, I shall ask you to be as quiet as possible,"
15 he began. "I don't know whether you fully understand that I have just been shot."

TR then unbuttoned his jacket to show the crowd the seeping bloodstain on his shirt.

"It takes more than that to kill a bull moose," he
20 said. He proceeded to finish the speech.

TR grew up to be a frontier-loving fighter, but he was born into a more privileged milieu. He grew up a sickly child in a wealthy society family. His father was a dashing Northerner who was politically allied with
25 the abolitionists, but who mostly loved to drink and dance. His mother was a Southern belle from a slave-owning family. She was fastidiously clean, taking more than one bath a day and covering her all-white clothes in veils and paper cuffs to keep dirt away. On the family's
30 European vacations, TR's father would toss cake crumbs to beggar children. The family would relish watching the impoverished children eat "like chickens."

Despite his early illnesses and the elitist nature of his social stratum, TR threw himself into life, risk, and
35 physical exertion as he got older. After Harvard, he went West to hunt buffalo and herd cattle like a cowboy, albeit in his own high-society way. He ordered pearl pistols and spurs from Louis Comfort Tiffany's fine jewelry shop. His fringe-lined leather shirts cost the equivalent of
40 thousands of today's dollars.

After returning to the New York political scene for a period, TR volunteered to fight in the Spanish-American war. He excelled in a suitably-named cavalry called the Rough Riders. The Rough Riders transcended social class;
45 the volunteer unit included Native Americans and Ivy-League bluebloods alike. TR led the cavalry to victory in the crucial Battle of San Juan, helping to shatter the Spanish Empire in the Americas. TR was eventually awarded the Medal of Honor for his leadership.

50 TR became vice president to William McKinley and, after McKinley was assassinated, he became president. Always the eccentric, TR kept ponies, snakes and a host of other animals in his White House. He drank copious amounts of coffee with sugar—his own
55 son said TR's coffee cup was "more in the nature of a bathtub." On a trip to Tennessee he observed that his cup of Maxwell House coffee was "good to the last drop." The company adopted his phrase as their slogan.

TR's political style reflected his personality; it was
60 brash and fiercely aggressive. His views mirrored his individualistic and frontier-oriented life. He promoted American power and exceptionalism while fighting against the business interests that squeezed poor and middle-class men. He brought large anti-trust lawsuits
65 against the Northern Securities Company, a railroad conglomerate helmed by J.P. Morgan. He pushed other anti-monopoly legislation through the Senate by appealing directly to citizens, using what he called "the bully pulpit." TR also fought for environmental
70 conservation, creating national forests, parks, and wildlife refuges throughout America.

TR was a radical, however, he remained a man of his time. He failed to address the deep currents of racism that seared through America. In some cases, he actively
75 perpetuated racism, as when he dishonorably discharged hundreds of black soldiers in response to the purported violence of a few. Like many men of his era and social class, TR did not regard the struggles of blacks and Native Americans as particularly pressing. Yet TR was also a
80 visionary, irrevocably shifting America's relationship to its landscape and business through the force of his ebullience and passion.

TR's Natural History Museum memorial is fitting. Its unabashed Imperialism is old-fashioned, but
85 the space is undeniably grand. Of the four quotes that frame the dinosaur, all of which belong to TR himself, his words on "The State" are particularly apt: "If I must choose between righteousness and peace, I choose righteousness."

18

11. The main function of the first paragraph is to:

   A. briefly explore the four subjects of nature, youth, manhood, and the state.
   B. introduce the main subject of the passage.
   C. demonstrate how ancient Theodore Roosevelt is.
   D. set a scene with which to launch a discussion.

12. The passage indicates that each of the following are true of TR's family EXCEPT that:

   F. his parents were members of an elite social class.
   G. his family at times interacted with people from a different social class.
   H. his family included many other politicians, including another president.
   J. his parents came from different political backgrounds.

13. It can be inferred from the passage that TR's attitude towards war included:

   A. the belief that war is not always the worst option.
   B. an openness to using war to preserve nature and wildlife.
   C. criticism of the military-industrial complex.
   D. enthusiasm based on his own experience volunteering in multiple cavalries.

14. The author describes the Rough Riders as:

   F. a cavalry that drafted men by force from across America.
   G. a cavalry that played an important role in the Spanish–American war.
   H. a cavalry that was led by a diverse swath of men.
   J. a cavalry that fought in many wars.

15. As the author relates it, TR's attitude toward the racism faced by blacks and Native Americans can be best described as:

   A. apathy.
   B. scorn.
   C. empathy.
   D. celebration.

16. In the context of the paragraph, TR's use of "the bully pulpit" (line 69) most likely means

   F. convincing legislators to pass bills using aggressive tactics.
   G. convincing citizens to pressure their representatives to pass legislation.
   H. appealing to citizens to donate to charitable causes.
   J. asking everyday Americans to become politicians.

17. The author most likely shares the story about the shooting of TR and TR's subsequent response in order to:

   A. evoke sympathy for TR's vulnerability.
   B. allude the violent nature of the times.
   C. depict TR's high tolerance for physical pain.
   D. give a sense of TR's remarkable resilience.

18. According to the passage, one policy championed by TR was:

   F. stimulus for small business owners.
   G. segregation for racial minorities.
   H. breaking up monopolies.
   J. placing more animals on the endangered species list.

19. The passage mentions which one of the following about TR?

   A. TR traveled to places beyond the United States.
   B. TR was indifferent toward animals.
   C. TR was an abolitionist.
   D. TR had a large brood of children.

20. The author most likely shares TR's quote on "The State" in lines 87–89 because the author views TR as:

   F. one of America's greatest presidents.
   G. a man with a passion for economic justice.
   H. someone driven by bold convictions and willing to risk harm.
   J. a president who emphasized the military over domestic matters.

18

PASSAGE 3

SOCIAL STUDIES: This passage is adapted from the article titled "Living with Lions: The Economics of Coexistence in the Gir Forests, India" by authors at the Wildlife Institute of India.

Rarely do forest-dwelling pastoral communities coexist in harmony with large predators, such as lions. This is not, however, for the reason you might think. Although large carnivores do sometimes kill humans, 5 the major conflict between species arises from large carnivores' preying on the livestock kept by forest-dwellers and the resulting threat to the economic security of pastoral communities.

Human communities react differently to this 10 conflict depending on their religious beliefs, customs, and cultures, as well as their actual and perceived magnitudes of economic losses. They also must factor into their response the legal status of carnivores, which are protected to varying degrees depending 15 on the country. Reactions of livestock owners living among large carnivores typically range from total extermination of the predators to occasional removal of problem animals. Rarely, however, does tolerant coexistence occur.

20 In the overwhelmingly rural country of India, home to approximately 1.2 billion people, forest resources have been part of traditional livelihoods for generations. The politics of ecology are contentious, with pro-economic groups arguing that conservation policies alienate 25 traditional forest-dwellers' access to forests and their resources, marginalizing these people by making it difficult for them to sustain their traditional livelihoods. The contrary view, held by preservationists, is that the fact that the forest-dwelling population is growing 30 means that catering to its interests is unsustainable and ultimately detrimental to the conservation of biodiversity.

Two-thirds of India's wildlife reserves are grazed by livestock, which are subject to predation by large 35 carnivores. It has long been understood that traditional cultural, ethical and religious reverence towards life forms, combined with recent legal protection, are important contributors to the continued survival of large carnivores in India. In particular, pastoral farming 40 communities in the country have displayed great tolerance regarding the presence of lions in the Gir forests.

At the onset of the nineteenth century, Asiatic lions (*Panthera leo persica*) became restricted to the Gir forests of Western India. Facing both hunting and loss of 45 habitat, they declined in population to near extinction, i.e. around 50 individuals. Subsequently, stringent protections legislated by the government reversed that trend. Today, Gir lions have increased to about 400 in number, and are dispersed across a large tract of agro-50 pastoral land adjacent to the Gir forests.

Meanwhile, the forests are also inhabited by semi-nomadic, pastoral communities called Maldharis and have been for over a century. These primarily Hindu communities have a strong ethical code regarding nature 55 and natural resources. They are primarily vegetarian, keeping livestock only for the sale of dairy products, on which they rely economically. The underlying mechanism that permits their coexistence with the Asiatic lions, however, is not solely their moral or religious beliefs.

60 It is economically more profitable for the Maldharis to live in the forests despite the lions, because Maldhari livestock within Gir obtain most of their forage requirements from the forest free of cost. Were they to live outside the forest, they would be required to feed 65 their livestock with food they purchased. Occasional predation by lions, therefore, is merely one cost of rearing livestock in the Gir forests, and one outweighed by the benefits. Maldhari and lions coexist in a stable situation, as the average annual financial loss of a Maldhari 70 household due to livestock predation by lions is minimal when offset by the freegrazing rights obtained by a family living in Gir.

Additional economic benefits to Maldhari families include fuel wood and minor forest products, forest 75 topsoil—which they are able to mix with dung and sell as manure—and free access to water.

The Maldhari's peaceful coexistence with lions demonstrates that when it comes to human beings living among large mammalian beasts, cultural, religious 80 and even legal circumstances are not the only relevant considerations. There are economic values at play as well, and these may be more important than people realize. Given the current reach and ongoing integration of the global economy into the most remote and rural parts of 85 the world, it is possible that economic considerations will ultimately determine the fate of large carnivores outside of Gir as well.

21. The main point that the author seeks to make in the passage is that:

   A. human beings coexist with large carnivores partly because of financial considerations.
   B. human beings typically do not live with large carnivores for myriad reasons, including religious and cultural considerations.
   C. human beings who live with large carnivores such as lions do so strictly because they benefit from doing so.
   D. human beings frequently live with large carnivores because of the economic benefits of doing so.

22. The author claims that the Maldharis continue to live in the Gir forests because of:

   F. their preference for rural life.
   G. their historic presence there.
   H. the relatively low cost of resources.
   J. the presence of lions.

23. The author asserts that the reason humans and lions so infrequently live together is that:

   A. lions kill people.
   B. lions kill livestock.
   C. people must compete with lions for critical sustenance.
   D. they thrive in distinct climates.

24. When the author uses *freegrazing rights* (line 71), she is referring to:

   F. the freedom that forest-dwellers experience outside of confined borders.
   G. the unrestricted area in which pastoral livestock roams.
   H. the legal right of forest-dwellers to raise cattle.
   J. the cost of feeding livestock for forest-dwellers.

25. According to the passage, around when did the population of Asiatic lions dwindle to a near catastrophic level?

   A. Late 1900s
   B. Early 1800s
   C. Late 1700s
   D. Early 1900s

26. As it is used in lines 66–67, *Occasional predation* most nearly means:

   F. lions consuming the livestock that belongs to the Maldhari.
   G. lions preying upon the Maldhari.
   H. lions chasing Maldhari livestock from the forest.
   J. the Maldhari livestock's greatest threat to survival.

27. According to the passage, the Maldhari would likely cease their coexistence with lions in the Gir forest for all of the following reasons EXCEPT:

   A. the forest became unable to sustain the Maldhari's livestock.
   B. the lions' predation of livestock increased.
   C. grazing costs of livestock outside of the Gir forest dropped significantly.
   D. the Gir forests became inhospitable to lions.

28. According the passage, most of India is:

   F. vegetarian.
   G. rural.
   H. Hindu.
   J. inhabited by large carnivores.

29. The passage states that the reason the Maldhari raise livestock is:

   A. to subsist on the sale of the meat.
   B. to subsist on the meat of the livestock.
   C. to subsist on the dairy provided by the livestock.
   D. to subsist on the sale of the dairy provided by the livestock.

30. In the passage, the "preservationists" mentioned in line 28 make the argument that:

   F. increasing the number of species in the forest requires passage laws to preserve it.
   G. a greater number of people living in the forests threatens the diversity of species there.
   H. conservation is more important than sustaining the traditional livelihoods of pastoral communities.
   J. the economy is best served by conservation of the forest.

PASSAGE 4

SOCIAL STUDIES: This passage is adapted from a book on the history of education and gender.

A Google image search for the word "teacher" yields a trove of similar pictures. The stock photo features a woman standing in front of a green chalkboard. She might be holding an apple, writing an equation, or

5 responding to a waving child's hand. She is almost always smiling.

The fact that men are noticeably absent from these photos is not based solely on popular perception of the gender of educators. Men are, in fact, largely absent from

10 the teaching profession itself. Today, more than three-quarters of America's schoolteachers are women. But this wasn't always the case. During the colonial era, men dominated the classroom. At the time, schools were one-room schoolhouses. Children of all ages learned together

15 in a large room led by a single—usually male—teacher. A few of these men were career teachers, but most were not. Rather, the majority of teachers were either local farmers or entrepreneurs who taught on the side, or were educated young men who viewed teaching as a stepping stone to a

20 more lucrative and prestigious career in another field.

The "feminization" of the classroom began in the mid-nineteenth century, and was the result of active campaigning on the part of reformers like Horace Mann. In a series of lectures on the power and duties

25 of women, Mann spoke against the women's rights movement, arguing that men and women have different, complementary roles. "Birds and fishes might as well attempt to exchange natures and elements. Sometimes, indeed, the bird does dive into the water, and sometimes

30 the fish flies for a moment through the air, but each must immediately return to its own element," he said.

The "element" of women, Mann believed, was nurturing and virtuous. Women, he argued, were natural caretakers and thus meant to aid the young,

35 the sick, the weak, and the poor. Since the education of young children was considered to be a moral as well as an academic task, women were viewed as perfect for the job: "as a teacher of schools ... how divinely does she come, her head encircled with a halo of heavenly light,"

40 Mann wrote.

However, there was more than an ethical dimensions involved. The push to put women in the classroom, however, was practical as well. "Common schools," a precursor to today's public school, were spreading across the United

45 States. America needed teachers. Women were available to work—and cheaply. Women's supposed moral superiority did not translate to superior financial compensation; in women, education reformers saw virtuous laborers who could be paid a pittance. "God seems to have made

50 woman peculiarly suited to guide and develop the infant mind, and it seems…very poor policy to pay a man 20 or 22 dollars a month, for teaching children the ABCs, when a female could do the work more successfully at one third of the price," noted a Massachusetts school

55 committee in 1849.

As women infiltrated the classroom, men began to leave. This result should not have surprised reformers. Teaching was being defined as work that women, who were still kept out of more prestigious fields like the law

60 and medicine, could do better than men. In an age when men's and women's roles were clearly defined, few men would choose to do work considered "women's work." By the turn of the twentieth, only a fourth of teachers were men. Still, some men stayed in education as

65 administrators; even as women took on more teaching roles, men kept most leadership positions.

The proportion of female teachers in the United States has not budged since, but the women's rights movement of the twentieth century changed the

70 relationship between the teaching profession and gender in other ways. The feminist and labor movements chipped away at and eventually erased the pay disparity between male and female teachers. Leadership positions in schools are still disproportionally filled by men in comparison to

75 the teaching pool, but a full 52% of principals today are women.

The women's rights movement may have had other unintentional effects on teaching. Some argue that feminism indirectly harmed the quality of con-

80 temporary teachers. Fifty years ago, America's highest-achieving women were barred from highest-powered professions. With their options limited, these women chose to teach. Today, faced with a wider array of pro-fessional options, these same women may avoid teach-

85 ing in favor of medicine, the law, academia, politics, or any number of more prestigious and better-paying posi-tions. As a result, today's teacher corps may be drawn from, on average, a pool of less academically accom-plished professionals than in the past. This has not,

90 however, been proven, and others argue that teachers have had remarkably consistent educational trajectories throughout the twentieth century.

31. One of the author's main points is that the relationship between the teaching profession and gender:

  A. is necessarily filled with discrimination.
  B. has changed over time.
  C. indicates that nurturing is an important component of teaching.
  D. reflects the fact that women make better teachers than men.

32. According to the author, Horace Mann believed:

  F. women to be inferior to men.
  G. men to be poor caretakers.
  H. education to be a moral as well as an intellectual task.
  J. education should focus on the study of birds and fishes.

33. The author most likely mentions the proportion of male administrators at the end of the twentieth century (lines 63–66) to make the point that:

  A. men still wanted to work in education.
  B. women preferred working in the classroom to working in an office.
  C. men received promotions at work while women did not.
  D. while classroom teaching was considered "women's work," school leadership was not.

34. When the Massachusetts school committee described women as "*peculiarly* suited to guide and develop the infant mind" in lines 50–51, the word "peculiarly" most likely was intended to mean that women are:

  F. *especially* suited.
  G. *oddly* suited.
  H. *not usually* suited.
  J. *financially* suited.

35. According to the passage, what was one effect of the feminist movement on the teaching profession?

  A. The proportion of female teachers went down.
  B. The quality of teachers unquestionably plummeted.
  C. The pay gap between male and female teachers went down.
  D. The number of female math and science teachers increased.

36. As it is used in line 56, the word *infiltrated* most precisely means:

  F. invaded.
  G. insinuated their way into.
  H. sneaked into.
  J. entered.

37. According to the passage, the idea that the women's movement has weakened the academic credentials of the American teaching pool:

  A. is a currently debated notion.
  B. has been thoroughly debunked.
  C. is an intentional effect of the movement.
  D. is the inevitable result of an increasing array of options before women.

38. The passage makes the claim that one reason many men left the teaching profession was that:

  F. men considered themselves morally and intellectually above "women's work."
  G. men did not want to participate in the spread of Common Schools.
  H. men wanted to move into more prestigious and financially remunerative professions.
  J. men felt that they were insufficiently skilled at nurturing young people.

39. In line 57, the sentence "This result should not have surprised reformers" most strongly reflects the belief that:

  A. gender discrimination at the time seemed latent but was in fact accepted by all.
  B. the effects of recruiting female teachers should have been more deeply questioned by the reformers.
  C. the reformers should have predicted that their approach would backfire.
  D. the notion that men and women were meant to fill different roles was entrenched at the time.

40. According to the passage, some mid-nineteenth century education reformers, such as Horace Mann, made the argument that:

  F. women were superior to men.
  G. the women's rights movement incorrectly collapsed the spheres of men and women.
  H. the teaching profession should be exclusively filled by women primarily in order to save the government money.
  J. women should work alongside men in many if not most professions.

18

MANHATTAN
PREP   791

PASSAGE 5

SOCIAL STUDIES: This passage is adapted from a 2014 article titled "Good Fences: The Importance of Setting Boundaries for Peaceful Coexistence."

Robert Frost's poem "Mending Wall" depicts two neighbors patching the stone wall between their properties. The first-person narrator questions the need for a wall, noting "Before I built a wall I'd ask to know/
5 What I was walling in or walling out / And to whom I was like to give offence."

That narrator was skeptical of the notion that good fences make good neighbors, but new research shows that the old proverb may indeed be true. While one study of
10 the phenomenon focused on Switzerland, the findings may prove applicable to global peace building.

Switzerland is recognized as a country of peace, stability and prosperity, which is surprising given its linguistic and religious diversity. This kind of diversity
15 has often led to conflict and violence in other countries across the world, but Switzerland has managed to maintain peaceful coexistence since becoming a federal state in 1848.

What makes Switzerland different than other
20 diverse countries? Peace within its national borders does not depend on integrated coexistence, but rather on well-defined topographical and political boundaries separating groups. In Switzerland, landscape elements separate linguistic groups, and political cantons (which
25 are similar to states) separate religious groups. These barriers allow for partial autonomy within a single country—they are both physical and metaphorical fences.

Mountains and lakes are an important feature of the boundaries that separate sharply defined linguistic
30 Swiss groups. The recent study looked at the three main language groups—German, French and Italian—which together comprised 91% of the total population in the 2000 census. The study considered the effect of physical boundaries due to lakes and mountain ranges specifically,
35 and determined the scale of these boundaries by using an edge detection algorithm that calculated topographical heights. The process identified where there was a sharp contrast in height, i.e., a cliff, or steep incline, that ran for a significant distance. This was deemed a natural
40 boundary.

The research demonstrated that a quiet reign of peace has persisted through the regions separated by these natural boundaries. Where such explicit boundaries do not exist, however, such as in mixed cantons where
45 alpine boundaries are absent, violence is more frequent. Indeed, in exactly one region where a porous mountain range does not adequately separate linguistic groups, there has been a history of conflict. That area once contained a sovereign French-speaking Roman Catholic
50 state. However, in 1815, the region was folded into the larger state of Bern, which had a large German-speaking Protestant population. In the ensuing centuries, the region experienced significant violent conflict, including arson, bombings and other terrorist attacks.

55 The conflict led to a referendum, and in 1979 the modern-day state of Jura was created out of a section of the north part of Bern for the French-speaking Catholic population. French-speaking Protestant citizens in southern Jura chose to remain in the northern part of
60 Bern (which had become the official "Bern"), despite that the population there speaking German, choosing to value similar religion over similar language. Part of the reason for this may have been economic, as Bern is a wealthier and more powerful region. However, because
65 of remaining religious tensions, the regional conflict did not end. A proposal to shift the French-speaking Protestant areas of Bern to join French-speaking Catholic Jura is currently being considered.

Political boundaries not accompanied by physical
70 boundaries have, however, been more successful in other parts of the world where they have aligned with ethnic, linguistic and cultural boundaries between groups. In the former Yugoslavia, during widespread ethnic violence, existing political boundaries did not generally coincide
75 with the linguistic and cultural boundaries between distinct groups. However, in the few areas where they *did,* peace prevailed.

The study of peace in Switzerland provides some assurance that theories linking boundaries to peace may
80 be useful in creating interventions designed to reduce violence in various parts of the world. In demographically diverse areas that lack physical barriers, political barriers similar to the ones in Yugoslavia could help temper local violence—though the evidence suggests that it will
85 be important to ensure that they align with linguistic, religious and cultural differences as well.

41. The principal purpose and style of the passage can best be classified as:

    A. polemical.
    B. narrative.
    C. journalistic.
    D. poetic.

42. The last paragraph differs from the paragraph immediately preceding it (lines 69–77) in that the last paragraph is more:

    F. analytical, while the preceding paragraph is more a reporting of facts.
    G. vague, while the preceding paragraph is more data-based.
    H. specific, while the preceding paragraph is more general.
    J. optimistic, while the preceding paragraph is foreboding.

43. The passage answers all of the following questions EXCEPT:

    A. why the modern-day state of Jura was created out of the north part of Bern.
    B. why the French-speaking Protestant population chose to remain in Bern.
    C. what languages were primarily spoken in Switzerland in 2000.
    D. how Switzerland became a federal state in 1848.

44. Among the following quotes from the passage, the one that best captures the author's views on the implications of her topic is:

    F. "new research shows that the old proverb may indeed be true" (lines 8–9).
    G. "Part of the reason for this may have been economic, as Bern is a wealthier and more powerful region" (lines 62–64).
    H. "In demographically diverse areas that lack physical barriers, political barriers similar to the ones in Yugoslavia could help temper local violence" (lines 81–84).
    J. "Switzerland is recognized as a country of peace, stability and prosperity, which is surprising, given its linguistic and religious diversity" (lines 12–14).

45. By the word *cantons* in line 24, the author most nearly means:

    A. nations.
    B. lakes.
    C. mountains.
    D. states.

46. The author suggests that in the former Yugoslavia, all of the following were true EXCEPT that:

    F. it was peaceful in the regions where certain categories of boundaries overlapped.
    G. it was racked by widespread ethnic violence.
    H. in general, political boundaries did not overlap with linguistic and cultural boundaries.
    J. in general, physical boundaries were responsible for the pockets of peace that did exist.

47. The example of the former Yugoslavia is used by the author to illustrate the concept that:

    A. political boundaries should coincide with other boundaries to be effective.
    B. political boundaries are not effective without physical boundaries.
    C. ethnic boundaries are more influential than other kinds.
    D. sometimes even the creation of well-planned political boundaries fails.

48. As it is used in line 10, *the phenomenon* most nearly means:

    F. that Frost was incorrect.
    G. that good fences make good neighbors.
    H. that walls divide.
    J. that walls as a metaphor apply to nation-building.

49. The author uses the statement "they are both physical and metaphorical fences" in line 27 most nearly to mean that:

    A. the boundaries being discussed have a dual role.
    B. the boundaries being discussed are marked by fences.
    C. the boundaries being discussed harken back to the Frost poem.
    D. the boundaries being discussed are more symbolic than literal.

50. One purpose of the Frost poem at the beginning of the passage is to:

    F. set the tone for the passage as literary.
    G. establish the point of view of the poem's narrator as the theme of the passage.
    H. introduce a metaphor that will be operative in developing the theme.
    J. state the conclusion of the passage in literary terms.

18

PASSAGE 6

SOCIAL STUDIES: This passage is adapted from an article titled, "A Propaganda Index for Reviewing Problem Framing in Articles and Manuscripts: An Exploratory Study."

When it comes to the reporting of research findings in the medical profession, there is an integrity problem. Rather than presenting findings from an unbiased approach with no agenda in mind, writers,
5 pharmaceutical companies, and even the government and scholars are often guilty of misconstruing actual results in order to make them more amenable to the marketing of particular products. For example, scientific articles are often "ghostwritten" by private companies
10 who are funding the research, rather than by scientists themselves. The express goal of private companies, of course, is different than it is for disinterested scientists. While scientists and researchers in all fields are theoretically independent parties on a quest for truth,
15 private companies by nature are primarily interested in selling a product.

Ghostwriting in the field of scientific reporting is not the only kind of ethically questionable behavior that occurs in scientific "reporting," however. Another
20 problem that often arises is a lack of sufficient, inde-pendent statistical analysis to support the conclusions that are drawn. Instead of confirming data taken from small sample studies with larger sample sizes, scientists merely report their conclusions as "true" without regard
25 to whether those conclusions hold across populations. Still another problem occurs when research on certain diseases is published in lieu of research on other diseases that are actually more common in the population. This disparity in funding is often due to the perception that
30 there is a profit to be made from the funded research.

Despite these concerns, advances have recently been made in creating guidelines designed to enhance reporting of research. For instance, recent years have seen increased transparency regarding conflicts of
35 interest created by funding, whereby authors must reveal in their reports if they have been paid by pharmaceutical or biotech companies, as well as any other kinds of financial ties they have with such industries (such as owning stock).

40 Even in scholarly journals, however, there is often silence when it comes to the controversial subject of "problem framing." Consider the various ways that the same issue could be framed in an academic journal—for example, how one might define social anxiety. One
45 researcher might frame the problem of social anxiety as follows: "Social anxiety is a *common anxiety disorder* associated with considerable social and occupational handicap that *may or may not* abate without treatment." Another might define it differently: "Social anxiety is
50 a *chronic and insidious psychiatric disorder* that has an early onset. Spontaneous recovery without treatment *is unlikely.*"

I needn't point out that the phrasing of the latter has a certain urgent tone lacking in the former.

55 In the fields of psychiatry and psychology, it is common to deploy such tactics, turning everyday problems into mental illness. And yet, in these disciplines' reporting guidelines, whose stated purpose is to improve the quality and fairness of research reporting, problem framing itself
60 is not even mentioned.

Red flags for hiding competing arguments include phrases such as, "Clearly …" and "It is generally agreed …" This kind of unchallenged repetition encourages "the woozle effect"; if we hear something enough times, we
65 assume that it is true. But it may not be true that social anxiety is "insidious," which means "harmful in a nearly undetectable way." That is a subjective term, a matter of opinion. Should it therefore be included in the medical definition of the diagnosis?

70 I strongly believe that editors of medical journals should be required to consider more carefully, from an evidentiary and conceptual point of view, the framing of concerns addressed in reports of research. They should require authors to reveal rather than hide controversies,
75 as well as to accurately describe well-argued alternatives to the views being promoted, including definitions. Authors should be required to avoid "weasel" words such as "common," which is too vague to be meaningful without a number attached to it. They should refrain
80 from using fear-mongering terms such as "insidious." And they should be required to describe quantitative data related to claims made (for example, sizes of effects in place of broad terms such as "most" and "few"). With these changes, society can more confidently rely on
85 medical research as it is presented in the journals that are intended to distribute true scholarship.

18

MANHATTAN
PREP

51. It can reasonably be inferred from the passage that the author of the passage feels which of the following about current standards for medical journals?

   A. They are too slack in certain fields but not in others.
   B. They have improved in recent years but remain excessively rigid in the fields of psychiatry and psychology.
   C. They should be revisited to provide more adequate guidelines as to how problems should be framed by researchers.
   D. They are not the source of the problem, which lies solely in the present-day structure of scientific funding.

52. The author can best be described as:

   F. an outside observer.
   G. a distant onlooker.
   H. someone who left academia long ago.
   J. someone personally invested in the subject.

53. The fourth paragraph (lines 40–52) primarily serves to:

   A. define the medical issue of social anxiety in more than one way.
   B. outline the central view to which the author is opposed.
   C. introduce and illustrate an important and controversial topic.
   D. point out the difficulty of defining complex phenomena.

54. Which of the following best summarizes the author's thoughts regarding how scientific research is funded?

   F. The author feels that it is one reason why medical reporting is unreliable.
   G. The author feels that it is the only cause of bias in medical reporting.
   H. The author believes that if funding did not come from private sources, medical research would be credible.
   J. The author is curious about how the funding sources of medical research affect its reliability.

55. The main function of the final paragraph related to the passage as a whole is to:

   A. require authors to address controversies openly, rather than bury them.
   B. argue that current medical reporting amounts to nothing more than propaganda.
   C. make recommendations for specific changes to standards in medical reporting.
   D. invite others to weigh in on what standards should govern medical reporting.

56. By use of the term *woozle effect* in line 64, the author most nearly intends to suggest that:

   F. reading a term like "clearly" often enough may make an argument seem clearer or otherwise better than it actually is.
   G. words that seem to mean one thing often mean something else entirely.
   H. the degree to which a term like "insidious" applies to a disease is generally subjective.
   J. the more often a person hears an opinion, the greater the likelihood that it is in fact true.

57. The two definitions of social anxiety in lines 46–52 differ in that:

   A. the first definition paints the diagnosis as more serious in terms of treatment, while the latter paints it as less so.
   B. the first definition paints the diagnosis as less serious in terms of treatment, while the latter paints it as more so.
   C. the first definition is academic, while the second is propaganda, according to the author.
   D. the first definition is literal, while the second is more figurative.

58. According to the passage, reporting guidelines in the fields of psychiatry and psychology are designed to:

   F. eliminate all bias in research reporting.
   G. improve the quality of research reporting.
   H. make research reporting less personal.
   J. incentivize researchers to be honest.

59. Which of the following words does the author NOT specifically mention as problematic when it appears in science reporting?

   A. Insidious
   B. Most
   C. Common
   D. Majority

60. The author attributes certain disparities in funding across various research projects to:

   F. the excitement in the scientific community for particular projects.
   G. the potential for certain research aims to result in socially beneficial outcomes.
   H. expectations about opportunities to make money.
   J. the belief that the most important areas of research will be the most profitable.

18

PASSAGE 7

SOCIAL STUDIES: This passage is adapted from an essay titled "From Mummies to Morgues: the Sociology of Death."

Death is life's only guarantee. Yet death's place—physically, morally, spiritually, and socially—changes dramatically across human cultures. How different societies treat the dying and the dead reflects and
5 reinforces ideas about illness, family, God, the afterlife, and life itself. For example, ancient Egyptians in the Old Kingdom mummified the bodies of their kings. Mummification included removing all of the deceased's internal organs except his heart; drying the body with
10 salt; stuffing the dried body to retain its human shape; and wrapping the body in cloths and amulets made of precious stones. The purpose of this elaborate and expensive process was to ensure entrance for the deceased to the eternal afterlife; only well-preserved bodies could
15 pass into the underworld. How different this ritual is from the simple burials of today.

One aspect of death that differs across cultures is the place of grief. Ancient Egyptians held lengthy funerary processions for the dead. Women were often
20 hired to lament loudly because it was believed that the cries of despondent mourners would echo through the hall of the afterworld. These echoes, in turn, would help the deceased gain entrance to it. Thus, grief in ancient Egypt, with its emphasis on the afterworld, focused on
25 taking care of the dead.

Jewish grief rituals, however, focus on the bereaved as much as they do the dead. Jews believe the dead do not pass to a heavenly afterworld, but to dust. Jews bury all of their dead in simple wooden coffins containing no
30 metal, including no nails, in order to ensure that the dead and their wrappings will fully decompose into the earth. The traditional Jewish funeral is relatively brief, but the rituals for the bereaved extend for a longer period of time. Following a Jewish burial, the family of the dead "sit shiva,"
35 during which family members stay home and light a slow-burning candle made of olive oil or paraffin to signify the dead; they cover their mirrors, wear no makeup, and do not shave or cook. During this period of rest and support, community members bring food and share in prayer.

40 While this built-in home-rest lasts only a week—after seven days, family members are expected to begin to re-enter normal society—the grieving process is extended in steps of decreasing intensity. For the thirty days after the burial, family members avoid parties and

45 other celebratory events, and for the rest of the year, family members say mourning prayers daily or weekly. Children of deceased parents are expected to continue to avoid celebratory events. After this year of proscribed mourning finishes, mourning is, interestingly, forbidden,
50 with the exception of a few anniversary days each year.

The graduated stages of grief within Judaism, ending with the figurative release of grief, foreshadowed later psychiatric attitudes towards grief. In 1969, psychiatrist Elisabeth Kubler-Ross introduced the "five
55 stages of grief" in her book *On Death and Dying*. The Kubler-Ross model became popular among Americans, although it has not been fully accepted by the psychiatric community. Kubler-Ross argued that while particular experiences of grief were subjective, there exists a useful
60 archetype. First, the bereaved enters Denial, a stage in which he or she tries to shut loss out of his or her mind. The stage of Denial is followed by Anger, which is followed by Bargaining, during which the bereaved makes deals with a higher power, him- or herself, or
65 loved ones, to try to undo aspects of the loss. The fourth stage, Depression, is the darkness that comes after the Bargaining inevitably fails. Only in the fifth stage does the bereaved arrive at Acceptance.

The medicalization of death and grief is one aspect
70 of contemporary American death rituals; our society is powerfully shaped by science as well as by notions of the afterlife. The American Psychiatric Association (APA), the professional group for mental health workers, stepped into controversy when it folded grief into clinical
75 depression. The APA defines mental illnesses in a manual called the Diagnostic Statistical Manual of Mental Disorders, or DSM. The DSM lists criteria that must be met for a patient to be diagnosed with, say, anorexic or bipolar disorders. The most recent edition, the DSM-V,
80 took out what was called the "bereavement exclusion" from its definition of depression. In the previous four editions, clinicians were instructed not to diagnose with major depressive disorder anyone who had lost a loved one in the previous two months. Now, they can.

85 The decision to allow clinicians to diagnose freshly bereaved individuals with a mental disorder was met with both criticism and praise. Some argued that it would enable individuals in pain to receive relief in the form of medication and other medical attention, while
90 others argued that the decision reflected an increasing tendency to define normal behavior as "illness" requiring expensive pills.

61. According to the passage, each of the following is true of the Kubler-Ross model EXCEPT that:

    A. the model includes both denial and acceptance.

    B. the model isn't entirely accepted.

    C. the model is popular throughout the world.

    D. the model was originally introduced in a book.

62. When the author says the "medicalization of death and grief" (line 69), she is most likely referring to the fact that:

    F. bodies can be donated to science.

    G. all grief takes place today in the context of hospitals and medicine.

    H. all symptoms of death and grief have been newly defined as illnesses requiring pharmaceutical treatment.

    J. Western medicine and hospital practices influence the experiences of death and grief.

63. The main purpose of the second paragraph (lines 17–25) is to:

    A. introduce a main theme of the essay and offer a specific example.

    B. continue a discussion of the primary culture on which the author focuses.

    C. describe a ritual that the author finds shockingly different from today's rituals.

    D. offer an anecdote that digresses from the main theme of the passage.

64. It can be inferred from the passage that the decision to remove the bereavement exclusion from the DSM:

    F. was supported by most medical professionals.

    G. was met with outrage by people resistant to the use of pharmaceuticals to treat mental illness.

    H. was a decision that remains controversial.

    J. was a mistake because normal behavior should not be pathologized.

65. Based on the passage, members of which of the following group are most likely to believe that human consciousness persists after death?

    A. Adherents of the Kubler-Ross model

    B. Contemporary American psychiatrists

    C. Ancient Egyptians

    D. Religious Jews

66. The main function of the fourth paragraph (lines 40–50) in relation to the whole passage is to:

    F. introduce the rituals of a specific culture.

    G. offer more detail about something described in the previous paragraph.

    H. rebut a point with which the author disagrees.

    J. describe a set of beliefs that have been adopted by the psychiatric community.

67. According to the passage, shiva includes:

    A. a year of wearing torn clothes.

    B. thirty days of staying home from work and praying.

    C. a period of fasting.

    D. a period in which mirrors are covered.

68. It can be inferred from the passage that one difference between ancient Egyptian and Jewish practices regarding death is that:

    F. Jews bury all bodies using similar rituals, while ancient Egyptians did not.

    G. Jews respect death, while ancient Egyptians did not.

    H. ancient Egyptians prepared dead bodies for burial, while Jews do not.

    J. ancient Egyptians grieved more loudly than Jews.

69. The author likely describes Jewish funerals as "relatively brief" (line 32) in order to highlight:

    A. the simplicity of these rituals.

    B. the contrast between the length of the service and the length of the traditional grieving process.

    C. the fact that Jewish rituals are the opposite of ancient Egyptian rituals.

    D. the Jewish belief in the afterlife.

70. The author thinks Jewish rituals around grief "foreshadowed later psychiatric attitudes" (lines 52–53) because:

    F. both feature a series of differentiated stages that end with a lessening of grief.

    G. both identify anger and acceptance as components of grief.

    H. both integrate community support into the grieving process.

    J. both define "right" and "wrong" ways to grieve.

MANHATTAN
PREP

PASSAGE 8

SOCIAL STUDIES: These passages are adapted excerpts from "Influence of Ethnolinguistic Diversity on the Sorghum Genetic Patterns in Subsistence Farming Systems in Eastern Kenya."

PASSAGE A

In the past, agriculture involved planting a variety of different plants, which was a practice that was important for providing a kind of insurance for the farmer. If a farmer only grows one crop, he risks that conditions in
5 a particular year might be disastrous for his yields; but if he grows several, he reduces that risk, simply because different species—both animals and plants—respond in different ways to changes in the environment. In parts of the world that are dependent on agriculture—most of
10 the world— crop diversity is thus very important.

There are several ways that social boundaries contribute to the evolution of crop diversity. They do so both directly, by determining seed flows, and indirectly, by shaping what kinds of seeds are commonly used
15 and what information is shared within a community or outside of it. Recent studies have revealed that diversification processes of crops, such as banana and sweet potatoes, are linked to human migration patterns. Today, the evolution of crops is still ongoing, particularly
20 in societies where smaller, household-based farming systems are prevalent.

Studying how people relate to each other and to their crops can help us better understand crop evolution. Farmers' varieties are relevant units for studying crop
25 diversity, because farmers name them. These names can be used as a marker of knowledge diffusion and exchanges across communities. So is the distribution of genetic diversity. Patterns can then be compared.

Research suggests that the ethnic organization
30 of farming communities plays an important role in determining what crop populations exist in a given area. For instance, sorghum is a cereal extensively cultivated in small-farming systems because of its ability to grow under harsh climatic conditions. Researchers hypothesized that
35 the spatial distribution of sorghum botanical races in Africa was related to that of the ethnic groups. In a study undertaken in Niger, they found that human ethnic diversity has probably had an even greater impact on sorghum diversity than environmental constraints—a
40 hugely significant finding.

PASSAGE B

Three ethnic groups, the Chuka, the Tharaka and the Mbeere, migrated to the same part of Kenya by the end of the 19th century. Since that time they have remained culturally distinct. This is not solely due
45 to hostility between them, however. The Mbeere and Chuka historically have existed in conflict with one another, while the Chuka and Tharaka maintain strong social ties and consider themselves kin. Intermarriage is common between the Chuka and Tharaka, while it
50 is uncommon between the Mbeere and Chuka, or the Mbeere and Tharaka.

The Mbeere households are located in the southern part of the region. The Tharaka are mostly on the northeastern side, and the Chuka reside on the
55 northwestern side. Consistent with the social relationships between groups, a clear spatial boundary exists between the Mbeere and both the Chuka and Tharaka, while the Chuka and Tharaka populations are more mixed, geographically.

60 The three ethnic groups manage cropping systems that are based on cereals and legumes—sorghum, cowpeas, maize and mungo bean, mainly. The different sorghum varieties are either grown in separate plots or mixed together in farmers' fields. In addition, farmers in all
65 three groups have adopted a number of genetically altered crop varieties, disseminated by the Kenyan Ministry of Agriculture. These improved varieties are cultivated together in the same field with the local varieties.

Of the local varieties supplied by the farmers, there
70 is variance in the genetics of the crops among the three groups, but not for the improved varieties supplied by the Ministry of Agriculture, which are the same across all three. When it comes to differences in the local varieties, however, the variation is not distributed equally. The two
75 groups that are friendly—Chuka and Tharaka—grow crops that are more genetically similar to one another's crops than to the crops grown by the Mbeere. Certain seed varieties are significantly less frequent in the Mbeere group than in the Chuka and Tharaka groups, while
80 another was significantly more frequent in the Mbeere group than in the other two.

This correlation between social interaction patterns and the extent of variation of crop diversity suggests that the two are related. It may be that increased social interaction
85 affects the genetics of the local crops that are planted.

71. According to the author of Passage A, sorghum is grown in small farming communities because:

   A. it is cheap to harvest.
   B. it can withstand extreme weather.
   C. the soil in the region is amenable to it.
   D. it is successful across ethnic groups.

72. In Passage A, the author's attitude toward crop diversity is that it is:

   F. critical to the majority of the planet's economic systems.
   G. vital to a small, rural segment of the world's population.
   H. important primarily to farmers to ensure annual yields.
   J. less important than maintaining ethnic diversity.

73. It can be reasonably inferred that the author of Passage A believes that in relation to environmental influences on sorghum diversity, human behavioral influences:

   A. function in a complementary way.
   B. operate independently.
   C. are less likely to make a difference.
   D. are likely to be more impactful.

74. By "local varieties" in lines 69 and 73, the author of Passage B most likely means:

   F. crops that differ equally among the groups discussed.
   G. crops genetically modified by local farmers.
   H. crops that are not genetically modified.
   J. crops genetically modified by the Kenyan Ministry of Agriculture.

75. Passage B indicates that of the three groups:

   A. the Mbeere, Tharaka, and Chuka are all isolated from one another both geographically and socially.
   B. the Mbeere and Tharaka get along, while the Chuka are hostile toward the Tharaka.
   C. the Chuka and Tharaka interact socially, while the Mbeere are more isolated.
   D. the Chuka and Mbeere have a long history of open war.

76. The main point of Passage B is that:

   F. superior crop yields are associated with increased levels of socializing among ethnic groups.
   G. greater interaction between groups is correlated with greater similarity in the varieties of crops harvested by those groups.
   H. genetically modified crops are not subject to the same effects of human behavior on crop genetics.
   J. boundaries between ethnic groups play a greater role in determining genetic information of crops than does any other factor.

77. How do Passages A and B differ?

   A. Passage A is more scholarly, while Passage B is more anecdotal.
   B. Passage A is more general, while Passage B is more specific.
   C. Passage A is opinionated, while Passage B is objective.
   D. Passage A presents controversial findings, while Passage B is irrefutable.

78. Compared to the author of Passage A, the author of Passage B:

   F. is more reserved in his interpretation of the finding that human behavior may affect crop diversity.
   G. is more enthusiastic about exploring the theme in the context of a multiple real communities.
   H. is more objective in his analysis of the study being discussed.
   J. is a greater advocate for further research than the author of the first passage.

79. It can reasonably be inferred that the authors of the two passages:

   A. generally agree about the nature of the causal mechanism being discussed.
   B. disagree regarding the significance of the causal mechanism being discussed.
   C. would be likely to disagree on most specifics of the issue being discussed.
   D. come from very different scholarly backgrounds.

18

PASSAGE 9

SOCIAL STUDIES: Passage A is adapted from a book on the history of nursing. Passage B is an excerpt from an American History textbook.

PASSAGE A

Vera Hay, a British nurse during World War II, was one of the first nurses to land at Normandy shortly after D-Day. Hay was stationed at the Chateau de Beaussy, a field hospital for British troops where major surgeries
5 were performed in order to stabilize patients so that they were safe to travel back to England. There, Hay cared for up to 200 injured soldiers a day, conducting triage on patients as they arrived. Those with more serious injuries were rushed straight through to surgery.

10 Fifty years later, at 92, Hay reflected on what stood out in her memory of that time. "The pain of the casualties, both our own troops and the German prisoners of war," she told the British newspaper *The Telegraph*. "They all were patients to us. They needed
15 rehydration, rest, morphine to keep them comfortable and we were using the new penicillin."

Over 425,000 Allied and German troops were killed, wounded or went missing during the Battle of Normandy.

20 Hay had completed her nursing training in August 1943 and promptly volunteered for the Queen Alexandra's Imperial Military Nursing Service. Less a year later, not even a week after D-Day, she found herself landing on Normandy's Gold Beach and traveling sixteen kilometers
25 to the hospital, a journey that took about twenty-four hours as she and the other nurses had to steer clear of pockets of German resistance along the way.

At the hospital, the nurses did not rotate. Everyone was required to work around the clock, sleeping only
30 when they had the chance. This meant that Hay usually slept for no more than one or two hours at a time.

On the other side of the English Channel, nurses like Mary Virginia Desmarais were waiting. "We received our first casualties on D plus 4," she recollects.
35 "They were fresh battle casualties in great pain that had been given only first aid in France and aboard the [boats] that brought them into Southampton, England." When the buses arrived with patients, an announcement would be called over the loudspeaker: "Man your stations until
40 further notice."

Desmarais writes, "There was no time for meals or rest. The line of casualties was endless, it seemed."

The English Channel, only 20 miles wide at its narrowest point, separated Hay and Desmarais. On both
45 sides of it, in the field hospitals of France and the city hospitals of England, both nurses worked tirelessly to save as many as they could of hundreds of thousands of injured men. They were true heroes behind the front lines.

PASSAGE B

The Battle of Normandy was not a battle that lasted
50 a day or even a few days. It lasted three months, from June 1944 to August 1944. The invasion continued into Germany, and ultimately led to Germany's surrender and the liberation of Europe from Nazi control.

The Battle itself, code-named "Operation Overlord,"
55 was launched on June 6th, 1944, also known as D-Day. The visual of the launch of Overlord has become iconic. More than 5,000 ships and landing craft carrying troops and supplies from England traversed the English Channel to France, while more than 11,000 aircraft
60 descended upon five beaches that ran along a 50-mile stretch of heavily fortified coast in France's Normandy region. Together, these crafts carried approximately 150,000 soldiers. These Allied Forces were composed of American, British and Canadian forces, constituting
65 one of the largest amphibious (on both land and water) military assaults in modern history.

To prepare an attack of such magnitude was a feat in itself and required planning for unexpected obstacles, such as the weather. Perhaps it should come as no
70 surprise that D-Day itself was not originally planned for June 6th. General Dwight D. Eisenhower had selected the date for the invasion as June 5th, but the weather from England over the English Channel was poor in the week leading up to it, and on the afternoon of the 4th,
75 it was still bad.

"The weather in this country is practically unpredictable," Eisenhower wrote, "For some days our experts have been meeting almost hourly and I have been holding Commander-in-Chief meetings once or twice a day
80 to consider the reports and tentative predictions." Fair predictions for the following day, however, led him to order the invasion on the 6th. He told the troops, "You are about to embark upon the Great Crusade, toward which we have striven these many months. The eyes of
85 the world are upon you."

Prior to D-Day, the Allies had conducted a large-scale deception campaign designed to mislead the Germans about the intended invasion target. As a result, the German response to the invasion was weak, and
90 by late August 1944, all of northern France had been liberated. By the spring of 1945 the Allies had defeated the Germans.

80. The main function of Passage A is to:

F. celebrate the contributions of two wartime nurses.

G. provide an overview of the medical teams that worked in the European theater in World War II.

H. establish a particular World War II nurse as a war hero.

J. offer a portrait of the most typical female profession in the early twentieth century.

81. All of the following are true of Hay and Desmarais EXCEPT that:

A. Hay was stationed in Normandy, France; Desmarais was stationed in Southampton, England.

B. neither Hay nor Desmarais rested very much during the relevant period.

C. both Hay and Desmarais recall particular medications administered to patients.

D. both Hay and Desmarais recall the pain experienced by the patients under their care.

82. By "D plus 4" in line 34, the nurse being quoted most nearly means:

F. June 6th, 1944.

G. June 10th, 1944.

H. June 6th, 1945.

J. June 10th, 1945.

83. According to the author of Passage B, the Battle of Normandy was also broadly referred to by those involved as:

A. D-Day.

B. Operation Overlord.

C. Great Crusade.

D. Allied Forces.

84. The author of Passage B would most likely agree that the success of the Battle of Normandy is due in part to:

F. the quality of the medical care provided by the nurses and doctors at the frontlines.

G. the number of British troops, specifically, involved in the battle.

H. the unfortunate turn of the weather in early June 1944 that delayed the campaign, ultimately for the better.

J. the degree to which the Germans were misled by the deception campaign leading up to D-Day.

85. As it is used in line 65, *amphibious* most nearly means:

A. related to water.

B. by boat.

C. that soldiers arrived in boats that could land and proceed forward on solid ground.

D. that the initial attack during the Battle of Normandy took place on both land and sea.

86. Based on the two passages, it can most reasonably be inferred that Vera Hay first arrived in Normandy in which of the following vehicles?

F. Boat or plane

G. Boat or submarine

H. Plane or bus

J. Boat or bus

87. Compared to the author of Passage A, the author of Passage B is more focused on:

A. on-the-ground reasons why certain tactical maneuvers were made.

B. executive levels of wartime decision making.

C. the personal stake of those enlisted in the battle.

D. the significant power of German resistance to Allied Forces during WWII.

88. It can reasonably be inferred that compared to the author of Passage B, the author of Passage A expressly feels that:

F. medical professionals such as Hay and Desmarais deserve high honors for their work during the campaign.

G. the nurses of World War II have received inadequate praise for their tireless service.

H. the great contributions of Vera Hay warrant unparalleled recognition today.

J. if not for nurses like Vera Hay and Mary Virginia Desmarais, Operation Overlord likely would not have succeeded.

18

Answer Keys

Write in whether you got each problem right or wrong (or left it blank). If your answer was correct, put a 1 in every blank to the right of that problem. Sum up each column and compare your total to the total possible "Out Of" points in each column.

Passage 1

Problem	Correct Answer	Right/ Wrong/Blank	Main Ideas/ Author's Approach	Details	Relationships	Meanings of Words	Generalizations
1	C		—				
2	J			—			
3	A			—			
4	H				—		
5	A					—	
6	G				—		
7	C				—		
8	J			—			
9	C				—		
10	H		—				
Total							
Out Of		10	2	3	4	1	0

Passage 2

Problem	Correct Answer	Right/ Wrong/Blank	Main Ideas/ Author's Approach	Details	Relationships	Meanings of Words	Generalizations
11	D		—				
12	H			—			
13	A				—		
14	G			—			
15	A			—			
16	G					—	
17	D		—				
18	H			—			
19	A			—			
20	H						—
Total							
Out Of		10	2	5	1	1	1

Passage 3

Problem	Correct Answer	Right/ Wrong/Blank	Main Ideas/ Author's Approach	Details	Relationships	Meanings of Words	Generalizations
21	A		—				
22	H				—		
23	B				—		
24	J					—	
25	B			—			
26	F					—	
27	D						—
28	G			—			
29	D			—			
30	G			—			
Total							
Out Of		10	1	4	2	2	1

Passage 4

Problem	Correct Answer	Right/ Wrong/Blank	Main Ideas/ Author's Approach	Details	Relationships	Meanings of Words	Generalizations
31	B		—				
32	H			—			
33	D			—			
34	F					—	
35	C			—			
36	J					—	
37	A				—		
38	H			—			
39	D				—		
40	G			—			
Total							
Out Of		10	1	5	2	2	0

Passage 5

Problem	Correct Answer	Right/ Wrong/Blank	Main Ideas/ Author's Approach	Details	Relationships	Meanings of Words	Generalizations
41	C						—
42	F		—				
43	D			—			
44	H		—				
45	D					—	
46	J			—			
47	A						—
48	G					—	
49	A					—	
50	H		—				
Total							
Out Of		10	3	2	0	3	2

Passage 6

Problem	Correct Answer	Right/ Wrong/Blank	Main Ideas/ Author's Approach	Details	Relationships	Meanings of Words	Generalizations
51	C		—				
52	J						—
53	C		—				
54	F				—		
55	C		—				
56	F					—	
57	B				—		
58	G			—			
59	D			—			
60	H				—		
Total							
Out Of		10	3	2	3	1	1

18

MANHATTAN
PREP

Passage 7

Problem	Correct Answer	Right/ Wrong/Blank	Main Ideas/ Author's Approach	Details	Relationships	Meanings of Words	Generalizations
61	C			—			
62	J					—	
63	A		—				
64	H				—		
65	C				—		
66	G		—				
67	D			—			
68	F				—		
69	B				—		
70	F					—	
Total							
Out Of		10	2	2	4	2	0

Passage 8

Problem	Correct Answer	Right/ Wrong/Blank	Main Ideas/ Author's Approach	Details	Relationships	Meanings of Words	Generalizations
71	B		—				
72	F						—
73	D				—		
74	H					—	
75	C				—		
76	G		—				
77	B						—
78	F		—				
79	A						—
Total							
Out Of		9	2	1	2	1	3

Passage 9

Problem	Correct Answer	Right/ Wrong/Blank	Main Ideas/ Author's Approach	Details	Relationships	Meanings of Words	Generalizations
80	F		—				
81	C			—			
82	G					—	
83	B			—			
84	J						—
85	D					—	
86	F			—			
87	B		—				
88	F		—				
Total							
Out Of		9	3	3	0	2	1

18

Social Studies Solutions

Passage 1 Solutions

1. **(C)** She sees the redesign as a positive step towards making courtrooms more accessible and comfortable, but is skeptical as to whether other courtrooms will follow suit.

Author's Approach

The author believes that courtrooms should make the law "accessible" and "understandable," and that courtrooms should make witnesses feel "comfortable enough … to be honest." She describes the redesign as accessible to parents and protective of children. Yet she also believes "it is unlikely" that standard courtrooms will follow suit (lines 62–64). This matches (C), which expresses both a positive view of the redesign and uncertainty as to whether other courts will make similar changes. Choice (A) is incorrect because the author believes the changes are relevant to standard courtrooms, even though she is not sure whether standard courtrooms will follow suit. (B) is incorrect because the author believes "the law can be respected while still being made accessible, understandable and, in courtrooms, comfortable enough for witnesses to be honest" (lines 83–85). (D) is incorrect because she does not connect this particular redesign to public spirit or politics.

2. **(J)** a raised platform for the judge and a divider separating the viewing area from the proceedings.

Details

The author describes standard courtrooms in the second paragraph: "In most courtrooms … the proceedings are separated from the viewing area by a wall or divider. The topography of the space—the judge seated on a raised platform—allows the judge to observe the room's activity from an elevated position" (lines 5–12). Choice (J) is correct.

3. **(A)** allow participants to view and testify at proceedings while in physically separate places.

Details

In lines 44–47, the author states, "The extensive use of video would be expected to allow a participant in any location within the complex to communicate with another participant anywhere else." This matches choice (A). Choice (C) is tempting because that same paragraph describes incarcerated parents. However, note that video enables incarcerated parents to participate in proceedings *without* being transported to the courthouse. Thus, choice (C) gives the opposite of what you are looking for.

4. **(H)** a hierarchical style of architecture in courtrooms is strongly ingrained in the United States.

Relationships

The author offers the Supreme Court as an example of the way courtroom architecture mirrors the standard reverence for the law and authority. "Perhaps the most striking example of hierarchical American courthouse architecture is the Supreme Court itself," she states in lines 74–76. Choice (H) describes hierarchical architecture as "ingrained," which means deeply embedded. This matches the example of the Supreme Court. Choice (F) is incorrect because the author does not assert that the law "must always" be given the utmost respect; rather, she believes the law *is* given the utmost respect. Choice (J) is tempting, but while this may be true, this detail does not express *why* the author offers this example. Lastly, the author is not making the point that the court is prestigious; she is suggesting that the Supreme Court reflects a broader trend about how architecture is used to convey hierarchy in United States courtrooms. Choice (G) is incorrect. Therefore, Choice (H) is correct.

MANHATTAN
PREP

5.   **(A)** Standard courtrooms will adopt a less hierarchical style.

Meaning of Words

"It is unlikely," follows the question, "Will standard courtrooms ever follow suit?" That is, will standard courtrooms ever incorporate the less hierarchical style of the Bexar County children's courtrooms? Choice (A) is correct because it captures that question. The author argues that the traditional, authority-respecting nature of the legal profession will inhibit major changes in courtroom architecture.

6.   **(G)** alienates and confuses many members of the general public.

Relationships

In lines 17–22, the author cites "legalese"—law-specific language—as an example of "why the public would find courtrooms less than welcoming" (lines 20–21) and says that it is "unfamiliar to many lay people" (line 17). This matches choice (G). The author does not connect jargon to authority, so choice (F) is incorrect. "Angry" is too extreme, so choice (H) is incorrect. (J) is incorrect because the author does not connect legal jargon to architectural terms.

7.   **(C)** The scholarship is valuable because we should examine how courtroom architecture reflects our values and facilitates justice.

Relationships

The author opens her essay by citing Mulcahy's work. She uses Mulcahy's scholarship as a launching pad for her discussion. She clearly respects the scholarship, so (B) must be incorrect. She never argues that "no one had pointed out the discrepancy between American legal ideals and the reality of the courtroom before," so (D) must be incorrect. Between choices (A) and (C), (A) offers a prescriptive vision (what courtrooms *should* be), while (C) is more reserved. (A) is incorrect because while the author believes courtrooms should be "accessible" and "understandable" (line 84), she never argues that they should be the "centers of spirited debate." Choice (C) is correct because it reflects the overall tone and spirit of the author's argument.

8.   **(J)** local residents believed that a special courtroom for childhood abuse cases was needed.

Details

The author states the idea "sprang from consensus in the county that a special courtroom to accommodate the high number of abused children was critical" (lines 29–32). This matches choice (J).

9.   **(C)** "Judges, statutes, and sacred, guiding documents, such as both state and federal constitutions, are given the utmost respect."

Relationships

The author describes the traditional hierarchical view of the law in this paragraph, offering robes as an example of this view. Choice (C) is correct. Choices (A) and (B) are incorrect because these quotes offer critiques of the hierarchical view of the law, while the use of robes aligns with the hierarchical view. Choice (D) is from the description of the alternative courtrooms. Again, the robes are standard rather than alternative, so (D) is incorrect.

10.   **(H)** underscore the point that courtrooms are not the open, democratic spaces people once dreamed them to be.

Author's Approach

This comparison comes during the author's description of standard courtrooms. The author describes contemporary courtrooms and their raised daises to illustrate Mulcahy's argument that today's courtrooms are "a far cry from the apolitical, public-spirited" places they were "once idealized to be" (lines 3–4). Choice (H) is correct. Choice (G) is the opposite of what you are looking for; the theatrical courtroom is the standard rather than an alternative design. Choice (F) is too literal. Choice (J) is incorrect because the author does not explore the judge's view or any "viewers."

Passage 2 Solutions

11.   **(D)** set a scene with which launch a discussion.

Author's Approach

The main focus of the passage is Theodore Roosevelt, but he isn't mentioned in the first paragraph. Choices (B) and (C), therefore, must be incorrect. The first paragraph instead describes TR's memorial, which includes objects and quotes that point to TR's personality. However, (A) is too specific; these subjects of nature, etc., are not even briefly explored. The function of this paragraph is to set the scene for the anecdotes that follow. (D) is correct.

12.   **(H)** his family included many other politicians, including another president.

Details

The author describes TR's family in the sixth paragraph. The family is described in lines 22–23 as "privileged" and "wealthy." Since this is an EXCEPT question, (F) must be incorrect. Choice (G) is incorrect, as the family vacationed in Europe, where they would interact with local poor children (lines 29–31). Choice (J) is incorrect because in the same paragraph, you are told that although TR's father was allied with abolitionists, his mother came from a slave-owning family. Choice (H) is never mentioned in the passage, which makes (H) what you are looking for.

13.   **(A)** the belief that war is not always the worst option.

Relationships

The author offers a few glimpses of TR's attitude towards war. You know that he volunteered to join the army as a young man. At the end of the passage, the author also offers a relevant quote: "If I must choose between righteousness and peace, I choose righteousness" (lines 87–89). This quote implies that TR was willing to go to war for righteousness, which matches choice (A). Answer choice (B) is too specific; no particular connection is made between TR's willingness to go to war and his interest in preserving nature. Choice (C) was never mentioned in the passage. Choice (D) is also incorrect; TR did not volunteer for "multiple" cavalries, as far as you know. Only one cavalry (the Rough Riders) is mentioned. Choice (A) is correct.

18

14. **(G)** a cavalry that played an important role in the Spanish–American war.

Details

The passage states, "TR led the [Rough Riders] cavalry to victory in the crucial Battle of San Juan, helping to shatter the Spanish Empire in the Americas" (lines 46–48). The word "crucial" means "important." Answer choice (G) is correct. You know that the Rough Riders was a "volunteer" unit, so (F) is incorrect. Also, while Rough Riders was composed of a diverse array of men, the passage does not suggest that they were *led* by a diverse group. Choice (H) is incorrect. Choice (J) is incorrect because the passage describes the Rough Riders in the context of the Spanish–American war. Other wars are not mentioned in connection with this cavalry.

15. **(A)** apathy.

Details

The passage states, "Like many men of his era and social class, TR did not regard the struggles of black and Native Americans as particularly pressing" (lines 77–79). This attitude can be captured in the word "apathy," which means "indifference, lack of caring." Therefore, choice (A) is correct.

16. **(G)** convincing citizens to pressure their representatives to pass legislation.

Meaning of Words

The passage tells you in lines 66–69 that TR used "the bully pulpit" to appeal "directly to citizens" in order to "push other anti-monopoly legislation through the Senate." TR was therefore going to the public to pressure the existing Senate indirectly. Choices (H) and (J) are incorrect because they do not connect to legislation. Choice (F) does not connect to the general public. Choice (G) is correct because it discusses using the public to pressure elected officials to pass legislation.

17. **(D)** give a sense of TR's remarkable resilience.

Main Ideas/Author's Approach

This story introduces TR as a strong person, one who could rebound from a possibly fatal injury almost instantly. The phrase "remarkable resilience," choice (D), captures this trait. Choice (C) is too literal (of course, TR had a high tolerance for pain, apparently, but the point of the story is broader), while (B) is too general (the "violent nature of the times" is not the topic of the passage). The story does not depict TR as weak or in need of sympathy, so (A) is incorrect.

18. **(H)** breaking up monopolies.

Details

The passage states, "[TR] brought large anti-trust lawsuits against the Northern Securities Company, a railroad conglomerate helmed by J.P. Morgan. He pushed other anti-monopoly legislation through the Senate by appealing directly to citizens" (lines 64–68). Choice (H) is correct. Neither (F), (G), nor (J) are supported by the passage.

19.   **(A)** TR traveled to places beyond the United States.

Details

While the passage mentions TR's son in line 55, the passage never informs the reader that TR had many children, so (D) is therefore incorrect. Choice (B) is incorrect as well; the passage informs the reader that TR kept animals in the White House. Choice (C) is never mentioned by the passage. The passage does, however, describe the Roosevelt family's "European vacations" (line 30). Choice (A) is correct.

20.   **(H)** someone driven by bold convictions and willing to risk harm.

Generalizations

The passage is filled with words like "brash," "passion," "ebullience" (which means "cheerfulness, exuberant energy"), and "aggressive." All of these words point to the author's view of TR as a forceful and driven man. The quote offered at the end of the passage mirrors this view. Choice (H) is correct. Choice (J) is incorrect because the author does not compare TR's leadership on military and domestic matters. Similarly, the passage never discusses economic justice, so answer choice (G) is incorrect. Choice (F) is too extreme; the author may admire TR, but she does not rank him as among the greatest when compared to other presidents.

Passage 3 Solutions

21.   **(A)** human beings coexist with large carnivores partly because of financial considerations.

Main Idea

The author's primary purpose in writing the passage is to stress that while human beings rarely coexist with large carnivores, one reason they do is because it's economically sensible to do so, so (A) is correct. She gives the example of the Gir forest, where "it is economically more profitable for the Maldharis to live in the forests" (lines 60–61). While (B) is true according to the author, it's not the main point. Choices (C) and (D) are both too extreme—"strictly" and "frequently" are both incorrect.

22.   **(H)** the relatively low cost of resources.

Relationships (Cause–Effect)

The reason it is more economically beneficial for the Maldharis to live in the forest despite the lions is that "Maldhari livestock within Gir obtain most of their forage requirements from the forest free of cost" (lines 61–63). This supports choice (H).

23.   **(B)** lions kill livestock.

Relationships (Cause–Effect)

The author writes in lines 5–6 that "the major conflict between species arises from large carnivores' preying on the livestock kept by forest-dwellers." Choice (B) is correct.

18

24. **(J)** the cost of feeding livestock for forest-dwellers.

Meaning of Words

The phrase *free grazing rights* refers to the idea that the livestock of the Maldhari graze, or eat, for free in the forest, whereas outside the forest, the Maldhari would have to purchase food for their livestock. Therefore, (J) is correct.

25. **(B)** Early 1800s

Details

In lines 42–45, the author tells you that it was at the onset of the nineteenth century when the lions nearly became extinct. The nineteenth century means the 1800s. Its onset would be at the beginning of the 1800s, so (B) is correct.

26. **(F)** lions consuming the livestock that belongs to the Maldhari.

Meaning of Words

The *occasional predation* refers to lions eating from time to time the livestock that belongs to the Maldhari, which is merely "one cost of rearing livestock in the Gir forests" (lines 66–67), so (F) is correct. Choice (J) is too extreme; you don't know that the occasional predation is necessarily the *greatest* threat to the livestock. Choice (G) is incorrect because the lions are not preying upon the Maldhari themselves. Choice (H) is incorrect because there isn't a suggestion that the issue is *chasing* the livestock away.

27. **(D)** the Gir forests became inhospitable to lions.

Generalizations

If the forest became unable to sustain the Maldhari's livestock, as (A) states, the Maldhari would no longer benefit from *freegrazing rights*. Choice (A) is therefore a reason they might leave the forest. Likewise, if the lions in the forest began to prey more heavily on the livestock, as (B) postulates, it may mean that the cost of living with the carnivores would be too great to warrant remaining there. Finally, if the grazing costs of raising livestock outside of the Gir forest dropped significantly, as (C) asserts, then the Maldhari would have less of a reason to endure the predation of lions by remaining in the forest. The only one of the choices that does *not* provide a reason for the Maldhari to cease coexisting with the lions is (D). The Maldhari would in fact benefit if the forests became inhospitable to lions. You are looking for this exception, so (D) is correct.

28. **(G)** rural.

Details

In line 20, you learn that the country of India is "overwhelmingly rural," which means that *most of it* is rural. Other choices may or may not be true in real life, but they are not supported by the passage as descriptions of the entire country. Therefore, (G) is correct.

29.   **(D)** to subsist on the sale of the dairy provided by the livestock.

Details

In lines 55–57, you're told that the Maldhari are "primarily vegetarian, *keeping livestock only for the sale of dairy products, on which they rely.*" This supports choice (D).

30.   **(G)** a greater number of people living in the forests threatens the diversity of species there.

Details

The preservationists argue that "the fact that the forest-dwelling population is growing means that catering to its interests *is unsustainable and ultimately detrimental to the conservation of biodiversity*" (lines 28–32). Choice (G) is a restatement of this idea.

Passage 4 Solutions

31.   **(B)** has changed over time.

Main Idea/Author's Approach

The passage offers a history of the American teaching profession in relation to gender. It points to various changes, including the transition from a majority-male teaching corps to a majority-female teaching corps. Choice (B) is correct. Choice (A) is too extreme; while the author does allude to discrimination when she discusses the pay gap between male and female teachers, she does not argue that the profession is *necessarily* discriminatory. That nurturing is an important component of teaching, choice (C), may have been suggested by reformers like Horace Mann, but the author herself never makes such claims. Choice (D), again, is an argument made by reformers, not by the author.

32.   **(H)** education to be a moral as well as an intellectual task.

Details

The author discusses Horace Mann's arguments in the third and fourth paragraphs. Mann pushed to put more women in the classroom because "the education of young children was considered to be a moral as well as an academic task" and he thought women were particularly suited to such tasks (lines 35–37). Choice (H) is correct.

33.   **(D)** while classroom teaching was considered "women's work," school leadership was not.

Details

Lines 64–66 come in the context of a discussion of the changing role of women in education. The author suggests that teaching was increasingly being defined as women's work and, as a result, men were leaving the classroom. The author contrasts the balance of women in the classroom with the balance of women in leadership positions. Men, who were flee-ing "feminine" classroom work, were staying in education as administrators. You can infer that leadership positions, even in education, were still considered "men's" work. While it's possible that the men were receiving promotions, that's never actually given as a reason for their presence in leadership roles, so (C) is incorrect. It is possible that the male leaders of schools were not hired from the ranks of the teachers, but rather brought in from outside. Choice (D) is correct.

18

MANHATTAN
PREP

34. **(F)** *especially* suited.

Meaning of Words

"Peculiar" has many meanings, including odd, unfamiliar, unusual, or exclusive to. In this context, "peculiarly" means "especially," or "particularly." The school board implies that women are good at guiding the infant mind, and especially so. The board does not see this as odd or unfamiliar; rather, they see women's ability as special. Choice (F) is correct.

35. **(C)** The pay gap between male and female teachers went down.

Details

The passage addresses the women's movement towards the end of the passage. The author acknowledges that the proportion of female teachers has remained the same through the movement, but suggests that feminism has had other effects. In particular, she notes, "The feminist and labor movements chipped away at and eventually erased the pay disparity between male and female teachers," (lines 71–73). Choice (C) is correct.

36. **(J)** entered.

Meaning of Words

Look back at the context of "infiltrated." The author describes the influx of female teachers into school classrooms. Nothing sinister is going on, so (F), (G), and (H) all strike an incorrectly negative tone. Rather, women are simply *entering* the teaching profession. The word "infiltrate" can have a negative connotation (e.g., in military contexts), but here it does not. Thus choice (J) is correct.

37. **(A)** is a currently debated notion.

Relationships

The passage presents two points of view on this question. "Some argue" that the women's movement has drawn talented women away from teaching. "Others" point to contradictory evidence. The author suggests that the assertion that feminism has thinned the contemporary pool of teachers "has not, however, been proven" (lines 89–90). Choice (A) points to disagreement and is correct.

38. **(H)** men wanted to move into more prestigious and financially remunerative professions.

Details

The author offers several reasons and scenarios in which men left the teaching profession. One reason was that men sought professions that offered more money and higher status. The author first mentions this point in the second paragraph, when she describes "educated young men who viewed teaching as a stepping stone to a more lucrative and prestigious career in another field" (lines 18–20). She alludes to this theme again in the sixth paragraph. Teaching had been defined as women's work, while men's work constituted "more prestigious fields like the law and medicine" (lines 59–60). The men who left teaching to do more male-orientated work presumably left the field for one of these "higher" professions. Choice (H) is correct.

39. **(D)** the notion that men and women were meant to fill different roles was entrenched at the time.

Relationships

This sentence articulates the bold claim that reformers *should* have anticipated the flight of male teachers from the classroom. Why would the author believe this phenomenon to have been predictable? First, remember that the author argues that men left teaching because men's work and women's work were seen as separate at the time. If this separation of work roles could have predictably resulted in men leaving teaching, then the separation must have been deeply rooted and apparent in social attitudes. Choice (D) is correct.

40. **(G)** the women's rights movement incorrectly collapsed the spheres of men and women.

Details

Support for the correct answer, choice (G), is in the third paragraph: "In a series of lectures on the power and duties of women, Mann spoke against the women's rights movement, arguing that *men and women have different, complementary roles*" (lines 24–27). *Exclusively* and *primarily* are too strong in (H), and (J) is likewise too extreme. Choice (F) is not stated in the text.

Passage 5 Solutions

41. **(C)** journalistic.

Generalizations

The tone of the passage is that of one who reports facts and then applies objective analysis to them. The intent of the passage as a whole is not to be strongly critical ("polemical"), to tell a story ("narrative"), or to evoke poetry, but to examine the significance and implications of a set of circumstances. Throughout the passage, facts are reported and objectively analyzed. This purpose and style can be characterized as "journalistic." Choice (C) is correct.

42. **(F)** analytical, while the preceding paragraph is more a reporting of facts.

Author's Approach

In the final paragraph, the author states that the findings of the research could potentially be used as a means to foster peace around the world. She is applying the logic of the information shared earlier in the passage, including in the preceding paragraph, in order to draw out implications and conclusions. The last paragraph could thus be regarded as "analytical," making choice (F) correct. The other choices do not set up appropriate distinctions between the two paragraphs.

43. **(D)** how Switzerland became a federal state in 1848.

Details

The passage mentions in lines 17–18 that Switzerland became a federal state in 1848, but it doesn't indicate *how*. In lines 55–58, you learn that the "modern-day state of Jura was created out of a section of the north part of Bern to ease conflict in the region," choice (A). Lines 58–62 state, "French-speaking Protestant citizens in southern Jura chose to remain in the northern part of Bern…choosing to value similar religion over similar language," choice (B). And in line 31, the passage indicates the languages spoken in Switzerland according to the 2000 census, choice (C). Therefore, choice (D) is not answered by the passage.

44.   **(H)** "In demographically diverse areas that lack physical barriers, political barriers similar to the ones in Yugoslavia could help temper local violence" (lines 81–84).

Author's Approach

According to the author, the significance of the studies on barriers and peace is that creating them could lead to peace. While choices (F) and (G) and (J) are true, they don't capture *implications*, the meaningful, important ideas that result from all the facts and analysis. Choice (H) is therefore correct.

45.   **(D)** states.

Meaning of Words

In lines 24–25, the passage reads "political cantons (*which are similar to states*)." Therefore, choice (D) is correct.

46.   **(J)**   in general, physical boundaries were responsible for the pockets of peace that did exist.

Details

In the second-to-last paragraph, the author describes the former Yugoslavia as a place with "widespread ethnic violence" (line 73), except that in a few places, it was peaceful. These were places where political boundaries overlapped with linguistic and cultural boundaries. Physical boundaries, however, are not mentioned as present in the former Yugoslavia. Therefore, (J) is correct.

47.   **(A)**   political boundaries should coincide with other boundaries to be effective.

Generalizations

In lines 81–86, the author explicitly states her purpose in choosing to include discussion of Yugoslavia: "In demographically diverse areas that lack physical barriers, political barriers similar to the ones in Yugoslavia could help temper local violence—though the evidence suggests that it will be important to ensure that [the political barriers] align with linguistic, religious and cultural differences as well." This idea is offered in choice (A).

48.   **(G)**   that good fences make good neighbors.

Meaning of Words

The phenomenon refers back to the previous sentence to express the idea that "good fences"—or boundaries—can make "good neighbors" (line 7–8) as in, make for more peaceful relations between neighboring groups. Choice (G) is correct.

49.   **(A)**   the boundaries being discussed have a dual role.

Meaning of Words

The referenced text is preceded by a description that provides the necessary context to understand it: "landscape elements separate linguistic groups, and political cantons (which are similar to states) separate religious groups. These barriers allow for partial autonomy within a single country" (lines 23–25). Therefore, you can conclude that the phrase physical and metaphorical fences refers to how these fences both separate groups literally—by putting mountains and lakes in between—and separate them figuratively, by distinguishing the groups conceptually from one another. Choice (A) is correct.

50. **(H)** introduce a metaphor that will be operative in developing the theme.

Author's Approach

The poem is used to introduce the metaphor of *fences*, or boundaries, which the author will discuss as a tool for fostering peace in Switzerland and elsewhere. This is reflected in choice (H), the correct answer. The correct answer, however, is not (G), because Frost's narrator indicates *reluctance* to erect fences, which is contradictory to the view of the author of the passage that fences or boundaries can be useful.

Passage 6 Solutions

51. **(C)** They should be revisited to provide more adequate guidelines as to how problems should be framed by researchers.

Main Idea

The author is very opinionated as to the state of standards for medical reporting, particularly around problem framing. In the final paragraph, he makes this especially clear when he says, "I strongly believe that editors of medical journals *should be required* to consider more carefully… *the framing* of concerns addressed in reports of research" (lines 70–73), and goes on to enumerate other standards he thinks should exist. Thus, choice (C) is correct.

52. **(J)** someone personally invested in the subject.

Generalizations

The author of this passage is clearly invested in what he is discussing. Phrases such as "I strongly believe" in line 70 indicate a passionate viewpoint. Evidently, the author feels he has a personal stake in the issue at hand. Choice (J) is correct.

53. **(C)** introduce and illustrate an important and controversial topic.

Main Idea

In the fourth paragraph, the author introduces an important and controversial topic, which is "problem framing" (line 42), the specific type of bias in medical reporting with which he takes issue in the passage. This topic is illustrated through the example of two definitions of a medical issue (namely, social anxiety). The answer is not (A) because those multiple definitions of social anxiety are not themselves the point of the paragraph. They're there to demonstrate the impact of how a problem is framed. Choice (B) is contradictory to the purpose of the paragraph, which does not outline a view to which the author is opposed. And (D) is incorrect because the point is not to illustrate the difficulty of defining complex phenomena, such as social anxiety, rather, the reason for providing the different definitions is to show how much difference there can be in the way that issues are framed, and how that difference might impact how seriously an issue is taken. Therefore, (C) is correct.

54.   **(F)** The author feels that it is one reason why medical reporting is unreliable.

Relationships (Cause–Effect)

Why are scientists "guilty of misconstruing actual results" of scientific research (lines 6–7)? According to the author, the reason is to make any associated products "more amenable to the marketing of particular products" (lines 7–8). The passage states in lines 8–11 that "scientific articles are often 'ghostwritten' by private companies who are funding the research, rather than by scientists themselves." The author then goes on to describe how private companies have a different goal than independent researchers. Thus, the author evidently feels that the funding of scientific research (particularly private funding) is one reason for distorted medical reporting. Choice (F) is the best answer. Choice (G) is too strong ("only" rules out any other possible causes of bias). Choice (H) is also extreme—there isn't a suggestion that if the research weren't privately funded, it would be credible. Finally, "curious" in (J) is not strong enough. The author does have an opinion on the effect that funding sources have on objectivity.

55.   **(C)** make recommendations for specific changes to standards in medical reporting.

Main Idea

In the final paragraph, the author enumerates specific recommendations that he feels should exist for the reporting of medical research—from particular words that should be used, to more general practices that should be adopted, such as noting alternative definitions of diagnoses. This is the main purpose of this paragraph. The paragraph itself cannot require anything of scientific authors, so (A) is out. Choice (B) goes too far: the author strongly dislikes current standards, but does not say that the practices result in "nothing more than propaganda" (which would be to say that the reports are worthless). Finally, the paragraph does not "invite others to weigh in" at all as in choice (D); the recommendations are specific and clear. Choice (C) is correct.

56.   **(F)** reading a term like "clearly" often enough may make an argument seem clearer or otherwise better than it actually is.

Meaning of Words

The author defines *woozle effect* as follows: "if we hear something enough times, we assume that it is true" (lines 64–65). This expression of the principle matches up well to choice (F). The other choices do not correspond to the definition given.

57.   **(B)** the first definition paints the diagnosis as less serious in terms of treatment, while the latter paints it as more so.

Relationships (Comparisons)

The first definition uses less serious terminology, calling social anxiety a "*common anxiety disorder*" (line 46) that "*may or may not* abate without treatment" (line 48). In contrast, the second definition calls social anxiety a "*chronic and insidious psychiatric disorder*" (line 50) and indicates that recovery without treatment "is unlikely" (lines 51–52). The author also then draws attention to this difference by noting the "urgent tone" of the second definition (line 54).

58.   **(G)** improve the quality of research reporting.

Details

Lines 58–59 of the passage tell you that the "stated purpose" of the reporting guidelines in these disciplines is to "improve the quality and fairness of research reporting." This matches choice (G). The other choices are unsupported: the guidelines are not intended to "eliminate all bias," nor to make the reporting "less personal." It is not clear how they would possibly "incentivize researchers to be honest." No incentives of any kind seem to be built into the guidelines.

59.   **(D)** Majority

Details

In the final paragraph, lines 70–86, the author lists particular words with which he takes issue. These include "common," "most" and "insidious," but "majority" is not mentioned and thus is the correct answer to this question, which asks for what he does *not* specifically mention. Choice (D) is correct.

60.   **(H)** expectations about opportunities to make money.

Relationships (Cause–Effect)

In lines 28–30, the author states: "This disparity in funding is *often due to the perception that there is a profit to be made from the funded research.*" Thus, the author is attributing the disparity, or difference, in funding to differing expectations about money-making opportunities. Choice (H) is a restatement of that idea. The other choices do not have support in the text.

Passage 7 Solutions

61.   **(C)** the model is popular throughout the world.

Details

Choice (A), the inclusion of denial and acceptance, can be found in lines 60–68. That the model isn't entirely accepted, choice (B), is stated in lines 57–58. Choice (D), that it was introduced in a book, is mentioned in lines 54–55. While the author tells you that the Kubler-Ross model is popular "among Americans" (line 56), the rest of the world is not mentioned. Choice (C) must be correct on this EXCEPT question.

62.   **(J)** Western medicine and hospital practices influence the experiences of death and grief.

Meaning of Words

The two final paragraphs of the passage connect to what the author refers to as the "medicalization" of grief (line 69). The author connects this trend to the impact of "science" (line 71) and to the increasing definition of behaviors in medical terms. Choice (G) is too extreme, however; the author never says that *all* grief occurs in a medical context. Choice (H) is also too extreme. The removal of the bereavement exclusion from the DSM does not mean that *all* symptoms of grief and death are labeled illnesses. Choice (F) is unsupported by the passage, which never discusses the "donation of

18

821

bodies to science." Choice (J) connects to the broader theme alluded to in these final paragraphs—namely, the way that death and grief fall under the umbrella of medicine in contemporary America.

63.   **(A)** introduce a main theme of the essay and offer a specific example.

Main Idea/Author's Approach

The passage moves through several themes and ideas, but focuses primarily on different attitudes towards grief. That focus is introduced in the second paragraph (lines 17–25). By way of introduction, the author offers a specific example of a grieving ritual, namely the ancient Egyptians' funerary processions. This introduction of a main theme and of an example of that theme matches Choice (A).

64.   **(H)** was a decision that remains controversial.

Relationships

In lines 85–87, the author says that the decision to eliminate the bereavement exclusion was met with "both criticism and praise." This points to controversy. The author never ties up this controversy with any kind of resolution or opinion. Choice (H) is therefore correct. Choice (F) is not supported by the passage. Choice (G) connects to the "criticism" described by the author, but is too extreme. Choice (J) offers an opinion never given by the author.

65.   **(C)** Ancient Egyptians

Relationships

The passage only describes Jewish and ancient Egyptian beliefs concerning the afterlife. Choices (A) and (B) are therefore unsupported by the passage. Choice (D) is the opposite of what you are looking for, since the author tells you that "Jews believe the dead do not pass to a heavenly afterworld, but to dust" (lines 27–28), implying that Jews see the dead as bodies rather than as continuing consciousnesses. Choice (C), however, is supported by the passage, since you know that ancient Egyptians believed the deceased to enter an afterworld. Ancient Egyptians therefore believed that at least some aspect of a person continues after his or her body perishes.

66.   **(G)** offer more detail about something described in the previous paragraph.

Main Point/Author's Approach

The author outlines aspects of Jewish grief rituals in the third paragraph and offers more detail in the fourth, focusing on the extended aspects of the grieving process. This is supported in choice (G). Choice (F) is incorrect because the author does not *introduce* Jewish death rituals here but continues a discussion already introduced. Choice (H) is incorrect because the passage is a synthesis of information, not an argument so there is nothing to "rebut," or argue against. Choice (J) is unsupported: psychiatric and religious beliefs remain separate in the passage. Choice (G) is correct.

67.   **(D)** a period in which mirrors are covered.

Details

According to the passage, "Following a Jewish burial, the family of the dead 'sit shiva,' during which family members … cover their mirrors" (lines 34–37). Choice (D) is correct.

68.   **(F)** Jews bury all bodies using similar rituals, while ancient Egyptians did not.

Relationships

The passage states that "ancient Egyptians in the Old Kingdom mummified the *bodies of their kings*" (lines 6–7), while "Jews bury *all* of their dead in simple wooden coffins containing no metal" (lines 28–30). Thus, choice (F) is supported. Choice (G) is not supported because the ancient Egyptians did respect death, as the first two paragraphs relate. Choice (H) is incorrect because the passage offers no evidence that Jews do not prepare bodies for burial. Choice (J) is incorrect because, while you know that the ancient Egyptians valued loud grief (lines 19–20), you do not know whether Jews also grieve loudly. Choice (F) is correct.

69.   **(B)** the contrast between the length of the service and the length of the traditional grieving process.

Relationships (Comparisons)

The author contrasts the brief funeral with the extended grief rituals using the word "but" within the same sentence (lines 32–33): "The traditional Jewish funeral is relatively brief, but the rituals for the bereaved extend for a longer period of time." Choice (B) is correct.

70.   **(F)** both feature a series of differentiated stages that end with a lessening of grief.

Meaning of Words

"Foreshadow" means "be an early indication of (something)." The author argues that Jewish grief rituals foreshadow psychiatric attitudes towards grief because, like the Kubler-Ross model that appeared in 1969, they include "graduated stages of grief … ending with the figurative release of grief" (lines 51–52). Choice (F) is correct.

Passage 8 Solutions

71.   **(B)** it can withstand extreme weather.

Details

In lines 32–34, the author states that "sorghum is a cereal *extensively cultivated in small-farming systems because of its ability to grow under harsh climatic conditions*." In other words, sorghum can withstand extreme weather. Choice (B) is correct.

72. **(F)** critical to the majority of the planet's economic systems.

Generalizations

The author states in lines 8–10, "In parts of the world that are dependent on agriculture—*most of the world*—*crop diversity is thus very important*." Choice (F), therefore, is the best answer. The other choices take a more restricted view on the importance of crop diversity.

73. **(D)** are likely to be more impactful.

Relationships (Comparisons)

In lines 37–40, it notes that researchers "found that human ethnic diversity *has probably had an even greater impact on sorghum diversity than environmental constraints*—a hugely significant finding." Choice (D) is supported directly by this text. Choices (A), (B), and (C) are incorrect because the author does not compare the impact of environmental factors to that of human behavioral factors apart from this statement.

74. **(H)** crops that are not genetically modified.

Meaning of Words

In lines 64–68, the passages states that "farmers in all three groups have adopted *a number of genetically altered crop varieties*, disseminated by the Kenyan Ministry of Agriculture. *These improved varieties* are cultivated *together in the same field with the local varieties*." The distinction implies that the local varieties are, in contrast to the "improved varieties," *not* genetically modified. Thus, choice (H) is correct.

75. **(C)** the Chuka and Tharaka interact socially, while the Mbeere are more isolated.

Relationships (Comparisons)

In lines 47–48, the passage states that "the Chuka and Tharaka maintain strong social ties." Lines 56–57 indicate that "a clear spatial boundary exists between the Mbeere and both the Chuka and Tharaka." These statements support choice (C). Choice (D) is too extreme because while the Chuka and the Mbeere "have existed in conflict" historically (line 46), you aren't told they've been engaged in open warfare for any period of time, let alone a long one. Choice (C) is correct.

76. **(G)** greater interaction between groups is correlated with greater similarity in the varieties of crops harvested by those groups.

Main Idea

The Chuka and Tharaka, who "maintain strong social ties" (lines 47–48), harvest local varieties of crops that are similar to each other but differ from the crops grown by the Mbeere, with whom the Chuka and Tharaka interact much less (lines 74–77). Choice (F) is incorrect because nothing indicates that any crops are "superior" to other crops. Choice (H) is wrong because it's not the main point of the passage (this idea only surfaces briefly in lines 71–73), and (J) is incorrect because it's too extreme. The author never goes so far as to suggest that ethnic boundaries are the *most* important factor in determining crop genetics. Choice (G) is correct.

77.   **(B)**   Passage A is more general, while Passage B is more specific.

Generalizations

The first and second passages cover the same topic—how human behavior affects the genetic diversity of crops—but Passage A discusses the issue more generally, with just a few brief examples, while Passage B examines the theme in detail and at length in a specific community in Africa. Choice (B) is correct.

78.   **(F)**   is more reserved in his interpretation of the finding that human behavior may affect crop diversity.

Author's Approach

In lines 37–40, the author of Passage A calls the finding that "human ethnic diversity has probably had an even greater impact on sorghum diversity than environmental constraints" a "hugely significant finding." At the end of Passage B (in lines 84–85), the author says, "It may be that increased social interaction affects the genetics of the local crops that are planted," expressing no opinion or valuation of this finding. Therefore, you can reasonably infer that the author of Passage B is more reserved in his interpretation of the finding than Passage A's author. Choice (F) is correct.

79.   **(A)**   generally agree about the nature of the causal mechanism being discussed.

Generalizations

Both authors write that the behavior of humans (for instance, patterns of social interaction) can have an effect on the diversity of crops grown by those humans. This is the "causal mechanism" being discussed, and the authors both report that research supports it. They therefore generally agree, so choice (A) is correct.

Passage 9 Solutions

80.   **(F)**   celebrate the contributions of two wartime nurses.

Main Ideas

The passage discusses two nurses, one in England and one in France, who aided in the treatment of soldiers injured in the Battle of Normandy. The final paragraph of Passage A celebrates these two nurses as "true heroes behind the front lines" (line 48). Notice that the passage does not establish just one of these nurses as a hero. Choice (F) is correct.

81.   **(C)**   both Hay and Desmarais recall particular medications administered to patients.

Details

This is an EXCEPT question. The locations in choice (A) correspond to where each nurse was stationed, so this choice is incorrect. In lines 15–16 and 38–39, both Hay and Desmarais recall the pain experienced by the patients under their care so (D) is incorrect. Neither one rested much, either, as is evident in lines 34–35 and in lines 45–46 so (B) is incorrect. However, while Hay recalls particular medications ("*morphine to keep them comfortable* and we were using *the new penicillin*" in lines 19–20), Desmarais does not mention any specific medicines by name in the passage, so choice (C) is correct.

18

82. **(G)** June 10th, 1944.

Meaning of Words

You learn in Passage B that D-Day was June 6th, 1944 (line 55). "D plus 4" means D-Day plus four days after it. This would be June 10th, 1944.

83. **(B)** Operation Overlord.

Details

In line 54, the passage states, "*The Battle itself*, code-named '*Operation Overlord*.'" Choice (B) is correct. While D-Day, choice (A), is a nickname for the day the battle was *launched*, it is not used to describe the Battle itself, which lasted much longer than a day (three months, in fact), as you are told in lines 49–50. Likewise, while General Eisenhower referred to the Battle just before it commenced as the "Great Crusade," the question asks for the term used broadly by *those involved*, not just by a single person at a particular time, so (C) is incorrect, choice (D) is also unsupported by the text.

84. **(J)** the degree to which the Germans were misled by the deception campaign leading up to D-Day.

Generalizations

In lines 86–91, the passage states that "the Allies *had conducted a large-scale deception campaign designed to mislead the Germans*" and "*As a result … by late August 1944, all of northern France had been liberated.*" Choice (J) is correct.

85. **(D)** that the initial attack during the Battle of Normandy took place on both land and sea.

Meaning of Words

Lines 64–66 indicate that it was *the assault itself* that was described as "amphibious," meaning on both land and sea: "… constituting *one of the largest amphibious (on both land and water) military assaults* in modern history." Choices (A) and (B) are incorrect. Therefore, (D), the initial attack is what was occurring on both land and sea. However, you cannot be sure that the actual *boats* in which the soldiers arrived were able to proceed forward on land, so (C) is incorrect.

86. **(F)** Boat or plane

Details

From England to France over the English Channel, soldiers, medical professionals and others would need to be carried by aircraft or boat, as described in the passage (lines 57–62): "More than 5,000 *ships and landing craft* carrying troops and supplies from England traversed the English Channel to France, while more than 11,000 *aircraft* descended…" It is reasonable to infer that Hay would have had to travel by one of these craft rather than by bus or any other land-based vehicle. Choice (F) is therefore correct.

MANHATTAN
PREP

87.   **(B)**   executive levels of wartime decision making.

Author's Approach

Passage B is primarily concerned with General Eisenhower's decision making leading up to D-Day, whereas Passage A is concerned with the day-to-day experiences and recollections of two of a great many nurses working on the ground during the Battle of Normandy. Choice (B) is correct because choices (A), (C), and (D) are inaccurate descriptions of Passage B.

88.   **(F)**   medical professionals such as Hay and Desmarais deserve high honors for their work during the campaign.

Author's Approach

In lines 46–48, the author of Passage A says that "both nurses worked tirelessly to save as many as they could of hundreds of thousands of injured men. *They were true heroes behind the frontlines.*" Choice (F) is correct. While (G) may be tempting, you don't know that the author believes that the nurses of World War II have received inadequate praise for their service. Choice (H) is too narrow in that it focuses solely on Vera Hay, who the author would not necessarily say warrants "unparalleled recognition" compared to others such as Desmarais. Finally, choice (J) is incorrect because no part of the text suggests that the author believes that without these nurses, the mission would have failed.

Chapter 19
of

5lb. Book of ACT® Practice Problems

Reading:

Humanities

In This Chapter...

Humanities Passages & Solutions

Chapter 19
Reading: Humanities

The Reading passages in this chapter are classified within the humanities, which include art, music, film, theater, television, and other artistic and media studies, as well as literary criticism, language, philosophy, and other studies traditionally connected with the term "humanities." A small amount of context is given at the start, but each passage is self-contained.

Various kinds of questions are asked about these passages, including the following:

1. Main Ideas/Author's Approach. Main idea or ideas of the passage (or a part of it); the approach, voice, point of view, method, or purpose of the author.

2. Details. Specific details mentioned in the passage.

3. Relationships. Comparisons, sequences of events, cause-effect relationships, or other relationships that are described or implied in the passage.

4. Meanings of Words. The meaning of a word or phrase, in its context, in the passage.

5. Generalizations. Broad observations that can be drawn from the passage.

How should you use this chapter? Here are some recommendations, according to the level you've reached in ACT Reading.

1. Fundamentals. Do a passage or two untimed to begin with. As you become more comfortable, put the clock on. In all cases, review the solutions closely, and articulate what you've learned. Reread the passage again to ensure that you fully understand it, and redo problems as necessary.

2. Fixes. Do one passage at a time under timed conditions. Examine the results, learn your lessons, then test yourself with more passages (one from each Reading chapter) at once.

3. Tweaks. Confirm your mastery by doing a few passages (one from each Reading chapter) at once under timed conditions. A full set of four is the ultimate goal. Aim to improve the speed and ease of your reading and solution process.

Good luck on the problems!

19

PASSAGE 1

HUMANITIES: This passage is from an essay by a museum director.

Most museum displays of ancient Greek sculptures are reveries in white. Marble Gods, nymphs, beasts, and men are uniformly monochromatic; their forms differ only in the curves of their muscles and contours of
5   their hair and fur. Yet ancient Greeks would have seen a very different kind of art. The sculptures we think of as so chromatically restrained were originally painted in bright—even garish—colors and patterns.

Contemporary art conservators have begun to
10 reconstruct how ancient statues were originally painted. A 2014 exhibit in Copenhagen, the result of collaboration among conservators, archeologists, and chemists, displayed ancient sculptures alongside replicas painted with the riotous color intended by the artists. A marble statue of a
15 lion, for example, acquired a yellow body, an electric blue mane and tail, and red decorative face-paint. A muscular male torso was leafed in gold. The rest of his body was painted white and patterned with blue and red shapes like oblong balloons tied with ribbons.

20 Determining how a statue was once painted begins by observing the statue with the ordinary eye. The researchers then slowly deepen their view of the sculpture by using magnifying eyeglasses and microscopes outfitted with bright lights that further magnify the marble 40
25 times over, and finally video microscopes that magnify it 160 times. They methodically document every inch of the stone surface in search of traces of metal leaf and pigment.

Next, team members use a variety of technologies to further confirm how the marble was painted. Sometimes,
30 they take tiny samples of the statue to examine how the paint was layered. To identify more deteriorated pigments and binders (binders are the materials in which pigments are suspended), conservators use infrared spectroscopy and ultraviolet photography. These techniques utilize
35 different wavelengths of light to illuminate individual materials. When hit by particular wavelengths, certain minerals fluoresce, or glow. Since paint colors are made of specific ground minerals and elements—for example, red is often iron oxide, while green is often malachite—
40 these techniques enable conservators to determine exactly which pigments were used.

Conservators can sometimes determine where colors were, even when no pigment remains. Different pigments, with their varying chemical compounds, decay at different

45 rates. Thus, certain parts of a statue become stripped of paint faster than other parts. As these parts of the statue erode more quickly than the others, a subtle relief emerges on the surface of the stone that traces the shapes of the original painted designs. Conservators can spot these reliefs
50 by shining a "raking light" parallel to the stone's surface.

Revealing aspects of ancient statues long forgotten raises new questions as to how to restore and display the art. Museums would not display as a painting a Renaissance "fresco" worn to a mere plaster wall. Why,
55 then, display bare marble as a statue? Some conservators argue that their job is to preserve the intended look of an artwork, even if that means re-fashioning large chunks of it. To these conservators, that the statues have persisted as cold monochromes for centuries matters less than the
60 original aesthetic intent of the artist.

Other conservators rightly acknowledge the passage of time. A ruin is a ruin, not a newly manufactured work. For these conservators, preservation is about protecting and repairing ancient artifacts, not creating new pieces,
65 even in the spirit of their original forms. They would argue that the ravages of time become a part of any artwork; in the case of ancient statues, that means the stripped marble becomes the piece's new skin.

The ancient Greeks themselves did not promote
70 the idea of "ruin value"—the idea that a work should be designed such that even its remains are beautiful. The principle behind "ruin value" is that the marking of time on the remains of fine art and architecture symbolizes bygone greatness. Nonetheless, the impressive nature of the
75 Greek ruins inspired the concept. Ancient statues today are artistry plus time, and the result is something that transcends artistic intent. Investigations into how they were originally painted are fascinating, and the painted replicas are stunning, if weird. The original statues, however, should
80 be left intact as ancient, weathered, creatures of stone.

1. The passage devotes the LEAST attention to which of the following topics?

    A. The environmental forces that caused ancient Greek statues to lose their paint

    B. The process by which conservators discover how statues were once painted

    C. The debate between those who believe the statues should be restored to their original form and those who disagree

    D. Descriptions of how ancient Greek statues originally appeared to viewers

MANHATTAN
PREP

2. The passage indicates that in order to ascertain the original painted ornamentation, if any, on a statue, all of the following devices may be used EXCEPT:

   F. video microscopes.
   G. magnifying glasses
   H. x-ray spectroscopy.
   J. ultraviolet photography.

3. The author describes "ruin value" (line 70) as:

   A. the intention of ancient Greek sculptors and architects to create work with enduring power.
   B. a concept inspired by ancient Greek ruins.
   C. a slowly growing respect for time's effects on art over the past several centuries.
   D. a deepening understanding of art and architecture's purpose in the world.

4. The author believes that the best course of action with regard to ancient Greek statues is to:

   F. restore them to their original state.
   G. leave them in their present-day state.
   H. use modern technologies to alter them.
   J. restore them to their ruin value.

5. The conservators discussed in lines 61–68 regard time as:

   A. a challenge to preserving art.
   B. a tool for understanding art.
   C. a reason to create art.
   D. a part of art.

6. In the context of the passage, "chromatically restrained" in line 7 most nearly means:

   F. dull to the average observer.
   G. opaque.
   H. black.
   J. singular in color.

7. By "Museums would not display as a painting a Renaissance 'fresco' worn to a mere plaster wall" in lines 53–54, the author intends to convey:

   A. the arguable absurdity of featuring the Greek statues without paint.
   B. the irrationality of displaying a painting so worn, its paint was gone.
   C. the double standard held by museums with regard to paintings and sculpture.
   D. the futility of attempting to compare frescos and sculptures.

8. The author most likely uses quotation marks around "raking light" in line 50 in order to mean that it is:

   F. not generally accepted as the device's name.
   G. a device whose name is not commonly known.
   H. a device that does not actually rake.
   J. not actually a light.

9. According to the passage, ancient Greek statues were sometimes adorned with which of the following?

   A. Pink paint
   B. Blue face paint
   C. Rubber balloons
   D. Gold leaf

10. The passage mentions which of the following as a particularly powerful instrument?

    F. Infrared spectroscopy
    G. Video microscopes
    H. Ultraviolet photography
    J. Raking lights

PASSAGE 2

HUMANITIES: This passage is from an article by an art critic.

How does the experience of looking at works of fine art in real life compare to looking at photographs of them, particularly in digital form?

In 2011, Google launched Art Project, an interactive
5 tool that allowed viewers to travel—virtually—through 17 of the world's most famous art museums—including London's Tate Gallery, New York City's Metropolitan Museum of Art, and Florence's Uffizi. Visitors could explore the layout of these museums and view, up close,
10 more than 1,000 pieces of art. By 2012, Google had expanded its network to 151 participating museums from 40 countries, featuring over 32,000 pieces of art.

There is no question that improving access to art through technology is, overall, a good thing. People
15 who will never be able to visit Italy can now not only see Botticelli's Birth of Venus, they can also study it millimeter by millimeter—the high-resolution images of particular pieces of art make possible such clinical examination. One could not get as close in person at the
20 Uffizi.

But what is lost in the translation from a physical painting to digital reproduction, even high-quality digital reproduction?

In her review of the project upon its launch, Roberta
25 Smith writes that while the Google Art Project offers the chance to become educated in "the way artists construct an image on a flat surface," which she calls "great practice for looking at actual works," the experience is "nothing like standing before the real, breathing thing."
30 It is a sentiment shared by Robin Williams' character, Sean, in the film *Good Will Hunting*, when he lectures the younger character Will, "If I asked you about art, you'd probably give me the skinny on every art book ever written. But I'll bet you can't tell me what it smells like
35 in the Sistine Chapel. You've never actually stood there and looked up at that beautiful ceiling."

What precisely is the difference between standing there looking up at it, and looking at it on a screen? To answer this question, you must begin with a broader one:
40 What is art, how do we define it?

In the classic text *Art as Experience*, John Dewey defines art not as an "expressive object" but rather the development of an experience—something in which the viewer's participation, perspective and context is

essential. While the object of art itself is the site for
45 the experience—or the "unifying occasion" for the experience—the "art" occurs when that object meets the active observer. Dewey's theory, which draws heavily on psychology, can be seen as a precursor to the
50 emerging field of neuroaesthetics—the use of imaging technologies to study how the brain responds to the viewing of art. Neuroaesthetics attempts to get a handle on the cognitive processes involved in the experience of art. A young discipline, it is nonetheless making great
55 strides in the world of art theory.

In his book *Experiencing Art*, psychologist Arthur Shimamura sets out his theory of how appreciation of the visual arts unfolds in the human mind. "The I-SKE model" takes into consideration how the intentions of
60 the artist are interpreted by the beholder on three levels: sensations, knowledge and emotions (hence the "SKE" in the model's name). According to Shimamura, art is not merely perceptual but viewed through these filters, which together constitute an experience that is greater
65 than the sum of its individual parts. He also goes deep into the details of the neural mechanisms that underlie this process.

Shimamura's research gets to the heart of what, if anything, is lacking in Google's Art Project and similar
70 attempts to digitalize the art of traditional painting. Art is not only the paint on the canvas, but what we, in encountering that paint on canvas, bring with us, as well as what our external circumstances are in that moment. For better or worse, sitting at home in front of
75 our computers is not going to be the same experience as standing in front of the Mona Lisa at the Louvre in Paris.

Indeed, we may not have the option in that case; several major world museums like the Louvre are omitted from the Art Project currently. One reason
80 for these museums' opting out is to avoid copyright issues, but the museum leadership may also be weighing additional considerations, those in line with Dewey's and Shimamura's work, reasons that go to the heart of why we look at art, what we hope to gain from it, and why it
85 is as important to us as it is.

11. The main purpose of the passage can be best described as an effort to:

   A. examine the nature of aesthetic experience.
   B. explore the benefits and shortcomings of a new tool.
   C. ruminate on the way the philosophy of art has changed over time.
   D. criticize a highly flawed new technology.

12. The author's attitude towards Shimamura's theories can be best characterized as:

   F. receptive.
   G. dismissive.
   H. ecstatic.
   J. frosty.

13. It can be reasonably inferred that the author sees the Mona Lisa as:

   A. an artwork that cannot be digitally represented.
   B. a two-dimensional work that can be well-captured by the computer screen.
   C. a piece that must be physically experienced to be fully understood.
   D. an artwork that only exists in the eye of the beholder.

14. According to the passage, one benefit that the Google Art Project offers is:

   F. the ability to fully experience artworks in far-flung places.
   G. the ability to see a thumbnail of a painting from any major museum.
   H. the ability to examine an artwork very closely.
   J. the ability to look at paintings next to other paintings by the same artist.

15. According to the passage, Roberta Smith believes the Google Art Project to be:

   A. a work of art.
   B. a useless endeavor.
   C. valuable as an educational tool.
   D. an instrument with which to practice making art.

16. When the author describes "considerations, those in line with Dewey's and Shimamura's work" (lines 82–83), the author is most likely referring to which of the following considerations?

   F. The importance of art to society
   G. The lessons that can be gleaned from the movie *Good Will Hunting*
   H. The value of creating multiple reproductions of any artwork
   J. The way that the viewer helps to create an aesthetic experience

17. The passage indicates that neuroaesthetics is:

   A. a field that unites science, psychology, and painting.
   B. a discipline that uses technology to understand how people look at art.
   C. a discipline founded by John Dewey.
   D. a set of ideas heavily drawn on by the Google Art Project.

18. According to the author, a reason museums have chosen not to participate in the Google Art Project is that:

   F. they want to boycott the project.
   G. they are worried about losing money to Google.
   H. they are protecting certain copyrights.
   J. they believe the project misunderstands the nature of sculpture.

19. The author most likely describes art as "what we, in encountering that paint on canvas, bring with us" in lines 71–72 because she believes art to be:

   A. an interaction between an object and its viewer.
   B. a purely psychological response.
   C. a highly filtered experience.
   D. entirely created in the viewer's eye.

20. As it is used in line 5, "travel" most nearly means:

   F. move through space and time.
   G. take an airplane.
   H. physically explore.
   J. metaphorically walk around.

19

PASSAGE 3

HUMANITIES: This passage is adapted from a director's essay about her life in film.

I was 18 when I first wanted to be a director, when I first decided—no, discovered—that I wanted to make films. It was while viewing *Citizen Kane* in my Intro to Film class, which was held in the same lecture hall where we had sat through freshman orientation three weeks earlier. The day of orientation, the first official day of college, I had dressed in a new outfit—yellow flats, cutoff shorts (so I wouldn't look like I was trying too hard), and one of the tee shirts my mother had ironed for me and folded in a perfect square, like they do with shirts in stores. When she handed me the stack to pack, I saw wet spots on the top one from where her tears had fallen. I couldn't recall ever seeing her cry over me. But I had never been away from home for more than three days, and I was moving across the country.

That morning, the morning of orientation, the shirt still had those creases, and my roommate asked if it was new.

"Yes," I answered, flattered, thinking I must look especially nice.

"It still has the store fold lines," she said, and I became self-conscious. As we walked across the quad to the lecture hall, I felt a surge of homesickness. My mom had flown to the east coast to help me move in and flown back the next day. It had been less than 24 hours, but I missed her.

I hardly recall what was said in the morning lecture. There was talk of ambition and aspiration, I recall. We were told we would make friends that would remain with us all of our lives. *But how will they recognize me?* I wondered. *I don't even know who I am.*

I was always the quiet child. I don't think I ever once spoke in class without raising my hand first and waiting for clear approval to proceed. My voice quivered the few times I had to speak publicly, and I declined my offer to give the valedictorian address because I so dreaded the attention. "Heady, not social," my aunt once called me, which crushed me with its truth. Despite my excellent grades, my star pupil status, my accolades from teachers, and my parents' unyielding adoration, I was a nervous bundle, perpetually terrified of being found out as a fraud. I figured I was just fooling everyone. When teachers wrote, "Insightful!" in the margins of my essays, internally I cowered in shame—I was just putting on a show, writing what would get me an A, playing the part of the good student, the good daughter. Who was I, really?

When I got to college, I was no different.

But three weeks into school came Orson Welles. As homework before the class at which the film would be screened, we were to read about his background. I gobbled it up. I was astounded that this film—directed, written, produced by and starring a single man, his *first* feature film—was nominated for Academy Awards in nine categories. He'd grown up in Wisconsin, too. His mother died when he was nine. His father died when he was 15. After his father's death, he traveled to Europe on the inheritance, and it is said that in Dublin, he strode into a theater and claimed he was a Broadway star. Welles made his stage debut at that very theater on October 13, 1931—a decade before making *Citizen Kane*. What bravery! I wanted to possess such courage, such self-assurance. I wanted to fake it and make it.

By the time the first scene of *Citizen Kane* opened on a "No Trespassing" sign clinging ominously to a chain-link fence, I was primed to love the film, for I already considered everything about its context remarkable. And still, I was surprised by my reaction. I cried. I cried because it was so good, and because I knew, watching it, what I wanted to do with my life. There was no question in my mind, and it had happened that fast—in an instant, from one shot on a wavy, pull-down screen in a chilly lecture hall. Before that moment, I didn't know, and after it, I did.

Over the past 20 years, I have made 13 feature-length films, and over a dozen shorts. My films are not like *Citizen Kane*, and I don't mean only in quality, although I am proud of my work (even if it hasn't won any Oscars … yet). I mean they lack its emotional tension, the grip and mystery of its arc. I make movies that are more intellectual games than anything else. I toy with logic, with our sense of what is real and what isn't. One might call my work heady, not social.

And yet my own films are not exclusively mental exercises (cerebral calisthenics). I always make sure that there is heart in my work, that at least one of the lead characters exhibits a moment of tenderness. These moments are rare in my films, but I think the rarity of an aching heart, a well-timed fleeting glimpse of it, makes the ache more beautiful, and more memorable. At least, that has been my experience.

21. The main purpose of the passage can best be described as an effort to:

    A. examine the trajectory of the author's career.
    B. recall the moment at which the author decided to pursue a particular career path.
    C. discuss the artistic evolution undergone by the artist.
    D. express a belief in the power of film as a genre.

22. The author's attitude toward the subject of the passage can best be characterized as:

    F. unabashed sadness.
    G. mild regret.
    H. suppressed joy.
    J. thoughtful nostalgia.

23. It can be reasonably inferred that the author believes *Citizen Kane* was:

    A. unworthy of the Oscar nominations it received.
    B. superior to the films that she has made as a director.
    C. the product of a writer and director who was overrated at the time of its release.
    D. a particularly intellectual film.

24. According to the author, compared to how she was as a child, as an adult she is:

    F. notably more social.
    G. less adventurous.
    H. similar in certain ways.
    J. more easily upset.

25. As described in the passage, the effect *Citizen Kane* had on the author can best be described as:

    A. affirmative.
    B. suggestive.
    C. transformative.
    D. temporary.

26. When the author states, "These moments are rare in my films" (lines 86–87), she most likely means that:

    F. few of her films contain moments of sentimentality.
    G. few of her films contain emotional elements.
    H. while all of her films can be described as tender, they are less so than they seem.
    J. emotional elements are present in almost all of her films, but in small amounts.

27. The passage suggests that the author's primary motivation in making films is:

    A. compulsion.
    B. fame.
    C. social justice.
    D. emotional exploration.

28. According to the author, her interest in Orson Welles prior to seeing his film was rooted in:

    F. his regional perspective coupled with his global experience.
    G. his brash willingness to present himself as what he wanted to be, even if he was not that, yet.
    H. his unlikely ability to overcome his tragic childhood.
    J. his artistic persistence in the face of powerful forces of resistance.

29. The author calls her films "heady, not social" in line 82 most likely to suggest that her films are:

    A. not meant for broad audiences.
    B. intended to educate more than to entertain.
    C. less emotional sagas than brainy explorations.
    D. written independently, without help from others.

30. The "rarity of an aching heart" that the author finds "more memorable" (lines 87–89) can be most reasonably seen to echo back to:

    F. the production of her first film.
    G. the one time she saw her mother cry.
    H. the day before she first saw *Citizen Kane*.
    J. her valedictorian address.

PASSAGE 4

19

HUMANITIES: This passage is adapted from an essay by a linguist on the power of words.

In 1940, Benjamin Lee Whorf wrote an article in M.I.T.'s Technology Review called "Science and Linguistics," in which he argued, among other things, that our mother tongue constrains our minds and prevents us
5 from being able to think certain thoughts. Whorf believed that if a language is missing the word for a particular concept, then its speakers should not be able to understand that concept. Accordingly, if a language doesn't have a past tense, its speakers shouldn't be able to think about the
10 past, and if it lacks a future tense, the speakers would lack the capacity to understand the future.

Whorf was ridiculed as laughably wrong. We are quite capable of thinking about the future and past even if we lack the terminology for it. Think, for instance, about
15 a child telling her mother that her brother kicked her, but not yet aware of the past tense: "He kick me," she says, clearly referring to the past, and with full understanding that the event has already happened. Recall the instances when you learned a word for something you had wished
20 you could express—before you knew what "nostalgia" meant, for example, you had probably felt it.

But twenty years after Whorf's fallible argument was published to little respect, much less acceptance, renowned linguist Roman Jakobson arrived at a related
25 but more nuanced conclusion. "Languages," Jakobson argued, "differ essentially in what they *must* convey and not in what they *may* convey." In other words, if language shapes how we think, it's by determining what we're *obligated* to think about rather than what we're
30 *allowed* to think about.

Consider this example offered by journalist Guy Deutscher in the *New York Times* in 2010, reflecting on the difference between English and Chinese: "If I want to tell you in English about a dinner with my neighbor, I
35 have to tell you something about the timing of the event: I have to decide whether we dined, have been dining, are dining, will be dining and so on. Chinese, on the other hand, does not oblige its speakers to specify the exact time of the action in this way, because the same verb
40 form can be used for past, present or future actions."

Deutscher stressed that this does not mean that a Chinese speaker would be unable to understand the concept of time, but that the person wouldn't *have* to articulate timing every time they wanted to tell a story

45 about a meal. Could this mean Chinese speakers think less about time than English speakers? Perhaps.

As another example of the phenomenon, consider how the use of the terms "partner" and "significant other" changed the nature of discussions about romantic
50 relationships. While previously, lack of gender-neutral terminology for one's romantic partner automatically conveyed the sex of a person—girlfriend and boyfriend, husband and wife—the emergence of neutral terms freed up the question of gender, removing it from its location
55 embedded within the very language we use to describe our lives. Before, language obliged us to reveal gender in our conversations. Afterward, it became necessary to ask further questions for clarification—"Do you mean a man or a woman?" To which one could say, if he or she
60 wished, "None of your business."

A very intriguing illustration of "linguistic obligation" is among speakers of the Australian Aboriginal language Guugu Yimithirr, which lacks coordinates related to the self such as "in front of,"
65 "behind," "left of," "right of," etc. The language strictly uses geographical coordinates to describe directions—that is, east, west, south, and north. But what happens when one doesn't know where north is?

That is the fascinating part, because it doesn't
70 happen. Native Guugu Yimithirr speakers do not have that problem—they *always* know where north is, even without a compass, and accordingly, they know where the other cardinal directions are as well. While a native English speaker, reliant on self-focused directional
75 terminology, will most certainly not develop the same intuitive sense of cardinal direction as one who was raised to rely solely on the geographical coordinates from birth, Guugu Yimithirr speakers are raised to be aware of cardinal directions at all times. As a result, they're as
80 aware of cardinal directions as an English speaker might be that her face is "in front" of her and her spine is "in back" of her lungs.

To an extent, then, Whorf was right. He may have missed the mark in assuming that we cannot imagine or
85 feel what we cannot say, but clearly, what we *must* say can leave us with modes of thinking and seeing that are far more influenced by language than we realize.

MANHATTAN
PREP

31. Which of the following is NOT mentioned in the passage as an illustration of the relationship between words and thought?

   A. Romantic status
   B. Cardinal directions
   C. The substance of meals
   D. Physical acts

32. The author's attitude toward Whorf in the second and third paragraphs (lines 12–30) can best be described as:

   F. unimpressed.
   G. irritated.
   H. scornful.
   J. delighted.

33. The statement "if language shapes how we think, it's by determining what we're *obligated* to think about" in lines 27–29 serves primarily to:

   A. undermine the author's position.
   B. restate the principal theme of the passage.
   C. elaborate on the central topic of the passage.
   D. state the main idea of the passage.

34. In lines 67–68, the author asks, "But what happens when one doesn't know where north is?" most likely to:

   F. raise a dilemma that current research is unable to solve.
   G. ask a rhetorical question to emphasize that she's already provided the answer.
   H. introduce an important attribute of a key example.
   J. propose a caveat to a theory.

35. The sixth and seventh paragraphs (lines 47–68) can be described in which of the following ways?

   A. The sixth paragraph provides an example of a phenomenon and the seventh paragraph introduces another example of the same phenomenon.
   B. The sixth paragraph provides an example of a phenomenon and the seventh paragraph provides an example of a different phenomenon.
   C. The sixth paragraph continues an example of a phenomenon and the seventh paragraph introduces a new phenomenon.
   D. The sixth paragraph introduces a phenomenon and the seventh paragraph provides an example of that phenomenon.

36. According to the passage, each of the following is true of the language Guugu Yimithirr EXCEPT that:

   F. it is spoken in Australia.
   G. it is an aboriginal language.
   H. it lacks a term for "south."
   J. it lacks a term for "in front of."

37. According to the passage, linguist Roman Jakobson is generally regarded:

   A. in low esteem.
   B. in high esteem.
   C. indifferently.
   D. with awed reverence.

38. By "its location" in line 54, the author most nearly means:

   F. its placement in typical sentences.
   G. its existence as a part of language.
   H. its status as a controversial subject.
   J. its scientific definition.

39. In the final paragraph, the author returns to a discussion of Whorf and his thesis most likely in order to:

   A. redeem him somewhat.
   B. assert that he was correct.
   C. ridicule him once more.
   D. credit him with new findings.

40. The author's tone in the final paragraph can best be described as:

   F. curious and intrigued.
   G. existential and deflated.
   H. carefree and whimsical.
   J. sympathetic and somber.

PASSAGE 5

HUMANITIES: This passage is adapted from a transcript from a radio show on a company called Genius, at that time known as Rap Genius.

The company Rap Genius has changed the way rappers and listeners alike think about rap. To understand why Rap Genius has been so important to rap, however, one must hearken back to rap's origins and the context
5 from which it emerged.

Blues musician and historian Elijah Wald has argued that the blues were being spoken as early as the 1920s, going so far as to call rap/hip hop "the living blues." Wald is not alone. While jazz, which unquestionably
10 grew out of the blues tradition, is often cited as a musical precursor to hip hop, its poetry also links the genres. John Sobol, jazz musician and poet who wrote *Digitopia Blues*, has noted as much, stressing both the substance and lyricism that carry over from jazz to rap.

15 As for the term "rap" itself, it was used to describe talking on records as early as 1971, on Isaac Hayes' album *Black Moses*, and by the 1980s, it was a thriving art form. While the modern genre has evolved dramatically over the decades of its existence, throughout its lifespan rappers
20 have used literary techniques that enrich the meaning of the music—double entendres, alliteration, and other forms of wordplay that are also found in classical poetry. Similes and metaphors are used extensively in rap lyrics—some artists have written whole verses in similes.

25 These poetic devices become linked to individual identity. While some rappers are known for the metaphorical content of their raps, others, such as Lupe Fiasco, are known for their complexity. Fiasco, along with others like Public Enemy, The Notorious B.I.G.
30 and, more recently, Jay-Z and Nas, are known for their sociopolitical subject matter.

Rap Genius, a website founded in 2009 on which rap lyrics, recordings and videos are posted for annotation by visitors, presented for the first time a place for rap to
35 be listened to, read, examined, annotated and discussed by anyone with an Internet connection. In bringing in a variety of interpretations of rap text, it elevates rap's significance as a rich cultural art form with sociopolitical depth.

Initially, the founders annotated lyrics themselves.
40 Gradually, they invited others to comment and eventually opened it up to the public. In a climactic moment for the growth of the company, the artists themselves were invited to annotate their own lyrics through "Verified

Accounts." Nas was the first to sign up. Soon after,
45 the RZA—a member of the American hip hop group Wu-Tang Clan—also joined.

But rappers have not been the only ones to bring authority to the public conversation about rap. The ACLU, in response to the line "Meanwhile the DEA teamed up
50 with CCA," in Kanye West's song "New Slaves," wrote a 170-word primer on the prison-industrial complex in the United States. While some celebrated the participation of such a well-known and well-regarded institution, its input was not universally well-received. One user opined
55 that the ACLU had missed the point of West's song entirely, and that its lengthy annotation demonstrated the flaw with Rap Genius' model. "Knowing what Kanye's referencing in one line tells you almost nothing about the meaning of 'New Slaves' as a song," he wrote.
60 "The problem with Rap Genius is its presupposition that language is logical."

Language may be logical, but rap, like poetry, is not always logical in the same sense. It's rhythmic; it's complex; it's full of literary devices with sub-textual
65 meanings; it's emotional. Still, this criticism misses the point. The beauty and power of Rap Genius is that it enables conversation. That requires, of course, staying and participating in that conversation.

There is no one definitive meaning to a piece of
70 text, and perhaps Rap Genius relies too heavily on the idea that there is only one meaning. However, the site's structure provides an opportunity for even that tenet to be debated, both explicitly and implicitly. If you don't like someone's interpretation, you can write your own,
75 or offer a direct criticism. If you don't like the way the conversation unfolds, you may make that comment, as well. Moderators maintain the site for quality control and to prevent trolling (posting deliberately offensive content), but generally, sincere remarks of all sorts are
80 allowed to remain; that is, after all, the intent.

So effective was Rap Genius at bringing people in to discuss the art form that eventually, people started adding explanations to all sorts of texts. The site now features the Bill of Rights, excerpts from the Bible and
85 other religious writing, and poetry by Emily Dickinson.

MANHATTAN
PREP

41. The passage pays the LEAST attention to which of the following topics?

   A. Variations in rap styles
   B. The role of production companies in promoting contemporary rap
   C. Rap's origins, according to historians
   D. New ways in which rap is being listened to and analyzed

42. Which of the following developments occurred first, chronologically, according to the passage?

   F. Isaac Hayes released his album, *Black Moses*.
   G. The blues became an established musical genre.
   H. Jazz became an established musical genre.
   J. Rap Genius was founded.

43. In the passage, who most directly expresses the opinion that no text has one definitive meaning?

   A. The ACLU
   B. The Rap Genius user quoted in the passage
   C. The author
   D. John Sobol

44. Viewed in the context of the passage, the terms "entirely" and "almost nothing" (line 58) in the seventh paragraph (line 56) convey a tone of:

   F. explicit disapproval.
   G. uncensored rage.
   H. informed agreement.
   J. mild indifference.

45. Information about Kanye West's song "New Slaves" in the passage indicates that the referenced text of the song is likely:

   A. illogical, despite being viewed as logical by one notable institution.
   B. subject to more than one interpretation, whether or not there is more than one accurate interpretation.
   C. less about slavery as a historical phenomenon and more about it as a metaphor applicable to contemporary life.
   D. more critical of the government than the ACLU captured in its annotation of the song.

46. The passage claims that jazz:

   F. is more poetic than rap.
   G. was the sole precursor to rap and hip hop.
   H. grew out of the blues.
   J. is essentially the same as the blues.

47. In describing Rap Genius, the author characterizes the company as generally being which of the following?

   A. A negative development for rap as a genre
   B. A positive development for rap as a genre
   C. A neutral development for rap as a genre
   D. A development whose consequences for rap as a genre are yet to be seen

48. Which of the following is NOT stated as a feature of Rap Genius?

   F. It contains excerpts of religious texts.
   G. It allows users to converse within bounds policed by people certified for that purpose.
   H. It treats the rappers who wish to annotate their own raps differently than other users.
   J. It discourages the participation of one-time users.

49. It can be most reasonably inferred from the passage that the author of the passage believes that rap is:

   A. inherently logical.
   B. invariably complex.
   C. notably poetic.
   D. deceptively simple.

50. The passage identifies which of the following rap artists as being a user of Rap Genius?

   F. Lupe Fiasco
   G. Kanye West
   H. Jay-Z
   J. The RZA

PASSAGE 6

HUMANITIES: This passage is adapted from an article about contemporary South Korean culture.

The term "Korean Wave" is reputed to have been coined in 1999 by Beijing journalists attempting to describe the rapid expansion of Korean culture across the globe. In Chinese, the words were different—they
5 referred to the phenomenon as "Hánliú," which is literally translated as "flow of Korea." The idea is the same, though and the Korean Wave as it is known today has continued to describe global interest in Korean pop culture, most notably in the music industry. "K-pop," a genre originating in
10 South Korea characterized by a wide variety of audiovisual elements, has become a worldwide phenomenon, with fans in nearly every country and of every age.

Modern K-pop was invented in 1992, when the group Seo Taiji & Boys integrated a variety of music
15 styles into their own. Their experimentation with this kind of mish-mash was hugely successful. Certainly due in no small part to their success, a paradigm shift in the South Korean music industry ensued. Foreign musical elements are now a standard feature of K-pop,
20 which thrives on its ability to connect with audiences overseas. Since around 2005, the K-pop music market has experienced growth rates in the double digits. In the first half of 2012, it grossed nearly $3.4 billion.

Recognized by *Time* magazine as "South Korea's
25 Greatest Export," K-pop is not an organic, sprawling enterprise, but a product designed, managed and promoted primarily by three large agencies: S.M. Entertainment, YG Entertainment and JYP Entertainment. Together, they are often referred to as the "Big Three" in South
30 Korea. In the 2000s, the record labels also began acting as agencies for the artists. Today, their responsibilities include recruiting, financing, training, marketing and publishing new artists as well as managing their activities and public relations.

35 However, K-pop has taken on greater significance than just being a widely popular form of entertainment. On May 25, 2010, the government of South Korea formally accused North Korea of launching the torpedo that exploded and sank the nation's warship, Cheonan,
40 in the Yellow Sea. Of the 104 crew members on board Cheonan, 46 died in the incident. South Korea declared "psychological warfare" on the North, setting up 11 speakers over which it planned to broadcast the newly released single of a popular K-pop group. The intent was

45 to send the tune over the Korean Demilitarized Zone that separates the countries so that it could be heard by North Korean soldiers stationed there. The stated goal of this "psychological warfare" was to promote peace and reunification, although how exactly this gesture would
50 promote peace remains unclear.

This wasn't the first time such tactics had been deployed. North and South Korea agreed in 2000 to dismantle the loudspeaker systems along the border and to stop radio transmissions. Since 2004, there had been
55 no blaring. According to South Korean media, while ultimately it never happened, the Ministry of Defense also considered setting up large TV screens on which to play music videos by several popular K-pop girl groups.

A question that has arisen lately in the media is
60 why K-pop bands tend to have so many members. They often will have eight or nine—even thirteen. According to Dr. Shin Dong Kim, a professor at Hallym University in South Korea, this, too, is a calculated decision by the companies to maximize popularity.

65 "As fans' taste and preferences are diverse, the more members a group has, the better it can serve the fans' tastes," he says. "You can find at least one or two boys or girls of your own taste from the large groups."

Such tactics seem to have paid off. In September
70 2014, the K-pop boy band INFINITE became the first Korean musicians to top the *Billboard* Twitter Emerging Artists chart when a video of their dancing (actually, practicing for their single, "Last Romeo") went viral. Journalist Natalie Moran says this almost never happens
75 with foreign acts. Moran says the ranking represents "a huge shift in American audiences—a willingness to finally acknowledge that K-pop is the amazing genre our country needs to diversify its tastes."

K-pop may or may not be a way to peace. One thing
80 is clear, though. It may have only been around since the '90s, but it's not going anywhere anytime soon.

51. The main purpose of the passage can be best described as an effort to:

   A. give details about a specific tactic for peace-building.
   B. relate the artistic merits of a particular musical movement.
   C. give an overview of the origins and future development of a cultural phenomenon.
   D. describe various aspects of a popular cultural movement.

52. The author's main attitude toward the subject of the passage can best be described as:

   F. unbridled enthusiasm.
   G. open curiosity.
   H. rational criticality.
   J. visceral wariness.

53. It can be reasonably inferred that the author believes the use of K-pop as a peace-building tool to be:

   A. a clever, if unusual, tactic.
   B. of uncertain effectiveness.
   C. an excellent way to promote quality music.
   D. a common practice in South Korea.

54. According to the seventh and eighth paragraphs (lines 65–78), the decision to create large K-pop bands:

   F. has contributed to the successful crossover of K-pop from Korea to other parts of the world.
   G. is the sole reason for K-pop's popularity.
   H. has enabled K-pop to break into Twitter.
   J. drives K-pop to include more diverse sounds.

55. As stated in the passage, the style of K-pop can be described as:

   A. a purely Korean aesthetic.
   B. a musical genre that incorporates elements of pop, reggae, and hip hop.
   C. a highly synthesized pop sound.
   D. a collage of various international musical styles.

56. The author's statement that "K-pop is not an organic, sprawling enterprise, but a product designed, managed and promoted primarily by three large agencies" (lines 25–27) can be best summarized by which of the following statements?

   F. K-pop was originally created by no more than three companies.
   G. K-pop spreads in a natural way.
   H. K-pop comes in three distinct styles.
   J. K-pop is a manufactured commodity.

57. The passage states that the South Korean Ministry of Defense has considered which one of the following?

   A. Naming K-pop the national style of music.
   B. Using K-pop musicians as international ambassadors.
   C. Projecting music videos featuring female musicians on large TV screens.
   D. Creating a national endowment for K-pop.

58. The author mentions each of the following about K-pop EXCEPT that:

   F. it includes visual elements.
   G. it has been used for non-musical purposes.
   H. it has exclusively gender-segregated groups.
   J. it arrived on the international scene as part of a larger spread of Korean culture.

59. The author most likely describes the decision to have large K-pop groups as "calculated" in line 63 because she believes:

   A. the decision was an intentional one made by K-pop musicians.
   B. K-pop to be the creation of a singular mastermind.
   C. the decision was the result of a great deal of number-crunching.
   D. the choice reflects the fundamentally commercial nature of K-pop.

60. The "tactics" mentioned in line 51 most directly refer to:

   F. the use of entertainment for non-entertainment purposes.
   G. the choice to make K-pop groups large.
   H. the use of K-pop to seduce North Korean soldiers.
   J. the release of music onto the American *Billboard* charts.

PASSAGE 7

HUMANITIES: This passage is adapted from an essay written in 2014 by an American novelist, in which she takes a strong position on a controversial issue.

I've wanted children since I was old enough to understand that I would eventually become an adult myself. My desire to be a mother has, of course, evolved. As a grown up, I stopped wanting a cuddly, miniature
5 creature to rule over and dress up and sling around by her hair and started wanting to experience the great swelling of love that I've watched wash over my friends and cousins and, most recently, my sister. When I met my nephew, I felt a version of that wave. It was, as they
10 say, a love like nothing I'd ever felt before.

But for the first time in my life, I am wondering if to have a child would be cruel, the wrong thing. I am wondering if to bring a person into the world at this moment in the planet's history is something that I can
15 stomach, ethically, and to be sure, I'm no Mother Teresa. I do not always return the extra change. I do not give to beggars. I went four years without paying my taxes in my early twenties (to be fair, that was a decade ago, and I wasn't completely aware of what I was doing). That is who I am.

20 Glaciers and ice shelves around the world are quickly melting. An immediate result will be a rise in sea levels, potentially up to more than 32 feet, which will mean that many coastal areas will completely disappear beneath the ocean, according to NASA. The shock to
25 ecosystems as the planet heats up will be catastrophic in places. Consider the recent drought in California; the tornadoes that ransacked Oklahoma; the hurricanes that become more frequent, and more destructive, by the year. Many ecosystems are very delicate—the slightest change
30 can kill off a species, and in doing so, also render extinct other species that depend on it. Since ecosystems are all interconnected, this kind of chain reaction of effects is inevitable. The questions are how dramatic the reactions will be, and which species will be affected in what ways
35 and when.

For all of these reasons, the human cost of global warming is hard to quantify—but it's not hard to predict, given how human beings act in crisis, natural or man-made. See Ferguson, Missouri. See New Orleans,
40 Louisiana after Katrina.

I am afraid that in the looming global climate crisis, panic and suffering are also inevitable. And where there is panic and suffering, there is conflict. And where there is conflict, there is more suffering—especially with
45 weapons involved.

But none of this is what makes me the most hesitant to become what I've always wanted to be—a mother. What makes me most hesitant is that this matter—the most important thing in all of our lives,
50 no matter who we are or where we live or what race or gender we are or whether we're the 1% or the 99% and whether we vote red or blue or green or not at all—has been deceitfully crafted into a false political question. Despite overwhelming scientific consensus that it is
55 happening and that there are actions we could be taking as a species to prevent it, those with stakes in manufacturing the illusion of a "counterargument" have successfully and criminally packaged and sold to the public the idea that global warming is perhaps
60 not all that bad and that regardless, we humans aren't to blame, and so there isn't much we should be doing about it. Earlier this summer, officials from the Reagan, Bush, and Nixon administrations (who, one might think, might behave otherwise) pushed
65 Congress to act on global warming, as it's becoming impossible to deny, yet the deniers are still too many.

The people who have invested in the creation and spread of this lie are fooling humanity into blindly accepting the demise of our species. They will go down
70 as the greatest criminals in human history.

In the meantime, when sea levels rise, when my home, Long Island, is forced to build sea walls as a sad, Band-Aid concession until it disappears, when homes are destroyed on all coasts by hurricanes too vicious for
75 our structures and infrastructures, when water becomes too scarce and too many lives are lost to sickness and violence and the lie is exposed, because it's too obvious to deny any longer: global warming is real, and it is killing us—I may or may not be here. But my children
80 would be.

So I'll avert my eyes when a homeless man asks me for a dollar, and I will cross my fingers that the IRS doesn't come knocking at my door, and I will feel slightly guilty about the extra five I kept when the clerk counted
85 incorrectly the other week. But I don't know about bringing a son or daughter into a world so fundamentally short-sighted that it is welcoming future generations into devastation and doing nothing about it. That person— her—I am not sure I can be.

MANHATTAN
PREP

61. The narrator of the passage can be best described as someone who is:

  A. deeply troubled by her own hypocrisy.
  B. examining a long-held belief.
  C. questioning whether she should act on a profound desire.
  D. concerned with the relationship between charity and motherhood.

62. According to the author, the politicization of global warming is:

  F. a reflection of human beings' tendency to panic following crisis.
  G. an unfortunate campaign that whitewashes hard truths.
  H. an exaggeration of minor disagreements among scientists.
  J. the result of intentionally malicious actions meant to harm the human species.

63. Which one of the following is an example of a result of global warming offered by the author?

  A. Wildfires in areas with droughts
  B. Increasingly intense hurricanes
  C. Tornadoes throughout the United States
  D. A 50-foot rise in sea levels

64. The author most strongly implies that her desire to be a mother:

  F. has disappeared as a result of global warming.
  G. is strengthened by witnessing her peers become mothers.
  H. includes the desire to play dress-up.
  J. is a feeling that comes and goes depending on her life experiences.

65. As it is used in line 36, the phrase *human cost* most nearly means:

  A. the exact number of people killed by global warming.
  B. the impact of global warming on global economies.
  C. the amount of money required of all people to fight global warming.
  D. the amount of human suffering caused by global warming.

66. The author would be most likely to make which one of the following assertions about those who deny climate change?

  F. They have an interest in convincing others that climate change is not real or man-made.
  G. They are breaking criminal laws.
  H. They are members of the Reagan, Bush, and Nixon administrations.
  J. They believe the rest of humanity to be foolish.

67. The author suggests that humans generally respond to crisis with:

  A. sea walls.
  B. sadness.
  C. panic.
  D. introspection.

68. In the context of the passage, the author likely cites the officials from the Reagan, Bush, and Nixon administrations (lines 63–64) in order to emphasize that:

  F. politicians are unable to stop global warming.
  G. economic inequality drives much of the political controversy around global warming.
  H. most climate change denialists are members of past presidential administrations.
  J. there should be less political controversy around the existence of global warming.

69. The author's description of herself as "no Mother Teresa" (line 15) most nearly means that:

  A. she pursues justice imperfectly.
  B. she is generally unconcerned with doing the "right" thing.
  C. she does not believe in morality.
  D. she dislikes moral posturing.

70. The author offers sea walls in Long Island as an example of:

  F. a completely futile attempt at protecting human infrastructure.
  G. the kind of action we should be taking to stem global warming.
  H. a stopgap measure that will have little long-term effect.
  J. a highly effective method for preventing damage to property.

PASSAGE 8

HUMANITIES: This passage is adapted from an essay published in a 2014 volume of a magazine about politics and literature.

"Live free or die," the New Hampshire state motto, is a mantra with historical roots that stretch back to both the American and French Revolutionary Wars. The precise phrase in English is credited to General John
5 Stark, New Hampshire's most famous soldier of the American Revolutionary War. He followed the phrase with, "Death is not the worst of evils."

The notion of freedom as a principle whose importance cannot be overstated undergirds not only the
10 struggle for American Independence but also the struggles of humankind throughout our species' history. It is freedom that inspires human beings to fight; it is freedom that inspires nations to wage war; it is freedom that compels teenagers from the safety of their homes into the
15 streets seeking autonomy and adventure.

And so, it is perhaps not a surprise that in recent decades, there has emerged in the United States a movement that seeks governmental and societal consent of a new kind of freedom—the liberty to choose the
20 gender with which one identifies. The movement toward "gender fluidity" is a manifestation of the same pursuit of freedom that has motivated human beings for generations.

"How does newness come into the world?" author
25 Salman Rushdie asks in his novel *The Satanic Verses*, and we might ask the same regarding the pursuit of freedom. For it is not without resistance that one moves from un-free to free; were the transfer frictionless, there would be no need for such a transfer in the first place.

30 Indeed, there are numerous individuals, organizations and institutions that reject the idea of gender fluidity—of gender choice—on the grounds that it is not traditional, or not conducive to a functional society. This opposition misses the fundamental driving force at work—liberty to
35 choose who one is.

Certainly, there are adjustments that must be made when newness is introduced into society. We must ask ourselves questions such as: What values do we value most highly? How do we respect minority
40 rights and interests while also respecting the majority's views? How do we evolve with the changing times while remaining true to the fundamental beliefs that anchor us? Ultimately, these questions lead to where they always

lead—to the dilemma of where to draw the boundaries
45 of freedom.

Of course, the freedom of the collective is not best served by utter lawlessness. This means that one person's "freedom" to act any way that he or she wishes occasionally must be constrained in order to preserve
50 the freedoms of his or her neighbors, and thereby the freedoms of society as a whole. I am not permitted to play my music as loudly as I wish during the wee hours when you are trying to sleep on the other side of my wall—there are noise ordinances dictating as much. I
55 may not drive on the left side of the road in America where people drive on the right side just because I feel like it—doing such a thing would be reckless, a death wish for both me and others. Our collective autonomy is preserved by reasonable restrictions, carefully considered
60 and decided upon, of individual autonomy.

But these restrictions have a limit. One's choice of gender identity is not like my playing music loudly at night, or your driving recklessly into oncoming traffic; it is not like these, because one's choice of gender does
65 not endanger or harm others. While individuals may be *offended* by one's decision to select a gender identity with which he or she was not born, we do not as a society consider mere offense to be a harm for purposes of legislation. If my being offended meant I needed
70 protection from that offense, no one could do anything, for it is certain that every possible action is capable of offending at least one other person.

The challenge of new ideas entering the world is the same as a bud pushing through soil—there is friction,
75 and force; there is obstacle; there is the risk of failure; there is no guarantee. But if the endeavor is successful, there is a blossoming. Whatever costs are incurred by a culture in transition, whatever pains it suffers, and on whomever the bulk of that suffering lands, there can
80 be no doubt that societal transitions such as the gender identity movement are not seamless affairs. They are difficult, as pursuits of freedom often—or, I would venture to say, invariably—are.

71. One of the main arguments the author is trying to make in the passage is that:

- **A.** death is preferable to life without freedom.
- **B.** a person should not play music so loudly that it keeps her neighbors awake.
- **C.** a person born female should be able to choose to become a male.
- **D.** a person who wishes to drive on the left side of the road in the U.S. should not be able to do so.

72. Given the information in the second, third, and fourth paragraphs (lines 8–29), which of the following is the most accurate description of how "gender fluidity" has been treated in recent decades in the United States?

- **F.** With resistance
- **G.** With disgust
- **H.** With curiosity
- **J.** With open arms

73. The author views "freedom" and "liberty" as:

- **A.** fleeting.
- **B.** self-contradicting.
- **C.** overlapping but different.
- **D.** synonymous.

74. Which of the following is mentioned in the passage as a reason for why some limits on freedom are necessary?

- **F.** The desire to exploit the powerless
- **G.** The need to prevent chaos
- **H.** The desire to ensure that the fewest number of people are offended
- **J.** The goal to preserve our collective autonomy

75. The author uses the term *blossoming* in line 77 to mean:

- **A.** the opening of minds.
- **B.** the discovery of beauty.
- **C.** the unleashing of freedom.
- **D.** the unveiling of oppression.

76. When the author says that "were the transfer frictionless, there would be no need for such a transfer in the first place" in lines 28–29, he most likely means that:

- **F.** if the process of becoming free were smooth, one would have been, to some extent, free to begin with.
- **G.** if, in the process of becoming free, one does not face resistance, one has not earned one's freedom.
- **H.** a person who does not value freedom takes it for granted.
- **J.** the transition from un-free to free is automatic.

77. The author implies that the reason for resistance to the gender fluidity movement is that:

- **A.** people lack empathy.
- **B.** people fear it.
- **C.** people are offended.
- **D.** people are angry.

78. According to the passage, *offense* constitutes all of the following EXCEPT:

- **F.** something that is impossible to wholly prevent.
- **G.** something that is not harm for legal purposes.
- **H.** something native solely to societies that lack freedom.
- **J.** something that some people may experience in response to gender fluidity.

79. The primary function of the first paragraph is to:

- **A.** introduce the main thesis of the passage.
- **B.** introduce the principle that supports the passage's thesis.
- **C.** present the author's opinion in abstract terms.
- **D.** present an idea to which the author is opposed.

80. It can most reasonably be inferred that:

- **F.** Salman Rushdie is a proponent of freedom at all expense.
- **G.** General John Stark was a founder of New Hampshire.
- **H.** "Live free or die" was also uttered during the French Revolutionary War.
- **J.** the gender fluidity movement will succeed.

PASSAGE 9

HUMANITIES: Passage A is from an essay on public broadcasting as an educational tool. Passage B is from a Social Studies textbook.

Passage A

Public broadcasting, also known as public television, exists in some form in most countries. While features of it vary across cultures, its purpose is to serve the public good. This is not to say that only governments fund it, however; in
5 some countries, such as the U.S., individual contributions and commercial financing are heavily involved.

Historically, public broadcasting was the *only* kind of television available in many countries. Commercial television—the airing of television for profit, via
10 advertisements or consumer pay—didn't emerge full-fledged in Europe until the late twentieth century, for example, while public television existed in the region since the 1940s. The United States is the exception in this regard; commercial TV came first. In line with
15 that tradition, in the U.S. today, television is still overwhelmingly commercial.

Nearly every home in the United States contains a TV. Household ownership of a television exceeds 95%, and most households possess more than one television. The
20 U.S.'s TV networks are the largest and most syndicated in the world. And yet, the U.S. spends only about $4 per capita on providing public television, compared to $30 to $134 for the largest European countries. Germany, for example, spends over $131 dollars per capita on public broadcasting,
25 which adds up to over 10 billion dollars spent annually.

It is unfortunate that U.S. television is primarily commercial, given that studies show public television improves political knowledge. Evaluating political knowledge across 14 western European countries,
30 researchers found that watching public broadcasting increased correct answers to political questions by roughly 12 percent. Additionally, further study has shown that not only does public broadcasting improve political knowledge generally, but it also reduces the knowledge
35 gap between "haves" and "have-nots."

The U.S. should take note. While it is unlikely that it will ever spend billions, like Germany, there is an undeniable opportunity to increase government funds for public broadcasting, in order to address the problems of
40 political apathy, indifference and ignorance that plague democracy in this country.

Passage B

Public broadcasting in the United States is a small but sprawling and decentralized entity. While it does receive some government support, that support is
45 minimal, and public broadcasting itself is not operated by the government. A large proportion of funding for public television comes from donations made by individuals and corporations.

For instance, the Public Broadcasting Service
50 (PBS), formerly National Educational Television, relies primarily on support from viewers. It does, however, accept commercial sponsorship of specific programs. On the sponsorship page of PBS's website, the organization offers information to prospective sponsors interested in
55 learning more about sponsorship opportunities, most notably audience demographics for particular shows. The audience for *Curious George*, for instance, is primarily composed of women with between one and five children. Sponsorship of the show includes two 15-second spots
60 during its daily Monday-to-Friday broadcast. Current sponsors include a children's shoe company and a children's educational website.

These types of sponsorship announcements (or "underwriting") have come to resemble standard "TV
65 commercials" so closely that one couldn't be faulted for questioning what, if any, difference exists between the two. Differences, however, do exist. Sponsorship spots on public television tend to be notably shorter than commercials on for-profit TV. They also differ in tone
70 and are disproportionately educational in nature.

The structure of the operations of public broadcasting is also complex. The first public broadcasting stations in the U.S. were operated by state colleges and universities; they were often run as part of the
75 schools' cooperative extension services. The Cooperative Extension System is a government agency that provides funding to universities with the mission of advancing "agriculture, the environment, human health and well-being, and communities" by supporting research,
80 education and extension programs. Public broadcasting thus fell under this rubric as a non-credit, education-based endeavor.

Today, public television stations are individual entities that license their content to one of several different
85 non-profit organizations, municipal or state governments, or universities. These licensees may distribute that content but do not own it.

MANHATTAN
PREP

90 So, the next time you turn on PBS to watch "Sesame Street" and wonder who is behind getting Big Bird to your screen, know that it is not one single entity or source of funding, but a web of players, all with various stakes in bringing you that quaint—but not forgotten—brand of media in our country: public television.

81. The primary function of the fourth paragraph (lines 26–35) in Passage A is:

   A. to introduce the reasons for the author's thesis as presented in the next paragraph.

   B. to convey the relevance of the essay to the reader's life.

   C. to demonstrate the few ways in which the U.S. is unlike Europe.

   D. to emphasize the many differences between the European and U.S. systems.

82. It can most reasonably be inferred that the author of Passage A believes that:

   F. the German model of public broadcasting is ideal.

   G. European citizens are more informed politically than U.S. citizens.

   H. the U.S. populace would benefit from increased governmental subsidies to public broadcasting.

   J. the European populace is exposed to more educational political media than is the U.S. populace.

83. The main idea of Passage A is that:

   A. nations vary in the extent to which they value public television.

   B. all nations should embrace the potential of public television.

   C. public television is more important to Europe than it is to the United States.

   D. the United States would benefit from increased public funding for public television.

84. Passage B indicates that in the United States, public broadcasting was originally operated by:

   F. the government.

   G. commercial entities.

   H. universities.

   J. a web of players.

85. When the author of Passage B says "quaint but not forgotten" in line 92, she most nearly means:

   A. remembered fondly.

   B. unusual but surviving.

   C. charming but impractical.

   D. archaic but unparalleled.

86. According to Passage B, "distributing" content on television is NOT necessarily the same as:

   F. publicizing it.

   G. owning it.

   H. featuring it.

   J. funding it.

87. The author of Passage B would most likely agree with the author of Passage A that:

   A. despite government funding, public television's commercial dependence in recent years has negatively affected its quality.

   B. public television in the U.S. should be more heavily subsidized by the government.

   C. politics in the U.S. would be less polarized if more people were watching public television.

   D. despite a degree of commercial funding, public television remains distinct from commercial television in at least several important ways.

88. Which of the following statements most accurately describes the tone of the two passages, respectively?

   F. Passage A is neutral, while Passage B is opinionated.

   G. Passage A is opinionated, while Passage B is neutral.

   H. Passage A is general, while Passage B is specific.

   J. Passage A is academic, while Passage B is colloquial.

89. The two passages both mention:

   A. non-government funding sources of public television.

   B. European practices.

   C. the potential of public television to enlighten citizens politically.

   D. the Cooperative Extension System.

Answer Keys

Write in whether you got each problem right or wrong (or left it blank). If your answer was correct, put a 1 in every blank to the right of that problem. Sum up each column and compare your total to the total possible "Out Of" points in each column.

Passage 1

Problem	Correct Answer	Right/ Wrong/Blank	Main Ideas/ Author's Approach	Details	Relationships	Meanings of Words	Generalizations
1	A						—
2	H			—			
3	B				—		
4	G		—				
5	D			—			
6	J					—	
7	A		—				
8	G		—				
9	D			—			
10	G			—			
Total							
Out Of		10	3	4	1	1	1

Passage 2

Problem	Correct Answer	Right/ Wrong/Blank	Main Ideas/ Author's Approach	Details	Relationships	Meanings of Words	Generalizations
11	B		—				
12	F				—		
13	C				—		
14	H			—			
15	C			—			
16	J					—	
17	B			—			
18	H			—			
19	A						—
20	J					—	
Total							
Out Of		10	1	4	2	2	1

Passage 3

Problem	Correct Answer	Right/ Wrong/Blank	Main Ideas/ Author's Approach	Details	Relationships	Meanings of Words	Generalizations
21	B		—				
22	J		—				
23	B						—
24	H				—		
25	C						—
26	J					—	
27	A		—				
28	G		—				
29	C		—				
30	G			—			
Total							
Out Of		10	5	1	1	1	2

Passage 4

Problem	Correct Answer	Right/ Wrong/Blank	Main Ideas/ Author's Approach	Details	Relationships	Meanings of Words	Generalizations
31	C			—			
32	F		—				
33	D		—				
34	H		—				
35	A		—				
36	H			—			
37	B			—			
38	G					—	
39	A		—				
40	F						—
Total							
Out Of		10	5	3	0	1	1

MANHATTAN
PREP

Passage 5

Problem	Correct Answer	Right/ Wrong/Blank	Main Ideas/ Author's Approach	Details	Relationships	Meanings of Words	Generalizations
41	B			—			
42	G			—			
43	C			—			
44	F					—	
45	B				—		
46	H			—			
47	B						—
48	J			—			
49	C				—		
50	J			—			
Total							
Out Of		10	0	6	2	1	1

Passage 6

Problem	Correct Answer	Right/ Wrong/Blank	Main Ideas/ Author's Approach	Details	Relationships	Meanings of Words	Generalizations
51	D		—				
52	G						—
53	B				—		
54	F			—			
55	D			—			
56	J					—	
57	C			—			
58	H			—			
59	D				—		
60	F					—	
Total							
Out Of		10	1	4	2	2	1

19

Passage 7

Problem	Correct Answer	Right/Wrong/Blank	Main Ideas/Author's Approach	Details	Relationships	Meanings of Words	Generalizations
61	C						—
62	G						—
63	B			—			
64	G				—		
65	D					—	
66	F				—		
67	C			—			
68	J		—				
69	A					—	
70	H			—			
Total							
Out Of		10	1	3	2	2	2

Passage 8

Problem	Correct Answer	Right/Wrong/Blank	Main Ideas/Author's Approach	Details	Relationships	Meanings of Words	Generalizations
71	C		—				
72	F						—
73	D					—	
74	J			—			
75	C					—	
76	F					—	
77	C				—		
78	H						—
79	B		—				
80	H			—			
Total							
Out Of		10	2	2	1	3	2

MANHATTAN
PREP

Passage 9

Problem	Correct Answer	Right/ Wrong/Blank	Main Ideas/ Author's Approach	Details	Relationships	Meanings of Words	Generalizations
81	A		—				
82	H		—				
83	D		—				
84	H			—			
85	B					—	
86	G			—			
87	D				—		
88	G						—
89	A			—			
Total							
Out Of		9	3	3	1	1	1

Humanities Solutions

Passage 1 Solutions

1. **(A)** The environmental forces that caused ancient Greek statues to lose their paint

Generalizations

The passage does not discuss the environmental forces that caused ancient Greek statues to lose their paint. Choice (A) is correct. The passage does, however, mention all the other choices: the process of discovering the original painted designs (third through fifth paragraphs), the debate over whether to restore those designs (sixth and seventh paragraphs), and descriptions of how the ancient statues originally appeared (first and second paragraphs). You are looking for the topic that is *not* mentioned. Therefore, choice (A) is the correct answer.

2. **(H)** x-ray spectroscopy

Details

There is no mention of x-ray spectroscopy being used. Choice (F), video microscopes, is mentioned in line 25, choice (G), magnifying glasses, is mentioned in line 23, and choice (J), ultraviolet photography, is mentioned in line 34. You are looking for the method that is *not* mentioned in the passage; choice (H) is correct.

3. **(B)** a concept inspired by ancient Greek ruins.

Relationships

In lines 74–75, the passage states that "the impressive nature of the Greek ruins inspired the concept" of ruin value, and yet, this wasn't the intent of their creators: "The ancient Greeks themselves did not promote the idea of 'ruin value'" (lines 69–70). Choice (B) is correct.

4. **(G)** leave them in their present-day state.

Author's Approach

In lines 79–80, the author states, "The original statues, however, should be left intact as ancient, weathered, creatures of stone." Choice (G) restates this language.

5. **(D)** a part of art.

Details

In lines 66–67, the passage states that these conservators believe that "the ravages of time become a part of any artwork." Choice (D) reflects this and is correct.

6.   **(J)** singular in color.

Meaning of Words

The passage is discussing the Ancient Greek statues that in their present form, displayed in museums, are "reveries in white" (line 2). That is, these statues now are singular in color, unlike their colorful original condition. Choice (J) is correct.

7.   **(A)** the arguable absurdity of featuring the Greek statues without paint.

Author's Approach

By drawing the comparison, the author is highlighting how one might view failure to restore the statues to their original, colorful states as preposterous—just as it would be preposterous to hang a painting on which the original paint has completely decayed, leaving only the canvas. Choice (A) is correct.

8.   **(G)** a device whose name is not commonly known.

Author's Approach

The author puts quotations around the term "raking light" in order to acknowledge to the reader that it is a specialized term in the field of art restoration and that, accordingly, the reader may not be familiar with it. Choice (G) is correct.

9.   **(D)** Gold leaf

Details

Lines 16–17 state, "A muscular male torso was leafed in gold." This supports choice (D). While balloons were *painted* on the statue, actual balloons, choice (C), were not used, nor was choice (B), blue face paint (although "red decorative face-paint" was mentioned). The passage does not mention choice (A), pink paint.

10.   **(G)** Video microscopes

Details

In lines 25–26, the author mentions "video microscopes that magnify [objects] by 160 times." This fact indicates that relative to other microscopes mentioned, including the ones that magnify objects 40 times, video microscopes are especially powerful. The author emphasizes this power by writing that the "researchers then slowly deepen their view of the sculpture by using . . . finally video microscopes" (lines 22–25). The sequence strongly implies that the last instruments mentioned provide the deepest or most powerful views. Choice (G) is correct.

MANHATTAN
PREP

Passage 2 Solutions

11. **(B)** explore the benefits and shortcomings of a new tool.

Main Idea

The passage examines the Google Art project, an "interactive tool" (lines 4–5). According to the author, this project "is, overall, a good thing" (line 14). However, the author also argues that it is still lacking because "sitting at home in front of our computers is not going to be the same experience as standing in front of the Mona Lisa" (lines 74–76). Choice (B) reflects the author's balanced view. Choice (A) is too broad, while choice (D) is too extreme. Choice (C) is not discussed by the passage.

12. **(F)** receptive.

Relationships

The author integrates Shimamura's thinking (detailed in the third-to-last paragraph) into her own discussion and evaluation of the Google Art Project. She says: "Shimamura's research gets to the heart of what, if anything is lacking in Google's Art Project" (lines 68–69). While the author is positive about Shimamura's theories, "ecstatic," choice (H), is too strong. The author is not "frosty," choice (J) or "dismissive," choice (G). Choice (F), "receptive," is more appropriate, and the correct choice.

13. **(C)** a piece that must be physically experienced to be fully understood.

Relationships

"Sitting at home on our computers is not going to be the same experience as standing in front of the Mona Lisa," says the author (lines 74–76). This sentiment is reflected in the language of choice (C). It is too extreme to say that the Mona Lisa *cannot* be digitally represented, so choice (A) is incorrect. Choice (B) offers the opposite of what you are looking for—the author believes the Mona Lisa is *not* captured well on the computer screen. Choice (D) interprets the author's statements about the interactions between the viewer and the art object too literally.

14. **(H)** the ability to examine an artwork very closely.

Details

In lines 14–19, the passage states that through technology-enabled access to art, "People who will never be able to visit Italy can now not only see Botticelli's Birth of Venus, they can also study it millimeter by millimeter—the high-resolution images of particular pieces of art make possible such clinical examination." Thus, choice (H) is correct.

15. **(C)** valuable as an educational tool.

Details

The passage describes Roberta Smith's argument about the Google Art Project: "The Google Art Project offers the chance to become educated in 'the way artists construct an image on a flat surface,' which she calls 'great practice for looking at actual works'" (lines 25–28). This would support choice (C).

16. **(J)** The way that the viewer helps to create an aesthetic experience.

Meaning of Words

Toward the end of the passage, the author finalizes her argument. Citing Dewey and Shimamura, she says, "Art is not only the paint on canvas, but what we, in encountering the paint on canvas, bring with us" (lines 71–72). She uses Dewey's ideas about art as experience to assist her argument, as well as Shimamura's theory that art is shaped by various filters. Both of these ideas point to the notion that the viewer's subjective experience helps to create an "aesthetic" experience (in which art is appreciated). Thus, choice (J) is correct.

17. **(B)** a discipline that uses technology to understand how people look at art.

Details

According to the passage, neuroaesthetics is "the use of imaging technologies to study how the brain responds to the viewing of art," (lines 50–52). Choice (B) restates this language. Choice (A) is unsupported—the author never says that neuroaesthetics actually "unites" the broad fields of science, psychology, and painting. Choice (C) is incorrect because while the author cites Dewey as a "precursor" to neuroaesthetics, she never argues that he founded the discipline. Choice (D) makes unwarranted connections between different parts of the passage; you do not know whether neuroaesthetics influenced the Google Art Project.

18. **(H)** they are protecting certain copyrights.

Details

The passage states that museums like the Louvre are opting out of the Google Art Project: "One reason for these museums' opting out is to avoid copyright issues" (lines 79–81). This matches choice (H).

19. **(A)** an interaction between an object and its viewer.

Generalization

This question connects to the author's overall argument. The author favorably describes Dewey's and Shimamura's works that characterize art as a shared experience between the object and the viewer. The author thus locates "art" in the spark that happens when object meets the eye. Choice (A) reflects this position. Choice (B) is too strong. While the author links the viewing of art to psychology, she never says it is "purely" psychological. The same issue infects choices (C) and (D)—*highly* filtered? *Entirely* created? These words are too extreme.

20. **(J)** metaphorically walk around.

Meaning of Words

In line 5, the author describes *virtual* travel rather than physical travel. After all, the word "virtually" is set off by dashes for emphasis. Choices (F), (G), and (H) are all too literal. Choice (J) correctly captures the author's description of digitally exploring museums.

Passage 3 Solutions

21. **(B)** recall the moment at which the author decided to pursue a particular career path.

Main Idea

While the entire passage is devoted to recalling the author's decision to become a director, lines 48–73 are solely devoted to the moment itself. Choice (B) is correct. Choice (A) is too broad in scope—you don't know about the whole trajectory of her career, other than that she made films. While she pays some attention to her career's overall features in lines 74–90, these features are presented in the context of her primary purpose, which is to describe why she became a director. Choice (C) is incorrect because she doesn't describe artistic evolution; she merely describes *deciding* to become an artist, then becoming one. Choice (D) may be true, but it is not her main purpose.

22. **(J)** thoughtful nostalgia.

Author's Approach

In lines 72–73, the author writes, "Before that moment, I didn't know, and after it, I did." The description leading up to the moment she's talking about involves careful recollection of details—what she was wearing, what people said, what she was thinking. She is nostalgically remembering an important experience in her life. She is thoughtful about it because she is taking care to describe the circumstances with precision. Thus, Choice (J) is correct. Choice (F) is not true—if anything, she is happy about her decision. Choice (G) has similar issues. Choice (H) is incorrect because if she feels joy about her choice, she's certainly not suppressing it. She is proud of her work (line 77).

23. **(B)** superior to the films that she has made as a director.

Generalizations

"My films are not like Citizen Kane, and I don't mean only in quality," she writes in lines 75–76. You know she views *Citizen Kane* as a remarkably good film, and so you can infer by these facts that she's saying that *Citizen Kane* is *superior* to hers in quality. This supports Choice (B). Choice (A) isn't supported at all. Choice (C) is not true, either. While he was a newcomer to flim, she gives no suggestion that she believes he was "overrated." If anything, she seems to believe he deserves the praise he received. Choice (D) is not something the author writes about *Citizen Kane*. She describes her *own* films as intellectual (line 80).

24. **(H)** similar in certain ways.

Relationships (Comparisons)

As a child, the author wasn't particularly social but "heady": "'Heady, not social,' my aunt once called me, which crushed me with its truth" (lines 37–38). As an adult, she makes films that she describes as heady, as well: "One might call my work heady, not social" (line 82). You can infer that this is because as an adult filmmaker she still retains, to some extent, the outlook she possessed as a child. Thus, Choice (H) is correct. Choice (F) is too extreme. While you may be able to infer that she's more comfortable speaking as an adult, you don't know how much more, and "notably" means quite a bit. Choice (G) isn't something for which you're given any evidence, nor is (J).

25. **(C)** transformative.

Generalizations

In lines 1–4, the author writers, "… when I first decided—no, discovered—that I wanted to make films. It was while viewing *Citizen Kane* in my Intro to Film class …" Viewing the movie was, for her, "transformative," choice (C). It wasn't "affirmative," (A), because there wasn't anything to *affirm* yet. She didn't know what she wanted to be until she saw the film. Seeing *Citizen Kane* wasn't "suggestive," (B), because it was more powerful than that word implies. And (D), "temporary," is incorrect; the effect of seeing the film has lasted her lifetime.

26. **(J)** emotional elements are present in most of her films, but in small amounts.

Meaning of Words

In lines 84–86, the author states: "but I always make sure that there is heart in my work, that at least one of the lead characters exhibits a moment of tenderness." You can infer that this means that in every movie, there is a moment of tenderness, or an "aching heart" (line 88) as she goes on to describe, although "these moments are rare" (lines 86–87). Choice (J) reflects this, but for this reason, (F) and (G) are incorrect. She isn't saying *few* of her films display emotion, but that emotional moments are rare yet present in *every* film, or almost every film, of hers.

27. **(A)** compulsion.

Main Idea

In lines 68–73, the author writes: "I knew, watching it, what I wanted to do with my life. *There was no question in my mind*, and it had happened that fast—in an instant, from one shot on a wavy, pull-down screen in a chilly lecture hall. Before that moment, I didn't know, and after it, I did." These lines strongly suggest that the author was *compelled* to make films, supporting choice (A). Choices (B) and (C) aren't at all mentioned as motivations, and (D) implies that she was more emotional than she was as a person. Choice A is correct.

28. **(G)** his brash willingness to present himself as what he wanted to be, even if he was not that, yet.

Author's Approach

"He strode into a theater and claimed he was a Broadway star … What bravery! I wanted to possess such courage, such self-assurance. I wanted to fake it and make it," the author writes in lines 57–62. Choice (G) is the closest match— Welles pretended to be an actor, then became one, and the author was drawn to that. Choice (F) isn't something she highlights as an interest or attraction, nor is (H). Choice (J) would be impossible to support because you don't get evidence of his facing much *resistance* to his artistic endeavors. On the contrary, he is quite well-received (all those Oscar nominations for his first film!).

29. **(C)** less emotional sagas than brainy explorations.

Author's Approach

Just before line 82, you've been told that her films are *not* like Welles' films in part because they "lack its emotional tension" (lines 78–79). In the next line, she tells you that her films are "more intellectual games" (line 80). These descriptions support (C). Being more intellectual, however, doesn't mean they're intended to educate; they can still be intellectual entertainment, so (B) is incorrect. Choices (A) and (D) are not answers for which the passage provides any evidence.

30.   **(G)**   the one time she saw her mother cry.

Details

In lines 11–13, the author writes: "I saw wet spots on the top one from where her tears had fallen. I couldn't recall ever seeing her cry over me." This single episode of her witnessing her mother's emotional reaction to her daughter's moving away was meaningful to the author, and lines referenced in this question harken back to it and make (G) the correct answer. Choices (F) and (H) refer to instances in the story that are not so emotional, or in fact do not exist, she never gave her valedictorian address, choice (J).

Passage 4 Solutions

31.   **(C)**   The substance of meals

Details

The *timing* of meals is discussed (lines 33–40) as an illustration of a difference between Chinese and English languages, but the substance of meals, (C), is never mentioned. The incorrect choices are all brought up somewhere in the passage: "Romantic status," (A), in lines 47–60, "Cardinal directions," (B), in lines 65–82, and "Physical acts," (D), such as kicking, in lines 14–18.

32.   **(F)**   unimpressed.

Author's Approach

The author describes Whorf's theory as "fallible" (line 22) and viewed as "laughably wrong" (line 12). She notes that his article was published to "little respect" (line 23). In the second paragraph, the author asserts her own position in opposition to Whorf ("We are quite capable of thinking about the future and past even if we lack the terminology for it" in lines 12–14). She then provides her own set of counterexamples to Whorf. This evidence all supports choice (F), that at this point in the passage, she is *unimpressed* with Whorf. Choice (H), "Scornful," and (G), "irritated," are too strong, however (there is already some redemption in the third paragraph, via Roman Jakobson's "related... conclusion"), and (J), "delighted," is not supported.

33.   **(D)**   state the main idea of the passage.

Main Idea

The idea that language shapes how we think by influencing what we *must* think about rather than what we *can* think about is the main point of the passage and is first stated here. The rest of the passage provides three extended examples, followed by a final paragraph that essentially reiterates the point. Therefore, (D) is correct. Choice (A) is incorrect because the author's position is not being undermined, or weakened. Choice (B) is incorrect because the main idea (or principal theme) is not being *restated*—while the text in question introduces the idea that language determines what we *must* think about, this is the first time the author says it.

34.　**(H)** introduce an important attribute of a key example.

Author's Approach

The author is posing a riddle ("What if you don't know which way north is?") that is actually likely to be on the mind of the reader at this point in the passage. That is, the author has not already provided the answer to this riddle. Therefore, the answer to the problem is not (G). The author then goes on to solve the riddle she has posed, however, so the answer is not (F). The riddle is solved by the fact that the native speakers of Guugu Yimithirr always know which way north is. The fact that the speakers of the language all know something (so this knowledge can be built into the language) is a key feature of this language that provides an important illustration of the main idea of the passage. Choice (H) is correct.

35.　**(A)** The sixth paragraph provides an example of a phenomenon and the seventh paragraph introduces another example of the same phenomenon.

Author's Approach

The sixth paragraph (lines 47–60) offers as an example of how language shapes thought—how we discuss romantic partners. Paragraph seven (lines 61–68) introduces a *new* example in the language of Guugu Yimithirr, which is offered as further support of the same idea. Choice (A) is correct.

36.　**(H)** it lacks a term for "south."

Details

In lines 62–65, you learn that Guugu Yimithirr is an "Australian Aboriginal language" which lacks coordinates related to the self such as 'in front of,' The language *does,* however, have a term for south (line 67). You are looking for an answer that is *not* true (namely, that it lacks this term), so (H) is correct.

37.　**(B)** in high esteem.

Details

Line 24 refers to "renowned linguist Roman Jakobson." Therefore, it's reasonable to infer that he is generally held in high esteem, (B). Choice (D) is too extreme ("awed reverence"). Choices (A) and (C) are the opposite of what you're looking for.

38.　**(G)** its existence as a part of language.

Meaning of Words

Lines 53–56 tell you that "the emergence of neutral terms freed up the question of gender, removing it from its location embedded within the very language we use to describe our lives." Therefore, you can infer that "location" here means "part of language." Choice (G) is correct.

MANHATTAN
PREP

39. (A) redeem him somewhat.

Author's Approach

In line 83, in the final paragraph, the author states: "To an extent, then, Whorf was right," which is "redemptive." That is, this statement brings Whorf back, to some degree, from his "ridiculed" position in line 12. However, she notes that he "may have missed the mark" in lines 83–84, and so she is not providing a complete redemption or a rescinding of her earlier critique. Choice (A) is correct.

40. (F) curious and intrigued.

Generalization

The author says in lines 85–87 that "clearly, what we *must* say can leave us with modes of thinking and seeing that are far more influenced by language than we realize." This is a forward-looking statement that acknowledges our lack of knowledge and invites further research into the subject. Choice (F), "Curious and intrigued," describes the attitude of the statement well.

Passage 5 Solutions

41. (B) The role of production companies in promoting contemporary rap

Details

This question is similar to an EXCEPT question. Eliminate answer choices concerning subjects the passage *does* pay attention to in order to identify the right answer. The author writes about "variations in rap styles" in the fourth paragraph (lines 25–31) so (A) must be incorrect. The origins of rap are discussed in the second and third paragraphs. That knocks out choice (C). The whole passage concerns choice (D); the author opens her discussion by saying, "The company Rap Genius has changed the way rappers and listeners alike think about rap" (lines 1–2). That leaves you with choice (B), which is never mentioned in the passage.

42. (G) blues became an established musical genre.

Details

The passage talks about history in the second and third paragraphs. Lines 7–8 state that "the blues were being spoken as early as the 1920s," which implies that the blues existed even before then. These spoken blues were precursors to rap and jazz. Since every other answer choice concerns jazz or rap, the origin of blues must chronologically be the first of the group. Choice (G) is correct.

43. (C) The author

Details

"There is no one definitive meaning to a piece of text," the passage states in lines 69–70. This opinion is not attributed to any other voice. It therefore must be in the author's voice, which matches choice (C).

MANHATTAN
PREF

44. (F) explicit disapproval.

Meaning of Words

These words are part of a criticism. A Rap Genius user criticizes, in clear terms, the ACLU's addition to an entry on a Kanye West song. "They know nothing! They entirely missed the point!" the user essentially says. Choices (H) and (J) are not negative enough. Choice (G) is too strong; this user expresses something closer to scorn than anger. Choice (F) correctly captures the emotion of "explicit disapproval" present in these lines.

45. (B) subject to more than one interpretation, whether or not there is more than one accurate interpretation.

Relationships

The passage discusses disagreement around West's "New Slaves." The ACLU connects the song to the "prison-industrial complex" (line 51) while a user interprets the song differently (lines 54–57). The author does not weigh in as to the correct interpretation, so the reader is left with multiple ways of looking at the song, as stated in choice (B).

46. (H) grew out of the blues.

Details

The answer to this question shows up in the second paragraph: "While jazz, which unquestionably grew out of the blues tradition, is often cited as a musical precursor to hip hop ..." (lines 9–11). This supports choice (H).

47. (B) A positive development for rap as a genre

Generalizations

The first sentence of the passage captures the author's point of view: "The company Rap Genius has changed the way rappers and listeners alike think about rap" (lines 1–2). The author also describes Rap Genius as "effective ... at bringing people in to discuss the art form" (lines 81–82). The author is a Rap Genius fan. Thus, choice (B) is correct.

48. (J) It discourages the participation of one-time users.

Details

This is an EXCEPT question, so a process of elimination is the best approach. Look for answer choices that *are* stated features of Rap Genius. Choice (F) is stated in lines 84–85. Choice (H) can be found in lines 42–44; rappers get "verified accounts" to annotate their own lyrics. Finally, choice (G) is present in lines 77–80. What is missing from the passage is any suggestion that the site discourages one-time users, so choice (J) is correct.

49. (C) notably poetic.

Relationships

The author subtly connects rap to poetry at various points in the passage. She says that the poetry and lyricism of jazz "link" to rap (lines 11–14) and that "rap, like poetry, is not always logical" (lines 62–63). Choice (A) is contradicted by this statement and is incorrect. Choice (B) is tempting, but the author never goes so far as to say that all rap is *invariably* complex, nor that all of it is deceptively simple, choice (D). Lines 26–31 showcase the author's balanced perspective here. Choice (C) is correct.

50. **(J)** The RZA

Details

"The RZA—a member of the American hip hop group Wu-Tang Clan—also joined [Rap Genius]" states the passage in lines 45–46. Choice (J) is correct.

Passage 6 Solutions

51. **(D)** describe various aspects of a popular cultural movement.

Main Idea

The passage describes various facets of K-pop. The author explores its sound, its origins, its size, and its use as a tool for psychological warfare and peace. This purpose matches choice (D). Choice (A) is too specific to describe the main purpose of the whole passage. The author doesn't detail the future development of K-pop or describe its artistic merits, so (B) and (C) are also incorrect.

52. **(G)** open curiosity.

Generalization

The author doesn't take a strong stance on K-pop. Rather, she offers a fairly neutral overview of its history. Choices (F), (H), and (J) contain words that are too emotionally strong; the author shows neither "unbridled enthusiasm" (too positive) nor "visceral wariness" (too negative). Even "rational criticality" is inappropriate, because little criticism of the K-pop genre is offered. The author does seem curious about the music, though; why else would she have written such a detailed article on the subject? Thus, choice (G) is correct.

53. **(B)** of uncertain effectiveness.

Relationships

In lines 47–50, the author states: "The stated goal of this 'psychological warfare' was to promote peace and reunification, although how exactly this gesture would promote peace remains unclear." That is, the author is unsure about how effective this kind of warfare is; to her, it is "of uncertain effectiveness," as in correct choice (B). Choice (A) is a bit off, because the author never implies that this decision was particularly clever or smart. Choice (C) is incorrect because the point of the maneuver was to promote reunification, not music. Choice (D) is unsupported—while these tactics had been used before, the author never implies that they were common.

54. **(F)** has contributed to the successful crossover of K-pop from Korea to other parts of the world.

Details

In these paragraphs (lines 65–78), the author connects the size of K-pop groups—which means the groups have something for everyone's taste—to K-pop's international success. More specifically, she connects it to K-pop's unusual breakthrough on the American *Billboard* chart ("Such tactics seem to have paid off" in line 69). This "successful crossover" matches choice (F). While the author does connect the size of K-pop brands to a variety of "tastes," she does not connect it to a diversity of sounds, so (J) is incorrect. Choice (G) is too extreme (*sole* reason?) and choice (H) confuses the *Billboard* Twitter charts with Twitter itself (moreover, "breaking into" an activity is different from "topping" the charts in that activity).

55. **(D)** a collage of various international musical styles.

Details

The passage describes K-pop as a "mish-mash" (line 16) of "a variety of music styles" (lines 14–15). In other words, K-pop is a collage, a combination of disparate elements, as described in choice (D). Choice (A) is too extreme—purity is a high standard—while choice (B) is too specific. The author never describes K-pop as synthesized, so choice (C) is also incorrect.

56. **(J)** K-pop is a manufactured commodity.

Meaning of Words

In lines 25–27, the author contrasts an "organic enterprise" with a "product" designed and promoted by "large" agencies. In other words, she contrasts something self-perpetuating and self-made with something manufactured for sale by big business. Choice (J) describes something manufactured, and a commodity—a good to be bought and sold. This matches the contrast set up by the author. Choice (F) is too extreme; while it's promoted *primarily* by three companies, there may be more involved.

57. **(C)** Projecting music videos featuring female musicians on large TV screens.

Details

The fifth paragraph states "the Ministry of Defense also considered setting up large TV screens on which to play music videos by several popular K-pop girl groups" (lines 56–58). Choice (C) restates this idea.

58. **(H)** it has exclusively gender-segregated groups.

Details

Choice (F) is mentioned in lines 10–11 (K-pop includes "audiovisual elements"). Choice (G) is described in the fourth and fifth paragraphs (about K-pop's use in psychological warfare). Choice (J) is stated in the opening lines of the passage. However, it is never asserted that K-pop has exclusively gender-segregated groups. There are hints at some degree of gender segregation (e.g., in line 58, "K-pop girl groups" are mentioned), but the author never claims that all K-pop groups are exclusively men or exclusively women. You are looking for what the author does *not* mention. Thus, (H) is correct.

59. **(D)** the choice reflects the fundamentally commercial nature of K-pop.

Relationships

The author emphasizes the way K-pop is a product manufactured by business, arguing "K-pop is not an organic, sprawling enterprise, but a product designed, managed and promoted primarily by three large agencies" (lines 25–27). Here and elsewhere, the author implies that the decision to create large K-pop groups is also a careful business decision because it is aimed at increasing K-pop's international appeal, and by extension, sales. Choice (D) essentially restates this idea: the very existence of these groups is commercialized. Choice (A) is incorrect because the decision was likely not made by musicians but by the large agencies mentioned earlier in the passage. Choices (B) and (C) interpret the term "calculating" in too extreme or literal a manner.

60. **(F)** the use of entertainment for non-entertainment purposes.

Meaning of Words

These tactics are described as the author discusses the use of K-pop as a tool for psychological warfare and peace-building. The author puts this maneuver in a larger context of how the South Korean government projects pop culture across the border to North Korea for political, that is, non-entertainment, purposes. At an abstract level, this matches choice (F). Choice (H) is incorrect because it is never stated that the purpose was to *seduce* North Korean soldiers, but rather to attack them psychologically.

Passage 7 Solutions

61. **(C)** questioning whether she should act on a profound desire.

Generalizations

The author discusses how the reality of global warming affects her desire to be a mother. Global warming and charity are not the same, so choice (D) is incorrect. Choice (A) is also incorrect; the author worries about global warming, not any internal contradictions she may have. "Questioning" and "examining" are both actions the author engages in, so you have to dig a little deeper into choices (B) and (C). Choice (C) describes a desire while choice (B) describes a belief. The author's yearning to be a mother is a desire, not a belief, so (C) is correct.

62. **(G)** an unfortunate campaign that whitewashes hard truths.

Generalizations

The politicization of global warming is described in the sixth and seventh paragraphs (lines 46–70). The author argues that global warming has been "deceitfully crafted into a false political question" (line 53). She says the deniers argue that "global warming is perhaps not all that bad and that regardless, we humans aren't to blame" (lines 59–62), a position she characterizes as a "lie." She sees the "false politicization" as a harmful illusion that masks difficult-to-face realities. Choice (G) matches this characterization. Choice (J) is extreme; while the author has harsh words for climate change denialists, she never says they are intentionally harming people. Choices (H) and (F) are unsupported.

63. **(B)** Increasingly intense hurricanes

Details

"The hurricanes that become more frequent, and more destructive, by the year" are mentioned in lines 27–28, so choice (B) is correct. The other choices are close but incorrect; for instance, "tornadoes that ransacked Oklahoma" (line 28) are mentioned, but they are not necessarily "throughout the United States," as choice (C) claims.

64. **(G)** is strengthened by witnessing her peers become mothers.

Relationships (Cause–Effect)

The author describes her desire to be a mother right at the beginning of the passage. She details how that desire has changed over time from a fantasy of playing dress-up to a yearning "to experience the great swelling of love that I've watched wash over my friends and cousins and, most recently, my sister" (lines 6–8). You can infer that witnessing this "swelling of love" increases the author's own desire for a child, as choice (G) indicates. Choice (H) is incorrect because that answer choice describes the desires of the author's younger self. Choice (J) is generally unsupported by the passage. Choice (F) is too extreme; global warming has caused the author to question her maternal desires, but it has not caused the disappearance of those desires.

65. **(D)** the amount of human suffering caused by global warming.

Meaning of Words

Reread lines 36–45. The author says "the human cost of global warming is hard to quantify—but it's not hard to predict." She goes on to describe that predicted human cost—"panic," "suffering," and "conflict" (line 43), all of which point to choice (D). Choice (A) is too specific; suffering includes but is not limited to death. Choices (B) and (C) interpret "cost" too literally.

66. **(F)** They have an interest in convincing others that climate change is not real or man-made.

Relationships (Cause–Effect)

Climate change denialists are not portrayed positively by this author, who describes them as "manufacturing an illusion" (line 57) and says that they "will go down as the greatest criminals in human history" (lines 69–70). This makes choice (G) a tempting answer choice, since (G) discusses crime. However, choice (G) is incorrect. The author uses "criminal" in the sense of "shameful" or "disgraceful"; she does not imply that denialists are breaking actual laws. Choice (H) is the opposite of what you are looking for, since those members were described as urging Congress to act against climate change. Choice (J) is not suggested by the passage. That leaves choice (F). The author describes climate change denialists as "*those with stakes in* manufacturing the illusion of a 'counterargument'" (lines 56–57) and as "*The people who have invested in* the creation and spread of this lie" (lines 67–68). They *have stakes* and *have invested in*; in other words, they have an interest in this argument. Choice (F) states this idea.

67.   **(C)** panic.

Details

The author speculates how humans will respond to future catastrophes wrought by global warming by discussing how they usually respond to crises. She suggests that "panic" is inevitable (line 42). Choice (C) is correct.

68.   **(J)** there should be less political controversy around the existence of global warming.

Author's Approach

These members of former presidential administrations urged Congress to act in the face of climate change. The author cites them as examples of politicians taking a correct position and avoiding the "false political question" (line 53) created by those who deny the "overwhelming scientific consensus" (line 54) that global warming is real. The author implies here that the political choice is false because there should be no debate, or at least less of it—we should listen to the voices of scientists. This idea is stated in choice (J).

69.   **(A)** she pursues justice imperfectly.

Meaning of Words

The examples of the ways the author is "no Mother Teresa" (line 15)—no saint—include failing to pay taxes and failing to give money to beggars. These are the "good deeds" of daily life. The author contrasts these deeds with her urgent sense of justice around climate change. In the final paragraph, she says, "So I'll avert my eyes when a homeless man asks me for a dollar … But I don't know about bringing a son or daughter into a world so fundamentally short-sighted that it is welcoming future generations into devastation and doing nothing about it" (lines 81–88). Thus, by describing herself as "no Mother Teresa," she is putting her passion about global warming into the context of her own ordinary imperfections. This idea is stated in choice (A).

70.   **(H)** a stopgap measure that will have little long-term effect.

Details

The author states: "In the meantime, when sea levels rise, when my home, Long Island, is forced to build sea walls as a sad, Band-Aid concession until it disappears …" (lines 71–73). A "Band-Aid concession" is a temporary solution, so choice (H) is correct.

Passage 8 Solutions

71.   **(C)** a person born female should be able to choose to become a male.

Main Idea

That people should have the freedom to choose their gender is the author's explicit opinion and the overall point of the passage. Choice (C) is correct. The issue is first broached in the third paragraph (lines 16–23) as a natural outgrowth of a more general pursuit of liberty; the rest of the passage is designed to provide logical support for the argument. The other answer choices are incorrect because while the author *may* agree with (A) and, in the cases of (B) and (D), does explicitly agree; they are not *main arguments* he is making.

72. **(F)** With resistance

Generalizations

In the fourth paragraph (lines 24–29), the author claims that when newness, or new freedoms, come into the world, they do not come "without resistance" (line 27). The fifth paragraph (lines 30–35) applies this general idea to the specific reaction of "numerous individuals, organizations, and institutions" (lines 30–31) to the idea of gender fluidity: they "reject" it (line 31). The word "resistance" in choice (F) captures this concept. "Disgust" in choice (G) is too strong a term (this is never implied in the passage), and "curiosity" in (H) and "open arms" in (J) are too positive.

73. **(D)** synonymous.

Meaning of Words

In the passage, the author uses "freedom" and "liberty" interchangeably, as for example, in line 19, where he says, "a new kind of *freedom—the liberty* to choose." Choice (D) is therfore correct. While he does believe that freedom can be *challenging* to secure, that's different than it being *fleeting* or temporary, so choice (A) is incorrect. There is no support given for choices (B) or (C).

74. **(J)** The goal to preserve our collective autonomy

Details

In lines 58–60, the author states, "*Our collective autonomy* is preserved by reasonable restrictions, carefully considered and decided upon, of individual autonomy." This idea of "reasonable restrictions" corresponds to that of "some limits on freedom" in the question. Choice (J) is correct.

75. **(C)** the unleashing of freedom.

Meaning of Words

In the last paragraph of the passage, the author is writing about the challenge of new ideas entering the world, specifically, freedom. It "*is the same as a bud pushing through soil … But if the endeavor is successful, there is a blossoming*" (lines 73–77). The blossoming is best understood as a metaphor for the realization, discovery, or creation of *freedom*. This is reflected in choice (C).

76. **(F)** if the process of becoming free were smooth, one would have been, to some extent, free to begin with.

Meaning of Words

"Frictionless" means "smooth," and in line 28 the author is discussing how anything new being brought into the world will face obstacles. If there are no obstacles, then it must *not be new*. Likewise, if you are free to move out of a jail cell,

MANHATTAN
PREP

then you were not really in jail; you were already free to go. Choice (F) is best because it is a restatement of the author's point: if freedom is easy to come by, one must already be free.

77. **(C)** people are offended.

Relationships (Cause–Effect)

The author writes in lines 64–65 that "one's choice of gender *does not endanger or harm others*." The author goes on to say that individuals "may be *offended* by one's decision to select a gender identity with which he or she was not born" (lines 65–67). Therefore, you can infer that the author believes that at least some of the resistance to gender fluidity results from the offense that some people take to the concept. Choice (C) is correct. Empathy, fear, and anger, noted in choices (A), (B), and (D), are not discussed.

78. **(H)** something native solely to societies that lack freedom.

Generalizations

In the eighth paragraph, lines 61–72, the author discusses how an offense is not a harm for legal purposes. Thus, choice (G) is wrong, because you are looking for what does not constitute offense. The author also states that "it is certain that every possible action is capable of offending at least one other person" (lines 71–72), and therefore is *impossible to wholly prevent*, as in choice (F). Finally, lines 65–67 state that some people may be offended by gender fluidity. The author never indicates, however, that offense is something that is *solely* native to societies that lack freedom (that is, that offense would only take place in non-free societies). Choice (H), therefore, is not part of what constitutes offense.

79. **(B)** introduce the principle that supports the passage's thesis.

Author's Approach

In the first paragraph, the author focuses on the phrase "Live free or die" (line 1), then provides a brief history of the phrase for the purpose of emphasizing the importance of freedom. This principle of the fundamental importance of freedom is what the author claims undergirds the passage's thesis, which is that gender fluidity is also a matter of freedom. That thesis is not, however, introduced until the third paragraph, so the first paragraph does not itself introduce the thesis. Thus, choice (B) is correct.

80. **(H)** "Live free or die" was also uttered during the French Revolutionary War.

Details

Lines 1–3 state that the quoted text "is a mantra with historical roots that stretch back to both the American and French Revolutionary Wars." You can infer, then, that it was uttered during the French Revolutionary War. Choice (H) is correct. The other choices are not supported by the passage.

Passage 9 Solutions

81. **(A)** to introduce the reasons for the author's thesis as presented in the next paragraph.

Main Idea

In lines 26–28, the author of Passage A says, "It is unfortunate that U.S. television is primarily commercial, given that studies show public television improves political knowledge." This is the first instance in which the author has expressed an opinion, and the previous text has been background for this opinion. Finally, this opinion leads to the primary point, or thesis, of the passage—that *the U.S. should take note*—in the next (and final) paragraph. Therefore, choice (A) is correct. While (C) and (D) may have some support, neither one is the *primary function* of the paragraph.

82. **(H)** the U.S. populace would benefit from increased governmental subsidies to public broadcasting.

Author's Approach

The final paragraph of the passage is where the author presents his thesis. He mentions the potential benefits of increasing public funding for public television and suggests that the U.S. "take note" (line 36) of the studies demonstrating these benefits. This evidence in the text supports choice (H). The other choices are not fully supported by the passage: the author never argues (F), that the German model is "ideal," nor (G), that European citizens are "more informed politically" (they just might gain more political knowledge from public television), nor (J), that Europeans are exposed to more "educational political media" (maybe U.S. citizens see more of such programs on commercial television or on the Internet).

83. **(D)** the United States would benefit from increased public funding for public television.

Main Idea

Line 36 introduces the final paragraph of the passage and says, "The U.S. should take note"; namely of the positive effects of public television, in particular on the political knowledge of the populace. In lines 26–27, the author says, "It is unfortunate that U.S. television is primarily commercial," and the core of the last sentence of the passage is that "there is an undeniable opportunity to increase government funds for public broadcasting" (lines 37–39). Thus, it is reasonable to conclude that the main idea of the passage is that the U.S. populace would benefit from such an increase in public funds. This is stated in choice (D).

84. **(H)** universities.

Details

Lines 72–74 state, "The first public broadcasting stations in the U.S. were operated by state colleges and universities." Choice (H) is therefore correct.

85. **(B)** unusual but surviving.

Meaning of Words

Public broadcasting is not as dominant as commercial television in the United States (line 43: it is *small*), but it remains in operation today. Choice (B) is therefore the best answer. Choice (A) makes it seem as if public broadcasting no longer exists. Choices (C) and (D) are too extreme—it is presented neither as impractical or unparalleled.

86.   **(G)**   owning it.

Details

In the second-to-last paragraph, lines 82–86, the passage states, "These licensees may *distribute that content but do not own it.*" Thus, choice (G) is correct.

87.   **(D)**   despite a degree of commercial funding, public television remains distinct from commercial television in at least several important ways.

Relationships (Comparisons)

The author of Passage B doesn't speak to choices (A), (B), or (C). However, in the third paragraph of Passage B (lines 63–70), the author indicates several ways in which public broadcasting differs from commercial TV. Likewise, Passage A's thesis relies on the two forms being different. For instance, Passage A's author says in lines 26–28, "It is unfortunate that U.S. television is primarily commercial, given that studies show public television improves political knowledge." Choice (D) is therefore correct.

88.   **(G)**   Passage A is opinionated, while Passage B is neutral.

Generalizations

The author of Passage A expresses a strong opinion in the final paragraph of the passage (that is, public television should be given more public funds), while Passage B, taken from a Social Studies textbook, provides more of a neutral overview. Thus, choice (G) is correct.

89.   **(A)**   non-government funding sources of public television.

Details

In lines 4–6, the author of Passage A mentions that "in some countries, such as the U.S., individual contributions and commercial financing are heavily involved." In Passage B, the same concept appears in lines 46–48: "A large proportion of funding for public television comes via donations from individuals and corporations." Thus, choice (A) is correct.

Chapter *of* 20

5lb. Book of ACT® Practice Problems

Reading:
Natural Sciences

In This Chapter...

Natural Sciences Passages & Solutions

Chapter 20
Reading: Natural Sciences

The Reading passages in this chapter are classified within natural sciences, which include biology, chemistry, physics, astronomy, ecology, technology, and other subjects that focus on nature and the universe. A small amount of context is given at the start, but each passage is self-contained.

Various kinds of questions are asked about these passages, including the following:

1. Main Ideas/Author's Approach. Main idea or ideas of the passage (or a part of it); the approach, voice, point of view, method, or purpose of the author.

2. Details. Specific details mentioned in the passage.

3. Relationships. Comparisons, sequences of events, cause-effect relationships, or other relationships that are described or implied in the passage.

4. Meanings of Words. The meaning of a word or phrase, in its context, in the passage.

5. Generalizations. Broad observations that can be drawn from the passage.

How should you use this chapter? Here are some recommendations, according to the level you've reached in ACT Reading.

1. Fundamentals. Do a passage or two untimed to begin with. As you become more comfortable, put the clock on. In all cases, review the solutions closely, and articulate what you've learned. Reread the passage again to ensure that you fully understand it, and redo problems as necessary.

2. Fixes. Do one passage at a time under timed conditions. Examine the results, learn your lessons, then test yourself with more passages (one from each Reading chapter) at once.

3. Tweaks. Confirm your mastery by doing a few passages (one from each Reading chapter) at once under timed conditions. A full set of four is the ultimate goal. Aim to improve the speed and ease of your reading and solution process.

Good luck on the problems!

PASSAGE 1

NATURAL SCIENCE: This passage is adapted from an essay on handedness in vertebrates, which are animals with backbones.

On the exterior, the human body seems symmetrical. Yet this appearance belies a deeply asymmetrical interior. Internally, the human heart is on the left side, the liver is on the right side, the spleen is left, the gallbladder is
5 right, and so on. Perhaps more importantly, this internal asymmetry extends to the brain. As the human brain has grown, it was thought that each side, or hemisphere, of the brain has become more specialized. Each hemisphere communicates with the other, and many tasks require the
10 use of both hemispheres working in concert, but others are accomplished primarily by one hemisphere or the other.

In the past, scientific consensus was that this separation of functions within the brain was a uniquely human trait. The theory was that as the human brain grew in
15 size, the connections between the two hemispheres could not grow at the same pace. As the connections became insufficient for efficient communication, each hemisphere evolved to become more self-sufficient until the tasks performed by one was separate from the other. When
20 humans began using tools and developing language, their brains expanded and specialization occurred.

Most humans openly prefer to use their left hemisphere in everyday activities. These people are in fact right-handed. About 90% of all humans are right-
25 handed, implying that the dominant hemisphere for motor functions of most humans is the left side. The tendency to prefer the left side of the brain for motor functions is so pronounced that scientists can monitor it at all stages of life. At least one study has shown that after only
30 12 weeks of gestation, a human fetus will move the right arm more than the left and a 15-week-old fetus will prefer to suck the thumb of his right hand rather than left. Clearly, there is some kind of genetic predisposition involving the separation of the hemispheres of the brain. One may ask
35 whether this separation is found similarly in all animals.

The idea that this preference is uniquely human persists despite many recent findings that animals can also be categorized as left- or right-handed. Captive gorillas and chimps all tend to be right-handed. Orangutans,
40 conversely, tend to be left-handed. The question scientists must answer is why. Apes are well known for mimicry. One of the reasons some have been able to communicate through sign language is because of this tendency to mirror what those around them are doing. If humans sign,
45 apes can as well. Possibly the preference for using their right hand comes, not from the brain, but simply from watching humans and observing a general preference for right-handedness. This theory is supported by the fact that when similar studies are conducted on apes in the
50 wild, there seems to be no particular preference for left- or right-hand dominance.

Other scientists argue that the inconclusive evidence from wild apes is a result of small sample sizes and inadequate observation. Instead, these scientists claim
55 that the specialization of brain hemispheres and the corresponding handedness has been part of life since vertebrates first emerged on Earth 500 million years ago. These scientists suggest that each brain hemisphere evolved not to further separate from each other, but
60 rather to maximize each species' survival potential.

What might the left and right hemispheres of the brain do differently in other vertebrates? One hypothesis is that the left side is used to complete simple, everyday tasks. In contrast, the right side is more adaptive, responding to
65 unusual situations quickly. The right side was therefore used more for dangerous and emotional circumstances, such as detecting and responding to a predator. However, the left side was more regularly dominant, resulting in a more planned, controlled reaction.

70 To test this hypothesis, scientists would need to evaluate animals that cannot show handedness. Through intensive study, they have determined that fishes, reptiles, and toads all tend to attack prey from the right side. They favor their right eye and right body to complete this
75 everyday action. Just as right-handedness indicates the left hemisphere of the brain is being used, this feeding pattern shows the preference for the left hemisphere. Birds show a similar slant toward right-sided feeding, and even whales have proven to be 75% right-jawed.

80 The evidence that a left-brained, right-handed preference for everyday activities occurs in nearly all vertebrates is mounting. However, no animal has shown as extreme a preference as humans. The source of this contradiction is probably a combination of factors. There
85 is certainly a genetic component to the differentiation of the brain hemispheres. Otherwise, right-handedness would not be so common among all vertebrates. Yet the use of tools and the continued reliance on fine motor skills for the everyday tasks of humans forced the right-
90 handed preference to become increasingly favored. Genetics may have started humans on the path to left-brained dominance, but other factors must have been important to produce such an extreme bias that we see present in human brains today.

MANHATTAN
PREP

1. The author of the passage is most likely to agree with which of the following?

    A. All species of animals are right-handed.
    B. Reliance on fine motor skills alone created the preference for right-handedness.
    C. Specialization of the brain is unique to humans.
    D. Handedness cannot be explained by purely genetic or purely learned factors.

2. As used in the passage, the word "concert" (line 10) most nearly means:

    F. harmony.
    G. discord.
    H. musicality.
    J. specialization.

3. Each of the following is named in the passage as a type of animal that tends to favor the left hemisphere of the brain for everyday activities EXCEPT:

    A. birds.
    B. humans.
    C. orangutans.
    D. toads.

4. The main point of the passage is that:

    F. studying handedness is crucial to understanding brain chemistry.
    G. the specialization of the hemispheres of the brain has a complex origin.
    H. all members of the ape family show either right- or left-handedness.
    J. genetic factors account for little if any of the specialization of the brain.

5. It can be inferred from the passage that no species has ever displayed:

    A. a preference for left-handedness.
    B. a 95% preference for right-handedness.
    C. a preference for using both hemispheres of the brain equally.
    D. the ability to change handedness.

6. An idea the author of the passage disagrees with is that:

    F. the specialization of the hemispheres of the brain is uniquely human.
    G. feeding methods can be used to evaluate use of left or right hemispheres of the brain.
    H. the right side of the brain is more responsive to unusual situations.
    J. the growth of the human brain was faster than the growth of the connections between the two hemispheres of the brain.

7. According to the passage, why do scientists believe that apes are not truly right- or left-handed?

    A. Some apes show a preference for right-handedness and others for left-handedness.
    B. Brain studies on apes have shown no specialization of the hemispheres.
    C. Apes in the wild have no preference for either left- or right-side dominance.
    D. Apes have the ability to mimic human sign language.

8. The two groups of scientists discussed in the passage most clearly disagree about:

    F. whether animals other than apes can show specialization in the brain's hemispheres.
    G. whether left- and right-handedness is linked to the different hemispheres of the brain.
    H. whether studies on wild apes were valid studies.
    J. whether there is an evolutionary impetus for handedness.

9. The purpose of the third paragraph (lines 22–35) is likely:

    A. to discuss studies that prove handedness in humans.
    B. to prove that the left hemisphere of the brain is always preferred for everyday activities in humans.
    C. to show an interesting finding related to handedness.
    D. to suggest that genetics play a role in the separation of the hemispheres of the brain.

10. According to the hypothesis about brain hemispheres in simple vertebrates, what might a scientist expect to observe?

    F. An animal that has a damaged left hemisphere is unable to communicate.
    G. An animal that has a damaged right hemisphere is unable to perform everyday tasks.
    H. An animal that has a damaged left hemisphere is unable to respond to an unexpected situation.
    J. An animal that has a damaged right hemisphere is unable to respond to an unexpected situation.

PASSAGE 2

NATURAL SCIENCE: This passage is adapted from an article on ancient scientific instruments.

A solar eclipse has been an awe-inspiring sight for centuries. When a solar eclipse occurs, the moon passes between the Earth and the sun. This creates the illusion that the sun has been momentarily blacked out. Before
5 the causes were understood, many cultures placed a strange significance on eclipses. Often, solar and lunar eclipses were thought of as omens. When they were seen as negative, they radically changed the behavior of many people in ancient times. One solar eclipse was said
10 to occur in the middle of a war in ancient Greece, and the effect of the image was so powerful that both sides stopped fighting and peace was declared.

In ancient China, although an eclipse was believed to be the result of a legendary dragon devouring the sun,
15 often consequences were nonetheless real. Solar eclipses were directly linked to an emperor's future, and it is believed that at least two ancient astrologers were killed for failing to predict an eclipse. With such importance placed on being able to predict these astrological events
20 and given such little understanding of their mechanisms, ancient cultures devised different ways to foresee when total eclipses would occur.

This drive to calculate the timing of solar eclipses has led to groundbreaking inventions. The earliest known
25 one is the Antikythera Mechanism. The Antikythera Mechanism was created near the end of the second century, B.C.E. by the ancient Greeks. Though it has been studied extensively since its discovery over 100 years ago, only in the last few decades have scientists determined
30 its function. It is believed to be a computing machine designed to predict eclipses, which it did, successfully.

Amazingly, the Antikythera Mechanism worked through a simple input-output method. To determine the next solar or lunar eclipse in a given time, the user would
35 turn the dial to the desired time frame, and the machine would turn a corresponding dial that indicated not only the date of the next eclipse, but the exact time of day. The order, arrangement and function of the predictive symbols remain a mystery to scientists.

40 The significance of this discovery cannot be overstated. In essence, it is the world's first computer. After it was created, it took nearly 1,000 years for similarly complex machines to be invented. Why was it considered so advanced? The physics involved in such a
45 prediction is intricate, especially considering the limited information available to the ancient Greeks. Only 300 years before the Antikythera Mechanism was created, all Greeks believed that the Earth was the center of the universe and the sun revolved around it.

50 Today, scientists understand more about the complexities of orbital rotation. We accept that the Earth rotates around the sun, but the orbit is elliptical, not circular. Each day, depending on the time of year, the Earth is gradually traveling nearer to or farther from the sun.
55 In early January, the Earth is only 147 million kilometers from the sun, but by early June, the distance between the two has grown to 152 million kilometers. The variation in distance adds to the difficulty of calculating when the Earth will be positioned to observe a solar eclipse.

60 Further contributing to the complexity is the rotation of the Earth on its axis. Relative to the sun, the Earth is tilted. A basketball spinning on an athlete's finger has no tilt relative to the athlete (until the ball begins to fall). If that basketball were tilted so that it kept spinning on the
65 athlete's finger, but was now leaning a little to the side, it would be more representative of the spin of the Earth. This tilt is the cause of the seasons—the hemisphere of the Earth that is tilted toward the sun experiences summer— and the source of another difficulty of predicting the
70 alignment needed for an eclipse.

These two difficulties pale in comparison to the intricacies of the moon's orbit, however. As the Earth revolves about the sun, the moon is simultaneously revolving around the Earth. The tricky part is that the
75 plane of the moon's revolution is not the same as the plane of the Earth's revolution. All calculations regarding the three must therefore be completed in three dimensions. The only way for an eclipse to occur is for all three bodies to align perfectly.

80 Today, we can account for all the different rotations and revolutions of the sun, moon, and Earth because we have carefully studied their movement using satellites, telescopes, and other high-tech equipment, none of which was available in ancient times. When the Antikythera
85 Mechanism was created, the sole source of information scientists had was what they observed by looking into the night sky. Yet they were able to create an impossible machine that accounts for the variables involved and predicts upcoming eclipses. As we study the Antikythera
90 Mechanism, we continue to make discoveries about ancient civilizations, their startling understanding of the universe, and their grasp of complex mathematical concepts.

MANHATTAN
PREP

11. According to the author, the biggest obstacle to predicting eclipses is:

   A. the difference between the moon's and the Earth's planes of revolution.
   B. the rotation of the Earth on its axis.
   C. the revolution of the Earth around the sun.
   D. the limited information available to modern-day scientists.

12. The author believes that each of the following is a reason the Antikythera Mechanism is an impressive achievement EXCEPT:

   F. the mistaken understanding ancient Greeks had of the universe.
   G. the simple input-output method it employs.
   H. the attitude scientists held at the time that such an invention was too difficult.
   J. the limited access to technology and information ancient Greeks had.

13. One effect of the tilt of the Earth, according to the passage, is:

   A. the creation of night and day.
   B. the different seasons.
   C. the formation of eclipses.
   D. the revolution of the moon on a different plane than the revolution of the Earth.

14. The sixth paragraph (lines 50–59) suggests that if the orbit of the Earth around the sun were circular rather than elliptical, then:

   F. eclipses would become less common.
   G. there would be no difference in the seasons.
   H. the Antikythera Mechanism would have been invented even earlier than it actually was.
   J. the Earth would always be the same distance from the sun.

15. Which of the following questions is NOT answered by the passage?

   A. Approximately when was the Antikythera Mechanism created?
   B. Approximately when was the Antikythera Mechanism lost?
   C. Approximately when was the Antikythera Mechanism found?
   D. Approximately when was the Antikythera Mechanism's purpose understood?

16. The main point of the fifth paragraph (lines 40–49) is:

   F. that Ancient Greeks mistakenly thought the sun rotated around the Earth before the Antikythera Mechanism was created.
   G. to emphasize that the Antikythera Mechanism has survived into modern times.
   H. that the Antikythera Mechanism was an important discovery.
   J. that scientists in ancient times had less information and fewer resources than scientists today.

17. The author implies that a solar eclipse is caused by:

   A. the moon passing between the sun and the Earth.
   B. a legendary dragon devouring the sun.
   C. the Antikythera Mechanism.
   D. the spin and revolution of the Earth.

18. According to the passage, in ancient times, a motivation to predict eclipses could have been:

   F. to stop a dragon from devouring the sun.
   G. to stop wars.
   H. to understand more about the nature of the universe.
   J. to gain insight into an emperor's future.

19. According to the author, one benefit to studying the Antikythera Mechanism is to:

   A. learn about how ancient civilizations viewed the universe.
   B. understand more about the rotation and revolution of the sun, moon, and Earth.
   C. determine the function of specific predictive symbols.
   D. predict the next solar eclipse.

20. The passage implies which of the following?

   F. Eclipses were nearly impossible to predict in ancient times.
   G. Calculations in three dimensions are more difficult than calculations in two dimensions.
   H. In ancient times, scientists did not believe the Earth was tilted relative to the sun.
   J. Without modern technology, we would not be able to predict eclipses.

PASSAGE 3

NATURAL SCIENCE: This passage is adapted from a magazine article titled "The World's Coolest Animal?"

Tardigrades, organisms with eight legs that are able to thrive in remarkably extreme conditions, are perhaps Earth's most resilient life form. Resembling bears (complete with claws that assist with locomotion), they
5 are less than a single millimeter long and nonetheless can withstand temperatures from just above absolute zero (–458 degrees Fahrenheit, or just one degree Kelvin), to those far above the boiling point of water. It is possible that they have survived the fatal pressures of
10 the greatest ocean trenches. They are able to withstand radiation in amounts that are hundreds of times greater than the lethal dose for human beings. Tardigrades can even survive for certain periods in the vacuum of outer space.

15 While genetic studies have revealed that they originally lived in freshwater environments before adapting to live on land, today these incredible critters have been found all over: in hot springs, under solid ice, in lakes, ponds, meadows—even on top of the
20 Himalayas.

"They are probably the most extreme survivors we know among animals," biologist Bob Goldstein says. "People talk about cockroaches surviving anything. I think long after the cockroaches would be killed,
25 we'd still have dried tardigrades that could be rehydrated."

How is this hardy creature capable of such feats?

One reason is that tardigrades, or "water bears" as they are occasionally called, are among only a few species
30 capable of reversibly suspending their metabolism in order to achieve a state of cryptobiosis—a state in which all metabolic processes in an organism come to a halt, prohibiting it from reproducing, developing or repairing itself. In such a state, an organism is able to sustain itself
35 through adverse environmental conditions that might ordinarily be fatal to it.

Tardigrades living in ordinary, terrestrial environments require a sheath of water on their bodies in order to perform standard life activities. But when
40 faced with adverse conditions, they enter cryptobiosis. In such a state, the tardigrade's metabolism decreases to 0.1% of its normal level, and its water content can

drop to 1% of its normal level. This process is not a simple one. At the molecular level, in a complex system,
45 many different components must work together as "bioprotectants" to guard the most important molecules within the cell.

There are various types of cryptobiosis, of which anhydrobiosis is the most studied form. It derives from
50 the Greek word for "life without water" and is used to describe organisms in a dry state of desiccation. The four other types are anoxybiosis, lacking oxygen; chemobiosis, a response to toxins; cryobiosis, a reaction to low temperature (or freezing); and osmobiosis, a response to
55 increased solute concentration. While various organisms are capable of one or several of these actions, tardigrades are unique in that they can undergo all five types of cryptobiosis.

In 2007 tardigrades became the first known animal
60 to survive in space after dehydrated tardigrades were carried into orbit on the FOTON-M3 mission. For ten days, the tardigrades were exposed to the oxygen vacuum of space; they also endured sub-freezing temperatures and strong solar winds. When the mission returned to
65 earth, the discovery was stunning—following a mere 30 minutes of rehydration, over 68% of the sample was revived, although few of them went on to produce viable embryos.

Only a few years later, a group of Italian scientists
70 returned to space with the critters via the final flight of space shuttle Endeavour with the goal of studying how the "hardiest animal on Planet Earth" is able to survive away from it. One of these projects, the Tardkiss experiment, exposed tardigrades to various levels of
75 radiation. The hope is that the Tardkiss study might help researchers create techniques to protect other organisms, not just micro ones, from extreme conditions found in space—perhaps, eventually, even human beings.

A reasonable prediction is that tardigrades will
80 affirm their status as one of our planet's hardiest living creatures. It is plausible that the Tardkiss experiment along with the other studies being conducted on the mission will result in the kind of scientific discovery that reveals unimagined possibilities for our species
85 and changes our planet. For now, we will have to wait and see. Who knows? Perhaps tardigrades hold the key to unlocking further exploration not only of the solar system, but of the deepest oceans.

21. The passage states that when entering a state of cryptobiosis, an animal's metabolism:

    A. accelerates.
    B. essentially stops.
    C. is repaired.
    D. is sustained.

22. What is the author's attitude toward the outcome of the "mission" (line 64)?

    F. The discovery was extremely disappointing, because most of the tardigrades had lost the ability to reproduce.
    G. The discovery was simultaneously exciting and disappointing, since the tardigrades had survived but had lost the ability to produce viable embryos.
    H. The discovery was exciting, because the tardigrades had survived while other species on the mission had not.
    J. The discovery was exciting, because tardigrades had done something no other animal had done before.

23. It can be best inferred from the passage that:

    A. today's tardigrades are different from the tardigrades that lived a long time ago.
    B. tardigrades would be able to thrive in outer space if brought there in large numbers.
    C. tardigrades spend much of their life in a state of cryptobiosis.
    D. tardigrades are genetically similar to bears.

24. The author states that one reason tardigrades are particularly hardy is that:

    F. they have lived in outer space for several centuries.
    G. they are capable of undergoing cryptobiosis.
    H. they do not need water to survive.
    J. they come from freshwater environments.

25. According to the passage, cryptobiosis:

    A. always involves the ability to live in a nearly oxygenless state.
    B. is complex because many molecular components must work together to guard specific molecules.
    C. is unique to tardigrades among terrestrial species.
    D. is required for animals to transition from freshwater to other environments.

26. According to the passage, researchers brought tardigrades to space a second time because:

    F. they wanted to see if tardigrades could produce viable embryos in space.
    G. they needed to replicate the results of the first study to prove its statistical significance.
    H. they wanted to learn from the tardigrades' ability to survive.
    J. they wanted to model how tardigrades would survive in the deepest oceans.

27. In the context of the passage as a whole, it is most reasonable to infer that that phrase "dehydrated tardigrades" (line 60), most likely refers specifically to:

    A. tardigrades in a state of cryptobiosis.
    B. tardigrades lacking oxygen.
    C. tardigrades that had been subjected to low temperatures.
    D. tardigrades that were near death.

28. The main purpose of the eighth and ninth paragraphs (lines 59–78) is:

    F. to introduce the idea of using tardigrades to explore the ocean.
    G. to prove that tardigrades are the key to future space travel.
    H. to support the thesis that tardigrades are among the hardiest creatures on earth.
    J. to introduce a counter-argument to the author's thesis.

29. What does the author suggest might be true of tardigrades?

    A. They no longer live in freshwater environments.
    B. They are significantly less hardy than cockroaches.
    C. They can withstand temperatures significantly below absolute zero.
    D. They have survived in ocean trenches.

30. According to the passage, tardigrades are different than humans in that:

    F. tardigrades are capable of withstanding significantly more radiation than humans are.
    G. tardigrades have various metabolic levels, while humans do not.
    H. tardigrades are not capable of movement, while humans are.
    J. tardigrades can live in the Himalayas, while humans cannot.

MANHATTAN
PREP   885

PASSAGE 4

NATURAL SCIENCE: This passage is adapted from a report on current developments in synthetic polymers, which are large molecules made by chemists out of smaller repeating units.

Macromolecules are large molecules made up of smaller ones. Polymers, both natural and synthetic, are one example of macromolecules commonly used because their traits differ from the traits of their smaller
5 component parts, called monomers. Monomers are normally identical or at least similar to one another. The unique properties of a polymer make it ideal for a variety of applications.

One type of synthetic polymer is known as a
10 thermoset polymer. These plastics are created as a liquid, poured into the desired form, and "cured." Curing is accomplished by heating the material or starting a chemical reaction. Through curing, the thermoset polymer is permanently set in position; it is unchangeable even if
15 heated again. The result is a very strong plastic perfect to use at high temperatures. Unfortunately, they also tend to be non-recyclable and very brittle.

Conversely, thermoplastic polymers are adaptable. Up to a certain temperature they are solid, but become
20 malleable past that temperature. Thermoplastic polymers are perfect for short-term applications and are easily recycled into a new form at a higher temperature. The reason for this stark difference in properties is that thermoset polymers are three-dimensional materials
25 with units that are chemically bound. Thermoplastic polymers are two-dimensional, and the sheets of material only associate with one another through intermolecular forces. Intermolecular forces can be easily broken with heating, whereas a chemical bond will require extreme
30 conditions to change. Despite the differences between synthetic polymers, they share certain limitations.

Naturally occurring polymers have properties that scientists have not been able to replicate. DNA and RNA are two well-known natural polymers. Even simple
35 natural polymers are part of our everyday life. Keratin is a protein that polymerizes to form the key structural component of hair, skin, and nails.

One of the biggest differences between natural and artificial polymers is that natural ones have the ability
40 to self-heal under certain conditions. A cut on the skin is not irreversible. DNA is damaged and repaired on an almost constant basis. Yet when a piece of plastic is broken, it cannot fix itself.

In the past, scientists have been able to provoke
45 a healing response in synthetic polymers through external stimulation. Generally, heat or light is required. Additionally, environmental conditions have to be precisely met. A thermoset polymer would require far too much energy to self-heal. Unfortunately, thermoset
50 polymers, because of their rigidity, are also the most brittle and so most prone to cracking.

To overcome these obstacles, scientists have developed a self-repair strategy using microcapsules. Each microcapsule is filled with monomers and added to a
55 polymer. The microcapsules are not part of the polymer framework, but are positioned throughout. When a polymer cracks, any microcapsules nearby will break open. The monomers inside the microcapsules will flow into the crack and polymerize. As they do so, the two
60 sides of the crack will be re-bind together, creating a "healed" polymer.

This strategy faces many challenges. The polymerization reaction is often carried out in high heat. In order for a self-healing polymer to be viable, the monomers would
65 have to react at room temperature. They would additionally have to be stable and unreactive before the appropriate time. The microcapsules themselves would also have to be stable for a long period, only responding after a crack had occurred. Moreover, in self-healing polymers, the number
70 of monomers used would be determined by the number of ruptured microcapsules. Controlling the number of ruptured microcapsules is impossible. Therefore, the reaction must continue to completion regardless of the quantities of materials available.

75 Because of these difficulties, success until recently has been limited to small ruptures in the polymer framework. However, a new design has shown promise. A system of capillaries can theoretically repair holes of up to 3 cm in width. Additional monomers will be delivered
80 to the breakage site as needed through the capillaries. The system works like the arteries within the circulatory system, delivering material where it is most needed. Though further study and research is necessary, this breakthrough may provide the groundwork needed to
85 manufacture fully self-healing polymers.

31. Which of the following is a characteristic of a thermoplastic, but not thermoset, polymer?

  A. Stability at high temperatures
  B. Comprised of monomers
  C. Ability to self-heal
  D. Easy recyclability at high temperatures

32. According to the passage, what is one significant difference between natural and synthetic polymers until recently?

  F. Synthetic polymers are made of closely bound monomers; natural ones are not.
  G. Natural polymers are adaptable; synthetic polymers are not.
  H. Natural polymers can self-heal; synthetic polymers cannot.
  J. Synthetic polymers are part of our everyday life; natural polymers are not.

33. Each of the following is named as a difficulty of creating self-healing polymers EXCEPT that:

  A. self-healing reactions must be carried out in high heat.
  B. microcapsules will have to be stable for long periods.
  C. monomers will have to be stable within the microcapsule.
  D. the reaction must progress without control over exact quantities.

34. The passage implies which of the following?

  F. Self-healing reactions have not yet been accomplished.
  G. Self-healing reactions of small ruptures have already been accomplished.
  H. Self-healing reactions of large ruptures will soon be accomplished.
  J. Self-healing reactions of small ruptures will soon be accomplished.

35. What does the author mean by "curing" (line 11)?

  A. Healing cracks
  B. Heating polymers
  C. Setting permanently
  D. Polymerizing monomers

36. Based on information given in the passage, which of the following would be most analogous to a polymer?

  F. A brick wall with identical bricks cemented into position
  G. A pile of bricks that are not held in place
  H. A wall that contains both wood and bricks cemented into specific positions
  J. A window that is framed with bricks

37. What is the purpose of the microcapsules in the self-healing process?

  A. To remove the cause of damage
  B. To insert additional monomers
  C. To prevent cracking
  D. To add strength in advance of ruptures

38. According to the passage, thermoset polymers are:

  F. natural polymers.
  G. a newly created set of polymers.
  H. unsuited to everyday use.
  J. stable at high temperatures.

39. Keratin, as described in the passage, is most likely which of the following?

  A. A monomer
  B. A polymer
  C. A component of DNA
  D. A component of RNA

40. The author's main point is that:

  F. polymers will soon replace metals for most tasks.
  G. self-healing polymers are one of the most important breakthroughs in recent science.
  H. despite difficulties in creating a synthetic self-healing polymer, scientists have made significant progress.
  J. microcapsules are an important part of creating self-healing polymers.

PASSAGE 5

NATURAL SCIENCE: This passage is adapted from an article about the magnetic field of the Earth.

The Earth's magnetic field is an invisible force that affects many aspects of the world we live in. Migratory animals, such as birds, use the magnetic field to guide their trajectory. Without it, they would likely be unable
5 to return to the same area each season. Humans similarly benefit from the effects of the magnetic field. For example, the sun's radiation is severe enough to cause significant damage to humans. However, the combination of the filtering effects of the atmosphere and the protective
10 barrier from the magnetic field enable us to safely work and live under the sun. This powerful natural force has gradually revealed a surprisingly complex history with not entirely reassuring implications for the future.

How did this magnetic field originate? It is unclear,
15 but the prominent theory is called the dynamo effect. The dynamo effect holds that the iron core in the center of the Earth generates the field. Heat from the radioactive decay forces the outermost part of the Earth's iron core to move. The iron is a conductive material and
20 its movement generates an electric current that interacts with magnetic forces, which creates a self-sustaining magnetic field.

Other forces also significantly influence the Earth's magnetic field. For example, Venus has an iron core
25 similar to that of Earth. If the core were the sole source of the magnetic field, Venus should experience similar magnetic effects. However, there is no magnetic field surrounding Venus. It is likely that the planet's rotation affects the field generation. Earth rotates on its axis once
30 every 24 hours, while Venus completes a rotation only every 116 Earth days.

If Earth's magnetic field were stable, it would be an interesting geological find, but would have relatively little immediate impact. Studies of iron deposits in rocks,
35 however, indicate that the field has undergone significant and ongoing changes. Iron is a magnetic substance, so it will align with nearby magnetic fields. This effect can be seen on a small scale by watching iron filings attracted to a simple magnet. On a larger scale, iron is present
40 in volcanic lava. When the lava is liquefied, the iron is free to move and orient in a natural position. After the lava hardens, the iron particles are unable to move. A lava rock that solidified at a particular point in time will therefore have iron particles oriented in the direction of
45 magnetic north at that time.

By studying lava rocks from various periods, scientists have determined that magnetic north has moved. Over the course of thousands of years, magnetic north shifted not only around the north pole, but also
50 around the south pole: the field has been shown to completely reverse itself. Thus while today our compass needles point toward the north pole, several thousand years ago, they would have been drawn south.

It was assumed that shifting the Earth's magnetic
55 field from one pole to another took thousands of years. Since we have been observing the field, however, there has been substantial movement from the geographic North Pole. Magnetic North is slowly drifting towards Siberia at an increasingly rapid pace. Since 1831, magnetic north
60 has moved 600 miles. Interestingly, the magnetic field is also significantly weakening. It is approximately 15% weaker than it was 200 years ago. This rapid movement combined with the reduced strength is forcing scientists to reevaluate their original timeline. Instead of several
65 thousand years, it is entirely possible that magnetic north can switch poles in only a few hundred years. Some scientists believe it can reverse in as few as 75 years.

If this is the case, magnetic north may move to the geographic south pole in the very near future.
70 This switch could have devastating effects on our way of life. Electrical grids use the Earth's magnetic field to function, and could become inoperable as the field weakens. The field is likely to continue to weaken until it reverses completely, and remain weak for some time
75 after. Through this entire period, our electrical systems would be at risk.

More disturbingly, our health could be directly affected. Because the magnetic field protects us from radiation, a weaker magnetic field creates more exposure
80 risk. Cancer and mutations, two results of increased radiation, are likely to rise. However, there is no evidence that any mass extinctions or cataclysmic events occurred during past field reversals. The true extent of the damage cannot yet be known.

MANHATTAN
PREP

41. According to the passage, the author expresses which of the following attitudes about the potential effects of a global magnetic field reversal?

   A. Skepticism
   B. Concern
   C. Hope
   D. Relief

42. It can be inferred from the passage that iron can be used to analyze the Earth's magnetic field because:

   F. iron is a magnetic substance.
   G. iron is the primary component of volcanic lava.
   H. iron is found only in certain places throughout the world.
   J. iron is relatively difficult to extract from solidified lava.

43. As described in the passage, the dynamo effect is:

   A. an accepted fact.
   B. a theory that is unlikely to be accepted.
   C. a mistaken conception scientists used to have.
   D. a theory that has yet to be proven.

44. Each of the following is identified as being affected by the Earth's magnetic field EXCEPT:

   F. cancer rates.
   G. migratory patterns of birds.
   H. volcanic eruptions.
   J. electrical grids.

45. According to the dynamo effect (lines 14–22), a critical component in generating the Earth's magnetic field is:

   A. radioactive decay.
   B. the rotation of the Earth.
   C. volcanic activity.
   D. the periodic reversal of magnetic north.

46. According to lines 24–31, if Venus had a magnetic field similar to Earth's, scientists would expect to observe:

   F. higher iron content in Venus's core.
   G. faster movement within Venus's core.
   H. additional radioactive decay on Venus.
   J. faster rotation on Venus's axis.

47. The sixth paragraph (lines 54–67) supports the general hypothesis that:

   A. the Earth's magnetic field is produced via the dynamo effect.
   B. a weak magnetic field could have devastating effects on our way of life.
   C. a reversal of the Earth's magnetic poles is possible in the near future.
   D. magnetic north is not where scientists would expect it to be.

48. Which of the following, if true, would most WEAKEN the idea that iron can be used to determine the magnetic field orientation at different historical times?

   F. Nickel, a magnetic metal, present in liquefied lava rocks orients in the same direction as iron does from the same period.
   G. Cobalt, a magnetic metal, present in liquefied lava rocks orients in a different direction than iron does from the same period.
   H. Magnesium, a nonmagnetic metal, present in liquefied lava rocks orients in the same direction as iron does from the same period.
   J. Aluminum, a nonmagnetic metal, present in liquefied lava rocks orients in a different direction than iron does from the same period.

49. Which of the following is a hypothesis that, according to the passage, was once believed by scientists but has now been cast into question?

   A. The Earth's magnetic field is a stable phenomenon.
   B. Venus has an Earth-like magnetic field.
   C. The movement of the Earth's iron core contributes to the Earth's magnetic field.
   D. The reversal of Earth's magnetic field takes thousands of years.

50. The main purpose of the passage is to:

   F. inform the public about an impending disaster.
   G. explain a natural phenomenon and its potential effects.
   H. argue that the dynamo effect is the most likely source of the Earth's magnetic field.
   J. discuss the importance of iron in scientific study.

MANHATTAN
PREF

PASSAGE 6

NATURAL SCIENCE: This passage is adapted from a report on infectious diseases around the world.

As the world's leading cause of infectious blindness, trachoma is an ongoing problem in 53 countries. Trachoma is caused by a bacterial infection that, over time, scars the upper eyelid. The scarring occurs when the eyelid turns
5 inward and scratches the eye. This condition is known as entropion. When this occurs, the eyelashes rub against the eye, causing irritation and discomfort. Over time, scarring causes visual impairment and blindness.

Despite its severe effects, trachoma is an easily
10 treatable disease when caught in its early stages. Often, a simple course of antibiotics will result in a complete cure with no long-term effects. Even in advanced stages, trachoma patients may experience relief with surgery. Entropion can be reversed through surgery on the eyelid.
15 This surgery limits and even stops any further damage to the eye and the sufferer's vision. Unfortunately, the visual impairment or blindness caused by entropion, if left uncorrected, is often irreversible.

The devastating effects of long-term untreated
20 exposure combined with the trachoma's inherent treatability have provoked a substantial response. The World Health Organization and other global health organizations have stepped in to educate and treat the affected population. The incidence of trachoma has been
25 significantly reduced by creating a four-part strategy referred to as SAFE: surgery, antibiotics, facial cleanliness, and environmental improvement. With the goal of eliminating trachoma by 2020, health organizations have seen a reduction from 84 million cases in 2003 to
30 21.4 million cases in 2012. However, not all aspects of the SAFE strategy are able to be effectively examined.

The use of antibiotics and surgery are easily monitored. Both require a doctor's care, so there is substantial information regarding the use and
35 effectiveness of antibiotics and treatment. However, prevention is much more difficult to observe. Trachoma is spread through physical contact. The irritation of the eye causes a discharge, which is transferred to the hand whenever the sufferer touches his or her eyes. If there
40 is insufficient hand and face washing, the discharge is spread from the hand to objects or other people. This contact spreads the bacteria. Prevention is difficult to evaluate because only those who have caught the bacteria are likely to seek medical attention.

45 The best preventative measures used are the second half of SAFE: facial cleanliness (F) and environmental improvement (E). Unfortunately, the studies on F and E have been inconsistent and imprecise. There is disagreement about the standards for measuring facial
50 cleanliness. For example, how important is it to wash ones face twice a day instead of just once a day? Is soap an essential component? Is towel sharing a source of contagion rather than cleaning? How do you define easy access to clean water? How do you define clean water?

55 To answer these questions, a recent study has examined the literature on the effectiveness and prevalence of the F and E. Finally, there are some definitive answers on the relationship between living conditions and the occurrence of trachoma. Previously, anecdotal evidence
60 suggested that improved *access* to water resulted in a lower occurrence of trachoma. However, this study found no evidence of that relationship. Instead, improved *quality* of water, especially water delivered through pipes rather than wells, correlated with a lower occurrence of the disease.

65 More important is the proportion of water devoted to personal hygiene. Those who allocate a larger portion of their household water to cleanliness have significantly lower levels of trachoma. This discovery correlates well with the evidence that facial cleaning is crucial. Those
70 who washed their face at least once a day reduced their likelihood of contracting trachoma. The risk was reduced even further when the facial cleaning was with soap. Surprisingly, the act of sharing a towel within a household, long believed to be a key source of trachoma
75 spread, did not seem to have any effect.

Unfortunately, this study has not had an immediate impact. Current education in trachoma prevention emphasizes facial washing and discontinued towel sharing. It does not focus on using soap during washings,
80 nor on water quality. Moreover, the current emphasis on increased access to water may be misplaced. High quality water is beneficial, yet access to nearby water does not seem to be statistically significant. Further studies are needed to assess definitively the importance of a nearby
85 water source.

While these findings represent significant progress in scientific understanding of trachoma and preventative measures, there is still a substantial gap between the current state and the goal of complete eradication of trachoma by
90 2020. Education and further study are both needed.

51. According to the passage, which of the following is an effective method for treating trachoma?

   A. Antibiotics
   B. Facial washing with soap
   C. Increased access to water
   D. Using water delivered through pipes rather than wells

52. Each of the following is a result of uncorrected entropion EXCEPT:

   F. visual impairment.
   G. scarring on the eye.
   H. irritation.
   J. bacterial infection.

53. According to the passage, why is it easier to monitor antibiotics and surgery than prevention?

   A. More studies have been done that include antibiotics and surgery.
   B. It is not clear which preventive measures work.
   C. Those who have prevented infection are unlikely to inform a doctor.
   D. There is no agreed upon set of standards for nearby water.

54. The author implies that a mistaken belief scientists held was that:

   F. trachoma could be eliminated by 2020.
   G. towel-sharing within a household increases the spread of trachoma.
   H. trachoma is caused by entropion.
   J. clean water is not a factor in the spread of trachoma.

55. What is the purpose of the second-to-last paragraph (lines 76–85)?

   A. To explain the relevance of this study
   B. To elaborate on the dangers of trachoma
   C. To emphasize the importance of soap
   D. To express concern about the incomplete studies on trachoma

56. The author of the passage is most likely to agree with which of the following?

   F. Trachoma is a devastating and frequently fatal disease.
   G. Trachoma is likely to be eliminated by 2020.
   H. Trachoma is not likely to be eliminated by 2020.
   J. It is possible, if not always simple, to prevent trachoma.

57. According to the passage, the spread of trachoma is caused by:

   A. proximity to an infected person.
   B. direct contact with the bacteria.
   C. contact with unclean animals.
   D. lack of nearby water sources.

58. As explained in the passage, trachoma is best described as:

   F. an infection spread by means other than physical contact.
   G. an infection that has largely been ignored worldwide.
   H. a clearly treatable infection.
   J. an unfortunately incurable infection.

59. The author would expect which of the following to result in a decrease in the incidence of trachoma?

   A. Corrections to the education about trachoma spread
   B. Increased access to antibiotics
   C. More public awareness of the disease
   D. Additional help from global health organizations

60. According to the passage, how is water most clearly related to the spread of trachoma?

   F. Increased access to water decreases the occurrence of trachoma.
   G. Increased percent of household water allocated to cleanliness decreases the occurrence of trachoma.
   H. Increased distance from water increases the occurrence of trachoma.
   J. Increased access to wells increases the occurrence of trachoma.

20

PASSAGE 7

NATURAL SCIENCE: This passage is adapted from an article titled "Protein Nanomachines" by M. Strong.

In 1959, Richard Feynman, a noted physicist, delivered what many now consider the first lecture on nanotechnology. This lecture prompted intense discussion about the possibilities of manipulating materials at the molecular level. At the time of his presentation, the manipulation of single molecules and single atoms seemed improbable. In fact, many scientists considered it impossible. Despite this skepticism, Feynman challenged his audience to consider a new field of physics. He envisioned a world in which individual molecules and atoms could be manipulated and controlled.

Feynman encouraged his listeners to reinterpret what they already knew. He pointed out that examples of highly successful "machines" at a tiny scale already existed. He emphasized the inherently dynamic properties of biological cells. Feynman dramatically noted that although cells are "very tiny," they are "very active. They manufacture various substances. They walk around. They wiggle. They do all kinds of wonderful things on a very small scale." Of course, many of the "wonderful things" that he was referring to are a result of the activities of proteins and protein complexes within each cell. By studying the mechanisms of protein interaction, Feynman predicted the development of synthetic nanostructures.

The field of nanotechnology has indeed emerged and blossomed since Feynman's 1959 lecture. Scientists from many disciplines are now taking a careful look at biological macromolecules that power cells. These "machines," such as DNA and proteins, are nanoscale size. They range in width from a few nanometers (nm) to over 20 nm. Over millions of years of evolution, they have been carefully refined into efficient factories. By modeling our nanoconstruction on these naturally occurring structures, we can take advantage of the techniques nature has perfected.

Protein pathways are particularly interesting. They are analogous to nanoscale "assembly lines." Protein pathways involve a series of proteins that act in sequential order to create a particular product or perform a particular function. These pathways provide cellular energy and are responsible for nearly all aspects of life. While these protein-based "assembly lines" are commonplace within biological cells, we have yet to synthesize them. This prompts two interesting questions with respect to the field of nanotechnology. First, can we mimic these multicomponent protein-based "assembly lines" on fabricated surfaces? Second, can we meet the challenge of tailoring these "nanoscale assembly lines" to perform new and unique tasks?

The first step in the creation of nanoscale protein machines is positioning individual proteins at the nanoscale level. Recently, there has been some success in using the pattern of DNA nanogrids. DNA strands form a double helix of protein interactions. The rigid structure enables specific orientation and position of interacting complexes. The structure forms a line of proteins that can be manipulated, changed, and used in reactions. The definitive positioning provides a model that makes it possible not only to place specific proteins, but also to alter them in controlled and systematic ways.

Already, this DNA nanogrid has been used to create a system of proteins. Under strictly controlled conditions, biotin proteins were created and held along the DNA nanogrid precisely 19 nm apart from each other. Upon that scaffold, researchers added streptavidin, a protein that has a strong binding affinity for biotin. The scaffold grew to two dimensions, with one layer of biotin and a second of streptavidin. The resulting array represents the first periodic, self-assembled DNA lattice in which individual protein molecules are precisely positioned into a periodic array with nanometer dimensions.

This work has opened up exciting new avenues in the field of nanotechnology. Theoretically, we can construct dynamic protein-based assemblies using DNA systems. Currently, we can only modify existing structures. Yet it is foreseeable that variations of these same DNA scaffolds will eventually be used for the design and construction of more complex protein-based assemblies. One day, we may have nanoscale assembly lines or periodic arrays of dynamic motor proteins. This work is important because it demonstrates not only that it is possible to create uniform arrays of proteins using biological scaffolds, but also emphasizes the important role that molecular biology will undoubtedly play as the field of nanotechnology matures.

As the field of nanotechnology continues to evolve, it is likely that we will see many more nanotechnology applications utilizing biological macromolecules. Toward the end of Richard Feynman's 1959 lecture, he quipped, "What are the possibilities of small but movable machines? They may or may not be useful, but they surely would be fun to make."

61. The main purpose of this passage is to:

   A. prove the idea that nanotechnology is possible.
   B. explain ways in which molecular biology could further nanotechnological development.
   C. discuss the ways in which a nanogrid involving biotin will further this field of study.
   D. question the existing methods of developing nanotechnology.

62. It can be inferred from the passage that before Richard Feynman's 1959 lecture:

   F. there had been little or no successful work on the development of synthetic nanostructures.
   G. molecular "assembly lines" did not yet exist.
   H. most scientists held Feynman's ideas in contempt.
   J. biological cells were not used to inspire any scientific design.

63. According to the passage, each of the following is a way in which biological systems have impacted nanotechnology EXCEPT by:

   A. providing a model for nanoconstruction.
   B. inspiring the attempt to create multicomponent systems on fabricated surfaces.
   C. enabling scientists to create a DNA-based nanogrid.
   D. suggesting the ability to change the function of a single protein.

64. The "DNA lattice" mentioned in line 69 is a significant creation because it:

   F. allows "assembly line" functionality at the nanoscale.
   G. associates biotin and streptavidin.
   H. is the first lattice of this type synthetically created on such a small scale.
   J. separated biotin proteins by precisely 19 nm.

65. The purpose of the second-to-last paragraph (lines 72–85) is to:

   A. explain the current status of nanotechnology research.
   B. discuss the limitations of nanotechnology research.
   C. predict the future developments likely to occur in nanotechnology.
   D. crystallize Richard Feynman's vision of nanotechnology.

66. According to the passage, an example of a biological macromolecule is a:

   F. nanoscale assembly line.
   G. protein.
   H. biotin-streptavidin lattice.
   J. cell.

67. Which of the following would be an example of a protein pathway as mentioned in line 36?

   A. Five different proteins, working sequentially, generate cellular energy.
   B. A protein, as it breaks down, generates cellular energy.
   C. Five proteins, working simultaneously, generate cellular energy.
   D. A single protein works to generate cellular energy.

68. According to the passage, Richard Feynman would be most likely to agree with the idea that:

   F. the manipulation of single atoms and molecules is improbable.
   G. nanotechnology is certain to be useful.
   H. cells have already perfected nanotechnology.
   J. there are natural examples of small-scale machines.

69. When comparing protein pathways to assembly lines, the author is most nearly illustrating his point that:

   A. nanotechnology is an inevitable scientific development.
   B. small but movable machines would be fun to make.
   C. biological macromolecules have been perfected over years of evolution.
   D. natural systems in which several nanoscale molecules work together to achieve a goal are already in existence.

70. According to the passage, a goal that scientists have not yet achieved but that they could, in theory, achieve one day is to:

   F. create dynamic protein-based assembly systems.
   G. create a self-assembled DNA lattice.
   H. tailor nanoscale assembly lines to provide cellular energy.
   J. manipulate and control individual atoms and molecules.

20

PASSAGE 8

NATURAL SCIENCE: This passage is adapted from Feinberg JA, Newman CE, Watkins-Colwell GJ, Schlesinger MD, Zarate B, et al. (2014) "Cryptic Diversity in Metropolis: Confirmation of a New Leopard Frog Species from New York City and Surrounding Atlantic Coast Regions."

Considerable focus has been targeted on identifying and cataloging new animal species over the past few decades. Because amphibians in particular are facing severe global declines and extinctions caused by threats
5 such as habitat destruction, research projects concerning these animals carry added urgency. Without proper identification, conservation efforts are unlikely to be successful. Most commonly, new undocumented species have been discovered in tropical areas. In contrast, far
10 less attention or discovery has been associated with well-documented regions. Urban areas tend to produce new species only rarely. For anurans, an order of amphibians that includes frogs and toads, this discovery pattern is particularly evident. Only two previously undetected
15 species of anurans have been reported from the continental United States and Canada since 1986. Anuran species are more commonly discovered in Mexico and southern areas of the US that are not well documented.

Unfortunately, identification of new species can
20 be complicated by the presence of cryptic species. A cryptic species is a species that is mistakenly grouped with a similar one. The species tend to look and behave similarly, and even have overlapping habitats. When a cryptic species is classified as a similar species,
25 known as a congener, the needs of both species can be misunderstood. Not only can conservation efforts be misdirected, but also it may be unclear that such efforts are even needed. A cryptic species discovery therefore can have important implications despite its difficulty. Both
30 the new species and congeners will be affected. Further, cryptic species can be found in unexpected locales and reflect surprisingly high levels of diversity.

Left undetected, cryptic species may remain well-concealed among other species. The grouped species may
35 seem common or widespread. However, the individual congeners could be range-restricted, rare, or even extinct. The most recently discovered anuran in the US was a cryptic species, the Atlantic Coast leopard frog. It was first identified in the New York City region in 2012. The
40 Atlantic Coast leopard frog is similar to the Southern and Northern leopard frogs, and has been mistakenly associated with both. The three congeners, however, are distinct from each other. The Atlantic Coast leopard frog call is acoustically unique. It also has notably different
45 genetics, habitat, and geographic distribution. Finally, it is visually distinct. In theory, its identification should have been straightforward. Yet it remained concealed until recently.

The Atlantic Coast leopard frog occupies parts
50 of the lower Northeast and mid-Atlantic US. It is primarily found within the densely populated and heavily industrialized Interstate-95 corridor. This is one of the largest human population centers on earth. The long-term concealment of a novel anuran here is both
55 surprising and significant. It raises potentially important conservation concerns. Amphibians can be sensitive to disease, contaminants, and environmental changes. Leopard frogs in particular have been subject to enigmatic declines and disappearances. Without an understanding
60 of the cause of the declines, it is unlikely we can take appropriate steps to halt or slow their occurrence. Cryptic species misclassified as their congeners make targeted conservation nearly impossible.

That a cryptic species was identified in the New
65 York City region is noteworthy. It provides an example of a new species discovery from one of the most developed, heavily settled, and well-inventoried places on earth. Novel and undescribed vertebrate species are unexpected here and thus carry considerable interest and value. The
70 last amphibian discovered in either New York or New England was the Fowler's toad, found in 1882. New York is a particularly rare place to find amphibians. Only seven have ever been described from that state. Before this discovery, the most recent amphibian discovered
75 there was the northern cricket frog in 1854.

Several other points warrant consideration. The discovery of the Atlantic Coast leopard frog demonstrates that human knowledge of the natural world remains incomplete even in the best-known locales. Second,
80 although new frog discoveries are generally uncommon north of Mexico, they do still occur periodically. Third, the two most recent examples are both cryptic species. Taken together, these points suggest that occasional future discoveries from well-cataloged areas
85 may continue, but probably in the form of additional cryptic species. Moreover, a single trait such as a unique vocalization pattern may play a critical role in a species discovery.

The Atlantic Coast leopard frog is a relatively
90 large, conspicuous species, and acoustically distinct

from its congeners. That it remained ill-defined and poorly documented within one of the largest population centers on earth is rather remarkable. Repeated acoustic misidentification may have played a role. Many colleagues
95 with whom we communicated recalled unusual calls from frog populations classified as Northern or Southern leopard frogs. Some attributed these calls to the unusual habitat. Others presumed the call variation was a new type of call within the species. None discovered the
100 presence of a new species. Given these examples and the species-specific nature of frog calls, we encourage greater scrutiny and examination of unexpected calls. This is especially vital when the calls are encountered and heard consistently across entire populations or regions. Such
105 efforts may reveal additional diversity.

71. It can be inferred from the passage that Fowler's toad was discovered

   A. by accident.
   B. in New York.
   C. in New England, but not in New York.
   D. the same way the Atlantic Coast leopard frog was.

72. According to the author, discovering cryptic species is important because it:

   F. enables targeted conservation efforts.
   G. furthers medical knowledge.
   H. allows scientists to differentiate frog calls.
   J. conceals diversity among species.

73. Which of the following is identified as a truth about all leopard frogs?

   A. They are cryptic species.
   B. They have been subject to disappearances.
   C. They are primarily located in the Northeast and mid-Atlantic US.
   D. They have a large population.

74. The passage implies that a cryptic species could be misidentified as its congener because:

   F. it is acoustically distinct.
   G. it is an unknown species.
   H. it resides primarily in an urban area.
   J. the two have similar behavior and appearance.

75. All of the species mentioned in the passage can be classified as each of the following EXCEPT:

   A. frogs.
   B. anurans.
   C. amphibians.
   D. animals.

76. The purpose of the final paragraph (lines 89–105) is most clearly:

   F. to discredit colleagues who misidentified cryptic species.
   G. to explain the differences between the Atlantic Coast leopard frog and other frog species.
   H. to discuss how a cryptic species remained undetected and what that implies for future study.
   J. to explain why the location of discoveries is important.

77. According to the final paragraph, the author recommends which of the following specific courses of action regarding further study?

   A. Conservation efforts should be intensified.
   B. Anurans should be the focus of ongoing investigations.
   C. More urban areas should be searched for amphibian species.
   D. Greater examination of unexpected calls should be conducted.

78. The term "novel" (line 68) most nearly means:

   F. literary.
   G. new.
   H. unnecessary.
   J. invented.

79. The primary purpose of the second paragraph (lines 19–32) is most clearly:

   A. to discuss the importance of correctly identifying cryptic species.
   B. to define congener species.
   C. to explain how cryptic species can remain unidentified for long periods.
   D. to introduce the Atlantic Coast leopard frog and its importance.

80. The author discusses Northern and Southern leopard frogs most likely to:

   F. provide examples of other endangered frog species.
   G. explain what Atlantic Coast leopard frogs were misidentified as.
   H. discuss the most recently identified frog species in the area.
   J. introduce similarities between frog species.

PASSAGE 9

NATURAL SCIENCE: Passage A is adapted from a general article on black holes. Passage B is adapted from a report on the process of detecting black holes.

PASSAGE A

Black holes have long been the topic of scientific debate. They were once considered a myth, then a theory that could never be proven, but we now have located an enormous number of black holes. In fact, recent studies
5 have indicated a new black hole could be forming every day, if not more often.

Black holes are created by the death of particularly large stars. Our own sun is approximately 20 times too small to form a black hole. In all stars, there are
10 dueling forces. Large masses create strong gravity pulling matter toward the center of the mass. However, nuclear reactions that occur within the star—hydrogen fusion, for example—create a pressure that drives matter away from the star. In a healthy star, the equilibrium between these
15 two forces will remain stable for billions of years.

With age, the equilibrium of the star can shift. The reactions become less common as the materials for hydrogen fusion and other reactions are used up, and the pressure subsequently decreases. Though the
20 gravity does not increase in absolute value, the loss of the corresponding pressure makes the effects of gravity far more pronounced. As a result, the star sheds its outer layers and begins to collapse in upon its own core.

If the star is small enough, like our sun, electron
25 degeneracy will eventually stop the collapse. Electron degeneracy is the resistance that electrons have to occupying each other's space. Once the electrons within the star are essentially bumping up against each other, the resulting dead star is known as a white dwarf.

30 Larger stars cannot reach this equilibrium. The electrons are present and resisting one another, but not strongly enough to offset the massive amount of gravity large stars create. Yet not all large stars result in black holes.

When an incredibly massive star sheds its outer
35 layers, the process is stunning. The outer layers are rejected so forcefully that their light can overpower an entire galaxy. This outcome is known as a supernova. If enough matter is ejected that the remaining core is left with insufficient mass, electron degeneracy can stabilize
40 the core. However, if the core contains the mass at least 2.5 times greater than the mass of the Earth's sun, the

gravitational force is too strong to be overpowered. The core compacts infinitely, becoming a black hole.

PASSAGE B

A black hole is defined as an area of space where
45 the force of gravity is so strong that not even light can escape. Unlike stars, which are generally found through observation, black holes cannot be seen. In order for an object to be visible, it must reflect or emit light. Because black holes only absorb light, they are invisible.

50 Yet scientists have located a number of black holes. How? Their effects. Just as you cannot see the wind but can determine it is windy by looking at the leaves on the trees, scientists can infer the presence of a black hole by observing deformities in the surrounding space.

55 One method for finding a black hole is studying the movement of stars. A body in space will orbit a nearby, larger object because that larger object has more mass and therefore more gravity. Black holes, despite their relatively small size, are so dense that they have a
60 greater mass than any object around them. The smallest black holes are roughly the size of a single atom, yet have the mass of a large mountain. More common are stellar black holes, which may be as large as ten miles but have the mass of up to 20 suns.

65 Because black holes have such a great mass, stars in their vicinity will orbit around them, just as the Earth orbits around the sun. Analyzing the motion of the star in its orbit and other stars rotating around the black hole can prove not only where the black hole is, but also how
70 strong and massive it is.

The sheer number of black holes in the universe forces them to sometimes move close to one another. When this occurs, the huge gravitational forces of the black holes will interact, resulting in the emission of
75 high-energy light that can be observed.

Finally, black holes strongly attract all matter, not just massive objects like stars and other black holes. Planets, moons, stellar bodies, and gases will all be caught up in the black holes' immense pull. These
80 interactions would be difficult to see from a distance, but they aggregate. The trapped matter quickly accelerates around the black hole as it spirals toward the center. Just before the matter crosses the point of no return, it releases strong X-rays. Though not visible to the eye,
85 this radiation can be detected by NASA telescopes, giving scientists more information about the location and properties of black holes.

81. According to Passage A, what could prevent a black hole from occurring when a large star dies?

    A. The use of massive amounts of gravity
    B. The presence of dueling forces
    C. The creation of a white dwarf
    D. The ejection of enough matter to reduce the core's mass

82. The word "resistance," as used in line 26, most nearly means:

    F. refusal.
    G. confrontation.
    H. struggle.
    J. endurance.

83. According to Passage A, a supernova is most specifically characterized by:

    A. the collapse of a star's core prior to creating a black hole.
    B. the creation of a black hole.
    C. the emission of a star's outer layer in a burst of light.
    D. the swirling of gas around a black hole.

84. The main purpose of Passage B is most nearly to:

    F. determine the consequences of the presence of a black hole.
    G. strategize more effective means of finding black holes.
    H. explain how black holes are formed.
    J. elaborate on methods scientists use to detect black holes.

85. X-ray light that is used to find black holes is generated by:

    A. matter spiraling into a black hole.
    B. telescopes used to detect black holes.
    C. stars orbiting around black holes.
    D. the force of gravity emanating from black holes.

86. Black holes are difficult to detect because they:

    F. are so far from Earth.
    G. absorb light without emitting any.
    H. have a gravitational pull.
    J. are more massive than stars.

87. The difference between the two passages can best be explained in which of the following ways?

    A. One views black holes as a major celestial event; the other views them as a mere matter of scientific interest.
    B. One is concerned with the process of forming a black hole; the other is focused on how to find a black hole.
    C. Both passages have the same focus.
    D. One is concerned with how people have historically viewed a black hole; the other is focused on current accepted scientific fact.

88. Each passage contains support for which of the following ideas?

    F. Electron repulsion can act to prevent the formation of black holes.
    G. If black holes did not absorb light, they would be easier to detect.
    H. Intense gravity is a fundamental property of black holes.
    J. A more massive star is more likely to create a black hole.

89. Which of the following is discussed by Passage A, but not by Passage B?

    A. Methods for discovering black holes
    B. The number of black holes in existence
    C. The emission of X-rays from matter falling into black holes
    D. How scientists have historically viewed black holes

Answer Keys

Write in whether you got each problem right or wrong (or left it blank). If your answer was correct, put a 1 in every blank to the right of that problem. Sum up each column and compare your total to the total possible "Out Of" points in each column.

Passage 1

Problem	Correct Answer	Right/ Wrong/Blank	Main Ideas/ Author's Approach	Details	Relationships	Meanings of Words	Generalizations
1	D		—				
2	F					—	
3	C			—			
4	G		—				
5	B						—
6	F		—				
7	C				—		
8	H				—		
9	D		—				
10	J			—			
Total							
Out Of		10	4	2	2	1	1

Passage 2

Problem	Correct Answer	Right/ Wrong/Blank	Main Ideas/ Author's Approach	Details	Relationships	Meanings of Words	Generalizations
11	A			—			
12	H			—			
13	B			—			
14	J				—		
15	B			—			
16	H		—				
17	A				—		
18	J			—			
19	A		—				
20	G						—
Total							
Out Of		10	2	5	2	0	1

Passage 3

Problem	Correct Answer	Right/Wrong/Blank	Main Ideas/Author's Approach	Details	Relationships	Meanings of Words	Generalizations
21	B			—			
22	J					—	
23	A				—		
24	G			—			
25	B			—			
26	H			—			
27	A					—	
28	H						—
29	D			—			
30	F			—			
Total							
Out Of		10	0	6	1	2	1

Passage 4

Problem	Correct Answer	Right/Wrong/Blank	Main Ideas/Author's Approach	Details	Relationships	Meanings of Words	Generalizations
31	D				—		
32	H			—			
33	A			—			
34	G						—
35	C					—	
36	F					—	
37	B				—		
38	J			—			
39	A						—
40	H		—				
Total							
Out Of		10	1	3	2	2	2

Passage 5

Problem	Correct Answer	Right/ Wrong/Blank	Main Ideas/ Author's Approach	Details	Relationships	Meanings of Words	Generalizations
41	B		—				
42	F			—			
43	D					—	
44	H			—			
45	A			—			
46	J				—		
47	C						—
48	G						—
49	D			—			
50	G		—				
Total							
Out Of		10	2	4	1	1	2

Passage 6

Problem	Correct Answer	Right/ Wrong/Blank	Main Ideas/ Author's Approach	Details	Relationships	Meanings of Words	Generalizations
51	A			—			
52	J			—			
53	C				—		
54	G			—			
55	A		—				
56	J		—				
57	B			—			
58	H					—	
59	A		—				
60	G			—			
Total							
Out Of		10	3	5	1	1	0

Passage 7

Problem	Correct Answer	Right/Wrong/Blank	Main Ideas/Author's Approach	Details	Relationships	Meanings of Words	Generalizations
61	B		—				
62	F						—
63	D			—			
64	H					—	
65	C		—				
66	G			—			
67	A					—	
68	J						—
69	D				—		
70	F			—			
Total							
Out Of		10	2	3	1	2	2

Passage 8

Problem	Correct Answer	Right/Wrong/Blank	Main Ideas/Author's Approach	Details	Relationships	Meanings of Words	Generalizations
71	C				—		
72	F						—
73	B			—			
74	J				—		
75	A						—
76	H		—				
77	D			—			
78	G					—	
79	A		—				
80	G		—				
Total							
Out Of		10	3	2	2	1	2

MANHATTAN
PREP

Passage 9

Problem	Correct Answer	Right/ Wrong/Blank	Main Ideas/ Author's Approach	Details	Relationships	Meanings of Words	Generalizations
81	D						—
82	F					—	
83	C			—			
84	J		—				
85	A				—		
86	G			—			
87	B				—		
88	H						—
89	D			—			
Total							
Out Of		9	1	3	2	1	2

20

Natural Sciences Solutions

Passage 1 Solutions

1.   **(D)** Handedness cannot be explained by purely genetic or purely learned factors.

Author's Approach

The final paragraph discusses a *"combination of factors"* (line 84). The author explains that "there is certainly a genetic component" (lines 84–85), but concludes that "other factors must have been important" (lines 92–93). The author does not believe that all species of animals are right-handed, as in choice (A). She even provides an example of a left-handed species; orangutans (lines 39–40). While fine motor skills forced humans to increasingly favor using the right hand (lines 87–90), the fine motor skills did not create the preference alone, as choice (B) says. Choice (C) is directly contradicted in the passage by a variety of examples of animals other than humans that have brain specialization.

2.   **(F)** harmony.

Meaning of Words

Reread the entire sentence in lines 8–11: "Each hemisphere communicates with the other, and many tasks require the use of both hemispheres working in concert, but others are accomplished primarily by one hemisphere or the other." The sentence contrasts tasks that are accomplished primarily by one hemisphere with hemispheres working in concert. If the task is not accomplished primarily by one, it must be accomplished by both. "Concert" must therefore mean working together; "harmony" is a good synonym. This matches choice (F). "Discord," choice (G), is the opposite meaning. Choice (H), "musicality," is unrelated to the context of the passage. "Specialization," (J), does not imply the two sides are working together.

3.   **(C)** orangutans.

Details

Orangutans are named as an animal that tend to be left-handed (lines 39–40). Combine that point with lines 22–24, "Most humans openly prefer to use their left hemisphere in everyday activities. These people are in fact right-handed," (lines 22–24). And you can infer that an animal that is right-handed is likely to favor the left hemisphere of the brain for everyday activities. Choices (A), (B), and (D)—birds (line 78), humans (line 24), and toads (line 73)—all favor the right side of their bodies, so they are likely to favor the left hemisphere of their brains. Thus, (C) is correct.

4.   **(G)** the specialization of the hemispheres of the brain has a complex origin.

Main Idea

Throughout the passage, the author discusses the two brain hemispheres. The first three paragraphs talk about the hemispheres of the human brain. After that, the author talks about other animals and their clear preference for one hemisphere over the other for everyday activities. In the concluding paragraph, the author discusses the potential sources for brain hemisphere specialization. Choice (G) is therefore the best answer. Choice (F) mistakenly emphasizes handedness. Handedness is used to determine which hemisphere of the brain is used for everyday activities, but it is not the main point of the passage. The second-to-last paragraph (lines 70–79) is the best example that handedness is secondary. That paragraph discusses animals that cannot display handedness, but still display a preference for the left hemisphere. Choice (H) focuses exclusively on the ape family and does not take into account the importance of brain hemisphere specialization. Choice (J) is contradicted by the passage. Genetic factors certainly contribute to the specialization (lines 84–86).

5.　**(B)**　a 95% preference for right-handedness.

Generalizations

In lines 82–83, the author states that "no animal has shown as extreme a preference as humans." Therefore, no other species could have a stronger preference for being right-handed. In the third paragraph the author states, "About 90% of all humans are right-handed" (line 24). You can therefore infer that no species has shown a preference for right-handedness greater than about 90%. Therefore, choice (B) is correct.

Choice (A) is contradicted by the fact that orangutans are left handed (lines 39–40). Though choice (C) is never directly contradicted, it is impossible to infer. There is ongoing study on the preference for hemispheres among different animals. Similarly, choice (D) has no support in the passage.

6.　**(F)**　the specialization of the hemispheres of the brain is uniquely human.

Author's Approach

The author provides numerous examples of specialization of hemispheres of the brain occurring in animals other than human. Lines 72–75 tell you that fish, reptiles, and toads all have specialization. All other answer choices are points that the author likely agrees with. Since you are looking for what the author disagrees with, choice (F) is correct.

7.　**(C)**　Apes in the wild have no preference for either left- or right-side dominance.

Relationships (Cause–Effect)

The fourth paragraph (lines 36–51) discusses the different theories regarding the handedness of apes. The first part gives evidence as to why they are right- or left-handed, but in line 44, the idea that they may not be truly right- or left-handed is introduced. Instead, they may just be mimicking what they see in humans. The support for this theory is given in lines 48–51: "This theory is supported by the fact that when similar studies are conducted on apes in the wild, there seems to be no particular preference for left- or right-hand dominance." This language matches choice (C). Another tempting answer may be (D) because it deals with mimicry specifically. However, the fact that apes have the ability to mimic human sign language is not used as evidence that the apes are not right- or left-handed. Sign language is only discussed to illustrate that mimicry is possible in apes. The actual evidence that handedness is unconnected to brain hemispheres comes from the study of wild apes.

8.   **(H)** whether studies on wild apes were valid studies.

Relationships (Comparisons)

The two groups of scientists are compared in the fourth and fifth paragraphs (lines 36–60). The theory introduced in the fourth paragraph is that apes do not show a true preference for handedness because "when similar studies are conducted on apes in the wild, there seems to be no particular preference for left- or-right hand dominance" (lines 49–51). The disagreeing scientists are introduced in the following paragraph. They claim that the lack of preference "is a result of small sample sizes and inadequate observation" (lines 53–54). The disagreement is therefore whether studies on wild apes were valid, which is stated in choice (H).

9.   **(D)** to suggest that genetics play a role in the separation of the hemispheres of the brain.

Main Idea

The third paragraph talks about humans showing a preference for right-handedness even before birth. It ends with a conclusion, "Clearly, there is some kind of genetic predisposition involving the separation of the brain hemispheres of the brain" (lines 32–34). This matches choice (D). Choice (B) can be ruled out as too extreme to be true, because the left-hemisphere is not always preferred. Choices (A) and (C) may be factually true, but they are not the purpose of the paragraph.

10.   **(J)** An animal that has a damaged right hemisphere is unable to respond to an unexpected situation.

Details

All the answer choices discuss the effects of damage to one brain hemisphere or the other. The hypothesis about brain hemispheres is introduced in the seventh paragraph (lines 61–69). The left side controls simple and everyday tasks, while the right side controls unusual situations. Therefore, damage to the right side would be likely to make it difficult for an animal to respond in an unexpected situation. This matches choice (J).

Passage 2 Solutions

11.   **(A)** the difference between the moon's and the Earth's planes of revolution.

Details

The author cites many obstacles to predicting eclipses. However, the biggest one is discussed in the second-to-last paragraph. The author says that the previous "difficulties pale in comparison to the intricacies of the moons orbit" (lines 71–72). The paragraph goes on to specify that the difficulty is that the two planes of revolution differ. This matches choice (A).

12.   **(H)** the attitude scientists held at the time that such an invention was too difficult.

Details

Each of the three wrong answer choices can be found in the passage. Choice (F) is found in lines 46–49, which notes that only 300 years ago, the Greeks believed the sun revolved around the Earth. The author also finds it amazing that "the Antikythera Mechanism worked through a simple input-output method" (lines 32–33). This eliminates choice (G). Finally, the principles behind the working of this advanced machine were "intricate, especially considering the limited information available to the ancient Greeks" (lines 45–46). This eliminates choice (J). The attitude of scientists at the time it was created is never discussed. Thus, choice (H) is the correct answer for this EXCEPT question.

13.   **(B)** the different seasons.

Details

The author tells you in line 67 that the "tilt is the cause of the seasons." Choice (B) is correct. None of the other answers are associated with the tilt of the Earth.

14.   **(J)** the Earth would always be the same distance from the sun.

Relationships (Cause–Effect)

The sixth paragraph (lines 50–59) explains that the Earth's orbit is elliptical and goes on to discuss the effects this has. The author states that "the Earth is gradually travelling nearer to or farther from the sun [each day]" (lines 53–54). Because of this fact, the distance between the Earth and the sun is variable. Presumably, if the Earth's orbit were not elliptical, these effects would not occur. Therefore, if the Earth's orbit were circular, the distance would likely be constant. This matches choice (J).

15.   **(B)** Approximately when was the Antikythera Mechanism lost?

Details

Because this question is asking what is *not* answered, you should be able to find answers for the three wrong answers. Lines 25–27 state "The Antikythera Mechanism was created at the end of the second century, B.C.E." Eliminate choice (A). The same paragraph states that it has been studied since its discovery "over 100 years ago" (line 28). Eliminate choice (C). Finally, its purpose was understood "only in the last few decades" (lines 29–30). Eliminate answer choice (D). However, the passage never discusses when the mechanism was lost, so choice (B) is correct.

16.   **(H)** that the Antikythera Mechanism was an important discovery.

Main Idea

Choices (F) and (J) are both stated in the paragraph, but neither are the main point of the paragraph. Instead, they are used to support the idea that the Antikythera Mechanism was a significant discovery, which is (H). Answer choice (G) is not even discussed in the paragraph. Thus, choice (H) is correct.

17.   **(A)** the moon passing between the sun and the Earth.

Relationships (Cause–Effect)

The first paragraph discusses the causes and different interpretations of solar eclipses. The author states, "When a solar eclipse occurs, the moon passes between the Earth and the sun. This creates the illusion that the sun has been momentarily blacked out" (lines 2–4). Choice (A) matches this description. Choice (B) is a misconception that used to be held. Choice (D) makes it hard to predict eclipses, and certainly contributes to their timing, but it is not the cause.

18.   **(J)** to gain insight into an emperor's future.

Details

Lines 15–16 explain that in ancient China, "Solar eclipses were directly linked to an emperor's future." This matches choice (J). The passage does refer to some of the other answer choices, but not as a motivation to predict eclipses. A dragon was believed to be devouring the sun during an eclipse, choice (F), but there was no discussion of trying to stop it. There was also an example of a solar eclipse stopping a war, choice (G), but it was not related to predicting eclipses. Choice (H), understanding more about the nature of the universe, is never discussed.

19.   **(A)** learn about how ancient civilizations viewed the universe.

Author's Approach

The final paragraph summarizes some of the benefits of studying the Antikythera Mechanism. It concludes that "we continue to make discoveries about ancient civilizations, their startling understanding of the universe, and their grasp of complex mathematical concepts" (lines 90–93). The other answer choices discuss what we might learn by studying solar eclipses or what ancient Greeks hoped to learn by creating the Antikythera Mechanism, but not what we can learn by studying it.

20.   **(G)** Calculations in three dimensions are more difficult than calculations in two dimensions.

Generalizations

The most challenging aspect of predicting eclipses is discussed in the second-to-last paragraph. The predictions are said to be particularly challenging because of differences in the planes of orbit of the Earth and the moon. It goes on to state, *"All calculations regarding the three must therefore be completed in three dimensions"* (lines 76–77). This implies that 3-D calculations are more difficult than 2-D calculations, making choice (G) the correct answer. Choices (F) and (J) are contradicted by the passage. Eclipses were predicted in ancient times, without modern technology. Choice (H) is not directly contradicted, but it is never supported by the passage.

Passage 3 Solutions

21.   **(B)** essentially stops.

Details

In lines 31–32, the passage describes cryptobiosis as "a state in which all metabolic processes in an organism come to a halt." In other words, metabolism stops. In lines 41–42, you learn that the stoppage is not 100%, but at only 0.1% of its normal level, metabolism essentially stops. Thus, choice (B) is correct. The other choices are not supported by the text.

22.   **(J)** The discovery was exciting, because tardigrades had done something no other animal had done before.

Meaning of Words

The passage expresses enthusiasm and curiosity about tardigrades. The author seems in awe of the animal's hardiness and notes in lines 59–60 that "tardigrades became the first known animal to survive in space." The author describes this discovery as "stunning" (line 65) because she is excited about it. Choices (F) and (G) express significant negativity about the discovery, but little such negativity is present in the passage. The inability of most of the survivors to produce viable embryos is presented as an afterthought, preceded by the word "although." Choice (H) is unsupported, since there were no other species on the mission.

23. (A) today's tardigrades are different from the tardigrades that lived a long time ago.

Relationships (Comparisons)

In lines 15–18, the author states, "While genetic studies have revealed that they originally lived in freshwater environments before adapting to live on land, today these incredible critters have been found all over." Thus, today's tardigrades are different from the ones that "originally lived in freshwater environments," the point made in choice (A). The other choices are too extreme and are not supported by the passage.

24. (G) they are capable of undergoing cryptobiosis.

Details

The author asks, "How is this hardy creature capable of such feats?" (line 27). She answers her own question: tardigrades "are among only a few species capable of reversibly suspending their metabolism in order to achieve a state of cryptobiosis" (lines 29–31). This is one reason why tardigrades are so hardy, according to the author, matching choice (G). The other choices are unsupported by the text of the passage.

25. (B) is complex because many molecular components must work together to guard specific molecules.

Details

The passage states, in regard to cryptobiosis, "This process is not a simple one. At the molecular level … many different components must work together as 'bioprotectants' to guard the most important molecules within the cell" (lines 43–47), language that corresponds to choice (B). Choice (A) is incorrect because an absence of oxygen is only one type of cryptobiosis. Choice (C) is incorrect because tardigrades can uniquely undergo all five *types* of cryptobiosis, but you are not told that they are the only species that can undergo the process. Choice (D) is incorrect because, while tardigrades did transition from freshwater to other environments, the passage offers no evidence that cryptobiosis was required for this transition.

26. (H) they wanted to learn from the tardigrades' ability to survive.

Details

The author states in lines 69–76 that "a group of Italian scientists returned to space with the critters … with the goal of studying how the 'hardiest animal on Planet Earth' is able to survive away from it … The hope is that the Tardkiss study might help researchers create techniques to protect other organisms." That is, these scientists were (and are) trying to learn from the tardigrades' ability to survive, as choice (H) puts it. Choices (F), (G), and (J) describe goals that were not stated in the passage.

27. (A) tardigrades in a state of cryptobiosis.

Meaning of Words

The state of cryptobiosis, which includes extreme dehydration, is the state that enables tardigrades to withstand extreme environments. You can infer that the tardigrades who were sent into the extreme environment of outer space were dehydrated into cryptobiosis. Some of the other features may also apply to those tardigrades (e.g., they also surely lacked oxygen in space), but "dehydrated" (which in normal circumstances just refers to the loss of water) here specifically indicates that the tardigrades were put into a cryptobiotic state before they were carried into orbit. Thus, choice (A) is correct.

28.   **(H)** to support the thesis that tardigrades are among the hardiest creatures on earth.

Generalizations

As stated right up front in lines 2–3, the author's main thesis is that tardigrades "are perhaps the Earth's most resilient life form." The description of the space experiments, which show the tardigrades withstanding conditions that no other animal has been known to withstand, supports this thesis, in line with choice (H). The other choices do not express the main purpose of these paragraphs.

29.   **(D)** They have survived in ocean trenches.

Details

In the first paragraph, the author states, "It is possible that they [tardigrades] have survived the fatal pressures of the greatest ocean trenches" in lines 9–10. None of the incorrect choices have this sort of textual support. Choice (D) is correct.

30.   **(F)** tardigrades are capable of withstanding significantly more radiation than humans are.

Details

When introducing the various attributes of tardigrades, the author states in lines 10–12 that the animals "are able to withstand radiation in amounts that are hundreds of times greater than the lethal dose for human beings." This is the only comparison from among the four choices supported by the passage. Choice (F) is correct.

Passage 4 Solutions

31.   **(D)** Easy recyclability at high temperatures

Relationships (Comparisons)

The second and third paragraphs describe thermoset and thermoplastic polymers respectively. Thermoset polymers "tend to be non-recyclable" (line 17), whereas thermoplastic polymers are "easily recycled into a new form at a higher temperature" (lines 21–22). This matches choice (D). The other choices are not supported by the text.

32.   **(H)** Natural polymers can self-heal; synthetic polymers cannot.

Details

The passage states: "One of the biggest differences between natural and artificial polymers is that natural ones have the ability to self-heal under certain conditions" (lines 38–40). This matches choice (H). The other choices are not supported by the text.

33.   **(A)** self-healing reactions must be carried out in high heat.

Details

The second-to-last paragraph (lines 62–74) lists numerous challenges involved in creating self-healing polymers. Each of the three wrong answer choices, (B), (C), and (D), are listed in this paragraph but you are looking for what is not there to answer this EXCEPT question. However, it also says "the monomers would have to react at room temperature" (lines 64–65). This means the reactions cannot be carried out in high heat. Thus, choice (A) is not mentioned and is therefore the correct answer.

34.   **(G)** Self-healing reactions of small ruptures have already been accomplished.

Generalizations

Each of the answer choices discusses whether self-healing reactions have been accomplished or if they soon will be. The sixth paragraph (lines 44–51) introduces the success that has already been achieved in the field. It is clear that some limited self-healing reactions have already been synthesized. Eliminate (F). Knowing that success has already been accomplished, eliminate (H) and (J). In the final paragraph it states that "success until recently has been limited to small ruptures in the polymer framework" (lines 75–77). This matches choice (G).

35.   **(C)** Setting permanently

Meaning of Words

Lines 13–15 state: "Through curing, the thermoset polymer is permanantely set in position; it is unchangeable even if heated again." Curing is unrelated to healing or heating the polymers, choices (A) and (B), or creating them in the first place, choice (D). Instead, it is setting them (i.e., having them take a solid shape.) Therefore, choice (C) is correct.

36.   **(F)** A brick wall with identical bricks cemented into position

Meaning of Words

To answer this question, you must determine what the author means by polymer. The author defines it as "one example of macromolecules" (line 3), which are themselves "large molecules made up of smaller ones" (lines 1–2). Polymers have "smaller component parts, called monomers. Monomers are normally identical or at least similar to one another" (lines 4–6). An analogy would be something that has smaller units that are similar to each other and positioned into a series. The closest match in the answer choices to that is a brick wall, which has a series of identical components, that is the bricks, held in place. The analogy isn't perfect, since a brick wall is rather like a brick, whereas you are told in lines 4–5 that the traits of polymers differ from those of the monomers. However, the cemented brick wall, choice (F), is the best analogy available to you.

37.   **(B)** To insert additional monomers

Relationships (Cause–Effect)

As described in lines 55–61, the microcapsules are filled with monomers that will be used to heal cracks in polymers. It is because of these microcapsules that self-healing is possible. Choice (B) is correct. The other choices are not supported in the text.

38. **(J)** stable at high temperatures.

Details

Thermoset polymers are created by curing, and they have several characteristics discussed in the passage. Specifically, they are "unchangeable even if heated again" (lines 14–15). Part of what makes them attractive materials is their stability at high temperatures, which matches choice (J). The other choices are not supported in the text.

39. **(A)** A monomer

Generalizations

Keratin is used when talking about examples of natural polymers. However, it is not a polymer itself. Instead, the passage states that keratin "is a protein that polymerizes to form the key structural component of hair, skin, and nails" (lines 36–37). That makes keratin a component of a polymer. The only components of polymers discussed are called monomers. Thus, choice (A) is correct.

40. **(H)** despite difficulties in creating a synthetic self-healing polymer, scientists have made significant progress.

Main Idea

The passage focuses on the challenges and successes of creating a self-healing polymer. It takes some time to develop this focus, because first you need to be told about polymers in general, then thermoset versus thermoplastic polymers. However, the final sentence of the passage captures the theme well: "Though further study and research is necessary, this breakthrough may provide the groundwork needed to manufacture fully self-healing polymers" (lines 83–85). This language is reflected in choice (H). There is no discussion of whether polymers will replace metals. Eliminate (F). The author is focusing on self-healing polymers, but there is no mention of how important self-healing polymers are compared to other breakthroughs. Eliminate (G). Microcapsules are an important component of self-healing polymers, but they are not the focus of the passage. Eliminate (J).

Passage 5 Solutions

41. **(B)** Concern

Author's Approach

Toward the end of the passage, the author begins discussing the direct effects of a global magnetic field reversal. She states: "This switch could have devastating effects on our way of life" (line 70–71). Hope, choice (C), and relief, choice (D), are certainly not reflected in that statement. Choice (A), "*Skepticism*" would mean that she is doubtful that the effects would occur or be serious. Although she acknowledges that the "true extent of the damage cannot yet be known" (lines 83–84), she is only expressing doubt about the degree of possible damage, not the risk itself. Instead, the author is expressing severe concern in her use of the word "devastating" earlier. Thus, choice (B) is correct.

42. **(F)** iron is a magnetic substance.

Details

The fourth paragraph discusses how iron can be used to monitor the magnetic field over time. Lines 36–37 explain: "iron is a magnetic substance, so it will align with nearby magnetic fields." By determining the orientation of the iron within volcanic rocks created at various times, the magnetic field at the time can be known. This point corresponds to choice (F). Choice (G) may be tempting because volcanic lava is part of the analysis. However, there are probably many substances in volcanic lava; you are not told that iron is the primary component. The reason that iron is singled out as a useful substance is that it orients toward magnetic north.

43. **(D)** a theory that has yet to be proven.

Meaning of Words

Each of these answer choices discuss whether the dynamo effect is true or false and how it is perceived. The author talks about the dynamo effect in the second paragraph. While most of the paragraph is a description of what this effect is, lines 14–15 talk about its validity as a theory. How the magnetic field originates is said to be "unclear, but the prominent theory is called the dynamo effect." Therefore, the author does not believe this effect is proven, but calls it the currently accepted idea. It is therefore neither a fact nor a mistaken conception. Eliminate (A) and (C). Because the dynamo effect is a prominent theory, the author implies that the theory has already been widely accepted. Eliminate (B). Thus, choice (D) is correct.

44. **(H)** volcanic eruptions.

Details

Because this is an EXCEPT question, you should be able to find evidence for the three wrong answers. You can then choose the remaining answer. Lines 78–81 tell you that a weaker magnetic field can lead to increased risk of cancer and mutations. Eliminate answer (F). Also, in the first paragraph, the author states: "Migratory animals, such as birds, use the magnetic field to guide their trajectory" (lines 2–4). Eliminate (G). Finally, "electrical grids use the Earth's magnetic field to function" (lines 71–72). Eliminate (J). There is no support for the idea that volcanic eruptions are affected by the magnetic field. You are looking for the idea that has no support in the passage. Therefore, choice (H) is correct.

45. **(A)** radioactive decay.

Details

The second paragraph explains the theory of the dynamo effect. It states: "Heat from the radioactive decay forces … the Earth's iron core to move … its movement generates an electric current … which creates a self-sustaining magnetic field" (lines 17–22). Choice (A) is correct.

46. **(J)** faster rotation on Venus's axis.

Relationships (Cause–Effect)

The third paragraph (lines 23–31) tells you that Venus's core is similar to Earth's, so a magnetic field should be generated on Venus. However, it isn't. The reason given is that "the planet's rotation affects the field generation" (lines 28–29). Venus's rotation is much slower than Earth's. Therefore, if a field were generated around Venus, you would expect the rotation to be more similar to Earth's. This matches choice (J).

47.   **(C)** a reversal of the Earth's magnetic poles is possible in the near future.

Generalizations

The sixth paragraph (lines 54–67) starts with the idea that a magnetic field reversal would take thousands of years. However, the author disagrees with this idea, and spends the rest of the paragraph providing evidence that suggests that the reversal could probably happen more rapidly. Moreover, there is a substantial discussion of signs that say the magnetic field is currently weakening. This would support choice (C).

48.   **(G)** Cobalt, a magnetic metal, present in liquefied lava rocks orients in a different direction than iron does from the same period.

Generalizations

Each of these answer choices talks about the orientation of different metals within lava. The metal discussed in the passage, iron, behaves very specifically in lava: "A lava rock that solidified at a particular point in time will therefore have iron molecules oriented in the direction of magnetic north at that time" (lines 42–45). To weaken this idea, you would need unexpected behavior. Metals that are not magnetic are irrelevant. Their orientation shouldn't rely on the Earth's magnetic field. Eliminate (H) and (J). Nickel and cobalt are both given as magnetic metals, so they should align with magnetic north. In order to weaken the idea that magnetic materials behave this way, scientists would need to find that magnetic materials align in a different direction than magnetic north for some reason. This would match choice (G).

49.   **(D)** The reversal of Earth's magnetic field takes thousands of years.

Details

The only theory that the author disagrees with is given in the sixth paragraph (lines 54–67). She states: "It was assumed that shifting the Earth's magnetic field from one pole to another took thousands of years" (lines 54–55). With more information, however, the author concludes that scientists are forced "to reevaluate their original timeline" (line 64). The original theory is cast into question. Thus, choice (D) is correct.

50.   **(G)** explain a natural phenomenon and its potential effects.

Main Idea

Throughout the passage, the author is concerned with explaining how the Earth's magnetic field works, what effects it has, and its potential reversal. The magnetic field is the "natural phenomenon" referred to in answer choice (G). The others can be eliminated. Even though the magnetic field may soon reverse, there is no certainty about an impending disaster, nor a call to action. Eliminate (F). Answer choice (H) is factually correct, but it is a minor point in the passage (only focused on in the second paragraph). Similarly, iron is discussed in the fourth paragraph, but it is not the main point of the passage. Eliminate (J).

Passage 6 Solutions

51. **(A)** Antibiotics

Details

The passage states: "Often, a simple course of antibiotics will result in a complete cure" (lines 10–12). The other three answers are mentioned, but never as a treatment for trachoma. At best, they are preventative measures. Answer choice (A) is correct.

52. **(J)** bacterial infection.

Details

As an EXCEPT question, you should find evidence for the three wrong answers in the passage. Entropion is described in the first paragraph. You learn that "the eyelashes rub against the eye, causing irritation and discomfort. Over time, scarring causes visual impairment and blindness" (lines 6–8). These lines eliminate answer choices (F), (G), and (H). The correct answer is (J).

53. **(C)** Those who have prevented infection are unlikely to inform a doctor.

Relationships (Comparison)

The fourth paragraph discusses both why it is easy to monitor antibiotics and surgery and why it is difficult to monitor prevention. The final sentences state: "Prevention is difficult to evaluate because only those who have caught the bacteria are likely to seek medical attention" (lines 42–44). You can infer that those who have not become infected will not seek medical attention. This matches choice (C).

54. **(G)** towel-sharing within a household increases the spread of trachoma.

Details

There are several mistaken beliefs that this passage disputes. However, only choice (G) is supported by the text: "Surprisingly, the act of sharing a towel within a household, long believed to be a key source of trachoma spread, did not seem to have any effect" (lines 73–75).

55. **(A)** To explain the relevance of this study

Main Idea

The second-to-last paragraph (lines 76–85) ties together the results of the study with the current status of trachoma work. It cites mistakes in the current process and what future research should pursue. Thus, this paragraph is explaining the relevance of the study, as is expressed in choice (A). The other choices can be eliminated. The dangers of trachoma are not specifically discussed in this paragraph. Eliminate (B). It is true that soap is an important step in prevention, but the purpose of the paragraph is not to focus on soap. Eliminate (C). The author does want further studies, but the paragraph talks more about how to change education and prevention measures. There are things that the author believes can and should be done in addition to further studies. Eliminate (D).

MANHATTAN
PREP

56.   **(J)**   It is possible, if not always simple, to prevent trachoma.

Author's Approach

The author talks about prevention of trachoma being difficult to measure, but she certainly believes it can be prevented. One clear example of this is in lines 45–47: "The best preventative measures used are the second half of SAFE: facial cleanliness (F) and environmental improvement (E)." If the author is discussing the best preventative measures, she clearly believes prevention is possible. The other choices are not supported; the author never claims that trachoma is fatal, nor does she take a position on the goal of eliminating trachoma by the year 2020 (i.e., whether this goal is likely or not to be achieved). Eliminate (F), (G), and (H).

57.   **(B)**   direct contact with the bacteria.

Details

The passage states: "Trachoma is spread through physical contact" (lines 36–37). The author states that trachoma causes discharge that can "spread from the hand to objects or other people. This contact spreads the bacteria" (lines 41–42). This matches choice (B). No other ways that spread trachoma are discussed, which eliminates choices (A), (C), and (D).

58.   **(H)**   a clearly treatable infection.

Meaning of Words

Trachoma can be identified as a treatable infection from a few lines. You know that "trachoma is an easily treatable disease" (lines 9–10) and it is "the world's leading cause of infectious blindness" (line 1). Thus, trachoma is clearly a treatable infection, so choice (H) is correct. Choices (F) and (G) are unsupported: you are told that trachoma *is* spread through physical contact (you don't know whether there are also other means of spreading the disease), and trachoma has "provoked a substantial response" (line 21) from several global health organizations. You can also eliminate (J).

59.   **(A)**   Corrections to the education about trachoma spread

Author's Approach

In the final paragraph, the author states: "Education and further study are both needed" (line 90) (to reach the goal of eradicating trachoma). The previous paragraph discusses errors in current educational efforts around trachoma. The author is clearly saying that correcting those educational errors could decrease trachoma spread. This matches choice (A).

60.   **(G)**   Increased percent of household water allocated to cleanliness decreases the occurrence of trachoma.

Details

The sixth and seventh paragraphs (lines 55–75) both discuss the relevance of water to trachoma spread: "Instead, improved *quality* of water, especially water delivered through pipes rather than wells, correlated with a lower occurrence of the disease" (lines 62–64). The author also states: "Those who allocate a larger portion of their household water to cleanliness have significantly lower levels of trachoma" (lines 66–68). This matches choice (G).

Passage 7 Solutions

61. **(B)** explain ways in which molecular biology could further nanotechnological development.

Main Idea

The passage repeatedly holds to the idea that naturally created molecules could be the inspiration and template for synthetic nanotechnology. The author crystallizes this idea in the final paragraph, stating: "As the field of nanotechnology continues to evolve, it is likely that we will see many more nanotechnology applications utilizing biological macromolecules" (lines 86–88). This fusion of biology and nanotechnology is best expressed in choice (B). Choice (A) can be eliminated because the passage supports but cannot "prove" (beyond a doubt) this idea. Nanogrids involving biotins are discussed as the first example of a synthetic nanogrid, but it is at best an example; the author does not intend to base the entire argument on this one case. Choice (C) can be eliminated. The author does not attempt to question existing methods, but rather suggests that biological macromolecules could be important. Eliminate (D).

62. **(F)** there had been little or no successful work on the development of synthetic nanostructures.

Generalizations

Richard Feynman introduced the idea of nanotechnology to the scientific world in "what many now consider the first lecture" on the subject (line 2). He discussed applying the systems already present in the natural world to synthesis and creation of nanotechnology. You can reasonably infer that synthetic nanostructures had not yet achieved significant success. This matches choice (F).

63. **(D)** suggesting the ability to change the function of a single protein.

Details

The three wrong answers should all be found in the passage for an EXCEPT question. Choice (A) is directly stated in lines 33–34: "By modeling our nanoconstruction on these naturally occurring structures ... " Eliminate (A). Answer choice (B) can be eliminated with this question the author asks about the inspiration of protein pathways: "First, can we mimic these multicomponent protein-based 'assembly lines' on fabricated surfaces" (lines 45–47). Finally, (C) is specifically discussed by saying that "there has been some success in using the pattern of DNA nanogrids" (lines 52–53). Thus, (D) is correct.

64. **(H)** is the first lattice of this type synthetically created on such a small scale.

Meaning of Words

The passage discusses this lattice because it is "the first periodic, self-assembled DNA lattice ... with nanometer dimensions" (lines 69–71). This matches choice (H).

65. **(C)** predict the future developments likely to occur in nanotechnology.

Author's Approach

The second-to-last paragraph (lines 72–85) is oriented around future developments that are discussed in an optimistic way. The author states: "This work has opened up exciting new avenues in the field of nanotechnology" (lines 72–73). In the rest of the paragraph, the author continues to talk about the future: "it is foreseeable … one day … it is possible … as the field of nanotechnology matures" (lines 76–85). Choice (C) matches this idea.

66. **(G)** protein.

Details

In the third paragraph, the author discusses how today's scientists are using biology for inspiration. She states: "Scientists from many disciplines are now taking a careful look at biological macromolecules that power cells" (lines 26–28). The author refers to these macromolecules as machines, and gives two examples: "DNA and proteins" (line 29). Thus, (G) is correct.

67. **(A)** Five different proteins, working sequentially, generate cellular energy.

Meaning of Words

Protein pathways are defined as "a series of proteins that act in sequential order to create a particular product or perform a particular function" (lines 38–40). All of the answer choices result in generating cellular energy, so they all create a particular product. The difference is whether there is a series of proteins working in sequential order. Only choice (A) demonstrates that relationship.

68. **(J)** there are natural examples of small-scale machines.

Generalizations

As the passage describes in the first two paragraphs, Richard Feynman introduced the idea of nanotechnology and envisioned modeling it on natural systems. He certainly doesn't believe this manipulation is improbable. Eliminate (F). It is likely that he believes or at least hopes that nanotechnology is useful, but he is not certain. In fact, in his speech he says "They may or may not be useful" (line 91). Eliminate (G). Feynman never claims that cells have perfected nanotechnology. He believes that cells are active and should be studied. Choice (H) is too extreme. He does believe, however, that those cells contain examples of small-scale machines. Choice (J) is correct.

69. **(D)** natural systems in which several nanoscale molecules work together to achieve a goal are already in existence.

Relationships (Comparison)

Throughout the essay, the author focuses on using biological systems to model nanotechnological innovations. After explaining protein pathways, the author comments that they "are commonplace within biological cells, [but] we have yet to synthesize them" (lines 42–43). Protein pathways are used to illustrate a natural nanoscale system. Thus, choice (D) is correct.

20

70. **(F)** create dynamic protein-based assembly systems.

Details

Only one answer choice is something that the passage states as possible, but not yet achieved. The author states: "theoretically, we can construct dynamic protein-based assemblies using DNA systems" (lines 73–75). Choices (G) and (J) have already been achieved (see lines 69–71), whereas (H) is never mentioned as a goal that could one day be achieved. Therefore, choice (F) is correct.

Passage 8 Solutions

71. **(C)** in New England, but not in New York.

Relationships (Comparisons)

Fowler's toad is identified as from "either New York or New England" (lines 70–71) and "found in 1882" (line 71). There is no mention of how it was found, so choices (A) and (D) are incorrect. Choices (B) and (C) raise the question of whether Fowler's toad was found in New York. Lines 70–71 don't indicate that, so you have to expand your search. The final sentence in the paragraph gives the only other example of an animal found in that region. The northern cricket frog was found in New York in 1854. Importantly, this was "the most recent amphibian discovered there" (lines 74–75). If Fowler's toad, found in 1882, had been discovered in New York, it would be more recent than the northern cricket frog. Therefore, Fowler's toad couldn't have been found in New York. Choice (C) is correct.

72. **(F)** enables targeted conservation efforts.

Generalizations

The author explains what happens when a cryptic species remains unidentified in the second paragraph. The passage states: "Not only can conservation efforts be misdirected, but also it may be unclear that such efforts are even needed" (lines 26–28). This implies that if cryptic species are found, the conservation efforts can be directed at the specific species. The author continues: "A cryptic species discovery therefore can have important implications" (lines 28–29). In other words, the discovery is important *because* it allows for targeted conservation efforts. This matches choice (F).

73. **(B)** They have been subject to disappearances.

Details

Though the passage talks about a variety of leopard frog species and their characteristics, with regard to leopard frogs in general, the passage asserts that they "have been subject to enigmatic declines and disappearances" (lines 58–59), as is stated in choice (B). Choices (A) and (C) are true of the *Atlantic Coast* leopard frog, but not necessarily of the other leopard frog species. As for choice (D), you are told nothing about the relative size of leopard frog populations (only that they are declining).

74.   **(J)**   the two have similar behavior and appearance.

Relationships (Comparisons)

Even though a cryptic species and its congener have significant differences that are discussed throughout the passage, there are similarities. They can be mistaken for one another because the "species tend to look and behave similarly, and even have overlapping habitats" (lines 22–23). This matches choice (J).

75.   **(A)**   frogs.

Generalizations

The species discussed in the passage are the Northern, Southern, and Atlantic Coast leopard frog, Fowler's toad, and the northern cricket frog. All of them are animals, amphibians, and anurans ("an order of amphibians that includes frogs and toads," according to lines 12–13). Fowler's toad, however, is not a frog; it's, well, a toad. The fact that frogs and toads are distinct is implied in the definition of anurans, which mentions the two separately. Choice (A) is correct.

76.   **(H)**   to discuss how a cryptic species remained undetected and what that implies for future study.

Author's Approach

The final paragraph gives theories as to why the Atlantic Coast leopard frog remained undiscovered for so long ("repeated acoustic misidentification," according to lines 93–94). The paragraph ends with methods for avoiding this problem in further investigations. This most closely matches choice (H). Though the author cites mistakes her colleagues made, her purpose is not to discredit them (i.e., deliberately damage their reputations), but rather to explain what happened. Eliminate (F). Choices (G) and (J) are not discussed in the final paragraph.

77.   **(D)**   Greater examination of unexpected calls should be conducted.

Details

In the final paragraph, the author gives a specific recommendation for future study. She states that "we encourage greater scrutiny and examination of unexpected calls" (lines 101–102), which matches choice (D). Choices (A) and (C) may seem plausible, but there are no recommendations in the final paragraph of these kinds. Choice (B) is too broad; you are asked for the *specific* recommendation the author gives.

78.   **(G)**   new.

Meaning of Words

Novel species are those that were previously undiscovered. Novel, in line 68 ("Novel and undescribed vertebrate species are unexpected"), most nearly means "new." Choice (G) is correct.

79. **(A)** to discuss the importance of correctly identifying cryptic species.

Author's Approach

In the second paragraph, the author introduces the definition of cryptic species. She uses this concept to illustrate why identifying a new species can be difficult, and also why it is important to do so correctly. Without correct classification, conservation efforts are difficult. These ideas point to choice (A). Choices (B) and (C) may be tempting, because cryptic species and their congeners are defined in this paragraph. However, the emphasis is not on defining congener species; that is an aside. Eliminate (B). Even though cryptic species are thoroughly discussed, there is no explanation of how they remain unidentified for long periods. Eliminate (C). Choice (D) should be eliminated because the Atlantic Coast leopard frog is not mentioned in this paragraph.

80. **(G)** explain what Atlantic Coast leopard frogs were misidentified as.

Author's Approach

After the author introduces cryptic species in the second paragraph, she first mentions all three types of leopard frogs in the third paragraph. Most of the passage focuses on analyzing the Atlantic Coast leopard frog, a cryptic species that was recently discovered. The Northern and Southern leopard frogs are mentioned as congeners of this cryptic species, which "has been mistakenly associated with both" (lines 41–42). Thus, choice (G) is correct.

Passage 9 Solutions

81. **(D)** The ejection of enough matter to reduce the core's mass

Generalizations

Passage A explains that a large star can create a black hole upon its death. Only one scenario is discussed that will prevent the black hole: "If enough matter is ejected that the remaining core is left with insufficient mass, electron degeneracy can stabilize the core" (lines 37–40). This matches choice (D). Choice (B) references forces that determine the equilibrium of a star. However, all stars have dueling forces. What prevents a black hole from occurring is a loss of matter great enough to allow electron degeneracy to prevent total collapse into a black hole (the scenario at the very end of Passage A).

82. **(F)** refusal.

Meanings of Words

The sentence in question is this: "Electron degeneracy is the resistance that electrons have to occupying each other's space" (lines 25–27). The closest synonym to *resistance* among the answer choices is "refusal": the electrons refuse to occupy the same space. "Confrontation," "struggle," and "endurance" can all mean "resistance" in other contexts, but they are imprecise synonyms here. Eliminate (G), (H), and (J).

83. **(C)** the emission of a star's outer layer in a burst of light.

Details

A supernova is defined in lines 35–37: "When an incredibly massive star sheds its outer layers … The outer layers are rejected so forcefully that their light can overpower an entire galaxy." This matches choice (C).

84. **(J)** elaborate on methods scientists use to detect black holes.

Main Idea

The author of Passage B discusses three different ways scientists have used to identify black holes and explains why finding black holes would be so difficult. The focus in Passage B is on the detection of black holes, as in fact the introduction to passage 9 indicates. This matches choice (J).

85. **(A)** matter spiraling into a black hole.

Relationships (Cause–Effect)

The X-ray radiation is generated when matter is quickly pulled into a black hole (lines 81–84). This matches choice (A).

86. **(G)** absorb light without emitting any.

Details

Passage B discusses the difficulty of tracking an invisible object. In order to be directly visible, an object must "reflect or emit light" (line 48). In contrast, "black holes only absorb light" (line 49). Therefore, (G) is correct.

87. **(B)** One is concerned with the process of forming a black hole; the other is focused on how to find a black hole.

Relationships (Comparisons)

The main purpose of the first passage is to explain how a black hole can be formed. The purpose of the second is to describe how to locate a black hole. This matches choice (B).

88. **(H)** Intense gravity is a fundamental property of black holes.

Generalizations

Passage A discusses gravity in terms of the formation of a black hole. As a star dies, the gravity in the core can create a black hole. Passage B does not talk about the formation of a black hole, but does talk about a black hole's gravitational pull on surrounding stars and other objects. Both authors discuss the immensely powerful gravitational forces that a black hole generates. Choice (H) is correct.

89. **(D)** How scientists have historically viewed black holes

Details

The introductory paragraph of Passage A talks about the evolving view of black holes: "They were once considered a myth, then a theory that could not be proven, but we now have located an enormous number of black holes" (lines 2–4). Passage B never touches on the history of how black holes have been viewed. Thus choice (D) is correct.

Chapter 21

of

5lb. Book of ACT® Practice Problems

Science:
Life Sciences

In This Chapter...

Life Sciences Passages & Solutions

Chapter 21

Science: Life Sciences

The Science passages in this chapter are classified within life sciences, which include cell biology, genetics, evolution, microbiology, botany, zoology, and other topics that could be studied in a Life Sciences or Biology course.

In the Science section, you'll encounter three types of passages, each with a corresponding question type.

1. Data Representation. A scientific article that contains charts and tables of information. Here, you will be asked Data Interpretation questions. That is, you'll need to interpret the data you're given.

2. Research Summary. A description of an experiment (or two). Here, you will be asked Scientific Investigation questions. In other words, you'll need to examine the experiment (the scientific investigation) critically: assessing its design, analyzing its outcomes, etc.

3. Conflicting Viewpoints. Two or more explanations or interpretations of a scientific phenomenon. These explanations always conflict. Here, you will be asked Evaluation of Models, Inferences, & Experimental Results questions, requiring you to compare, contrast, or otherwise evaluate the explanations given.

How should you use this chapter? Here are some recommendations, according to the level you've reached in ACT Science.

1. Fundamentals. Do a passage or two untimed to begin with. As you become more comfortable, put the clock on. In all cases, review the solutions closely, and articulate what you've learned. Reread the passage again to ensure that you fully understand it, and redo problems as necessary.

2. Fixes. Do one passage at a time under timed conditions. Examine the results, learn your lessons, then test yourself with more passages (one or two from each Science chapter) at once.

3. Tweaks. Confirm your mastery by doing several passages (a couple from each Science chapter) at once under timed conditions. A set of five or six passages (doing all seven questions per passage) or seven passages (doing about six questions per passage) is ideal. Aim to improve the speed and ease of your reading and solution process.

Good luck on the problems!

PASSAGE 1

The functioning of the cardiovascular system can be monitored by measuring the blood pressure, heart rate, and breathing rate.

Blood pressure, the force that blood exerts on the vessels of the cardiovascular system, can be measured using a *sphygmomanometer* and a stethoscope. The sphygmomanometer, shown in Figure 1, consists of an inflatable arm cuff, a pressure gauge, and an inflation pump.

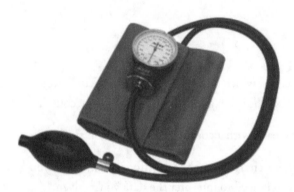

Figure 1

In order to take a measurement, the arm band is placed around a subject's arm, while the experimenter listens to the forearm with a stethoscope. Although the normal flow of blood has no sound, the sound of the subject's pulse (i.e., the heart beat) disappears after the arm cuff is tightened and the artery becomes fully compressed. After the pulse disappears, the experimenter slowly deflates the arm cuff. As blood starts to squirt through the partially compressed artery in the arm, the experi-

menter will hear a sound and take the corresponding pressure reading on the pressure gauge of the sphygmomanometer. This pressure is called the *systolic pressure,* with a normal value of 120 mmHg or less. When the squirting sound disappears and blood flow returns to normal, a second pressure reading is taken. This is called the *diastolic pressure,* with a normal value of 80 mmHg or less.

Heart rate, the number of times a heart beats per minute, can be measured by putting a hand over the chest and counting the number of beats in one minute. Heart rate is measured in beats per minute (BPM), with a normal resting heart rate of between 60 and 100 BPM.

Breathing rate, the number of breaths taken in one minute, is measured by placing a hand on the chest of the subject and counting the number of *inspirations,* or inhaled breaths, in one minute. Breathing rate is measured in breaths per minute, with a normal resting breathing rate of 8 to 16 breaths per minute.

To test the effects of different activities on the cardiovascular system, a 20-year-old student was administered various tests of cardiovascular function. First, the student's measurements were taken and recorded to establish baseline values. Next the student ran on a treadmill for 15 minutes, and the measurements were taken again. Finally, the student meditated for 10 minutes while listening to soothing music, and her measurements were taken afterward. The results are summarized in Table 1.

Table 1

Measurement Time	Heart Rate (BPM)	Blood Pressure (mmHg, Systolic/Diastolic)	Breathing Rate (breaths per minute)
Baseline measurements (at rest)	74	118/75	12
After 15 minutes on the treadmill	179	117/76	44
After 10 minutes of meditation	63	110/70	8

1. Which of the following can be measured with no additional instruments?

    A. Heart rate only
    B. Breathing rate only
    C. Blood pressure only
    D. Both heart rate and breathing rate

2. Approximately how many times per second was the student's heart beating after the period of exercise?

    F. 60 times per second
    G. 30 times per second
    H. 3 times per second
    J. 1 time per second

3. How could the blood pressure of this student at rest be described?

    A. Systolic pressure was higher than normal, and diastolic pressure was normal.
    B. Diastolic pressure was higher than normal, and systolic pressure was normal.
    C. Both systolic and diastolic pressures were normal.
    D. Both systolic and diastolic pressures were higher than normal.

4. It can be inferred from the passage that, with just a stethoscope, an experimenter listening to a normal, living patient's forearm:

    F. would be able to hear a pulse.
    G. would not be able to hear a pulse.
    H. would be able to hear the squirting of blood.
    J. would hear various sounds, depending on the circumstances, but there is not enough information to tell what sounds would be heard.

5. In a patient with normal blood pressure, what might be the pressure exerted by an arm cuff of a sphygmo-manometer at which the sound of a pulse disappears entirely?

    A. 160 mmHg
    B. 120 mmHg
    C. 80 mmHg
    D. 60 mmHg

6. Based on Table 1, what conclusion can be drawn about the student after a period of exercise?

    F. The student has a dangerously high heart rate after a period of exercise.
    G. The student has a dangerously low heart rate after a period of exercise.
    H. The student is in the normal range for heart rate after a period of exercise.
    J. There is not enough information provided about heart rate after exercise to draw a conclusion.

7. Blood pressure is directly proportional both to the amount of blood flow and to the *total peripheral resistance* (TPR) of the blood vessels. If every heartbeat delivers the same amount of blood flow, what can be concluded about the heart after a period of exercise?

    A. TPR must have increased after exercise.
    B. TPR must have decreased after exercise.
    C. Amount of blood flow must have decreased after exercise.
    D. Systolic pressure must have increased after exercise.

PASSAGE 2

The *forced swim test* is a behavioral test that is used to measure depression-like symptoms in a mouse. In the test, a mouse is put into a beaker of distilled water and observed, as indicated in Figure 1. The beaker of water is not a familiar environment for the mouse, and so it triggers a *stress response*, which is mediated by the stress hormone *cortisol*.

In the test, the mouse will always try to swim for some amount of time, during which it uses all four legs to move around the vat. After some time, it may then begin a period of *struggling,* during which the mouse uses some of its four legs but not all of them. Swimming and struggling are both stress responses. Finally, the animal may progress to *floating*, during which the mouse does not move at all.

Figure 1

Experiment 1

A mouse was exposed to the forced swim test and its behavior was recorded in Table 1.

Table 1

Minute of Experiment	Behavior Observed
1	Swimming
2	Swimming
3	Struggling
4	Struggling
5	Struggling
6	Floating
7	Floating
8	Floating
9	Floating
10	Floating

Experiment 2

A mouse was administered 1 mg/kg of the drug *fluoxetine* and was exposed to the forced swim test. Its behavior was recorded in Table 2.

Table 2

Minute of Experiment	Behavior Observed
1	Swimming
2	Swimming
3	Swimming
4	Swimming
5	Struggling
6	Struggling
7	Swimming
8	Swimming
9	Struggling
10	Floating

Experiment 3

A mouse was administered 1 mg/kg of the drug *oxycodone* and was exposed to the forced swim test. Its behavior was recorded in Table 3.

Table 3

Minute of Experiment	Behavior Observed
1	Swimming
2	Struggling
3	Floating
4	Floating
5	Floating
6	Floating
7	Floating
8	Floating
9	Floating
10	Floating

8. Which graph represents the number of minutes that the mouse spends in each stage before the administration of any drug?

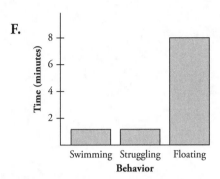

F.

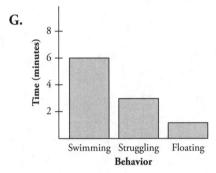

G.

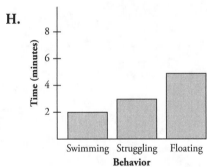

H.

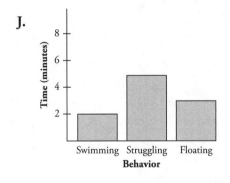

J.

9. In Experiment 1, if the mouse had been observed for a longer period of time, which behavior would the mouse likely exhibit after 12 minutes?

   A. Swimming
   B. Struggling
   C. Floating
   D. Kicking

10. All of the following situations would be predicted to result in increased cortisol levels EXCEPT:

    F. a mouse being nursed by its mother.
    G. a mouse being hanged by its tail from a great height.
    H. a mouse in an extremely cold environment.
    J. a mouse running away from a large predator.

11. According to Experiment 3, *oxycodone* presumably had what effect on cortisol levels?

    A. Oxycodone increased cortisol levels, since the animal showed an increased stress response.
    B. Oxycodone increased cortisol levels, since the animal showed a decreased stress response.
    C. Oxycodone decreased cortisol levels, since the animal showed an increased stress response.
    D. Oxycodone decreased cortisol levels, since the animal showed a decreased stress response.

21

12. Which of the following graphs accurately represents the amount of time the mouse spent in each of the three states after the administration of *fluoxetine,* as demonstrated in Experiment 2?

F.

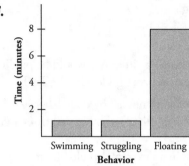

G.

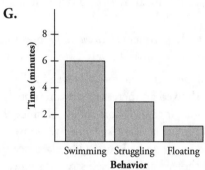

H.

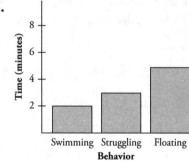

J.

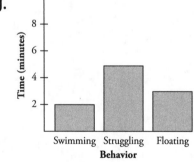

MANHATTAN
PREP

13. Depression is a mental disorder that is characterized by a decreased stress response during exposure to a stressful environment. A researcher hypothesizes that fluoxetine has antidepressant qualities in mice. Do these data support this hypothesis?

A. Yes, since fluoxetine decreased the amount of time swimming and struggling and increased the amount of time floating for the mouse.

B. Yes, since fluoxetine increased the amount of time swimming and struggling and decreased the amount of time floating for the mouse.

C. No, since fluoxetine decreased the amount of time swimming and struggling and increased the amount of time floating for the mouse.

D. No, since fluoxetine increased the amount of time swimming and struggling and decreased the amount of time floating for the mouse.

14. Which of the following is NOT a valid criticism of the experimental setup?

F. The same test was repeated on one mouse, and this repetition could have had lasting effects on the mouse.

G. The mouse would eventually begin floating, no matter what conditions were imposed.

H. The behavior of the mouse may have changed more frequently than was measured at the 1-minute intervals at which behavior was recorded.

J. The very act of administering the drugs could have had an effect on the stress response, regardless of the mechanism of action of the drug itself.

21

PASSAGE 3

In biology, *cell theory* is a scientific theory that describes the properties of cells. The three components of cell theory are the following:

1. All living organisms are composed of one or more cells.
2. The cell is the fundamental unit of living things.
3. All cells arise from pre-existing, living cells.

Aside from these ideas of cell theory, cells vary from one organism to another. Bacterial cells lack a nucleus, and, for this reason, they are referred to as *prokaryotic cells*. *Eukaryotic cells,* or cells that contain a nucleus, are functionally more evolved and make up all multi-cellular organisms on Earth.

Endosymbiotic theory states that 1.5 billion years ago, a primitive eukaryotic cell engulfed a smaller prokaryotic cell, and the two entered a mutually beneficial, or *symbiotic*, relationship. According to this theory, various *organelles*, or functional components of the modern cell, initially existed as independent organisms before they were absorbed by bigger cells. Three scientists discuss their points of view on endosymbiotic theory.

Scientist 1

Relatively small organelles such as mitochondria were engulfed by larger cells via *phagocytosis,* a process in which the cell engulfs a smaller organism. According to recent biochemical research, the two-layered outer membrane of the mitochondria is structurally very similar to the cell membrane itself. This suggests that mitochondria could have existed on their own. Additionally, mitochondria have their own set of DNA, suggesting that they could have, at one point, contained the genetic information required to sustain life. Furthermore, the DNA within mitochondria is similar to that of bacteria, indicating that mitochondria were originally independent, prokaryotic organisms.

Scientist 2

Endosymbiosis is readily observable in the world today. Free-living algae form symbiotic relationships with coral, which allow the coral to perform photosynthesis. Additionally, free-living protists engulf bacteria or yeast with numerous functional benefits. Finally, *chloroplasts*, the organelles responsible for photosynthesis in plants, contain a membrane similar to that of plant cells and have their own set of DNA (just as mitochondria contain their own DNA), implying that chloroplasts could have been functionally independent before endosymbiosis occurred.

Scientist 3

Although chloroplasts and mitochondria contain DNA, the majority of the cell's instructions come from the larger and more complex nucleus. Analysis of the functioning of a human cell, for instance, indicates that nuclear instructions are necessary for both chloroplasts and mitochondria to function. Proteins are transported from the cytoplasm to the organelle, where they act with proteins formed from the DNA of the organelle. Because of this range of events, we cannot explain the function of organelles independently outside of the host cell. Furthermore, if one were to isolate a mitochondrion in culture, the mitochondrion will not, on its own, survive, grow, or reproduce. Therefore, it is not considered alive.

15. Which correctly lists the following in order of increasing size?
    A. Mitochondria, nucleus, eukaryotic cell
    B. Mitochondria, eukaryotic cell, nucleus
    C. Nucleus, mitochondria, eukaryotic cell
    D. Nucleus, eukaryotic cell, mitochondria

16. On which of the following do all three scientists agree?
    F. Mitochondria were engulfed by ancient cells.
    G. Chloroplasts were engulfed by ancient cells.
    H. Mitochondria contain their own DNA.
    J. Chloroplasts would be able to survive, grow, and reproduce on their own.

MANHATTAN
PREP

17. From the information provided in Scientist 2's argument, it can be implied that algae:

   A. is a prokaryotic organism.
   B. contains chloroplasts.
   C. is a unicellular organism.
   D. is larger than coral.

18. Scientist 3 implicitly defines life as having all of the following features EXCEPT:

   F. survival.
   G. growth.
   H. response to stimuli.
   J. reproduction.

19. A pea plant would be made up of which of the following types of cells?

   A. Mitochondria
   B. Chloroplasts
   C. Prokaryotic
   D. Eukaryotic

20. Suppose that new information led to the discovery that mitochondrial DNA, on its own, contains enough information to sustain life. The arguments of which scientist(s) would be weakened?

   F. Scientist 1 only
   G. Scientist 3 only
   H. Scientist 1 and Scientist 2
   J. Scientist 1 and Scientist 3

21. Imagine a molecule in the center of a mitochondrion. If that molecule were delivered from its starting point directly to the outside of a cell, how many membrane layers would it have to pass through?

   A. 1
   B. 2
   C. 4
   D. 8

21

MANHATTAN
PREP   935

PASSAGE 4

A group of students created a classification chart for the organisms living in a communal greenhouse.

Table 1

Step	Trait	Appearance	Result
1	Reproductive unit	spores	Go to Step 2
		seeds	Go to Step 5
2	Root, stem, leaves	not present	*Algae*
		present	Go to Step 3
3	*Vascular system,* or conducting tubules for nutrients	not present	*Hornwort*
		present	Go to Step 4
4	*Megaphyllis,* or leaves with developed vascular system	not present	*Club Moss*
		present	*Fern*
5	Flower or fruit	not present	*Gymnosperm*
		present	Go to Step 6
6	Appearance of flower or fruit	Flower parts in 3 units; fruit contains 3 chambers; 1 embryonic seed leaf	*Monocot*
		Flower parts in 4 or 5 units; fruit contains 4 or 5 chambers; 2 embryonic seed leaves	*Dicot*

22. Table 1 could be used to identify organisms that belong to which of the following kingdoms?

   F. Archaebacteria
   G. Fungi
   H. Plants
   J. Animals

23. Based on Table 1, which of the following would NOT be true of a strawberry plant?

   A. It utilizes spores as a reproductive unit.
   B. It contains embryonic seed leaves.
   C. It contains a flower.
   D. It utilizes seeds as a reproductive unit.

24. Based on Table 1, which of the following would NOT be true of a fern?

   F. It contains a stem.
   G. It utilizes seeds as a reproductive unit.
   H. It contains a vascular system.
   J. It contains megaphyllis.

25. The picture below is taken from a cross-section of the flower of a *Gladiolus* plant. How could *Gladiolus* be classified?

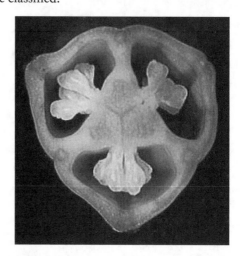

   A. Fern
   B. Gymnosperm
   C. Monocot
   D. Dicot

26. According to Table 1, hornwort and club moss both have which of the following traits?

   F. They utilize seeds as a reproductive unit.
   G. They contain a vascular system.
   H. They contain megaphyllis.
   J. They contain leaves.

27. Organisms that contain flowers or fruits are referred to as *angiosperms*. Which of the following would both be considered angiosperms?

   A. Algae and hornwort
   B. Gymnosperm and fern
   C. Club moss and gymnosperm
   D. Monocot and dicot

28. Which of the following is most likely to be a reason that the existence of a flower could be considered evolutionarily advantageous (that is, increasing the chances of successful reproduction)?

   F. A flower guarantees more seeds per organism.
   G. A flower could attract a mobile animal to help spread the seeds of an organism.
   H. A flower improves the vascular system of an organism.
   J. The colors of a flower help attract more sunlight.

PASSAGE 5

The bacterium *Salmonella enterica* is found throughout the world in the environment and in animals. Many illnesses such as food poisoning and typhoid fever have been tied to *S. enterica*. *S. enterica* is a *motile* bacteria, meaning that it is able to move freely due to the action of its numerous tails, or *flagella*, around its body.

Kirby-Bauer testing is a laboratory method for testing the efficacy of numerous antibiotic drugs in stopping the replication of bacteria. In Kirby-Bauer testing, discs containing antibiotics are placed on agar plates with growing colonies of healthy bacteria. After a waiting period, antibiotic effectiveness can be observed by the consistency of the agar around each disc—a cloudy appearance indicates that there is a prevalence of bacteria and that the antibiotic is not effective, while a clear area indicates that bacteria have been destroyed and that the antibiotic is effective.

The antibiotic *penicillin* is used in a Kirby-Bauer test of *S. enterica* and two other types of bacteria (Bacteria X and Bacteria Y). The results are shown in Figure 1. The scientist Paul Ehrlich predicted the discovery of antibiotics and referred to them as *magic bullets*, or compounds that destroy or prevent the normal functioning of bacterial cells but do not destroy or interfere with animal cells. Three students discuss their viewpoints on the mechanism of action of penicillin on this Kirby-Bauer test.

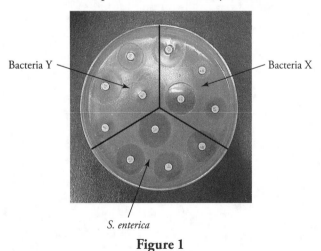

S. enterica

Figure 1

Student 1

Penicillin paralyzes bacterial flagella, limiting cell motility. A paralyzed cell cannot move around to obtain the nutrients it needs for survival; therefore, penicillin causes bacterial cells to waste away and inhibits their ability to reproduce. Since human cells can be motile, penicillin can also destroy human cells.

Student 2

Penicillin destroys bacterial cell walls causing *lysis*, or the destruction of the cell due to an influx of water. Since animal cells do not have cell walls, the penicillin targets bacterial cells only.

Student 3

Penicillin does not destroy bacteria but instead prevents them from multiplying. Since bacteria have different reproductive processes from animal cells, penicillin does not disrupt the normal functioning of animal cells.

Student 4

A clear circle in Kirby-Bauer test does not indicate that the bacteria are being destroyed. Any motile bacteria could simply be moving to an area that is farther away from the antibiotic disc, leaving a clear circle around the disc.

29. Which bacteria seem to be the most resistant to penicillin?
    - **A.** *S. enterica*
    - **B.** Bacteria X
    - **C.** Bacteria Y
    - **D.** None of the bacteria appear resistant at all to penicillin.

30. *Bacteriocidal* antibiotics destroy bacteria, while *bacteriostatic* antibiotics simply limit their reproduction. Which student(s) support the idea that penicillin is a bacteriocidal antibiotic?
    - **F.** Student 1 only
    - **G.** Students 1 and 2 only
    - **H.** Student 3 only
    - **J.** Students 2 and 4 only

31. The view(s) of which student(s) is(are) consistent with Ehrlich's theory of magic bullets?

   A. Student 1 only
   B. Student 2 only
   C. Students 2 and 3 only
   D. Students 1, 2, and 3 only

32. It can be inferred that the function of agar is to:

   F. destroy bacteria by paralyzing them.
   G. destroy bacteria via lysis.
   H. provide nutrients for bacteria so that they can grow.
   J. prevent the reproduction of bacteria.

33. Microscopic analysis of *S. enterica* on the agar reveals numerous irregularities and holes in the normally continuous cell wall. Which student's point of view is most supported by this observation?

   A. Student 1
   B. Student 2
   C. Student 3
   D. Student 4

34. Which of the following designs could be created to test the theory of Student 4?

   F. Re-create the experiment using a different antibiotic.
   G. Re-create the experiment using a non-motile strain of bacteria.
   H. Re-create the experiment using a non-agar substance.
   J. Re-create the experiment using fewer bacteria.

35. Which additional observation would strengthen the point of view of Student 4?

   A. The observation that *S. enterica* have an extremely short reproductive cycle
   B. The existence of multiple flagella on a single *S. enterica* cell
   C. A higher density of bacteria on the edges of the clear circle surrounding the antibiotic disc
   D. The observation that *S. enterica* have an extremely long reproductive cycle

PASSAGE 6

Origin of Life

Scientists believe that the Earth was formed about 4.5 billion years ago (BYA). All life on Earth is DNA-based, so DNA is found in the cells of all living plants on Earth. The earliest undisputed evidence of life is dated about 3.5 BYA, though the manner that this life developed is a source of constant debate. Below, scientists discuss their theories about *abiogenesis*, or the process of life developing from non-living matter.

Scientist 1

By creating conditions similar to those of early Earth—namely, creating an atmosphere of water (H_2O), methane (CH_4), ammonia (NH_3), and hydrogen (H_2)—abiogenesis can be replicated in the laboratory.

The chemicals are sealed inside an array of glass flasks connected in a continuous loop, with one glass half-full of liquid water and another flask containing a pair of electricity-inducing *electrodes*. The water is heated to simulate evaporation and then cooled so the water could condense back onto the flask. This cycle was repeated.

If this process is instituted for two weeks, roughly 2% of the carbon will form *amino acids*, which are the building blocks of proteins in living organisms. Sugars and hydrocarbons will also be formed, although nucleic acids (which are part of DNA) are not. Since proteins are integral to the normal functioning of life as we know it, this experiment indicates that abiogenesis could have occurred naturally on Earth without the intervention of any other source, although the prominence of ultraviolet (UV) radiation in Earth's early atmosphere delayed the formation of these biomolecules significantly.

Scientist 2

The early Earth's atmosphere consisted of methane (CH_4), ammonia (NH_3), water (H_2O), hydrogen sulfide (H_2S), carbon dioxide (CO_2), carbon monoxide (CO),

and phosphate (PO_4^{3-}). The existence of zinc sulfide (ZnS) was also integral to the formation of life. As part of the *zinc-world hypothesis,* ZnS was formed in *hydrothermic ducts* in the Earth's oceans. It has been shown that ZnS has integral roles in the normal functioning of DNA, RNA, and protein; thus, a ZnS precursor to DNA-based life must have existed. Since ZnS could not have formed without large amounts of radiation, the prevalence of UV radiation was integral to the eventual formation of life.

36. According to the information in the passage, how long did it take for life to develop on Earth?
    F. 100,000 years
    G. 1,000,000 years
    H. 100,000,000 years
    J. 1,000,000,000 years

37. On which of the following would both scientists agree?
    A. The prevalence of UV light hindered the formation of life.
    B. Zinc was an important precursor element to the formation of life.
    C. A great deal of UV light was present in Earth's early atmosphere.
    D. A great deal of carbon monoxide was present in Earth's early atmosphere.

38. Which of the following is a weakness of the explanation proposed by Scientist 1?
    F. It does not offer an explanation for the formation of nucleic acids.
    G. It does not provide a complete list of the compounds present in Earth's early atmosphere.
    H. It does not sufficiently reproduce the process of water evaporation in the atmosphere.
    J. It does not sufficiently reproduce the process of water condensation in the atmosphere.

39. Which of the following best resembles the experimental setup of flasks described by Scientist 1?

A.

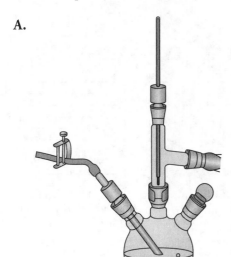

D.

B.

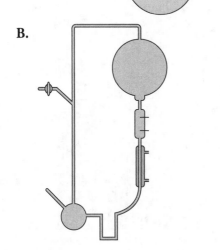

C.

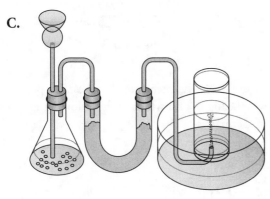

40. Suppose there was evidence that carbon dioxide did not form on Earth until 2.5 BYA. The argument of which scientist(s) would be weakened by this information?

F. Scientist 1 only
G. Scientist 2 only
H. Both Scientist 1 and Scientist 2
J. Neither Scientist 1 nor Scientist 2

41. Which of the following elements would Scientist 2 NOT expect to find in DNA?

A. Carbon
B. Helium
C. Hydrogen
D. Oxygen

42. It can be inferred that the electric discharge of the electrodes in the experiment described by Scientist 1 replicate which early Earth phenomenon?

F. Rainfall
G. Batteries
H. Lightning
J. Thunder

21

21

PASSAGE 7

Demography is the statistical study of human populations. Demographers analyze various rates affecting population, including birth, death, fertility, immigration, and emigration, in order to understand population sizes and predict future changes. One tool that demographers use to make predictions on future changes to populations is a *population pyramid*, a type of graph that shows the distribution of a population by gender over various age groups. All ages and age bands are in years.

Figure 1 shows the population pyramid of three different countries (the Democratic Republic of Congo, the United States, and Germany) in 2006. Figure 2 shows the population pyramid for the United Kingdom in 2001 and 2011, according to census data. Figure 3 shows the percentage of the total population in Lane County, Oregon, over 75 years old in 1930, 1970, and 1990.

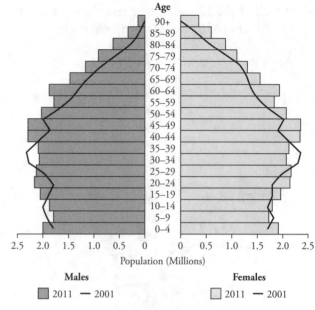

Figure 2

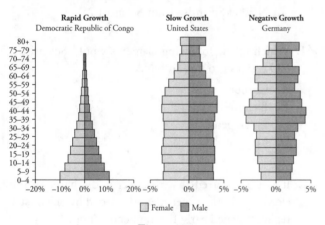

Figure 1

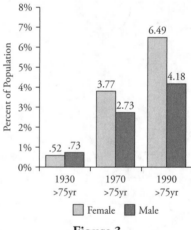

Figure 3

43. In Figure 1, the percentage of the total population was the highest for which of the following age groups in Germany?

    A. 5–9

    B. 20–24

    C. 40–44

    D. 75–79

44. In Figure 2, each of the following demographics in the United Kingdom increased in total population between 2001 and 2011 EXCEPT:

   F. males 0–4
   G. males 60–64
   H. females 30–34
   J. females 55–59

45. Based on the information given in Figure 3, which of the following can be properly inferred about the population of Lane County, Oregon?

   A. The number of females over 75 was greater in 1990 than in 1930.
   B. The number of females over 75 was greater than the number of males over 75 in 1930.
   C. The number of females over 75 was greater than the number of males over 75 in 1970.
   D. The number of people over 75 was greater in 1990 than in 1970.

46. In Figure 2, which of the following age groups made up the largest percentage of the population in the United Kingdom in 2001?

   F. 5–9
   G. 20–24
   H. 35–39
   J. 45–49

47. If the total population of the United States in 2006 was approximately 300 million people, how many children between the ages of 0 and 4 were living there at the time?

   A. Less than 8 million
   B. Between 8 and 16 million
   C. Between 16 and 24 million
   D. Between 24 and 30 million

48. If Lane County, Oregon, was experiencing rapid population growth in 1930, which of the following population pyramids would be most likely to represent the age distribution in that county at that time?

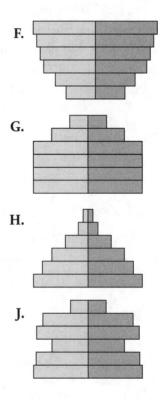

49. Compared to a country that has a much higher percentage of people in the post-reproductive stages of life than the pre-reproductive stages of life, a country that has a much higher percentage of people in the pre-reproductive stages of life than the post-reproductive would be more likely to see:

   A. an immediate sharp increase in population.
   B. an eventual sharp increase in population.
   C. an immediate sharp decrease in population.
   D. an eventual sharp decrease in population.

PASSAGE 8

Auxin is a plant hormone known to transmit signals involved in numerous aspects of plant development, including stem elongation, leaf patterning, and fruit development. Brassinosteroids (BRs) are a separate class of hormones that promote many of the same aspects of development through less well-understood mechanisms. To identify the genes underlying these similarities, researchers created *Arabidopsis* lines in which a single gene (either AXR3 or TIR1) was deleted. These genes are known to be involved in the auxin response. Seeds from these plants and seeds from the non-mutated "wild type" (WT) version were sprouted in the presence of varied concentrations of *brassinolide*, a potent BR, for 3 days. Afterwards, the emerging *hypocotyl* (stem) length was measured. The hypocotyl lengths at 3 days are shown in Figure 1.

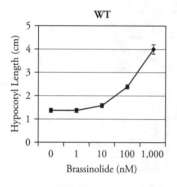 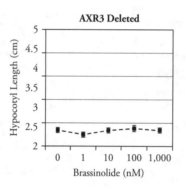 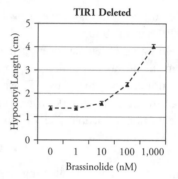

Figure 1

To understand the overlap in the effects of auxin and BR, the researchers then treated WT seedlings with BR or auxin and quantified a broad panel of approximately 22,000 genes. After treatment by one or both hormones, 596 genes in this panel were *upregulated* (increased in amount). The Venn diagram in Figure 2 shows the counts of genes that became upregulated after treatment by BR only, auxin only, or both BR and auxin.

the effects following separate treatments. WT seedlings were sprouted for 24 hours in the presence of either auxin, BR, or a combination of auxin and BR. The increase in expression of these genes, in copies per cell compared to untreated seedlings, is shown in Table 1.

Table 1

Gene	Auxin	BR	Auxin + BR
AHP1	30	10	35
BXF7	55	120	300
NYN4	80	190	320
PLD9	140	150	220
SVM2	200	190	190

Figure 2

Four genes that were upregulated by both auxin and BR were selected for an analysis of *synergism* between the two hormones. Synergism occurs when two compounds given together have an effect greater than the sum of

MANHATTAN PREP

50. A plant had a hypocotyl length of 4 cm after 3 days of brassinolide treatment. According to Figure 1, which of the following could describe the plant?

   F. TIR1 deleted, grown in 1,000 nM brassinolide
   G. WT, grown in 100 nM brassinolide
   H. AXR3 deleted, grown in 1,000 nM brassinolide
   J. WT, grown in 10 nM brassinolide

51. How much longer will the hypocotyl of a WT plant treated with 1,000 nM brassinolide be than that of a WT plant treated with 10 nM brassinolide, on average?

   A. 1.0 cm
   B. 1.5 cm
   C. 2.0 cm
   D. 2.5 cm

52. Which of the following best describes the impact of AXR3 and TIR1 deletions on the effect of brassinolide treatment on hypocotyl growth?

   F. Neither AXR3 nor TIR1 deletion affects plants' response to brassinolide.
   G. AXR3 deletion increases the effect, whereas TIR1 deletion decreases it.
   H. AXR3 deletion eliminates the effect, whereas TIR1 deletion does not affect it.
   J. AXR3 deletion increases the effect of brassinolide, but not as much as TIR1 deletion does.

53. Which of the following statements accurately reflects the effects of AXR3 deletion at 3 days following sprouting?

   A. AXR3 deletion has no impact on hypocotyl growth.
   B. In the absence of brassinolide, AXR3 deletion increases average length of hypocotyls relative to WT plants.
   C. In the absence of brassinolide, AXR3 deletion decreases average length of hypocotyls relative to WT plants.
   D. AXR3 deletion increases hypocotyl length compared to WT, but ONLY at 100 nM brassinolide or greater.

54. Approximately what fraction of auxin-upregulated genes were also upregulated following treatment with BR?

   F. 10%
   G. 20%
   H. 75%
   J. 98%

55. How many of the genes in Table 1 demonstrated a synergistic effect of auxin and BR?

   A. 2
   B. 3
   C. 4
   D. 5

56. Which of the following hypotheses on the relationship between auxin-induced upregulation, BR-induced gene upregulation, and auxin–BR synergy is most strongly suggested by the data in Table 1?

   F. Auxin and BR always have synergistic effects on genes strongly upregulated by both treatments.
   G. Auxin and BR usually have synergistic effects, EXCEPT on genes strongly upregulated by BR.
   H. Auxin and BR have synergistic effects on genes more strongly upregulated by auxin.
   J. Auxin and BR have synergistic effects on genes more strongly upregulated by BR.

21

PASSAGE 9

Many plants have growth and reproductive responses that are adapted to seasonal changes in climate, a characteristic known as *seasonality*. Two of the major signals of seasonal change are temperature and duration of light exposure.

To evaluate the effects of these two stimuli on flowering, a researcher transplanted 20 newly sprouted soybean seedlings into each of 8 different temperature- and light-controlled boxes. The seedlings were kept at a constant temperature, either 20°C or 30°C, and exposed to a regulated amount of light: either 8, 12, 16, or 20 consecutive hours in each 24-hour day. Following 7 weeks of growth, the number of plants with one or more open flowers was counted in each group. These numbers are shown in Table 1.

Table 1

Light Exposure (h)	Temperature	
	20°C	**30°C**
8	15	19
12	16	20
16	7	12
20	3	4

To study the genetic basis of the observed responses to temperature and light exposure, the researcher identified two genes suspected to be involved in the response to these stimuli in other plant species. The researcher then created two soybean *lines*, A and B, each carrying an inactivating mutation in one of these genes. These mutant lines differed from the original *parental* line only in the targeted gene.

Twenty seedlings from each of these mutant lines were subjected to the same sets of temperature- and light-exposure conditions as in the first experiment. After 7 weeks of growth, the number of plants with one or

more open flowers was counted in each group. These numbers are shown in Table 2.

Table 2

Light Exposure (h)	Mutant A		Mutant B	
	20°C	**30°C**	**20°C**	**30°C**
8	16	20	5	20
12	17	18	6	19
16	15	19	3	13
20	16	20	0	3

57. In the first experiment, flowering of the parental soybean line at 7 weeks was at a maximum under which of the following conditions?
    A. Light for 16 hours or more, at 20°C
    B. Light for 16 hours or more, at 30°C
    C. Light for 12 hours or fewer, at 20°C
    D. Light for 12 hours or fewer, at 30°C

58. Which of the following statements best describes the effect of temperature on the flowering of the parental line at 7 weeks?
    F. Flowering is unaffected by temperature.
    G. At all levels of light exposure, more plants will flower at 20°C than at 10° warmer.
    H. At all levels of light exposure, more plants will flower at 30°C than at 20°C.
    J. Increasing temperature from 20°C to 30°C increases flowering in only plants exposed to 12 or more hours of light per day.

59. If the researcher had planted 100 seedlings of the parental line, and then subjected these plants to 16 hours of light per day at 30°C, approximately how many plants would be expected to have one or more open flowers after 7 weeks?
    A. 20
    B. 40
    C. 60
    D. 80

60. The flowering data for the mutant lines is plotted on the graph below. Select the answer choice matching the line for Mutant A at 20°C.

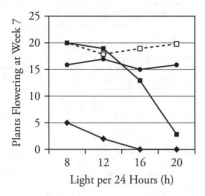

F. -●-
G. -□-
H. -◆-
J. -■-

61. Compared to the parental line, Mutant A is:

 A. less affected by light exposure.
 B. more affected by light exposure.
 C. less affected by temperature.
 D. more affected by temperature.

62. Which of the following conclusions is best supported by the data presented in Tables 1 and 2?

 F. Neither Mutant A nor Mutant B affects soybean flowering at 20°C.
 G. Compared to the parental line, Mutant B has an abnormal response to light exposure at 30°C.
 H. The gene inactivated in Mutant B may play a role in seasonal response to temperature changes.
 J. It is not possible to affect responses to light exposure through genetic mechanisms.

63. If 200 seedlings of the parental line had been exposed to 21 hours of light at 20°C, which of the following is the most likely number that would be expected to flower?

 A. 0
 B. 20
 C. 50
 D. 100

PASSAGE 10

Cell Structure

All living things, or *organisms*, are made up of cells; thus, the cell is commonly referred to as the fundamental unit of life. *Prokaryotic* cells, cells that lack a nucleus, were the first forms of life on Earth, as they developed 3.5 billion years ago (BYA). All bacteria are prokaryotic cells and unicellular. *Eukaryotic* cells, or cells that contain a nucleus, evolved from prokaryotic cells and are comparatively much more complex. Since eukaryotic cells contain a nucleus, they are referred to as *nucleated*. The first eukaryotic cell formed roughly 2 BYA, and about 1 billion years after the first eukaryotic cell was formed, multiple eukaryotes joined together to form the first multicellular organisms. All the cells of plants, fungi, and animals are eukaryotic, and these organisms are consequently referred to as *eukaryotes*.

The size of various prokaryotic and eukaryotic cells is found in Table 1, with diameters given in micrometers (μm), or millionths of a meter.

Cell	Approximate Diameter
Escherichia coli (bacterium)	0.5 μm
Human erythrocyte (red blood cell)	7 μm
Human ovum (egg cell)	100 μm
Streptococcus pneumoniae (bacterium)	1 μm
Root cell from oak tree	80 μm

Table 1

Numerous differences can be observed among cells in fungi, plants, and animals. Each of these cells contains a boundary around the cell called a *cell membrane*, which separates the inside of the cell from the outside of the cell. Some cells also maintain a *cell wall*, a more rigid barrier to maintain composure. Plants have cell walls made of *cellulose,* a material that is not found in animal cells. Bacteria generally have cell walls made of *peptidoglycan*, and animal cells lack cell walls entirely. Animal cells, plant cells, and bacterial cells all contain *ribosomes,* which use heredity information to create proteins.

Table 2

Cell	Cell Membrane	Cell Wall	Ribosomes	Cellulose	Peptido-glycan
Eschericia coli (bacterium)	Yes	Yes	Yes, Type 1	No	Yes
Human erythrocyte (red blood cell)	Yes	No	Yes, Type 2	No	No
Human ovum (egg cell)	Yes	No	Yes, Type 2	No	No
Streptococcus pneumoniae (bacterium)	Yes	Yes	Yes, Type 1	No	Yes
Root cell from oak tree (plant cell)	Yes	Yes	Yes, Type 2	Yes	No

64. According to the information above, which of these words would generally NOT be associated with eukaryotes or eukaryotic cells in comparison with prokaryotic cells?

    F. Multicellular
    G. Evolved
    H. Simple
    J. Nucleated

65. According to the information above, when did the first living things composed of multiple cells form?

    A. 4 BYA
    B. 3 BYA
    C. 2 BYA
    D. 1 BYA

MANHATTAN
PREP

66. A student swabs his inner cheek for cells and observes them under a microscope. Which of the following would be an unlikely trait of this student's cheek cells?

   F. They contain cellulose.
   G. They contain a nucleus.
   H. They contain a cell membrane.
   J. They are eukaryotic.

67. Which hypothesis is supported by Table 1?

   A. Larger cells are usually part of unicellular organisms.
   B. Smaller cells are usually part of multicellular organisms.
   C. Eukaryotic cells are usually larger than prokaryotic cells.
   D. Prokaryotic cells are usually larger than eukaryotic cells.

68. According to Table 2, which of the following appear(s) to be present in the greatest variety of living organisms?

   F. Cellulose
   G. Type 2 ribosomes
   H. Proteins
   J. Cell walls

69. Suppose someone were to try and design a medicine that targets and destroys bacteria but not eukaryotic cells. What would be an appropriate target for this drug?

   A. Cell membrane
   B. Proteins
   C. Type 1 ribosomes
   D. Cellulose

70. Which of the following is NOT a form of hereditary information?

   F. DNA
   G. RNA
   H. Proteins
   J. These are all forms of hereditary information.

21

PASSAGE 11

All cells arise from the division of pre-existing cells. The *cell cycle* is a distinct progression of stages that occurs in between the time a cell divides and the time the resulting two cells, or *daughter cells*, also divide.

The cell cycle has two major portions: *interphase* and the *mitotic stage.* During interphase, the cell prepares for division. Interphase can be further divided into three parts: the G_1 phase, during which the cell grows enormously in size, the S phase, during which genetic material replicates, and the G_2 phase, during which the cell creates proteins that are essential for cell division.

The mitotic stage includes four distinct stages called prophase, metaphase, anaphase, and telophase. During *prophase*, genetic material condenses and becomes visible in the form of x-shaped *chromosomes*. Prophase is followed by *metaphase*, during which the chromosomes are aligned at the equator of the cell along an imaginary middle line called the *metaphase plate*. Following metaphase, in *anaphase*, the chromosomes split and move towards the two poles of the cell, and in *telophase*, the nuclei of the daughter cells are formed.

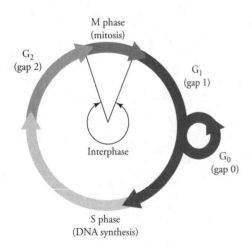

Figure 1

While going through the cell cycle, certain cells become specialized and no longer replicate. These cells stay in what can be termed the G_0 phase permanently. This phase can be considered either an extended G_1 phase or a separate phase outside of the normal cell cycle. Cells in the G_0 phase include mature muscle cells, nerve cells, and liver cells. On the other hand, certain cells go through the cell cycle repeatedly and continually throughout an organism's life, and these cells are generally referred to as *stem cells*.

Experiment 1

A student cuts a thin slice of onion, stains the slice, and views it under the microscope. She counts the number of cells in her sample that were in each phase of the cell cycle and charts her results in Figure 2.

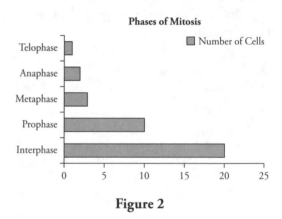

Figure 2

Experiment 2

A student cultures three different types of cells in a petri dish and stores them in an incubator at 37°C with nutrients to replicate the conditions of the human body. Table 1 displays the counts of each cell type after various periods of time.

Table 1

Cell Type	Time		
	0 hr	12 hr	24 hr
A	50	99	200
B	50	74	102
C	50	50	50

MANHATTAN
PREP

71. According to the passage, 10 cells that each go through one phase of mitosis would produce how many daughter cells?

    A. 5
    B. 10
    C. 20
    D. 100

72. If a cell were unable to complete G_2 phase, what would presumably happen?

    F. The cell would not grow.
    G. The cell would not synthesize a new copy of chromosomes.
    H. The cell would not become specialized and would stay in the G_0 stage.
    J. The cell would be unable to replicate because it lacked the necessary proteins for division.

73. A student repeats Experiment 1 with a sample that includes 75 onion cells. Approximately how many of these cells would she expect to find in prophase?

    A. 10
    B. 20
    C. 40
    D. 60

74. In Experiment 2, which type of cell is type C least likely to be?

    F. Nerve cell
    G. Stem cell
    H. Muscle cell
    J. Liver cell

75. In Experiment 2, after 36 hours, how many cells of type A would you expect to find?

    A. 200
    B. 300
    C. 400
    D. 800

76. According to Figure 2, which of the following phases of the mitotic stage is presumably the shortest in duration?

    F. Telophase
    G. Anaphase
    H. Metaphase
    J. Prophase

77. An animal cell undergoing mitosis is pictured below. In which phase of mitosis is this cell?

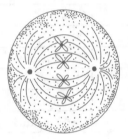

    A. Prophase
    B. Metaphase
    C. Anaphase
    D. Telophase

PASSAGE 12

Viruses are simple structures that are composed of genetic information, coded in the form of *deoxyribonucleic acid* (DNA) or *ribonucleic acid* (RNA), surrounded by a protein coat. *Bacteriophages* are viruses that invade and attack bacteria. Viruses cannot reproduce without a host cell, and bacteriophages use bacteria as hosts to fuel viral reproduction.

When a bacteriophage infects a bacterial cell, it uses *adhesion proteins* to attach itself to the surface of the bacterium. The virus then injects its hereditary information into the bacterium, and the hereditary information makes its way to the bacterial nucleus, where it directs the production of thousands of new viruses. The bacterial cell eventually *lyses*, or ruptures, releasing the virus and its new copies.

Experiment 1

Students researched the classification of numerous viruses, the diseases they caused, and the size of these viruses. They discovered that viruses are assigned to a group based primarily on the size and the hereditary material that they use. The students' findings are summarized in Table 1.

Table 1

Virus	Group	Hereditary Material	Disease	Size (diameter)
Poliovirus	Picornavirus	RNA	Poliomyelitis	100 nm
Coxsackie	Picornavirus	RNA	Meningitis	?
Rhinovirus	Picornavirus	RNA	Common Cold	300 nm
Measles	Paramyxovirus	DNA	Measles	1,000 nm
Influenza	Orthomyxovirus	DNA	Influenza	80 nm

Experiment 2

Students researched the classification of numerous bacteria, the diseases they caused, and the size of these bacteria. Their findings are summarized in Table 2.

Students classified the shape as *cocci*, which are spheres that often attach to each other; *bacilli*, which are straight, thin rods; or *spirochetes*, which are spiral-shaped rods.

Table 2

Bacteria	Shape	Disease	Size (diameter)
Streptococcus pneumoniae	Cocci	Pneumonia	1,250 nm
Staphylococcus aureus	Cocci	Skin infection	600 nm
Bacillus anthracis	Bacilli	Anthrax	1,300 nm
Salmonella typhi	Bacilli	Food poisoning	5,000 nm
Treponema pallidum	Spirochete	Syphilis	15,000 nm

Experiment 3

To identify the type of hereditary material used in bacteria, students labeled a protein coat of a bacteriophage with ^{35}S (a radioactive isotope of sulfur) and the DNA of another virus with ^{32}P (a radioactive isotope of phosphorus). After the bacteriophage entered a bacterial cell, they checked each bacterial cell for radioactive material. They discovered that the bacteria invaded by ^{35}S-labeled protein capsules had no radioactive material inside, while the bacteria invaded by viruses with ^{32}P-labeled DNA did have radioactive material inside. This experiment is illustrated in Figure 1.

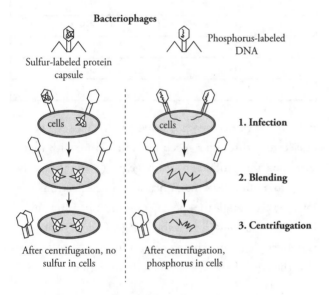

Figure 1

78. Which of the following is the most likely size of the Coxsackie virus?

   F. 10 nm
   G. 150 nm
   H. 800 nm
   J. 1,200 nm

79. According to Table 1 and Table 2, which is NOT true about viruses?

   A. All bacteria are larger than all viruses.
   B. Some viruses are capable of inserting their genetic information into bacteria.
   C. A virus is responsible for the common cold.
   D. Viruses can be as small as 80 nm.

80. A bacteriophage is found to have DNA as a hereditary material and a size of roughly 900 nm. Which group would you classify this bacteriophage under?

   F. Picornavirus
   G. Paramyxovirus
   H. Orthomyxovirus
   J. Cocci

81. In Experiment 3, why, presumably, did the students use radioactive material?

   A. To allow the material to enter the bacteria
   B. To lengthen the life cycle of the virus
   C. To destroy the bacteria
   D. To trace where the material went

82. A new drug is developed that destroys the adhesion proteins of a bacteriophage. What would be the likely effect of this drug on this bacteriophage?

   F. It would cause the bacteria to lyse.
   G. It would cause the virus to lyse.
   H. It would not allow the bacterium to adhere to and enter the virus.
   J. It would not allow the virus to adhere to and enter the bacteria.

83. The drawing below was obtained from a student's lab notebook. Which type of bacteria in Table 2 could these be?

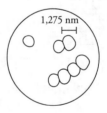

   A. *Streptococcus pneumoniae*
   B. *Staphylococcus aureus*
   C. *Bacillus anthracis*
   D. *Salmonella typhi*

84. According to the results of Experiment 3, what could students conclude?

   F. Genetic material of bacteria is in the form of proteins and contains sulfur.
   G. Genetic material of bacteria is in the form of DNA and contains sulfur.
   H. Genetic material of bacteria is in the form of proteins and contains phosphorus.
   J. Genetic material of bacteria is the form of DNA and contains phosphorus.

PASSAGE 13

A *compound light microscope* (CLM) uses a series of lenses to magnify an image. To prepare an image for viewing, a transparent specimen is placed on the stage. Light, which can be controlled by the *diaphragm*, passes through the image and is first magnified by the *objective lens*, a simple high-powered magnifying glass near the specimen. Light then passes through the objective lens to the *ocular lens*, another high-powered magnifying glass nearest the viewer's eye. The compound light microscope is a relatively simple way of obtaining a magnified image, but it cannot increase the size of an image more than 1000×.

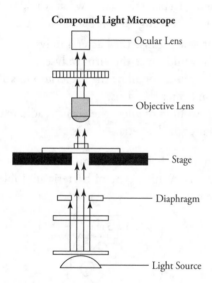

Figure 1

The total magnification of the image in a CLM can be obtained with the following equation.

(Magnification of objective lens) × (Magnification of ocular lens) = Total magnifying power

Table 1 shows the magnifying power of various objective lenses on a particular CLM. Table 2 shows the real-size field of view related to numerous settings of total magnifying power.

Table 1

Color of Objective Lens	Magnification Power
Red	4×
Yellow	10×
Orange	20×
Blue	40×
Green	100×

Table 2

Total Magnifying Power	Field of View Diameter (mm)
4×	4.5
10×	1.8
20×	0.9
40×	0.45
100×	0.18

A *transmission electron microscope* (TEM) passes a beam of electrons through a specimen, interacting with that specimen and producing an image on a viewing screen of up to 5,000,000× magnification. Since electrons must pass through the specimen, it must be ultra-thin in order to produce a viewable image. Consequently, it is impossible to view living objects in a TEM. Additionally, the cost of a TEM is generally very high.

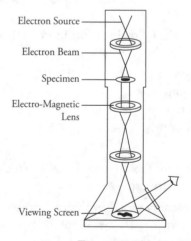

Figure 2

85. Which would have the greatest total magnification power in a CLM?

   A. 4× objective lens, 10× ocular lens
   B. 10× objective lens, 4× ocular lens
   C. 10× objective lens, 10× ocular lens
   D. 40× objective lens, 5× ocular lens

86. According to the passage, which of the following is a disadvantage of using a CLM?

   F. The amount of light passing through the diaphragm can damage the viewer's eye.
   G. It only has a maximum magnification of 100×.
   H. The cost of a CLM is extremely high.
   J. It requires a sample that allows light to pass through it.

87. What is one advantage of using a TEM over a CLM?

   A. It is less costly.
   B. You can view living images.
   C. You can obtain a much higher magnification.
   D. You can use different varieties of objective lenses.

88. In his lab notebook, a student drew the following image of a live amoeba. Which magnification technique did he most likely use?

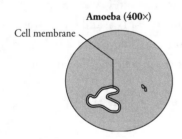

Amoeba (400×)

Cell membrane

   F. CLM with 10× ocular lens and red objective lens
   G. CLM with 10× ocular lens and yellow objective lens
   H. CLM with 10× ocular lens and blue objective lens
   J. TEM

89. Suppose a 5× magnifying glass is placed on top of the ocular lens of a CLM that had a 10× ocular lens and a 4× objective lens. What would be the predicted total magnification power of these three lenses combined?

   A. 19×
   B. 30×
   C. 45×
   D. 200×

The following two questions apply to the scenario below. A student using a CLM with a 10× ocular lens and a yellow objective lens from Table 1 observes a linear arrangement of plant cells and sketches them below.

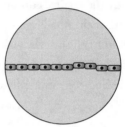

90. Approximately how large is each cell?

   F. 18 mm
   G. 1.8 mm
   H. 0.18 mm
   J. 0.018 mm

91. If the student were to switch to an orange objective lens while using the same ocular lens, how many cells would she expect to see?

   A. 1
   B. 5
   C. 10
   D. 20

PASSAGE 14

An animal cell is filled with solution and surrounded by a *semipermeable membrane*, an outer layer that allows some materials to enter the cell but not others. Relatively large or charged materials generally cannot pass through the membrane unless they are guided by specialized membrane proteins that allow them to pass. Water can move in and out of membrane proteins by *osmosis*, the diffusion (or random mixing and spreading) of water from an area of low solute concentration to an area of high solute concentration.

In animal cells, the movement of water into and out of a cell is determined by the relative concentration of solute inside and outside the cell. As a large amount of water moves out of a cell, the cell shrivels, which is referred to as *crenation*. As a large amount of water moves into a cell, the cell swells and can eventually burst, which is referred to as *lysis*.

The terms hypertonic, hypotonic, and isotonic are used to compare the relative concentration of solute between two solutions. A *hypertonic* solution has a higher solute concentration when compared to another solution. Therefore, water will diffuse towards the hypertonic solution as indicated in Figure 1.

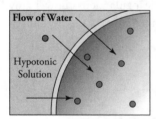
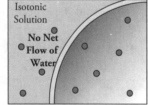
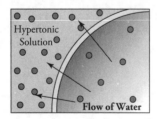

Figure 1

A *hypotonic* solution has a lower concentration of solute when compared to another solution. Therefore, water will diffuse away from hypotonic solution. *Isotonic* solutions have the same concentration as one another, and there is no noticeable change in the diffusion of water among isotonic solutions.

Osmotic concentration is a numerical measure of the amount of solute in a given volume of solution, allowing for the comparison of solutions to determine osmotic behavior. The formula for osmotic concentration is:

$$\text{Osmotic concentration} = \frac{\text{Osmoles of the solute}}{\text{Liters of the solution}}$$

An *osmole* of a solute is 1 mole of the solute in dissolved form.

Experiment 1

Students prepared 4 solutions. Solution A was created by dissolving a total of 0.3 moles of sodium ions (Na^+) and chloride ions (Cl^-) in water to create a 1.0 L solution, Solution B was created by dissolving a total of 0.3 moles of Na^+ ions and Cl^- ions in water to create a 0.5 L solution, Solution C was created by dissolving an unknown amount of Na^+ and Cl^- in water to create a 1.0 L solution, and Solution D was created by dissolving 0.6 moles of the protein *globulin* in water to create a 2.0 L solution.

Experiment 2

Students placed red blood cells into beakers filled with the 4 solutions, waited for 10 minutes, and observed the cells under a microscope.

Solution That Blood Cells Were Placed In	Process Observed
A	No change
B	Crenation
C	Lysis
D	No Change

MANHATTAN
PREP

92. Which of the following is a true statement?

    F. Diffusion is a form of osmosis.
    G. Osmosis is a form of diffusion.
    H. Hypertonic solutions have the same concentration as each other.
    J. Hypotonic solutions have the same concentration as each other.

93. What is the osmotic concentration of Solution D?

    A. 2.6 osmol/L
    B. 1.2 osmol/L
    C. 0.6 osmol/L
    D. 0.3 osmol/L

94. Based on the results of Experiment 2, what is the osmotic concentration of the blood cells?

    F. 0.3 osmol/L
    G. 0.6 osmol/L
    H. 1.2 osmol/L
    J. 2.6 osmol/L

95. Which of the following correctly describes Solution B and Solution C?

    A. Solution B is isotonic to the blood cells; Solution C is hypertonic to the blood cells.
    B. Solution B is hypertonic to the blood cells; Solution C is hypotonic to the blood cells.
    C. Solution B is hypotonic to the blood cells; Solution C is hypertonic to the blood cells.
    D. Solution B is hypotonic to the blood cells; Solution C is isotonic to the blood cells.

96. Which of the following lists Solutions A, B, and C in order of decreasing osmotic concentration?

    F. Solution A, Solution B, Solution C
    G. Solution B, Solution A, Solution C
    H. Solution B, Solution C, Solution A
    J. Solution C, Solution A, Solution B

97. Suppose a blood sample from a fish is taken, and the osmolarity of these fish cells was 0.2 osmol/L. What would you expect to happen if these cells were dropped in Solution B?

    A. The cells would lyse because they are hypertonic to Solution B.
    B. The cells would crenate because they are hypertonic to Solution B.
    C. The cells would lyse because they are hypotonic to Solution B.
    D. The cells would crenate because they are hypotonic to Solution B.

98. The *Biuret Test* involves using sodium hydroxide and hydrated copper (II) sulfate as an indicator for peptide bonds, usually formed between amino acids to create proteins. In the presence of these peptide bonds, the Biuret reagent turns from blue to pink. Which solution would you expect to produce a positive (pink) Biuret test?

    F. Solution A
    G. Solution B
    H. Solution C
    J. Solution D

MANHATTAN
PREP

Answer Keys

Write in whether you got each problem right or wrong (or left it blank). If your answer was correct, put a 1 in every blank to the right of that problem. Sum up each column and compare your total to the total possible "Out Of" points in each column.

Passage 1

Problem	Correct Answer	Right/ Wrong/Blank	Interpretation of Data	Scientific Investigation	Evaluation of Models, Inferences, and Experimental Results
1	D			—	
2	H			—	
3	C			—	
4	F			—	
5	A			—	
6	J			—	
7	B			—	
Total					
Out Of	7		0	7	0

Passage 2

Problem	Correct Answer	Right/ Wrong/Blank	Interpretation of Data	Scientific Investigation	Evaluation of Models, Inferences, and Experimental Results
8	H		—		
9	C		—		
10	F		—		
11	D		—		
12	G		—		
13	B		—		
14	G		—		
Total					
Out Of	7	7	0	0	

MANHATTAN
PREP

Passage 3

Problem	Correct Answer	Right/ Wrong/Blank	Interpretation of Data	Scientific Investigation	Evaluation of Models, Inferences, and Experimental Results
15	A				—
16	H				—
17	B				—
18	H				—
19	D				—
20	G				—
21	C				—
Total					
Out Of		7	0	0	7

Passage 4

Problem	Correct Answer	Right/ Wrong/Blank	Interpretation of Data	Scientific Investigation	Evaluation of Models, Inferences, and Experimental Results
22	H		—		
23	A		—		
24	G		—		
25	C		—		
26	J		—		
27	D		—		
28	G		—		
Total					
Out Of		7	7	0	0

Passage 5

Problem	Correct Answer	Right/ Wrong/Blank	Interpretation of Data	Scientific Investigation	Evaluation of Models, Inferences, and Experimental Results
29	C				—
30	G				—
31	C				—
32	H				—
33	B				—
34	G				—
35	C				—
Total					
Out Of	7	7	0	0	7

Passage 6

Problem	Correct Answer	Right/ Wrong/Blank	Interpretation of Data	Scientific Investigation	Evaluation of Models, Inferences, and Experimental Results
36	J				—
37	C				—
38	F				—
39	B				—
40	G				—
41	B				—
42	H				—
Total					
Out Of	7	7	0	0	7

21

MANHATTAN
PREP

Passage 7

Problem	Correct Answer	Right/ Wrong/Blank	Interpretation of Data	Scientific Investigation	Evaluation of Models, Inferences, and Experimental Results
43	C			—	
44	H			—	
45	C			—	
46	H			—	
47	C			—	
48	H			—	
49	B			—	
Total					
Out Of		7	0	7	0

Passage 8

Problem	Correct Answer	Right/ Wrong/Blank	Interpretation of Data	Scientific Investigation	Evaluation of Models, Inferences, and Experimental Results
50	F			—	
51	D			—	
52	H			—	
53	B			—	
54	G			—	
55	A			—	
56	J			—	
Total					
Out Of		7	0	7	0

Passage 9

Problem	Correct Answer	Right/ Wrong/Blank	Interpretation of Data	Scientific Investigation	Evaluation of Models, Inferences, and Experimental Results
57	D			—	
58	H			—	
59	C			—	
60	F			—	
61	A			—	
62	H			—	
63	B			—	
Total					
Out Of	7		0	7	0

Passage 10

Problem	Correct Answer	Right/ Wrong/Blank	Interpretation of Data	Scientific Investigation	Evaluation of Models, Inferences, and Experimental Results
64	H		—		
65	D		—		
66	F		—		
67	C		—		
68	H		—		
69	C		—		
70	H		—		
Total					
Out Of	7	7		0	0

Passage 11

Problem	Correct Answer	Right/ Wrong/Blank	Interpretation of Data	Scientific Investigation	Evaluation of Models, Inferences, and Experimental Results
71	C			—	
72	J			—	
73	B			—	
74	G			—	
75	C			—	
76	F			—	
77	B			—	
Total					
Out Of	7		0	7	0

Passage 12

Problem	Correct Answer	Right/ Wrong/Blank	Interpretation of Data	Scientific Investigation	Evaluation of Models, Inferences, and Experimental Results
78	G			—	
79	A			—	
80	G			—	
81	D			—	
82	J			—	
83	A			—	
84	J			—	
Total					
Out Of	7		0	7	0

Passage 13

Problem	Correct Answer	Right/ Wrong/Blank	Interpretation of Data	Scientific Investigation	Evaluation of Models, Inferences, and Experimental Results
85	D		—		
86	J		—		
87	C		—		
88	H		—		
89	D		—		
90	J		—		
91	B		—		
Total					
Out Of		7	7	0	0

Passage 14

Problem	Correct Answer	Right/ Wrong/Blank	Interpretation of Data	Scientific Investigation	Evaluation of Models, Inferences, and Experimental Results
92	G			—	
93	D			—	
94	F			—	
95	B			—	
96	G			—	
97	D			—	
98	J			—	
Total					
Out Of		7	0	7	0

Life Sciences Solutions

Passage 1 Solutions

1. **(D)** Both heart rate and breathing rate

Scientific Investigation

According to the passage, the blood pressure requires a sphygmomanometer and a stethoscope. However, the heart rate and breathing rate only require the placement of a hand over the chest without any additional instrument. The correct answer is (D).

2. **(H)** 3 times per second

Scientific Investigation

Looking at Table 1, the student's heart rate after 15 minutes on the treadmill was 179 beats per minute. Since there are 60 seconds for every minute, the student's heart would beat approximately 3 times every second. The correct answer is (H).

3. **(C)** Both systolic and diastolic pressures were normal.

Scientific Investigation

The passage states that the normal resting blood pressures are less than 120 mmHg (systolic) and less than 80 mmHg (diastolic). Using Table 1, the baseline (rest) blood pressure of the student was 118 mmHg (systolic) and 75 mmHg (diastolic), both under the normal limit. The correct answer is (C).

4. **(F)** would be able to hear a pulse.

Scientific Investigation

The passage states that "[a]lthough the normal flow of blood has no sound, the sound of the subject's pulse (i.e., the heart beat) disappears after the arm cuff is tightened …" If the sound of the pulse disappears, then the pulse must be able to be heard before that point. The correct answer is (F).

5. **(A)** 160 mmHg

Scientific Investigation

The passage states that the arm cuff is tightened until the sound of the pulse disappears, then the systolic pressure, which normally is equal to or less than 120 mmHg, is recorded when the sound of the squirting blood is heard. Finally, the diastolic pressure, which normally is equal to or less than 80 mmHg, is recorded when the sound of squirting blood disappears again. Thus, the sound of the pulse must disappear at a pressure above the systolic pressure, or above 120 mmHg. The correct answer is (A).

6.   **(J)** There is not enough information provided about heart rate after exercise to draw a conclusion.

Scientific Investigation

According to Table 1, the student's heart rate after a period of exercise was 179 BPM. While the passage states that the normal resting heart rate is between 60 BPM and 100 BPM, the passage provides no information about the normal heart rate after a period of exercise, so no conclusion can be drawn regarding the student's heart rate after a period of exercise. The correct answer is (J).

7.   **(B)** TPR must have decreased after exercise.

Scientific Investigation

Looking at Table 1, the student's systolic and diastolic pressures remained approximately the same at rest and after a period of exercise. However, because the heart rate increased from 74 BPM to 179 BPM, and each heart beat delivers the same amount of blood flow, the total blood flow also increased. Since the blood pressure is directly proportional both to the amount of blood flow and to the TPR, if the blood flow increases, then the TPR must have decreased by the same factor in order for the blood pressure to remain the same. The correct answer is (B).

Passage 2 Solutions

8.   **(H)** Graph H

Interpretation of Data

According to Table 1, the mouse before administration of any drug spends 2 minutes swimming, 3 minutes struggling, and 5 minutes floating. Graph C is the only one that correctly represents this data. The correct answer is (H).

9.   **(C)** Floating

Interpretation of Data

The introduction suggests that the "floating" stage is the last one in this test. Looking at Table 1, the mouse reaches the floating stage after minute 6, and does not appear to recover from it. You can conclude that the mouse will probably still be floating after 12 minutes. The correct answer is (C).

10.   **(F)** a mouse being nursed by its mother.

Interpretation of Data

The introduction states that the "beaker of water is not a familiar environment for the mouse, and so it triggers a *stress response*," indicating that stress responses are triggered in unfamiliar environments. Since cortisol mediates the stress response, it would not be expected to be increased in a familiar environment. Answer choices (G), (H), and (J) are all unfamiliar or stressful environments and are expected to result in higher cortisol levels, while answer choice (F) is a familiar environment, so cortisol levels are not expected to rise. The correct answer is (F).

11. **(D)** Oxycodone decreased cortisol levels, since the animal showed a decreased stress response.

Interpretation of Data

If you look at Experiment 3, you can see that the mouse displayed swimming and struggling for a much shorter time (2 minutes) compared to Experiment 1 (5 minutes), indicating that it had a decreased stress response when administered oxycodone. Decreased stress response correlates to decreased cortisol levels. The correct answer is (D).

12. **(G)** Graph G

Interpretation of Data

According to Table 2, the mouse after administration of fluoxetine spends 6 minutes swimming, 3 minutes struggling, and 1 minute floating. Graph G is the only one that correctly represents this data. The correct answer is (G).

13. **(B)** Yes, since fluoxetine increased the amount of time swimming and struggling and decreased the amount of time floating for the mouse.

Interpretation of Data

Looking at Experiment 2, you can see that the mouse that was administered fluoxetine was swimming or struggling for 9 minutes, which is a longer time than for the control in Experiment 1. As a result, you can conclude that that the mouse had an increased stress response when it is administered fluoxetine. Thus, this drug may be helpful to counter the decreased stress response experienced in depression. The correct answer is (B).

14. **(G)** The mouse would eventually begin floating, no matter what conditions were imposed.

Interpretation of Data

Answer choice (F) is a valid criticism, because you would not know whether the results observed in Experiments 2 and 3 were only caused by the administration of the drug. The results may have been impacted by the previous experiments. Answer choice (H) is also a valid criticism, because if there were changes in behavior between the 1-minute intervals, you might draw different conclusions about cortisol levels in the mouse. Finally, answer choice (J) is a valid criticism, because you would not be able to rely on the experimental results if the results were due to the "placebo" effect of administering the drugs rather than the drugs themselves. In contrast, choice (G) introduces an irrelevant criticism. The fact that the mouse always begins floating does not undermine the experimental results. The question is not whether the mouse begins floating, but when. The correct answer is (G).

Passage 3 Solutions

15. **(A)** Mitochondria, nucleus, eukaryotic cell

Evaluation of Models, Inferences, and Experimental Results

The passage defines a eukaryotic cell as a cell that contains a nucleus, so the nucleus is smaller than the eukaryotic cell. In addition, Scientist 3 states: "Although … mitochondria contain DNA, the majority of the cell's instructions come from the larger and more complex nucleus," so mitochondria are smaller than the nucleus. The correct answer is (A).

16. **(H)** Mitochondria contain their own DNA.

Evaluation of Models, Inferences, and Experimental Results

All three scientists agree that mitochondria contain their own DNA, because this point is stated by all three. Scientist 1 explicitly states that "mitochondria have their own set of DNA," and Scientist 3 states that "chloroplasts and mitochondria contain DNA." Scientist 2 mentions as an aside that mitochondria contain DNA. The correct answer is (H).

17. **(B)** contains chloroplasts.

Evaluation of Models, Inferences, and Experimental Results

Scientist 2 states that algae's symbiotic relationship with coral allows coral to perform photosynthesis, implying that coral cannot perform photosynthesis on its own. In addition, Scientist 2 states that chloroplasts are the organelles that are responsible for photosynthesis. In order for algae to allow coral to perform photosynthesis, it can be inferred that algae has chloroplasts. The correct answer is (B).

18. **(H)** response to stimuli.

Evaluation of Models, Inferences, and Experimental Results

Scientist 3 states that a "mitochondrion will not, on its own, survive, grow, or reproduce. Therefore, it is not considered alive." The scientist argues that the mitochondrion cannot be living because of its inability to survive, grow, and reproduce, implying that these abilities (survival, growth, and reproduction) are features of a living organism. However, Scientist 3 never mentions or alludes to a cell's response to stimuli as a feature of life. The correct answer is (H).

19. **(D)** Eukaryotic

Evaluation of Models, Inferences, and Experimental Results

Mitochondria and chloroplasts are organelles within a eukaryotic cell but are not cells by themselves. Because a pea plant is a multi-cellular organism, then, according to the passage, it is made of eukaryotic cells (as the definition of this term asserts). The correct answer is (D).

MANHATTAN
PREP

20. **(G)** Scientist 3 only

Evaluation of Models, Inferences, and Experimental Results

Both Scientists 1 and 2 hypothesize that mitochondria were once functionally independent prokaryotic organisms and may have been, at one point, considered living. However, Scientist 3 argues that mitochondria cannot survive, grow, or reproduce on their own, and could never live independently. That said, if it were discovered that mitochondrial DNA can in fact sustain life, then it would be possible for mitochondria to survive on their own, weakening the argument of Scientist 3. The correct answer is (G).

21. **(C)** 4

Evaluation of Models, Inferences, and Experimental Results

In order for this molecule to go from the center of a mitochondrion to the outside of a cell, it must pass through the membrane of the mitochondrion, and then the membrane of the cell. Scientist 1 states that "the two-layered outer membrane of the mitochondria is structurally very similar to the cell membrane itself," suggesting that both the mitochondria membrane and cell membrane are two-layered. Thus, the molecule would have to pass through a total of 4 membrane layers to travel outside the cell. The correct answer is (C).

Passage 4 Solutions

22. **(H)** Plants

Data Interpretation

All of the organisms listed are part of the plant kingdom. The correct answer is (H).

23. **(A)** It utilizes spores as a reproductive unit.

Data Interpretation

All of the plants in Steps 5 and 6 use seeds as a reproductive unit, according to Step 1 (which sorts plants into those using spores and those using seeds). The key is to recognize that a strawberry plant must contain fruit, since strawberries are a kind of fruit. A strawberry plant contains fruit, contains embryonic seed leaves, and contains a flower. It certainly does not use spores as a reproductive unit, as only the plants in Steps 1–4 use spores. The correct answer is (A).

24. **(G)** It utilizes seeds as a reproductive unit.

Data Interpretation

All of the plants in Steps 5 and 6 use seeds as a reproductive unit, while the plants in Steps 1–4 use spores as a reproductive unit. Since the fern is listed under Step 4, it does not use seeds as a reproductive unit. Ferns contain a stem, a vascular system, and megaphyllis, as listed in Steps 2, 3 and 4. The correct answer is (G).

25. **(C)** Monocot

Data Interpretation

This image is the cross-section of a flower with 3 distinct subunits. This description fits the one for monocot, as described in Step 6. The correct answer is (C).

26. **(J)** They contain leaves.

Data Interpretation

According to the classification tree, both hornwort and club moss contain roots, stems, and leaves. What separates them is the existence of a vascular system, but this distinction is further down the classification tree than the existence of roots, stems, and leaves. The correct answer is (J).

27. **(D)** Monocot and dicot

Data Interpretation

According to the classification tree, both monocots and dicots are classified under plants that have the appearance of a fruit or flower (Step 6). Thus, they are both angiosperms. The correct answer is (D).

28. **(G)** A flower could attract a mobile animal to help spread the seed of an organism.

Data Interpretation

This question requires an inference. It should seem unlikely that flowers would guarantee more seeds per organism or that they would necessarily help attract more sunlight (in fact, sunlight does not have much to do with reproduction). It should also seem unlikely that flowers would improve the vascular system of an organism. Rather, a flower could attract a mobile animal to spread the flower's genetic material and help overcome the major difficulty that plants have in reproducing with other plants—an inability to move. Other animals could facilitate the mixing of DNA between different plants, which is also considered evolutionarily advantageous. The correct answer is (G).

Passage 5 Solutions

29. **(C)** Bacteria Y

Evaluation of Models, Inferences, and Experimental Results

The Kirby-Bauer test pictured in Figure 1 shows that Bacteria X and *S. enterica* are largely destroyed by the penicillin discs (as indicated by the clear areas), while Bacteria Y is much less affected (the areas around the discs are much cloudier). Thus, Bacteria Y seems to be the most resistant to penicillin. The correct answer is (C).

30.   **(G)** Students 1 and 2 only

Evaluation of Models, Inferences, and Experimental Results

Student 1 states that "penicillin causes bacterial cells to waste away," which can be thought of as slow-motion destruction (since the bacteria cannot gain nutrients). The lack of mobility also limits bacterial reproduction, but preventing the bacteria from feeding is certainly destruction. Student 3 says that "[p]enicillin does not destroy bacteria but instead prevents them from multiplying." Student 4 states that a "clear circle … does not indicate that the bacteria are being destroyed." Student 2 most clearly argues the case that penicillin is bacteriocidal, claiming that penicillin "destroys bacterial cell walls causing … the destruction of the cell." Thus, Students 1 and 2 suggest that penicillin is bacteriocidal, directly destroying the bacteria. Note that you do not have the choice of Student 2 alone, and Student 1 is clearly closer to the bacteriocidal position than Student 4. The correct answer is (G).

31.   **(C)** Students 2 and 3 only

Evaluation of Models, Inferences, and Experimental Results

The passage mentions that Ehrlich's theory of magic bullets states there are compounds that "destroy or prevent the normal functioning of bacterial cells but do not destroy or interfere with animal cells." Student 1 suggests that while penicillin "causes bacterial cells to waste away and inhibits their ability to reproduce," it can also "destroy human cells," which are animal cells, so Student 1's point of view does not support the theory of magic bullets. Student 2 states that "[s]ince animal cells do not have cell walls, the penicillin targets bacterial cells only," and supports the theory of magic bullets. Student 3 says that penicillin "prevents [bacteria] from multiplying. Since bacteria have different reproductive processes from animal cells, penicillin does not disrupt the normal functioning of animal cells," supporting the magic bullet theory. Student 4 argues that bacteria are not actually being destroyed, so there is no support for the magic bullet theory. The correct answer is (C).

32.   **(H)** provide nutrients for bacteria so that they can grow.

Evaluation of Models, Inferences, and Experimental Results

In describing the Kirby-Bauer test, the passage states that "discs containing antibiotics are placed on agar plates with growing colonies of healthy bacteria." This text suggests that the agar helps the colonies of bacteria grow, and does not destroy the bacteria. The correct answer is (H).

33.   **(B)** *Student 2*

Evaluation of Models, Inferences, and Experimental Results

If irregularities and holes were observed on the normally continuous cell wall of the bacteria, this observation would suggest that the antibiotic contributed to weakening the cell walls. Student 2 hypothesizes that "[p]enicillin destroys bacterial cell walls," which is supported by this observation. The correct answer is (B).

34. **(G)** Re-create the experiment using a non-motile strain of bacteria.

Evaluation of Models, Inferences, and Experimental Results

Student 4 suggests that "[a]ny motile bacteria could simply be moving to an area that is farther away from the antibiotic disc," so that the bacteria are not in fact destroyed. If this is indeed the case, then you would want to repeat the experiment with bacteria that could not move away from the antibiotic and see whether these bacteria survive or not. The correct answer is (G).

35. **(C)** A higher density of bacteria on the edges of the clear circle surrounding the antibiotic disc

Evaluation of Models, Inferences, and Experimental Results

If the suggestion by Student 4 is that the bacteria are simply "moving to an area that is farther away from the antibiotic disc," then you would expect to observe many more bacteria around the area of the clear circle than there were before the discs were placed on the agar, as these bacteria "flee" the area of the discs. The correct answer is (C).

Passage 6 Solutions

36. **(J)** 1,000,000,000 years

Evaluation of Models, Inferences, and Experimental Results

The passage states that the Earth was formed 4.5 billion years ago, and the first evidence of life was found 3.5 billion years ago. According to this information, it took 1 billion years, or 1,000,000,000 years, for life to develop. The correct answer is (J).

37. **(C)** A great deal of UV light was present in Earth's early atmosphere.

Evaluation of Models, Inferences, and Experimental Results

Both scientists say that there was a "prominence" or a "prevalence" of UV radiation. While Scientist 1 says that this UV "delayed the formation of these biomolecules significantly," Scientist 2 suggests that this UV "was integral to the eventual formation of life." Only Scientist 2 describes the possible role of zinc in the formation of life and mentions that carbon monoxide was in the early Earth's atmosphere. The correct answer is (C).

38. **(F)** It does not offer an explanation for the formation of nucleic acids.

Evaluation of Models, Inferences, and Experimental Results

Scientist 1 states that using the experiment setup that simulates the early Earth's conditions, amino acids and sugars were observed to form, but not nucleic acids. This is a significant weakness because nucleic acids make up DNA (as Scientist 1 admits), and the passage states that "all life on Earth is DNA-based." Scientist 1's account does list the components of the early Earth atmosphere, and has a process to mimic water evaporation and condensation. The correct answer is (F).

39. **(B)** Setup B

Evaluation of Models, Inferences, and Experimental Results

According to Scientist 1, this experimental setup requires two glass flasks connected in a continuous loop. Setup B is the only one that has two flasks in a continuous loop. The correct answer is (B).

40. **(G)** Scientist 2 only

Evaluation of Models, Inferences, and Experimental Results

Scientist 1 does not list carbon dioxide as a component of the early Earth's atmosphere, but Scientist 2 does. If carbon dioxide did not form until 2.5 BYA, then it would not be available in abiogenesis, so the argument by Scientist 2 would be weakened. The correct answer is (G).

41. **(B)** Helium

Evaluation of Models, Inferences, and Experimental Results

Scientist 2's model suggests that elements available in the compounds present in the early Earth could be used in the formation of life, including carbon, hydrogen, nitrogen, oxygen, sulfur, phosphorus, and zinc. However, Scientist 2 never mentions helium as being present and available to form DNA. The correct answer is (B).

42. **(H)** Lightning

Evaluation of Models, Inferences, and Experimental Results

Scientist 1 states that the electrodes were "electricity-inducing." This is used to simulate natural electricity-inducing phenomena, such as lightning. Rainfall and thunder are not electricity-inducing phenomena, and batteries are not natural objects and were not available in the early Earth. The correct answer is (H).

Passage 7 Solutions

43. **(C)** 40–44

Scientific Investigation

If you take a look at the population pyramid graph for Germany in Figure 1, the widest bars, which represent the age group with the greatest percent of the population, correspond to the 40- to 44-year-old age group. The correct answer is (C).

44. **(H)** females 30–34.

Scientific Investigation

If you look at Figure 2, the line represents the population for each demographic in 2001, and the bar represents the population for each demographic in 2011. For the females in the 30- to 34-year-old group, the line has a larger value than the bar, so the population for that demographic decreased between 2001 and 2011. The correct answer is (H).

45. **(C)** The number of females over 75 was greater than the number of males over 75 in 1970.

Scientific Investigation

In Figure 3, the graph represents the percent of the total population in each demographic. However, because you do not know the total population in each year, you cannot compare the number of people in one year with the number in another year. That said, you can make comparisons within one year. In 1930, the percent of females older than 75 is less than the percent of males over 75, while in 1970, the percent of females older than 75 is more than the percent of males over 75. The correct answer is (C).

46. **(H)** 35–39

Scientific Investigation

Examining Figure 2, you want to look at the widest point of the line for both males and females, which is for the age group between 35 and 39. The correct answer is (H).

47. **(C)** Between 16 and 24 million

Scientific Investigation

From Figure 1, the percent of the population that was male ages 0–4 is about 3%, and the percent that was female ages 0–4 is also about 3%, so around 6% of the total population was between 0 and 4 years old. If the total population of the United States in 2006 was 300 million, then the age group between 0 and 4 years of age represented 6% of 300 million, or around 18 million people. The correct answer is (C).

48. **(H)** Graph H

Scientific Investigation

According to the examples presented in the passage (Figure 1 and Figure 2), the convention of the population pyramid is to put the oldest part of the population on top. Additionally, in a rapid-growth scenario, the youngest part of the population (on the bottom of the pyramid) should be the widest part of the pyramid, and there should be a relatively smooth transition from the top to the bottom. These features eliminate all choices but graph H. The correct answer is (H).

49. **(B)** an eventual sharp increase in population.

Scientific Investigation

If a population has a much higher percentage of people in the pre-reproductive stages of life, then after a few years, a greater amount of reproduction is likely to take place, resulting in a greater number of children and increasing the population sharply. A population that has a higher percentage of people in the post-reproductive stages of life will have a greater number of deaths in the next few years, perhaps resulting in a decrease in the population. The sharp increase in population will not take place immediately because the reproduction will not all take place right away. The correct answers (B).

Passage 8 Solutions

50. **(F)** TIR1 deleted, grown in 1,000 nM brassinolide

Scientific Investigation

Figure 1 presents the lengths of hypocotyls under various genetic and treatment conditions. TIR1-deleted plants grown in 1,000 nM brassinolide had hypocotyl lengths near 4 cm. None of the other options produce hypocotyl lengths anywhere close to 4 cm. The correct answer is (F).

51. **(D)** 2.5 cm

Scientific Investigation

The data in Figure 1 for WT plants show that plants treated with 10 and 1,000 nM brassinolide will have hypocotyls of 1.5 and 4 cm, respectively. The difference between these measurements is 2.5 cm. The correct answer is (D).

52. **(H)** AXR3 deletion eliminates the effect, whereas TIR1 deletion does not affect it.

Scientific Investigation

The data in Figure 1 show that at each concentration of brassinolide, the growth of TIR1-deleted and WT plants is roughly the same. Thus, TIR1 deletion does not affect the growth response to brassinolide. AXR deletion, on the other hand, results in a near-identical hypocotyl length in plants treated with 1,000 nM brassinolide and untreated plants, eliminating the effect of brassinolide. The correct answer is (H).

53. **(B)** In the absence of brassinolide, AXR3 deletion increases average length of hypocotyls relative to WT plants.

Scientific Investigation

The data in Figure 1 show that plants not treated with brassinolide (0 nM on the graph) have hypocotyl lengths in WT and AXR3-deleted plants of 1.5 and 2.5 cm, respectively. Although WT plants have greater hypocotyl length when treated with 1000 nM brassinolide, AXR3-deleted plants that are not treated with brassinolide have longer hypocotyls than WT plants that are similarly untreated. The correct answer is (B).

54. (G) 20%

Scientific Investigation

Determining the percentage of auxin-upregulated genes that were also upregulated following treatment with BR, requires this calculation:

$$\frac{\text{Number of genes upregulated following auxin} + \text{BR}}{\text{Number of genes upregulated following auxin alone or auxin} + \text{BR}} \times 100\%$$

$$\frac{82\,(\text{from overlap in Figure 2})}{418\,(\text{adding both auxin only numbers})} \times 100\%$$

$$\text{approximately } \frac{1}{5} \times 100\%$$
$$\text{approximately } 20\%$$

The correct answer is (G).

55. (A) 2

Scientific Investigation

To determine whether auxin and BR treatment have synergistic effects on the genes in Table 1, add the effects of the individual treatments and compare that sum to the effect of the combined treatment. If the effect of the combined treatment is greater than the sum, the treatments are said to be synergistic.

AHP1: 30 + 10 = 40, which is greater than 35, therefore NOT synergistic.

BXF7: 55 + 12 = 175, which is less than 300, therefore synergistic.

NYN4: 80 + 190 = 270, which is less than 320, therefore synergistic.

PLD9: 140 + 150 = 290, which is greater than 220, therefore NOT synergistic.

SVM2: 200 + 190 = 390, which is greater than 190, therefore NOT synergistic.

Of the 5 genes, only 2 were synergistic. The correct answer is (A).

56. (J) Auxin and BR have synergistic effects on genes more strongly upregulated by BR.

Scientific Investigation

The two genes affected synergistically by auxin and BR are BXF7 and NYN4. For these two genes, BR treatment by itself had more than twice the effect of auxin treatment by itself. For example, for BXF7, auxin treatment by itself led to an increase of 55, while BR treatment by itself led to an increase of 120. As for the three genes NOT affected synergistically by auxin and BR together, BR treatment by itself did NOT have such a greater impact than auxin treatment by itself (the numbers in the first two columns are much more similar for those three genes). Thus, it is reasonable to hypothesize that the effect of BR relative to auxin (that is, the greater impact of BR alone) may impact synergism. The correct answer is (J).

Passage 9 Solutions

57.   **(D)** Light for 12 hours or fewer, at 30°C

Scientific Investigation

Table 1 shows that the parental line's flowering at 7 weeks was at a maximum at 30°C, with either 8 or 12 hours of light per day. The correct answer is (D).

58.   **(H)** At all levels of light exposure, more plants will flower at 30°C than at 20°C

Scientific Investigation

Comparing the 20°C and 30°C columns in Table 1 line by line shows that the number in the 30°C column is greater than the number in the 20°C column in all cases. Consequently, temperature has a distinct effect on flowering. The correct answer is (H).

59.   **(C)** 60

Scientific Investigation

Under the same conditions, you would expect the same proportion of plants to flower. In the actual experiment, 12 of 20 plants flowered. In the hypothetical experiment, 5 times more seedlings were planted, so 5 times more seedlings would be expected to flower: $5 \times 12 = 60$.

This can also be set up as a proportion and solved algebraically by cross-multiplying:

$$\frac{12}{20} = \frac{x}{100}$$
$$x = 60$$

The correct answer is (C).

60.   **(F)** Line F.

Scientific Investigation

Mutant A at 20°C has 16, 17, 15, and 16 flowering plants at 8, 12, 16, and 20 hours of light per day. Curve F matches these data points. The correct answer is (F).

61.   **(A)** less affected by light exposure.

Scientific Investigation

Flowering of the parental line is sharply reduced when light is increased beyond 12 hours per day, whereas flowering of Mutant A is the same at 8 or 20 hours of light. If choice (B) were correct, a greater difference in flowering would be seen as light exposure increased. For instance, a greater drop in flowering would be seen between 12 and 16 hours. Choices (C) and (D) are not correct because the effect of temperature on Mutant A is nearly the same as on the parental line: decreasing the temperature from 30°C to 20°C results in approximately 1/4 fewer flowering plants. The correct answer is (A).

62.   **(H)** The gene inactivated in Mutant B may play a role in seasonal response to temperature changes.

Scientific Investigation

The strongest effect of Mutant B is a drastic loss of flowering at lower temperatures, but normal flowering in response to light exposure. In fact, even though the maximal flowering is reduced (at 8 and 12 hours of light per day), the decrease from 12 to 16 hours is proportionally the same in the original parental-line plants as it is in Mutant B at 30°C. This pattern strongly suggests that the effect of the gene inactivated in Mutant B only affects responses to temperature. Both Mutant A and Mutant B have altered flowering at 20°C, eliminating answer choice (F). Mutant B's response to light is almost identical to the parental line's response at 30°C, eliminating choice (G). Mutant A demonstrates that choice (J) is incorrect. The reduction of flowering with increased light exposure has been eliminated by genetic manipulation in that mutant strain. The correct answer is (H).

63.   **(B)** 20

Scientific Investigation

Extrapolating on the trend from Table 1, you could conclude that with 21 hours of light (just a little more than 20 hours), slightly fewer than 3 seeds out of every 20 would be expected to flower. If there are 200 seeds, then slightly fewer than 30 out of 200 would be expected to flower. Choice (B) is the only answer choice that is slightly fewer than 30. Nothing in the data suggests that immediately beyond 20 hours of light, the proportion of seeds that flower should drop all the way to 0% as choice (A) would indicate. The correct answer is (B).

Passage 10 Solutions

64.   **(H)** Simple

Interpretation of Data

The passage states, "Eukaryotic cells are … comparatively much more complex" than prokaryotic cells. Thus, simple would not be an appropriate word to describe them in comparison with prokaryotic cells. The correct answer is (H).

65.   **(D)** 1 BYA

Interpretation of Data

According to the passage, the first event was the development of prokaryotic cells, 3.5 billion years ago. Then, roughly 2 billion years ago, eukaryotic cells formed, and finally, 1 billion years later (that is, $2 - 1 = 1$ billion years ago), the first multicellular organisms formed out of eukaryotic cells. The correct answer is (D).

66.   **(F)** They contain cellulose.

Interpretation of Data

According to the passage, cellulose is found in plant cell walls, and no animal cells have cell walls (notice that cell walls are different from cell membranes). The correct answer is (F).

67.   **(C)** Eukaryotic cells are usually larger than prokaryotic cells.

Interpretation of Data

According to Table 1, the largest three cells listed (the red blood cell, the egg cell, and the oak tree cell) are all part of animals (humans) or plants, and so they are eukaryotic. The smallest two cells are both bacteria, so they are prokaryotic. The correct answer is (C).

68.   **(H)** Proteins

Interpretation of Data

Choice (F), cellulose, is only present in plant cells. Choice (G), type 2 ribosomes, seem only to be present in animal and plant cells, not bacteria. Choice (J), cell walls, are only present in bacteria and plants, not in animals. However, some kind of ribosome appears to be present in all five entries in Table 1. In fact, as the passage states, "Animal cells, plant cells, and bacterial cells all contain ribosomes, which use hereditary information to create proteins." Thus, proteins (which are created in all of these kinds of cells) are present in the greatest variety of living organisms. The correct answer is (H).

69.   **(C)** Type 1 ribosomes

Interpretation of Data

All bacterial cells in Table 2 have Type 1 ribosomes, while eukaryotic cells have Type 2 ribosomes. Thus, Type 1 ribosomes would be a distinctive target for a medicine that would attack bacteria but not eukaryotic cells. Cell membranes and proteins are universal (they are found in eukaryotic cells as well as in bacteria). Cellulose is only found in plant cells and is irrelevant to the situation presented above. The correct answer is (C).

70. **(H)** Proteins

Interpretation of Data

This is a rare question that tests outside knowledge of biology. Both DNA and RNA are types of nucleic acids, whose function is to store hereditary (genetic) information that is passed from organisms to their offspring. Proteins are made from the information contained in DNA and RNA, but they are not a form of hereditary information themselves. The correct answer is (H).

Passage 11 Solutions

71. **(C)** 20

Scientific Investigation

Each cell that goes through one phase of mitosis will produce 2 daughter cells. Thus, if 10 cells go through mitosis, 20 cells will result. The correct answer is (C).

72. **(J)** The cell would be unable to replicate because it lacked the necessary proteins for division.

Scientific Investigation

According to the passage, G_2 is the phase during which the cell creates proteins that are essential for cell division. Thus, if the cell were unable to complete this phase, it would be unable to replicate or divide. The correct answer is (J).

73. **(B)** 20

Scientific Investigation

Experiment 1 examines 36 cells, as you can see by adding up the bars ($1 + 2 + 3 + 10 + 20 = 36$). Thus, if someone were to repeat the investigation with 75 cells, which is a little more than twice 36, all of the numbers would be roughly double those in Experiment 1. Since there are 10 cells in prophase in Experiment 1, there would be roughly 20 cells in prophase in the 75-cell experiment. The correct answer is (B).

74. **(G)** Stem cell

Scientific Investigation

According to Table 1, cell C does not increase in number over time. Thus, you can conclude that it is not dividing and replicating. The passage says that certain cells generally do not replicate, such as nerve cells, liver cells, and muscle cells. Stem cells, on the other hand, replicate often. Thus, cell type C is unlikely to be a stem cell. The correct answer is (G).

75. (C) 400

Scientific Investigation

According to Table 1, the count of cell type A doubles roughly every 12 hours (as the number grows from 50 to 99 and finally to 200). Since there were 200 cells at $t = 24$ hours, then you would expect there to be double the amount of cells, or 400 cells, at $t = 36$ hours. The correct answer is (C).

76. (F) Telophase

Scientific Investigation

In a random sampling of cells, the phase in which you see the greatest number of cells should be the longest, while the phase in which we see the least number of cells should be the shortest. Since the student observes the least number of cells in telophase, this phase is presumably the shortest. The correct answer is (F).

77. (B) Metaphase

Scientific Investigation

According to the passage, metaphase is the phase in which x-shaped chromosomes line up along the equator of the cell. Thus, the pictured cell is in metaphase. The correct answer is (B).

Passage 12 Solutions

78. (G) 150 nm

Scientific Investigation

Since each virus group has the same type of genetic information and is roughly the same size, you would expect the Coxsackie virus to be roughly the same size as the other picornaviruses (Poliovirus = 100 nm; Rhinovirus = 300 nm). The only answer that is relatively close to those sizes is 150nm. The correct answer is (G).

79. (A) All bacteria are larger than all viruses.

Scientific Investigation

According to Table 1, the measles virus is 1,000 nm in size, and according to Table 2, *staphylococcus aureus* is 600 nm in size. Thus, not all bacteria are larger than all viruses. The correct answer is (A).

80. (G) Paramyxovirus

Scientific Investigation

Since viruses are classified according to size and the type of hereditary material, look at the group of a virus or viruses that are roughly the same size (900 nm) and use DNA as a hereditary material. Measles virus, which is a paramyxovirus, is closest in its features. The correct answer is (G).

MANHATTAN
PREP

81. **(D)** To trace where the material went

Scientific Investigation

While sulfur and phosphorus occur naturally in cells, radioactive labeling of these elements makes them easy to trace. This way, the students could follow the material they were interested in and see where it wound up. The correct answer is (D).

82. **(J)** It would not allow the virus to adhere to and enter the bacteria.

Scientific Investigation

According to the passage, adhesion proteins allow a virus to attach to a bacterial cell before injecting its genetic information into the bacterial cell. Thus, if the adhesion proteins were damaged, the virus would not be able to attach to the bacteria. The correct answer is (J).

83. **(A)** Streptococcus pneumoniae

Scientific Investigation

The image shows cocci (sphere-shaped bacteria) that are roughly 1,275 nm. These observations most closely match the description of *Streptococcus pneumoniae* from Table 2. The correct answer is (A).

84. **(J)** Genetic material of bacteria is in the form of DNA and contains phosphorus.

Scientific Investigation

In the experiment, the radioactive phosphorus entered the bacteria, while the radioactive sulfur did not. Thus, the genetic material of the bacteria contains phosphorus and not sulfur. Since the phosphorus was initially used to labeled DNA, it must be DNA, and not protein, that is entering the bacteria. Thus, the students can conclude that genetic material is DNA and contains phosphorus. The correct answer is (J).

Passage 13 Solutions

85. **(D)** 40× objective lens, 5× ocular lens

Interpretation of Data

From the formula for total magnification power, this combination would give you a total magnification power of (40)(5) = 200×. Answer choice (A) would give you a total magnification power of 40×, answer choice (B) would give you 40×, and answer choice (C) would give you 100×. The correct answer is (D).

86. **(J)** It requires a sample that allows light to pass through it.

Interpretation of Data

According to the passage, a CLM can only be used to examine a "transparent" specimen; that is, one that allows light to pass through it. Since you cannot use a CLM with opaque materials, the restriction to transparent specimens would be considered a disadvantage. The correct answer is (J).

87. **(C)** You can obtain a much higher magnification.

Interpretation of Data

According to the passage, a CLM can obtain a magnification of 1000×, while a TEM can obtain a magnification of up to 5,000,000×. Thus, a TEM can obtain a much higher magnification. The correct answer is (C).

88. **(H)** CLM with 10× ocular lens and blue objective lens

Interpretation of Data

According to the passage, a TEM cannot be used with live specimens. Thus, you can conclude that a CLM was used. Since the magnification of 400× was noted, you can deduce that the student used an 10× ocular lens and a blue objective lens (40×) to obtain a total magnification of 400×. The correct answer is (H).

89. **(D)** 200×

Interpretation of Data

From the formula of total magnification power, you can reasonably deduce that if you multiply together all the individual magnification powers of the lenses, you can calculate the total magnification power of several lenses working in unison. Thus, you can determine (5)(10)(4) = 200× total magnification power. The correct answer is (D).

90. **(J)** 0.018 mm

Interpretation of Data

According to the description of the experimental setup, you know that the total magnification power in this experiment is 100×. Table 2 tells you that the field of view at this total magnification power is 0.18 mm in diameter. Since there are 10 cells in the field of view, each cell is roughly 0.18 mm ÷ 10, or 0.018 mm. The correct answer is (J).

91. **(B)** 5

Interpretation of Data

By switching to the orange objective lens, the magnification would be doubled (from 10× to 20×) and the size of the field of view would be halved (this result can be deduced by comparing values in Table 2: as the magnifying power increases down the table, the field of view shrinks by exactly the same factors). If the size of the field of view is halved, you would expect to see half as many, or 5 cells. The correct answer is (B).

Passage 14 Solutions

92. **(G)** Osmosis is a form of diffusion.

Scientific Investigation

According to the passage, osmosis is the diffusion of water from an area of low solute concentration to an area of high solute concentration. Thus, osmosis is a form of diffusion, which is parenthetically defined as "random mixing and spreading." Isotonic solutions, not hypertonic or hypotonic, have the same concentrations as one another. The correct answer is (G).

93. **(D)** 0.3 osmol/L

Scientific Investigation

The formula for osmotic concentration tells you that you need the concentration of the solute divided by the number of liters of solution. According to Experiment 1, you have 0.6 moles of solute divided by 2 liters of solution. 0.6 divided by 2 equals 0.3 osmol/L. The correct answer is (D).

94. **(F)** 0.3 osmol/L

Scientific Investigation

The osmotic concentration of blood cells can be deduced by observing the environments in which blood cells are placed in isotonic solutions and, consequently, they neither crenate nor lyse. Thus, you can deduce the osmotic concentration of red blood cells by calculating the osmotic concentration of Solution A or Solution D. Solution A has 0.3 osmoles of Na^+ and Cl^- and 1L of solution, so the osmotic concentration is 0.3 osmol/L. Thus, the osmotic concentration of the red blood cells is also 0.3 osmol/L. The correct answer is (F).

95. **(B)** Solution B is hypertonic to the blood cells; Solution C is hypotonic to the blood cells.

Scientific Investigation

According to the passage, if a solution is hypertonic to cells, water will flow out of the cells into the solution and the cells will crenate. If a solution is hypotonic to cells, water will flow from the solution into the cells and the cells will lyse. Since the cells crenate in Solution B, Solution B is hypertonic. Since the cells lyse in Solution C, Solution C is hypotonic. The correct answer is (B).

96. **(G)** Solution B, Solution A, Solution C

Scientific Investigation

Osmotic concentration is calculated by dividing the osmoles of solute by the liters of solution. The osmotic concentration of Solution A is 0.3/1.0 = 0.3 osmol/L; the osmotic concentration of Solution B is 0.3/0.5 = 0.6 osmol/L; the osmotic concentration of Solution C is unknown, but since red blood cells lysed in it, you know that the osmotic concentration must be less than 0.3 osmol/L. Thus, Solution B has the largest osmotic concentration, followed by Solution A, followed by Solution C. The correct answer is (G).

MANHATTAN
PREP

97.   **(D)** The cells would crenate because they are hypotonic to solution B.

Scientific Investigation

The osmotic concentration of Solution B is calculated by dividing the number of osmoles of solute by the number of liters of solution. For Solution B, the osmotic concentration is $0.3 \div 0.5 = 0.6$ osmol/L. If fish cells have a concentration of 0.2 osmol/L, then they are hypotonic to Solution B. Thus, water would flow from the cells outward toward Solution B, and the cells would crenate. The correct answer is (D).

98.   **(J)**   Solution D

Scientific Investigation

Amino acids and peptide bonds are the building blocks of proteins. Solutions A, B, and C contain only sodium and chloride ions and water. Solution D is the only one that contains protein; thus, you would expect a positive (pink) Biuret test. The correct answer is (J).

Chapter *of* 22

5lb. Book of ACT® Practice Problems

Science:

Physical Sciences

In This Chapter...

Physical Sciences Passages & Solutions

Chapter 22

Science: Physical Sciences

The Science passages in this chapter are classified within physical sciences, which include properties of matter, acids & bases, reaction kinetics, organic chemistry, thermodynamics, mechanics, electromagnetism, and other topics that could be studied in a Physical Sciences, Chemistry, or Physics course.

In the Science section, you'll encounter three types of passages, each with a corresponding question type.

1. Data Representation. A scientific article that contains charts and tables of information. Here, you will be asked Data Interpretation questions. That is, you'll need to interpret the data you're given.

2. Research Summary. A description of an experiment (or two). Here, you will be asked Scientific Investigation questions. In other words, you'll need to examine the experiment (the scientific investigation) critically: assessing its design, analyzing its outcomes, etc.

3. Conflicting Viewpoints. Two or more explanations or interpretations of a scientific phenomenon. These explanations always conflict. Here, you will be asked Evaluation of Models, Inferences, & Experimental Results questions, requiring you to compare, contrast, or otherwise evaluate the explanations given.

How should you use this chapter? Here are some recommendations, according to the level you've reached in ACT Science.

1. Fundamentals. Do a passage or two untimed to begin with. As you become more comfortable, put the clock on. In all cases, review the solutions closely, and articulate what you've learned. Reread the passage again to ensure that you fully understand it, and redo problems as necessary.

2. Fixes. Do one passage at a time under timed conditions. Examine the results, learn your lessons, then test yourself with more passages (one or two from each Science chapter) at once.

3. Tweaks. Confirm your mastery by doing several passages (a couple from each Science chapter) at once under timed conditions. A set of five or six passages (doing all seven questions per passage) or seven passages (doing about six questions per passage) is ideal. Aim to improve the speed and ease of your reading and solution process.

Good luck on the problems!

22

PASSAGE 1

The term *atom* is used to describe the fundamental unit of matter of which the matter on Earth is made. Since the atom is too small to be directly observed, scientists throughout history have proposed models about the structure of the atom. Three of these models are presented below.

Model 1

All matter is made of solid spherical particles known as atoms. Any attempt to separate atoms into smaller parts will be unsuccessful, as atoms are indivisible and indestructible. There are different types of atoms called elements, and all atoms of a given element are identical and have the same properties, such as size and mass.

Model 2

Atoms are composed of a positively charged solid sphere and negatively charged fundamental particles called *electrons* that are randomly distributed throughout the sphere. The electrons are set within the sphere and are immobile. An atom is considered neutral if the amount of positive charge in the solid sphere is equal to the amount of negative charge in all of the electrons. If the amount of positive and negative charges is unequal, the atom is referred to as an *ion*.

Model 3

Atoms are made of three smaller particles that are themselves fundamental and indivisible. The nucleus, which is the center of the atom, is composed of positively charged *protons* and the uncharged *neutrons*, each with a mass of approximately 1 *atomic mass unit (amu)**.

The negatively charged *electrons,* which are very small with negligible mass, occupy the rest of space of the atom outside the nucleus. Because the electrons are so small compared to the size of the atom, the vast majority of the atom is empty space.

* 1 atomic mass unit is approximately 1.66×10^{-24} kg.

If an atom has the same number of protons and electrons, the atom is neutral. An ion is formed when the number of protons and electrons are unequal: the atom is positively charged if there are more protons than electrons, and an atom is negatively charged if there are more electrons than protons.

1. In which model would an atom most closely resemble a marble, a spherical solid with no smaller sub-units?
    A. Model 1
    B. Model 2
    C. Model 3
    D. None of the models presented support an atom that resembles a marble.

2. Which model(s) would best be able to explain why some atoms have an electrical charge?
    F. Model 1 only
    G. Models 1 and 2 only
    H. Models 2 and 3 only
    J. Model 3 only

3. A scientist isolates a sample of sodium and hypothesizes that the typical sodium atom has 11 protons, 11 electrons, and 12 neutrons. According to the theory presented in Model 3, what is the approximate mass of the typical sodium atom?
    A. 11 amu
    B. 12 amu
    C. 22 amu
    D. 23 amu

4. Research of the living world confirms that there are multiple different forms of carbon in the world: one with a mass of 12 amu, another with a mass of 13 amu, and another with a mass of 14 amu. This information most directly refutes which model?
    F. Model 1
    G. Model 2
    H. Model 3
    J. This information does not refute any of the models.

5. In 1911, Ernest Rutherford conducted an experiment in which he fired a beam of helium atoms at a sheet of solid gold foil (which is also made of atoms). He found that while some of the fired atoms were reflected back towards the location from where they were fired and others were deflected at an angle, most of the helium atoms actually passed right through the sheet of foil. Which model(s) is(are) most directly refuted by the results of this experiment?

A. Model 1 only
B. Models 1 and 2 only
C. Models 1 and 3 only
D. Models 2 and 3 only

6. Recent research has shown that protons and neutrons can be further analyzed as being composed of even smaller particles called *quarks*. With which model, as presented above, does this new research fit?

F. Model 1
G. Model 2
H. Model 3
J. None of the models

7. Which of the following illustrations most nearly represents Model 2?

A.

B.

C.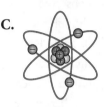

D.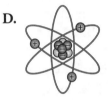

22

PASSAGE 2

A *gas chromatograph* is used to monitor the quantities of reagents at specific times during a reaction. Students monitor the progress of the reaction of methane (CH_4) and fluorine (F_2) to tetrafluoromethane (CF_4) and hydrogen gas (H_2) under specific conditions.

$$CH_4 + 2F_2 \longrightarrow CF_4 + 2H_2$$

It takes 1 hour for the reaction to progress to completion. During that time, the students observed the side products trifluoromethane (CHF_3), difluoromethane (CH_2F_2), and fluoromethane (CH_3F). Table 1 measures the amount of reactant present during the reaction. Table 2 shows the amount of the products created until the reaction completes. Table 3 indicates the heat released in kilojoules (kJ) during the reaction every 10 minutes and the cumulative heat released.

Table 1: Gas Chromatograph Results
Number of Moles of Reactants

Time (minutes)	Amount of CH_4	Amount of F_2
0	10	20
10	8	19
20	5	17
30	3	13
40	2	10
50	0	1
60	0	0

Table 2: Gas Chromatograph Results
Number of Moles of Products

Time (minutes)	CF_4	CHF_3	CH_2F_2	CH_3F	H_2
0	0	0	0	0	0
10	0	0	0	2	1
20	0	0	1	4	3
30	0	2	3	2	7
40	3	2	1	0	15
50	8	2	0	0	19
60	10	0	0	0	20

Table 3: Calorimetry Results
Amount of Heat Released

Time (minutes)	Heat Released (kJ)	Cumulative Heat Released (kJ)
0	0	0
10	318.06	318.06
20	695.59	1,013.65
30	1,678.06	2,691.71
40	1,819.93	4,511.64
50	1,781.33	6,292.97
60	2,290.33	8,583.3

8. According to Table 2, for approximately how many minutes does each of the side products exist?

   F. 10 minutes
   G. 20 minutes
   H. 30 minutes
   J. 40 minutes

9. According to Tables 1 and 3, by the time there was no more methane present in the reaction, the cumulative amount of heat released was:

    A. 1,781.33 kJ.
    B. 6,292.97 kJ.
    C. 2,290.33 kJ.
    D. 8,583.3 kJ.

10. According to Table 2, at 40 minutes into the experiment, all of the side products were present EXCEPT:

    F. tetrafluoromethane.
    G. trifluoromethane.
    H. difluoromethane.
    J. fluoromethane.

11. If the students continued their experiment for an additional hour, they would be likely to observe:

    A. no change in the amount of any chemical.
    B. an increase in side products.
    C. an increase in CH_4 and F_2.
    D. a decrease in CH_4 and F_2.

12. When the students observed 3 moles of CH_2F_2, the amount of heat that they observed the reaction release at that time was:

    F. 318.06 kJ.
    G. 1,678.06 kJ.
    H. 1,781.33 kJ.
    J. 2,290.33 kJ.

13. The interval that displays the most rapid decline in the amount of F_2 is between:

    A. the 10-minute mark and the 20-minute mark.
    B. the 30-minute mark and the 40-minute mark.
    C. the 40-minute mark and the 50-minute mark.
    D. the 50-minute mark and the 60-minute mark.

14. Though fluorine (F_2), chlorine (Cl_2), and bromine (Br_2) gases will all react with methane, the rates of reaction will differ. Fluorine is the most reactive of the three, while bromine is the least reactive. If 10 moles of CH_4 is reacted with 20 moles of each of these elements, and the results are analyzed via gas chromatograph, which is the most plausible table of the results after 1 hour?

F	Moles of F_2	0	G	Moles of F_2	20
	Moles of Cl_2	2		Moles of Cl_2	15
	Moles of Br_2	5		Moles of Br_2	10
H	Moles of F_2	5	J	Moles of F_2	10
	Moles of Cl_2	2		Moles of Cl_2	15
	Moles of Br_2	0		Moles of Br_2	20

22

PASSAGE 3

In order to determine the ideal reaction conditions of using the reactants calcium chloride ($CaCl_2$) and copper bromide ($CuBr_2$) to create the products calcium bromide ($CaBr_2$) and copper chloride ($CuCl_2$), students observed the following reaction over the course of 24 hours under various conditions:

$$CaCl_2 + CuBr_2 \rightarrow CaBr_2 + CuCl_2$$

The reactions were observed with and without a *catalyst* (that typically accelerates reactions), at three different temperatures (258 K, 298 K, and 313 K), and in both dilute and concentrated solutions. The students recorded the percent of reaction completed every 10 minutes under the different conditions for the first 3 hours. The percents indicate the proportion of reactants that have been fully converted to products.

Table 1 shows the reaction progression of the dilute solution over the course of 3 hours. Table 2 shows the reaction progression of the concentrated solution over the course of 3 hours. Figure 1 records the progress of the reactions in dilute conditions over a period of 24 hours.

Table 1: Percent Conversions to Products in Dilute Solution

Time (min)	Reactions without a Catalyst			Reactions with a Catalyst		
	258 K	298 K	313 K	258 K	298 K	313 K
10	0%	0%	2%	1%	20%	42%
20	0%	1%	4%	1%	30%	67%
30	0%	1%	8%	2%	36%	78%
40	1%	2%	14%	2%	43%	80%
50	1%	3%	18%	2%	49%	81%
60	1%	4%	23%	2%	52%	81%
70	1%	4%	27%	3%	54%	82%
80	1%	5%	30%	3%	56%	82%
90	1%	7%	33%	3%	57%	82%
100	1%	8%	37%	3%	58%	83%
110	2%	8%	39%	4%	58%	83%
120	2%	10%	42%	4%	59%	83%
130	2%	10%	45%	4%	59%	83%
140	2%	13%	48%	4%	59%	84%
150	2%	14%	54%	5%	60%	84%
160	2%	19%	60%	5%	60%	84%
170	2%	20%	63%	5%	60%	84%
180	2%	23%	68%	5%	60%	84%

MANHATTAN
PREP

Table 2: Percent Conversions to Products in Concentrated Solution

Time (min)	Reactions without a Catalyst			Reactions with a Catalyst		
	258 K	298 K	313 K	258 K	298 K	313 K
10	0%	2%	10%	1%	26%	56%
20	0%	4%	20%	2%	42%	80%
30	1%	6%	29%	3%	50%	92%
40	1%	8%	37%	3%	56%	96%
50	1%	10%	45%	4%	61%	97%
60	1%	12%	51%	4%	65%	97%
70	2%	15%	57%	5%	69%	98%
80	2%	18%	62%	5%	71%	98%
90	2%	21%	66%	5%	72%	98%
100	2%	25%	68%	6%	72%	98%
110	3%	28%	69%	6%	73%	98%
120	3%	30%	70%	6%	73%	98%
130	3%	34%	70%	6%	73%	98%
140	4%	37%	71%	7%	74%	98%
150	4%	41%	71%	7%	74%	98%
160	4%	45%	72%	7%	75%	98%
170	5%	50%	72%	7%	75%	98%
180	5%	53%	73%	8%	75%	98%

Figure 1: Percent Conversions in Dilute Conditions

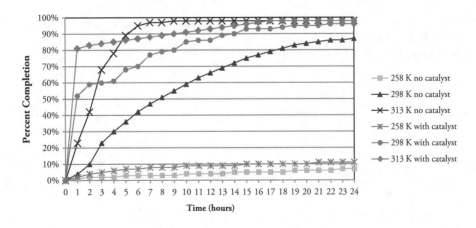

15. Based on the data in Tables 1 and 2, which of the following most accurately represents the distribution of products and reactants after 3 hours in a concentrated solution at 313 K without a catalyst?

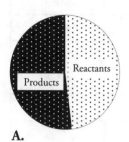

A.

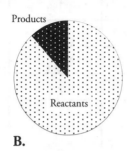

Products

B.

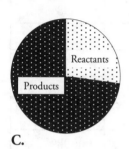

C.

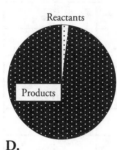

Reactants

D.

16. If the trends displayed in Figure 1 continue, which of the following is most likely to have the largest increase in percent conversion from hour 24 to hour 25?

  F. The reaction at 298 K with no catalyst

  G. The reaction at 313 K with no catalyst

  H. The reaction at 313 K with a catalyst

  J. The reaction at 298 K with a catalyst

17. If the students hope to obtain the highest percent conversions in the shortest amount of time, they should:

  A. decrease the temperature and include a catalyst.

  B. increase the temperature and include a catalyst.

  C. decrease the temperature and do not include a catalyst.

  D. increase the temperature and do not include a catalyst.

18. According to Tables 1 and 2, the condition that, by itself, would have the largest effect in the first 10 minutes on the rate of the reaction at 298 K without a catalyst and in dilute solution would be:

  F. raising the temperature to 313 K.

  G. making the solution concentrated.

  H. adding a catalyst.

  J. lowering the temperature to 258 K.

19. If the reaction can only proceed to 98% conversion to products, at what point in time was the reaction completed under the following conditions: 313 K, in concentrated solution, and with a catalyst?

  A. 70 minutes

  B. 140 minutes

  C. 180 minutes

  D. 240 minutes

20. According to Figure 1, at what point did the two reactions performed in dilute solution and at 313 K first have equal percent conversions?

  F. 1 hour

  G. 5 hours

  H. 10 hours

  J. 17 hours

21. If the students wanted to stop the reaction when it reaches 66% conversion, under which of the following conditions should the experiment be performed and at what time should the reaction be stopped?

  A. 313 K, dilute solution, with catalyst, stopped at 30 minutes

  B. 313 K, concentrated solution, with catalyst, stopped at 20 minutes

  C. 313 K, dilute solution, no catalyst, stopped at 150 minutes

  D. 313 K, concentrated solution, no catalyst, stopped at 90 minutes

MANHATTAN
PREP

PASSAGE 4

The reaction of hydrochloric acid with silver hydroxide produces water and silver chloride, as summarized in the following chemical equation:

$$HCl + AgOH \rightarrow AgCl + H_2O$$

Silver chloride is a solid that precipitates out of solution as it is formed. The reaction is irreversible and will proceed to completion within seconds. Three students attempted to isolate the silver chloride formed after the reaction using different methods of separation.

Experiment 1

The apparatus shown in Figure 1 was used to remove the water from the reaction container via distillation. Hydrochloric acid and silver hydroxide were added to the round-bottomed flask and the reaction was allowed to progress to completion. The round-bottomed flask was then attached to the distillation apparatus. Water was cycled through the condenser and heat was applied to the flask, causing the water from the reaction to evaporate into the top of the condenser, precipitate towards the bottom of the condenser, and collect as liquid into the conical flask. The volume of this liquid was then measured. The silver chloride and any impurities from the reaction remained in the round-bottomed flask. These solids were removed, and their mass was measured.

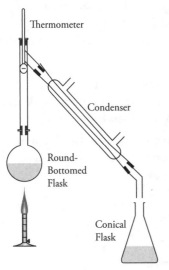

Figure 1

Experiment 2

The reaction of hydrochloric acid with silver hydroxide proceeded in a test tube. After the reaction had completed, the student applied vacuum pressure to the filter flask, inserted filter paper into the Buchner funnel, and poured the contents of the test tube onto the filter paper as shown in Figure 2. The water from the reaction was pulled into the conical flask through vacuum filtration, and the volume of this liquid was measured. The silver chloride and any solid impurities were left on the filter paper in the Buchner funnel. The mass of the dried solids was measured, after subtracting the weight of the filter paper.

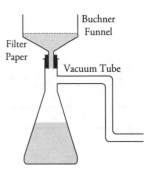

Figure 2

Experiment 3

As in Experiment 2, the reaction occurred in a test tube. Once the reaction was completed, the student inserted filter paper into the funnel, and poured the contents of the test tube onto the filter paper as shown in Figure 3. The water from the reaction drained through the conical funnel into the flask, and the volume of this liquid was measured. The silver chloride and any solid impurities remained on the filter paper inside the funnel. The mass of the dried solids was measured, after subtracting the weight of the filter paper.

Figure 3

The results of the three experiments were collected in Table 1. The actual volume represents the measured volume of water collected at the end of the separation, while the actual mass represents the measured mass of the solid separated from the liquid.

Table 1

	Expected Volume (mL)	**Expected Mass (g)**	**Actual Volume (mL)**	**Actual Mass (g)**
Experiment 1	18	143	16.2	145
Experiment 2	18	143	17.7	134
Experiment 3	18	143	16.7	129

22. Why might the actual mass collected in Experiment 1 be higher than the expected mass?

   F. Because the reaction did not run to completion

   G. Because of the additional weight of the filter paper

   H. Because applying heat caused the products to increase their mass

   J. Because of impurities within the product

23. If Experiment 2 is run again, what volume of water is likely to be collected if the expected volume is 90 mL?

   A. 76 mL

   B. 34 mL

   C. 88 mL

   D. 53 mL

24. Why might the actual mass collected in Experiments 2 and 3 be lower than the expected mass, even though the reaction progressed to completion?

   F. Because heat was applied

   G. Because the reaction was transferred from one container to another

   H. Because the liquid collected contained the missing grams of product

   J. Because of the presence of impurities

25. After reacting hydrochloric acid and silver hydroxide, but before separating the liquid and solid products, each of the students was likely to see a:

   A. mixture of both solid and liquid.

   B. solution that was entirely liquid.

   C. solid powder.

   D. thick gel.

26. If Experiment 1 is continued for 10 minutes after all the water has been collected in the conical flask, the student observes that the material in the round-bottomed flask turns a purple color. This effect could most reasonably be due to:

    F. the reaction of boiling water with silver.
    G. the reaction of chloride with hydrogen.
    H. the reaction of hydroxide with silver.
    J. the reaction of silver with heat.

27. According to Table 1, in the majority of experiments, the amount of product collected was:

    A. higher than the amount of product expected.
    B. lower than the amount of product expected.
    C. the same as the amount of product expected.
    D. independent of the amount of product expected.

28. The only piece of equipment that all three experiments used was:

    F. the Buchner funnel.
    G. the condenser.
    H. the conical flask.
    J. the filter paper.

22

PASSAGE 5

Atomic absorption spectrometry (AAS) can identify the elements and their concentrations in a sample using the element's characteristic wavelength. The unknown sample is collected in the *nebulizer*, which then sprays it through a flame (Figure 1).

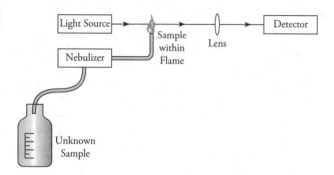

Figure 1

As the sample travels through the flame, a light source projects light at specific wavelengths through the sample. Light at some of those wavelengths is absorbed by the sample. The light with wavelengths that are not absorbed are transmitted through lens and recorded by a detector.

The *absorbance* is a measurement of the percent of light of a particular wavelength that is absorbed by the sample: an absorbance of 1.0 indicates that the sample absorbed 90% of the light at that wavelength. Readings with lower absorbance are more prone to error.

Table 1 shows the characteristic flame emission wavelengths (i.e., the wavelengths at which the element has the highest absorbance, or its peak absorbance) for various metals. Table 2 shows the analysis of 5 unknown samples, giving the range of wavelengths of their greatest absorbance. Figure 2 shows the absorbance across a range of wavelengths for Sample 1.

Note: Samples contain only the metals listed in Table 1.

Table 1

Name	Atomic Symbol	Flame Emission Wavelength (nm)
Aluminum	Al	396.1
Calcium	Ca	422.7
Copper	Cu	327.4
Gold	Au	267.6
Iridium	Ir	380.0
Iron	Fe	372.0
Lithium	Li	670.8
Magnesium	Mg	285.2
Manganese	Mn	403.1
Mercury	Hg	253.7
Potassium	K	766.5
Rhodium	Rh	369.2
Silver	Ag	328.1
Sodium	Na	589.0
Tin	Sn	284.0
Titanium	Ti	399.8
Tungsten	W	400.9
Zinc	Zn	213.9

Table 2

Sample	Wavelength Range (nm)	Absorbance
1	395–410	0.99
2	240–260	0.45
3	575–595	0.27
4	280–290	0.33
5	395–405	0.75

MANHATTAN
PREP

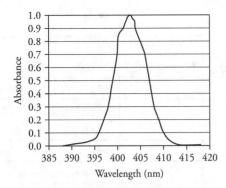

Figure 2

29. The information contained in Tables 1 and 2 supports the conclusion that Sample 3 contains:

    A. lithium.
    B. silver.
    C. sodium.
    D. tin.

30. Sample 1 could represent how many of the elements in Table 1?

    F. 1
    G. 2
    H. 3
    J. 4

31. Based on Figure 2, which of the following is most likely the metal contained in Sample 1?

    A. Aluminum
    B. Magnesium
    C. Manganese
    D. Titanium

32. Based only on the information in Table 2, which sample can be identified with the least certainty?

    F. Sample 2
    G. Sample 3
    H. Sample 4
    J. Sample 5

33. If Sample 5 contained two different metals, based on the information in Tables 1 and 2, which of the following could be those two metals?

    A. Al and Mg
    B. Li and Mn
    C. Mn and Ti
    D. Sn and W

34. If every sample contains only one metal and no two metals are the same, which of the following could be contained in Sample 5, on the basis of all information given?

    F. Gold
    G. Iridium
    H. Manganese
    J. Titanium

35. Based on Table 1, which of the following pairs of elements is most difficult to differentiate by AAS?

    A. Ag and Na
    B. Fe and Ir
    C. Li and K
    D. Ti and W

22

PASSAGE 6

The decomposition of hydrogen peroxide (H_2O_2) is an irreversible reaction that produces water (H_2O) and oxygen gas (O_2). Though slow under normal conditions, the reaction proceeds quickly when catalyzed with potassium iodide (KI). Two students performed the reaction using different experimental setups and recorded their observations.

Experiment 1

A 50 mL graduated cylinder filled with 30 mL of 30% H_2O_2 solution, and 4.0 g of solid KI pellets are added as shown in Figure 1. A student records his observations in Table 1.

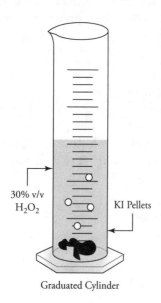

30% v/v H_2O_2

KI Pellets

Graduated Cylinder

Figure 1

Table 1

Time (sec)	Volume Liquid (mL)	Observations
0	30.0	Added KI to cylinder.
10	29.6	Large number of bubbles rose through liquid.
20	29.2	Bubbles continued to rise.
30	28.8	Bubbles continued to rise.
40	28.4	Few bubbles observed.
50	28.0	No more bubbles created.
60	28.0	No change.

Experiment 2

An empty thick-walled glass syringe was fitted to a test tube opening. Volume measurements were taken by observing the gauge on the syringe. A student placed 6 mL of 3% H_2O_2 solution and 2.0 g of solid KI pellets in the test tube, as shown in Figure 2. She immediately placed a rubber stopper on the test tube to prevent the escape of gases. The observations from the time the experiment began are shown in Table 2.

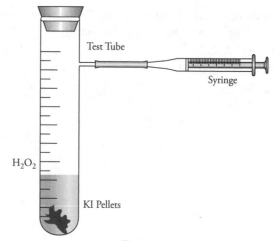

Test Tube

Syringe

H_2O_2

KI Pellets

Figure 2

Table 2

Time (sec)	Volume Gas (mL)	Observations
0	0.0	Added KI to test tube.
3	20.0	Small number of bubbles rose through liquid.
6	34.0	Bubbles continued to rise.
9	52.0	Bubbles continued to rise.
12	68.0	Bubbles continued to rise.
15	80.0	Very few bubbles observed.
18	94.5	No more bubbles created.
21	94.5	No change.

36. When potassium iodide is added to hydrogen peroxide, a decomposition reaction occurs. Which of the following equations correctly represents this reaction?

    F. $H_2O_2 \rightarrow H_2 + O_2$
    G. $H_2O_2 \rightarrow H_2O + 2\ O_2$
    H. $2H_2O_2 \rightarrow 2\ H_2O + O_2$
    J. $2H_2O_2 \rightarrow H_2O + O_2$

37. Approximately how long did it take for Experiment 2 to reach completion?

    A. 18 seconds
    B. 21 seconds
    C. 50 seconds
    D. 60 seconds

38. The bubbles observed during both reactions were most likely which of the following?

    F. O_2
    G. H_2O
    H. KI
    J. H_2O_2

39. Which experiment took more time to reach completion?

    A. Experiment 1, because more H_2O_2 was present.
    B. Experiment 1, because more KI catalyst was present.
    C. Experiment 2, because less KI catalyst was present.
    D. Experiment 2, because less H_2O_2 was present.

40. In Experiment 1, some of the observed loss in volume was most reasonably due to:

    F. the creation of oxygen gas.
    G. the evaporation of KI.
    H. the conversion of liquid H_2O_2 into gaseous H_2O_2.
    J. the inherent properties of a decomposition reaction.

41. If Experiment 2 had been conducted at constant volume, the result would likely be:

    A. that no reaction could take place.
    B. an increase in final pressure.
    C. a much slower reaction.
    D. a decrease in final temperature.

42. If the student running Experiment 2 had accidently used the 30% H_2O_2 solution used in Experiment 1, what would the most likely result be?

    F. The reaction would not occur.
    G. A different reaction would occur.
    H. A significantly larger volume of gas would be produced.
    J. A significantly smaller volume of gas would be produced.

22

PASSAGE 7

Though identical in most properties, *isotopes* of an element have different atomic masses. A *gas centrifuge* is an apparatus often used to separate isotopes of an element. A centrifuge takes advantage of centripetal force as it spins, forcing heavier atoms toward the outside and lighter ones inward as illustrated in Figure 1. A mixture of isotopes is inserted through the input tube, and as the centrifuge spins, heavier isotopes are collected through Output Tube A. Lighter isotopes are forced toward the center, so they are removed through Output Tube B.

The natural abundances of several zinc isotopes, their atomic masses, and some of their uses are listed in Table 1. Once zinc is converted into gaseous diethyl zinc, it can be processed through a gas centrifuge.

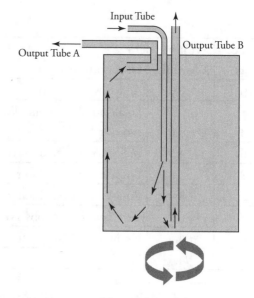

Figure 1

Table 1

Isotope	Atomic Mass	Natural Abundance	Common Use
Zn-64	64 amu	48.63%	Measurement of neutron spectra
Zn-66	66 amu	27.90%	Production of copper-67 (Cu-67), gallium-67 (Ga-67), and gallium-68 (Ga-68)
Zn-67	67 amu	4.10%	Studies of zinc uptake in the body
Zn-68	68 amu	18.75%	Production of copper-67 (Cu-67) for therapeutic uses
Zn-70	70 amu	0.62%	Research into super-heavy elements

Experiment 1

A sample of diethyl zinc was purified so that it contained only the three heaviest isotopes of zinc. To accomplish this, a student used a gas centrifuge, collecting the lighter isotopes and setting them aside, then re-purified the heavier collection. The numbers of millimoles inserted through the input tube and collected from each output tube after each run are listed in Table 2.

Table 2

	Total Input (millimoles)	Output Tube A (millimoles)	Output Tube B (millimoles)
Run 1	100	63	37
Run 2	63	34	29
Run 3	34	22	12

Experiment 2

In order to work exclusively with Zn-70, a student determines how many runs through the gas centrifuge a sample with a naturally occurring distribution of zinc isotopes would need in order to isolate the desired isotope. She carefully measures the isotopic composition of the sample collected from Output Tube A after each run and charts the percent Zn-70 in Figure 2.

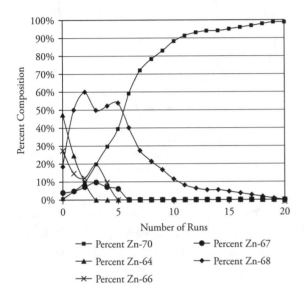

Figure 2

43. According to Table 1 and Figure 2, if a student wanted to research super-heavy elements using a zinc sample with naturally occurring isotope distribution, approximately how many times should the sample be run to have a sample that is at least 98% pure?

A. 1
B. 3
C. 10
D. 19

44. According to Tables 1 and 2 and Figure 2, which isotope most likely represented the largest percentage of the collection from Output Tube B after Run 1?

F. Zn-64
G. Zn-66
H. Zn-67
J. Zn-68

45. If the radioactive isotope Zn-69 were included in the sample of naturally occurring zinc being run through the gas centrifuge, where would it more likely be collected after Run 1?

A. Input Tube
B. Output Tube A
C. Output Tube B
D. Impossible to determine

46. According to Figure 2, which isotope was the first to be completely removed from the sample collection?

F. Zn-70
G. Zn-68
H. Zn-66
J. Zn-64

47. If a student wanted a sample that was approximately 50% Zn-70 and 50% Zn-68, approximately how many times should a sample with a naturally occurring isotope distribution be purified on the gas centrifuge via the method in Experiment 2?

A. 2
B. 3
C. 5
D. 10

48. In Experiment 1, what was the total amount of sample that the student collected through Output Tube B?

F. 100 millimoles
G. 78 millimoles
H. 66 millimoles
J. 37 millimoles

49. If a student collected and purified the sample emitted through Output Tube B, which isotope is least likely to be observed after 8 runs?

A. Zn-64
B. Zn-66
C. Zn-68
D. Zn-70

PASSAGE 8

Adsorption chromatography (AC) is a technique used to separate components of a solution. In AC, a solution that may contain different compounds is passed through a column that contains a solid silica gel (Figure 1). Highly polar compounds that pass through the silica gel are more strongly adsorbed, or bound, to the silica gel, than less polar compounds, and therefore, highly polar compounds pass through the silica gel more slowly. The components of a solution can thus be separated by measuring the time it takes each component to pass through the column.

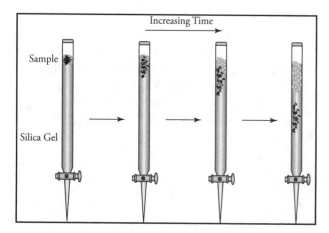

Figure 1

The polarity index of eight compounds is given in Table 1. A compound with a higher polarity index is more polar.

Table 1

Compound	Polarity Index
Hexane	0.0
Cyclohexane	0.2
Carbon tetrachloride	1.6
Xylene	2.5
Benzene	2.7
Chloroform	4.1
Ethanol	5.2
Acetonitrile	5.8

Experiment 1

A student prepares a column and passes through samples of each of the eight compounds in Table 1. The time that it takes for each compound to pass through the column, or the *retention time*, is shown in Figure 2.

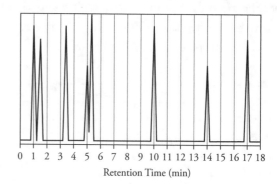

Figure 2

Experiment 2

AC is performed on three unknown samples, labeled A, B, and C. The graph of the retention time for Unknowns A, B, and C are shown in Figures 3, 4, and 5, respectively.

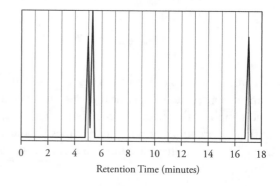

Figure 3

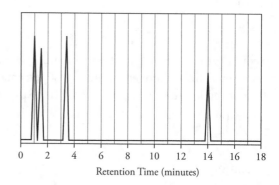

Figure 4

MANHATTAN
PREP

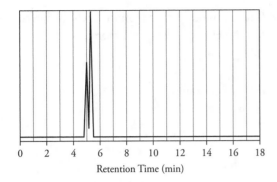

Figure 5

50. According to Table 1 and Figure 2, which compound most likely has a retention time of 3.5 minutes?

   F. Acetonitrile
   G. Carbon tetrachloride
   H. Chloroform
   J. Hexane

51. According to Table 1 and Figures 2–5, which substance is likely in none of the unknown mixtures?

   A. Chloroform
   B. Cyclohexane
   C. Ethanol
   D. Xylene

52. Which of the following is most likely in Unknown B but not in Unknown C?

   F. Acetonitrile
   G. Carbon tetrachloride
   H. Chloroform
   J. Xylene

53. If an additional compound were introduced with a polarity index of 2.3, it would most likely have a retention time that is:

   A. longer than carbon tetrachloride but shorter than xylene.
   B. longer than cyclohexane but shorter than hexane.
   C. longer than xylene but shorter than carbon tetrachloride.
   D. longer than hexane but shorter than cyclohexane.

54. If a student mixed Unknowns A and B and recorded the retention time through AC using the same method as the student in Experiment 2, the resulting graph would most likely look like which of the following?

F.

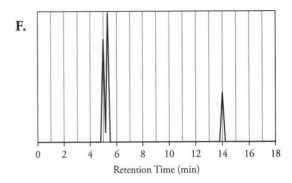

G.

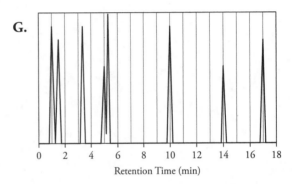

H.

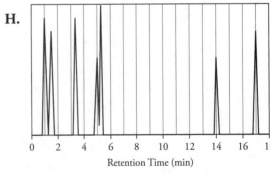

J.

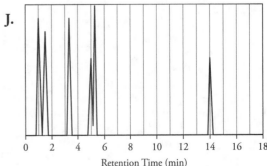

55. All of the following compounds appear only in one of the three unknown samples EXCEPT:

    A. acetonitrile.
    B. benzene.
    C. cyclohexane.
    D. ethanol.

56. One compound that is most likely in Unknown A but in neither Unknown B nor C is:

    F. acetonitrile.
    G. ethanol.
    H. cyclohexane.
    J. xylene.

22

PASSAGE 9

Students studied the motion of objects on inclined planes, or ramps, in a series of experiments.

Experiment 1

A student positioned two inclined planes oriented toward each other as illustrated in Figure 1.

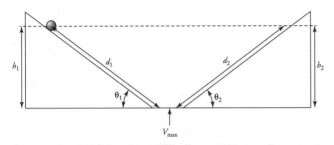

Figure 1

The angles of incline were altered in four trials, as illustrated in Figure 2. A circular disk was released from a height of 10 meters, and its motion as it rolled down one inclined plane and up the other was observed. The friction between the disk and the surfaces is negligible, other than that required to rotate the disk, and the rotational inertia of the disk is also negligible (i.e., it takes very little energy to get the disk spinning).

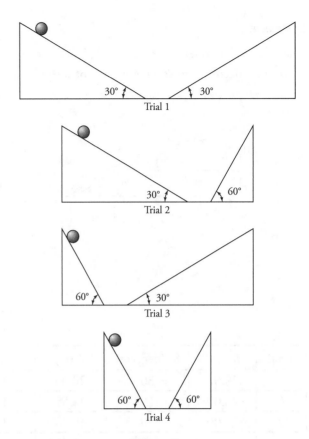

Figure 2

The heights on the inclined planes to which the disk reached (h_1 and h_2), the angles of incline of each inclined plane (θ_1 and θ_2), the distances traveled by the disk over each inclined plane (d_1 and d_2), the acceleration of the disk during its motion over each inclined plane (a_1 and a_2, with a negative value representing deceleration), and the velocity of the disk between the inclined planes (v_{max}) were measured and recorded in Table 1.

Table 1

Trial	h_1 (m)	θ_1 (degrees)	d_1 (m)	a_1 (m/s²)	v_{max} (m/s)	h_2 (m)	θ_2 (degrees)	d_2 (m)	a_2 (m/s²)
1	10.00	30	20.00	4.9	14	10.00	30	20.00	−4.9
2	10.00	30	20.00	4.9	14	10.00	60	11.55	−8.5
3	10.00	60	11.55	8.5	14	10.00	30	20.00	−4.9
4	10.00	60	11.55	8.5	14	10.00	60	11.55	−8.5

Experiment 2

A second student oriented the inclined planes so one downhill trajectory had varying degrees of steepness as shown in Figure 2.

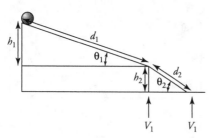

Figure 2

The two angles of incline were varied, and measurements from a circular disk rolling downhill were recorded in Table 2. The velocities (v_1 and v_2) were measured at the bottom of each inclined plane. The friction between the disk and the surfaces is negligible.

Table 2

Trial	h_1 (m)	θ_1 (degrees)	d_1 (m)	v_1 (m/s)	h_2 (m)	θ_2 (degrees)	d_2 (m)	v_2 (m/s)
5	10.00	30	20.00	14.0	15.00	60	17.32	22.1
6	10.00	60	11.55	14.0	5.00	30	10.00	17.1
7	20.00	30	40.00	19.8	5.00	30	10.00	22.1
8	10.00	60	11.55	14.0	5.00	60	5.77	17.1

57. Based on the data collected from both experiments, as the angle of the inclined plane increases, the distance traveled by the circular disk along that plane, while not changing the initial height,:

A. increases.
B. decreases.
C. remains constant.
D. doubles.

58. According to Table 1, the height the circular disk reaches of the second inclined plane (h_2) may only be affected by:

F. the acceleration of the disk over the first inclined plane (a_1).
G. the angle of incline of the first inclined plane (θ_1).
H. the distance the disk travels over the first inclined plane (d_1).
J. the height from which the disk was released from the first inclined plane (h_1).

59. The circular disk traveled the furthest total distance over the inclined planes in:

A. Trial 1.
B. Trial 3.
C. Trial 5.
D. Trial 7.

60. In Trial 7, which of these hypothetical changes would be expected to result in the greatest velocity at the bottom of the first inclined plane (v_1)?

F. Decreasing the angle of incline (θ_1) while lowering the initial height (h_1)
G. Decreasing the angle of incline (θ_1) while raising the initial height (h_1)
H. Increasing the angle of incline (θ_1) while keeping the same initial height (h_1)
J. Increasing the angle of incline (θ_1) while lowering the initial height (h_1)

61. If there were significant friction between the disk and the inclined planes in the trials for Experiment 1 but all other conditions remained the same, you would expect to see:

A. a decrease in final height (h_2).
B. a decrease in initial height (h_1).
C. an increase in initial height (h_1).
D. an increase in final height (h_2).

62. Based on the setup in Experiment 2, the final velocity (v_2) seems dependent on the:

F. height of the first inclined plane only (h_1).
G. height of the second inclined plane only (h_2).
H. total distance traveled over both inclined planes ($d_1 + d_2$).
J. total height of both inclined planes ($h_1 + h_2$).

63. In Trial 1, which of the following would NOT be expected to increase if the initial height were raised to 20.0 m while keeping the angle of incline at 30°?

A. The acceleration of the disk down the first inclined plane (a_1)
B. The distance traveled by the disk down the first inclined plane (d_1)
C. The final height of the disk (h_2)
D. The velocity at the bottom of the inclined plane (v_{max})

22

PASSAGE 10

Various forces can act on objects, including the normal force, which is directly related to the object's mass, and the frictional force, which depends on both mass and the type of material being used. Once all forces acting on an object are known, the resulting overall force, or net force, can be calculated. The forces acting on a box on an inclined plane are illustrated in Figure 1.

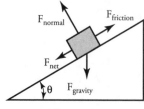

Figure 1

Study 1

Students calculated the normal, frictional, and net forces of different boxes that were placed on different inclined planes. They varied both the material of the boxes and the material of the inclined plane. In all cases, the angle θ of the inclined plane is 30°, and the mass of the box is 200 grams (g).

The results are listed in Table 1. All forces are measured in newtons (N). If the net force was positive, the box started sliding down the plane from rest. The higher the positive net force, the faster the box accelerated as it slid down the incline. If the net force was negative, the box stayed at rest and did not slide down the plane. In those cases, if the box was given a push down the plane, the box decelerated and came to a halt.

Table 1

Box Material	Incline Material	Normal Force (N)	Frictional Force (N)	Net Force (N)
Glass	Glass	1.697	1.697	−0.717
Copper	Steel	1.697	0.900	0.080
Steel	Copper	1.697	0.900	0.080
Glass	Nickel	1.697	1.324	−0.344
Nickel	Glass	1.697	1.324	−0.344
Ice	Ice	1.697	0.034	0.946
Ice	Steel	1.697	0.051	0.929
Steel	Ice	1.697	0.051	0.929

Study 2

Students attempted to prevent a copper box from sliding down a steel incline by varying the mass of the box. The results are listed in Table 2.

Table 2

Mass of Box (g)	Angle of Incline	Normal Force (N)	Frictional Force (N)	Net Force (N)
350	30°	2.970	1.574	0.141
150	30°	1.273	0.675	0.060
50	30°	0.424	0.225	0.020
25	30°	0.212	0.112	0.010

Study 3

Using a 200-gram glass box and a nickel incline, students measured the effect of varying the angle of incline. The results are listed in Table 3.

Table 3

Angle of Incline	Normal Force (N)	Frictional Force (N)	Net Force (N)
35°	1.606	1.252	−0.128
40°	1.501	1.171	0.089
45°	1.386	1.081	0.305
50°	1.260	0.983	0.519

64. According to Table 2, as the mass of an object decreases in this situation, how do frictional force and net force change?

	$F_{friction}$	F_{net}
F.	increase	increase
G.	increase	decrease
H.	decrease	increase
J.	decrease	decrease

65. In which of the following trials during Study 1 and Study 3 did students observe the box remaining at rest on the incline?

   A. 200-g nickel box, glass 30° incline
   B. 350-g copper box, steel 30° incline
   C. 25-g copper box, steel 30° incline
   D. 200-g glass box, nickel 50° incline

66. Which of the following conditions is most likely to result in the box not sliding down the incline from rest?

   F. Increased frictional force, increased angle
   G. Increased frictional force, decreased angle
   H. Decreased frictional force, increased angle
   J. Decreased frictional force, decreased angle

67. All else being equal, which of the following pairs of materials is likely to result in the least force of friction?

   A. Glass and iron
   B. Steel and iron
   C. Ice and iron
   D. Nickel and iron

68. If the box is made of material X and the incline is made of material Y, then what can be reasonably concluded about the net force?

   F. The net force will be greater than if the box is made of material Y and the incline is made of material X.
   G. The net force will be less than if the box is made of material Y and the incline is made of material X.
   H. The net force will be the same as in the case when the box is made of material Y and the incline is made of material X.
   J. No conclusion can be reasonably drawn about the net force.

69. For which of the following pairs of materials is the ratio of the frictional force to the normal force the greatest at 30° of incline?

   A. Glass box and glass incline
   B. Steel box and copper incline
   C. Nickel box and glass incline
   D. Ice box and steel incline

70. According to the studies the students conducted, the normal force on the box depends on:

   F. the mass and material of the box.
   G. the angle and material of the incline.
   H. the mass of the box and the angle of the incline.
   J. the material of both the box and the incline.

PASSAGE 11

Newton's Law of Universal Gravitation states that any two bodies of mass in the universe attract each other with a force that is directly proportional to their masses and inversely proportional to the square of the distances between them. The force of this attraction between the two bodies can be calculated by the following formula:

$$F = G\frac{m_1 \times m_2}{d^2}$$

F is the force that each body exerts on the other body, G is a gravitational constant, m_1 is the mass of the first object, m_2 is the mass of the second object, and d is the distance between the two objects.

Newton's Law of Universal Gravitation can also be used to calculate the force of attraction between planetary bodies. The attributes of selected planets in the solar system are given in Table 1. An *equinox* occurs when the length of day (with light from the sun hitting any particular point on the planet) and the length of night (with that point on the planet shaded) would theoretically be approximately equal (if the planet were hypothetically spun once very quickly on its axis). A spring equinox occurs halfway across the planet's full orbit around the sun from an autumnal equinox. A full day can be defined as one natural rotation of the planet on its own axis, resulting in one period of light and one period of darkness.

Table 1

Planet	Approximate Mass ($\times 10^{21}$ kg)	Spring Equinox/ Autumnal Equinox	Length of Full Day (Full Earth days)	Approximate Distance from Sun (millions of km)
Venus	5,000	June 25/August 21	244	100
Earth	6,000	March 21/June 21	1.0	150
Jupiter	1,900,000	1997/2000	0.4	800
Saturn	568,000	1980/1987	0.4	1,500
Uranus	86,800	1922/1943	0.7	3,000
Neptune	102,000	1880/1921	0.7	4,500

71. Approximately how many times per revolution around the sun does the Earth experience an equinox?

    A. 1
    B. 2
    C. 4
    D. 183

72. According to the information above, how many times as long does it take for Saturn to make one revolution around the sun as it takes for Earth to make one revolution around the sun?

    F. Saturn takes the same amount of time to revolve around the sun.
    G. Saturn takes 14 times as long to revolve around the sun.
    H. Saturn takes 28 times as long to revolve around the sun.
    J. Saturn takes 42 times as long to revolve around the sun.

73. What is the relationship between a planet's distance from the sun and that planet's mass?

   A. The farther a planet is from the sun, the more massive it is.
   B. The farther a planet is from the sun, the less massive it is.
   C. As the distance increases, the mass of the planet falls, then rises.
   D. There is no predictable relationship between a planet's distance from the sun and its mass.

74. Suppose you calculated that Mars has a mass of roughly 600×10^{21} kg. Based on the information in Table 1, what could be concluded about the force that the sun exerts on Mars?

   F. The force the sun exerts on Mars is roughly 10 times the force of gravity the sun exerts on Earth.
   G. The force the sun exerts on Mars is roughly $1/10^{th}$ the force of gravity the sun exerts on Earth.
   H. The force the sun exerts on Mars is roughly $1/100^{th}$ the force of gravity the sun exerts on Earth.
   J. The force the sun exerts on Mars cannot be compared to the force the sun exerts on the Earth without the distance between Mars and the sun.

75. Which of the planets listed above takes the longest amount of time to revolve around the sun?

   A. Venus
   B. Jupiter
   C. Uranus
   D. Neptune

76. Suppose a student standing in the middle of a room with a 10-kg blue chair exactly 5 m to her right and a 20-kg green chair exactly 5 m to her left. Which of the following statements is true?

   F. The green chair exerts a gravitational force on the student that is exactly twice the force of the blue chair.
   G. The green chair exerts a gravitational force on the student that is exactly one-half the force of the blue chair.
   H. The green chair exerts a gravitational force on the student that is exactly 4 times the force of the blue chair.
   J. Neither of the chairs exerts a gravitational force on the student.

77. Suppose a new planet, Planet X, is discovered that has the same mass as Saturn and is the same distance from the sun as Neptune is. How would the sun's gravitational force on Planet X compare to the sun's gravitational force on Saturn?

   A. The force of the sun on Planet X would be 9 times the force on Saturn since gravitational force is directly related to the square of the distance from the sun.
   B. The force of the sun on Planet X would be 3 times the force on Saturn since gravitational force is directly proportional to the distance from the sun.
   C. The force of the sun on Planet X would be $1/9^{th}$ the force on Saturn since gravitational force is inversely proportional to the distance from the sun.
   D. The force of the sun on Planet X would be $1/3^{rd}$ the force on Saturn since gravitational force is inversely proportional to the square of the distance from the sun.

PASSAGE 12

Period 3 of the Periodic Table comprises the 8 elements listed in the third row of the Periodic Table, as shown

in Figure 1: sodium (Na), magnesium (Mg), aluminum (Al), silicon (Si), phosphorus (P), sulfur (S), chlorine (Cl), and argon (Ar).

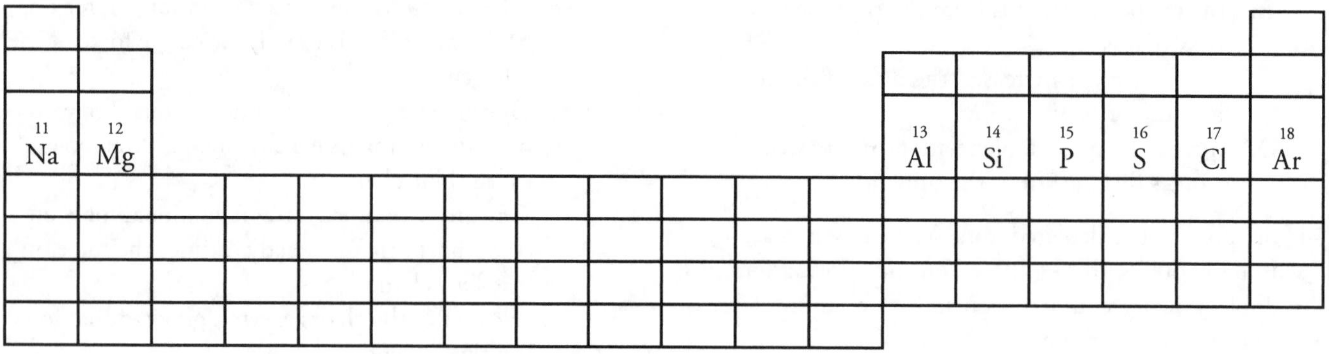

11 Na	12 Mg											13 Al	14 Si	15 P	16 S	17 Cl	18 Ar

Figure 1

Characteristics of an element include:

- *Atomic number*: the number of *protons*, or positively charged particles, in an atom of that element. An atom is neutral if it has equal numbers of protons and electrons.
- *Atomic radius*: the distance from the center to the edge of an atom of the element. Atoms are small spheres
- *Electronegativity*: the tendency of an element to attract electrons. The values for electronegativity are given on a scale that ranges from 0.7 for slightly electronegative elements (the element does

not attract electrons easily) to 4.0 for the most electronegative elements (the element strongly attracts electrons).

- *Valence electrons*: the electrons in the outer shell of an atom; they can range from 1 to 8. Atoms have a tendency to lose or gain electrons until they have 8 valence electrons and have a complete outer shell.
- *Ionization energy*: the amount of energy required to remove one valence electron from an atom.

The data for these characteristics of elements in Period 3 are given in Table 1.

Table 1

Atomic Number	Element Name	Element Symbol	Atomic Radius (pm)	Electronegativity	Number of Valence Electrons	Ionization Energy (eV)
11	Sodium	Na	190	0.93	1	5.14
12	Magnesium	Mg	145	1.31	2	7.65
13	Aluminum	Al	118	1.61	3	5.99
14	Silicon	Si	111	1.90	4	8.15
15	Phosphorus	P	98	2.19	5	10.49
16	Sulfur	S	88	2.58	6	10.36
17	Chlorine	Cl	79	3.16	7	12.97
18	Argon	Ar	71	–	8	15.76

78. According to Table 1, which of the following graphs best represents the relationship between number of valence electrons and ionization energy in Period 3?

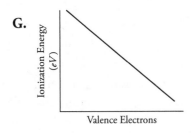

79. How many electrons does a neutral atom of sodium contain?

   A. 11
   B. 12
   C. 15
   D. 16

80. An atom of which element has the largest atomic radius?

   F. Argon
   G. Chlorine
   H. Magnesium
   J. Sodium

81. According to Table 1, to which element in Period 3 would electrons be *most* attracted?

   A. Chlorine
   B. Silicon
   C. Sodium
   D. Sulfur

82. How many electrons would phosphorus have to gain in order for it to have a complete outer shell?

   F. 3
   G. 4
   H. 5
   J. 8

83. Which of the following correctly lists the elements in order of increasing ionization energy?

   A. Ar < Mg < S < Na
   B. Ar < S < Mg < Na
   C. Na < Mg < S < Ar
   D. Na < S < Mg < Ar

84. Based on the information provided in the passage, which of the following is the most likely reason that argon's electronegativity is not given?

   F. Argon has an atomic radius that is too small to measure with the scale used in Table 1.
   G. Argon has an atomic radius that is too large to measure with the scale used in Table 1.
   H. Argon has 8 valence electrons and does not attract further electrons, so its electronegativity is too small to be determined with the scale used in Table 1.
   J. Argon has 8 valence electrons and does not attract further electrons, so its electronegativity is too large to be determined with the scale used in Table 1.

PASSAGE 13

Solid materials were examined for their maximum solubility levels in water at various temperatures. Figure 1 shows the grams of solute for various chemical compounds in a saturated solution with 100 g of H_2O solvent at temperatures between 0°C and 100°C.

$$\text{Solubility} = \frac{\text{Grams of solute in a saturated solution}}{\text{Grams of solvent}}$$

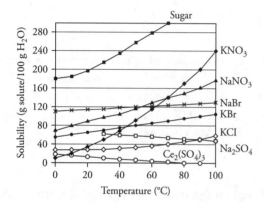

Figure 1

85. Approximately how many grams of KBr could be dissolved in 100 g H_2O at 60°C?

   A. 85 grams
   B. 100 grams
   C. 115 grams
   D. 130 grams

86. Which of the following solutes shows the greatest increase in solubility as the temperature increases from 0°C to 100°C?

   F. KCl
   G. NaBr
   H. $NaNO_3$
   J. KNO_3

87. Which type of solute, according to Figure 1, has a lower solubility at higher temperatures?

   A. Bromides, whose formulas contain Br
   B. Nitrates, whose formulas contain NO_3
   C. Sulfates, whose formulas contain SO_4
   D. Chlorides, whose formulas contain Cl

88. Which of the following compounds appears NOT to be soluble in water at 100°C?

   F. KCl
   G. $Ce_2(SO_4)_3$
   H. NaBr
   J. Sugar

89. Approximately how many grams of $NaNO_3$ could be dissolved in 25 g H_2O at 90°C?

   A. 0 grams
   B. 40 grams
   C. 80 grams
   D. 160 grams

90. A supersaturated solution is one that contains more dissolved solute at a given temperature than would be expected from the solubility charts. Assuming no solute precipitates out during the temperature change, which of the following actions is the most likely to result in a supersaturated solution?

   F. Decreasing the temperature of a saturated solution of Na_2SO_4
   G. Increasing the temperature of a saturated solution of KNO_3
   H. Decreasing the temperature of a saturated solution of KBr
   J. Increasing the temperature of a saturated solution of NaBr

91. Which compound shown in the figure demonstrates the greatest percent increase in solubility from 20°C to 30°C?

   A. Sugar
   B. $NaNO_3$
   C. NaBr
   D. KNO_3

MANHATTAN
PREP

PASSAGE 14

For a pure liquid solvent, the *vapor pressure* under normal atmospheric conditions at 20°C is a characteristic value. (The vapor pressure is the pressure of gaseous particles of the solvent that have evaporated from the solvent's surface.) Similarly, the melting and boiling points of the pure solvent are constant. However, if the solvent is mixed with a solute or another solvent, the vapor pressure and the melting and boiling points change. If the solute is non-volatile, the changes depend only on the number of moles of solute mixed. If the solute

or solvent is volatile, the interactions are more complex. The vapor pressure of the mixture depends on both the particular solvents mixed and the ratio of the solvents.

Table 1 displays standard values for several solvents. Table 2 lists the changes when a non-volatile solute is mixed with various solvents from Table 1. Table 3 lists changes when certain pairs of volatile solvents from Table 1 are mixed. All vapor pressures are measured at 20°C under normal atmospheric conditions.

22

Table 1 Characteristic Values for Various Solvents

Solvent Name	Formula	Vapor Pressure (hPa)	Boiling Point (°C)	Melting Point (°C)
Benzene	C_6H_6	101	80.1	5.5
Chloroform	$CHCl_3$	210	61.2	−63.5
Ethanol	C_2H_6O	59	78.5	−114.1
Ether	$C_4H_{10}O$	587	34.6	−116.3
Water	H_2O	17.5	100.0	0.0

Table 2 Properties of Mixtures with Non-Volatile Solutes

Solvent	Moles Solvent	Moles Solute	Vapor Pressure Mixture (hPa)	Boiling Point Mixture (°C)	Melting Point Mixture (°C)
$CHCl_3$	150	5	203.23	62.21	−64.81
$CHCl_3$	200	5	204.88	61.95	−64.48
$CHCl_3$	150	1	208.61	61.40	−63.76
H_2O	300	5	17.21	100.47	−1.72
H_2O	100	5	16.67	101.42	−5.16
H_2O	300	1	17.44	100.09	−0.34
C_2H_6O	100	2	57.84	79.03	−114.97
C_2H_6O	200	2	58.42	78.76	−114.53
C_2H_6O	100	5	56.19	79.82	−116.27

Table 3 Vapor Pressures of Mixtures at 20°C with Volatile Solutes

Solvent A	Moles Solvent A	Solvent B	Moles Solvent B	Vapor Pressure Mixture (hPa)
C_6H_6	100	C_2H_6O	100	80
C_6H_6	200	C_2H_6O	50	93
C_2H_6O	100	H_2O	100	38
C_2H_6O	200	H_2O	100	45
C_2H_6O	100	H_2O	20	52
$CHCl_3$	100	$C_4H_{10}O$	100	399
$CHCl_3$	50	$C_4H_{10}O$	100	461
$CHCl_3$	100	$C_4H_{10}O$	300	493

92. When chloroform ($CHCl_3$) and ether ($C_4H_{10}O$) are mixed in a 1 : 2 ratio by moles, the vapor pressure is:

   F. 210 hPa.
   G. 587 hPa.
   H. 399 hPa.
   J. 461 hPa.

93. The boiling point of 100 moles of water (H_2O), when mixed with 5 moles of a non-volatile solute, increases by:

   A. 0.47°C.
   B. 1.42°C.
   C. 1.72°C.
   D. 5.16°C.

94. According to Tables 1 and 3, when two different volatile solvents mix, the resulting vapor pressure is:

   F. higher than the vapor pressure of either of the individual solvents.
   G. lower than the vapor pressure of either of the individual solvents.
   H. higher than the vapor pressure of one of the individual solvents, but lower than the other.
   J. independent of the vapor pressure of the individual solvents.

95. According to Tables 1 and 2, when a non-volatile solute is mixed with a solvent, the boiling and melting points of the solvent change in which of the following ways?

   A. The boiling point and the melting point both increase.
   B. The boiling point decreases, while the melting point increases.
   C. The boiling point increases, while the melting point decreases.
   D. The boiling point and the melting point both decrease.

96. One of the effects of dissolving salt (which is non-volatile) in water while boiling the water is that:

   F. the vapor pressure increases.
   G. the boiling point increases.
   H. the melting point increases.
   J. the mixture becomes more volatile.

MANHATTAN
PREP

97. If 100 moles of ethanol (C_2H_6O) is mixed with 50 moles of water (H_2O), the resulting vapor pressure of the mixture will likely be:

    A. 45 hPa.
    B. 52 hPa.
    C. 59 hPa.
    D. 70 hPa.

98. According to the data provided, mixing benzene (C_6H_6) and chloroform ($CHCl_3$) in a 1 : 1 ratio by moles would most likely result in a vapor pressure between:

    F. 100 and 110 hPa.
    G. 120 and 130 hPa.
    H. 150 and 160 hPa.
    J. 180 and 190 hPa.

22

PASSAGE 15

Carbohydrates are molecules composed entirely of carbon, hydrogen, and oxygen that are used for energy and structure in organisms. The fundamental unit of a carbohydrate is a *monosaccharide,* which is a one-ring structure. Figure 1 shows the monosaccharide glucose. *Disaccharides* are composed of two monosaccharides linked together, while *polysaccharides* are composed of three or more monosaccharides linked together.

CH₂OH

Figure 1

Benedict's Reagent is a solution that becomes an orange color in the presence of monosaccharides or disaccharides. In the absence of monosaccharides or disaccharides, Benedict's Reagent is blue. Similarly, *iodine* can be used as an indicator of large polysaccharides. In the absence of large polysaccharides, iodine is brown, whereas in the presence of large polysaccharides, iodine turns black.

The features of numerous carbohydrates are listed in Table 1.

Experiment 1

Students taste test numerous carbohydrates and describe their taste as bitter or sweet.

Table 1

Carbohydrate	Structure	Taste
Glucose	Monosaccharide	Sweet
Fructose	Monosaccharide	Sweet
Maltose	Disaccharide	Sweet
Lactose	Disaccharide	Sweet
Starch	Polysaccharide	Bitter
Chitin	Polysaccharide	Bitter

Experiment 2

A sac of *dialysis tubing*, a semipermeable membrane (one that allows some molecules to pass but not others) is filled with a mixture of glucose, starch, and water (the last of which provides most of the mass of the mixture). Then, the sac is tied shut on both ends. The sac is dropped into a beaker containing a brown solution of iodine in water, and the beaker is heated to 40°C. After 10 minutes, observations were recorded in Table 2.

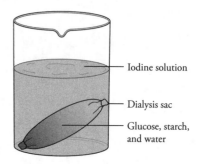

— Iodine solution

— Dialysis sac

— Glucose, starch, and water

Table 2

Time	Color of Iodine Solution	Mass of Bag (g)
0	Brown	15.9
10	Brown	8.2

99. Which of the following could the structure above represent?

   A. Fructose
   B. Maltose
   C. Starch
   D. Chitin

100. Many predators in the animal kingdom have a preferential taste for sweetness. On the basis of this fact, which of the following would be an advantageous carbohydrate for an insect to build a shell from, and for what reason?

   F. Chitin, because it is bitter.
   G. Chitin, because it is a large molecule.
   H. Fructose, because it is sweet.
   J. Fructose, because it is a small molecule.

101. In Experiment 2, the mass of the bag decreased by approximately:

   A. 8%.
   B. 25%.
   C. 50%.
   D. 100%.

102. According to the results of Experiment 2, which is known to be true about the conditions of the solution in the beaker before the sac was inserted?

   F. It contained no iodine.
   G. It contained disaccharides.
   H. It contained monosaccharides.
   J. It contained no large polysaccharides.

103. Based on the information presented in Table 1, which of the following reactions would be most likely to happen?

   A. Glucose + Fructose → Maltose
   B. Fructose + Maltose → Glucose
   C. Maltose + Lactose → Fructose
   D. Maltose + Glucose → Lactose

104. In Experiment 2, it can be concluded that the microscopic holes in the dialysis tubing are:

   F. large enough for starch and water to pass through.
   G. large enough for starch to pass through, but not for water to pass through.
   H. large enough for glucose to pass through, but not for water to pass through.
   J. large enough for water to pass through, but not for starch to pass through.

105. If the solution outside the sac contained Benedict's Reagent instead of iodine, then a possible outcome and corresponding explanation of Experiment 2 would be that:

   A. the outside solution turns from orange to blue, indicating that glucose was unable to pass through the semipermeable membrane.
   B. the outside solution stays orange, indicating that glucose was unable to pass through the semipermeable membrane.
   C. the outside solution stays blue, indicating that glucose was able to pass through the semipermeable membrane.
   D. the outside solution turns from blue to orange, indicating that glucose was able to pass through the semipermeable membrane.

PASSAGE 16

When a liquid is placed in a closed container, some of the liquid evaporates. The pressure of the vapor is called the *vapor pressure*. Two students conduct experiments to investigate how adding *solutes* (substances that are dissolved in the liquid) affects the vapor pressure of the liquid.

Experiment 1

A student measures the vapor pressure of solutions in which various amounts of NaCl (which has a molar mass of 58.4 g/mol) and sucrose (which has a molar mass of 342 g/mol) are dissolved in 100 mL water at 25°C. The results are listed in Table 1.

Table 1

Trial	Solute	Mass of Solute (g)	Vapor Pressure (mm Hg)
1	None (water only)	–	24.0
2	NaCl	5.0 g	23.2
3	NaCl	10.0 g	22.6
4	NaCl	15.0 g	21.9
5	NaCl	20.0 g	21.3
6	NaCl	25.0 g	20.7
7	Sucrose	20.0 g	23.7
8	Sucrose	40.0 g	23.5
9	Sucrose	60.0 g	23.2
10	Sucrose	80.0 g	23.0
11	Sucrose	100.0 g	22.8

Experiment 2

A student measures the vapor pressure of solutions in which 20.0 g of NaCl are dissolved in 100 mL water at various temperatures. The results are listed in Table 2.

Table 2

Trial	Solute	Mass of Solute (g)	Temperature (°C)	Vapor Pressure (mm Hg)
1	None (water only)	–	10	9.0
2	None (water only)	–	30	31.5
3	None (water only)	–	50	92.3
4	NaCl	20.0g	10	8.0
5	NaCl	20.0g	30	28.0
6	NaCl	20.0g	50	82.1

MANHATTAN
PREP

106. Which of the following factors was NOT directly controlled by the student in Experiment 1?

   F. Amount of solute dissolved
   G. Temperature
   H. Volume of the water
   J. Vapor pressure of the solution

107. Based on the results of Experiments 1 and 2, which of the following changes can increase the vapor pressure of a solution, if every other factor is held constant?

   A. Dissolve the solute in 50 mL of water instead of 100 mL of water
   B. Increase the mass of dissolved solute in the solution
   C. Increase the temperature of the solution
   D. Use a solute with a lower molar mass

108. Based on the data collected in Experiment 1, what can be concluded about the relationship between the molar mass of the solute and the vapor pressure when equal masses of solutes are dissolved at constant temperature?

   F. A solute with a smaller molar mass lowers the vapor pressure more than a solute with a greater molar mass.
   G. A solute with a smaller molar mass lowers the vapor pressure less than a solute with a greater molar mass.
   H. The molar mass of the solute does not affect the vapor pressure.
   J. No conclusion can be drawn because the solutes tested have the same molar masses.

109. The vapor pressure of a 100 mL sample of water was found to be 20.0 mm Hg. Using the information from Experiments 1 and 2, the temperature of this sample is closest to:

   A. 12°C.
   B. 22°C.
   C. 32°C.
   D. 42°C.

110. Based on the results of Experiment 2, which of the following can be concluded about how the vapor pressure of pure water changes with temperature, as compared with how the vapor pressure changes with temperature for an NaCl solution? As the temperature is increased:

   F. the vapor pressure of pure water increases less than that of the NaCl solution.
   G. the vapor pressure of pure water increases more than that of the NaCl solution.
   H. the vapor pressure of pure water increases the same as that of the NaCl solution.
   J. the vapor pressure of pure water increases more than that of the NaCl at lower temperatures, but increases less at higher temperatures.

111. Suppose a solution is prepared with both NaCl and sucrose dissolved in 100 mL of water at 25°C so that the vapor pressure of the solution is 21.0 mm Hg. Which of the following could be the masses of each solute? Assume that the effect of combining solutes on the vapor pressure is additive.

   A. 10.0 g NaCl and 20.0 g sucrose
   B. 10.0 g NaCl and 40.0 g sucrose
   C. 20.0 g NaCl and 20.0 g sucrose
   D. 20.0 g NaCl and 40.0 g sucrose

112. Suppose an experiment was conducted using $CaCl_2$ dissolved in water instead of NaCl or sucrose. Which of the following would be expected to have the highest vapor pressure?

   F. 0 g $CaCl_2$ at 30°C
   G. 0 g $CaCl_2$ at 50°C
   H. 20.0 g $CaCl_2$ at 30°C
   J. 20.0 g $CaCl_2$ at 50°C

PASSAGE 17

The *retina* is the part of the human eye that transmits light into visual information when its specialized cells fire, or send, signals in the presence of light. The retina contains two specialized types of cells: *rod cells* transmit black-and-white vision and *cone cells* fire in response to colored light to transmit color information. Humans possess three different types of cone cells. The rates of firing of rod cells and of three types of cone cells in the presence of different types of light are indicated below.

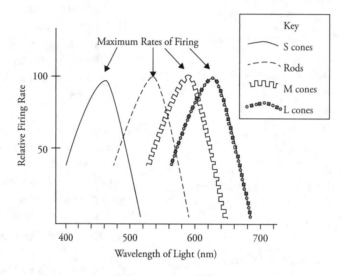

Figure 1

(Note: *Relative firing rate* is a function that compares the rate of firing of a particular type of rod or cone cell to the maximum firing rate for that cell, in response to any type of light.)

Typical wavelengths and frequencies for different colors of light are reflected in Table 1.

Table 1

Color of Light	Frequency $(10_{14}\ Hz)$	Wavelength (nm)
Violet	7.2	400 nm
Blue	6.3	475 nm
Green	5.7	510 nm
Yellow	5.4	550 nm
Orange	5.0	590 nm
Red	4.5	650 nm

113. According to Table 1, as the wavelength of light increases, the frequency of that light:

    A. increases only.
    B. decreases only.
    C. increases, then decreases.
    D. decreases, then increases.

114. *Infrared light* is a type of radiation that has a longer wavelength than roughly 700 nm. Based on the information provided in Table 1 and in Figure 1, what would be the expected relative rate of response for L cones in the presence of infrared light?

    F. Less than 5
    G. Between 5 and 10
    H. Between 10 and 50
    J. Greater than 50

MANHATTAN
PREP

115. Figure 1 includes a representation of all of the rods and cones that are found in the human eye. According to Figure 1, how many different types of rod cells do humans have?

   A. 0
   B. 1
   C. 2
   D. 3

116. Which type of cell would be most active in the presence of blue light?

   F. Rod cell
   G. L cone
   H. M cone
   J. S cone

117. Certain types of color blindness result from genetic mutations that change the shape of one specific type of cone cell, rendering that type of cone cell completely unable to fire. Which of the following could represent the firing spectrum for the eyes of an individual with such a mutation?

A.

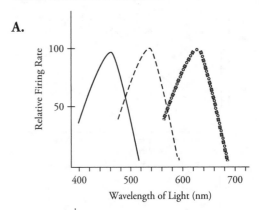

B.

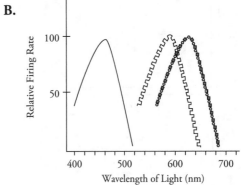

C.

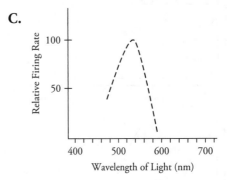

D.

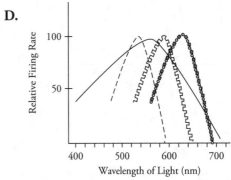

118. The speed of light (V) can be calculated using the equation $V = f\lambda$, where f is equal to the frequency of the light and λ is equal to the wavelength of that light. Which of the following best approximates the speed of light graphed against its frequency?

F.

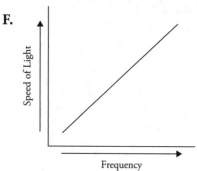

G.

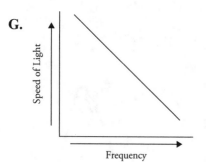

H.

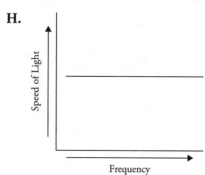

J.

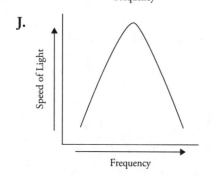

119. The difference in wavelength between the point at which rods and M cones have identical relative firing rates and the point at which M cones and L cones have identical relative firing rates is approximately:

A. 5 nm.

B. 18 nm.

C. 27 nm.

D. 50 nm.

PASSAGE 18

A *photovoltaic cell* is a device that generates electrical current when light falls upon it. The current generated can be used to measure the *intensity*, or apparent brightness, of the light (Figure 1).

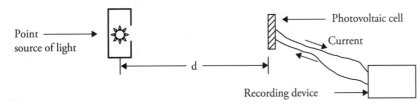

Figure 1

Table 1 shows the light intensity measured at different distances from a point source of light with three brightness settings.

Table 1

Brightness	Distance d (cm)	Intensity (lux)
Low	10	3.25
Medium	10	7.29
High	10	9.20
Low	20	0.81
Medium	20	1.82
High	20	2.30
Low	30	0.36
Medium	30	0.81
High	30	1.02

Polarizers are semi-transparent filters that transmit only light vibrating in certain directions (Figure 2).

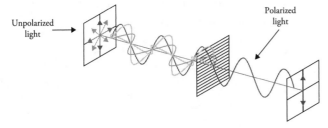

Figure 2

Table 2 shows the light intensity measured at different distances from the point source on a constant brightness setting with and without a single polarizer inserted between the photovoltaic cell and the point source.

Table 2

Polarizer	Distance d (cm)	Intensity (lux)
With	10	2.55
Without	10	7.29
With	20	0.64
Without	20	1.82
With	30	0.28
Without	30	0.81

Table 3 shows the light intensity measured at 20 centimeters from the point source on the high brightness setting when two polarizers are inserted at varying angles to each other.

Table 3

Angle between Polarizers	Intensity (lux)
0°	0.81
30°	0.60
45°	0.40
60°	0.20
90°	0.00

120. For a given brightness setting, which of the following graphs best illustrates the relationship between the distance and the light intensity listed in Table 1?

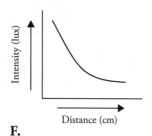

F.

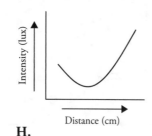

H.

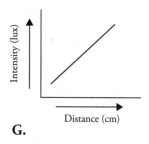

G.

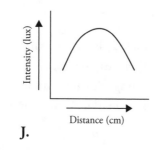

J.

121. Tables 1 and 2 correspond to the same experimental setup when no polarizer is present. Based on this information, the brightness setting in effect when Table 2 was generated:

A. was high.
B. was medium.
C. was low.
D. cannot be determined.

122. Based on the data in Table 2, the presence of a single polarizer reduced the intensity of light by approximately:

F. 15%.
G. 40%.
H. 65%.
J. 90%.

123. The angle between two polarizers that transmits approximately half of the intensity as is transmitted at 0° is:

A. 30°.
B. 45°.
C. 60°.
D. 90°.

124. Based on the given data, the lowest intensity would be expected under which of the following experimental conditions?

F. Low brightness, 10 cm distance, 1 polarizer
G. Medium brightness, 20 cm distance, 2 polarizers at an angle of 0°
H. Medium brightness, 30 cm distance, 2 polarizers at an angle of 45°
J. High brightness, 20 cm distance, 2 polarizers at an angle of 90°

125. With no polarizers, at a distance of 40 cm from the point source on the high brightness setting, the photovoltaic cell would be expected to register an intensity:

A. between 0 and 1 lux.
B. between 1 and 2 lux.
C. between 2 and 3 lux.
D. between 3 and 4 lux.

126. The experimental conditions that would be expected to produce the same intensity as low brightness, 20 cm distance, and no polarizers are:

F. high brightness, 30 cm distance, and 1 polarizer.
G. medium brightness, 10 cm distance, and 2 polarizers at an angle of 0°.
H. medium brightness, 30 cm distance, and no polarizers.
J. low brightness, 10 cm distance, and 2 polarizers at an angle of 60°.

MANHATTAN
PREP

PASSAGE 19

Students analyzed an unknown mixture of at least eight metallic or semi-metallic elements using techniques of *emission spectroscopy*. The mixture was subjected to excitement through the input of energy, and as the atoms of these elements relaxed, they emitted specific wavelengths of light to carry away the excess energy. The intensity of these emissions at different wavelengths was observed; however, these spectral results (Figure 1) were too complex to analyze thoroughly. In this and all subsequent figures, the wavelengths of the light are measured in nanometers (nm) along the horizontal axis, while the relative intensity of the light (or average power transmitted over a unit area) is measured in dimensionless units along the vertical axis.

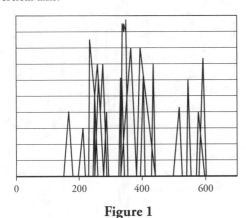

Figure 1

Study 1

A student determined that the mixture contained silicon, sodium, magnesium, and aluminum. She removed all four of these elements, and the remaining materials created an emission spectrum, shown in Figure 2.

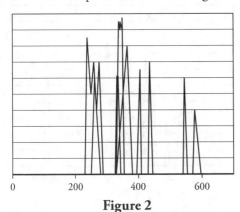

Figure 2

Study 2

A second student determined the mixture also contained hafnium and titanium. He removed both of those elements, as well as magnesium and aluminum, from the original mixture. The emission spectrum resulting from the remaining mixture is shown in Figure 3.

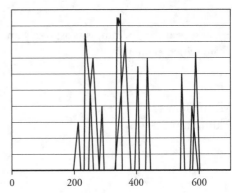

Figure 3

Study 3

Finally, a student determined zirconium and mercury were present. She removed both of those elements, as well as magnesium, from the original mixture. The spectrum resulting from the remaining mixture is shown in Figure 4.

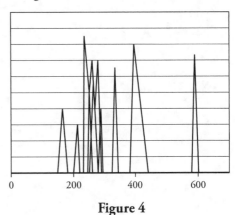

Figure 4

127. The highest peak that appears around 600 nm could indicate the presence of:

   A. sodium.
   B. aluminum.
   C. magnesium.
   D. zirconium.

128. All of the mixtures analyzed in the three studies are missing a peak shown in the initial spectrum approximately located at:

   F. 200 nm.
   G. 300 nm.
   H. 500 nm.
   J. 600 nm.

129. The earliest peak, at 167 nm, is most likely an emission from which element?

   A. Iron
   B. Mercury
   C. Magnesium
   D. Aluminum

130. If iron were also known to be in the original mixture, which of the following could be the emission spectrum if iron, hafnium, titanium, magnesium, and aluminum were all removed?

F.

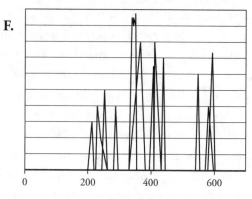

G.

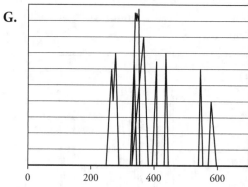

H.

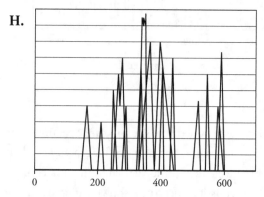

J.

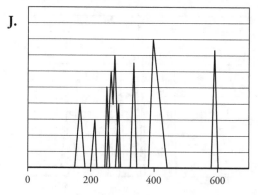

MANHATTAN
PREP

131. The broad peak located around 340 nm that is absent from the spectrum observed in Study 3 is most likely either:

    A. mercury or zirconium.
    B. magnesium or mercury.
    C. magnesium or zirconium.
    D. magnesium or hafnium.

132. The clearest emission spectrum could most likely be obtained by:

    F. removing mercury.
    G. removing mercury and two other elements.
    H. removing mercury, magnesium, and two other elements.
    J. removing all but two of the elements.

133. If the mixture had not been excited by an energy input, students would be likely to observe:

    A. a radically different emission spectrum.
    B. little or no emission.
    C. a change in the emission wavelengths.
    D. less intense peaks.

22

PASSAGE 20

In order to determine the identity of unknown metals qualitatively, electron emissions are often observed. The unknown materials are excited by heat or other means, causing electrons to change energy levels. As the electron relaxes back to the ground state, light with specific colors is emitted. The most common colors emitted by several metals are listed in Table 1.

Table 1

Metal	Emission Color
Li	Red
Na	Orange
K	Violet
Rb	Red-Violet
Cs	Blue-Purple
Ca	Orange-Red
Sr	Red
Ba	Pale green
Pb	Light grey
Fe	Yellow-Orange

In both Study 1 and Study 2, the identities of the unknown metals are limited to those listed in Table 1. The wavelengths of light that produce a particular color in the visible spectrum are listed in Table 2.

Table 2

Wavelength (nm)	Color
400–424	Violet
424–491	Blue
491–570	Green
570–585	Yellow
585–647	Orange
647–700	Red

Study 1

Five unknown samples were studied by means of a *flame test*. A student used a platinum wire, which had been cleaned in acid and with heat. This process is known to eliminate virtually all background emissions from the platinum. The student placed a small sample of each unknown on the wire, one at a time, and subjected the unknown on the wire to a flame. He recorded the colors observed on each in Table 3.

Table 3

Unknown	Emission Color
A	Blue-Purple
B	Pale green
C	Red
D	Red-Violet
E	Violet

Study 2

A student found an additional six unknown samples. She did not know whether any were the same as the ones studied by the first student. She subjected them to a similar test as described above. However, instead of platinum wire, she used nichrome wire. The nichrome wire is made of a nickel-chromium alloy and is known to emit a trace of orange when excited. Her results are listed in Table 4.

Table 4

Unknown	Emission Color
F	Red-Orange
G	Blue-Purple
H	Red-Orange
I	Pale green-Orange
J	Grey-Orange
K	Orange-Red

Because Unknowns F, H, and K were so similar, the student made an additional note: "Unknowns F and H produced different shades of red from one another, so they were unlikely to be the same material, but in both cases, the orange was very light and barely detectable. Unknown K had a vibrant orange. The orange was actually more pronounced than the red."

134. According to Tables 1 and 3, the most likely identity of Unknown B is most likely:

   F. Cs.
   G. Pb.
   H. Ba.
   J. Fe.

135. According to Tables 1 and 3, Unknown C is most likely either:

   A. Li or Sr.
   B. Rb or K.
   C. Li or Ca.
   D. Ca or Rb.

136. Which of the following samples could most reasonably be the same material?

   F. Unknowns F and K
   G. Unknowns D and E
   H. Unknowns F and H
   J. Unknowns C and F

137. Nichrome wire is least helpful in evaluating samples that contain:

   A. a sample that emits a wavelength between 400 and 424 nm.
   B. a sample that emits a wavelength between 491 and 570 nm.
   C. a sample that emits a wavelength between 585 and 647 nm.
   D. a sample that emits a wavelength between 647 and 700 nm.

138. According to Tables 1 and 2, which of the following is most likely to emit a wavelength at approximately 415 nm and another wavelength at approximately 675 nm?

   F. Rb
   G. Cs
   H. K
   J. Sr

139. According to Table 2, a metal that emitted a wavelength of light at exactly 491 nm is likely to appear as which of the following?

   A. Blue
   B. Blue-green
   C. Green
   D. Green-yellow

140. Each of the following was likely present in the unknown samples of exactly one of the two studies EXCEPT:

   F. Pb.
   G. Cs.
   H. Ca.
   J. K.

22

PASSAGE 21

Matter on Earth exists predominantly in three different states: solid, liquid, or gas. *Solids* contain molecules that are tightly packed, usually in a regular pattern, and do not move freely. *Liquids* contain molecules that are tightly packed but move freely past each other in no regular pattern. *Gases* contain molecules that are widely separated and that move freely in no particular pattern.

Assuming a standard pressure of 1 atmosphere (atm), the temperature at which a substance turns from solid to liquid is called the *melting point,* and the temperature at which a substance turns from liquid to gas is called the *boiling point.* These temperatures are typically measured in degrees Celsius (°C).

The *latent heat of melting* is defined as the amount of energy required to convert 1 kilogram of a substance from solid to liquid at the melting point. The *latent heat of vaporization* is the amount of energy required to convert 1 kilogram of a substance from liquid to gas at the boiling point. These heats are often measured in kilojoules (kJ) per kilogram (kg) of the substance.

The melting point, boiling point, latent heat of melting, latent heat of vaporization, and molecular weight of several substances are listed in Table 1 below.

Table 1

Substance	Melting Point (°C)	Latent Heat of Melting (kJ/kg)	Boiling Point (°C)	Latent Heat of Vaporization (kJ/kg)	Molecular Weight (g/mol)
Water	0	335	100	2,272	18
Mercury	−38.8	11	357	295	200
Lead	328	23	1,750	859	207
Silver	962	111	1,950	2,356	108
Aluminum	659	399	2,327	10,530	27
Copper	1,083	207	2,595	4,730	64

A *phase-change diagram* at constant pressure displays the temperature and phase of a substance as heat is added to it. The phase change diagram for a mystery substance (which is listed in Table 1) is outlined below in Figure 1.

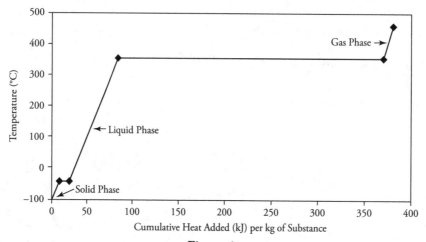

Figure 1

MANHATTAN
PREP

141. *Condensed phases* are the phases in which molecules are placed close together. Which of the following are condensed phases?

   A. Solid only
   B. Liquid only
   C. Liquid and solid only
   D. Solid and gas only

142. According to Table 1, what is the relationship between molecular weight and boiling point?

   F. There is a direct relationship: as molecular weight increases, boiling point increases.
   G. There is an inverse relationship: as molecular weight increases, boiling point decreases.
   H. There is a U-shaped relationship: as molecular weight increases, boiling point first decreases, then increases
   J. There is no clear relationship between molecular weight and boiling point.

143. At 1 atm of pressure and 1,000°C, in what phase are copper and silver?

   A. Copper is solid, while silver is liquid.
   B. Copper is solid, while silver is gas.
   C. Copper is liquid, while silver is solid.
   D. Copper and silver are both gas.

144. What is the mystery substance whose phase-change diagram is displayed in Figure 1?

   F. Water
   G. Mercury
   H. Silver
   J. Copper

145. According to Figure 1, while the substance is transforming from liquid to gas at the boiling point, one can infer that the heat being added:

   A. increases temperature of the substance only.
   B. changes the phase of the substance only.
   C. increases the temperature of the substance and changes the phase of the substance.
   D. decreases the temperature of the substance and changes the phase of the substance.

146. If 20 kJ of heat could be added every second, approximately how long would it take, at 659°C, to turn 1 kg of solid aluminum into a liquid?

   F. 1 second
   G. 10 seconds
   H. 20 seconds
   J. 40 seconds

147. The latent heat of vaporization is always greater than the latent heat of melting for any pure substance, but the ratio of the two latent heats can differ. Which of the following substances has the lowest ratio of its latent heat of vaporization to its latent heat of melting?

   A. Aluminum
   B. Lead
   C. Mercury
   D. Water

PASSAGE 22

Suppose a sample of a liquid is placed in a closed container. Some molecules in this sample have enough energy to escape the liquid phase, as shown in Figure 1. This evaporated gas is called the *vapor*. The *vapor pressure* is the pressure of this gas at a given temperature.

Figure 1

Figure 2 shows the vapor pressures of diethyl ether, ethanol, and water from 0°C to 100°C. The *boiling point* of a liquid is the temperature when the vapor pressure of the liquid is the same as the atmospheric pressure. For example, if the atmospheric pressure is 760 torr, the boiling point of diethyl either is 35°C because that is

the temperature at which the vapor pressure of diethyl ether is 760 torr. Table 1 shows the energy required for samples of various masses of each liquid to completely vaporize at their respective boiling points. Table 2 shows data for the three substances.

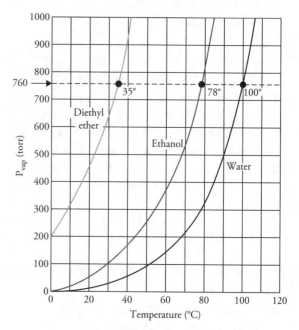

Figure 2

Table 1

Substance	Boiling Point	Mass of Sample				
		10 g	20 g	30 g	40 g	50 g
Diethyl ether	35°C	3.5 kJ	7.1 kJ	11 kJ	14 kJ	18 kJ
Ethanol	78°C	8.4 kJ	17 kJ	25 kJ	34 kJ	42 kJ
Water	100°C	23 kJ	45 kJ	68 kJ	90. kJ	110 kJ

MANHATTAN
PREP

Table 2

	Chemical Formula	Molar Mass (g/mol)
Diethyl ether	$C_4H_{10}O$	74.1
Ethanol	C_2H_5OH	46.1
Water	H_2O	18.0

148. Based on the graph in Figure 2, a sample of which liquid would have the highest vapor pressure at 50°C?

   F. Diethyl ether
   G. Ethanol
   H. Water
   J. It depends on the mass of the sample.

149. Given the information in Table 1, approximately what mass of ethanol can be vaporized at its boiling point if 10 kJ of energy is absorbed?

   A. 8.4 g
   B. 10 g
   C. 12 g
   D. 30 g

150. From the data given in Tables 1 and 2, a student concludes that substances with a smaller molar mass have higher boiling points. Which of the following facts refutes this hypothesis?

   F. Acetone, with a molar mass of 58.1 g/mol, has a boiling point of 56°C.
   G. Isopropyl alcohol, with a molar mass of 60.1 g/mol, has a boiling point of 83°C.
   H. Pentane, with a molar mass of 72.2 g/mol, has a boiling point of 36°C.
   J. Propanal, with a molar mass of 58.1 g/mol, has a boiling point of 48°C.

151. From the information in Figure 2 and Table 1, which of the following can be concluded?

   A. Substances that have a particular vapor pressure at a lower temperature have higher boiling points.
   B. Substances that have higher vapor pressures at a given temperature have higher boiling points.
   C. Substances that have lower vapor pressures at a given temperature have higher boiling points.
   D. None of these conclusions can be drawn.

152. Suppose samples of all three liquids were placed in a bell jar at 40°C in which the atmospheric pressure can be lowered by pumping out air. To what level should the air pressure be lowered so that only one liquid remains?

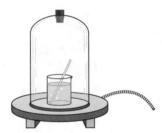

   F. 1,000 torr
   G. 400 torr
   H. 100 torr
   J. 10 torr

153. Suppose 100 g samples of each liquid are placed in separate closed containers at their respective boiling points. The graph below shows the mass of each liquid as they are heated with constant energy input. Using the data from Table 1, which liquid is represented by each line on the graph below?

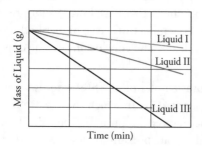

Liquid I	Liquid II	Liquid III
A. Diethyl ether	Ethanol	Water
B. Diethyl ether	Water	Ethanol
C. Water	Diethyl ether	Ethanol
D. Water	Ethanol	Diethyl ether

154. Based on Figure 2, which of the following explains the relationship between temperature and vapor pressure of a substance?

F. As the temperature increases, the vapor pressure decreases because more molecules in the gas phase are returning to the liquid.

G. As the temperature increases, the vapor pressure decreases because the attraction between molecules in the liquid increases.

H. As the temperature increases, the vapor pressure increases because more molecules are moving with enough energy to escape the liquid phase.

J. As the temperature increases, the vapor pressure increases because the substance boils at a higher temperature.

MANHATTAN
PREP

PASSAGE 23

Conductivity is a measurement of the ability of something to conduct electrical current. The conductivity of a solution can be determined by measuring the resistance when a current is passed through the solution. A conductivity meter is used to measure resistance, which can then be used to calculate the conductivity of the solution. Conductivity measurements in the following reactions are all given in micro-Siemens per centimeter (μS/cm).

When placed in water, many compounds dissociate, or break up, into ions, which are electrically charged atoms or molecules. The movement of these ions constitutes electrical current. Generally, the more ions present in solution, the higher the conductivity observed.

Study 1

A researcher measured the conductivity of a variety of solutions at 25°C using a standard conductivity meter. Because conductivity is dependent on concentration, she repeated the experiment at seven different concentrations for each solution. The concentrations are measured in mg/L. The results are listed in Table 1.

Table 1: Conductivity (μS/cm) at 25°C

	Concentration (mg/L)						
	1	**10**	**100**	**300**	**1,000**	**3,000**	**10,000**
HCl	11.7	116	1,140	3,390	11,100	32,200	103,000
H_2SO_4	8.8	85.6	805	2,180	6,350	15,800	48,500
H_3PO_4	3.9	36.5	342	890	2,250	4,820	10,500
NH_4OH	4.1	17	58	102	189	329	490
NaCl	2.2	21.4	210	617	1,990	5,690	17,600

Study 2

A second researcher repeated the experiment of Study 2, but varied the temperature instead of the concentrations. He performed the experiment at two different concentrations; 1 mg/L and 100 mg/L. The results are listed in Tables 2 and 3.

Table 2: Conductivity (μS/cm) at 1 mg/L

	Temperature			
	0°C	**18°C**	**25°C**	**50°C**
HCl	7.7	10.4	11.7	16.0
H_2SO_4	5.8	7.7	8.8	12.1
NaCl	1.2	1.9	2.2	3.5

Table 3: Conductivity (μS/cm) at 100 mg/L

	Temperature			
	0°C	**18°C**	**25°C**	**50°C**
HCl	752.4	1,014.6	1,140	1,561.8
H_2SO_4	531.3	700.35	805	1,110.9
NaCl	111.3	180.6	210	329.7

155. According to Table 1, as the concentration of each solution increased, the conductivity:

    A. generally increased.
    B. increased without exception.
    C. decreased without exception.
    D. generally decreased.

156. According to the two studies, under what conditions would a solution likely be least conductive?

  F. Low temperatures and low concentrations
  G. Low temperatures and high concentrations
  H. High temperatures and low concentrations
  J. High temperatures and high concentrations

157. Which of the following has the highest level of conductivity?

  A. 1 mg/L solution of H_2SO_4 at 25°
  B. 1 mg/L solution of H_2SO_4 at 50°
  C. 100 mg/L solution of H_2SO_4 at 25°
  D. 100 mg/L solution of H_2SO_4 at 50°

158. Which of the following graphs best represents the results of Study 2?

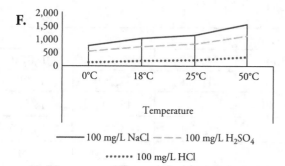

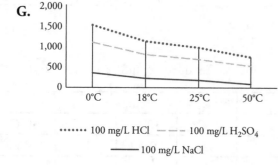

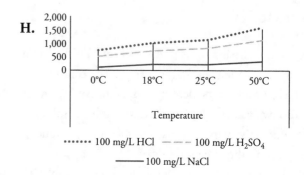

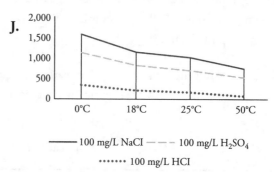

159. The conductivity of NH_4OH follows the trends seen in Experiment 1 up to very high concentrations. At those high concentrations, the conductivity starts to decrease. Why might this be?

  A. At very high concentrations of NH_4OH, more ions are available to conduct electrical current.
  B. At very high concentrations of NH_4OH, the temperature of the solution also increases.
  C. At very high concentrations of NH_4OH, water's ability to allow particles such as ions to flow is reduced.
  D. At very high concentrations of NH_4OH, positive and negative ions form neutral pairs that do not conduct electricity.

MANHATTAN
PREP

160. Based on the results from the two studies, if an analysis was carried out on ammonium hydroxide (NH_4OH) at 18°C and a concentration of 100 mg/L, the conductivity would most likely be close to:

   F. 17 μS/cm

   G. 51 μS/cm

   H. 58 μS/cm

   J. 102 μS/cm

161. An increased level of conductivity is generally associated with a larger number of the ions within solution. All other conditions being equal, why might a certain number of molecules of H_2SO_4, which can in theory dissociate into three ions ($2\ H^+$ and $1\ SO_4^{-2}$) show higher conductivity than an equal number of molecules of H_3PO_4, which can in theory dissociate into four ions ($3\ H^+$ and $1\ PO_4^{-3}$)?

   A. Because the phosphate ion (PO_4^{-3}) is less conductive than the sulfate ion SO_4^{-2}.

   B. Because hydrogen ions (H^+) are too small and light to contribute to conductivity.

   C. Because H_2SO_4 more completely dissociates in solution than H_3PO_4.

   D. Because H_3PO_4 creates a greater number of ions in solution than H_2SO_4.

22

PASSAGE 24

The density of a material is calculated by dividing the mass of the material by the volume of the material. Numerous methods may be employed for determining the density of solids. Measuring the mass of a solid is generally straightforward, but the volume of irregular objects or powders can be more difficult. Two students tested different methods for measuring the volume of solids.

Study 1

One student analyzed various solids through *volume displacement*. In this procedure, the solid was introduced into a sample of water of known volume. The water was displaced by the solid, and the total volume increased to include both the solid and the liquid, as illustrated in Figure 1.

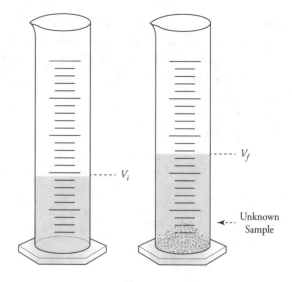

Figure 1

The volume of the solid can be determined by subtracting the initial volume from the displaced volume. This method is limited to solids that are more dense than the liquid into which they are inserted and that do not interact with the liquid. The results of the student's study are listed in Table 1.

Table 1

Sample Name	Chemical Formula	Initial Volume (mL)	Final Volume (mL)	Sample Mass (g)	Calculated Density (g/mL)	Actual Density (g/mL)	Percent Error
Magnesium	Mg	20	23.50	6	1.71	1.70	−1%
Aluminium	Al	20	26.20	17	2.74	2.70	−2%
Copper	Cu	20	21.30	11	8.46	8.30	−2%
Gold	Au	20	21.30	25	19.23	19.30	0%
Iron	Fe	20	22.60	20	7.69	7.80	1%
Coarse Salt	NaCl	20	20.20	5	25.00	0.80	−3,021%
Fine Salt	NaCl	20	20.18	10	55.56	1.20	−4,526%
Powdered Sugar	$C_{12}H_{22}O_{11}$	20	20.10	3	30.00	0.80	−3,645%
Granulated Sugar	$C_{12}H_{22}O_{11}$	20	20.15	8	53.33	0.85	−6,182%

Study 2

A second student analyzed the volume of the same solids using *gas pycnometry*. The student inserted the samples into a sealed container of known volume (V_C). The container was filled with gas, and the initial pressure (P_I) was measured with a *manometer*. The gas was then allowed to interact with a reference chamber that had a known pressure (P_R) and volume. The final pressure (P_F) was measured. The volume of the sample (V_S) was determined using the following equations:

$$V_S = V_C + \frac{V_R}{1 - P_{RATIO}}$$

$$P_{RATIO} = \frac{P_I - P_R}{P_F - P_R}$$

The accuracy of this method is limited to solids that do not deteriorate under pressure, are non-volatile, and are not extremely fine powders. Fine, powdered material can be drawn into the reference cell, resulting in miscalculations of volume. The apparatus is illustrated in Figure 2 and the student's results are listed in Table 2.

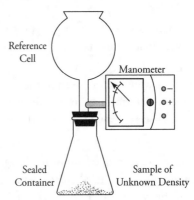

Figure 2

Table 2: Gas Pycnometry

Sample Name	Chemical Formula	Pressure Ratio	Sample Volume (mL)	Sample Mass (g)	Calculated Density (g/mL)	Actual Density (g/mL)	Percent Error
Magnesium	Mg	0.67	60.00	90	1.50	1.70	12%
Aluminium	Al	1.54	11.43	30	2.63	2.70	3%
Copper	Cu	0.56	52.50	450	8.57	8.30	−3%
Gold	Au	4.30	26.97	500	18.54	19.30	4%
Iron	Fe	10.00	28.89	230	7.96	7.80	−2%
Coarse Salt	NaCl	0.26	43.51	35	0.80	0.80	0%
Fine Salt	NaCl	0.57	53.33	150	2.81	1.20	−134%
Powdered Sugar	$C_{12}H_{22}O_{11}$	4.00	26.67	200	7.50	0.80	−836%
Granulated Sugar	$C_{12}H_{22}O_{11}$	0.80	80.00	70	0.88	0.85	−3%

162. The most dense material studied, according to Tables 1 and 2, is:

  F. powdered Sugar.
  G. gold.
  H. iron.
  J. copper.

163. The density of water is 1.00 g/mL. Which of the following materials is likely to float based solely on its known density?

  A. Magnesium
  B. Gold
  C. Coarse salt
  D. Fine salt

164. The four materials with the largest percent error in Study 1 were inaccurate most likely because:

  F. the solids dissolved in the water.
  G. the solids were less dense than the water.
  H. the solids deteriorated under pressure.
  J. the solids were drawn into the reference cell.

165. The two materials with the largest percent error in Study 2 were inaccurate most likely because:

  A. the solids dissolved in the water.
  B. the solids were less dense than the water.
  C. the solids deteriorated under pressure.
  D. the solids were drawn into the reference cell.

166. A student decided to determine the density of a silver sample using volume displacement. The initial volume of the water was 50 mL. When 21 grams of silver was added to the water, the volume rose to 52 mL. Approximately what would the calculated density be?

  F. 2.5 g/mL
  G. 10.5 g/mL
  H. 21 g/mL
  J. 52 g/mL

167. Which bar graph best represents the calculated densities of Study 2 (all values are in g/mL)?

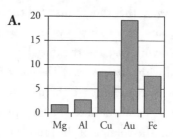

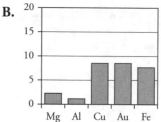

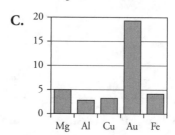

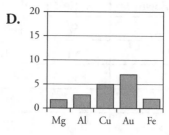

168. After 5.1 grams of magnesium are added to 50 mL of water in a graduated cylinder, approximately what would be the final volume in the graduated cylinder?

  F. 50 mL
  G. 51 mL
  H. 52 mL
  J. 53 mL

PASSAGE 25

Many chemical reactions are either *endothermic,* meaning they absorb heat, or *exothermic*, meaning they release heat. Two students set out to study the following reaction:

$$Pb(NO_3)_2 + CaCl_2 \rightarrow PbCl_2 + Ca(NO_3)_2$$

To monitor the reaction, the students created identical solutions for each study. One solution was created by mixing 330 mg of $Pb(NO_3)_2$ with 50 mL of water. A second solution was created by mixing 110 mg of $CaCl_2$ with 50 mL of water. When the two solutions were mixed together, the reaction began. $PbCl_2$ is a white solid, while the other reactants and products were all dissolved in solution.

Experiment 1

Using an *isobaric calorimeter*, a student analyzed the heat transfer during the reaction. An isobaric calorimeter operates by monitoring the temperature change within a closed system as illustrated in Figure 1.

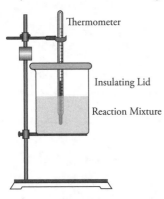

Figure 1

The temperature of the reaction was monitored for 1 hour, and the results are recorded on Figure 2. The reaction was expected to release 556 Joules. However, using this data, the student determined the heat released by the reaction was 501 Joules.

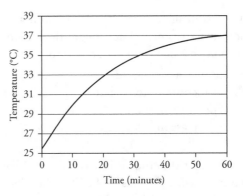

Figure 2

Experiment 2

A second student repeated the Experiment 1 to determine the percent yield of the reaction, or the percent of the expected product that is observed in experimental conditions. After mixing the two solutions described above, the student allowed the reaction to progress for 1 hour. After an hour, the student filtered the white solid and determined its mass. His results are in Table 1.

Table 1: $PbCl_2$

Expected	Actual
280 g	250 g
1 mmol	0.9 mmol

169. In Experiment 1, the approximate temperature change of the reaction after 1 hour, according to Figure 2, is:

   A. 60°C.
   B. 37°C.
   C. 25.5°C.
   D. 11.5°C.

170. At the end of Experiment 2, the student discarded the aqueous solution but retained the white solid. Each of the following would also have been discarded EXCEPT:

   F. lead nitrate.
   G. calcium chloride.
   H. lead chloride.
   J. calcium nitrate.

171. If the student had continued monitoring the reaction in Experiment 1 for longer than 1 hour, it is possible that he would have observed:

    A. an increase in liquid.
    B. an increase in temperature.
    C. a decrease in solid.
    D. a decrease in heat.

172. Why might the student in Experiment 2 have chosen to measure the mass of $PbCl_2$ rather than any of the other materials?

    F. Because the color change was observable.
    G. Because $PbCl_2$ dissolves easily in water.
    H. Because it is easy to measure a liquid.
    J. Because it is easier to separate a solid from a liquid than a liquid from another liquid.

173. Which of the following would accurately describe the reaction studied?

    A. Acid-base
    B. Oxidation-reduction
    C. Endothermic
    D. Exothermic

174. The percent yield of the reaction after 1 hour, according to both experiments, was:

    F. 100%.
    G. 90%.
    H. 75%.
    J. 50%.

175. Each of the following might explain why the heat of reaction was lower than expected in Experiment 1 EXCEPT that:

    A. the reaction takes longer than 1 hour to reach completion.
    B. some heat was lost to the surroundings.
    C. material was lost during the purification process.
    D. human error was present.

MANHATTAN
PREP

PASSAGE 26

Though elephant ivory was once a prized collector item, it is now known that hunting elephants for their ivory has led to a dramatic decline in the animal's population. As a result, ivory trade is strictly regulated. It is important for a collector to determine the age of each piece of ivory as one step in verifying that the ivory is legal to own and sell.

Analyzing the radioactive isotopes within an ivory sample can provide estimations of when the ivory was harvested. Carbon-14 (C-14) dating is regularly used to determine the age of organic material that is several thousand years old. It can also be used to analyze samples down to the decade and even the year, since there is enough annual variation in C-14 that we can pinpoint when a sample was harvested. Figure 1 illustrates the activity of C-14 per gram of carbon for samples of ivory with known dates of origin.

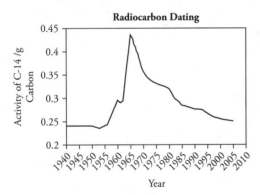

Figure 1

To resolve any ambiguity in when a sample was collected, two other studies are commonly performed. Strontium-90 (Sr-90) is associated with calcium (Ca) that is present in organic life forms mainly due to nuclear weapon testing. Since nuclear testing did not occur before 1955, any sample harvested before this time should have an activity level of Sr-90 per gram of Ca of nearly zero. The highest levels are seen in samples originating between 1960 and 1980. Since nuclear testing dramatically decreased after 1980, any samples harvested later than those decades would also have small

activity levels of Sr-90. However, the process of Sr-90 testing must be completed in a sterile room. Otherwise, samples with minimal levels of strontium can become contaminated and show artificially inflated activity levels of Sr-90.

The second study commonly performed to determine the collection date of a sample determines the ratio of thorium-228 (Th-228) atoms to thorium-232 (Th-232) atoms. If the death of the sample occurred in the recent past, the ratio of the Th-228 to Th-232 activities should be significantly higher than 1. That ratio decreases steadily for approximately 50 years, at which time the ratio nears the value of 1.

In 2010, a facility was given six samples of ivory harvested during unknown years. The facility ran analyses on the activity levels of carbon, strontium, and thorium. The results are displayed in Figures 2, 3, and 4.

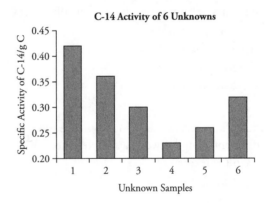

Figure 2

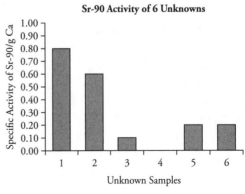

Figure 3

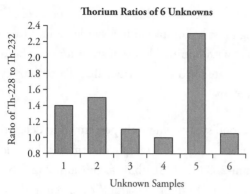

Figure 4

176. Based on Figure 3, which sample is likely to be from ivory obtained prior to 1955?

  F. Sample 1
  G. Sample 2
  H. Sample 4
  J. Sample 6

177. According to Figures 1 and 2, which of the following pairs of samples could be from 1965–1980?

  A. Samples 2 and 6
  B. Samples 2 and 4
  C. Samples 1 and 5
  D. Samples 4 and 6

178. Strontium activity analysis would be most useful in differentiating between a sample taken in 1950 and a sample formed in:

  F. 1940.
  G. 1954.
  H. 1970.
  J. 1990.

179. Based on Figures 1, 2, and 4, the most likely time when Unknown 5 originated was:

  A. 1955.
  B. 1960.
  C. 1980.
  D. 2000.

180. If a sample of ivory was harvested in 2000, but the sample was not analyzed until 2050, the thorium ratio would be most near to:

  F. 2.5.
  G. 2.0.
  H. 1.5.
  J. 1.0.

181. If the strontium analysis was not completed in a clean room, the results most likely to be obscured are those from:

  A. Samples 1 and 2.
  B. Samples 3 and 4.
  C. Samples 1 and 5.
  D. Samples 2 and 6.

182. If a sample created in 1958 were analyzed in 2015, it would likely have which of the following results for C-14 activity and Th ratio?

	C-14 activity	Th ratio
F.	0.28	1.0
G.	0.28	1.8
H.	0.22	1.8
J.	0.22	0.5

PASSAGE 27

Color changes—or the absence of a color change—can be used to identify a variety of chemical properties and transformations. By observing color changes, researchers can monitor the onset of a chemical reaction, differentiate similar compounds, and determine which product is formed if multiple options are available. It should be noted that these observations are typically qualitative, not numeric. They can be misleading if multiple compounds have similar colors or if one color is strong enough to overpower other colors that are less intense.

Color change can be used to monitor the use of iodide in the following aqueous (water-based) reactions:

Reaction 1:

$$HgCl_{2(aq)} + 2\ KI_{(aq)} \rightarrow HgI_{2(s)} + 2\ KCl_{(aq)}$$

Reaction 2 (in the presence of KI and acid):

$$I_{2(s)} + C_6H_{10}O_{5(aq)} \rightarrow I_2 \bullet C_6H_{10}O_{5(aq)}$$

Mercury chloride ($HgCl_2$), potassium iodide (KI), and starch ($C_6H_{10}O_5$) are all soluble in water; that is, they all dissolve completely. Each of these compounds forms a colorless solution. Iodine (I_2) is a dark solid that, by itself, is only slightly soluble in water. If potassium iodide is present, the iodine will become more soluble and actually dissolve enough into solution for the reaction to progress.

The products are brightly colored. Mercury iodide (HgI_2) is a bright orange salt that is insoluble in water, so it will precipitate, or fall, out of solution. When iodine forms a complex with starch ($I_2 \bullet C_6H_{10}O_5$), a deep blue-black solution is produced.

Study 1

A student attempted to determine how the reactions would progress if performed in the same reaction vessel as shown in Figure 1.

Figure 1

Mercury chloride and potassium iodide are added to the solution at the same time. The student performs the experiment several times, each time adding different amounts of the reagents, as measured in millimoles (mmol). The amounts for each trial are shown in Table 1.

Table 1

Trial	Number of mmols			
	$HgCl_2$	KI	I_2	$C_6H_{10}O_5$
1	10	20	10	10
2	10	100	10	10
3	100	20	10	10
4	10	20	100	10
5	10	20	10	100
6	0	20	10	10

The color changes the student noted for each trial are shown in Table 2.

Table 2

Trial	After 5 Seconds	After 10 Seconds
1	orange precipitate	orange precipitate
2	orange precipitate	dark blue solution
3	orange precipitate	orange precipitate
4	orange precipitate	orange precipitate
5	orange precipitate	orange precipitate
6	no change	dark blue solution

183. In Trial 1, what is the most likely product formed?
   A. Potassium iodide
   B. Iodine-starch complex
   C. Mercury iodide
   D. Mercury chloride

184. What did the color changes most likely indicate in Trial 2?
   F. The creation first of mercury iodide, then of an iodine-starch complex
   G. The creation first of the iodide ion, then of mercury iodide
   H. The creation first of an iodine-starch complex, then of mercury iodide
   J. The creation first of the iodide ion, then of an iodine-starch complex

185. Trial 6 was the only one that did not display an orange precipitate after 5 seconds most likely because:
   A. the absence of mercury made the creation of mercury iodide impossible.
   B. Reaction 2 progressed more quickly than Reaction 1 under these conditions.
   C. the excess potassium iodide favors the formation of the starch-iodine complex.
   D. the activation energy to complete Reaction 1 was insurmountable under these conditions.

186. What can be concluded about the relative rates of Reaction 1 and Reaction 2, under the conditions applied in the experiment?
   F. The two reactions proceed at the same rate.
   G. Reaction 1 takes place faster than Reaction 2.
   H. Reaction 2 takes place faster than Reaction 1.
   J. Nothing can be concluded about the relative rates of the two reactions.

187. Reaction 1 is irreversible in aqueous solution most likely because:
   A. chloride bonds more strongly with mercury than does iodide.
   B. the activation energy of the reverse reaction is too low.
   C. the presence of starch prohibits reversals.
   D. mercury iodide is insoluble in aqueous solution.

188. When the two reactions compete, as they do in Figure 1, which condition allows both to progress?
   F. The presence of excess starch
   G. The presence of no mercury chloride
   H. The presence of excess potassium iodide
   J. The presence of excess iodine

189. What is the most likely reason that a dark blue color was not observed in Trial 1?
   A. There was insufficient starch to form the iodine starch complex.
   B. There was insufficient potassium iodide remaining after the precipitation reaction.
   C. There was insufficient mercury chloride in the aqueous solution.
   D. There was insufficient potassium to complete the reaction.

PASSAGE 28

Combustion is a process that breaks down compounds called *hydrocarbons*, substances made entirely of hydrogen and carbon. Combustion can be used to determine the percent composition of the carbon and hydrogen in an unknown hydrocarbon. The general equation for combustion is:

$$C_xH_y + \text{excess } O_2 \rightarrow xCO_2 + (y/2)H_2O$$

where x represents the moles of carbon atoms present in the unknown and y represents the moles of hydrogen atoms. *Moles* are a unit used to quantify the number of atoms in a given mass of a sample:

$$1 \text{ mole} = 6.02 \times 10^{23} \text{ atoms}$$

Different elements have different masses per mole. For example, there are 12 g of carbon in 1 mole of carbon atoms, and there is 1 g of hydrogen in 1 mole of hydrogen atoms. Thus, it is said that the *molar mass* of carbon is 12 grams/mole, and the molar mass of hydrogen is 1 gram/mole. Therefore, 1 mole of a hydrocarbon contains multiple moles of both carbon and hydrogen, and this is denoted by the subscript next to each element. For example, 1 mole of decane $(C_{10}H_{22})$ contains 10 moles of carbon and 22 moles of hydrogen.

As the unknown combusts, the resulting carbon dioxide and water is collected in the apparatus shown in Figure 1.

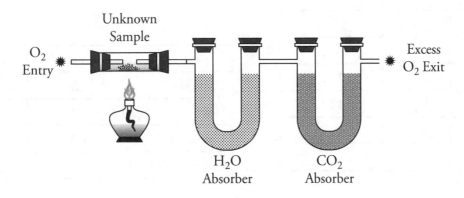

Figure 1

The mass of the carbon dioxide and water is calculated by subtracting the mass of each absorber before combustion begins from its mass after combustion is complete.

Experiment 1

A student combusted five unknowns and analyzed the resulting amount of carbon dioxide and water. He calculated the number of grams and of moles of both carbon and hydrogen. The results are represented in Table 1.

The student narrowed down his list of possible unknowns to those listed in Table 2.

Table 1

	Mass C (g)	Mass H (g)	Moles C	Moles H
Unknown A	24	5	2	5
Unknown B	12	2	1	2
Unknown C	36	3	3	3
Unknown D	60	11	5	11
Unknown E	36	7	3	7

Table 2

Compound Name	Formula	Ratio of C to H atoms
Propane	C_3H_8	3 : 8
Butane	C_4H_{10}	2 : 5
Pentane	C_5H_{12}	5 : 12
Hexane	C_6H_{14}	3 : 7
Cyclohexane	C_6H_{12}	1 : 2
Benzene	C_6H_6	1 : 1
Octane	C_8H_{18}	4 : 9
Decane	$C_{10}H_{22}$	5 : 11

Study 2

A second student combusted three unknowns and analyzed the products via the same method but did not calculate the number of moles of carbon or hydrogen, only the grams of each element. She was similarly restricted to those hydrocarbons listed in Table 2. The results are shown in Table 3.

Table 3

	Mass C (g)	Mass H (g)
Unknown W	12	2
Unknown X	12	1
Unknown Y	60	12
Unknown Z	36	6

190. What percent of the mass of Unknown B is composed of carbon?

  F. 14%
  G. 16%
  H. 65%
  J. 86%

191. Which of the following samples could be the same compound?

  A. Unknown A and Unknown X
  B. Unknown B and Unknown W
  C. Unknown C and Unknown Y
  D. Unknown D and Unknown Z

MANHATTAN
PREP

192. How many moles of hydrogen are present in Unknown Z?

   F. 0.5
   G. 1
   H. 6
   J. 12

193. According to Tables 1 and 2, how many moles of decane was Unknown D composed of?

   A. 0.5
   B. 1.0
   C. 5.0
   D. 11.0

194. Based on the results of Study 1, a possible identity of Unknown A is:

   F. pentane.
   G. butane.
   H. propane.
   J. octane.

195. The ratio of moles of carbon to moles of hydrogen in Unknown X is:

   A. 12 : 1.
   B. 44 : 17.
   C. 11 : 3.
   D. 1 : 1.

196. Excess oxygen is used in these experiments most likely so that:

   F. the reaction will proceed with the correct ratios.
   G. the reaction will be spontaneous.
   H. the reaction will be observable.
   J. the reaction will proceed to completion.

22

Answer Keys

Write in whether you got each problem right or wrong (or left it blank). If your answer was correct, put a 1 in every blank to the right of that problem. Sum up each column and compare your total to the total possible "Out Of" points in each column.

Passage 1

Problem	Correct Answer	Right/ Wrong/Blank	Interpretation of Data	Scientific Investigation	Evaluation of Models, Inferences, and Experimental Results
1	A		—		
2	H		—		
3	D		—		
4	F		—		
5	B		—		
6	J		—		
7	B		—		
Total					
Out Of	7	7		0	0

Passage 2

Problem	Correct Answer	Right/ Wrong/Blank	Interpretation of Data	Scientific Investigation	Evaluation of Models, Inferences, and Experimental Results
8	H		—		
9	B		—		
10	J		—		
11	A		—		
12	G		—		
13	C		—		
14	F		—		
Total					
Out Of	7	7		0	0

Passage 3

Problem	Correct Answer	Right/ Wrong/Blank	Interpretation of Data	Scientific Investigation	Evaluation of Models, Inferences, and Experimental Results
15	C		—		
16	F		—		
17	B		—		
18	H		—		
19	A		—		
20	G		—		
21	D		—		
Total					
Out Of		7	7	0	0

Passage 4

Problem	Correct Answer	Right/ Wrong/Blank	Interpretation of Data	Scientific Investigation	Evaluation of Models, Inferences, and Experimental Results
22	J		—		
23	C		—		
24	G		—		
25	A		—		
26	J		—		
27	B		—		
28	H		—		
Total					
Out Of		7	7	0	0

Passage 5

Problem	Correct Answer	Right/ Wrong/Blank	Interpretation of Data	Scientific Investigation	Evaluation of Models, Inferences, and Experimental Results
29	C		—		
30	J		—		
31	C		—		
32	G		—		
33	C		—		
34	J		—		
35	D		—		
Total					
Out Of		7	7	0	0

Passage 6

Problem	Correct Answer	Right/ Wrong/Blank	Interpretation of Data	Scientific Investigation	Evaluation of Models, Inferences, and Experimental Results
36	H		—		
37	A		—		
38	F		—		
39	A		—		
40	F		—		
41	B		—		
42	H		—		
Total					
Out Of		7	7	0	0

Passage 7

Problem	Correct Answer	Right/ Wrong/Blank	Interpretation of Data	Scientific Investigation	Evaluation of Models, Inferences, and Experimental Results
43	D		—		
44	F		—		
45	B		—		
46	J		—		
47	C		—		
48	G		—		
49	D		—		
Total					
Out Of		7	7	0	0

Passage 8

Problem	Correct Answer	Right/ Wrong/Blank	Interpretation of Data	Scientific Investigation	Evaluation of Models, Inferences, and Experimental Results
50	G			—	
51	A			—	
52	G			—	
53	A			—	
54	H			—	
55	B			—	
56	F			—	
Total					
Out Of		7	0	7	0

MANHATTAN
PREP

Passage 9

Problem	Correct Answer	Right/ Wrong/Blank	Interpretation of Data	Scientific Investigation	Evaluation of Models, Inferences, and Experimental Results
57	B			—	
58	J			—	
59	D			—	
60	G			—	
61	A			—	
62	J			—	
63	A			—	
Total					
Out Of		7	0	7	0

Passage 10

Problem	Correct Answer	Right/ Wrong/Blank	Interpretation of Data	Scientific Investigation	Evaluation of Models, Inferences, and Experimental Results
64	J			—	
65	A			—	
66	G			—	
67	C			—	
68	H			—	
69	A			—	
70	H			—	
Total					
Out Of		7	0	7	0

MANHATTAN
PREP

Passage 11

Problem	Correct Answer	Right/ Wrong/Blank	Interpretation of Data	Scientific Investigation	Evaluation of Models, Inferences, and Experimental Results
71	B			—	
72	G			—	
73	D			—	
74	J			—	
75	D			—	
76	F			—	
77	C			—	
Total					
Out Of		7	0	7	0

Passage 12

Problem	Correct Answer	Right/ Wrong/Blank	Interpretation of Data	Scientific Investigation	Evaluation of Models, Inferences, and Experimental Results
78	F		—		
79	A		—		
80	J		—		
81	A		—		
82	F		—		
83	C		—		
84	H		—		
Total					
Out Of		7	7	0	0

Passage 13

Problem	Correct Answer	Right/ Wrong/Blank	Interpretation of Data	Scientific Investigation	Evaluation of Models, Inferences, and Experimental Results
85	A		—		
86	J		—		
87	C		—		
88	G		—		
89	B		—		
90	H		—		
91	D		—		
Total					
Out Of		7	7	0	0

Passage 14

Problem	Correct Answer	Right/ Wrong/Blank	Interpretation of Data	Scientific Investigation	Evaluation of Models, Inferences, and Experimental Results
92	J		—		
93	B		—		
94	H		—		
95	C		—		
96	G		—		
97	A		—		
98	H		—		
Total					
Out Of		7	7	0	0

MANHATTAN PREP

Passage 15

Problem	Correct Answer	Right/ Wrong/Blank	Interpretation of Data	Scientific Investigation	Evaluation of Models, Inferences, and Experimental Results
99	B			—	
100	F			—	
101	C			—	
102	J			—	
103	A			—	
104	J			—	
105	D			—	
Total					
Out Of		7	0	7	0

Passage 16

Problem	Correct Answer	Right/ Wrong/Blank	Interpretation of Data	Scientific Investigation	Evaluation of Models, Inferences, and Experimental Results
106	J			—	
107	C			—	
108	F			—	
109	B			—	
110	G			—	
111	C			—	
112	G			—	
Total					
Out Of		7	0	7	0

Passage 17

Problem	Correct Answer	Right/ Wrong/Blank	Interpretation of Data	Scientific Investigation	Evaluation of Models, Inferences, and Experimental Results
113	B			—	
114	F			—	
115	B			—	
116	J			—	
117	A			—	
118	H			—	
119	D			—	
Total					
Out Of	7	0	7	0	

Passage 18

Problem	Correct Answer	Right/ Wrong/Blank	Interpretation of Data	Scientific Investigation	Evaluation of Models, Inferences, and Experimental Results
120	F		—		
121	B		—		
122	H		—		
123	B		—		
124	J		—		
125	A		—		
126	H		—		
Total					
Out Of	7	7	0	0	

MANHATTAN
PREP

Passage 19

Problem	Correct Answer	Right/ Wrong/Blank	Interpretation of Data	Scientific Investigation	Evaluation of Models, Inferences, and Experimental Results
127	A			—	
128	H			—	
129	D			—	
130	G			—	
131	A			—	
132	J			—	
133	B			—	
Total					
Out Of	7	0	7	0	

Passage 20

Problem	Correct Answer	Right/ Wrong/Blank	Interpretation of Data	Scientific Investigation	Evaluation of Models, Inferences, and Experimental Results
134	H			—	
135	A			—	
136	J			—	
137	C			—	
138	F			—	
139	B			—	
140	G			—	
Total					
Out Of	7	0	7	0	

Passage 21

Problem	Correct Answer	Right/ Wrong/Blank	Interpretation of Data	Scientific Investigation	Evaluation of Models, Inferences, and Experimental Results
141	C		—		
142	J		—		
143	A		—		
144	G		—		
145	B		—		
146	H		—		
147	D		—		
Total					
Out Of	7	7	0	0	

Passage 22

Problem	Correct Answer	Right/ Wrong/Blank	Interpretation of Data	Scientific Investigation	Evaluation of Models, Inferences, and Experimental Results
148	F		—		
149	C		—		
150	G		—		
151	C		—		
152	H		—		
153	D		—		
154	H		—		
Total					
Out Of	7	7	0	0	

MANHATTAN
PREP

Passage 23

Problem	Correct Answer	Right/ Wrong/Blank	Interpretation of Data	Scientific Investigation	Evaluation of Models, Inferences, and Experimental Results
155	B			—	
156	F			—	
157	D			—	
158	H			—	
159	D			—	
160	G			—	
161	C			—	
Total					
Out Of	7	0	7	0	

Passage 24

Problem	Correct Answer	Right/ Wrong/Blank	Interpretation of Data	Scientific Investigation	Evaluation of Models, Inferences, and Experimental Results
162	G			—	
163	C			—	
164	F			—	
165	D			—	
166	G			—	
167	A			—	
168	J			—	
Total					
Out Of	7	0	7	0	

Passage 25

Problem	Correct Answer	Right/ Wrong/Blank	Interpretation of Data	Scientific Investigation	Evaluation of Models, Inferences, and Experimental Results
169	D			—	
170	H			—	
171	B			—	
172	J			—	
173	D			—	
174	G			—	
175	C			—	
Total					
Out Of		7	0	7	0

Passage 26

Problem	Correct Answer	Right/ Wrong/Blank	Interpretation of Data	Scientific Investigation	Evaluation of Models, Inferences, and Experimental Results
176	H		—		
177	A		—		
178	H		—		
179	D		—		
180	J		—		
181	B		—		
182	F		—		
Total					
Out Of		7	7	0	0

MANHATTAN
PREP

Passage 27

Problem	Correct Answer	Right/ Wrong/Blank	Interpretation of Data	Scientific Investigation	Evaluation of Models, Inferences, and Experimental Results
183	C			—	
184	F			—	
185	A			—	
186	G			—	
187	D			—	
188	H			—	
189	B			—	
Total					
Out Of	7		0	7	0

Passage 28

Problem	Correct Answer	Right/ Wrong/Blank	Interpretation of Data	Scientific Investigation	Evaluation of Models, Inferences, and Experimental Results
190	J			—	
191	B			—	
192	H			—	
193	A			—	
194	G			—	
195	D			—	
196	J			—	
Total					
Out Of	7		0	7	0

Physical Sciences Solutions

Passage 1 Solutions

1. **(A)** Model 1

Interpretation of Data

In Model 2, the atom has smaller sub-particles—the electron. In Model 3, not only are there sub-particles (protons, neutrons, and electrons), but the atom is mostly empty space, rather than a solid sphere. The correct answer is (A).

2. **(H)** Models 2 and 3 only

Interpretation of Data

In Model 1, there is no mention that an atom can have electrical charge. Model 2 mentions that an ion is formed if the number of positive charges (from the atom) and negative charges (from the electrons) are not equal. Model 3 states that an ion is formed if the numbers of protons and electrons are not equal. The correct answer is (H).

3. **(D)** 23 amu

Interpretation of Data

According to Model 3, the mass of the proton and neutron are both approximately 1 amu. Since the electron has negligible (virtually no) mass, you can ignore it when finding the sodium atom's mass. With 11 protons and 12 neutrons, the mass is 11 amu + 12 amu = 23 amu. The correct answer is (D).

4. **(F)** Model 1

Interpretation of Data

Model 1 states that all atoms of an element are identical and have the same properties, such as mass. However, according to the question stem, there are different kinds of carbon atoms with different masses, which directly refutes Model 1. The correct answer is (F).

5. **(B)** Models 1 and 2 only

Interpretation of Data

While it makes sense for atoms to deflect when they hit each other, the surprising finding stated in the question is that most of the helium atoms actually passed through the sheet of foil, indicating that atoms are probably not solid spheres, but rather empty space. Both Models 1 and 2 state that the atom is a solid sphere, and thus would not explain Rutherford's findings. Model 3, however, states that outside the nucleus, the atom is empty space, supporting Rutherford's observations that the atoms usually pass through each other. The correct answer is (B).

6.   **(J)** None of the models

Interpretation of Data

The atom presented in Model 1 has no smaller sub-particles. Models 2 and 3 describe the electron as a subatomic, fundamental particle, and Model 3 describes the electron, the neutron, and the proton as subatomic particles "that are themselves fundamental and indivisible." However, the new research shows that protons and neutrons are composed of even smaller particles, a finding that directly conflicts with Model 3. Models 1 and 2 do not even mention protons and neutrons, so the new research does not fit well with either of them. The correct answer is (J).

7.   **(B)** Illustration B.

Interpretation of Data

Model 2 states that the atom is a solid positive sphere with small negatively charged electrons distributed throughout. Answer choice (A) does not show that the sphere is positively charged or that the atom contains negatively charged electrons. Answer choices (C) and (D) are not correct because Model 2 does not present a nucleus in the atom. The correct answer is (B).

Passage 2 Solutions

8.   **(H)** 30 minutes

Interpretation of Data

The three side products are CHF_3, CH_2F_2, and CH_3F. If you look at the CH_3F column in Table 2, it is present at the 10-minute, 20-minute, and 30-minute marks, so it is present for about 30 minutes. Likewise, CH_2F_2 is present at the 20-minute, 30-minute, and 40-minute marks, so it is also present for about 30 minutes. Finally, CHF_3 is present at the 30-minute, 40-minute, and 50-minute marks, so it is also present for about 30 minutes. All of these side products are present for approximately 30 minutes. The correct answer is (H).

9.   **(B)** 6,292.97 kJ.

Interpretation of Data

You need to first look at Table 1 to figure out when no more methane (CH_4) was present: at the 50-minute mark, there are 0 moles of CH_4 in the reaction mixture. The question asks for the total amount of heat released, which refers to the cumulative heat released in Table 3. At 50 minutes, 6,292.97 kJ of heat has been released. The correct answer is (B).

10. **(J)** fluoromethane.

Interpretation of Data

If you look at Table 1, at the 40-minute mark there were 2 moles of CH4 present. Likewise, if you look at Table 2, at the 40-minute marks there were 3 moles of CH_4, 2 moles of CHF_3, 1 mole of CH_2F_2, and 15 moles of H_2. However, there are 0 moles of CH_3F, which is named fluoromethane according to the passage. The correct answer is (J).

11.   **(A)**   no change in the amount of any chemical.

Interpretation of Data

If you look at Table 1, there are no more moles of the reactants CH_4 and F_2 at the 60-minute mark. Also, if you look at Table 2, there are no side products (CHF_3, CH_2F_2, and CH_3F) present at the 60-minute mark. Since only the products (CF_4 and H_2) are present in the reaction mixture, the reaction can no longer proceed, and the students would expect to see no change in the reaction mixture. The correct answer is (A).

12.   **(G)**   1,678.06 kJ.

Interpretation of Data

If you look at Table 2, there are 3 moles of CH_2F_2 present at the 30-minute mark. At the 30-minute mark on Table 3, 1,678.06 kJ of energy is released *at that time* (not cumulatively). The correct answer is (G).

13.   **(C)**   the 40-minute mark and the 50-minute mark.

Interpretation of Data

You can determine when the most rapid decline in the amount of F_2 occurs by examining the rightmost column in Table 1. In that column, compare numbers that are right next to each other and look for the greatest difference. The most rapid decline is from the 40-minute mark (10 moles present) to the 50-minute mark (only 1 mole present). The correct answer is (C).

14.   **(F)**   Table F.

Interpretation of Data

If you look at Tables 1 and 2, you can see that the reaction with fluorine has reached completion after 1 hour. Thus, the remaining moles of fluorine should be practically 0. Because chlorine and bromine are less reactive than fluorine, the reactions with those chemicals would likely not be completed after 1 hour, so some moles of both chemicals would remain. Because bromine is the least reactive, it should have the most remaining material that has not yet undergone the chemical reaction. The correct answer is (F).

Passage 3 Solutions

15.   **(C)**   Graph C

Interpretation of Data

According to Table 2 (which shows the conversions in concentrated solution), the percent conversion into products is 73% after 3 hours under the conditions specified (313 K, no catalyst). That is, 73% of the reactants have been converted into products, leaving 100% − 73% = 27%. The graph that best shows these percents (73% is just a little less than three-quarters of the circle) is the third graph. The correct answer is (C).

MANHATTAN
PREP

16.   **(F)** The reaction at 298 K with no catalyst

Interpretation of Data

Looking at Figure 1, you can see that several of the reactions have progressed to stable levels after 24 hours. The two reactions performed at 313 K and the reaction at 298 K with a catalyst are all close to 100% complete. Even if they continued to 100% complete, the increase in percent conversion couldn't be more than 5%, and the three graphs are almost completely horizontal. However, the reaction at 298 K with no catalyst is likely to continue to progress, because the conversion is still below 90%. Although this reaction is slowing down in its 25th hour, the rate of change of the conversion percentage appears to be somewhat greater than the rates of the other reactions at this point in time. The correct answer is (F).

17.   **(B)** increase the temperature and include a catalyst.

Interpretation of Data

Looking at both Tables and Figure 1, you can see that the percent conversions increase dramatically when the temperature is increased. When you compare reactions at the same temperature with and without a catalyst, those performed with a catalyst almost always have a higher percent conversion at any point in time. Thus, combining high temperature and a catalyst would result in the highest percent conversion in the lowest amount of time. The correct answer is (B).

18.   **(H)** adding a catalyst.

Interpretation of Data

At 298 K without a catalyst and in dilute solution (Table 1), the conversion percentage is 0%. In other words, the reaction has not progressed at all. Which change, by itself, would alter this conversion percentage the most? Raising the temperature to 313 K only changes the percent conversion to 2%; likewise, making the solution concentrated changes the percent conversion to 2%. In contrast, adding a catalyst changes the percent conversion to 20%. Thus, the addition of a catalyst (at the given conditions) has the largest individual effect on the rate of reaction. The correct answer is (H).

19.   **(A)** 70 minutes.

Interpretation of Data

Table 2 contains the data for concentrated reactions. At 313 K with a catalyst, the first time the reaction reaches 98% completion is at 70 minutes. The correct answer is (A).

20.   **(G)** 5 hours

Interpretation of Data

The two reactions performed in dilute solution and at 313 K differ in one respect: whether the catalyst is present or not. Compare the lines labeled "313 K no catalyst" and "313 K with catalyst." The first time that these two lines intersect in Figure 1 is the first time the two reactions have equal percent conversions. That point occurs at just before the 5-hour mark. The correct answer is (G).

21.   **(D)** no catalyst, stopped at 90 minutes

Interpretation of Data

In the reaction that occurs at 313 K, in concentrated solution (Table 2) without a catalyst, the percent conversion reaches 66% at the 90-minute mark. The other options would all result in a percent conversion that is either too high or too low. The correct answer is (D).

22 Passage 4 Solutions

22.   **(J)** Because of impurities within the product

Interpretation of Data

In the description for Experiment 1, you learn that the round-bottomed flask will contain both silver chloride and any solid impurities that were not evaporated into the conical flask with the water. The solid mass of silver chloride would include any impurities, making the experimental mass too high. The correct answer is (J).

23.   **(C)** 88 mL

Interpretation of Data

In Experiment 2, the volume collected (17.7 mL) is only slightly lower than the expected volume (18 mL). (Technically, there is less than a 2% error.) Thus, you would expect the collected volume to be only slightly lower than the expected volume of 90 mL, so 88 mL is the best answer. All the other values are far too low. The correct answer is (C).

24.   **(G)** Because the reaction was transferred from one container to another.

Interpretation of Data

A common source of experimental error occurs during transfer of materials. When you move material from one container to another, some material is almost always left behind. In both Experiments 2 and 3, the actual volume and mass are both lower than the expected because of the residue left on the original reaction container. Experiment 1 is different because the reaction vessel was directly used to separate the solid and liquid. Neither experiment used heat (only Experiment 1 did), so answer choice (F) is incorrect.

If the liquid contained the missing solid, the volume of the liquid would be higher than expected, not lower. Moreover, the solid cannot pass through the filter paper, so answer choice (H) is incorrect. If impurities were present, the mass would be greater than expected, not lower. The correct answer is (G).

25. **(A)** mixture of both solid and liquid.

Interpretation of Data

The reaction of hydrochloric acid and silver hydroxide will create water and silver chloride. Silver chloride is insoluble in water, so students are likely to see a solid (silver chloride) within a liquid (water). The different experiments focused on separating this suspension. The correct answer is (A).

26. **(J)** the reaction of silver with heat.

Interpretation of Data

After all the water has been removed, the only remaining compound in the round-bottomed flask is silver chloride. Use process of elimination. There is no remaining water, so answer choice (F) is incorrect. There is no hydrogen present, so answer choices (G) and (H) are incorrect. However, the flame is still present, so the reaction of silver with heat is possible. The correct answer is (J).

27. **(B)** lower than the amount of product expected.

Interpretation of Data

Looking at Table 1, the expected mass and volume were higher than the actual mass and volume in two of the three experiments. The only exception was that in Experiment 1, the actual mass was higher than the expected mass. However, in the other two experiments (the majority of the three experiments), the amount of product collected was lower than expected. The correct answer is (B).

28. **(H)** the conical flask.

Interpretation of Data

Looking at the three figures, you'll see that the Buchner Funnel is used only in Experiment 2, so answer choice (F) is incorrect. The condenser is used only in Experiment 1, so answer choice (G) is incorrect. Filter paper is used in both Experiments 2 and 3, but not in Experiment 1, so answer choice (J) is incorrect. The conical flask, however, is used to collect the water in all three experiments. The correct answer is (H).

Passage 5 Solutions

29. **(C)** sodium.

Interpretation of Data

Looking at Table 2, the peak absorbance for Sample 3 takes place at wavelengths between 575 nm and 595 nm. Looking at the various elements in Table 1, the only element with a characteristic flame emission wavelength in that range is sodium, which absorbs light at 589.0 nm. Lithium (670.8 nm), silver (328.1 nm), and tin (284.0 nm) do not have characteristic wavelengths between 575 nm and 595 nm. The correct answer is (C).

30. (J) 4

Interpretation of Data

According to Table 2, the peak absorbance for Sample 1 takes place between wavelengths of 395 nm and 410 nm. Elements in Table 1 with a characteristic flame emission wavelength in that range include aluminum (396.1 nm), manganese (403.1 nm), titanium (399.8 nm), and tungsten (400.9 nm). The correct answer is (J).

31. (C) Manganese

Interpretation of Data

In Figure 2, you want to look for the wavelength that has the greatest absorbance, or the highest point of the graph. This highest point is between 400 nm and 405 nm, or around 403 nm. This corresponds to manganese, which on Table 1 has a characteristic flame emission wavelength of 403.1 nm. Aluminum (396.1 nm), magnesium (285.2 nm), and titanium (399.8 nm) do not have characteristic flame emission wavelengths that are as close to 403 nm. The correct answer is (C).

32. (G) Sample 3

Interpretation of Data

The passage states: "Readings with lower absorbance are more prone to error." Looking at the absorbance of the samples in Table 2, you can see that Sample 3 has the lowest absorbance (0.27) and is therefore less reliable than the other samples. The correct answer is (G).

33. (C) Mn and Ti

Interpretation of Data

Looking at Table 2, the peak absorbance for Sample 5 is between 395 nm and 405 nm. In Table 1, four elements have characteristic flame emission wavelengths in that range: aluminum (396.1 nm), manganese (403.1 nm), titanium (399.8 nm), and tungsten (400.9 nm). Magnesium (285.2 nm), lithium (670.8 nm), and tin (284.0 nm) do not fall in this range. The elements in answer choice (C), Mn and Ti, are both possible. The correct answer is (C).

34. (J) Titanium

Interpretation of Data

The peak absorbance of Sample 5 takes place between 395 nm and 405 nm. Thus, of the answer choices, only manganese (403.1 nm) and titanium (400.9 nm) have characteristic flame emission wavelengths in that range. Looking at Figure 2, you can see that the peak absorbance of Sample 1 takes place around 403 nm, so Sample 1 is likely manganese. If no two samples contain the same element, then Sample 5 must contain titanium. The correct answer is (J).

35. **(D)** Ti and W.

Interpretation of Data

Elements that are difficult to differentiate would have very similar characteristic flame emission wavelengths. Since titanium (399.8 nm) and tungsten (400.9 nm) have characteristic wavelengths that differ by about 1 nm, this pair of elements is the most difficult of the choices to differentiate; the other pairs have larger differences in their characteristic wavelengths. The correct answer is (D).

Passage 6 Solutions

36. **(H)** $2H_2O_2 \rightarrow 2H_2O + O_2$

Interpretation of Data

The introduction states that hydrogen peroxide decomposes to form water and oxygen gas, so answer choice (F) is not correct. In a balanced chemical equation, the number of atoms of each element in the reactants is equal to that in the products. In answer choice (G), the number of oxygen atoms is different, and in answer choice (J), the number of hydrogen and oxygen atoms are different. The correct answer is (H).

37. **(A)** 8 seconds

Interpretation of Data

The data for Experiment 2 is shown in Table 2. The reaction reaches completion when the bubbles stop forming. At 18 seconds, no additional bubbles are observed, so the reaction was completed at around 18 seconds. The correct answer is (A).

38. **(F)** O_2

Interpretation of Data

The bubbles indicate a gas that is formed as a product. The introduction states that in the reaction, oxygen is a gas that is formed. It is not H_2O_2, which is a reactant and a solution. The bubbles are not KI, which is a solid and a catalyst. The bubbles are not likely to be water, which is a liquid at room temperature. The correct answer is (F).

39. **(A)** Experiment 1 because more H_2O_2 was present.

Interpretation of Data

If you compare the observations from Table 1 and Table 2, you can see that it took 50 seconds in Experiment 1 and 18 seconds in Experiment 2 before no more bubbles were observed, so Experiment 1 took more time to reach completion. If Experiment 1 had more catalyst, this would speed up the reaction rather slow it down, so (B) is not correct. Since there was more H_2O_2 in Experiment 1 (it used a greater volume more highly concentrated H_2O_2 than Experiment 2), it took a longer time before all the H_2O_2 would decompose. The correct answer is (A).

40. **(F)** the creation of oxygen gas.

Interpretation of Data

One of the products created is oxygen. As it is released, the reaction progresses and hydrogen peroxide is used up. The only explanation for the reduced volume is the completion of the reaction, shown by the creation of oxygen. There is no evidence in the passage that potassium iodide evaporates. Answer choice (G) is incorrect. Hydrogen peroxide is reacted, not converted from a liquid form to a gaseous form, so answer (H) is incorrect. Not all decomposition reactions necessarily result in a reduced volume, so answer choice (J) is incorrect. The correct answer is (F).

41. **(B)** an increase in final pressure.

Interpretation of Data

As the reaction progresses in Experiment 2, gaseous oxygen is created. This additional gas will build up in the reaction vessel if the volume is kept constant. The pressure will increase as more gas is created. Answer choice (B) is correct.

42. **(H)** A significantly larger volume of gas would be produced.

Interpretation of Data

A 30% solution of H_2O_2 would contain much more reactant than an equivalent volume of 3% solution, and thus the amount of oxygen produced would also increase. There is no reason to believe the reaction would not occur or that a different reaction would occur. Answer choice (H) is correct.

Passage 7 Solutions

43. **(D)** 19

Interpretation of Data

According to Table 1, Zn-70 is the isotope that is used for research of super-heavy elements. You need to figure out how many runs are required to have a sample in which at least 98% is the Zn-70 isotope. Looking at Figure 2, track the "Percent Zn-70" line, which continually rises across the graph. The sample is around 5% Zn-70 after 1 run, 20% after 3 runs, 90% after 10 runs, and over 98% after 19 runs. The correct answer is (D).

44. **(F)** Zn-64

Interpretation of Data

Output Tube B emits the lightest isotopes in the sample. According to Table 1, if a 100-millimole sample of zinc is placed in the centrifuge, the abundance of each isotope is the approximate amount of that isotope in the sample. Because the abundance for the lightest isotope, Zn-64, is 48.63%, you can expect the 100-millimole sample to contain approximately 49 millimoles of Zn-64. Looking at Table 2, you can see that Output Tube B after Run 1 contains the 37 millimoles of the lightest isotopes. Since the percent composition of Zn-64 fell the most in Output Tube A after Run 1 (in Figure 2), the largest percentage of the atoms emitted from Output Tube B are expected to be Zn-64. The correct answer is (F).

45. **(B)** Output Tube A

Interpretation of Data

According to Table 1, Zn-69 would be among the heaviest isotopes, second to Zn-70. When a sample is run through the centrifuge, the heavier atoms are collected from Output Tube A. After just 1 run, the Zn-69 would be expected to exit Output Tube A with Zn-70, since the abundance of Zn-70 is so small (0.62%). The graph for Zn-69 would behave much like that for Zn-68: growing at first as the lighter isotopes are removed, and then eventually falling after several more runs (allowing Zn-70 to dominate in the end). The correct answer is (B).

46. **(J)** Zn-64

Interpretation of Data

To find the isotope to first be completely removed, look for which isotope will reach 0% of the sample in the fewest number of runs. According to Figure 2, Zn-64 (the lightest isotope) reaches 0% at run 3, before any other isotope. The correct answer is (J).

47. **(C)** 5

Interpretation of Data

Looking at Figure 2, follow the data for Zn-68 and Zn-70. At 5 runs, the mixture is approximately 54% Zn-68, 40% Zn-70, and 6% Zn-67 (all other isotopes appear to be negligible). This is the point at which Zn-68 and Zn-70 are closest to 50%. An argument could be made for 6 times as another close approximation, but that option isn't available in the choices. The correct answer is (C).

48. **(G)** 78 millimoles

Interpretation of Data

To find the total amount of the sample collected through Output Tube B, sum up the amount of the sample from that tube after each run: 37 millimoles after Run 1, plus 29 millimoles after Run 2, plus 12 millimoles after Run 3 = 78 millimoles. Alternatively, the amount of the sample that was collected from Output Tube A after Run 3 (100 millimoles total − 22 millimoles in Output Tube A after Run 3) also gives the total amount collected through Output Tube B through the experiment. The correct answer is (G).

49. **(D)** Zn-70

Interpretation of Data

Output Tube B emits the lightest isotopes. While it is possible for heavier atoms to also be collected through Output Tube B, the possibility of that happening decreases as more runs are done. Since Zn-70 is the heaviest isotope, it is unlikely to remain after collecting the sample through Output Tube B after 8 runs. The correct answer is (D).

Passage 8 Solutions

50. **(G)** Carbon tetrachloride

Scientific Investigation

In Figure 2, each peak represents a different compound. Compounds that are less polar (have a lower polarity index) pass through more quickly, or have a shorter retention time. That is, the smaller the polarity index, the further to the left in the graph its peak appears. The compound with a retention time of approximately 3.5 minutes is the third peak from the left, so it is the third least polar compound. From Table 1, the third least polar compound is carbon tetrachloride. At this point, it would probably be useful to label the peaks on Figure 2 with the compounds in Table 1 (either their names or their positions from #1 to #8). The correct answer is (G).

51. **(A)** Chloroform

Scientific Investigation

If you compare each of the graphs for Unknowns A, B, and C (Figures 3–5) to Figure 2, all of the peaks show up except for the one that has a retention time of 10 minutes. This has the third-highest retention time, and therefore, the third most polar. Using Table 1, the compound with the third-highest polarity index is chloroform. The correct answer is (A).

52. **(G)** Carbon tetrachloride

Scientific Investigation

Comparing the graphs between Unknowns B (Figure 4) and C (Figure 5), you can see that there are no overlapping peaks between them. That means these solutions do not have common compounds. So you are really asking, *What are the compounds in Unknown B?* According to Figure 4, Unknown B has peaks at 1.0 min, 1.5 min, 3.3 min, and 14.0 min, which (according to Table 1 and Figure 2) corresponds to hexane, cyclohexane, carbon tetrachloride, and ethanol, respectively. The correct answer is (G).

53. **(A)** longer than carbon tetrachloride but shorter than xylene.

Scientific Investigation

Looking at Table 1, the additional compound with a polarity index of 2.3 is between carbon tetrachloride (with a polarity index of 1.6) and xylene (with a polarity index of 2.5). Since the new compound is more polar than carbon tetrachloride and is less polar than xylene, it would have a retention time longer than carbon tetrachloride but shorter than xylene. The correct answer is (A).

54. **(H)** Graph H

Scientific Investigation

If Unknowns A and B were combined, then the peaks from both solutions would be observed. According to Figure 3, Unknown A has peaks at 4.0 min, 4.3 min, and 17.0 min, while in Figure 4, Unknown B has peaks at 1.0 min, 1.5 min, and 3.3 min. In other words, the mixture would have every peak but #6 (at 10 minutes). The graph with all of those peaks corresponds to the third graph. The correct answer is (H).

55. **(B)** benzene.

Scientific Investigation

When combining the graphs for Unknowns A, B, and C (which are Figures 3, 4, and 5, respectively), you have peaks at 1.0 min (Unknown B), 1.5 min (Unknown B), 3.3 min (Unknown B), 5.0 min (Unknowns A and C), 5.3 min (Unknowns A and C), 14.0 min (Unknown B), and 17.0 min (Unknown A). The compounds that correspond to 5.0 min and 5.3 min appear in more than one unknown solution. These correspond to xylene and benzene, respectively. Only benzene is available as an answer choice. The correct answer is (B).

56. **(F)** acetonitrile.

Scientific Investigation

From Figure 3, Unknown A has peaks at 5.0 min, 5.3 min, and 17.0 min. Looking at Figures 4 and 5, only Unknown C has overlapping peaks at 5.0 min and 5.3 min. So acetonitrile, corresponding to the peak in Unknown A at 17.0 min, is only in Unknown A. The correct answer is (F).

Passage 9 Solutions

57. **(B)** decreases.

Scientific Investigation

Examine two trials that differ only in the angle of incline. If you compare Trials 1 and 3, these two trials begin at the same height (h_1), 10.00 m. However, as the angle of incline (θ_1) increases from 30° to 60°, the distance that the disk travels (d_1) decreases from 20.00 m to 11.55 m. The correct answer is (B).

58. **(J)** the height from which the disk was released from the first inclined plane (h_1).

Scientific Investigation

Looking at Table 1, you can see that the disk reaches 10.00 m up the inclined plane for all four trials. As a result, if a particular quantity changes in those trials, that quantity does not affect the final height. In Experiment 1, the acceleration of the disk over the first inclined plane (a_1), the angle of the first inclined plane (θ_1), and the distance the disk travels over the first inclined plane (d_1) all change between trials, but these factors do not affect the final height (h_2). Only the initial height (h_1) is unchanged. The correct answer is (J).

59.   (D) Trial 7.

Scientific Investigation

To find the total distance traveled over the inclined planes, add the distance traveled over each inclined plane $(d_1 + d_2)$ for each of the trials:

Trial 1: 20.00 m + 20.00 m = 40.00 m
Trial 3: 11.55 m + 20.00 m = 31.55 m
Trial 5: 20.00 m + 17.32 m = 37.32 m
Trial 7: 40.00 m + 10.00 m = 50.00 m

Trial 7 has the longest total distance traveled. The correct answer is (D).

60.   (G) Decreasing the angle of incline (θ_1) while raising the initial height (h_1)

Scientific Investigation

Consider in general how changing the angle of incline and the initial height affect the ending velocity. If you compare Trials 6 and 8, the first inclined plane has the same initial height (h_1), angle of incline (θ_1), and distance traveled (d_1). However, on the second inclined plane, as the angle of incline (θ_2) increases from 30° to 60°, the ending velocity (v_2) remains the same, 17.1 m/s. Changing the angle of incline does not affect the final velocity. If you compare Trials 6 and 7, the initial height (h_1) is raised from 10.00 m to 20.00 m, and the final velocity (v_2) also increases from 17.1 m/s to 22.1 m/s. When the initial height (h_1) is raised, the final velocity (v_2) will increase. The correct answer is (G).

61.   (A) a decrease in final height (h_2).

Scientific Investigation

The question states that "all other conditions remained the same," so the initial height would not be changed. To choose between the remaining two options, you need to draw on a little outside knowledge and experience of friction. Friction slows down an object in motion, dissipating its "kinetic energy" (energy of motion) as heat. If the friction between the circular disk and the inclined planes is considered, then the disk would travel more slowly down the first inclined plane and have less kinetic energy to move up the second inclined plane. The disk would reach a lower final height than it would without friction. The correct answer is (A).

62.   (J) total height of both inclined planes $(h_1 + h_2)$.

Scientific Investigation

You want to compare two experiments to see which quantity, when changed, results in a corresponding change in the final velocity (v_2). Looking at Table 2, if you compare Trials 5 and 6 in which the initial height (h_1) is unchanged, the final velocity (v_2) changes from 22.1 m/s to 17.1 m/s. The initial height (h_1) by itself does not change the final velocity, so choice (F) is not correct. If you compare Trials 6 and 7, the height of the second inclined plane (h_2) remains the same, but the final velocity changes (v_2). Thus, the height of the second plane by itself does not affect the velocity, and choice (G) is not correct. If you compare Trials 5 and 7, the total distance traveled $(d_1 + d_2)$ are 37.32 m in Trial 5 and 50.00 m

MANHATTAN
PREP

in Trial 7; however, the final velocities remained the same and are unaffected by the total distance, so (H) is not correct. Finally, looking at the total height ($h_1 + h_2$), you can see that there is a corresponding change in the final velocity:

Trial 5: Total height of 10.00 m + 15.00 m = 25.00 m results in a final velocity of 22.1 m/s.
Trial 7: Total height of 20.00 m + 5.00 m = 25.00 m results in a final velocity of 22.1 m/s.
Trial 6: Total height of 10.00 m + 5.00 m = 15.00 m results in a final velocity of 17.1 m/s.
Trial 8: Total height of 10.00 m + 5.00 m = 15.00 m results in a final velocity of 17.0 m/s.

The correct answer is (J).

63. **(A)** The acceleration of the disk down the first inclined plane (a_1)

Scientific Investigation

If the initial height (h_1) were raised while keeping the same angle of incline, the distance the disk would travel (d_1) must also be longer. You can see this fact by drawing similar triangles. Thus, choice (B) is not correct. From Trials 1–4, the initial height of the disk (h_1) is the final height the disk reaches on the second inclined plane (h_2), so raising the initial height would also be expected to increase the final height, and (C) is not correct. From the trials in Experiment 2, when the disk starts at a higher point ($h_1 + h_2$), the final velocity increases, so (D) is not correct. Finally, if you look at the trials in Experiment 1, the acceleration (a_1) changes with the angle of incline (θ_1), but when the angle is the same, the acceleration is the same. So the acceleration will not increase if the angle of incline remains the same. The correct answer is (A).

Passage 10 Solutions

64. **(J)** decrease, decrease

Scientific Investigation

The mass of the box (first column) decreases as you move down the table. Both the frictional force and the net force (last two columns) decrease as well as you move down the table. Thus, both forces decrease as the mass decreases. The correct answer is (J).

65. **(A)** 200-g nickel box, glass 30° incline

Scientific Investigation

For the box to remain at rest on the incline, the calculated net force needs to be negative, according to the description of Study 1. The only trial for which the net force is negative is the trial from Study 1 in which a 200-gram nickel box is placed on a glass 30° incline. In this case, the net force is −0.344 newtons. The correct answer is (A).

66. **(G)** Increased frictional force, decreased angle

Scientific Investigation

The box doesn't slide down the incline from rest when the calculated net force is negative. Looking at Table 1, you can see that the net force is negative when the frictional force is large (rows 1, 4, and 5). Looking at Table 3, you can see that the net force is negative when the angle is the smallest (row 1). Together, these patterns indicate that when the frictional force is increased and the angle is decreased, the conditions are best for preventing the box from sliding down the incline. The correct answer is (G).

67.   **(C)** Ice and iron

Scientific Investigation

You do not have data on iron from any study, so you have to make an inference from the patterns you observe in Table 1, which displays the frictional force resulting from various pairs of materials. If you scan the table, you can see that the smallest frictional forces by far are in the last three rows, all of which involve ice as one or both of the materials. Thus, it is reasonable to conclude that of the four possible pairs, ice and iron will result in the least force of friction. The correct answer is (C).

68.   **(H)** The net force will be the same as in the case when the box is made of material Y and the incline is made of material X.

Scientific Investigation

This question is essentially asking you what happens when the box material and the incline material are switched. If you study Table 1, you can see several such pairs: copper and steel (rows 2 and 3), glass and nickel (rows 4 and 5), and ice and steel (the last two rows). The copper-steel combination gives the same results as the steel-copper combination. The same is true for the other two pairs for which you have data both ways (X–Y and Y–X). Thus, you can conclude that the net force will be the same in both situations: box X + incline Y and box Y + incline X. The correct answer is (H).

69.   **(A)** Glass box and glass incline

Scientific Investigation

Table 1 shows the frictional force and the normal force for various pairs of materials at 30° of incline, so this is the table to investigate. You need the greatest ratio of one force (frictional) to another force (normal). Since the normal force is the same in all cases, you can just look for the greatest frictional force. The greatest frictional force is in row 1, glass box and glass incline. The correct answer is (A).

70.   **(H)** the mass of the box and the angle of the incline.

Scientific Investigation

Table 2 demonstrates that the normal force changes with the mass of the box. Table 3 demonstrates that the normal force changes with the angle of the incline. In contrast, Table 1 shows that the materials out of which the box and the incline are made do not affect the normal force. The correct answer is (H).

Passage 11 Solutions

71. (B) 2

Scientific Investigation

The passage states that the two equinoxes occur when they are halfway across from each other. For any orbit, a planet will experience exactly one spring equinox and one autumnal equinox in every revolution around the sun (and in the case of Earth, a full revolution around the sun takes 1 year). The correct answer is (B).

72. (G) Saturn takes 14 times as long to revolve around the sun.

Scientific Investigation

It takes 1 year for Earth to make one revolution around the sun. According to Table 1, Saturn experiences its spring and autumnal equinoxes at 1980 and 1987. That is, Saturn makes half an orbit in approximately 7 years, so it will take about 14 years to make a full revolution. This period is 14 times the revolution period of Earth. The correct answer is (G).

73. (D) There is no predictable relationship between a planet's distance from the sun and its mass.

Scientific Investigation

Table 1 lists the selected planets in order of their distance away from the sun. However, their masses vary greatly and non-uniformly as the distance increases: even though Jupiter is not the furthest planet from the sun, it has by far the greatest mass. There is no obvious, predictable relationship between a planet's distance from the sun and its mass. The correct answer is (D).

74. (J) The force the sun exerts on Mars cannot be compared to the force the sun exerts on the Earth without the distance between Mars and the sun.

Scientific Investigation

According to the formula given by Newton's Law of Universal Gravitation, the force of attraction between two bodies can be determined if you know the mass of both bodies and their distance from each other. Since the gravitational force is directly related to the masses, if a planet is 1/10th as massive as Earth, then it experiences 1/10th the gravitational attraction to the sun, assuming that Mars is the same distance from the sun as Earth. However, you are not given the distance of Mars from the sun, so you cannot determine the gravitational force on Mars by the sun. The correct answer is (J).

75. (D) Neptune

Scientific Investigation

A planet with a longer time of revolution will also have a longer time between its equinoxes because the equinoxes represent half of a planet's orbit. The planet listed with the longest time between equinoxes is Neptune, with equinoxes separated by 41 years. The correct answer is (D).

76. **(F)** The green chair exerts a gravitational force on the student that is exactly twice the force of the blue chair.

Scientific Investigation

According to the formula for Newton's Law of Gravitation, the gravitation force is directly related to the masses and inversely related to the square of the distances between two objects. Because both chairs are the same distance away from the student, you need to compare the masses of the chairs. Because the green chair has twice the mass of the blue chair, it will exert twice the gravitational force as the blue chair. The correct answer is (F).

77. **(C)** The force of the sun on Planet X would be 1/9*th* the force on Saturn since gravitational force is inversely proportional to the square of the distance from the sun.

Scientific Investigation

The formula for Newton's Law of Gravitation states that the force of attraction between two objects is directly related to the masses and inversely related to the square of the distance between two objects. If Planet X has the same mass as Saturn, then you just need to compare the distance between the sun and Planet X to the distance between the sun and Saturn. If Planet X is the same distance from the sun as Neptune (4,500 million km), then it is approximately 3 times farther away from the sun as Saturn (1500 million km). If Planet X is 3 times as far from the sun as Saturn is (and they have the same mass), then Planet X will experience a gravitational force that is 1/9th (the inverse of 3^2) the force experienced by Saturn. The correct answer is (C).

Passage 12 Solutions

78. **(F)** Graph F

Interpretation of Data

In Table 1, the elements are listed in increasing number of valence electrons (e.g., sodium has 1 valence electron, magnesium has 2, aluminum has 3, etc.). As the number of valence electrons increase, the ionization energy also increases from sodium with 5.14 eV to argon with 15.76 eV. Notice that although this is not entirely linear (e.g., aluminum has a smaller ionization energy than magnesium even though it has more valence electrons), it does describe the *general* trend between these two variables. Select the only graph with a positive relationship (i.e., positive slope). The correct answer is (F).

79. **(A)** 11

Interpretation of Data

The introduction states that in a neutral atom, the numbers of protons and electrons are equal. If you look in Table 1 at the row containing sodium, you can see that sodium has 11 protons (its atomic number is 11), so it also has 11 electrons. The correct answer is (A).

80. **(J)** Sodium

Interpretation of Data

If you look at the atomic radius column of Table 1, sodium has an atomic radius of 190 pm, which is the largest of all the elements listed. The correct answer is (J).

81. **(A)** Chlorine

Interpretation of Data

The introduction defines electronegativity as the tendency of an atom to attract elements, so you want to look for the element with the highest electronegativity. In the electronegativity column of Table 1, chlorine, with a value of 3.16, has the highest electronegativity of all the elements. The correct answer is (A).

82. **(F)** 3

Interpretation of Data

The description of valence electrons states that an atom has a complete outer shell when it has 8 valence electrons. According to Table 1, phosphorus already has 5 valence electrons, so it needs to gain 3 more electrons to complete its outer shell. The correct answer is (F).

83. **(C)** $Na < Mg < S < Ar$

Interpretation of Data

According to the ionization energy column of Table 1, the ionization energies for sodium, magnesium, sulfur, and argon are 5.14 eV, 7.65 eV, 10.36 eV, and 15.76 eV, respectively. Thus, these ionization energies increase in this order. The correct answer is (C).

84. **(H)** Argon has 8 valence electrons and does not attract further electrons, so its electronegativity is too small to be determined with the scale used in Table 1.

Interpretation of Data

The description of valence electrons states that an atom has a complete outer shell when it has 8 valence electrons. Table 1 shows that argon already has 8 valence electrons and does not need any more to complete its outer shell, so its tendency to attract electrons, or electronegativity, is negligible and too small to be determined. The correct answer is (H).

Passage 13 Solutions

85. **(A)** 85 grams

Interpretation of Data

First, verify what the question is asking for. You need to figure out how much (in grams) of a certain compound can be dissolved in a certain amount of H_2O at a certain temperature. By studying the chart, you can see how to plug in your inputs. The temperature is along the horizontal axis. Each compound has its own data series. The chart is standardized for 100 g of H_2O solvent, which is fortunately the same amount as in the question, so you don't have to adjust what the chart gives you. Finally, the result is along the vertical axis: grams of solute per 100 grams of water solvent. The compound in the question, KBr, is in the middle of the list on the right side, so the correct series is represented by small filled-in circles. Next, find the data point corresponding to 60°C. The point is between 80 g and 120 g, but it is obviously much closer to 80 g than to 120 g. Of the possible answers, only 85 grams is possible. The correct answer is (A).

86. **(J)** KNO_3

Interpretation of Data

An increase in solubility with rising temperature corresponds to a rising data series on the chart. The compound with the greatest increase over some temperature range must have a data series that rises sharply from a low number to a high number, so that the difference between those numbers—the increase—is the greatest. By inspecting the graph for each of the compounds in the answer choices, you can see that the data series for KNO_3 makes the sharpest rise. KNO_3's solubility increases from about 10 grams per 100 g H_2O to about 240 grams per 100 g H_2O. Thus, the increase is $240 - 10 = 230$ grams per 100 g H_2O. No other compound listed shows a comparable increase over the same temperature range. The correct answer is (J).

87. **(C)** Sulfates, whose formulas contain SO_4

Interpretation of Data

Temperature (on the horizontal axis) increases to the right on the chart, while solubility (on the vertical axis) increases upward. Therefore, in order for the solubility to be lower as the temperature rises, a data series must fall as it moves to the right. The only two data series that fall as they move to the right are those for Na_2SO_4 and for $Ce_2(SO_4)_3$. Thus, the type of solute that the question asks for is the type that contains SO_4 (sulfates). The correct answer is (C).

88. **(G)** $Ce_2(SO_4)_3$

Interpretation of Data

Solubility, as shown on the chart, measures how soluble a compound is in water. For something *not* to be soluble at a certain temperature, its solubility must be 0. At 100°C (on the far right of the chart), there is no data point with a 0 y-value (which would place that point on the horizontal axis). However, the data series for $Ce_2(SO_4)_3$ is very low and decreases as the temperature increases, ending at 0 g of solubility at 90°C. Therefore, it is very reasonable to expect that at 100°C, this compound also has a solubility of 0 g per 100 g of H_2O. The correct answer is (G).

MANHATTAN
PREP

89. **(B)** 40 grams

Interpretation of Data

At first blush, this question seems to be very similar to the first question asked on this passage—and in fact, the two questions are very similar. The tricky part of this question, however, is that the relevant amount of H_2O solvent is not 100 g, the standard amount that the chart is based on. So you cannot just read off the answer from the chart, as you did before; rather, you must adjust your answer. The question asks for how much solute can be dissolved in 25 grams of H_2O, which is only ¼ as much as the standard 100 grams (¼ = 25 ÷ 100). Thus, you should take only ¼ of the amount you read from the chart. At 90°C (along the horizontal axis), the series for $NaNO_3$ is second from the top (filled-in triangles). The point in question is at approximately 160 grams of solute. Again, however, this number is not the final answer—you must divide it by 4: 160 ÷ 4 = 40 grams of solute. The correct answer is (B).

22

90. **(H)** Decreasing the temperature of a saturated solution of KBr

Interpretation of Data

In the question, a supersaturated solution is defined as one that contains more than the typical maximum amount of dissolved solute. The issue at hand is how to create such a solution. By studying the answer choices, you can see that all of them involve raising or lowering the temperature of a saturated solution. Since the solubility curves on the chart generally change with temperature, you should think about which way you want the curve to go, in order to make a supersaturated solution. Take the first answer choice: decreasing the temperature of a saturated solution of Na_2SO_4. Imagine that you start at 100°C. From the chart, you can see that a saturated solution at that temperature contains about 50 grams of dissolved solute in 100 grams of water. What happens if you decrease the temperature? The solubility of Na_2SO_4 goes up as you lower the temperature, so more than 50 grams can normally be dissolved. This result is the opposite of what you want—you want the solubility to *decrease*, so that you are only supposed to be able to dissolve less than 50 grams. This way, your 50-gram solution would be magically supersaturated. Since the solubility of Na_2SO_4 increases with a fall in temperature, you don't get supersaturation. Thus, this answer is incorrect. sSimilarly, the other wrong answers all result in increasing the solubility. The correct answer, in contrast, results in a decrease of solubility. The KBr curve slopes up to the right, so when you decrease the temperature (moving left), you decrease the solubility. This action is the one most likely to result in a supersaturated solution. The correct answer is (H).

91. **(D)** KNO_3

Interpretation of Data

The key to this question is to notice the specific wording: "greatest percent increase." This means that you are not looking for the greatest *absolute* increase in solubility, which is the difference between the 20°C solubility and the 30°C solubility. Rather, you need to calculate that absolute increase, then divide it by the original solubility (at 20°C) and multiply by 100%. The number you get is the percent increase. An absolute increase in solubility corresponds to a steep upward slope of the data series on the chart. Inspect the differences between the 20°C solubilities and the 30°C solubilities for the four compounds in the answer choices. You should see that both sugar and KNO_3 have much bigger increases over this range of temperatures than $NaNO_3$ and NaBr do. The issue is that the increase for sugar and the increase for KNO_3 are about the same: around 15–20 grams. In fact, sugar's increase may be slightly higher. However, the right answer is definitely KNO_3. The reason is that for KNO_3, the starting point is much lower—about 35 grams. An increase of 15–20 grams on top of a base of only 35 grams is around 50% in percent terms. In contrast, the same absolute increase on top of sugar's base of almost 200 grams is only around 10% in percent terms. Thus, KNO_3 has the greatest percent increase in solubility over this temperature range. The correct answer is (D).

Passage 14 Solutions

92. **(J)** 461 hPa.

Interpretation of Data

The relevant table is Table 3, which lists the vapor pressures of mixtures. Look in the first and third columns for the solvents you want (chloroform, or $CHCl_3$, and ether, or $C_4H_{10}O$). The last three rows of the table each contain this pair of solvents. Finally, look for the row that contains the ratio of moles that you want (1 : 2). Columns 2 and 4 contain the molar amounts of each solvent. The second-to-last row lists 50 moles of $CHCl_3$ and 100 moles of $C_4H_{10}O$, which corresponds to the right ratio (50 : 100 = 1 : 2). The last column lists the vapor pressure of the mixture: 461 hPa. The correct answer is (J).

93. **(B)** 1.42°C.

Interpretation of Data

The first table to consult is Table 2, which lists the properties of mixtures of solvents with non-volatile solutes. The solvent in question is water, so you should study the middle three rows. The particular row to focus on is the one that matches the facts in the question: 100 moles of water and 5 moles of solute. Since the question asks about how the boiling point of that mixture changes, find the boiling point of the mixture: 101.42°C. Finally, you have to return to Table 1 to get the normal boiling point of water, which is 100°C. Thus, the boiling point of the mixture has increased by 101.42 − 100.0 = 1.42°C. The correct answer is (B).

94. **(H)** higher than the vapor pressure of one of the individual solvents, but lower than the other.

Interpretation of Data

The question is asking about a general pattern that you can extract from Tables 1 and 3. The answer choices should lead you to compare the vapor pressure of a mixture of two solvents (Table 3) with the vapor pressures of each of the solvents by itself (Table 1). Any pair of solvents from Table 3 will do. For instance, consider the first row of Table 3. A 1 : 1 mixture of C_6H_6 and C_2H_6O gives you a vapor pressure of 80 hPa. Now look up the characteristic vapor pressures of those two solvents in Table 1. C_6H_6 has a vapor pressure of 101 hPa, while C_2H_6O has a vapor pressure of 59 hPa. Since 80 is between 59 and 101, and the pattern must be universal (or the question would not be well-formed), you can conclude that the resulting vapor pressure of the mixture is between the vapor pressures of the pure solvents (according to the data you are given). The correct answer is (H).

95. **(C)** The boiling point increases, while the melting point decreases.

Interpretation of Data

As in the previous question, you are asked to generalize a pattern from data given to you in Tables 1 and 2. Since the answer choices do not make room for any exceptions, you can generalize from any one example. Water is the most familiar solvent in the tables; moreover, pure water has very simple boiling and melting points (100.0°C and 0.0°C, respectively), so the changes to those numbers are easier to track. Scan the middle three rows of Table 2, which involve water as the solvent. The boiling points are all higher than 100.0°C, while the melting points are all lower than 0.0°C. Thus, the boiling point increases but the melting point decreases when a solute is added. The correct answer is (C).

96. **(G)** the boiling point increases.

Interpretation of Data

As in the previous problem, you need to extrapolate a general pattern from specific data. The solution to the prior problem showed how the data on water in Tables 1 and 2 indicate an increase in the boiling point when you add a non-volatile solute. This question tells you that salt is non-volatile, so in this particular case, the boiling point must increase as well. The correct answer is (G).

97. **(A)** 45 hPa.

Interpretation of Data

The middle row of Table 3 is the one you want. It contains the right chemicals, and although the numbers of moles aren't exactly the same as those given in the question, the ratio of moles is the same (200 : 100 = 100 : 50). Thus, you would expect that the vapor pressure of this mixture would be 45 hPa, the value given in the last column. As the passage indicates, the vapor pressure of a pure solvent (under standard conditions) is a characteristic of that solvent; in other words, the value of that characteristic vapor pressure does not depend on the amount of the solvent. Thus, you would expect the same kind of result for a mixture: what matters is the ratio of the two solvents, not their absolute amounts. The correct answer is (A).

98. **(H)** 150 and 160 hPa.

Interpretation of Data

This question is tough because the pair of solvents isn't listed in Table 3. The best approach is to study another pair of solvents that are also in a 1 : 1 ratio. For instance, consider the first row of Table 3. A 1 : 1 molar mixture of benzene (C_6H_6) and ethanol (C_2H_6O) has a vapor pressure of 80 hPa. How does that number compare to the vapor pressures of each pure solvent? From Table 1, benzene has a vapor pressure of 101 hPa, while ethanol has a vapor pressure of 59 hPa. The mixture's pressure (80) is exactly halfway between the other two pressures (101 and 59, which average to 80). Other pairs of solvents in Table 3 produce the same kind of results: the pressure of a 1 : 1 mixture is the simple average of the two solvents' individual pressures. Extrapolating to the case at hand, you can make a solid prediction that a 1 : 1 mixture of benzene (vapor pressure = 101 hPa) and chloroform (vapor pressure = 210) would have a vapor pressure of 155.5 hPa, which is between 150 and 160 hPa. The correct answer is (H).

MANHATTAN
PREP

Passage 15 Solutions

99. **(B)** Maltose

Scientific Investigation

The structure shown has two rings. The first paragraph of the passage describes monosaccharides as having a one-ring structure, while disaccharides are composed of two monosaccharides linked together. Thus, disaccharides have two rings in their structures, and you are looking for a disaccharide. From Table 1, you can see that maltose and lactose are disaccharides, while fructose is a monosaccharide, and both starch and chitin are polysaccharides (three or more monosaccharides linked together). The only possibility among the answer choices is maltose. The correct answer is (B).

100. **(F)** Chitin, because it is bitter.

Scientific Investigation

According to Experiment 1, the taste of various carbohydrates can be described as either sweet or bitter. You are told in the question stem that many predators prefer sweet tastes. Thus, it would be advantageous as a defense mechanism to make a shell out of a bitter molecule. Chitin is listed in Table 1 as bitter, whereas fructose is described as sweet. Thus, chitin should be used, because it is bitter. It may have other advantages, too—for instance, it may be easier to build sturdy shells out of large molecules than out of small ones—but on the basis of the evidence you have about predators (and their taste for sweetness), you would pick chitin *because* it is bitter. The correct answer is (F).

101. **(C)** 50%.

Scientific Investigation

The mass of the bag decreased by $15.9 - 8.2 = 7.7$ grams. To find the percent change, take this absolute change, divide by the original mass, and multiply by 100%:

7.7 grams $\div$ 15.9 grams $\approx 0.48 \times 100\% = 48\%$.

The closest choice by far is 50%. The correct answer is (C).

102. **(J)** It contained no large polysaccharides.

Scientific Investigation

In the setup for the experiment, you are told that the solution in the beaker contains "a brown solution of iodine in water." With this fact alone, you can rule out all the wrong choices, in fact. You know the solution contains iodine, and you would have to be told whether there was something else meaningful in the beaker (besides iodine and water) before the sac is dropped in. Table 2 reminds you that the color of the iodine solution is brown at time 0. According to an earlier paragraph describing iodine and Benedict's Reagent, iodine is brown when there are no large polysaccharides around. The brown color of the iodine is further proof that the solution contains no large polysaccharides. The correct answer is (J).

103. (A) Glucose + Fructose → Maltose

Scientific Investigation

Table 1 tells you that both glucose and fructose are monosaccharides. That is, they each have just one ring (as you are told in the first paragraph of the passage). Meanwhile, maltose is a disaccharide, which is composed of two monosaccharides. Thus, a reasonable chemical reaction that might actually happen is one in which two monosaccharides—for instance, glucose and fructose, each with a single ring—come together to make a disaccharide—for instance, maltose, with two rings. None of the other reactions in the answer choices preserve the number of rings. The correct answer is (A).

104. (J) large enough for water to pass through, but not for starch to pass through.

Scientific Investigation

If starch were able to pass through the membrane of the dialysis tubing (from inside the sac to outside), then the iodine in the beaker would turn black. However, Table 2 tells you that the color of the iodine solution remains brown, so you know that the starch cannot pass through the membrane. Conversely, you know that water *can* pass through the membrane. How? The mass of the sac has dropped by about a half. Since the starch can't leave the sac, it must have been one or both of the other components that left (glucose and/or water). Moreover, because you are told that water "provides most of the mass of the mixture" inside the sac, you can conclude that a 50% drop in the mass of the sac must have been largely due to water leaving the sac. Thus, the membrane must allow water to pass through. The correct answer is (J).

105. (D) the outside solution turns from blue to orange, indicating that glucose was able to pass through the semipermeable membrane.

Scientific Investigation

The second paragraph of the passage tells you that Benedict's Reagent is blue when there is no glucose around, but orange when there is glucose. Since the solution in the beaker would just be Benedict's Reagent and water, the solution would start with a blue (no glucose) color. At this point, you can eliminate two of the three wrong answer choices.

The experiment could then go two ways:

1. Glucose passes through the membrane, leaving the sac and entering the solution outside. With glucose around, the Benedict's Reagent turns orange (indicating glucose).
2. Glucose does not pass through the membrane; instead, it remains trapped inside the sac. As a result, the Benedict's Reagent stays blue.

Answer choice (D) corresponds to the first situation (which, in fact, is the real one). Choice (C) does not correspond to the second situation, however. If the solution stays blue, then the glucose is *unable* to pass through the membrane and escape the sac. The correct answer is (D).

Passage 16 Solutions

106. (J) Vapor pressure of the solution

Scientific Investigation

The result that the student is measuring is the vapor pressure, so this is the variable not under direct control. These measurements are the outputs of the experiment and are listed in the rightmost column of Table 1. The student does directly control the amount of solute dissolved (as listed in Table 1), the temperature (25°C), and the volume of the water (100 mL). These factors are some of the inputs to the experiment (along with the identity of any solutes). The correct answer is (J).

107. (C) Increase the temperature of the solution

Scientific Investigation

In Table 2, Trials 4, 5, and 6 demonstrate that as you increase the temperature of an NaCl solution from 10°C to 30°C and finally to 50°C, the vapor pressure of the solution increases (in this case, from 8.0 mmHg to 28.0 mmHg and finally 82.1 mmHg). All of the other proposed changes would actually lower the vapor pressure of the solution. Dissolving the solute in less water is equivalent to increasing the mass of the solute—both raise the concentration of the solute, and as Table 1 demonstrates, more solute in a constant amount of water lowers the vapor pressure. Finally, using the same mass of a different solute with a lower molar mass lowers the vapor pressure. You can see this effect by comparing Trial 5 and Trial 7 in Table 1. The same mass of solute is used in each case (20.0 g), but the solute with a lower molar mass (NaCl) produces a solution with lower vapor pressure. The correct answer is (C).

108. (F) A solute with a smaller molar mass lowers the vapor pressure more than a solute with a greater molar mass.

Scientific Investigation

As in the previous problem, compare Trial 5 and Trial 7 in Table 1. The same mass of solute is used in each case (20.0 g) and the temperature is constant (25°C), but the solute with a lower molar mass (NaCl) produces a solution with lower vapor pressure. Both solutes reduce the vapor pressure from that of pure water (24.0 mmHg), but 20.0 g of NaCl decreases the vapor pressure all the way to 21.3 mmHg (a decrease of 2.7 mmHg), while the same mass of sucrose only decreases the vapor pressure to 23.7 mmHg (a decrease of 0.3 mmHg). The correct answer is (F).

109. (B) 22°C.

Scientific Investigation

Table 2 shows the relationship between temperature and vapor pressure for pure water at various temperatures: 10°C, 30°C, and 50°C. The corresponding vapor pressures are 9.0 mm Hg, 31.5 mm Hg, and 92.3 mm Hg, respectively. The relationship does not appear to be exactly linear—the vapor pressure increases more rapidly in the upper range of temperature—but you can very reasonably conclude that a pressure of 20 mm Hg would correspond to a temperature between 10°C (which gives 9.0 mm Hg of pressure) and 30°C (which gives 31.5 mm Hg). Only two of the answers are between 10°C and 30°C, namely 12°C and 22°C. The first of these possibilities is very unlikely, since the pressure in mm Hg would have to jump from 9 to 20 in just 2 degrees, then slow down and increase from 20 to 31.5 over the next 18 degrees, then leap from 31.5 to 92.3 over the next 20 degrees (from 30°C to 50°C). It's much more probable that the pressure goes from 9 to 20 over 12 degrees, then increases from 20 to 31.5 over the next 8 degrees, reflecting the acceleration that you observe in the next temperature range. Table 1 also gives you a good benchmark. The vapor pressure of water at 25°C is 24.0 mm Hg. To get a vapor pressure of 20.0 mm Hg, which is just a little less than 24.0, you would expect the temperature to be just a little less than 25°C. The temperature of 22°C fits well. The correct answer is (B).

110. **(G)** the vapor pressure of pure water increases more than that of the NaCl solution.

Scientific Investigation

Using Table 2, pick a temperature range for both pure water and the NaCl solution—say, 10°C to 30°C). For pure water, the vapor pressure in mmHg increases from 9.0 to 31.5, for an increase of 31.5 – 9.0 = 22.5 mmHg. For the NaCl solutions, the vapor pressure in mmHg increases from 8.0 to 28.0, for an increase of 28.0 – 8.0 = 20.0 mmHg. The increase for pure water is greater than it is for the NaCl solution. This pattern holds true for any other temperature range you choose. The correct answer is (G).

111. **(C)** 20.0 g NaCl and 20.0 g sucrose

Scientific Investigation

According to the question stem, you are looking for the vapor pressure of this solution to be 21.0 mmHg. Since the vapor pressure of pure water at the same temperature is 24.0 mmHg, the decrease that you want is 24.0 – 21.0 = 3.0 mmHg. You are to assume that "the effect of combining solutes on the vapor pressure is additive"—in other words, you will get part of the 3.0 mmHg decrease from the NaCl solute and the rest of the decrease from the sucrose, and you'll add those two parts together to get a 3.0 mmHg decrease. This question demands some quick mental math, as you scan down the last column of Table 1. You need to compute the difference between 24.0 mmHg (pure water's vapor pressure at 25°C) and the numbers you see corresponding to 10 g or 20 g NaCl or to 20 g or 40 g sucrose. The right combination is 20 g NaCl (which gives you a decrease of 24.0 – 21.3 = 2.7 mmHg) and 20 g sucrose (which gives you a decrease of 24.0 – 23.7 = 0.3 mmHg), since 2.7 + 0.3 = 3.0 mmHg. The correct answer is (C).

112. **(G)** 0 g $CaCl_2$ at 50°C

Scientific Investigation

You are not given direct information about $CaCl_2$ as a solute, but you can extrapolate the patterns you've observed in the tables. First, study the answer choices to identify the comparisons at stake. One variable is how much solute to use: 0 g (none!) or 20 g. The other variable is temperature: lower (30°C) or higher (50°C). By now, you know the effect of both variables. Introducing any solute lowers the vapor pressure, as Table 1 demonstrates, so you should choose 0 g over 20 g of $CaCl_2$. Increasing the temperature increases the vapor pressure, as Table 2 demonstrates, so you should choose 50°C over 30°C. The correct answer is (G).

Passage 17 Solutions

113. **(B)** decreases only.

Scientific Investigation

In the third column of Table 1, the wavelength of light increases as you read down the table. The second column lists the corresponding frequency. The numbers always decrease (7.2 drops to 6.3, then to 5.7, etc.) as the wavelength increases. The correct answer is (B).

114. **(F)** Less than 5.

Scientific Investigation

According to the question stem, the wavelength of infrared light is greater than 700 nm. If you examine the right side of Figure 1, no curve extends all the way to 700 nm, but you can extrapolate the L cone curve (the closest one) and conclude that even this type of cell will have a firing rate that is very close to 0 at 700 nm or above. Logically, no cell can have a negative firing rate, so these curves cannot extend below 0, but effectively they must become nearly indistinguishable from 0 at 700 nm. Even a low firing rate of 5 (one-tenth of the height of 50) is too high at 700 nm. The correct answer is (F).

115. **(B)** 1

Scientific Investigation

The first paragraph tells you that the human eye contains 3 types of cone cells, and in Figure 1, you see 3 separate curves for cones. These curves correspond to S, M, and L cones, according to the legend. In contrast, only 1 type of curve is visible and labeled in the legend: "Rods." Thus, you can conclude that there is exactly 1 type of rod cell in the human eye. The correct answer is (B).

116. **(J)** S cone

Scientific Investigation

Table 1 tells you that blue light has a typical wavelength of 475 nm. Go to Figure 1 and carefully trace upward from where 475 would hit (slightly to the left of the hash mark at 480 nm, the one before the 500 nm label). You can see that the S cone curve (solid) is clearly above the rod curve (dashed). Alternatively, you can see that the intersection of those two curves (where the activity or firing rate of the two types of cells would be the same) is clearly between 480 nm and 500 nm. 475 nm is below that intersection point, so the S cones must be more active. The correct answer is (J).

117. **(A)** Graph A

Scientific Investigation

The first diagram displays a set of three curves, corresponding to Figure 1 in all ways but one: one of the cone curves (that for M cones) is missing. Since the mutation makes one type of cone cell completely unable to fire, according to the question stem, a diagram in which a cone curve is completely missing would represent the firing spectrum for someone with that mutation. In the other diagrams, either the rod curve is missing, or all three cone curves are missing, or one cone curve is distorted in shape (actually increasing its firing range). None of these sensibly represent a situation in which exactly one type of cone cell doesn't work at all. The correct answer is (A).

118. **(H)** Graph H

Scientific Investigation

Using the given equation $V = f\lambda$, you can compute the speed of light by multiplying a frequency given in Table 1 by the corresponding wavelength (in the same row). If you do this for a few different rows, you get almost exactly the same number, differing by only a few percentage points (well within rounding error). The smallest number is 2,880, while the largest number is 2,993. If you plotted all of these numbers against the frequency, you would get very close to a constant horizontal line. That is, the speed of light is constant as you change the frequency. The correct answer is (H).

119. **(D)** 50 nm.

Scientific Investigation

According to Figure 1, the rod curve (dashed) and the M cone curve (square zigzag) cross at approximately 555 nm, just below the hash mark at 560 nm. Meanwhile, the M cone curve and the L cone curve (dotted) cross at approximately 605 nm. Your estimates may be slightly different, but the difference would still come out to approximately 605 – 555 = 50 nm. The closest answer choice (27 nm) is only about half as big, and the other choices are even smaller. The correct answer is (D).

Passage 18 Solutions

120. **(F)** Graph F

Interpretation of Data

Pick a brightness setting (say, high), and look up the corresponding intensities in Table 1. Note that these values are not right next to each other.

As the distance increases on the graph, the intensity falls. The only graph that always falls is in choice (F). The shape of the graph is also correct: the decrease is sharp at first (from 9.20 to 2.30), then not as sharp (from 2.30 to 1.02). The correct answer is (F).

121. **(B)** was medium.

Interpretation of Data

Pick a distance (say, 10 cm), and look up the corresponding "without" intensity in Table 2. In this case, you get 7.29 lux. Now look at Table 1 in the three rows for the same distance (10 cm). Medium brightness gives you the same intensity. You would get the same result if you picked 20 cm or 30 cm as your distance. The correct answer is (B).

122. (H) 65%.

Interpretation of Data

Pick a distance (say, 10 cm), and compare the "with" and "without" intensities.

The "with" intensity is 4.74 lux less (= 7.29 – 2.55) than the "without" intensity. This decrease of 4.74 lux corresponds to a percent decrease of 4.74 ÷ 7.29 ≈ 65%. You would get the same result if you picked any other distance. The correct answer is (H).

123. (B) 45°.

Interpretation of Data

In Table 3, under a given set of conditions, the intensity at 0° is 0.81 lux. Half of that value is 0.405 lux, and the angle with the closest intensity is 45°. The correct answer is (B).

124. (J) High brightness, 20 cm distance, 2 polarizers at an angle of 90°

Interpretation of Data

The key to this problem lies in Table 3. Notice that the intensity of the light drops all the way to *zero* when the angle between the polarizers is 90°. You can reasonably expect the same pattern to hold for any distance or brightness setting, even a close distance and high brightness. No other value in any table goes as low, so it is most logical to conclude that the lowest intensity occurs with the combination of settings in choice (J), the correct answer.

125. (A) between 0 and 1 lux.

Interpretation of Data

The lack of polarizers tells you to use Table 1. You must extrapolate the "high" figures out to 40 cm. Since the intensity falls as the distance increases, you would expect the intensity to be less than 1.02 lux, the intensity at 30 cm. The only reasonable answer is choice (A), which is correct.

126. (H) medium brightness, 30 cm distance, and no polarizers.

Interpretation of Data

Table 1 shows the most data with no polarizers, so start there. The intensity corresponding to low brightness, 20 cm distance, and no polarizers is 0.81 lux. Where else does that particular intensity appear? Three places: once in another row of Table 1, once in Table 2, and once in Table 3. The row in Table 1 corresponds to medium brightness, 30 cm distance, and no polarizers. That's choice (H), so you're done. Incidentally, Table 3's entry of 0.81 lux almost fits choice (G), but according to the text, every setting in Table 3 is at 20 cm, not 10 cm. Moreover, Table 2's entry of 0.81 lux just repeats Table 1's entry, in effect. None of the answer choices besides (H) would give you an intensity close to 0.81 lux. The correct answer is (H).

Passage 19 Solutions

127. **(A)** sodium.

Scientific Investigation

A good approach for this entire passage is to make a chart tracking which elements are in and which are out for each of the studies. Taking the time to make such a chart from the descriptions of each study will pay off across the whole set of questions. Of course, use abbreviations in your own version, for speed.

	Silicon	Sodium	Magnesium	Aluminum	Hafnium	Titanium	Zirconium	Mercury
Original	Yes	Y	Y	Y	Y	Y	Y	Y
Study 1	—	—	—	—	Y	Y	Y	Y
2	Y	Y	—	—	—	—	Y	Y
3	Y	Y	—	Y	Y	Y	—	—

Identify the highest peak around 600 nm in the original diagram (all the way to the right, over 7 units tall). Then look for that peak in the remaining three diagrams. It is missing from Figure 2 (Study 1), but it is present in the figures for Studies 2 and 3. The two elements that follow this same pattern of presence and absence are silicon and sodium. Only sodium is among the answer choices. The correct answer is (A).

128. **(H)** 500 nm.

Scientific Investigation

You need to find a peak in the original diagram that is missing in all three of the other diagrams. Rather than glance back and forth between the four charts, use the answer choices to focus your analysis. Working through the answer choices, you can see that an original peak at or just above 200 nm (3 units tall) is present in Figure 3, so 200 nm is not correct. There does not seem to be a peak exactly at 300 nm in the original diagram, an observation that would cast doubt on this choice; even choosing a nearby peak (such as the tallest one on the chart), you can see that this peak appears in other diagrams. The original gap at 300 nm is repeated in the studies, so the nearby peaks are left in place. Next, at 500 nm, a broad peak in the original (slightly over 4 units tall) is omitted from all of the remaining diagrams. This is the pattern you are looking for; you can stop at this point. The correct answer is (H).

129. **(D)** Aluminum

Scientific Investigation

Examine the diagrams to see which one or ones this peak shows up in besides the original. The peak is missing from Studies 1 and 2, but it is present in Study 3. Using the chart created in the solution for the first problem, you can see that the only element on the chart that follows the same pattern of presence and absence is aluminum. The correct answer is (D).

130. (G) Graph G

Scientific Investigation

First, determine which study is closest to the proposed experiment. Study 2 fits the bill: the four elements removed in Study 2 are all removed as part of the experiment proposed in the question stem. The only difference is that one more element is removed as well, namely iron, which has not been removed from any other study. So you are looking for a diagram that resembles Study 2's diagram, with nothing new added, and with some peaks (representing iron) missing. The diagram that best obeys these constraints is the second option. Notice, for instance, that in choice (F), there are three large peaks at and just above 400 nm, whereas in Study 2, one of those peaks has been removed. Likewise, in choices (H) and (J), the broad, short peak at about 170 nm (to the left) is present, but that peak is missing from Study 2. The correct answer is (G).

131. (A) mercury or zirconium.

Scientific Investigation

The broad peak in question (at 340 nm) is the tallest one on the original diagram. Notice that it is present in Studies 1 and 2 but absent from Study 3. Thus, the element generating that peak would also be present in Studies 1 and 2 and absent from Study 3. According to the chart in the solution to the first problem, the only elements fitting this pattern are zirconium and mercury. The correct answer is (A).

132. (J) removing all but two of the elements.

Scientific Investigation

The most cluttered spectrum, with many peaks jostling against each other, is the one associated with the original mixture of many elements. By removing elements, the students doing the studies made the results simpler to follow—there are fewer overlapping peaks. Of the options described in the answer choices, the one that would provide the clearest spectrum is the one with the fewest elements contributing peaks: namely, just two elements. All of the other choices would leave at least four elements in the mixture, making for more confusing diagrams. The correct answer is (J).

133. (B) little or no emission.

Scientific Investigation

The first paragraph describes the process of analyzing a mixture of elements via emission spectroscopy. The second sentence strongly implies that the "excitement through the input of energy" that the mixture undergoes is crucial to the process. Without this excitation, the atoms of the mixture would not emit specific wavelengths of light "to carry away the excess energy." Thus, you can deduce that there would be no emission of these wavelengths in the absence of the energy input. The correct answer is (B).

Passage 20 Solutions

134. (H) Ba.

Scientific Investigation

Table 3 tells you that Unknown B emitted a pale green color during a flame test. Cross-referencing with Table 1, you can see that the only metal on the list that emits pale green is Ba. The correct answer is (H).

135. (A) Li or Sr.

Scientific Investigation

Unknown C emitted a red color during Study 1, according to Table 3. In Table 1, the only metals that emit red light are Li and Sr. The correct answer is (A).

136. (J) Unknowns C and F

Scientific Investigation

The wrong answers contain some tricky pairs. Unknowns F and H are both "red-orange" according to Table 4, but the student notes that their shades of red are different, so "they were unlikely to be the same material." Unknowns D and E have overlapping but distinct colors (red-violet and violet, respectively), and the platinum wire used in this study contributed no additional color, so these different results make the two samples unlikely to be the same metal. Finally, Unknowns F and K display both red and orange, but of different intensities; in fact, the student notes that in Unknown K, "the orange was actually more pronounced than the red." The nichrome wire used in Study 2 would only have contributed "a trace of orange"; moreover, it was used with both F and K, so the different results would indicate that the unknowns were different materials. The only pair that could be the same material is Unknowns C and F. Unknown C emits a red color, while Unknown F emits a red-orange color. However, the orange "was very light and barely detectable" for Unknown F, and it is reasonable to suspect that the nichrome wire was the source of this color. The correct answer is (J).

137. (C) a sample that emits a wavelength between 585 and 647 nm.

Scientific Investigation

According to the description of Study 2, nichrome wire can introduce a "trace of orange" into the results. As a result, this kind of wire is least useful in determining whether the sample contains something that emits orange. You would not know whether an orange result came from the original sample or from the nichrome wire. According to Table 2, orange light has a wavelength between 585 and 647 nm. The correct answer is (C).

138. (F) Rb

Scientific Investigation

First, look up the colors that these wavelengths correspond to. According to Table 2, 415 nm is in the violet range, while 675 nm is in the red range. Thus, the metal you are looking for emits a red-violet color. In Table 1, only Rb is labeled as red-violet. The correct answer is (F).

139. (B) Blue-green

Scientific Investigation

Since 491 nm is *both* at the high end of blue's range and at the low end of green's range, according to Table 2, the light would be seen as blue-green. It's easy to spot 491 in the blue range and pick "Blue" quickly; be wary of numbers at the ends of ranges. The correct answer is (B).

140. (G) Cs.

Scientific Investigation

This problem demands a careful process of elimination. The right answer will be the only choice that is either in both studies or in neither. Use Table 1 to get the colors of the answer choices: Pb is light grey, Cs is blue-purple, Ca is orange-red, and K is violet. Pb is not in Study 1, but it is probably in Study 2 (Unknown J). Likewise, Ca is only in Study 2 (Unknown K), while element K (potassium) is in Study 1 (Unknown E) but not in Study 2. In contrast, Cs's unique blue-purple shows up in both Study 1 (Unknown A) and Study 2 (Unknown G). The correct answer is (G).

Passage 21 Solutions

141. (C) Liquid and solid only

Interpretation of Data

In the question stem, condensed phases are defined as those "in which molecules are placed close together." The first paragraph of the passage defines both solid and liquid phases as ones in which molecules are "tightly packed"—in other words, the molecules are placed close together. So both the liquid phase and the solid phase are condensed. In contrast, in the gas phase, molecules are "widely separated"; thus, the gas phase is not condensed. The correct zanswer is (C).

142. (J) There is no clear relationship between molecular weight and boiling point.

Interpretation of Data

In Table 1, the boiling point (fourth column) increases as you scan downward. It does not rise in a steady fashion, but each number is bigger than all the numbers above it. In contrast, the molecular weight (last column on the right) displays no corresponding pattern. It jumps up, then falls back down, only to rise again. Thus, there is no clear relationship between the two quantities. The correct answer is (J).

MANHATTAN
PREP

143. **(A)** Copper is solid, while silver is liquid.

Interpretation of Data

To solve this problem, compare the given temperature to the melting points and boiling points of the two substances. 1,000°C is below the melting point of copper (1,083°C), so copper is a solid at 1,000°C. In contrast, 1,000°C is above the melting point of silver (962°C) but below the boiling point of silver (1,950°C), so at 1,000°C, silver is a liquid. The correct answer is (A).

144. **(G)** Mercury

Interpretation of Data

The fastest way to match up the phase-change diagram to the right substance in Table 1 is to identify the flat parts of the diagram. The horizontal transition between solid and liquid phase represents the melting process, so the vertical position of that transition corresponds to the melting point. By inspecting the diagram, you can see that the melting point of the substance is between −100°C and 0°C, probably around −40°C. The only substance in Table 1 with a melting point around this value is mercury. As a check, you can see that the boiling point, which separates the liquid phase from the gas phase, is between 300°C and 400°C. Mercury's boiling point is 357°C, according to Table 1, and no other boiling point is even close. The correct answer is (G).

145. **(B)** changes the phase of the substance only.

Interpretation of Data

At the boiling point, between the liquid phase and the gas phase, the graph is horizontal. That is, as heat is being added (as you move to the right on the graph), the temperature is not going up or down. So the heat being added is not going into increasing the temperature of the substance. The most reasonable inference you can make (from among those available to you in the answer choices) is that the heat goes into changing the phase of the substance only. The correct answer is (B).

146. **(H)** 20 seconds

Interpretation of Data

You want to turn 1 kg of solid aluminum into a liquid; in other words, you want to melt it. The temperature in the question (659°C) is in fact the melting point of aluminum. The other piece of information that you have about the process of melting aluminum is the "latent heat of melting," which the passage defines as "the amount of energy required to convert 1 kilogram of a substance from solid to liquid at the melting point." In Table 1, this number is listed as 399 kJ/kg for aluminum. In other words, it would take 399 kJ of energy to melt 1 kilogram of aluminum. The question tells you that you are adding 20 kJ of heat every second to the aluminum. How long will it take you to add a total of 399 kJ? Divide 399 by 20 to get approximately 20 seconds. The correct answer is (H).

147. (D) Water

Interpretation of Data

Since you do not have access to a calculator during this portion of the exam, you'll need to estimate the ratios in question. The ratio of X to Y is $X \div Y$, so the ratio of the latent heat of vaporization (column 5 of Table 1) to the latent heat of melting (column 3 of Table 1) is column 5 divided by column 3. You're looking for the smallest number. Go ahead and round drastically to get a rough estimate; you can also use benchmarks to get a lower or upper bound. (You can ignore copper and silver, because they aren't in the answer choices.)

Aluminum: $10,530 \div 399 > 10,000 \div 400 = 100 \div 4 = 25$
Lead: $859 \div 23 > 800 \div 25 = 32$
Mercury: $295 \div 11 \approx 300 \div 10 = 30$
Water: $2,272 \div 335 \approx 2,100 \div 300 = 7$

In other words, for water, the number in column 5 is only about 7 times as big as the number in column 3, whereas for all the other possibilities, the number in column 5 is 25 or more times as big as the number in column 3. These ratios are far enough apart that you can be confident that water has the lowest ratio. (So you know, the real ratios are 26.4, 37.3, 26.8, and 6.8, respectively.) The correct answer is (D).

Passage 22 Solutions

148. (F) Diethyl ether

Interpretation of Data

Figure 2 shows the vapor pressure at various temperatures. At 50°C, the substances the vapor pressure for diethyl ether is higher than what is shown on the graph, while the vapor pressures of ethanol and water are much lower, approximately 250 torr and 100 torr, respectively. The correct answer is (F).

149. (C) 12 g

Interpretation of Data

Table 1 shows the energy required to vaporize various masses of each substance. It takes 8.4 kJ of energy to vaporize 10 g of ethanol, and 17 kJ of energy to vaporize 20 g of ethanol. Therefore, 10 kJ of energy will vaporize between 10 g and 20 g of ethanol. The correct answer is (C).

150. (G) Isopropyl alcohol, with a molar mass of 60.1 g/mol, has a boiling point of 83°C.

Interpretation of Data

Even though isopropyl alcohol has a greater molar mass than ethanol (46.1 g/mol), it has a higher boiling point than ethanol (78°C). The correct answer is (G).

151. **(C)** Substances that have lower vapor pressures at a given temperature have higher boiling points.

Interpretation of Data

Figure 2 shows the vapor pressures of the substances at various temperatures. At any temperature, the substances from highest to lowest vapor pressures are diethyl ether, ethanol, and water. According to Table 1, the substances from lowest to highest boiling points are diethyl ether, ethanol, and water. The correct answer is (C).

152. **(H)** 100 torr

Interpretation of Data

Using Figure 2, you can see that positions to the left of the curve where it intersects a horizontal constant-torr line are below the substance's boiling point at that pressure (so the substance is primarily in its liquid state), while positions to the right of the curve along a horizontal constant-torr line are above the boiling point, so the substance is primarily in gas state.

When the temperature is 40°C and the pressure is 100 torr, only water is in liquid state, while diethyl ether and ethanol are both in gas state. The correct answer is (H).

153. **(D)** Water, Ethanol, Diethyl ether

Interpretation of Data

According to Table 1, for any given mass, diethyl ether requires the least energy to vaporize, while water requires the most energy to vaporize. Therefore, the mass of diethyl either will decrease at the fastest rate (Liquid III), while the mass of water will decrease at the slowest rate (Liquid I). The correct answer is (D).

154. **(H)** As the temperature increases, the vapor pressure increases because more molecules are moving with enough energy to escape the liquid phase.

Interpretation of Data

For each substance in Figure 2, the vapor pressure increases as the temperature increases. The introduction of the passage explains that vapor pressure is due to molecules that have enough energy to escape the liquid phase, so when the temperature increases, more molecules have the energy required to escape the liquid phase. The correct answer is (H).

Passage 23 Solutions

155. **(B)** increased without exception.

Scientific Investigation

In Table 1, the concentration of the solutions (as shown in the column headers) increases to the right. The conductivity measurements of each solution, shown in each row, increase to the right as well. There are no exceptions to this pattern. The correct answer is (B).

156. (F) Low temperatures and low concentrations

Scientific Investigation

The conductivity of solutions increases as concentration increases, according to Table 1. Thus, low concentrations would be likely to result in low conductivity. Tables 2 and 3 demonstrate that conductivity increases with temperature (both increase to the right on the tables). Thus, for low conductivity, you would want low temperatures. The correct answer is (F).

157. (D) 100 mg/L solution of H_2SO_4 at 50°

Scientific Investigation

All of the answer choices feature the same chemical, so you can just pay attention to the concentration and the temperature. For the highest conductivity, you want the higher concentration (100 mg/L) at the higher temperature (50°C). You can look up the specific conductivities and compare them, but since the trends do not have exceptions on the tables, you can save yourself time by applying the trends. The correct answer is (D).

158. (H) Graph H

Scientific Investigation

You should quickly rule out the graphs on which the conductivity falls to the right, since the conductivities increase with temperature. Thus, choices (G) and (J) are incorrect. The concentrations shown in the legends are all 100 mg/L, so you should examine Table 3, which shows the conductivities for solutions of that concentration. The highest conductivity is that of HCl, so the top line on the graph should correspond to HCl, not NaCl as in choice (F). The correct answer is (H).

159. (D) At very high concentrations of NH_4OH, positive and negative ions form neutral pairs that do not conduct electricity.

Scientific Investigation

In the introductory section, you are given a small amount of background about how conductivity works in solutions. In water, certain compounds dissociate into ions, which are charged atoms or molecules. Since the movement of these ions constitutes electricity, it should make sense that the more ions there are in solution, the greater the conductivity of that solution. However, you need to choose a reasonable explanation for a seemingly contradictory case: at very high concentrations, the conductivity of solutions of a particular compound actually starts to decrease. The best approach here is to eliminate unreasonable answers. Choice (A) states that more ions are available to conduct electrical current, but if that were the case, then you would still expect higher conductivity, not lower. There is no reason to suspect that the temperature would change, so choice (B) should be eliminated. As for choice (C), why would water lose its ability to flow, or to allow particles it contains to flow, at high concentrations of a compound? This option should strike you as unlikely, given everyday experience with water. Only choice (D) offers a sensible explanation: if the positive and negative ions form neutral pairs at very high concentrations, and those neutral pairs do not conduct electricity, then it makes sense that these very high concentrations actually lead to lower conductivity. The correct answer is (D).

160. (G) 51 µS/cm

Scientific Investigation

Be sure to read the conditions carefully. The combination of temperature and concentration does not exist on the table for ammonium hydroxide. However, you can see in Table 3, which contains other solutions at 100 mg/L of concentration, that the decrease in temperature from 25°C to 18°C leads to a decrease of roughly 10–15%. HCl's conductivity falls from 1,140 µS/cm to 1,014.6 µS/cm, a decrease of 125 (slightly more than 10%). The other compounds follow similar patterns. Applying a 10–15% decrease to the 25°C, 100 mg/L number for ammonium hydroxide (which is 58 µS/cm) gives you about 51 µS/cm.

22

You do not need to calculate this number precisely. All you have to realize is that you need to reduce 58 by a small amount, proportionally, to account for the slight decrease in temperature. There is only one reasonable option among the choices; all the others are too far away. The correct answer is (G).

161. (C) Because H_2SO_4 more completely dissociates in solution than H_3PO_4.

Scientific Investigation

You are looking for a sensible rationale for the phenomenon in question, given that you know the basic principle from the introduction: the more ions in solution, the more conductive it is. The phenomenon seems to contradict this principle: H_2SO_4 can dissociate into *fewer* ions per molecule but can show *higher* conductivity. The proper rationale should resolve the seeming paradox. Choices (A) and (B) make bold claims that lack support: why should any particular ion be less conductive than another in solution? If choice (D) were true, then you would expect H_3PO_4 solutions to be more conductive. The right explanation is the one that stays true to the larger principle: H_3PO_4 may be able to dissociate into more ions in theory, but H_2SO_4 *more completely* dissociates, or breaks up, into ions in actual solutions. So that's why H_2SO_4 can create more conductive solutions. The correct answer is (C).

Passage 24 Solutions

162. (G) gold.

Scientific Investigation

According to Tables 1 and 2, gold has a density of 19.30 g/mL, which is the largest density of all the materials listed. The correct answer is (G).

163. (C) Coarse salt

Scientific Investigation

According to the passage, solids will float if they are placed in liquids with a higher density. The only solid in the answer choices with a density of less than 1.00 g/mL is coarse salt, with a density of 0.80 g/mL. (In actuality, this coarse salt would dissolve in the water, but you are directed to consider only the density.) The correct answer is (C).

164. **(F)** the solids dissolved in the water.

Scientific Investigation

The four materials with the largest percent error are coarse salt, fine salt, powdered sugar, and granulated sugar. These are materials that are soluble in water, and the dissolving process can change the chemical bonds of the materials, altering their calculated densities. Additionally, none of the other answer choices fit—the setup of Study 1 does not include a reference cell, not all of the solids are less dense than water, and there was no pressure applied to make the solids deteriorate. The correct answer is (F).

165. **(D)** the solids were drawn into the reference cell.

Scientific Investigation

According to the passage, fine materials (such as fine salt and powdered sugar, the two materials with the largest percent error in Study 2) are at risk of being drawn into the reference cell. Additionally, none of the other answer choices fit—the setup of Study 1 does not include water, not all of the solids are less dense than water, and there was no reason to think that pressure would make solids deteriorate. The correct answer is (D).

166. **(G)** 10.5 g/mL.

Scientific Investigation

According to the passage, density is calculated by dividing mass by volume. In this case, the mass is 21 grams, and the volume is 52 mL – 50 mL = 2 mL. Therefore, the density is 21 grams ÷ 2 mL = 10.5 g/mL. The correct answer is (G).

167. **(A)** Graph A.

Scientific Investigation

The densities according to Study 2 are Mg = 1.50 g/mL; Al = 2.63 g/mL; Cu = 8.57 g/mL; Au = 18.54 g/mL; Fe = 7.96 g/mL. Graph A is the only one to accurately represent all of these values. The correct answer is (A).

168. **(J)** 53 mL

Scientific Investigation

Density is equal to mass divided by volume. The actual density of magnesium is 1.70 g/mL. If the mass of magnesium added to the water is 5.1 g, you can calculate the volume of magnesium using the formula:

$$1.70\frac{g}{mL} = \frac{5.1g}{x\ mL}$$

$$x\ mL = \frac{5.10}{1.70}$$

$$x\ mL = 3\ mL$$

Since the starting volume of the water is 50 mL, an additional 3 mL of magnesium (which does not dissolve in water) would make the final volume 53 mL. The correct answer is (J).

Passage 25 Solutions

169. **(D)** 11.5°C.

Scientific Investigation

The initial temperature is 25.5°C. When time equals 60 minutes on the *x*-axis, the graph reads 37°C on the *y*-axis. The difference between the temperature at 60 minutes and the starting temperature is 11.5°C. The correct answer is (D).

170. **(H)** lead chloride.

Scientific Investigation

According to the passage, $PbCl_2$ (lead chloride) is a white solid. Since everything was discarded except the solid, then lead chloride was retained. The correct answer is (H).

171. **(B)** an increase in temperature.

Scientific Investigation

According to the trend in Figure 2, as time increases, the temperature of the mixture increases. While the increase is leveling off, the slope is not yet completely horizontal, and so it is reasonable to conclude that the temperature would have increased at least a little more if the experiment were left to proceed for more than an hour. The correct answer is (B).

172. **(J)** Because it is easier to separate a solid from a liquid than a liquid from another liquid.

Scientific Investigation

Since PbCl2 is the only solid, it is the easiest one to mass because it can be filtered out of the liquid. This makes it the best candidate for the student to take the mass of. The correct answer is (J).

173. **(D)** Exothermic

Scientific Investigation

According to the passage, an exothermic reaction is a reaction that releases heat. Since this reaction releases 501 Joules of heat, it would be considered an exothermic reaction. The correct answer is (D).

174. **(G)** 90%.

Scientific Investigation

The percent yield can be calculated by dividing the observed yield by the expected yield. According to Study 1, the observed yield (of heat) is 501 joules and the expected yield is 565 joules. Therefore, 501 divided by 565 is equal to approximately 90%. In Study 2, the observed yield is 250 g and the expected yield is 280 g. Thus, 250 divided by 280 is also equal to approximately 90%. The correct answer is (G).

175. **(C)** material was lost during the purification process.

Scientific Investigation

According to the passage, there was no mention of a purification process, and there is no reason to think that this affected the heat of reaction. Even if lead chloride had been lost during the isolation of the solid, this would not have affected the predicted calculation of heat of reaction (which involves the reactants only) nor the observed heat of reaction (which is a measurement). The other answer choices all provide plausible explanations—if the reaction takes longer than 1 hour to reach completion, you would not observe the full value of heat released. If heat were lost to surroundings, you would measure a decreased heat of reaction. Human error could also affect the reading of any measurement or any other aspect of the experiment. The correct answer is (C).

Passage 26 Solutions

176. **(H)** Sample 4

Interpretation of Data

According to the passage, Sr-90 levels of samples from before 1955 should be essentially 0. The only sample that has a Sr-90 level of 0 is Sample 4. The correct answer is (H).

177. **(A)** Samples 2 and 6

Interpretation of Data

Figures 1 and 2 both measure C-14 activity. According to Figure 1, C-14 activity is above 0.3 between the years 1965 and 1980. According to Figure 2, Samples 2 and 6 both have C-14 activity that is above 0.3. Sample 1 also has C-14 activity above 0.3, but Sample 5 does not, so choice (C) is incorrect. The correct answer is (A).

178. **(H)** 1970.

Interpretation of Data

Strontium activity before 1955 was essentially 0, while strontium activity in the years 1960–1980 was extremely high. Therefore, this test could accurately determine the difference between a sample from 1950 (Sr level of 0) and a sample from 1970 (high Sr level). The correct answer is (H).

179. **(D)** 2000.

Interpretation of Data

From Figure 4, you can tell that Unknown 5 has a high ratio of Th-228 to Th-232. This means that death occurred in the recent past. Additionally, Figure 2 tells you that the C-14 activity is just above 0.25, and the only answer choice with that C-14 activity in Figure 1 is the year 2000. The correct answer is (D).

180. **(J)** 1.0.

Interpretation of Data

According to the passage, the ratio of Th-228 to Th-232 in recently deceased samples is significantly higher than 1. The ratio decreases steadily for approximately 50 years, at which time the ratio nears 1. Thus, if a sample harvested in 2000 is not analyzed until 2050, which is 50 years later, you would expect the thorium ratio to be about 1. The correct answer is (J).

181. **(B)** Samples 3 and 4.

Interpretation of Data

According to the passage, samples with minimal levels of strontium can become contaminated if the testing is not completed in a clean room. The two samples with the lowest level of strontium are Samples 3 and 4. The correct answer is (B).

182. **(F)** 0.28; 1.0

Interpretation of Data

According to Figure 1, a sample from 1958 would have a C-14 ratio of slightly more than 0.25, or roughly 0.28. Since the sample was created over 50 years before 2015, you would expect the Th-228 to Th-232 ratio to be about 1. The correct answer is (F).

Passage 27 Solutions

183. **(C)** Mercury iodide

Scientific Investigation

Table 2 indicates that in Trial 1, an orange precipitate is present at both 5 seconds and 10 seconds. Since mercury iodide is a bright orange salt that is insoluble in water, this chemical is most likely the product. The correct answer is (C).

184. **(F)** The creation first of mercury iodide, then of an iodine-starch complex

Scientific Investigation

According to Table 2, in Trial 2 an orange precipitate was present at 5 seconds. This means that mercury iodide (an orange insoluble salt) was first formed. Next, a dark blue color was observed in the solution at 10 seconds. Since the iodine-starch complex turns solutions a deep blue-black, the observation indicates that this complex was formed after the mercury iodide. The correct answer is (F).

185. **(A)** the absence of mercury made the creation of mercury iodide impossible.

Scientific Investigation

No orange precipitate was observed in Trial 6. This precipitate is composed of mercury iodide, which is bright orange and insoluble in water. To make a compound with mercury in it (such as mercury iodide), you need to start with something that contains mercury. Since no mercury chloride was used in Trial 6, it makes sense that no mercury iodide was created. The correct answer is (A).

186. **(G)** Reaction 1 takes place faster than Reaction 2.

Scientific Investigation

Reaction 1 creates mercury iodide (HgI_2), the orange precipitate. Reaction 2 creates the iodine-starch complex, which produces a deep blue-black solution. If you study Table 2, you notice that if the orange precipitate is going to be formed at all, it is always formed by the 5-second mark. However, Trial 6 demonstrates that the iodine-starch complex on its own takes more time to form (somewhere between 5 and 10 seconds). When both reactions take place, as in Trial 2, this order is preserved: first Reaction 1, then Reaction 2. Thus, it can be concluded that under the conditions applied in the experiment, Reaction 1 takes place faster than Reaction 2. The correct answer is (G).

187. **(D)** mercury iodide is insoluble in aqueous solution.

Scientific Investigation

You are told in the question stem that Reaction 1 is irreversible in aqueous solution—that is, this reaction cannot be reversed, or run backwards, in water. What is the most likely reason for this fact? In the passage, you are told that mercury iodide (the bright orange precipitate) is insoluble in water—that is, it does not dissolve in water, but rather falls out of solution as a solid. Since this solid cannot be dissolved in water, it makes sense that it cannot participate in a reaction that takes place in aqueous solution. Choices (A) and (B) would give reasons why the reaction could hypothetically be reversed (not why it can't). Choice (C) lacks support; it provides no logical connection to anything else in the passage. The correct answer is (D).

188. **(H)** The presence of excess potassium iodide

Scientific Investigation

The only trial in which it is clear that both reactions took place is Trial 2, when both color changes were observed. What is unique about Trial 2? If you study Table 1, the pattern becomes clear: Trial 2 is the only one in which the amount of KI (potassium iodide) added was much higher (100 mmol) than normal (20 mmol). Thus, you can infer that the condition that allows both reactions to progress is the presence of excess (extra) potassium iodide. The correct answer is (H).

189. **(B)** There was insufficient potassium iodide remaining after the precipitation reaction.

Scientific Investigation

Notice that Reaction 1 (which is the precipitation reaction, forming mercury iodide precipitate) uses up KI, potassium iodide. You are told in the passage that if potassium iodide is present, the iodine will become more soluble and actually dissolve enough for the iodine-starch reaction (Reaction 2) to happen. So if too much potassium iodide is used up in Reaction 1, then the iodine can't dissolve easily and form the iodine-starch complex. In other words, under those conditions, Reaction 2 cannot happen. The correct answer is (B).

Passage 28 Solutions

190. **(J)** 86%

Scientific Investigation

There are 12 g of carbon and 2 g of hydrogen in Unknown B. To calculate the percent mass, take the mass of carbon divided by the total mass, which is 12 g ÷ 14 g, or 6/7. This equals 86%. You don't have a calculator on this part of the exam, but you should be able to estimate 1/7, which is about 14%, and so 6/7 is equal to 100% minus about 14%, which is approximately 86%. The correct answer is (J).

191. **(B)** Unknown B and Unknown W.

Scientific Investigation

The same compound would have the same ratios of carbon to hydrogen. Unknown B and Unknown W both have 12 grams of carbon and 2 grams of hydrogen, while all of the other pairs have different ratios of carbon to hydrogen. The correct answer is (B).

192. **(H)** 6

Scientific Investigation

According to Table 3, there are 6 g of hydrogen in Unknown Z. Since the molar mass of hydrogen is 1 mole per gram, there are also 6 moles of hydrogen in Unknown Z. You can verify this result by examining Table 1: the number of grams and the number of moles are always equal for hydrogen. The correct answer is (H).

193. **(A)** 0.5

Scientific Investigation

According to the passage, one mole of decane consists of 10 moles of carbon and 22 moles of hydrogen. Since Unknown D is composed of 5 moles of carbon and 11 moles of hydrogen, this sample must be exactly half of 1 mole. The correct answer is (A).

194. **(G)** butane.

Scientific Investigation

According to Table 1, Unknown A contains 2 moles of carbon and 5 moles of hydrogen. The only answer choice that contains carbon to hydrogen in a molar ratio of 2 to 5 is butane. The correct answer is (G).

195. **(D)** 1 : 1.

Scientific Investigation

While the mass of carbon in Unknown X is 12g and the mass of hydrogen is 1g, the number of moles of carbon is 1 (there are 12 grams of carbon in 1 mole) and the number of moles of hydrogen is also 1 (there is 1 gram of H in 1 mole). Thus, the molar ratio is 1 : 1. The correct answer is (D).

196. **(J)** the reaction will proceed to completion.

Scientific Investigation

This question requires a bit of outside knowledge. Reactions are limited by whichever reactant (starting material) is depleted first. By using an "excess" amount of oxygen, you ensure that you are not limited by the amount of oxygen in the sample and that all the carbon undergoes the reaction. Thus, you are ensuring that the reaction will proceed to completion. The amount of oxygen does not affect the ratio of the products, the spontaneity of the reaction, or the ability to observe the reaction. The correct answer is (J).

Chapter 23

of

5lb. Book of ACT® Practice Problems

Science:
Earth Sciences

In This Chapter...

Earth Sciences Passages & Solutions

Chapter 23
Earth Sciences

The Science passages in this chapter are classified within earth sciences, which include environmental science, geology, meteorology, oceanography, and other topics that could be studied in an Earth Sciences course.

In the Science section, you'll encounter three types of passages, each with a corresponding question type.

1. Data Representation. A scientific article that contains charts and tables of information. Here, you will be asked Data Interpretation questions. That is, you'll need to interpret the data you're given.

2. Research Summary. A description of an experiment (or two). Here, you will be asked Scientific Investigation questions. In other words, you'll need to examine the experiment (the scientific investigation) critically: assessing its design, analyzing its outcomes, etc.

3. Conflicting Viewpoints. Two or more explanations or interpretations of a scientific phenomenon. These explanations always conflict. Here, you will be asked Evaluation of Models, Inferences, and Experimental Results questions, requiring you to compare, contrast, or otherwise evaluate the explanations given.

How should you use this chapter? Here are some recommendations, according to the level you've reached in ACT Science.

1. Fundamentals. Do a passage or two untimed to begin with. As you become more comfortable, put the clock on. In all cases, review the solutions closely, and articulate what you've learned. Reread the passage again to ensure that you fully understand it, and redo problems as necessary.

2. Fixes. Do one passage at a time under timed conditions. Examine the results, learn your lessons, then test yourself with more passages (one or two from each Science chapter) at once.

3. Tweaks. Confirm your mastery by doing several passages (a couple from each Science chapter) at once under timed conditions. A set of five or six passages (doing all seven questions per passage) or seven passages (doing about six questions per passage) is ideal. Aim to improve the speed and ease of your reading and solution process.

Good luck on the problems!

PASSAGE 1

Latitude is a horizontal measure of location on the globe. The widest part of the Earth is referred to as the *equator* and has been given the value of 0°. North latitudes extend up to the North Pole (90° N) and South latitudes extend down to the South Pole (90° S).

The seasonal fluctuations of temperature on Earth are largely a result of the tilt of the Earth with relation to the sun and the number of daylight hours. At locations near the equator (0°), the sun is almost directly overhead at noon all year. This results in tremendous amounts of solar energy and consequently higher temperatures.

The *tropical zone* of Earth is located between 23.5° N and 23.5° S latitudes. On either side of the tropical zone, between 23.5° and 66.5°, are the Earth's *temperate zones*. Beyond the temperate zones are the *polar zones*, between 66.5° and 90° of latitude. Polar, temperate, and tropical zones are shown in Figure 1. Figure 1 depicts the day on which the most direct sunlight strikes a longitude of 23.5° S. This scenario occurs on December 21 each year. The most direct sunlight strikes 23.5° N on June 21.

As the Earth revolves around the sun, the angle at which solar radiation strikes the Earth changes. The areas that get the most direct sunlight have longer days and warmer temperatures. The areas that receive less direct sunlight have shorter days and colder temperatures. A particular location refers to the season with the highest relative temperatures and longest days as summer, while the season with the lowest relative temperatures and shortest days are winter. Fall is between summer and winter, while spring is between winter and summer.

Temperature data at a particular degree of latitude can be quantified in numerous ways. The average temperature and precipitation of City X over a year are shown in Figure 2. The average temperature and precipitation of City Y over most of a year are shown in Table 1.

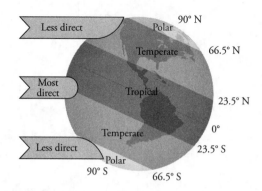

Figure 1

Average Temperature and Precipitation in City X

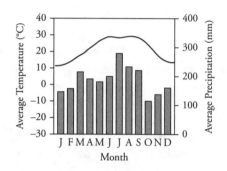

Figure 2

Average Temperature and Precipitation in City Y

Table 1

Month	Average Temperature (°C)	Average Precipitation (mm)
Jan.	−8.2	38.2
Feb.	−6.3	28.0
Mar.	−4.0	30.8
Apr.	3.4	35.7
May	9.0	45.9
Jun.	13.9	65.5
Jul.	16.5	81.3
Aug.	14.3	88.9
Sep.	9.6	58.5
Oct.	4.0	63.6
Nov.	−3.8	50.8

1. The variation in seasonal temperature at a particular location is primarily a result of:
   A. the distance of the location from the sun.
   B. the angular rotation of the sun.
   C. the angle and degree of sunlight hitting the location.
   D. the degree of longitude.

2. The equator lies in which zone?
   F. Tropical
   G. North Temperate
   H. South Temperate
   J. Polar

3. For the time sampled, how many months have a higher average precipitation in City Y than in City X?
   A. 0
   B. 2
   C. 10
   D. 12

4. Which season(s) has(have) highest amount of precipitation for the two cities sampled?

	City X	City Y
F.	Spring	Summer
G.	Summer	Summer
H.	Summer	Winter
J.	Winter	Spring

5. A city with a latitude measure of 80° S lies in which zone?
   A. South tropical
   B. North temperate
   C. South temperate
   D. Polar

6. Which of the following is most likely to be the average temperature in City Y during December?
   F. −6°C
   G. −3°C
   H. 8°C
   J. 44°C

7. When the equator is getting the most direct sunlight of any location on Earth, which season is it in the Northern Hemisphere?
   A. Winter
   B. Summer
   C. Winter or summer
   D. Spring or fall

23

PASSAGE 2

The *greenhouse effect* is a phenomenon in which certain gases in a planet's atmosphere called *greenhouse gases* absorb thermal radiation and re-emit that radiation in all directions. Since some of that energy is radiated back towards the surface of a planet, this effect leads to a higher surface temperature than would be expected if these specific gases were not present. Greenhouse gases on Earth include carbon dioxide (CO_2), nitrous oxide (N_2O), methane (CH_4), and carbon monoxide (CO). The concentration over time of numerous greenhouse gases in the Earth's atmosphere is shown in Figure 1.

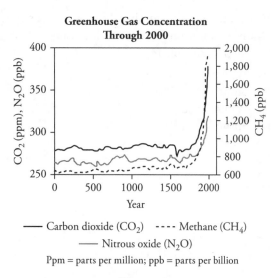

Figure 1

Since light has many characteristics of a wave, we can take measurements of the waves of different types of light. The *frequency* is the number of oscillations that each type of light exhibits per second, and the *wavelength* is the distance between successive oscillations. A large portion of light from the sun that strikes the Earth falls in the visible part of the *electromagnetic spectrum*. The Earth re-emits this energy as infrared light, which has a lower frequency and a longer wavelength than red light. The listing of all forms of light in the electromagnetic spectrum, as well as the frequency and wavelength of each type of light, is shown in Figure 2.

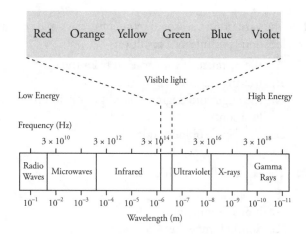

Figure 2

8. Using a *spectrometer*, a tool to measure wavelengths and frequencies of light, a student finds light with a frequency of 3×10^{12} Hz. Which type of light is this?

    F. Infrared
    G. Red light
    H. Purple light
    J. Ultraviolet

9. According to the passage, which of the following is true?

    A. As the concentration of greenhouse gases increases, the greenhouse effect is increased, and the average surface temperature of Earth decreases.
    B. As the concentration of greenhouse gases increases, the greenhouse effect is decreased, and the average surface temperature of Earth decreases.
    C. As the concentration of greenhouse gases increases, the greenhouse effect is increased, and the average surface temperature of Earth increases.
    D. As the concentration of greenhouse gases increases, the greenhouse effect is decreased, and the average surface temperature of Earth increases.

10. Given the information presented in the passage, in which year would one expect the average surface temperature of the Earth to be highest?

    F. 0
    G. 1500
    H. 2000
    J. 2100

MANHATTAN
PREP

11. It is generally accepted that exposure to light with a smaller wavelength can be a health hazard. Thus, exposure to which type of light is most dangerous?

    A. Infrared
    B. Gamma rays
    C. Radio waves
    D. Microwaves

12. Which of the following would NOT presumably increase the average surface temperature of the Earth?

    F. A decrease in the number of plants, leading to an increased amount of CO_2 in the atmosphere
    G. An increase in motor traffic, leading to an increased amount of CO_2 in the atmosphere
    H. A mass extinction and decrease in the number of animals globally, increasing the amount of O_2 in the atmosphere
    J. An increase in coal mining, leading to an increased amount of CH_4 in the atmosphere

13. Which of the following was found in the highest concentration in the Earth's atmosphere in the year 2000?

    A. CO_2
    B. N_2O
    C. CH_4
    D. It is impossible to determine.

14. The speed of light can be calculated via the equation $v = f\lambda$, where v is the speed of light, f is the frequency of that light, and λ is the wavelength of that light. What happens to v as the frequency of light increases?

    F. v increases.
    G. v decreases.
    H. v remains the same.
    J. v increases and then decreases.

23

PASSAGE 3

Students were studying two known fossils, labeled as Fossil H and Fossil G, that were found together in a single sedimentary rock layer of Earth. As the nearby areas were further examined, scientists discovered a wealth of fossils in nearby layers. Fossils that are found in the same layer are from approximately the same time. The fossils discovered are displayed in Figure 1. Layer 1 is closest to the surface, while Layer 6 is deepest in the ground. Table 1 indicates the names of different epochs and their time spans.

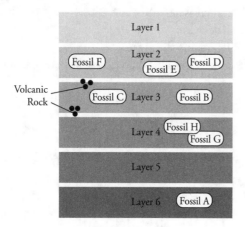

Figure 1

Table 1

Epoch	Years ago (million)	Age of
Permian	245–286	
Pennsylvanian	286–320	Amphibians
Mississippian	320–360	
Devonian	360–408	
Silurian	408–438	Fishes
Ordovician	438–505	Marine
Cambrian	505–545	Invertebrates

Volcanic rock was discovered between the layer containing the known fossils and the layer containing Fossils B and C. Volcanic rock was also found immediately above the layer containing Fossils B and C, but below the highest layer in which fossils were discovered (Layer 2).

Study 1

Relative dating can be used to estimate the age of a fossil found in rocks if it can be compared to a fossil of a known age. Sedimentary rock layers are created vertically. The lowest layer is the oldest, and as the layers get closer to the surface of the Earth, the layers contain increasingly recent fossils. In extremely rare instances, a layer or multiple layers can invert because of geological movement. An *inversion* results in the oldest fossils being deposited nearest the surface, and the most recent fossils being deposited deeper in the Earth. When this occurs, significant cracking and breaking is generally observed in the layer.

A student analyzed the cracking and breaking levels in the area of rock containing the fossils and found no evidence of inversion. She therefore dated Fossils A through F relative to the known Fossils H and G, both of which were known to be approximately 500 million years old.

Study 2

Volcanic lava, once solidified, creates igneous rock. The lava contains no lead (Pb-207), but it does contain radioactive uranium (U-235). Over time U-235 decays and becomes Pb-207 as the lava solidifies. By comparing the amount of U-235 to the amount of Pb-207 within igneous rock, researchers can estimate the age of the rock. This method is known as radiometric dating.

A student evaluated both the upper and lower layer of volcanic rock for U-235 and Pb-207. The lower layer had approximately 45.5% as much Pb-207 as U-235, indicating the age of the rock is 440 million years. The upper layer had 40.7% as much Pb-207 as U-235, so its age was calculated at 407 million years. The student then predicted the relative age of the fossils based on the known age of the volcanic rock.

MANHATTAN
PREP

15. Based on Study 1, what can the student conclude about the age of Fossil A?

   A. It is older than 500 million years.
   B. It is younger than 500 million years.
   C. It is between 407 and 440 million years old.
   D. It is younger than 407 million years.

16. According to Study 2, approximately how old is Fossil C?

   F. It is younger than 407 million years.
   G. It is between 407 and 440 million years old.
   H. It is between 440 and 704 million years old.
   J. It is older than 704 million years.

17. What is the earliest epoch that Fossil E could be from, according to these studies?

   A. Ordovician
   B. Devonian
   C. Pennsylvanian
   D. Permian

18. If Layers 2, 3, 4, and 5 had inverted as described in Study 1, students would be likely to observe:

   F. Fossil A appearing in a layer closer to the surface of the Earth than Fossil C.
   G. Fossils D and E appearing in separate layers.
   H. the volcanic rock appearing around Layer 5.
   J. Fossil C appearing in a layer closer to the surface of the Earth than Fossil F.

19. If the students performing Study 1 found volcanic rock immediately below Fossil A that was dated at 550 million years old, what could they conclude, assuming their conclusion is the narrowest date range available to the study?

   A. Fossil A is older than 550 million years.
   B. Fossil A is between 500 and 550 million years old.
   C. Fossil A is between 407 and 550 million years old.
   D. Fossil A is between 440 and 550 million years old.

20. Each of the following is a possible reason why there might be more fossils discovered in Layer 2 than Layer 6 EXCEPT that:

   F. over time, fossils tend to break down and be more difficult to discover.
   G. materials deeper in the Earth are generally harder to discover.
   H. inversion caused fossils that may have been in Layer 6 to shift layers.
   J. there may have been fewer plants and animals in this area of the world at the time when Layer 6 was being created.

21. If there had been 42% as much Pb-207 as U-235 in a volcanic rock studied, it is most likely that the age of the volcanic rock would be approximately:

   A. 398 million years old.
   B. 418 million years old.
   C. 458 million years old.
   D. 508 million years old.

PASSAGE 4

Burning coal is known to increase the acidity of the atmosphere. One reason for this is that most coal contains sulfur (S). As it burns, the sulfur is oxidized to become sulfur dioxide (SO_2). Many types of bacteria can decompose SO_2 into sulfide (S_{-2}), which is used in maintaining biological systems. When excess SO_2 is produced, however, it reacts with ozone or hydrogen peroxide in the atmosphere. This reaction creates sulfuric acid (H_2SO_4). Sulfuric acid is a major cause of acid rain.

Study 1

A closed system containing 10 L of air was used to study the effect of burning coal on both the levels of SO_2 in the atmosphere and the resulting pH of the atmosphere. (The lower the pH, the higher the acidity.) Various quantities of coal were measured. The results are displayed in Table 1.

Table 1

Amount Coal Burned (mg)	SO_2 Increase in Air (mg/L)	pH
100	0.020	3.77
90	0.018	3.82
80	0.016	3.87
70	0.014	3.93
60	0.012	3.99
50	0.010	4.07
40	0.008	4.16
30	0.006	4.28
20	0.004	4.45
10	0.002	4.72
0	0.000	5.60

Study 2

Collection stations are positioned throughout the United States to monitor the levels of various minerals in rainwater. Figure 1 shows the results from the station with the highest SO_2 content in various states over four years.

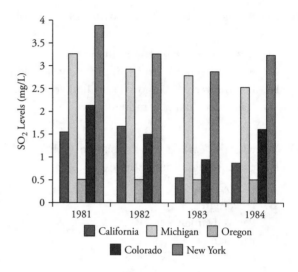

Figure 1

Several states had multiple collection stations throughout the state. Figure 2 shows the levels at different collection stations within Michigan over the same time range.

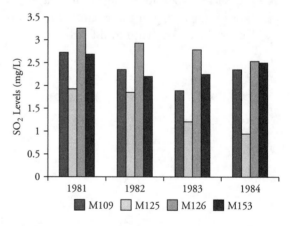

Figure 2

The change in SO_2 levels is best measured over the long term. Figure 3 illustrates the change of both SO_2 concentrations and pH at a single collection station in California over time.

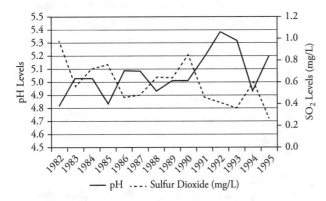

Figure 3

22. According to Table 1, as more coal is burned, which of the following is true about sulfur dioxide levels and pH?

	SO_2 levels	pH
F.	increase	increase
G.	increase	decrease
H.	decrease	increase
J.	decrease	decrease

23. Of the states compared in Figure 1, the state that recorded the highest SO_2 levels in all years from 1981 to 1984 was:

   A. California.
   B. New York.
   C. Michigan.
   D. Oregon.

24. According to Figure 3, the SO_2 level at the collection station monitored in 1993 was approximately:

   F. 0.36 mg/L.
   G. 0.6 mg/L.
   H. 4.8 mg/L.
   J. 5.3 mg/L.

25. According to Figure 2, the collection station that showed the largest decrease in SO_2 content from 1981 to 1984 was:

   A. MI09.
   B. MI25.
   C. MI26.
   D. MI53.

26. Assuming the trends discovered in Study 1 hold true generally, which of the following is likely to have the lowest pH?

   F. MI26 in 1981
   G. MI25 in 1984
   H. New York in 1981
   J. Oregon in 1983

27. Based on Figure 1, which of the following conclusions can be properly drawn for the years 1983 and 1984?

   A. The New York collection station had a higher SO_2 content than any station in California, Michigan, Oregon, or Colorado.
   B. The California collection station had a higher SO_2 content than any station in New York, Michigan, Oregon, or Colorado.
   C. The Oregon collection station had a lower SO_2 content than any station in California, New York, Michigan, or Colorado.
   D. The Colorado collection station had a lower SO_2 content than any station in California, New York, Michigan, or Oregon.

28. Which of the following is most likely to result in an increase in the pH of rain water?

   F. Keeping all coal burning localized to one state.
   G. Using low-carbon coal.
   H. Using coal that contains additional sulfur.
   J. Using coal that contains no sulfur.

PASSAGE 5

The *hydrologic cycle* is the process by which water on Earth continually moves and changes phase. Throughout the hydrologic cycle, the amount of water on Earth remains relatively unchanged over time, though water continually moves from one *reservoir*, or storing place, to another. Major reservoirs on Earth include oceans, glaciers, lakes, the atmosphere, and rivers. The *average reservoir time* measures, on average, how long a water molecule stays in a particular reservoir before moving to another reservoir. Table 1 shows different types of water reservoirs, their average reservoir time, and the approximate percent of total water on Earth that each of these reservoirs contains at any given time.

Table 1 The Earth's Water Reservoirs

Reservoir	Average Reservoir Time	% of Total Water on Earth
Oceans	3,200 years	97
Glaciers	20 years	2
Lakes	50 years	0.8
Atmosphere	9 days	0.1
Rivers	0.5 years	0.02

Water moves from one reservoir to another by physical processes that include precipitation, melting, evaporation, transpiration, condensation, collection, and infiltration. *Precipitation* is the process of water falling from the atmosphere to the Earth's surface. Most precipitation is in the form of rain (roughly 500,000 km³ per year globally), but it also includes snow, hail, and sleet (roughly 1,000 km³ per year globally). *Melting* is the transformation of water from the solid to the liquid phase and *evaporation* is the transformation of water from liquid to gas phases as it moves from the Earth's surface to its atmosphere. Rates of melting and evaporation are elevated in reservoirs with higher temperatures, larger surface areas, and more wind. *Transpiration* is the release of water vapor from plants and soil into the air. The transformation of water vapor to liquid water

droplets in the air is called *condensation*, which is responsible for the formation of clouds and fog. *Collection* refers to the gathering of water in a particular reservoir. *Infiltration* is the flow of water from the surface into the ground. The continual interaction of these processes, shown in Figure 1, constitutes the hydrologic cycle.

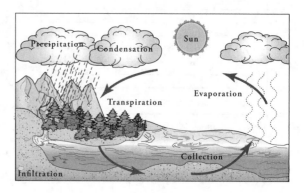

Figure 1

29. As the volume of a lake decreases during the summer months, the rate of which process is increased in that lake?
   A. Transpiration
   B. Evaporation
   C. Condensation
   D. Precipitation

30. Which process would likely be decreased most by the destruction of rainforest?
   F. Transpiration
   G. Evaporation
   H. Condensation
   J. Precipitation

31. Roughly what percent of global precipitation falls as rain annually?
   A. 0.2%
   B. 2.0%
   C. 98.0%
   D. 99.8%

32. A student finds that 78% of all precipitation occurs over the ocean, although 71% of the Earth's surface is covered by ocean. What conclusion can be drawn from these facts?

   F. Precipitation falls randomly over the Earth's surface.

   G. Precipitation is less likely to fall on land than in oceans.

   H. Precipitation is more likely to fall on land than in oceans.

   J. No conclusion about precipitation can be drawn.

33. A single water molecule has completed 2 full hydrological cycles in the past month. In which type of reservoir would the water molecule have most likely been stored?

   A. Ocean

   B. Glacier

   C. Lake

   D. Atmosphere

34. A decrease in ozone in the atmosphere has caused the amount of UV light entering the atmosphere to increase. Since UV light is known to break chemical bonds, which of the following elements would you expect to find at a increased level as a result of the presence of atmospheric water and increased UV light?

   F. Nitrogen

   G. Carbon

   H. Oxygen

   J. Helium

35. Which of the following statements accurately describes the effect that rising temperatures on a global scale would have on the average reservoir time of water in glaciers?

   A. Decrease in average reservoir time because of higher rates of melting and evaporation

   B. Increase in average reservoir time because of higher rates of melting and evaporation

   C. Decrease in average reservoir time because of lower rates of melting and evaporation

   D. Increase in average reservoir time because of lower rates of melting and evaporation

23

PASSAGE 6

A *Charpy V-notch test* (Figure 1) is used to determine the relative toughness of materials at various temperatures. A hammer is swung on a pendulum towards a metal specimen that is anchored to an anvil for support. The specimen is typically cut into a rectangular prism of that measures 10 mm × 10 mm × 55 mm. One side of the specimen has a 2 mm notch cut into it as shown in Figure 2.

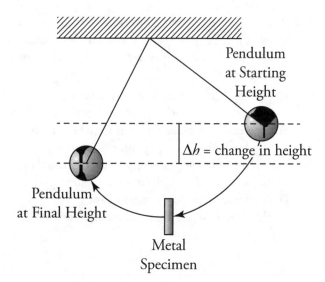

Figure 1

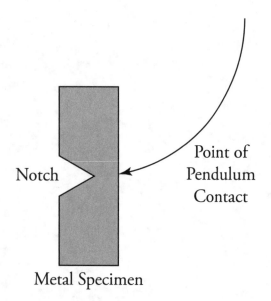

Figure 2

When the hammer reaches the metal specimen, energy is transferred to the specimen. This is known as *impact energy* (I). The specimen breaks along the notch. The higher the amount of energy needed to break the specimen, the *tougher* the metal is considered to be. Impact energy is calculated by observing the difference in height of the pendulum at the beginning of the test and after collision with the specimen, then applying the following equation:

Change in energy = mass of pendulum × force of gravity × change in height

$$\Delta E = m \times g \times \Delta h$$

The energy lost from the pendulum is transferred to the metal specimen, so ΔE = impact energy.

A study was performed on steel that was tempered under varying conditions. Low-energy steel was heated to between 300°C and 400°C and held at that temperature for 6 hours. High-energy steel was heated to approximately 600°C for the same amount of time. Heating steel allows the final product to be more uniform and dramatically increases its toughness. This higher-toughness steel is often used in construction of buildings that must withstand extreme conditions.

Both low-energy and high-energy steel were subjected to the Charpy V-notch test. The measurements are displayed in Table 1, and the calculated impact energy is illustrated over various temperatures in Figure 3. The mass of the pendulum in all trials was 100 kg, and the starting height was 30 cm. The metals were not tested at all temperatures.

Table 1

Temperature (°C)	Final Height (cm)	
	High-Energy Specimen	Low-Energy Specimen
−200	28.2	
−175	28.0	
−150	27.3	
−125	26.4	
−100	24.5	
−75	21.4	28.9
−50	20.0	28.7
−25	19.6	28.4
0	19.2	28.0
25	19.0	27.4
50	18.9	27.0
75		26.8
100		26.7
125		26.7

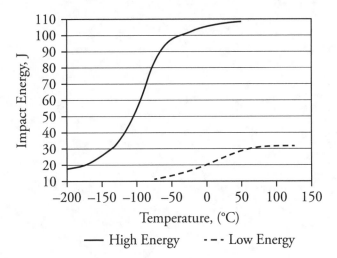

— High Energy   - - - Low Energy

Figure 3

36. Based on Figure 3, approximately how much energy is required to break a high-energy sample at −50°C?

    F. 98 J
    G. 62 J
    H. 47 J
    J. 13 J

37. According to Figure 3, as the temperature increases, the samples tend to:

    A. increase in toughness.
    B. decrease in toughness.
    C. increase in height.
    D. decrease in height.

38. According to Figure 3, the impact energy of a high-energy sample at 0°C is approximately how many times more than the impact energy of a low-energy sample at 0°C?

    F. 2
    G. 6
    H. 10
    J. 20

39. If a building was being constructed to withstand extremely low temperatures, the steel used in construction should most likely be:

    A. cooled to −200°C.
    B. created in a low-energy environment.
    C. kept at the lowest reasonable height.
    D. heated to 600°C and held at that temperature for at least 6 hours.

40. Based on Figure 1 and Table 1, if a low-energy metal specimen were tested at 0°C under identical conditions except that the initial height of the pendulum was increased to 40 cm, the final height of the pendulum would most likely be:

    F. 38.0 cm.
    G. 29.2 cm.
    H. 28.0 cm.
    J. 19.2 cm.

41. Assuming the toughness of any metal tends to remain the same past a certain temperature, the maximum impact energy needed to break a 10 mm × 10 mm × 55 mm sample of low-energy steel is approximately:

    A. 10 J.
    B. 32 J.
    C. 57 J.
    D. 100 J.

42. The impact energy of a sample should remain constant regardless of the properties of the pendulum used in the study. If the mass of the pendulum were tripled, but all other conditions remained the same, the studies would most likely show:

  F. an increase in the final height.
  G. an increase in the change in height.
  H. a decrease in the change in energy.
  J. a decrease in the impact energy.

PASSAGE 7

Hanford, Washington, is considered by many to be one of the most contaminated places in the Western Hemisphere. Hanford was the site of plutonium enrichment and decades of nuclear weapon production, and consequently, the groundwater in many areas is polluted. Additionally, the nearby Columbia River has shown increased levels of toxic chemicals at many sites.

Table 1

	Aquatic Water Quality Criteria	Drinking Water Standard
Chromium	10 µg/L	100 µg/L
Nitrate	N/A	45 mg/L
Strontium-90	8 pCi/L	8 pCi/L
Tritium	20,000 pCi/L	20,000 pCi/L

Maximum safe values of different chemicals in drinking water.

The maximum safe concentrations established for both aquatic water quality and drinking water are listed in Table 1. Concentrations are given in µg/L (1 µg = 10^{-6} g), in mg/L (1 mg = 10^{-3} g), and in pCi/L (1 pCi = 10^{-12} Ci, or curies, which technically are units of radioactivity). Strontium-90 has a specific activity, or radioactivity per gram, of 138 curies per gram, while tritium, which is a radioactive isotope of hydrogen, has a specific activity of 9,650 curies per gram. Researchers have been monitoring the concentrations of each of these contaminants at different sites along the Columbia River. Table 2 lists the measured concentrations in a variety of areas in both 2008 and 2010.

Table 2

| Site | Material | Maximum Concentration | |
		2008	2010
100-B/C	Chromium	12.4 µg/L	18 µg/L
	Nitrate	6.6 mg/L	2.2 mg/L
	Strontium-90	2.16 pCi/L	1.8 pCi/L
	Tritium	2,680 pCi/L	1,800 pCi/L
100-K	Chromium	62.6 µg/L	72 µg/L
	Nitrate	6.6 mg/L	7.1 mg/L
	Tritium	3,250 pCi/L	680 pCi/L
100-N	Chromium	7.7 µg/L	11 µg/L
	Nitrate	14.7 mg/L	4.7 mg/L
	Tritium	5,800 pCi/L	4,000 pCi/L
100-D	Chromium	11.3 µg/L	54 µg/L
	Nitrate	4.2 mg/L	3.4 mg/L
	Strontium-90	0.107 pCi/L	1.3 pCi/L
	Tritium		6,200 pCi/L
100-H	Chromium	33.7 µg/L	37 µg/L
	Nitrate	15.7 mg/L	6.9 mg/L
	Strontium-90	6.76 pCi/L	3 pCi/L
	Tritium	2,110 pCi/L	1,600 pCi/L
Hanford town site	Chromium	0.738 µg/L	2.7 µg/L
	Nitrate	6.2 mg/L	5.2 mg/L
	Tritium	14,300 pCi/L	20,000 pCi/L

All four contaminants are considered toxic above the standards established in Table 1. Tritium and strontium-90 are both radioactive. Nitrate is present naturally, but at high concentrations, can be dangerous. Chromium easily dissolves in water and is highly toxic to living organisms.

Note: all figures adapted from Hanford.gov; Hanford Site Groundwater Monitoring Report

43. According to Table 2, the concentration of strontium-90 increased from 2008 to 2010 in which of the following sites?

  A. 100-B/C
  B. 100-K
  C. 100-D
  D. 100-H

44. According to Tables 1 and 2, the chromium concentration was within safe levels for aquatic water quality in 2008, but had become unsafe by 2010 at which of the following sites?

   F. 100-B/C
   G. 100-K
   H. 100-N
   J. 100-D

45. The Hanford town site, if it had not been evacuated prior to 2010, would have been most likely to cause health problems in 2010 because:

   A. radioactive tritium had reached unsafe levels in drinking water.
   B. increasing chromium levels would soon reach unsafe levels in drinking water.
   C. nitrate levels were decreasing below what was needed to sustain crops.
   D. strontium-90 levels were below the detection limit.

46. Which of the following represents the change in tritium levels at four of the sites between 2008 and 2010?

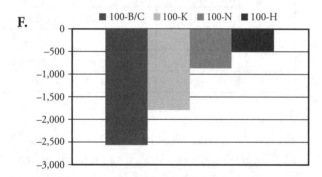

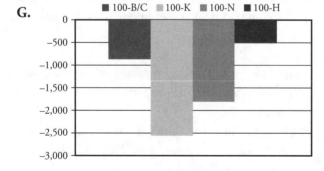

H.
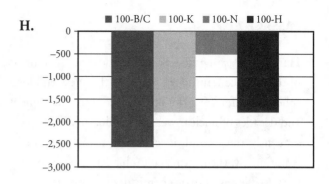

J.
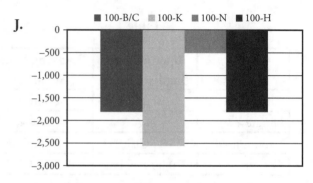

47. Which of the following can be present in the greatest mass concentrations in drinking water before it exceeds safety limits?

   A. Chromium
   B. Nitrate
   C. Strontium
   D. Tritium

48. Assuming clean-up efforts have not been able to reduce the levels of tritium in the environment, each of the following could account for a reduction in the concentrations of tritium found at various sites EXCEPT that:

   F. tritium was naturally converted into chromium.
   G. tritium decayed naturally to its non-radioactive isotope.
   H. tritium was washed downstream, increasing the concentration at unrecorded sites.
   J. animals moving through the area ingested materials containing tritium and moved it offsite.

49. There is no direct leakage from the radioactive sites to the Columbia River. Which of the following is the most likely reason that so many positions along the Columbia River show high levels of contamination?

A. Contaminated materials evaporate from the reactor site and are deposited through rain into the Columbia River

B. Wildlife visits the reactor site and transfers radioactive materials from the site to the Columbia River.

C. Some leaks from radioactive sites have yet to be detected.

D. Contaminated materials leak into the ground and are transferred through the soil to the Columbia River.

23

Answer Keys

Write in whether you got each problem right or wrong (or left it blank). If your answer was correct, put a 1 in every blank to the right of that problem. Sum up each column and compare your total to the total possible "Out Of" points in each column.

Passage 1

Problem	Correct Answer	Right/ Wrong/Blank	Interpretation of Data	Scientific Investigation	Evaluation of Models, Inferences, and Experimental Results
1	C		—		
2	F		—		
3	A		—		
4	G		—		
5	D		—		
6	F		—		
7	D		—		
Total					
Out Of	7	7		0	0

Passage 2

Problem	Correct Answer	Right/ Wrong/Blank	Interpretation of Data	Scientific Investigation	Evaluation of Models, Inferences, and Experimental Results
8	F		—		
9	C		—		
10	J		—		
11	B		—		
12	H		—		
13	A		—		
14	H		—		
Total					
Out Of	7	7		0	0

MANHATTAN
PREP

Passage 3

Problem	Correct Answer	Right/ Wrong/Blank	Interpretation of Data	Scientific Investigation	Evaluation of Models, Inferences, and Experimental Results
15	A		—		
16	G		—		
17	B		—		
18	J		—		
19	B		—		
20	H		—		
21	B		—		
Total					
Out Of		7	7	0	0

Passage 4

Problem	Correct Answer	Right/ Wrong/Blank	Interpretation of Data	Scientific Investigation	Evaluation of Models, Inferences, and Experimental Results
22	G			—	
23	B			—	
24	F			—	
25	B			—	
26	H			—	
27	A			—	
28	J			—	
Total					
Out Of		7	0	7	0

Passage 5

Problem	Correct Answer	Right/ Wrong/Blank	Interpretation of Data	Scientific Investigation	Evaluation of Models, Inferences, and Experimental Results
29	B		—		
30	F		—		
31	D		—		
32	G		—		
33	D		—		
34	H		—		
35	A		—		
Total					
Out Of		7	7	0	0

Passage 6

Problem	Correct Answer	Right/ Wrong/Blank	Interpretation of Data	Scientific Investigation	Evaluation of Models, Inferences, and Experimental Results
36	F		—		
37	A		—		
38	G		—		
39	D		—		
40	F		—		
41	B		—		
42	F		—		
Total					
Out Of		7	7	0	0

Passage 7

Problem	Correct Answer	Right/ Wrong/Blank	Interpretation of Data	Scientific Investigation	Evaluation of Models, Inferences, and Experimental Results
43	C		—		
44	H		—		
45	A		—		
46	G		—		
47	B		—		
48	F		—		
49	D		—		
Total					
Out Of		7	7	0	0

Earth Sciences Solutions

Passage 1 Solutions

1. **(C)** the angle and degree of sunlight hitting the location.

Interpretation of Data

According to the passage, the seasonal fluctuations of temperature on Earth are largely a result of the tilt of the Earth with relation to the sun and the number of daylight hours. Another way of saying this point is that the angle of sunlight hitting the location causes the temperature to be higher or lower. The correct answer is (C).

2. **(F)** Tropical

Interpretation of Data

According to Figure 1, the equator (the line at 0°C) lies in the middle of the tropical zone. The correct answer is (F).

3. **(A)** 0

Interpretation of Data

According to Figure 2, the average precipitation in City X is greater than 100 mm for each month. According to Table 1, not a single month in City Y has more than 100 mm of precipitation on average. Thus, there are no months in which the average precipitation of City Y is higher than the average precipitation of City X. The correct answer is (A).

4. **(G)** Summer; Summer

Interpretation of Data

The highest average precipitation for each city can be found by consulting Figure 2 and Table 1. For both cities, the highest average precipitation numbers are in June, July, and August. These months also have the highest temperatures and are the subsequently defined as the summer months. The correct answer is (G).

5. **(D)** Polar

Interpretation of Data

According to Figure 1, a city with a latitude measure of 80° S is below the line shown of 66.5° S. This puts the city in the polar zone. The correct answer is (D).

6.   **(F)** −6°C

Interpretation of Data

The average temperatures within a city are relatively continuous. That is, the average temperature for any month (with the exception of the very coldest and the very warmest month) falls in between the temperature of the preceding month and the temperature of the next month. Since the average November temperature in City Y is −3.8°C and the average January temperature in City Y is −8.1°C, any value that is between −3.8 and −8.1 would make the most sense. The only answer choice in that range is −6°C. The correct answer is (F).

7.   **(D)** Spring or fall

Interpretation of Data

As indicated in Figure 1 and the passage, the most direct sunlight strikes 23.5° S on December 21 and strikes 23.5° N on June 21. The most direct sunlight is over the equator exactly midway between these dates, or roughly March 21 or September 21. In the Northern Hemisphere, these dates correspond to spring or fall, respectively. The correct answer is (D).

Passage 2 Solutions

8.   **(F)** Infrared

Interpretation of Data

According to Figure 2, light with a frequency of 3×10^{12} Hz is infrared light. The correct answer is (F).

9.   **(C)** As the concentration of greenhouse gases increases, the greenhouse effect is increased, and the average surface temperature of Earth increases.

Interpretation of Data

According to the passage, the greenhouse effect results from the deflection of light by gases present in a planet's atmosphere. Thus, the more greenhouse gases present, the greater the greenhouse effect. Since the greenhouse effect involves the reflection of light towards a planet's surface, this effect causes an increase in temperature. The correct answer is (C).

10.   **(J)** 2100

Interpretation of Data

Temperature is directly correlated to the level of greenhouse gases present in the atmosphere. According to Figure 1, the number of greenhouse gases has risen tremendously in the past 500 years, and given the current trend, you would expect the number to continue to rise. Thus, 2100 would be expected to have the highest temperature of the years listed. The correct answer is (J).

11. **(B)** Gamma rays

Interpretation of Data

The types of light with the shortest wavelength are on the right of the table in Figure 2 (remember that 10^{-11} is much smaller than 10^{-1}). Thus, gamma rays have the smallest wavelength and would be considered the most dangerous. The correct answer is (B).

12. **(H)** A mass extinction and decrease in the number of animals globally, increasing the amount of O2 in the atmosphere.

Interpretation of Data

Since oxygen is not a greenhouse gas, increasing the amount of O_2 in the atmosphere would not increase the average surface temperature of the planet. All of the other answer choices describe events that would increase the amount of a greenhouse gas, thereby strengthening the greenhouse effect and raising the average surface temperature. The correct answer is (H).

13. **(A)** CO_2

Interpretation of Data

Since CO_2 levels are reported in parts per million, whereas the other two gases are reported in parts per billion, the concentration of CO_2 is actually much higher than the other two gases. A CO_2 level of 350 parts per million, for example, would equal 350,000 parts per billion. Thus, although the graph seems to show similar numbers for CO_2 and CH_4 in the year 2000, careful study of the scales reveals that the concentration of CO_2 was much higher (arousnd 350 parts per million) than the concentration of CH_4 (around 1,800 parts per *billion*, or only around 1.8 parts per million). The correct answer is (A).

14. **(H)** v remains the same.

Interpretation of Data

As wavelength increases, frequency decreases proportionally. For example, when the frequency of a particular light is 3×10^{10}, the wavelength is 10^{-2} (Table 1), and $v = 3 \times 10^8$. A different light has a frequency of 3×10^{16} and a wavelength of 10^{-8}, yet v is still 3×10^8. Thus, the speed of light remains unchanged regardless of the frequency or the wavelength. The correct answer is (H).

Passage 3 Solutions

15.   **(A)** It is older than 500 million years.

Interpretation of Data

Fossils that are in lower layers are older than the ones that are found above them. Since the passage tells you that Fossil H and Fossil G are approximately 500 million years old, and since Fossil A is below those, Fossil A must be older than 500 million years old. The correct answer is (A).

16.   **(G)** It is between 407 and 440 million years old.

Interpretation of Data

Fossil C is between the two layers of volcanic rock. The upper layer of volcanic rock, you are told in Study 2, is 407 million years old. The lower layer of volcanic rock is 440 million years old. Thus, Fossil C is between 407 and 440 million years old. The correct answer is (G).

17.   **(B)** Devonian

Interpretation of Data

The upper layer of volcanic rock is 407 million years old. Anything that is above that is less than 407 million years old, so it could theoretically be 406 million years old (or 389 million years old, for example). Both of these are in the Devonian period, and any of the earlier epochs would be impossible. The correct answer is (B).

18.   **(J)** Fossil C appearing in a layer closer to the surface of the Earth than Fossil F.

Interpretation of Data

Since there is no reason to think layers have inverted (it is extremely rare and there was no cracking observed), you can conclude that Fossil C is older than Fossil F. According to the passage, the inversion of layers would cause older fossils (Fossil C) to appear closer to the surface of the Earth than younger ones (Fossil F). The correct answer is (J).

19.   **(B)** Fossil A is between 500 and 550 million years old.

Interpretation of Data

Since Fossil H and Fossil G (in a younger, higher layer than the one Fossil A is in) are dated at 500 million years old, and the volcanic rock mentioned in the question is 550 million years old, you could conclude that Fossil A is between 500 and 550 million years old. This is the narrowest possible date range with the given information. The correct answer is (B).

MANHATTAN
PREP

20. **(H)** inversion caused fossils that may have been in Layer 6 to shift layers.

Interpretation of Data

Inversion does not affect the likelihood of discovering fossils, nor is there any reason to think that inversion occurred, since it is extremely rare and no noticeable cracking was observed. Moreover, no mechanism is described that could cause fossils to move from one layer to another (inversion just turns the pattern of layers upside down). All of the other answer choices provide plausible explanations for finding more fossils in Layer 2 than in Layer 6. The correct answer is (H).

21. **(B)** 418 million years old.

Interpretation of Data

The second paragraph of Study 2 tells you that uranium slowly turns to lead as lava turns to rock and ages. Thus, the more lead in a sample, the older the sample. Since a value of 40.7% lead is found in samples 407 million years old, and a value of 45.5% lead is found in samples 440 million years old, a value of 42% lead must be between 407 and 440 million years old. The only answer choice between those values is 418 million years old. The correct answer is (B).

Passage 4 Solutions

22. **(G)** increase; decrease

Scientific Investigation

Table 2 is organized by decreasing SO_2 level, so the readings with the highest concentrations of SO_2 are actually on top. The highest values of SO_2 are associated with the lowest pH values on the chart, and the lowest values of SO_2 are associated with the highest pH values. Thus, as the SO_2 level increases for a particular reading, the pH decreases. The correct answer is (G).

23. **(B)** New York.

Scientific Investigation

In Figure 1, the highest column for each year is the right most column, which represents New York. Thus, New York has the highest SO_2 levels in each year. The correct answer is (B).

24. **(F)** 0.36 mg/L.

Scientific Investigation

Figure 3 shows a lighter, dotted line that represents sulfur dioxide levels. If you go to 1993 on the x-axis and look for the correlated point on the light line, you get a reading of just under 0.4 mg/L (be careful to read the units on the right, which are for sulfur dioxide, rather than the ones on the left, which are for pH). The correct answer is (F).

25. **(B)** MI25.

Scientific Investigation

The largest decrease in SO_2 content is represented by the biggest change in column height from 1981 to 1984. The biggest drop or difference between the two columns is for MI25, where SO_2 levels dropped about 1.0 mg/L. The correct answer is (B).

26. **(H)** New York in 1981

Scientific Investigation

This question requires you to obtain fairly exact values for SO_2 concentrations from both Figure 1 and Figure 2, and to see which value is highest (since high SO_2 concentration means low pH, from Table 1). New York in 1981 has the highest value of SO_2 of the presented answer choices, with a SO_2 value of roughly 3.8 mg/L. The correct answer is (H).

27. **(A)** The New York collection station had a higher SO_2 content than any station in California, Michigan, Oregon, or Colorado.

Scientific Investigation

According to Figure 1, the value of SO_2 levels in New York was roughly 2.8 mg/L in 1983 and 3.2 mg/L in 1984. These readings are higher than those of any station in California, Michigan, Oregon, or Colorado during those two years. As you can see, the two New York columns are higher than any other columns for those two years. The correct answer is (A).

28. **(J)** Using coal that contains no sulfur.

Scientific Investigation

You can tackle this problem by process of elimination. Keeping all coal burning localized to one state will still affect rainwater, as the coal would still increase sulfur dioxide levels in the air (which spreads across state lines) and lower the pH (Table 1). Using low-carbon coal (whatever that might mean, since the term is not defined) does not mean that sulfur levels, the main driver of pH change, will be affected at all. Using coal that contains additional sulfur would decrease pH, as the amount of sulfur and pH are inversely correlated (Table 1). Using coal that contains no sulfur would decrease sulfur dioxide levels in the air and subsequently increase pH (Table 1). The correct answer is (J).

Passage 5 Solutions

29. **(B)** Evaporation

Interpretation of Data

During the summer months, the temperature is higher than normal. According to the passage, the rate of evaporation is increased in environments with higher temperature, so the rate of evaporation is increased. This increased rate explains the decrease in volume of the lake. The correct answer is (B).

30. **(F)** Transpiration

Interpretation of Data

According to the passage, transpiration is the release of water vapor from plants and soil into the air. Since the amount of rainforest is directly related to the number of plants, destruction of the rainforest would most likely result in decrease in transpiration. The correct answer is (F).

31. **(D)** 99.8%

Interpretation of Data

According to the passage, 500,000 km³ of water fall annually in the form of rain, while 1,000 km³ of water fall annually in other forms. The fraction of rain can be represented as

$$\frac{Amount\ of\ rain\ fall}{Total\ precipitation}$$

$$\frac{500,000}{501,000}$$

$$\frac{500}{501}$$

$$0.9980$$

$$99.8\%$$

An exact calculation is not required, as the fraction 500/501 is larger than 99/100, and there is only one answer choice that is larger than 99%. The correct answer is (D).

32. **(G)** Precipitation is less likely to fall on land than in oceans.

Interpretation of Data

The Earth's surfaces include ocean and land. If precipitation were to fall randomly on the Earth's surfaces, you would expect that 71% of precipitation would occur over the ocean, since you are told that the ocean represents 71% of the surface of the Earth. The fact that 78% (that is, more than 71%) of precipitation actually occurs over ocean means that, for some reason, precipitation is more likely to occur over the ocean than land. Another way of saying this is that precipitation is less likely to fall on land than in oceans. The correct answer is (G).

33. **(D)** Atmosphere

Interpretation of Data

The average reservoir time describes how long, on average, a molecule of water stays in a particular reservoir before moving to another reservoir. If a molecule of water has completed 2 full hydrological cycles in one month, the reservoir of that water molecule should have an average reservoir time of significantly less than a month. While glaciers, oceans, rivers, and lakes have much higher average reservoir times, the atmosphere has the lowest average reservoir time of just 9 days. The correct answer is (D).

34. **(H)** Oxygen.

Interpretation of Data

If UV light is breaking down chemical bonds, it will release elements that are in water. This requires a tiny bit of outside knowledge: that the chemical formula of water is H_2O. If the bonds between hydrogen and oxygen are broken, then you would expect higher volumes of hydrogen and oxygen. Since hydrogen is not an answer choice, the answer is oxygen. The correct answer is (H).

35. **(A)** Decrease in average reservoir time because of higher rates of melting and evaporation

Interpretation of Data

According to the passage, the rate of melting and evaporation increase with higher temperatures. The average reservoir time, which is defined as the amount of time a water molecule spends in a particular reservoir, would be decreased since water molecules change reservoirs more often in higher temperatures. The correct answer is (A).

Passage 6 Solutions

36. **(F)** 98 J

Interpretation of Data

In Figure 3, find −50°C on the *x*-axis. Read the corresponding point on the darker line, which represents low-energy samples. The *y*-value of that point is slightly less than 100 J, or roughly 98 J. The correct answer is (F).

37. **(A)** increase in toughness.

Interpretation of Data

According to the passage, the higher the amount of energy needed to break the specimen, the tougher the metal is considered to be. According to Figure 3, an increase in temperature results in a higher impact energy, since both curves increase to the right. Thus, an increase in temperature leads to an increase in toughness. It doesn't make sense to say that the samples themselves increase or decrease in height. Rather, you could say that the pendulum's final height increases or decreases under various conditions, but the samples themselves do not change height. The correct answer is (A).

38. **(G)** 6

Interpretation of Data

In Figure 3, find the point at 0°C on the *x*-axis. Find the *y*-value of the low-energy line at 0°C (just under 20 J) and the *y*-value of the high-energy line (just above 100 J). This is a bit more than 5 times the impact energy of the low-energy line, and 6 is the only answer choice that is close. The correct answer is (G).

39. **(D)** heated to 600°C and held at that temperature for at least 6 hours.

Interpretation of Data

According to the passage, steel that is to withstand extreme conditions should be heated to 600°C and held at that temperature for at least 6 hours. This increases the toughness of the steel and makes it suitable for extremely low temperatures. The correct answer is (D).

40. **(F)** 38.0 cm.

Interpretation of Data

According to the passage, the formula for impact energy, or change in energy, is as follows:

Change in Energy = mass of pendulum × force of gravity × change in height

If none of these conditions are changed, you know that the change in height in the new experimental setup must be the same as in the original experimental setup. In the original experiment, the initial height = 30 cm (passage) and the final height = 28 cm (Table 1), so the change in height = −2 cm (final height – initial height). If you have a new initial height of 40 cm, then the new final height must be 38 cm to preserve the change in height of −2 cm. The correct answer is (F).

41. **(B)** 32 J.

Interpretation of Data

An analysis of Figure 3 reveals that the low-energy (lighter) line levels off and becomes relatively constant at a y-value of just over 30 J. Thus, 32 J is the only reasonable answer choice. The correct answer is (B).

42. **(F)** an increase in the final height.

Interpretation of Data

According to the passage, the formula for change in energy (also known as impact energy) is:

Change in energy = mass of pendulum × force of gravity × change in height

Since you are told that impact energy does not change, eliminate answer (J), and since impact energy is the same as change in energy, eliminate answer (H). If mass of the pendulum is increased, one or both of the other two factors on the right side of the equation (force of gravity or change in height) must decrease to compensate for it. Since you need a decrease in the change of height to compensate for the increased mass of the pendulum, eliminate answer (G), which says exactly the opposite. If there is an increase in the final height, there is actually a decrease in the change in height (since change in height = initial height – final height). Thus, an increase in the final height would compensate for an increase in the mass of the pendulum to keep the value of the change in energy the same. The correct answer is (F).

Passage 7 Solutions

43. **(C)** 100-D

Interpretation of Data

According to Table 2, the concentration of strontium-90 at site 100-D was 0.107 pCi/L in 2008 and 1.03 pCi/L in 2010. Thus, the concentration of strontium-90 increased from 2008 to 2010 at that site. At every other site, the concentration of strontium-90 fell. The correct answer is (C).

44. **(H)** 100-N

Interpretation of Data

According to Table 1, safe levels of chromium for aquatic water quality are below 10 µg/L. For site 100-N, the chromium level in 2008 was 7.7 µg/L, while the chromium level in 2010 was 11 µg/L. Thus, the chromium concentration was within safe levels in 2008 and had become unsafe by 2010. The correct answer is (H).

45. **(A)** radioactive tritium had reached unsafe levels in drinking water.

Interpretation of Data

According to the Table 1, safe levels of tritium for drinking water standards are below 20,000 pCi/L. According to Table 2, the levels of tritium in 2010 were 20,000 pCi/L. Thus, tritium, which is radioactive according to the passage, had reached unsafe levels in drinking water in 2010. The correct answer is (A).

46. **(G)** Graph G

Interpretation of Data

Pick any individual site to calculate the change in tritium levels. At site 100-B/C, the tritium level in 2008 is 2,680 pCi/L, and the tritium level in 2010 is 1800 pCi/L, a change of −820 pCi/L over the two years. The only graph on which 100-B/C has a change of −820 pCi/L is graph G. A similar procedure can be followed for any of the four sites pictured in the graphs. The correct answer is (G).

47. **(B)** Nitrate

Interpretation of Data

The maximum safe values of each contaminant can be found in Table 1. Since the units of each contaminant are different, pay attention to which unit is largest. According to the passage, mg (milligrams, or thousandths of a gram) are larger than µg (micrograms, or millionths of a gram). The pCi unit is a little trickier, but note that a pCi is 10_{-12} curies, or one trillionth of a curie, which is very small. In theory, you can use the specific activities of strontium-90 and of tritium to convert the pCi limits to mass limits in grams, but just studying the numbers, you can see that the limit on strontium-90 would be much less than a picogram, and the limit on tritium would be just around 2 picograms. These limits are far smaller than even the microgram limit on chromium, let alone the milligram limit on nitrate. Thus, the nitrate limit of 45 mg/L is larger than the limit for any of the other contaminants. The correct answer is (B).

48.   **(F)** tritium was naturally converted into chromium.

Interpretation of Data

It is very unlikely that tritium, an isotope of hydrogen, the first element on the periodic table, would be spontaneously converted into a distant element such as chromium. Although radioactive decay can change the identity of elements, the typical pathway is to lower atomic numbers on the periodic table, and hydrogen is already at the lowest atomic number. All of the other answer choices provide more plausible explanations for the reduction in tritium levels. The correct answer is (F).

49.   **(D)** Contaminated materials leak into the ground and are transferred through the soil to the Columbia River.

Interpretation of Data

This question requires inferring a plausible mechanism for radioactive contamination. By process of elimination, you can eliminate answers that are unlikely explanations. Evaporation is an unlikely mechanism, since the evaporation of contaminated materials are unlikely to be deposited specifically back into the Columbia River. They would rather be distributed throughout the environment. Eliminate answer (A). Wildlife is unlikely to transfer radioactive materials since those materials are harmful to wildlife and this behavior would not be sustainable—it would kill the wildlife. Thus, eliminate answer (B). There is no reason to think leaks have yet to be detected, and the question stem mentions that there is no direct leakage from the radioactive sites to the Columbia River. Eliminate answer (C). It is, however, mentioned in the passage that groundwater is contaminated, and contamination of the soil, which in turn contaminates the river, is a plausible method of *indirect* contamination of the river. The correct answer is (D).

Chapter 24

of

5lb. Book of ACT® Practice Problems

Writing (Optional)

In This Chapter...

Chapter 24
Writing (Optional)

Check with Your Colleges First

Before you go any further in this chapter, recognize the key difference between the Writing section and the other four sections of the exam (English, Math, Reading, and Science): *the Writing section is optional*. Only about half of students take the "ACT Plus Writing," assuming that the ACT's figures from a few years ago still hold. You have to decide in advance whether to take the Writing section, and you pay more for the privilege.

So why take the Writing section? Some colleges recommend—or even require—that you take this section of the test. Other colleges don't care. Start by listing all of the schools you may be applying to, even if you haven't made a final decision yet. Then check with each school's admissions office directly to find out whether the ACT Writing is required. As a backup, you can also look on the ACT's website for a page called "What Colleges Have Decided about the Writing Test." As of press time, the page was located at the following address:

https://actapps.act.org/writPrefRM/

However, the best source of information is always the admissions offices themselves. They can also provide you with more information about the Writing scores of admitted students, such as the average score. Unfortunately, a super-high Writing score probably won't give you a big leg up, but a score much lower than average might be seen as a flaw. The good news is that with a little work, you can probably get to at least the average for your target schools.

How the Writing Section Works

The Writing section appears at the end of the test, after the other four sections. In this section, you write a 30 minute essay by hand. You are asked for your opinion on a yes-no question, which typically relates to high school life. The sample question at www.actstudent.org/writing/sample is a good example: "In your opinion, should high school be extended to five years?" Since everyone taking the ACT is in high school, the test-makers want every test-taker to be able to write from his or her own experience.

There is no right or wrong answer to the question. The test is asking for your opinion, after all. You can take either side (or even come up with a more complex position on the topic) and do perfectly well on this task.

The Writing section does not affect your overall composite score. Rather, you'll get two additional scores: a separate score for Writing alone (ranging from 2 to 12) and another combined English/Writing score (ranging from 1 to 36). Two people independently—and very rapidly—grade your essay on a scale from 1 to 6, and these two scores are added to produce the Writing score between 2 and 12.

The graders know that you have just half an hour to outline and write the essay, so they don't pore over your essay with red pens. By the time they finish reading your essay (in just a few minutes), they will have already scored it, drawing on their experience with hundreds of other students' essays.

Admissions officers also know that you have only spent half an hour on this essay. From their point of view, the real test of your writing skills is in the application—the essays that you write for the schools themselves. If you have to take the ACT Writing section, then you should prepare, but don't over-prepare. Just work your way through the rest of this chapter.

What the ACT Wants

According to the ACT, you need to do five things with your essay. Call these the "Five Factors."

1. Express judgment. That is, give your opinion on the topic. Make that opinion clear throughout the essay.

2. Maintain focus. That is, stay on topic. Avoid changing terms accidentally and answering a slightly different question that you might be more comfortable with.

3. Develop your position. That is, support your opinion with good logic. You should have two or three reasons for your opinion ("I believe that high school should not be extended to five years because of X. Another reason is Y. Yet another reason is Z."). These reasons should be illustrated with specific, concrete examples. The essay should go somewhere—that is, the reader should consistently encounter new thoughts that reinforce your argument.

4. Organize your ideas. That is, make it easy for the reader to follow the thinking in your writing. Write an introductory paragraph, then a couple of body paragraphs (one for each reason or key example), and finally a conclusion paragraph. Use signpost words and phrases.

5. Use language well. That is, write clearly and effectively, with few mistakes. Choose appropriate words. Build your sentences with purpose.

These Five Factors tend to show up—or not show up—together. High-scoring essays exhibit all five. Low-scoring essays exhibit few or none.

MANHATTAN
PREP

What the ACT Also Secretly Wants

The ACT has published many sample essays with various scores. If you study these essays closely, you will find the presence (or absence) of the Five Factors, just as you would expect.

However, you will also discover that, consciously or not, the ACT's graders want your essay to do two more things. Call these the "Secret Factors."

6. Use lots of words. Essays that are too short, no matter how polished, simply do not get high scores. Likewise, the published essays with 5's and 6's are all long. Of course, writing nonsense to boost your word count won't work, but a good rule of thumb is this:

> For a score of 4, write 400 words.
> For a 5, write 500 words.
> For a 6, write 600 words.

That is, write 600 *good* words, arranged suitably in 6–7 paragraphs, and exhibiting the Five Factors listed above.

7. Hit a higher grade level on "readability." "See Spot run. He runs fast. I like Spot." Unfortunately, as friendly as that little story is, it's too easy for the ACT: both the words and the sentences are too short. You need to aim for more sophistication in your word choice and sentence structure. Of course, you should use longer words and sentences naturally, in order to express your sophisticated ideas in clever, powerful ways. Avoid using sesquipedalian (long-winded) words for their own sake, and don't glue sentences together into unwieldy monstrosities. Look for a middle ground, somewhere style between Dr. Seuss and a technical manual on nuclear weapons.

Many word-processing programs and even some websites can calculate the "Flesch-Kincaid Grade Level" of a piece of text using sentence length and syllable counts. Here's a rule of thumb for grade level:

> For a score of 4, reach grade 8 on the Flesch-Kincaid scale.
> For a 5, reach grade 9.
> For a 6, reach grade 10.

Again, this factor is just one of seven. The grade level alone of your essay won't guarantee you any score. Your essay needs to have enough words, and it needs those Five Factors (judgment, focus, etc.) described earlier.

How to Prepare

Here's how to get ready for the ACT Writing section.

1. Read All Six Sample Essays Published for Free Online by the ACT.

Go to www.actstudent.org/writing/sample (the Web address as this book goes to print) for the full sample prompt. Then read the six samples, starting with the essay that earned a 1 and working your way up to the one that earned a 6. Read the scoring explanations as well. When you finish reading each essay, ask yourself these questions:

1. In 30 minutes, could I write an essay at least as good as this one?
2. What can I learn from this essay?

Put your answers below.

Sample Essay	In 30 minutes, could I write an essay at least as good as this one?	What can I learn from this essay?
Score of 1		
Score of 2		
Score of 3		
Score of 4		
Score of 5		
Score of 6		

If you don't think you can write an essay that will earn the score you want, carefully study the corresponding sample essay. Rewrite it by hand, so that the words and structures pass through your brain and hand. Analyze particularly interesting moves that the writer made—good logical arguments, skillful constructions of a sentence, even nifty turns of phrase. Adopt them for your own. Just as an aspiring basketball player might study LeBron James or an aspiring singer might study Carrie Underwood, so too should you study the work of better writers. The goal is the same: to borrow good moves.

Remember, another student wrote that sample essay. With some practice, you can write similar essays.

2. Write a Sample Essay under Exam Conditions.

Use either of the sample prompts in the next part of this chapter. Make sure you won't be interrupted, and give yourself exactly 30 minutes. Handwrite your essay on normal lined paper.

Take just a few minutes at the beginning of your allotted 30 to outline your thoughts. Articulate your position and come up with 2–3 reasons. Then start writing your essay. Here's a quick general outline:

Introductory paragraph: restate the question, state your position, and name your reasons for your position.

Body paragraphs: discuss one reason per paragraph. Include specific example(s) to support the reason.

Conclusion paragraph: acknowledge the other side of the argument briefly, then restate your position with even more conviction.

Don't stop early to edit and polish. Pace yourself as you write so that you are finishing the last paragraph with just a minute or two to spare. Remember that the ACT rewards the word count, so when in doubt, write it out. Just keep putting words on the page.

3. Score Yourself on the Five Factors.

Put down your pencil, get up, and walk around. Step away from your essay for at least a few minutes.

Then (or later on), reread your essay and judge it on each of the Five Factors. For each factor, give yourself 0–2 points according to the following rules:

> 0 points = Low, like the sample essays that scored 1 or 2.
>
> 1 point = Medium, like the sample essays that scored 3 or 4.
>
> 2 points = High, like the sample essays that scored 5 or 6.

After each prompt, there's a worksheet in which to record your points. The worksheet explains how to add up the points, divide by 2, and add 1 to determine a single score.

The result is your Five-Factor Score (which may be a decimal, such as 3.5). This score focuses on general principles of good persuasive writing—and it measures the factors that the ACT claims to measure.

However, this score is obviously subjective. Consciously or unconsciously, you may be too easy on yourself—or too hard. You are not a trained grader of these essays.

For these reasons, you should also take the next step, which will give you an objective measure to balance against the Five-Factor Score.

4. Compute the Secret-Factor Score.

The secret factors involve word count and readability, which are measured objectively. Retype your essay into a word-processing program, such as Microsoft Word. In and of itself, this process will be revealing to you—you'll see aspects of your writing that you wouldn't notice otherwise.

Most word-processing programs (except for bare-bones editors such as Notepad or Wordpad) contain a word count tool. Run that tool and put the number of words into the Secret-Factor worksheet.

You'll also need to compute a readability metric. Earlier, the Flesch-Kincaid Grade Level was described. A similar metric is called Flesch Reading Ease, and it turns out that this metric is slightly more predictive of ACT Writing scores. Flesch Reading Ease is usually between 0 and 100, and it goes down as the text gets harder (longer words, longer sentences). An overall rule of thumb is that a Reading Ease of 65–70 corresponds to a score of 4, a 60–65 corresponds to a 5, and a 55–60 corresponds to a 6.

If you run Microsoft Word's grammar checker and enable statistics, you'll get the Flesch Reading Ease. It might be easiest, however, just to cut and paste your essay into an online tool, such as this one:

> www.readability-score.com

At this site, for any chunk of text, you instantly get not only the Flesch Reading Ease score, but also the Flesch-Kincaid Reading Level, the word count, and several other metrics to boot. Of course, you can start with this online tool, but be sure to save your essay in a separate file, so that you have it stored in electronic form.

On the Secret-Factor scoring worksheet, you'll run a couple of computations with the Flesch Reading Ease number and the word count in order to generate a Secret-Factor Score.

5. Finally, Compare and Combine the Five-Factor Score and the Secret-Factor Score.

Compare the two scores. Are they very different? Which is higher?

If your Five-Factor Score is substantially higher, face the fact that you simply need to generate more words (and perhaps increase the grade level of your writing). Take advantage of the numerous opportunities you surely have at school, such as on timed tests and quizzes, to increase your "throughput"—the pace at which you write good prose.

Conversely, if your Secret-Factor Score is substantially higher, analyze which of the Five Factors are holding you back. Make a plan to improve these aspects of your timed writing—again, using the many chances you have on history quizzes, English tests, etc.

Finally, put your two scores together by taking their average. Sum them up and divide by 2. This is your best estimate of the Writing score you'd earn today.

If you are happy with this estimate—that is, if it's at or above the average score for your target schools—then you're done. Go into the test confidently.

If you're not happy with the estimate, however, redo the writing exercise with the other prompt. In addition, talk to your English teacher. Bring your essay to him or her and ask for feedback. Your teacher should be able to diagnose the issues and give you a few specific ideas on how to improve. If you're having any kind of issue with your writing, there's no substitute for the guidance of a teacher. Moreover, you'll impress your teacher with your initiative, and who knows what benefits that might yield for you?

MANHATTAN
PREP

Sample Prompts

Prompt 1

Doctors, psychologists, and educators have debated whether participation in team sports, not just general physical education, should be required for all high school students. Some people think that team sports build personal strengths in unique ways, leading to better physical and educational outcomes. Other people think that students will resent the requirement, weakening the value of the experience for all concerned. In your opinion, should team sports be required for all high school students?

In your essay, take a position on this question. You may write about either one of the two points of view given, or you may present a different point of view on this question. Use specific reasons and examples to support your position.

Take 30 minutes to write your essay on separate sheets of lined paper. Maintain exam-like conditions.

When you are done, score yourself using the following worksheets.

Five-Factor Score

On each factor, give yourself 0 points for Low performance, like the sample essays online that scored 1 or 2. Give yourself 1 point for Medium performance, like the essays that scored 3 or 4. Give yourself 2 points for High performance, like the essays that scored 5 or 6.

Factor	Points (0–2)
1. Express judgment. Is my opinion clear throughout the essay?	_____
2. Maintain focus. Does the essay stay on topic? Does it answer the question asked?	_____
3. Develop my position. Does the essay support my opinion with good logic? Are there 2–3 good reasons, expressed clearly? Are these reasons illustrated with specific, relevant examples?	_____
4. Organize my ideas. Is it easy for the reader to follow the thinking in my writing? Is the essay structure clear? Are signpost words and phrases used often and appropriately?	_____
5. Use language well. Is the writing clear and effective? Are there few mistakes? Are words chosen well? Are sentences constructed with purpose?	_____
Add up the points.	Total =
Divide total by 2.	÷ 2 =
Add 1 to get your Five-Factor Score.	+ 1 =

Secret-Factor Score

Retype your essay into a program or website that can calculate both the word count and the Flesch Reading Ease of the text. As mentioned earlier, a website that fits the bill as of press time is www.readability-score.com.

Secret Factor	Number
6. Use lots of words. How many words are in my essay?	Word Count =
Divide the word count by 153. Call this number **X**.	÷ 153 =
7. Hit a higher grade level on readability. What is the Flesch Reading Ease of my essay? The number will probably be between 50 (hard) and 100 (easy). Note: This is not the Flesch-Kincaid Grade Level.	Flesch Reading Ease =
Divide the Flesch Reading Ease by 21. Call this number **Y**.	÷ 21 =
Subtract **Y** from **X**. Round to 1 decimal place.	X – Y =
Add 4.4.	+ 4.4 =

Combined Score

Finally, combine the Five-Factor Score and Secret-Factor Score to determine your Combined Score.

Five-Factor Score	
Secret-Factor Score	
Add up the scores.	Total =
Divide the total by 2 to get your **Combined Score**.	÷ 2 =

MANHATTAN
PREP

Prompt 2

In some high schools, students are required to declare a major and commit to a specialized course of study, often to prepare for a particular industry or career. Some people think majors are a good requirement, because they think students benefit from the focus provided by majors. Other people think schools should not require majors, because students need a broad course of study to prepare for many possible careers. In your opinion, should students be required to declare majors in high school?

In your essay, take a position on this question. You may write about either one of the two points of view given, or you may present a different point of view on this question. Use specific reasons and examples to support your position.

Take 30 minutes to write your essay on separate sheets of lined paper. Maintain exam-like conditions.

When you are done, score yourself using the following worksheets.

Five-Factor Score

On each factor, give yourself 0 points for Low performance, like the sample essays online that scored 1 or 2. Give yourself 1 point for Medium performance, like the essays that scored 3 or 4. Give yourself 2 points for High performance, like the essays that scored 5 or 6.

Factor	Points (0–2)
1. Express judgment. Is my opinion clear throughout the essay?	_____
2. Maintain focus. Does the essay stay on topic? Does it answer the question asked?	_____
3. Develop my position. Does the essay support my opinion with good logic? Are there 2–3 good reasons, expressed clearly? Are these reasons illustrated with specific, relevant examples?	_____
4. Organize my ideas. Is it easy for the reader to follow the thinking in my writing? Is the essay structure clear? Are signpost words and phrases used often and appropriately?	_____
5. Use language well. Is the writing clear and effective? Are there few mistakes? Are words chosen well? Are sentences constructed with purpose?	_____
Add up the points.	Total =
Divide total by 2.	÷ 2 =
Add 1 to get your Five-Factor Score.	+ 1 =

MANHATTAN
PREP

Secret-Factor Score

Retype your essay into a program or website that can calculate both the word count and the Flesch Reading Ease of the text. As mentioned earlier, a website that as of press time fits the bill is www.readability-score.com.

Secret Factor	Number
6. Use lots of words. How many words are in my essay?	Word Count =
Divide the word count by 153. Call this number **X**.	÷ 153 =
7. Hit a higher grade level on readability. What is the Flesch Reading Ease of my essay? The number will probably be between 50 (hard) and 100 (easy). Note: This is not the Flesch-Kincaid Grade Level.	Flesch Reading Ease =
Divide the Flesch Reading Ease by 21. Call this number **Y**.	÷ 21 =
Subtract **Y** from **X**. Round to 1 decimal place.	X – Y =
Add 4.4.	+ 4.4 =

Combined Score

Finally, combine the Five-Factor Score and Secret-Factor Score to determine your Combined Score.

Five-Factor Score	
Secret-Factor Score	
Add up the scores. Total =	
Divide total by 2 to get your **Combined Score**.	÷ 2 =

MANHATTAN
PREP

Appendix A
of
5lb. Book of ACT® Practice Problems

Citations

Citations

All questions, answers, and solutions are the original work of Manhattan Prep. All passages, unless otherwise cited below, are the original work of Manhattan Prep, including cases in which outside sources are referred to for pedagogical reasons, and/or adapted from the public domain.

Passages cited below either are in the public domain (as U.S. government publications so deemed) or are open-access articles distributed under the terms of the Creative Commons Attribution license (CC BY 2.0), which permits unrestricted use, distribution, and reproduction in any medium, provided the original author and source are credited. In all cases of the passages cited below, changes were made to adapt the content of the original passages for educational and pedagogical purposes, and all applicable copyrights are retained by the authors of the original passages. For more information, see http://creativecommons.org/licenses/by/2.0/legalcode.

Chapter 18, Passage 4: Banerjee K, Jhala YV, Chauhan KS, Dave CV (2013) *Living with Lions: The Economics of Coexistence in the Gir Forests, India.* PLoS ONE 8(1): e49457. doi:10.1371/journal.pone.0049457

Chapter 18, Passage 5: Rutherford A, Harmon D, Werfel J, Gard-Murray AS, Bar-Yam S, et al. (2014) *Good Fences: The Importance of Setting Boundaries for Peaceful Coexistence.* PLoS ONE 9(5): e95660. doi:10.1371/journal.pone.0095660

Chapter 18, Passage 6: Gambrill E, Reiman A (2011) *A Propaganda Index for Reviewing Problem Framing in Articles and Manuscripts: An Exploratory Study.* PLoS ONE 6(5): e19516. doi:10.1371/journal.pone.0019516

Chapter 18, Passage 8: Labeyrie V, Deu M, Barnaud A, Calatayud C, Buiron M, et al. (2014) *Influence of Ethnolinguistic Diversity on the Sorghum Genetic Patterns in Subsistence Farming Systems in Eastern Kenya.* PLoS ONE 9(3): e92178. doi:10.1371/journal.pone.0092178

Chapter 20, Passage 7: Strong M (2004) *Protein Nanomachines.* PLoS Biol 2(3): e73. doi:10.1371/journal.pbio.0020073

Chapter 20, Passage 8: Feinberg JA, Newman CE, Watkins-Colwell GJ, Schlesinger MD, Zarate B, et al. (2014) *Cryptic Diversity in Metropolis: Confirmation of a New Leopard Frog Species (Anura: Ranidae) from New York City and Surrounding Atlantic Coast Regions.* PLoS ONE 9(10): e108213. doi:10.1371/journal.pone.0108213

Chapter 21, Passage 7, Figure 1: United Nations, Department of Economic and Social Affairs, Population Division (2007). *World Population Prospects: The 2006 Revision, Highlights, Working Paper No. ESA/P/WP.202,* via http://www.prb.org/Publications/Lesson-Plans/HumanPopulation/Change.aspx

MANHATTAN
PREP

Chapter 21, Passage 7, Figure 2: 2011 Census: Population Estimates for the United Kingdom, 27 March 2011. Figure 3: *UK Population by sex and five-year age group.* Census - Office for National Statistics, Northern Ireland Statistics and Research Agency, National Records of Scotland, via http://www.ons.gov.uk/ons/rel/census/2011-census/population-and-household-estimates-for-the-united-kingdom/stb-2011-census--population-estimates-for-the-united-kingdom.html#tab-The-structure-of-the-population-of-the-United-Kingdom.

Chapter 21, Passage 8, data and charts: Nemhauser JL, Mockler TC, Chory J (2004) *Interdependency of Brassinosteroid and Auxin Signaling in Arabidopsis.* PLoS Biol 2(9): e258. doi:10.1371/journal.pbio.0020258

Chapter 23, Passage 7, data and charts: *Hanford Site Groundwater Monitoring Reports for 2008 and for 2010,* U.S. Department of Energy, Richland Operations Office (DOE/RL-2008-66 and DOE/RL-2011-01), via http://www.hanford.gov/page.cfm/SoilGroundwaterAnnualReports

DON'T FORGET TO REGISTER YOUR BOOK ONLINE TO GET ACCESS TO:

SUPPLEMENTAL QUESTION BANKS

Take your studies even further with our question banks. These banks include extra ACT practice problems fine-tuned by our curriculum team to simulate real exam questions. Every question comes with a detailed answer explanation. These problems are an excellent practice resource for dedicated ACT students.

SCIENCE VOCABULARY LIST

This list features over 150 terms that have been used in official ACT Science passages. Many of these terms are not defined within the passage, so you must know them in advance. Other terms in our list are defined within the passage, but the more familiar you are with the specialized vocabulary that is typically used in Science passages, the faster you'll go and the better you'll do on this section of the ACT.

ONLINE UPDATES TO THE CONTENT IN THIS BOOK

The content presented in this book is updated periodically to ensure that it reflects the ACT's most current trends. You may view all updates, including any known errors or changes, upon registering for online access.

REGISTER NOW!

The above resources can be found in your Student Center at manhattanprep.com/act/studentcenter